OCA/OCP
Oracle Database 12c
All-in-One Exam Guide

(Exams 1Z0-061, 1Z0-062, & 1Z0-063)

About the Authors

John Watson (Oxford, UK) is an Oracle Certified Master DBA, with many other accreditations for Oracle technologies. He works for Skillbuilders Corporation, teaching and consulting throughout Europe and North America. He was with Oracle Corporation for several years in Johannesburg working for Internal Support and Oracle University. He speaks regularly at Oracle User Group meetings and has written several books on Oracle technologies. John has 30 years of experience in IT and first came across Oracle with database release 5, installing it on IBM PCs.

Roopesh Ramklass (Canada) is an Oracle Certified Master with expertise in infrastructure, middleware, and database architecture. He has worked for Oracle Global Support, Advanced Customer Services, and Oracle University. He has run an IT consultancy and is experienced with infrastructure system, software development, and systems integration. He has spoken at numerous Oracle Users Group conferences and is the author of several technology books.

Bob Bryla (Wisconsin) is an Oracle 9*i,* 10*g,* 11*g,* and 12*c* Certified Professional with more than 20 years of experience in database design, database application development, training, and Oracle database administration. He is the lead Oracle DBA and systems engineer at Epic in Verona, Wisconsin. In his spare time, he has authored several Oracle DBA books such as *Oracle Database 12*c: *The Complete Reference* and *Oracle Database 12*c *DBA Handbook*. In addition, he has authored several certification study guides for Oracle Database 11*g* and 12*c*. He has also been known to watch science-fiction movies and dabble in videography in his spare time.

Oracle Press™

OCA/OCP
Oracle Database 12*c*
All-in-One Exam Guide

(Exams 1Z0-061, 1Z0-062, & 1Z0-063)

John Watson
Roopesh Ramklass
Bob Bryla

New York   Chicago   San Francisco
Athens   London   Madrid   Mexico City
Milan   New Delhi   Singapore   Sydney   Toronto

Cataloging-in-Publication Data is on file with the Library of Congress

McGraw-Hill Education books are available at special quantity discounts to use as premiums and sales promotions, or for use in corporate training programs. To contact a representative, please visit the Contact Us pages at www.mhprofessional.com.

OCA/OCP Oracle Database 12c All-in-One Exam Guide (Exams 1Z0-061, 1Z0-062, & 1Z0-063)

6 7 8 9 10 11 QVS/QVS 23 22 21 20 19

ISBN: Book p/n 978-0-07-183006-5 and CD p/n 978-0-07-182805-5
of set 978-0-07-182808-6

MHID: Book p/n 0-07-183006-5 and CD p/n 0-07-182805-2
of set 0-07-182808-7

Sponsoring Editor Timothy Green	**Indexer** James Minkin
Editorial Supervisor Jody McKenzie	**Production Supervisor** James Kussow
Project Manager Raghavi Khullar, Cenveo® Publisher Services	**Composition** Cenveo Publisher Services
Acquisitions Coordinator Amy Stonebraker	**Illustration** Cenveo Publisher Services
Copy Editor Kim Wimpsett	**Art Director, Cover** Jeff Weeks
Proofreader Lisa McCoy	

Thank you to Silvia, for making life worth living.
—John

All my love to Ameetha, for a journey of a lifetime.
—Roopesh

The kids and the dog and the rest of the family…I do this for y'all!
—Bob

CONTENTS AT A GLANCE

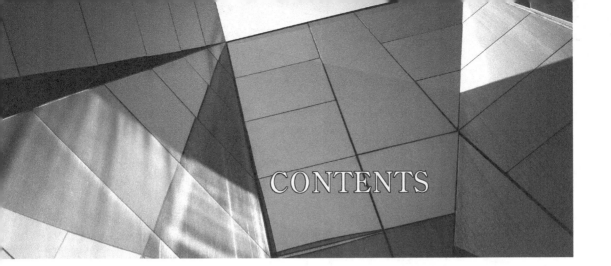

CONTENTS

Part V   Upgrades and Multitenant

INTRODUCTION

There is an ever-increasing demand for staff with IT industry certification. The benefits to employers are significant (they can be certain that staff have a certain level of competence), and the benefits to the individuals, in terms of demand for their services, are equally great. Many employers require technical staff to have certifications, and many IT purchasers will not buy from firms that do not have certified staff. The Oracle certifications are among the most sought after. But apart from rewards in a business sense, studying for the exams is an enjoyable process that may allow you to investigate aspects of the database that you might not usually use.

Your initiation into the wonderful world of Oracle database administration is about to begin. You can study this for the rest of your life. Enjoy!

Oracle Certification

There are several Oracle certification tracks; this book is concerned with the Oracle Database Administration certification track, specifically for release 12*c* of the database. There are three levels of DBA certification: Oracle Certified Associate (OCA), Oracle Certified Professional (OCP), and Oracle Certified Master (OCM). The OCA qualification is based on two examinations; the OCP qualification requires passing a third examination. You can take these examinations at any Pearson VUE Center, in any order. The OCM qualification requires completing a further two-day evaluation at an Oracle testing center, involving simulations of complex environments and use of advanced techniques that are not covered in this book.

To prepare for the OCA/OCP examinations, you can attend Oracle University instructor-led training courses, you can study Oracle University online learning material, or you can read this book. In all cases, you should also refer to the Oracle Documentation Library for details of syntax. This book will be a valuable addition to other study methods, but it is also sufficient by itself. It has been designed with the examination objectives in mind, though it also includes a great deal of information that will be useful in the course of your work.

Study the material and experiment, and as you work through the exercises and sample questions and become more familiar with the Oracle environment, you will realize that there is one golden rule:

"When in doubt, try it out."

In a multitude of cases, you will find that a simple test that takes a couple of minutes can save hours of speculation and poring through manuals. If anything is ever unclear, construct an example and see what happens. Note that this book was developed using Windows and Linux, but to carry out the exercises and your further investigations, you can use any platform for which the database is available.

The Examination

Here are some suggestions for approaching the exam.

An OCA/OCP exam will consist of multiple-choice questions, but it is multiple choice on steroids. The questions are not always "choose the best answer." Sometimes the questions will ask you to "choose all correct answers" or "put the answers in the correct order." Some questions are easy, some are hard, and some are confusing. You might be asked (for example) to "choose the best answer" and you will think, "All the answers are wrong!" or perhaps "But two of the answers are correct!" In that case, read the question carefully, and you may eventually see what they are wanting; the questions are often precisely worded.

The questions are fair and do not require feats of memory. You will not (for example) be asked if a view name is V$DATAFILE or V$DATA_FILE. But you might be asked whether V$DATAFILE or DBA_DATA_FILES is visible when the database is in mount mode. Fair enough: you should know whether a view is populated from the instance, from the controlfile, or from the data dictionary; you should know which of these structures is available in mount mode. This is not a matter of spelling; it is something you can work out.

The exam technique you should follow is to go through all the questions as quickly as possible, answering the ones you know and marking the ones you don't (there is an option to do that). That first run-through will take you half the time. Then spend the rest of the time going over the questions you marked, again and again. At the end, there may still be a few questions where you have no idea. In those cases, just guess—there are no deductions for errors. The mistake you must not make is to try to do the questions in order because you will run out of time. And there might have been some easy questions at the end that you never looked at.

All the detail of how to book an exam is available on the Oracle University web site, http://education.oracle.com/certification.

Prerequisite Knowledge and Environment

This book was developed using Windows and Linux, from which come all the examples. To carry out the exercises and your further investigations, you can use any platform on which the Oracle database can be installed. Note that you cannot install Oracle on any 32-bit operating system. Do not get too hung up on whether your platform is supported. For example, Oracle does not support the database on any "home" edition of Windows or on Centos Linux—but these should work for learning purposes, no problem.

Clearly, you must be familiar with whatever command-line interface and graphical admin tools your environment offers. Oracle University uses Linux in the classroom, and some exam questions do have a Linux feel to them, so if at all possible, try to do at least some preparation on a Linux machine.

The releases of the database used for developing this book were 12.1.0.0 (a beta release, as you may notice in some screenshots), 12.1.0.1 (the first production release), and 12.1.0.2. You should download and install whatever the latest release currently available to you happens to be. Oracle University validates the exams against the first production release. When a new release (perhaps 12.2.0.1) is issued, Oracle University will revalidate all questions against the new release and adjust or remove any questions where changes in behavior could affect the answer. So, for exam purposes, it should not matter what release you use—but for practical purposes, you want to be on the latest one.

A Word on Unauthorized Sample Questions (aka Brain Dumps)

The chapter review and practice exam questions that come with this book are not actual Oracle exam questions; that would be illegal. However, they do cover the knowledge you should have. There is no point in memorizing the questions and answers. Treat them merely as a check of whether you have grasped the material. Some students like to go through many simulation exams (which you can buy or perhaps download for free—though the legality of these should be confirmed) repeatedly until they have a perfect score. We strongly believe that this is poor preparation technique. It proves nothing more than that you can pass a particular simulated exam. The only value of such material is if you question the answers, that is, you work out why the supposedly correct answer is correct and why the wrong answers are wrong. That is the way to address all the questions in this book. If you really feel the need to do a trial exam, why not simply schedule the real thing? You never know, you might pass the first time.

On the CD-ROM

For more information on the CD-ROM, please see the "About the CD-ROM" appendix at the back of the book.

Objectives Maps

Here you will find an objectives map for each of the three exams. The maps have been constructed to allow you to cross-reference the official exam objectives with the objectives as they are presented and covered in this book. The objectives are listed as presented by the certifying body with the corresponding chapter reference.

Exam 1Z0-061

Exam 1Z0-062

Exam 1Z0-063

PART I

Getting Started

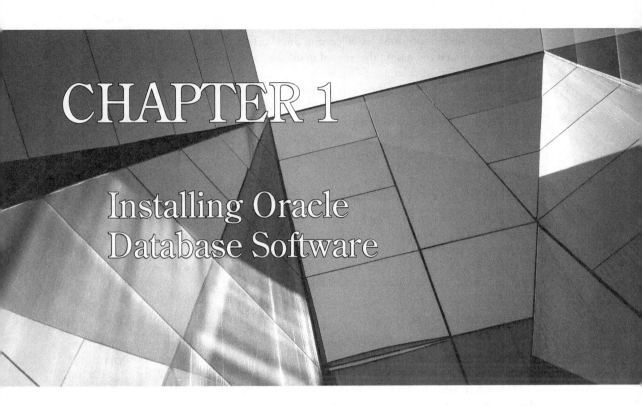

CHAPTER 1

Installing Oracle Database Software

Exam Objectives

In this chapter, you will learn to

- 062.2.2.1 Plan for an Oracle Database Software Installation
- 062.2.4.1 Install the Oracle Database Software

The Oracle Database software is installed with the Oracle Universal Installer (OUI). OUI is an Oracle product in its own right that is used to manage the installation and maintenance of many other products. The installation of Oracle software has, as far as possible, been standardized for all products on all platforms—but there are platform and product variations. Before installing anything, it is essential that you read the product's release notes for the platform concerned. This chapter goes through the process of planning the installation and then installing the Oracle Database 12c software, with examples from Linux and Windows.

Plan for an Oracle Database Software Installation

The install process requires a number of prerequisites, and principal among them are the availability of the software and a suitable machine. Once these are in place, the actual installation is straightforward and, depending on hardware, should take about 15 minutes. Ideally, students will have their own installation on their own PC so that they can practice as much as desired. That is the environment described here.

Supported Platforms

Historically, the Oracle Database was supported on an extraordinarily wide range of platforms, which was one reason for the product's pre-eminence in the relational database management software (RDBMS) market. In recent years, the number of platforms considered commercially viable has decreased, so Oracle Corporation has reduced support accordingly. Linux is always the first platform for release. The platforms most commonly available to students are Linux and Microsoft Windows, so these are the platforms most commonly referenced in the exams and in this guide.

Obtain the Oracle Database Software

Oracle Corporation has made the software available for public download without the need to buy a license. However, this public license is restricted. You can download and install the product on your own machine only for the purposes of application development and self-tuition. This is made clear in the license agreement. There are also legal restrictions on downloading in (or subsequently transferring to) certain countries. Furthermore, usually only the base release is publicly available. To obtain patches of any kind, it is necessary to have a support agreement. The base release is adequate for training purposes, though not necessarily for production use.

The two commonly used sources for software download are the Oracle Technology Network (OTN) and the Oracle Software Delivery Cloud. To reach the OTN download site, go to www.oracle.com, navigate through the Downloads tab to Oracle Database, and select the latest available release. To use the Oracle Software Delivery Cloud, go to http://edelivery.oracle.com and select the Oracle Database product pack. In either site, it is necessary to log on to an Oracle account (or create a new Oracle account) and then accept the license agreement. The software is in the form of ZIP files, and four are needed: two files for the Oracle Database software and two for the Grid Infrastructure software. Unzip them (one directory for the Oracle Database software and a second directory for the Grid Infrastructure), and you are ready to go.

User Accounts

On any version of Unix or Linux, it is not possible to install the software as the root user. It is necessary to create accounts that will own the software. Best practice is to create one account that will own the database software and a second account that will own the Grid Infrastructure software. This permits separation of the duties between the database administration domain and the system administration domain. For the purposes of education, one account can be used for both functions. Traditionally, this account is named oracle and given the primary group of oinstall. A secondary group will be dba. These groups should be created before installing and should be assigned to the oracle account.

On Windows, it is not uncommon to install Oracle software under an account with Administrator privileges. Although this is certainly bad from a security perspective and should never be done on a production system, it will not cause a problem on a training system. The installer will create all necessary operating groups named ORA_DBA and assign it to the account from which the installer is run.

Disk Space and Directories

The installation requires about 5GB for the database Oracle Home. An Oracle Home is the location of an Oracle product installation—a set of files in a directory structure. Note that variations in size because of the platform, the type of file system, and the options selected may be substantial. The directory may be on a local file system or a clustered file system, but it must be a "cooked" file system—that is, not an Automatic Storage Management (ASM) disk group or a raw device.

The recommended directory structure is known as Optimal Flexible Architecture (OFA). OFA is intended to ease the process of organizing multiple software installations. The general idea is that each product should be installed into its own Oracle Home, beneath an Oracle Base. The Oracle Base is a directory that will contain one or more Oracle Homes as well as various other directories for administration purposes and also the actual databases. The directory containing the OUI inventory exists outside the Oracle Base, which makes sense because it should be independent of any other product.

The recommended naming convention of Oracle Base is based on three variables:

/pm/s/u

And for each Oracle Home, add a literal and more variables:

/pm/s/u/product/v/type_[n]

The files that make up each database are in the Oracle Base, plus two variables:

/pm/s/u/q/d

Table 1-1 shows the variables and suggested values.
Here are some examples:

- An Oracle Base of D:\app\oracle is an indication that all Oracle-related files exist on drive D: in a directory called \app and that the installs were done by Windows user oracle.

- An Oracle Home of /u01/app/oracle/product/12.1.0/dbhome_1 suggests that the Oracle Base is /u01/app/oracle and that this directory contains the first installation of the 12c release 1 database software on this machine.

Variable	Description	Typical Values
pm	Mount point	Linux: /u01 Windows: D:\
s	Standard directory name	app
u	Operating system (OS) installer account	oracle
v	Software version	12.1.0
type	Type of product	dbhome
n	Install counter	1
q	Indication of the contents	oradata
d	Database name	orcl

Table 1-1 The OMF Naming Convention

- The path D:\app\oracle\oradata\orcl is the directory beneath Oracle Base containing the files of a database named orcl.
- The path /u01/app/oraInventory is the location of the OUI inventory files, next to the Oracle Base.

It is not essential to conform to the OFA directory structure, but OFA does make a database administrator's life easier. Many database administrators (DBAs), and some products, assume that OFA is in place, which means deviating from OFA may cause confusion.

The Prerequisite Checks

The installation release notes for each platform list the prerequisites. These will usually be hardware requirements (disk space and random access memory), operating system versions, availability of certain utilities, security settings, kernel resource limits, and patch levels. Generally speaking, at this level Windows installations are simpler than Linux. This is because Windows is a tightly controlled environment, and OUI can make many assumptions. Similarly, if the Linux distribution is Oracle Enterprise Linux, it is likely that a standard installation will fulfill all the prerequisites. A Red Hat, SUSE, or CentOS distribution may not conform by default and may therefore need some work before Oracle can be installed.

There are prerequisites for running OUI and more prerequisites for particular products. The OUI prerequisites are coded in the file oraparam.ini and are basic. Search for this file in the unzipped software. The following is from release 12.1.0.1.0 for 64-bit Linux:

```
[Generic Prereqs]
TEMP_SPACE=500
SWAP_SPACE=150
MIN_DISPLAY_COLORS=256
[end code]
```

OUI will refuse to run if these conditions are not met. Then there are prerequisites for the product actually being installed. These are coded into the cvu_prereq.xml file and are checked by OUI as part of the installation. It is possible to ignore failures to meet the prerequisites and proceed with installation, but if you do so, there is no guarantee the installation will actually function correctly.

 TIP Often the problem with prereq failures is not that the products won't work; it is deciding whether they matter. For example, on Linux, some of the kernel settings and packages are not really needed for an entry-level installation. However, a problem may occur with support. If you ever raise a service request (an SR, which is passed to Oracle Support Services through My Oracle Support) and your system does not conform to the prereqs, the support analysts might refuse to help you. Therefore, if you have to break one of the rules to get an installation through, be sure to fix it as soon as possible afterward.

Install the Oracle Database Software

OUI gives several options for installation. The suggested installation, discussed next, will be suitable for any studies up to the Oracle Certified Professional level. The Oracle Certified Master curriculum includes RAC, the installation of which is not covered here. One option is whether to chain the installation of the software with the creation of a database. This option is not going to be taken here, however, because creating a database is dealt with as a separate topic.

The OUI Inventory

OUI creates an inventory, which is a set of Extensible Markup Language (XML) files that record exactly what Oracle products have been installed on the machine, with details of where the Oracle Homes are. To prevent this inventory from being corrupted, a locking mechanism prevents running OUI (or the Opatch patching routine) concurrently in two or more sessions. Whenever OUI or Opatch is run, the first thing it does is locate the inventory and check whether it is already locked. The location of the inventory and the operating system group that owns it are stored in a pointer file. The pointer file has a platform-specific name and location. On Linux, it is /etc/oracle/oraInst.loc, as in this example, which shows that the inventory is located in the /u01/app/oraInventory directory:

```
db121a $
db121a $ cat /etc/oraInst.loc
inventory_loc=/u01/app/oraInventory
inst_group=oinstall
db121a $
```

On Solaris or AIX, the pointer file resides in the /var/opt/oracle directory. On Windows, the inventory location is defined in a registry key.

HKEY_LOCAL_MACHINE/SOFTWARE/ORACLE/inst_loc

OUI is written in Java, using JDK 1.5, which is included in the product. This means that OUI is the same on all platforms, with the exception of certain trivial variations in the Java user interface, such as whether windows have square or rounded corners. OUI can be installed as a self-contained product in its own Oracle Home, but this is not usually necessary because it is shipped with every other Oracle product and can be launched from the product installation CD (or DVD); it will install itself into the Oracle Home along with the product. There are different versions of OUI, and if a product comes with a version earlier than the one already installed on the machine, it's usually a good idea (and may indeed be necessary) to install the product using the already-installed version from the existing Oracle Home. When OUI prompts for the location of the products.xml file, specify the DVD or directory with the product you want to install.

TIP Always use the latest version of OUI you have available. There can be issues with updating the OUI inventory if you try to revert to earlier versions after using a later version. Also note that some products (such as the WebLogic server) still do not use OUI and are installed independently. You can download the latest OUI from the Oracle Technology Network.

The OUI Dialog: Interactive Install

To launch OUI, run the runInstaller.sh shell script (Linux) or the setup.exe program (Windows) from the root of the directory in which the software was unzipped. For an interactive install, a graphical terminal must be available. For Windows, this is no problem. For Linux, it means an X terminal of some kind. If you are logged on to the console through one of the standard Linux X Window managers (such as Gnome), OUI will run straightaway. If you are connecting remotely, you will have to use a connection method that allows display of graphics, such as a VNC desktop or an X Window server. There is nothing special about this; any Linux tutorial or experienced Linux user can explain it. However, this topic is beyond the scope of an Oracle tutorial.

The use of the OUI dialog is detailed in the exercise at the end of this chapter. In summary, here is the information requested by the 12 steps of the installer on Linux (Windows is slightly different):

1. **Configure Security Updates** Give login credentials for My Oracle Support (optional).

2. **Download Software Updates** Enable automatic downloads of CPUs or PSUs (optional).

3. **Select Installation Option** Choose whether to chain the install to creating or upgrading a database.

4. **Grid Installation Options** Create an installation for single instance, RAC, or RAC One Node.

5. **Select Product Languages** By default, only English is selected.

6. **Select Database Edition** Choose Enterprise Edition, Standard Edition, or Standard Edition 1.

7. **Specify Installation Location** Specify the Oracle Base and Oracle Home directories.

8. **Privileged Operating System Groups** Nominate the groups that will manage the Oracle Home.

9. Perform Prerequisite Checks   Validate the environment.

10. Summary   Read the summary of the dialog.

11. Install Product   View the progress.

12. Finish   You have successfully completed the OUI dialog.

Step 9 may fail on some tests. This is unlikely on Windows, but on Linux (if you're not using an Oracle-validated version of Linux, such as OEL 5.8), you may face a number of issues. Typically, these involve kernel parameter settings and the availability of certain RPM package managers (RPMs). Every issue will be flagged as "warning" or "critical." Clicking the Fix And Check Again button will generate a script and prompt you to run it as root, which will fix many "fixable" issues (such as kernel limits). However, it cannot fix all of them. Therefore, any unfixable issues (such as missing critical RPMs) should be addressed before proceeding. If it is not possible to fix the issues, clicking the Ignore All check box will allow you to proceed, but with no guarantee that the installation will succeed.

Step 11, on Linux, includes a prompt to run the script root.sh as the root user. This script accomplishes certain tasks that require root privileges, such as creating files in /etc and changing ownership and access modes on certain files in the Oracle Home.

Silent Install and Response Files

Running OUI interactively is fine for a one-off install. However, if you are installing on multiple machines or perhaps designing a repeatable and automated procedure, it is necessary to use another technique: driving OUI with a response file. A response file is read by OUI and contains answers to all the questions posed by the interactive dialog. When using a response file, you'll usually want to disable all graphical output. This allows you to carry out installations on systems where no graphical terminal device is available, such as blade servers with no console attached.

Creating a response file from scratch is beyond the capability of most junior DBAs. However, a template response file is provided: the file db_install.rsp in the /response/ directory beneath the root of the installation software. It is well documented, with descriptions of every value required. But even veteran DBAs will try to avoid writing a response file by hand. And there is no need to because you can generate one with an interactive run of OUI. Launch OUI and go through the dialog. On the final screen you'll see a check box next to the question "Generate response file?" At this point you nominate a location for an automatically generated response file based on the preceding dialog and then cancel the install.

To run a silent install later (perhaps on a different machine), edit the generated file to match the environment and then launch OUI with the following syntax (for Windows):

```
setup.exe -silent -responseFile db_install.rsp
```

You can pass many other command-line switches to the installer. This is how to display them all in Linux:

```
./runInstaller -help
```

A particularly useful switch is –ignoreSysPrereqs, which allow a silent or interactive install to proceed even if the prerequisite checks fail.

Windows and Linux Variations

Discussing the details of platform variations is beyond the scope of the Oracle Certified Professional (OCP) syllabus. However, because it is possible that students may find the differences confusing, here is a summary of the principal differences:

- **User ID on Linux** An operating system user who will own the software must be precreated and must be a member of operating system groups to be used to own the Oracle Home and for database administration. It is customary to name the user oracle and the groups oinstall and dba. Run OUI as this user; you cannot run the OUI as root.

- **User ID on Windows** OUI must be run as a user with administration privileges, and it prompts for the user who owns the Oracle Home. If the user does not exist, it will be created.

- **Operating system groups on Linux** At least one group must be precreated, the OSDBA group. You can call it anything you want, but dba is the customary group name, and the user running the installer must be a member of this group. A second group, customarily called oinstall, should be the primary group of the user running OUI.

- **Operating system groups on Windows** The names are hard-coded and will be created by OUI. The nominated user will be made a member of these groups automatically.

- **Root scripts on Linux** At the end of the installation, a shell script must be run as the root user. This script makes certain changes that require root privileges. Execute it when prompted. Windows does not require this step because the OUI must itself have been run as a user with administration rights.

Exercise 1-1: Install the Oracle Database Software In this exercise, you will install an Oracle Home, but you won't create a database at this point.

Prepare your training system by creating appropriate directories and a user; then launch OUI and follow the wizard. The steps and prompts are slightly different between the Windows and Linux dialogs, but overall the process is similar and self-explanatory, with context-sensitive assistance available via the Help button. The following is an example of the OUI dialog for Windows, followed by a dialog from a Linux install. Of course, you must adjust the process to your own circumstances. You can use these two examples to assist you in your installation.

The Windows installation dialog was captured by running the OUI setup.exe file on a 64-bit Windows 8.0 machine. You may need to adjust the suggested responses to your environment.

1. **Configure Security Updates** Deselect the I Wish To Receive Security Updates check box. Leave the other fields blank, click Next, and then click Yes when warned about not providing an e-mail address.

2. **Download Software Update** Select the Skip Software Updates radio button and then click Next.

3. **Select Installation Option** Select the Install Database Software Only radio button and then click Next.

4. **System Class**   Select the Server Class radio button. This has no technical significance but does ensure that you will subsequently see all possible options. Click Next.

5. **Grid Installation Options**   Select the Single Instance Database Installation radio button and then click Next.

6. **Select Install Type**   Select the Advanced Install radio button and then click Next.

7. **Select Product Languages**   Add any languages you need and then click Next.

8. **Select Database Edition**   Select the Enterprise Edition radio button and then click Next.

9. **Specify Oracle Home User**   Enter the name and password of either an existing user who will own the installation or a new user to be created by OUI. A commonly used username is oracle (in all lowercase). Click Next.

10. **Specify Installation Location**   Enter an Oracle Base directory, such as C:\app\oracle, and a software location, such as C:\app\oracle\product\12.1.0\dbhome_1. Click Next.

11. **Perform Prerequisite Checks**   OUI will perform its checks. Fix any issues.

12. **Summary**   A summary of the installation will be displayed. It is possible to make changes here or to navigate back through the dialog with the Back button. Click Install to proceed.

The Linux installation dialog was captured by running the OUI runInstaller.sh file on a 64-bit Linux 5.8 machine. You may need to adjust the suggested responses to your environment.

1. **Configure Security Updates**   Deselect the I Wish To Receive Security Updates check box. Leave the other fields blank, click Next, and then click Yes when warned about not providing an e-mail address.

2. **Download Software Update**   Select the Skip Software Updates radio button and then click Next.

3. **Select Installation Option**   Select the Install Database Software Only radio button and then click Next.

4. **Grid Installation Options**   Select the Single Instance Database Installation radio button and then click Next.

5. **Select Product Languages**   Add any languages you need and then click Next.

6. **Select Database Edition**   Select the Enterprise Edition radio button and then click Next.

7. **Specify Installation Location**   Enter an Oracle Base directory on which your Linux user has full permissions, such as /u01/apporacle, and a software location within it, such as /u01/app/oracle/product/12.1.0/dbhome_1. Click Next.

8. **Privileged Operating System Groups**   Select an operating system group from each drop-down box. The list will be dependent on the group membership of the user under which you are running the OUI. Selecting dba, if available, is usually a good choice. Click Next.

9. **Perform Prerequisite Checks** OUI will perform its checks. Fix any issues.

10. **Summary** A summary of the installation will be displayed. It is possible to make changes here or to navigate back through the dialog with the Back button. Click Install to proceed.

11. **Install Product** OUI copies the software into the Oracle Home, links it, and runs various configuration scripts.

12. **Execute Configuration Scripts** A pop-up window (make sure it is not hiding behind another window!) will prompt you to run a shell script as root. Run this, accepting defaults for all the prompted values. Then click OK in the pop-up window. The installation is now complete; click Close to exit from the installer.

Two-Minute Drill

Plan for an Oracle Database Software Installation

- Create operating system groups and users.
- Create a directory beneath which the Oracle Base will exist.
- Download the appropriate version of the installation DVDs.

Install the Oracle Database Software

- Launch OUI: setup.exe (Windows) or runInstaller.sh (Linux).
- Follow the OUI dialog.

Self Test

1. Which statement best describes the relationship between the Oracle Base and the Oracle Home? (Choose the best answer.)

   A. The Oracle Base exists inside the Oracle Home.

   B. The Oracle Base can contain Oracle Homes for different products.

   C. One Oracle Base is required for each product, but versions of the product can exist in their own Oracle Homes within their Oracle Base.

   D. The Oracle Base is created when you run the orainstRoot.sh script, and it contains a pointer to the Oracle Home.

2. What does Optimal Flexible Architecture describe? (Choose the best answer.)

   A. A directory structure

   B. Distributed database systems

   C. A multitier processing architecture

   D. All of the above

3. What environment variable must be set on Linux before running the Oracle Universal Installer for an interactive installation? (Choose the best answer.)

   A. ORACLE_HOME

   B. ORACLE_BASE

   C. ORACLE_SID

   D. DISPLAY

4. If the OUI detects that a prerequisite has not been met, what can you do? (Choose the best answer.)

   A. You must cancel the installation, fix the problem, and launch OUI again.

   B. A silent install will fail; an interactive install will continue.

   C. Instruct OUI to continue (at your own risk).

   D. The options will depend on how far into the installation OUI is when the problem is detected.

5. What type of devices can OUI install an Oracle Home onto? (Choose all that apply.)

   A. Regular file systems

   B. Clustered file systems

   C. Raw devices

   D. ASM disk groups

6. Which command-line switch can be used to prevent the OUI from stopping when prerequisite tests fail? (Choose the best answer.)

   A. –silent

   B. –record

   C. –responsefile

   D. –ignoresysprereqs

7. When does an OUI inventory get created? (Choose the best answer.)

   A. Every time a new Oracle Home is created

   B. Every time a new Oracle Base is created

   C. Before the first run of the OUI

   D. During the first run of the OUI

Self Test Answers

1. ☑   B. The Oracle Base directory contains all the Oracle Homes, which can be any versions of any products.
   ☒   A, C, and D are incorrect. A is incorrect because it inverts the relationship. C is incorrect because there is no requirement for a separate base for each product. D is incorrect because it misunderstands the purpose of the orainstRoot.sh script, which is to create the oraInst.loc file, not to create the Oracle Base directory.

2. ☑ **A**. The rather grandly named Optimal Flexible Architecture is nothing more than a naming convention for directory structures.
   ☒ **B, C**, and **D** are incorrect. These answer choices are incorrect because they go way beyond OFA.

3. ☑ **D**. Without a DISPLAY set, the OUI will not be able to open any windows.
   ☒ **A, B**, and **C** are incorrect. These answer choices are incorrect because although they can be set before the OUI is launched, the OUI will prompt for values for them.

4. ☑ **C**. Perhaps not advisable, but you can certainly do this.
   ☒ **A, B**, and **D** are incorrect. **A** is incorrect because while it might be a good idea, it is not something you have to do. **B** is incorrect because the interactive installation will halt. **D** is incorrect because all prerequisites are checked at the same time.

5. ☑ **A** and **B**. The Oracle Home must exist on a file system, but it can be local or clustered.
   ☒ **C** and **D** are incorrect. Raw devices and ASM devices can be used for databases, but not for an Oracle Home.

6. ☑ **D**. The –ignoresysprereqs switch stops OUI from running the tests.
   ☒ **A, B**, and **C** are incorrect. **A** is incorrect because this switch will suppress generation of windows, not running tests. **B** is incorrect because this is the switch to generate a response file. **C** is incorrect because this is the switch to read a response file.

7. ☑ **D**. If the OUI cannot find an inventory, it will create one.
   ☒ **A, B**, and **C** are incorrect. **A** and **B** are incorrect because one inventory can manage any number of Homes in any Base. **C** is incorrect because the inventory is created at the end of the process, not the beginning.

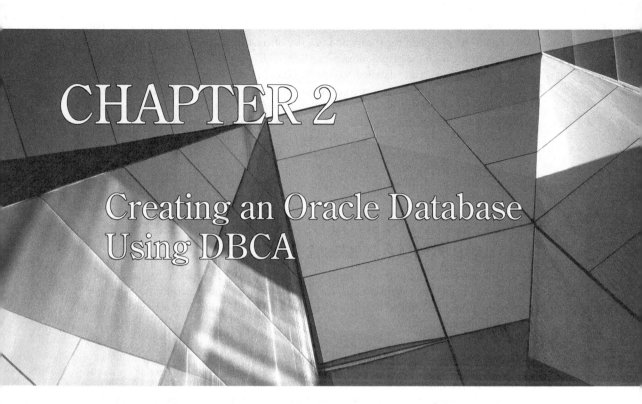

CHAPTER 2

Creating an Oracle Database Using DBCA

Exam Objectives

In this chapter, you will learn to

- 062.2.5.1 Create a Database by Using the Database Configuration Assistant (DBCA)
- 062.2.5.2 Generate Database Creation Scripts by Using DBCA
- 062.2.5.3 Manage Database Design Templates by Using DBCA
- 062.2.5.4 Configure Database Options by Using DBCA

This chapter goes through the theory and practice of creating a database—through the mechanics of creation using both the graphical user interface (GUI) and the command line. This chapter also describes how to create database templates. However, one objective that must be dealt with immediately is to demystify the process: creating a database is no big deal. Furthermore, you really do not have to worry about getting it right. Hardly anything is fixed at database-creation time. It certainly makes sense to think about how your database will be structured, its purpose, and its environment at creation time, but with one exception: everything can be changed afterward (although some changes may be awkward). As a general rule, keep things as simple as possible at this stage.

Create a Database by Using the Database Configuration Assistant

Creating a database is not difficult. The process can be quick and simple: It may take less than ten minutes, and a single two-word command will do it. However, there are some concepts you should understand before proceeding with the creation process, namely, the instance, the database, and the data dictionary.

The Instance, the Database, and the Data Dictionary

An Oracle server is an instance and a database; the two are separate but connected. The *instance* is composed of memory structures and processes in your random access memory (RAM) and on your central processing units (CPUs). Its existence is transient; it can be started and stopped. The *database* is composed of files on disk; once created, it persists until it is deleted. Creating an instance is nothing more than building the memory structures and starting the processes. Creating a database is done by the instance as a once-off operation, and the instance can then subsequently open and close the database many times. The database is inaccessible without the instance.

Within the database is a set of tables and other objects called the *data dictionary*. The data dictionary describes all the logical and physical structures in the database, including all the segments that store user data. The database creation process involves creating the bare minimum of physical structures needed to support the data dictionary and then creating the data dictionary within them.

An instance is defined by an instance parameter file. The parameter file contains directives that define (among other things) how the instance should be built in memory, including the size of the memory structures and the behavior of the background processes. After the instance has been built, it is said to be in *no mount* mode. In no mount mode, the instance exists but has not connected to a database. Indeed, the database may not have been created at this point.

All parameters, either specified by the parameter file or set implicitly, have defaults, except for the DB_NAME parameter. This parameter names the database to which the instance will connect. This name is also embedded in the controlfile. One parameter, CONTROL_FILES, tells the instance the location of the controlfile. This parameter defines the connection between the instance and the database. When the instance reads the controlfile (which it will find by reading the CONTROL_FILES parameter or by relying on the default value), if there is a mismatch in database names, the database will not mount. In mount mode, the instance has successfully connected to the controlfile. If the controlfile is damaged or nonexistent, it will be impossible to mount the database. The controlfile is small but vital.

Within the controlfile are pointers to the other files (the online redo log files and the datafiles) that make up the rest of the database. Having mounted the database, the instance can open the database by locating and opening these other files. An open database is a database where the instance has opened all the available online redo log files and datafiles. Also within the controlfile is a mapping of datafiles to tablespaces. This lets the instance identify the datafiles that make up the SYSTEM tablespace. In the SYSTEM tablespace, it will find the data dictionary. The data dictionary lets the instance resolve references to objects referred to in Structured Query Language (SQL) code to the segments in which they reside and work out where, physically, the objects are.

The creation of a database server must therefore involve these steps:

1. Create the instance.

2. Create the database.

3. Create the data dictionary.

In practice, though, there is a fourth step.

4. Make the database usable.

The data dictionary, as initially created with the database, is fully functional but unusable. It has the capability for defining and managing user data but cannot be used by normal human beings because its structure is too abstruse. Before users (or database administrators) can actually use the database, a set of views must be created on top of the data dictionary that will present it in a human-understandable form. Also, many PL/SQL packages are required to add functionality.

The data dictionary itself is created by running a set of SQL scripts that exist in the ORACLE_HOME/rdbms/admin directory. These are called by the CREATE DATABASE command. The first is sql.bsq, which then calls several other scripts. These scripts issue a series of commands that create all the tables and other objects that make up the data dictionary.

The views and other objects that make the database usable are generated with more scripts in the ORACLE_HOME/rdbms/admin directory and have a *cat* prefix. Examples of these are catalog.sql and catproc.sql, which should always be run immediately after database creation. There are many other optional "cat" scripts that will enable certain features—some of these can be run at creation time; others might be run subsequently to install the features at a later date.

Using the Database Configuration Assistant to Create a Database

These are the steps to follow to create a database:

1. Create a parameter file and (optionally) a password file.

2. Use the parameter file to build an instance in memory.

3. Issue the CREATE DATABASE command. This will generate, at a minimum, a controlfile, two online redo log files, one datafile each for the SYSTEM and SYSAUX tablespaces, and a data dictionary. The syntax does allow a lot more to be done at this point.

4. Run SQL scripts to generate the data dictionary views and the supplied PL/SQL packages.

5. Run SQL scripts to generate the code that implements Enterprise Manager Database Express as well as any options (such as Java) the database will require.

6. On Windows systems, there is an additional step because Oracle runs as a Windows service. Oracle provides a utility, oradim.exe, to assist you in creating this service.

These steps can be executed interactively from the SQL*Plus prompt or through a GUI tool, the Database Configuration Assistant (DBCA). Alternatively, you can automate the process by using scripts or DBCA with a response file.

Regardless of the platform you are running on, the easiest way to create a database is through DBCA. It creates a parameter file and a password file and then generates scripts that will start the instance, create the database, and generate the data dictionary and the data dictionary views. Alternatively, you can create the parameter file and password file by hand and then do the rest from a SQL*Plus session. Many database administrators (DBAs) combine the two techniques: They use DBCA to generate the files and scripts and then look at them and perhaps edit them before running them from SQL*Plus.

To launch DBCA on Windows, take the shortcut on the Start menu. This is an example of the navigation path: Start | Programs | Oracle – OraDB12Home1 | Configuration and Migration Tools | Database Configuration Assistant.

Note that the precise path will vary depending on the name given to the Oracle Home at install time. Alternatively, run the dbca.bat script from a CMD prompt. Following a standard installation, it will be included in your Windows search path.

To launch DBCA on Linux, first set the environment variables that should always be set for any Linux DBA session: DISPLAY, ORACLE_BASE, ORACLE_HOME, and PATH. Here is an example of a script that will do this:

```
export DISPLAY=myhost:0.0
export ORACLE_BASE=/u01/app/oracle
export ORACLE_HOME=$ORACLE_BASE/product/12.1.0/dbhome_1
export PATH=$ORACLE_HOME/bin:$PATH
```

Note that the Base and Home will vary according to choices made at install time. The variables also exist in a Windows environment but are usually defined as registry variables set by the Oracle Universal Installer (OUI) rather than shell variables. The DISPLAY variable must be set to the address of your X server. To launch DBCA, run the dbca shell script, which is located in the $ORACLE_HOME/bin directory.

 TIP Be sure to have the $ORACLE_HOME/bin directory at the start of your search path in case there are any Linux executables with the same name as Oracle executables. A well-known case in point is rman, which is the name of both an Oracle tool and a SUSE Linux utility.

Remember that (with one exception) every choice made at database creation time can be changed later but that some changes are awkward and will involve downtime. Therefore, it is not vital to get everything right—but the more you can get right, the better.

The DBCA Dialog

The DBCA dialog consists (depending on options) of about 13 steps.

Step 1: Database Operation

The radio buttons available in this first step allow you to select the type of operation you want to perform.

- **Create Database**   You can launch a dialog that will prompt you to create an instance and a database.
- **Configure Database Options**   You can adjust an existing database, perhaps by installing additional capabilities.
- **Delete Database**   You can remove any existing instances and databases.
- **Manage Templates**   A template is a stored, preconfigured database. Some templates are supplied, or you can create your own from an existing database.
- **Manage Pluggable Databases**   Pluggable databases are a new feature in 12*c* and are beyond the scope of the Oracle Certified Associate (OCA) curriculum.

Step 2: Creation Mode

The Create A Database With Default Configuration option gives you access to a small subset of DBCA's capabilities. The Advanced Mode option, on the other hand, gives you access to all the possibilities.

Step 3: Database Template

A template is a stored version of a preconfigured database from which you can generate a new database. Creating a database from a template is much faster than creating it from nothing, but not all options are configurable. Oracle supplies two demonstration templates: a general-purpose template, which is configured for nothing in particular, and a data warehouse template, which is supposedly optimized for query processing rather than transaction processing. The Custom Database option generates a dialog that will give you complete freedom in how the database is configured, with no predefined limits.

Step 4: Database Identification

The database must have a global database name. The global name consists of a database name and, optionally, a database domain. The database name is embedded in the controlfile, will be specified as the DB_NAME instance parameter, and must be unique on the server machine. The name may be up to eight characters long, including alphanumeric characters, underscores (_), number signs (#), and dollar signs ($), and the first character must be alphabetic. Case sensitivity may vary from one platform to another. The database name is an example of a value you want to get right; it can be changed later, but doing so requires downtime.

The database domain may be up to 128 characters long, including alphanumeric characters and the number sign (#). Dots can be used as separators for the different elements of the domain. The domain is used for the DB_DOMAIN instance parameter. Note that although it is possible to construct a global name that resembles the fully qualified domain names (FQDNs) used on Transmission Control Protocol (TCP) networks, there is no relationship between them.

The second required value is the system identifier (SID). This is the name of the Oracle instance to be created and is used for the ORACLE_SID parameter. There is no reason for this to be the same as the DB_NAME value, but for the sake of your sanity, you will usually keep it the same. It must be unique on the database server machine.

TIP Using global names with a domain may help distinguish databases on different machines that happen to have the same DB_NAME. Many DBAs will append the machine's FQDN as the DB_DOMAIN for this purpose. But there is no need to use a DB_DOMAIN at all. Some DBAs consider domains to be a liability, possibly because they can cause confusion due to their impact on database links and the database global name.

Step 5: Management Options

Use of Oracle Enterprise Manager (OEM) is entirely optional. If you want to use it, you have two possibilities: Enterprise Manager Database Express and Enterprise Manager Cloud Control. Enterprise Manager Database Express is a version of OEM that is configured within the one managed database. If you install a second database, you will require a separate instance of Database Express, configured within that database. Enterprise Manager Cloud Control is Oracle's universal management system, which usually runs on a dedicated machine (or machines) with agents running on each target server. If you have a Cloud Control installation available, DBCA needs to know how to log on to it.

Step 6: Database Credentials

In this step you provide passwords for the SYS and SYSTEM schemas. SYS is the schema that owns the data dictionary itself, and the password is written out to the external password file. The SYS user is very special, and the password may be required for some critical functions (such as startup and shutdown). The SYSTEM schema is really just a user like any other, but it is given many powerful privileges.

Oracle best practice is that these passwords should be at least eight characters, including a mix of upper- and lowercase letters and at least one digit. The characters are any included in your database character set (detailed later in the chapter). If you specify a password that is considered too simple, DBCA will complain but will let you proceed nonetheless.

A Windows variation at this point is that you will be prompted for the password of the operating system account that owns the Oracle Home.

TIP It is often considered best practice to stick to a small range of characters for the passwords (upper- and lowercase letters, digits, and the more common punctuation marks) and to begin with a leading alphabetic character. Some command shell interpreters may have problems with the more unusual characters.

Step 7: Storage Locations

The database may be created on either an Automatic Storage Management disk group or in a file system directory. Either way, you can nominate the destination or let DBCA decide where to store the database files, based on its derived value for the ORACLE_BASE environment variable. Both storage types can also optionally use Oracle Managed Files (OMF). OMF lets Oracle take control of naming all your database files and constructing a suitable directory structure within which to store them.

The Recovery Related Files section of this step lets you nominate a Fast Recovery Area to be used as a default location for backups and other files related to recovery and also to enable the archive log mode of operation. Most (if not all) production databases will run in archive log mode, but it can be enabled at any time subsequent to database creation.

Step 8: Database Options

Various options are separately licensed and should be selected or deselected according to your license. The Sample Schemas tab will cause DBCA to install the demonstration schemas into their own tablespace.

Step 9: Initialization Parameters

There are more than 300 publicly visible initialization parameters and thousands more so-called hidden parameters. DBCA provides prompts for the bare minimum, with a link to an editor where you can see its defaults for the others and set any you want. Step 9 of the DBCA dialog prompts either for an overall total for memory to be used by the instance or to specify values for the System Global Area (SGA) and the Program Global Area (PGA). SGA is used by the instance and is accessible from all sessions; it is divided into many substructures, some of which can be individually tuned. PGA is divided into private memory areas for each connected session and process. This stage of the DBCA dialog sets some of the memory parameters.

The Sizing tab shows two parameters: DB_BLOCK_SIZE (although the prompt is just Block Size) and PROCESSES. DB_BLOCK_SIZE is critical; it is the one parameter that can never be changed after database creation. This is because it specifies the size of the blocks into which the SYSTEM tablespace datafile is formatted. The SYSTEM tablespace stores the data dictionary, and changing it would require re-creating the data dictionary, which would be equivalent to creating a new database. The default DB_BLOCK_SIZE is 8KB. The legal values are 2KB, 4KB, 8KB, 16KB, and (on some platforms) 32KB.

The Character Sets tab lets you choose the database character set and the alternative national character set. The database character set is used for the data dictionary and all character data types except NVARCHAR2, NCHAR, and NCLOB, which use the national character set. It is theoretically possible to change the character set at any time after database creation, but this is a potentially dangerous process and not one on which to embark lightly. Many DBAs believe that best practice is not to use the default (which is derived from your operating system) but to use Unicode—specifically, AL32UTF8.

The Connection Mode tab lets you configure the shared server. This topic is discussed in Chapter 14.

TIP No DBA has ever been fired for choosing 8KB, the default value, as the DB_BLOCK_SIZE value. There is rarely any reason to use anything else. But the default character set may well be inappropriate, particularly if you are ever likely to have clients using languages other than American English.

Step 10: Creation Options

In this step, the Create Database check box will launch the actual creation. The Save As A Database Template check box will generate a stored template based on the preceding dialog, which can subsequently be used many times (this is selected at step 3). Finally, the Generate Database Creation Scripts check box will generate and save a set of scripts that can be run manually to create the database.

Step 11: Prerequisite Checks

DBCA runs a few brief "sanity checks" to confirm that the creation will work. If there are any failures, they really should be addressed before proceeding. However, you can choose to ignore them and proceed regardless.

TIP The DBCA validation checks are not comprehensive. Errors may show up only during step 13. Typical of these are memory issues. For instance, if at step 9 you specify Automatic Memory Management with a total that is more than the shared memory configured on your system, you will not get an error at this point.

Step 12: Summary

The Summary window shows what DBCA intends to do. Scan through the report, and if you see anything you do not like, this is a good time to use the Back button and make changes.

Step 13: Progress Page

The Progress Page window shows the creation of the scripts (if they were requested) and then the various stages of database creation. This may take 10 minutes, or it may take an hour or more. The difference is largely dependent on whether a template was used, what options were selected, and the hardware specifications.

Exercise 2-1: Create a Database with DBCA Using the graphical DBCA tool, create a database. Repeat the exercise as many times as you can, deleting any previously created databases first if you are short on RAM or disk space. It is important to become comfortable with the process and to experiment with the various options presented by the dialog.

Some of the responses will vary depending on whether the platform is Windows, Linux, or something else. The variations will be obvious, and most commonly have to do with directory naming conventions. Here are the steps to follow:

1. Log on to the server machine.

   Connect to the server as the operating system user who did the installation. The standard account name is oracle.

2. Launch DBCA.

From a command shell, make sure you have the appropriate environment variables set. The following is a typical dialog on a Linux system using the bash shell:

```
db121a $
db121a $ export DISPLAY=192.168.56.1:0.0
db121a $ xclock
db121a $ export ORACLE_BASE=/u01/app/oracle
db121a $ export ORACLE_HOME=$ORACLE_BASE/product/12.1.0/dbhome_1
db121a $ export PATH=$ORACLE_HOME/bin:$PATH
db121a $ which dbca
/u01/app/oracle/product/12.1.0/dbhome_1/bin/dbca
db121a $ dbca
```

The DISPLAY variable is set to point to the address of your X server (typically your PC). Test it by running any X program, such as the X-Clock. If you are running on the console or perhaps in a VNC desktop, this will not be necessary. Next, the ORACLE_BASE value is set and assumes an Optimal Flexible Architecture (OFA) installation (binaries owned by user oracle). ORACLE_HOME and PATH continue the OFA standard. Using the which utility confirms that dbca is on the search path, so launch it.

On Windows, it may be possible to find a link to DBCA in the Start menu and run it relying on variables set in the registry. Alternatively, you could control everything manually from a command prompt, like so:

```
c:\> set ORACLE_BASE=c:\app\oracle
c:\> set ORACLE_HOME=%ORACLE_BASE%\product\12.1.0\dbhome_1
c:\> set PATH=%ORACLE_HOME%\bin;%PATH%
c:\> where dbca
c:\app\oracle\product\12.1.0\dbhome_1\BIN\dbca.bat
c:\> dbca
```

3. Respond to the prompts as follows:

A. Select the Create Database radio button. Click Next.

B. Select the Advanced Mode radio button. Click Next.

C. Select the Custom Database radio button. Click Next.

Note that, at this point, depending on whether the Grid Infrastructure product has already been installed on the server, you may get a prompt regarding Oracle Restart. Ignore this and continue.

D. Specify both the Global Database Name and SID values as orcl121. Click Next.

E. Select the Configure Enterprise Manager (EM) Database Express check box. Click Next.

F. Select the radio button Use The Same Administrative Password For All Accounts and enter **Oracle121**. Click Next.

G. Select File System in the Storage Type drop-down box, and select the radio button Use Database File Locations From Template. Leave everything else at the default. This will cause DBCA to create both the database and the Fast Recovery Area beneath the ORACLE_BASE. Click Next.

H. On the Database Components tab, leave everything at the default. Click the Sample Schemas tab and select the Sample Schemas check box. Click Next.

I. Acceptable memory settings will depend on your environment, and the default may or may not be suitable. These values usually work, even on very low-spec systems. On the Memory tab, select the Typical radio button, set the value of Memory Size (SGA and PGA) to 640MB, and deselect the Use Automatic Memory Management check box.

On the Character Sets tab, select the Use Unicode (AL32UTF8) radio button. Click Next.

J. Select the check boxes for both Create Database and Generate Database Creation Scripts. Note the directory where the scripts will be created. Click Next.

K. This should not require any input.

L. Study the summary. Click Finish.

M. The scripts will be generated, followed by a small modal window telling you where they are (if you don't see this window, make sure that it isn't hiding beneath something else). Click OK.

As the wizards run, you will notice that the first two, which create the instance and the database, complete in just a few minutes. The others, which create the data dictionary views and the various components, will take much longer.

On completion, you will be presented with a success window that shows the uniform resource locator (URL) for accessing Enterprise Manager Database Express. It will resemble this:

http://db121a.example.com:5500/em

Note this URL for future use.

4. After the installation, confirm that you can log on to the newly created database using SQL*Plus.

From an operating system prompt, set your ORACLE_SID environment variable to the name of the database instance, and then log on and off, as in this example for Windows:

```
c:\> set ORACLE_SID=orcl121
c:\> sqlplus / as sysdba
SQL*Plus: Release 12.1.0.0.2 Beta on Sat Apr 6 12:10:42 2013
Copyright (c) 1982, 2012, Oracle.  All rights reserved.
Connected to:
Oracle Database 12c Enterprise Edition Release 12.1.0.0.2 - 64bit Beta
With the Partitioning, OLAP, Data Mining and Real Application Testing
options
SQL> exit
Disconnected from Oracle Database 12c Enterprise Edition
Release 12.1.0.0.2 - 64bit Beta
With the Partitioning, OLAP, Data Mining and Real Application Testing
options
c:\>
```

Alternatively, use this example for Linux:

```
db121a orcl121$ db121a orcl121$ export ORACLE_SID=orcl121
db121a orcl121$ sqlplus / as sysdba
SQL*Plus: Release 12.1.0.0.2 Beta on Sat Apr 6 14:08:35 2013
Copyright (c) 1982, 2012, Oracle.  All rights reserved.
Connected to:
Oracle Database 12c Enterprise Edition Release 12.1.0.0.2 - 64bit Beta
With the Partitioning, OLAP, Data Mining and Real Application Testing
options
SQL> exit
Disconnected from Oracle Database 12c Enterprise Edition
Release 12.1.0.0.2 - 64bit Beta
With the Partitioning, OLAP, Data Mining and Real Application Testing
options
db121a orcl121$
```

5. Repeat *ad infinitum.*

Go through this exercise as often as you can, making your own variations, until you are happy with all the options. At Step 1: Database Operation, you may want to select the Delete Database radio button to remove the previous creation.

Generate Database Creation Scripts by Using DBCA

There is no reason not to create a database interactively with DBCA, but in many situations it is better to create a database from the command line. Why? Perhaps for one of the following reasons:

- The server machine may not have graphics capability.
- Change control procedures may require tested scripts.
- You may have to create a dozen identical databases.
- You do not want to sit in front of a screen responding to prompts.

Whatever the reason, it is straightforward to create a database manually, if you have the scripts. The easiest way to write the scripts is to let DBCA do it for you.

Generating the Scripts

To generate the scripts, launch DBCA and go through the dialog, taking whatever options are appropriate. At step 10, select the appropriate check box and choose a directory. The default location is beneath ORACLE_BASE. The typical location for a database named orcl121 on Windows would be as follows:

```
c:\app\oracle\admin\orcl121\scripts
```

On Linux, the typical location would be as follows:

```
/u01/app/oracle/admin/orcl121/scripts
```

Whatever the platform, the scripts have the same structure: shell script named after the database (for example, orcl121.sh for Linux, orcl121.bat for Windows) that does some operating system (OS) work and then launches SQL*Plus to run a SQL script (called oracle121.sql). The SQL script drives the rest of the database creation. Studying these scripts and the scripts they call is instructive.

The Creation Scripts

The starting point is the shell script. Take a look at a Linux example:

```
#!/bin/sh
OLD_UMASK='umask'
umask 0027
mkdir -p /u01/app/oracle/admin/orcl121/adump
mkdir -p /u01/app/oracle/admin/orcl121/dpdump
mkdir -p /u01/app/oracle/admin/orcl121/pfile
mkdir -p /u01/app/oracle/audit
mkdir -p /u01/app/oracle/cfgtoollogs/dbca/orcl121
mkdir -p /u01/app/oracle/fast_recovery_area
mkdir -p /u01/app/oracle/fast_recovery_area/orcl121
mkdir -p /u01/app/oracle/oradata/orcl121
mkdir -p /u01/app/oracle/product/12.1.0/dbhome_1/dbs
umask ${OLD_UMASK}
ORACLE_SID=orcl121; export ORACLE_SID
PATH=$ORACLE_HOME/bin:$PATH; export PATH
echo You should Add this entry in the /etc/oratab:
orcl121:/u01/app/oracle/product/12.1.0/dbhome_1:Y
/u01/app/oracle/product/12.1.0/dbhome_1/bin/sqlplus /nolog
@/u01/app/oracle/admin/orcl121/scripts/orcl121.sql
```

This creates a few directories, using values calculated from the ORACLE_BASE and ORACLE_HOME environment variables, provided in the DBCA dialog, or from defaults with appropriate access permissions. It then concludes with the call to SQL*Plus to launch the SQL script orcl121.sql. A variation on Windows will be calls to the ORADIM utility that creates the Windows service under which the instance will run.

The driving SQL script will vary greatly, depending on the options taken in the DBCA dialog. Here is one example:

```
set verify off
ACCEPT sysPassword CHAR PROMPT 'Enter new password for SYS: ' HIDE
ACCEPT systemPassword CHAR PROMPT 'Enter new password for SYSTEM: ' HIDE
host /u01/app/oracle/product/12.1.0/dbhome_1/bin/orapwd file=/u01/app/oracle/
product/12.1.0/dbhome_1/dbs/orapworcl121

force=y extended=y
@/u01/app/oracle/admin/orcl121/scripts/CreateDB.sql
@/u01/app/oracle/admin/orcl121/scripts/CreateDBFiles.sql
@/u01/app/oracle/admin/orcl121/scripts/CreateDBCatalog.sql
@/u01/app/oracle/admin/orcl121/scripts/sampleSchema.sql
@/u01/app/oracle/admin/orcl121/scripts/apex.sql
@/u01/app/oracle/admin/orcl121/scripts/postDBCreation.sql
@/u01/app/oracle/admin/orcl121/scripts/lockAccount.sql
```

The ACCEPT commands prompt for passwords for the SYS and SYSTEM schemas. Then the script invokes a host shell to run the orapwd utility. This utility creates the external password file with a name that is platform specific. On Linux, it will be $ORACLE_HOME/dbs/ orapw<DBNAME> (where <DBNAME> is the name of the database), and on Windows, it will be %ORACLE_HOME%\database\PWD<DBNAME>.ora.

Following this is a set of calls to other SQL scripts, beginning with CreateDB.sql.

```
SET VERIFY OFF
connect "SYS"/"&&sysPassword" as SYSDBA
set echo on
spool /u01/app/oracle/admin/orcl121/scripts/CreateDB.log append
startup nomount pfile="/u01/app/oracle/admin/orcl121/scripts/init.ora";
CREATE DATABASE "orcl121"
MAXINSTANCES 8
MAXLOGHISTORY 1
MAXLOGFILES 16
MAXLOGMEMBERS 3
MAXDATAFILES 100
DATAFILE '/u01/app/oracle/oradata/orcl121/system01.dbf' SIZE 700M
REUSE AUTOEXTEND ON NEXT  10240K MAXSIZE UNLIMITED
EXTENT MANAGEMENT LOCAL
SYSAUX DATAFILE '/u01/app/oracle/oradata/orcl121/sysaux01.dbf' SIZE 550M
REUSE AUTOEXTEND ON NEXT  10240K MAXSIZE UNLIMITED
SMALLFILE DEFAULT TEMPORARY TABLESPACE TEMP

TEMPFILE '/u01/app/oracle/oradata/orcl121/temp01.dbf' SIZE 20M
REUSE AUTOEXTEND ON NEXT  640K MAXSIZE UNLIMITED
SMALLFILE UNDO TABLESPACE "UNDOTBS1"

DATAFILE  '/u01/app/oracle/oradata/orcl121/undotbs01.dbf' SIZE 200M
REUSE AUTOEXTEND ON NEXT  5120K MAXSIZE UNLIMITED
CHARACTER SET AL32UTF8
NATIONAL CHARACTER SET AL16UTF16
LOGFILE GROUP 1 ('/u01/app/oracle/oradata/orcl121/redo01.log') SIZE 51200K,
GROUP 2 ('/u01/app/oracle/oradata/orcl121/redo02.log') SIZE 51200K,
GROUP 3 ('/u01/app/oracle/oradata/orcl121/redo03.log') SIZE 51200K
USER SYS IDENTIFIED BY "&&sysPassword"

USER SYSTEM IDENTIFIED BY "&&systemPassword";
spool off
```

The second line connects as user SYS using the supplied password. The fifth line starts the database in no mount mode using a parameter file named init.ora. This file will be populated with parameters set by default or specified in the DBCA dialog. The next command (which continues to the end of the file) creates the database.

NOTE Remember the modes: The nomount command means "build the memory structures and start the processes."

Following the CREATE DATABASE "orcl121" line are some settings for limits (such as MAXDATAFILES=100, meaning that this database will be restricted to 100 datafiles) and then clauses for four tablespaces:

- The SYSTEM tablespace (where the data dictionary lives) will be in a datafile named system01.dbf with a size of 700MB.

- The SYSAUX tablespace (objects that are not associated with the data dictionary but are closely related) will be in a datafile named sysaux01.dbf with a size of 550MB.

- A default temporary tablespace (for temporary data—space needed by sessions for, one hopes, only a brief period) named TEMP will be in tempfile temp01.dbf, with a size of 20MB. An undo tablespace (used for undo segments, which are necessary to ensure transactional consistency) named UNDOTBS1 will use the datafile undotbs01.dbf, with a size of 200MB.

Then the character sets for the database and national language are specified. In the example, they are Unicode. The LOGFILE section specifies that the database should have three online log file groups, each consisting of one file (the log file member) that's 50MB in size. Finally, the passwords for SYS and SYSTEM are set.

This database creation command takes only a couple minutes to run. All it does is create the minimal structures necessary for a database, most importantly the data dictionary. Control then returns to the calling SQL script, which (in the example) launches more scripts.

- CreateDBFiles.sql creates a tablespace called USERS, to be used as the default tablespace for storing permanent objects (such as tables).

- CreateDBCatalog.sql calls a set of scripts to generate the required views onto the data dictionary and the various supplied PL/SQL packages.

- Several scripts (JServer.sql through apex.sql) then generate various options that were selected in the DBCA dialog.

- postDBCreation.sql runs anything necessary immediately after creation, such as applying bundled patches and converting the pfile to an spfile.

- lockAccount.sql locks all preseeded accounts (with a few exceptions) and finally restarts the database.

The scripts generated and their contents vary greatly, depending on the DBCA dialog. For example, if at step 3 you chose to create a database from a template, the whole process is much simpler because the database does not need to be created, and most of the work is done via calls to the RMAN Recovery Manager procedures, which in effect restore a database from a backup in the template.

The Initialization Parameter File

To start the database instance, DBCA must create an initialization parameter file. This is generated whether you select the option to create a database or to generate scripts. The file is generated in the same directory as the other scripts and is nominated on the STARTUP command in the CreateDB.sql script.

```
startup nomount pfile="/u01/app/oracle/admin/orcl121/scripts/init.ora";
```

Here is the file generated by the dialog from Exercise 2-1 (comment lines removed for brevity):

```
db_block_size=8192
open_cursors=300
db_domain=""
db_name="orcl121"
control_files=("/u01/app/oracle/oradata/orcl121/control01.ctl",
"/u01/app/oracle/fast_recovery_area/orcl121/control02.ctl")
db_recovery_file_dest="/u01/app/oracle/fast_recovery_area"
db_recovery_file_dest_size=5061476352
compatible=12.0.0.0.0
diagnostic_dest=/u01/app/oracle
processes=300
sga_target=503316480
audit_file_dest="/u01/app/oracle/admin/orcl121/adump"
audit_trail=db
remote_login_passwordfile=EXCLUSIVE
dispatchers="(PROTOCOL=TCP) (SERVICE=orcl121XDB)"
pga_aggregate_target=167772160
undo_tablespace=UNDOTBS1
```

All these parameters will be covered in later chapters. The file has just 16 parameters specified out of hundreds and is the bare minimum needed to get a typical database running. Many more parameters will usually be added subsequently according to the requirements for the environment, scale, and performance.

Exercise 2-2: Generate Database Creation Scripts by Using DBCA   Use DBCA to generate several sets of database creation scripts. Perform as many iterations of this as you want, supplying a different database name and SID each time and selecting different options. Here are the steps to follow:

1. Launch DBCA. Respond to the prompts as follows:

    A. Select the Create Database radio button. Click Next.

    B. Select the radio button Advanced Mode. If you select Create A Database With Default Configuration, you do not get a prompt to generate scripts. Click Next.

    C. Select the radio button General Purpose Or Transaction Processing. Click Next.

    D. Specify the value **gpdb** for both Global Database Name and SID. Click Next.

    E. Deselect everything. Click Next.

    F. Enter the passwords as **Oracle121**. Click Next.

    G. Choose Storage Type: File System. Leave everything else at the default. Click Next.

    H. Leave everything at the default. Click Next.

    I. Leave everything at the default. Click Next.

    J. Deselect the check boxes Create Database and Save As A Database Template. Select the check box Generate Database Creation Scripts. Note the destination directory. Click Next.

    K. No input needed.

    L. Study the summary. Note that the install from a template will include all the options that were prompted for in the previous exercise and will also have values for various parameters. Click Finish.

    M. The scripts will be generated. Click OK and then Close.

2. Study the scripts.

Attempt to reverse-engineer the creation process. Note that the process is much simpler when using a template. Compare the scripts generated by this exercise with those generated by the previous exercise.

3. Repeat.

And repeat again, with variations. It is vital to become familiar with the DBCA dialog and with the scripts that it generates.

Manage Database Design Templates by Using DBCA

A *template* is a stored definition of a database. This definition can be subsequently used to create any number of databases, and it's portable across platforms. Templates come in one of two forms:

- **Structure only** A structure-only template contains the structural information (database options selected, storage details, initialization parameters) but does not include the actual datafiles. When this template is used, the database will be created from nothing. It is not possible for any user-defined data to be included.

- **Structure and data** A structure-and-data template also includes the datafiles. Databases created from this template will be identical to the database from which the template was generated, as of the time of generation.

Templates are managed through DBCA. If at step 1 of the DBCA dialog you choose the radio button for Manage Templates, you will be prompted whether to delete a template or create one from one of three sources:

- An already existing template
- An existing database, structure only
- An existing database, structure and data

The template or database must already exist on the machine from which DBCA is running. Note that the template creation from a running database will require a restart of the source database if the template includes datafiles, but not if it is structure only.

The DBCA dialog is perfectly straightforward. You are prompted for the source and type of the template and, if it includes datafiles, for the location of the file that will store the compressed database. Once the template has been created, it will be visible as a source for a new database at step 3 of the DBCA dialog.

The underlying storage for a template is from files in the ORACLE_HOME/assistants/dbca/templates directory. Copying these files to another Oracle Home will make the template available there.

Exercise 2-3: Manage Database Design Templates by Using DBCA   Use DBCA to create a template from the database created in this chapter's first exercise. These are the steps to follow:

1. Launch DBCA. Respond to the prompts as follows:

   A. Select the Manage Templates radio button. Click Next.

   B. Select the radio buttons Create A Database Template and From An Existing Database (Structure As Well As Data). Click Next.

   C. Select orcl121 from the Database Instance drop-down box. Click Next.

   D. Give the template a name and description. Note that the name is used for the name of the template datafile in ORACLE_HOME/assistants/dbca/templates. Click Next.

   E. Select the radio button for converting the file locations to use OFA structure. This is usually the best option because it makes it simpler to use the template on another machine with a different file system. Click Next.

   F. Note the summary information. Click Finish.

   G. The template will be created, restarting the source database if it is running. This is necessary for the copy of the datafiles to be consistent; the copy is made with the database in mount mode. Click OK and then Close.

2. Use the template.

   Use the template (if you want) to create a database. Launch DBCA and respond to the prompts as follows:

   A. Select the radio button Create Database. Click Next.

   B. Select the radio button Advanced Mode. Click Next.

   C. The list of templates presented will include the newly created template. Note that it does include datafiles. Select its radio button, and click the Show Details button. This will generate the equivalent of the summary information previously displayed when the source database was created. Study this and then dismiss the window.

3. Exit DBCA. Click the Cancel button and then confirm to exit.

Configure Database Options by Using DBCA

The final topic on database creation is modifying databases subsequent to creation. The concept to hang onto is that a database option, generally speaking, is a combination of executable code in the Oracle Home and necessary objects (such as tables and PL/SQL procedures) in the database. The software installation will have installed the executable code. But for any one database running off that Home, the options will be enabled only if the objects have been created. The DBCA database creation prompts for which options to install, which determines the scripts called by the driving database creation script. It will by now be apparent why when using a template with datafiles it is not possible to control the options: They either will or will not have existed in the database from which the template was generated.

Using DBCA to configure options causes DBCA to generate calls to scripts that will install options in the database. It is not possible to uninstall options through DBCA. To see the installed options, log on to the database and query the DBA_REGISTRY view. This is an example:

```
orcl121> select comp_name,version,status from dba_registry order by 1;
COMP_NAME                             VERSION           STATUS
------------------------------------- ----------------- ------
OLAP Catalog                          12.1.0.0.2        VALID
Oracle Application Express            4.1.1.00.23       VALID
Oracle Database Catalog Views         12.1.0.0.2        VALID
Oracle Database Packages and Types    12.1.0.0.2        VALID
Oracle Expression Filter              12.1.0.0.2        VALID
5 rows selected.
orcl121>
```

Exercise 2-4: Configure Database Options by Using DBCA   In this exercise, you'll use DBCA to add an option that was not selected for the original database creation. Here are the steps to follow:

1. Confirm the list of options installed.

   From an operating system prompt, log on to the database and run this query:

   ```
   select comp_name from dba_registry;
   ```

2. Launch DBCA. Respond to the prompts as follows:

   A. Select the Configure Database Options radio button. Click Next.

   B. Select the radio button for the orcl21 database. Click Next.

   C. DBCA presents the list of components given at creation time with those previously selected grayed out and any remaining available for selection. Note that it is not possible to add the sample schemas with this method.

   Select the check box Oracle Label Security. Click Next.

   D. Deselect the check box Oracle Database Vault. Click Next.

   E. Leave everything at the default. Click Next.

   F. The summary will show what is to be installed. Click Finish.

   G. The option will install. Click OK and Close.

3. Confirm the installation.

   Rerun the query against DBA_REGISTRY and note that Label Security is now an installed component.

Two-Minute Drill

Create a Database by Using the Database Configuration Assistant

- DBCA is written in Java and requires a graphical display.
- The dialog prompts for all necessary information to create an instance and a database.
- At the conclusion of the creation, the database is ready for use.

Generate Database Creation Scripts by Using DBCA

- The generation includes a shell script that calls a set of SQL scripts.
- Also generated are a parameter file and a password file.
- The scripts can optionally be edited and then run manually.

Manage Database Design Templates by Using DBCA

- A template is a saved database definition from which more databases can be created.
- Templates include structural information and, optionally, datafiles.
- A structure-only template cannot include references to user objects.
- A structure-and-data template permits only minimal changes at creation time.

Configure Database Options by Using DBCA

- Options are installed by running scripts against an existing database.
- It is not possible to uninstall options through DBCA.

Self Test

1. Which of these operations can be accomplished with DBCA? (Choose all that apply.)
   - A. Create a database
   - B. Remove a database
   - C. Upgrade a database
   - D. Add database options
   - E. Remove database options

2. To create a database, in what mode must the instance be? (Choose the best answer.)
   - A. Not started
   - B. Started in NOMOUNT mode
   - C. Started in MOUNT mode
   - D. Started in OPEN mode

3. Several actions are necessary to create a database. Place these in the correct order:

   1. Create the data dictionary views.

   2. Create the parameter file.

   3. Create the password file.

   4. Issue the CREATE DATABASE command.

   5. Issue the STARTUP command.

   (Choose the best answer.)

   A. 2, 3, 5, 4, 1

   B. 3, 5, 2, 4, 1

   C. 5, 3, 4, 2, 1

   D. 2, 3, 1, 4, 5

4. What instance parameter cannot be changed after database creation? (Choose the best answer.)

   A. All instance parameters can be changed after database creation.

   B. All instance parameters can be changed after database creation if it is done while the instance is in MOUNT mode.

   C. CONTROL_FILES.

   D. DB_BLOCK_SIZE.

5. What files are created by the CREATE DATABASE command? (Choose all that apply.)

   A. The controlfile

   B. The server parameter file

   C. The online redo log files

   D. The password file

   E. The static initialization parameter file

   F. The SYSAUX tablespace datafile

   G. The SYSTEM tablespace datafile

6. What will happen if you do not run the catalog.sql and catproc.sql scripts after creating a database? (Choose the best answer.)

   A. It will not be possible to open the database.

   B. It will not be possible to create any user tables.

   C. It will not be possible to use PL/SQL.

   D. It will not be possible to query the data dictionary views.

   E. It will not be possible to connect as any user other than SYS.

7. What tools can be used to manage templates?(Choose the best answer.)

   A. The Database Configuration Assistant

   B. The Database Upgrade Assistant

   C. SQL*Plus

   D. Database Express

   E. The Oracle Universal Installer

8. At what point can you not choose or change the database character set? (Choose the best answer.)

   A. At database creation time, if you are using a DBCA template

   B. At database creation time, if you are using a DBCA template that includes datafiles

   C. At database creation time, if you are not using a DBCA template

   D. After database creation, using DBCA to install options

9. If there are several databases created off the same Oracle Home, how will Database Express be configured? (Choose the best answer.)

   A. Database Express will give access to all the databases created from the one Oracle Home through one URL.

   B. Database Express will give access to each database through different ports.

   C. Database Express needs to be configured in only one database and can then be used to connect to all of them.

   D. Database Express can manage only one database per Oracle Home.

10. The SYSAUX tablespace is mandatory. What will happen if you attempt to issue a CREATE DATABASE command that does not specify a datafile for the SYSAUX tablespace? (Choose the best answer.)

    A. The command will fail.

    B. The command will succeed, but the database will be inoperable until the SYSAUX tablespace is created.

    C. A default SYSAUX tablespace and datafile will be created.

    D. The SYSAUX objects will be created in the SYSTEM tablespace.

11. What files are generated when you choose the option Generate Database Creation Scripts in the Database Configuration Assistant? (Choose all that apply.)

    A. A shell script

    B. SQL scripts

    C. A parameter file

    D. A password file

    E. A response file

Self Test Answers

1. ☑ **A**, **B**, and **D**. DBCA can create and remove databases and also install options into existing databases.

☒ **C** and **E** are incorrect. A database upgrade would require the Database Upgrade Assistant (DBUA), not DBCA. Removing options cannot be done through any wizard. It is a manual process.

2. ☑ **B**. The instance must be running before you create a database.

☒ **A**, **C**, and **D** are incorrect. The instance must be started, but it cannot be mounted (because there is no controlfile) or opened (because there are no datafiles).

3. ☑ **A**. This is the correct sequence (although 2 and 3 could be done the other way round).

☒ **B**, **C**, and **D** are incorrect. Those sequences are not possible.

4. ☑ **D**. This is the one parameter that can never be changed after creation.

☒ **A**, **B**, and **C** are incorrect. **A** and **B** are incorrect because DB_BLOCK_SIZE cannot be changed no matter when you try to do it. **C** is incorrect because the CONTROL_FILES parameter can certainly be changed, although this will require a shutdown and restart.

5. ☑ **A**, **C**, **F**, and **G**. All of these will always be created, by default, if they are not specified.

☒ **B**, **D**, and **E** are incorrect. **B** and **D** are incorrect because these should exist before the instance is started. **E** is incorrect because the conversion of the static parameter file to a dynamic parameter file occurs, optionally, only after the database is created.

6. ☑ **D**. The database will function, but without the data dictionary views and PL/SQL packages created by these scripts, it will be unusable.

☒ **A**, **B**, **C**, and **E** are incorrect. **A** is incorrect because the database will open; in fact, it must be open to run the scripts. **B** is incorrect because tables and other objects can certainly be created. **C** is incorrect because PL/SQL will be available; it is the supplied packages that will be missing. **E** is incorrect because although the scripts need to be run by SYS, you can connect as other users.

7. ☑ **A**. DBCA is the only tool that can manage templates.

☒ **B**, **C**, **D**, and **E** are incorrect. These are all incorrect because only DBCA offers template management.

8. ☑ **D**. It is not possible to change character sets after database creation with DBCA. Character sets are not installed as options.

☒ **A**, **B**, and **C** are incorrect. **A** and **B** are incorrect because templates are not relevant. If the template includes datafiles, DBCA will change the character set behind the scenes. **C** is incorrect because creation without a template gives you complete control, including your choice of character set.

9. ☑ **B.** Database Express can be used for each database and will be configured with a different port for each one.

☒ **A, C,** and **D** are incorrect. **A** is incorrect because this would require Cloud Control. **C** is incorrect because Database Express must be installed in every database that will use it. **D** is incorrect because although a Database Express instance is for only one database, every database can have its own.

10. ☑ **C.** There are defaults for everything, including the SYSAUX tablespace and datafile definitions.

☒ **A, B,** and **D** are incorrect. **A** is incorrect because the command will succeed. **B** and **D** are incorrect because these are not the way the defaults work.

11. ☑ **A, B, C,** and **D.** One shell script is generated that calls a set of SQL scripts. There is also a password file to allow SYSDBA connections and a parameter file to start the instance.

☒ **E** is incorrect because response files are generated by the Oracle Universal Installer, not by the Configuration Assistant.

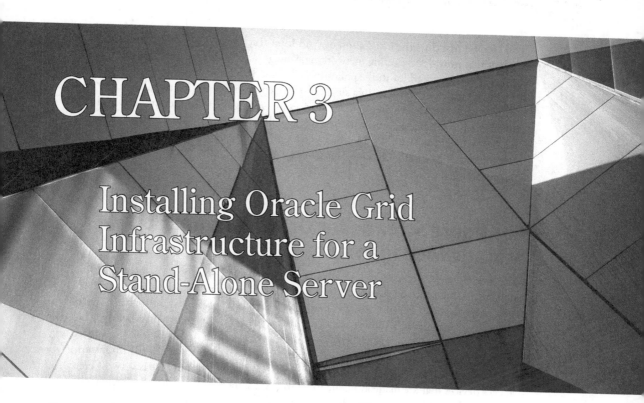

CHAPTER 3

Installing Oracle Grid Infrastructure for a Stand-Alone Server

Exam Objectives

In this chapter, you will learn to

- 62.2.4.1   Configure Storage for Oracle Automatic Storage Management (ASM)
- 62.2.2.2   Install Oracle Grid Infrastructure for a Stand-Alone Server

This chapter describes the installation of Grid Infrastructure (GI). GI is a separately installed product that provides clustering, networking, storage, and high-availability services for Oracle databases. It is required for Real Application Clusters (RAC) databases and can also be used with single-instance databases. In a single-instance environment, GI is usually used to provide Automatic Storage Management (ASM) devices for storing database files (as described in this chapter) and to provide an automatic restart capability in the event of failures (as described in Chapter 4). The treatment of GI in the Oracle Certified Associate (OCA) syllabus is limited to using the restart capability in a single-instance environment, although concepts of ASM may also be examined.

Configure Storage for Oracle Automatic Storage Management

Grid Infrastructure includes the ASM capability to manage storage to be used for Oracle database files. In earlier releases (up to release 11.1.x), ASM was shipped as part of the database software, but from 11.2.x onward, it is part of GI. GI is a set of processes that run as part of the operating system: on Windows, services that run with Administrator privileges; on Linux, daemons that run with root privileges. The GI processes start an ASM instance. In some ways, an ASM instance resembles the relational database management system (RDBMS) instance with which all database administrators (DBAs) are familiar, but its purpose is very different: it manages devices that are made available to RDBMS instances for file storage. These devices must be configured by the system administrator before installing GI.

GI Architecture

GI consists of a set of processes, all of which are protected against failure. The core process is the High Availability Services daemon, the OHASD. This is protected by the operating system. If it fails, the operating system (OS) will restart it. The OHASD then starts and monitors a set of other processes, which in turn will start and monitor resources used by database instances. These resources are ASM and database listeners.

 TIP   You can run database listeners from a database home or from a GI home. It is considered best practice to run only one listener (from the GI home if GI has been installed).

GI maintains a registry of resources that run under its control. These resources may include any or all of the following:

- Database listeners
- Virtual Internet Protocol (IP) addresses
- An ASM instance (one only)
- ASM disk groups

- Database instances
- Third-party products

The registry exists in a file called the Oracle Local Registry (OLR). The location of the OLR is specified by a platform-specific pointer. On Linux, the pointer is the file /etc/oracle/olr.loc. On Windows, it is the registry key HKEY_LOCAL_MACHINE/SOFTWARE/Oracle/olr/olrconfig_loc.

Resources are registered in the OLR using the crsctl utility. These registrations include details of how to start and stop the resources, the operating accounts under which they should run, and what to do if they fail. The GI daemons make use of this information to manage the resources.

The crsctl utility is also used to stop and start the GI processes, including the OHASD, and to administer registered resources. An alternative administration tool is the srvctl utility. srvctl can manage Oracle resources, not any third-party products that may have been registered and placed under GI control. It is generally much easier to use syntactically (and is less prone to error) than the crsctl utility.

 EXAM TIP GI processes and any resources can be administered with the crsctl utility. The srvctl utility can manage only Oracle resources; it cannot manage GI or third-party resources.

ASM Architecture

ASM is a logical volume manager (LVM) that can be used to configure striped and mirrored volumes for storing Oracle database files. These volumes are known as *disk groups*. Disk groups are not formatted with a file system that is visible to the operating system; they can be used only for Oracle database files, and these files can be managed only with Oracle products and utilities.

To understand the relationship between an ASM file and an Oracle database file, study the entity-relationship diagram presented in Figure 3-1.

ASM files reside on a disk group, consisting of one or more ASM disks. The ASM disks are formatted into allocation units (AUs). AUs are grouped into file extents, and a file consists of one or more file extents. There is, in effect, a many-to-many relationship between ASM files and ASM disks. One file can be spread across many disks, and one disk can hold parts of many files. As good relational engineers, we do not permit many-to-many relationships; this one is resolved in two ways: by the disk group entity and by the file extent and AU route. Any one file extent consists of consecutive AUs on one ASM disk. An ASM file is defined by its *extent map*—that is, the list of pointers to the physical locations of its file extents.

ASM is managed by the ASM instance. The ASM instance consists of memory components and background processes; it is a lightweight structure that manages the ASM environment. It tracks the extent maps that define file locations, adding or removing file extents to or from files according to demands from the RDBMS instance using the file.

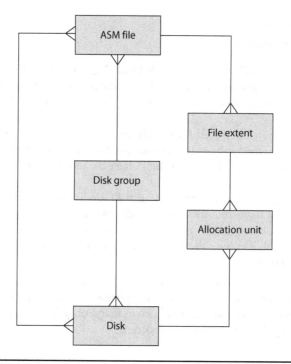

Figure 3-1 The ASM storage model

The ASM instance has a System Global Area (SGA), and it accepts sessions in the same way that an RDBMS instance does, but it is never in any mode other than nomount. An ASM instance never mounts a controlfile; it has no data dictionary. Therefore, the only way to log on is by using operating system authentication or password file authentication.

The ASM bootstrap does the following:

1. The operating system starts the GI processes.

2. GI starts the ASM instance.

3. The ASM instance locates the ASM disk devices.

4. The ASM instance mounts the disk groups and registers them with GI.

5. The RDBMS instance starts.

6. The RDBMS instance needs a file that is on an ASM disk group.

7. The RDBMS requests the ASM instance address from GI.

8. The RDBMS instance logs on to the ASM instance and requests access to the ASM file.

9. The ASM instance returns the file's extent map.

10. The RDBMS instance opens the file.

In summary, when opening an ASM file, GI facilitates the connection between the RDBMS and ASM instances, and then the ASM instance facilitates the connection between the RDBMS instance and the file.

 EXAM TIP   No data ever passes through an ASM instance. All I/O is between the RDBMS instance and the file. The ASM instance is only a control structure.

An ASM disk group can store only database files, but it is a broad definition of database files and incudes these file types:

- Controlfiles
- Datafiles
- Tempfiles
- Online logfiles
- Archive logfiles
- Server parameter file, the spfile
- Password file
- RMAN backups
- Data Pump dump files

These file types cannot be stored on an ASM disk group:

- The Oracle Home
- Trace files or the alert log
- A pfile initialization file
- User-managed backups

ASM Disks

The term *ASM disk* is a little misleading because the devices are not actually disks. The following are the possibilities:

- Partitions of directly attached storage (DAS) devices
- Storage area network (SAN) devices
- Network-attached storage (NAS) devices

DAS devices are disks physically attached to the server. Typically, this means SCSI disks or some variation thereof. In earlier releases, it was possible to give the entire, raw disk to ASM to use as an ASM disk. This was rarely advisable and is no longer possible. It is now required that the disks have a partition table, even if this defines only one partition covering the entire disk. The partition is then presented to ASM.

SAN devices will usually be striped (and possibly mirrored) volumes managed by a storage array and attached to the server over a fiber-optic channel. They will be presented to ASM as logical unit numbers (LUNs). There is no practical limit to the size that these volumes may be. Striping the volumes with whatever RAID algorithm is considered appropriate will improve performance. Mirroring can be enabled at the SAN level or managed by ASM.

NAS devices will typically be iSCSI volumes or NFS files. An iSCSI device is exported to the network by an iSCSI target machine and mounted on the database server by an iSCSI initiator. NFS files will exist as large zero-filled files on an NFS volume exported from an NFS server and mounted by the database server. The underlying storage for NAS devices may, of course, be a RAID device; the NAS layer will conceal this from ASM. The local area network connection between the database server and storage server should be high speed and dedicated to this function. Multipathing is advisable to add bandwidth and resilience against network failures.

DAS, SAN, or iSCSI devices (which should not be formatted with any file system) are identified by their device drivers. NFS files are identified by their fully qualified filename. Either way, the ASM instance needs to determine what devices it should use. An ASM instance is controlled by a parameter file, in the same way as an RDBMS instance. One critical parameter is ASM_DISKSTRING. This is a comma-separated list of values (which may include wildcard characters) that identify the ASM disks. The manner of naming the devices, and therefore the values to include in the ASM_DISKSTRING, is platform specific. These are the default values for some popular operating systems:

AIX	/dev/rhdisk*
HP-UX	/dev/rdisk/*
Solaris	/dev/rdsk/*
Windows	\\.\ORCLDISK*
Linux	/dev/raw/*
On Linux if using ASMLib Kernel Driver	ORCL:*

It is important to note that the default value may find disks that are not intended for ASM's use. If this is the case, it is imperative to set the parameter such that it will find only appropriate devices.

Creating ASM Disks

Disk creation will be done by your system administrator. Subsequently, each disk device will be accessed through a device driver. Device drivers are created by the operating system as it boots. During boot-up, the operating system scans the various I/O buses and creates a device driver for each device it finds. Because this is a dynamic process, it is possible that any one device may be assigned to a different device driver on each boot. Furthermore, following creation, the device drivers will be root owned.

To make devices usable by ASM, it is necessary that the names be persistent across system restarts and that the drivers be readable and writeable by the Oracle processes. On Linux, there are three techniques for this.

- **The ASMLib kernel library** This library is available for some Linux distributions, depending on your Linux license.

- **The ASM Filter Driver** This facility is provided from release 12.1.0.2 and can replace the ASMLib. It adds functionality that will prevent any non-Oracle process from writing to the ASM disks.

- **The udev facility** This facility runs scripts written by your system administrator that identify devices and set appropriate ownership and permissions.

To configure devices on Windows, Oracle supplies the asmtool.exe utility. Other operating systems will have their own platform-specific techniques for managing device ownership and name persistence.

If you are using NFS files as ASM disks, create them with commands such as these, which create a 1TB file and give access to the Oracle owner:

```
dd if=/dev/zero of=/asm/disk1 bs=1048576 count=1048576
chown oracle:dba /asm/disk1
chmod 660 /asm/disk1
```

The details of creating ASM disks are beyond the scope of the OCA examination, and there are many platform variations.

Install Oracle Grid Infrastructure for a Stand-Alone Server

GI is installed into a dedicated Oracle Home. The release of GI must be greater than or equal to the release of any database that intends to use the GI services. It is, for example, possible for a 12.1.*x* GI installation to service an 11.2.*x* database—but not the other way around. GI must always be running on the same nodes as the database instances. It is, however, possible in a clustered environment to configure Flex ASM, where only a small number of nodes (by default, three) run ASM instances.

The GI installation media include a copy of the Oracle Universal Installer (OUI). Run this (the executable is the runInstaller.sh shell script on Unix and is the setup.exe file on Windows) and follow the prompts. These are the major choices:

- **Download Software Updates** Choose whether to register the installation with My Oracle Support to facilitate downloading patches and updates.

- **Select Installation Option** What type of dialog box should the OUI present? The options are as follows:
  - Install and Configure Oracle Grid Infrastructure for a Cluster
  - Install and Configure Oracle Grid Infrastructure for a Standalone Server

- Upgrade Oracle Grid Infrastructure or Oracle Automatic Storage Management
- Install Oracle Grid Infrastructure Software Only
- **Create ASM Disk Group** Set the ASM_DISKSTRING discovery path and choose disks to be used for a disk group.

Figure 3-2 shows the window that prompts for creating a disk group. This window is part of the dialog box presented by the Install and Configure installation options.

In the figure, note that by default Redundancy is set to Normal, meaning that unless specified otherwise, every extent of every file created on this disk group will be mirrored. This means that the group must consist of at least two disks because there would be little point in creating a mirror copy on the same device as the primary copy, and ASM will not permit this. The other radio buttons are High, meaning that three copies will be made of each extent (and at least three disks are required), and External, meaning that ASM will not mirror at all but rather rely on fault tolerance provided by the storage medium.

The allocation unit size defaults to 1MB. This has a knock-on effect on the file extent size. The first 20,000 extents of any file are one AU, the next 20,000 extents are four AUs, and

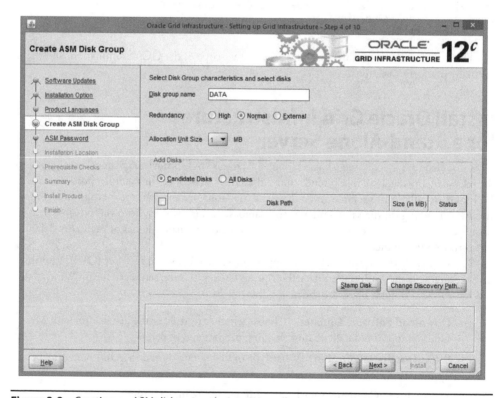

Figure 3-2 Creating an ASM disk group during GI install

beyond that they are 16 AUs. AU size can be set to 1, 2, 4, 8, 16, 32, or 64MB. It applies to all files on the disk group and can never be changed after disk group creation.

TIP Opinion is tending toward 4MB being the optimal AU size for large systems and is recommended by Oracle for Exadata installations. But in the context of ASM, "large" does mean "very large indeed." In fact, 1MB will be fine for most installations.

In Figure 3-2, no disks are shown. This is because the default search path has not detected any and no disk string has yet been set. Clicking the Change Discovery Path button will prompt for the location of the prepared ASM disks, which will then (if configured correctly) be listed as candidates for members of the disk group.

If you are using OUI to perform an upgrade, the OUI will detect the existing installation and transfer its configuration to the newly installed GI home. It is not possible to have two instances of GI running on one machine concurrently, and the installation wizards will take care of disabling the previous version.

It is considered best practice to install GI under a different operating system user than the database software. This is to allow separation of duties: one OS user can manage GI's storage and high-availability features, making them available to several DBAs who each have their own OS account. At a small site, where the GI administrator and the DBA are the same person, there is no necessity to follow this rule. Nonetheless, the operating system will always separate these roles through the use of operating system groups. The GI administrator must be a member of the OSASM group. The name of this group is hard-coded on Windows as ORA_ASMDBA, and the group is created implicitly. On Unix, the group can be named anything and must be created before running OUI.

Exercise 3-1: Install Grid Infrastructure   In this exercise, you will install the GI software and configure it for use. It is assumed that the software has been downloaded and unzipped. The routine is slightly different on Windows and Linux.

1. Follow these steps on Windows:

    A. Launch the OUI dialog box by running the setup.exe file. You will need to do this from a command prompt started with the Run As Administrator privilege.

    B. In the Download Software Updates window, select the Skip Software Updates radio button. Click Next.

    C. In the Select Installation Option window, select the Install Grid Infrastructure Software Only radio button. Click Next.

    D. In the Select Install Type window, select the Install Oracle Grid Infrastructure For A Standalone Server radio button. Click Next.

    E. In the Select Product Languages window, choose any languages you want. Click Next.

    F. In the Specify Installation Location, adjust the directory if you want (the default is usually fine). Click Next.

G. In the Perform Prerequisite Checks window, any "failed" checks should be addressed and a decision made about whether they are likely to matter in your case. Warnings (for example, regarding Windows security issues) can usually be ignored. Check the Ignore All box, and click Next.

H. In the Summary window, click Install.

I. After the install completes, the Finish window, shown next, will prompt you to run the operating system command necessary to configure GI for a stand-alone server:

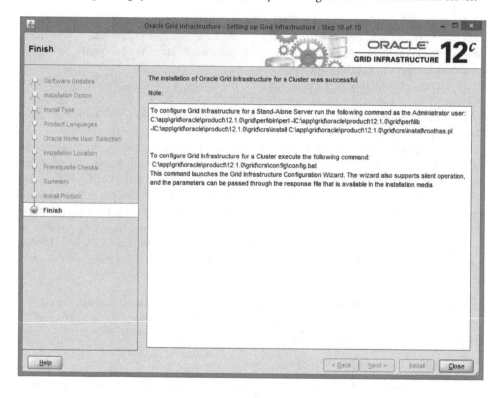

In the illustration, the command, which must be run as Administrator, is one long command with no line breaks (copy/paste will be useful).

```
C:\app\grid\oracle\product\12.1.0\grid\perl\bin\perl
-IC:\app\grid\oracle\product\12.1.0\grid\perl\lib
-IC:\app\grid\oracle\product\12.1.0\grid\crs\install
C:\app\grid\oracle\product\12.1.0\grid\crs\install\roothas.pl
```

After running the command, click Close to exit from the installer.

2. Follow these steps on Linux:

A. Launch the OUI dialog box in a graphical session by running the runInstaller shell script. This cannot be done as the root user. Using the same account that was used for the Oracle software install will be fine (although for a production site, you would usually create a separate OS user to install GI).

B. In the Download Software Updates window, select the Skip Software Updates radio button. Click Next.

C. In the Select Installation Option window, select the Install Grid Infrastructure Software Only radio button. Click Next.

D. In the Select Product Languages window, choose any languages you want. Click Next.

E. In the Privileged Operating System Groups window, if you are running the installer as the same user who installed the Oracle software, select the group dba for all three groups (OSASM, OSDBA for ASM, and OSOPER for ASM).

F. In the Specify Installation Location window, adjust the directory if you want (the default is usually fine). Click Next.

G. In the Perform Prerequisite Checks window, you can usually ignore warnings. Any "failed" checks should be addressed. For instance, a failure of the test for an NTP daemon will not matter; a failure on file permissions would. Check the Ignore All box, and click Next.

H. In the Summary window, click Install.

I. Execute Configuration Scripts is a pop-up window that will prompt you to run a script named something like /u01/app/12.1.0.grid/root.sh as root. Execute this script from a root session, accepting the defaults for any prompts. The following illustration shows the result of a typical run:

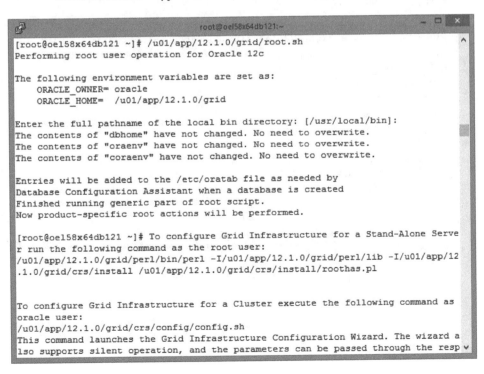

J. Still in your root session, run the command generated by the root.sh script that will complete the configuration for a stand-alone server. This is one long command, with no line breaks. In the preceding illustration, the command is as follows:

```
/u01/app/12.1.0/grid/perl/bin/perl
-I/u01/app/12.1.0/grid/perl/lib
-I/u01/app/12.1.0/grid/crs/install
/u01/app/12.1.0/grid/crs/install/roothas.pl
```

Following completion, return to the OUI window and click OK and Close.

3. To confirm the successful installation, use the crsctl utility. This will be in the bin directory beneath the directory chosen for the installation. Here is an example on Windows:

```
cd \app\grid\oracle\product\12.1.0\grid\bin
crsctl config has
crsctl status resource
```

Here is an example on Linux:

```
cd /u01/app/12.1.0/grid/bin
./crsctl config has
./crsctl status resource
```

These commands will show that the High Availability Service (HAS) is enabled and that the Event Management Daemon is running, as shown in the following illustration:

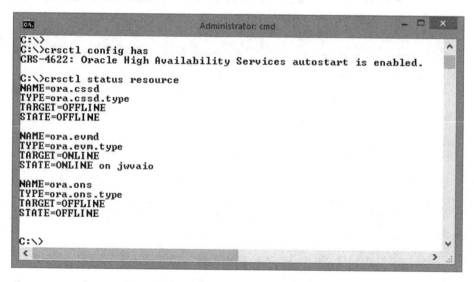

4. Investigate the automatic startup of the GI processes.

A. On Windows, GI is launched by a Windows service. Check its configuration and status with the sc utility, as shown in this illustration:

```
c:\>sc qc OracleOHService
[SC] QueryServiceConfig SUCCESS

SERVICE_NAME: OracleOHService
        TYPE               : 10   WIN32_OWN_PROCESS
        START_TYPE         : 2    AUTO_START
        ERROR_CONTROL      : 1    NORMAL
        BINARY_PATH_NAME   : C:\app\grid\oracle\product\12.1.0\grid\bin\ohasd.exe
        LOAD_ORDER_GROUP   :
        TAG                : 0
        DISPLAY_NAME       : OracleOHService
        DEPENDENCIES       :
        SERVICE_START_NAME : LocalSystem

c:\>sc query OracleOHService

SERVICE_NAME: OracleOHService
        TYPE               : 10   WIN32_OWN_PROCESS
        STATE              : 4    RUNNING
                                  (STOPPABLE, PAUSABLE, ACCEPTS_SHUTDOWN)
        WIN32_EXIT_CODE    : 0    (0x0)
        SERVICE_EXIT_CODE  : 0    (0x0)
        CHECKPOINT         : 0x0
        WAIT_HINT          : 0x0

c:\>
```

B. On Linux, GI is launched through the rc system. Look for the file /etc/rc.d/init.d/ init.ohasd and links to it in the various rc directories. There will also be an entry in /etc/inittab that will respawn the init.ohasd process if it fails.

Two-Minute Drill

Configure Storage for Oracle Automatic Storage Management

- An ASM disk group stores only database files; it has no normal file system.
- ASM disks are unformatted DAS, SAN, or NAS devices.
- The ASM instance is a control structure only; no data passes through it.

Install Oracle Grid Infrastructure for a Stand-Alone Server

- GI must be installed into its own Oracle Home.
- Configuring GI requires root (Linux) or Administrator (Windows) privileges.
- The ASM disk search string can be set at install time or changed later.
- The GI daemons are launched by the operating system on boot-up.

Self Test

1. What file types and directories can be stored with ASM? (Choose all that apply.)

   A. Alert log

   B. Controlfiles

   C. Datafiles

   D. Online redo log files

   E. Oracle Home directory

   F. Tempfiles

2. Which of the following recovery files can be stored with ASM? (Choose all that apply.)

   A. Archive redo log files

   B. RMAN backup sets

   C. RMAN image copies

   D. User-managed backups

   E. The flash recovery area

3. What are the default characteristics of ASM files? (Choose the best answer.)

   A. The files will be striped for performance but not mirrored for safety.

   B. The files will be mirrored for safety but not striped for performance.

   C. The files will be both striped and mirrored.

   D. The files will be neither striped nor mirrored.

4. What statement is correct about ASM and logical volume managers (LVMs)? (Choose the best answer.)

   A. ASM is itself an LVM and cannot work with a third-party LVM.

   B. ASM can use LVM volumes if they are formatted with a file system.

   C. You can use ASM for striping and the LVM for mirroring.

   D. You can use ASM for mirroring and the LVM for striping.

5. How can you connect to an ASM instance? (Choose the best answer.)

   A. By using operating system authentication only

   B. By using password file authentication only

   C. By using data dictionary authentication only

   D. By using either operating system or password file authentication

6. What does ASM stripe? (Choose the best answer.)

   A. Files across all disk groups

   B. Disks across all disk groups

   C. Disk groups across all disks

   D. Files across all disks in a group

7. You want to make Grid Infrastructure services available to your database. Where can the software be installed? (Choose the best answer.)

   A. Into the database Oracle Home if it is the same release

   B. Into an Oracle Home on a machine accessible to all databases over a network

   C. Into a dedicated Oracle Home on each machine running a database

   D. All of the above

8. What utilities can you use to start and stop the GI High Availability Services? (Choose two correct answers.)

   A. crsctl

   B. SQL*Plus

   C. srvctl

   D. Windows net start utility

Self Test Answers

1. ☑ **B**, **C**, **D**, and **F**. You can use ASM for database files, such as the controlfile, the datafiles, the tempfiles, and the online log files.
   ☒ **A** and **E** are incorrect. **A** is incorrect because the alert and trace files must be on conventional storage, and **E** is incorrect because your Oracle Home must be on conventional storage as well.

2. ☑ **A**, **B**, **C**, and **E**. Archive logs, RMAN backups and image copies, and indeed the whole flash recovery area can be on ASM.
   ☒ **D** is incorrect. You cannot direct user-managed backups to ASM because operating system utilities cannot write to ASM devices.

3. ☑ **C**. By default, files are both striped and mirrored because this is the default when creating a disk group and will be applied to all files unless specified otherwise.
   ☒ **A**, **B**, and **D** are incorrect. **A** is incorrect because normal redundancy mirroring is the default. **B** and **D** are incorrect because while you can disable mirroring by using the EXTERNAL REDUNDANCY option, you cannot disable striping (and you would not want to).

4. ☑ **C**. This is probably the best way to use ASM: to rely on an LVM to provide fault tolerance and ASM to provide Oracle-aware striping.
   ☒ **A**, **B**, and **D** are incorrect. **A** is incorrect because an LVM can be used to create the disks presented to ASM. **B** is incorrect because LVMs must be presented as raw devices, not as "cooked" file systems. **D** is incorrect because you can (and should) use two layers if striping: first at the hardware level over physical volumes, then ASM will stripe on top of these.

5. ☑ **D**. Both password file and operating system authentication will work.
   ☒ **A**, **B**, and **C** are incorrect. **A** and **B** are incorrect because both techniques can be used. **C** is incorrect because an ASM instance has no data dictionary.

6. ☑ **D**. ASM stripes files across all disks in the group.
☒ **A**, **B**, and **C** are incorrect. **A** is incorrect because one file can exist only in one group. **B** and **C** are incorrect because it is file extents that are striped, not disks or diskgroups.

7. ☑ **C**. GI must be installed into its own home directory.
☒ **A**, **B**, and **D** are incorrect. **A** is incorrect because it is not possible for the GI and database binaries to coexist in one Oracle Home. **B** and **D** are incorrect because it is not possible for a database to contact GI over a network connection.

8. ☑ **A** and **D**. crsctl is the Oracle-provided tool that can manage the GI processes, and on Windows the service manager can also be used.
☒ **B** and **C** are incorrect. **B** is incorrect because SQL*Plus can manage an ASM instance, but not GI. **C** is incorrect because srvctl can manage GI registered resources, but not GI itself.

CHAPTER 4

Using Oracle Restart

Exam Objectives

In this chapter, you will learn to

- 62.2.5.1 Use Oracle Restart to Manage Components

This chapter details the use of Oracle Restart, which is the nonclustered version of Grid Infrastructure. It provides the ability to manage a range of Oracle resources. Once placed under GI control, the resources can be started and stopped with the GI utilities and restarted automatically in the event of failure.

Use Oracle Restart to Manage Components

Oracle Restart is a service provided by GI. It consists of a set of processes started and monitored by the operating system. Some of these processes run with root (or Administrator) privileges, and others run as the user under which GI was installed. Oracle Restart can be configured to start automatically or manually.

A *resource* is, in this context, something that can be managed by GI. All resources are registered in the Oracle Local Registry (OLR). Once registered, they are under the control of Oracle Restart. Some configuration tools will implicitly register resources if they detect the presence of an Oracle Restart configuration; others will not. In the latter case, the resource must be explicitly registered. Once registered, a resource can be started or stopped either with GI utilities (which also will take care of stopping or starting any dependent resources) or with the utilities native to the resource.

Of great importance is the high-availability capability. GI includes an event-monitoring mechanism that will detect any state change for a registered resource, propagate messages regarding state changes, and, if necessary, attempt an automatic restart of failed resources.

Administering the Oracle Restart Processes

Following the installation of GI, the Oracle Restart processes will be started automatically on booting the server. On Linux, the core process is the init.ohasd daemon. This is launched through an rc script, with monitoring and respawn enabled by an entry in the /etc/inittab file. Should the daemon die (or be killed), init will restart it. On Windows, the same function is provided by the OracleOHService Windows service, which launches, monitors, and restarts the ohasd.exe process.

To control Oracle Restart manually, use the crsctl utility. Figure 4-1 shows the use of the most frequently used crsctl commands for administering Oracle Restart on a Windows system. The commands are syntactically identical on Linux. Note that most of these commands can be executed only by a user with Administrator (Windows) or root (Linux) privileges.

These are the commands used in Figure 4-1:

Command	Description
crsctl config has	Oracle Restart is configured to start on boot-up.
crsctl check has	Oracle Restart is currently running.
crsctl stop has	Stop the Oracle Restart process.
crsctl start has	Start the Oracle Restart process.

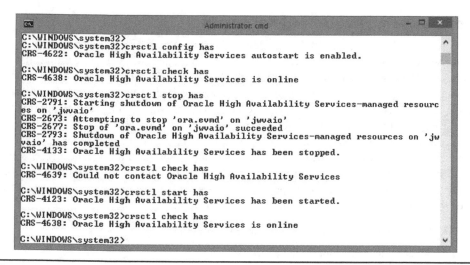

Figure 4-1   Using the crsctl utility to manage Oracle Restart (Windows)

Figure 4-2 shows some more crsctl commands, this time on a Linux system.
These are the commands used in Figure 4-2:

Command	Description
crsctl query softwareversion	The software that is installed.
crsctl config has	Oracle Restart is not configured to start on boot-up.
crsctl enable crs	From now on, Oracle Restart will start on boot-up.
crsctl disable crs	It is now disabled again.

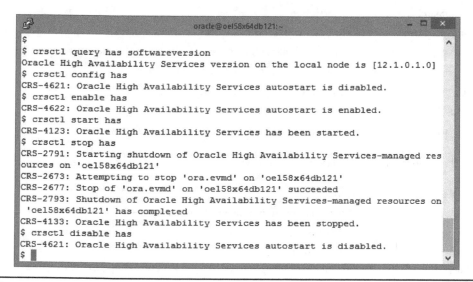

Figure 4-2   Using the crsctl utility to manage Oracle Restart (Linux)

Administering Registered Resources

Resources must be registered with Oracle Restart if it is to provide a high-availability service for them. Some tools will register resources as they are created; others will not. For example, if you create a database with the Database Configuration Assistant (DBCA) utility, it will detect the presence of Oracle Restart and run commands to register the database. You can see these commands in the scripts that DBCA generates. If you create the database with SQL*Plus, you must register it yourself. If you create a listener with the Net Configuration Assistant, it will be registered; if you create one with the Net Manager, it will not be registered. If GI has been installed after other products have already been installed, all previously created resources must be explicitly registered.

It is possible to register resources with the crsctl utility, but this is a general-purpose tool and the syntax for adding a resource is, to put it mildly, awkward. When registering a resource, you need to give Oracle Restart, at a minimum, this information:

- Exactly how to start, stop, and monitor the resource
- What to do if the resource fails
- On what other resources it may depend

Furthermore, the nature of the information needed will be different for different types of resources. A much better alternative when working with Oracle resources is to use the srvctl utility. This is preconfigured with commands for working with all the resources that a DBA is likely to need. It is, however, limited to Oracle resources; you cannot use it to (for example) register an Apache web listener as a managed resource.

The general syntax of the srvctl utility is as follows:

```
srvctl <command> <object> <options>
```

The commonly used commands are as follows:

Command	Description
add | remove	Register or deregister a resource
enable | disable	Allow or disallow Oracle Restart to manage the resource
start | stop	Start or stop a registered (and enabled) resource
config	Show the configuration of the resource
modify	Adjust the configuration of the resource
status	Show whether the resource is started or stopped

The commonly used objects are as follows:

Object	Description
database	A database, including the instance that opens it
service	A database service
listener	A database listener
asm	The node's Automatic Storage Management (ASM) instance
diskgroup	An ASM disk group

The options used in an srvctl command depend on the command and the nature of the object.

TIP   The srvctl utility has a superb help facility. Run `srvctl -help`, and you will see the full syntax of every command for every resource type. Unfortunately, you can't do this when taking the exam.

To register a database, use a command such as this:

```
srvctl add database -db orclz -oraclehome /u01/db_home1
```

The first option is the DB_UNIQUE_NAME of the database, which will (usually) be the DB_NAME. The second option is the Oracle Home off which the instance that opens the database will run. Other not infrequently used options let you specify required disk groups, nominate the spfile and the password file, and control the automatic start. By default, the database will be configured such that Oracle Restart will start it in OPEN mode automatically. To show the configuration of the database orclz, use this command:

```
srvctl config database -db orclz -all
```

This is how to start, stop, and check the status of a database:

```
srvctl start database -db orclz -startoption open
srvctl stop database -db orclz -stopoption immediate
srvctl status database -db orclz
```

The arguments STARTOPTION and STOPOPTION default to OPEN and IMMEDIATE (as shown). Other possible STARTOPTION values are NOMOUNT, MOUNT, and READONLY. Other STOPOPTION values are NORMAL, TRANSACTIONAL, and ABORT.

EXAM TIP   The srvctl utility is installed in both a database Oracle Home and the GI Oracle Home and can be run from either. The crsctl utility is available only in the GI Oracle Home.

The Restart Capability

When a resource is placed under the control of Oracle Restart, it will be monitored by GI and restarted in the event of failure. A controlled shutdown of the resource (whether with the srvctl utility or with a tool native to the resource) will not trigger a restart.

EXAM TIP   There is no "reality check" when using SRVCTL ADD. The fact that a database is successfully registered in the OLR does not mean that it actually exists.

Restart behavior is determined by the POLICY argument passed to the SRVCTL ADD command or to the SRVCTL MODIFY command subsequently. The default value is to enable automatic restart.

```
-POLICY AUTOMATIC | MANUAL | NORESTART
```

Exercise 4-1: Configure a Database for Oracle Restart   In this exercise, you register your database with Oracle Restart. It is assumed that Exercise 3-1 has been completed.

1. From an operating system prompt, confirm that the OHASD is configured and running. Note that you will need Administrator or root privileges, and ensure that your search path includes the bin directory in the GI home. Then use the crsctl utility as follows:

```
crsctl config has
crsctl check has
```

2. Demonstrate that the GI process that implements Oracle Restart is itself protected against failure by the operating system. On Linux, as the root user, identify the process number of the daemon and then kill it. Use these commands, substituting whatever the process number of your init.ohasd process is for 12345:

```
ps -ef | grep init.ohasd
kill -9 12345
ps -ef | grep init.ohasd
```

On Windows, use the Task Manager to locate the ohasd.exe process and then click the End Task button to kill it.

Observe that the process is restarted, with a different process ID, within seconds.

3. Use the srvctl utility to register your database with Oracle Restart. You can rely on defaults for all arguments except the database unique name and the Oracle Home. If you have the ORACLE_HOME environment variable set to the database home, you can use it. Here is an example on Linux with a database named orclz:

```
srvctl add database -d orclz -oraclehome $ORACLE_HOME
```

4. Confirm that the database has been successfully registered and then check its status.

```
srvctl config database -d orclz
srvctl status database -d orclz
```

The database will be reported as "not running," whether it is or not. This is because it has not been started since it was registered.

5. Force GI to perform a reality check by issuing a start command and then check the status again.

```
srvctl start database -db orclz
srvctl status database -db orclz
```

The following illustration shows steps 2 through 4 on a Windows system:

```
C:\>
C:\>srvctl add database -db orclz -oraclehome c:\app\oracle\product\12.1.0\dbhome_1

C:\>srvctl config database -db orclz -all
Database unique name: orclz
Database name:
Oracle home: c:\app\oracle\product\12.1.0\dbhome_1
Oracle user: oracle
Spfile:
Password file:
Domain:
Start options: open
Stop options: immediate
Database role: PRIMARY
Management policy: AUTOMATIC
Database instance: orclz
Disk Groups:
Services:
Database is enabled

C:\>srvctl status database -db orclz
Database is not running.

C:\>srvctl start database -db orclz

C:\>srvctl status database -db orclz
Database is running.

C:\>_
```

6. Experiment with startup and shutdown commands, both with srvctl and with SQL*Plus. Check the status each time.
7. While the database is running, demonstrate the restart capability. On Linux, use the ps command to identify the smon background process and then kill it. This will terminate the instance immediately. On Windows, use the Task Manager End Task button to kill the oracle.exe process.

   Observe that the instance will restart within seconds.

   The following illustration shows the instance restart test on Linux:

```
$
$ srvctl status database -db orclz
Database is running.
$
$ ps -ef | grep smon
oracle     9454     1  0 22:14 ?        00:00:00 ora_smon_orclz
oracle     9599  2958  0 22:14 pts/1    00:00:00 grep smon
$
$ kill -9 9454
$
$ srvctl status database -db orclz
Database is not running.
$
$ srvctl status database -db orclz
Database is running.
$
$ ps -ef | grep smon
oracle     9812     1  0 22:16 ?        00:00:00 ora_smon_orclz
oracle     9945  2958  0 22:17 pts/1    00:00:00 grep smon
$
```

Oracle Restart can protect resources other than databases, including both Oracle-supplied services and third-party services. If Oracle Restart is already installed, then most Oracle services installed subsequently will be registered during their installation. If this has not been done, they can be registered later.

Exercise 4-2: Register a Listener as a Managed Resource   Place your database listener under Oracle Restart control and demonstrate its effectiveness. The command you will need (no line breaks) is as follows:

```
srvctl add listener
[ -listener <lsnr_name> ]
[ -oraclehome <path> ]
[ -endpoints "<port>" ]
```

The default values for the arguments assume that the listener is named LISTENER, that the listening endpoint is 1521, and that the Oracle Home is the GI home (which will not be correct if you have followed the exercises so far). Then check its configuration and status, stop and start the listener, and observe the effect of killing the listener process with an operating system utility.

The following are possible commands (with a Windows Oracle Home):

```
srvctl add listener -listener listener -oraclehome c:\app\oracle\
product\12.1.0\dbhome_1
srvctl config listener -listener listener
srvctl stop listener -listener listener
srvctl start listener -listener listener
```

This is one way to simulate a failure on Windows:

```
net stop OracleOraDB12Home1TNSListener
```

On Linux, find the process ID of the tnslsnr process and kill it.
Note that the listener will restart in a few seconds.

Two-Minute Drill

Use Oracle Restart to Manage Components

- Control Oracle Restart with the crsctl utility.
- Administer Oracle Restart–managed resources with the srvctl utility.
- The OHASD process is protected by the operating system.
- Protected components may be databases, database listeners, the ASM instance, and ASM disk groups.
- If dependencies have been configured (such as between a database and a disk group), Oracle Restart will stop and start them in an appropriate sequence.

Self Test

1. Under what circumstances will Oracle Restart restart a database? (Choose two answers.)

   A. If it is stopped with SQL*Plus

   B. If it fails after being started with SQL*Plus

   C. If it fails after being started with the srvctl utility

   D. If it is stopped with the crsctl utility

2. There are several techniques for registering a database with Oracle Restart. Which of these techniques will not result in a successful registration?

   A. Use the SRVCTL ADD DATABASE command from the database home to add the database to the OLR and then create the database with SQL*Plus.

   B. Create the database with DBCA.

   C. Create a database and leave it running and then install GI and run the GI configuration scripts.

   D. Create the database with SQL*Plus and then use the SRVCTL ADD DATABASE command from the Grid Infrastructure home to add the database to the OLR.

3. Following a standard installation, the GI processes will start automatically when a machine is booted. How can you change this behavior such that they must be started manually? (Choose the best answer.)

   A. Use the srvctl utility:

   ```
   srvctl config has -startoption manual
   ```

   B. Use the crsctl utility:

   ```
   crsctl disable has
   ```

   C. Edit the /etc/inittab file to remove the entry that launches the OHASD.

   D. Use the DBCA graphical utility to adjust the start mode.

4. Your database uses the ASM disk groups DATA and FRA for its storage. You register the database with this command:

   ```
   srvctl add database -db orcl -diskgroup DATA,FRA \
   -oraclehome $ORACLE_HOME
   ```

   Which of the following statements is correct? (Choose the best answer.)

   A. If you attempt to use srvctl to start the database before the ASM instance has mounted the disk groups, the database will not start.

   B. If you attempt to use srvctl to start the database before the ASM instance has started, the ASM instance will start automatically.

   C. The $ORACLE_HOME variable must be set to the ASM home so that the database instance can find the ASM instance.

   D. The registration command will fail if the database does not exist.

Self Test Answers

1. ☑ **B** and **C**. Oracle Restart will restart automatically after any failure, no matter how the database was started.

   ☒ **A** and **D** are incorrect. These are incorrect because Oracle Restart will not restart a database that is stopped in an orderly fashion, no matter what utility is used for this.

2. ☑ **C**. The GI installation and configuration does not include any facility for detecting and registering databases, whether or not they are running at the time.

   ☒ **A**, **B**, and **D** are incorrect. **B** is incorrect because if DBCA detects the presence of GI, it will generate and run appropriate commands. **A** and **D** are incorrect because registration in the OLR can be done before or after database creation, running the utility from either home.

3. ☑ **B**. The crsctl utility is the supported technique for disabling the autostart of the GI processes.

   ☒ **A**, **C**, and **D** are incorrect. **A** is incorrect because the srvctl utility can manage an Oracle Restart–registered resource, not Oracle Restart itself. **C** is incorrect because although you could hack at the operating system inittab and rc files, it is not a supported technique. **D** is incorrect because DBCA cannot manage any GI components, only databases.

4. ☑ **B**. Oracle Restart is aware of dependencies, and it will start ASM and mount any required disk groups.

   ☒ **A**, **C**, and **D** are incorrect. **A** is incorrect because registered dependencies will take care of this. **C** is incorrect because when you are registering a database, the ORACLE_ HOME argument must point to the home off which the RDBMS instance will run. **D** is incorrect because there is no "reality" check when adding entries to the OLR; the errors will come later.

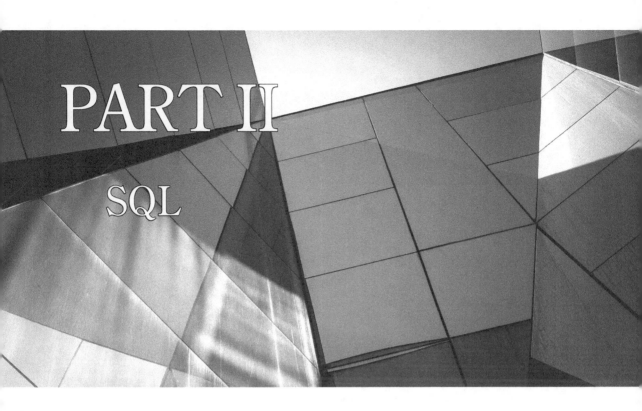

PART II

SQL

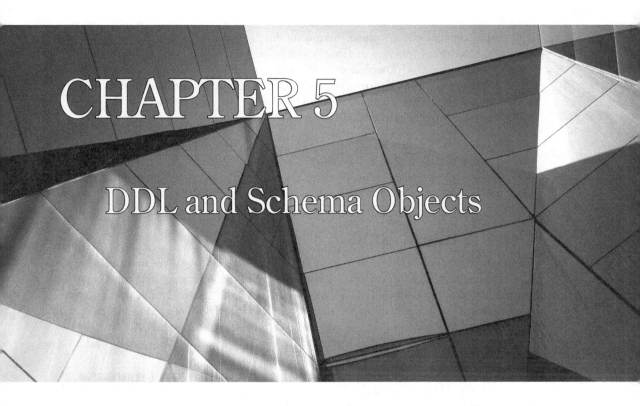

CHAPTER 5

DDL and Schema Objects

Exam Objectives

In this chapter, you will learn to

This chapter contains several sections that are not directly tested by the exam but are considered prerequisite knowledge for every student. Two tools used extensively for exercises are SQL*Plus and SQL Developer, which are covered in this chapter. Oracle specialists use these every day in their work. The exercises and many of the examples are based on two demonstration sets of data, known as the HR and OE schemas, supplied by Oracle. There are instructions on how to launch the tools and create the demonstration schemas.

The primitive data types and the standard heap-organized table structure are the first topics in this chapter that are directly measured in the exam. The chapter moves on to defining the object types that are dependent on tables (indexes, constraints, and views) and then sequences and synonyms. All of these object types will be used throughout the remainder of this book.

Use the Client Tools

Numerous tools can be used to connect to an Oracle database. Two of the most basic are SQL*Plus and SQL Developer. These are provided by Oracle Corporation and are adequate for much of the work that a developer or a database administrator needs to do. The choice between them is a matter of personal preference, partly to do with the environment and partly to do with functionality. SQL Developer undoubtedly offers far more functionality than SQL*Plus, but it is more demanding in that it needs a graphical terminal, whereas SQL*Plus can be used on character mode devices.

The tool that has lasted longest is SQL*Plus, and even though Oracle Corporation is promoting SQL Developer strongly as a replacement, technical people working in the Oracle environment will be well advised to become familiar with SQL*Plus.

SQL*Plus

SQL*Plus is a client-server tool for connecting to a database and issuing ad hoc SQL commands. It can also be used for creating PL/SQL code and has facilities for formatting results. It is available on all platforms to which the database has been ported; the sections that follow give some detail on using SQL*Plus on Linux and Windows. There are no significant differences with using SQL*Plus on any other platform.

In terms of architecture, SQL*Plus is a user process written in C. It establishes a session against an instance and a database over the Oracle Net protocol. The platforms for the client and the server can be different. For example, there is no reason not to use SQL*Plus on a Windows PC to connect to a database running on a Unix server (or the other way round), provided that Oracle Net has been configured to make the connection.

SQL*Plus on Linux

The SQL*Plus executable file on a Linux installation is sqlplus. The location of this file will be installation specific, but will typically be something like this:

```
/u01/app/oracle/product/12.1.0/db_1/bin/sqlplus
```

Your Linux account should be set up appropriately to run SQL*Plus, but you will need to set some environment variables. These are as follows:

ORACLE_HOME
PATH
LD_LIBRARY_PATH

The ORACLE_HOME variable points to the Oracle Home. An Oracle Home is the Oracle software installation, in other words, the set of files and directories containing the executable code and some of the configuration files. The PATH must include the bin directory contained within the Oracle Home. The LD_LIBRARY_PATH should include the lib directory, also contained within the Oracle Home, but in practice you may get away without setting this. Figure 5-1 shows a Linux terminal window and some tests to see whether the environment is correct.

In Figure 5-1, first the echo command checks whether the three variables have been set up correctly. There is an ORACLE_HOME, and the bin and lib directories in it have been set as the last element of the PATH and the first element of the LD_LIBRARY_PATH variables, respectively. Then, the which command confirms that the SQL*Plus executable file really is available in the PATH. Finally, SQL*Plus is launched with a username, a password, and a connect identifier passed to it on the command line. If the tests do not return acceptable results and SQL*Plus fails to launch, you should discuss this with your system administrator and your database administrator. Some common errors with the logon itself are described in the section "Creating and Testing a Database Connection" later in this chapter.

The format of the logon string is the database username followed by a forward slash character as a delimiter, then a password followed by an @ symbol as a delimiter, and finally an Oracle Net connect identifier. In this example, the username is system, whose password is admin123, and the database is identified by coda.

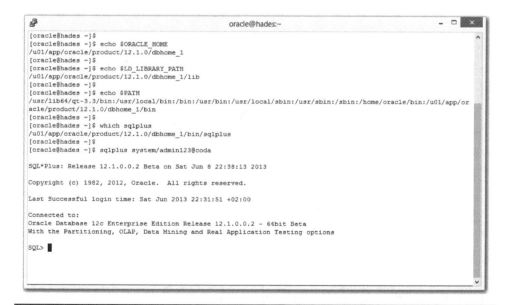

Figure 5-1   Checking the Linux session setup

Following the logon, the next lines of text display the version of SQL*Plus being used, which is 12.1.0.0.2; the version of the database to which the connection has been made (which happens to be the same as the version of the SQL*Plus tool); and which options have been installed within the database. The last line is the prompt to the user, SQL>, at which point the user can enter any SQL*Plus or SQL command. If the logon does not succeed with whatever username (probably not system) you have been allocated, you should discuss this with your database administrator.

SQL*Plus on Windows

Historically, there were always two versions of SQL*Plus for Microsoft Windows: the character version and the graphical version. The character version was (and still is) the executable file sqlplus.exe, and the graphical version was sqlplusw.exe. With the current release and 11g, the graphical version no longer exists, but many developers will prefer to use it, and the versions shipped with earlier releases are perfectly good tools for working with a 12c database. There are no problems with mixing versions; a 12c SQL*Plus client can connect to a 10g database, and a 10g SQL*Plus client can connect to a 12c database. Following a default installation of either an Oracle database or just an Oracle client on Windows, SQL*Plus will be available as a shortcut on the Windows Start menu. The location of the executable file launched by the shortcut will typically be something like the following:

```
D:\app\oracle\product\12.1.0\dbhome_1\BIN\sqlplus.exe
```

However, the exact path will be installation specific. Figure 5-2 shows a logon to a database with SQL*Plus, launched from the shortcut. The first line of text shows the version of

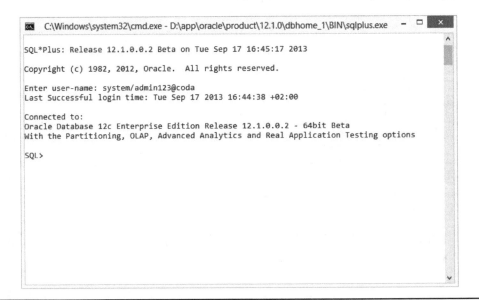

Figure 5-2 A database logon with SQL*Plus for Windows

SQL*Plus, which is the 12.1.0.0.2 release, and the time the program was launched. The third line of text is a logon prompt.

```
Enter user-name:
```

This is followed by the logon string entered manually, which is as follows:

```
system/admin123@coda
```

A change some people like to make to the shortcut that launches SQL*Plus is to prevent it from immediately presenting a logon prompt. To do this, add the nolog switch to the end of the command.

```
sqlplus /nolog
```

There is no reason not to launch SQL*Plus from an operating system prompt rather than from the Start menu shortcut; simply open a command window and run it. The program will immediately prompt for a logon, unless you invoke it with the nolog switch described earlier.

Creating and Testing a Database Connection

SQL*Plus does not have any way of storing database connection details. Each time a user wants to connect to a database, the user must tell SQL*Plus who they are and where the database is. There are variations depending on site-specific security facilities, but the most common means of identifying yourself to the database is by presenting a username and a case-sensitive password. There are two typically used forms of connect identifier for identifying the database: either by providing an alias that is resolved into the full connect details or by entering the full details.

From an operating system prompt, these commands will launch SQL*Plus and connect as database user SCOTT whose password is tiger using each technique:

```
sqlplus scott/tiger@orcl
```

```
sqlplus scott/tiger@ocp12c.oracle.com:1521/orcl.oracle.com
```

The first example uses an alias, orcl, to identify the database. This must be *resolved* into the full connect details. The usual techniques for this name resolution are to use a locally stored text file called the tnsnames.ora file (typically contained within the network/admin subdirectory of the ORACLE_HOME) or to contact an LDAP directory such as Microsoft's Active Directory or Oracle's Oracle Internet Directory (OID).

The second example provides all the connect details inline. The connect details needed are the hostname of the computer on which the database instance is running, the Transmission Control Protocol (TCP) port on which the Oracle Net database listener can be contacted, and the database service to which the user wants the database listener to connect him. The first technique, where the user needs to enter only an alias, requires the database administrator to configure a name resolution mechanism; the second technique can work only if the user knows the connect details.

There are a number of circumstances that will cause a SQL*Plus connection attempt to fail. Figure 5-3 illustrates some of the more common problems.

Figure 5-3

Some common logon problems

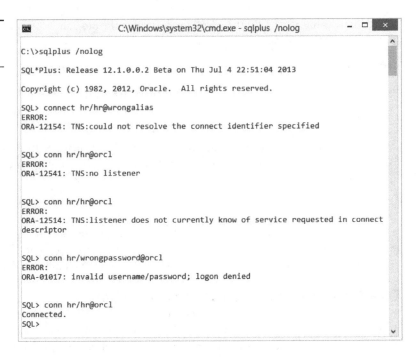

```
C:\>sqlplus /nolog

SQL*Plus: Release 12.1.0.0.2 Beta on Thu Jul 4 22:51:04 2013

Copyright (c) 1982, 2012, Oracle.  All rights reserved.

SQL> connect hr/hr@wrongalias
ERROR:
ORA-12154: TNS:could not resolve the connect identifier specified


SQL> conn hr/hr@orcl
ERROR:
ORA-12541: TNS:no listener


SQL> conn hr/hr@orcl
ERROR:
ORA-12514: TNS:listener does not currently know of service requested in connect
descriptor


SQL> conn hr/wrongpassword@orcl
ERROR:
ORA-01017: invalid username/password; logon denied


SQL> conn hr/hr@orcl
Connected.
SQL>
```

First, the user launches SQL*Plus from a Windows operating system prompt, using the NOLOG switch to prevent the immediate logon prompt. No problem so far.

Second, from the SQL> prompt, the user issues a connection request, which fails with a well-known error:

```
ORA-12154: TNS: could not resolve the connect identifier specified
```

This error is because the connect identifier given, wrongalias, cannot be resolved into database connection details by the Transparent Network Substrate (TNS) layer of Oracle Net. The name resolution method to be used and its configuration are matters for the database administrator. In this case, the error is obvious: The user entered the wrong connect identifier.

The second connect attempt gives the correct identifier, orcl. This fails with the following:

```
ORA-12541: TNS:no listener
```

This indicates that the connect identifier has resolved correctly into the address of a database listener but that the listener is not actually running. Note that another possibility would be that the address resolution is faulty and is sending SQL*Plus to the wrong address. Following this error, the user should contact the database administrator and ask him or her to start the listener. Then try again.

The third connect request fails with the following:

```
ORA-12514: TNS:listener does not currently know of service requested in
connect descriptor
```

This error is generated by the database listener. SQL*Plus has found the listener with no problems, but the listener cannot make the onward connection to the database service. The most likely reason for this is that the database instance has not been started, so the user should ask the database administrator to start it and then try again.

The fourth connect request fails with the following:

```
ORA-01017: invalid username/password; logon denied
```

To receive this message, the user must have contacted the database. The user has gotten through all the possible network problems, the database instance is running, and the database itself has been opened by the instance. The user just has the password or username wrong. Note that the message does not state whether it is the password or the username that is wrong; if it were to do so, it would be giving out information to the effect that the other one was right.

Finally, the fifth connect attempt succeeds.

TIP The preceding example demonstrates a problem-solving technique you will use frequently. If something fails, work through what it is doing step by step. Read every error message.

SQL Developer

SQL Developer is a tool for connecting to an Oracle database (or, in fact, some non-Oracle databases too) and issuing ad hoc SQL commands. It can also manage PL/SQL objects. Unlike SQL*Plus, it is a graphical tool with wizards for commonly needed actions. SQL Developer is written in Java and requires a Java Runtime Environment (JRE) to run.

Being written in Java, SQL Developer is available on all platforms that support the appropriate version of the JRE. There are no significant differences between platforms.

Installing and Launching SQL Developer

SQL Developer is not installed with the Oracle Universal Installer, which is used to install all other Oracle products. It does not exist in an Oracle Home, but is a completely self-contained product. The latest version can be downloaded from Oracle Corporation's web site.

TIP An installation of the 12c database will include a copy of SQL Developer, but it will not be the current version. Even if you happen to have an installation of the database, you will usually want to install the current version of SQL Developer as well.

To install SQL Developer, unzip the ZIP file. That's all. It does require a JDK, the Java Runtime Environment, to be available; this comes from Oracle. But if an appropriate JDK is not already available on the machine being used, there are downloadable versions of SQL Developer for Windows that include it. For platforms other than Windows, the JDK must be preinstalled. Download it from Oracle's web site and install according to the platform-specific directions. To check that the JDK is available with the correct version, from an operating system prompt, run the following command:

```
java -version
```

This should return something like the following:

```
java version "1.7.0_71"
Java(TM) SE Runtime Environment (build 1.7.0_71-b14)
Java HotSpot(TM) 64-Bit Server VM (build 24.71-b01, mixed mode)
```

If it does not, using the which java command may help identify the problem; the search path could be locating an incorrect version.

Once SQL Developer has been unzipped, change your current directory to the directory in which SQL Developer was unzipped and launch it. On Windows, the executable file is sqldeveloper.exe. On Linux, it is the sqldeveloper.sh shell script. Remember to check that the DISPLAY environment variable has been set to a suitable value (such as 127.0.0.1:0.0, if SQL Developer is being run on the system console) before running the shell script.

Any problems with installing the JRE and launching SQL Developer should be referred to your system administrator.

The SQL Developer User Interface

Figure 5-4 shows the SQL Developer user interface after connecting to a database.

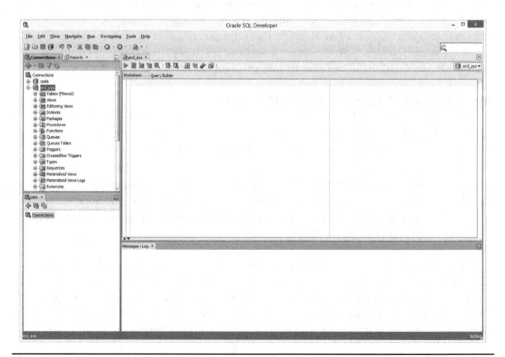

Figure 5-4   The SQL Developer user interface

The general layout of the SQL Developer window is a left pane for navigation around objects and a right pane to display and enter information.

In the figure, the left pane shows that a connection has been made to a database. The connection is called orcl_sys. This name is just a label chosen when the connection was defined, but most developers will use some sort of naming convention—in this case, the name chosen is the database identifier, which is orcl, and the name of the user the connection was made as, which was sys. The branches beneath list all the possible object types that can be managed. Expanding the branches would list the objects themselves. The right pane has an upper part prompting the user to enter a SQL statement and a lower part that will display the result of the statement. SQL Developer can be a useful tool because it is highly customizable. Experiment with it, read the Help, and set up the user interface the way that works best for you.

Creating a Database Connection

Database connections can be created and saved for reuse. The window where connections can be defined can be reached by choosing the + symbol visible on the Connections tab shown previously in Figure 5-4.

The name for the connection is arbitrary. The username and password must both be supplied, but only the username will be saved unless the Save Password check box is selected. Saving a password means that future connections can be made without any password prompt. This is convenient but highly dangerous if there is any possibility that the computer you are working on is not secure. In effect, you are delegating the authentication to your local operating system; if you can log on to that, you can log on to the database.

Assuming that you are using SQL Developer to connect to an Oracle database rather than to a third-party database, select the Oracle tab.

The Role drop-down box gives you the option to connect as *sysdba*. A sysdba connection is required before certain particularly serious operations (such as database startup and shutdown) can be carried out. It will never be needed for the exercises covered in this book.

The Connection Type radio buttons let you choose from five options:

- **Basic**   This prompts for the machine name of the database server, the port on which the database listener will accept connection requests, and the instance (the session identifier [SID]) or the service to which the connection will be made.

- **TNS**   If a name resolution method has been configured, then an alias for the database can be selected (from the local tnsnames.ora file) or entered, rather than the full details needed by the Basic option.

- **LDAP**   Database service definitions and their connection details that are stored in a Lightweight Directory Access Protocol (LDAP) directory service may be queried by specifying the LDAP server details.

- **Advanced**   This allows entry of a full Java Database Connectivity (JDBC) connect string. This is completely Oracle independent and could be used to connect to any database that conforms to the JDBC standard.

- **Local/Bequeath**   If the database is running on the same machine as your SQL Developer client, this option allows you to connect directly to a server process, bypassing the network listener.

Selecting Basic requires the user to know how to connect to the database; selecting TNS requires some configuration to have been done on the client machine by the database administrator so that the alias can be resolved into the full connection details.

Categorize the Main Database Objects

Various object types can exist within a database, many more with the current release than with earlier versions. All objects have names, and all objects are owned by someone. The "someone" is a database user, such as HR. The objects the user owns are their *schema*. An object's name must conform to certain rules.

Object Types

This query lists the count by object type for the objects that happen to exist in this particular database:

```
SQL> select object_type, count(object_type)
     from dba_objects
     group by object_type
     order by object_type;
```

OBJECT_TYPE	COUNT(OBJECT_TYPE)	OBJECT_TYPE	COUNT(OBJECT_TYPE)
CHAIN	1	PACKAGE	1321
CLUSTER	10	PACKAGE BODY	1259
CONSUMER GROUP	20	PROCEDURE	196
CONTEXT	10	PROGRAM	10
DESTINATION	2	QUEUE	30
DIMENSION	5	RESOURCE PLAN	13
DIRECTORY	14	RULE	3
EDITION	1	RULE SET	22
EVALUATION CONTEXT	16	SCHEDULE	4
FUNCTION	350	SCHEDULER GROUP	4
INDEX	4514	SEQUENCE	273
INDEX PARTITION	492	SYNONYM	37018
INDEXTYPE	8	TABLE	2603
JAVA CLASS	30942	TABLE PARTITION	408
JAVA DATA	325	TABLE SUBPARTITION	32
JAVA RESOURCE	979	TRIGGER	611
JAVA SOURCE	2	TYPE	2527
JOB	29	TYPE BODY	226
JOB CLASS	15	UNDEFINED	17
LIBRARY	224	UNIFIED AUDIT POLICY	7
LOB	921	VIEW	6189
LOB PARTITION	15	WINDOW	9
MATERIALIZED VIEW	2	XML SCHEMA	49
OPERATOR	55		

47 rows selected.

This query addresses the view DBA_OBJECTS, which has one row for every object in the database. The numbers are low because the database is a small one used only for teaching. A database used for a business application generally has many more objects. You may not be able to see the view DBA_OBJECTS because it depends on which permissions have been granted to your account. Alternative views are USER_OBJECTS, which will show all the objects owned by you, and ALL_OBJECTS, which will show all the objects to which you have been granted access (including your own). All users have access to these views. In a 12c database, an additional layer of views prefixed with CDB_ has been added to facilitate the new multitenant database feature that logically separates a traditional database into one container and optionally multiple pluggable databases.

The objects of greatest interest to a SQL programmer are those that contain, or give access to, data. These include tables, views, synonyms, indexes, and sequences.

Tables basically store data in rows segmented by columns. A view is a stored SELECT statement that can be referenced as though it were a table. It is nothing more than a named query. Instead of running the statement, the user issues a SELECT statement against the view. In effect, the user is selecting from the result of another selection. A synonym is an alias for a table (or a view). Users can execute SQL statements against the synonym, and the database will map them into statements against the object to which the synonym points. Indexes are a means of improving access times to rows in tables. If a query requires only one row, then rather than scanning the entire table to find the row, an index can provide a pointer to the row's exact location. Of course, the index itself must be searched, but this is often faster than scanning the table. A sequence is a construct that generates numbers. Sequences issue numbers in order on demand.

The remaining object types are less commonly relevant to a SQL programmer. Their use falls more within the realm of PL/SQL programmers and database administrators.

Users and Schemas

Many people use the terms *user* and *schema* interchangeably. In the Oracle environment, you can get away with this (though not necessarily with other database management systems). A *user* is a person who can connect to the database. The user will have a username and a password. A *schema* is a container for the objects owned by a user. When a user is created, their schema is created too. A schema is the objects owned by a user; initially, it will be empty.

Some schemas will always be empty; users will never create any objects because they do not need to and (if set up correctly) will not have the necessary privileges anyway. Users such as this will have been granted permissions, either through direct privileges or through roles, to use code and access data in other schemas owned by other users. Other users may be the reverse of this; they will own many objects but will never actually log on to the database. They might not even have been granted the CREATE SESSION privilege, so the account is effectively disabled (or indeed it can be locked); these schemas are used as repositories for code and data accessed by others.

Schema objects are objects with an owner. The unique identifier for an object of a particular type is not its name; it is its name prefixed with the name of the schema to which it belongs. Thus, the table HR.REGIONS is a table called REGIONS, which is owned by user HR. There could be another table named SYSTEM.REGIONS, which would be a completely different table (perhaps different in both structure and contents) owned by user SYSTEM and residing in their schema.

A number of users (and their associated schemas) are created automatically at database creation time. Principal among these are SYS and SYSTEM. User SYS owns the data dictionary, which is a set of tables (in the SYS schema) defining the database and its contents. SYS also owns several hundred PL/SQL packages, which consist of code that is provided for the use of database administrators and developers. Objects in the SYS schema should never be modified with data manipulation language (DML) commands. If you were to execute DML against the data dictionary tables, you would run the risk of corrupting the data dictionary, with disastrous results. You update the data dictionary by running DDL commands (such as CREATE TABLE), which provide a layer of abstraction between you and the data dictionary. The SYSTEM schema stores various additional objects used for administration and monitoring.

Depending on the options selected during database creation, there may be more users created. These users store code and data required by various database options. For example, the user MDSYS stores the objects used by Spatial, an option that extends the capabilities of an Oracle database to manage geographical information.

Naming Schema Objects

A schema object is owned by a user and must conform to certain rules:

- The name may be between 1 and 30 characters long (with the exception of database link names that may be up to 128 characters long).
- Reserved words (such as SELECT) cannot be used as object names.
- All names must begin with a letter of the alphabet.
- Object names can only include letters, numbers, the underscore (_), the dollar sign ($), or the hash symbol (#).
- Lowercase letters will be automatically converted to uppercase.

By enclosing the name within double quotes, all these rules (with the exception of the length) can be broken, but to get to the object subsequently, it must always be specified with double quotes, as in the examples in Figure 5-5. Note that the same restrictions also apply to column names.

NOTE Object names must be no longer than 30 characters. The characters can consist of letters and digits, as well as the underscore, dollar, and hash symbols.

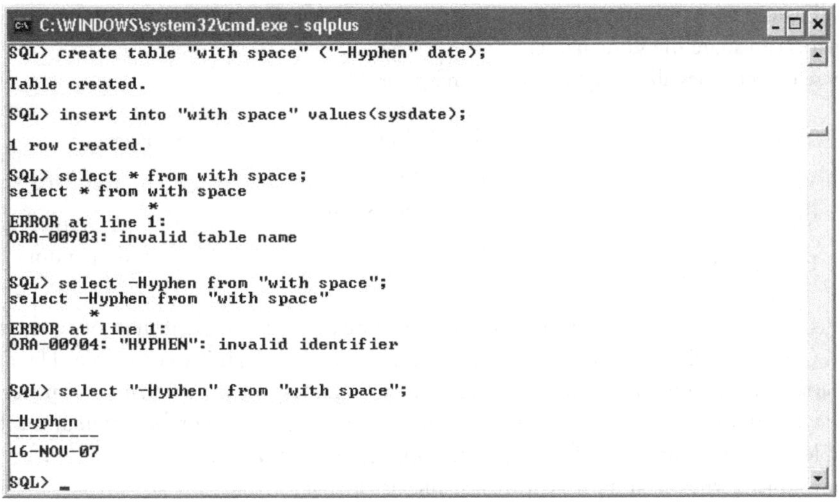

```
C:\WINDOWS\system32\cmd.exe - sqlplus

SQL> create table "with space" ("-Hyphen" date);

Table created.

SQL> insert into "with space" values(sysdate);

1 row created.

SQL> select * from with space;
select * from with space
                   *
ERROR at line 1:
ORA-00903: invalid table name


SQL> select -Hyphen from "with space";
select -Hyphen from "with space"
       *
ERROR at line 1:
ORA-00904: "HYPHEN": invalid identifier


SQL> select "-Hyphen" from "with space";

-Hyphen
---------
16-NOV-07

SQL> _
```

Figure 5-5   Using double quotes to use nonstandard names

Although tools such as SQL*Plus and SQL Developer will automatically convert lowercase letters to uppercase unless the name is enclosed within double quotes, remember that object names are always case sensitive. In this example, the two tables are completely different:

```
create table lower (c1 date);
Table created.

create table "lower" (col1 varchar2(2));
Table created.

select table_name
from user_tables
where lower(table_name) = 'lower';

TABLE_NAME
------------------------------
lower
LOWER
```

TIP   Although it is possible to use lowercase names and nonstandard characters (even spaces), it is considered bad practice because of the confusion it can cause.

Object Namespaces

Generally speaking, the unique identifier for an object is its name, which is dot prefixed with the schema name. However, for a full understanding of object naming, it is necessary to introduce the concept of a *namespace*. A namespace defines a group of object types, within which all names must be uniquely identified by schema and name. Objects in different namespaces can share the same name.

These object types all share the same namespace:

- Tables
- Views
- Sequences
- Private synonyms

- Stand-alone procedures
- Stand-alone stored functions

- Packages
- Materialized views
- User-defined types and operators

Thus, it is impossible to create a view with the same name as a table if they are in the same schema. Once created, SQL statements can address a view as though it were a table. The fact that tables, views, and private synonyms share the same namespace means that you can set up several layers of abstraction between what the users see and the actual tables, which can be invaluable for both security and for simplifying application development.

These object types each have their own namespace:

- Constraints
- Clusters

- Database triggers
- Private database links

- Dimensions

Thus, it is possible (though perhaps not a very good idea) for an index to have the same name as a table, even within the same schema.

 EXAM TIP   Within a schema, tables, views, and synonyms cannot have the same name.

Exercise 5-1: Determine What Objects Are Accessible to Your Session   In this exercise, query various data dictionary views as user HR to determine what objects belong to the HR schema and what objects in other schemas are accessible to HR. Please follow the instructions outlined in Chapter 7 to create the HR schema if it is absent from your database.

1. Connect to the database with SQL*Plus or SQL Developer as user HR.

2. Determine how many objects of each type are in the HR schema.

   ```
   select object_type, count(*)
   from user_objects
   group by object_type;
   ```

   The USER_OBJECTS view lists all objects owned by the schema to which the current session is connected, in this case HR.

3. Determine how many objects in total HR has permissions on.

   ```
   select object_type, count(*)
   from all_objects
   group by object_type;
   ```

   The ALL_OBJECTS view lists all objects to which the user has some sort of access.

4. Determine who owns the objects HR can see.

```
select distinct owner
from all_objects;
```

List the Data Types that Are Available for Columns

When creating tables, each column must be assigned a data type, which determines the nature of the values that can be inserted into the column. These data types are also used to specify the nature of the arguments for PL/SQL procedures and functions. When selecting a data type, you must consider the data you need to store and the operations you will want to perform upon it. Space is also a consideration. Some data types are fixed length, taking up the same number of bytes no matter what data is actually in it; others are variable. If a column is not populated, then Oracle will not give it any space at all. If you later update the row to populate the column, then the row will get bigger, no matter whether the data type is fixed length or variable. In a 12*c* database, a new system parameter, MAX_STRING_SIZE, allows string data types to be much larger than in previous versions when it is changed from its default value of STANDARD to EXTENDED.

The following are the data types for alphanumeric data:

- **VARCHAR2**   Variable-length character data, from 1 byte to 4,000 bytes if MAX_STRING_SIZE=STANDARD and up to 32,767 bytes if MAX_STRING_SIZE=EXTENDED. The data is stored in the database character set.

- **NVARCHAR2**   Like VARCHAR2, but the data is stored in the alternative national language character set, one of the permitted Unicode character sets.

- **CHAR**   Fixed-length character data, from 1 byte to 2,000 bytes, in the database character set. If the data is not the length of the column, then it will be padded with spaces.

   TIP   For compliance with the International Organization for Standardization (ISO) and the American National Standards Institute (ANSI), you can specify a VARCHAR data type, but any columns of this type will be automatically converted to VARCHAR2.

The following is the data type for binary data:

- **RAW**   Variable-length binary data, from 1 byte to 4,000 bytes if MAX_STRING_SIZE=STANDARD and up to 32,767 bytes if MAX_STRING_SIZE=EXTENDED. Unlike the CHAR and VARCHAR2 data types, RAW data is not converted by Oracle Net from the database's character set to the user process's character set on SELECT or the other way on INSERT.

The following are the data types for numeric data, all variable length:

- **NUMBER**   Numeric data, for which you can specify precision and scale. The precision can range from 1 to 38, and the scale can range from –84 to 127.

- **FLOAT**   An ANSI data type, floating-point number with a precision of 126 binary (or 38 decimal). Oracle also provides BINARY_FLOAT and BINARY_DOUBLE as alternatives.

- **INTEGER**   Equivalent to NUMBER, with scale zero.

The following are the data types for date and time data, all fixed length:

- **DATE**   This is either length zero, if the column is empty, or 7 bytes. All DATE data includes century, year, month, day, hour, minute, and second. The valid range is from January 1, 4712 BC, to December 31, 9999 AD.

- **TIMESTAMP**   This is length zero if the column is empty, or up to 11 bytes, depending on the precision specified. This is similar to DATE, but with a precision of up to nine decimal places for the seconds and six places by default.

- **TIMESTAMP WITH TIMEZONE**   This is like TIMESTAMP, but the data is stored with a record kept of the time zone to which it refers. The length may be up to 13 bytes, depending on precision. This data type lets Oracle determine the difference between two times by normalizing them to Coordinated Universal Time (UTC), even if the times are for different time zones.

- **TIMESTAMP WITH LOCAL TIMEZONE**   This is like TIMESTAMP, but the data is normalized to the database time zone on saving. When retrieved, it is normalized to the time zone of the user process selecting it.

- **INTERVAL YEAR TO MONTH**   This is used for recording a period in years and months between two DATEs or TIMESTAMPs.

- **INTERVAL DAY TO SECOND**   This is used for recording a period in days and seconds between two DATEs or TIMESTAMPs.

The following are the large object data types:

- **CLOB**   Character data stored in the database character set. The size is effectively unlimited: 4GB minus 1 multiplied by the database block size.

- **NCLOB**   Like CLOB, but data is stored in the alternative national language character set, one of the permitted Unicode character sets.

- **BLOB**   Like CLOB, but binary data that will not undergo character set conversion by Oracle Net.

- **BFILE**   A locator pointing to a file stored on the operating system of the database server. The size of the files is limited to 2 to the power of 64 minus 1, though your operating system may have other ideas.

- **LONG**   Character data in the database character set, up to 2GB minus 1. All the functionality of LONG (and more) is provided by CLOB; LONGs should not be used in a modern database, and if your database has any columns of this type, they should be converted to CLOB. There can be only one LONG column in a table.

- **LONG RAW**   Like LONG, but binary data that will not be converted by Oracle Net. Any LONG RAW columns should be converted to BLOBs.

The following is the ROWID data type:

- **ROWID**   This is a value coded in base 64 that is the pointer to the location of a row in a table. It is encrypted. Within it is the exact physical address. ROWID is an Oracle proprietary data type that is not visible unless specifically selected.

EXAM TIP   For the exam you will be expected to know about these data types: VARCHAR2, CHAR, NUMBER, DATE, TIMESTAMP, INTERVAL, RAW, LONG, LONG RAW, CLOB, BLOB, BFILE, and ROWID. Detailed knowledge will also be needed of VARCHAR2, NUMBER, and DATE.

The VARCHAR2 data type must be qualified with a number indicating the maximum length of the column. If a value is inserted into the column that is less than this, it is not a problem. The value will take up only as much space as it needs. If the value is longer than this maximum, the INSERT will fail with an error. If the value is updated to a longer or shorter value, the length of the column (and therefore the row itself) will change accordingly. If it is not entered at all or is updated to NULL, then it will take up no space at all.

The NUMBER data type may optionally be qualified with a precision and a scale. The precision sets the maximum number of significant decimal digits, where the most significant digit is the left-most nonzero digit and the least significant digit is the right-most known digit in the number. The scale is the number of digits from the decimal point to the least significant digit. A positive scale is the number of significant digits to the right of the decimal point to (and including) the least significant digit. A negative scale is the number of significant digits to the left of the decimal point to (but not including) the least significant digit.

The DATE data type always includes century, year, month, day, hour, minute, and second—even if all these elements are not specified at insert time. Year, month, and day must be specified; if the hours, minutes, and seconds are omitted, they will default to midnight. Using the TRUNC function on a date also has the effect of setting the hours, minutes, and seconds to midnight.

Exercise 5-2: Investigate the Data Types in the HR Schema   In this exercise, find out what data types are used in the tables in the HR schema, using two techniques.

1. Connect to the database as user HR with SQL*Plus or SQL Developer.

2. Use the DESCRIBE command to show the data types in some tables.

   ```
   describe employees;
   describe departments;
   ```

3. Use a query against a data dictionary view to show what columns make up the EMPLOYEES table, like the DESCRIBE command would.

   ```
   select column_name, data_type, nullable, data_length, data_precision,
   data_scale
   from user_tab_columns
   where table_name='EMPLOYEES';
   ```

   The view USER_TAB_COLUMNS shows the detail of every column in every table in the current user's schema.

Create a Simple Table

Tables can be stored in the database in several ways. The simplest is the *heap* table. A heap consists of variable-length rows in random order. There may be some correlation between the order in which rows are entered and the order in which they are stored, but this is a matter of luck. More advanced table structures, such as the following, may impose ordering and grouping on the rows or force a random distribution:

- **Index organized tables**   These store rows in the order of an index key.

- **Index clusters**   These can denormalize tables in parent-child relationships so that related rows from different tables are stored together.

- **Hash clusters**   These force a random distribution of rows, which will break down any ordering based on the entry sequence.

- **Partitioned tables**   These store rows in separate physical structures, the partitions, and allocate rows according to the value of a column.

Using the more advanced table structures has no effect whatsoever on SQL. Every SQL statement executed against tables defined with these options will return the same results as though the tables were standard heap tables, so using these features will not affect code. But while their use is transparent to programmers, they do give enormous benefits in performance.

Creating Tables with Column Specifications

To create a standard heap table, use this syntax:

```
CREATE TABLE [schema.]table [ORGANIZATION HEAP]
(column datatype [DEFAULT expression]
[,column datatype [DEFAULT expression]…);
```

At a minimum, specify the table name (it will be created in your own schema if you don't specify someone else's) and at least one column with a data type. There are few developers who ever specify ORGANIZATION HEAP because this is the default and is industry-standard SQL. The DEFAULT keyword in a column definition lets you provide an expression that will generate a value for the column when a row is inserted if a value is not provided by the INSERT statement.

Consider this statement:

```
create table scott.emp
(empno number(4),
ename varchar2(10),
hiredate date default trunc(sysdate),
sal number(7,2),
comm number(7,2) default 0.03);
```

This will create a table called EMP in the SCOTT schema. Either user SCOTT himself has to issue the statement (in which case nominating the schema would not actually be necessary), or another user could issue it if he has been granted permission to create tables in another user's schema. Taking the columns one by one, here is a breakdown:

- EMPNO can be four digits long, with no decimal places. If any decimals are included in an INSERT statement, they will be rounded (up or down) to the nearest integer.

- ENAME can store any characters at all, up to ten of them.

- HIREDATE will accept any date, optionally with the time, but if a value is not provided, today's date will be entered as midnight.

- SAL, intended for the employee's salary, will accept numeric values with up to seven digits. A maximum of five digits may be to the left of the decimal point. If any digits over two are to the right of the decimal point, they will be rounded.

- COMM (for commission percentage) has a default value of 0.03, which will be entered if the INSERT statement does not include a value for this column.

Following creation of the table, these statements insert a row and select the result:

```
insert into scott.emp (empno, ename, sal)
values (1000, 'John', 1000.789);
1 row created.

select *
from scott.emp;

     EMPNO ENAME      HIREDATE        SAL       COMM
---------- ---------- --------- ---------- ----------
      1000 John       19-NOV-13    1000.79        .03
```

Note that values for the columns not mentioned in the INSERT statement have been generated by the DEFAULT clauses. Had those clauses not been defined in the table definition, the columns would have been NULL. Also note the rounding of the value provided for SAL.

TIP The DEFAULT clause can be useful, but it is of limited functionality. You cannot use a subquery to generate the default value; you can specify only literal values or functions or sequences.

Creating Tables from Subqueries

Rather than creating a table from nothing and then inserting rows into it (as in the previous section), tables can be created from other tables by using a subquery. This technique lets you create the table definition and populate the table with rows with just one statement. Any query at all can be used as the source of both the table structure and the rows. The syntax is as follows:

CREATE TABLE [*schema.*]*table* AS *subquery*;

All queries return a two-dimensional set of rows; this result is stored as the new table. Here is a simple example of creating a table with a subquery:

```
create table employees_copy as
select *
from employees;
```

This statement will create a table EMPLOYEES_COPY, which is an exact copy of the EMPLOYEES table, identical in both definition and the rows it contains. Any not null and check constraints on the columns will also be applied to the new table, but any primary key, unique, or foreign key constraints will not be. (Constraints are discussed later.) This is because these three types of constraints require indexes that might not be available or desired.

The following is a more complex example:

```
create table emp_dept as
select last_name ename, department_name dname, round(sysdate - hire_date)
service
from employees
natural join departments
order by dname, ename;
```

The rows in the new table will be the result of joining the two source tables, with two of the selected columns having their names changed. The new SERVICE column will be populated with the result of the arithmetic that computes the number of days since the employee was hired. The rows will be inserted in the order specified. This ordering will not be maintained by subsequent DML, but assuming the standard HR schema data, the new table will look like this:

```
select *
from emp_dept
where rownum < 10;
```

ENAME	DNAME	SERVICE
Gietz	Accounting	4203
De Haan	Executive	4713
Kochhar	Executive	3001
Chen	Finance	2994
Faviet	Finance	4133
Popp	Finance	2194
Sciarra	Finance	2992
Urman	Finance	2834
Austin	IT	3089

```
9 rows selected.
```

The subquery can, of course, include a WHERE clause to restrict the rows inserted into the new table. To create a table with no rows, use a WHERE clause that will exclude all rows:

```
create table no_emps as
select *
from employees
where 1=2;
```

The WHERE clause 1=2 can never return TRUE, so the table structure will be created, ready for use, but no rows will be inserted at creation time.

Altering Table Definitions After Creation

There are many alterations that can be made to a table after creation. Those that affect the physical storage fall into the domain of the database administrator, but many changes are purely logical and will be carried out by the SQL developers. The following are examples (for the most part self-explanatory):

- Adding columns:

```
alter table emp
add (job_id number);
```

- Modifying columns:

```
alter table emp
modify (comm number(4,2) default 0.05);
```

- Dropping columns:

```
alter table emp
drop column comm;
```

- Marking columns as unused:

```
alter table emp
set unused column job_id;
```

- Renaming columns:

```
alter table emp
rename column hiredate to recruited;
```

- Marking the table as read-only:

```
alter table emp
read only;
```

All of these changes are data definition language (DDL) commands with the built-in COMMIT. They are therefore nonreversible and will fail if there is an active transaction against the table. They are also virtually instantaneous, with the exception of dropping a column. Dropping a column can be a time-consuming exercise because as each column is dropped, every row must be restructured to remove the column's data. The SET UNUSED command, which makes columns nonexistent as far as SQL is concerned, is often a better alternative, followed, when convenient, by the following lines, which will drop all the unused columns in one pass through the table:

```
ALTER TABLE tablename
DROP UNUSED COLUMNS;
```

Marking a table as read-only will cause errors for any attempted DML commands. But the table can still be dropped. This can be disconcerting, but is perfectly logical when you think it through. A DROP command doesn't actually affect the table; it affects the tables in the data dictionary that define the table, and these are not read-only.

Dropping and Truncating Tables

The TRUNCATE TABLE command has the effect of removing every row from a table, while leaving the table definition intact. DROP TABLE is more drastic in that the table definition is removed as well. The syntax is as follows:

DROP TABLE [*schema.*]*tablename* ;

If *schema* is not specified, then the table called *tablename* in your currently logged-on schema will be dropped.

As with a TRUNCATE, SQL will not produce a warning before the table is dropped, and furthermore, as with any DDL command, it includes a COMMIT. But there are some restrictions; if any session (even your own) has a transaction in progress that includes a row in the table, then the DROP will fail, and it is also impossible to drop a table that is referred to in a foreign key constraint defined for another table. This table (or the constraint) must be dropped first.

 TIP Oracle 12c includes a recycle bin option that is enabled by default. This allows any dropped table to be restored unless it was dropped with the PURGE option or unless the recycle bin option has been disabled.

Exercise 5-3: Create Tables In this exercise, use SQL Developer to create a heap table, insert some rows with a subquery, and modify the table. Do some more modifications with SQL*Plus and then drop the table.

1. Connect to the database as user HR with SQL Developer.

2. Right-click the Tables branch of the navigation tree and click New Table.

3. Name the new table EMPS and use the Add Column button to set it up, as in the following illustration:

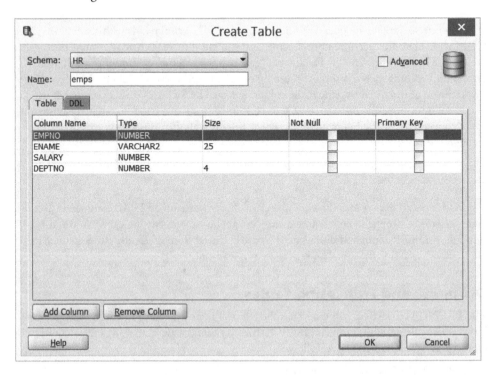

4. Click the DDL tab to see the statement has been constructed. It should look like this:

```
CREATE TABLE EMPS
(
EMPNO NUMBER
,ENAME VARCHAR2(25)
,SALARY NUMBER
,DEPTNO NUMBER(4, 0)
);
```

Return to the Table tab (as in the preceding illustration) and click OK to create the table.

5. Run this statement:

```
insert into emps
select employee_id, last_name, salary, department_id
from employees;
```

and commit the insert:

```
commit;
```

6. Right-click the EMPS table in the SQL Developer navigator and click Column and Add.

7. Define a new column HIRED, of type DATE, as in the following illustration; click Apply to create the column.

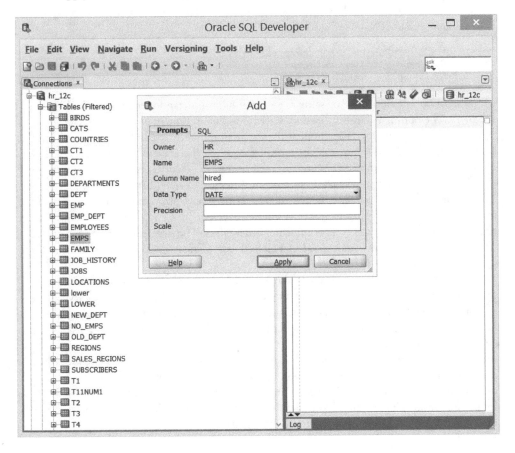

8. Connect to the database as HR with SQL*Plus.

9. Define a default for the HIRED column in the EMPS table:

```
alter table emps
modify (hired default sysdate);
```

10. Insert a row without specifying a value for HIRED and check that the new row does have a HIRED date but that the other rows do not:

```
insert into emps (empno, ename)
values (99, 'Newman');

select hired, count(1)
from emps
group by hired;
```

11. Tidy up by dropping the new table:

```
drop table emps;
```

Create and Use Temporary Tables

A *temporary* table has a definition that is visible to all sessions, but the rows within it are private to the session that inserted them. Programmers can use them as a private storage area for manipulating large amounts of data. The syntax is as follows:

```
CREATE GLOBAL TEMPORARY TABLE temp_tab_name
(column datatype [,column datatype] )
[ON COMMIT {DELETE | PRESERVE} ROWS] ;
```

The column definition is the same as a regular table and can indeed be supplied from a subquery. The optional clause at the end determines the lifetime of any rows inserted. The default is to remove the rows the moment the transaction that inserted them completes, but this behavior can be changed to preserve them until the session that inserted them ends. Whichever option is chosen, the data will be private to each session; different users can insert their own rows into their own copy of the table, and they will never see each other's rows.

In many ways, a temporary table is similar to a permanent table. You can execute any DML or SELECT command against it. It can have indexes, constraints, and triggers defined. It can be referenced in views and synonyms or joined to other tables. The difference is that the data is transient and private to the session and that all SQL commands against it will be far faster than commands against permanent tables.

The first reason for the speed is that temporary tables are not segments in permanent tablespaces. The table gets written out to a temporary segment in the user's temporary tablespace. I/O on temporary tablespaces is much faster than I/O on permanent tablespaces because it does not go via the database buffer cache; it is all performed directly on disk by the session's server process.

A second reason for speed is that DML against temporary tables does not generate redo. Since the data persists only for the duration of a session (perhaps only for the duration of a transaction), there is no purpose in generating a redo. This gives the dual benefit of fast DML for the session working on the table and taking the strain off the redo generation system, which can be a bad point of contention on busy multiuser databases.

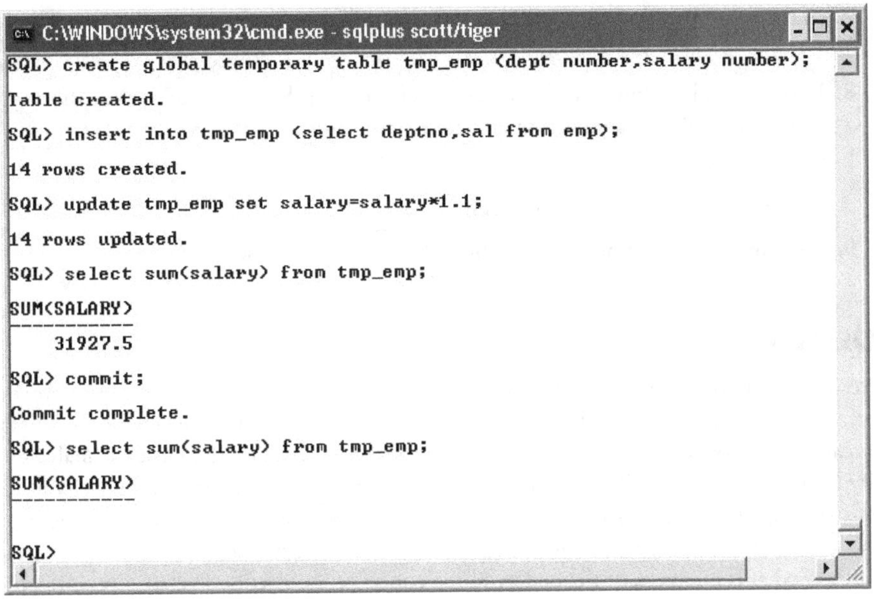

```
C:\WINDOWS\system32\cmd.exe - sqlplus scott/tiger
SQL> create global temporary table tmp_emp (dept number,salary number);
Table created.
SQL> insert into tmp_emp (select deptno,sal from emp);
14 rows created.
SQL> update tmp_emp set salary=salary*1.1;
14 rows updated.
SQL> select sum(salary) from tmp_emp;

SUM(SALARY)
-----------
    31927.5
SQL> commit;
Commit complete.
SQL> select sum(salary) from tmp_emp;

SUM(SALARY)
-----------

SQL>
```

Figure 5-6   Creation and use of a temporary table

Figure 5-6 shows the creation and use of a temporary table with SQL*Plus. The Database Control Table Creation Wizard can also create temporary tables.

Exercise 5-4: Create and Use Temporary Tables   In this exercise, create a temporary table to be used for reporting on current employees. Demonstrate, by using two SQL*Plus sessions, that the data is private to each session.

1. Connect to your database with SQL*Plus as user HR.

2. Create a temporary table as follows:
   ```
   create global temporary table tmp_emps on commit preserve rows as
   select * from employees where 1=2;
   ```

3. Insert some rows and commit them.
   ```
   insert into tmp_emps select * from employees where department_id=30;
   commit;
   ```

4. Start a second SQL*Plus session as HR.

5. In the second session, confirm that the first insert is not visible, even though it was committed in the first session, and insert some different rows.
   ```
   select count(*) from tmp_emps;
   insert into tmp_emps select * from employees where department_id=50;
   commit;
   ```

6. In the first session, truncate the table.
   ```
   truncate table tmp_emps;
   ```

7. In the second session, confirm that there are still rows in that session's copy of the table.

```
select count(*) from tmp_emps;
```

8. In the second session, demonstrate that terminating the session does clear the rows. This will require disconnecting and connecting again.

```
disconnect;
connect hr/hr
select count(*) from tmp_emps;
```

9. Tidy up the environment by dropping the tables in both sessions.

Indexes

Indexes have two functions: to enforce primary key and unique constraints and to improve performance. An application's indexing strategy is critical for performance. There is no clear demarcation of whose domain index management lies within. When the business analysts specify business rules that will be implemented as constraints, they are in effect specifying indexes. The database administrators will be monitoring the execution of code running in the database and will make recommendations for indexes. The developer, who should have the best idea of what is going on in the code and the nature of the data, will also be involved in developing the indexing strategy.

Why Indexes Are Needed

Indexes are part of the constraint mechanism. If a column (or a group of columns) is marked as a table's primary key, then every time a row is inserted into the table, Oracle must check that a row with the same value in the primary key does not already exist. If the table has no index on the columns, the only way to do this would be to scan right through the table, checking every row. Although this might be acceptable for a table of only a few rows, for a table with thousands or millions (or billions) of rows, this is not feasible. An index gives (near) immediate access to key values, so the check for existence can be made virtually instantaneously. When a primary key constraint is defined, Oracle will automatically create an index on the primary key columns, if one does not exist already.

A unique constraint also requires an index. It differs from a primary key constraint in that the columns of the unique constraint can be left null. This does not affect the creation and use of the index. Foreign key constraints are enforced by indexes, but the index must exist on the parent table, not necessarily on the table for which the constraint is defined. A foreign key constraint relates a column in the child table to the primary key or to a unique key in the parent table. When a row is inserted in the child table, Oracle will do a lookup on the index on the parent table to confirm that there is a matching row before permitting the insert. However, you should always create indexes on the foreign key columns within the child table for performance reasons; a DELETE on the parent table will be much faster if Oracle can use an index to determine whether there are any rows in the child table referencing the row that is being deleted.

Indexes are critical for performance. When executing any SQL statement that includes a WHERE clause, Oracle has to identify which rows of the table are to be selected or modified. If there is no index on the columns referenced in the WHERE clause, the only way to do this is with a *full table scan*. A full table scan reads every row of the table in order to find the relevant rows. If the table has many rows, this can take a long time. If there is an index on the relevant columns, Oracle can search the index instead. An index is a sorted list of key values, structured in a manner that makes the search very efficient. With each key value is a pointer to the row in the table. Locating relevant rows via an index lookup is far faster than using a full table scan, if the table is over a certain size and the proportion of the rows to be retrieved is below a certain value. For small tables or for a WHERE clause that will retrieve a large fraction of the table's rows, a full table scan will be quicker. You can (usually) trust Oracle to make the correct decision regarding whether to use an index based on statistical information the database gathers about the tables and the rows within them.

A second circumstance where indexes can be used is for sorting. A SELECT statement that includes the ORDER BY, GROUP BY, or UNION keyword (and a few others) must sort the rows into order—unless there is an index, which can return the rows in the correct order without needing to sort them first.

A third circumstance when indexes can improve performance is when tables are joined, but again Oracle has a choice. Depending on the size of the tables and the memory resources available, it may be quicker to scan tables into memory and join them there, rather than use indexes. The *nested loop join* technique passes through one table using an index on the other table to locate the matching rows; this is usually a disk-intensive operation. A *hash join* technique reads the entire table into memory, converts it into a hash table, and uses a hashing algorithm to locate matching rows; this is more memory and CPU intensive. A *sort merge join* sorts the tables on the join column and then merges them together; this is often a compromise among disk, memory, and CPU resources. If there are no indexes, then Oracle is severely limited in the join techniques available.

TIP   Indexes assist SELECT statements and also any UPDATE, DELETE, or MERGE statements that use a WHERE clause, but they will slow down INSERT statements.

Types of Indexes

Oracle supports several types of indexes, each with several variations. The two index types of concern here are the B*Tree index, which is the default index type, and the bitmap index. As a general rule, indexes will improve performance for data retrieval but reduce performance for DML operations. This is because indexes must be maintained. Every time a row is inserted into a table, a new key must be inserted into every index on the table, which places an additional strain on the database. For this reason, on transaction processing systems it is customary to keep the number of indexes as low as possible (perhaps no more than those needed for the constraints) and on query-intensive systems such as a data warehouse to create as many as might be helpful.

B*Tree Indexes

A B*Tree index (the *B* stands for "balanced") is a tree structure. The root node of the tree points to nodes at the second level, which can point to nodes at the third level, and so on. The necessary depth of the tree will be largely determined by the number of rows in the table and the length of the index key values.

TIP The B*Tree structure is very efficient. If the depth is greater than three or four, then either the index keys are very long or the table has billions of rows. If neither of these is the case, then the index is likely to benefit from a rebuild.

The leaf nodes of the index tree store the rows' keys, in order, each with a pointer that identifies the physical location of the row. So to retrieve a row with an index lookup, if the WHERE clause is using an equality predicate on the indexed column, Oracle navigates down the tree to the leaf node containing the desired key value and then uses the pointer to find the row location. If the WHERE clause is using a nonequality predicate (such as LIKE, BETWEEN, >, or <), then Oracle can navigate down the tree to find the first matching key value and then navigate across the leaf nodes of the index to find all the other matching values. As it does so, it will retrieve the rows from the table in order.

The pointer to the row is the *rowid*. The rowid is an Oracle-proprietary pseudocolumn, which every row in every table has. Encrypted within it is the physical address of the row. Because rowids are not part of the SQL standard, they are never visible to a normal SQL statement, but you can see them and use them if you want. This is demonstrated in Figure 5-7.

The rowid for each row is globally unique. Every row in every table in the entire database will have a different rowid. The rowid encryption provides the physical address of the row; Oracle can use this to calculate which operating system file, and where in the file, the row is and go straight to it.

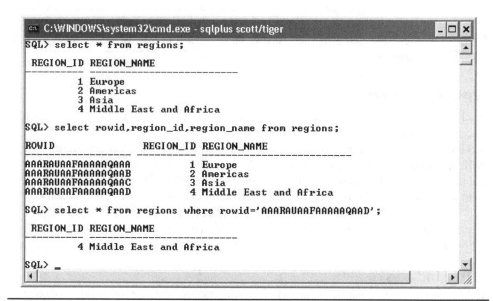

Figure 5-7 Displaying and using rowids

B*Tree indexes are an efficient way of retrieving rows if the number of rows needed is low in proportion to the total number of rows in the table and if the table is large. Consider this statement:

```
select count(*) from employees
where last_name between 'A%' and 'Z%';
```

This WHERE clause is sufficiently broad in that it will include every row in the table. It would be much slower to search the index to find the rowids and then use the rowids to find the rows than to scan the whole table. After all, it is the whole table that is needed. Another example is that if the table is small enough that one disk read can scan it in its entirety, there is no point in reading an index first.

It is often said that if the query is going to retrieve more than 2 to 4 percent of the rows, then a full table scan will be quicker. A special case is if the value specified in the WHERE clause is NULL. NULLs do not go into B*Tree indexes, so a query such as the following will always result in a full table scan:

```
select * from employees
where last_name is null;
```

There is little value in creating a B*Tree index on a column with few unique values because it will not be sufficiently selective; the proportion of the table that will be retrieved for each distinct key value will be too high. In general, B*Tree indexes should be used if the following items are true:

- The cardinality (the number of distinct values) in the column is high.

- The number of rows in the table is high.

- The column is used in WHERE clauses or JOIN conditions.

Bitmap Indexes

In many business applications, the nature of the data and the queries is such that B*Tree indexes are not of much use. Consider a table of sales for a chain of supermarkets that stores one year of historical data, which can be analyzed in several dimensions. Figure 5-8 shows a simple entity-relationship diagram, with just four of the dimensions.

Figure 5-8
A fact table with four dimensions

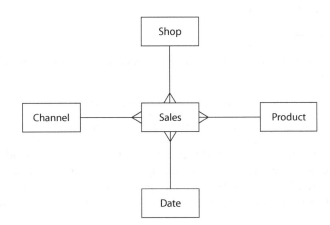

The cardinality of each dimension could be quite low. Make these assumptions:

SHOP	There are four shops.
PRODUCT	There are 200 products.
DATE	There are 365 days.
CHANNEL	There are two channels (walk-in and delivery).

Assuming an even distribution of data, only two of the dimensions (PRODUCT and DATE) have a selectivity that is better than the commonly used criterion of 2 percent to 4 percent, which makes an index worthwhile. But if queries use range predicates (such as counting sales in a month or of a class of ten or more products), then not even these will qualify. This is a simple fact: B*Tree indexes are often useless in a data warehouse environment. A typical query might want to compare sales between two shops by walk-in customers of a certain class of product in a month. There could well be B*Tree indexes on the relevant columns, but Oracle would ignore them as being insufficiently selective. This is what bitmap indexes are designed for.

A bitmap index stores the rowids associated with each key value as a bitmap. The bitmaps for the CHANNEL index might look like this:

```
WALK-IN     110101110001010111100010101.....
DELIVERY    001010001110101000101000010.....
```

This indicates that the first two rows were sales to walk-in customers, the third sale was a delivery, the fourth sale was a walk-in, and so on.

The bitmaps for the SHOP index might be as follows:

```
LONDON      11001001001001101000010000.....
OXFORD      00100010010000010001001000.....
READING     00010000000100000100100010.....
GLASGOW     00000100100010000010000101.....
```

This indicates that the first two sales were in the London shop, the third was in Oxford, the fourth in Reading, and so on. Now if this query is received:

```
select count(*) from sales
where channel='WALK-IN'
and shop='OXFORD';
```

Oracle can retrieve the two relevant bitmaps and add them together with a Boolean AND operation.

```
WALK-IN          110101110001010111100010101.....
OXFORD           00100010010000010001001000.....
WALK-IN & OXFORD 00000010000000010000000000.....
```

The result of the bitwise AND operation shows that only the seventh and sixteenth rows qualify for selection. This merging of bitmaps is fast and can be used to implement complex Boolean operations with many conditions on many columns using any combination of AND, OR, and NOT operators. A particular advantage that bitmap indexes have over B*Tree indexes is that they include NULLs. As far as the bitmap index is concerned, NULL is just another distinct value, which will have its own bitmap.

In general, bitmap indexes should be used if the following are true:

- The cardinality (the number of distinct values) in the column is low.
- The number of rows in the table is high.
- The column is used in Boolean algebra operations.

 TIP If you knew in advance what the queries would be, then you could build B*Tree indexes that would work, such as a composite index on SHOP and CHANNEL. But usually you don't know, which is where the dynamic merging of bitmaps provides great flexibility.

Index Type Options

There are six commonly used options that can be applied when creating indexes:

- Unique or nonunique
- Reverse key
- Compressed
- Composite
- Function based
- Ascending or descending

All six variations apply to B*Tree indexes, but only the last three can be applied to bitmap indexes.

A *unique* index will not permit duplicate values. Nonunique is the default. The unique attribute of the index operates independently of a unique or primary key constraint; the presence of a unique index will not permit insertion of a duplicate value even if there is no such constraint defined. A unique or primary key constraint can use a nonunique index; it will just happen to have no duplicate values. This is in fact a requirement for a constraint that is deferrable because there may be a period (before transactions are committed) when duplicate values do exist. Constraints are discussed in the next section.

A *reverse key* index is built on a version of the key column with its bytes reversed. Rather than indexing *John,* it will index *nhoJ.* When a SELECT is done, Oracle will automatically reverse the value of the search string. This is a powerful technique for avoiding contention in multiuser systems. For instance, if many users are concurrently inserting rows with primary keys based on a sequentially increasing number, all their index inserts will concentrate on the high end of the index. By reversing the keys, the consecutive index key inserts will tend to be spread over the whole range of the index. Even though *John* and *Jules* are close together, *nhoJ* and *seluJ* will be quite widely separated.

A *compressed* index stores repeated key values only once. The default is not to compress, meaning that if a key value is not unique, it will be stored once for each occurrence, each having a single rowid pointer. A compressed index will store the key once, followed by a string of all the matching rowids.

A *composite* index is built on the concatenation of two or more columns. There are no restrictions on mixing data types. If a search string does not include all the columns, the index can still be used, but if it does not include the leftmost column, Oracle will have to use a skip-scanning method that is much less efficient than if the left-most column is included.

A *function-based* index is built on the result of a function applied to one or more columns, such as UPPER(last_name) or TO_CHAR(startdate, 'ccyy-mm-dd'). A query will have to apply the same function to the search string, or Oracle may not be able to use the index.

By default, an index is *ascending,* meaning that the keys are sorted in order of lowest value to highest. A descending index reverses this. In fact, the difference is often not important. The entries in an index are stored as a doubly linked list, so it is possible to navigate up or down with equal celerity, but this will affect the order in which rows are returned if they are retrieved with an index full scan.

Creating and Using Indexes

Indexes are created implicitly when primary key and unique constraints are defined if an index on the relevant columns does not already exist. The basic syntax for creating an index explicitly is as follows:

```
CREATE [UNIQUE | BITMAP] INDEX [ schema.]indexname
ON [schema.]tablename (column [, column...] ) ;
```

The default type of index is a nonunique, noncompressed, non-reverse-key B*Tree index. It is not possible to create a unique bitmap index (and you wouldn't want to if you could—think about the cardinality issue). Indexes are schema objects, and it is possible to create an index in one schema on a table in another, but most people would find this somewhat confusing. A *composite* index is an index on several columns. Composite indexes can be on columns of different data types, and the columns do not have to be adjacent in the table.

 TIP   Many database administrators do not consider it good practice to rely on implicit index creation. If the indexes are created explicitly, the creator has full control over the characteristics of the index, which can make it easier for the database administrator (DBA) to manage subsequently.

Consider this example of creating tables and indexes and then defining constraints:

```
create table dept(deptno number,  dname varchar2(10));
create table emp (empno number, surname varchar2 (10),
 forename varchar2(10), dob date, deptno number);
create unique index dept_i1 on dept(deptno);
create unique index emp_i1 on emp(empno);
create index emp_i2 on emp(surname,forename);
create bitmap index emp_i3 on emp(deptno);
alter table dept add constraint dept_pk primary key (deptno);
alter table emp add constraint emp_pk primary key (empno);
alter table emp add constraint emp_fk
foreign key (deptno) references dept(deptno);
```

The first two indexes created are flagged as UNIQUE, meaning that it will not be possible to insert duplicate values. This is not defined as a constraint at this point but is true nonetheless.

The third index is not defined as UNIQUE and will therefore accept duplicate values; this is a composite index on two columns. The fourth index is defined as a bitmap index because the cardinality of the column is likely to be low in proportion to the number of rows in the table.

When the two primary key constraints are defined, Oracle will detect the preexisting indexes and use them to enforce the constraints. Note that the index on DEPT.DEPTNO has no purpose for performance because the table will in all likelihood be so small that the index will never be used to retrieve rows (a scan will be quicker), but it is still essential to have an index to enforce the primary key constraint.

Once created, indexes are used completely transparently and automatically. Before executing a SQL statement, the Oracle server will evaluate all the possible ways of executing it. Some of these ways may involve using whatever indexes are available; others may not. Oracle will make use of the information it gathers on the tables and the environment to make an intelligent decision about which (if any) indexes to use.

TIP   The Oracle server should make the best decision about index use, but if it is getting it wrong, it is possible for a programmer to embed instructions, known as *optimizer hints,* in code that will force the use (or not) of certain indexes.

Modifying and Dropping Indexes

The ALTER INDEX command cannot be used to change any of the characteristics described in this chapter, including the type (B*Tree or bitmap) of the index, the columns, and whether it is unique or nonunique. The ALTER INDEX command lies in the database administration domain and is typically used to adjust the physical properties of the index, not the logical properties that are of interest to developers. If it is necessary to change any of these properties, the index must be dropped and re-created. Continuing the example in the preceding section, to change the index EMP_I2 to include the employees' birthdays, you use this:

```
drop index emp_i2;
create index emp_i2 on emp(surname,forename,dob);
```

This composite index now includes columns with different data types. The columns happen to be listed in the same order that they are defined in the table, but this is by no means necessary.

When a table is dropped, all the indexes and constraints defined for the table are dropped as well. If an index was created implicitly by creating a constraint, then dropping the constraint will also drop the index. If the index had been created explicitly and the constraint created later, then if the constraint were dropped, the index would survive.

Exercise 5-5: Create Indexes   In this exercise, create, populate, and add some indexes to the CUSTOMERS table.

   1. Connect to the HR schema and create the CUSTOMERS, ORDERS, ORDER_ITEMS, and PRODUCTS tables as follows:

```
create table customers(customer_id number(8,0) not null,
   join_date date not null,customer_status varchar2(8) not null,
   customer_name varchar2(20) not null,creditrating varchar2(10));
```

```
create table orders (order_id number(8), order_date date, order_status
varchar2(8), order_amount number(10,2),
customer_id number(8));

create table order_items (order_item_id number(8),
order_id number(8), product_id number(8));

create table products(product_id number(8),
product_description varchar2(20), product_status varchar2(8),
price number (10,2), price_date date, stock_count number(8));
```

2. Create a compound B*Tree index on the customer names and status.

```
create index cust_name_i on customers (customer_name, customer_status);
```

3. Create bitmap indexes on a low-cardinality column.

```
create bitmap index creditrating_i on customers(creditrating);
```

4. Determine the name and some other characteristics of the indexes just created by running this query:

```
select index_name,column_name,index_type,uniqueness
from user_indexes natural join user_ind_columns
where table_name='CUSTOMERS';
```

Constraints

Table constraints are a means by which the database can enforce business rules and guarantee that the data conforms to the entity-relationship model determined by the systems analysis that defines the application data structures. For example, the business analysts of your organization may have decided that every customer and every order must be uniquely identifiable by number, that no orders can be issued to a customer before that customer has been created, and that every order must have a valid date and a value greater than zero. These would be implemented by creating primary key constraints on the CUSTOMER_ID column of the CUSTOMERS table and the ORDER_ID column of the ORDERS table, a foreign key constraint on the ORDERS table referencing the CUSTOMERS table, a not-null constraint on the DATE column of the ORDERS table (the DATE data type will itself ensure that any dates are valid automatically—it will not accept invalid dates), and a check constraint on the ORDER_AMOUNT column on the ORDERS table.

If any DML executed against a table with constraints defined violates a constraint, then the whole statement will be rolled back automatically. Remember that a DML statement that affects many rows might partially succeed before it hits a constraint problem with a particular row. If the statement is part of a multistatement transaction, then the statements that have already succeeded will remain intact but uncommitted.

 EXAM TIP   A constraint violation will force an automatic rollback of the entire statement that hit the problem, not just the single action within the statement and not the entire transaction.

The Types of Constraints

The constraint types supported by Oracle Database are as follows:

- UNIQUE
- NOT NULL
- PRIMARY KEY
- FOREIGN KEY
- CHECK
- REF

Constraints have names. It is good practice to specify the names with a standard naming convention, but if they are not explicitly named, Oracle will generate names. A discussion of REF constraints that are typically used in object-relational interactions is beyond the scope of this guide.

Unique Constraints

A *unique* constraint nominates a column (or combination of columns) for which the value must be different for every row in the table. If the constraint is based on a single column, this is known as the *key* column. If the constraint is composed of more than one column (known as a *composite key* unique constraint), the columns do not have to be the same data type or be adjacent in the table definition.

An oddity of unique constraints is that it is possible to enter a NULL value into the key columns; it is indeed possible to have any number of rows with NULL values in their key columns. This is because NULL is not equal to anything, not even to another NULL. So, selecting rows on a key column will guarantee that only one row is returned—unless you search for NULL, in which case all the rows where the key columns are NULL will be returned.

 EXAM TIP   It is possible to insert many rows with NULLs in a column with a unique constraint. This is not possible for a column with a primary key constraint.

Unique constraints are enforced by an index. When a unique constraint is defined, Oracle will look for an index on the key columns, and if one does not exist, it will be created. Then whenever a row is inserted, Oracle will search the index to see whether the values of the key columns are already present; if they are, it will reject the insert. The structure of these indexes (known as *B*Tree indexes*) does not include NULL values, which is why many rows with NULL are permitted; they simply do not exist in the index. While the first purpose of the index is to enforce the constraint, it has a secondary effect: improving performance if the key columns are used in the WHERE clauses of SQL statements. However, selecting WHERE *key_column* IS NULL cannot use the index (because it doesn't include the NULLs) and will therefore always result in a scan of the entire table.

Not-Null Constraints

The *not-null* constraint forces values to be entered into the key column. Not-null constraints are defined per column and are sometimes called *mandatory columns*; if the business requirement is that a group of columns should all have values, you cannot define one not-null constraint for the whole group but must define a not-null constraint for each column.

Any attempt to insert a row without specifying values for the not-null-constrained columns results in an error. It is possible to bypass the need to specify a value by including a DEFAULT clause on the column when creating the table, as discussed in the earlier section "Creating Tables with Column Specifications."

Primary Key Constraints

The *primary key* is the means of locating a single row in a table. The relational database paradigm includes a requirement that every table should have a primary key, namely, a column (or combination of columns) that can be used to distinguish every row. Oracle Database deviates from the paradigm (as do some other RDBMS implementations) by permitting tables without primary keys.

The implementation of a primary key constraint is in effect the union of a unique constraint and a not-null constraint. The key columns must have unique values, and they may not be null. As with unique constraints, an index must exist on the constrained columns. If one does not exist already, an index will be created when the constraint is defined. A table can have only one primary key. Try to create a second, and you will get an error. A table can, however, have any number of unique constraints and not-null columns, so if there are several columns that the business analysts have decided must be unique and populated, one of these can be designated the primary key and the others made unique and not null. An example could be a table of employees, where e-mail address, Social Security number, and employee number are all required and unique.

 EXAM TIP Unique and primary key constraints need an index. If one does not exist, one will be created automatically.

Foreign Key Constraints

A *foreign key* constraint is defined on the child table in a parent-child relationship. The constraint nominates a column (or columns) in the child table that corresponds to the primary key columns in the parent table. The columns do not need to have the same names, but they must be of the same data type. Foreign key constraints define the relational structure of the database, that is, the many-to-one relationships that connect the table, in their third normal form.

If the parent table has unique constraints as well as (or instead of) a primary key constraint, these columns can be used as the basis of foreign key constraints, even if they are nullable.

 EXAM TIP A foreign key constraint is defined on the child table, but a unique or primary key constraint must already exist on the parent table.

Just as a unique constraint permits null values in the constrained column, so does a foreign key constraint. You can insert rows into the child table with null foreign key columns—even if there is not a row in the parent table with a null value. This creates *orphan* rows and can cause dreadful confusion. As a general rule, all the columns in a unique constraint and all the columns in a foreign key constraint are best defined with not-null constraints as well; this will often be a business requirement.

Attempting to insert a row in the child table for which there is no matching row in the parent table will give an error. Similarly, deleting a row in the parent table will give an error if there are already rows referring to it in the child table. There are two techniques for changing this behavior. First, the constraint may be created as ON DELETE CASCADE. This means that if a row in the parent table is deleted, Oracle will search the child table for all the matching rows and delete them too. This will happen automatically. A less drastic technique is to create the constraint as ON DELETE SET NULL. In this case, if a row in the parent table is deleted, Oracle will search the child table for all the matching rows and set the foreign key columns to null. This means that the child rows will be orphaned but will still exist. If the columns in the child table also have a not-null constraint, then the deletion from the parent table will fail.

It is not possible to drop or truncate the parent table in a foreign key relationship, even if there are no rows in the child table. This still applies if the ON DELETE SET NULL or ON DELETE CASCADE clause was used.

A variation on the foreign key constraint is the *self-referencing* foreign key constraint. This defines a condition where the parent and child rows exist in the same table. An example is a table of employees that includes a column for the employee's manager. The manager is an employee and must exist in the table. So if the primary key is the EMPLOYEE_ID column and the manager is identified by a column MANAGER_ID, then the foreign key constraint will state that the value of the MANAGER_ID column must refer back to a valid EMPLOYEE_ID. If an employee is his own manager, then the row would refer to itself.

Check Constraints

A *check* constraint can be used to enforce simple rules, such as that the value entered in a column must be within a range of values. The rule must be an expression that will evaluate to TRUE or FALSE. The rules can refer to absolute values entered as literals or to other columns in the same row, and they may make use of some functions. As many check constraints as you want can be applied to one column, but it is not possible to use a subquery to evaluate whether a value is permissible or to use functions such as SYSDATE.

TIP The not-null constraint is in fact implemented as a preconfigured check constraint.

Defining Constraints

Constraints can be defined when creating a table or added to the table later. When defining constraints at table creation time, the constraint can be defined inline with the column to which it refers or at the end of the table definition. There is more flexibility to using the latter technique. For example, it is impossible to define a foreign key constraint that refers to two columns or a check constraint that refers to any column other than that being constrained if the constraint is defined inline, but both these are possible if the constraint is defined at the end of the table.

For the constraints that require an index (the unique and primary key constraints), the index will be created with the table if the constraint is defined at table creation time.

Consider these two table creation statements (to which line numbers have been added):

```
1    create table dept (
2    deptno number(2,0) constraint dept_deptno_pk primary key
3    constraint dept_deptno_ck check (deptno between 10 and 90),
4    dname  varchar2(20) constraint dept_dname_nn not null
5    create table emp  (
6    empno     number(4,0) constraint emp_empno_pk primary key,
7    ename     varchar2(20) constraint emp_ename_nn not null,
8    mgr       number (4,0) constraint emp_mgr_fk references emp (empno),
9    dob       date,
10    hiredate date,
11   deptno    number(2,0) constraint emp_deptno_fk references dept(deptno)
12    on delete set null,
13    email varchar2(30) constraint emp_email_uk unique,
14    constraint emp_hiredate_ck check (hiredate >= dob + 365*16),
15    constraint emp_email_ck
16    check ((instr(email,'@') > 0) and (instr(email,'.') > 0)));
```

Taking these statements line by line, here is the process:

1. The first table created is DEPT, intended to have one row for each department.

2. DEPTNO is numeric, two digits, no decimals. This is the table's primary key. The constraint is named DEPT_DEPTNO_PK.

3. A second constraint applied to DEPTNO is a check limiting it to numbers in the range 10 to 90. The constraint is named DEPT_DEPTNO_CK.

4. The DNAME column is variable-length characters, with a constraint DEPT_DNAME_NN making it not nullable.

5. The second table created is EMP, intended to have one row for every employee.

6. EMPNO is numeric, up to four digits with no decimals. Constraint EMP_EMPNO_PK marks this as the table's primary key.

7. ENAME consists of variable-length characters, with a constraint EMP_ENAME_NN making it not nullable.

8. MGR is the employee's manager, who must himself be an employee. The column is defined in the same way as the table's primary key column of EMPNO. The constraint EMP_MGR_FK defines this column as a self-referencing foreign key, so any value entered must refer to an already existing row in EMP (though it is not constrained to be not null, so it can be left blank).

9. DOB, the employee's birthday, is a date and not constrained.

10. HIREDATE is the date the employee was hired and is not constrained. At least, not yet.

11. DEPTNO is the department with which the employee is associated. The column is defined in the same way as the DEPT table's primary key column of DEPTNO, and the constraint EMP_DEPTNO_FK enforces a foreign key relationship; it is not possible to assign an employee to a department that does not exist. This is nullable, however.

12. The EMP_DEPTO_FK constraint is further defined as ON DELETE SET NULL, so if the parent row in DEPT is deleted, all matching child rows in EMPNO will have DEPTNO set to NULL.

13. EMAIL is variable-length character data and must be unique if entered (though it can be left empty).

14. This defines an additional table-level constraint EMP_HIREDATE_CK. The constraint checks for use of child labor by rejecting any rows where the date of hiring is not at least 16 years later than the birthday. This constraint could not be defined inline with HIREDATE because the syntax does not allow references to other columns at that point.

15. An additional constraint EMP_EMAIL_CK is added to the EMAIL column, which makes two checks on the e-mail address. The INSTR functions search for the at (@) sign and dot (.) characters (which will always be present in a valid e-mail address); if it can't find both of them, the check condition will return FALSE, and the row will be rejected.

The preceding examples show several possibilities for defining constraints at table creation time. Further possibilities not covered include the following:

- Controlling the index creation for the unique and primary key constraints

- Defining whether the constraint should be checked at insert time (which it is by default) or later, when the transaction is committed

- Stating whether the constraint is in fact being enforced at all (which is the default) or is disabled

It is possible to create tables with no constraints and then to add them later with an ALTER TABLE command. The end result will be the same, but this technique does make the code less self-documenting because the complete table definition will then be spread over several statements rather than being in one.

Constraint State

At any time, every constraint is either enabled or disabled and validated or not validated. Any combination of these is syntactically possible:

- **ENABLE VALIDATE** It is not possible to enter rows that will violate the constraint, and all rows in the table conform to the constraint.

- **DISABLE NOVALIDATE** Any data (conforming or not) can be entered, and there may already be nonconforming data in the table.

- **ENABLE NOVALIDATE** There may already be nonconforming data in the table, but all data entered now must conform.

- **DISABLE VALIDATE** All data in the table conforms to the constraint, but new rows need not. The index is also dropped on the constraint.

The ideal situation (and the default when a constraint is defined) is ENABLE VALIDATE. This will guarantee that all the data is valid, and no invalid data can be entered. The other extreme, DISABLE NOVALIDATE, can be useful when uploading large amounts of data into a table. It may well be that the data being uploaded does not conform to the business rules, but rather than have a large upload fail because of a few bad rows, putting the constraint in this state will allow the upload to succeed. Immediately following the upload, transition the constraint into the ENABLE NOVALIDATE state. This will prevent the situation from deteriorating further while the data is checked for conformance before transitioning the constraint to the ideal state.

As an example, consider this script, which reads data from a source table of live data into a table of archive data. The assumption is that there is a NOT NULL constraint on a column of the target table that may not have been enforced on the source table.

```
alter table sales_archive modify constraint sa_nn1 disable novalidate;
insert into sales_archive
select * from sales_current;
alter table sales_archive modify constraint sa_nn1 enable novalidate;
update sales_archive set channel='NOT KNOWN' where channel is null;
alter table sales_archive modify constraint sa_nn1 enable validate;
```

Constraint Checking

Constraints can be checked as a statement is executed (an IMMEDIATE constraint) or when a transaction is committed (a DEFERRED constraint). By default, all constraints are IMMEDIATE and not deferrable. An alternative approach to the previous example would have been possible had the constraint been created as deferrable.

```
set constraint sa_nn1 deferred;
insert into sales_archive
select * from sales_current;
update sales_archive set channel='NOT KNOWN' where channel is null;
commit;
set constraint sa_nn1 immediate;
```

For the constraint to be deferrable, it must have been created with the appropriate syntax.

```
alter table sales_archive add constraint sa_nn1
check (channel is not null) deferrable initially immediate;
```

It is not possible to make a constraint deferrable later if it was not created that way. The constraint SA_NN1 will, by default, be enforced when a row is inserted (or updated), but the check can be postponed until the transaction commits. A common use for deferrable constraints is with foreign keys. If a process inserts or updates rows in both the parent and child tables, then if the foreign key constraint is not deferred, the process may fail if rows are not processed in the correct order.

Changing the status of a constraint between ENABLED/DISABLED and VALIDATE/NOVALIDATE is an operation that will affect all sessions. The status change is a data dictionary update. Switching a deferrable constraint between IMMEDIATE and DEFERRED is session specific, though the initial state will apply to all sessions.

 EXAM TIP By default, constraints are enabled and validated, and they are not deferrable.

Exercise 5-6: Manage Constraints   In this exercise, define and adjust some constraints on the table created in Exercise 5-5.

1. In SQL Developer, navigate to the HR schema and click the CUSTOMERS table.

2. Go to the Constraints tab to view the four NOT NULL constraints that were created with the table. Note that their names are not helpful—this will be fixed in step 8.

3. Click the Actions button and choose Constraints: Add Primary Key.

4. In the Add Primary Key window, name the constraint PK_CUSTOMER_ID, choose the CUSTOMER_ID column, and click Apply.

5. Choose the Show SQL tab to see the constraint creation statement and then click the Apply button to run the statement.

6. Connect to your database as user HR with SQL*Plus.

7. Run this query to find the names of the constraints:

```
select constraint_name, constraint_type, column_name
from user_constraints natural join user_cons_columns
where table_name='CUSTOMERS';
```

8. Rename the constraints to something more meaningful using the original constraint names retrieved in step 7, with ALTER TABLE commands.

```
ALTER TABLE CUSTOMERS RENAME CONSTRAINT old_name TO new_name ;
```

9. Add the following constraints to the HR schema:

```
alter table orders add constraint pk_order_id primary key(order_id);
alter table products add constraint pk_product_id primary key(product_id);
alter table order_items add constraint fk_product_id foreign key(product_id)
references products(product_id);
alter table order_items add constraint fk_order_id foreign key(order_id)
references orders(order_id);
alter table orders add constraint fk_customer_id foreign key(customer_id)
references customers(customer_id);
```

Views

To the user, a view looks like a table, in other words, a two-dimensional structure of rows of columns against which the user can run SELECT and DML statements. The programmer knows the truth: A view is just a named SELECT statement. Any SELECT statement returns a two-dimensional set of rows. If the SELECT statement is saved as a view, then whenever the users query or update rows in the view (under the impression that it is a table), the statement runs, and the result is presented to users as though it were a table. The SELECT statement on which a view is based can be anything. It can join tables, perform aggregations, or do sorts; absolutely any legal SELECT command can be used as the basis for a view.

 EXAM TIP   Views share the same namespace as tables. Anywhere that a table name can be used, a view name is also syntactically correct.

Why Use Views at All?

Possible reasons include providing security, simplifying user SQL statements, preventing errors, improving performance, and making data comprehensible. Table and column names are often long and pretty meaningless. The view and its columns can be much more obvious.

Views to Enforce Security

It may be that users should see only certain rows or columns of a table. There are several ways of enforcing this, but a view is often the simplest. Consider the HR.EMPLOYEES table. This includes personal details that should not be visible to staff outside the personnel department. But finance staff will need to be able to see the costing information. This view will depersonalize the data.

```
create view hr.emp_fin as
select hire_date,job_id,salary,commission_pct,department_id from hr.employees;
```

Note the use of schema qualifiers for the table as the source of the data (often referred to as either the *base* or the *detail* table) and the view; views are schema objects and can draw their data from tables in the same schema or in other schemas. If the schema is not specified, it will, of course, be in the current schema.

Finance staff can then be given permission to see the view but not the table and can issue statements such as this:

```
select * from emp_fin where department_id=50;
```

They will see only the five columns that make up the view, not the remaining columns of EMPLOYEES with the personal information. The view can be joined to other tables or aggregated as though it were a table.

```
select department_name, sum(salary) dept_sal
from departments natural join emp_fin
group by department_name;
```

A well-constructed set of views can implement a whole security structure within the database, giving users access to data they need to see while concealing data they do not need to see.

Views to Simplify User SQL

It will be much easier for users to query data if the hard work (such as joins or aggregations) is done for them by the code that defines the view. In the previous example, the user had to write code that joined the EMP_FIN view to the DEPARTMENTS table and summed the salaries per department. This could all be done in a view.

```
create view dept_sal as
select d.department_name, sum(e.salary) dept_sal
from departments d left outer join employees e on d.department_id=e.department_id
group by department_name order by department_name;
```

Then the users can select from DEPT_SAL without needing to know anything about joins or even how to sort the results.

```
select * from dept_sal;
```

In particular, they do not need to know how to make sure that all departments are listed, even those with no employees. The example in the preceding section would have missed these.

Views to Prevent Errors

It is impossible to prevent users from making errors, but well-constructed views can prevent some errors arising from a lack of understanding of how data should be interpreted. The preceding section already introduced this concept by constructing a view that will list all departments, whether or not they currently have staff assigned to them.

A view can help to present data in a way that is unambiguous. For example, many applications never actually delete rows. Consider this table:

```
create table emp  ( empno number constraint emp_empno_pk primary key,
ename  varchar2(10), deptno number, active varchar2(1) default 'Y');
```

The column ACTIVE is a flag indicating that the employee is currently employed and will default to Y when a row is inserted. When a user, through the user interface, "deletes" an employee, the underlying SQL statement will be an update that sets ACTIVE to N. If users who are not aware of this query the table, they may severely misinterpret the results. It will often be better to give them access to a view.

```
create view current_staff as select * from emp where active='Y';
```

Queries addressed to this view cannot possibly see "deleted" staff members.

Views to Make Data Comprehensible

The data structures in a database will be normalized tables. It is not reasonable to expect users to understand normalized structures. To take an example from the Oracle E-Business Suite, a "customer" in the Accounts Receivable module is, in fact, an entity consisting of information distributed across the tables HZ_PARTIES, HZ_PARTY_SITES, HZ_CUST_ACCTS_ALL, and many more. All these tables are linked by primary key–to–foreign key relationships, but these are not defined on any identifiers visible to users (such as a customer number). They are based on columns the users never see that have values generated internally from sequences. The forms and reports used to retrieve customer information never address these tables directly; they all work through views.

As well as presenting data to users in a comprehensible form, the use of views to provide a layer of abstraction between the objects seen by users and the objects stored within the database can be invaluable for maintenance work. It becomes possible to redesign the data structures without having to recode the application. If tables are changed, then adjusting the view definitions may make any changes to the SQL and PL/SQL code unnecessary. This can be a powerful technique for making applications portable across different databases.

Views for Performance

The SELECT statement behind a view can be optimized by programmers so that users don't need to worry about tuning code. There may be many possibilities for getting the same result, but some techniques can be much slower than others. For example, when joining two tables, there is usually a choice between the *nested loop* join and the *hash* join. A nested loop join uses an index to get to individual rows; a hash join reads the whole table into memory. The choice between the two will be dependent on the state of the data and the hardware resources available.

Theoretically, you can always rely on the Oracle optimizer to work out the best way to run a SQL statement, but there are cases where the optimizer gets it wrong. If the programmers know which technique is best, they can instruct the optimizer. This example forces use of the hash technique:

```
create view dept_emp as
select /*+USE_HASH (employees departments)*/ department_name, last_name
from departments natural join employees;
```

Whenever users query the DEPT_EMP view, the join will be performed by scanning the detail tables into memory. The users do not need to know the syntax for forcing use of this join method. You do not need to know it, either; this is beyond the scope of the Oracle Certified Professional (OCP) examination, but the concept of tuning with view design should be known.

Simple and Complex Views

For practical purposes, classification of a view as *simple* or *complex* is related to whether DML statements can be executed against it. Simple views can (usually) accept DML statements; complex views cannot. The strict definitions are as follows:

- A simple view draws data from one detail table, uses no functions, and does no aggregation.
- A complex view can join detail tables, use functions, and perform aggregations.

Applying these definitions shows that of the four views used as examples in the preceding section, the first and third are simple, and the second and fourth are complex.

It is not possible to execute INSERT, UPDATE, or DELETE commands against a complex view. The mapping of the rows in the view back to the rows in the detail tables cannot always be established on a one-to-one basis, which is necessary for DML operations. It is usually possible to execute DML against a simple view, but not always. For example, if the view does not include a column that has a NOT NULL constraint, then an INSERT through the view cannot succeed (unless the column has a default value). This can produce a disconcerting effect because the error message will refer to a table and a column that are not mentioned in the statement, as demonstrated in the first example in Figure 5-9.

The first view in the figure, RNAME_V, does conform to the definition of a simple view, but an INSERT cannot be performed through it because it is missing a mandatory column. The second view, RUPPERNAME_V, is a complex view because it includes a function. This makes an INSERT impossible because there is no way the database can work out what should actually be inserted. It can't reverse-engineer the effect of the UPPER function in a deterministic fashion. But the DELETE succeeds because that is not dependent on the function.

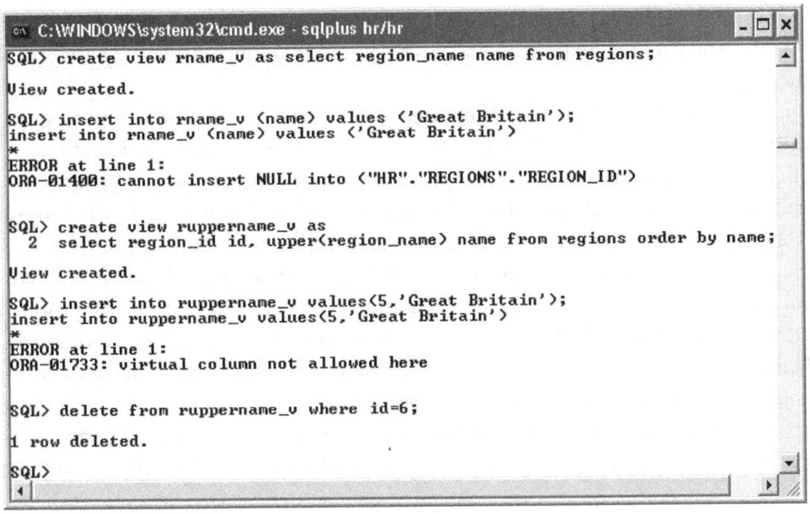

```
C:\WINDOWS\system32\cmd.exe - sqlplus hr/hr

SQL> create view rname_v as select region_name name from regions;

View created.

SQL> insert into rname_v (name) values ('Great Britain');
insert into rname_v (name) values ('Great Britain')
*
ERROR at line 1:
ORA-01400: cannot insert NULL into ("HR"."REGIONS"."REGION_ID")

SQL> create view ruppername_v as
  2  select region_id id, upper(region_name) name from regions order by name;

View created.

SQL> insert into ruppername_v values(5,'Great Britain');
insert into ruppername_v values(5,'Great Britain')
*
ERROR at line 1:
ORA-01733: virtual column not allowed here

SQL> delete from ruppername_v where id=6;

1 row deleted.

SQL>
```

Figure 5-9   DML against simple and complex views

CREATE VIEW, ALTER VIEW, and DROP VIEW

The syntax to create a view is as follows:

```
CREATE [OR REPLACE] [FORCE | NOFORCE] VIEW
[schema.]viewname [(alias [,alias]...)]
AS subquery
[WITH CHECK OPTION [CONSTRAINT constraintname]]
[WITH READ ONLY [CONSTRAINT constraintname]] ;
```

Note that views are schema objects. There is no reason not to have a view owned by one user referencing detail tables owned by another user. By default, the view will be created in the current schema. The optional keywords, none of which have been used in the examples so far, are as follows:

- **OR REPLACE**   If the view already exists, it will be dropped before being created.

- **FORCE or NOFORCE**   The FORCE keyword will create the view even if the detail tables in the subquery do not exist. NOFORCE is the default and will cause an error if the detail table does not exist.

- **WITH CHECK OPTION**   This has to do with DML. If the subquery includes a WHERE clause, then this option will prevent insertion of rows that wouldn't be seen in the view or updates that would cause a row to disappear from the view. By default, this option is not enabled, which can give disconcerting results.

- **WITH READ ONLY**   This prevents any DML through the view.

- **CONSTRAINT** *constraintname*   This can be used to name the WITH CHECK OPTION and WITH READ ONLY restrictions so that error messages when the restrictions cause statements to fail will be more comprehensible.

In addition, a set of alias names can be provided for the names of the view's columns. If not provided, the columns will be named after the table's columns or with aliases specified in the subquery.

The main use of the ALTER VIEW command is to compile the view. A view must be compiled successfully before it can be used. When a view is created, Oracle will check that the detail tables and the necessary columns on which the view is based do exist. If they do not, the compilation fails, and the view will not be created—unless you use the FORCE option. In that case, the view will be created but will be unusable until the tables or columns to which it refers are created and the view is successfully compiled. When an invalid view is queried, Oracle will attempt to compile it automatically. If the compilation succeeds because the problem has been fixed, users won't know there was ever a problem—except that their query may take a little longer than usual. Generally speaking, you should manually compile views to make sure they do compile successfully, rather than having users discover errors.

It is not possible to adjust a view's column definitions after creation in the way that a table's columns can be changed. The view must be dropped and re-created. The DROP command is as follows:

```
DROP VIEW [schema.]viewname ;
```

By using the OR REPLACE keywords with the CREATE VIEW command, the view will be automatically dropped (if it exists at all) before being created.

Exercise 5-7: Create Views   In this exercise, you will create some simple and complex views using data in the HR schema. Either SQL*Plus or SQL Developer can be used.

1. Connect to your database as user HR.

2. Create views on the EMPLOYEES and DEPARTMENT tables that remove all personal information.

```
create view emp_anon_v as
select hire_date, job_id,salary,commission_pct,department_id from employees;
create view dept_anon_v as
select department_id,department_name,location_id from departments;
```

3. Create a complex view that will join and aggregate the two simple views. Note that there is no reason you cannot have views of views.

```
create view dep_sum_v as
select e.department_id, count(1) staff, sum(e.salary) salaries,
d.department_name from emp_anon_v e join dept_anon_v d
on e.department_id=d.department_id
group by e.department_id,d.department_name;
```

4. Confirm that the view works by querying it.

Synonyms

A *synonym* is an alternative name for an object. If synonyms exist for objects, then any SQL statement can address the object either by its actual name or by its synonym. This may seem trivial. It isn't. Use of synonyms means that an application can function for any user, irrespective of which schema owns the views and tables or even in which database the tables reside. Consider this statement:

```
select * from hr.employees@prod;
```

The user issuing the statement must know that the employees table is owned by the HR schema in the database identified by the database link PROD (do not worry about database links—they are a means of accessing objects in a database other than that onto which you are logged). If a public synonym has been created with this statement:

```
create public synonym emp for hr.employees@prod;
```

then all the user (any user!) needs to enter is the following:

```
select * from emp;
```

This gives both data independence and location transparency. The user must have privileges to access the underlying object in order for the synonym-based reference to succeed. Tables and views can be renamed or relocated without ever having to change code; only the synonyms need to be adjusted.

As well as SELECT statements, DML statements can address synonyms as though they were the object to which they refer.

Private synonyms are schema objects. Either they must be in your own schema or they must be qualified with the schema name. Public synonyms exist independently of a schema. A public synonym can be referred to by any user to whom permission has been granted to see it without the need to qualify it with a schema name. Private synonyms must have unique names within their schema. Public synonyms can have the same name as schema objects. When executing statements that address objects without a schema qualifier, Oracle will first look for the object in the local schema, and only if it cannot be found will it look for a public synonym. Thus, in the preceding example, if the user happened to own a table called EMP, it would be this that would be seen, not the table pointed to by the public synonym.

The syntax to create a synonym is as follows:

```
CREATE [PUBLIC] SYNONYM synonym FOR object ;
```

A user will need to have been granted permission to create private synonyms and further permission to create public synonyms. Usually, only the database administrator can create (or drop) public synonyms. This is because their presence (or absence) will affect every user.

 EXAM TIP The *public* in *public synonym* means that it is not a schema object and cannot therefore be prefixed with a schema name. It does not mean that everyone has permissions against it.

To drop a synonym, do this:

```
DROP [PUBLIC] SYNONYM synonym ;
```

If the object to which a synonym refers (the table or view) is dropped, the synonym continues to exist. Any attempt to use it will return an error. In this respect, synonyms behave in the same way as views. If the object is re-created, the synonym must be recompiled before use. As with views, this will happen automatically the next time the synonym is addressed, or it can be done explicitly with this:

```
ALTER SYNONYM synonym COMPILE;
```

Exercise 5-8: Create and Use Synonyms   In this exercise, you will create and use private synonyms using objects in the HR schema. You can use either SQL*Plus or SQL Developer.

1. Connect to your database as user HR.

2. Create synonyms for the three views created in Exercise 5-7.

```
create synonym emp_s for emp_anon_v;
create synonym dept_s for dept_anon_v;
create synonym dsum_s for dep_sum_v;
```

3. Confirm that the synonyms are identical to the underlying objects.

```
describe emp_s;
describe emp_anon_v;
```

4. Confirm that the synonyms work (even to the extent of producing the same errors) by running the statements in Exercise 5-7 against the synonyms instead of the views.

```
select * from dsum_s;
insert into dept_s values    (99,'Temp Dept',1800 );
insert into emp_s values    (sysdate,'AC_MGR',10000,0,99);
update emp_s set salary=salary*1.1;
rollback;
select max(salaries / staff) from dsum_s;
```

5. Drop two of the views.

```
drop view emp_anon_v;
drop view dept_anon_v;
```

6. Query the complex view that is based on the dropped views.

```
select * from dep_sum_v;
```

Note that the query fails.

7. Attempt to recompile the broken view.

```
alter view dep_sum_v compile;
```

This fails as well.

8. Drop the DEP_SUM_V view.

```
drop view dep_sum_v;
```

9. Query the synonym for a dropped view.

```
select * from emp_s;
```

This fails.

10. Recompile the broken synonym.

```
alter synonym emp_s compile;
```

Note that this does not give an error, but rerun the query from step 9. It is definitely still broken.

11. Tidy up by dropping the synonyms.

```
drop synonym emp_s;
drop synonym dept_s;
drop synonym dsum_s;
```

Sequences

A sequence is a structure for generating unique integer values. Only one session can read the next value and thus force it to increment. This is a point of serialization, so each value generated will be unique.

Sequences are an invaluable tool for generating primary keys. Many applications will need automatically generated primary key values. Examples in everyday business data processing are customer numbers and order numbers. The business analysts will have stated that every order must have a unique number, which should continually increment. Other applications may not have such a requirement in business terms, but it will be needed to enforce relational integrity. Consider a telephone billing system. In business terms, the unique identifier of a telephone is the telephone number (which is a string), and the unique identifier of a call will be the source telephone number and the time the call began (which is a timestamp). These data types are unnecessarily complex to use as primary keys for the high volumes that go through a telephone switching system. While this information will be recorded, it will be much faster to use simple numeric columns to define the primary and foreign keys. The values in these columns can be sequence based.

The sequence mechanism is independent of tables, the row locking mechanism, and commit or rollback processing. This means that a sequence can issue thousands of unique values a minute—far faster than any method involving selecting a column from a table, updating it, and committing the change.

Figure 5-10 shows two sessions selecting values from a sequence called SEQ1.

Note that in the figure each selection of SEQ1.NEXTVAL generates a unique number. The numbers are issued consecutively in order of the time the selection was made, and the number increments globally, not just within one session.

Creating Sequences

The full syntax for creating a sequence is as follows:

```
CREATE SEQUENCE [schema.]sequencename
[INCREMENT BY number]
[START WITH number]
[MAXVALUE number | NOMAXVALUE]
[MINVALUE number | NOMINVALUE]
[CYCLE | NOCYCLE]
[CACHE number | NOCACHE]
[ORDER | NOORDER] ;
```

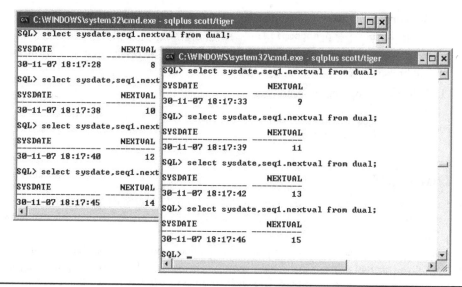

Figure 5-10 Use of a sequence by two sessions concurrently

You can see that creating a sequence can be simple. For example, the sequence used in Figure 5-6 was created with this:

```
create sequence seq1;
```

The options are shown in the following table:

INCREMENT BY	This sets how much higher (or lower) than the last number a number will be. This defaults to +1 but can be any positive number (or negative number for a descending sequence).
START WITH	This is the starting point for the sequence, in other words, the number issued by the first selection. It defaults to 1 but can be anything.
MAXVALUE	This is the highest number an ascending sequence can go to before generating an error or returning to its START WITH value. The default is no maximum.
MINVALUE	This is the lowest number a descending sequence can go to before generating an error or returning to its START WITH value. The default is no minimum.
CYCLE	This controls the behavior on reaching MAXVALUE or MINVALUE. The default behavior is to give an error, but if CYCLE is specified, the sequence will return to its starting point and repeat.
CACHE	For performance, Oracle can preissue sequence values in batches and cache them for issuing to users. The default is to generate and cache the next 20 values.
ORDER	This is relevant only for a clustered database: ORDER forces all instances in the cluster to coordinate incrementing the sequence so that numbers issued are always in order even when issued to sessions against different instances.

Appropriate settings for INCREMENT BY, START WITH, and MAXVALUE or MINVALUE will come from your business analysts.

It is rare for CYCLE to be used because it lets the sequence issue duplicate values. If the sequence is being used to generate primary key values, CYCLE makes sense only if there is a routine in the database that will delete old rows faster than the sequence will reissue numbers.

Caching sequence values is vital for performance. Selecting from a sequence is a point of serialization in the application code; only one session can do this at once. The mechanism is efficient. It is much faster than locking a row, updating the row, and then unlocking it with a COMMIT. But even so, selecting from a sequence can be a cause of contention between sessions. The CACHE keyword instructs Oracle to pregenerate sequence numbers in batches. This means that they can be issued faster than if they had to be generated on demand.

TIP   The default number of values to cache is only 20. Experience shows that this is usually not enough. If your application selects from the sequence 10 times a second, then set the cache value to 50,000. Don't be shy about this.

Using Sequences

To use a sequence, a session can select either the next value with the NEXTVAL pseudocolumn, which forces the sequence to increment, or the last (or "current") value issued to that session with the CURRVAL pseudocolumn. The NEXTVAL will be globally unique. Each session that selects it will get a different, incremented value for each SELECT. The CURRVAL will be constant for one session until it selects NEXTVAL again. There is no way to find out what the last value issued by a sequence was. You can always obtain the next value by incrementing it with NEXTVAL, and you can always recall the last value issued to your session with CURRVAL, but you cannot find the last value issued.

EXAM TIP   The CURRVAL of a sequence is the last value issued to the current session, not necessarily the last value issued. You cannot select the CURRVAL until after selecting the NEXTVAL.

A typical use of sequences is for primary key values. This example uses a sequence CUST_SEQ to generate unique customer numbers, ORDER_SEQ to generate unique order numbers, and LINE_SEQ to generate unique line numbers for the line items of the order. First create the sequences, which is a once-off operation.

```
create sequence order_seq start with 10;
create sequence line_seq start with 10;
```

Then insert the orders with their lines as a single transaction.

```
insert into orders (order_id, order_date, customer_id)
values (order_seq.nextval, sysdate, '1000' );
insert into order_items (order_id, order_item_id, product_id)
values (order_seq.currval, line_seq.nextval, 'A111');
insert into order_items (order_id, order_item_id, product_id)
values (order_seq.currval, line_seq.nextval, 'B111');
commit;
```

The first INSERT statement raises an order with a unique order number drawn from the sequence ORDER_SEQ for customer number 1000. The second and third statements insert the two lines of the order, using the previously issued order number from ORDER_SEQ as the foreign key to connect the line items to the order, and the next values from LINE_SEQ to generate a unique identifier for each line. Finally, the transaction is committed.

A sequence is not tied to any one table. In the preceding example, there would be no technical reason not to use one sequence to generate values for the primary keys of the order and of the lines.

A COMMIT is not necessary to make the increment of a sequence permanent. It is permanent and made visible to the rest of the world the moment it happens. It can't be rolled back, either. Sequence updates occur independently of the transaction management system. For this reason, there will always be gaps in the series. The gaps will be larger if the database has been restarted abnormally and the CACHE clause was used. All numbers that have been generated and cached but not yet issued will be lost when the database is aborted. At the next restart, the current value of the sequence will be the last number generated, not the last issued. So, with the default CACHE of 20, every shutdown abort or instance failure will lose up to 20 numbers.

If the business analysts have stated that there must be no gaps in a sequence, then another means of generating unique numbers must be used. For the preceding example of raising orders, the current order number could be stored in this table and initialized to 10:

```
create table current_on(order_number number);
insert into current_on values(10);
commit;
```

Then the code to create an order would have to become the following:

```
update current_on set order_number=order_number + 1;
insert into orders (order_number,order_date,customer_number)
values ((select order_number from current_on),sysdate,'1000');
commit;
```

This will certainly work as a means of generating unique order numbers, and because the increment of the order number is within the transaction that inserts the order, it can be rolled back with the insert if necessary. There will be no gaps in order numbers, unless an order is deliberately deleted. But it is far less efficient than using a sequence, and code like this is famous for causing dreadful contention problems. If many sessions try to lock and increment the one row containing the current number, the whole application will hang as the sessions queue up to take their turn.

After creating and using a sequence, you can modify it. The syntax is as follows:

```
ALTER SEQUENCE sequencename
[INCREMENT BY number]
[START WITH number]
[MAXVALUE number | NOMAXVALUE]
[MINVALUE number | NOMINVALUE]
[CYCLE | NOCYCLE]
[CACHE number | NOCACHE]
[ORDER | NOORDER] ;
```

This ALTER command is the same as the CREATE command, with one exception: There is no way to set the starting value. If you want to restart the sequence, the only way is to drop it and re-create it. To adjust the cache value from the default to improve the performance of the preceding order entry example, do the following:

```
alter sequence order_seq cache 1000;
```

However, if you want to reset the sequence to its starting value, the only way is to drop it and create it again.

```
drop sequence order_seq;
```

Exercise 5-9: Create and Use Sequences   In this exercise, you will create and use some sequences. You will need two concurrent sessions, either SQL Developer or SQL*Plus.

1. Log on to your database twice as HR in separate sessions. Consider one to be your A session and the other to be your B session.

2. In your A session, create a sequence as follows:

   ```
   create sequence seq1 start with 10 nocache maxvalue 15 cycle;
   ```

   The use of NOCACHE is deleterious to performance. If MAXVALUE is specified, then CYCLE will be necessary to prevent errors when MAXVALUE is reached.

3. Execute the following commands in the appropriate session in the correct order to observe the use of NEXTVAL and CURRVAL and the cycling of the sequence:

Step	In Your A Session	In Your B Session
1	select seq1.nextval from dual;	
2		select seq1.nextval from dual;
3	select seq1.nextval from dual;	
4		select seq1.nextval from dual;
5	select seq1.currval from dual;	
6		select seq1.nextval from dual;
7	select seq1.nextval from dual;	
8		select seq1.currval from dual;
9	select seq1.nextval from dual;	
10		select seq1.nextval from dual;

4. Create a table with a primary key.

   ```
   create table seqtest(c1 number,c2 varchar2(10));
   alter table seqtest add constraint seqtest_pk primary key (c1);
   ```

5. Create a sequence to generate primary key values.

   ```
   create sequence seqtest_pk_s;
   ```

6. In your A session, insert a row into the new table and commit.

   ```
   insert into seqtest values (seqtest_pk_s.nextval,'first');
   commit;
   ```

7. In your B session, insert a row into the new table and do not commit it.

```
insert into seqtest values (seqtest_pk_s.nextval,'second');
```

8. In your A session, insert a third row and commit.

```
insert into seqtest values (seqtest_pk_s.nextval,'third');
commit;
```

9. In your B session, roll back the second insertion.

```
rollback;
```

10. In your B session, see the contents of the table.

```
select * from seqtest;
```

This demonstrates that sequences are incremented and the next value is published immediately, outside the transaction control mechanism.

11. Tidy up.

```
drop table seqtest;
drop sequence seqtest_pk_s;
drop sequence seq1;
```

12. Connect to the HR schema with either SQL Developer or SQL*Plus and create three sequences that will be used in later exercises.

```
create sequence prod_seq;
create sequence cust_seq;
create sequence order_seq;
```

Two-Minute Drill

Categorize the Main Database Objects

- Some objects contain data, principally tables and indexes.
- Programmatic objects such as stored procedures and functions are executable code.
- Views and synonyms are objects that give access to other objects.
- Tables are two-dimensional structures, storing rows defined with columns.
- Tables exist within a schema. The schema name together with the table name makes a unique identifier.

List the Data Types that Are Available for Columns

- The most common character data types are VARCHAR2, NUMBER, and DATE.
- There are many other data types.

Create a Simple Table

- Tables can be created from nothing or with a subquery.
- After creation, column definitions can be added, dropped, or modified.
- The table definition can include default values for columns.

Create and Use Temporary Tables

- Rows in a temporary table are visible only to the session that inserted them.
- DML on temporary tables does not generate redo.
- Temporary tables exist only in sessions' Program Global Areas (PGAs) or in temporary segments.
- A temporary table can keep rows for the duration of a session or of a transaction, depending on how it was created.

Indexes

- Indexes are required for enforcing unique and primary key constraints.
- NULLs are not included in B*Tree indexes but are included in bitmap indexes.
- B*Tree indexes can be unique or nonunique, which determines whether they can accept duplicate key values.
- B*Tree indexes are suitable for high-cardinality columns; bitmap indexes are for low-cardinality columns.
- Bitmap indexes can be compound, function based, or descending; B*Tree indexes can also be unique, compressed, and reverse key.

Constraints

- Constraints can be defined at table creation time or added later.
- A constraint can be defined inline with its column or at the table level after the columns.
- Table-level constraints can be more complex than those defined inline.
- A table may have only one primary key but can have many unique keys.
- A primary key is functionally equivalent to unique plus not null.
- A unique constraint does not stop insertion of many null values.
- Foreign key constraints define the relationships between tables.

Views

- A simple view has one detail (or base) table and uses neither functions nor aggregation.
- A complex view can be based on any SELECT statement, no matter how complicated.
- Views are schema objects. To use a view in another schema, the view name must be qualified with the schema name.
- A view can be queried exactly as though it were a table.
- Views can be joined to other views or to tables, they can be aggregated, and in some cases they can accept DML statements.
- Views exist only as data dictionary constructs. Whenever you query a view, the underlying SELECT statement must be run.

Synonyms

- A synonym is an alternative name for a view or a table.

- Private synonyms are schema objects; public synonyms exist outside user schemas and can be used without specifying a schema name as a qualifier.

- Synonyms share the same namespace as views and tables and can therefore be used interchangeably with them.

Sequences

- A sequence generates unique values—unless either MAXVALUE or MINVALUE and CYCLE have been specified.

- Incrementing a sequence need not be committed and cannot be rolled back.

- Any session can increment the sequence by reading its next value. It is possible to obtain the last value issued to your session but not the last value issued.

Self Test

1. If a table is created without specifying a schema, in which schema will it be? (Choose the best answer.)

   A. It will be an *orphaned* table, without a schema.

   B. The creation will fail.

   C. It will be in the SYS schema.

   D. It will be in the schema of the user creating it.

   E. It will be in the PUBLIC schema.

2. Several object types share the same namespace and therefore cannot have the same name in the same schema. Which of the following object types is not in the same namespace as the others? (Choose the best answer.)

   A. Index

   B. PL/SQL stored procedure

   C. Synonym

   D. Table

   E. View

3. Which of these statements will fail because the table name is not legal? (Choose two answers.)

   A. `create table "SELECT" (col1 date);`

   B. `create table "lowercase" (col1 date);`

   C. `create table number1 (col1 date);`

   D. `create table 1number(col1 date);`

   E. `create table update(col1 date);`

4. What are distinguishing characteristics of heap tables? (Choose two answers.)

    A. A heap table can store variable-length rows.

    B. More than one table can store rows in a single heap.

    C. Rows in a heap are in random order.

    D. Heap tables cannot be indexed.

    E. Tables in a heap do not have a primary key.

5. Which of the following data types are variable length? (Choose all that apply.)

    A. BLOB

    B. CHAR

    C. LONG

    D. NUMBER

    E. RAW

    F. VARCHAR2

6. Study these statements:

```
create table tab1 (c1 number(1), c2 date);
alter session set nls_date_format='dd-mm-yy';
insert into tab1 values (1.1,'31-01-07');
```

Will the insert succeed? (Choose the best answer.)

    A. The insert will fail because the 1.1 is too long.

    B. The insert will fail because the '31-01-07' is a string, not a date.

    C. The insert will fail for both reasons A and B.

    D. The insert will succeed.

7. Which of the following is not supported by Oracle as an internal data type? (Choose the best answer.)

    A. CHAR

    B. FLOAT

    C. INTEGER

    D. STRING

8. Consider this statement:

```
create table t1 as select * from regions where 1=2;
```

What will be the result? (Choose the best answer.)

    A. There will be an error because of the impossible condition.

    B. No table will be created because the condition returns FALSE.

    C. The table T1 will be created, but no rows will be inserted because the condition returns FALSE.

    D. The table T1 will be created, and every row in REGIONS will be inserted because the condition returns a NULL as a row filter.

9. When a table is created with a statement such as the following:

```
create table newtab as select * from tab;
```

will there be any constraints on the new table? (Choose the best answer.)

   A. The new table will have no constraints because constraints are not copied when creating tables with a subquery.

   B. All the constraints on TAB will be copied to NEWTAB.

   C. Primary key and unique constraints, but not check and not-null constraints, will be copied.

   D. Check and not-null constraints, but not unique or primary keys, will be copied.

   E. All constraints will be copied, except foreign key constraints.

10. Which types of constraints require an index? (Choose all that apply.)

   A. CHECK

   B. NOT NULL

   C. PRIMARY KEY

   D. UNIQUE

11. A transaction consists of two statements. The first succeeds, but the second (which updates several rows) fails partway through because of a constraint violation. What will happen? (Choose the best answer.)

   A. The whole transaction will be rolled back.

   B. The second statement will be rolled back completely, and the first will be committed.

   C. The second statement will be rolled back completely, and the first will remain uncommitted.

   D. Only the one update that caused the violation will be rolled back; everything else will be committed.

   E. Only the one update that caused the violation will be rolled back; everything else will remain uncommitted.

12. Which of the following statements is correct about indexes? (Choose the best answer.)

   A. An index can be based on multiple columns of a table, but the columns must be of the same data type.

   B. An index can be based on multiple columns of a table, but the columns must be adjacent and specified in the order that they are defined in the table.

   C. An index cannot have the same name as a table, unless the index and the table are in separate schemas.

   D. None of these statements is correct.

13. Which of the following options can be applied to B*Tree indexes but not to bitmap indexes? (Choose all correct answers.)

   A. Compression

   B. Descending order

C. Function-based key expressions

D. Reverse key indexing

E. Uniqueness

F. Use of compound keys

14. Data in temporary tables has restricted visibility. If a user logs on as HR and inserts rows into a temporary table, to whom will the rows be visible?

    A. To no session other than the one that did the insert

    B. To all sessions connected as HR

    C. To all sessions, until the session that inserted them terminates

    D. To all sessions, until the session that inserted them commits the transaction

15. Where does the data in a temporary table get written to disk? (Choose the best answer.)

    A. It is never written to disk.

    B. To the user's temporary tablespace.

    C. To the temporary tablespace of the user in whose schema the table resides.

    D. To a disk local to the session's user process.

16. Which of these is a defining characteristic of a complex view, rather than a simple view? (Choose all correct answers.)

    A. Restricting the projection by selecting only some of the table's columns

    B. Naming the view's columns with column aliases

    C. Restricting the selection of rows with a WHERE clause

    D. Performing an aggregation

    E. Joining two tables

17. Consider these three statements:
    ```
    create view v1 as select department_id,department_name,last_name from
    departments join employees using (department_id);
    select department_name,last_name from v1 where department_id=20;
    select d.department_name,e.last_name from departments d, employees e
    where d.department_id=e.department_id and
    d.department_id=20;
    ```
    Why will the first query be quicker than the second? (Choose the best answer.)

    A. The view has already done the work of joining the tables.

    B. The view uses ISO standard join syntax, which is faster than the Oracle join syntax used in the second query.

    C. The view is precompiled, so the first query requires less dynamic compilation than the second query.

    D. There is no reason for the first query to be quicker.

18. Study this view creation statement:

```
create view dept30 as
select department_id,employee_id,last_name from employees
where department_id=30 with check option;
```

What might make the following statement fail? (Choose the best answer.)

```
update dept30 set department_id=10 where employee_id=114;
```

A. Unless specified otherwise, views will be created as WITH READ ONLY.

B. The view is too complex to allow DML operations.

C. The WITH CHECK OPTION will reject any statement that changes the DEPARTMENT_ID.

D. The statement will succeed.

19. There is a simple view SCOTT.DEPT_VIEW on the table SCOTT.DEPT. This insert fails with an error:

```
SQL> insert into dept_view values('SUPPORT','OXFORD');
insert into dept_view values('SUPPORT','OXFORD')
*
ERROR at line 1:
ORA-01400: cannot insert NULL into ("SCOTT"."DEPT"."DEPTNO")
```

What might be the problem? (Choose the best answer.)

A. The INSERT violates a constraint on the detail table.

B. The INSERT violates a constraint on the view.

C. The view was created as WITH READ ONLY.

D. The view was created as WITH CHECK OPTION.

20. What are the distinguishing characteristics of a public synonym rather than a private synonym? (Choose two correct answers.)

A. Public synonyms are always visible to all users.

B. Public synonyms can be accessed by name without a schema name qualifier.

C. Public synonyms can be selected from without needing any permissions.

D. Public synonyms can have the same names as tables or views.

21. Consider these three statements:

```
create synonym s1 for employees;
create public synonym s1 for departments;
select * from s1;
```

Which of the following statements is correct? (Choose the best answer.)

A. The second statement will fail because an object S1 already exists.

B. The third statement will show the contents of EMPLOYEES.

C. The third statement will show the contents of DEPARTMENTS.

D. The third statement will show the contents of the table S1, if such a table exists in the current schema.

22. A view and a synonym are created as follows:

```
create view dept_v as select * from dept;
create synonym dept_s for dept_v;
```

Subsequently the table DEPT is dropped. What will happen if you query the synonym DEPT_S? (Choose the best answer.)

A. There will not be an error because the synonym addresses the view, which still exists, but there will be no rows returned.

B. There will not be an error if you first recompile the view with the command ALTER VIEW DEPT_V COMPILE FORCE;.

C. There will be an error because the synonym will be invalid.

D. There will be an error because the view will be invalid.

E. There will be an error because the view will have been dropped implicitly when the table was dropped.

23. A sequence is created as follows:

```
create sequence seq1 maxvalue 50;
```

If the current value is already 50, when you attempt to select SEQ1.NEXTVAL, what will happen? (Choose the best answer.)

A. The sequence will cycle and issue 0.

B. The sequence will cycle and issue 1.

C. The sequence will reissue 50.

D. There will be an error.

24. You create a sequence as follows:

```
create sequence seq1 start with 1;
```

After selecting from it a few times, you want to reinitialize it to reissue the numbers already generated. How can you do this? (Choose the best answer.)

A. You must drop and re-create the sequence.

B. You can't. Under no circumstances can numbers from a sequence be reissued once they have been used.

C. Use the command ALTER SEQUENCE SEQ1 START WITH 1; to reset the next value to 1.

D. Use the command ALTER SEQUENCE SEQ1 CYCLE; to reset the sequence to its starting value.

Self Test Answers

1. ☑   **D.** The schema will default to the current user.

☒   **A**, **B**, **C**, and **E** are incorrect. **A** is incorrect because all tables must be in a schema. **B** is incorrect because the creation will succeed. **C** is incorrect because the SYS schema is not a default schema. **E** is incorrect because while there is a notional user PUBLIC, he does not have a schema at all.

2. ☑ **A.** Indexes have their own namespace.
   ☒ **B, C, D,** and **E** are incorrect. Stored procedures, synonyms, tables, and views exist in the same namespace.

3. ☑ **D** and **E. D** violates the rule that a table name must begin with a letter, and **E** violates the rule that a table name cannot be a reserved word. Both rules can be bypassed by using double quotes.
   ☒ **A, B,** and **C** are incorrect. These are incorrect because all will succeed (though **A** and **B** are not exactly sensible).

4. ☑ **A** and **C.** A heap is a table of variable-length rows in random order.
   ☒ **B, D,** and **E** are incorrect. **B** is incorrect because a heap table can be only one table. **D** and **E** are incorrect because a heap table can (and usually will) have indexes and a primary key.

5. ☑ **A, C, D, E,** and **F.** All these are variable-length data types.
   ☒ **B** is incorrect. CHAR columns are fixed length.

6. ☑ **D.** The number will be rounded to one digit, and the string will be cast as a date.
   ☒ **A, B,** and **C** are incorrect. Automatic rounding and typecasting will correct the "errors," though ideally they would not occur.

7. ☑ **D.** STRING is not an internal data type.
   ☒ **A, B,** and **C** are incorrect. CHAR, FLOAT, and INTEGER are all internal data types, though not as widely used as some others.

8. ☑ **C.** The condition applies only to the rows selected for insert, not to the table creation.
   ☒ **A, B,** and **D** are incorrect. **A** is incorrect because the statement is syntactically correct. **B** is incorrect because the condition does not apply to the DDL, only to the DML. **D** is incorrect because the condition will exclude all rows from selection.

9. ☑ **D.** Check and not-null constraints are not dependent on any structures other than the table to which they apply and so can safely be copied to a new table.
   ☒ **A, B, C,** and **E** are incorrect. **A** is incorrect because not-null and check constraints will be applied to the new table. **B, C,** and **E** are incorrect because these constraints need other objects (indexes or a parent table) and so are not copied.

10. ☑ **C** and **D.** Unique and primary key constraints are enforced with indexes.
    ☒ **A** and **B** are incorrect. Check and not-null constraints do not rely on indexes.

11. ☑ **C.** A constraint violation will force a rollback of the current statement but nothing else.
    ☒ **A, B, D,** and **E** are incorrect. **A** is incorrect because all statements that have succeeded remain intact. **B** and **D** are incorrect because there is no commit of anything until it is specifically requested. **E** is incorrect because the whole statement, not just the failed row, will be rolled back.

12. ☑ **D.** All the statements are incorrect.
    ☒ **A, B,** and **C** are incorrect. **A** is incorrect because compound indexes need not be on columns of the same datatype. **B** is incorrect because the columns in a compound index need not be physically adjacent. **C** is incorrect because indexes and tables do not share the same namespace.

13. ☑   **A**, **D**, and **E**. Compression, reverse key, and unique can be applied only to B*Tree indexes.
    ☒   **B**, **C**, and **F** are incorrect. Descending, function-based, and compound indexes can be either B*Tree or bitmap.

14. ☑   **A**. Rows in a temporary table are visible only to the inserting session.
    ☒   **B**, **C**, and **D** are incorrect. All these incorrectly describe the scope of visibility of rows in a temporary table.

15. ☑   **B**. If a temporary table cannot fit in a session's PGA, it will be written to the session's temporary tablespace.
    ☒   **A**, **C**, and **D** are incorrect. **A** is incorrect because temporary tables can be written out to temporary segments. **C** is incorrect because the location of the temporary segment is session specific, not table specific. **D** is incorrect because it is the session server process that writes the data, not the user process.

16. ☑   **D** and **E**. Aggregations and joins make a view complex and make DML impossible.
    ☒   **A**, **B**, and **C** are incorrect. Selection and projection or renaming columns does not make the view complex.

17. ☑   **D**. Sad but true. Views will not help performance, unless they include tuning hints.
    ☒   **A**, **B**, and **C** are incorrect. **A** is incorrect because a view is only a SELECT statement; it doesn't prerun the query. **B** is incorrect because the Oracle optimizer will sort out any differences in syntax. **C** is incorrect because although views are precompiled, this doesn't affect the speed of compiling a user's statement.

18. ☑   **C**. The WITH CHECK OPTION will prevent DML that would cause a row to disappear from the view.
    ☒   **A**, **B**, and **D** are incorrect. **A** is incorrect because views are, by default, created read-write. **B** is incorrect because the view is a simple view. **D** is incorrect because the statement cannot succeed because the CHECK option will reject it.

19. ☑   **A**. There is a NOT NULL or PRIMARY KEY constraint on DEPT.DEPTNO.
    ☒   **B**, **C**, and **D** are incorrect. **B** is incorrect because constraints are enforced on detail tables, not on views. **C** and **D** are incorrect because the error message would be different.

20. ☑   **B** and **D**. Public synonyms are not schema objects and so can be addressed directly only. They can have the same names as schema objects.
    ☒   **A** and **C** are incorrect. These are incorrect because users must be granted privileges on a public synonym before they can see it or select from it.

21. ☑   **B**. The order of priority is to search the schema namespace before the public namespace, so it will be the private synonym (to EMPLOYEES) that will be found.
    ☒   **A**, **C**, and **D** are incorrect. **A** is incorrect because a synonym can exist in both the public namespace and the schema namespace. **C** is incorrect because the order of priority will find the private synonym first. **D** is incorrect because it would not be possible to have a table and a private synonym in the same schema with the same name.

22. ☑ **D.** The synonym will be fine, but the view will be invalid. Oracle will attempt to recompile the view, but this will fail.

☒ **A, B, C,** and **E** are incorrect. **A** is incorrect because the view will be invalid. **B** is incorrect because the FORCE keyword can be applied only when creating a view (and it would still be invalid, even so). **C** is incorrect because the synonym will be fine. **E** is incorrect because views are not dropped implicitly (unlike indexes and constraints).

23. ☑ **D.** The default is NOCYCLE, and the sequence cannot advance further.

☒ **A, B,** and **C** are incorrect. **A** and **B** are incorrect because CYCLE is disabled by default. If it were enabled, the next number issued would be 1 (not 0) because 1 is the default for START WITH. **C** is incorrect because under no circumstances will a sequence issue repeating values.

24. ☑ **A.** It is not possible to change the next value of a sequence, so you must re-create it.

☒ **B, C,** and **D** are incorrect. **B** is incorrect because while a NOCYCLE sequence can never reissue numbers, there is no reason why a new sequence (with the same name) cannot do so. **C** is incorrect because START WITH can be specified only at creation time. **D** is incorrect because this will not force an instant cycle; it will affect what happens only when the sequence reaches its MAXVALUE or MINVALUE.

CHAPTER 6

DML and Concurrency

Exam Objectives

In this chapter, you will learn to

- 061.9.1   Describe Each Data Manipulation Language (DML) Statement
- 061.9.2   Insert Rows into a Table
- 061.9.3   Update Rows in a Table
- 061.9.4   Delete Rows from a Table
- 061.9.5   Control Transactions
- 062.9.1   Explain DML and Undo Data Generation
- 062.9.2   Monitor and Administer Undo Data
- 062.9.3   Describe the Difference between Undo Data and Redo Data
- 062.9.4   Configure Undo Retention
- 062.10.1   Describe the Locking Mechanism and Data Concurrency Management
- 062.10.2   Monitor and Resolve Locking Conflicts

Data in a relational database is managed with the Data Manipulation Language (DML) commands of SQL. These are INSERT, UPDATE, DELETE, and, with more recent versions of SQL, MERGE. This chapter discusses what happens in memory and on disk when you execute INSERT, UPDATE, or DELETE statements—the manner in which changed data is written to blocks of table and index segments and the old version of the data is written out to blocks of an undo segment. The theory behind this, summarized as the ACID test, which every relational database must pass, is explored, and you will see the practicalities of how undo data is managed.

The transaction control statements COMMIT and ROLLBACK, which are closely associated with DML commands, are also explained. The chapter ends with a detailed examination of concurrent data access and table and row locking.

Describe Each Data Manipulation Language Statement

Strictly speaking, there are five DML commands:

- SELECT
- INSERT
- UPDATE
- DELETE
- MERGE

In practice, most database professionals never include SELECT as part of DML. It is considered a separate language in its own right, which is not unreasonable when you consider that the next five chapters are dedicated to describing it. The MERGE command is often dropped as well, not because it isn't clearly a data manipulation command, but because it doesn't do anything that cannot be done with other commands. You can think of MERGE as a shortcut for executing either an INSERT or an UPDATE or a DELETE, depending on some condition. A command often considered with DML is TRUNCATE. This is actually a Data Definition Language (DDL) command, but because the effect for end users is the same as for a DELETE (though its implementation is totally different), it does fit with DML.

INSERT

Oracle stores data in the form of rows in tables. Tables are *populated* with rows (just as a country is *populated* with people) in several ways, but the most common method is with the INSERT statement. SQL is a set-oriented language, so any one command can affect one row or a set of rows. It follows that one INSERT statement can insert an individual row into one table or many rows into many tables. The basic versions of the statement do insert just one row, but more complex variations can, with one command, insert multiple rows into multiple tables.

TIP   There are much faster techniques than INSERT for populating a table with large numbers of rows. The SQL*Loader utility can upload data from files produced by an external feeder system, and Data Pump can transfer data in bulk from one Oracle database to another, either via disk files or through a network link.

EXAM TIP   An INSERT command can insert one row, with column values specified in the command, or can insert a set of rows created by a SELECT statement.

The simplest form of the INSERT statement inserts one row into one table, using values provided inline as part of the command. The syntax is as follows:

```
INSERT INTO table [(column [,column...])] VALUES (value [,value...]);
```

Here's an example:

```
insert into hr.regions values (10,'Great Britain');
insert into hr.regions (region_name, region_id) values ('Australasia',11);
insert into hr.regions (region_id) values (12);
insert into hr.regions values (13,null);
```

The first of the preceding commands provides values for both columns of the REGIONS table. If the table had a third column, the statement would fail because it relies upon *positional notation*. The statement does not say which value should be inserted into which column; it relies on the position of the values, namely, their ordering in the command. When the database receives a statement using positional notation, it will match the order of the values to the order in which the columns of the table are defined. The statement would also fail if the column order was wrong; the database would attempt the insertion but would fail because of data type mismatches.

The second command nominates the columns to be populated and the values with which to populate them. Note that the order in which columns are mentioned now becomes irrelevant—as long as the order of the columns is the same as the order of the values.

The third example lists one column and therefore only one value. All other columns will be left null. This statement will fail if the REGION_NAME column is not nullable. The fourth example will produce the same result, but because there is no column list, some value (even a NULL) must be provided for each column.

TIP   It is often considered good practice not to rely on positional notation and instead always to list the columns. This is more work but makes the code self-documenting (always a good idea!) and also makes the code more resilient against table structure changes. For instance, if a column is added to a table, all the INSERT statements that rely on positional notation will fail until they are rewritten to include a NULL for the new column. INSERT code that nominates the columns will continue to run.

To insert many rows with one INSERT command, the values for the rows must come from a query. The syntax is as follows:

```
INSERT INTO table [column [, column...] ] subquery;
```

Note that this syntax does not use the VALUES keyword. If the column list is omitted, then the subquery must provide values for every column in the table. To copy every row from one table to another, if the tables have the same column structure, a command such as this is all that is needed:

```
insert into regions_copy select * from regions;
```

This presumes that the table REGIONS_COPY does exist. The SELECT subquery reads every row from the source table, which is REGIONS, and the INSERT inserts them into the target table, which is REGIONS_COPY.

 EXAM TIP Any SELECT statement, specified as a subquery, can be used as the source of rows passed to an INSERT. This enables insertion of many rows. Alternatively, using the VALUES clause will insert one row. The values can be literals or prompted for as substitution variables.

To conclude the description of the INSERT command, it should be mentioned that it is possible to insert rows into several tables with one statement. This is not part of the Oracle Certified Professional (OCP) examination, but for completeness, here is an example:

```
insert all
when 1=1 then
  into emp_no_name (department_id,job_id,salary,commission_pct,hire_date)
  values (department_id,job_id,salary,commission_pct,hire_date)
when department_id <> 80 then
  into emp_non_sales (employee_id,department_id,salary,hire_date)
  values (employee_id,department_id,salary,hire_date)
when department_id = 80 then
  into emp_sales (employee_id,salary,commission_pct,hire_date)
  values (employee_id,salary,commission_pct,hire_date)
select employee_id,department_id,job_id,salary,commission_pct,hire_date
from employees where hire_date > sysdate - 30;
```

To read this statement, start at the bottom. The subquery retrieves all employees recruited in the last 30 days. Then go to the top. The ALL keyword means that every row selected will be considered for insertion into all the tables following, not just into the first table for which the condition applies. The first condition is 1=1, which is always true, so every source row will create a row in EMP_NO_NAME. This is a copy of the EMPLOYEES table with the personal identifiers removed. The second condition is DEPARTMENT_ID <> 80, which will generate a row in EMP_NON_SALES for every employee who is not in the sales department; there is no need for this table to have the COMMISSION_PCT column. The third condition generates a row in EMP_SALES for all the salespeople; there is no need for the DEPARTMENT_ID column because they will all be in department 80.

This is a simple example of a multitable insert, but it should be apparent that with one statement, and therefore only one pass through the source data, it is possible to populate many target tables. This can take an enormous amount of strain off the database.

Exercise 6-1: Use the INSERT Command   In this exercise, use various techniques to insert rows into a table.

1. Connect to the HR schema with either SQL Developer or SQL*Plus.

2. Query the PRODUCTS, ORDERS, and ORDER_ITEMS tables created in Exercise 5-5 to confirm what data is currently stored.

```
select * from products;
select * from orders;
select * from order_items;
```

3. Insert two rows into the PRODUCTS table, providing the values inline.

```
insert into products values (prod_seq.nextval, '12c SQL Exam Guide',
'ACTIVE',60,sysdate, 20);
insert into products
values (prod_seq.nextval, '12c All-in-One Guide',
'ACTIVE',100,sysdate, 40);
```

4. Insert two rows into the ORDERS table, explicitly providing the column names.

```
insert into orders (order_id, order_date, order_status, order_amount,
customer_id)
values (order_seq.nextval, sysdate, 'COMPLETE', 3, 2);
insert into orders (order_id, order_date, order_status, order_amount,
customer_id)
values (order_seq.nextval, sysdate, 'PENDING', 5, 3);
```

5. Insert three rows into the ORDER_ITEMS table, using substitution variables.

```
insert into order_items values (&item_id, &order_id, &product_id,
&quantity);
```

When prompted, provide these values: {1, 1, 2,5}, {2,1,1,3}, and {1,2,2,4}.

6. Insert a row into the PRODUCTS table, calculating the PRODUCT_ID to be 100 higher than the current high value. This will need a scalar subquery.

```
insert into products values ((select max(product_id)+100 from products),
'12c DBA2 Exam Guide', 'INACTIVE', 40, sysdate-365, 0);
```

7. Confirm the insertion of the rows.

```
select * from products;
select * from orders;
select * from order_items;
```

8. Commit the insertions.

```
commit;
```

The following illustration shows the results of the exercise, using SQL*Plus:

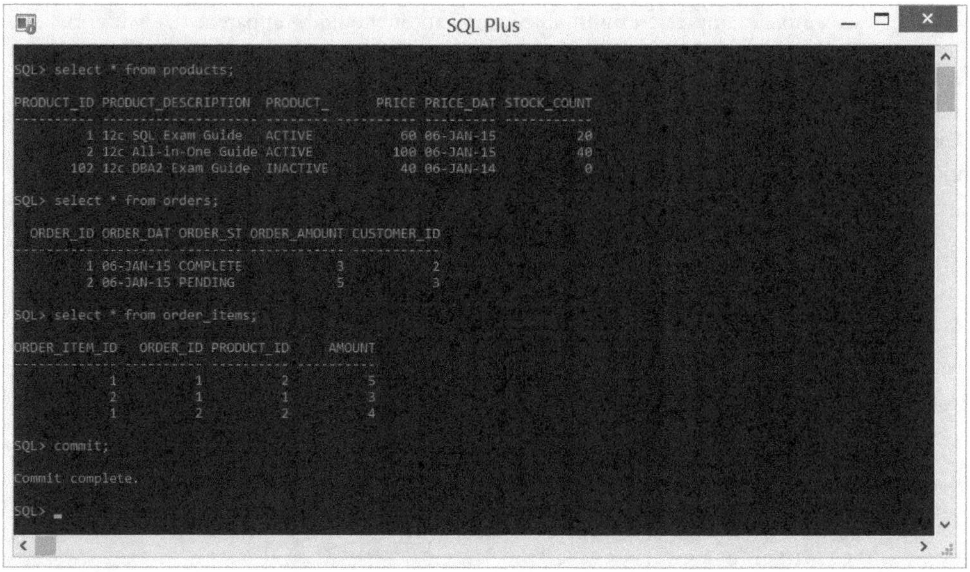

UPDATE

The UPDATE command is used to change rows that already exist—rows that have been created by an INSERT command or possibly by a tool such as Data Pump. As with any other SQL command, an UPDATE can affect one row or a set of rows. The size of the set affected by an UPDATE is determined by a WHERE clause, in exactly the same way that the set of rows retrieved by a SELECT statement is defined by a WHERE clause. The syntax is identical. All the rows updated will be in one table; it is not possible for a single UPDATE command to affect rows in multiple tables.

When updating a row or a set of rows, the UPDATE command specifies which columns of the rows to update. It is not necessary (or indeed common) to update every column of the row. If the column being updated already has a value, then this value is replaced with the new value specified by the UPDATE command. If the column was not previously populated—which is to say, its value was NULL—then it will be populated after the UPDATE with the new value.

A typical use of UPDATE is to retrieve one row and update one or more columns of the row. The retrieval will be done using a WHERE clause that selects a row by its primary key, which is the unique identifier that will ensure that only one row is retrieved. Then the columns that are updated will be any columns other than the primary key column. It is unusual to change the value of the primary key. The lifetime of a row begins when it is inserted and then may continue through several updates, until it is deleted. Throughout this lifetime, it will not usually change its primary key.

To update a set of rows, use a less restrictive WHERE clause than the primary key. To update every row in a table, do not use any WHERE clause at all. This set behavior can be disconcerting when it happens by accident. If you select the rows to be updated with any column other than the primary key, you may update several rows, not just one. If you omit the WHERE clause completely, you will update the whole table—perhaps millions of rows updated with just one statement—when you meant to change just one.

 EXAM TIP One UPDATE statement can change rows in only one table, but it can change any number of rows in that table.

An UPDATE command must honor any constraints defined for the table, just as the original INSERT would have. For example, it will not be possible to update a column that has been marked as mandatory to a NULL value or to update a primary key column so that it will no longer be unique. The basic syntax is the following:

```
UPDATE table SET column=value [,column=value...] [WHERE condition];
```

The more complex form of the command uses subqueries for one or more of the column values and for the WHERE condition. Figure 6-1 shows updates of varying complexity, executed from SQL*Plus.

```
                              SQL Plus                        _  □   ×

SQL> UPDATE employees
  2    SET salary=10000
  3    WHERE employee_id=206;

1 row updated.

SQL> UPDATE employees
  2    SET salary=salary*1.1
  3    WHERE last_name='Cambrault';

2 rows updated.

SQL> UPDATE employees
  2    SET salary=salary*1.1
  3    WHERE department_id IN
  4    (SELECT department_id
  5     FROM departments
  6     WHERE department_name LIKE '%&Which_department%');
Enter value for which_department: IT
old   6:   WHERE department_name LIKE '%&Which_department%')
new   6:   WHERE department_name LIKE '%IT%')

5 rows updated.

SQL> UPDATE employees
  2    SET department_id=80,
  3        commission_pct=
  4    (SELECT min(commission_pct)
  5     FROM employees
  6     WHERE department_id=80)
  7    WHERE employee_id=206;

1 row updated.

SQL> _
```

Figure 6-1 Examples of using the UPDATE statement

The first example is the simplest. One column of one row is set to a literal value. Because the row is chosen with a WHERE clause that uses the equality predicate on the table's primary key, there is an absolute guarantee that, at most, only one row will be affected. No row will be changed if the WHERE clause fails to find any rows at all.

The second example shows use of arithmetic and an existing column to set the new value, and the row selection is not done on the primary key column. If the selection is not done on the primary key or if a nonequality predicate (such as BETWEEN) is used, then the number of rows updated may be more than one. If the WHERE clause is omitted entirely, the update will be applied to every row in the table.

The third example in Figure 6-1 introduces the use of a subquery to define the set of rows to be updated. A minor additional complication is the use of a replacement variable to prompt the user for a value to use in the WHERE clause of the subquery. In this example, the subquery (lines 3 and 4) will select every employee who is in a department whose name includes the string 'IT' and will increment their current salary by 10 percent (unlikely to happen in practice).

It is also possible to use subqueries to determine the value to which a column will be set, as in the fourth example. In this case, one employee (identified by primary key in line 5) is transferred to department 80 (the sales department), and then the subquery in lines 3 and 4 sets his commission rate to whatever the lowest commission rate in the department happens to be.

The syntax of an update that uses subqueries is as follows:

```
UPDATE table
SET column=[subquery] [,column=subquery...]
WHERE column = (subquery) [AND column=subquery...] ;
```

There is a rigid restriction on the subqueries using update columns in the SET clause. The subquery must return a *scalar* value. A scalar value is a single value of whatever data type is needed; the query must return one row, with one column. If the query returns several values, the UPDATE will fail. Consider these two examples:

```
update employees
set salary=(select salary from employees where employee_id=206);
update employees
set salary=(select salary from employees where last_name='Abel');
```

The first example, using an equality predicate on the primary key, will always succeed. Even if the subquery does not retrieve a row (as would be the case if there were no employee with EMPLOYEE_ID equal to 206), the query will still return a scalar value: a null. In that case, all the rows in EMPLOYEES would have their SALARY set to NULL, which might not be desired but is not an error as far as SQL is concerned. The second example uses an equality predicate on LAST_NAME, which is not guaranteed to be unique. The statement will succeed if there is only one employee with that name, but if there were more than one, it would fail with the error "ORA-01427: single-row subquery returns more than one row." For code that will work reliably, no matter what the state of the data, it is vital to ensure that the subqueries used for setting column values are scalar.

TIP A common fix for making sure that queries are scalar is to use MAX or MIN. This version of the statement will always succeed:

```
update employees set salary=
(select max(salary) from employees where last_name='Abel');
```

However, just because it will work doesn't necessarily mean that it does what is wanted.

The subqueries in the WHERE clause must also be scalar if it is using the equality predicate (as in the preceding examples) or the greater/less than predicates. If it is using the IN predicate, then the query can return multiple rows, as in this example that uses IN:

```
update employees
set salary=10000
where department_id in (select department_id from departments
where department_name like '%IT%');
```

This will apply the update to all employees in a department whose name includes the string 'IT'. There are several of these. But even though the query can return several rows, it must still return only one column.

Exercise 6-2: Use the UPDATE Command   In this exercise, use various techniques to update rows in a table. It is assumed that the HR.PRODUCTS table is as shown in the illustration at the end of Exercise 6-1. If not, adjust the values as necessary.

1. Connect to the HR schema using SQL Developer or SQL*Plus.

2. Update a single row, identified by primary key.

```
update products set product_description='DBA1 Exam Guide'
where product_id=102;
```

This statement should return the message "1 row updated."

3. Update a set of rows, using a subquery to select the rows and to provide values.

```
update products
set product_id=(1+(select max(product_id) from products where prod-
uct_id <> 102))
where product_id=102;
```

This statement should return the message "1 row updated."

4. Confirm the state of the rows.

```
select * from products;
```

5. Commit the changes made.

```
commit;
```

DELETE

Previously inserted rows can be removed from a table with the DELETE command. The command will remove one row or a set of rows from the table, depending on a WHERE clause. If there is no WHERE clause, every row in the table will be removed (which can be a little disconcerting if you left out the WHERE clause by mistake).

TIP   There are no "warning" prompts for any SQL commands. If you instruct the database to delete a million rows, it will do so. Immediately. There is none of that "Are you sure?" business that some environments offer.

A deletion is all or nothing. It is not possible to nominate columns. When rows are inserted, you can choose which columns to populate. When rows are updated, you can choose which columns to update. But a deletion applies to the whole row—the only choice is which rows in which table. This makes the DELETE command syntactically simpler than the other DML commands. The syntax is as follows:

```
DELETE [FROM] table [WHERE condition];
```

This is the simplest of the DML commands, particularly if the condition is omitted. In that case, every row in the table will be removed with no prompt. The only complication is in the condition. This can be a simple match of a column to a literal.

```
delete from employees where employee_id=206;
delete from employees where last_name like 'S%';
delete from employees where department_id=&Which_department;
delete from employees where department_id is null;
```

The first statement identifies a row by primary key. Only one row will be removed—or no row at all, if the value given does not find a match. The second statement uses a nonequality predicate that could result in the deletion of many rows, namely, every employee whose surname begins with an uppercase *S*. The third statement uses an equality predicate but not on the primary key. It prompts for a department number with a substitution variable, and all employees in that department will go. The final statement removes all employees who are not currently assigned to a department.

The condition can also be a subquery.

```
delete from employees where department_id in
(select department_id from departments where location_id in
  (select location_id from locations where country_id in
    (select country_id from countries where region_id in
      (select region_id from regions where region_name='Europe')
    )
  )
)
```

This example uses a subquery for row selection that navigates the HR geographical tree (with more subqueries) to delete every employee who works for any department that is based in Europe. The same rule for the number of values returned by the subquery applies as for an UPDATE command: If the row selection is based on an equality predicate (as in the preceding example), the subquery must be scalar, but if it uses IN, the subquery can return several rows.

If the DELETE command finds no rows to delete, this is not an error. The command will return the message "0 rows deleted" rather than an error message because the statement did complete successfully—it just didn't find anything to do.

Exercise 6-3: Use the DELETE Command   In this exercise, use various techniques to delete rows in a table. It is assumed that the HR.PRODUCTS table has been modified during the previous two exercises. If not, adjust the values as necessary.

1. Connect to the HR schema using SQL Developer or SQL*Plus.

2. Remove one row, using the equality predicate on the primary key.

   ```
   delete from products where product_id=3;
   ```

   This should return the message "1 row deleted."

3. Attempt to remove every row in the table by omitting a WHERE clause.

```
delete from products;
```

This will fail due to a constraint violation because there are child records in the ORDER_ITEMS table that reference PRODUCT_ID values in the PRODUCTS table via the foreign key constraint FK_PRODUCT_ID.

4. Commit the deletion.

```
commit;
```

To remove rows from a table, there are two options: the DELETE command and the TRUNCATE command. DELETE is less drastic, in that a deletion can be rolled back, whereas a truncation cannot. DELETE is also more controllable in that it is possible to choose which rows to delete, whereas a truncation always affects the whole table. DELETE is, however, a lot slower and can place a lot of strain on the database. TRUNCATE is virtually instantaneous and effortless.

TRUNCATE

The TRUNCATE command is not a DML command; it is a DDL command. The difference is enormous. When DML commands affect data, they insert, update, and delete rows as part of transactions. Transactions are defined later in this chapter, in the section "Control Transactions." For now, let it be said that a transaction can be controlled, in the sense that the user has the choice of whether to make the work done in a transaction permanent or whether to reverse it. This is useful but forces the database to do additional work behind the scenes that the user is not aware of. DDL commands are not user transactions (though within the database, they are, in fact, implemented as transactions—but developers cannot control them), and there is no choice about whether to make them permanent or to reverse them. Once executed, they are done. However, in comparison to DML, they are very fast.

EXAM TIP   Transactions, consisting of INSERT, UPDATE, and DELETE (or even MERGE) commands, can be made permanent (with a COMMIT) or reversed (with a ROLLBACK). A TRUNCATE command, like any other DDL command, is immediately permanent. It can never be reversed.

From the user's point of view, a truncation of a table is equivalent to executing a DELETE of every row; it's a DELETE command without a WHERE clause. But whereas a deletion may take some time (possibly hours, if there are many rows in the table), a truncation will go through instantly. It makes no difference whether the table contains one row or billions; a TRUNCATE will be virtually instantaneous. The table will still exist, but it will be empty.

TIP   DDL commands, such as TRUNCATE, will fail if there is any DML command active on the table. A transaction will block the DDL command until the DML command is terminated with a COMMIT or a ROLLBACK.

EXAM TIP   TRUNCATE completely empties the table. There is no concept of row selection like there is with a DELETE.

One part of the definition of a table as stored in the data dictionary is the table's physical location. When first created, a table is allocated a single area of space of a fixed size in the database's datafiles. This is known as an *extent* and will be empty. Then, as rows are inserted, the extent fills up. Once it is full, more extents will be allocated to the table automatically. A table therefore consists of one or more extents, which hold the rows. As well as tracking the extent allocation, the data dictionary tracks how much of the space allocated to the table has been used. This is done with the *high water mark*. The high water mark is the last position in the last extent that has been used; all space below the high water mark has been used for rows at one time or another, and none of the space above the high water mark has been used yet.

Note that it is possible for there to be plenty of space below the high water mark that is not being used at the moment; this is because of rows having been removed with a DELETE command. Inserting rows into a table pushes up the high water mark. Deleting them leaves the high water mark where it is; the space they occupied remains assigned to the table but is freed up for inserting more rows.

Truncating a table resets the high water mark. Within the data dictionary, the recorded position of the high water mark is moved to the beginning of the table's first extent. Because Oracle assumes that there can be no rows above the high water mark, this has the effect of removing every row from the table. The table is emptied and remains empty until subsequent insertions begin to push the high water mark back up again. In this manner, one DDL command, which does little more than make an update in the data dictionary, can annihilate billions of rows in a table.

The syntax to truncate a table couldn't be simpler.

```
TRUNCATE TABLE table;
```

MERGE

There are many occasions where you want to take a set of data (the source) and integrate it into an existing table (the target). If a row in the source data already exists in the target table, you may want to update the target row, you may want to replace it completely, or you may want to leave the target row unchanged. If a row in the source does not exist in the target, you will want to insert it. The MERGE command lets you do this. A MERGE passes through the source data for each row attempting to locate a matching row in the target. If no match is found, a row can be inserted; if a match is found, the matching row can be updated. The release 10g enhancement means that the target row can even be deleted after being matched and updated. The end result is a target table into which the data in the source has been merged.

A MERGE operation does nothing that could not be done with INSERT, UPDATE, and DELETE statements—but with one pass through the source data, it can do all three. Alternative code without a MERGE would require three passes through the data, one for each command.

The source data for a MERGE statement can be a table or any subquery. The condition used for finding matching rows in the target is similar to a WHERE clause. The clauses that update or insert rows are as complex as an UPDATE or an INSERT command. It follows that MERGE is the most complicated of the DML commands, which is not unreasonable because it is (arguably) the most powerful. Using MERGE is not on the OCP syllabus, but for completeness, here is a simple example:

```
merge into employees e using new_employees n
  on (e.employee_id = n.employee_id)
when matched then
  update set e.salary=n.salary
```

```
when not matched then
  insert (employee_id,last_name,salary)
  values (n.employee_id,n.last_name,n.salary);
```

The preceding statement uses the contents of a table NEW_EMPLOYEES to update or insert rows in EMPLOYEES. The situation could be that EMPLOYEES is a table of all staff, and NEW_EMPLOYEES is a table with rows for new staff and for salary changes for existing staff. The command will pass through NEW_EMPLOYEES and, for each row, attempt to find a row in EMPLOYEES with the same EMPLOYEE_ID. If there is a row found, its SALARY column will be updated with the value of the row in NEW_EMPLOYEES. If there is not such a row, one will be inserted. Variations on the syntax allow the use of a subquery to select the source rows, and it is even possible to delete matching rows.

DML Statement Failures

Commands can fail for many reasons, including the following:

- Syntax errors
- References to nonexistent objects or columns
- Access permissions
- Constraint violations
- Space issues

Figure 6-2 shows several attempted executions of a statement with SQL*Plus.

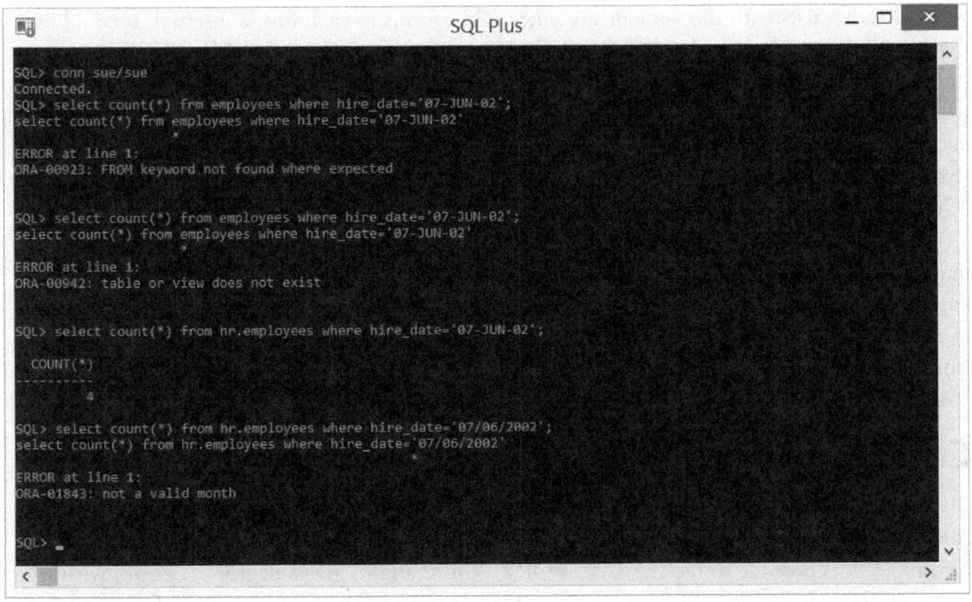

Figure 6-2 Some examples of statement failure

In Figure 6-2, a user connects as SUE (password, SUE—not an example of good security) and queries the EMPLOYEES table. The statement fails because of a simple syntax error, correctly identified by SQL*Plus. Note that SQL*Plus never attempts to correct such mistakes, even when it knows exactly what you meant to type. Some third-party tools may be more helpful, offering automatic error correction.

The second attempt to run the statement fails with an error stating that the object does not exist. This is because it does not exist in the current user's schema; it exists in the HR schema. Having corrected that, the third run of the statement succeeds—but only just. The value passed in the WHERE clause is a string, "07-JUN-2002," but the column HIRE_DATE is not defined in the table as a string; it is defined as a date. To execute the statement, the database had to work out what the user really meant and cast the string as a date. In the last example, the type casting fails.

If a statement is syntactically correct and has no errors with the objects to which it refers, it can still fail because of access permissions. If the user attempting to execute the statement does not have the relevant permissions on the tables to which it refers, the database will return an error identical to that which would be returned if the object did not exist. As far as the user is concerned, it does not exist.

Errors caused by access permissions are a case where SELECT and DML statements may return different results. It is possible for a user to have permission to see the rows in a table but not to insert, update, or delete them. Such an arrangement is not uncommon; it often makes business sense. Perhaps more confusingly, permissions can be set up in such a manner that it is possible to insert rows that you are not allowed to see. And, perhaps worst of all, it is possible to delete rows that you can neither see nor update. However, such arrangements are not common.

A constraint violation can cause a DML statement to fail. For example, an INSERT command can insert several rows into a table, and for every row the database will check whether a row already exists with the same primary key. This occurs as each row is inserted. It could be that the first few rows (or the first few million rows) go in without a problem, and then the statement hits a row with a duplicate value. At this point it will return an error, and the statement will fail. This failure will trigger a reversal of all the insertions that had already succeeded. This is part of the SQL standard; a statement must succeed in total or not at all. The reversal of the work is a *rollback*. The mechanisms of a rollback are described in the next section of this chapter, "Control Transactions."

If a statement fails because of space problems, the effect is similar. A part of the statement may have succeeded before the database ran out of space. The part that did succeed will be automatically rolled back. Rollback of a statement is a serious matter. It forces the database to do a lot of extra work and will usually take at least as long as the statement has taken already (sometimes much longer).

Control Transactions

The concepts behind a *transaction* are part of the relational database paradigm. A transaction consists of one or more DML statements, followed by either a ROLLBACK or a COMMIT command. It is possible to use the SAVEPOINT command to give a degree of control within the transaction. Before going into the syntax, it is necessary to review the concept of a transaction. A related topic is read consistency; this is automatically implemented by the Oracle server, but to a certain extent, programmers can manage it by the way they use the SELECT statement.

Database Transactions

Oracle's mechanism for assuring transactional integrity is the combination of undo segments and redo log files. This mechanism is undoubtedly the best of any database yet developed and conforms perfectly with the international standards for data processing. Other database vendors comply with the same standards with their own mechanisms but with varying levels of effectiveness. In brief, any relational database must be able to pass the ACID test; it must guarantee atomicity, consistency, isolation, and durability.

A is for Atomicity

The principle of atomicity states that either all parts of a transaction must complete or none of them complete. For example, if your business analysts have said that every time you change an employee's salary, you must also change his grade, then the atomic transaction will consist of two updates. The database must guarantee that both go through or neither do. If only one of the updates were to succeed, you would have an employee on a salary that was incompatible with his grade, which is a data corruption in business terms. If anything (anything at all!) goes wrong before the transaction is complete, the database itself must guarantee that any parts that did go through are reversed; this must happen automatically. But although an atomic transaction sounds small (like an atom), it could be enormous. To take another example, it is logically impossible in accountancy terms for the nominal ledger of an accounting suite to be half in August and half in September. The end-of-month rollover is therefore (in business terms) one atomic transaction, which may affect millions of rows in thousands of tables, as well as take hours to complete (or to roll back, if anything goes wrong). The rollback of an incomplete transaction is the reversal process and may be manual (as when you issue the ROLLBACK command), but it must be automatic and unstoppable in the case of an error.

C is for Consistency

The principle of consistency states that the results of a query must be consistent with the state of the database at the time the query started. Imagine a simple query that averages the value of a column of a table. If the table is large, it will take many minutes to pass through the table. If other users are updating the column while the query is in progress, should the query include the new or old values? Should it include rows that were inserted or deleted after the query started? The principle of consistency requires that the database ensure that changed values are not seen by the query; it will give you an average of the column as it was when the query started, no matter how long the query takes or what other activity is occurring on the tables concerned.

Through the use of undo segments, Oracle guarantees that if a query succeeds, the result will be consistent. However, if your undo segments are incorrectly configured, the query may not succeed. The famous Oracle error "ORA-1555: snapshot too old" is raised. This used to be a difficult problem to fix with earlier releases of the database, but from release 9*i* onward, you should always be able to avoid it.

I is for Isolation

The principle of isolation states that an incomplete (that is, uncommitted) transaction must be invisible to the rest of the world. While the transaction is in progress, only the one session that is executing the transaction is allowed to see the changes. All other sessions must see the unchanged data, not the new values. The logic behind this is, first, that the full transaction might not go through (remember the principle of atomicity?), and therefore no other users should be allowed to see changes that might be reversed. And, second, during the progress of a transaction, the data is (in business terms) inconsistent; there is a short time when the employee has had their salary changed, but not their grade. Transaction isolation requires that the database must conceal transactions in progress from other users. They will see the pre-update version of the data until the transaction completes, when they will see all the changes as a consistent set.

Oracle guarantees transaction isolation, consistency, and atomicity through the use of undo segments.

D is for Durability

The principle of durability states that once a transaction completes, it must be impossible for the database to lose it. During the time that the transaction is in progress, the principle of isolation requires that no one (other than the session concerned) can see the changes it has made so far. But the instant the transaction completes, it must be broadcast to the world, and the database must guarantee that the change is never lost because a relational database is not allowed to lose data. Oracle fulfills this requirement through the use of log files. Log files come in two forms—online redo log files and archive redo log files—that store a record of every change applied to the database. Of course, data can be lost through user error, such as using inappropriate DML and dropping objects. But as far as Oracle and the database administrator (DBA) are concerned, such events are transactions like any other. According to the principle of durability, they are absolutely nonreversible.

Executing SQL Statements

The entire SQL language consists of only a dozen or so commands. The ones you are concerned with here are SELECT, INSERT, UPDATE, and DELETE.

Executing a SELECT Statement

The SELECT command retrieves data. The execution of a select statement is a staged process. The server process executing the statement will first check whether the blocks containing the data required are already in memory in the database buffer cache. If they are, then execution can proceed immediately. If they are not, the server process must locate them on disk and copy them into the database buffer cache.

 EXAM TIP Always remember that server processes read blocks from datafiles into the database buffer cache; DBW*n* writes blocks from the database buffer cache to the datafiles.

Once the data blocks required for the query are in the database buffer cache, any further processing (such as sorting or aggregation) is carried out in the Program Global Area (PGA) of the session. When the execution is complete, the result set is returned to the user process.

How does this relate to the ACID test just described? For consistency, if the query encounters a block that has been changed since the time the query started, the server process will go to the undo segment that protected the change, locate the old version of the data, and, for the purposes

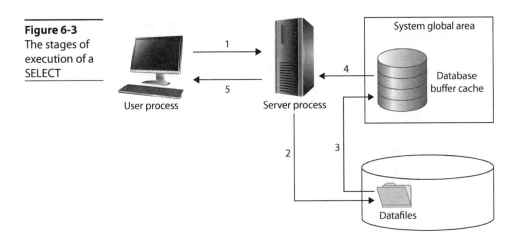

Figure 6-3
The stages of execution of a SELECT

System global area

Database buffer cache

User process

Server process

Datafiles

PART II

of the current query only, roll back the change. Thus, any changes initiated after the query commenced will not be seen. A similar mechanism guarantees transaction isolation, though this is based also on whether the change has been committed, not only on whether the data has been changed. Clearly, if the data needed to do this rollback is no longer in the undo segments, this mechanism will not work. That is when you get the "snapshot too old" error.

Figure 6-3 shows a representation of the way a SELECT statement is processed.

In the figure, step 1 is the transmission of the SELECT statement from the user process to the server process. The server will search the database buffer cache to determine whether the necessary blocks are already in memory and, if they are, proceed to step 4. If they are not, step 2 is to locate the blocks in the datafiles, and step 3 is to copy them into the database buffer cache. Step 4 transfers the data to the server process, where there may be some further processing before step 5 returns the result of the query to the user process.

Executing an UPDATE Statement

For any DML operation, it is necessary to work on both data blocks and undo blocks and also to generate redo: the A, C, and I of the ACID test require generation of undo; the D requires generation of redo.

EXAM TIP Undo is not the opposite of redo! Redo protects all block changes, no matter whether it is a change to a block of a table segment, an index segment, or an undo segment. As far as redo is concerned, an undo segment is just another segment, and any changes to it must be made durable.

The first step in executing DML is the same as executing SELECT; the required blocks must be found in the database buffer cache or copied into the database buffer cache from the datafiles. The only change is that an empty (or *expired*) block of an undo segment is needed too. From then on, things are a bit more complicated.

First, locks must be placed on any rows and associated index keys that are going to be affected by the operation. This is covered later in this chapter.

Then the redo is generated; the server process writes to the log buffer the change vectors that are going to be applied to the data blocks. This generation of redo is applied both to table block changes and to undo block changes. If a column of a row is to be updated, then the rowid and the new value of the column are written to the log buffer (which is the change that will be applied to the table block) and also the old value (which is the change that will be applied to the undo block). If the column is part of an index key, then the changes to be applied to the index are also written to the log buffer, together with a change to be applied to an undo block to protect the index change.

Having generated the redo, the update is carried out in the database buffer cache; the block of table data is updated with the new version of the changed column, and the old version of the changed column is written to the block of the undo segment. From this point until the update is committed, all queries from other sessions addressing the changed row will be redirected to the undo data. Only the session that is doing the update will see the actual current version of the row in the table block. The same principle applies to any associated index changes.

Executing INSERT and DELETE Statements

Conceptually, INSERT and DELETE are managed in the same fashion as an UPDATE. The first step is to locate the relevant blocks in the database buffer cache or to copy them into it if they are not there.

Redo generation is the same. All change vectors to be applied to data and undo blocks are first written out to the log buffer. For an INSERT, the change vector to be applied to the table block (and possibly index blocks) consists of the bytes that make up the new row (and possibly the new index keys). The vector to be applied to the undo block is the rowid of the new row. For a DELETE, the change vector to be written to the undo block is the entire row.

A crucial difference between INSERT and DELETE is in the amount of undo generated. When a row is inserted, the only undo generated is writing out the new rowid to the undo block. This is because to roll back an INSERT, the only information Oracle requires is the rowid so that this statement can be constructed:

```
delete from table_name where rowid=rowid_of_the_new_row ;
```

Executing this statement will reverse the original change.

For a DELETE, the whole row (which might be several kilobytes) must be written to the undo block so that the deletion can be rolled back if need be by constructing a statement that will insert the complete row back into the table.

The Start and End of a Transaction

A session begins a transaction the moment it issues any DML. The transaction continues through any number of further DML commands until the session issues either a COMMIT or a ROLLBACK statement. Only committed changes will be made permanent and become visible to other sessions. It is impossible to nest transactions. The SQL standard does not allow a user to start one transaction and then start another before terminating the first. This can be done with PL/SQL (Oracle's proprietary third-generation language) but not with industry-standard SQL.

The explicit transaction control statements are COMMIT, ROLLBACK, and SAVEPOINT. There are also circumstances other than a user-issued COMMIT or ROLLBACK that will implicitly terminate a transaction.

- Issuing a DDL or Data Control Language (DCL) statement
- Exiting from the user tool (SQL*Plus or SQL Developer or anything else)
- If the client session dies
- If the system crashes

If a user issues a DDL (CREATE, ALTER, or DROP) or DCL (GRANT or REVOKE) command, the transaction in progress (if any) will be committed; it will be made permanent and become visible to all other users. This is because the DDL and DCL commands are themselves transactions. As it is not possible to nest transactions in SQL, if the user already has a transaction running, the statements the user has run will be committed implicitly before the statement that makes up the DDL or DCL command executes.

If you start a transaction by issuing a DML command and then exit from the tool you are using without explicitly issuing either a COMMIT or a ROLLBACK, the transaction will terminate—but whether it terminates with a COMMIT or a ROLLBACK is entirely dependent on how the tool is written. Many tools will have different behavior, depending on how the tool is exited. (For instance, in the Microsoft Windows environment, it is common to be able to terminate a program either by selecting File | Exit from a menu on the top left of the window or by clicking an X in the top-right corner. The programmers who wrote the tool may well have coded different logic into these functions.) In either case, it will be a controlled exit, so the programmers should issue either a COMMIT or a ROLLBACK, but the choice is up to them.

If a client's session fails for some reason, the database will always roll back the transaction. Such failure could be for a number of reasons. The user process can die or be killed at the operating system level, the network connection to the database server may go down, or the machine where the client tool is running can crash. In any of these cases, there is no orderly issue of a COMMIT or ROLLBACK statement, and it is up to the database to detect what has happened. The behavior is that the session is killed and an active transaction is rolled back. The behavior is the same if the failure is on the server side. If the database server crashes for any reason, when it next starts up, all transactions from any sessions that were in progress will be rolled back.

Transaction Control: COMMIT, ROLLBACK, SAVEPOINT, SELECT FOR UPDATE

Oracle's implementation of the relational database paradigm begins a transaction implicitly with the first DML statement. The transaction continues until a COMMIT or ROLLBACK statement. The SAVEPOINT command is not part of the SQL standard and is really just an easy way for programmers to back out some statements in reverse order. It need not be considered separately because it does not terminate a transaction.

COMMIT

Commit processing is where many people (and even some experienced DBAs) show an incomplete, or indeed completely inaccurate, understanding of the Oracle architecture. When you say COMMIT, all that happens physically is that LGWR flushes the log buffer to disk. DBW*n* does absolutely nothing. This is one of the most important performance features of an Oracle database.

EXAM TIP What does DBW*n* do when you issue a COMMIT command? Answer: absolutely nothing.

To make a transaction durable, all that is necessary is that the changes that make up the transaction are on disk; there is no need whatsoever for the changed table data to be on disk in the datafiles. If the changes are on disk in the form of multiplexed redo log files, then in the event of damage to the database, the transaction can be reinstantiated by restoring the datafiles from a backup taken before the damage occurred and applying the changes from the logs. This process is covered in detail in later chapters—for now, just hang on to the fact that a COMMIT involves nothing more than flushing the log buffer to disk and flagging the transaction as complete. This is why a transaction involving millions of updates in thousands of tables over many minutes or hours can be committed in a fraction of a second. Because LGWR writes in nearly real time, virtually all the transaction's changes are on disk already. When you say COMMIT, LGWR actually does write in real time; your session will hang until the write is complete. This delay will be the length of time it takes to flush the last bit of redo from the log buffer to disk, which will take milliseconds. Your session is then free to continue, and from then on all other sessions will no longer be redirected to the undo blocks when they address the changed table, unless the principle of consistency requires it.

The change vectors written to the redo log are all the change vectors: those applied to data blocks (tables and indexes) and those applied to undo segments.

EXAM TIP The redo log stream includes all changes, including those applied to data segments and to undo segments, for both committed and uncommitted transactions.

Where there is often confusion is that the stream of redo written out to the log files by LGWR will contain changes for both committed and uncommitted transactions. Furthermore, at any given moment, DBW*n* may or may not have written out changed blocks of data segments or undo segments to the datafiles for both committed and uncommitted transactions. So in principle, your database on disk is corrupted. The datafiles may well be storing uncommitted work and be missing committed changes. But in the event of a crash, the stream of redo on disk always has enough information to reinstantiate any committed transactions that are not in the datafiles (by use of the changes applied to data blocks) and to reinstantiate the undo segments (by use of the changes applied to undo blocks) needed to roll back any uncommitted transactions that are in the datafiles.

EXAM TIP Any DDL command, or a GRANT or REVOKE, will commit the current transaction.

ROLLBACK

While a transaction is in progress, Oracle keeps an image of the data as it was before the transaction. This image is presented to other sessions that query the data while the transaction is in progress. It is also used to roll back the transaction automatically if anything goes wrong or deliberately if the session requests it. The syntax to request a rollback is as follows:

```
ROLLBACK [TO SAVEPOINT savepoint] ;
```

The optional use of savepoints is detailed in the section following.

The state of the data before the rollback is that the data has been changed, but the information needed to reverse the changes is available. This information is presented to all other sessions in order to implement the principle of isolation. The rollback will discard all the changes by restoring the prechange image of the data; any rows the transaction inserted will be deleted, any rows the transaction deleted will be inserted back into the table, and any rows that were updated will be returned to their original state. Other sessions will not be aware that anything has happened at all; they never saw the changes. The session that did the transaction will now see the data as it was before the transaction started.

SAVEPOINT

Savepoints allow a marker to be set in a transaction that can be used to control the effect of the ROLLBACK command. Rather than rolling back the whole transaction and terminating it, it becomes possible to reverse all changes made after a particular point but leave changes made before that point intact. The transaction itself remains in progress: still uncommitted, still able to be rolled back, and still invisible to other sessions.

The syntax is as follows:

```
SAVEPOINT savepoint;
```

This creates a named point in the transaction that can be used in a subsequent ROLLBACK command. Table 6-1 illustrates the number of rows in a table at various stages in a transaction. The table is a simple table called TAB, with one column.

The example in the table shows two transactions: the first terminated with a COMMIT, the second with a ROLLBACK. It can be seen that the use of savepoints is visible only within the transaction; other sessions see nothing that is not committed.

SELECT FOR UPDATE

One last transaction control statement is SELECT FOR UPDATE. Oracle, by default, provides the highest possible level of concurrency. Readers do not block writers, and writers do not block readers. Or, in plain language, there is no problem with one session querying data that another session is updating or one session updating data that another session is querying. However, there are times when you may want to change this behavior and prevent changes to data that is being queried.

It is not unusual for an application to retrieve a set of rows with a SELECT command, present them to a user for perusal, and prompt them for any changes. Because Oracle is a

Command	Rows Visible to the User	Rows Visible to Others
`truncate table tab;`	0	0
`insert into tab values ('one');`	1	0
`savepoint first;`	1	0
`insert into tab values ('two');`	2	0
`savepoint second;`	2	0
`insert into tab values ('three');`	3	0
`rollback to savepoint second;`	2	0
`rollback to savepoint first;`	1	0
`commit;`	1	1
`delete from tab;`	0	1
`rollback;`	1	1

Table 6-1   Read Consistency and Savepoints

multiuser database, it is not impossible that another session has also retrieved the same rows. If both sessions attempt to make changes, there can be some rather odd effects. The following table depicts such a situation.

First User	Second User
`select * from regions;`	`select * from regions;`
	delete from regions where region_id=5;
	commit;
update regions set region_name='GB' where region_id=5;	

This is what the first user will see from a SQL*Plus prompt:

```
SQL> select * from regions;
 REGION_ID REGION_NAME
---------- ------------------------
         5 UK
         1 Europe
         2 Americas
         3 Asia
         4 Middle East and Africa
SQL> update regions set region_name='GB' where region_id=5;
0 rows updated.
```

This is a bit disconcerting. One way around this problem is to lock the rows in which one is interested.

```
select * from regions for update;
```

The FOR UPDATE clause will place a lock on all the rows retrieved. No changes can be made to them by any session other than that which issued the command, and therefore the subsequent updates will succeed; it is not possible for the rows to have been changed. This means that one session will have a consistent view of the data (it won't change), but the price to be paid is that other sessions will hang if they try to update any of the locked rows (they can, of course, query them).

The locks placed by a FOR UPDATE clause will be held until the session issuing the command issues a COMMIT or ROLLBACK. This must be done to release the locks, even if no DML commands have been executed.

The So-Called Autocommit

To conclude this discussion of commit processing, it is necessary to remove any confusion about what is often called *autocommit* or sometimes *implicit commit*. You will often hear it said that in some situations Oracle will autocommit. One of these situations is when doing DDL, which is described in the preceding section; another is when you exit from a user process such as SQL*Plus.

Quite simply, there is no such thing as an automatic commit. When you execute a DDL statement, there is a perfectly normal COMMIT included in the source code that implements the DDL command. But what about when you exit from your user process? If you are using SQL*Plus on a Windows terminal and you issue a DML statement followed by an EXIT, your transaction will be committed. This is because built into the SQL*Plus EXIT command there is a COMMIT statement. But what if you click in the top-right corner of the SQL*Plus window? The window will close, and if you log in again, you will see that the transaction has been rolled back. This is because the programmers who wrote SQL*Plus for Microsoft Windows included a ROLLBACK statement in the code that is executed when you close the window. The behavior of SQL*Plus on other platforms may well be different; the only way to be sure is to test it. So, whether you get an "autocommit" when you exit from a program in various ways is entirely dependent on how your programmers wrote your user process. The Oracle server will simply do what it is told to do.

The SQL*Plus command SET AUTOCOMMIT ON will cause SQL*Plus to modify its behavior; it will append a COMMIT to every DML statement issued. So, all statements are committed immediately as soon as they are executed and cannot be rolled back. But this is happening purely on the user process side; there is still no autocommit in the database, and the changes made by a long-running statement will be isolated from other sessions until the statement completes. Of course, a disorderly exit from SQL*Plus in these circumstances, such as killing it with an operating system utility while the statement is running, will be detected by PMON, and the active transaction will always be rolled back.

Exercise 6-4: Explain DML and Undo Data Generation   In this exercise, you will demonstrate transaction isolation and control. Use two SQL*Plus sessions (or SQL Developer if you prefer), each connected as user SYSTEM. Run the commands in the steps that follow in the two sessions in the correct order.

Step	In Your First Session	In Your Second Session
1	`create table t1 as select * from all_users;`	
2	`select count(*) from t1;`	`select count(*) from t1;`

The results are the same in both sessions.

Step	In Your First Session	In Your Second Session
3	delete from t1;	
4	`select count(*) from t1;`	`select count(*) from t1;`

The results differ because transaction isolation conceals the changes.

Step	In Your First Session	In Your Second Session
5	`rollback;`	
6	`select count(*) from t1;`	`select count(*) from t1;`

The results are the same in both sessions.

Step	In Your First Session	In Your Second Session
7	`delete from t1;`	
8	`select count(*) from t1;`	`select count(*) from t1;`
9	`create view v1 as select * from t1;`	
10	`select count(*) from t1;`	`select count(*) from t1;`
11	`rollback;`	
12	`select count(*) from t1;`	`select count(*) from t1;`

Oh dear! The DDL statement committed the DELETE, so it can't be rolled back.

Step	In Your First Session	In Your Second Session
13	`drop view v1;`	
14	`drop table t1;`	

Explain DML and Undo Data Generation

Undo data is the information needed to reverse the effects of DML statements. It is often referred to as *rollback data,* but try to avoid that term. In earlier releases of Oracle, the terms *rollback data* and *undo data* were used interchangeably, but from 9*i* onward they are different. Their function is the same, but their management is not. The old mechanism of rollback segments is long outdated, and all databases should use *automatic undo management,* which uses undo segments to store undo data.

Rolling back a transaction means to use data from the undo segments to construct an image of the data as it was before the transaction occurred. This is usually done automatically to satisfy the requirements of the ACID test, but the Flashback Query capability (detailed in the section "Flashback Query and Undo Retention") leverages the power of the undo mechanism by giving you the option of querying the database as it was at some time in the past. And, of course, any user can use the ROLLBACK command interactively to back out any DML statements that were issued and not committed.

The ACID test requires, first, that the database should keep preupdate versions of data in order that incomplete transactions can be reversed—either automatically in the case of an error or on demand through the use of the ROLLBACK command. This type of rollback is permanent and published to all users. Second, for consistency, the database must be able to present a query with a version of the database as it was at the time the query started. The server process running the query will go to the undo segments and construct what is called a *read-consistent* image of the blocks being queried, if they were changed after the query started. This type of rollback is temporary and visible only to the session running the query. Third, undo segments are also used for transaction isolation. This is perhaps the most complex use of undo data. The principle of isolation requires that no transaction can be in any way dependent upon another incomplete transaction. In effect, even though a multiuser database will have many transactions in progress at once, the end result must be as though the transactions were executing one after another. The use of undo data combined with row and table locks guarantees transaction isolation, which means the impossibility of incompatible transactions. Even though several transactions may be running concurrently, isolation requires that the end result must be as if the transactions were serialized.

 EXAM TIP   Use of undo segments is incompatible with use of rollback segments; it is one or the other, depending on the setting of the UNDO_ MANAGEMENT parameter.

Exercise 6-5: Monitor and Administer Undo Data   In this exercise, you will investigate the undo configuration and usage in your database. Use either SQL*Plus or SQL Developer.

1. Connect to the database as user SYSTEM.

2. Determine whether the database is using undo segments or rollback segments with this query:

   ```
   select value from v$parameter where name='undo_management';
   ```

   This should return the value AUTO. If it does not, issue this command and then restart the instance:

   ```
   alter system set undo_management=auto scope =spfile;
   ```

3. Determine what undo tablespaces have been created and which one is being used with these two queries:

   ```
   select tablespace_name from dba_tablespaces where contents='UNDO';
   select value from v$parameter where name='undo_tablespace';
   ```

4. Determine what undo segments are in use in the database and how big they are.

   ```
   select tablespace_name,segment_name,segment_id,status from dba_rollback_segs;
   select usn,rssize from v$rollstat;
   ```

   Note that the identifying number for a segment has a different column name in the two views.

5. Find out how much undo data was being generated in your database in the recent past.

   ```
   alter session set nls_date_format='dd-mm-yy hh24:mi:ss';
   select begin_time, end_time,
   (undoblks * (select value from v$parameter where  name='db_block_size'))
   undo_bytes from  v$undostat;
   ```

Monitor and Administer Undo Data

A major feature of undo segments is that they are managed automatically, but you must set the limits within which Oracle will do its management. After considering the nature and volume of activity in your database, you set certain instance parameters and adjust the size of your undo tablespace in order to achieve your objectives.

Error Conditions Related to Undo

The principles are simple. First, there should always be sufficient undo space available to allow all transactions to continue. Second, there should always be sufficient undo data available for all queries to succeed. The first principle requires that your undo tablespace must be large enough to accommodate the worst case for undo demand. It should have enough space allocated for the peak usage of active undo data generated by your transaction workload. Note that this might not be during the highest number of concurrent transactions; it could be that during normal running you have many small transactions, but the total undo they generate might be less than that generated by a single end-of-month batch job. The second principle requires that there be additional space in the undo tablespace to store unexpired undo data that might be needed for read consistency.

If a transaction runs out of undo space, it will fail with the error "ORA-30036: unable to extend segment in undo tablespace." The statement that hit the problem is rolled back, but the rest of the transaction remains intact and uncommitted. The algorithm that assigns space within the undo tablespace to undo segments means that this error condition will arise only if the undo tablespace is absolutely full of active undo data.

 EXAM TIP   If a DML statement runs out of undo space, the portion of it that had already succeeded will be rolled back. The rest of the transaction remains intact and uncommitted.

If a query encounters a block that has been changed since the query started, it will go to the undo segment to find the pre-update version of the data. If, when it goes to the undo segment, that bit of undo data has been overwritten, the query will fail with the famous Oracle error "ORA-1555: snapshot too old."

If the undo tablespace is undersized for the transaction volume and the length of queries, Oracle has a choice: Either let transactions succeed and risk queries failing with ORA-1555 or let queries succeed and risk transactions failing with ORA-30036. The default behavior is to let the transactions succeed to allow them to overwrite unexpired undo.

Parameters for Undo Management

The following four parameters control undo:

- UNDO_MANAGEMENT
- UNDO_TABLESPACE
- UNDO_RETENTION (discussed in the section "Configure Undo Retention")
- TEMP_UNDO_ENABLED (discussed in the section "Temporary Undo")

UNDO_MANAGEMENT defaults to AUTO. It is possible to set this to MANUAL, meaning that Oracle will not use undo segments at all. This is for backward compatibility, and if you use this, you will have to do a vast amount of work creating and tuning rollback segments. Don't do it. Oracle Corporation strongly advises setting this parameter to AUTO to enable use of undo segments. This parameter is static, meaning that if it is changed, the change will not come into effect until the instance is restarted. The other parameters are dynamic—they can be changed while the instance is running.

If you are using UNDO_MANAGEMENT=AUTO (as you should), you should also specify UNDO_TABLESPACE. This parameter nominates a tablespace, which must have been created as an undo tablespace, as the active undo tablespace. All the undo segments within it will be brought online (that is, made available for use) automatically.

Sizing and Monitoring the Undo Tablespace

The undo tablespace should be large enough to store the worst case of all the undo generated by concurrent transactions, which will be active undo plus enough unexpired undo to satisfy the longest-running query. In an advanced environment, you may also have to add space to allow for flashback queries. The algorithm is simple: Calculate the rate at which undo is being generated at your peak workload and multiply by the length of your longest query. There is a view, V$UNDOSTAT, that will tell you all you need to know.

Making your undo datafiles autoextensible will ensure that transactions will never run out of space, but Oracle will not extend them merely to meet the UNDO_RETENTION target; it is therefore still possible for a query to fail with "snapshot too old." However, you should not rely on the autoextend capability; your tablespace should be the correct size to begin with.

Figure 6-4 shows the undo configuration and usage using SQL*Plus. The same information is available in graphical format in Database Express. On the database home page, select the Undo Management link on the Storage drop-down menu.

Figure 6-4 Undo configuration and activity	

```
oracle@oel58x64db121:~

orclz> alter session set nls_date_format='hh24:mi:ss';

Session altered.

orclz> show parameters undo

NAME                                 TYPE        VALUE
------------------------------------ ----------- ------------------------------
temp_undo_enabled                    boolean     FALSE
undo_management                      string      AUTO
undo_retention                       integer     900
undo_tablespace                      string      UNDOTBS1
orclz> select begin_time,end_time,undoblks,activeblks,unexpiredblks,
  2    maxquerylen,txncount from v$undostat;

BEGIN_TI END_TIME   UNDOBLKS ACTIVEBLKS UNEXPIREDBLKS MAXQUERYLEN  TXNCOUNT
-------- --------  --------- ---------- ------------- ----------- ---------
20:31:12 20:33:52          1        160        540256        1393        17
20:21:12 20:31:12     256344       4000        281952        1092       605
20:11:12 20:21:12     281117        160           328         490       908
20:01:12 20:11:12        130        160           280         945       846
19:51:12 20:01:12         42        160             8         345       388

orclz> select blocks from dba_data_files where tablespace_name='UNDOTBS1';

   BLOCKS
----------
   540800
```

The first statement in the figure sets the session's date display format to show hours, minutes, and seconds. Then the SQL*Plus SHOW command shows the settings for the four instance parameters that include the string "undo" in their name. All four are set to their default: Temporary undo is disabled, undo management is automatic (using undo segments, not antiquated rollback segments), the retention target is 900 seconds, and the undo tablespace is UNDOTBS1, which is the tablespace created when using DBCA to create a database. A query against V$UNDOSTAT shows undo activity captured in 10-minute intervals. During the half-hour shown, undo generation peaked at 281,117 blocks in one 10-minute interval and generated 908 transactions. The longest query was 1,393 seconds. Finally, querying DBA_DATA_FILES shows that the undo tablespace datafile is 540,800 blocks, which is about 4GB, assuming that the database was created using the default block size of 8KB.

Doing some simple arithmetic shows that the undo generation rate peaks at about 500 blocks a second, so if the longest query is about 1,000 seconds (which is pretty close to the undo_retention setting), you would need an undo tablespace of about half a million blocks to ensure that undo can always be kept for as long as the longest query. This database would appear to have undo configuration that is well matched to the workload.

The V$UNDOSTAT view is often referred to as the *undo advisor* because it lets you predict how long undo data can be kept for a given workload. Database Express represents this nicely, as shown in Figure 6-5.

The curve in the undo advisor window shows that if the undo tablespace were 5GB, it would be able to store undo data for between about 1,500 and 4,000 seconds (depending on activity). Larger or smaller sizes would increase or decrease the time for which undo would be kept.

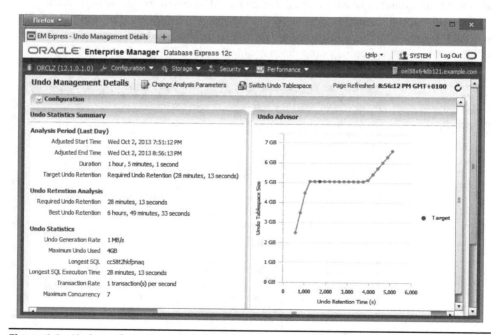

Figure 6-5   Undo configuration in Database Express

Temporary Undo

Temporary undo segments are used for storing undo data generated by DML against global temporary tables. A global temporary table is a table whose definition may be visible to all sessions (*global*) but whose rows are private to the session that inserted them. The duration of the rows is either until COMMIT or until the session terminates (*temporary*).

Global temporary tables are often useful to developers. They offer a storage location for data that may be useful for interim result sets, without any need to worry about clearing the data when it is no longer needed or ensuring that sessions will not interfere with (or even see) data created by another session. From the database's point of view, global temporary tables are easy to manage. They exist as segments created (and dropped) automatically in a temporary tablespace.

The performance on temporary tables is usually superior to the performance of permanent tables. This is for two reasons.

- *The I/O is direct.* The session reads and writes its temporary segment without going through the buffer cache and without involving the database writer.

- *No redo is generated on global temporary tables.* There would be no reason. The purpose of redo is to make changes persistent, and global temporary tables do not store persistent data.

Undo data is generated by DML against temporary tables. This is necessary because the usual transactional rules apply. And it follows that redo is generated because even though the table may be a temporary segment, the undo segment is not. In earlier releases, this caused these two problems:

- A performance hit because of undo segment input/output (I/O) going via the buffer cache and generating associated redo

- The impossibility of transactions against temporary tables in a read-only database; the table might not exist in a read/write tablespace, but the undo segment does

Release 12*c* has a facility that permits the creation of temporary undo segments in a temporary tablespace. This may significantly improve the performance of transactions against temporary tables without compromising the transactional integrity, and it also means that transactions can be run against read-only databases, such as a Data Guard physical standby database.

Creating and Managing Undo Tablespaces

As far as datafile management is concerned, an undo tablespace is the same as any other tablespace; files can be added, resized, taken online and offline, and moved or renamed. But it is not possible to specify any options regarding storage. You cannot specify automatic segment space management, and you cannot specify a uniform extent size. To create an undo tablespace, use the keyword UNDO.

```
CREATE UNDO TABLESPACE tablespace_name
DATAFILE datafile_name SIZE size [ M | G | T ]
 [ RETENTION NOGUARANTEE | GUARANTEE ] ;
```

By default, the tablespace will not guarantee undo retention. This characteristic can be specified at tablespace creation time or set later.

```
ALTER TABLESPACE tablespace_name
retention [ GUARANTEE | NOGUARANTEE ] ;
```

 EXAM TIP Unless specified at creation time in the datafile clause, the datafiles of an undo tablespace will not be set to autoextend. But if your database is created with the Database Configuration Assistant (DBCA), it will enable automatic extension for the undo tablespace's datafile with maximum size unlimited. Automatic extension can be enabled or disabled at any time, like it can be for any datafile.

It is not possible to create segments in an undo tablespace, other than the undo segments that will be created automatically. Initially, there will be a pool of ten undo segments created in an undo tablespace. More will be created if there are more than ten concurrent transactions. Oracle will monitor the concurrent transaction rate and adjust the number of segments as necessary.

No matter how many undo tablespaces there may be in a database, generally speaking, only one will be in use at a time. The undo segments in this tablespace will have a status of online (meaning that they are available for use); the segments in any other undo tablespaces will have a status of offline, indicating that they will not be used. If the undo tablespace is changed, all the undo segments in the old undo tablespace will be taken offline and those in the new undo tablespace will be brought online. There are two exceptions to this:

- In a Real Application Cluster (RAC) database, every instance opening the database must have its own undo tablespace. This can be controlled by setting the UNDO_TABLESPACE parameter to a different value for each instance. Each instance will bring its own undo segments online.

- If the undo tablespace is changed by changing the UNDO_TABLESPACE parameter, any segments in the previously nominated tablespace that were supporting a transaction at the time of the change will remain online until the transaction finishes.

Exercise 6-6: Work with Undo Tablespaces   In this exercise, you will create an undo tablespace and bring it into use. Here are the steps to follow:

1. Connect to your instance as user SYSTEM with SQL*Plus.

2. Create an undo tablespace.
   ```
   create undo tablespace undo2 datafile 'a_path_and_filename'
   size 100m;
   ```
   For the datafile's path and name, use anything suitable for your environment.

3. Run the following query, which will return one row for each tablespace in your database.
   ```
   select tablespace_name,contents,retention from dba_tablespaces;
   ```

Note that your new tablespace has contents UNDO, meaning that it can be used only for undo segments and that retention is NOGUARANTEE.

4. Run the following query, which will return one row for each rollback or undo segment in your database:

```
select tablespace_name, segment_name, status
from dba_rollback_segs;
```

Note that ten undo segments have been created automatically in your new undo tablespace, but they are all offline.

5. Adjust your instance to use the new undo tablespace. Use a SCOPE clause to ensure that the change will not be permanent.

```
alter system set undo_tablespace=undo2 scope=memory;
```

6. Rerun the query from step 4. You will see that the undo segments in the new tablespace have been brought online and those in the previously active undo tablespace are offline.

7. Tidy up by setting the undo_tablespace parameter back to its original value and then dropping the new undo tablespace. Remember to use the INCLUDING CONTENTS AND DATAFILES clause.

Describe the Difference Between Undo Data and Redo Data

This topic gets a special mention because many mistakes are made by many people when describing undo and redo. Here is a set of contrasts:

- *Undo is transient, whereas redo is permanent.* Undo data persists for at least the duration of the transaction that generates it, but possibly for no longer. Eventually, it will always be overwritten. Redo persists indefinitely, first in the online log files and then in the archive log files.

- *Undo operates at the logical level, whereas redo operates at the physical level.* Undo data is row oriented; changes are grouped according to the transaction that made them, and within an undo segment all the entries are related to rows of the same transaction. Redo is physically oriented. Change vectors are related to physical locations in blocks by the row ID pointer. There is no relationship between consecutive change vectors in the log buffer or the log files.

- *Undo can reverse changes, whereas redo can repeat changes.* Undo data provides the ability to reverse committed transactions. Redo provides the ability to replay work that has been lost.

- *Undo resides in tablespaces, whereas redo resides in files.* Undo data is a segment structure within the database. Redo is written out to operating system files.

- *Undo are redo are not opposites.* They have different functions. Undo is about transactional integrity, whereas redo is about preventing data loss.

Configure Undo Retention

Automatic undo management will always keep undo data for as long as possible. This is usually all that is required. However, there are two cases where DBA action may be necessary: if it is necessary to ensure that queries will always succeed, even if this means that DML may fail, and if flashback queries are being used extensively.

Configuring Undo Retention to Support Long-Running Queries

UNDO_RETENTION, set in seconds, is usually optional. It specifies a target for keeping inactive undo data and determines when it becomes classified as expired rather than unexpired. If, for example, your longest-running query is 30 minutes, you would set this parameter to 1800. Oracle will then attempt to keep all undo data for at least 1,800 seconds after COMMIT, and your query should therefore never fail with ORA-1555. If, however, you do not set this parameter or set it to zero, Oracle will still keep data for as long as it can anyway. The algorithm controlling which expired undo data is overwritten first will always choose to overwrite the oldest bit of data; therefore, UNDO_RETENTION is always at the maximum allowed by the size of the tablespace.

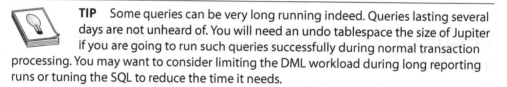

TIP   Some queries can be very long running indeed. Queries lasting several days are not unheard of. You will need an undo tablespace the size of Jupiter if you are going to run such queries successfully during normal transaction processing. You may want to consider limiting the DML workload during long reporting runs or tuning the SQL to reduce the time it needs.

Where the UNDO_RETENTION parameter is not optional is if you have configured guaranteed undo retention. The default mode of operation for undo is that Oracle will favor transactions over queries. If the sizing of the undo tablespace is such that a choice has to be made between the possibility of a query failing with ORA-1555 and the certainty of a transaction failing with ORA-30036, Oracle will choose to let the transaction continue by overwriting undo data that a query might need. In other words, the undo retention is only a target that Oracle will try to achieve. But there may be circumstances when successful queries are considered more important than successful transactions. An example might be the end-of-month billing run for a utilities company, when it might be acceptable to risk transactions being blocked for a short time while the reports are generating. Another case is if you are making use of flashback queries, which rely on undo data.

Guaranteed undo retention, meaning that undo data will never be overwritten until the time specified by the undo retention has passed, is enabled at the tablespace level. This attribute can be specified at tablespace creation time, or an undo tablespace can be altered later to enable it. Once you activate an undo tablespace for which retention guarantee has been specified, all queries will complete successfully, provided they finish within the undo retention time; you will never have "snapshot too old" errors again. The downside is that transactions may fail for lack of undo space.

If the UNDO_RETENTION tablespace parameter has been set and the datafile (or datafiles) making up the undo tablespace is set to autoextend, then Oracle will increase the size of the datafile automatically if necessary to keep to the undo retention target. This combination of guaranteed undo retention and autoextending datafiles means that both queries and transactions will always succeed—assuming you have enough disk space. If you don't, the automatic extension will fail.

Flashback Query and Undo Retention

Flashback Query can place additional demands on the undo system. Flashback Query is a facility that allows users to see the database as it was at a time in the past. There are several methods of making flashback queries, but the simplest is a straightforward SELECT statement with an AS OF clause. Here is an example:

```
select * from scott.emp as of timestamp (systimestamp - 10/1440);
```

This statement will return all the rows in the SCOTT.EMP table that were there 10 minutes ago. Rows that have been deleted will be seen, rows that have been inserted will not be seen, and rows that have been updated will be seen with their old values. This is the case whether or not the DML statements have been committed. To execute flashback queries, undo data is used to roll back all the changes. The rows that have been deleted are extracted from the undo segments and inserted back into the result set; rows that have been inserted are deleted from the result set. A query such as the preceding one that attempts to go back 10 minutes will probably succeed. A query that tries to go back a week would almost certainly fail because the undo data needed to reconstruct a version of the table as it was a week ago will have been overwritten.

Flashback Query can be a valuable tool. For example, if because of some mistake a deletion has occurred (and has been committed) at some time in the last hour, this command will reverse it by inserting all deleted rows back into the table:

```
insert into scott.emp
(select * from scott.emp as of timestamp (systimestamp - 1/24)
minus
select * from scott.emp);
```

If Flashback Query is likely to be used, then you must configure the undo system to handle it by setting the UNDO_RETENTION parameter to an appropriate value. If you want the ability to flash back a day, it must be set to 86,400 seconds. The undo tablespace must be appropriately sized. Then to be certain of success, either enable automatic extension for the undo tablespace's datafiles or enable the retention guarantee for the tablespace.

Exercise 6-7: Work with Transactions and Flashback Query   In this exercise, you'll demonstrate the manner in which undo data is used to provide transaction isolation and rollback, as well as to implement Flashback Query. Use the REGIONS table in the HR demonstration schema. Here are the steps to follow:

1. Connect to the HR schema with two sessions concurrently. These can be two SQL*Plus sessions, two SQL Developer sessions, or one of each. The table that follows lists the steps to follow in each session:

Step	In Your First Session	In Your Second Session
1	`select * from regions;`	`select * from regions;`
Both sessions see the same data.		
2	`insert into regions` `values(100,'UK');`	`insert into regions` `values(101,'GB');`
3	`select * from regions;`	`select * from regions;`
Both sessions see different results: the original data plus their own changes.		
4	`commit;`	
5	`select * from regions;`	`select * from regions;`
One transaction has been published to the world, the other is still visible to only one session.		
6	`rollback;`	`rollback;`
7	`select * from regions;`	`select * from regions;`

The committed transaction was not reversed because it has already been committed, but the uncommitted one is now completely gone, having been terminated by the rolling back of the change. With all transactions terminated, both sessions see a consistent view of the table.

2. Demonstrate the use of Flashback Query using one session connected as user HR.

   A. Adjust your time display format to include seconds.

   ```
   alter session set nls_date_format='dd-mm-yy hh24:mi:ss';
   ```

   B. Query and record the current time.

   ```
   select sysdate from dual;
   ```

   C. Delete the row inserted previously and then commit the deletion.

   ```
   delete from regions where region_id=100;
   commit;
   ```

   D. Query the table as it was before the row was deleted.

   ```
   select * from regions as of timestamp
   to_timestamp('time_from_step_2','dd-mm-yy hh24:mi:ss');
   ```

The deleted row for region 100 will be listed, having been retrieved from an undo segment.

Describe the Locking Mechanism and Data Concurrency Management

There are many types of locks. Most are internal to the server, such as locks necessary for serializing execution of certain critical sections of code or for protecting certain memory structures. The Oracle Certified Associate (OCA) exam does not cover these, although they are often important for tuning. The topics covered are locks that are used at the application layer, such as locks taken and released as SQL statements execute. These locks are applied either to rows or to entire tables, automatically or manually (if developers really need to do this).

Serialization of concurrent access is accomplished by record- and table-locking mechanisms. Locking in an Oracle database is completely automatic. Generally speaking, problems arise only if software tries to interfere with the automatic locking mechanism with poorly written code or if the business analysis is faulty and thus results in a business model where sessions will collide.

Shared and Exclusive Locks

The standard level of locking in an Oracle database guarantees the highest possible level of concurrency. This means that if a session is updating one row, the one row is locked and nothing else. Furthermore, the row is locked only to prevent other sessions from updating it; other sessions can read it at any time. The lock is held until the transaction completes, either with a COMMIT or with a ROLLBACK. This is an exclusive lock; the first session to request the lock on the row gets it, and any other sessions requesting write access must wait. Read access is permitted—although if the row has been updated by the locking session, as will usually be the case, then any reads will involve the use of undo data to make sure that reading sessions do not see any uncommitted changes.

 EXAM TIP Locked rows cannot be updated or deleted by another session, but any other session can still read them.

Only one session can take an exclusive lock on a row, or a whole table, at a time—but *shared* locks can be taken on the same object by many sessions. It would not make any sense to take a shared lock on one row because the only purpose of a row lock is to gain the exclusive access needed to modify the row. Shared locks are taken on whole tables, and many sessions can have a shared lock on the same table. The purpose of taking a shared lock on a table is to prevent another session from acquiring an exclusive lock on the table. You cannot get an exclusive lock if anyone else already has a shared lock. Exclusive locks on tables are required to execute DDL statements. You cannot issue a statement that will modify an object (for instance, dropping a column of a table) if any other session already has a shared lock on the table.

To execute DML on rows, a session must acquire exclusive locks on the rows to be changed, as well as shared locks on the tables containing the rows. If another session already has exclusive locks on the rows, the session will hang until the locks are released by a COMMIT or a ROLLBACK. If another session already has a shared lock on the table and exclusive locks on other rows, that is not a problem. An exclusive lock on the table could be a problem, but the default locking mechanism does not lock whole tables unless this is necessary for DDL statements.

 TIP It is possible to demand an exclusive lock on a whole table, but this has to be specifically requested, and programmers would need a good reason for doing it.

All DML statements require at least two locks: an exclusive lock on each row affected and a shared lock on the table containing the row. The exclusive lock prevents another session from interfering with the row, and the shared lock prevents another session from changing the table definition with a DDL statement. These locks are requested automatically. If a DML statement cannot acquire the exclusive row locks it needs, it will hang until it gets them.

Executing DDL commands requires an exclusive lock on the object concerned. This cannot be obtained until all DML transactions against the table have finished, thereby releasing both their exclusive row locks and their shared table locks. The exclusive lock required by any DDL statement is requested automatically, but if it cannot be obtained—typically because another session already has the shared lock granted for DML—then the statement will terminate with an error immediately.

 EXAM TIP Any uncommitted insert, update, or delete of a row will cause any attempted DDL on the table to fail immediately.

The Enqueue Mechanism

Requests for locks are queued. If a session requests a lock and cannot get it because another session already has the row or object locked, the session will wait. It may be that several sessions are waiting for access to the same row or object—in that case, Oracle will keep track of the order in which the sessions requested the lock. When the session with the lock releases it, the next session will be granted the lock, and so on. This is known as the *enqueue mechanism.*

If you do not want a session to queue up if it cannot get a lock, the only way to avoid this is to use the WAIT or NOWAIT clause of the SELECT...FOR UPDATE command. A normal SELECT will always succeed because SELECT does not require any locks, but a DML statement will hang. The SELECT...FOR UPDATE command will select rows and lock them in exclusive mode. If any of the rows are locked already, the SELECT...FOR UPDATE statement will be queued, and the session will hang until the locks are released, just like a DML statement would. To avoid sessions hanging, use either SELECT...FOR UPDATE NOWAIT or SELECT...FOR UPDATE WAIT <n>, where <n> is a number of seconds. Having obtained the locks with either of the SELECT...FOR UPDATE options, you can then issue the DML commands with no possibility of the session hanging.

 TIP It is possible to append the keywords SKIP LOCKED to a SELECT FOR UPDATE statement, which will return and lock only rows that are not already locked by another session.

Automatic and Manual Locking

Whenever any DML statement is executed, as part of the execution, the session will automatically take a shared lock on the table and exclusive locks on the affected rows. This automatic locking is perfect for virtually all operations. It offers the highest possible level of concurrency (minimizing the possibilities for contention) and requires no programmer input whatsoever. These locks are released, also automatically, when the transaction is completed with either COMMIT or ROLLBACK.

Whenever any DDL statement is executed, the session will automatically take an exclusive lock on the entire object. This lock persists for the duration of the DDL statement and is released automatically when the statement completes. Internally, what is happening is that the

DDL is, in fact, DML statements against rows in tables in the data dictionary. If one could see the source code of, for example, the DROP TABLE command, this would be clear. It will (among other things) be deleting a number of rows from the SYS.COL$ table, which has one row for every column in the database, and one row from the SYS.TAB$ table, which has one row for every table, followed by COMMIT. Most DDL statements are quick to execute, so the table locks they require will usually not be noticed by users.

Manually locking objects can be done. The syntax is as follows:

```
lock table table_name in mode_name mode;
```

Five modes are possible, each of which may or may not be compatible with another lock request of a certain mode from another session:

- ROW SHARE
- ROW EXCLUSIVE
- SHARE
- SHARE ROW EXCLUSIVE
- EXCLUSIVE

The following table shows the lock compatibilities. If one session has taken the lock type listed across the top of the table, another session will (Y) or will not (N) be able to take the type of lock listed in the first column.

	Row Share	Row Exclusive	Share	Share Row Exclusive	Exclusive
Row Share	Y	Y	Y	Y	N
Row Exclusive	Y	Y	N	N	N
Share	Y	N	Y	N	N
Share Row Exclusive	Y	N	N	N	N
Exclusive	N	N	N	N	N

For example, if a session has taken a ROW SHARE lock on a table, other sessions can take any type of lock except EXCLUSIVE. On the other hand, if a session has an EXCLUSIVE lock on the object, no other session can take any lock at all. A ROW SHARE lock permits DML by other sessions but will prevent any other session from taking an EXCLUSIVE lock on the table. An EXCLUSIVE lock is needed (and requested automatically) in order to drop the table. ROW SHARE will therefore ensure that the table is not dropped by another session. In practice, the only type of lock that is ever likely to be taken manually is the EXCLUSIVE lock. This will prevent any other sessions from performing any DML against the table.

Whenever a session does any DML against a table, it will (automatically) take a table lock in ROW EXCLUSIVE mode. Because this is not incompatible with other sessions taking a ROW EXCLUSIVE mode lock, many sessions can perform DML concurrently—as long as they do not attempt to update the same rows.

Monitor and Resolve Locking Conflicts

When a session requests a lock on a row or object and cannot get it because another session has an exclusive lock on the row or object, it will hang. This is *lock contention,* and it can cause the database performance to deteriorate appallingly as sessions queue up waiting for locks. Some lock contention may be inevitable as a result of normal activity; the nature of the application may be such that different users will require access to the same data. But in many cases, lock contention is caused by program and system design.

The Oracle database provides utilities for detecting lock contention, and it is also possible to solve the problem in an emergency. A special case of lock contention is the *deadlock,* which is always resolved automatically by the database.

 TIP   Lock contention is a common reason for an application that performs well under test to grind to a halt when it goes production and the number of concurrent users increases.

The Causes of Lock Contention

It may be that the nature of the business is such that users do require write access to the same rows at the same time. If this is a limiting factor in the performance of the system, the only solution is business process reengineering to develop a more efficient business model. However, although some locking is a necessary part of business data processing, some faults in application design can exacerbate the problem.

Long-running transactions will cause problems. An obvious case is where a user updates a row and then does not commit the change. Perhaps they even go off to lunch, leaving the transaction unfinished. You cannot stop this from happening if users have access to the database with tools such as SQL*Plus, but it should never occur with well-written software. The application should take care that a lock is imposed only just before an update occurs and then released (with a COMMIT or ROLLBACK) immediately afterward.

Poorly written batch processes can also cause problems if they are coded as long transactions. Consider the case of an accounting suite nominal ledger. It is a logical impossibility in accountancy terms for the ledger to be partly in one period and partly in another, so the end-of-month rollover to the next period is one business transaction. This transaction may involve updating millions of rows in thousands of tables and take hours to complete. If the rollover routine is coded as one transaction with a COMMIT at the end, millions of rows will be locked for hours—but in accountancy terms, this is what should happen. Good program design would avoid the problem by updating the rows in groups, with regular commits, but the programmers will also have to take care of simulating read consistency across transactions and handle the situation where the process fails partway through. If it were one transaction, this wouldn't be a problem; the database would roll it back. If it involves many small transactions, they will have to manage a ledger that is half in one period and half in another. These considerations should not be a problem. Your programmers should bear in mind long transactions' impact on the usability of the system and design their systems accordingly.

Third-party user process products may impose excessively high locking levels. For example, some application development tools always do a SELECT...FOR UPDATE to avoid the necessity of requerying the data and checking for changes. Some other products cannot do row-level locking. If a user wants to update one row, the tool locks a group of rows—perhaps dozens or even hundreds. If your application software is written with tools such as these, the Oracle database will simply do what it is told to do; it will impose numerous locks that are unnecessary in business terms. If you suspect that the software is applying more locks than necessary, investigate whether it has configuration options to change this behavior.

Lastly, make sure your programmers are aware of the capabilities of the database. A common problem is repeatable reads. Consider this example:

```
SQL> select * from regions;
 REGION_ID REGION_NAME
---------- ------------------------
         1 Europe
         2 Americas
         3 Asia
         4 Middle East and Africa
SQL> select count(*) from regions;
  COUNT(*)
----------
         5
```

How can this be possible? The first query (the detail report) shows four rows, but then the second query (the summary report) shows five. The problem is that during the course of the first query, another session inserted and committed the fifth row. One way out of this would be to lock the table while running the reports, thus causing other sessions to hang. A more sophisticated way would be to use the SET TRANSACTION READ ONLY statement. This will guarantee (without imposing any locks) that the session does not see any DML on any tables, committed or not, until it terminates the read-only transaction with a COMMIT or ROLLBACK. The mechanism is based on the use of undo segments.

Detecting Lock Contention

Certain views will tell you what is going on with locking in the database, and Database Express offers a graphical interface for lock monitoring. Lock contention is a natural consequence of many users accessing the same data concurrently. The problem can be exacerbated by badly designed software, but in principle, lock contention is part of normal database activity. It is therefore not possible for DBAs to resolve it completely; they can identify only that it is a problem and suggest to system and application designers that they bear in mind the impact of lock contention when designing data structures and programs.

Lock contention can be seen in the V$SESSION view. This view has one row for each currently logged-on session. The unique identifier is the column session identifier (SID). If a session is blocked by another session, the SID of the blocking session is shown in the column BLOCKING_SESSION. Figure 6-6 shows a query that joins V$SESSION to itself, using the SID and BLOCKING_SESSION columns. The only sessions listed are those that are blocked; all other sessions will have BLOCKING_SESSION=NULL and will therefore not be included.

In the figure, user MILLER is blocking two other sessions: JW and KING. User SCOTT is blocking user SYSTEM. To identify lock contention in Database Express, click the Performance

Figure 6-6
Finding and
killing blocking
sessions

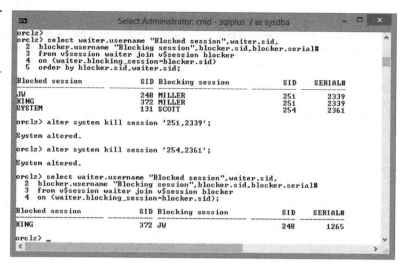

tab, click the link for Performance Hub, and then click the Current ADDM Findings tab. This
will show current detected issues, with details visible if you click the Impact bar. Figure 6-7
shows a situation where one session, SID=256, is blocking two other sessions (SID=15 and
SID=251) with row lock enqueues. It is also possible to understand the queue: Session SID=15
is blocked by both sessions 251 and 256, so killing 256 (which is suggested as Recommendation 1)

Findings ⓘ

Finding	Scope	Priority	Number of Recommendations	Impact
⊟ Unresolved hangs or session wait chains	🗄	◉		▬▬▬▬▬▬
Unresolved hangs or session wait chains	🗄	◯	1	▬▬▬▬▬▬
SQL statements consuming significant database time	🗄	◉		▬▬▬▬▬▬

Details ⓘ

Recommendations

Recommendation 1   Kill the session with ID [1:256,3723]. The session runs as operating system process 9076.

Finding Details

🔧 Kill Session

Session ID	Blocker Type	Process	Blockers	Event
1:15,1541		Foreground	1:251,3059 | 1:256,3723	enq: TX - row lock contention
1:251,3059		Foreground	1:256,3723	enq: TX - row lock contention
1:256,3723	🔒	Foreground		SQL *Net message from client

Figure 6-7   Lock contention as displayed in Database Express

will not be enough to free it. However, killing session 256 will free up session 251. This will allow 251 to complete its work, which may then free up session 15. All the sessions are identified by a three-faceted session ID, consisting of the instance number (which is always 1 because this is not a clustered database), the SID, and the SERIAL#.

Solving Lock Contention

In most circumstances, such blocks will be very short lived. The blocking sessions will commit their transactions, and the blocked sessions will then be able to work. In an emergency, however, it is possible for the DBA to solve the problem—by terminating the session (or sessions) holding too many locks for too long. When a session is terminated forcibly, any locks it holds will be released as its active transaction is rolled back. The blocked sessions will then become free and can continue.

To terminate a session, use the ALTER SYSTEM KILL SESSION command. It takes the SID and SERIAL# of the session to identify which session to kill. The SID is unique at any given moment, but as users log on and off, SIDs will be reused. The SID plus SERIAL# is guaranteed to be unique for the lifetime of the instance, and both must be specified when a session is killed.

```
ALTER SYSTEM KILL SESSION ' sid , serial# ';
```

Deadlocks: A Special Case

It is possible to construct a position where two sessions block each other in such a fashion that both will hang, each waiting for the other to release its lock. This is a *deadlock*. Deadlocks are caused by bad program design and are resolved automatically by the database. Information regarding deadlocks is written out to the alert log, with full details in a trace file—part of your daily monitoring will pick up the occurrence of deadlocks and inform your developers that they are happening.

If a deadlock occurs, both sessions will hang, but only for a brief moment. One of the sessions will detect the deadlock within seconds, and it will roll back the statement that caused the problem. This will free up the other session, returning the message "ORA-00060 Deadlock detected." This message must be trapped by your programmers in their exceptions clauses, which should take appropriate action.

 EXAM TIP   You can do nothing about deadlocks other than report them; they are resolved automatically by the database.

It must be emphasized that deadlocks are a program design fault. They occur because the code attempts to do something that is logically impossible. Well-written code will always request locks in a sequence that cannot cause deadlocks to occur or will test whether incompatible locks already exist before requesting them.

Exercise 6-8: Describe the Locking Mechanism and Data Concurrency Management   In the first part of this exercise, you will use SQL*Plus to cause a problem and then detect and resolve it. In the second part, you will learn how to handle deadlocks.

Here are the steps to follow to demonstrate lock contention:

1. Using SQL*Plus, connect to your database with three sessions as user SYSTEM.

2. In the first session, create a table.

   ```
   create table lockdemo as select * from all_users;
   ```

3. In the second session, update a row.

   ```
   update lockdemo set user_id=99 where username='SYS';
   ```

4. In the third session, issue the same statement as in step 2. The session will hang.

5. In the first session, run this query to identify which session is blocked:

   ```
   select username,sid,blocking_session from v$session
   where blocking_session is not null;
   ```

   Then run this query to retrieve the necessary details of the blocking session:

   ```
   select username,sid,serial# from v$session
   where sid=&blocking_session;
   ```

   When prompted, enter the blocking session's SID.

6. In the first session, kill the blocking session.

   ```
   alter system kill session '&blocking_sid,&serial';
   ```

   When prompted, enter the blocking session's SID and SERIAL#.

7. Tidy up.

   A. In the second session, attempt to run any SQL statement. You will receive the message "ORA-00028: your session has been killed."

   B. In the third session, the update will now have succeeded and completed. Terminate the transaction with COMMIT or ROLLBACK.

Here are the steps to follow to demonstrate deadlocks:

1. In your first session, update a row.

   ```
   update lockdemo set user_id=99 where username='SYS';
   ```

2. In your third session, update a second row.

   ```
   update lockdemo set user_id=99 where username='SYSTEM';
   ```

3. In your first session, attempt to update the second row.

   ```
   update lockdemo set user_id=99 where username='SYSTEM';
   ```

   This will hang because the row is already locked.

4. Set up the deadlock by updating the first row in the third session.

   ```
   update lockdemo set user_id=99 where username='SYS';
   ```

   This will hang, but within three seconds the first session will become free with the message "ORA-00060: deadlock requested while waiting for resource."

5. Retrieve information about the deadlock from the alert log and trace files.

   A. From an operating system prompt, open the alert log in the database's trace directory. The location can be found with this query:

   ```
   select value from v$diag_info where name='Diag Trace';
   ```

   and the file will be called alert_*SID*.ora. The last entry in the file will be something like this (a Windows example):

   ```
   Sat Jan 10 22:32:54 2015
   ORA-00060: Deadlock detected. More info in file D:\APP\ORACLE\diag\
   rdbms\coda\coda\trace\coda_ora_8364.trc.
   ```

   B. Open the trace file with an editor. Toward the top of the file will be this critical message:

   ```
   *** 2015-01-10 22:32:54.817
   DEADLOCK DETECTED ( ORA-00060 )

   [Transaction Deadlock]

   The following deadlock is not an ORACLE error. It is a
   deadlock due to user error in the design of an application
   or from issuing incorrect ad-hoc SQL.
   ```

   Note that this message places the responsibility firmly on the developers. Look lower down in the file, and you will find the SIDs of the sessions involved and the statements they executed that caused the deadlock.

6. Tidy up. In the first session, issue a ROLLBACK to roll back the update that did succeed. This will free up the third session, where you can now also issue a ROLLBACK. Drop the LOCKDEMO table.

Two-Minute Drill

Describe Each Data Manipulation Language Statement

- INSERT enters rows into a table.
- UPDATE adjusts the values in existing rows.
- DELETE removes rows.
- MERGE can combine the functions of INSERT, UPDATE, and DELETE.
- Even though TRUNCATE is not DML, it does remove all rows in a table.
- It is possible for an INSERT to enter rows into multiple tables.
- Subqueries can be used to generate the rows to be inserted, updated, or deleted.
- An INSERT, UPDATE, or DELETE is not permanent until it is committed.
- TRUNCATE removes every row from a table.
- A TRUNCATE is immediately permanent; it cannot be rolled back.

Control Transactions

- A transaction is a logical unit of work, possibly comprising several DML statements.
- Transactions are invisible to other sessions until committed.
- Until committed, transactions can be rolled back.
- A SAVEPOINT lets a session roll back part of a transaction.

Explain DML and Undo Data Generation

- All DML commands generate undo and redo.
- Redo protects all changes to segments—undo segments as well as data segments.
- Server processes read from datafiles; DBW*n* writes to datafiles.

Monitor and Administer Undo Data

- An instance will use undo segments in one nominated undo tablespace.
- More undo tablespaces may exist, but only one will be used at a time.
- The undo tablespace should be large enough to take account of the maximum rate of undo generation and the longest-running query.
- Undo tablespace datafiles are datafiles like any others.

Describe the Difference Between Undo Data and Redo Data

- Undo protects transactions, whereas redo protects block changes. They are not opposites; they are complementary.

Configure Undo Retention

- Undo data will always be kept until the transaction that generated it completes with a COMMIT or a ROLLBACK. This is active undo.
- Undo data will be retained for a period after it becomes inactive to satisfy any read consistency requirements of long-running queries; this is unexpired undo.
- Expired undo is data no longer needed for read consistency and may be overwritten at any time as space in undo segments is reused.
- Configure undo retention by setting a target with the undo_retention parameter. This is only a target, and if the undo tablespace has insufficient space, it will not be attained— unless you set the tablespace to RETENTION GUARANTEE, which risks transactions failing for lack of undo space.

Describe the Locking Mechanism and Data Concurrency Management

- The default level of locking is row level.
- Locks are required for all DML commands and are optional for SELECT.
- A DML statement requires shared locks on the objects involved and exclusive locks on the rows involved.
- A DDL lock requires an exclusive lock on the object it affects.

Monitor and Resolve Locking Conflicts

- Blocking caused by row locks can be identified by querying the V$SESSION view or through Database Express.
- Resolve lock contention either by terminating blocking transactions or by killing the blocking session.
- Deadlocks are resolved automatically.

Self Test

1. Which of the following commands can be rolled back? (Choose all that apply.)

   A. COMMIT

   B. DELETE

   C. INSERT

   D. MERGE

   E. TRUNCATE

   F. UPDATE

2. If an UPDATE or DELETE command has a WHERE clause that gives it a scope of several rows, what will happen if there is an error partway through execution? The command is one of several in a multistatement transaction. (Choose the best answer.)

   A. The command will skip the row that caused the error and continue.

   B. The command will stop at the error, and the rows that have been updated or deleted will remain updated or deleted.

   C. Whatever work the command had done before hitting the error will be rolled back, but work done already by the transaction will remain.

   D. The whole transaction will be rolled back.

3. Study the result of this SELECT statement:

```
SQL> select * from t1;
       C1         C2         C3         C4
---------- ---------- ---------- ----------
        1          2          3          4
        5          6          7          8
```

If you issue this statement:

```
insert into t1 (c1,c2) values(select c1,c2 from t1);
```

why will it fail? (Choose the best answer.)

A. Because values are not provided for all the table's columns. There should be NULLs for C3 and C4.

B. Because the subquery returns multiple rows. It requires a WHERE clause to restrict the number of rows returned to one.

C. Because the subquery is not scalar. It should use MAX or MIN to generate scalar values.

D. Because the VALUES keyword is not used with a subquery.

E. It will succeed, inserting two rows with NULLs for C3 and C4.

4. You want to insert a row and then update it. What sequence of steps should you follow? (Choose the best answer.)

A. INSERT, UPDATE, COMMIT

B. INSERT, COMMIT, UPDATE, COMMIT

C. INSERT, SELECT FOR UPDATE, UPDATE, COMMIT

D. INSERT, COMMIT, SELECT FOR UPDATE, UPDATE, COMMIT

5. Which of these commands will remove every row in a table? (Choose all correct answers.)

A. A DELETE command with no WHERE clause

B. A DROP TABLE command

C. A TRUNCATE command

D. An UPDATE command, setting every column to NULL and with no WHERE clause

6. User JOHN updates some rows and asks user ROOPESH to log in and check the changes before he commits them. Which of the following statements is true? (Choose the best answer.)

A. ROOPESH can see the changes but cannot alter them because JOHN will have locked the rows.

B. ROOPESH will not be able to see the changes.

C. JOHN must commit the changes so that ROOPESH can see them and, if necessary, roll them back.

D. JOHN must commit the changes so that ROOPESH can see them, but only JOHN can roll them back.

7. There are several steps involved in executing a DML statement. Place these in the correct order:

   A. Apply the change vectors to the database buffer cache.

   B. Copy blocks from datafiles into buffers.

   C. Search for the relevant blocks in the database buffer cache.

   D. Write the change vectors to the log buffer.

8. When a COMMIT is issued, what will happen? (Choose the best answer.)

   A. All the change vectors that make up the transaction are written to disk.

   B. DBW*n* writes the change blocks to disk.

   C. LGWR writes the log buffer to disk.

   D. The undo data is deleted so that the changes can no longer be rolled back.

9. What types of segments are protected by redo? (Choose all that apply.)

   A. Index segments

   B. Table segments

   C. Temporary segments

   D. Undo segments

10. Which of these commands will terminate a transaction? (Choose all that apply.)

    A. CREATE

    B. GRANT

    C. SAVEPOINT

    D. SET AUTOCOMMIT ON

11. Locks are needed to stop sessions from working on the same data at the same time. If one user updates a row without specifying any locking, what will be the effect on other sessions?

    A. Others will be able to read and write other rows but not the affected rows.

    B. Others will be able to read the affected rows but not write to them.

    C. Others will be able to read and write the affected rows, but a COMMIT will hang until the first session has been committed or rolled back.

    D. Others will not be able write any rows because, by default, the first session will have taken a lock on the entire table.

12. Which of these commands will prevent other sessions from reading rows in the table? (Choose the best answer.)

    A. LOCK TABLE SCOTT.EMP IN EXCLUSIVE MODE;

    B. LOCK TABLE SCOTT.EMP IN ROW EXCLUSIVE MODE;

    C. SELECT * FROM SCOTT.EMP FOR UPDATE;

    D. DELETE FROM SCOTT.EMP;

    E. Oracle does not provide a lock that will prevent others from reading a table.

13. If several sessions request an exclusive lock on the same row, what will happen? (Choose the best answer.)

    A. The first session will get the lock; after it releases the lock, there is a random selection of the next session to get the lock.

    B. The first session will get an exclusive lock, and the other sessions will get shared locks.

    C. The sessions will be given an exclusive lock in the sequence in which they requested it.

    D. Oracle will detect the conflict and roll back the statements that would otherwise hang.

14. If a programmer does not request a type of lock when updating many rows in one table, what lock or locks will they be given? (Choose the best answer.)

    A. No locks at all. The default level of locking is NONE in order to maximize concurrency.

    B. An exclusive lock on the table. This is the fastest method when many rows are being updated.

    C. Shared locks on the table and on each row. This is the safest (although not the fastest) method.

    D. An exclusive lock on each row and a shared lock on the table. This maximizes concurrency safely.

15. What happens if two sessions deadlock against each other? (Choose the best answer.)

    A. Oracle will roll back one session's statement.

    B. Oracle will roll back both sessions' statements.

    C. Both sessions will hang indefinitely.

    D. Oracle will terminate one session.

    E. Oracle will terminate both sessions.

16. When a DML statement executes, what happens? (Choose the best answer.)

    A. Both the data and the undo blocks on disk are updated, and the changes are written out to the redo stream.

    B. The old version of the data is written to an undo segment, and the new version is written to the data segments and the redo log buffer.

    C. Both data and undo blocks are updated in the database buffer cache, and the updates also go to the log buffer.

    D. The redo log buffer is updated with information needed to redo the transaction, and the undo blocks are updated with information needed to reverse the transaction.

17. If you suspect that undo generation is a performance issue, what can you do to reduce the amount of undo data generated? (Choose the best answer.)

    A. Convert from use of rollback segments to automatic undo management.

    B. Set the UNDO_MANAGEMENT parameter to NONE.

    C. Reduce the size of the undo segments.

    D. There is nothing you can do because all DML statements must generate undo.

18. First, user JOHN initiates a query. Second, user ROOPESH updates a row that will be included in the query. Third, JOHN's query completes. Fourth, ROOPESH commits his change. Fifth, JOHN runs his query again. Which of the following statements are correct? (Choose all that apply.)

    A. The principle of consistency means that both of JOHN's queries will return the same result set.

    B. When ROOPESH commits, the undo data is flushed to disk.

    C. When ROOPESH commits, the undo becomes inactive.

    D. JOHN's first query will use undo data.

    E. JOHN's second query will use undo data.

    F. The two queries will be inconsistent with each other.

19. If an undo segment fills up, what will happen? (Choose the best answer.)

    A. Another undo segment will be created automatically.

    B. The undo segment will increase in size.

    C. The undo tablespace will extend if its datafiles are set to autoextend.

    D. Transactions will continue in a different undo segment.

20. Which of the following statements are correct about undo? (Choose all that apply.)

    A. One undo segment can protect many transactions.

    B. One transaction can use many undo segments.

    C. One database can have many undo tablespaces.

    D. One instance can have many undo tablespaces.

    E. One undo segment can be cut across many datafiles.

    F. Undo segments and rollback segments cannot coexist.

21. Your undo tablespace has 10 undo segments, but during a sudden burst of activity you have 20 concurrent transactions. What will happen? (Choose the best answer.)

    A. Oracle will create another ten undo segments.

    B. The transactions will be automatically balanced across the ten undo segments.

    C. Ten transactions will be blocked until the first ten commit.

    D. What happens will depend on your UNDO_RETENTION setting.

22. Your users are reporting "ORA-1555: Snapshot too old" errors. What might be the cause of this? (Choose the best answer.)

   A. You are not generating snapshots frequently enough.

   B. The undo data is too old.

   C. There is not enough undo data.

   D. Your undo tablespace is retaining data for too long.

23. Examine this query and result set:

```
SQL> select BEGIN_TIME,END_TIME,UNDOBLKS,MAXQUERYLEN
from V$UNDOSTAT;
BEGIN_TIME        END_TIME           UNDOBLKS MAXQUERYLEN
----------------  ----------------   -------- -----------
02-01-08:11:35:55 02-01-08:11:41:33    14435          29
02-01-08:11:25:55 02-01-08:11:35:55   120248         296
02-01-08:11:15:55 02-01-08:11:25:55   137497          37
02-01-08:11:05:55 02-01-08:11:15:55   102760        1534
02-01-08:10:55:55 02-01-08:11:05:55   237014         540
02-01-08:10:45:55 02-01-08:10:55:55   156223        1740
02-01-08:10:35:55 02-01-08:10:45:55   145275         420
02-01-08:10:25:55 02-01-08:10:35:55    99074         120
```

The block size of the undo tablespace is 4KB. Which of the following would be the optimal size for the undo tablespace? (Choose the best answer.)

   A. 1GB

   B. 2GB

   C. 3GB

   D. 4GB

24. When do changes get written to the log buffer? (Choose all that apply.)

   A. When a table block is updated

   B. When an index block is updated

   C. When an undo block is updated

   D. During rollback operations

   E. On COMMIT

   F. When queries are run that access blocks with uncommitted changes

25. Even though you are using automatic undo segments, users are still getting "snapshot too old" errors. What could you do? (Choose all that apply.)

   A. Increase the UNDO_RETENTION parameter.

   B. Set the RETENTION_GUARANTEE parameter.

   C. Tune the queries to make them run faster.

   D. Increase the size of the undo tablespace.

   E. Enable RETENTION GUARANTEE.

   F. Increase the size of your undo segments.

Self Test Answers

1. ☑ **B, C, D**, and **F**. These are the DML commands; they can all be rolled back.
   ☒ **A** and **E** are incorrect. COMMIT terminates a transaction, which can then never be rolled back. TRUNCATE is a DDL command and includes a built-in COMMIT.

2. ☑ **C**. This is the expected behavior: The statement is rolled back, and the rest of the transaction remains uncommitted.
   ☒ **A, B**, and **D** are incorrect. **A** is incorrect because while this behavior is, in fact, configurable, it is not enabled by default. **B** is incorrect because while this is, in fact, possible in the event of space errors, it is not enabled by default. **D** is incorrect because only the one statement will be rolled back, not the whole transaction.

3. ☑ **D**. The syntax is incorrect; use either the VALUES keyword or a subquery, but not both. Remove the VALUES keyword, and it will run. C3 and C4 would be populated with NULLs.
   ☒ **A, B, C**, and **E** are incorrect. **A** is incorrect because there is no need to provide values for columns not listed. **B** and **C** are incorrect because an INSERT can insert a set of rows, so there is no need to restrict the number with a WHERE clause or by using MAX or MIN to return only one row. **E** is incorrect because the statement is not syntactically correct.

4. ☑ **A**. This is the simplest (and therefore the best) way.
   ☒ **B, C**, and **D** are incorrect. All these will work, but they are all needlessly complicated. No programmer should use unnecessary statements.

5. ☑ **A** and **C**. The TRUNCATE will be faster, but the DELETE will get there too.
   ☒ **B** and **D** are incorrect. **B** is incorrect because this will remove the table as well as the rows within it. **D** is incorrect because the rows will still be there—even though they are populated with NULLs.

6. ☑ **B**. The principle of isolation means that only JOHN can see his uncommitted transaction.
   ☒ **A, C**, and **D** are incorrect. **A** is incorrect because transaction isolation means that no other session will be able to see the changes. **C** and **D** are incorrect because a committed transaction can never be rolled back.

7. ☑ **C, B, D**, and **A**. This is the sequence. All others are incorrect.

8. ☑ **C**. A COMMIT is implemented by placing a COMMIT record in the log buffer and LGWR flushing the log buffer to disk.
   ☒ **A, B**, and **D** are incorrect. **A** is incorrect because many of the change vectors (perhaps all of them) will be on disk already. **B** is incorrect because DBW*n* does not participate in commit processing. **D** is incorrect because the undo data may well persist for some time; a COMMIT is not relevant to this.

9. ☑ **A, B**, and **D**. Changes to any of these will generate redo.
   ☒ **C** is incorrect. Changes to temporary segments do not generate redo.

10. ☑   **A** and **B**. Both DDL and access control commands include a COMMIT.
☒   **C** and **D** are incorrect. **C** is incorrect because a savepoint is only a marker within a transaction. **D** is incorrect because this is a SQL*Plus command that acts locally on the user process; it has no effect on an active transaction.

11. ☑   **B**. By default, a row exclusive lock will protect the row against write but not read.
☒   **A**, **C**, and **D** are incorrect. **A** is incorrect because reading the updated row (in its pre-update form) will always be possible. **C** is incorrect because it is DML that will be blocked, not COMMIT. **D** is incorrect because the default exclusive lock is on the affected row only.

12. ☑   **E**. Readers are never blocked.
☒   **A**, **B**, **C**, and **D** are incorrect. **A** is incorrect because it will lock all rows against update, and **B** is incorrect because it will lock any updated rows. Neither will block readers. **C** and **D** are incorrect because they will take shared locks on the table and exclusive locks on the rows. Again, neither can prevent reads.

13. ☑   **C**. This correctly describes the operation of the enqueue mechanism.
☒   **A**, **B**, and **D** are incorrect. **A** is incorrect because locks are granted sequentially, not randomly. **B** is incorrect because the shared locks apply to the object; row locks must be exclusive. **D** is incorrect because this is more like a description of how deadlocks are managed.

14. ☑   **D**. This correctly describes the DML locking mechanism: a shared lock to protect the table definition and exclusive locks to protect the rows.
☒   **A**, **B**, and **C** are incorrect. **A** is incorrect because locks are always imposed. **B** is incorrect because exclusive table locks are applied only if the programmer requests them. **C** is incorrect because exclusive locks must always be taken on rows.

15. ☑   **A**. One of the statements will be automatically rolled back, allowing the session to continue.
☒   **B**, **C**, **D**, and **E** are incorrect. **B** is incorrect because only one statement will be rolled back. The other will remain in effect, blocking its session. **C** is incorrect because this is exactly the effect that is avoided. **D** and **E** are incorrect because the deadlock-resolution mechanism does not terminate sessions, only statements.

16. ☑   **C**. All DML occurs in the database buffer cache, and changes to both data blocks and undo blocks are protected by redo.
☒   **A**, **B**, and **D** are incorrect. **A** is incorrect because writing to disk is independent of executing the statement. **B** and **D** are incorrect because they are incomplete: Redo protects changes to both data blocks and undo blocks.

17. ☑   **D**. All DML generates undo, so the only way to reduce undo generation would be to redesign the application.
☒   **A**, **B**, and **C** are incorrect. **A** is incorrect because although automatic undo is more efficient, it cannot reduce undo. **B** is incorrect because there is no parameter setting that can switch off undo. **C** is incorrect because the size of the segments will affect only how quickly they are reused, not how much undo is generated.

18. ☑ **C, D,** and **F. C** is correct because undo becomes inactive on commit (although it does not necessarily expire). **D** is correct because the query will need undo data to construct a result consistent with the state of the data at the start of the query. **F** is correct because Oracle guarantees consistency within a query, not across queries.

   ☒ **A, B,** and **E** are incorrect. **A** is incorrect because Oracle guarantees consistency within a query, not across queries. **B** is incorrect because there is no correlation between a COMMIT and a write to the datafiles. **E** is incorrect because the second query is against a table that is not changed during the course of the query.

19. ☑ **B.** Undo segments extend as a transaction generates more undo data.

   ☒ **A, C,** and **D** are incorrect. **A** is incorrect because another undo segment will be created only if there are more concurrent transactions than segments. **C** confuses the effect of a segment filling up with that of the tablespace filling up. **D** is impossible because one transaction can be protected by only one undo segment.

20. ☑ **A, C, E. A** is correct, although Oracle will try to avoid this. **C** is correct, although only one will be made active at any moment by the instance. **E** is correct because when it comes to storage, an undo segment is like any other segment: The tablespace abstracts the physical storage from the logical storage.

   ☒ **B, D,** and **F** are incorrect. **B** is incorrect because one transaction is protected by one undo segment. **D** is incorrect because one instance can use only one undo tablespace. **F** is incorrect because undo and rollback segments can coexist, but a database can use only one or the other.

21. ☑ **A.** Undo segments are spawned according to demand.

   ☒ **B, C,** and **D** are incorrect. **B** is incorrect because more segments will be created. **C** is incorrect because there is no limit imposed by the number of undo segments. **D** is incorrect because this parameter is not relevant to transactions, only to queries.

22. ☑ **C.** An "ORA-1555: snapshot too old" error is a clear indication that undo data is not being kept for long enough to satisfy the query workload. There is not enough undo data available.

   ☒ **A, B,** and **D** are incorrect. **A** is incorrect because it doesn't refer to undo at all—it refers to snapshots, which existed in earlier versions of the database but are now called materialized views. **B** and **D** are both incorrect because they describe the opposing situation, where undo data is being retained for longer than necessary. This is not a problem, but it may be a waste of space.

23. ☑ **C.** To calculate this, take the largest figure for UNDBLKS, which is for a 10-minute period. Divide by 600 to get the rate of undo generation in blocks per second, and multiply by the block size to get the figure in bytes. Multiply by the largest figure for MAXQUERYLEN to find the space needed if the highest rate of undo generation coincided with the longest query, and then divide by a billion to get the answer in gigabytes:
237,014 / 600 * 4,096 * 1,740 = 2.6GB (approximately).

   ☒ **A, B,** and **D** are incorrect. These figures are derived from an incorrect understanding of the undo arithmetic (detailed for **C**).

24. ☑   **A, B, C,** and **D.** Changes to all data blocks are protected by redo. A rollback operation changes blocks and therefore also generates redo.

☒   **E** and **F** are incorrect. COMMIT does not write changes because they have already been written. Queries never read or write redo, although they may well read undo.

25. ☑   **C, D,** and **E.** Answer **C** is correct because making the queries complete faster will reduce the likelihood of "snapshot too old." **D** is correct because it will allow more unexpired undo to be stored. **E** will solve the problem completely, although it may cause problems with transactions.

☒   **A, B,** and **F** are incorrect. **A** is incorrect because it won't help by itself—it is just a target, unless combined with **E. B** is incorrect because there is no such parameter (although it is a clause that can be applied to an undo tablespace). **F** is incorrect because this cannot be done manually—Oracle will already be doing its best automatically.

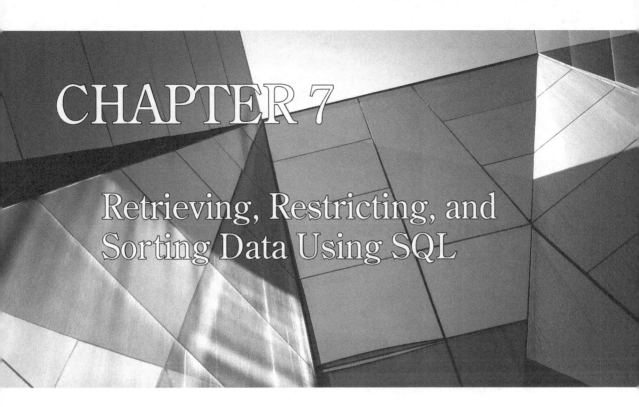

CHAPTER 7

Retrieving, Restricting, and Sorting Data Using SQL

Exam Objectives

In this chapter, you will learn to

- 061.1.1 Explain the Capabilities of SQL SELECT Statements
- 061.1.2 Execute a Basic SELECT Statement
- 061.2.1 Limit the Rows Retrieved by a Query
- 061.2.2 Sort the Rows Retrieved by a Query
- 061.2.3 Use Ampersand Substitution to Restrict and Sort Output at Runtime

This chapter discusses the relational paradigm, normalizing data into relational structures, and retrieving data stored in relational tables using the SELECT statement. The statement is introduced in its basic form and is progressively built on to extend its core functionality. This chapter also discusses the WHERE clause, which specifies one or more conditions that the Oracle server evaluates to restrict the rows returned by the statement. The chapter examines the ORDER BY clause, which provides data-sorting capabilities, and the new SQL row-limiting clause; the chapter closes by discussing ampersand substitution, which is a mechanism that provides a way to reuse the same statement to execute different queries by substituting query elements at run-time.

Explain the Capabilities of SQL SELECT Statements

Knowing how to retrieve data in a set format using a query language is the first step toward understanding the capabilities of SELECT statements. Describing the relations involved provides a tangible link between the theory of how data is stored in tables and the practical visualization of the structure of these tables. These topics form an important precursor to the discussion of the capabilities of the SELECT statement. The three primary areas explored are as follows:

- Introducing the SQL SELECT statement
- Introducing the DESCRIBE table command
- Exploring the capabilities of the SELECT statement

Introducing the SQL SELECT Statement

The SELECT statement from the Structured Query Language (SQL) has to be the single most powerful nonspoken language construct. It is an elegant, flexible, and highly extensible mechanism created to retrieve information from a database table. A database would serve little purpose if it could not be queried to answer all sorts of interesting questions. For example, you may have a database that contains personal financial records such as your bank statements, your utility bills, and your salary statements. You could easily ask the database for a date-ordered list of your electrical utility bills for the last six months or query your bank statement for a list of payments made to a certain account over the same period. The beauty of the SELECT statement is encapsulated in its simple, English-like format that allows questions to be asked of the database in a natural manner.

The DESCRIBE Table Command

To get the answers you seek, you must ask the correct questions. An understanding of the terms of reference, which in this case are relational tables, is essential for the formulation of the correct questions. A structural description of a table is useful to establish what questions can be asked of it. The Oracle server stores information about all tables in a special set of relational tables called the *data dictionary* in order to manage them. The data dictionary is quite similar to a regular language dictionary. It stores definitions of database objects in a centralized, ordered, and structured format. The data dictionary was described in Chapter 2.

A clear distinction must be drawn between storing the definition and the contents of a table. The definition of a table includes information such as the table name, table owner, details about the columns that compose the table, and its physical storage size on disk. This information is also referred to as *metadata*. The contents of a table are stored in rows and are referred to as *data*.

You can obtain the structural metadata of a table by querying the database for the list of columns that compose it using the DESCRIBE command. The general form of the syntax for this command is as follows:

```
DESC[RIBE] <SCHEMA>.tablename
```

This command will be systematically unpacked. The DESCRIBE keyword can be shortened to DESC. All tables belong to a schema or owner. If you are describing a table that belongs to the schema to which you have connected, you can omit the <SCHEMA> portion of the command. Figure 7-1 shows how the EMPLOYEES table is described from SQL*Plus after connecting to the database as the HR user with the DESCRIBE EMPLOYEES command and how the DEPARTMENTS table is described using the shorthand notation: DESC HR .DEPARTMENTS. The HR. notational prefix could be omitted since the DEPARTMENTS table belongs to the HR schema. The HR schema (and every other schema) has access to a

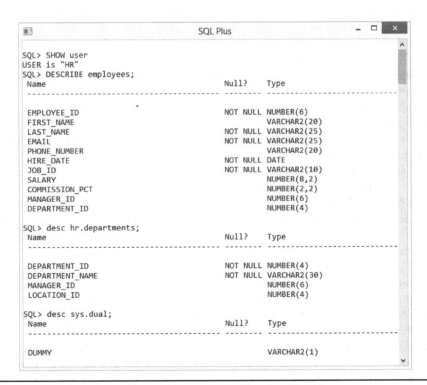

Figure 7-1   Describing the EMPLOYEES, DEPARTMENTS, and DUAL tables

special table called DUAL, which belongs to the SYS schema. This table can be structurally described with the command describe sys.dual.

Describing tables yields interesting and useful results. You know which columns of a table can be selected since their names are exposed. You also know the nature of the data contained in these columns since the column data type is exposed. Chapter 5 detailed column types.

Mandatory columns, which are forced to store data for each row, are exposed by the Null? column output produced by the DESCRIBE command having the value NOT NULL. You are guaranteed that any column restricted by the NOT NULL constraint contains some data. It is important to note that NULL has special meaning for the Oracle server. NULL refers to an absence of data. Blank spaces do not count as NULL since they are present in the row and have some length even though they are not visible.

Capabilities of the SELECT Statement

Relational database tables are built on a mathematical foundation called *relational theory*. In this theory, relations or tables are operated on by a formal language called *relational algebra*. Relational algebra uses some specialized terms: Relations store tuples, which have attributes. Or in Oracle-speak, tables store rows, which have columns. SQL is a commercial interpretation of the relational algebra constructs. Three concepts from relational theory encompass the capabilities of the SELECT statement: projection, selection, and joining.

Projection refers to the restriction of columns selected from a table. When requesting information from a table, you can ask to view all the columns. You can retrieve all data from the HR.DEPARTMENTS table with a simple SELECT statement. This query will return DEPARTMENT_ID, DEPARTMENT_NAME, MANAGER_ID, and LOCATION_ID information for every department record stored in the table. What if you wanted a list containing only the DEPARTMENT_NAME and MANAGER_ID columns? Well, you would request just those two columns from the table. This restriction of columns is called *projection*.

Selection refers to the restriction of the rows selected from a table. It is often not desirable to retrieve every row from a table. Tables may contain many rows, and instead of requesting all of them, selection provides a means to restrict the rows returned. Perhaps you have been asked to identify only the employees who belong to department 30. With *selection* it is possible to limit the results set to those rows of data with a DEPARTMENT_ID value of 30.

Joining, as a relational concept, refers to the interaction of tables with each other in a query. *Third normal form* presents the notion of separating different types of data into autonomous tables to avoid duplication and maintenance anomalies and to associate related data using primary and foreign key relationships. These relationships provide the mechanism to join tables with each other (discussed in Chapter 10).

Assume there is a need to retrieve the e-mail addresses for employees who work in the Sales department. The EMAIL column belongs to the EMPLOYEES table, while the DEPARTMENT_NAME column belongs to the DEPARTMENTS table. *Projection* and *selection* from the DEPARTMENTS table may be used to obtain the DEPARTMENT_ID value that corresponds to the Sales department. The matching rows in the EMPLOYEES table may be *joined* to the DEPARTMENTS table based on this common DEPARTMENT_ID value. The EMAIL column may then be *projected* from this set of results.

The SQL SELECT statement is mathematically governed by these three tenets. An unlimited combination of projections, selections, and joins provides the language to extract the relational data required.

EXAM TIP   The three concepts of projection, selection, and joining, which form the underlying basis for the capabilities of the SELECT statement, are usually measured in the exam. You may be asked to choose the correct three fundamental concepts or to choose a statement that demonstrates one or more of these concepts.

Data Normalization

This section introduces several real-world data organization scenarios to discuss the relational paradigm and introduce some practical modeling techniques. Critical to an understanding of SQL is an understanding of the relational paradigm and the ability to *normalize* data into relational structures. Normalization is the work of systems analysts because they model business data into a form suitable for storing in relational tables. It is a science that can be studied for years, and there are many schools of thought that have developed their own methods and notations.

Real-World Scenarios

This guide uses several hypothetical scenarios, including the two canned scenarios called HR and OE provided by Oracle and frequently used as the context for exam questions to illustrate various SQL concepts. The following scenarios evolve further as new concepts are discussed.

Car Dealership   Sid runs a car dealership and needs a system to keep track of the cars that she buys and sells. She has noticed business taking a dive and wants to move into the 21st century and create a web site that advertises available stock. She needs a system to keep records of the cars she has bought and sold and the details of these transactions.

Geological Cores   Core samples of the earth have been collected by your local geological survey agency. To ensure scientific rigor, the developers at GeoCore have determined that the system must track the exact geographical location, the elemental content of the core samples, and the dates of collection.

Order Entry   The order entry (OE) scenario provided as a sample by Oracle contains information for a fictitious commercial system that tracks the products, the customers, and the sales orders that have been placed.

Human Resources   The human resources (HR) scenario provided as a sample by Oracle records employees, departments, office locations, and job-related information for a typical HR department.

Although the hypothetical scenarios described vary in complexity, they share several characteristics, including a potential data growth that may eventually overwhelm a paper-based or spreadsheet-based data organization solution, as well as a requirement for data to be manipulated (inserted, updated, and deleted) and retrieved in an efficient manner. The challenge of producing an efficient data organization design (also known as a *data model*) may be overcome with both an understanding of how the data being organized is likely to be utilized and a few basic data modeling techniques. The goal is to achieve an optimal balance between data storage and data access, which will provide long-term downstream cost-saving benefits.

Data Modeling

Various formalized data modeling approaches are available, such as the Zachman framework and the Rational Unified Process, that ultimately seek to provide a systematic, standards-based approach to representing objects in an enterprise. There are a multitude of notations available to model entities and their relationships. A popular notation adopted by Oracle in its computer-aided software engineering (CASE) tools and more recently in SQL Developer is the crow's foot notation, which will be discussed in this chapter. Other notations, such as Relational Schema notation and Universal Markup Language (UML), are also popular, but you must choose a notation that is comfortable and sensible for you.

Logical modeling is based on conceptualizing objects of interest as *entities* and their interactions with each other as *relationships*. There are many approaches to entity-relationship diagrams, each with their benefits and limitations. A brief discussion of entity-relationship diagrams and their notation follows.

Entities and Relations

Many Oracle professionals have adopted a framework that consists of three modeling stages for relational database modeling. A logical model is conceived when high-level constructs called *entities,* comprising various *attributes* and their *relationships,* are typically represented together in a diagram. Entities in logical models are usually depicted as rectangles with rounded corners, which comprise attributes or identifiers, sometimes denoted by an "o" symbol. Attributes that uniquely identify an instance of an entity are designated as primary keys and are sometimes denoted by the "#*" characters. Data typing the attributes may be done at this stage, but it is generally not reflected in the design.

The logical model is then turned into a relational model by translating the entities into *relations,* commonly referred to as tables. The idea here is that sets of instances of the entities are collectively modeled as a table. The attributes are turned into table *columns.* Each instance of an entity is reflected as a *tuple* or *row* of data, each having values for its different attributes or columns. The number of "rows in the table" is the "cardinality of the tuples." Usually the attributes that are unique for each row are called *unique keys,* and typically a unique key is chosen to be the *primary key* (which is discussed later). The relationships between the entities are often modeled as *foreign keys,* which will also be explored in this chapter.

Relations in relational models are usually depicted as rectangles. At this stage there is typically more detail in terms of data typing for the attributes, and primary and foreign key attributes are also reflected with a *P* and an *F,* respectively, in the relational model. Finally, the relational model is engineered into a physical model by implementing the design in a relational database.

Figure 7-2
A single car
dealership
entity

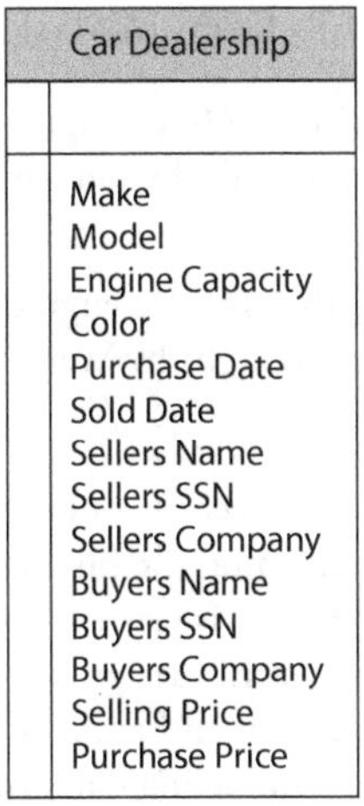

Car Dealership
Make
Model
Engine Capacity
Color
Purchase Date
Sold Date
Sellers Name
Sellers SSN
Sellers Company
Buyers Name
Buyers SSN
Buyers Company
Selling Price
Purchase Price

Crow's foot notation is often used to depict relationships in logical and relational data models. The relationships between the entities can be one of the following and will be explored in the context of the car dealership scenario:

- **1:N** One-to-many
- **N:1** Many-to-one
- **1:1** One-to-one
- **M:N** Many-to-many

Consider the scenario of Sid's car dealership introduced earlier. You could model the likely data as an entity consisting of the following car-related attributes: Make, Model, Engine Capacity, and Color. Information regarding the buying and selling of cars is also required, so you could add Purchase Date, Sold Date, Sellers Name, Sellers SSN (for Social Security number), Sellers Company, the same details for the buyer, and finally Purchase Price and Selling Price, as in Figure 7-2.

Sample transactional data stored in a table based on this entity may look like Figure 7-3, which shows three rows of data in a table comprising 14 columns called CAR_DEALERSHIP. The commands to create tables and populate them with data will be discussed later in this book. For now, there are several more fundamental important things to notice. Tables store data in rows, also called records. Each data element is found at the intersection of a row, and a column, also called a cell. It is fairly intuitive and much like a spreadsheet.

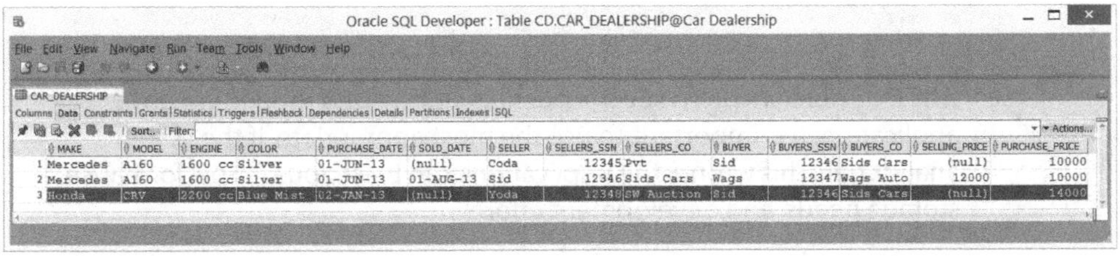

	MAKE	MODEL	ENGINE	COLOR	PURCHASE_DATE	SOLD_DATE	SELLER	SELLERS_SSN	SELLERS_CO	BUYER	BUYERS_SSN	BUYERS_CO	SELLING_PRICE	PURCHASE_PRICE
1	Mercedes	A160	1600 cc	Silver	01-JUN-13	(null)	Coda	12345	Pvt	Sid	12346	Sids Cars	(null)	10000
2	Mercedes	A160	1600 cc	Silver	01-JUN-13	01-AUG-13	Sid	12346	Sids Cars	Wags	12347	Wags Auto	12000	10000
3	Honda	CRV	2200 cc	Blue Mist	02-JAN-13	(null)	Yoda	12348	GW Auction	Sid	12346	Sids Cars	(null)	14000

Figure 7-3 Sample data in the CAR_DEALERSHIP table

The first two records in the CAR_DEALERSHIP table include the following information:

- A silver Mercedes A160 with a 1600cc engine capacity that belonged to Coda, a private seller with SSN 12345, was bought by Sid with SSN 12346 from Sid's Cars, for $10,000 on June 1, 2013.

- A silver Mercedes A160 with a 1600cc engine capacity that belonged to Sid, with SSN 12346, from Sid's Cars, was bought by Wags, with SSN 12347, from Wags Auto, for $12,000 on August 1, 2013.

Notice the repetition of data. Each record contains duplicate information for the cars being bought or sold and for the customer doing the buying or selling. Unnecessary duplication of data usually indicates poor design since it is wasteful and often requires needless maintenance. If this maintenance is not carefully done, this design allows errors (sometimes referred to as *insert update and deletion anomalies*) to creep in and reduces the overall integrity of the data.

Database normalization refers to modeling data using multiple entities with relationships between them, which may reduce or entirely eliminate data redundancy. There are many types of normal forms that have been defined theoretically, but relational database design primarily focuses on the following three:

- First normal form (1NF) deals with the issue of eliminating unnecessary repeating groups of data. An example of a repeating group in Figure 7-3 would be the first four columns on the first two rows where descriptive information about the car is repeated. You could define a new Cars entity that uniquely identifies a specific car using the Car ID primary key attribute as well as the Make, Model, Engine Capacity, and Color attributes. The Car ID identifier is then used in the related Transactions entity to avoid repeating groups of data.

- Second normal form removes attributes from the entity (1NF) that are not dependent on the primary key. In the proposed Cars entity described earlier, the Color attribute is not dependent on a specific car. You could define a new Colors entity that uniquely identifies a specific color using the Color ID primary key attribute. The Color ID can then be referenced by the Cars entity.

- Third normal form removes all interdependent attributes from a 2NF entity. The buyers and sellers of cars each have a uniquely identifying Social Security number (SSN). Their names, however, are interdependent on the SSN attribute. You could define a new Customers entity that uniquely identifies a customer using the Customer ID primary key attribute where interdependent information such as the customer's name and company are stored.

NOTE   There are often several possible normalized models for an application. It is important to use the most appropriate. If the systems analyst gets this wrong, the implications can be serious for performance, storage needs, and development effort.

Note that in the context of performance tuning it is intentional and acceptable to duplicate data in entities. When data is normalized across multiple entities instantiated as multiple tables that must be joined together, the Oracle server processes need to physically fetch data from multiple tables and join them in memory buffers to produce the required results set. The extra input/output (IO) required to query or manipulate normalized data sometimes justifies denormalizing data models to reduce disk IO operations and hence increase performance. This is common in data warehouses (DWHs) and decision support systems (DSSs), but is an exception rather than the rule in online transaction processing (OLTP) systems.

Consider the logical data model in Figure 7-4. The car-related data has been modeled as the Cars entity. The customer (buyers and sellers) information is essentially the same, so customers have been modeled as the Customers entity with the Customer Type attribute to differentiate between Purchasers and Sellers. The sales and purchases are recorded in the Transactions entity, while a *lookup* entity called Colors keeps track of different colors.

There are several advantages to conceptualizing this design as four interrelated entities. First, the data has been normalized, and there is no duplication of data. A practical benefit of multiple

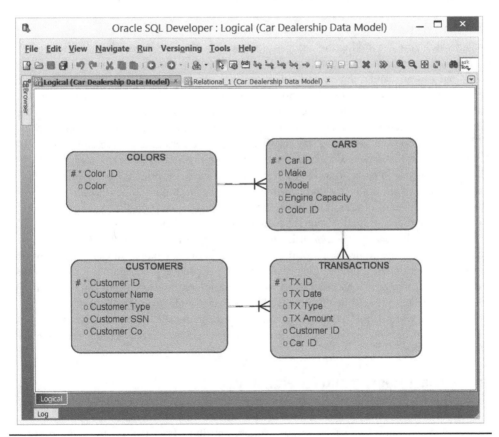

Figure 7-4 The car dealership entity-relationship diagram

entities, each tracking a single construct such as Cars, Customers, Colors, and even Transactions, is the ease of data maintenance. New colors can be added, each with a unique code, and as new cars are purchased, these colors, defined and maintained in one place, can be used to describe multiple cars with the same color. You could improve the sophistication of this model by defining entities for tires, security systems, tracking devices, or audiovisual add-ons. You could equally enhance the details collected for each car, such as the vehicle identification numbers (VINs) and engine numbers, or for each customer, such as address and bank details, but this hypothetical scenario serves to illustrate several concepts and obviously cannot be used in a production application scenario without further enhancements.

Primary Keys

Each entity in Figure 7-4 has a primary key attribute that uniquely identifies a tuple or row of data denoted by "#*" adjacent to the attribute name. Each value of the Car ID primary key is unique in the entity. Multiple rows cannot share the same primary key value. Similarly, Color ID uniquely identifies each row in the Colors entity, as do Customer ID and Transaction ID in the Customers and Transactions entities, respectively.

Relationships

The lines in Figure 7-4 linking the various entities are known as *relations*. The crow's foot notation expresses the cardinality of the relationships between the entities—one-to-one, one-to-many, many-to-one, and many-to-many. The crow's foot notation explicitly illustrates the entity with the *many* side of the relationship with multiple "feet," while the entity on the *one* side has one foot. Attributes in a one-to-one relationship are identical, while many-to-many relationships indicate that multiple tuples in entity A have the same attribute values as many tuples in entity B. Both one-to-one and many-to-many relationships are not common and sometimes point to flaws in the relational model. One-to-many and many-to-one relationships occur frequently when modeling relational entities. They relate attributes in two entities in a *master-detail* relationship. From the point of view of the relationship between the Cars and Colors entities (the order is significant), for example, *many* records in the Cars entity will be *one* Color. Many cars could have the same single Color ID attribute, indicating they are the same color. The Colors entity is the *master* or *lookup* entity, while the Cars entity is the *detail* entity in this relationship. From the point of view of the relationship between Colors and Cars, *one* Color can be associated with *many* Cars. So, it is just a matter of perspective whether a relationship is one-to-many or many-to-one; it all depends on which direction of the relationship you consider. The other relationships indicated by the crow's feet show that a single car can be bought and sold multiple times, which is the reason for the one-to-many relationship between the Cars and Transactions entities and that one customer can perform many transactions (such as buying and selling many cars).

Referential Integrity and Foreign Keys

These relationships introduce the concept of referential integrity, which ensures data consistency and integrity by guaranteeing that an attribute (say attribute A) belonging to the entity on the *one* side of the relationship must be unique, while the attribute (say attribute B) on the entity on the *many* side must have a value that is in the set of unique values described by attribute A. Attribute B is called a foreign key since it has a referential dependency on attribute A. Consider the Colors-Cars relationship based on the Color ID attribute. Referential integrity ensures that the Color ID attribute in each tuple in the Cars entity must have a value that is identical to exactly one instance of the Color ID attribute in the Colors entity. This guarantee is central to relational modeling since the *joining* of the Cars and Colors entities on the Color ID attribute allows the Colors.Color (this is *dot notation*) attribute to be matched with a related tuple in the Cars entity. The Color ID attribute in the Cars entity is the foreign key that is related to the unique key, which is the Color ID attribute in the Colors entity, where it also happens to be the primary key. It is common that foreign keys in an entity are based on primary keys in a related entity, but this is not the rule.

 TIP Foreign keys in an entity are based on unique keys in a related entity, but those unique keys do not have to be the primary key; they just have to be unique.

The logical model in Figure 7-4 would typically evolve into a relational model with more data typing details and clearer primary and foreign keys, as shown in Figure 7-5.

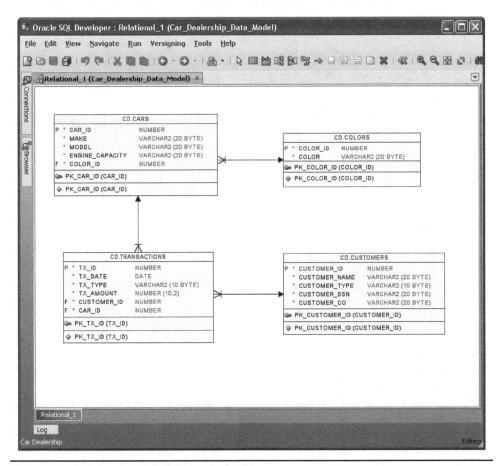

Figure 7-5 Relational model of the car dealership

The relational model could be engineered into a physical model where actual tables and other database constructs (discussed later in this chapter) are created. The sample data in Figure 7-3 transferred into the physical model built from the relational model described earlier would produce four datasets, as in Figure 7-6.

The first two rows of data in the Transactions dataset can be interpreted as follows:

- A transaction with TX ID 100 describes the purchase of a car with Car ID 1 by Sid's dealership from a customer with Customer ID 2 for $10,000 on June 1, 2013. You *look up* Customer ID 2 and see it was a sale from Coda, a private seller with SSN 12345. You *look up* Car ID 1 and determine that it was a 2001-A160 Mercedes with Color ID 1, which you further resolve to be Silver.

- A transaction with TX ID 101 describes the sale of Car ID 1 to Customer ID 4, which you resolve to be a dealer called Wags from Wags Auto with SSN 12347, for $12,000 on August 1, 2013.

Based on the earlier descriptions offered in a single entity design, nothing has been lost by organizing the sample data across the four-entity design. However, much has been gained.

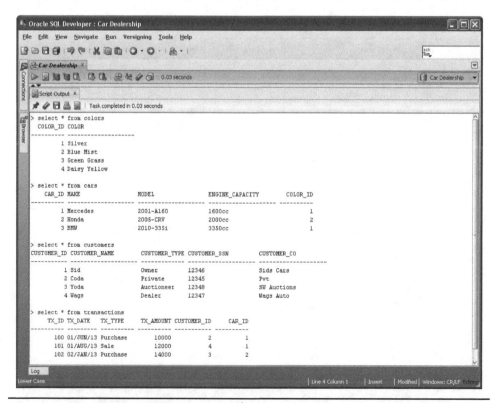

Figure 7-6   Sample data using the car dealership relational model

There is no duplication of data. There is a clarity and elegance that will facilitate ease of maintenance of this data as new cars are bought and sold and as new customers transact with Sid's dealership.

Rows and Tables

The relational paradigm models data as two-dimensional tables. A table consists of a number of rows, each consisting of a set of columns. Within a table, all the rows have the same column structure, though it is possible that in some rows some columns may have nothing in them. An example of a table would be a list of one's employees, each employee being represented by one row. The columns might be an employee number, a name, and a code for the department in which the employee works. Any employees not currently assigned to a department would have that column blank. Another table could represent the departments, with one row per department and with columns for the department's code and the department's name.

Relational tables conform to certain rules that constrain and define the data. At the column level, each column must be of a certain data type, such as numeric, date-time, or character. The character data type is the most general, in that it can accept any type of data. At the row level, usually each row must have some uniquely identifying characteristic. This could be the value of one column, such as the employee number and department number in the preceding examples, which cannot be repeated in different rows. There may also be rules that define links between the tables, such as a rule that every employee must be assigned a department code that can be matched to a row in the departments table. Tables 7-1 through 7-4 are examples of the tabulated data definitions (a subset of data and structures from the sample schema known as SCOTT provided by Oracle).

Looking at the layout of the DEPT and EMP tables in Tables 7-1 and 7-2, the two-dimensional structure is clear. Each row is of fixed length, each column is of fixed length (padded with spaces when necessary), and the rows are delimited with a new line. Table 7-3 shows the rows in the DEPT table stored in DEPTNO order, but this is a matter of chance, not design: Relational tables do not impose any particular ordering on their rows. Table 7-4 shows that department number 10 has one

Column Name	Description	Data Type	Length
DEPTNO	Department number	Numeric	2
DNAME	Department name	Character	14

Table 7-1   The DEPT Table

Column Name	Description	Data Type	Length
EMPNO	Employee number	Numeric	4
ENAME	Employee name	Character	10
DEPTNO	Department number	Numeric	2

Table 7-2   The EMP Table

DEPTNO	DNAME
10	ACCOUNTING
20	RESEARCH
30	SALES
40	OPERATIONS

Table 7-3   Row Data from the DEPT Table

EMPNO	ENAME	DEPTNO
7369	SMITH	20
7499	ALLEN	30
7521	WARD	30
7566	JONES	20
7654	MARTIN	30
7698	BLAKE	30
7782	CLARK	10
7788	SCOTT	20

Table 7-4   Row Data from the EMP Table

employee, and department number 40 has none. Changes to data are usually very efficient with the relational model. New employees can be appended to the employees table, or they can be moved from one department to another simply by changing the DEPTNO value in their row.

Consider an alternative structure, where the data is stored according to the hierarchical paradigm. The hierarchical model was developed before the relational model, for technology reasons. In the early days of computing, storage devices lacked the capability for maintaining the many separate files that were needed for the many relational tables. Note that this problem is avoided in the Oracle database by abstracting the physical storage (files) from the logical storage (tables); there is no direct connection between tables and files and certainly not a one-to-one mapping. In effect, many tables can be stored in a few files.

A hierarchical structure stores all related data in one unit. For example, the record for a department would include all that department's employees. The hierarchical paradigm can be very fast and very space efficient. One file access may be all that is needed to retrieve all the data needed to satisfy a query. The employees and departments listed previously could be stored hierarchically as follows:

```
10,ACCOUNTING,7782,CLARK
20,RESEARCH,7369,SMITH,7566,JONES,7788,SCOTT
30,SALES,7499,ALLEN,7521,WARD,7654,MARTIN,7698,BLAKE
40,OPERATIONS
```

In this example layout, the rows and columns are of variable length. Columns are delimited with a comma, and rows are delimited with a new line. Data retrieval is typically very efficient if the query can navigate the hierarchy. If you know an employee's department, you can find the employee quickly. If you don't, the retrieval may be slow. Changes to data can be a problem if the change necessitates movement. For example, to move employee 7566, JONES from RESEARCH to SALES would involve considerable effort on the part of the database because the move has to be implemented as a removal from one line and an insertion into another. Note that in this example while it is possible to have a department with no employees (the OPERATIONS department), it is absolutely impossible to have an employee without a department. There is nowhere to put him or her. This is excellent if there is a business rule stating that all employees must be in a department, but not so good if that is not the case.

The relational paradigm is highly efficient in many respects for many types of data, but it is not appropriate for all applications. As a general rule, a relational analysis should be the first approach taken when modeling a system. Only if it proves inappropriate should you resort to nonrelational structures. Applications where the relational model has proven highly effective include virtually all OLTP and DSS systems. The relational paradigm can be demanding in its hardware requirements and in the skill needed to develop applications around it, but if the data fits, it has proved to be the most versatile model. There can be, for example, problems caused by the need to maintain the indexes that maintain the links between tables and the space requirements of maintaining multiple copies of the indexed data in the indexes themselves and in the tables in which the columns reside. Nonetheless, relational design is, in most circumstances, the optimal model.

A number of software publishers have produced database management systems that conform (with varying degrees of accuracy) to the relational paradigm; Oracle is only one. IBM was perhaps the first company to commit major resources to it, but its product (which later developed into DB2) was not ported to non-IBM platforms for many years. Microsoft SQL Server is another relational database that has been limited by the platforms on which it runs. Oracle databases, by contrast, have always been ported to every major platform from the first release. It may be this that gave Oracle the edge in the relational database management system (RDBMS) marketplace.

A note on terminology: Confusion can arise when discussing relational databases with people used to working with Microsoft products. SQL is a language, and SQL Server is a database, but in the Microsoft world, the term *SQL* is often used to refer to either.

Create the Demonstration Schemas

Throughout this book, there are examples of SQL code. For the most part, the examples use tables in two demonstration schemas provided by Oracle: the HR schema, which is sample data that simulates a simple human resources application, and the OE schema, which simulates a more complicated order entry application.

These schemas can be created when the database is created; it is an option presented by the Database Configuration Assistant (DBCA). If they do not exist, they can be created later by running some scripts that will exist in the database Oracle Home.

PART II

TIP   An earlier demonstration schema was SCOTT (password tiger). This schema is simpler than HR or OE. Many people with extensive experience with Oracle still prefer to use this. The creation script is still supplied; it is utlsampl.sql.

Users and Schemas

In Oracle parlance, a database *user* is a person who can log on to the database. A database *schema* is all the objects in the database owned by one user. The two terms can often be used interchangeably because there is a one-to-one relationship between users and schemas. Note that while there is, in fact, a CREATE SCHEMA command, this does not actually create a schema—it is only a quick way of creating objects in a schema. A schema is initially created empty when a user is created with the CREATE USER command.

Schemas are used for storing objects. These may be data objects such as tables or programmatic objects such as PL/SQL stored procedures. User logons are used to connect to the database and access these objects. By default, users have access to the objects in their own schema and to no others, but most applications change this. Typically, one schema may be used for storing data that is accessed by other users who have been given permission to use the objects, even though they do not own them. In practice, few users will ever have objects in their own schema or permission to create them. They will have access rights (which will be strictly controlled) only to objects in another schema. These objects will be used by all users who run the application whose data that schema stores. Conversely, the users who own the data-storing schemas may never, in fact, log on; the only purpose of their schemas is to contain data used by others.

It is impossible for a data object to exist independently of a schema. In other words, all tables must have an owner. The owner is the user in whose schema the table resides. The unique identifier for a table (or any other schema object) is the username, followed by the object name. It follows that it is not possible for two tables with the same name to exist in the same schema but that two tables with the same name (though possibly different structures or contents) can exist in different schemas. If an object does not exist in one's own schema, to access it a user must qualify its name with the name of the schema in which it resides. For example, HR.EMPLOYEES is the table called EMPLOYEES in user HR's schema. Unless synonyms are available, only a user connected as HR could get to the table by referring to EMPLOYEES without a schema name qualifier. A synonym is a construct that makes an object accessible to other users without requiring its schema name as a prefix.

The HR and OE Schemas

The HR demonstration schema consists of seven tables, linked by primary key–to–foreign key relationships. Figure 7-7 illustrates the relationships between the tables as an entity-relationship diagram.

Two of the relationships shown in Figure 7-7 may not be immediately comprehensible. First, there is a many-to-one relationship from EMPLOYEES to EMPLOYEES. This is what is known as a *self-referencing foreign key*. This means that many employees can be connected to one employee, and it's based on the fact that many employees may have one manager, but the manager is also an employee. The relationship is implemented by the column manager_id being a foreign key to employee_id, which is the table's primary key.

Figure 7-7
The HR entity-
relationship
diagram

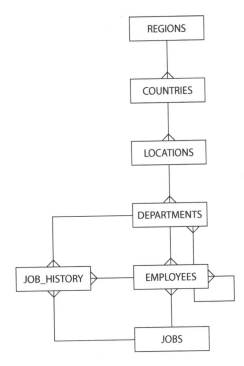

The second relationship that may require explanation is between DEPARTMENTS and EMPLOYEES, which is bidirectional. The one-department-to-many-employees relationship simply states that there may be many staff members in each department, based on the EMPLOYEES dept_id column being a foreign key to the DEPARTMENTS primary key dept_id column. The one-employee-to-many-departments relationship shows that one employee could be the manager of several departments and is implemented by the manager_id column in DEPARTMENTS being a foreign key to the primary key employee_id column in EMPLOYEES.

Table 7-5 shows the columns of each table in the HR schema, using the notation described in the earlier section "Data Normalization" to indicate primary keys (#), foreign keys (\), and whether columns are optional (o) or mandatory (*).

The tables are as follows:

- REGIONS has rows for major geographical areas.

- COUNTRIES has rows for each country, which are optionally assigned to a region.

- LOCATIONS includes individual addresses, which are optionally assigned to a country.

- DEPARTMENTS has a row for each department, optionally assigned to a location and optionally with a manager (who must exist as an employee).

- EMPLOYEES has a row for every employee, each of whom must be assigned to a job and optionally to a department and to a manager. The managers must themselves be employees.

Table	Columns	
REGIONS	#*	region_id
	o	region_name
COUNTRIES	#*	country_id
	o	country_name
	\o	region_id
LOCATIONS	#*	location_id
	o	street_address
	o	postal_code
	*	city
	o	state_province
	\o	country_id
DEPARTMENTS	#*	department_id
	*	department_name
	\o	manager_id
	\o	location_id
EMPLOYEES	#*	employee_id
	o	first_name
	*	last_name
	*	e-mail
	o	phone_number
	*	hire_date
	*	job_id
	o	salary
	o	commission_pct
	\o	manager_id
	\o	department_id
JOBS	#*	job_id
	*	job_title
	o	min_salary
	o	max_salary
JOB_HISTORY	#*	employee_id
	#*	start_date
	*	end_date
	*	job_id
	\o	department_id

Table 7-5   The Tables and Columns on the HR Schema

- JOBS lists all possible jobs in the organization. It is possible for many employees to have the same job.

- JOB_HISTORY lists previous jobs held by employees, uniquely identified by employee_id and start_date; it is not possible for an employee to hold two jobs concurrently. Each job history record will refer to one employee, who will have had one job at that time and may have been a member of one department.

This HR schema is used for most of the exercises and many of the examples embedded in the chapters of this book and does need to be available.

 CAUTION   There are rows in EMPLOYEES that do not have a matching parent row in DEPARTMENTS. This could be by design, but might well be a design mistake that is possible because the DEPARTMENT_ID column in EMPLOYEES is not mandatory. There are similar possible errors in the REGIONS–COUNTRIES–LOCATIONS hierarchy, which really does not make a lot of sense.

The OE schema is considerably more complex than the HR schema. The table structures are much more complicated; they include columns defined as nested tables, user-defined data types, and Extensible Markup Language (XML) data types. The objects referred to are described as they are used.

Demonstration Schema Creation

If the database you are using was created specifically for studying for the SQL examination, the demonstration schemas should have been created already. They are an option presented by the Database Configuration Assistant when it creates a database. After database creation, the schemas may have to be unlocked and their passwords set; by default, the accounts are locked, which means you cannot log on to them. These commands, which could be issued from SQL*Plus or SQL Developer, will make it possible to log on as users HR and OE using the passwords hr and oe:

```
alter user hr account unlock identified by hr;
alter user oe account unlock identified by oe;
```

These alter user commands can be issued only when connected to the database as a user with database administrator (DBA) privileges, such as the user SYSTEM.

If the schemas were not created at database creation time, they can be created later by running scripts installed into the Oracle Home of the database. If these scripts are not present, you may download and install the Oracle Database Examples software from Oracle. These scripts will need to be run from SQL*Plus or SQL Developer as a user with SYSDBA privileges. The script will prompt for certain values as it runs. For example, on Linux, first launch SQL*Plus from an operating system prompt.

```
sqlplus / as sysdba
```

There are various options for this connection, but the preceding syntax will usually work if the database is running on the same machine where you are running SQL*Plus. Then invoke the script from the SQL> prompt.

```
SQL> @?/demo/schema/human_resources/hr_main.sql
```

The ? character is a variable that SQL*Plus will expand into the path to the Oracle Home directory. The script will prompt for HR's password, default tablespace, and temporary tablespace; the SYS password; and a destination for a log file of the script that is running. Typical values for the default tablespace and temporary tablespace are USERS and TEMP, but these will need to have been created already. After completion, you will be connected to the database as the new HR user. To verify this, run these statements:

```
SQL> show user;
```

You will see that you are currently connected as HR; then run the following:

```
SQL> select table_name from user_tables;
```

You will see a list of the seven tables in the HR schema.

To create the OE schema, follow the same process, nominating the script.

```
?/demo/schema/order_entry/oe_main.sql
```

The process for creating the schemas on Windows is identical, except for the path delimiters—where most operating systems use forward slashes, Windows uses backslashes. So, the path to the Windows HR creation script becomes the following:

```
@?\demo\schema\human_resources\hr_main.sql
```

Note that running these schema creation scripts will *drop* the schemas first if they already exist. Dropping a schema means removing every item in it and then removing the user. This should not be a problem, unless the schema has been used for some development work that needs to be kept.

 CAUTION   The demonstration schemas should not exist in production databases. It is not good, for security reasons, to have unnecessary schemas in a database that have well-known usernames, capabilities, and (possibly) passwords.

Execute a Basic SELECT Statement

The practical capabilities of the SELECT statement are realized in its execution. The key to executing any query language statement is a thorough understanding of its syntax and the rules governing its usage. You will learn more about this topic first, then about the execution of a basic query, and finally about expressions and operators, which exponentially increase the utility of data stored in relational tables. Next, the concept of a null value is demystified, as its pitfalls are exposed. These topics are covered in the following four sections:

- The syntax of the primitive SELECT statement
- The rules meant to be followed
- SQL expressions and operators
- NULL, meaning nothing

Syntax of the Primitive SELECT Statement

In its most primitive form, the SELECT statement supports the projection of columns and the creation of arithmetic, character, and date expressions. It also facilitates the elimination of duplicate values from the results set. The basic SELECT statement syntax is as follows:

```
SELECT *|{[DISTINCT] column|expression [alias],...}
FROM table;
```

The special keywords or reserved words of the SELECT statement syntax appear in uppercase. When using the commands, however, the case of the reserved words in your query statement does not matter. Reserved words cannot be used as column names or other database object names. SELECT, DISTINCT, and FROM are three keywords. A SELECT statement always contains two or more clauses. The two mandatory clauses are the SELECT clause and the FROM clause. The pipe symbol (|) is used to denote OR. So, you can read the first form of the preceding SELECT statement as follows:

```
SELECT *
FROM table;
```

In this format, the asterisk (*) is used to denote all columns. SELECT * is a succinct way of asking Oracle to return all possible columns. It is used as a shorthand, time-saving symbol instead of typing in SELECT *column1, column2, column3, column4,...,columnX*, to select all the columns. The FROM clause specifies which table to query to fetch the columns requested in the SELECT clause.

You can issue the following SQL command to retrieve all the columns and all the rows from the REGIONS table in the HR schema:

```
select * from regions;
```

When this command is executed, it returns all the rows of data and all the columns belonging to this table. Use of the asterisk in a SELECT statement is sometimes referred to as a *blind* query because the exact columns to be fetched are not specified.

The second form of the basic SELECT statement has the same FROM clause as the first form, but the SELECT clause is different.

```
SELECT {[DISTINCT] column|expression [alias],...}FROM table;
```

This SELECT clause can be simplified into two formats. Here's the first:

```
SELECT column1 (possibly other columns or expressions) [alias optional]
```

Here's the second:

```
SELECT DISTINCT column1 (possibly other columns or expressions)
[alias optional]
```

An *alias* is an alternative name for referencing a column or expression. Aliases are typically used for displaying output in a user-friendly manner. They also serve as shorthand when referring to columns or expressions to reduce typing. Aliases will be discussed in detail later in this chapter. By explicitly listing only the relevant columns in the SELECT clause, you, in effect, *project* the exact subset of the results you want to retrieve. The following statement will return just the REGION_NAME column of the REGIONS table:

```
select region_name from regions;
```

You may be asked to obtain all the job roles in the organization that employees have historically fulfilled. For this you can issue the command SELECT * FROM JOB_HISTORY. However, in addition, the SELECT * construct returns the EMPLOYEE_ID, START_DATE, and END_DATE columns. The uncluttered results set containing only the JOB_ID and DEPARTMENT_ID columns can be obtained with the following statement:

```
select job_id,department_id from job_history;
```

Using the DISTINCT keyword allows duplicate rows to be eliminated from the results set. In numerous situations a unique set of rows is required. It is important to note that the criterion employed by the Oracle server in determining whether a row is unique or distinct depends entirely on what is specified after the DISTINCT keyword in the SELECT clause. Selecting distinct JOB_ID values from the JOB_HISTORY table with the following query will return the eight distinct job types:

```
select distinct job_id from job_history;
```

An important feature of the DISTINCT keyword is the elimination of duplicate values from *combinations* of columns.

Rules Are Meant to Be Followed

SQL is a fairly strict language in terms of syntax rules, but it remains simple and flexible enough to support a variety of programming styles. This section discusses some of the basic rules governing SQL statements.

Uppercase or Lowercase

It is a matter of personal taste about the case in which SQL statements are submitted to the database. Many developers, including the authors of this book, prefer to write their SQL statements in lowercase. There is also a common misconception that SQL reserved words need to be specified in uppercase. Again, this is up to you. Adhering to a consistent and standardized format is advised.

There is one caveat regarding case sensitivity. When interacting with literal values, case does matter. Consider the JOB_ID column from the JOB_HISTORY table. This column contains rows of data that happen to be stored in the database in uppercase, as in SA_REP and ST_CLERK. When requesting that the results set be restricted by a literal column, the case is critical. The Oracle server treats the request for the rows in the JOB_HISTORY table that contain a value of St_Clerk in the JOB_ID column differently from the request for rows that have a value of ST_CLERK in the JOB_ID column.

Metadata about different database objects is stored by default in uppercase in the data dictionary. If you query a database dictionary table to return a list of tables owned by the HR schema, it is likely that the table names returned will be stored in uppercase. This does not mean a table cannot be created with a lowercase name; it can be. It is just more common and is the default behavior of the Oracle server to create and store tables, columns, and other database object metadata in uppercase in the database dictionary.

 EXAM TIP You can submit SQL statements to the database in any case. You must pay careful attention to case when interacting with character literal data and aliases. Requesting a column called JOB_ID or job_id returns the same column, but asking for rows where the JOB_ID value is PRESIDENT is different from asking for rows where the value is President.

Statement Terminators

Semicolons are generally used as SQL statement terminators. SQL*Plus always requires a statement terminator, and usually a semicolon is used. A single SQL statement, or even groups of associated statements, are often saved as script files for future use. Individual statements in SQL scripts are commonly terminated by a line break (or carriage return) and a forward slash on the next line, instead of a semicolon. You can create a SELECT statement, terminate it with a line break, include a forward slash to execute the statement, and save it in a script file. The script file can then be called from within SQL*Plus. Note that SQL Developer does not require a statement terminator if only a single statement is present, but it will not object if one is used. It is good practice to always terminate your SQL statements with a semicolon. Several examples of SQL*Plus statements follow:

```
select country_name, country_id, location_id from countries;

select city, location_id,
       state_province, country_id
from locations
/
```

The first example demonstrates two important rules. First, the statement is terminated by a semicolon. Second, the entire statement is written on one line. It is entirely acceptable for a SQL statement either to be written on one line or to span multiple lines as long as no words in the statement span multiple lines. The second sample of code demonstrates a statement that spans three lines that is terminated by a new line and executed with a forward slash.

Indentation, Readability, and Good Practice

Consider the following query:

```
select city, location_id,
       state_province, country_id
from locations
/
```

This example highlights the benefits of indenting your SQL statement to enhance the readability of your code. The Oracle server does not object if the entire statement is written on one line without indentation. However, it is good practice to separate different clauses of the SELECT statement onto different lines. When an expression in a clause is particularly complex, it often enhances readability to separate that term of the statement onto a new line. When developing SQL to meet your reporting needs, the process is often iterative. The SQL interpreter is far more useful during development if complex expressions are isolated on separate lines since errors are usually thrown in the format of "ERROR at line X:" This makes the debugging process much simpler.

Exercise 7-1: Answer Your First Questions with SQL   In this step-by-step exercise, you make a connection using SQL*Plus as the HR user to answer two questions using the SELECT statement.

Question 1: How many unique departments have employees currently working in them?

1. Start SQL*Plus and connect to the HR schema.

2. You may initially be tempted to find the answer in the DEPARTMENTS table. A careful examination reveals that the question asks for information about employees. This information is contained in the EMPLOYEES table.

3. The word *unique* should guide you to use the DISTINCT keyword.

4. Combining steps 2 and 3, you can construct the following SQL statement:
   ```
   select distinct department_id
   from employees;
   ```

5. This query returns 12 rows. Notice that the third row is empty. This is a null value in the DEPARTMENT_ID column.

6. The answer to the first question is therefore as follows: Eleven unique departments have employees working in them, but at least one employee has not been assigned to a department.

Question 2: How many countries are there in the Europe region?

1. This question comprises two parts. Consider the REGIONS table, which contains four regions, each uniquely identified by a REGION_ID value, and the COUNTRIES table, which has a REGION_ID column indicating which region a country belongs to.

2. The first query needs to identify the REGION_ID value of the Europe region. This is accomplished by the SQL statement, which shows that the Europe region has a REGION_ID value of 1.
   ```
   select * from regions;
   ```

3. To identify which countries have 1 as their REGION_ID value, you can execute the following SQL query:

```
select region_id, country_name from countries;
```

4. Manually counting the country rows with a REGION_ID of 1 returned shows that there are eight countries in the Europe region as far as the HR data model is concerned.

SQL Expressions and Operators

The general form of the SELECT statement introduced the notion that columns and expressions may be projected. An expression usually consists of an operation being performed on one or more column values or expressions. The operators that can act upon values to form an expression depend on the underlying data type. They are the four cardinal arithmetic operators (addition, subtraction, multiplication, and division) for numeric columns, the concatenation operator for character or string columns, and the addition and subtraction operators for date and timestamp columns. As in regular arithmetic, there is a predefined order of evaluation (operator precedence) when more than one operator occurs in an expression. Round brackets have the highest precedence. Division and multiplication operations are next in the hierarchy and are evaluated before addition and subtraction, which have lowest precedence.

Operators with the same level of precedence are evaluated from left to right. Round brackets may therefore be used to enforce nondefault operator precedence. Using brackets generously when constructing complex expressions is good practice and is encouraged. It leads to readable code that is less prone to error. Expressions expose a large number of useful data manipulation possibilities.

Arithmetic Operators

Consider the JOB_HISTORY table, which stores the start date and end date of an employee's term in a previous job role. It may be useful for tax or pension purposes to calculate how long an employee worked in that role. This information can be obtained using an arithmetic expression. Several elements of both the SQL statement and the results returned from Figure 7-8 warrant further discussion.

The SELECT clause specifies five elements. The first four are regular columns of the JOB_HISTORY table, while the latter provides the source information required to calculate the number of days that an employee filled a particular position. Consider employee number 176 on the ninth row of output. This employee started as a sales manager on January 1, 2007, and ended employment on December 31, 2007. Therefore, this employee worked for exactly one year, which, in 2007, consisted of 365 days.

The number of days for which an employee was employed can be calculated by using the fifth element in the SELECT clause, which is an expression. This expression demonstrates that arithmetic performed on columns containing date information returns numeric values that represent a certain number of days.

To enforce operator precedence of the subtraction operation, the subexpression *end_date-start_date* is enclosed in round brackets. Adding 1 makes the result inclusive of the first day.

Figure 7-8
Arithmetic
expression
to calculate
number of
days worked

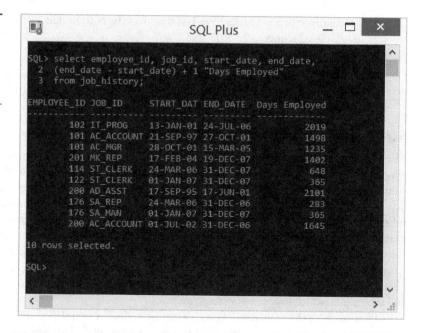

```
SQL> select employee_id, job_id, start_date, end_date,
  2  (end_date - start_date) + 1 "Days Employed"
  3  from job_history;

EMPLOYEE_ID JOB_ID     START_DAT END_DATE  Days Employed
----------- ---------- --------- --------- -------------
        102 IT_PROG    13-JAN-01 24-JUL-06          2019
        101 AC_ACCOUNT 21-SEP-97 27-OCT-01          1498
        101 AC_MGR     28-OCT-01 15-MAR-05          1235
        201 MK_REP     17-FEB-04 19-DEC-07          1402
        114 ST_CLERK   24-MAR-06 31-DEC-07           648
        122 ST_CLERK   01-JAN-07 31-DEC-07           365
        200 AD_ASST    17-SEP-95 17-JUN-01          2101
        176 SA_REP     24-MAR-06 31-DEC-06           283
        176 SA_MAN     01-JAN-07 31-DEC-07           365
        200 AC_ACCOUNT 01-JUL-02 31-DEC-06          1645

10 rows selected.

SQL>
```

TIP As you practice SQL on your test database environment, you may encounter two infamous Oracle errors: "ORA-00923: FROM keyword not found where expected" and "ORA-00942: table or view does not exist." These often indicate spelling or punctuation errors, such as missing enclosing quotes around character literals.

Expression and Column Aliasing

Figure 7-8 introduced a new concept called column aliasing. Notice that the expression has a meaningful heading named Days Employed. This heading is an alias. An *alias* is an alternative name for a column or an expression. If this expression did not make use of an alias, the column heading would be (END_DATE-START_DATE)+1, which is not very user friendly. Aliases are especially useful with expressions or calculations and may be implemented in several ways. There are a few rules governing the use of column aliases in SELECT statements. The alias "Days Employed" in Figure 7-8 was specified by leaving a space and entering the alias in double quotation marks. These quotation marks are necessary for two reasons. First, this alias consists of more than one word. Second, case preservation of an alias is possible only if the alias is double quoted. If a multiworded, space-separated alias is specified, an "ORA-00923: FROM keyword not found where expected" error is returned if it is not double quoted. SQL offers a more formalized way of inserting aliases by inserting the *AS* keyword between the column or expression and the alias, as shown in the first line of this query:

```
SELECT EMPLOYEE_ID AS "Employee ID",
       JOB_ID AS "Occupation",
       START_DATE, END_DATE,
       (END_DATE-START_DATE)+1 "Days Employed"
FROM JOB_HISTORY;
```

Character and String Concatenation Operator

The double pipe symbols (||) represent the character *concatenation* operator. This operator is used to join character expressions or columns together to create a larger character expression. Columns of a table may be linked to each other or to strings of literal characters to create one resultant character expression.

The concatenation operator is flexible enough to be used multiple times and almost anywhere in a character expression. Consider the following query:

```
SELECT 'THE '||REGION_NAME||' region is on Planet Earth' "Planetary Location",
FROM REGIONS;
```

Here, the character literal *The* is concatenated to the contents of the REGION_NAME column. This new string of characters is further concatenated to the character literal *region is on Planet Earth,* and the entire expression is aliased with the friendly heading *Planetary Location.*

Literals and the DUAL Table

Literals are commonly used in expressions and refer to numeric, character, or date and time values found in SELECT clauses that do not originate from any database object. Concatenating character literals to existing column data can be useful, but what about processing literals that have nothing to do with existing column data? To ensure relational consistency, Oracle offers a clever solution to the problem of using the database to evaluate expressions that have nothing to do with any tables or columns. To get the database to evaluate an expression, a syntactically legal SELECT statement must be submitted. What if you wanted to know the sum of two numeric literals? Oracle solves the problem of relational interaction with the database operating on literal expressions by providing a special single-rowed, single-columned table called DUAL.

Recall that the DUAL table described earlier contains one column called DUMMY of the character data type. You can execute the query SELECT * FROM DUAL, and the data value "X" is returned as the contents of the DUMMY column. Testing complex expressions during development by querying the dual table is an effective method to evaluate whether these expressions are correct. Literal expressions can be queried from any table, but remember that the expression will be processed for every row in the table, while querying the DUAL table returns only one row.

```
select 'literal '||'processing using the REGIONS table'
from regions;

select 'literal '||'processing using the DUAL table'
from dual;
```

The first statement will return four lines in the results set since there are four rows of data in the REGIONS table, while the second returns only one row.

Two Single Quotes or the Alternative Quote Operator

The literal character strings concatenated so far have been singular words prepended and appended to column expressions. These character literals are specified using single quotation marks. Here's an example:

```
select 'I am a character literal string' from dual;
```

What about character literals that contain single quotation marks? Plurals pose a particular problem for character literal processing. Consider the following statement:

```
select 'Plural's have one quote too many' from dual;
```

Executing this statement causes an Oracle error to be generated: So, how are words that contain single quotation marks dealt with? There are essentially two mechanisms available. The most popular of these is to add an additional single quotation mark next to each naturally occurring single quotation mark in the character string. The following statement demonstrates how the previous error is avoided by replacing the character literal *'Plural's* with the literal *'Plural''s*:

```
select 'Plural''s have one quote too many' from dual;
```

Using two single quotes to handle each naturally occurring single quote in a character literal can become messy and error prone as the number of affected literals increases. Oracle offers a neat way to deal with this type of character literal in the form of the alternative quote (q) operator. The problem is that Oracle chose the single quote character as the special symbol with which to enclose or wrap other character literals. These character-enclosing symbols could have been anything other than single quotation marks.

Bearing this in mind, consider the alternative quote (q) operator. The q operator enables you to choose from a set of possible pairs of wrapping symbols for character literals as alternatives to the single quote symbols. The options are any single-byte or multibyte character or the four brackets: (round brackets), {curly braces}, [square brackets], or <angle brackets>. Using the q operator, the character delimiter can effectively be changed from a single quotation mark to any other character, as shown here:

```
SELECT q'<Plural's can also be specified with alternate quote operators>'
FROM DUAL;

SELECT  q'[Even square brackets [] can be used for Plural's]' FROM DUAL;

SELECT  q'XWhat about UPPER CASE X for Plural's ?X'
FROM DUAL;
```

The syntax of the alternative quote operator is as follows, where *delimiter* can be any character or bracket:

```
q'delimiter character literal which may include single quotes delimiter'
```

The first and second examples show the use of angle and square brackets as character delimiters, while the third example demonstrates how an uppercase *X* has been used as the special character delimiter symbol through the alternative quote operator. Note that the *X* character can itself be included in the string—so long as it is not followed by a quotation mark.

NULL Is Nothing

Null refers to an absence of data. A row that contains a null value lacks data for that column. Null is formally defined as a value that is unavailable, unassigned, unknown, or inapplicable. Failure to heed the special treatment that null values require will almost certainly lead to an error or, worse, an inaccurate answer. This section focuses on interacting with null column data with the SELECT statement and its impact on expressions.

Not Null and Nullable Columns

Tables store rows of data that are divided into one or more columns. These columns have names and data types associated with them. Some of them are constrained by database rules to be mandatory columns. It is compulsory for some data to be stored in the NOT NULL columns in each row. When columns of a table, however, are not compelled by the database constraints to hold data for a row, these columns run the risk of being empty.

CAUTION   Any arithmetic calculation with a NULL value always returns NULL.

Oracle offers a mechanism for interacting arithmetically with NULL values using the general functions discussed in Chapter 8. Division by a null value results in null, unlike division by zero, which results in an error. When a null is encountered by the character concatenation operator, however, it is simply ignored. The character concatenation operators ignore null, while the arithmetic operations involving null values always result in null.

Foreign Keys and Nullable Columns

Data model design sometimes leads to problematic situations when tables are related to each other via a primary and foreign key relationship but the column that the foreign key is based on is nullable.

The DEPARTMENTS table has, as its primary key, the DEPARTMENT_ID column. The EMPLOYEES table has a DEPARTMENT_ID column that is constrained by its foreign key relationship to the DEPARTMENT_ID column in the DEPARTMENTS table. This means that no record in the EMPLOYEES table is allowed to have in its DEPARTMENT_ID column a value that is not in the DEPARTMENTS table. This referential integrity forms the basis for third normal form and is critical to overall database integrity.

But what about NULL values? Can the DEPARTMENT_ID column in the DEPARTMENTS table contain nulls? The answer is *no*. Oracle insists that any column that is a primary key be implicitly constrained to be mandatory. But what about implicit constraints on foreign key columns? This is a quandary for Oracle since in order to remain flexible and cater to the widest audience, it cannot insist that columns related through referential integrity constraints must be mandatory. Further, not all situations demand this functionality.

The DEPARTMENT_ID column in the EMPLOYEES table is actually nullable. Therefore, the risk exists that there are records with null DEPARTMENT_ID values present in this table. In fact, there are such records in the EMPLOYEES table. The HR data model allows employees, correctly or not, to belong to no department. When performing relational joins between tables, it is entirely possible to miss or exclude certain records that contain nulls in the join column. Chapter 10 discusses ways to deal with this challenge.

Exercise 7-2: Construct Expressions   In this exercise, you will construct a query using expressions and aliases to display results from the HR schema in a more user-friendly manner.

1. Query the HR.JOBS table and return a single expression of the form *The Job Id for the* <job_title's> *job is*: <job_id>. Take note that the job_title should have an apostrophe and an *s* appended to it to read more naturally. A sample of this output for the organization president is as follows: *The Job Id for the President's job is: AD_PRES*. Alias this column expression: Job Description using the AS keyword. There are multiple solutions to this problem. The approach chosen here is to handle the naturally occurring single quotation mark with an additional single quote. You could make use of the alternative quote operator to delimit the naturally occurring quote with another character.

2. A single expression aliased as Job Description is required; you may construct it by concatenating the literal 'The Job Id for the' to the JOB_TITLE column. This string is then concatenated to the literal '''s job is: ' , which is further concatenated to the JOB_ID column. An additional single quotation mark is added to yield the SELECT statement that follows:

```
select 'The Job Id for the '||job_title||'''s job is: '||job_id
AS "Job Description" from jobs;
```

Limit the Rows Retrieved by a Query

One of the cornerstone principles in relational theory is selection. Selection is actualized using the WHERE clause of the SELECT statement, sometimes referred to as the *predicate*. Conditions that restrict the dataset returned take many forms and operate on columns as well as expressions. Only rows that conform to these conditions are returned. Conditions restrict rows using comparison operators in conjunction with columns and literal values. Boolean operators provide a mechanism to specify multiple conditions to restrict the rows returned. Boolean, conditional, concatenation, and arithmetic operators are discussed to establish their order of precedence when they are encountered in a SELECT statement.

The WHERE Clause

The WHERE clause extends the SELECT statement by providing the ability to restrict rows returned based on one or more conditions. Querying a table with just the SELECT and FROM clauses results in every row of data stored in the table being returned. Using the DISTINCT keyword, duplicate values are excluded, and the resultant rows are restricted to some degree. What if very specific information is required from a table, for example, only the data where a column contains a specific value? How would you retrieve the countries that belong to the Europe region from the COUNTRIES table? What about retrieving just those employees who work as sales representatives? These questions are answered using the WHERE clause to specify exactly which rows must be returned. The format of the SQL SELECT statement that includes the WHERE clause is as follows:

```
SELECT *|{[DISTINCT] column|expression [alias],...}
FROM table
[WHERE condition(s)];
```

The WHERE clause always follows the FROM clause. The square brackets indicate that the WHERE clause is optional. One or more conditions may be simultaneously applied to restrict the results set. A condition is specified by comparing two terms using a conditional operator. These terms may be column values, literals, or expressions. The *equality* operator is most commonly used to restrict result sets. An example of using a WHERE clause is shown next:

```
select country_name
from countries
where region_id=3;
```

This example projects the COUNTRY_NAME column from the COUNTRIES table. Instead of selecting every row, the WHERE clause restricts the rows returned to only those containing a 3 in the REGION_ID column.

Numeric-Based Conditions

Conditions must be formulated appropriately for different column data types. The conditions restricting rows based on numeric columns can be specified in several different ways. Consider the SALARY column in the EMPLOYEES table. This column has a data type of NUMBER(8,2). The SALARY column can be restricted as follows:

```
select last_name, salary from employees where salary = 10000;
```

The LAST_NAME and SALARY values of the employees who earn $10,000 are retrieved since the data types on either side of the operator match and are compatible.

A numeric column can be compared to another numeric column in the same row to construct a WHERE clause condition, as the following query demonstrates:

```
select last_name, salary from employees
where salary = department_id;
```

This WHERE clause is too restrictive and results in no rows being selected because the range of SALARY values is 2100 to 24000, and the range of DEPARTMENT_ID values is 10 to 110. Since there is no overlap in the range of DEPARTMENT_ID and SALARY values, there are no rows that satisfy this condition and therefore nothing is returned.

WHERE clause conditions can also be used to compare numeric columns and expressions or to compare expressions to other expressions.

```
select last_name, salary from employees
where salary = department_id*100;
```

```
select last_name, salary from employees
where salary/10 = department_id*10;
```

The first example compares the SALARY column with DEPARTMENT_ID*100 for each row. The second example compares two expressions. Notice that the conditions in both examples are algebraically identical, and the same dataset is retrieved when both are executed.

Character-Based Conditions

Conditions determining which rows are selected based on character data are specified by enclosing character literals in the conditional clause, within single quotes. The JOB_ID column in the EMPLOYEES table has a data type of VARCHAR2(10). Suppose you wanted a list of the LAST_NAME values of those employees currently employed as sales representatives. The JOB_ID value for a sales representative is SA_REP. The following statement produces such a list:

```
select last_name from employees where job_id='SA_REP';
```

If you tried specifying the character literal without the quotes, an Oracle error would be raised. Remember that character literal data is case sensitive, so the following WHERE clauses are not equivalent:

```
Clause 1: where job_id=SA_REP
Clause 2: where job_id='Sa_Rep'
Clause 3: where job_id='sa_rep'
```

Clause 1 generates an "ORA-00904: 'SA_REP': invalid identifier" error since the literal SA_REP is not wrapped in single quotes. Clause 2 and Clause 3 are syntactically correct but not equivalent. Further, neither of these clauses yields any data since there are no rows in the EMPLOYEES table having JOB_ID column values that are either Sa_Rep or sa_rep.

Character-based conditions are not limited to comparing column values with literals. They may also be specified using other character columns and expressions. Character-based expressions may form either one or both parts of a condition separated by a conditional operator. These expressions can be formed by concatenating literal values with one or more character columns. The following four clauses demonstrate some of the options for character-based conditions:

```
Clause 1: where 'A '||last_name||first_name = 'A King'
Clause 2: where first_name||' '||last_name = last_name||' '||first_name
Clause 3: where 'SA_REP'||'King' = job_id||last_name
Clause 4: where job_id||last_name ='SA_REP'||'King'
```

Clause 1 concatenates the string literal *A* to the LAST_NAME and FIRST_NAME columns. This expression is compared to the literal *A King*. Clause 2 demonstrates that character expressions may be placed on both sides of the conditional operator. Clause 3 illustrates that literal expressions may also be placed on the left of the conditional operator. It is logically equivalent to clause 4, which has swapped the operands in clause 3 around. Both clauses 3 and 4 identically restrict the results.

Date-Based Conditions

DATE columns are useful for storing date and time information. Date literals must be enclosed in single quotation marks just like character data. When used in conditional WHERE clauses, date columns may be compared to other date columns, literals, or expressions. The literals are automatically converted into DATE values based on the default date format, which is DD-MON-RR. If a literal occurs in an expression involving a DATE column, it is automatically converted into a date value using the default format mask. DD represents days, MON represents the first three letters of a month, and RR represents a Year 2000–compliant year (that is, if RR is between 50 and 99, then the Oracle server returns the previous century, or else it returns the current century). The full four-digit year, YYYY, can also be specified. Consider the following four WHERE clauses:

```
Clause 1: where start_date = end_date
Clause 2: where start_date = '01-JAN-2001'
Clause 3: where start_date = '01-JAN-01'
Clause 4: where start_date = '01-JAN-99'
```

The first clause tests equality between two DATE columns. Rows that contain the same values in their START_DATE and END_DATE columns will be returned. Note, however, that DATE values are equal to each other only if there is an exact match between all their components, including day, month, year, hours, minutes, and seconds. Chapter 8 discusses the details of storing DATE values. Until then, don't worry about the hours, minutes, and seconds components. In the second WHERE clause, the START_DATE column is compared to this character literal: '01-JAN-2001'. The entire four-digit year component (YYYY) has been specified. This is acceptable to the Oracle server. The third condition is equivalent to the second, since the literal '01-JAN-01' is converted to the date value 01-JAN-2001. This is because of the RR component being less than 50, so the current (21st) century, 20, is prefixed to the year RR component to provide a century value. The century component for the literal '01-JAN-99' becomes the previous century (19) and is converted to a date value of 01-JAN-1999 for the fourth condition since the RR component, 99, is greater than 50.

Date arithmetic using the addition and subtraction operators is supported. An expression like END_DATE – START_DATE returns the number of days between START_DATE and END_DATE. START_DATE + 30 returns a date 30 days later than START_DATE.

EXAM TIP Conditional clauses compare two terms using comparison operators. Knowing the data types of the terms is important so that they can be enclosed in single quotes, if necessary.

Comparison Operators

The *equality* operator is generally used to illustrate the concept of restricting rows using a WHERE clause. There are several alternative operators that may also be used. The *inequality* operators like "less than" or "greater than or equal to" may be used to return rows conforming to inequality conditions. The BETWEEN operator facilitates range-based comparison to test whether a column value lies between two values. The IN operator tests set membership, so a row is returned if the column value tested in the condition is a member of a set of literals. The pattern matching comparison operator LIKE is extremely powerful, allowing components of character column data to be matched to literals conforming to a specific pattern. The last comparison operator discussed in this section is the IS NULL operator, which returns rows where the column value contains a null value. These operators may be used in any combination in the WHERE clause.

Equality and Inequality

Limiting the rows returned by a query involves specifying a suitable WHERE clause. If the clause is too restrictive, then few or no rows are returned. If the conditional clause is too broadly specified, then more rows than are required are returned. Exploring the different available operators should equip you with the language to request exactly those rows you are interested in. Testing for *equality* in a condition is both natural and intuitive. Such a condition is formed using the "is equal to" (=) operator. A row is returned if the equality condition is true for that row. Consider the following query:

```
select last_name, salary from employees where job_id='SA_REP';
```

The JOB_ID column of every row in the EMPLOYEES table is tested for equality with the character literal SA_REP. For character information to be equal, there must be an exact case-sensitive match. When such a match is encountered, the values for the projected columns, LAST_NAME and SALARY, are returned for that row. Note that although the conditional clause is based on the JOB_ID column, it is not necessary for this column to be projected by the query.

Inequality-based conditions enhance the WHERE clause specification. Range and pattern matching comparisons are possible using inequality and equality operators, but it is often preferable to use the BETWEEN and LIKE operators for these comparisons. Table 7-6 describes the inequality operators.

Inequality operators allow range-based queries to be fulfilled. You may be required to provide a set of results where a column value is *greater than* another value. The following query may be issued to obtain a list of LAST_NAME and SALARY values for employees who earn more than $5,000:

```
select last_name, salary from employees where salary > 5000;
```

The *composite inequality operators* (made up of more than one symbol) are utilized in the following clauses:

```
Clause 1: where salary <= 3000
Clause 2: where salary <> department_id
```

Clause 1 returns those rows that contain a SALARY value that is less than or equal to 3000. Clause 2 demonstrates one of the two forms of the "not equal to" operators. Clause 2 returns the rows that have SALARY column values that are not equal to the DEPARTMENT_ID values.

Numeric inequality is naturally intuitive. The comparison of character and date terms, however, is more complex. Testing character inequality is interesting because the strings being compared on either side of the inequality operator are converted to a numeric representation of

Table 7-6 Inequality Operators	Operator	Description
	<	Less than
	>	Greater than
	<=	Less than or equal to
	>=	Greater than or equal to
	<>	Not equal to
	!=	Not equal to

its characters. Based on the database character set and National Language Support (NLS) settings, each character string is assigned a numeric value. These numeric values form the basis for the evaluation of the inequality comparison. Consider the following statement:

```
select last_name from employees where last_name < 'King';
```

The character literal 'King' is converted to a numeric representation. Assuming a US7ASCII database character set with AMERICAN NLS settings, the literal 'King' is converted into its ordinal character values: K (75), i (105), n (110), and g (103). For each row in the EMPLOYEES table, the LAST_NAME column data is similarly converted into numeric values for each character, which are then compared in turn with the numeric values of the characters in the literal 'King'. For example, the row with LAST_NAME='Kaufling' is compared as follows: The first character in both strings is 'K' with an equal ordinal value of 75. So, the second character (i=105) is compared with (a=97). Since (97 < 105) or (a < i), 'Kaufling' < 'King', and the row is selected. The same process for comparing numeric data using the inequality operators applies to character data. The only difference is that character data is converted implicitly by the Oracle server to a numeric value based on certain database settings.

Inequality comparisons operating on date values follow a similar process to character data. The Oracle server stores dates in an internal numeric format, and these values are compared within the conditions.

Range Comparison with the BETWEEN Operator

The BETWEEN operator tests whether a column or expression value falls within a range of two boundary values. The item must be at least the same as the lower boundary value or' at most' the same as the higher boundary value or fall within the range for the condition to be true.

Suppose you want the last names of employees who earn a salary in the range of $3,400 and $4,000. A possible solution using the BETWEEN operator is as follows:

```
select last_name from employees where salary between 3400 and 4000;
```

Conditions specified with the BETWEEN operator can be equivalently denoted using two inequality-based conditions.

```
select last_name from employees where salary >=3400 and salary <=4000;
```

It is shorter and simpler to specify the range condition using the BETWEEN operator.

Set Comparison with the IN Operator

The IN operator tests whether an item is a member of a set of literal values. The set is specified by comma-separating the literals and enclosing them in round brackets. If the literals are character or date values, then these must be delimited using single quotes. You may include as many literals in the set as you want. Consider the following example:

```
select last_name from employees where salary in (1000,4000,6000);
```

The SALARY value in each row is compared for equality to the literals specified in the set. If the SALARY value equals 1,000; 4,000; or 6,000; the LAST_NAME value for that row is returned. The following two statements demonstrate the use of the IN operator with DATE and CHARACTER data:

```
select last_name from employees
where last_name in ('King','Kochhar');

select last_name from employees
where hire_date in ('30-JAN-2004','21-SEP-2005');
```

Pattern Comparison with the LIKE Operator

The LIKE operator is designed exclusively for character data and provides a powerful mechanism for searching for letters or words. LIKE is accompanied by two wildcard characters: the percentage symbol (%) and the underscore character (_). The percentage symbol is used to specify zero or more wildcard characters, while the underscore character specifies one wildcard character. A wildcard may represent any character.

You can use the following query to provide a list of employees whose first names begin with the letter *A*:

```
select first_name from employees where first_name like 'A%';
```

The character literal that the FIRST_NAME column is compared to is enclosed in single quotes like a regular character literal. In addition, it has a percentage symbol, which has a special meaning in the context of the LIKE operator. The percentage symbol substitutes zero or more characters appended to the letter *A*. The wildcard characters can appear at the beginning, the middle, or the end of the character literal. They can even appear alone, as follows:

```
where first_name like '%';
```

In this case, every row containing a FIRST_NAME value that is not null will be returned. Wildcard symbols are not mandatory when using the LIKE operator. In such cases, LIKE behaves as an equality operator testing for exact character matches; so, the following two WHERE clauses are equivalent:

```
where last_name like 'King';
where last_name = 'King';
```

The underscore wildcard symbol substitutes exactly one other character in a literal. Consider searching for employees whose last names are four letters long, begin with a *K*, have an unknown second letter, and end with an *ng*. You may issue the following statement:

```
where last_name like 'K_ng';
```

As Figure 7-9 shows, the two wildcard symbols can be used independently, together, or even multiple times in a single WHERE condition. The first query retrieves those records where COUNTRY_NAME begins with the letter *I* followed by one or more characters, one of which must be a lowercase *a*.

The second query retrieves those countries whose names contain the letter *i* as its fifth character. The length of the COUNTRY_NAME values and the letter they begin with are unimportant. The four underscore wildcard symbols preceding the lowercase *i* in the WHERE

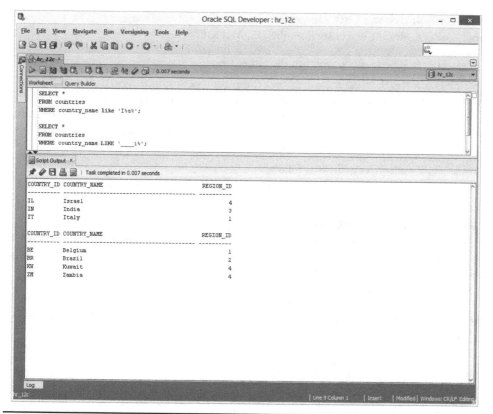

Figure 7-9 The wildcard symbols of the LIKE operator

clause represent exactly four characters (which could be any characters). The fifth letter must be an *i*, and the percentage symbol specifies that the COUNTRY_NAME can have zero or more characters from the sixth character onward.

What about when you are searching for a literal that contains a percentage or underscore character? A naturally occurring underscore character may be escaped (or treated as a regular nonspecial symbol) using the ESCAPE identifier in conjunction with an ESCAPE character. In the following example, any JOB_ID values that begin with the three characters *SA_* will be returned:

```
select job_id from jobs
where job_id like 'SA\_%' escape '\';
```

Traditionally, the ESCAPE character is the backslash symbol, but it does not have to be. The following statement is equivalent to the preceding one but uses a dollar symbol as the ESCAPE character instead:

```
select job_id from jobs
where job_id like 'SA$_%' escape '$';
```

The percentage symbol may be similarly escaped when it occurs naturally as character data.

Exercise 7-3: Use the LIKE Operator   Construct a query to retrieve a list of department names that end with the letters *ing* from the DEPARTMENTS table.

1. Start SQL*Plus and connect to the HR schema.

2. The WHERE clause must perform a comparison between the DEPARTMENT_NAME column values and a pattern beginning with zero or more characters but ending with three specific characters, *ing*. The operator enabling character pattern matching is the LIKE operator. The pattern the DEPARTMENT_NAME column must conform to is '%ing'.

3. Thus, the correct query is as follows:

```
select department_name from departments where department_name like '%ing';
```

NULL Comparison with the IS NULL Operator

NULL values inevitably find their way into database tables. It is sometimes required that only those records that contain a NULL value in a specific column are sought. The IS NULL operator selects only the rows where a specific column value is NULL. Testing column values for equality to NULL is performed using the IS NULL operator instead of the "is equal to" operator (=).

Consider the following query, which fetches the LAST_NAME column from the EMPLOYEES table for those rows that have NULL values stored in the COMMISSION_PCT column:

```
select last_name from employees
where commission_pct is null;
```

This WHERE clause reads naturally and retrieves only the records that contain NULL COMMISSION_PCT values.

Boolean Operators

Boolean or *logical* operators enable multiple conditions to be specified in the WHERE clause of the SELECT statement. This facilitates a more refined data extraction capability. Consider isolating those employee records with FIRST_NAME values that begin with the letter *J* and that earn a COMMISSION_PCT greater than 10 percent. First, the data in the EMPLOYEES table must be restricted to FIRST_NAME values like J%, and second, the COMMISSION_PCT values for the records must be tested to ascertain if they are larger than 10 percent. These two separate conditions may be associated using the Boolean AND operator and are applied consecutively in a WHERE clause. A result set conforming to any or all conditions or to the negation of one or more conditions may be specified using the OR, AND, and NOT Boolean operators, respectively.

The AND Operator

The AND operator merges conditions into one large condition to which a row must conform to be included in the results set. If two conditions specified in a WHERE clause are joined with an AND operator, then a row is tested consecutively for conformance to both conditions before being retrieved. If it conforms to neither or only one of the conditions, the row is excluded. Employee records with FIRST_NAME values beginning with the letter *J* and COMMISSION_PCT greater than 10 percent can be retrieved using the following query:

```
select first_name, last_name, commission_pct, hire_date from employees
where first_name like 'J%' and commission_pct > 0.1;
```

Notice that the WHERE clause now has two conditions but only one WHERE keyword. The AND operator separates the two conditions. To specify further mandatory conditions, simply add them and ensure that they are separated by additional AND operators. You can specify as many conditions as you want. Remember, though, the more AND conditions specified, the more restrictive the query becomes.

The OR Operator

The OR operator separates multiple conditions, at least one of which must be satisfied by the row selected to warrant inclusion in the results set. If two conditions specified in a WHERE clause are joined with an OR operator, then a row is tested consecutively for conformance to either or both conditions before being retrieved. Conforming to just one of the OR conditions is sufficient for the record to be returned. If it conforms to none of the conditions, the row is excluded. Retrieving employee records having FIRST_NAME values beginning with the letter *B* or those with a COMMISSION_PCT greater than 35 percent can be written as follows:

```
select first_name, last_name, commission_pct, hire_date from employees
where first_name like 'B%' or commission_pct > 0.35;
```

Notice that the two conditions are separated by the OR keyword. All employee records with FIRST_NAME values beginning with an uppercase *B* will be returned regardless of their COMMISSION_PCT values, even if they are NULL. Records with COMMISSION_PCT values greater than 35 percent (regardless of what letter their FIRST_NAME begins with) are also returned.

Further, OR conditions may be specified by separating them with an OR operator. The more OR conditions you specify, the less restrictive your query becomes.

The NOT Operator

The NOT operator negates conditional operators. A selected row must conform to the logical opposite of the condition in order to be included in the results set. Conditional operators may be negated by the NOT operator, as shown by the WHERE clauses listed in Table 7-7.

Positive	Negative
where last_name='King'	where NOT (last_name='King')
where first_name LIKE 'R%'	where first_name NOT LIKE 'R%'
where department_id IN (10,20,30)	where department_id NOT IN (10,20,30)
where salary BETWEEN 1 and 3000	where salary NOT BETWEEN 1 and 3000
where commission_pct IS NULL	where commission_pct IS NOT NULL

Table 7-7   Conditions Negated by the NOT Operator

The NOT operator negates the comparison operator in a condition, whether it's an equality, inequality, range-based, pattern matching, set membership, or null testing operator.

Precedence Rules

Arithmetic, character, comparison, and Boolean expressions were examined in the context of the WHERE clause. But how do these operators interact with each other? Table 7-8 shows the precedence hierarchy for the previously mentioned operators.

Operators at the same level of precedence are evaluated from left to right if they are encountered together in an expression. When the NOT operator modifies the LIKE, IS NULL, and IN comparison operators, their precedence level remains the same as the positive form of these operators.

Consider the following SELECT statement that demonstrates the interaction of various different operators:

```
select last_name,salary,department_id,job_id,commission_pct
from employees
where last_name like '%a%' and salary > department_id * 200
or
job_id in ('MK_REP','MK_MAN') and commission_pct is not null
```

The LAST_NAME, SALARY, DEPARTMENT_ID, JOB_ID, and COMMISSION_PCT columns are projected from the EMPLOYEES table based on two discrete conditions. The first condition retrieves the records containing the character *a* in the LAST_NAME field AND with a SALARY value greater than 200 times the DEPARTMENT_ID value. The product of DEPARTMENT_ID and 200 is processed before the inequality operator since the precedence of multiplication is higher than the inequality comparison.

The second condition fetches those rows with JOB_ID values of either MK_MAN or MK_REP in which COMMISSION_PCT values are not null. For a row to be returned by this query, either the first *or* second conditions need to be fulfilled. Changing the order of the

Precedence Level	Operator Symbol	Operation
1	()	Parentheses or brackets
2	/, *	Division and multiplication
3	+, -, ||	Addition, subtraction, and concatenation
4	=, !=, <, >, <=, >=	Equality and inequality comparison
5	IS [NOT] NULL, LIKE, [NOT] IN [NOT] BETWEEN, EXISTS, IS OF *type*	Null, pattern, set, range, and type comparison
6	NOT	NOT logical condition
7	AND	AND logical condition
8	OR	OR logical condition

Table 7-8 Operator Precedence Hierarchy

conditions in the WHERE clause changes its meaning because of the different precedence of the operators. Consider the following query:

```
select last_name,salary,department_id,job_id,commission_pct
from employees
where last_name like '%a%' and salary > department_id * 100 and commission_pct
is not null
or
job_id = 'MK_MAN'
```

There are two composite conditions in this query. The first condition retrieves the records with the character *a* in the LAST_NAME field AND a SALARY value greater than 100 times the DEPARTMENT_ID value AND where the COMMISSION_PCT value is not null. The second condition fetches those rows with JOB_ID values of MK_MAN. A row is returned by this query if it conforms to either condition 1 OR condition 2, but not necessarily to both.

EXAM TIP The Boolean operators OR and AND allow multiple WHERE clause conditions to be specified, while the NOT operator negates a conditional operator and may be used several times within the same condition. The equality, inequality, BETWEEN, IN, and LIKE comparison operators test two terms within a single condition. Only one comparison operator is used per conditional clause.

Sort the Rows Retrieved by a Query

The usability of the retrieved datasets may be significantly enhanced with a mechanism to order or sort the information. Information may be sorted alphabetically, numerically, and chronologically in ascending or descending order. Further, the data may be sorted by one or more columns, including columns that are not listed in the SELECT clause. Sorting is usually performed once the results of a SELECT statement have been fetched. The sorting parameters do not influence the records returned by a query, just the presentation of the results. Exactly the same rows are returned by a statement including a sort clause as are returned by a statement excluding a sort clause. Only the ordering of the output may differ. Sorting the results of a query is accomplished using the ORDER BY clause.

The ORDER BY Clause

The ORDER BY clause is usually the last clause in a SELECT statement. The format of the ORDER BY clause in the context of the SQL SELECT statement is as follows:

```
SELECT *|{[DISTINCT] column|expression [alias],...}
FROM table
[WHERE condition(s)]
[ORDER BY {col(s)|expr|numeric_pos} [ASC|DESC] [NULLS FIRST|LAST]];
```

Ascending and Descending Sorting

Ascending sort order is natural for most types of data and is therefore the default sort order used whenever the ORDER BY clause is specified. An ascending sort order for numbers is lowest to highest, while it is earliest to latest for dates and alphabetically for characters. The first form of the ORDER BY clause shows that results of a query may be sorted by one or more columns or expressions.

```
ORDER BY col(s)|expr;
```

Suppose that a report is requested that must contain an employee's LAST_NAME, HIRE_DATE, and SALARY information, sorted alphabetically by the LAST_NAME column for all sales representatives and marketing managers. This report could be extracted with the following:

```
select last_name, hire_date, salary from employees
where job_id in ('SA_REP','MK_MAN')
order by last_name;
```

The data selected may be ordered by any of the columns from the tables in the FROM clause, including those that do not appear in the SELECT list. By appending the keyword DESC to the ORDER BY clause, rows are returned sorted in descending order. The optional NULLS LAST keywords specify that if the sort column contains null values, then these rows are to be listed last after sorting the remaining NOT NULL values. To specify that rows with null values in the sort column should be displayed first, append the NULLS FIRST keywords to the ORDER BY clause. A dataset may be sorted based on an expression as follows:

```
select last_name, salary, hire_date, sysdate-hire_date tenure
from employees order by tenure;
```

The smallest TENURE value appears first in the output since the ORDER BY clause specifies that the results will be sorted by the expression alias. Note that the results could be sorted by the explicit expression and the alias could be omitted, but using aliases renders the query easier to read.

Several implicit default options are selected when you use the ORDER BY clause. The most important of these is that unless DESC is specified, the sort order is assumed to be ascending. If null values occur in the sort column, the default sort order is assumed to be NULLS LAST for ascending sorts and NULLS FIRST for descending sorts. If no ORDER BY clause is specified, the same query executed at different times may return the same set of results in different row order, so no assumptions should be made regarding the default row order.

Positional Sorting

Oracle offers an alternative, shorter way to specify the sort column or expression. Instead of specifying the column name, the position of the column as it occurs in the SELECT list is appended to the ORDER BY clause. Consider the following example:

```
select last_name, hire_date, salary from employees order by 2;
```

The ORDER BY clause specifies the numeric literal 2. This is equivalent to specifying ORDER BY HIRE_DATE since that is the second column in the SELECT clause. *Positional sorting* applies only to columns in the SELECT list.

Composite Sorting

Results may be sorted by more than one column using *composite sorting*. Multiple columns may be specified (either literally or positionally) as the composite sort key by comma-separating them in the ORDER BY clause. To fetch the JOB_ID, LAST_NAME, SALARY, and HIRE_DATE values from the EMPLOYEES table such that the results must be sorted in reverse alphabetical order by JOB_ID first, then in ascending alphabetical order by LAST_NAME, and finally in numerically descending order based on the SALARY column, you can run the following query:

```
select job_id, last_name, salary, hire_date from employees
where job_id in ('SA_REP','MK_MAN') order by job_id desc, last_name, 3 desc;
```

Exercise 7-4: Use the ORDER BY Clause   The JOBS table contains descriptions of different types of jobs an employee in the organization may occupy. It contains the JOB_ID, JOB_TITLE, MIN_SALARY, and MAX_SALARY columns. You are required to write a query that extracts the JOB_TITLE, MIN_SALARY, and MAX_SALARY columns, as well as an expression called VARIANCE, which is the difference between the MAX_SALARY and MIN_SALARY values for each row. The results must include only JOB_TITLE values that contain either the word *President* or *Manager*. Sort the list in descending order based on the VARIANCE expression. If more than one row has the same VARIANCE value, then, in addition, sort these rows by JOB_TITLE in reverse alphabetic order.

1. Start SQL Developer and connect to the HR schema.

2. Sorting is accomplished with the ORDER BY clause. Composite sorting is required using both the VARIANCE expression and the JOB_TITLE column in descending order.

3. Executing this statement returns a set of results matching the request:

```
SELECT JOB_TITLE, MIN_SALARY, MAX_SALARY, (MAX_SALARY - MIN_SALARY) VARIANCE
FROM JOBS WHERE JOB_TITLE LIKE '%President%' OR JOB_TITLE LIKE '%Manager%'
ORDER BY VARIANCE DESC, JOB_TITLE DESC;
```

The SQL Row-Limiting Clause

Many analytic queries require only a portion of a dataset, such as the top three salespeople in an organization or the four most recently employed staff members. The row-limiting clause of the SELECT statement allows a dataset to be segmented in various ways. The format of the row-limiting clause in the context of the SQL SELECT statement is as follows:

```
SELECT *|{[DISTINCT] column|expression [alias],...}
FROM table
[WHERE condition(s)]
[ORDER BY order_by_clause]
[OFFSET offset { ROW|ROWS}]
[FETCH {FIRST | NEXT } [{ number_of_rows | percent percentage_of_rows }]
{ ROW | ROWS } {ONLY | WITH TIES }];
```

The OFFSET clause specifies the number of rows to skip to get to the start position in a results set. OFFSET defaults to 0 in the absence of an OFFSET clause or if a NULL, negative, or offset that is larger than the total rows in a results set is provided. The ROW and ROWS keywords have identical meaning, and both singular and plural forms are provided to make your OFFSET clause read more naturally.

The FETCH clause specifies either an exact *number_of_rows* or a *percentage_of_rows* to return. In the absence of this clause, the entire result set is returned, starting from row number OFFSET+1 to the last row. The FIRST and NEXT keywords also serve to clarify semantics but have identical meaning. Fetching the FIRST 2 rows from OFFSET 100 in a dataset retrieves the same two rows as fetching the NEXT 2 rows from OFFSET 100.

The *number_of_rows* option of the FETCH clause defaults to 0 if a NULL or negative row count is specified. Mixed fractions provided as *number_of_rows* are truncated, and only the whole number portion is used as this parameter. If the *number_of_rows* value is larger than the number of rows remaining starting from position OFFSET + 1, all rows in a results set are returned. The *percentage_of_rows* option must be a number, and a NULL or negative value defaults to 0. This option specifies the percentage of the result set to retrieve.

The ROW or ROWS keywords again have identical meaning, and both singular and plural forms are provided to make your FETCH clause read more naturally.

The keywords ONLY or WITH TIES should be read together with the ROW/ROWS keywords. ROWS ONLY retrieves the exact number or percentage of rows specified. Retrieving ROWS WITH TIES fetches any additional rows with the same sort key as the last row retrieved but has any effect only if an ORDER BY clause is specified.

As Figure 7-10 shows, the first query fetches the 7 rows after it retrieves all 107 rows from the EMPLOYEES table sorted in default ascending order by salary, skips 100 rows because of

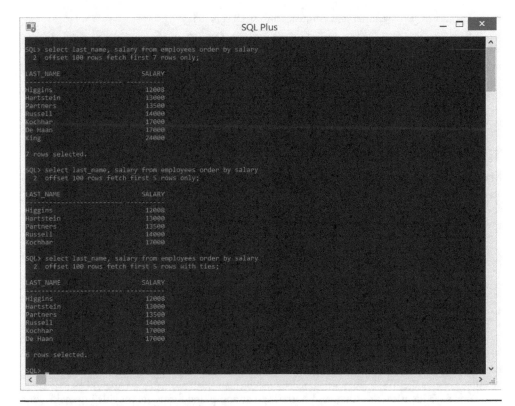

Figure 7-10 The SQL row-limiting clause

the offset clause, and finally returns the last names and salaries of the top 7 highest-paid employees. The second query prunes this list by fetching the first 5 of these 7 rows starting at row 101 (OFFSET + 1). Note how the final query returns an additional row to the second query since employees De Haan and Kochhar both earn the same salary ($17,000) and are thus tied with the same sort key.

Ampersand Substitution

As you develop and perfect SQL statements, you can save them for future use. It is sometimes desirable to have a generic form of a statement that has a variable or placeholder defined that can be substituted at run-time. SQL*Plus offers this functionality in the form of *ampersand substitution*. Every element of the SELECT statement may be substituted, and the reduction of queries to their core elements to facilitate reuse can save you hours of tedious and repetitive work. This section examines substitution variables and the DEFINE and VERIFY commands.

Substitution Variables

Substitution variables may be regarded as placeholders. A SQL query is composed of two or more clauses. Each clause can be divided into subclauses, which are in turn made up of character text. Any text, subclause, or clause element is a candidate for substitution.

Single Ampersand Substitution

The most basic and popular form of SQL element is *single ampersand substitution*. The ampersand character (&) is the symbol chosen to designate a substitution variable in a statement and precedes the variable name with no spaces between them. When the statement is executed, the SQL*Plus client processes the statement, notices a substitution variable, and attempts to resolve this variable's value in one of two ways. First, it checks whether the variable is *defined* in the user session. (The DEFINE command is discussed later in this chapter.) If the variable is not defined, the user process prompts for a value that will be substituted in place of the variable. Once a value is submitted, the statement is complete and is executed by the Oracle server. The *ampersand substitution* variable is resolved at execution time and is sometimes known as *run-time binding* or *run-time substitution*.

You may be required to look up contact information like PHONE_NUMBER data given either LAST_NAME or EMPLOYEE_ID values. This generic query may be written as follows:

```
select employee_id, last_name, phone_number from employees
where last_name = '&LASTNAME' or employee_id = &EMPNO;
```

When running this query, SQL*Plus prompts you to input a value for the variable called LASTNAME. You enter an employee's last name, if you know it, for example, King. If you don't know the last name but know the employee ID number, you can type in any value and press the ENTER key to submit the value. Oracle then prompts you to enter a value for the EMPNO variable. After typing in a value, for example, 0, and hitting ENTER, there are no remaining substitution variables for Oracle to resolve, and the following statement is executed:

```
select employee_id, last_name, phone_number from employees
where last_name = 'King' or employee_id = 0;
```

Variables can be assigned any alphanumeric name that is a valid identifier name. The literal you substitute when prompted for a variable must be an appropriate data type for that context; otherwise, an "ORA-00904: invalid identifier" error is returned. If the variable is meant to substitute a character or date value, the literal needs to be enclosed in single quotes. A useful technique is to enclose the *ampersand substitution* variable in single quotes when dealing with character and date values. In this way, the user is required to submit a literal value without worrying about enclosing it in quotes.

Double Ampersand Substitution

When a substitution variable is referenced multiple times in the same query, Oracle will prompt you to enter a value for every occurrence of the single ampersand substitution variable. For complex scripts, this can be inefficient and tedious. The following statement retrieves the FIRST_NAME and LAST_NAME data from the EMPLOYEES table for those rows that contain the same set of characters in both these fields:

```
select first_name, last_name from employees
where last_name like '%&SEARCH%' and first_name like '%&SEARCH%';
```

The two conditions are identical but apply to different columns. When this statement is executed, you are first prompted to enter a substitution value for the SEARCH variable used in the comparison with the LAST_NAME column. Thereafter, you are prompted to enter a substitution value for the SEARCH variable used in the comparison with the FIRST_NAME column. This poses two problems. First, it is inefficient to enter the same value twice, but second and more important, typographical errors may confound the query since Oracle does not verify that the same literal value is entered each time substitution variables with the same name are used. In this example, the logical assumption is that the contents of the variables substituted should be the same, but the fact that the variables have the same name has no meaning to the Oracle server, and it makes no such assumption. The first example in Figure 7-11 shows the results of running the preceding query and submitting two distinct values for the SEARCH substitution variable. In this particular example, the results are incorrect since the requirement was to retrieve FIRST_NAME and LAST_NAME pairs that contained the identical string of characters.

When a substitution variable is referenced multiple times in the same query and your intention is that the variable must have the same value at each occurrence in the statement, it is preferable to make use of *double ampersand substitution*. This involves prefixing the first occurrence of the substitution variable that occurs multiple times in a query with two ampersand symbols instead of one. When Oracle encounters a double ampersand substitution variable, a session value is defined for that variable, and you are not prompted to enter a value to be substituted for this variable in subsequent references.

The second example in Figure 7-11 demonstrates how the SEARCH variable is preceded by two ampersands in the condition with the LAST_NAME column and thereafter is prefixed by one ampersand in the condition with the FIRST_NAME column. When the statement is executed, you are prompted to enter a value to be substituted for the SEARCH variable only once for the condition with the LAST_NAME column. This value is then automatically resolved from the session value of the variable in subsequent references to it, as in the condition with the FIRST_NAME column. To undefine the SEARCH variable, you need to use the UNDEFINE command described later in this chapter.

Figure 7-11
Double
ampersand
substitution

```
SQL Plus                                        _ □ ×

SQL> SELECT first_name, last_name
  2  FROM employees
  3  WHERE last_name LIKE '%&SEARCH%'
  4  AND first_name LIKE '%&SEARCH%';
Enter value for search: K
old    3: WHERE last_name LIKE '%&SEARCH%'
new    3: WHERE last_name LIKE '%K%'
Enter value for search: S
old    4: AND first_name LIKE '%&SEARCH%'
new    4: AND first_name LIKE '%S%'

FIRST_NAME           LAST_NAME
-------------------- ------------------------
Steven               King
Sundita              Kumar

SQL> SELECT first_name, last_name
  2  FROM employees
  3  WHERE last_name LIKE '%&&SEARCH%'
  4  AND first_name LIKE '%&&SEARCH%';
Enter value for search: G
old    3: WHERE last_name LIKE '%&&SEARCH%'
new    3: WHERE last_name LIKE '%G%'
old    4: AND first_name LIKE '%&&SEARCH%'
new    4: AND first_name LIKE '%G%'

FIRST_NAME           LAST_NAME
-------------------- ------------------------
Girard               Geoni

SQL>
```

> **TIP**   Whether you work as a developer, database administrator, or business
> end user, all SQL queries you encounter may be broadly classified as either
> ad hoc or repeated queries. Ad hoc queries are usually one-off statements
> written during some data investigation exercise that are unlikely to be reused. The
> repeated queries are those that are run frequently or periodically, which are usually saved
> as script files and run with little to no modification whenever required. Reuse prevents
> costly redevelopment time and allows these consistent queries to potentially benefit
> from Oracle's native automatic tuning features geared toward improving query
> performance.

Substituting Column Names

Literal elements of the WHERE clause have been the focus of the discussion on substitution
thus far, but virtually any element of a SQL statement is a candidate for substitution. In the
following statement, the FIRST_NAME and JOB_ID columns are static and will always be
retrieved, but the third column selected is variable and specified as a substitution variable named
COL. The result set is further sorted by this variable column in the ORDER BY clause.

```
select first_name, job_id, &&col
from employees
where job_id in ('MK_MAN','SA_MAN')
order by &col;
```

Unlike character and date literals, column name references do not require single quotes either when explicitly specified or when substituted via ampersand substitution.

Substituting Expressions and Text

Almost any element of a SQL statement may be substituted at run-time. The constraint is that Oracle requires at least the first word to be static. In the case of the SELECT statement, at a minimum, the SELECT keyword is required, and the remainder of the statement may be substituted as follows:

```
select &rest_of_statement;
```

When the statement is executed, you are prompted to submit a value for the variable called REST_OF_STATEMENT, which, when appended to the SELECT keyword, is any legitimate query. Useful candidates for ampersand substitution are statements that are run multiple times and differ slightly from each other.

Define and Verify

Double ampersand substitution is used to avoid repetitive input when the same variable occurs multiple times in a statement. When a double ampersand substitution occurs, the variable is stored as a session variable. As the statement executes, all further occurrences of the variable are automatically resolved using the stored session variable. Any subsequent executions of the statement within the same session automatically resolve the substitution variables from stored session values. This is not always desirable and indeed limits the usefulness of substitution variables. Oracle does, however, provide a mechanism to undefine these session variables. The VERIFY command is specific to SQL*Plus and controls whether substituted elements are echoed on the user's screen prior to executing a SQL statement that uses substitution variables.

The DEFINE and UNDEFINE Commands

Session-level variables are implicitly created when they are initially referenced in SQL statements using double ampersand substitution. They persist or remain available for the duration of the session or until they are explicitly undefined. A session ends when the user exits their client tool like SQL*Plus or when the user process is terminated.

The problem with persistent session variables is they tend to detract from the generic nature of statements that use ampersand substitution variables. Fortunately, these session variables can be removed with the UNDEFINE command. Within a script or at the command line of SQL*Plus or SQL Developer, the syntax to undefine session variables is as follows:

```
UNDEFINE variable;
```

Consider a simple generic example that selects a static and variable column from the EMPLOYEES table and sorts the output based on the variable column.

```
select last_name, &&COLNAME
from employees where department_id=30 order by &COLNAME;
```

The first time this statement executes, you are prompted to supply a value for the COLNAME variable. Assume you enter SALARY. This value is substituted, and the statement executes. A subsequent execution of this statement within the same session does not prompt for any COLNAME values since it is already defined as SALARY in the context of this session and can be undefined only with the UNDEFINE COLNAME command. Once the variable has been undefined, the next execution of the statement prompts the user for a value for the COLNAME variable.

The DEFINE command serves two purposes. It can be used to retrieve a list of all the variables currently defined in your SQL session; it can also be used to explicitly define a value for a variable referenced as a substitution variable by one or more statements during the lifetime of that session. The syntaxes for the two variants of the DEFINE command are as follows:

```
DEFINE;
DEFINE variable=value;
```

Support of session-persistent variables may be switched off and on as required using the SET DEFINE OFF command. The SET command is not a SQL language command, but rather a SQL environment control command. When you specify SET DEFINE OFF, the client tool (for example, SQL*Plus) does not save session variables or attach special meaning to the ampersand symbol. This allows the ampersand symbol to be used as an ordinary literal character if necessary. The SET DEFINE ON|OFF command therefore determines whether ampersand substitution is available in your session. The following query uses the ampersand symbol as a literal value. When it is executed, you are prompted to submit a value for the bind variable SID.

```
select 'Coda & Sid' from dual;
```

By turning off the ampersand substitution functionality, this query can be executed without prompts.

```
SET DEFINE OFF
select 'Coda & Sid' from dual;
SET DEFINE ON
```

Once the statement executes, you can use the SET DEFINE ON command to switch the substitution functionality back on. If DEFINE is OFF and the context that an ampersand is used in a statement cannot be resolved literally, Oracle returns an error.

The VERIFY Command

Two categories of commands are available when dealing with the Oracle server: SQL language commands and the SQL client control commands. The SELECT statement is a language command, while the SET command controls the SQL client environment. There are many different language and control commands available, but the control commands relevant to substitution are DEFINE and VERIFY.

The VERIFY command controls whether the substitution variable submitted is displayed onscreen so that you can verify that the correct substitution has occurred. A message is displayed showing the *old* clause followed by the *new* clause containing the substituted value. The VERIFY command is switched ON and OFF with the command SET VERIFY ON|OFF. If

VERIFY is first switched OFF and a query that uses ampersand substitution is executed, you are prompted to input a value. The value is then substituted, the statement runs, and its results are displayed. If VERIFY is then switched ON and the same query is executed, once you input a value but before the statement commences execution, Oracle displays the clause containing the reference to the substitution variable as the *old* clause with its line number, and, immediately below this, the *new* clause displays the statement containing the substituted value.

Exercise 7-5: Using Ampersand Substitution   You are required to write a reusable query using the current tax rate and the EMPLOYEE_ID number as inputs and return the EMPLOYEE_ID, FIRST_NAME, SALARY, ANNUAL SALARY (SALARY * 12), TAX_RATE, and TAX (TAX_RATE * ANNUAL SALARY) information for use by the HR department clerks.

1. Start SQL*Plus and connect to the HR schema.

2. The select list must include the four specified columns as well as two expressions. The first expression, aliased as ANNUAL SALARY, is a simple calculation, while the second expression, aliased as TAX, depends on the TAX_RATE value. Since TAX RATE may vary, this value must be substituted at run-time.

3. A possible solution is as follows:

```
SELECT &&EMPLOYEE_ID, FIRST_NAME, SALARY, SALARY * 12 AS "ANNUAL SALARY",
&&TAX_RATE, (&TAX_RATE * (SALARY * 12)) AS "TAX"
FROM EMPLOYEES WHERE EMPLOYEE_ID = &EMPLOYEE_ID;
```

4. The double ampersand preceding EMPLOYEE_ID and TAX_RATE in the SELECT clause stipulates to Oracle that when the statement is executed, the user must be prompted to submit a value for each substitution variable that will be used wherever they are subsequently referenced as &EMPLOYEE_ID and &TAX_RATE, respectively.

Two-Minute Drill

Explain the Capabilities of SQL SELECT Statements

- The three fundamental operations that SELECT statements are capable of are projection, selection, and joining.

- Projection refers to the restriction of columns selected from a table. Using projection, you retrieve only the columns of interest and not every possible column.

- Selection refers to the extraction of rows from a table. Selection includes the further restriction of the extracted rows based on various criteria or conditions. This allows you to retrieve only the rows that are of interest and not every row in the table.

- Joining involves linking two or more tables based on common attributes. Joining allows data to be stored in third normal form in discrete tables instead of in one large table.

- The DESCRIBE command lists the names, data types, and nullable status of all columns in a table.

Execute a Basic SELECT Statement

- The SELECT clause determines the *projection* of columns. In other words, the SELECT clause specifies which columns are included in the results returned.

- The DISTINCT keyword preceding items in the SELECT clause causes duplicate combinations of these items to be excluded from the returned results set.

- Expressions and regular columns may be aliased by using the AS keyword or by leaving a space between the column or expression and the alias.

- Naturally occurring single quotes in a character literal can be selected by making use of either an additional single quote per naturally occurring quote or the alternative quote operator.

Limit the Rows Retrieved by a Query

- One or more conditions constitute a WHERE clause. These conditions specify rules to which the data in a row must conform to be eligible for selection.

- For each row tested in a condition, there are terms on the left and right of a comparison operator. Terms in a condition can be column values, literals, or expressions.

- Comparison operators may test two terms in many ways. Equality and inequality tests are common, but range, set, and pattern comparisons are also available.

- Boolean operators include the AND, OR, and NOT operators. The AND and OR operators enable multiple conditional clauses to be specified. These are sometimes referred to as multiple WHERE clauses.

- The NOT operator negates the comparison operator involved in a condition.

Sort the Rows Retrieved by a Query

- Results are sorted using the ORDER BY clause. Rows retrieved may be ordered according to one or more columns by specifying either the column names or their numeric position in the SELECT clause.

- The sorted output may be arranged in descending or ascending order using the DESC or ASC modifier after the sort terms in the ORDER BY clause.

- The row-limiting clause allows a portion of a dataset to be fetched. An optional OFFSET may be provided to indicate the start position of the row-limited set. Either an absolute number or a percentage of rows may be requested. If the WITH TIES option is specified, all rows with the same sort keys as the last row of the row-limited set will additionally be fetched.

Ampersand Substitution

- Ampersand substitution facilitates SQL statement reuse by providing a means to substitute elements of a statement at run-time. The same SQL statement may therefore be run multiple times with different input parameters.

- Session-persistent variables may be set explicitly using the DEFINE command. The UNDEFINE command may be used to unset both implicitly (double ampersand substitution) and explicitly defined session variables.

- The VERIFY environmental setting controls whether SQL*Plus displays the old and new versions of statement lines that contain substitution variables.

Self Test

1. Which query will create a projection of the DEPARTMENT_NAME and LOCATION_ ID columns from the DEPARTMENTS table? (Choose the best answer.)

   A. SELECT DISTINCT DEPARTMENT_NAME, LOCATION_ID FROM DEPARTMENTS;

   B. SELECT DEPARTMENT_NAME, LOCATION_ID FROM DEPARTMENTS;

   C. SELECT DEPT_NAME, LOC_ID FROM DEPT;

   D. SELECT DEPARTMENT_NAME AS "LOCATION_ID" FROM DEPARTMENTS;

2. After describing the EMPLOYEES table, you discover that the SALARY column has a data type of NUMBER(8,2). Which SALARY values will not be permitted in this column? (Choose the best answers.)

   A. SALARY=12345678

   B. SALARY=123456.78

   C. SALARY=1234567.8

   D. SALARY=123456

   E. SALARY=12.34

3. After describing the JOB_HISTORY table, you discover that the START_DATE and END_DATE columns have a data type of DATE. Consider the expression END_ DATE – START_DATE. Choose two correct statements regarding this expression.

   A. A value of DATE data type is returned.

   B. A value of type NUMBER is returned.

   C. A value of type VARCHAR2 is returned.

   D. The expression is invalid since arithmetic cannot be performed on columns with DATE data types.

   E. The expression is valid since arithmetic can be performed on columns with DATE data types.

4. Which statement reports on unique JOB_ID values from the EMPLOYEES table? (Choose the best answer.)

   A. SELECT JOB_ID FROM EMPLOYEES;

   B. SELECT UNIQUE JOB_ID FROM EMPLOYEES;

   C. SELECT DISTINCT JOB_ID, EMPLOYEE_ID FROM EMPLOYEES;

   D. SELECT DISTINCT JOB_ID FROM EMPLOYEES;

5. Choose the two illegal statements. The two correct statements produce identical results. The two illegal statements will cause an error to be raised.

   A. SELECT DEPARTMENT_ID|| ' represents the '|| DEPARTMENT_NAME||' Department' as "Department Info" FROM DEPARTMENTS;

   B. SELECT DEPARTMENT_ID|| ' represents the || DEPARTMENT_NAME||' Department' as "Department Info" FROM DEPARTMENTS;

   C. select department_id|| ' represents the '||department_name|| ' Department' "Department Info" from departments;

   D. SELECT DEPARTMENT_ID represents the DEPARTMENT_NAME Department as "Department Info" FROM DEPARTMENTS;

6. Which two clauses of the SELECT statement facilitate selection and projection? (Choose the best answer.)

   A. SELECT, FROM

   B. ORDER BY, WHERE

   C. SELECT, WHERE

   D. SELECT, ORDER BY

7. Choose the WHERE clause that extracts the DEPARTMENT_NAME values containing the character literal *er* from the DEPARTMENTS table. The SELECT and FROM clauses are SELECT DEPARTMENT_NAME FROM DEPARTMENTS. (Choose the best answer.)

   A. WHERE DEPARTMENT_NAME IN ('%e%r');

   B. WHERE DEPARTMENT_NAME LIKE '%er%';

   C. WHERE DEPARTMENT_NAME BETWEEN 'e' AND 'r';

   D. WHERE DEPARTMENT_NAME CONTAINS 'e%r'

8. Which of the following conditions are equivalent to each other? (Choose all that apply.)

   A. WHERE SALARY <=5000 AND SALARY >=2000

   B. WHERE SALARY IN (2000,3000,4000,5000)

   C. WHERE SALARY BETWEEN 2000 AND 5000

   D. WHERE SALARY > 2000 AND SALARY < 5000

   E. WHERE SALARY >=2000 AND <=5000

9. Choose two false statements about the ORDER BY clause. (Choose the best answer.)

   A. When using the ORDER BY clause, it must always be accompanied by a row-limiting clause.

   B. The ORDER BY clause may appear in a SELECT statement that does not contain a WHERE clause.

   C. The ORDER BY clause specifies one or more terms by which the retrieved rows are sorted. These terms can only be column names.

   D. Positional sorting is accomplished by specifying in the ORDER BY clause the numeric position of a column as it appears in the SELECT list.

10. When using ampersand substitution variables in the following query, how many times will you be prompted to input a value for the variable called JOB the first time this query is executed?

    SELECT FIRST_NAME, '&JOB'
    FROM EMPLOYEES
    WHERE JOB_ID LIKE '%'||&JOB||'%'
    AND '&&JOB' BETWEEN 'A' AND 'Z';

    (Choose the best answer.)

    A. 0

    B. 1

    C. 2

    D. 3

11. When using a row-limiting clause in the following query, what employee information is returned?

    SELECT employee_id, first_name
    FROM employees
    ORDER BY employee_id
    OFFSET 5 ROWS FETCH NEXT 5 ROWS ONLY;

    (Choose the best answer.)

    A. The five employees with the highest employee_id

    B. The five employees with the lowest employee_id

    C. The five employees with the 6th to 10th lowest employee_id

    D. The five employees with the 6th to 10th highest employee_id

    E. The ten employees with the lowest employee_id

    F. None of the above

Self Test Answers

1. ☑ **B**. A projection is an intentional restriction of the columns returned from a table.
   ☒ **A, C,** and **D** are incorrect. **A** is eliminated since the question has nothing to do with duplicates, distinctiveness, or uniqueness of data. **C** incorrectly selects nonexistent columns called DEPT_NAME and LOC_ID from a nonexistent table called DEPT. **D** returns just one of the requested columns: DEPARTMENT_NAME. Instead of additionally projecting the LOCATION_ID column from the DEPARTMENTS table, it attempts to alias the DEPARTMENT_NAME column as LOCATION_ID.

2. ☑ **A** and **C**. Columns with the NUMBER(8,2) data type can store, at most, eight digits, of which, at most, two of those digits are to the right of the decimal point. Although **A** and **C** are the correct answers, note that since the question is phrased in the negative, these values are *not* allowed to be stored in such a column. **A** and **C** are not allowed because they contain eight and seven whole number digits, respectively, but the data type is constrained to store six whole number digits and two fractional digits.
   ☒ **B, D,** and **E** are incorrect. **B, D,** and **E** can legitimately be stored in this data type and, therefore, are the incorrect answers to this question. **D** shows that numbers with no fractional part are legitimate values for this column, as long as the number of digits in the whole number portion does not exceed six digits.

3. ☑ **B** and **E**. The result of arithmetic between two date values represents a certain number of days.
   ☒ **A, C,** and **D** are incorrect. It is a common mistake to expect the result of arithmetic between two date values to be a date as well, so **A** may seem plausible, but it is false.

4. ☑ **D**. Unique JOB_ID values are projected from the EMPLOYEES table by applying the DISTINCT keyword to just the JOB_ID column.
   ☒ **A, B,** and **C** are incorrect. **A** returns an unrestricted list of JOB_ID values including duplicates, **B** makes use of the UNIQUE keyword in the incorrect context, and **C** selects the distinct combination of JOB_ID and EMPLOYEE_ID values. This has the effect of returning all the rows from the EMPLOYEES table, since the EMPLOYEE_ID column contains unique values for each employee record. Additionally, **C** returns two columns, which is not what was originally requested.

5. ☑ **B** and **D**. **B** and **D** represent the two illegal statements that will return syntax errors if they are executed. This is a tricky question because it asks for the illegal statements and not the legal statements. **B** is illegal because it is missing a single quote enclosing the character literal *represents the*. **D** is illegal because it does not make use of single quotes to enclose its character literals.
   ☒ **A** and **C** are incorrect. **A** and **C** are the legal statements and, therefore, in the context of the question, are the incorrect answers. **A** and **C** appear to be different, since the SQL statements differ in case and **A** uses the alias keyword AS, whereas **C** just leaves a space between the expression and the alias. Yet both **A** and **C** produce identical results.

6. ☑ **C.** The SELECT clause facilitates projection by specifying the list of columns to be projected from a table, while the WHERE clause facilitates selection by limiting the rows retrieved based on its conditions.

 ☒ **A**, **B**, and **D** are incorrect. **A**, **B**, and **D** are incorrect because the FROM clause specifies the source of the rows being projected and the ORDER BY clause is used for sorting the selected rows.

7. ☑ **B.** The LIKE operator tests the DEPARTMENT_NAME column of each row for values that contain the characters *er*. The percentage symbols before and after the character literal indicate that any characters enclosing the *er* literal are permissible.

 ☒ **A**, **C**, and **D** are incorrect. **A** and **C** are syntactically correct. **A** uses the IN operator, which is used to test set membership. **C** tests whether the alphabetic value of the DEPARTMENT_NAME column is between the letter *e* and the letter *r*. Finally, **D** uses the word *contains,* which cannot be used in this context.

8. ☑ **A and C.** Each of these conditions tests for SALARY values in the range of $2,000 to $5,000.

 ☒ **B**, **D**, and **E** are incorrect. **B** excludes values like $2,500 from its set. **D** excludes the boundary values of $2,000 and $5,000, and **E** is illegal since it is missing the SALARY column name reference after the AND operator.

9. ☑ **A and C.** A row-limiting clause is optional and the terms specified in an ORDER BY clause can include column names, positional sorting, numeric values, and expressions.

 ☒ **B** and **D** are incorrect because they are true.

10. ☑ **D.** The first time this statement is executed, two single ampersand substitution variables are encountered before the third double ampersand substitution variable. If the first reference on the first line of the query contained a double ampersand substitution, you would be prompted to input a value only once.

 ☒ **A**, **B**, and **C** are incorrect. These are incorrect since you are prompted three times to input a value for the JOB substitution variable. In subsequent executions of this statement in the same session, you will not be prompted to input a value for this variable.

11. ☑ **C.** The results are sorted from lowest to highest employee_id. The OFFSET 5 clause limits the rows returned to the second set of five employee records.

 ☒ **A**, **B**, **D** and **E** are incorrect. The OFFSET and ORDER_BY clauses determine which segment of the results set is extracted and the sort order, while the FETCH clause determines how many rows are ultimately retrieved.

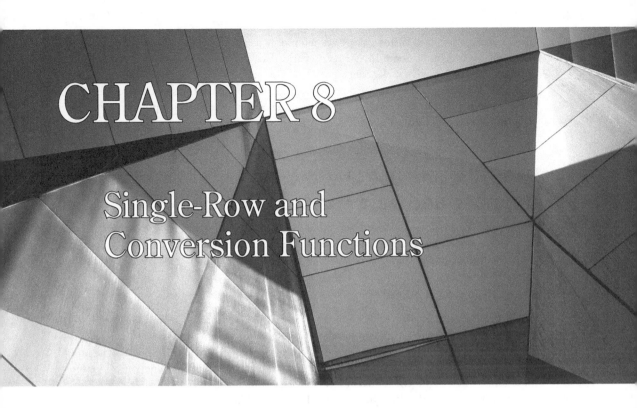

CHAPTER 8

Single-Row and Conversion Functions

Exam Objectives

In this chapter, you will learn to

- 061.3.1   Describe Various Types of Functions Available in SQL
- 061.3.2   Use Character, Number, and Date Functions in SELECT Statements
- 061.4.1   Describe Various Types of Conversion Functions That Are Available in SQL
- 061.4.2   Use the TO_CHAR, TO_NUMBER, and TO_DATE Conversion Functions
- 061.4.3   Apply Conditional Expressions in a SELECT Statement

The functions discussed in this chapter are commonly used built-in PL/SQL programs, packaged and supplied by Oracle. Some operate on numeric, date, and character data, while others convert data between the different scalar data types. Functions can be nested, and some functions are aimed at simplifying interactions with NULL. The conditional functions CASE and DECODE have the ability to display different results depending on data values, which provide *if-then-else* logic in the context of a SQL query.

Describe and Use Character, Number, and Date Functions in SQL

SQL functions are broadly divided into those that calculate and return a value for every row in a dataset and those that return a single aggregated value for all rows. The character case conversion functions will be examined, followed by the character manipulation, numeric, and date functions.

Defining a Function

A *function* is a program written to optionally accept input parameters, perform an operation, and return a single value. A function returns only one value per execution.

Three important components form the basis of defining a function. The first is the input parameter list. It specifies zero or more arguments that may be passed to a function as input for processing. These arguments or parameters may be optional and of differing data types. The second component is the data type of its resultant value. Upon execution, only one value of a predetermined data type is returned by the function. The third encapsulates the details of the processing performed by the function and contains the program code that optionally manipulates the input parameters, performs calculations and operations, and generates a return value.

A function is often described as a *black box* that takes an input, performs a calculation, and returns a value. Instead of focusing on their implementation details, it is more useful to concentrate on the features that built-in functions provide.

Functions may be *nested* within other functions, such as F1(x, y, F2(a, b), z), where F2 takes two input parameters, a and b, and forms the third of four parameters submitted to F1. Functions can operate on any data type; the most common are character, date, and numeric data. These operands may be columns or expressions.

As an example, consider a function that calculates a person's age. The AGE function takes one date input parameter, which is their birthday. The result returned by the AGE function is a number representing a person's age. The black-box calculation involves obtaining the difference in years between the current date and the birthday input parameter.

Types of Functions

Functions can be broadly divided into two categories: those that operate on a single row at a time and those that process multiple rows. This distinction is vital to understanding the broader context in which functions are used.

Single-Row Functions

There are several categories of *single-row* functions, including character, numeric, date, conversion, and general. These are functions that operate on one row of a dataset at a time. If a query selects ten rows, the function is executed ten times, once per row with the values from that row as input to the function.

This query selects two columns of the REGIONS table along with an expression using the LENGTH function with the REGION_NAME column:

```
select region_id, region_name, length(region_name) from regions;
```

The length of the REGION_NAME column is calculated for each of the four rows in the REGIONS table; the function executes four separate times, returning one result per row.

Single-row functions manipulate the data items in a row to extract and format them for display purposes. The input values to a single-row function can be user-specified constants or literals, column data, variables, or expressions optionally supplied by other nested single-row functions. The nesting of single-row functions is a commonly used technique. Functions can return a value with a different data type from its input parameters. The preceding query shows how the LENGTH function accepts one character input parameter and returns a numeric output.

Apart from their inclusion in the SELECT list of a SQL query, single-row functions may be used in the WHERE and ORDER BY clauses.

Multiple-Row Functions

As the name suggests, this category of functions operates on more than one row at a time. Typical uses of *multiple-row* functions include calculating the sum or average of the numeric column values or counting the total number of records in sets. These are sometimes known as *aggregation* or *group* functions and are explored in Chapter 9.

Using Case Conversion Functions

Numerous sources, including application interfaces and batch programs, may save character data in tables. It is not safe to assume that character data has been entered in a case-consistent manner. The character *case conversion* functions serve two important purposes. They may be used, first, to modify the appearance of a character data item for display purposes and, second, to render them consistently for comparison operations. It is simpler to search for a string using a consistent case format instead of testing every permutation of uppercase and lowercase characters that could match the string. Remember that these functions do not alter the data stored in tables. They still form part of the read-only SQL query.

These functions expect string parameters that may consist of string literals, character column values, character expressions, or numeric and date values (which are implicitly converted into strings).

The LOWER Function

The LOWER function replaces the uppercase characters in a string with their lowercase equivalents. Its syntax is LOWER(*s*). The following query illustrates the usage of this function:

```
select lower(100+100), lower('SQL'), lower(sysdate) from dual;
```

Assume that the current system date is 17-DEC-2014. The strings 200, sql, and 17-dec-2014 are returned. Note that date results may vary based on the session parameters. The numeric and date expressions are evaluated and implicitly converted into character data before the LOWER function is executed.

The LOWER function is used in the following condition to locate the records with the letters *U* and *R*, in any case, adjacent to each other in the LAST_NAME field:

```
select first_name, last_name, lower(last_name) from employees
where lower(last_name) like '%ur%';
```

Consider writing an alternative query to return the same results without using a case conversion function. It could be done as follows:

```
select first_name, last_name from employees
where last_name like '%ur%' or last_name like '%UR%'
or last_name like '%uR%' or last_name like '%Ur%'
```

This query works but is cumbersome, and the number of OR clauses required increases exponentially as the length of the search string increases.

The UPPER Function

The UPPER function is the logical opposite of the LOWER function and replaces the lowercase characters in a given string with their uppercase equivalents. Its syntax is UPPER(*s*). The following query illustrates the usage of this function:

```
select * from countries where upper(country_name) like '%U%S%A%';
```

This query extracts the rows from the COUNTRIES table where the COUNTRY_NAME values contain the letters *U*, *S*, and *A* (in any case) in that order.

The INITCAP Function

The INITCAP function converts a string of characters into capitalized case. It is often used for data presentation purposes. The first letters of each word in the string are converted to their uppercase equivalents, while the remaining letters of each word are converted to their lowercase equivalents. A word is usually a string of adjacent characters separated by a space or underscore, but other characters such as the percentage symbol, exclamation mark, or dollar sign are valid word separators. Punctuation or special characters are regarded as valid word separators.

The INITCAP function can take only one parameter. Its syntax is INITCAP(*s*). The following query illustrates the usage of this function:

```
select initcap('init cap or init_cap or init%cap') from dual
```

The query returns Init Cap Or Init_Cap Or Init%Cap.

Exercise 8-1: Use the Case Conversion Functions   Construct a query to retrieve a list of all FIRST_NAME and LAST_NAME values from the EMPLOYEES table where FIRST_NAME contains the character string li.

1. Start SQL Developer or SQL*Plus and connect to the HR schema.

2. The WHERE clause must compare the FIRST_NAME column values with a pattern of characters containing all possible case combinations of the string li. Therefore, if the FIRST_NAME contains the character strings LI, Li, lI, or li, that row must be retrieved.

3. The LIKE operator is used for character matching, and four combinations can be extracted with four WHERE clauses separated by the OR keyword. However, the case conversion functions can simplify the condition. If the LOWER function is used on the FIRST_NAME column, the comparison can be done with one WHERE clause condition. The UPPER or INITCAP functions could also be used.

4. Executing this statement returns employees' names containing the characters li:

```
select first_name, last_name from employees where lower(first_name)
like '%li%';
```

Using Character Manipulation Functions

The *character manipulation* functions are possibly some of the most powerful features to emerge from Oracle. Their usefulness in data manipulation is almost without peer, and many seasoned technical professionals whip together a quick script to massage data items using these functions. Nesting these functions is common. The concatenation operator (||) is generally used instead of the CONCAT function. The LENGTH, INSTR, SUBSTR, and REPLACE functions are often used together, as are RPAD, LPAD, and TRIM.

The CONCAT Function

The CONCAT function joins two character literals, columns, or expressions to yield one larger character expression. The CONCAT function takes two parameters. Its syntax is CONCAT(*s1*, *s2*), where *s1* and *s2* represent string literals, character column values, or expressions resulting in character values. The following query illustrates the usage of this function:

```
select concat('Today is:',SYSDATE) from dual;
```

The second parameter to the CONCAT function is SYSDATE, which returns the current system date. This value is implicitly converted to a string to which the literal in the first parameter is concatenated. If the system date is 17-DEC-2014, the query returns the string Today is:17-DEC-2014.

Consider using the CONCAT function to join three terms to return one character string. Since CONCAT takes only two parameters, it is only possible to join two terms with one instance of this function. One solution is to nest the CONCAT function within another CONCAT function, as shown here:

```
select concat('Outer1 ', concat('Inner1',' Inner2')) from dual;
```

The first CONCAT function has two parameters; the first is the literal Outer1, while the second is a nested CONCAT function. The second CONCAT function takes two parameters: the first is the literal Inner1, while the second is the literal Inner2. This query results in the following string: Outer1 Inner1 Inner2. Nested functions are described in a later section. The concatenation operator || discussed in Chapter 7 may also be used to join these terms.

The LENGTH Function

The LENGTH function returns the number of characters that constitute a character string. Blank spaces, tabs, and special characters are all counted by the LENGTH function. The LENGTH function takes only one string parameter. Its syntax is LENGTH(*s*). Consider the following query:

```
select * from countries where length(country_name) > 10;
```

The LENGTH function is used to extract the COUNTRY_NAME values with lengths greater than ten characters from the COUNTRIES table.

The LPAD and RPAD Functions

The LPAD and RPAD functions, also known as *left pad* and *right pad functions,* return a string padded with a specified number of characters to the left or right of a given string, respectively. The character strings used for padding include character literals, column values, expressions, blank spaces (the default), tabs, and special characters.

The LPAD and RPAD functions take three parameters. Their syntaxes are LPAD(s, n, p) and RPAD(s, n, p), where s represents the source string, n represents the final length of the string returned, and p specifies the character string to be used as padding. If LPAD is used, the padding characters p are added to the left of the source string s until it reaches length n. If RPAD is used, the padding characters p are added to the right of the source string s until it reaches length n. Note that if the parameter n is smaller than or equal to the length of the source string s, then no padding occurs and only the first n characters of s are returned. Consider the queries shown in Figure 8-1.

The first query does not pad the data, and the results are not as readable as the output from the second query. RPAD is used to add spaces where necessary to the concatenation of first_name and last_name until each name is 18 characters long, while LPAD adds spaces to the beginning of the salary value until each salary is 6 characters long.

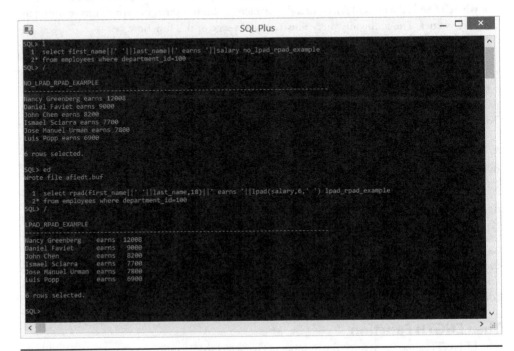

Figure 8-1   Using the LPAD and RPAD functions

The TRIM Function

The TRIM function removes characters from the beginning or end of character values to yield a potentially shorter item. The TRIM function takes a parameter made up of a mandatory component and an optional one. Its syntax is TRIM([*trailing*|*leading*|*both*] *trimstring* from *s*). The string to be trimmed (*s*) is mandatory. The following points list the rules governing the use of this function:

- TRIM(*s*) removes spaces from both sides of the input string.

- TRIM(trailing *trimstring* from *s*) removes all occurrences of *trimstring* from the end of string *s* if it is present.

- TRIM(leading *trimstring* from *s*) removes all occurrences of *trimstring* from the beginning of string *s* if it is present.

- TRIM(both *trimstring* from *s*) and TRIM(*trimstring* from *s*) remove all occurrences of *trimstring* from the beginning and end of string *s* if it is present.

  ```
  select trim(both '*' from '****Hidden****'),
  trim(leading '*' from '****Hidden****'),
  trim(trailing '*' from '****Hidden****') from dual;
  ```

The preceding query returns the strings Hidden, Hidden****, and ****Hidden. Note that although one trim character is specified, multiple occurrences will be trimmed if they are consecutively present.

The INSTR Function (In-String)

The INSTR function locates the position of a search string within a given string. It returns the numeric position at which the *n*th occurrence of the search string begins, relative to a specified start position. If the search string is not present, the INSTR function returns zero.

The INSTR function takes two optional and two mandatory parameters. The syntax is INSTR(*source string*, *search string*, [*search start position*], [*nth occurrence*]). The default value for the *search start position* is 1, or the beginning of the *source string*. The default value for the *nth* occurrence is 1, or the first occurrence. Consider the following queries:

```
Query 1: select instr('1#3#5#7#9#', '#') from dual;
Query 2: select instr('1#3#5#7#9#', '#' ,5) from dual;
Query 3: select instr('1#3#5#7#9#', '#', 3, 4) from dual;
```

Query 1 searches from the start of the source string for the first occurrence of the hash and returns position 2. Query 2 searches for the hash from position 5 and finds the next occurrence at position 6. Query 3 searches for the hash from position 3 and finds the fourth occurrence at position 10.

TIP   The INSTR function is often used in combination with the SUBSTR function in utility programs designed to extract encoded data from electronic data streams.

The SUBSTR Function (Substring)

The SUBSTR function extracts a substring of a specified length from the source string beginning at a given position. If the start position is larger than the length of the source string, null is returned. If the number of characters to extract from a given start position is greater than the length of the source string, the segment returned is the substring from the start position to the end of the string.

The SUBSTR function takes three parameters, with the first two being mandatory. Its syntax is SUBSTR(*source string, start position, [number of characters to extract]*). The default number of characters to extract is equal to the number of characters from the *start position* to the end of the *source string*. Consider the following queries:

```
Query 1: select substr('1#3#5#7#9#', 5) from dual;
Query 2: select substr('1#3#5#7#9#', 5, 3) from dual;
Query 3: select substr('1#3#5#7#9#', -3, 2) from dual;
```

Query 1 extracts the substring beginning at position 5. Since the third parameter is not specified, the default extraction length is equal to the number of characters from the start position to the end of the source string, which is 6. Accordingly, for query 1, the substring returned is 5#7#9#. Query 2 returns the three characters occupying positions 5–7, which form the substring 5#7. Query 3 starts at position –3. The negative start position parameter instructs Oracle to commence searching three characters from the end of the string. Therefore, the start position is three characters from the end of the string, which is position 8. The third parameter is 2, which results in the substring #9 being returned.

The REPLACE Function

The REPLACE function replaces all occurrences of a search item in a source string with a replacement term. If the length of the replacement term is different from that of the search item, then the lengths of the returned and source strings will be different. If the search string is not found, the source string is returned unchanged. The REPLACE function takes three parameters, with the first two being mandatory. Its syntax is REPLACE(*source string, search item, [replacement term]*). If the *replacement term* parameter is omitted, each occurrence of the *search item* is removed from the *source string*. In other words, the *search item* is replaced by an empty string. Consider the following queries:

```
Query 1: select replace('1#3#5#7#9#','#','->') from dual;
Query 2: select replace('1#3#5#7#9#','#') from dual;
```

The hash in query 1 is specified as the search character, and the replacement string is specified as ->. The hash symbol occurs five times in the source, and the resultant string is 1->3->5->7->9->. Query 2 does not specify a replacement string. The default behavior is therefore to replace the search string with an empty string; this, in effect, removes the search character completely from the source, resulting in the string 13579 being returned.

Using Numeric Functions

There is a range of built-in *numeric functions* provided by Oracle that rivals the mathematical toolboxes of popular spreadsheet packages. A significant differentiator between numeric and other functions is that they accept and return only numeric data. Oracle provides numeric functions for solving trigonometric, exponentiation, and logarithmic problems, among others. This guide focuses on three *numeric single-row functions*: ROUND, TRUNC, and MOD.

The Numeric ROUND Function

The ROUND function performs a rounding operation on a numeric value based on the decimal precision specified. The value returned is rounded either up or down, depending on the numeric value of the significant digit at the specified decimal precision position. If the specified decimal precision is n, the digit significant to the rounding is found $(n + 1)$ places to the RIGHT of the decimal point. If it is negative, the digit significant to the rounding is found n places to the LEFT of the decimal point. If the numeric value of the significant digit is greater than or equal to 5, a "round up" occurs; otherwise, a "round down" occurs.

The ROUND function takes two parameters. Its syntax is ROUND(*source number, decimal precision*). The source number parameter represents any numeric value. The decimal precision parameter specifies the degree of rounding and is optional. If the decimal precision parameter is absent, the default degree of rounding is zero, which means the source is rounded to the nearest whole number.

Consider the decimal degrees listed in Table 8-1 for the number 1601.916. The negative decimal precision values are located to the left of the decimal point, while the positive values are found to the right.

If the decimal precision parameter is one, then the source number is rounded to the nearest tenth. If it is two, then the source is rounded to the nearest hundredth, and so on. The following queries illustrate the usage of this function:

```
Query 1: select round(1601.916, 1) from dual;
Query 2: select round(1601.916, 2) from dual;
Query 3: select round(1601.916, -3) from dual;
Query 4: select round(1601.916) from dual;
```

Query 1 has a decimal precision parameter (n) of 1, which implies that the source number is rounded to the nearest tenth. Since the hundredths ($n + 1$) digit is 1 (less than 5), rounding down occurs, and the number returned is 1601.9. The decimal precision parameter in query 2 is 2, so the source number is rounded to the nearest hundredth. Since the thousandths unit is 6

Decimal Precision	Significant Rounding Digit for Number: 1601.916	Decimal Position
−4	1	Thousands ($n \times 1000$)
−3	6	Hundreds ($n \times 100$)
−2	0	Tens ($n \times 10$)
−1	1	Units ($n \times 1$)
1	9	Tenths ($n \div 10$)
2	1	Hundredths ($n \div 100$)
3	6	Thousandths ($n \div 1000$)

Table 8-1   Decimal Precision Descriptions

(greater than 5), rounding up occurs, and the number returned is 1601.92. The decimal precision parameter of the query 3 is –3. Since it is negative, the digit significant for rounding is found 3 places to the left of the decimal point, at the hundreds digit, which is 6. Since the hundreds unit is 6, rounding up occurs, and the number returned is 2000. Query 4 has dispensed with the decimal precision parameter. This implies that rounding is done to the nearest whole number. Since the tenth unit is 9, the number is rounded up, and 1602 is returned.

The Numeric TRUNC Function (Truncate)

The TRUNC function performs a truncation operation on a numeric value based on the decimal precision specified. A numeric truncation is different from rounding in that it drops the numbers beyond the decimal precision specified and does not attempt to round up or down if the decimal precision is positive. However, if the decimal precision (n) is negative, the input value is zeroed down from the nth decimal position.

The TRUNC function takes two parameters. Its syntax is TRUNC(*source number, decimal precision*). The source number represents any numeric value. The decimal precision specifies the degree of truncation and is optional. If the decimal precision parameter is absent, the default decimal precision is zero, which means the source number is truncated to an integer value.

If the decimal precision parameter is 1, then the source number is truncated at its tenths unit. If it is 2, it is truncated at its hundredths unit, and so on. The following queries illustrate the usage of this function:

```
Query 1: select trunc(1601.916, 1) from dual;
Query 2: select trunc(1601.916, 2) from dual;
Query 3: select trunc(1601.916, -3) from dual;
Query 4: select trunc(1601.916) from dual;
```

Query 1 has a decimal precision parameter of 1, which implies that the source number is truncated at its tenths unit, and the number returned is 1601.9. The decimal precision parameter (n) in query 2 is 2, so the source number is truncated at its hundredths unit, and the number returned is 1601.91. Note that this result would be different if a rounding operation were performed since the digit in position ($n + 1$) is 6 (greater than 5). Query 3 specifies a negative number (–3) as its decimal precision. Three places to the left of the decimal point implies that the truncation happens at the hundreds digit, as shown earlier in Table 8-1. Therefore, the source number is zeroed down from its hundreds digit (6), and the number returned is 1000. Finally, query 4 does not have a decimal precision parameter, implying that truncation is done at the whole-number degree of precision. The number returned is 1601.

The MOD Function (Modulus)

The MOD function returns the numeric remainder of a division operation. Two numbers, the dividend (number being divided) and the divisor (number to divide by), are provided, and a division operation is performed. If the divisor is a factor of the dividend, MOD returns zero since there is no remainder. If the divisor is zero, no division by zero error is returned, and the MOD function returns the dividend instead. If the divisor is larger than the dividend, then the MOD function returns the dividend as its result. This is because it divides zero times into the divisor, leaving the remainder equal to the dividend.

The MOD function takes two parameters. Its syntax is MOD(*dividend, divisor*). The *dividend* and *divisor* parameters represent a numeric literal, column, or expression, which may be negative or positive. The following queries illustrate the usage of this function:

```
Query 1: select mod(6, 2) from dual;
Query 2: select mod(5, 3) from dual;
Query 3: select mod(7, 35) from dual;
Query 4: select mod(5.2, 3) from dual;
```

Query 1 divides 6 by 2 perfectly, yielding 0 as the remainder. Query 2 divides 5 by 3, yielding 1 with remainder 2. Query 3 attempts to divide 7 by 35. Since the *divisor* is larger than the *dividend*, the number 7 is returned as the modulus value. Query 4 has a decimal fraction as the *dividend*. Dividing 5.2 by 3 yields 1 with remainder 2.2.

TIP　Any even number divided by 2 naturally has no remainder, but odd numbers divided by 2 always have a remainder of 1. Therefore, the MOD function is often used to distinguish between even and odd numbers.

Working with Dates

The *date* functions provide a convenient way to solve date-related problems without needing to keep track of leap years or the number of days in particular months. We first describe storage of dates and the default date format masks before examining the SYSDATE function. We then discuss date arithmetic and the *date manipulation functions*: ADD_MONTHS, MONTHS_BETWEEN, LAST_DAY, NEXT_DAY, ROUND, and TRUNC.

Date Storage in the Database

The database stores dates internally in a numeric format that supports the storage of century, year, month, and day details, as well as time information such as hours, minutes, and seconds. When accessing date information from a table, the default format of the results comprises two digits that represent the day, a three-letter abbreviation of the month, and two digits representing the year component. To avoid anomalies that arise with automatic type casting, the literal dates in the following queries have been converted to dates by a TO_DATE conversion function discussed later in this chapter. Exact results may vary due to NLS session parameter differences.

The SYSDATE Function

The SYSDATE function takes no parameters and returns the current system date and time according to the database server. If the database server is installed with AMERICAN as the default language, the SYSDATE function returns the DD-MON-RR components of the current server system date. If the database server is located in a different time zone from a client querying the database, the date and time returned by SYSDATE will differ from the local time on the client machine. Here is a query to retrieve the database server date:

```
select sysdate from dual;
```

Date Arithmetic

The following equation illustrates an important principle regarding *date arithmetic*:

$Date1 - Date2 = Num1$.

A date can be subtracted from another date. The difference between two date items represents the number of days between them. Any number, including fractions, may be added to or subtracted from a date item. In this context, the number represents a number of days. The sum or difference between a number and a date item always returns a date item. This principle implies that adding, multiplying, or dividing two date items is not permitted.

The MONTHS_BETWEEN Function

The MONTHS_BETWEEN function returns the number of months between two mandatory date parameters. Its syntax is MONTHS_BETWEEN(*date1, date2*). The function computes the difference in 31-day months between *date1* and *date2*. If *date1* occurs before *date2*, a negative number is returned. The difference between the two date parameters may consist of a whole number that represents the number of months between the two dates and a fractional component that represents the days and time remaining (based on a 31-day month) after the integer difference between years and months is calculated. A whole number with no fractional part is returned if the day components of the dates being compared are either the same or the last day of their respective months.

The following query illustrates the MONTHS_BETWEEN function:

```
select months_between(sysdate, sysdate-31) from dual;
```

Assume that the current date is 16-APR-2009. This query returns 1 as the number of months between 16-APR-2009 and 16-MAR-2009.

 EXAM TIP A common mistake is to assume that the return data type of single-row functions is the same as the category the function belongs to. This is true only of the numeric functions. Character and date functions can return values of any data type. For example, the INSTR character function and the MONTHS_BETWEEN date function both return a number. It is also common to erroneously assume that the difference between two dates is a date, when in fact it is a number.

The ADD_MONTHS Function

The ADD_MONTHS function returns a date item calculated by adding a specified number of months to a given date value. The ADD_MONTHS function takes two mandatory parameters. Its syntax is ADD_MONTHS(*start date, number of months*). The function computes the target date after adding the specified number of months to the *start date*. The number of months may be negative, resulting in a target date earlier than the start date being returned. The number of months may be fractional, but the fractional component is ignored, and the integer component is used. These three queries illustrate the ADD_MONTHS function:

```
Query 1: select add_months(to_date('07-APR-2009','DD-MON-YYYY'), 1) from dual;
Query 2: select add_months(to_date('31-DEC-2008','DD-MON-YYYY'), 2.5) from dual;
Query 3: select add_months(to_date('07-APR-2009','DD-MON-YYYY'), -12) from dual;
```

Query 1 returns 07-MAY-2009, since the day component remains the same if possible and the month is incremented by one. The second query has two interesting dimensions. The parameter specifying the number of months to add contains a fractional component, which is ignored. Adding two months to the date 31-DEC-2008 should return the date 31-FEB-2009, but there is no such date, so the last day of the month, 28-FEB-2009, is returned. Since the number of months added in the third query is –12, the date 07-APR-2008 is returned, which is 12 months prior to the start date.

The NEXT_DAY Function

The NEXT_DAY function returns the date when the next occurrence of a specified day of the week occurs. It takes two mandatory parameters and has the syntax NEXT_DAY(*start date, day of the week*). The function computes the date on which the *day of the week* parameter next occurs after the *start date*. The *day of the week* parameter must be a valid character value as determined by the NLS_DATE_LANGUAGE session parameter. For NLS_DATE_LANGUAGE=AMERICAN, the default values are at least the first three characters of the day name. The character values representing the days of the week may be specified in any case. The short name may be longer than three characters; for example, Sunday may be referenced as sun, sund, sunda, or Sunday. Consider the following queries:

```
Query 1: select next_day(to_date('01-JAN-2009','DD-MON-YYYY'), 'tue') from dual;
Query 2: select next_day(to_date('01-JAN-2009','DD-MON-YYYY'), 'WEDNE') from dual;
```

Here, 01-JAN-2009 is a Thursday. Therefore, the next time a Tuesday occurs will be five days later, on 06-JAN-2009. The second query specifies the character literal WEDNE, which is interpreted as Wednesday. The next Wednesday after 01-JAN-2009 is 07-JAN-2009.

The LAST_DAY Function

The LAST_DAY function returns the date of the last day in the month to which the given day belongs. It takes a single mandatory parameter and has the syntax LAST_DAY(*start date*). The function extracts the month that the *start date* parameter belongs to and calculates the date of the last day of that month. The following query returns the date 31-JAN-2009:

```
select last_day(to_date('01-JAN-2009','DD-MON-YYYY')) from dual;
```

The Date ROUND Function

The date ROUND function performs a rounding operation on a value based on a specified date precision format. The value returned is rounded either up or down to the nearest date precision format. This function takes one mandatory parameter and one optional parameter and has the syntax ROUND(*source date, [date precision format]*). The *source date* parameter represents any date item. The *date precision format* parameter specifies the degree of rounding and is optional. If it is absent, the default degree of rounding is *day*. The *date precision formats* include *century* (CC), *year* (YYYY), *quarter* (Q), *month* (MM), *week* (W), *day* (DD), *hour* (HH), and *minute* (MI).

Rounding up to *century* is equivalent to adding one to the current century. Rounding up to the next month occurs if the *day* component is greater than 16, or else rounding down to the beginning of the current month occurs. If the month falls between one and six, then rounding to *year* returns the date at the beginning of the current year; if not, it returns the date at the beginning of the following year. Consider the following query and its results:

```
SQL> select round(sysdate) day, round(sysdate,'w') week,
  2         round(sysdate,'month') month, round(sysdate,'year') year
  3  from dual;

DAY        WEEK       MONTH      YEAR
---------  ---------  ---------  ---------
17-APR-09  15-APR-09  01-MAY-09  01-JAN-09
```

Assume this query was run on 17-APR-2009 at 00:05. The first item rounds the date to the nearest day. Since the time is 00:05, which is after midnight, the date is not rounded up. The second item rounds the date to the same day of the week as the first day of the month. Since 01-APR-2009 is a Wednesday, the date returned is the Wednesday of the week in which this date occurs. Remember that, by default, the first day of the week is a Sunday. Therefore, the first Wednesday in the week beginning 12-APR-2009 is 15-APR-2009. The third item rounds the date to the beginning of the following month since the day component is 17 and returns 01-MAY-2009. The fourth item is rounded up to the date at the beginning of the current year since the month component is 4, and 01-JAN-2009 is returned.

The Date TRUNC Function

The date TRUNC function performs a truncation operation on a date value based on a specified date precision format.

The date TRUNC function takes one mandatory parameter and one optional parameter. Its syntax is TRUNC(*source date*, [*date precision format*]). The *source date* parameter represents any date item. The *date precision format* parameter specifies the degree of truncation and is optional. If it is absent, the default degree of truncation is *day*. This means that any time component of the *source date* is set to midnight or 00:00:00 (00 hours, 00 minutes, and 00 seconds). Truncating at the month level sets the date of the *source date* to the first day of the month. Truncating at the year level returns the date at the beginning of the current year. The following query and results show four items in the SELECT list, each truncating a date literal to a different degree of precision:

```
SQL> select trunc(sysdate) day, trunc(sysdate,'w') week,
  2         trunc(sysdate,'month') month, trunc(sysdate,'year') year
  3  from dual;

DAY        WEEK       MONTH      YEAR
---------  ---------  ---------  ---------
17-APR-09  15-APR-09  01-APR-09  01-JAN-09
```

Assume this query was run on 17-APR-2009 at 12:05 A.M. The first item sets the time component of 00:05 to 00:00 and returns the current day. The second item truncates the date to the same day of the week as the first day of the month (Wednesday) and returns the Wednesday in its week: 15-APR-2009. The third item truncates the date to the beginning of the current month and returns 01-APR-2009. The fourth item truncates the date to the beginning of the current year and returns 01-JAN-2009.

Exercise 8-2: Use the Character Manipulation Functions   Connect to the OE schema and construct a query that extracts the unique e-mail hostname from the CUSTOMERS .CUST_EMAIL column.

1. Start SQL Developer and connect to the OE schema.

2. A typical CUSTOMERS.CUST_EMAIL entry looks as follows:

   firstname.lastname@hostname.EXAMPLE.COM. The hostname begins immediately after the @ symbol and ends before the EXAMPLE.COM. The SUBSTR function may be used to extract this value. However, the start position and the length are still unknown. The INSTR function may be used to locate the position of the first occurrence of the @ symbol and the characters EXAMPLE.COM.

3. A possible solution is as follows:

```
select distinct substr(cust_email, instr(cust_email,'@')+1,
instr(cust_email, '.EXAMPLE.COM')-instr(cust_email,'@')-1)
hostname from customers;
```

Describe Various Types of Conversion Functions Available in SQL

SQL conversion *functions* are single-row functions designed to alter the nature of the data type of a column value, expression, or literal. *TO_CHAR, TO_NUMBER,* and *TO_DATE* are the three most widely used conversion functions. TO_CHAR converts numeric and date information into characters, while TO_NUMBER and TO_DATE convert character data into numbers and dates, respectively.

Conversion Functions

Oracle allows columns to be defined with ANSI, DB2, and SQL/DS data types. These are converted internally to Oracle data types. Each column has an associated data type that constrains the nature of the data it can store. A NUMBER column cannot store character information. A DATE column cannot store random characters or numbers. However, the character equivalents of both number and date information can be stored in a VARCHAR2 field.

If a function that accepts a character input parameter finds a number instead, Oracle automatically converts it into its character equivalent. If a function that accepts a number or a date parameter encounters a character value, there are specific conditions under which automatic data type conversion occurs. Although implicit data type conversions are available, it is generally more reliable to explicitly convert values from one data type to another using single-row conversion functions.

Implicit Data Type Conversion

Values that do not share identical data types with function parameters are *implicitly converted* to the required format if possible. VARCHAR2 and CHAR data types are collectively referred to as character types. Character fields are flexible and allow the storage of almost any type of information. Therefore, DATE and NUMBER values can easily be converted to their character equivalents. These conversions are known as *number to character* and *date to character* conversions. Consider the following queries:

```
Query 1: select length(1234567890) from dual;
Query 2: select length(SYSDATE) from dual;
```

Both queries use the LENGTH function, which takes a character string parameter. The number 1234567890 in query 1 is implicitly converted into a character string, '1234567890', before being evaluated by the LENGTH function, which returns 10. Query 2 first evaluates the SYSDATE function, which is assumed to be 07-APR-38. This date is implicitly converted into the character string '07-APR-38', and the LENGTH function returns the number 9.

It is uncommon for character data to be implicitly converted into numeric data types, since the only condition under which this can occur is if the character data represents a valid number. The character string '11' will be implicitly converted to a number, but '11.123.456' will not be, as the following queries demonstrate:

```
Query 3: select mod('11', 2) from dual;
Query 4: select mod('11.123', 2) from dual;
Query 5: select mod('11.123.456', 2) from dual;
Query 6: select mod('$11', 2) from dual;
```

Queries 3 and 4 implicitly convert the character strings '11' and '11.123' into the numbers 11 and 11.123, respectively, before the MOD function evaluates them and returns the results 1 and 1.123. Query 5 returns the error "ORA-1722: invalid number" when Oracle tries to perform an implicit *character to number* conversion because the string '11.123.456' is not a valid number. Query 6 also fails with the invalid number error since the dollar symbol cannot be implicitly converted into a number.

Implicit *character to date* conversion is possible when the character string conforms to the following date patterns: [D|DD] *separator1* [MON|MONTH] *separator2* [R|RR|YY|YYYY]. D and DD represent single-digit and two-digit days of the month. MON is a three-character abbreviation, while MONTH is the full name for a month. R and RR represent single- and two-digit years. YY and YYYY represent two- and four-digit years, respectively. The *separator1* and *separator2* elements may be most punctuation marks, spaces, and tabs. Table 8-2 demonstrates

Function Call	Format	Results
`add_months('24-JAN-09', 1)`	DD-MON-RR	24/FEB/09
`add_months('1\january/8'', 1)`	D\MONTH/R	01/FEB/08
`months_between('13*jan*8', '13/feb/2008')`	DD*MON*R, DD/MON/YYYY	−1
`add_months('01$jan/08', 1)`	DD$MON/RR	01/FEB/08
`add_months('13!jana08', 1)`	JANA is an invalid month	ORA-1841: (full) year must be between − 4713 and +9999 and not be 0
`add_months('24-JAN-09 18:45', 1)`	DD-MON-RR HH24:MI	ORA-1830: date format picture ends before converting entire input string

Table 8-2   Examples of Implicit Character to Date Conversion

implicit character to date conversion, listing several function calls and the results SQL Developer returns. These results assume that your system makes use of the American session defaults.

CAUTION Although implicit data type conversions are available, it is more reliable to convert values explicitly from one data type to another using single-row conversion functions. Converting character information to NUMBER and DATE relies on format masks.

Explicit Data Type Conversion

Functions that convert items from one data type to another are known as *explicit* data type conversion functions. These return a value guaranteed to be the type required and offer a safe and reliable method of converting data items.

NUMBER and DATE items can be converted explicitly into character items using the TO_CHAR function. A character string can be explicitly changed into a NUMBER using the TO_NUMBER function. The TO_DATE function is used to convert character strings into DATE items. Oracle's format masks enable a wide range of control over character-to-number and character-to-date conversions.

EXAM TIP Your understanding of commonly used format models or masks will be practically tested with questions like "Predict the result of a function call such as TO_CHAR(TO_DATE('01-JAN-00','DD-MON-RR'),'Day')."

Use the TO_CHAR, TO_NUMBER, and TO_DATE Conversion Functions

This certification objective contains a systematic description of the TO_NUMBER, TO_DATE, and TO_CHAR functions, with examples. The discussion of TO_CHAR is divided into the conversion of date items to characters and numbers to characters. This separation is warranted by the availability of different format masks for controlling conversion to character values. These conversion functions exist alongside many others but are the most widely used.

Using the Conversion Functions

Many situations demand the use of conversion functions. They may range from formatting DATE fields in a report to ensuring that numeric digits extracted from character fields are correctly converted into numbers before applying them in an arithmetic expression.

Table 8-3 illustrates the syntax of the single-row explicit data type conversion functions.

`TO_NUMBER(char1, [format mask], [nls_parameters]) = num1`	`TO_CHAR(num1, [format mask], [nls_parameters]) = char1`
`TO_DATE(char1, [format mask], [nls_parameters]) = date1`	`TO_CHAR(date1, [format mask], [nls_parameters]) = char1`

Table 8-3 Syntax of Explicit Data Type Conversion Functions

Optional national language support (NLS) parameters (nls_parameters) are useful for specifying the language and format in which the names of date and numeric elements are returned. These parameters are usually absent, and the default values for elements such as day or month names and abbreviations are used. As Figure 8-2 shows, there is a publicly available view called NLS_ SESSION_PARAMETERS that contains the NLS parameters for your current session. The default NLS_CURRENCY value is the dollar symbol, but this can be changed at the user session level. For example, to change the currency to the three-character string GBP, you can issue the following command:

```
ALTER SESSION set NLS_CURRENCY='GBP';
```

Converting Numbers to Characters Using the TO_CHAR Function

The TO_CHAR function returns an item of data type VARCHAR2. When applied to items of type NUMBER, several formatting options are available. Its syntax is as follows:

```
TO_CHAR(num, [format], [nls_parameter])
```

Figure 8-2 National language support session parameters

The *num* parameter is mandatory and must be a numeric value. The optional *format* parameter may be used to specify numeric formatting information such as width, currency symbol, position of a decimal point, and group (or thousands) separators and must be enclosed in single quotation marks. There are other formatting options for numbers being converted into characters, some of which are listed in Table 8-4. Consider the following two queries:

```
Query 1: select to_char(00001)||' is a special number' from dual;
Query 2: select to_char(00001, '0999999')||' is a special number' from dual;
```

Query 1 evaluates the number 00001, removes the leading zeros, converts the number 1 into the character '1', and returns the character string '1 is a special number'. Query 2 applies the numeric format mask '0999999' to the number 00001, converting it into the character

Format Element	Description of Element	Format	Number	Character Result
9	Numeric width	9999	12	12
0	Displays leading zeros	09999	0012	00012
.	Position of decimal point	09999.999	030.40	00030.400
D	Decimal separator position (period is default)	09999D999	030.40	00030.400
,	Position of comma symbol	09999,999	03040	00003,040
G	Group separator position (comma is default)	09999G999	03040	00003,040
$	Dollar sign	$099999	03040	$003040
L	Local currency	L099999	03040	GBP003040 if nls_currency is set to GBP
MI	Position of minus sign for negatives	99999MI	-3040	3040-
PR	Wrap negatives in parentheses	99999PR	-3040	<3040>
EEEE	Scientific notation	99.99999EEEE	121.976	1.21976E+02
U	nls_dual_currency	U099999	03040	CAD003040 if nls_dual_currency is set to CAD
V	Multiplies by 10n times (n is the number of nines after V)	9999V99	3040	304000
S	+ or – sign is prefixed	S999999	3040	+3040

Table 8-4   Numeric Format Masks

string '0000001'. After concatenation to the character literals, the string returned is '0000001 is a special number'. The zero and the six nines in the format mask indicate to the TO_CHAR function that leading zeros must be displayed and that the display width must be set to seven characters. Therefore, the string returned by the TO_CHAR function contains seven characters.

TIP   Converting numbers into characters is a reliable way to ensure that functions and general SQL syntax, which expects character input, do not return errors when numbers are encountered. Converting numbers into character strings is common when numeric data must be formatted for reporting purposes. The format masks that support currency, thousands separators, and decimal point separators are frequently used when presenting financial data.

Converting Dates to Characters Using the TO_CHAR Function

You can take advantage of a variety of format models to convert DATE items into almost any character representation of a date using TO_CHAR. Its syntax is as follows:

```
TO_CHAR(date1, [format], [nls_parameter])
```

Only the *date1* parameter is mandatory; it must take the form of a value that can be implicitly converted to a date. The optional *format* parameter is case sensitive and must be enclosed in single quotes. The format mask specifies which date elements are extracted and whether the element should be described by a long or an abbreviated name. The names of days and months are automatically padded with spaces. These may be removed using a modifier to the format mask called the fill mode (*fm*) operator. By prefixing the format model with the letters *fm*, you instruct Oracle to trim all spaces from the names of days and months. There are many formatting options for dates being converted into characters, some of which are listed in Table 8-5. Consider the following three queries:

```
Query 1: select to_char(sysdate)||' is today''s date' from dual;
Query 2: select to_char(sysdate,'Month')||'is a special time' from dual;
Query 3: select to_char(sysdate,'fmMonth')||'is a special time' from dual;
```

If the current system date is 03/JAN/09 and the default display format is DD/MON/RR, then query 1 returns the character string '03/JAN/09 is today's date'. There are two notable components in query 2. First, only the month component of the current system date is extracted for conversion to a character type. Second, since the format mask is case sensitive and 'Month' appears in title case, the string returned is 'January is a special time'. There is no need to add a space in front of the literal 'is a special time', since the TO_CHAR function automatically pads the name of the month with a space. If the format mask in query 2 was 'MONTH', the string returned would be 'JANUARY is a special time'. The *fm* modifier is applied to query 3, and the resultant string is 'Januaryis a special time'. Note there is no space between January and the literal 'is a special time'. In Table 8-5, assume the elements are operating on the date 02-JUN-1975 and the current year is 2009.

The date format elements pertaining to weeks, quarters, centuries, and other less commonly used format masks are listed in Table 8-6. The result column is obtained by evaluating the

Format Element	Description	Result
Y	Last digit of year	5
YY	Last two digits of year	75
YYY	Last three digits of year	975
YYYY	Four-digit year	1975
RR	Two-digit century-aware year	75
YEAR, year, Year	Case-sensitive English spelling of year	NINETEEN SEVENTY FIVE, nineteen seventy five, Nineteen Seventy Five
MM	Two-digit month	06
MON, mon, Mon	Three-letter abbreviation of month	JUN, jun, Jun
MONTH, month, Month	Case-sensitive English spelling of month	JUNE, june, June
D	Day of the week	2
DD	Two-digit day of month	02
DDD	Day of the year	153
DY, dy, Dy	Three-letter abbreviation of day	MON, mon, Mon
DAY, day, Day	Case-sensitive English spelling of day	MONDAY, monday, Monday

Table 8-5   Date Format Masks for Days, Months, and Years

Format Element	Description	Result
W	Week of month	4
WW	Week of year	39
Q	Quarter of year	3
CC	Century	10
S preceding CC, YYYY, or YEAR	If date is BC, a minus is prefixed to result	–10, –1000, or –ONE THOUSAND
IYYY, IYY, IY, I	ISO dates of four, three, two, and one digit, respectively	1000, 000, 00, 0
BC, AD, B.C. and A.D.	BC or AD and period-spaced B.C. or A.D.	BC
J	Julian day—days since 31 December 4713 BC	1356075
IW	ISO standard week (1 to 53)	39
RM	Roman numeral month	IX

Table 8-6   Less Commonly Used Date Format Masks

Format Element	Description	Result
AM, PM, A.M., and P.M.	Meridian indicators	PM
HH, HH12, and HH24	Hour of day, 1–12 hours, and 0–23 hours	09, 09, 21
MI	Minute (0–59)	35
SS	Second (0–59)	13
SSSSS	Seconds past midnight (0–86399)	77713

Table 8-7 Date Format Mask for Time Components

TO_CHAR function using the date 24-SEP-1000 BC, with the format mask from the format element column in the table.

The time component of a date time data type is extracted using the format models in Table 8-7. The result is obtained by evaluating the TO_CHAR function using the date, including its time component 27-JUN-2010 21:35:13, with the format mask in the Format Element column in Table 8-7.

Table 8-8 lists several miscellaneous elements that may be used in date time format models. Punctuation marks are used to separate format elements. Three types of suffixes exist to format components of date time elements. Furthermore, character literals may be included in a date format model if they are enclosed in double quotation marks. The results in Table 8-8 are obtained by applying the TO_CHAR function using the date 12/SEP/08 14:31 with the format masks listed in the Description and Format Mask column.

The JOB_HISTORY table keeps track of jobs occupied by employees in the company. The query in Figure 8-3 retrieves a descriptive sentence about the quitting date for each employee based on their END_DATE, EMPLOYEE_ID, and JOB_ID fields. A character expression is concatenated to a TO_CHAR function call with a format model of 'fmDay "the" ddth "of" Month YYYY'. The *fm* modifier is used to trim blank spaces that trail the names of the shorter days and shorter months. The two character literals enclosed in double quotation marks are the words "the" and "of". The 'th' format model is applied to the 'dd' date element to create an ordinal day such as the 17th or 31st. The 'Month' format model displays the full name of the month element of the END_DATE column in title case. Finally, the YYYY format mask retrieves the four-digit year component.

Format Element	Description and Format Mask	Result
− / . , ? # !	Punctuation marks: 'MM.YY'	09.08
"any character literal"	Character literals: '"Week" W "of" Month'	Week 2 of September
TH	Positional or ordinal text: 'DDth "of" Month'	12TH of September
SP	Spelled-out number: 'MmSP Month Yyyysp'	Nine September Two Thousand Eight
THSP or SPTH	Spelled-out positional or ordinal number: 'hh24SpTh'	Fourteenth

Table 8-8 Miscellaneous Date Format Masks

Figure 8-3   TO_CHAR function with dates

Although the century component of a date is not displayed by default, it is stored in the database when the date value is inserted or updated and is available for retrieval. The DD-MON-RR format mask is the default for display and input. When inserting or updating date values, the century component is obtained from the SYSDATE function if it is not supplied. The RR date format mask differs from the YY format mask in that it may be used to specify different centuries based on the current and specified years. The century component assigned to a date with its year specified with the RR date format may be better understood by considering the following principles:

- If the two digits of the current year and the specified year lie between 0 and 49, the current century is returned. Suppose the present date is 02-JUN-2007. The century returned for the date 24-JUL-04 in DD-MON-RR format is 20.

- If the two digits of the current year lie between 0 and 49 and the specified year falls between 50 and 99, the previous century is returned. Suppose the current date is 02-JUN-2007. The century returned for 24-JUL-94 is 19.

- If the two digits of the current and specified years lie between 50 and 99, the current century is returned by default. Suppose the current date is 02-JUN-1975; the century returned for 24-JUL-94 is 19.

- If the two digits of the current year lie between 50 and 99 and the specified year falls between 0 and 49, the next century is returned. Suppose the current date is 02-JUN-1975; the century returned for 24-JUL-07 is 20.

Converting Characters to Dates Using the TO_DATE Function

The TO_DATE function returns an item of type DATE. Character strings converted to dates may contain all or just a subset of the date time elements composing a DATE. When strings with only a subset of the date time elements are converted, Oracle provides default values to construct a complete date. Components of character strings are associated with different date time elements using a format model or mask. Its syntax is as follows:

```
TO_DATE(string1, [format], [nls_parameter])
```

Only *string1* is mandatory, and if no format mask is supplied, *string1* must be implicitly convertible into a date. The optional *format* parameter is almost always used and is specified in single quotation marks. The format masks are identical to those listed in Tables 8-5, 8-6, and 8-7. The TO_DATE function has an *fx* modifier, which is similar to *fm* used with the TO_CHAR function. The *fx* modifier specifies an exact match for *string1* and the format mask. When the *fx* modifier is specified, character items that do not exactly match the format mask yield an error. Consider the following five queries:

```
Query 1: select to_date('25-DEC-2010') from dual;
Query 2: select to_date('25-DEC') from dual;
Query 3: select to_date('25-DEC', 'DD-MON') from dual;
Query 4: select to_date('25-DEC-2010 18:03:45', 'DD-MON-YYYY
HH24:MI:SS') from dual;
Query 5: select to_date('25-DEC-10', 'fxDD-MON-YYYY') from dual;
```

Query 1 evaluates the string 25-DEC-2010 and has sufficient information to convert it implicitly into a DATE item with a default mask of DD-MON-YYYY. The hyphen separator could be substituted with another punctuation character. Since no time components are provided, the time for this converted date is set to midnight, or 00:00:00. Query 2 cannot implicitly convert the string into a date because there is insufficient information and an ORA-01840: input value is not long enough for the date format; an error is returned. By supplying a format mask DD-MON to the string 25-DEC in query 3, Oracle can match the number 25 to DD and the abbreviated month name DEC to the MON component. Year and time components are absent, so the current year returned by the SYSDATE function is used and the time is set to midnight. If the current year is 2009, query 3 returns the date 25/DEC/09 00:00:00. Query 4 performs a complete conversion of a string with all the date time elements present, and no default values are supplied by Oracle. Query 5 uses the *fx* modifier in its format mask. Since the year component of the string is

10 and the corresponding format mask is YYYY, the *fx* modifier results in an ORA-01862 error being returned: "the numeric value does not match the length of the format item."

Converting Characters to Numbers Using the TO_NUMBER Function

The TO_NUMBER function returns an item of type NUMBER. Character strings converted into numbers must be suitably formatted so that any nonnumeric components are translated or stripped away with an appropriate format mask. The syntax is as follows:

```
TO_NUMBER(string1, [format], [nls_parameter])
```

Only the *string1* parameter is mandatory and if no *format* mask is supplied, it must be a value that can be implicitly converted into a number. The optional *format* parameter is specified in single quotation marks. The format masks are identical to those listed in Table 8-4. Consider the following two queries:

```
Query 1: select to_number('$1,000.55') from dual;
Query 2: select to_number('$1,000.55','$999,999.99') from dual;
```

Query 1 cannot perform an implicit conversion to a number because of the dollar sign, comma, and period; it returns the error ORA-1722: invalid number. Query 2 matches the dollar symbol, comma, and period from the string to the format mask, and although the numeric width is larger than the string width, the number 1000.55 is returned.

 EXAM TIP   The TO_NUMBER function converts character items into numbers. If you convert a number using a shorter format mask, an error is returned. If you convert a number using a longer format mask, the original number is returned. Be careful not to confuse TO_NUMBER conversions with TO_CHAR. For example, TO_NUMBER(123.56,'999.9') returns an error, while TO_CHAR(123.56,'999.9') returns 123.6.

Apply Conditional Expressions in a SELECT Statement

Nested functions were introduced earlier, but we offer you a formal discussion of this concept in this section. We also describe conditional functions that work with NULL values and support conditional logic in expressions.

Nested Functions

Nested functions use the output from one function as the input to another. Functions always return exactly one result. Therefore, you can reliably consider a function call in the same way as you would a literal value when providing input parameters to a function. Single-row functions can be nested to any level of depth. The general form of a function is as follows:

```
Function1(parameter1, parameter2,...) = result1
```

Substituting function calls as parameters to other functions may lead to an expression such as the following:

```
F1( param1.1, F2( param2.1, param2.2, F3( param3.1)), param1.3)
```

Nested functions are first evaluated before their return values are used as parametric input to other functions. They are evaluated from the innermost to outermost levels. The preceding expression is evaluated as follows:

1. F3(*param3.1*) is evaluated, and its return value provides the third parameter to function F2 and may be called *param2.3*.

2. F2(*param2.1, param2.2, param2.3*) is evaluated, and its return value provides the second parameter to function F1 and is *param1.2*.

3. F1(*param1.1, param1.2, param1.3*) is evaluated, and the result is returned to the calling program.

Function F3 is nested three levels deep in this example.

Consider the following query:

```
select next_day(last_day(sysdate)-7, 'tue') from dual;
```

There are three functions in the SELECT list, which, from inner to outer levels, are SYSDATE, LAST_DAY, and NEXT_DAY. The query is evaluated as follows:

1. The innermost function is evaluated first. SYSDATE returns the current date. Assume that today's date is 28-OCT-2009.

2. The second innermost function is evaluated next. LAST_DAY('28-OCT-2009') returns the date of the last day in October, which is 31-OCT-2009.

Finally, the NEXT_DAY('24-OCT-2009', 'tue') function is evaluated, and the query returns the number of the last Tuesday of the month, which in this example is 27-OCT-2009.

 TIP It is tempting to dive in and construct a complex expression comprising many nested function calls, but this approach evolves with practice and experience. Conceptualize a solution to a query and break it down into the component function calls. The DUAL table is useful for ad hoc testing and debugging of separate function calls. Test and debug smaller components and iteratively assemble these until the final expression is formed.

Conditional Functions

Conditional logic, also known as *if-then-else* logic, refers to choosing a path of execution based on data values meeting certain conditions. *Conditional functions* return different values based on evaluating comparison conditions. Functions within this category simplify working with null values and include the *NVL, NVL2, NULLIF,* and *COALESCE* functions. Generic conditional logic is implemented by the DECODE function and the CASE expression. The DECODE function is specific to Oracle, while the CASE expression is ANSI SQL compliant.

The NVL Function

The NVL function evaluates whether a column or expression of any data type is null. If the term is null, it returns an alternative not-null value; otherwise, the original term is returned.

The NVL function takes two mandatory parameters; its syntax is *NVL(original, ifnull)*, where *original* represents the term being tested and *ifnull* is the result returned if the *original* term evaluates to null. The data types of the *original* and *ifnull* parameters must always be compatible. Either they must be of the same type or it must be possible to implicitly convert *ifnull* to the type of the *original* parameter. The NVL function returns a value with the same data type as the *original* parameter. Consider the following three queries:

```
Query 1: select nvl(1234) from dual;
Query 2: select nvl(null, 1234) from dual;
Query 3: select nvl(substr('abc', 4), 'No substring exists') from dual;
```

Since the NVL function takes two mandatory parameters, query 1 returns the error ORA-00909: invalid number of arguments. Query 2 returns 1234 after the null keyword is tested and found to be null. Query 3 involves a nested SUBSTR function that attempts to extract the fourth character from a three-character string that returns null, leaving the outer function NVL(null,'No substring exists') to execute, which then returns the string 'No substring exists'.

 TIP The NVL function is invaluable for converting null numeric values to zero so that arithmetic on them doesn't return null.

The NVL2 Function

The NVL2 function provides an enhancement to NVL but serves a similar purpose. It evaluates whether a column or expression of any data type is null or not. If the first term is not null, the second parameter is returned, or else the third parameter is returned. Recall that the NVL function is different since it returns the original term if it is not null.

The NVL2 function takes three mandatory parameters with the syntax NVL2(*original, ifnotnull, ifnull*), where *original* represents the term being tested. *ifnotnull* is returned if *original* is not null, and *ifnull* is returned if *original* is null. The data types of the *ifnotnull* and *ifnull* parameters must be compatible, and they cannot be of type LONG. Either they must be of the same type or it must be possible to convert *ifnull* to the type of the *ifnotnull* parameter. The data type returned by the NVL2 function is the same as that of the *ifnotnull* parameter. Consider the following queries:

```
Query 1: select nvl2(1234, 1, 'a string') from dual;
Query 2: select nvl2(null, 1234, 5678) from dual;
Query 3: select nvl2(substr('abc', 2), 'Not bc', 'No substring') from dual;
```

The *ifnotnull* term in query 1 is a number, and the *ifnull* parameter is a string. Since there is a data type incompatibility between them, an "ORA-01722: invalid number" error is returned. Query 2 returns the *ifnull* parameter, which is 5678. Query 3 extracts the characters bc using the SUBSTR function and the NVL2('bc','Not bc','No Substring') function is evaluated and the *ifnotnull* parameter, 'Not bc', is returned.

The NULLIF Function

The NULLIF function tests two terms for equality. If they are equal, the function returns a null, or else it returns the first of the two terms tested.

The NULLIF function takes two mandatory parameters of any data type. Its syntax is NULLIF(*ifunequal, comparison_term*), where the parameters *ifunequal* and *comparison_term* are compared. If they are identical, then NULL is returned. If they differ, the *ifunequal* parameter is returned. Consider the following queries:

```
Query 1: select nullif(1234, 1234) from dual;
Query 2: select nullif('24-JUL-2009', '24-JUL-09') from dual;
```

Query 1 returns a null since the parameters are identical. The character literals in query 2 are not implicitly converted to DATE items and are compared as two character strings by the NULLIF function. Since the strings are of different lengths, the *ifunequal* parameter 24-JUL-2009 is returned.

Figure 8-4 shows how NULLIF is nested as a parameter to the NVL2 function. The NULLIF function itself has the SUBSTR and UPPER character functions embedded in the expression used as its *ifunequal* parameter. The EMAIL column is compared with an expression, formed by concatenating the first character of the FIRST_NAME to the uppercase equivalent of the LAST_NAME column, for employees with four-character first names. When these terms are equal, NULLIF returns a null, or else it returns the evaluated *ifunequal* parameter. This is used as a parameter to NVL2. The NVL2 function provides descriptive text classifying rows as matching the pattern or not.

The COALESCE Function

The COALESCE function returns the first not-null value from its parameter list. If all its parameters are null, then null is returned.

The COALESCE function takes two mandatory parameters and any number of optional parameters. The syntax is COALESCE(*expr1, expr2, . . . , exprn*), where *expr1* is returned if it is not null, else *expr2* if it is not null, and so on. COALESCE is a general form of the NVL function, as the following two equations illustrate:

```
COALESCE(expr1, expr2) = NVL(expr1, expr2)
COALESCE(expr1,expr2,expr3) = NVL(expr1,NVL(expr2,expr3))
```

The data type returned by COALESCE, if a not-null value is found, is the same as that of the first not-null parameter. To avoid an "ORA-00932: inconsistent data types" error, all not-null parameters must have data types compatible with the first not-null parameter. Consider the following three queries:

```
Query 1: select coalesce(null, null, null, 'a string') from dual;
Query 2: select coalesce(null, null, null) from dual;
Query 3: select coalesce(substr('abc', 4), 'Not bc', 'No
substring') from dual;
```

Query 1 returns the fourth parameter, which is a string since this is the first not-null parameter encountered. Query 2 returns null because all its parameters are null. Query 3

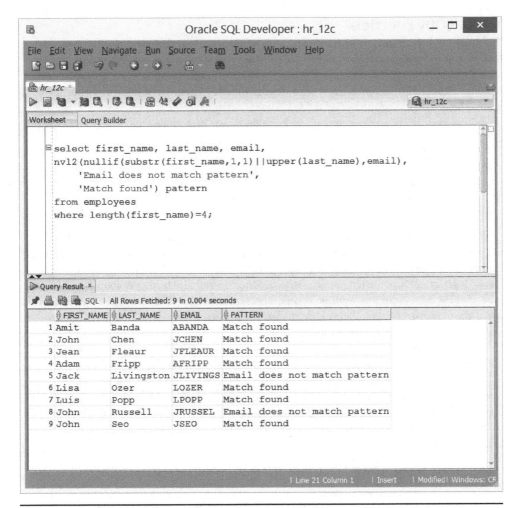

Figure 8-4 The NVL2 and NULLIF functions

evaluates its first parameter, which is a nested SUBSTR function, and finds it to be null. The second parameter is not null, so the string 'Not bc' is returned.

EXAM TIP The parameters of the general function NVL2 can be confusing if you are already familiar with NVL. NVL(*original, ifnull*) returns *original* if it is not null, or else *ifnull* is returned. The NVL2(*original, ifnotnull, ifnull*) function returns *ifnotnull* if *original* is not null, or else *ifnull* is returned. The confusion may arise because the second parameter in the NVL function is *ifnull,* while the second parameter in the NVL2 function is *ifnotnull*. Be mindful of the meaning of the parameter positions in functions.

The DECODE Function

The DECODE function implements *if-then-else* conditional logic by testing its first two terms for equality and returns the third if they are equal and optionally returns another term if they are not.

The DECODE function takes at least three mandatory parameters, but it can take many more. The syntax of the function is DECODE(*expr1, comp1, iftrue1,* [*comp2, iftrue2* . . . [*compN, iftrueN*]], [*iffalse*]). These parameters are evaluated as shown in the following pseudocode example:

```
If expr1 = comp1 then return iftrue1
      else if expr1 = comp2 then return iftrue2
          ...
          ...
              else if expr1 = compN then return iftrueN
      else return null | iffalse;
```

Here, *expr1* is compared with *comp1.* If they are equal, then *iftrue1* is returned. If *expr1* is not equal to *comp1,* then what happens next depends on whether the optional parameters *comp2* and *iftrue2* are present. If they are, then *expr1* is compared to *comp2.* If they are equal, then *iftrue2* is returned. If not, what happens next depends on whether further *compn, iftrueN* pairs exist, and the cycle continues until no comparison terms remain. If no matches have been found and if the *iffalse* parameter is defined, then *iffalse* is returned. If the *iffalse* parameter does not exist and no matches are found, a null is returned.

All parameters to the DECODE function may be expressions. The return data type is the same as that of the first matching comparison item. The expression *expr1* is implicitly converted to the data type of the first comparison parameter *comp1.* As the other comparison parameters *comp2* . . . *compn* are evaluated, they too are implicitly converted to the same data type as *comp1.* DECODE considers two nulls to be equivalent, so if *expr1* is null and *comp3* is the first null comparison parameter encountered, then the corresponding result parameter *iftrue3* is returned. Consider the following queries:

```
Query 1: select decode(1234, 123, '123 is a match') from dual;
Query 2: select decode(1234, 123, '123 is a match', 'No match') from dual;
Query 3: select decode('search', 'comp1', 'true1', 'comp2', 'true2',
'search', 'true3', substr('2search', 2, 6), 'true4', 'false') from dual;
```

Query 1 compares the number 1234 with the first comparison term 123. Since they are not equal, the first result term cannot be returned. Further, as there is no default *iffalse* parameter defined, a null is returned. Query 2 is identical to the first except that an *iffalse* parameter is defined. Therefore, since 1234 is not equal to 123, the string 'No match' is returned. Query 3 searches through the comparison parameters for a match. The strings comp1 and comp2 are not equal to search, so the results true1 and true2 are not returned. A match is found in the third comparison term *comp3* (parameter 6), which contains the string search. Therefore, the third result term *iftrue3* (parameter 7) containing the string 'true3' is returned. Note that since a match has been found, no further searching takes place. So, although the fourth comparison term (parameter 8) is also a match to *expr1,* this expression is never evaluated because a match was found in an earlier comparison term.

The CASE Expression

Virtually all third- and fourth-generation programming languages implement a *case* construct. Like the DECODE function, the CASE expression facilitates *if-then-else* conditional logic. There are two variants of the CASE expression. The *simple* CASE expression lists the conditional search item once, and equality to the search item is tested by each comparison expression. The *searched* CASE expression lists a separate condition for each comparison expression.

The CASE expression takes at least three mandatory parameters but can take many more. Its syntax depends on whether a simple or a searched CASE expression is used. The syntax for the simple CASE expression is as follows:

```
CASE search_expr
 WHEN comparison_expr1 THEN iftrue1
 [WHEN comparison_expr2 THEN iftrue2
 ...
 WHEN comparison_exprN THEN iftrueN
 ELSE iffalse]
END
```

The simple CASE expression is enclosed within a CASE . . . END block and consists of at least one WHEN . . . THEN statement. In its simplest form, with one WHEN . . . THEN statement, the *search_expr* is compared with the *comparison_expr1*. If they are equal, then the result *iftrue1* is returned. If not, a null value is returned unless an ELSE component is defined, in which case the default *iffalse* value is returned. When more than one WHEN . . . THEN statement exists in the CASE expression, searching for a matching comparison expression continues until a match is found.

The search, comparison, and result parameters can be column values, expressions, or literals but must all be of the same data type. Consider the following query:

```
select
 case substr(1234, 1, 3)
  when '134' then '1234 is a match'
  when '1235' then '1235 is a match'
  when concat('1', '23') then concat('1', '23')||' is a match'
  else 'no match'
 end
from dual;
```

The search expression derived from the SUBSTR(1234, 1, 3) is the character string 123. The first WHEN . . . THEN statement compares the string 134 with 123. Since they are not equal, the result expression is not evaluated. The second WHEN . . . THEN statement compares the string 1235 with 123, and again, they are not equal. The third WHEN . . . THEN statement compares the results derived from the CONCAT('1','23') expression, which is 123, to the search expression. Since they are identical, the third results expression, '123 is a match', is returned.

The LAST_NAME and HIRE_DATE columns for employees with DEPARTMENT_ID values of 100 are retrieved along with two numeric expressions and one CASE expression, as shown in Figure 8-5.

Assume that SYSDATE is 27-JAN-2015. The numeric expression aliased as YEARS returns a truncated value obtained by dividing the months of service by 12. Five categories of loyalty

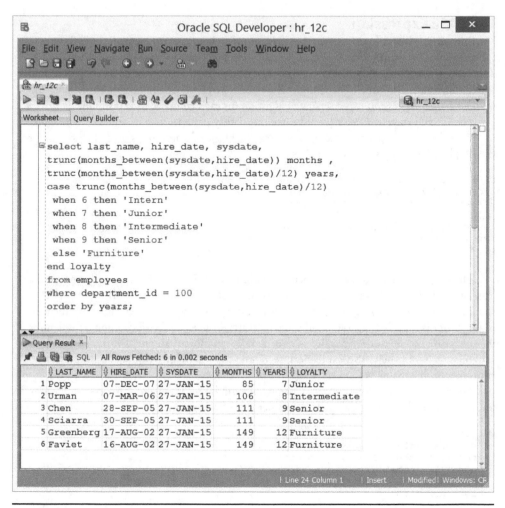

Figure 8-5 The simple CASE expression

classification based on years of service are defined. This forms the search expression in the CASE statement. None of the rows in the dataset matches the comparison expression in the first WHEN . . . THEN statement, but as Figure 8-5 shows, four rows met the remaining WHEN . . . THEN statements and two rows are caught by the ELSE statement.

The syntax for the searched CASE expression is as follows:

```
CASE
 WHEN condition1 THEN iftrue1
 [WHEN condition2 THEN iftrue2
 ...
 WHEN conditionN THEN iftrueN
 ELSE iffalse]
END
```

The searched CASE expression is enclosed within a CASE . . . END block and consists of at least one WHEN . . . THEN statement. In its simplest form with one WHEN . . . THEN statement, *condition1* is evaluated; if it is true, then the result *iftrue1* is returned. If not, a null value is returned unless an ELSE component is defined, in which case the default *iffalse* value is returned. When more than one WHEN . . . THEN statement exists in the CASE expression, searching for a matching comparison expression continues until one is found. The query to retrieve the identical set of results to those obtained in Figure 8-5, using a searched CASE expression, is as follows:

```
select last_name, hire_date, sysdate,
trunc(months_between(sysdate, hire_date)) months,
trunc(months_between(sysdate, hire_date)/12) years,
case
 when trunc(months_between(sysdate, hire_date)/12) < 7 then 'Intern'
 when trunc(months_between(sysdate, hire_date)/12) < 8 then 'Junior'
 when trunc(months_between(sysdate, hire_date)/12) < 9 then 'Intermediate'
 when trunc(months_between(sysdate, hire_date)/12) < 10 then 'Senior'
 else 'Furniture'
end Loyalty
from employees
where department_id = 100
order by years;
```

Exercise 8-3: Use the DECODE Function   Query the HR.LOCATIONS table for rows with the value US in the COUNTRY_ID column. An expression aliased as LOCATION_INFO is required to evaluate the STATE_PROVINCE column values and returns different information as per the following table. Sort the output based on the LOCATION_INFO expression.

If STATE_PROVINCE Is	The Value Returned Is
Washington	The string 'Headquarters'
Texas	The string 'Oil Wells'
California	The CITY column value
New Jersey	The STREET_ADDRESS column value

1. Start SQL Developer or SQL*Plus and connect to the HR schema.

2. The LOCATION_INFO expression may be calculated in several different ways. This includes using a CASE expression or a DECODE function. This solution uses a CASE expression:

```
select case state_province
 when 'Washington' then 'Headquarters'
 when'Texas' then 'Oil Wells'
 when 'California' then city
 when 'New Jersey' then street_address
end location_info, state_province, city, street_address, country_id
from locations where country_id='US' order by location_info;
```

Two-Minute Drill

Describe Various Types of Conversion Functions Available in SQL

- Explicit conversion occurs when a function like TO_CHAR is invoked to change the data type of a value. The TO_CHAR function performs date-to-character and number-to-character data type conversions.

- Character items are explicitly transformed into date values using the TO_DATE conversion function.

- Character items are changed into number values using the TO_NUMBER conversion function.

Use the TO_CHAR, TO_NUMBER, and TO_DATE Conversion Functions

- The TO_CHAR function returns an item of type VARCHAR2.

- Format models or masks prescribe patterns that character strings must match to facilitate accurate and consistent conversion into number or date items.

- Character terms, like month and day names, extracted from dates with the TO_CHAR function are automatically padded with spaces that may be trimmed by prefixing the format mask with the *fm* modifier.

- The TO_DATE function has an *fx* modifier that specifies an exact match for the character string to be converted and the date format mask.

Apply Conditional Expressions in a SELECT Statement

- Nested functions use the output from one function as the input to another.

- The NVL function returns either the original item unchanged or an alternative item if the initial term is null.

- The NVL2 function returns a new *if-null* item if the original item is null or an alternative *if-not-null* item if the original term is not null.

- The NULLIF function tests two terms for equality. If they are equal, the function returns null, or else it returns the first of the two terms tested.

- The COALESCE function returns the first not-null value from its parameter list. If all its parameters are null, then a null is returned.

- The DECODE function and the simple CASE and searched CASE expressions are used to facilitate *if-then-else* conditional logic.

Self Test

1. Which statements regarding single-row functions are true? (Choose all that apply.)

   A. They may return more than one value.

   B. They execute once for each row processed.

   C. They may have zero or more input parameters.

   D. They must have at least one mandatory parameter.

2. What value is returned after executing the following statement?

   ```
   SELECT SUBSTR('How_long_is_a_piece_of_string?', 5, 4) FROM DUAL;
   ```

   (Choose the best answer.)

   A. long

   B. _long

   C. ring?

   D. None of the above

3. What value is returned after executing the following statement?

   ```
   SELECT INSTR('How_long_is_a_piece_of_string?','_', 5, 3) FROM DUAL;
   ```

   (Choose the best answer.)

   A. 4

   B. 14

   C. 12

   D. None of the above

4. What value is returned after executing the following statement?

   ```
   SELECT MOD(14, 3) FROM DUAL;
   ```

   (Choose the best answer.)

   A. 3

   B. 42

   C. 2

   D. None of the above

5. What value is returned after executing the following statement? Take note that 01-JAN-2009 occurred on a Thursday.

   ```
   SELECT NEXT_DAY('01-JAN-2009', 'wed') FROM DUAL;
   ```

   (Choose the best answer.)

   A. 07-JAN-2009

   B. 31-JAN-2009

   C. Wednesday

   D. None of the above

6. Assuming SYSDATE=30-DEC-2007, what value is returned after executing the following statement?

```
SELECT TRUNC(SYSDATE, 'YEAR') FROM DUAL;
```

(Choose the best answer.)

   A. 31-DEC-2007

   B. 01-JAN-2008

   C. 01-JAN-2007

   D. None of the above

7. Choose any incorrect statements regarding conversion functions. (Choose all that apply.)

   A. TO_CHAR may convert date items to character items.

   B. TO_DATE may convert character items to date items.

   C. TO_CHAR may convert numbers to character items.

   D. TO_DATE may convert date items to character items.

8. If SYSDATE returns 12-JUL-2009, what is returned by the following statement?

```
SELECT TO_CHAR(SYSDATE, 'fmDDth MONTH') FROM DUAL;
```

(Choose the best answer.)

   A. 12TH JULY

   B. 12th July

   C. TWELFTH JULY

   D. None of the above

9. What value is returned after executing the following statement?

```
SELECT NVL2(NULLIF('CODA', 'SID'), 'SPANIEL', 'TERRIER') FROM DUAL;
```

(Choose the best answer.)

   A. SPANIEL

   B. TERRIER

   C. NULL

   D. None of the above

10. If SYSDATE returns 12-JUL-2009, what is returned by the following statement?

```
SELECT DECODE(TO_CHAR(SYSDATE, 'MM'), '02', 'TAX DUE', 'PARTY') FROM DUAL;
```

(Choose the best answer.)

   A. TAX DUE

   B. PARTY

   C. 02

   D. None of the above

Self Test Answers

1. ☑ **B** and **C**. Single-row functions execute once for every record selected in a dataset and may take either no input parameters, like SYSDATE, or many input parameters.
☒ **A** and **D** are incorrect. **A** is incorrect because a function, by definition, returns only one result, and **D** is incorrect because there are many functions with no parameters.

2. ☑ **A**. The SUBSTR function extracts a four-character substring from the given input string starting with and including the fifth character. The characters at positions 1 to 4 are How_. Starting with the character at position 5, the next four characters form the word *long*.
☒ **B**, **C**, and **D** are incorrect. **B** is a five-character substring beginning at position 4, while ring?, which is also five characters long, starts five characters from the end of the given string.

3. ☑ **B**. The INSTR function returns the position that the *n*th occurrence of the search string may be found after starting the search from a given start position. The search string is the underscore character, and the third occurrence of this character starting from position 5 in the source string occurs at position 14.
☒ **A**, **C**, and **D** are incorrect. They are incorrect since position 4 is the first occurrence of the search string and position 12 is the third occurrence if the search began at position 1.

4. ☑ **C**. When 14 is divided by 3, the answer is 4 with remainder 2.
☒ **A**, **B**, and **D** are incorrect because the MOD function returns the remainder of a division.

5. ☑ **A**. Since the first of January 2009 falls on a Thursday, the date of the following Wednesday is six days later.
☒ **B**, **C**, and **D** are incorrect. **B** returns the last day of the month in which the given date falls, and **C** returns a character string instead of a date.

6. ☑ **C**. The date TRUNC function does not perform rounding, and since the degree of truncation is YEAR, the day and month components of the given date are ignored and the first day of the year it belongs to is returned.
☒ **A**, **B**, and **D** are incorrect. **A** returns the last day in the month in which the given date occurs, and **B** returns a result achieved by rounding instead of truncation.

7. ☑ **D**. Dates are converted into character strings using TO_CHAR only, not the TO_DATE function.
☒ **A**, **B**, and **C** are incorrect. **A**, **B**, and **C** are correct statements.

8. ☑ **A**. The DD component returns the day of the month in uppercase. Since it is a number, it does not matter, unless the th mask is applied, in which case that component is specified in uppercase. MONTH returns the month spelled out in uppercase.
☒ **B**, **C**, and **D** are incorrect. **B** would be returned if the format mask was 'fmddth Month', and **C** would be returned if the format mask was 'fmDDspth MONTH'.

9. ☑ **A.** The NULLIF function compares its two parameters, and since they are different, the first parameter is returned. The NVL2('CODA', 'SPANIEL', 'TERRIER') function call returns SPANIEL, since its first parameter is not null.

☒ **B, C,** and **D** are incorrect. **B** would be correct if the NULLIF function returned a NULL, which would only happen if its two parameters were identical, and they are not. **C** would be correct if the second parameter to NVL2 was NULL, but it is not.

10. ☑ **B.** The innermost function TO_CHAR(SYSDATE, 'MM') results in the character string 07 being returned. The outer function is DECODE('07','02','TAX DUE','PARTY'). Since 07 is not equal to 02, the else component PARTY is returned.

☒ **A, C,** and **D** are incorrect. **A** would be returned only if the month component extracted from SYSDATE was 02. **C** and **D** are not options for output in the DECODE function parameter list.

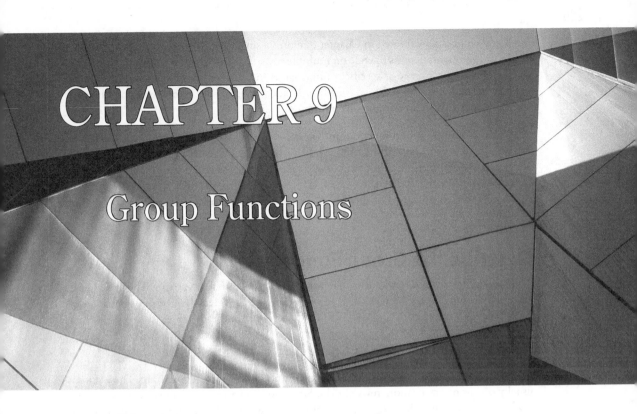

CHAPTER 9

Group Functions

Exam Objectives

In this chapter, you will learn to

- 061.5.1 Identify the Available Group Functions
- 061.5.2 Describe the Use of Group Functions
- 061.5.3 Group Data by Using the GROUP BY Clause
- 061.5.4 Include or Exclude Grouped Rows by Using the HAVING Clause

Single-row functions, explored in Chapter 8, return a single value for each row in a set of results. *Group* or *aggregate* functions operate on multiple rows. They are used to count the number of rows or to find the average of specific column values in a dataset. Many statistical operations, such as calculating standard deviation, medians, and averages, depend on executing functions against grouped data and not just single rows.

You will examine group functions in two stages. A discussion of their purpose and syntax precedes a detailed analysis of the AVG, SUM, MIN, MAX, COUNT, LISTAGG, STDDEV, and VARIANCE functions. Grouping or aggregating data based on one or more column values is examined before the GROUP BY clause is introduced. The WHERE clause restricts rows in a dataset before grouping, while the HAVING clause restricts them after grouping. This chapter concludes with a discussion of the HAVING clause.

Describe the Group Functions

This section defines SQL *group functions* and discusses the different variants. The syntax and examples demonstrating the selected group functions are provided along with a discussion of their data types and the effect of the DISTINCT keyword and null values.

Definition of Group Functions

Group functions operate on aggregated data and return a single result per group. These groups usually consist of one or more rows of data. Single-row functions are defined with the formula $F(x, y, z, \ldots)$ = result, where x, y, z . . . are input parameters. The function F executes on one row of the dataset at a time and returns a result for each row. Group functions can be defined using the following formula:

$$F(g1, g2, g3, \ldots, gn) = result1, result2, result2, \ldots, resultn;$$

The group function executes once for each cluster of rows and returns a single result per group. The rows within these groups are associated using a common value or attribute. If a table is presented as one group to the *group function* in its entirety, then one result is returned. One or more group functions may appear in the SELECT list as follows:

```
SELECT group_function(column or expression),...
FROM table [WHERE ...] [ORDER BY...]
```

Consider the EMPLOYEES table. There are 107 rows in this table. Groups may be created based on the common values that rows share. For example, the rows that share the same DEPARTMENT_ID value may be clustered together. Thereafter, *group functions* are executed separately against each unique group.

Figure 9-1 shows 12 distinct DEPARTMENT_ID values in the EMPLOYEES table, including a null value. The rows are distributed into 12 groups based on common DEPARTMENT_ID values. The COUNT function executes 12 times, once for each group. Notice that the distinct groups do not contain the same number of rows.

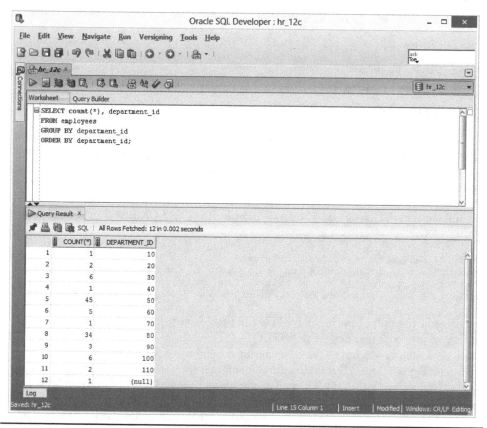

Figure 9-1   Group functions operating on 12 groups

> **NOTE**   *Group functions* aggregate a number of values from multiple rows
> into a single result. They are widely used for reporting purposes, providing
> sum totals, averages, and counts. They are also known as summary or
> aggregate functions.

Using Group Functions

AVG, SUM, MIN, MAX, COUNT, STDDEV, and VARIANCE demonstrate the practical
application of *group functions*. These group functions all return numeric results. Additionally,
the MIN and MAX functions may return character and date results. These functions operate on
non-null values, but unlike the others, the COUNT function call also counts rows with null
values under certain conditions.

The COUNT Function

The COUNT function counts the number of rows in a group. Its syntax is as follows:

```
COUNT({*|[DISTINCT|ALL] expr})
```

This syntax may be deconstructed into the following forms:

- `COUNT(*)`
- `COUNT(DISTINCT expr)`
- `COUNT(ALL expr)`
- `COUNT(expr)`

When COUNT(*) is invoked, all rows in the group, including those with nulls or duplicate values, are counted. When COUNT(DISTINCT *expr*) is executed, only unique occurrences of *expr* are counted for each group. The ALL keyword is part of the default syntax, so COUNT(ALL *expr*) and COUNT(*expr*) are equivalent. If *expr* is based on named columns, then nulls are ignored, but if *expr* is based on anything else, it will be evaluated for every row, whether there are null values in the row or not. The data type of *expr* may be NUMBER, DATE, CHAR, or VARCHAR2. Consider these queries:

```
Query 1: select count(*) from employees;
Query 2: select count(commission_pct), count(1) from employees;
Query 3: select count(distinct salary) from employees;
Query 4: select count(hire_date), count(manager_id) from employees;
```

Query 1 counts the rows in the EMPLOYEES table and returns the integer 107. Query 2 counts the rows with non-null COMMISSION_PCT values and returns 36. It also counts the literal expression 1, which is not based on a named column and is therefore evaluated for every row, returning 107. Query 3 considers the 107 non-null rows, determines the number of unique SALARY values, and returns 58. Query 4 demonstrates how the COUNT function is used on both a DATE column and a NUMBER column. The integers 107 and 106 are returned, since there are 107 non-null HIRE_DATE values and 106 non-null MANAGER_ID values in the group.

 EXAM TIP The COUNT of a literal, like COUNT(1), is internally rewritten to COUNT(*) and counts every row regardless of the presence of nulls.

The SUM Function

The SUM function returns the aggregated total of the non-null numeric values in a group. It has this syntax:

```
SUM([DISTINCT|ALL] expr)
```

This syntax may be deconstructed into the following forms:

- `SUM(DISTINCT expr)`
- `SUM(ALL expr)`
- `SUM(expr)`

SUM(DISTINCT *expr*) provides a total by adding all the unique values returned after *expr* is evaluated for each row in the group. SUM(*expr*) and SUM(ALL *expr*) provide a total by adding *expr* for each row in the group. Null values are ignored. The *expr* parameter must be a numeric value. Consider the following queries:

```
Query 1: select sum(2) from employees;
Query 2: select sum(salary) from employees;
Query 3: select sum(distinct salary) from employees;
Query 4: select sum(commission_pct) from employees;
```

There are 107 rows in the EMPLOYEES table. Query 1 adds the number 2 across 107 rows and returns 214. Query 2 takes the SALARY column value for every row in the group, which in this case is the entire table, and returns the total salary amount of 721166. Query 3 returns a total of 417158, since many employees get paid the same salary, and the DISTINCT keyword only adds unique values in the column to the total. Query 4 returns 7.9 after adding the non-null COMMISSION_PCT values.

The AVG Function

The *average* value of a column or expression is obtained by dividing the sum by the number of non-null rows in the group. The AVG function has this syntax:

```
AVG([DISTINCT|ALL] expr)
```

This syntax may be deconstructed into the following forms:

- AVG(DISTINCT *expr*)
- AVG(ALL *expr*)
- AVG(*expr*)

When AVG(DISTINCT *expr*) is invoked, the distinct values of *expr* are summed and divided by the number of unique occurrences of *expr*. AVG(ALL *expr*) and AVG(*expr*) add the non-null values of *expr* for each row and divide the sum by the number of non-null rows in the group. The *expr* parameter must be a numeric value. Consider these queries:

```
Query 1: select avg(2) from employees;
Query 2: select avg(salary) from employees;
Query 3: select avg(distinct salary) from employees;
Query 4: select avg(commission_pct) from employees;
```

There are 107 rows in the EMPLOYEES table. Query 1 adds the number 2 across 107 rows and divides the total by the number of rows to return the number 2. Numeric literals submitted to the AVG function are returned unchanged. Query 2 adds the SALARY value for each row to obtain the total salary amount of 721166, which is divided by the rows with non-null SALARY values (107) to return the average 6739.86916. There are 58 unique salary values, which, when added, yield a total of 417158. Dividing 417158 by 58 returns 7192.37931 as the average of the distinct salary values, which is returned by the third query. Adding the non-null COMMISSION_PCT values produces a total of 7.9. Dividing this by the employee records with non-null COMMISSION_PCT values (36) yields 0.219444444, which is returned by query 4.

The STDDEV and VARIANCE Functions

The *standard deviation* is a measure of the spread or distribution of the values in a column or expression. It is obtained by calculating the square root of the variance. The *variance* refers to the sum of the squared differences between the actual value and the average value divided by N-1 or N depending on whether variance is being established for a sample or the entire population. The VARIANCE function establishes variance for a sample and therefore divides the sum of squared differences between the actual and average values by N-1. For more information, look up the VAR_POP and VAR_SAMP functions, which are beyond the scope of this exam.

Variance is calculated by first calculating the average of the values in the set. Then for each number, subtract the average value and square the result. This is the squared difference. The variance is then the sum of all the squared differences divided by N-1. The STDDEV and VARIANCE functions have two forms, an aggregate form and an analytic form that is beyond the scope of the exam. The aggregate form has this syntax:

```
STDDEV([DISTINCT|ALL] expr)
VARIANCE([DISTINCT|ALL] expr)
```

Consider the queries in Figure 9-2.

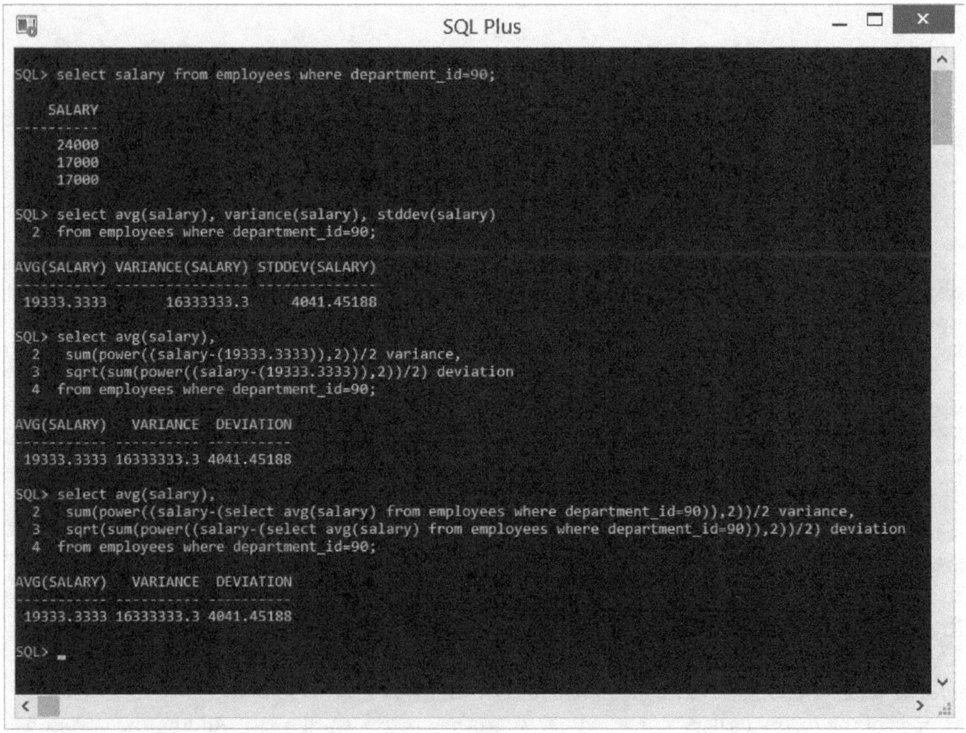

Figure 9-2 The VARIANCE and STDDEV functions

There are three employees who belong to department 90 with salary values of 24000, 17000, and 17000. The average salary is 19333.3333 as returned by query 2, which shows the variance and standard deviation. For the statistically inclined, queries 3 and 4 show alternative ways to calculate variance and standard deviation. These are nonexaminable and provided to exemplify the descriptions of these functions. Query 3 uses the *power* function, which raises (salary – average salary) to power 2, giving you the squared differences, which are summed using the sum function and divided by 2 (N-1). It also uses the sqrt function to calculate standard deviation. Remember, N is 3 because there are three salary values in the sample set. The average salary, 19333.3333, is hard-coded in query 3, while query 4 uses a nested subquery (details in Chapter 11) to dynamically fetch the average salary value.

The MAX and MIN Functions

The MAX and MIN functions return the maximum (largest) and minimum (smallest) *expr* value in a group. The MAX and MIN functions operate on NUMBER, DATE, CHAR, and VARCHAR2 data types. They return a value of the same data type as their input arguments, which are either the largest or smallest items in the group. When applied to DATE items, MAX returns the latest date, and MIN returns the earliest one. Character strings are converted to numeric representations of their constituent characters based on the NLS settings in the database. When the MIN function is applied to a group of character strings, the word that appears first alphabetically is returned, while MAX returns the word that appears last. The MAX and MIN functions have this syntax:

MAX([DISTINCT|ALL] expr); MIN([DISTINCT|ALL] expr)

This syntax may be deconstructed into the following forms:

- MAX(DISTINCT expr); MIN(DISTINCT expr)
- MAX(ALL expr); MIN(ALL expr)
- MAX(expr); MIN(expr);

MAX(*expr*), MAX(ALL *expr*), and MAX(DISTINCT *expr*) examine the values for *expr* in a group of rows and return the largest value. Null values are ignored. MIN(*expr*), MIN(ALL *expr*), and MIN(DISTINCT *expr*) examine the values for *expr* in a group of rows and return the smallest value. Consider these queries:

```
Query 1: select min(commission_pct), max(commission_pct) from employees;
Query 2: select min(start_date),max(end_date) from job_history;
Query 3: select min(job_id),max(job_id) from employees;
```

Query 1 returns 0.1 and 0.4 for the minimum and maximum COMMISSION_PCT values in the EMPLOYEES table. Notice that null values for COMMISSION_PCT are ignored. Query 2 evaluates a DATE column and indicates that the earliest START_DATE in the JOB_HISTORY table is 17-SEP-1995 and the latest END_DATE is 07-JAN-2015. Query 3 returns AC_ACCOUNT and ST_MAN as the JOB_ID values appearing first and last alphabetically in the EMPLOYEES table.

The LISTAGG Function

The LISTAGG function returns a string aggregation of column values. If an ORDER BY clause is present, values are sorted and concatenated. This function operates as a single-set aggregate function that operates on all rows and returns a single output row or as a group-set aggregate function that returns an output row for each group in the GROUP BY clause (discussed in the next section). The LISTAGG function has this syntax:

```
LISTAGG(expr, ['delimiter']) WITHIN GROUP (ORDER_BY_CLAUSE)
```

The *expr* parameter can be any valid expression. Null values are ignored. The *delimiter* specifies the optional string to separate the *expr*. The ORDER BY clause determines the order in which the concatenated values are returned. Consider the queries in Figure 9-3.

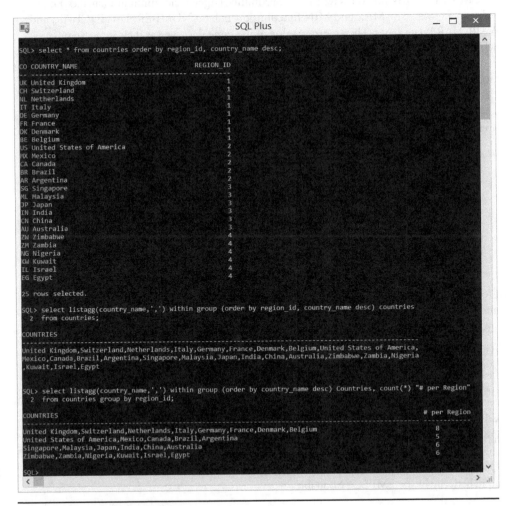

Figure 9-3 The LISTAGG function

Query 1 returns the familiar output format listing countries sorted by REGION_ID and reverse alphabetically by COUNTRY_NAME. Query 2 demonstrates the single-set aggregate form of the LISTAGG function, and a single row that concatenates the COUNTRY_NAME values in a comma-delimited list is returned. Query 3 shows the group-set aggregate form, and a comma-delimited concatenated list of COUNTRY_NAME values are returned for each grouping by REGION_ID along with a COUNT of the number of items per group.

 EXAM TIP   There are two fundamental rules to remember when studying group functions. First, they always operate on a single group of rows at a time. The group can be one of many groups a dataset has been segmented into, or it can be an entire table. The group function executes once per group. Second, rows with nulls occurring in group columns or expressions are ignored by all group functions, except the COUNT(*) and COUNT(*literal*) forms of the COUNT function.

Exercise 9-1: Use the Group Functions   The COUNTRIES table stores a list of COUNTRY_NAME values. You are required to calculate the average length of all the country names. Any fractional components must be rounded to the nearest whole number.

1. Start SQL*Plus or SQL Developer and connect to the HR schema.

2. The length of the country name value for each row is to be calculated using the LENGTH function. The average length may be determined using the AVG function. It may be rounded to the nearest whole number using the ROUND function. The following is a possible solution:

```
select round(avg(length(country_name))) average_country_name_length
from countries;
```

3. Executing this statement shows that the average length of all the country names in the COUNTRIES table is eight characters.

Group Data Using the GROUP BY Clause

The *group functions* discussed earlier use groups of rows making up the entire table. This section explores partitioning a set of data into groups using the *GROUP BY* clause. Group functions may be applied to these subsets or clusters of rows.

Creating Groups of Data

A table has at least one column and zero or more rows of data. In many tables, data requires analysis to transform it into useful information. It is a common reporting requirement to calculate statistics from a set of data divided into groups using different attributes. Previous examples using group functions operated against all the rows in a table. The entire table was treated as one large group. Groups of data within a set are created by associating rows with common attributes with each other. Thereafter, group functions can execute against each of these groups. Groups of data include entire rows and not specific columns.

Consider the EMPLOYEES table. It comprises 11 columns and 107 rows. You could create groups of rows that share a common DEPARTMENT_ID value. The SUM function can then be used to create salary totals per department. Another possible set of groups may share common JOB_ID column values. The AVG group function can then be used to identify the average salary paid to employees in different jobs.

A group is defined as a subset of the entire dataset sharing one or more common attributes. These attributes are typically column values but can also be expressions. The number of groups created depends on the distinct values present in the common attribute.

As Figure 9-4 shows, there are 12 unique DEPARTMENT_ID values in the EMPLOYEES table. If rows are grouped using common DEPARTMENT_ID values, there will be 12 groups. If a group function is executed against these groups, there will be 12 values returned because it will execute once for each group.

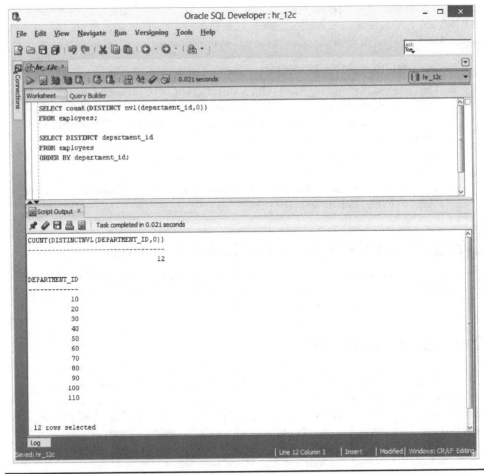

Figure 9-4 Unique DEPARTMENT_ID values in the EMPLOYEES table

NOTE Grouping data and using summary functions are widely utilized for reporting purposes. It is valuable to practice the segmentation of a set of data into different groups. Oracle provides the analytical language to deconstruct datasets into groups, divide these into further subgroups, and so on. Aggregate grouping functions can then be executed against these groups and subgroups.

The GROUP BY Clause

The SELECT statement is enhanced by the addition of the GROUP BY clause. This clause facilitates the creation of groups. It appears after the WHERE clause but before the ORDER BY clause, as follows:

```
SELECT column|expression|group_function(column|expression [alias]),...}
FROM table
[WHERE condition(s)]
[GROUP BY {col(s)|expr}]
[ORDER BY {col(s)|expr|numeric_pos} [ASC|DESC] [NULLS FIRST|LAST]];
```

The column or expression specified in the GROUP BY clause is also known as the *grouping attribute* and is the component that rows are grouped by. The dataset is segmented according to the grouping attribute. Consider the following query:

```
select department_id, max(salary), count(*)
from employees
group by department_id
order by department_id;
```

The grouping attribute in this example is the DEPARTMENT_ID column. The dataset, on which the group functions in the SELECT list must operate, is divided into 12 groups, one for each department. For each group (department), the maximum salary value and the number of rows are returned. Since the results are sorted by DEPARTMENT_ID, the third row in the set of results contains the values 11000 and 6. This indicates that 6 employees have the same DEPARTMENT_ID value (which you happen to know is 30). Of these 6, the highest earner has a SALARY value of 11000. This query demonstrates that the grouping attribute does not have to be included in the SELECT list.

It is common to see the grouping attribute in the SELECT list alongside grouping functions. If an item that is not a group function appears in the SELECT list and there is no GROUP BY clause, an "ORA-00937: not a single-group group function" error is raised. If a GROUP BY clause is present but that item is not a grouping attribute, then an "ORA-00979: not a GROUP BY expression" error is returned.

EXAM TIP Any item in the SELECT list that is not a group function must be a grouping attribute of the GROUP BY clause.

If a group function is placed in a WHERE clause, an "ORA-00934: group function is not allowed here" error is returned. Imposing group-level conditions is achieved using the HAVING clause discussed later in this chapter. Group functions may, however, be used as part of the ORDER BY clause.

The first query in Figure 9-5 raises an error because the END_DATE column is in the SELECT list with a group function and there is no GROUP BY clause. An ORA-00979 error is returned from the second query, since the START_DATE item is listed in the SELECT clause, but it is not a grouping attribute.

The third query divides the JOB_HISTORY rows into groups based on the four-digit year component from the END_DATE column. Four groups are created using this grouping attribute. These represent different years when employees ended their jobs. The COUNT shows the number of employees who quit their jobs during each of these years. The results are listed in descending order based on the "Number of Employees" expression. Note that the COUNT group function is present in the ORDER BY clause.

EXAM TIP A dataset is divided into groups using the GROUP BY clause. The grouping attribute is the common key shared by members of each group. The grouping attribute is usually a single column, but may be multiple columns or an expression that cannot be based on group functions. Note that only grouping attributes and group functions are permitted in the SELECT clause when using GROUP BY.

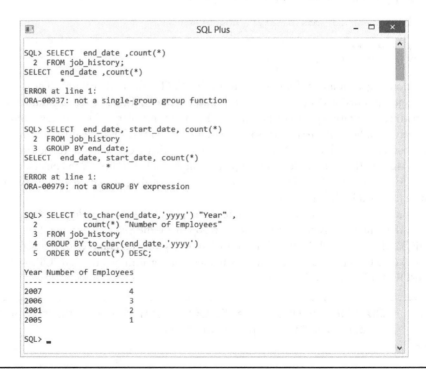

Figure 9-5 The GROUP BY clause

Grouping by Multiple Columns

A powerful extension to the GROUP BY clause uses multiple grouping attributes. Oracle permits datasets to be partitioned into groups and allows these groups to be further divided into subgroups using a different grouping attribute. Consider the following two queries:

```
Query 1: select department_id, sum(commission_pct)
from employees where commission_pct is not null
group by department_id;
Query 2: select department_id, job_id, sum(commission_pct)
from employees where commission_pct is not null
group by department_id, job_id;
```

Query 1 restricts the rows returned from the EMPLOYEES table to the 35 rows with non-null COMMISSION_PCT values. These rows are then divided into two groups: 80 and NULL based on the DEPARTMENT_ID grouping attribute. The result set contains two rows, which return the sum of the COMMISSION_PCT values for each group.

Query 2 is similar to the first one except it has an additional item: JOB_ID in both the SELECT and GROUP BY clauses. This second grouping attribute decomposes the two groups by DEPARTMENT_ID into the constituent JOB_ID components belonging to the rows in each group. The distinct JOB_ID values for rows with DEPARTMENT_ID=80 are AC_ACCOUNT, SA_REP, and SA_MAN. The distinct JOB_ID value for rows with a null DEPARTMENT_ID is SA_REP. Therefore, query 2 returns two groupings: one that consists of three subgroups, and the other with only one, as shown in Figure 9-6.

Exercise 9-2: Group Data Based on Multiple Columns   Analysis of staff turnover is a common reporting requirement. You are required to create a report that contains the number of employees who left their jobs, grouped by the year in which they left. The jobs they performed is

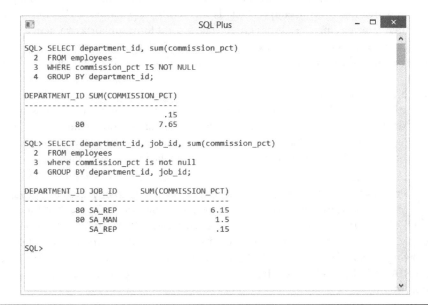

Figure 9-6   The GROUP BY clause with multiple columns

also required. The results must be sorted in descending order based on the number of employees in each group. The report must list the year, the JOB_ID, and the number of employees who left a particular job in that year.

1. Start SQL Developer and connect to the HR schema.

2. The JOB_HISTORY table contains the END_DATE and JOB_ID columns, which constitute the source data for this report.

3. The year component may be extracted using the TO_CHAR function. The number of employees who quit a particular job in each year may be obtained using the COUNT(*) function.

4. Executing the following statement returns the staff turnover report as requested:

```
select  to_char(end_date,'yyyy') "Year" ,job_id,
count(*) "Number of Employees"
from job_history
group by to_char(end_date,'yyyy'), job_id
order by count(*) desc;
```

Nested Group Functions

Recall that single-row functions may be nested or embedded to any level of depth. Group functions can be nested only two levels deep. Three formats using group functions are shown here:

G1(*group_item*) = result
G1(G2(*group_item*)) = result
G1(G2(G3(*group_item*))) is NOT allowed.

Group functions are represented by the letter *G* followed by a number. The first simple form contains no nested functions. Examples include the SUM(*group_item*) and AVG(*group_item*) functions that return a single result per group. The second form supports two nested group functions, like SUM(AVG(*group_item*)). In this case, a GROUP BY clause is necessary because the average value of the *group_item* per group is calculated before being aggregated by the SUM function.

The third form is disallowed by Oracle. Consider an expression that nests three group functions. If the MAX function is applied to the previous example, the expression MAX(SUM(AVG(*group_item*))) is formed. The two inner group functions return a *single value* representing the sum of a set of average values. This expression becomes MAX(*single value*), which is not sensible since a group function cannot be applied to a single value.

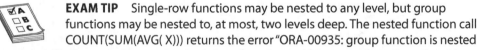

EXAM TIP   Single-row functions may be nested to any level, but group functions may be nested to, at most, two levels deep. The nested function call COUNT(SUM(AVG(X))) returns the error "ORA-00935: group function is nested too deeply." It is acceptable to nest single-row functions within group functions. Consider the following query: SELECT SUM(AVG(LENGTH(LAST_NAME))) FROM EMPLOYEES GROUP BY DEPARTMENT_ID. It calculates the sum of the average length of LAST_NAME values per department.

Include or Exclude Grouped Rows Using the HAVING Clause

Creating groups of data and applying aggregate functions are useful. A refinement to these features is the ability to include or exclude results based on group-level conditions. This section introduces the HAVING clause. A clear distinction is made between the WHERE clause and the HAVING clause.

Restricting Group Results

WHERE clause conditions restrict rows returned by a query. Rows are included if they fulfill the conditions listed and are sometimes known as *row-level results.* Clustering rows using the GROUP BY clause and applying an aggregate function to these groups returns results often referred to as *group-level results.* The HAVING clause restricts group-level results.

The following query limits the rows retrieved from the JOB_HISTORY table by specifying a WHERE condition based on the DEPARTMENT_ID column values.

```
select department_id
from job_history
where department_id in (50,60,80,110);
```

This query returns seven rows. If the WHERE clause were absent, all ten rows would be retrieved. Suppose you want to know how many employees were previously employed in each of these departments. There are seven rows that can be manually grouped and counted. However, if there are a large number of rows, an aggregate function like COUNT may be used, as shown in the following query:

```
select department_id, count(*)
from job_history
where department_id in (50,60,80,110)
group by department_id;
```

This query adds to the previous statement. The aggregate function COUNT was added to the SELECT list, and a GROUP BY DEPARTMENT_ID clause was also added. Four rows with their aggregate row count are returned, and it is clear that the original seven rows restricted by the WHERE clause were clustered into four groups based on common DEPARTMENT_ID values, as shown in the following table:

DEPARTMENT_ID	COUNT(*)
50	2
60	1
80	2
110	2

Suppose you wanted to restrict this list to only those departments with more than one employee. The HAVING clause limits or restricts the group-level rows as required.

This query must perform the following steps:

1. Consider the entire row-level dataset.

2. Limit the dataset by any WHERE clause conditions.

3. Segment the data into one or more groups using the grouping attributes specified in the GROUP BY clause.

4. Apply any aggregate functions to create a new group-level dataset. Each row may be regarded as an aggregation of its source row-level data based on the groups created.

5. Limit or restrict the group-level data with a HAVING clause condition. Only group-level results matching these conditions are returned.

 NOTE Choosing the appropriate context to use a WHERE or a HAVING clause depends on whether actual rows or group-level rows are to be restricted. When actual (physical) rows are restricted, one or more conditions are imposed using a WHERE clause. When these rows are grouped together, one or more aggregate functions may be applied, yielding one or more group-level rows that may be restricted using a HAVING clause.

The HAVING Clause

The general form of the SELECT statement is further enhanced by the addition of the HAVING clause and becomes the following:

```
SELECT column|expression|group_function(column|expression [alias]),...}
FROM table
[WHERE condition(s)]
[GROUP BY {col(s)|expr}]
[HAVING group_condition(s)]
[ORDER BY {col(s)|expr|numeric_pos} [ASC|DESC] [NULLS FIRST|LAST]];
```

An important difference between the HAVING clause and the other SELECT statement clauses is that it may be specified only if a GROUP BY clause is present. This dependency is sensible since group-level rows must exist before they can be restricted. The HAVING clause can occur before the GROUP BY clause in the SELECT statement. However, it is more common to place the HAVING clause after the GROUP BY clause. All grouping is performed and group functions are executed prior to evaluating the HAVING clause.

The following query shows how the HAVING clause is used to restrict an aggregated dataset. Records from the JOB_HISTORY table are divided into four groups. The rows that meet the HAVING clause condition (contributing more than one row to the group row count) are returned:

```
select department_id, count(*)
from job_history
where department_id in (50,60,80,110)
group by department_id
having count(*)>1;
```

Three rows with DEPARTMENT_ID values of 50, 80, and 110, each with a COUNT(*) value of 2, 2, and 3, are returned, respectively.

Figure 9-7 shows three queries. Query 1 divides the 107 records from the EMPLOYEES table into 19 groups based on common JOB_ID values. The average salary for each JOB_ID group and the aggregate row count are computed. Query 2 refines the results by conditionally excluding those aggregated rows where the average salary is less than or equal to 12000, using a

```
                          SQL Plus                    _  □   ×

SQL> SELECT job_id, avg(salary), count(*)
  2  FROM employees
  3  GROUP BY job_id;

JOB_ID     AVG(SALARY)   COUNT(*)
---------- -----------  ----------
IT_PROG           5760          5
AC_MGR           12008          1
AC_ACCOUNT        8300          1
ST_MAN            7280          5
PU_MAN           11000          1
AD_ASST           4400          1
AD_VP            17000          2
SH_CLERK          3215         20
FI_ACCOUNT        7920          5
FI_MGR           12008          1
PU_CLERK          2780          5
SA_MAN           12200          5
MK_MAN           13000          1
PR_REP           10000          1
AD_PRES          24000          1
SA_REP            8350         30
MK_REP            6000          1
ST_CLERK          2785         20
HR_REP            6500          1

19 rows selected.

SQL> SELECT job_id, avg(salary), count(*)
  2  FROM employees
  3  GROUP BY job_id
  4  HAVING avg(salary) > 10000;

JOB_ID     AVG(SALARY)   COUNT(*)
---------- -----------  ----------
AC_MGR           12008          1
PU_MAN           11000          1
AD_VP            17000          2
FI_MGR           12008          1
SA_MAN           12200          5
MK_MAN           13000          1
AD_PRES          24000          1

7 rows selected.

SQL> SELECT job_id, avg(salary), count(*)
  2  FROM employees
  3  GROUP BY job_id
  4  HAVING avg(salary) > 10000
  5  AND count(*) >1;

JOB_ID     AVG(SALARY)   COUNT(*)
---------- -----------  ----------
AD_VP            17000          2
SA_MAN           12200          5

SQL> _
```

Figure 9-7   The HAVING clause

HAVING clause. Query 3 demonstrates that the Boolean operators may be used to specify multiple HAVING clause conditions.

 EXAM TIP The HAVING clause can be specified only when a GROUP BY clause is present. A GROUP BY clause can be specified without a HAVING clause.

Exercise 9-3: Use the HAVING Clause The company is planning a recruitment drive and wants to identify which days of the week 20 or more staff members were hired. Your report must list the days and the number of employees hired on each of them.

1. Start SQL*Plus or SQL Developer and connect to the HR schema.

2. Divide EMPLOYEES records into groups based on the day component of the HIRE_DATE column. You can obtain the number of employees per group using the COUNT function. Use the HAVING clause to restrict these rows to only those where the count is greater than or equal to 20.

3. A possible solution is the following statement, which returns the days of the week on which 20 or more employees were hired:

```
select to_char(hire_date,'Day') hire_day, count(*)
from employees
group by to_char(hire_date,'Day')
having count(*)>=20;
```

Two-Minute Drill

Describe the Group Functions

- Group functions are also known as multiple-row, aggregate, or summary functions. They execute once for each group of data and aggregate the data from multiple rows into a single result for each group.

- Groups can be entire tables or portions of a table grouped together by a common grouping attribute.

- The COUNT of a column or an expression returns an integer value representing the number of rows in a group, where the specified column or expression is not null.

- The SUM function returns an aggregated total of all the non-null numeric values in a group.

- The AVG function divides the sum of a column or expression by the number of non-null rows in a group.

- The MAX and MIN functions operate on NUMBER, DATE, CHAR, and VARCHAR2 data types. They return a value that is either the largest or smallest item in the group.

Group Data Using the GROUP BY Clause

- The GROUP BY clause specifies the grouping attribute rows must have in common for them to be clustered together.

- The GROUP BY clause facilitates the creation of groups within a selected set of data and appears after the WHERE clause but before the ORDER BY clause.

- Any item on the SELECT list that is not a group function must be a grouping attribute.

- Group functions may not be placed in a WHERE clause.

- Datasets may be partitioned into groups and further divided into subgroups based on multiple grouping attributes.

- The LISTAGG function returns a concatenated string of sorted column values, sorted by the ORDER BY expression specified after the WITHIN GROUP clause.

Include or Exclude Grouped Rows Using the HAVING Clause

- Clustering rows using a common grouping attribute with the GROUP BY clause and applying an aggregate function to each of these groups returns *group-level results*.

- The HAVING clause provides the language to limit the group-level results returned.

- The HAVING clause can be specified only if there is a GROUP BY clause present.

- All grouping is performed and group functions are executed prior to evaluating the HAVING clause.

Self Test

1. What result is returned by the following statement?

```
SELECT COUNT(*) FROM DUAL;
```

(Choose the best answer.)

A. NULL

B. 0

C. 1

D. None of the above

2. Choose one correct statement regarding group functions.

A. Group functions can be used only when a GROUP BY clause is present.

B. Group functions can operate on multiple rows at a time.

C. Group functions operate on only a single row at a time.

D. Group functions can execute multiple times within a single group.

3. What value is returned after executing the following statement?

```
SELECT SUM(SALARY) FROM EMPLOYEES;
```

Assume there are ten employee records and each contains a SALARY value of 100, except for one, which has a null value in the SALARY field. (Choose the best answer.)

A. 900

B. 1000

C. NULL

D. None of the above

4. Which values are returned after executing the following statement?

```
SELECT COUNT(*), COUNT(SALARY) FROM EMPLOYEES;
```

Assume there are ten employee records and each contains a SALARY value of 100, except for one, which has a null value in the SALARY field. (Choose all that apply.)

A. 10 and 10

B. 10 and NULL

C. 10 and 9

D. None of the above

5. What value is returned after executing the following statement?

```
SELECT AVG(NVL(SALARY,100)) FROM EMPLOYEES;
```

Assume there are ten employee records and each contains a SALARY value of 100, except for one employee, who has a null value in the SALARY field. (Choose the best answer.)

A. NULL

B. 90

C. 100

D. None of the above

6. What value is returned after executing the following statement?

```
SELECT SUM((AVG(LENGTH(NVL(SALARY,0)))))
FROM EMPLOYEES
GROUP BY SALARY;
```

Assume there are ten employee records and each contains a SALARY value of 100, except for one, which has a null value in the SALARY field. (Choose the best answer.)

A. An error

B. 3

C. 4

D. None of the above

7. How many rows are returned by the following query?

```
SELECT SUM(SALARY), DEPARTMENT_ID FROM EMPLOYEES
GROUP BY DEPARTMENT_ID;
```

Assume there are 11 non-null and 1 null unique DEPARTMENT_ID values. All records have a non-null SALARY value. (Choose the best answer.)

A. 12

B. 11

C. NULL

D. None of the above

8. What values are returned after executing the following statement?

```
SELECT JOB_ID, MAX_SALARY FROM JOBS GROUP BY MAX_SALARY;
```

Assume that the JOBS table has ten records with the same JOB_ID value of DBA and the same MAX_SALARY value of 100. (Choose the best answer.)

A. One row of output with the values DBA, 100

B. Ten rows of output with the values DBA, 100

C. An error

D. None of the above

9. How many rows of data are returned after executing the following statement?

```
SELECT DEPT_ID, SUM(NVL(SALARY,100)) FROM EMP
GROUP BY DEPT_ID HAVING SUM(SALARY) > 400;
```

Assume the EMP table has ten rows and each contains a SALARY value of 100, except for one, which has a null value in the SALARY field. The first five rows have a DEPT_ID value of 10, while the second group of five rows, which includes the row with a null SALARY value, has a DEPT_ID value of 20. (Choose the best answer.)

A. Two rows

B. One row

C. Zero rows

D. None of the above

10. How many rows of data are returned after executing the following statement?

```
SELECT DEPT_ID, SUM(SALARY) FROM EMP GROUP BY DEPT_ID HAVING
SUM(NVL(SALARY,100)) > 400;
```

Assume the EMP table has ten rows and each contains a SALARY value of 100, except for one, which has a null value in the SALARY field. The first five rows have a DEPT_ID value of 10, while the second five rows, which include the row with a null SALARY value, have a DEPT_ID value of 20. (Choose the best answer.)

A. Two rows

B. One row

C. Zero rows

D. None of the above

11. Choose two statements that are true.

   A. The STDDEV function returns the square root of the VARIANCE.

   B. The VARIANCE function returns the square root of the STDDEV.

   C. The AVG function works on date and numeric data.

   D. The LISTAGG function returns a total numeric sum of a list of data.

   E. LISTAGG returns the concatenated values of the measure column.

12. How many rows of data are returned after executing the following statement?

```
select listagg(last_name) within group
(order by department_id)
from employees;
```

Assume the EMPLOYEES table has ten distinct DEPARTMENT_ID values and 107 rows. (Choose the best answer.)

   A. 0

   B. 1

   C. 10

   D. 107

   E. None of the above

Self Test Answers

   1. ☑   **C.** The DUAL table has one row and one column. The COUNT(*) function returns the number of rows in a table or group.
   ☒   **A, B**, and **D** are incorrect. **A** is incorrect because a table can have zero or more rows, but never NULL rows. **B** is incorrect since the DUAL table has one row. **D** is incorrect because the correct answer is **C**.

   2. ☑   **B.** By definition, group functions can operate on multiple rows at a time, unlike single-row functions.
   ☒   **A, C**, and **D** are incorrect. **A** is incorrect because a group function can be used without a GROUP BY clause. In this case, the entire dataset is operated on as a group. **C** is incorrect because group functions are often executed against an entire table, which is treated as one group. **D** is incorrect because once a dataset has been partitioned into different groups, any group functions execute once per group.

   3. ☑   **A.** The SUM aggregate function ignores null values and adds non-null values. Since nine rows contain the SALARY value 100, 900 is returned.
   ☒   **B, C**, and **D** are incorrect. **B** would be returned if SUM(NVL(SALARY,100)) were executed. **C** is a tempting choice since regular arithmetic with NULL values returns a NULL result. However, the aggregate functions, except for COUNT(*), ignore NULL values. **D** is incorrect because the correct answer is **A**.

4. ☑ **C.** COUNT(*) considers all rows, including those with NULL values, while COUNT(SALARY) only considers the non-null rows.

   ☒ **A, B,** and **D** are incorrect.

5. ☑ **C.** The NVL function converts the one NULL value into 100. Thereafter, the average function adds the SALARY values and obtains 1000. Dividing this by the number of records returns 100.

   ☒ **A, B,** and **D** are incorrect. **B** would be returned if AVG(NVL(SALARY,0)) were selected. It is interesting to note that if AVG(SALARY) were selected, 100 would have also been returned, since the AVG function would sum the non-null values and divide the total by the number of rows with non-null SALARY values. So, AVG(SALARY) would be calculated as 900/9=100.

6. ☑ **C.** The dataset is segmented by the SALARY column. This creates two groups: one with SALARY values of 100 and the other with a null SALARY value. The average length of SALARY value 100 is 3 for the rows in the first group. The NULL salary value is first converted into the number 0 by the NVL function, and the average length of SALARY is 1. The SUM function operates across the two groups adding the values 3 and 1, returning 4.

   ☒ **A, B,** and **D** are incorrect. **A** seems plausible since group functions may not be nested more than two levels deep. Although there are four functions, only two are group functions, while the others are single-row functions evaluated before the group functions. **B** would be returned if the expression SUM(AVG(LENGTH(SALARY))) were selected. **D** is incorrect because the correct answer is **C**.

7. ☑ **A.** There are 12 distinct DEPARTMENT_ID values. Since this is the grouping attribute, 12 groups are created, including 1 with a null DEPARTMENT_ID value. Therefore, 12 rows are returned.

   ☒ **B, C,** and **D** are incorrect. **B** is incorrect because the null DEPARTMENT_ID is a valid unique value by which the group is partitioned. **C** is incorrect because 12 rows are returned. **D** is incorrect because the correct answer is **A**.

8. ☑ **C.** For a GROUP BY clause to be used, a group function must appear in the SELECT list.

   ☒ **A, B,** and **D** are incorrect. These are incorrect since the statement is syntactically inaccurate and is disallowed by Oracle. Do not mistake the column named MAX_SALARY for the MAX(SALARY) function.

9. ☑ **B.** Two groups are created based on their common DEPT_ID values. The group with DEPT_ID values of 10 consists of five rows with SALARY values of 100 in each of them. Therefore, the SUM(SALARY) function returns 500 for this group, and it satisfies the HAVING SUM(SALARY) > 400 clause. The group with DEPT_ID values of 20 has four rows with SALARY values of 100 and one row with a NULL SALARY. SUM(SALARY) only returns 400, and this group does not satisfy the HAVING clause.

   ☒ **A, C,** and **D** are incorrect. Beware of the SUM(NVL(SALARY,100)) expression in the SELECT clause. This expression selects the format of the output. It does not restrict or limit the dataset in any way. **A** would be correct if the HAVING clause determined there to be two groups to which the aggregate function would be applied. **C** is incorrect because there is one set to be aggregated, which results in one row being returned. **D** is incorrect because the correct answer is **B**.

10. ☑ **A**. Two groups are created based on their common DEPT_ID values. The group with DEPT_ID values of 10 consists of five rows with SALARY values of 100 in each of them. Therefore, the SUM(NVL(SALARY,100)) function returns 500 for this group and satisfies the HAVING SUM(NVL(SALARY,100))>400 clause. The group with DEPT_ID values of 20 has four rows with SALARY values of 100 and one row with a null SALARY. SUM(NVL(SALARY,100)) returns 500, and this group satisfies the HAVING clause. Therefore, two rows are returned.

☒ **B, C**, and **D** are incorrect. Although the SELECT clause contains SUM(SALARY), which returns 500 and 400 for the two groups, the HAVING clause contains the SUM(NVL(SALARY,100)) expression, which specifies the inclusion or exclusion criteria for a group-level row. **B** would be correct if the HAVING clause determined there to be one group to which the aggregate function would be applied. **C** is incorrect because there are two sets to be aggregated, which results in two rows being returned. **D** is incorrect because the correct answer is **A**.

11. ☑ **A** and **E**. The standard deviation is mathematically defined as the square root of its variance. The LISTAGG function sorts the measure using the ORDER BY in the WITHIN GROUP clause and returns an ordered concatenated string.

☒ **B, C**, and **D** are incorrect. All these statements are false.

12. ☑ **B**. The dataset is not divided into groups by a GROUP BY clause, and the LISTAGG function therefore operates on the entire table as a single dataset. One long row consisting of a concatenated list on LAST_NAME values is returned.

☒ **A, C, D,** and **E** are incorrect. **A** is incorrect because LISTAGG returns at least one row. **C** and **D** would be correct if the dataset was divided into 10 and 107 groups, respectively. **E** is incorrect because the correct answer is **B**.

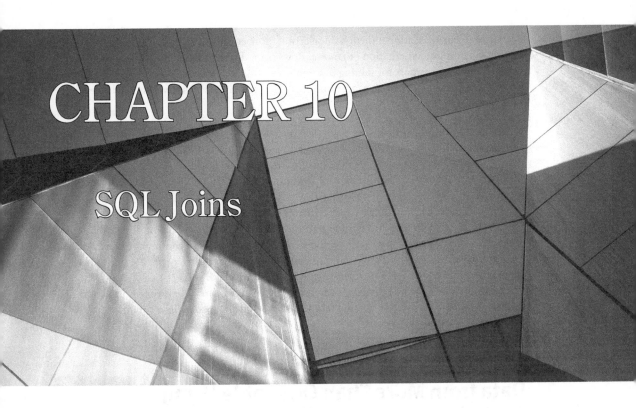

CHAPTER 10

SQL Joins

Exam Objectives

- 061.6.1 Write SELECT Statements to Access Data from More Than One Table Using Equijoins and Nonequijoins
- 061.6.2 Join a Table to Itself Using a Self-Join
- 061.6.3 View Data that Does Not Meet a Join Condition Using Outer Joins
- 061.6.4 Generate a Cartesian Product of Two or More Tables

The three pillars of relational theory are selection, projection, and joining. This chapter focuses on the practical implementation of *joining*. Rows from different tables are associated with each other using *joins*. Support for joining has implications for the way data is stored in database tables. Many data models such as third normal form or star schemas have emerged to exploit this feature.

Tables can be joined in several ways. The most common technique is called an *equijoin*. A row is associated with one or more rows in another table based on the *equality* of column values or expressions. Tables can also be joined using a *nonequijoin*. In this case, a row is associated with one or more rows in another table if its column values fall into a range determined by inequality operators.

A less common technique is to associate rows with other rows in the same table. This association is based on columns with logical and usually hierarchical relationships with each other. This is called a *self-join*. Rows with null or differing entries in common *join columns* are excluded when equijoins and nonequijoins collectively known as *inner joins* are performed. An *outer join* is available to fetch these *one-legged* or *orphaned* rows if necessary.

A *cross join* or *Cartesian product* is formed when every row from one table is joined to all rows in another. This join is often the result of missing or inadequate join conditions but is occasionally intentional.

Write SELECT Statements to Access Data from More Than One Table Using Equijoins and Nonequijoins

This certification objective receives extensive coverage in this chapter. It is crucial to learning the concepts and language for performing joins. This section introduces different types of joins in their primitive forms and outlines the broad categories that are available. This section then discusses the various join clauses. The chapter discusses modern American National Standards Institute (ANSI)–compliant and traditional Oracle syntaxes, with emphasis on the modern syntax. This section concludes with a discussion of nonequijoins and additional join conditions. Joining is described by focusing on the following eight areas:

- Types of joins
- Joining tables using ANSI SQL syntax
- Qualifying ambiguous column names
- The NATURAL JOIN clause
- The JOIN USING clause
- The JOIN ON clause
- N-way joins and additional join conditions
- Nonequijoins

Types of Joins

Two basic joins are the *equijoin* and the *nonequijoin*. Equijoins are probably more frequently used. Joins can be performed between multiple tables, but much of the following discussion will use two hypothetical tables to illustrate the concepts and language of joins. The first table is called the *source*, and the second is called the *target*. Rows in the source and target tables comprise one or more columns. As an example, assume that the *source* and *target* are the COUNTRIES and REGIONS tables from the HR schema, respectively.

The COUNTRIES table contains three columns named COUNTRY_ID, COUNTRY_ NAME, and REGION_ID. The REGIONS table is composed of two columns named REGION_ID and REGION_NAME. The data in these two tables is related to each other based on the common REGION_ID column. Consider the following queries:

```
Query 1: SELECT *
         FROM countries
         WHERE country_id='CA';

Query 2: SELECT region_name
         FROM regions
         WHERE region_id=2;
```

The name of the region to which a country belongs may be determined by obtaining its REGION_ID value. This value is used to join it with the row in the REGIONS table with the same REGION_ID. Query 1 retrieves the column values associated with the row from the COUNTRIES table where the COUNTRY_ID='CA'. The REGION_ID value of this row is 2. Query 2 fetches the Americas REGION_NAME from the REGIONS table for the row with REGION_ID=2. Equijoining facilitates the retrieval of column values from multiple tables using a single query.

The source and target tables can be swapped, so the REGIONS table could be the source and the COUNTRIES table could be the target. Consider the following two queries:

```
Query 1: SELECT *
         FROM regions
         WHERE region_name='Americas';

Query 2: SELECT country_name
         FROM countries
         WHERE region_id=2;
```

Query 1 fetches one row with a REGION_ID value of 2. Joining in this reversed manner allows the following question to be asked: What countries belong to the Americas region? The answers from Query 2 are five COUNTRY_NAME values: Argentina, Brazil, Canada, Mexico, and the United States of America. These results can be obtained from a single query that joins the tables together. The language to perform equijoins, nonequijoins, outer joins, and cross joins is introduced next, along with a discussion of the traditional Oracle join syntax.

Inner Joins

The inner join is implemented using three possible *join clauses* that use the following keywords in different combinations: NATURAL JOIN, USING, and ON.

When the source and target tables share identically named columns, it is possible to perform a natural join between them without specifying a join column. In this scenario, columns with the same names in the source and target tables are automatically associated with each other. Rows with matching column values in both tables are retrieved. The REGIONS and COUNTRIES table both share the REGION_ID column. They may be naturally joined without specifying join columns, as shown in the first two queries in Figure 10-1.

The NATURAL JOIN keywords instruct Oracle to identify columns with identical names between the source and target tables. Thereafter, a join is implicitly performed between them. In the first query, the REGION_ID column is identified as the only commonly named column in both tables. REGIONS is the source table and appears after the FROM clause. The target table is therefore COUNTRIES. For each row in the REGIONS table, a match for the REGION_ID value is sought from all the rows in the COUNTRIES table. An interim result set is constructed containing rows matching the join condition. This set is then restricted by the WHERE clause. In this case, because the COUNTRY_NAME value must be Canada, a REGION_NAME of Americas is returned.

Figure 10-1 Natural joins and other inner joins

The second query shows a natural join where COUNTRIES is the source table. The REGION_ID value for each row in the COUNTRIES table is identified. The set of rows from the REGIONS table to be used in the matching exercise with the COUNTRIES table is first pruned by the WHERE condition to only those with Americas as their REGION_NAME value. The COUNTRY_NAME values from rows with Americas as their REGION_NAME are returned from the COUNTRIES table.

Sometimes more control must be exercised regarding which columns to use for joins. When there are identical column names in the source and target tables you want to exclude as join columns, you can use the JOIN . . . USING format. Remember that Oracle does not impose any rules stating that columns with the same name in two discrete tables must necessarily have any relationship with each other. The third query explicitly specifies that the REGIONS table be joined to the COUNTRIES table based on common values in their REGION_ID columns. This syntax allows inner joins to be formed on specific columns instead of on all commonly named columns.

The fourth query demonstrates the JOIN . . . ON format of the inner join, which allows join columns to be explicitly stated. This format does not depend on the columns in the source and target tables having identical names. This form is more general and is the most widely used inner join format.

TIP   Be wary when using natural joins since database designers can assign the same name to key or unique columns. These columns can have names like ID or SEQ_NO. If a natural join is attempted between such tables, ambiguous and unexpected results may be returned.

Outer Joins

Not all tables share a perfect relationship, where every record in the source table can be matched to at least one row in the target table. It is occasionally required that rows with nonmatching join column values also be retrieved by a query. This may seem to defeat the purpose of joins but has some practical benefits.

Suppose the EMPLOYEES and DEPARTMENTS tables are joined with common DEPARTMENT_ID values. EMPLOYEES records with null DEPARTMENT_ID values are excluded along with values absent from the DEPARTMENTS table. An *outer join* fetches these rows.

Cross Joins

A *cross join* or *Cartesian product* derives its names from mathematics, where it is also referred to as a *cross product* between two sets or matrices. This join creates one row of output for every combination of source and target table rows.

If the source and target tables have three and four rows, respectively, a cross join between them results in $(3 \times 4 = 12)$ rows being returned. Consider the row counts retrieved from the queries in Figure 10-2.

The first two row counts are performed on the COUNTRIES and REGIONS tables yielding 25 and 4 rows, respectively. Query 3 counts the number of rows returned from a cross join of these tables and yields 100. Query 4 would return 100 records if the WHERE clause

Figure 10-2 Cross join

was absent. Each of the four rows in the REGIONS table is joined to the one row from the COUNTRIES table. Each row returned contains every column from both tables.

Oracle Join Syntax

A proprietary Oracle join syntax has evolved that is stable and understood by millions of users. This traditional syntax is supported by Oracle and is present in software systems across the world. You will no doubt encounter the traditional Oracle join syntax that is now making way for the standardized ANSI-compliant syntax discussed in this chapter.

The traditional Oracle join syntax supports inner joins, outer joins, and Cartesian joins, as shown in the following queries:

```
Query 1: SELECT regions.region_name, countries.country_name
         FROM regions, countries
         WHERE regions.region_id=countries.region_id;

Query 2: SELECT last_name, department_name
         FROM employees, departments
         WHERE employees.department_id (+) = departments.department_id;

Query 3: SELECT *
         FROM regions,countries;
```

Query 1 performs an inner join by specifying the join as a condition in the WHERE clause. This is the most significant difference between the traditional and ANSI SQL join syntaxes. Take note of the column aliasing using the TABLE.COLUMN_NAME notation to disambiguate the identical column names. This notation is discussed in detail later in this chapter. Query 2 specifies the join between the source and target tables as a WHERE condition. There is a plus (+) symbol enclosed in brackets to the *left* of the equal sign that indicates to Oracle that a *right outer join* must be performed. This query returns employees' LAST_NAME and their matching DEPARTMENT_NAME values. In addition, the outer join retrieves DEPARTMENT_NAME from the rows with DEPARTMENT_ID values not currently assigned to any employee records. Query 3 performs a Cartesian or cross join by excluding the join condition.

> **TIP** The traditional Oracle join syntax is widely used. However, the exam assesses your understanding of joins and the ANSI SQL forms of its syntax. Be prepared, though; some questions may tap your knowledge of the traditional syntax. This knowledge is useful since traditional Oracle syntax is deeply embedded across software systems worldwide.

Joining Tables Using ANSI SQL Syntax

Prior to Oracle 9*i*, the traditional join syntax was the only language available to join tables. Since then, Oracle has introduced a new language that is compliant with the latest ANSI standards. It offers no performance benefits over the traditional syntax. Inner, outer, and cross joins can be written using both ANSI SQL and traditional Oracle SQL.

The general form of the SELECT statement using ANSI SQL syntax is as follows:

SELECT *table1.column, table2.column*
FROM *table1*
[NATURAL JOIN *table2*] |
[JOIN *table2* USING (*column_name*)] |
[JOIN *table2* ON (*table1.column_name = table2.column_name*)] |
[LEFT | RIGHT | FULL OUTER JOIN *table2*
ON (*table1.column_name = table2.column_name*)] |
[CROSS JOIN *table2*];

The following sections explain this syntax and provide examples. The general form of the traditional Oracle-proprietary syntax relevant to joins is as follows:

SELECT *table1.column, table2.column*
FROM *table1, table2*
[WHERE (*table1.column_name = table2.column_name*)] |
[WHERE (*table1.column_name(+)= table2.column_name*)] |
[WHERE (*table1.column_name)= table2.column_name*) (+)] ;

If no joins or fewer than N-1 joins are specified in the WHERE clause conditions, where N refers to the number of tables in the query, then a Cartesian or cross join is performed. If an adequate number of join conditions is specified, then the first optional conditional clause specifies an inner join, while the second two optional clauses specify the syntax for right and left outer joins.

Qualifying Ambiguous Column Names

Columns with the same names may occur in tables involved in a join. The columns named DEPARTMENT_ID and MANAGER_ID are found in both the EMPLOYEES and DEPARTMENTS tables. The REGION_ID column is present in both the REGIONS and COUNTRIES tables. Listing such columns in a query becomes problematic when Oracle cannot resolve their origin. Columns with unique names across the tables involved in a join cause no ambiguity because Oracle can easily resolve their source table.

The problem of ambiguous column names is addressed with dot notation. A column can be prefixed by its table name and a dot or period symbol to designate its origin. This differentiates it from a column with the same name in another table. Dot notation can be used in queries involving any number of tables. Referencing some columns using dot notation does not imply that all columns must be referenced in this way.

Dot notation is enhanced with table aliases. A *table alias* provides an alternative, usually shorter name, for a table. A column may be referenced as TABLE_NAME.COLUMN_NAME or TABLE_ALIAS.COLUMN_NAME. Consider the query shown in Figure 10-3.

The EMPLOYEES table is aliased with the short name EMP, while the DEPARTMENTS table is not. The SELECT clause references the EMPLOYEE_ID and MANAGER_ID columns as EMP.EMPLOYEE_ID and EMP.MANAGER_ID. The MANAGER_ID column from the

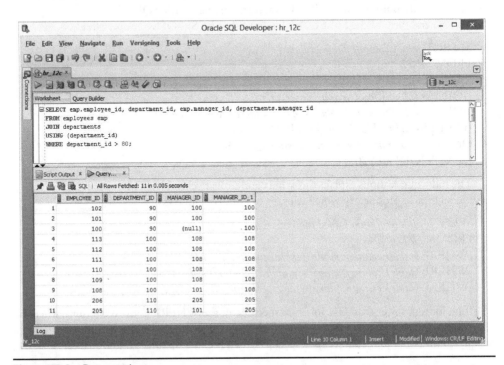

Figure 10-3 Dot notation

DEPARTMENTS table is referred to as DEPARTMENTS.MANAGER_ID. Qualifying the EMPLOYEE_ID column using dot notation is unnecessary because there is only one column with this name between the two tables. Therefore, there is no ambiguity.

The MANAGER_ID column must be qualified to avoid ambiguity because it is featured in both tables. Since the JOIN . . . USING format is applied, only DEPARTMENT_ID is used as the join column. If a NATURAL JOIN was employed, both the DEPARTMENT_ID and MANAGER_ID columns would be used. If the MANAGER_ID column was not qualified, an "ORA-00918: column ambiguously defined" error would be returned. If DEPARTMENT_ID was aliased, an "ORA-25154: column part of USING clause cannot have qualifier" error would be raised.

SQL Developer provides the heading MANAGER_ID to the first reference made in the SELECT clause. The string "_1" is automatically appended to the second reference, creating the heading MANAGER_ID_1.

 TIP Qualifying column references with dot notation to indicate a column's table of origin has a performance benefit. Time is saved because Oracle is directed instantaneously to the appropriate table and does not have to resolve the table name.

The NATURAL JOIN Clause

The general syntax for the NATURAL JOIN clause is as follows:

SELECT *table1.column, table2.column*
FROM *table1*
NATURAL JOIN *table2;*

The natural join identifies the columns with common names in *table1* and *table2* and implicitly joins the tables using all these columns. The columns in the SELECT clause can be qualified using dot notation unless they are one of the join columns. Consider the following queries:

```
Query 1: SELECT *
         FROM locations
         NATURAL JOIN countries;

Query 2: SELECT *
         FROM locations, countries
         WHERE locations.country_id = countries.country_id;

Query 3: SELECT *
         FROM jobs
         NATURAL JOIN countries;

Query 4: SELECT *
         FROM jobs, countries;
```

The natural join identifies columns with common names between the two tables. In Query 1, COUNTRY_ID occurs in both tables and becomes the join column. Query 2 is written using traditional Oracle syntax and retrieves the same rows as Query 1. Unless you are familiar with the columns in the source and target tables, natural joins must be used with caution because join conditions are automatically formed between all columns with shared names.

Query 3 performs a natural join between the JOBS and COUNTRIES tables. There are no columns with identical names, resulting in a Cartesian product. Query 4 is equivalent to Query 3, and a Cartesian join is performed using traditional Oracle syntax.

The natural join is simple but prone to a fundamental weakness. It suffers the risk that two columns with the same name might have no relationship and may not even have compatible data types. In Figure 10-4, the COUNTRIES, REGIONS, and SALES_REGIONS tables are

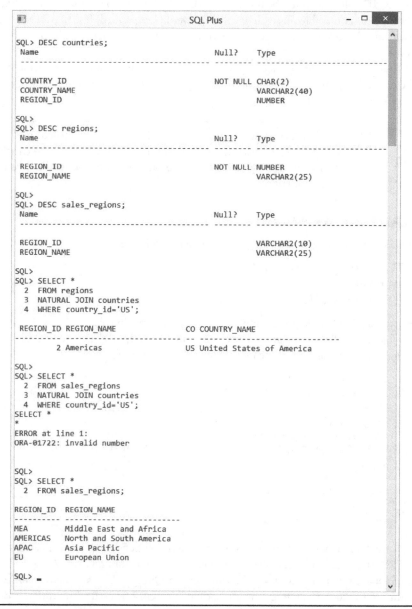

Figure 10-4 The natural join

described. The SALES_REGIONS table was constructed to illustrate the following important point: Although it has REGION_ID in common with the COUNTRIES table, it cannot be naturally joined to it because their data types are incompatible. The data types of the COUNTRIES.REGION_ID and SALES_REGIONS.REGION_ID columns are NUMBER and VARCHAR2, respectively. The character data cannot be implicitly converted into numeric data, and an "ORA-01722: invalid number" error is raised. The REGIONS.REGION_ID column is of type NUMBER, and its data is related to the data in the COUNTRIES table. Therefore, the natural join between the REGIONS and COUNTRIES table works perfectly.

Exercise 10-1: Using the NATURAL JOIN The JOB_HISTORY table shares three identically named columns with the EMPLOYEES table: EMPLOYEE_ID, JOB_ID, and DEPARTMENT_ID. You are required to describe the tables and fetch the EMPLOYEE_ID, JOB_ID, DEPARTMENT_ID, LAST_NAME, HIRE_DATE, and END_DATE values for all rows retrieved using a natural join. Alias the EMPLOYEES table as EMP and the JOB_HISTORY table as JH and use dot notation where possible.

1. Start SQL*Plus and connect to the HR schema.

2. The tables are described using the commands DESC EMPLOYEES and DESC JOB_HISTORY, and the columns with identical names and their data types can be examined.

3. The FROM clause is as follows:

   ```
   FROM JOB_HISTORY JH
   ```

4. The JOIN clause is as follows:

   ```
   NATURAL JOIN EMPLOYEES EMP
   ```

5. The SELECT clause is as follows:

   ```
   SELECT EMPLOYEE_ID, JOB_ID, DEPARTMENT_ID,
   EMP.LAST_NAME, EMP.HIRE_DATE, JH.END_DATE
   ```

6. Executing this statement returns a single row with the same EMPLOYEE_ID, JOB_ID, and DEPARTMENT_ID values in both tables.

The JOIN USING Clause

The format of the syntax for the JOIN USING clause is as follows:

SELECT *table1.column, table2.column*
FROM *table1*
JOIN *table2* USING (*join_column1, join_column2...*);

While the natural join contains the NATURAL keyword in its syntax, the JOIN . . . USING syntax does not. An error is raised if the keywords NATURAL and USING occur in the same join clause. The JOIN . . . USING clause allows one or more equijoin columns to be explicitly specified in brackets after the USING keyword. This avoids the shortcomings associated with the natural join. Many situations demand that tables be joined only on certain columns, and this format caters for this requirement. Consider the following queries:

```
Query 1: SELECT *
         FROM locations
         JOIN countries
         USING (country_id);
```

```
Query 2: SELECT *
         FROM locations, countries
         WHERE locations.country_id = countries.country_id;
```

Query 1 specifies that the LOCATIONS and COUNTRIES tables must be joined on common COUNTRY_ID column values. All columns from these tables are retrieved for the rows with matching join column values. Query 2 shows a traditionally specified query that retrieves the same rows as Query 1. The join columns specified with the JOIN . . . USING syntax cannot be qualified using table names or aliases when they are referenced in the SELECT and JOIN clauses. Since this join syntax potentially excludes some columns with identical names from the join clause, these must be qualified if they are referenced to avoid ambiguity.

As Figure 10-5 shows, the JOB_HISTORY and EMPLOYEES tables were joined based on the presence of equal values in their JOB_ID and EMPLOYEE_ID columns. Rows conforming to this join condition are retrieved. These tables share three identically named columns. In this example, only two of these are specified as join columns. Notice that although the third identically named column is DEPARTMENT_ID, it is qualified with a table alias to avoid ambiguity, while the join columns specified in the SELECT clause cannot be qualified with table aliases.

The JOIN ON Clause

The format of the syntax for the JOIN ON clause is as follows:

SELECT *table1.column, table2.column*
FROM *table1*
JOIN *table2* ON (*table1.column_name = table2.column_name*);

The natural join and the JOIN . . . USING clauses depend on join columns with identical column names. The JOIN . . . ON clause allows the explicit specification of join columns, regardless of their column names. This is the most flexible and widely used form of the join clauses.

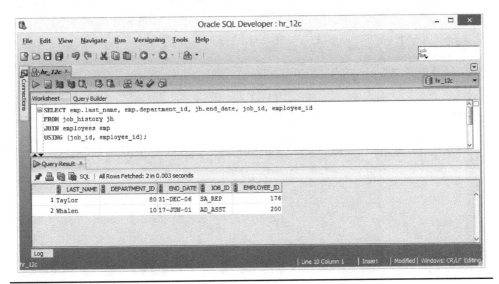

Figure 10-5   Natural join using the JOIN...USING clause

The ON and NATURAL keywords cannot appear together in a join clause. The equijoin columns are fully qualified as *table1.column1 = table2.column2* and are optionally specified in brackets after the ON keyword. The following queries illustrate the JOIN . . . ON clause:

```
Query 1: SELECT *
         FROM departments d
         JOIN employees e ON (e.employee_id=d.department_id);

Query 2: SELECT *
         FROM employees e, departments d
         WHERE e.employee_id=d.department_id;
```

Query 1 retrieves all column values from both the DEPARTMENTS and EMPLOYEES tables for the rows that meet an equijoin condition. This condition is fulfilled by EMPLOYEE_ID values matching DEPARTMENT_ID values in the DEPARTMENTS table. The traditional Oracle syntax in Query 2 returns the same results as Query 1. Notice the similarities between the traditional join condition specified in the WHERE clause and the join condition specified after the ON keyword.

The START_DATE column in the JOB_HISTORY table is joined to the HIRE_DATE column in the EMPLOYEES table in Figure 10-6. This equijoin retrieves the details of employees who worked for the organization and changed jobs.

Exercise 10-2: Using the NATURAL JOIN . . . ON Clause Each record in the DEPARTMENTS table has a MANAGER_ID column matching an EMPLOYEE_ID value in

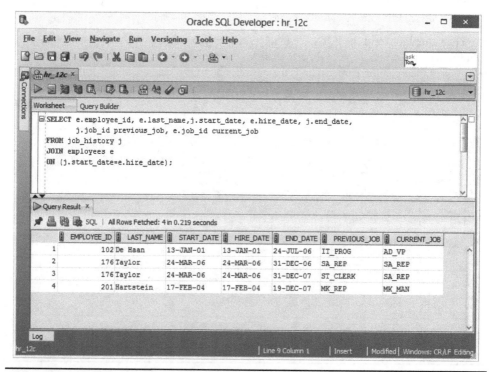

Figure 10-6   Inner join using the JOIN . . . ON clause

the EMPLOYEES table. You are required to produce a report with one column aliased as Managers. Each row must contain a sentence of the following format: FIRST_NAME LAST_NAME is manager of the DEPARTMENT_NAME department. Alias the EMPLOYEES table as E and the DEPARTMENTS table as D and use dot notation where possible.

1. Start SQL Developer and connect to the HR schema.

2. The Managers column can be constructed by concatenating the required items and separating them with spaces.

3. The SELECT clause is as follows:

```
SELECT E.FIRST_NAME||' '||E.LAST_NAME||' is manager of the '||
D.DEPARTMENT_NAME||' department.' "Managers"
```

4. The FROM clause is as follows:

```
FROM EMPLOYEES E
```

5. The JOIN . . . ON clause is as follows:

```
JOIN DEPARTMENTS D
ON (E. EMPLOYEE_ID=D.MANAGER_ID)
```

6. Executing this statement returns 11 rows describing the managers of each department, as shown in the following illustration:

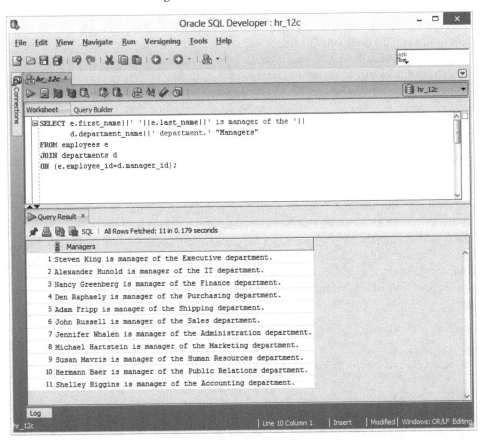

N-Way Joins and Additional Join Conditions

The joins just discussed were demonstrated using two tables. There is no restriction on the number of tables that can be joined. Third normal form consists of a set of tables connected through a series of primary and foreign key relationships. Traversing these relationships using joins enables consistent and reliable retrieval of data. However, there are instances when primary and foreign key relationships are not defined between tables. These tables can also be joined, but the results do not benefit from referential integrity being enforced by the database. When multiple joins exist in a statement, they are evaluated from left to right. Consider the following query using a mixture of natural joins and Oracle joins:

```
SELECT r.region_name, c.country_name, l.city, d.department_name
FROM departments d
NATURAL JOIN locations l,
countries c, regions r;
```

The natural join between DEPARTMENTS and LOCATIONS creates an interim result set consisting of 27 rows since they are implicitly joined on the LOCATION_ID column. This set is then Cartesian joined to the COUNTRIES table since a join condition is not implicitly or explicitly specified. The 27 interim rows are joined to the 25 rows in the COUNTRIES table, yielding a new interim results set with 675 (27 × 25) rows and three columns: DEPARTMENT_NAME, CITY, and COUNTRY_NAME. This set is then joined to the REGIONS table. Once again, a Cartesian join occurs because the REGION_ID column is absent from any join condition. The final result set contains 2700 (675 × 4) rows and four columns. Using natural joins mixed with Oracle joins is error prone and not recommended since join conditions may sometimes be erroneously omitted.

The JOIN . . . USING and JOIN . . . ON syntaxes are better suited for joining multiple tables. The following query joins four tables using the natural join syntax:

```
SELECT region_id, country_id, c.country_name, l.city, d.department_name
FROM departments d
NATURAL JOIN locations l
NATURAL JOIN countries c
NATURAL JOIN regions r;
```

This query correctly yields 27 rows in the final results set since the required join columns are listed in the SELECT clause. The following query demonstrates how the JOIN . . . ON clause is used to fetch the same 27 rows. A join condition can reference only columns in its scope. In the following example, the join from DEPARTMENTS to LOCATIONS may not reference columns in the COUNTRIES or REGIONS tables, but the join between COUNTRIES and REGIONS may reference any column from the four tables involved in the query.

```
SELECT r.region_name, c.country_name, l.city, d.department_name
FROM departments d
JOIN locations l ON (l.location_id=d.location_id)
JOIN countries c ON (c.country_id=l.country_id)
JOIN regions r ON (r.region_id=c.region_id);
```

The JOIN . . . USING clause can also be used to join these four tables as follows:

```
SELECT r.region_name, c.country_name, l.city, d.department_name
FROM departments d
JOIN locations l USING (location_id)
JOIN countries c USING (country_id)
JOIN regions r USING (region_id);
```

The WHERE clause is used to specify conditions that restrict the results set of a query whether it contains joins or not. The JOIN . . . ON clause is also used to specify conditions that limit the results set created by the join. Consider the following two queries:

```
Query 1:  SELECT d.department_name
          FROM departments d
          JOIN locations l
          ON (l.LOCATION_ID=d.LOCATION_ID)
          WHERE d.department_name LIKE 'P%';

Query 2:  SELECT d.department_name
          FROM departments d
          JOIN locations l
          ON (l.LOCATION_ID=d.LOCATION_ID
          AND d.department_name like 'P%');
```

Query 1 uses a WHERE clause to restrict the 27 rows created by equijoining the DEPARTMENTS and LOCATIONS tables based on their LOCATION_ID values to the three that contain DEPARTMENT_ID values beginning with the letter *P*. Query 2 implements the condition within the brackets of the ON subclause and returns the same three rows.

Five tables are joined in Figure 10-7, resulting in a list describing the top-earning employees and geographical information about their departments.

 TIP There are three equijoin or inner join formats. The natural join uses the NATURAL JOIN clause and joins two tables based on all columns with shared names. The other two formats use the JOIN . . . USING and JOIN . . . ON clauses. Pay attention to the syntax since a join clause such as SELECT * FROM TABLE1 NATURAL JOIN TABLE2 USING (COLUMN) may appear correct but is, in fact, syntactically incorrect. Remember the USING, ON, and NATURAL keywords are mutually exclusive in the context of the same join clause.

Nonequijoins

Nonequijoins match column values from different tables based on an inequality expression. The value of the join column in each row in the source table is compared to the corresponding values in the target table. A match is found if the expression used in the join, based on an inequality operator, evaluates to true. When such a join is constructed, a nonequijoin is performed.

A nonequijoin is specified using the JOIN . . . ON syntax, but the join condition contains an inequality operator instead of an equal sign.

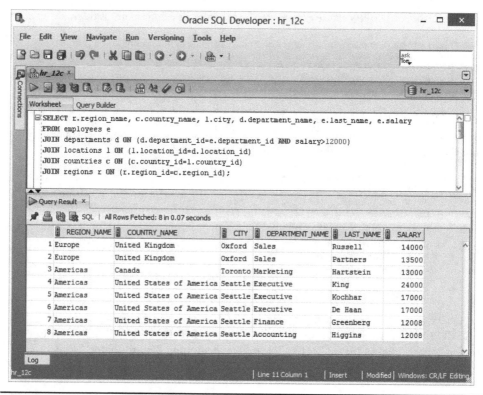

Figure 10-7   N-way joins and additional join conditions

The format of the syntax for a nonequijoin clause is as follows:

SELECT *table1.column, table2.column*
FROM *table1*
[JOIN *table2* ON (*table1.column_name* < *table2.column_name*)]|
[JOIN *table2* ON (*table1.column_name* > *table2.column_name*)]|
[JOIN *table2* ON (*table1.column_name* <= *table2.column_name*)]|
[JOIN *table2* ON (*table1.column_name* >= *table2.column_name*)]|
[JOIN *table2* ON (*table1.column* BETWEEN *table2.col1* AND *table2.col2*)]

Consider the 16 rows returned by the query in Figure 10-8. The EMPLOYEES table is nonequijoined to the JOBS table based on the inequality join condition (2*E.SALARY < J.MAX_SALARY). The JOBS table stores the salary range for different jobs in the organization. The SALARY value for each employee record is doubled and compared with all MAX_SALARY values in the JOBS table. If the join condition evaluates to true, the row is returned.

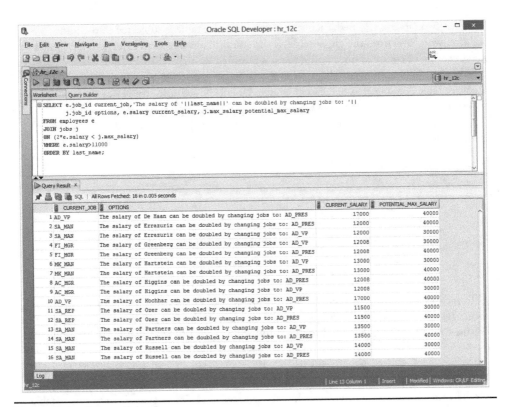

Figure 10-8   Nonequijoins

> **TIP**   Nonequijoins are not as commonly used as equijoins. The BETWEEN
> range operator often appears with nonequijoin conditions. It is simpler to
> use one BETWEEN operator in a condition than two nonequijoin conditions
> based on the less than or equal to (<=) operator and the greater than or equal to (>=)
> operator.

Join a Table to Itself Using a Self-Join

Storing hierarchical data in a single relational table may be accomplished by allocating at least
two columns per row. One column stores an identifier of the row's parent record, and the second
stores the row's identifier. Associating rows with each other based on a hierarchical relationship
requires Oracle to join a table to itself. This *self-join* technique is discussed in the next section.

Joining a Table to Itself Using the JOIN . . . ON Clause

Suppose you need to store a family tree in a relational table; you could take several approaches.
One option is to use a table called FAMILY with columns named ID, NAME, MOTHER_ID,
and FATHER_ID, where each row stores a person's name, a unique ID number, and the ID
values for their parents.

When two tables are joined, each row from the source table is subjected to the join condition with rows from the target table. If the condition evaluates to true, then the joined row, consisting of columns from both tables, is returned.

When the join columns originate from the same table, a self-join is required. Conceptually, the source table is duplicated to create the target table. The self-join works like a regular join between these tables. Note that, internally, Oracle does not duplicate the table, and this description is merely provided to explain the concept of self-joining. Consider the following three queries:

```
Query 1: SELECT id, name, father_id
         FROM family;

Query 2: SELECT name
         FROM family
         WHERE id=&father_id;

Query 3: SELECT f1.name Dad, f2.name Child
         FROM family f1
         JOIN family f2
         ON(f1.id=f2.father_id);
```

To identify a person's father in the FAMILY table, you could use Query 1 to get that person's ID, NAME, and FATHER_ID value. In Query 2, the FATHER_ID value obtained from the first query could be substituted to obtain the father's NAME value. Notice that both Queries 1 and 2 source information from the FAMILY table.

Query 3 performs a self-join with the JOIN . . . ON clause by aliasing the FAMILY table as f1 and f2. Oracle treats these as different tables even though they point to the same physical table. The first occurrence of the FAMILY table, aliased as f1, is designated as the source table, while the second occurrence, aliased as f2, is assigned as the target table. The join condition in the ON clause is of the format *source.child_id=target.parent_id*. Figure 10-9 shows a sample of FAMILY data and demonstrates a three-way self-join to the same table.

Exercise 10-3: Performing a Self-Join   There is a hierarchical relationship between employees and their managers. For each row in the EMPLOYEES table, the MANAGER_ID column stores the EMPLOYEE_ID of every employee's manager. Using a self-join on the EMPLOYEES table, you are required to retrieve the employee's LAST_NAME, EMPLOYEE_ID, MANAGER_ID, manager's LAST_NAME, and employee's DEPARTMENT_ID for the rows with DEPARMENT_ID values of 10, 20, or 30. Alias the EMPLOYEES table as E and the second instance of the EMPLOYEES table as M. Sort the results based on the DEPARTMENT_ID column.

1. Start SQL Developer and connect to the HR schema.

2. The SELECT clause is as follows:

```
SELECT E.LAST_NAME EMPLOYEE, E.EMPLOYEE_ID, E.MANAGER_ID,
M.LAST_NAME MANAGER, E.DEPARTMENT_ID
```

3. The FROM clause with source table and alias is as follows:

```
FROM EMPLOYEES E
```

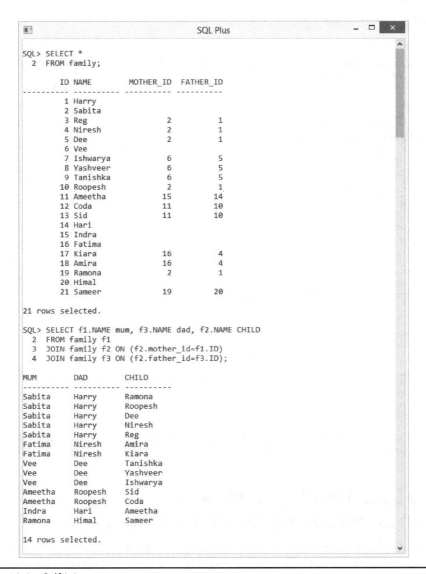

```
                                    SQL Plus                    _  □  ×

SQL> SELECT *
  2  FROM family;

        ID NAME        MOTHER_ID  FATHER_ID
---------- ---------- ---------- ----------
         1 Harry
         2 Sabita
         3 Reg                 2          1
         4 Niresh              2          1
         5 Dee                 2          1
         6 Vee
         7 Ishwarya            6          5
         8 Yashveer            6          5
         9 Tanishka            6          5
        10 Roopesh             2          1
        11 Ameetha            15         14
        12 Coda               11         10
        13 Sid                11         10
        14 Hari
        15 Indra
        16 Fatima
        17 Kiara              16          4
        18 Amira              16          4
        19 Ramona              2          1
        20 Himal
        21 Sameer             19         20

21 rows selected.

SQL> SELECT f1.NAME mum, f3.NAME dad, f2.NAME CHILD
  2  FROM family f1
  3  JOIN family f2 ON (f2.mother_id=f1.ID)
  4  JOIN family f3 ON (f2.father_id=f3.ID);

MUM        DAD        CHILD
---------- ---------- ----------
Sabita     Harry      Ramona
Sabita     Harry      Roopesh
Sabita     Harry      Dee
Sabita     Harry      Niresh
Sabita     Harry      Reg
Fatima     Niresh     Amira
Fatima     Niresh     Kiara
Vee        Dee        Tanishka
Vee        Dee        Yashveer
Vee        Dee        Ishwarya
Ameetha    Roopesh    Sid
Ameetha    Roopesh    Coda
Indra      Hari       Ameetha
Ramona     Himal      Sameer

14 rows selected.
```

Figure 10-9   Self-join

4. The JOIN . . . ON clause with aliased target table is as follows:

```
JOIN EMPLOYEES M ON (E.MANAGER_ID=M.EMPLOYEE_ID)
```

5. The WHERE clause is as follows:

```
WHERE E.DEPARTMENT_ID IN (10,20,30)
```

6. The ORDER BY clause is as follows:

```
ORDER BY E.DEPARTMENT_ID
```

7. Executing this statement returns nine rows describing the managers of each employee in these departments.

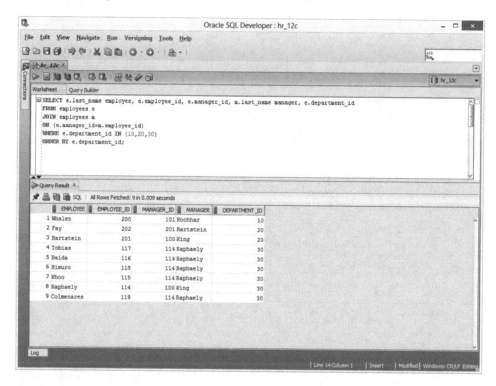

View Data That Does Not Meet a Join Condition by Using Outer Joins

Equijoins match rows between two tables based on the equality of the column data stored in each table. Nonequijoins rely on matching rows between tables based on a join condition containing an inequality expression. Target table rows with no matching join column in the source table are usually not required. When they are required, however, an *outer join* is used to fetch them. Several variations of outer joins can be used depending on whether join column data is missing from the source or target tables or both. These outer join techniques are described in the following topics:

- Inner versus outer joins
- Left outer joins
- Right outer joins
- Full outer joins

Inner versus Outer Joins

When equijoins and nonequijoins are performed, rows from the source and target tables are matched using a join condition formulated with equality and inequality operators, respectively. These are referred to as *inner joins*. An *outer join* is performed when rows, which are not retrieved by an inner join, are returned.

Two tables sometimes share a *master-detail* or *parent-child* relationship. In the sample HR schema there are several pairs of tables with such a relationship. One pair is the DEPARTMENTS and EMPLOYEES tables. The DEPARTMENTS table stores a master list of DEPARTMENT_NAME and DEPARTMENT_ID values. Each EMPLOYEES record has a DEPARTMENT_ID column constrained to be either a value that exists in the DEPARTMENTS table or null. This leads to one of the following three scenarios. The fourth scenario could occur if the constraint between the tables was removed.

1. An employee row has a DEPARTMENT_ID value that matches a row in the DEPARTMENTS table.

2. An employee row has a null value in its DEPARTMENT_ID column.

3. There are rows in the DEPARTMENTS table with DEPARTMENT_ID values that are not stored in any employee records.

4. An employee row has a DEPARTMENT_ID value that is not featured in the DEPARTMENTS table.

The first scenario describes an inner join between the two tables. The second and third scenarios cause many problems. Joining the EMPLOYEES and DEPARTMENTS tables on the DEPARTMENT_ID column may result in rows with null DEPARTMENT_ID values being excluded. An outer join can be used to include these orphaned rows in the results set. The fourth scenario should rarely occur in a well-designed database because foreign key constraints would prevent the insertion of child records with no parent values. Since this row will be excluded by an inner join, it can be retrieved using an outer join.

A left outer join between the source and target tables returns the results of an inner join as well as rows from the source table excluded by that inner join. A right outer join between the source and target tables returns the results of an inner join as well as rows from the target table excluded by that inner join. If a join returns the results of an inner join as well as rows from both the source and target tables excluded by that inner join, then a full outer join has been performed.

Left Outer Joins

The format of the syntax for the LEFT OUTER JOIN clause is as follows:

```
SELECT table1.column, table2.column
FROM table1
LEFT OUTER JOIN table2
ON (table1.column = table2.column);
```

A left outer join performs an inner join of *table1* and *table2* based on the condition specified after the ON keyword. Any rows from the table on the *left* of the JOIN keyword excluded for not fulfilling the join condition are also returned. Consider the following two queries:

```
Query 1: SELECT e.employee_id, e.department_id EMP_DEPT_ID,
                d.department_id DEPT_DEPT_ID, d.department_name
         FROM departments d
         LEFT OUTER JOIN employees e
         ON (d.DEPARTMENT_ID=e.DEPARTMENT_ID)
         WHERE d.department_name like 'P%';

Query 2: SELECT e.employee_id, e.department_id EMP_DEPT_ID,
                d.department_id DEPT_DEPT_ID, d.department_name
         FROM departments d
         JOIN employees e
         ON (d.DEPARTMENT_ID=e.DEPARTMENT_ID)
         WHERE d.department_name like 'P%';
```

Queries 1 and 2 are identical except for the join clauses, which have the keywords LEFT OUTER JOIN and JOIN, respectively. Query 2 performs an inner join, and seven rows are returned. These rows share identical DEPARTMENT_ID values in both tables. Query 1 returns the same seven rows and one additional row. This extra row is obtained from the table to the left of the JOIN keyword, which is the DEPARTMENTS table. It is the row containing details of the Payroll department. The inner join does not include this row since no employees are currently assigned to the department.

Figure 10-10 shows a left outer join. The inner join produces 27 rows with matching LOCATION_ID values in both tables. There are 43 rows in total, which implies that 16 rows were retrieved from the LOCATIONS table, which is on the *left* of the JOIN keyword. None of the rows from the DEPARTMENTS table contains any of these 16 LOCATION_ID values.

Right Outer Joins

The format of the syntax for the RIGHT OUTER JOIN clause is as follows:

SELECT *table1.column, table2.column*
FROM *table1*
RIGHT OUTER JOIN *table2*
ON (*table1.column = table2.column*);

A right outer join performs an inner join of *table1* and *table2* based on the join condition specified after the ON keyword. Rows from the table to the *right* of the JOIN keyword, excluded by the join condition, are also returned. Consider the following query:

```
SELECT e.last_name, d.department_name
FROM departments d
RIGHT OUTER JOIN employees e
ON (e.department_id=d.department_id)
WHERE e.last_name LIKE 'G%';
```

The inner join produces seven rows containing details for the employees with LAST_NAME values that begin with the letter *G*. The EMPLOYEES table is to the *right* of the JOIN keyword.

```
SQL Plus                                              _  □  ×

SQL> SELECT city, l.location_id "l.location_id", d.location_id "d.location_id"
  2  FROM locations l
  3  LEFT OUTER JOIN departments d
  4  ON (l.location_id=d.location_id);

CITY                            l.location_id d.location_id
------------------------------ ------------- -------------
Roma                                    1000
Venice                                  1100
Tokyo                                   1200
Hiroshima                               1300
Southlake                               1400          1400
South San Francisco                     1500          1500
South Brunswick                         1600
Seattle                                 1700          1700
Seattle                                 1700          1700
Seattle                                 1700          1700
Seattle                                 1700          1700
Seattle                                 1700          1700
Seattle                                 1700          1700
Seattle                                 1700          1700
Seattle                                 1700          1700
Seattle                                 1700          1700
Seattle                                 1700          1700
Seattle                                 1700          1700
Seattle                                 1700          1700
Seattle                                 1700          1700
Seattle                                 1700          1700
Seattle                                 1700          1700
Seattle                                 1700          1700
Seattle                                 1700          1700
Seattle                                 1700          1700
Seattle                                 1700          1700
Seattle                                 1700          1700
Toronto                                 1800          1800
Whitehorse                              1900
Beijing                                 2000
Bombay                                  2100
Sydney                                  2200
Singapore                               2300
London                                  2400          2400
Oxford                                  2500          2500
Stretford                               2600
Munich                                  2700          2700
Sao Paulo                               2800
Geneva                                  2900
Bern                                    3000
Utrecht                                 3100
Mexico City                             3200

43 rows selected.
```

Figure 10-10   Left outer join

Any employee records that do not conform to the join condition are included, provided they conform to the WHERE clause condition. In addition, the right outer join fetches one EMPLOYEE record with a LAST_NAME of Grant. This record currently has a null DEPARTMENT_ID value. The inner join excludes the record since no DEPARTMENT_ID is assigned to this employee.

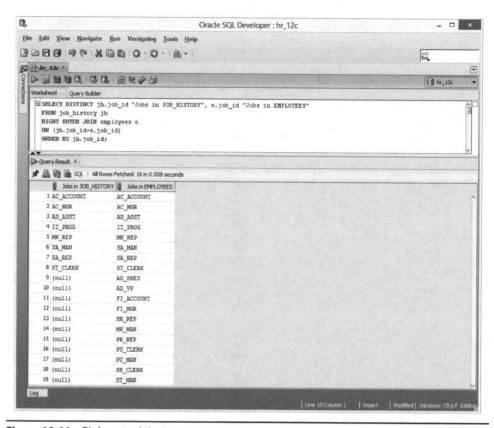

Figure 10-11 Right outer join

Figure 10-11 shows a right outer join between the JOB_HISTORY and EMPLOYEES tables. The EMPLOYEES table is on the right of the JOIN keyword. The DISTINCT keyword eliminates duplicate combinations of JOB_ID values from the tables. The results show the jobs that employees have historically left. The jobs that no employees have left are also returned. These have a null value in the "Jobs in JOB_HISTORY" column.

TIP There are three types of outer join formats. Each of them performs an inner join before including rows the join condition excluded. If a left outer join is performed, then rows excluded by the inner join, to the left of the JOIN keyword, are also returned. If a right outer join is performed, then rows excluded by the inner join, to the right of the JOIN keyword, are returned as well. The full outer join performs an inner join as well as a left and right outer join.

Full Outer Joins

The format of the syntax for the FULL OUTER JOIN clause is as follows:

SELECT *table1.column, table2.column*
FROM *table1*
FULL OUTER JOIN *table2*
ON (*table1.column = table2.column*);

A *full outer join* returns the combined results of a left and right outer join. An inner join of *table1* and *table2* is performed before rows excluded by the join condition from both tables are merged into the results set.

The traditional Oracle join syntax does not support a full outer join, which is typically performed by combining the results from a left and right outer join using the UNION set operator described in Chapter 11. Consider the full outer join shown in Figure 10-12. The WHERE clause restricting the results to rows with NULL DEPARTMENT_ID values shows the orphan rows in both tables. There is one record in the EMPLOYEES table that has no DEPARTMENT_ID values, and there are 16 departments to which no employees belong.

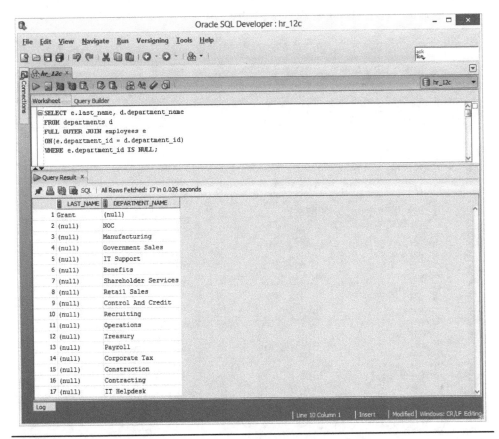

Figure 10-12   Full outer join

Exercise 10-4: Performing an Outer Join   The DEPARTMENTS table contains details of all departments in the organization. You are required to retrieve the DEPARTMENT_NAME and DEPARTMENT_ID values for those departments to which no employees are currently assigned.

1. Start SQL*Plus and connect to the HR schema.

2. The SELECT clause is as follows:

   ```
   SELECT D.DEPARTMENT_NAME, D.DEPARTMENT_ID
   ```

3. The FROM clause with source table and alias is as follows:

   ```
   FROM DEPARTMENTS D
   ```

4. The LEFT OUTER JOIN clause with aliased target table is as follows:

   ```
   LEFT OUTER JOIN EMPLOYEES E ON
   E.DEPARTMENT_ID=D.DEPARTMENT_ID
   ```

5. The WHERE clause is as follows:

   ```
   WHERE E.DEPARTMENT_ID IS NULL
   ```

6. Executing this statement returns 16 rows describing the departments to which no employees are currently assigned, as shown in the following illustration:

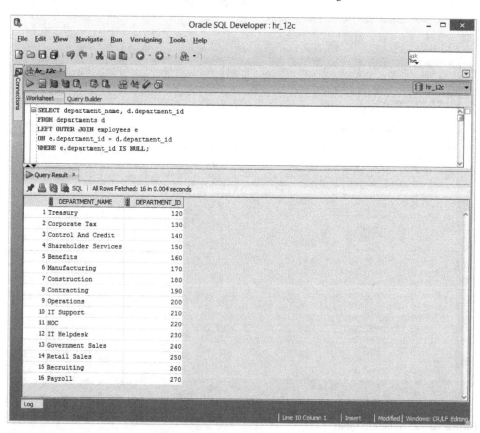

Generate a Cartesian Product of Two or More Tables

A Cartesian product of two tables may be conceptualized as joining each row of the source table with every row in the target table. The number of rows in the result set created by a Cartesian product is equal to the number of rows in the source table multiplied by the number of rows in the target table. Cartesian products can be formed intentionally using the ANSI SQL cross join syntax. This technique is described in the next section.

Creating Cartesian Products Using Cross Joins

Cartesian product is a mathematical term. It refers to the set of data created by merging the rows from two or more tables together. *Cross join* is the syntax used to create a Cartesian product by joining multiple tables. Both terms are often used synonymously. The format of the syntax for the CROSS JOIN clause is as follows:

SELECT *table1*.column, *table2*.column
FROM *table1*
CROSS JOIN *table2*;

It is important to observe that no join condition is specified using the ON or USING keyword. A Cartesian product freely associates the rows from *table1* with every row in *table2*. Conditions that limit the results are permitted in the form of WHERE clause restrictions. If *table1* and *table2* contain *x* and *y* number of rows, respectively, the Cartesian product will contain *x* times *y* number of rows. The results from a cross join can be used to identify orphan rows or generate a large dataset for use in application testing. Consider the following queries:

```
Query 1: SELECT *
         FROM jobs
         CROSS JOIN job_history;

Query 2: SELECT *
         FROM jobs j
         CROSS JOIN job_history jh
         WHERE j.job_id='AD_PRES';
```

Query 1 takes the 19 rows and 4 columns from the JOBS table and the 10 rows and 5 columns from the JOB_HISTORY table and generates one large set of 190 records with 9 columns. SQL*Plus presents any identically named columns as headings. SQL Developer appends an underscore and number to each shared column name and uses it as the heading. The JOB_ID column is common to both the JOBS and JOB_HISTORY tables. The headings in SQL Developer are labeled JOB_ID and JOB_ID_1, respectively. Query 2 generates the same Cartesian product as the first, but the 190 rows are constrained by the WHERE clause condition, and only 10 rows are returned.

TIP   When using the cross join syntax, a Cartesian product is intentionally generated. Inadvertent Cartesian products are created when there are insufficient join conditions in a statement. Joins that specify fewer than N-1 join conditions when joining N tables or that specify invalid join conditions may inadvertently create Cartesian products. A natural join between two tables sharing no identically named columns results in a Cartesian join since two tables are joined but less than one condition is available.

Figure 10-13
The cross
join

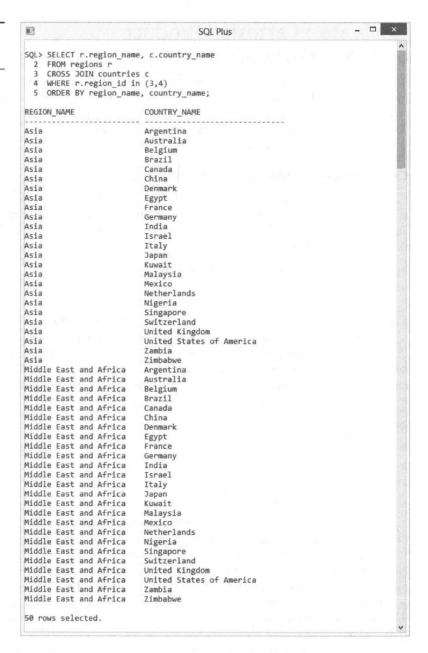

```
SQL> SELECT r.region_name, c.country_name
  2  FROM regions r
  3  CROSS JOIN countries c
  4  WHERE r.region_id in (3,4)
  5  ORDER BY region_name, country_name;

REGION_NAME                COUNTRY_NAME
------------------------   ------------------------
Asia                       Argentina
Asia                       Australia
Asia                       Belgium
Asia                       Brazil
Asia                       Canada
Asia                       China
Asia                       Denmark
Asia                       Egypt
Asia                       France
Asia                       Germany
Asia                       India
Asia                       Israel
Asia                       Italy
Asia                       Japan
Asia                       Kuwait
Asia                       Malaysia
Asia                       Mexico
Asia                       Netherlands
Asia                       Nigeria
Asia                       Singapore
Asia                       Switzerland
Asia                       United Kingdom
Asia                       United States of America
Asia                       Zambia
Asia                       Zimbabwe
Middle East and Africa     Argentina
Middle East and Africa     Australia
Middle East and Africa     Belgium
Middle East and Africa     Brazil
Middle East and Africa     Canada
Middle East and Africa     China
Middle East and Africa     Denmark
Middle East and Africa     Egypt
Middle East and Africa     France
Middle East and Africa     Germany
Middle East and Africa     India
Middle East and Africa     Israel
Middle East and Africa     Italy
Middle East and Africa     Japan
Middle East and Africa     Kuwait
Middle East and Africa     Malaysia
Middle East and Africa     Mexico
Middle East and Africa     Netherlands
Middle East and Africa     Nigeria
Middle East and Africa     Singapore
Middle East and Africa     Switzerland
Middle East and Africa     United Kingdom
Middle East and Africa     United States of America
Middle East and Africa     Zambia
Middle East and Africa     Zimbabwe

50 rows selected.
```

Figure 10-13 shows a cross join between the REGIONS and COUNTRIES tables. There are 4 rows in REGIONS and 25 rows in COUNTRIES. Since the WHERE clause limits the REGIONS table to 2 of 4 rows, the Cartesian product produces 50 (25 × 2) records. The results are sorted alphabetically, first on the REGION_NAME and then on the COUNTRY_NAME. The first record has the pair of values Asia and Argentina. When the REGION_NAME changes, the first record has the following pair of values: Middle East and Africa and Argentina. Notice that the COUNTRY_NAME values are repeated for every REGION_NAME.

Exercise 10-5: Performing a Cross Join   You are required to obtain the number of rows in the EMPLOYEES and DEPARTMENTS tables as well as the number of records that would be created by a Cartesian product of these two tables. Confirm your results by explicitly counting and multiplying the number of rows present in each of these tables.

1. Start SQL*Plus and connect to the HR schema.

2. The SELECT clause to find the number of rows in the Cartesian product is as follows:
   ```
   SELECT COUNT(*)
   ```

3. The FROM clause is as follows:
   ```
   FROM EMPLOYEES
   ```

4. The Cartesian product is performed using the following:
   ```
   CROSS JOIN DEPARTMENTS
   ```

5. Explicit counts of the rows present in the source tables are performed using the following:
   ```
   SELECT COUNT(*) FROM EMPLOYEES;
   SELECT COUNT(*) FROM DEPARTMENTS;
   ```

6. Explicit multiplication of the values resulting from the previous queries may be performed by querying the DUAL table.

7. Executing these statements reveals that there are 107 records in the EMPLOYEES table, 27 records in the DEPARTMENTS table, and 2,889 records in the Cartesian product of these two datasets, as shown in the following illustration:

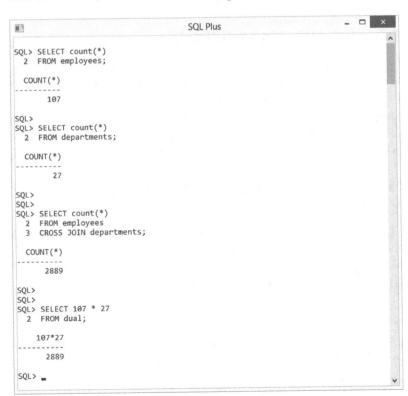

Two-Minute Drill

Write SELECT Statements to Access Data from More Than One Table Using Equijoins and Nonequijoins

- Equijoining occurs when one query fetches column values from multiple tables in which the rows fulfill an equality-based join condition.

- A natural join is performed using the NATURAL JOIN syntax when the source and target tables are implicitly equijoined using all identically named columns.

- The JOIN . . . USING syntax allows an inner join to be formed on specific columns with shared names.

- Dot notation refers to qualifying a column by prefixing it with its table name and a dot or period symbol. This designates the table a column originates from and differentiates it from identically named columns from other tables.

- The JOIN . . . ON clause allows the explicit specification of join columns regardless of their column names. This provides a flexible joining format.

- The ON, USING, and NATURAL keywords are mutually exclusive and therefore cannot appear together in a join clause.

- A nonequijoin is performed when the values in the join columns fulfill the join condition based on an inequality expression.

Join a Table to Itself Using a Self-Join

- A self-join is required when the join columns originate from the same table. Conceptually, the source table is duplicated, and a target table is created. The self-join then works as a regular join between two discrete tables.

- Storing hierarchical data in a relational table requires a minimum of two columns per row. One column stores an identifier of the row's parent record, and the second stores the row's identifier.

View Data that Does Not Meet a Join Condition Using Outer Joins

- When equijoins and nonequijoins are performed, rows from the source and target tables are matched. These are referred to as inner joins.

- An outer join is performed when rows, which are not retrieved by an inner join, are included for retrieval in addition to the rows retrieved by the inner join.

- A left outer join between the source and target tables returns the results of an inner join and the missing rows it excluded from the source table.

- A right outer join between the source and target tables returns the results of an inner join and the missing rows it excluded from the target table.

- A full outer join returns the combined results of a left outer join and right outer join.

Generate a Cartesian Product of Two or More Tables

- A Cartesian product is sometimes called a cross join. It is a mathematical term that refers to the set of data created by merging the rows from two or more tables.

- The count of the rows returned from a Cartesian product is equal to the number of rows in the source table multiplied by the number of rows in the target table.

- Joins that specify fewer than N-1 join conditions when joining N tables, or that specify invalid join conditions, inadvertently create Cartesian products.

Self Test

The following questions will help you measure your understanding of the material presented in this chapter. Read all the choices carefully because there may be more than one correct answer. Choose all the correct answers for each question.

1. The EMPLOYEES and DEPARTMENTS tables have two identically named columns: DEPARTMENT_ID and MANAGER_ID. Which of these statements joins these tables based only on common DEPARTMENT_ID values? (Choose all that apply.)

   A. SELECT * FROM EMPLOYEES NATURAL JOIN DEPARTMENTS;

   B. SELECT * FROM EMPLOYEES E NATURAL JOIN DEPARTMENTS D ON E.DEPARTMENT_ID=D.DEPARTMENT_ID;

   C. SELECT * FROM EMPLOYEES NATURAL JOIN DEPARTMENTS USING (DEPARTMENT_ID);

   D. None of the above

2. The EMPLOYEES and DEPARTMENTS tables have two identically named columns: DEPARTMENT_ID and MANAGER_ID. Which statements join these tables based on both column values? (Choose all that apply.)

   A. SELECT * FROM EMPLOYEES NATURAL JOIN DEPARTMENTS;

   B. SELECT * FROM EMPLOYEES JOIN DEPARTMENTS USING (DEPARTMENT_ID,MANAGER_ID);

   C. SELECT * FROM EMPLOYEES E JOIN DEPARTMENTS D ON E.DEPARTMENT_ID=D.DEPARTMENT_ID AND E.MANAGER_ID=D.MANAGER_ID;

   D. None of the above

3. Which join is performed by the following query? (Choose the best answer.)
   ```
   SELECT E.JOB_ID,J.JOB_ID FROM EMPLOYEES E
   JOIN JOBS J ON (E.SALARY < J.MAX_SALARY);
   ```

   A. Equijoin

   B. Nonequijoin

   C. Cross join

   D. Outer join

4. Which of the following statements are syntactically correct? (Choose all that apply.)

A. SELECT * FROM EMPLOYEES E JOIN DEPARTMENTS D USING (DEPARTMENT_ID);

B. SELECT * FROM EMPLOYEES JOIN DEPARTMENTS D USING (D.DEPARTMENT_ID);

C. SELECT D.DEPARTMENT_ID FROM EMPLOYEES JOIN DEPARTMENTS D USING (DEPARTMENT_ID);

D. None of the above

5. Which of the following statements are syntactically correct? (Choose all that apply.)

A. SELECT E.EMPLOYEE_ID, J.JOB_ID PREVIOUS_JOB, E.JOB_ID CURRENT_JOB FROM JOB_HISTORY J CROSS JOIN EMPLOYEES E ON (J.START_DATE=E.HIRE_DATE);

B. SELECT E.EMPLOYEE_ID, J.JOB_ID PREVIOUS_JOB, E.JOB_ID CURRENT_JOB FROM JOB_HISTORY J JOIN EMPLOYEES E ON (J.START_DATE=E.HIRE_DATE);

C. SELECT E.EMPLOYEE_ID, J.JOB_ID PREVIOUS_JOB, E.JOB_ID CURRENT_JOB FROM JOB_HISTORY J OUTER JOIN EMPLOYEES E ON (J.START_DATE=E.HIRE_DATE);

D. None of the above

6. Choose one correct statement regarding the following query:

```
SELECT * FROM EMPLOYEES E
JOIN DEPARTMENTS D ON (D.DEPARTMENT_ID=E.DEPARTMENT_ID) JOIN LOCATIONS
L ON (L.LOCATION_ID =D.LOCATION_ID);
```

A. Joining three tables is not permitted.

B. A Cartesian product is generated.

C. The JOIN . . . ON clause can be used for joins between multiple tables.

D. None of the above.

7. How many rows are returned after executing the following statement? (Choose the best answer.)

```
SELECT * FROM REGIONS R1 JOIN REGIONS R2 ON (R1.REGION_ID=LENGTH(R2.
REGION_NAME)/2);
```

The REGIONS table contains the following row data:

REGION_ID	REGION_NAME
1	Europe
2	Americas
3	Asia
4	Middle East and Africa

A. 2

B. 3

C. 4

D. None of the above

8. Choose one correct statement regarding the following query:

```
SELECT C.COUNTRY_ID
FROM LOCATIONS L RIGHT OUTER JOIN COUNTRIES C
ON (L.COUNTRY_ID=C.COUNTRY_ID) WHERE L.COUNTRY_ID is NULL;
```

   A. No rows in the LOCATIONS table have the COUNTRY_ID values returned.

   B. No rows in the COUNTRIES table have the COUNTRY_ID values returned.

   C. The rows returned represent the COUNTRY_ID values for all the rows in the LOCATIONS table.

   D. None of the above.

9. Which of the following statements are syntactically correct? (Choose all that apply.)

   A. SELECT JH.JOB_ID FROM JOB_HISTORY JH RIGHT OUTER JOIN JOBS J ON JH.JOB_ID=J.JOB_ID;

   B. SELECT JOB_ID FROM JOB_HISTORY JH RIGHT OUTER JOIN JOBS J ON (JH.JOB_ID=J.JOB_ID);

   C. SELECT JOB_HISTORY.JOB_ID FROM JOB_HISTORY OUTER JOIN JOBS ON JOB_HISTORY.JOB_ID=JOBS.JOB_ID;

   D. None of the above

10. If the REGIONS table, which contains 4 rows, is cross joined to the COUNTRIES table, which contains 25 rows, how many rows appear in the final results set? (Choose the best answer.)

   A. 100 rows

   B. 4 rows

   C. 25 rows

   D. None of the above

Self Test Answers

1. ☑   **D.** All the queries are incorrect, so **D** is the correct choice.
   ☒   **A**, **B**, and **C** are incorrect. **A** is incorrect because the query performs a natural join that implicitly joins the two tables on all columns with identical names, which, in this case, are DEPARTMENT_ID and MANAGER_ID. **B** and **C** are incorrect because the queries incorrectly contain the NATURAL keyword. If this is removed, they will join the DEPARTMENTS and EMPLOYEES tables based on the DEPARTMENT_ID column.

2. ☑ **A**, **B**, and **C**. These clauses demonstrate different techniques to join the tables on both the DEPARTMENT_ID and MANAGER_ID columns.

☒ **D** is incorrect because there are correct answers given.

3. ☑ **B**. The join condition is an expression based on the *less than* inequality operator. Therefore, this join is a nonequijoin.

☒ **A**, **C**, and **D** are incorrect. **A** would be correct if the operator in the join condition expression was an equality operator. The CROSS JOIN keywords or the absence of a join condition would result in **C** being true. **D** would be true if one of the OUTER JOIN clauses was used instead of the JOIN . . . ON clause.

4. ☑ **A**. This statement demonstrates the correct usage of the JOIN . . . USING clause.

☒ **B**, **C**, and **D** are incorrect. **B** is incorrect since only nonqualified column names are allowed in the brackets after the USING keyword. **C** is incorrect because the column in brackets after the USING keyword cannot be referenced with a qualifier in the SELECT clause. **D** is incorrect since there is a correct answer.

5. ☑ **B** demonstrates the correct usage of the JOIN . . . ON clause.

☒ **A**, **C**, and **D** are incorrect. **A** is incorrect since the CROSS JOIN clause cannot contain the ON keyword. **C** is incorrect since the OUTER JOIN keywords must be preceded by the LEFT, RIGHT, or FULL keyword. **D** is incorrect since there is a correct answer.

6. ☑ **C**. The JOIN…ON clause and the other join clauses can all be used for joins between multiple tables. The JOIN . . . ON and JOIN . . . USING clauses are better suited for N-way table joins.

☒ **A**, **B**, and **D** are incorrect. **A** is incorrect since you can join as many tables as you want. **B** is incorrect since a Cartesian product is not created since there are two join conditions and three tables. **D** is incorrect since there is a correct answer.

7. ☑ **B**. Three rows are returned. The REGIONS table is being joined to itself. For the row with a REGION_ID value of 2 in the table aliased as R1, a match is found with the row in the table aliased as R2 where the REGION_NAME value is Asia, because half the length of the REGION_NAME value is also 2. Therefore, this row is returned. The same logic results in the rows with REGION_ID values of three and four and matching REGION_NAME values of Europe and Americas being returned.

☒ **A**, **C**, and **D** are incorrect because exactly three rows are returned.

8. ☑ **A**. The right outer join fetches the COUNTRIES rows that the inner join between the LOCATIONS and COUNTRIES tables has excluded in addition to the inner join results. The WHERE clause then restricts the results by eliminating these inner join results. This leaves the rows from the COUNTRIES table with which no records from the LOCATIONS table records are associated.

☒ **B**, **C**, and **D** are incorrect. **B** is incorrect because it is rows from the COUNTRIES table that are returned. **C** is incorrect because these are the rows included by the inner join, but eliminated by the WHERE clause. **D** is incorrect because **A** is the correct answer.

9. ☑ **A.** This statement demonstrates the correct use of the RIGHT OUTER
JOIN . . . ON clause.
☒ **B, C,** and **D** are incorrect. The JOB_ID column in the SELECT clause in **B** is
not qualified and is therefore ambiguous since the table from which this column comes
is not specified. **C** uses an OUTER JOIN without the keywords LEFT, RIGHT, and
FULL. **D** is incorrect since there is a correct answer.

10. ☑ **A.** The cross join associates every four rows from the REGIONS table 25 times
with the rows from the COUNTRIES table yielding a result set that contains 100 rows.
☒ **B, C,** and **D** are incorrect. **B** and **C** would be returned if the product of the
number of rows in each table were 4 or 25. **D** is incorrect since **A** is the correct answer.

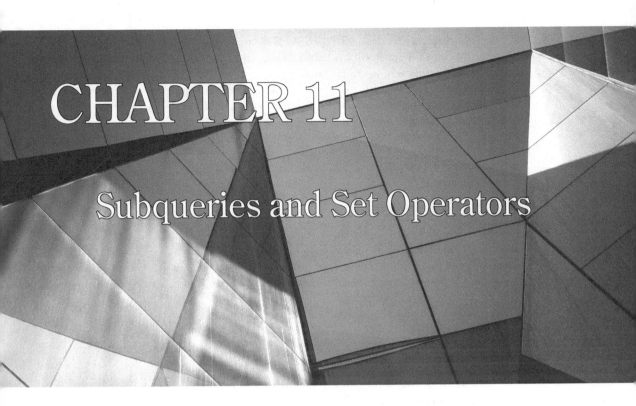

CHAPTER 11

Subqueries and Set Operators

Exam Objectives

In this chapter, you will learn to

- 061.7.1 Define Subqueries
- 061.7.2 Describe the Types of Problems that the Subqueries Can Solve
- 061.7.3 Describe the Types of Subqueries
- 061.7.4 Write Single-Row and Multiple-Row Subqueries
- 061.8.1 Describe Set Operators
- 061.8.2 Use a Set Operator to Combine Multiple Queries into a Single Query
- 061.8.3 Control the Order of Rows Returned

The previous chapters have dealt with the SELECT statement in considerable detail, but in every case the SELECT statement has been a single, self-contained command. This chapter is the first of two that show how you can combine two or more SELECT commands into one statement. The first technique (covered in this chapter) is the use of *subqueries*. A subquery is a SELECT statement whose output is used as input to another SELECT statement (or indeed to a data manipulation statement [DML] statement, as done in Chapter 6). The second technique is the use of set operators, where the results of several SELECT commands are combined into a single result set.

Define Subqueries

A subquery is a query that is nested inside a SELECT, INSERT, UPDATE, or DELETE statement or inside another subquery. A subquery can return a set of rows or just one row to its parent query. A *scalar* subquery is a query that returns exactly one value: a single row, with a single column. Scalar subqueries can be used in most places in a SQL statement where you could use an expression or a literal value.

The places in a query where a subquery can be used are as follows:

- In the SELECT list used for column projection
- In the FROM clause
- In the WHERE clause
- In the HAVING clause

A subquery is often referred to as an *inner* query, and the statement within which it occurs is then called the *outer* query. There is nothing wrong with this terminology, except that it may imply that you can have only two levels, inner and outer. In fact, the Oracle implementation of subqueries does not impose any practical limits on the level of nesting. The depth of subquery nesting permitted is unlimited in the FROM clause and is capped at 255 levels in the WHERE clause.

 EXAM TIP   Subqueries can be nested to an unlimited depth in a FROM clause but to "only" 255 levels in a WHERE clause. They can be used in the SELECT list and in the FROM, WHERE, and HAVING clauses of a query.

A subquery can have any of the usual clauses for selection and projection. The following are required clauses:

- A SELECT list
- A FROM clause

The following are optional clauses:

- WHERE
- GROUP BY
- HAVING

The subquery (or subqueries) within a statement must be executed before the parent query that calls it so that the results of the subquery can be passed to the parent.

Exercise 11-1: Explore Types of Subqueries   In this exercise, you will write code that demonstrates the places where subqueries can be used. Use either SQL*Plus or SQL Developer. All the queries should be run when connected to the HR schema.

1. Log on to your database as user HR.

2. Write a query that uses subqueries in the column projection list. The query will report on the current numbers of departments and staff.

```
select sysdate Today,
(select count(*) from departments) Dept_count,
(select count(*) from employees) Emp_count
from dual;
```

3. Write a query to identify all the employees who are managers. This will require using a subquery in the WHERE clause to select all the employees whose EMPLOYEE_ID appears as a MANAGER_ID.

```
select last_name from employees where
(employee_id in (select manager_id from employees));
```

4. Write a query to identify the highest salary paid in each country. This will require using a subquery in the FROM clause.

```
select max(salary),country_id from
  (select e.salary,department_id,location_id,l.country_id
   from employees e join departments d using (department_id)
                    join locations l using (location_id))
group by country_id;
```

Describe the Types of Problems that the Subqueries Can Solve

There are many situations where you will need the result of one query as the input for another.

Use of a Subquery Result Set for Comparison Purposes

Which employees have a salary that is less than the average salary? This could be answered by two statements or by a single statement with a subquery. The following example uses two statements:

```
select avg(salary) from employees;
select last_name from employees where salary < result_of_previous_query ;
```

Alternatively, the following example uses one statement with a subquery:

```
select last_name from employees
where salary < (select avg(salary)from employees);
```

In this example, the subquery is used to substitute a value into the WHERE clause of the parent query; it returns a single value, used for comparison with the rows retrieved by the parent query.

The subquery could return a set of rows. For example, you could use the following to find all departments that have one or more employees assigned to them:

```
select department_name from departments where department_id in
(select distinct(department_id) from employees);
```

In the preceding example, the subquery is used as an alternative to an inner join. You could achieve the same result with the following:

```
select department_name from departments join employees
on employees.department_id = departments.department_id
group by department_name;
```

If the subquery is going to return more than one row, then the comparison operator must be able to accept multiple values. These operators are IN, NOT IN, ANY, and ALL. If the comparison operator is any of the scalar equality or inequality operators (which each can accept only one value), the parent query will fail.

 TIP Using NOT IN is fraught with problems because of the way SQL handles NULLs. As a general rule, do not use NOT IN unless you are certain that the result set will not include a NULL.

Star Transformation

An extension of the use of subqueries as an alternative to a join is to enable the *star transformation* often needed in data warehouse applications. Consider the large SALES table in the demo SH schema used for recording sales transactions. Each row captures a particular product sold to a particular customer through a particular channel. These attributes are identified by lookup codes used as foreign keys to dimension tables with rows that describe each product, customer, and channel. To identify all sales of an item called Comic Book Heroes to customers in the city of Oxford through Internet orders, you could run the following query:

```
SELECT count(quantity_sold)
FROM sales s, products p, customers c, channels ch
WHERE s.prod_id=p.prod_id
AND s.cust_id=c.cust_id
AND s.channel_id=ch.channel_id
AND p.prod_name='Comic Book Heroes'
AND c.cust_city='Oxford'
AND ch.channel_desc='Internet';
```

This query uses the WHERE clause to join the tables and then to filter the results. The following is an alternative query that will yield the same result:

```
SELECT count(quantity_sold)
FROM sales
WHERE prod_id IN
```

```
(SELECT prod_id
 FROM products
 WHERE prod_name='Comic Book Heroes')
AND cust_id IN
 (SELECT cust_id
 FROM customers
 WHERE cust_city='Oxford')
AND channel_id IN
 (SELECT channel_id
 FROM channels
 WHERE channel_desc='Internet');
```

The rewrite of the first statement to the second is the star transformation. Apart from being an inherently more elegant structure (most SQL developers with any sense of aesthetics will agree with that), there are technical reasons why the database may be able to execute it more efficiently than the original query. Also, star queries are easier to maintain; it is simple to add more dimensions to the query or to replace the single literals (`'Comic Book Heroes'`, `'Oxford'`, and `'Internet'`) with lists of values.

TIP   There is an instance initialization parameter, STAR_TRANSFORMATION_ ENABLED, that (if set to true) will permit the Oracle query optimizer to rewrite code into star queries.

Generate a Table from Which to SELECT

Subqueries can also be used in the FROM clause where they are sometimes referred to as *inline views*. Consider the following problem based on the HR schema: Employees are assigned to a department, and departments have a location. Each location is in a country. How can you find the average salary of staff in a country, even though they work for different departments? Here's the answer:

```
SELECT avg(salary),country_id
FROM (SELECT salary, country_id
      FROM employees
      NATURAL JOIN departments
      NATURAL JOIN locations)
GROUP BY country_id;
```

The subquery conceptually constructs a table with every employee's salary and the country in which their department is based. The parent query then addresses this table, averaging the SALARY and grouping by COUNTRY_ID.

Generate Values for Projection

The third place a subquery can be used is in the SELECT list of a query. How can you identify the highest salary and the highest commission rate and thus what the maximum commission paid would be if the highest salaried employee also had the highest commission rate? Here's the answer, with two subqueries:

```
SELECT (SELECT max(salary) FROM employees) *
       (SELECT max(commission_pct) FROM employees) / 100
FROM dual;
```

In this usage, the SELECT list used to project columns is being populated with the results of the subqueries. A subquery used in this manner must be scalar or the parent query will fail with an error.

Generate Rows to Be Passed to a DML Statement

DML statements are covered in detail in Chapter 10. For now, consider these examples:

```
INSERT INTO sales_hist
SELECT *
FROM sales
WHERE date > sysdate-1;

UPDATE employees
SET salary = (SELECT avg(salary)
              FROM employees);

DELETE FROM departments
WHERE department_id NOT IN
(SELECT department_id
 FROM employees
 WHERE department_id is not null);
```

The first example uses a subquery to identify a set of rows in one table that will be inserted into another. The second example uses a subquery to calculate the average salary of all employees and passes this value (a scalar quantity) to an update statement. The third example uses a subquery to retrieve all DEPARTMENT_IDs that are in use and passes the list to a DELETE command, which will remove all departments that are not in use. Note the use of the additional WHERE clause in the subquery to ensure that no NULL values are returned by the subquery. If this clause were absent, no rows would be deleted.

 EXAM TIP A subquery can be used to select rows for insertion, but not in a VALUES clause of an INSERT statement.

Note that it is not legal to use a subquery in the VALUES clause of an insert statement. The following is fine:

```
INSERT INTO dates
SELECT sysdate
FROM dual;
```

But this is not:

```
INSERT INTO dates (date_col)
VALUES
 (SELECT sysdate
  FROM dual);
```

Exercise 11-2: Explore Complex Subqueries   In this exercise, you will write more complex subqueries. Use either SQL*Plus or SQL Developer. All the queries should be run when connected to the HR schema.

1. Log on to your database as user HR.

2. Write a query that will identify all employees who work in departments located in the United Kingdom. This will require three levels of nested subqueries.

```
SELECT last_name
FROM employees
WHERE department_id IN
  (SELECT department_id
   FROM departments
   WHERE location_id IN
     (SELECT location_id
      FROM locations
      WHERE country_id =
        (SELECT country_id
         FROM countries
         WHERE country_name='United Kingdom')
    )
  );
```

3. Check that the result from step 2 is correct by running the subqueries independently. First, find the COUNTRY_ID for the United Kingdom.

```
SELECT country_id
FROM countries
WHERE country_name='United Kingdom';
```

The result will be UK. Then find the corresponding locations.

```
SELECT location_id
FROM locations
WHERE country_id = 'UK';
```

The LOCATION_IDs returned will be 2400, 2500, and 2600. Then find the DEPARTMENT_IDs of departments in these locations.

```
SELECT department_id
FROM departments
WHERE location_id IN (2400,2500,2600);
```

The result will be two departments, 40 and 80. Finally, find the relevant employees.

```
SELECT last_name
FROM employees
WHERE department_id IN (40,80);
```

4. Write a query to identify all the employees who earn more than the average and who work in any of the IT departments. This will require two subqueries, not nested.

```
SELECT last_name
FROM employees
WHERE department_id IN
  (SELECT department_id
   FROM departments
   WHERE department_name LIKE 'IT%')
AND salary > (SELECT avg(salary)
              FROM employees);
```

Describe the Types of Subqueries

There are three broad divisions of subqueries:

- Single-row subqueries
- Multiple-row subqueries
- Correlated subqueries

Single- and Multiple-Row Subqueries

The *single-row* subquery returns one row. A special case is the scalar subquery, which returns a single row with one column. Scalar subqueries are acceptable (and often useful) in virtually any situation where you could use a literal value, a constant, or an expression. *Multiple-row* subqueries return sets of rows. These queries are commonly used to generate result sets that will be passed to a DML or SELECT statement for further processing. Both single-row and multiple-row subqueries will be evaluated once, before the parent query is run.

Single- and multiple-row subqueries can be used in the WHERE and HAVING clauses of the parent query, but there are restrictions on the legal comparison operators. If the comparison operator is any of the ones in the following table, the subquery must be a single-row subquery:

Symbol	Meaning
=	Equal
>	Greater than
>=	Greater than or equal
<	Less than
<=	Less than or equal
<>	Not equal
!=	Not equal

If any of the operators in the preceding table are used with a subquery that returns more than one row, the query will fail. The operators in the following table can use multiple-row subqueries:

Symbol	Meaning
IN	Equal to any member in a list
NOT IN	Not equal to any member in a list
ANY	Returns rows that match any value in a list
ALL	Returns rows that match all the values in a list

EXAM TIP   The comparison operators valid for single-row subqueries are =, >, >=, <, <=, and <>. The comparison operators valid for multiple-row subqueries are IN, NOT IN, ANY, and ALL.

Correlated Subqueries

A *correlated subquery* has a more complex method of execution than single- and multiple-row subqueries and is potentially much more powerful. If a subquery references columns in the parent query, then its result will be dependent on the parent query. This makes it impossible to evaluate the subquery before evaluating the parent query. Consider this statement, which lists all employees who earn less than the average salary:

```
SELECT last_name
FROM employees
WHERE salary <
 (SELECT avg(salary)
  FROM employees);
```

The single-row subquery needs to be executed only once, and its result will be substituted into the parent query. But now consider a query that will list all employees whose salary is less than the average salary of their department. In this case, the subquery must be run for each employee to determine the average salary for her department; it is necessary to pass the employee's department code to the subquery. This can be done as follows:

```
SELECT p.last_name, p.department_id
FROM employees p
WHERE p.salary <
 (SELECT avg(s.salary)
  FROM employees s
  WHERE s.department_id=p.department_id);
```

In this example, the subquery references a column, `p.department_id`, from the select list of the parent query. This is the signal that rather than evaluating the subquery once, it must be evaluated for every row in the parent query. To execute the query, Oracle will look at every row in EMPLOYEES and, as it does so, run the subquery using the DEPARTMENT_ID of the current employee row.

The flow of execution is as follows:

1. Start at the first row of the EMPLOYEES table.

2. Read the DEPARTMENT_ID and SALARY values of the current row.

3. Run the subquery using the DEPARTMENT_ID value from step 2.

4. Compare the result of step 3 with the SALARY value from step 2, and return the row if the SALARY value is less than the result.

5. Advance to the next row in the EMPLOYEES table.

6. Repeat from step 2.

A single-row or multiple-row subquery is evaluated once, before evaluating the outer query; a correlated subquery must be evaluated once for every row in the outer query. A correlated subquery can be a single- or multiple-row subquery, if the comparison operator is appropriate.

TIP Correlated subqueries can be an inefficient construct because of the need for repeated execution of the subquery. Always try to find an alternative approach.

Exercise 11-3: Investigate the Different Types of Subqueries In this exercise, you will demonstrate problems that can occur with different types of subqueries. Use either SQL*Plus or SQL Developer. All the queries should be run when connected to the HR schema; it is assumed that the EMPLOYEES table has the standard sets of rows.

1. Log on to your database as user HR.

2. Write a query to determine who earns more than Mr. Tobias.

```
select last_name from employees where
salary > (select salary from employees where last_name='Tobias')
order by last_name;
```

This will return 86 names, in alphabetical order.

3. Write a query to determine who earns more than Mr. Taylor.

```
select last_name from employees where
salary > (select salary from employees where last_name='Taylor')
order by last_name;
```

This will fail with the error "ORA-01427: single-row subquery returns more than one row." Determine why the query in step 2 succeeded but the one in step 3 failed. The answer lies in the data.

```
select count(last_name) from employees where last_name='Tobias';
select count(last_name) from employees where last_name='Taylor';
```

The use of the "greater than" operator in the queries for steps 2 and 3 requires a single-row subquery, but the subquery used can return any number of rows, depending on the search predicate used.

4. Fix the code in steps 2 and 3 so that the statements will succeed no matter what LAST_NAME is used. Here are two possible solutions: one uses a different comparison operator that can handle a multiple-row subquery; the other uses a subquery that will always be a single-row subquery.

Here's the first solution:

```
select last_name from employees where
salary > all (select salary from employees where last_name='Taylor')
order by last_name;
```

Here's the second solution:

```
select last_name from employees where
salary > (select max(salary) from employees where last_name='Taylor')
order by last_name;
```

Write Single-Row and Multiple-Row Subqueries

The following are examples of single- and multiple-row subqueries. They are based on the HR demonstration schema.

How would you figure out which employees have a manager who works for a department based in the United Kingdom? Here is a possible solution using multiple-row subqueries:

```
select last_name from employees
where manager_id in
(select employee_id from employees where department_id in
 (select department_id from departments where location_id in
  (select location_id from locations where country_id='UK')));
```

In the preceding example, subqueries are nested three levels deep. Note that the subqueries use the IN operator because it is possible that the queries could return several rows.

You have been asked to find the job with the highest average salary. This can be done with a single-row subquery.

```
select job_title from jobs natural join employees group by job_title
having avg(salary) =
(select max(avg(salary)) from employees group by job_id);
```

The subquery returns a single value: the average salary of the department with the highest average salary. It is safe to use the equality operator for this subquery because the MAX function guarantees that only one row will be returned.

The ANY and ALL operators are supported syntax, but their function can be duplicated with other more commonly used operators combined with aggregations. For example, these two statements, which retrieve all employees whose salary is greater than anyone in department 80, will return identical result sets:

```
select last_name from employees where salary > all
(select salary from employees where department_id=80);
select last_name from employees where salary >
(select max(salary) from employees where department_id=80);
```

The following table summarizes the equivalents for ANY and ALL:

Operator	Meaning
< ANY	Less than the highest
> ANY	More than the lowest
= ANY	Equivalent to IN
> ALL	More than the highest
< ALL	Less than the lowest
<>ALL	Equivalent to NOT IN

Using the EXISTS Condition

The EXISTS condition tests the existence of rows in a subquery and returns TRUE if one or more rows exist; otherwise, it returns FALSE. Consider the query that lists only the departments that have employees.

```
select department_name from departments d where EXISTS
(select * from employees e where d.department_id=e.department_id);
```

Eleven departments are returned. Some departments currently have no employees that belong to them. These 16 departments are easily identified by using the NOT EXISTS condition.

```
select department_name from departments d where NOT EXISTS
(select * from employees e where d.department_id=e.department_id);
```

Null Results in a Subquery

Be wary of the operators being used when comparing expressions to subquery results. If one of the values returned by a subquery is a null, the entire query may return a null. Conditions that compare a null value result in a null being returned. Therefore, if null values are likely to be part of the results set of a subquery, avoid using the NOT IN operator since this is equivalent to <> ALL. Consider these statements:

```
select last_name, employee_id, manager_id from employees where employee_id
not in (select manager_id from employees);
select last_name, employee_id, manager_id from employees where employee_id
not in (select manager_id from employees where manager_id is not null);
select last_name, employee_id, manager_id from employees where employee_id in
(select manager_id from employees);
```

There is one row in the EMPLOYEES table with a null MANAGER_ID. The first statement compares whether EMPLOYEE_ID <> ALL, and since a NULL is present in the subquery, the statement returns no rows. You can ensure that no nulls are returned in the subquery by using a WHERE clause, as in the second statement that returns the 89 employees who are not managers. The IN operator is equivalent to =ANY. There is no problem with null values in the result set, and the third statement returns the 18 employees who are managers.

Describe the Set Operators

All SELECT statements return a set of rows. The set operators take as their input the results of two or more SELECT statements and from these generate a single result set. This is known as a *compound query*. Oracle provides three set operators: UNION, INTERSECT, and MINUS. UNION can be qualified with ALL. There is a significant deviation from the International Organization for Standardization (ISO) standard for SQL here, in that ISO SQL uses EXCEPT where Oracle uses MINUS, but the functionality is identical. The set operators used in compound queries are as follows:

- **UNION**   Returns the combined rows from two queries, sorting them and removing duplicates
- **UNION ALL**   Returns the combined rows from two queries without sorting or removing duplicates

- **INTERSECT** Returns only the rows that occur in both queries' result sets, sorting them and removing duplicates

- **MINUS** Returns only the rows in the first result set that do not appear in the second result set, sorting them and removing duplicates

These commands are equivalent to the standard operators used in mathematics set theory, often depicted graphically as Venn diagrams.

Sets and Venn Diagrams

Consider groupings of living creatures, classified as follows:

- **Creatures with two legs** Humans, parrots, bats

- **Creatures that can fly** Parrots, bats, bees

- **Creatures with fur** Bears, bats

Each classification is known as a *set,* and each member of the set is an *element.* The *union* of the three sets is humans, parrots, bats, bees, and bears. This is all the elements in all the sets, without the duplications. The *intersection* of the sets is all elements that are common to all three sets, again removing the duplicates. In this simple example, the intersection has just one element: bats. The intersection of the two-legged set and the flying set has two elements: parrots and bats. The *minus* of the sets is the elements of one set without the elements of another, so the two-legged creatures set, minus the flying creatures set, minus the furry creatures set, results in a single element: humans.

These sets can be represented graphically as the Venn diagram shown in Figure 11-1. (Venn diagrams are named after John Venn, who formalized the theory at Cambridge University in the nineteenth century.)

The circle in the top left of the figure represents the set of two-legged creatures, the circle at the top right consists of creatures that can fly, and the bottom circle is furry animals. The unions, intersections, and minuses of the sets are immediately apparent by observing the elements in the various parts of the circles that do or do not overlap. The diagram in the figure also includes the universal set, represented by the rectangle. The universal set is all elements that exist, including those that are not members of the defined sets. In this case, the universal set would be defined as all living creatures, including those that did not develop fur, two legs, or the ability to fly (such as fish).

That's enough school math; now proceed to the implementation within SQL.

Set Operator General Principles

All set operators make compound queries by combining the result sets from two or more queries. If a SELECT statement includes more than one set operator (and therefore more than two queries), they will be applied in the order the programmer specifies: top to bottom and left to right. Although enhancements to the SQL 2011 standard give INTERSECT a higher priority than the others, currently all Oracle set operators have equal precedence. To override this possible future change in precedence, based on the order in which the operators appear, you can use

Figure 11-1
A Venn diagram
showing three
sets and the
universal set

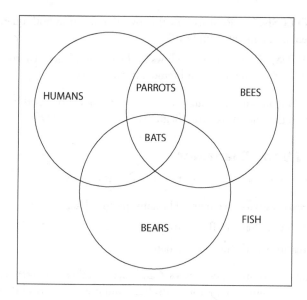

parentheses; operators within brackets will be evaluated before passing the results to operators outside the brackets.

TIP Given the pending change in operator priority, it may be good practice always to use parentheses. This will ensure that the code's function won't change when run against a later version of the database.

Each query in a compound query will project its own list of selected columns. These lists must have the same number of elements, be nominated in the same sequence, and be of broadly similar data type. They do not need to have the same names (or column aliases), nor do they need to come from the same tables (or subqueries). If the column names (or aliases) are different, the result set of the compound query will have columns named as they were in the first query.

EXAM TIP The columns in the queries that make up a compound query can have different names, but the output result set will use the names of the columns in the first query.

While the projected column lists do not have to be the same data type, they must be from the same data type group. For example, the columns selected by one query could be of data types DATE and NUMBER, and those from the second query could be TIMESTAMP and INTEGER. The result set of the compound query will have columns with the higher level of precision; in this case, they would be TIMESTAMP and NUMBER. Other than accepting data types from the same group, the set operators will not do any implicit type casting. If the second query retrieved columns of type VARCHAR2, the compound query would throw an error even if the string variables could be resolved to legitimate date and numeric values.

 EXAM TIP   The corresponding columns in the queries that make up a compound query must be of the same data type group.

UNION, MINUS, and INTERSECT will always combine the results sets of the input queries and then sort the results to remove duplicate rows. The sorting is based on all the columns, from left to right. If all the columns in two rows have the same value, then only the first row is returned in the compound result set. A side effect of this is that the output of a compound query will be sorted. If the sort order (which is ascending, based on the order in which the columns happen to appear in the select lists) is not the order you want, it is possible to put a single ORDER BY clause at the end of the compound query. It is not possible to use ORDER BY in any of the queries that make up the whole compound query because this would disrupt the sorting that is necessary to remove duplicates.

 EXAM TIP   A compound query will, by default, return rows sorted across all the columns, from left to right. The only exception is UNION ALL, where the rows will not be sorted. The only place where an ORDER BY clause is permitted is at the end of the compound query.

UNION ALL is the exception to the sorting-no-duplicates rule; the result sets of the two input queries will be concatenated to form the result of the compound query. But you still can't use ORDER BY in the individual queries; it can appear only at the end of the compound query where it will be applied to the complete result set.

Exercise 11-4: Describe the Set Operators   In this exercise, you will see the effect of the set operators. Either SQL*Plus or SQL Developer can be used.

1. Connect to your database as user HR.

2. Run this query:

```
SELECT region_name
FROM regions;
```

Note the result, in particular the order of the rows. If the table is as originally created, there will be four rows returned. The order will be Europe, Americas, Asia, Middle East, and Africa.

3. Query the Regions table twice, using UNION.

```
SELECT region_name
FROM regions
UNION
SELECT region_name
FROM regions;
```

The rows returned will be like for step 1 but sorted alphabetically.

4. This time, use UNION ALL.

```
SELECT region_name
FROM regions
UNION ALL
SELECT region_name
FROM regions;
```

There will be double the number of rows, and they will not be sorted.

5. An intersection will retrieve rows common to two queries.

```
SELECT region_name
FROM regions
INTERSECT
SELECT region_name
FROM regions;
```

All four rows are common, and the result is sorted.

6. A MINUS will remove common rows.

```
SELECT region_name
FROM regions
MINUS
SELECT region_name
FROM regions;
```

The second query will remove all the rows in the first query. The result is that no rows are left.

Use a Set Operator to Combine Multiple Queries into a Single Query

Compound queries are two or more queries, linked with one or more set operators. The end result is a single result set.

The examples that follow are based on two tables, OLD_DEPT and NEW_DEPT. The table OLD_DEPT is intended to represent a table created with an earlier version of Oracle, when the only data type available for representing date and time data was DATE, the only option for numeric data was NUMBER, and character data was fixed-length CHAR. The table NEW_DEPT uses the more closely defined INTEGER numeric data type (which Oracle implements as a NUMBER of up to 38 significant digits but no decimal places), the more space-efficient VARCHAR2 for character data, and the TIMESTAMP data type, which can, by default, store date and time values with six decimals of precision on the seconds. There are two rows in each table.

The UNION ALL Operator

A UNION ALL takes two result sets and concatenates them into a single result set. The result sets come from two queries that must select the same number of columns, and the corresponding columns of the two queries (in the order in which they are specified) must be of the same data type group. The columns do not need to have the same names.

Figure 11-2 demonstrates a UNION ALL operation from two tables. The UNION ALL of the two tables converts all the values to the higher level of precision; the dates are returned as timestamps (the less precise DATEs padded with zeros), the character data is the more efficient

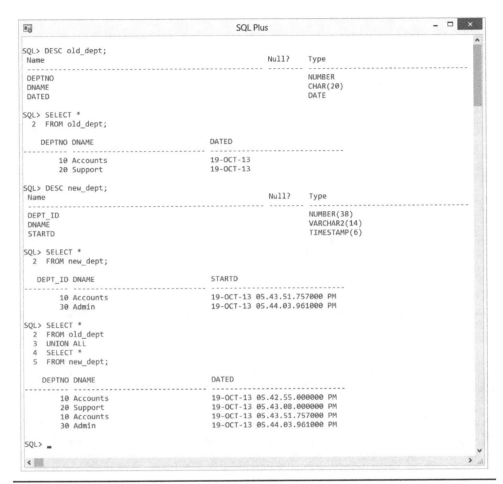

Figure 11-2   A UNION ALL with data type conversions

VARCHAR2 with the length of the longer input column, and the numbers (though this is not obvious because of the nature of the data) will accept decimals. The order of the rows is the rows from the first table in whatever order they happen to be stored, followed by the rows from the second table in whatever order they happen to be stored.

The UNION Operator

A UNION performs a UNION ALL and then sorts the result across all the columns and removes duplicates. The first query in Figure 11-3 returns all four rows because there are no duplicates. However, the rows are now in order. It may appear that the first two rows are not in order because of the values in DATED, but they are. The DNAME in the table OLD_DEPTS is 20 bytes long (padded with spaces), whereas the DNAME in NEW_DEPT, where it is a VARCHAR2, is only as

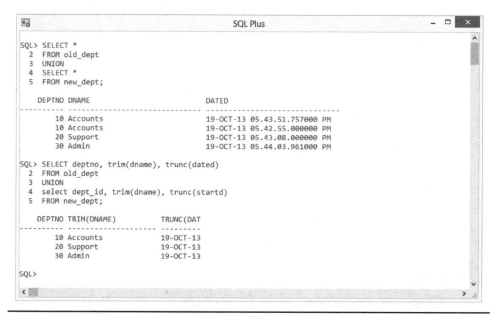

Figure 11-3 UNION compound queries

long as the name itself. The spaces give the row from OLD_DEPT a higher sort value, even though the date value is less.

EXAM TIP A UNION ALL will return rows grouped from each query in their natural order. This behavior can be modified by placing a single ORDER BY clause at the end.

The second query in Figure 11-3 removes any leading or trailing spaces from the DNAME columns and chops off the time elements from DATED and STARTD. Two of the rows thus become identical, so only one appears in the output.

Because of the sort, the order of the queries in a UNION compound query makes no difference to the order of the rows returned.

TIP If you know that there can be no duplicates between two tables, then always use UNION ALL. It saves the database from doing a lot of sorting. Your DBA will not be pleased with you if you use UNION unnecessarily.

The INTERSECT Operator

The intersection of two sets is the rows that are common to both sets, as shown in Figure 11-4.

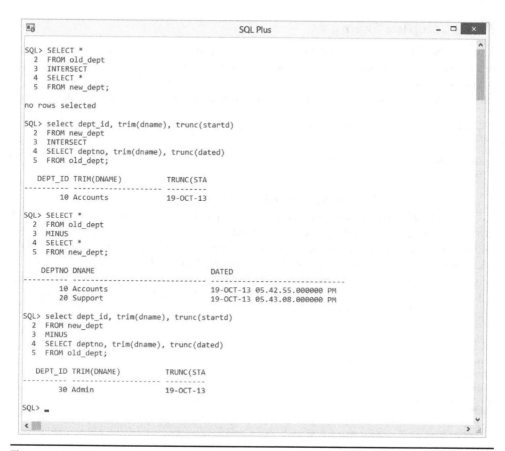

Figure 11-4   INTERSECT and MINUS

The first query shown in Figure 11-4 returns no rows because every row in the two tables is different. Next, applying functions to eliminate some of the differences returns the one common row. In this case, only one row is returned; had there been several common rows, they would be in order. The order in which the queries appear in the compound query has no effect on this.

The MINUS Operator

A MINUS runs both queries, sorts the results, and returns only the rows from the first result set that do not appear in the second result set.

The third query in Figure 11-4 returns all the rows in OLD_DEPT because there are no matching rows in NEW_DEPT. The last query forces some commonality, causing one of the rows to be removed. Because of the sort, the rows will be in order irrespective of the order in which the queries appear in the compound query.

More Complex Examples

If two queries do not return the same number of columns, it may still be possible to run them in a compound query by generating additional columns with NULL values. For example, consider a classification system for animals: All animals have a name and a weight, but the birds have a wingspan, whereas the cats have a tail length. The following is a query to list all the birds and cats:

```
SELECT name, tail_length, NULL
FROM cats
UNION ALL
SELECT name, NULL, wingspan
FROM birds;
```

Note the use of NULL to generate the missing values.

A compound query can consist of more than two queries, in which case operator precedence can be controlled with parentheses. Without parentheses, the set operators will be applied in the sequence in which they are specified. Consider the situation where there is a table PERMSTAFF with a listing of all permanent staff members and a table CONSULTANTS with a listing of consultant staff. There is also a table BLACKLIST of people blacklisted for one reason or another. The following query will list all the permanent and consulting staff in a certain geographical area, removing those on the blacklist:

```
SELECT name
FROM permstaff
WHERE location = 'Germany'
UNION ALL
SELECT name
FROM consultants
WHERE work_area = 'Western Europe'
MINUS
SELECT name
FROM blacklist;
```

Note the use of UNION ALL because it is assumed that no one will be in both the PERMSTAFF table and the CONSULTANTS table; a UNION would force an unnecessary sort. The order of precedence for set operators is the order specified by the programmer, so the MINUS operation will compare the BLACKLIST value with the result of the UNION ALL operation. The result will be all staff (permanent and consulting) who do not appear on the blacklist. If the blacklisting could be applied only to consulting staff and not to permanent staff, there would be two possibilities. First, the queries could be listed in a different order.

```
SELECT name
FROM consultants
WHERE work_area = 'Western Europe'
MINUS
SELECT name
FROM blacklist
UNION ALL
SELECT name
FROM permstaff
WHERE location = 'Germany';
```

This would return consultants who are not blacklisted and then append all permanent staff. Alternatively, parentheses could control the precedence explicitly.

```
SELECT name
FROM permstaff
WHERE location = 'Germany'
UNION ALL
  (SELECT name
   FROM consultants
   WHERE work_area = 'Western Europe'
   MINUS
   SELECT name
   FROM blacklist);
```

This query will list all permanent staff and then append all consultant staff who are not blacklisted.

These two queries will return the same rows, but the order will be different because the UNION ALL operations list the PERMSTAFF and CONSULTANTS tables in a different sequence. To ensure that the queries return identical result sets, there would need to be an ORDER BY clause at the foot of the compound queries.

 CAUTION The two preceding queries will return the same rows, but the second version could be considered better code because the parentheses make it more self-documenting. Furthermore, relying on implicit precedence based on the order of the queries works at the moment, but future releases of SQL may include set operator precedence.

Control the Order of Rows Returned

By default, the output of a UNION ALL compound query is not sorted at all; the rows will be returned in groups in the order of which query was listed first and within the groups in the order that they happen to be stored. The output of any other set operator will be sorted in ascending order of all the columns, starting with the first column named.

It is not syntactically possible to use an ORDER BY clause in the individual queries that make up a compound query. This is because the execution of most compound queries has to sort the rows, which would conflict with the ORDER BY. It might seem theoretically possible that a UNION ALL (which does not sort the rows) could take an ORDER BY for each query, but the Oracle implementation of UNION ALL does not permit this.

There is no problem with placing an ORDER BY clause at the end of the compound query, however. This will sort the entire output of the compound query. The default sorting of rows is based on all the columns in the sequence they appear. A specified ORDER BY clause has no restrictions; it can be based on any columns (and functions applied to columns) in any order. Here's an example:

```
SELECT deptno, trim(dname) name
FROM old_dept
UNION
SELECT dept_id, dname
```

```
FROM new_dept
ORDER BY name;
    DEPTNO NAME
---------- -------------------
        10 Accounts
        30 Admin
        20 Support
```

Two-Minute Drill

Define Subqueries

- A subquery is a SELECT statement embedded within another SQL statement.
- Subqueries can be nested within each other.
- With the exception of the correlated subquery, subqueries are executed before the outer query within which they are embedded.

Describe the Types of Problems that the Subqueries Can Solve

- Selecting rows from a table with a condition that depends on the data within the table can be implemented with a subquery.
- Complex joins can sometimes be replaced with subqueries.
- Subqueries can add values to the outer query's output that are not available in the tables the outer query addresses.

Describe the Types of Subqueries

- Multiple-row subqueries can return several rows, possibly with several columns.
- Single-row subqueries return one row, possibly with several columns.
- A scalar subquery returns a single value; it is a single-row, single-column subquery.
- A correlated subquery is executed once for every row in the outer query.

Write Single-Row and Multiple-Row Subqueries

- Single-row subqueries should be used with single-row comparison operators.
- Multiple-row subqueries should be used with multiple-row comparison operators.
- The ALL and ANY operators can be alternatives to use of aggregations.

Describe the Set Operators

- UNION ALL concatenates the results of two queries.
- UNION sorts the results of two queries and removes duplicates.

- INTERSECT returns only the rows common to the result of two queries.

- MINUS returns the rows from the first query that do not exist in the second query.

Use a Set Operator to Combine Multiple Queries into a Single Query

- The queries in the compound query must return the same number of columns.

- The corresponding columns must be of compatible data type.

- The set operators have equal precedence and will be applied in the order they are specified.

Control the Order of Rows Returned

- It is not possible to use ORDER BY in the individual queries that make a compound query.

- An ORDER BY clause specifying a column number or alias can be appended to the end of a compound query.

- The rows returned by a UNION ALL will be in the order they occur in the two source queries.

- The rows returned by a UNION will be sorted across all their columns, left to right.

Self Test

1. Consider this generic description of a SELECT statement:

```
SELECT select_list
FROM table
WHERE condition
GROUP BY expression_1
HAVING expression_2
ORDER BY expression_3 ;
```

Where could subqueries be used? (Choose all correct answers.)

A. select_list

B. table

C. condition

D. expression_1

E. expression_2

F. expression_3

2. A query can have a subquery embedded within it. Under what circumstances could there be more than one subquery? (Choose the best answer.)

   A. The outer query can include an inner query. It is not possible to have another query within the inner query.

   B. It is possible to embed a single-row subquery inside a multiple-row subquery, but not the other way around.

   C. The outer query can have multiple inner queries, but they must not be embedded within each other.

   D. Subqueries can be embedded within each other with no practical limitations on depth.

3. Consider this statement:

```
SELECT employee_id, last_name
FROM employees
WHERE salary >
  (SELECT avg(salary)
   FROM employees);
```

   When will the subquery be executed? (Choose the best answer.)

   A. It will be executed before the outer query.

   B. It will be executed after the outer query.

   C. It will be executed concurrently with the outer query.

   D. It will be executed once for every row in the EMPLOYEES table.

4. Consider this statement:

```
SELECT o.employee_id, o.last_name
FROM employees o
WHERE o.salary >
  (SELECT avg(i.salary)
   FROM employees i
   WHERE i.department_id=o.department_id);
```

   When will the subquery be executed? (Choose the best answer.)

   A. It will be executed before the outer query.

   B. It will be executed after the outer query.

   C. It will be executed concurrently with the outer query.

   D. It will be executed once for every row in the EMPLOYEES table.

5. Consider the following statement:

```
SELECT last_name
FROM employees
JOIN departments
ON employees.department_id = departments.department_id
WHERE department_name='Executive';
```

Also consider this statement:

```
SELECT last_name
FROM employees
WHERE department_id IN
 (SELECT department_id
  FROM departments
  WHERE department_name='Executive');
```

What can be said about the two statements? (Choose two correct answers.)

A. The two statements should generate the same result.

B. The two statements could generate different results.

C. The first statement will always run successfully; the second statement will error if there are two departments with DEPARTMENT_NAME='Executive'.

D. Both statements will always run successfully, even if there are two departments with DEPARTMENT_NAME='Executive'.

6. What are the distinguishing characteristics of a scalar subquery? (Choose two correct answers.)

A. A scalar subquery returns one row.

B. A scalar subquery returns one column.

C. A scalar subquery cannot be used in the SELECT LIST of the parent query.

D. A scalar subquery cannot be used as a correlated subquery.

7. Which comparison operator cannot be used with multiple-row subqueries? (Choose the best answer.)

A. ALL

B. ANY

C. IN

D. NOT IN

E. All the above can be used.

8. Consider this statement:

```
SELECT last_name, (SELECT count(*)
                   FROM departments)
FROM employees
WHERE salary = (SELECT salary
               FROM employees);
```

What is wrong with it? (Choose the best answer.)

A. Nothing is wrong—the statement should run without error.

B. The statement will fail because the subquery in the SELECT list references a table that is not listed in the FROM clause.

C. The statement will fail if the second query returns more than one row.

D. The statement will run but is extremely inefficient because of the need to run the second subquery once for every row in EMPLOYEES.

9. Which of the following statements are equivalent? (Choose two answers.)

   A.
   ```
   SELECT employee_id
   FROM employees
   WHERE salary < ALL
     (SELECT salary
      FROM employees
      WHERE department_id=10);
   ```

   B.
   ```
   SELECT employee_id
   FROM employees
   WHERE salary <
     (SELECT min(salary)
      FROM employees
      WHERE department_id=10);
   ```

   C.
   ```
   SELECT employee_id
   FROM employees
   WHERE salary NOT >= ANY
     (SELECT salary
      FROM employees
      WHERE department_id=10);
   ```

   D.
   ```
   SELECT employee_id
   FROM employees e
    JOIN departments d
   ON e.department_id=d.department_id
   WHERE e.salary <
     (SELECT min(salary)
      FROM employees)
   AND d.department_id=10;
   ```

10. Consider this statement, which is intended to prompt for an employee's name and then find all employees who have the same job as the first employee:

    ```
    SELECT last_name,employee_id
    FROM employees
    WHERE job_id =
     (SELECT job_id
      FROM employees
      WHERE last_name = '&Name');
    ```

    What would happen if a value were given for &Name that did not match with any row in EMPLOYEES? (Choose the best answer.)

    A. The statement would fail with an error.

    B. The statement would return every row in the table.

    C. The statement would return no rows.

    D. The statement would return all rows where JOB_ID is NULL.

11. Which of these set operators will not sort the rows? (Choose the best answer.)

    A. INTERSECT

    B. MINUS

    C. UNION

    D. UNION ALL

12. Which of these operators will remove duplicate rows from the final result? (Choose all that apply.)

    A. INTERSECT

    B. MINUS

    C. UNION

    D. UNION ALL

13. If a compound query contains both a MINUS operator and an INTERSECT operator, which will be applied first? (Choose the best answer.)

    A. The INTERSECT, because INTERSECT has higher precedence than MINUS.

    B. The MINUS, because MINUS has a higher precedence than INTERSECT.

    C. The precedence is determined by the order in which they are specified.

    D. It is not possible for a compound query to include both MINUS and INTERSECT.

14. There are four rows in the REGIONS table. Consider the following statements, and choose how many rows will be returned for each: 0, 4, 8, or 16:

    A.
```
SELECT *
FROM regions
UNION
SELECT *
FROM regions;
```

    B.
```
SELECT *
FROM regions
UNION ALL
SELECT *
FROM regions;
```

    C.
```
SELECT *
FROM regions
MINUS
SELECT *
FROM regions;
```

    D.
```
SELECT *
FROM regions
INTERSECT
SELECT *
FROM regions;
```

15. Consider this compound query:

```
SELECT empno, hired
FROM emp
UNION ALL
SELECT emp_id,hired,fired
FROM ex_emp;
```

The columns EMP.EMPNO and EX_EMP.EMP_ID are integer, the column EMP
.HIRED is timestamp, and the columns EX_EMP.HIRED and EX_EMP.FIRED are
date. Why will the statement fail? (Choose the best answer.)

A. Because the columns EMPNO and EMP_ID have different names.

B. Because the columns EMP.HIRED and EX_EMP.HIRED are different data types.

C. Because there are two columns in the first query and three columns in the second
query.

D. For all the reasons above.

E. The query will succeed.

16. Which line of this statement will cause it to fail? (Choose the best answer.)

A. `select ename, hired from current_staff`

B. `order by ename`

C. `minus`

D. `select ename, hired from current staff`

E. `where deptno=10`

F. `order by ename;`

17. Study this statement:

```
select ename from emp union all select ename from ex_emp;
```

In what order will the rows be returned? (Choose the best answer.)

A. The rows from each table will be grouped and within each group will be sorted on
ENAME.

B. The rows from each table will be grouped but not sorted.

C. The rows will not be grouped but will all be sorted on ENAME.

D. The rows will be neither grouped nor sorted.

Self Test Answers

1. ☑ **A, B, C,** and **E.** Subqueries can be used at all these points.
☒ **D** and **F** are incorrect. A subquery cannot be used in the GROUP BY and
ORDER BY clauses of a query.

2. ☑ **D.** Subquery nesting can be done to many levels.
   ☒ **A, B,** and **C** are incorrect. **A** and **C** are incorrect because subqueries can be nested. **B** is incorrect because the number of rows returned is not relevant to nesting subqueries, only to the operators being used.

3. ☑ **A.** The result set of the inner query is needed before the outer query can run.
   ☒ **B, C,** and **D** are incorrect. **B** and **C** are not possible because the result of the subquery is needed before the parent query can start. **D** is wrong because the subquery is run only once.

4. ☑ **D.** This is a correlated subquery that must be run for every row in the table.
   ☒ **A, B,** and **C** are incorrect. The result of the inner query is dependent on a value from the outer query; it must therefore be run once for every row.

5. ☑ **A** and **D.** The two statements will deliver the same result, and neither will fail if the name is duplicated.
   ☒ **B** and **C** are incorrect. **B** is incorrect because the statements are functionally identical, though syntactically different. **C** is incorrect because the comparison operator used, IN, can handle a multiple-row subquery.

6. ☑ **A** and **B.** A scalar subquery can be defined as a query that returns a single value.
   ☒ **C** and **D** are incorrect. **C** is incorrect because a scalar subquery is the only subquery that can be used in the SELECT LIST. **D** is incorrect because scalar subqueries can be correlated.

7. ☑ **E.** ALL, ANY, IN, and NOT IN are the multiple-row comparison operators.
   ☒ **A, B, C,** and **D** are incorrect. All of these can be used.

8. ☑ **C.** The equality operator requires a single-row subquery, and the second subquery could return several rows.
   ☒ **A, B,** and **D** are incorrect. **A** is incorrect because the statement will fail in all circumstances except the unlikely case where there is zero or one employee. **B** is incorrect because this is not a problem; there doesn't need to be a relationship between the source of data for the inner and outer queries. **D** is incorrect because the subquery will run only once; it is not a correlated subquery.

9. ☑ **A** and **B.** These are identical.
   ☒ **C** and **D** are incorrect. **C** is logically the same as **A** and **B** but syntactically is not possible; it will give an error. **D** will always return no rows, because it asks for all employees who have a salary lower than all employees. This is not an error but can never return any rows. The filter on DEPARTMENTS is not relevant.

10. ☑ **C.** If a subquery returns NULL, the comparison will also return NULL, meaning that no rows will be retrieved.
    ☒ **A, B,** and **D** are incorrect. **A** is incorrect because this would not cause an error. **B** is incorrect because a comparison with NULL will return nothing, not everything. **D** is incorrect because a comparison with NULL can never return anything, not even other NULLs.

11. ☑ **D**. UNION ALL returns rows in the order that they are delivered by the two queries from which the compound query is made up.
☒ **A, B**, and **C** are incorrect. INTERSECT, MINUS, and UNION all use sorting as part of their execution.

12. ☑ **A, B**, and **C**. INTERSECT, MINUS, and UNION all remove duplicate rows.
☒ **D** is incorrect. UNION ALL returns all rows, duplicates included.

13. ☑ **C**. All set operators have equal precedence, so the precedence is determined by the sequence in which they occur.
☒ **A, B**, and **D** are incorrect. **A** and **B** are incorrect because set operators have equal precedence—though this may change in future releases. **D** is incorrect because many set operators can be used in one compound query.

14. ☑ **A** = 4; **B** = 8; **C** = 0; **D** = 4.
☒ Note that 16 is not used; that would be the result of a Cartesian product query.

15. ☑ **C**. Every query in a compound query must return the same number of columns.
☒ **A, B, D**, and **E** are incorrect. **A** is incorrect because the columns can have different names. **B** is incorrect because the two columns are of the same data type group, which is all that was required. It therefore follows that **D** and **E** are also incorrect.

16. ☑ **B**. You cannot use ORDER BY for one query of a compound query; you can place only a single ORDER BY clause at the end.
☒ **A, C, D, E**, and **F** are incorrect. All these lines are legal.

17. ☑ **B**. The rows from each query will be together, but there will be no sorting.
☒ **A, C**, and **D** are incorrect. **A** is not possible with any syntax. **C** is incorrect because that would be the result of a UNION, not a UNION ALL. **D** is incorrect because UNION ALL will return the rows from each query grouped together.

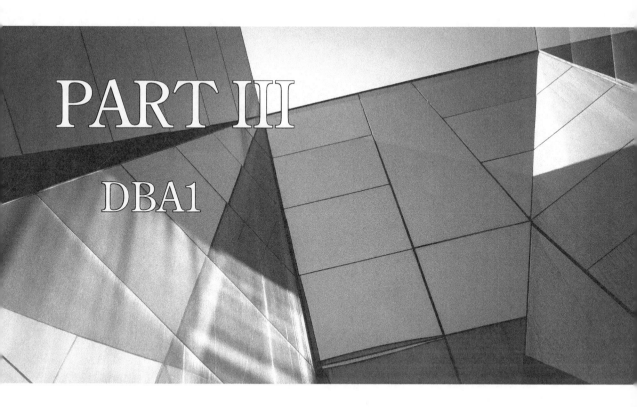

PART III

DBA1

CHAPTER 12

Architectural Overview of Oracle Database 12*c*

Exam Objectives

- 062.2.1 List the Architectural Components of an Oracle Database
- 062.1.2 Explain the Memory Structures
- 062.1.3 Describe the Process Structures
- 062.1.4 Explain the Relationship Between Logical and Physical Storage Structures

An Oracle server consists of two entities: the instance and the database. The instance consists of memory structures and processes, whereas the database consists of files on disk. Within the Oracle server there is complete abstraction of logical storage from physical storage. The logical structures that programmers see (such as tables) are not directly related to the physical structures (datafiles) that system administrators see. The relationship between the two is maintained by structures within the controlfile and the data dictionary.

List the Architectural Components of an Oracle Database

For the most part in this book, you will be dealing with the simplest database environment: one instance on one computer, opening a database stored on local disks. The more complex distributed architectures, involving multiple instances and multiple databases, are beyond the scope of the Oracle Certified Professional (OCP) examination (although not the Oracle Certified Master [OCM] qualification), although you may realistically expect to see high-level summary questions on distributed architecture.

Single-Instance Database Architecture

The instance consists of memory structures and processes. Its existence is transient, in your random access memory (RAM) and on your central processing units (CPUs). When you shut down the running instance, all trace of its existence goes away at the same time. The database consists of physical files on disk. Whether the instance is running or stopped, these files remain. Thus, the lifetime of the instance is only as long as it exists in memory; it can be started and stopped. By contrast, the database, once created, persists indefinitely—that is, until you deliberately delete the files that are associated with the database.

The processes that make up the instance are known as *background processes* because they are present and running at all times while the instance is active. These processes are for the most part completely self-administering, although in some cases it is possible for the database administrator (DBA) to influence the number of them and their operation. The memory structures, which are implemented in shared memory segments provided by the operating system, are known as the *System Global Area* (SGA). The SGA is allocated at instance startup and released on shutdown. Within certain limits, the SGA in the 12c instance and the components within it can be resized while the instance is running, either automatically or in response to the DBA's instructions.

User sessions consist of a user process running locally to the user machine connecting to a server process running locally to the instance on the server machine. The technique for launching the server processes, which are started on demand for each session, is covered in Chapter 13. The connection between user process and server process is usually across a local area network (LAN) and uses Oracle's proprietary Oracle Net protocol layered on top of an industry-standard protocol (usually Transmission Control Protocol [TCP]). The user-process/server-process split implements the client-server architecture; user processes generate SQL, and server processes execute SQL. The server processes are sometimes referred to as *foreground processes,* in contrast with the background processes that make up the instance. Associated with each server process is an area of nonshareable memory, called the *Program Global Area* (PGA). This is private to the session, unlike the SGA, which is available to all the foreground and background processes. Note that background processes also have a PGA. The size of any one session's PGA will vary according to the memory needs of the session at any one time; the DBA can define an upper limit for the total of all the PGAs, and Oracle manages the allocation of this to sessions dynamically.

TIP You will sometimes hear the term *shadow process*. Be cautious of using this term. Some people use it to refer to foreground processes; others use it to refer to background processes. Never mind which is correct—just make sure you know what they are talking about.

Memory management in 12c can be totally automatic. The DBA need do nothing more than specify an overall memory allocation for both the SGA and the PGA and then let Oracle manage this memory as it thinks best. Alternatively, the DBA can control memory allocations. As an in-between technique, the DBA can define certain limits on what the automatic management can do.

EXAM TIP SGA memory is shared across all background and foreground processes; PGA memory can be accessed only by the foreground process of the session to which it has been allocated. Both SGA and PGA memory can be automatically managed.

The physical structures that make up an Oracle database are the datafiles, the online redo log files, and the controlfile. Within the physical structures of the database, which the system administrators see, are the logical structures that the end users see. The Oracle architecture guarantees abstraction of the logical from the physical; there is no way a programmer can determine where, physically, a bit of data is located. Programmers address only logical structures, such as tables. Similarly, it is impossible for system administrators to know what bits of data are in any physical structure. All they can see is the operating system files, not what is within them. It is only you, the database administrator, who is permitted (and required) to see both sides of the story.

The abstraction of logical storage from physical storage is part of the relational database management (RDBMS) standard. If it were possible for a programmer to determine the physical location of a row, then successful execution of the code would be totally dependent on the one environment for which it was written. Changing the platform, moving the datafiles, and even renaming a file would break the application. It is, in fact, possible to determine where a table (and even one row within a table) actually is, but not through standard SQL. The language does not permit it. Tools are supplied for the database administrator's use for doing this, should it ever be necessary.

Data is stored in datafiles. There is no practical limit to the number or size of datafiles, and the abstraction of logical storage from physical storage means that datafiles can be moved or resized and more datafiles can be added without the application developers being aware of this. The relationship between physical and logical structures is maintained and documented in the data dictionary, which contains metadata describing the whole database. By querying certain views in the data dictionary, the DBA can determine precisely where every part of each table resides.

The data dictionary is a set of tables stored within the database. There is a recursive problem here: The instance needs to be aware of the physical and logical structures of the database, but the information describing this is itself within the database. The solution to this problem lies in the staged startup process, which is detailed in Chapter 13.

A requirement of the RDBMS standard is that the database must not lose data. This means it must be backed up; furthermore, any changes made to data between backups must be captured in a manner such that they can be applied to a restored backup. This is the forward recovery process. Oracle implements the capture of changes through the *redo log*, which is a sequential record of all *change vectors* applied to data. A change vector is the alteration made by a Data Manipulation Language (DML) statement (such as INSERT, UPDATE, DELETE, or MERGE, discussed in Chapter 6). Whenever a user session makes any changes, the data in the data block is changed, and the change vector is written out sideways to the redo log, in a form that makes it repeatable. Then, in the event of damage to a datafile, a backup of the file can be restored, and Oracle will extract the relevant change vectors from the redo log and apply them to the data blocks within the file. This ensures that work will never be lost—unless the damage to the database is so extensive as to lose not only one or more datafiles but also either their backups or the redo log.

The controlfile stores the details of the physical structures of the database and is the starting point for the link to the logical structures. When an instance opens a database, it does so by first reading the controlfile. Within the controlfile is information the instance can then use to connect to the rest of the database and the data dictionary within it.

The architecture of a single-instance database, represented graphically in Figure 12-1, can be summarized as consisting of four interacting components:

- A user interacts with a user process.

- A user process interacts with a server process.

- A server process interacts with an instance.

- An instance interacts with a database.

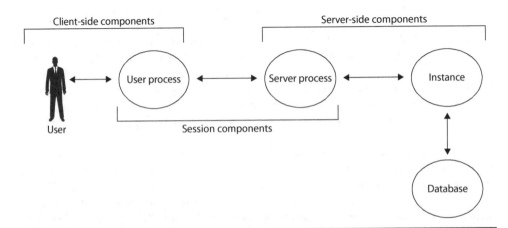

Figure 12-1   The indirect connection between a user and a database

The *user process* is the user interface software. It could be a simple tool, such as SQL*Plus, or something more complicated, such as Microsoft Access plus the ODBC driver, something written in C, or a Java process running on an application server. Whatever it is, it is the tool with which the user interacts on the client side. It is absolutely impossible for any client-side process to have any contact with the database. The client-server split is between the user process (which generates SQL) and the server process (which executes it).

Distributed Systems Architectures

In the single-instance environment, one instance opens one database. In a distributed environment, there are various possibilities for grouping instances and databases.

- **Real Application Clusters (RAC)**   Multiple instances open one database.

- **Streams or GoldenGate**   Multiple Oracle servers propagate transactions between each other.

- **Data Guard**   A primary database updates one or more standby databases to keep them all synchronized.

Combinations of these options can deliver a distributed system that can achieve the goal of 100 percent uptime and zero data loss, with limitless scalability and performance.

Exercise 12-1: Identify the Components of the Database Server   In this exercise you will run queries to determine whether the database is a self-contained system or is part of a larger distributed environment, and you will also identify the major components.

Connect to the database using SQL*Plus as user SYSTEM and then follow these steps:

1. Determine whether the instance is part of a RAC database.

   ```
   select parallel from v$instance;
   ```

   This will return NO for a single-instance database.

2. Determine whether the database is protected against data loss by a Data Guard standby database.

   ```
   select protection_level from v$database;
   ```

   This will return UNPROTECTED if the database is indeed unprotected.

3. Determine whether Streams has been configured in the database.

   ```
   select * from dba_streams_administrator;
   ```

   This will return no rows if Streams has never been configured.

4. Identify the physical structures of the database.

   ```
   select name,bytes from v$datafile;select name,bytes from v$tempfile;
   select member from v$logfile;
   select * from v$controlfile;
   ```

   Can you deduce any file and directory naming standards?

PART III

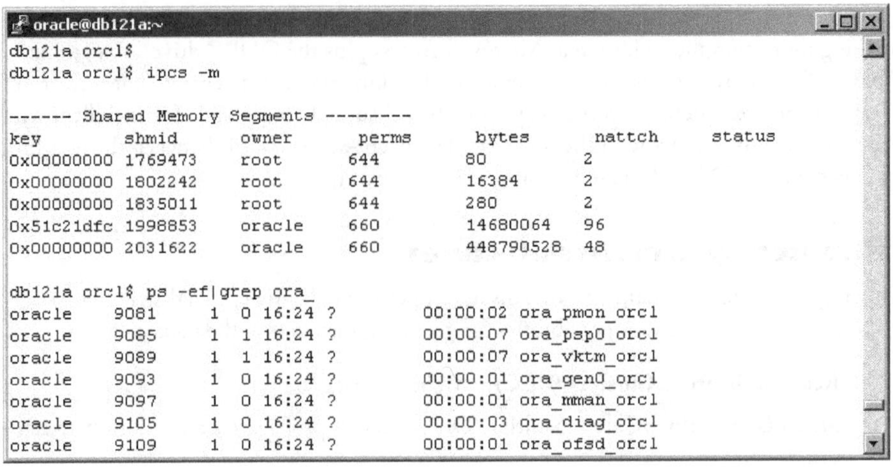

```
oracle@db121a:~                                                    _ □ X
db121a orcl$
db121a orcl$ ipcs -m

------ Shared Memory Segments --------
key         shmid      owner      perms      bytes       nattch    status
0x00000000 1769473     root       644        80          2
0x00000000 1802242     root       644        16384       2
0x00000000 1835011     root       644        280         2
0x51c21dfc 1998853     oracle     660        14680064    96
0x00000000 2031622     oracle     660        448790528   48

db121a orcl$ ps -ef|grep ora_
oracle      9081    1  0 16:24 ?        00:00:02 ora_pmon_orcl
oracle      9085    1  1 16:24 ?        00:00:07 ora_psp0_orcl
oracle      9089    1  1 16:24 ?        00:00:07 ora_vktm_orcl
oracle      9093    1  0 16:24 ?        00:00:01 ora_gen0_orcl
oracle      9097    1  0 16:24 ?        00:00:01 ora_mman_orcl
oracle      9105    1  0 16:24 ?        00:00:03 ora_diag_orcl
oracle      9109    1  0 16:24 ?        00:00:01 ora_ofsd_orcl
```

Figure 12-2   SGA and processes, as seen in Linux

5. Identify the memory and process structures.

For a Linux environment, from an operating system prompt use the ipcs command to display shared memory segments and the ps command to show the oracle processes.

```
ipcs -m
ps -ef|grep ora_
```

Figure 12-2 shows some sample output. ipcs shows two blocks of shared memory owned by user oracle that make up the SGA, and ps shows the background processes of an instance called orcl. Your output will vary depending on how your database instance was named.

For a Windows environment, launch Windows Task Manager. Search for an image named oracle.exe and adjust the column display to show the number of threads within the process and the committed memory. The threads are the background processes, and the committed memory is the total of SGA and PGA for the instance.

Explain the Memory Structures

An Oracle instance consists of a block of shared memory (the SGA) and a number of background processes. At a minimum, the SGA will contain three data structures:

- The database buffer cache default pool
- The log buffer
- The shared pool

It may, optionally, also contain the following:

- A large pool
- A Java pool

- A streams pool
- Additional buffer cache pools

User sessions also need memory on the server side. This is the nonshareable PGA. Each session will have its own private PGA.

 EXAM TIP Which SGA structures are required, and which are optional? The database buffer cache, log buffer, and shared pool are required; the large pool, Java pool, and streams pool are optional.

The Database Buffer Cache

The database buffer cache is Oracle's work area for executing SQL. When updating data, users' sessions don't directly do so on disk. The data blocks containing the data of interest are first copied into the database buffer cache. Changes (such inserting new rows and deleting or modifying existing rows) are applied to these copies of the data blocks in the database buffer cache. The blocks will remain in the cache for some time afterward, until the buffer they are occupying is needed for caching another block.

When querying data, it also goes via the cache. The session works out which blocks contain the rows of interest and copies them into the database buffer cache; the projected columns of relevant rows are then transferred into the session's PGA for further processing. Again, the blocks remain in the database buffer cache for some time afterward.

Take note of the term *block.* Datafiles are formatted into fixed-sized blocks. Table rows and other data objects such as index keys are stored in these blocks. The database buffer cache is formatted into memory buffers, each sized to hold one block. Unlike blocks, rows are of variable length; the length of a row will depend on the number of columns defined for the table, whether the columns actually have anything in them, and, if so, what. Depending on the size of the blocks (which is chosen by the DBA) and the size of the rows (which is dependent on the table design and usage), there may be several rows per block, or possibly a row may stretch over several blocks. The structure of a data block will be described in the section "The Datafiles" later in this chapter.

Ideally, all the blocks containing data that is frequently accessed will be in the database buffer cache, thus minimizing the need for disk input/output (I/O). As a typical use of the database buffer cache, consider an end user retrieving an employee record and updating it with these statements:

```
select last_name, salary, job_id from employees where employee_id=100;
update employees set salary=salary * 1.1 where employee_id=100;
commit;
```

The user process will have prompted the user for the employee number and constructed the SELECT statement. The SELECT retrieves some details to be sent to the user process, where they will be formatted for display. To execute this statement, the session's server process will read the data block containing the relevant row from a datafile into a buffer. The user process will then initiate a screen dialog to prompt for some change to be made and verified; then the

UPDATE statement and the COMMIT statement will be constructed and sent to the server process for execution. Provided that an excessive period of time has not elapsed, the block with the row will still be available in the cache when the UPDATE statement is executed. In this example, the buffer cache hit ratio will be 50 percent: two accesses of a block in the cache but only one read of the block from disk. A well-tuned database buffer cache can result in a cache hit ratio well over 90 percent.

A buffer storing a block whose image in the cache is not the same as the image on disk is often referred to as a *dirty* buffer. A buffer will be "clean" when a block is first copied into it. At that point, the block image in the buffer is the same as the block image on disk. The buffer will become dirty when the block in it is updated. Eventually, dirty buffers must be written back to the datafiles, at which point the buffer will be clean again. Even after being written to disk, the block remains in memory; it is possible that the buffer will not be overwritten with another block for some time.

Note that there is no correlation between the frequency of updates to a buffer (or the number of COMMITs) and when it gets written back to the datafiles.

EXAM TIP Changed blocks may be written to datafiles before or after COMMIT. In the course of normal running, it is not unusual for uncommitted data to be written to the datafiles or for committed changes not to have been written.

The size of the database buffer cache is critical for performance. The cache should be sized adequately for caching all the frequently accessed blocks (whether clean or dirty) but not so large that it caches blocks that are rarely needed. An undersized cache will result in excessive disk activity, as frequently accessed blocks are continually read from disk, used, overwritten by other blocks, and then read from disk again. An oversized cache is not so bad (so long as it is not so large that the operating system has to swap pages of virtual memory in and out of real memory) but can cause problems; for example, the startup of an instance is slower if it involves formatting a massive database buffer cache.

EXAM TIP The size of the database buffer cache can be adjusted dynamically, and it can be automatically managed.

The database buffer cache is allocated at instance startup time and can be resized up or down at any time. This resizing can be either manual or automatic, according to the workload, if the automatic mechanism has been enabled.

The Log Buffer

The log buffer is a small, short-term staging area for change vectors before they are written to the redo log on disk. A *change vector* is a modification applied to something; executing DML statements generates change vectors applied to data. The redo log is the database's guarantee that data will never be lost. Whenever a data block is changed, the change vectors applied to the block are written out to the redo log, from where they can be extracted and applied to datafile backups if it is ever necessary to restore a datafile. Thus, the datafile can be brought up to date.

Redo is not written directly to the redo log files by session server processes. If it were, the sessions would have to wait for disk I/O operations to complete whenever they executed a DML statement. Instead, sessions write redo to the log buffer in memory. This is much faster than writing to disk. The log buffer (which will contain change vectors from many sessions, interleaved with each other) is then written out to the redo log files. One write of the log buffer to disk may therefore be a batch of many change vectors from many transactions. Even so, the change vectors in the log buffer are written to disk in very nearly real time—and when a session issues a COMMIT statement, the log buffer write really does happen in real time. The writes are done by the log writer background process, the LGWR.

EXAM TIP   What does LGWR do when you COMMIT? It flushes the entire log buffer to disk. What does the DBW*n* do on COMMIT? Nothing.

The log buffer is small (in comparison with other memory structures) because it is a short-term storage area. Change vectors are inserted into it and are streamed to disk in near real time. There is no need for it to be more than a few megabytes at the most, and indeed making it much bigger than the default value can be seriously bad for performance. The default is determined by the Oracle server and is based on the number of CPUs on the server node. The default is usually correct.

Understanding COMMIT processing is vital. When a COMMIT statement is issued, part of the commit processing involves writing the contents of the log buffer to the redo log files on disk. This write occurs in real time, and while it is in progress, the session that issued the COMMIT will hang. The guarantee that a committed transaction will never be lost is based on that the commit-complete message is not returned to the session until the data blocks in the cache have been changed (which means that the transaction has been completed) and the change vectors have been written to the redo log on disk (and therefore the transaction could be recovered, if necessary).

The log buffer is allocated at instance startup, and it can never be resized subsequently without restarting the instance. It is a circular buffer. As server processes write change vectors to it, the current write address moves around. The log writer process writes the vectors out in batches, and as it does so, the space they occupied becomes available and can be overwritten by more change vectors. It is possible that at times of peak activity, change vectors will be generated faster than the log writer process can write them out. If this happens, all DML activity will cease (for a few milliseconds) while the log writer clears the buffer.

The process of flushing the log buffer to disk is one of the ultimate bottlenecks in the Oracle architecture. You cannot do DML faster than the LGWR can flush the change vectors to the online redo log files.

EXAM TIP   The size of the log buffer is static, fixed at instance startup. It cannot be automatically managed.

The Shared Pool

The shared pool is the most complex of the SGA structures. It is divided into hundreds of substructures, all of which are managed internally by the Oracle server. This discussion of architecture will mention only three of the shared pool components briefly:

- The library cache
- The data dictionary cache
- The SQL query and PL/SQL function result cache

Some other structures will be described in later chapters. All the structures within the shared pool are automatically managed. Their size will vary according to the pattern of activity against the instance, within the overall size of the shared pool. The shared pool itself can be resized dynamically, either in response to the DBA's instructions or through being managed automatically.

The Library Cache

The library cache is a memory area for storing recently executed code in its parsed form. The library cache caches all code: SQL, PL/SQL, and Java. Parsing is the conversion of code written by programmers into something executable, and it is a process that Oracle does on demand. Because parsed code is cached in the shared pool so that it can be reused without reparsing, performance can be greatly improved. Parsing SQL code takes time. Consider this simple SQL statement:

```
select * from employees where last_name='KING';
```

Before this statement can be executed, the Oracle server has to work out what it means and how to execute it. To begin with, what is *employees*? Is it a table, a synonym, or a view? Does it even exist? Then there is the asterisk (*). What are the columns that make up the EMPLOYEES table (if it is a table)? Does the user have permission to see the table? Answers to these questions and many others have to be found by querying the data dictionary.

 TIP The algorithm used to find SQL in the library cache is based on the American Standard Code for Information Interchange (ASCII) values of the characters that make up the statement. The slightest difference (even something as trivial as SELECT instead of select) means that the statement will not match and will therefore be parsed again. Code that is not reusable is bad for performance.

Having worked out what the statement actually means, the server has to decide how best to execute it. Is there an index on the last_name column? If so, would it be quicker to use the index to locate the row or to scan the whole table? More queries against the data dictionary are needed. It is quite possible for a simple one-line query against a user table to generate dozens of queries against the data dictionary and for the parsing of a statement to take many times longer than eventually executing it. The purpose of the library cache of the shared pool is to store statements in their parsed form, ready for execution. The first time a statement is issued, it has to be parsed before execution; the second time, it can be executed immediately. In a well-designed application, it is possible that statements may be parsed once and executed millions of times. This saves a huge amount of time.

The Data Dictionary Cache
The data dictionary cache is sometimes referred to as the *row cache*. Whichever term you prefer, it stores recently used object definitions, including descriptions of tables, indexes, users, and other metadata definitions. Keeping such definitions in memory in the SGA, where they are immediately accessible to all sessions rather than each session having to read them repeatedly from the data dictionary on disk, enhances parsing performance. The cached object definitions can be used to parse many different statements.

The data dictionary cache stores object definitions so that when statements do have to be parsed, they can be parsed fast—without having to query the data dictionary. Consider what happens if these statements are issued consecutively:

```
select sum(salary) from employees;
select * from employees where last_name='KING';
```

Both statements must be parsed because they are different statements, but parsing the first SELECT statement will have loaded the definition of the EMPLOYEES table and its columns into the data dictionary cache, so parsing the second statement will be faster than it would otherwise have been because no data dictionary access will be needed.

 TIP   Shared pool tuning is usually oriented toward making sure that the library cache is the right size. This is because the algorithms Oracle uses to allocate memory in the SGA are designed to favor the dictionary cache, so if the library cache is correct, the dictionary cache will already be correct.

The SQL Query and PL/SQL Function Result Cache
In many applications, the same query is executed many times, by either the same session or many different sessions. Creating a result cache lets the Oracle server store the results of such queries in memory. The next time the query is issued, rather than running the query, the server can retrieve the cached result. The result cache mechanism is intelligent enough to track whether the tables against which the query was run have been updated. If this has happened, the query results will be invalidated, and the next time the query is issued, it will be rerun. There is therefore no danger of ever receiving an out-of-date cached result.

The PL/SQL result cache uses a similar mechanism. When a PL/SQL function is executed, its return value can be cached, ready for the next time the function is executed. If the parameters passed to the function or the tables that the function queries are different, the function will be reevaluated, but otherwise the cached value will be returned.

By default, use of the SQL query and PL/SQL function result cache is disabled, but if enabled programmatically, it can often dramatically improve performance. The cache is within the shared pool; unlike the other memory areas described previously, it does afford DBAs some control in that they can specify a maximum size.

Sizing the Shared Pool

Sizing the shared pool is critical for performance. It should be large enough to cache all the frequently executed code and frequently needed object definitions (in the library cache and the data dictionary cache) but not so large that it caches statements that have been executed only once. An undersized shared pool cripples performance because server sessions have repeatedly had to grab space in it for parsing statements, which are then overwritten by other statements and therefore have to be parsed again when they are reexecuted. An oversized shared pool can impact badly on performance because it takes too long to search it. If the shared pool is less than the optimal size, performance will degrade. However, there is a minimum size below which statements will fail.

Memory in the shared pool is allocated according to a least recently used (LRU) algorithm. When the Oracle server needs space in the shared pool, it will overwrite the object that has not been used for the longest time. If the object is later needed again, it will have to be reloaded—possibly overwriting another object.

The shared pool is allocated at instance startup time. Prior to release 9*i* of the database, it was not possible to resize the shared pool subsequently without restarting the database instance, but from 9*i* onward it can be resized up or down at any time. This resizing can be either manual or (from release 10*g* onward) automatic, according to workload, if the automatic mechanism has been enabled.

The Large Pool

The large pool is an optional area that, if created, will be used automatically by various processes that would otherwise take memory from the shared pool. One major use of the large pool is by shared server processes, described in Chapter 14 in the discussion of the shared (or multithreaded) server architecture. Parallel execution servers will also use the large pool, if there is one. In the absence of a large pool, these processes will use memory from the shared pool. This can cause bad contention for the shared pool. If shared servers or parallel servers are being used, a large pool should always be created. Some I/O processes may also make use of the large pool, such as the processes used by the Recovery Manager when it is backing up to a tape device.

The Java Pool

The Java pool is required only if your application is going to run Java stored procedures within the database. It is used for the heap space needed to instantiate the Java objects. However, a number of Oracle options are written in Java, so the Java pool is considered standard nowadays. Note that Java code is not cached in the Java pool; it is cached in the shared pool, in the same way that PL/SQL code is cached.

The Streams Pool

Oracle Streams uses the streams pool, which is an advanced tool that is beyond the scope of the OCP examinations or this book, but for completeness a short description follows.

The mechanism used by Streams involves extracting change vectors from the redo log and from these reconstructing the statements that were executed—or statements that would have the same effect. These statements are executed at the remote database. The processes that extract changes from redo and the processes that apply the changes need memory; this memory is the streams pool. From database release 10*g* onward, it is possible to create and resize the streams pool after instance startup; this creation and sizing can be completely automatic. With earlier releases, it had to be defined at startup and was a fixed size.

 EXAM TIP The size of the shared, large, Java, and streams pools is dynamic and can be automatically managed.

Exercise 12-2: Investigate the Memory Structures of the Instance In this exercise, you will run queries to determine the current sizing of various memory structures that make up the instance. Here are the steps:

1. Connect to the database as user SYSTEM.

2. Use the SHOW SGA command to display summarized information.

3. Show the current, maximum, and minimum sizes of the SGA components that can be dynamically resized, like so:

```
select component, current_size, min_size, max_size
from v$sga_dynamic_components;
```

Figure 12-3 shows the results from a demonstration database. Note that the buffer cache is 150MB, consisting of a 134MB default pool plus a 16MB shared I/O pool (this last component is a section of the cache used for LOBs), and that no components have been resized since startup.

```
 oracle@db121a:~                                                        _ □ X
orcl> show sga

Total System Global Area  459304960 bytes
Fixed Size                  2261592 bytes
Variable Size             297799080 bytes
Database Buffers          150994944 bytes
Redo Buffers                8249344 bytes
orcl> select component, current_size,min_size,max_size from v$sga_dynamic_components;

COMPONENT                    CURRENT_SIZE   MIN_SIZE    MAX_SIZE
---------------------------- ------------ ---------- ----------
shared pool                     289406976  289406976  289406976
large pool                        4194304    4194304    4194304
java pool                         4194304    4194304    4194304
streams pool                            0          0          0
DEFAULT buffer cache            134217728  134217728  134217728
KEEP buffer cache                       0          0          0
RECYCLE buffer cache                    0          0          0
DEFAULT 2K buffer cache                 0          0          0
DEFAULT 4K buffer cache                 0          0          0
DEFAULT 8K buffer cache                 0          0          0
DEFAULT 16K buffer cache                0          0          0
DEFAULT 32K buffer cache                0          0          0
Shared IO Pool                   16777216   16777216   16777216
Data Transfer Cache                     0          0          0
ASM Buffer Cache                        0          0          0

15 rows selected.
```

Figure 12-3 Example of SGA configuration

4. Determine how much memory has been, and is currently, allocated to PGAs.

```
select name,value from v$pgastat where name in
('maximum PGA allocated','total PGA allocated');
```

Describe the Background Processes

The instance background processes are the processes that are launched when the instance is started and run until it is terminated. Five background processes have a long history with Oracle and are the first five described in the sections that follow: System Monitor (SMON), Process Monitor (PMON), Database Writer (DBWn), Log Writer (LGWR), and Checkpoint Process (CKPT). A number of others have been introduced with the more recent releases; notable among these are Manageability Monitor (MMON) and Memory Manager (MMAN). There are also some that are not essential but will exist in most instances. These include the Archiver (ARCn) and Recoverer (RECO) processes. Others will exist only if certain options have been enabled. This last group includes the processes required for RAC and Streams. Additionally, some processes exist that are not properly documented (or are not documented at all). The processes described here are those that every OCP candidate will be expected to know.

First, though, a platform variation must be cleared up before discussing processes. On Linux and Unix, all the Oracle processes are separate operating system processes, each with a unique process number. On Windows, there is one operating system process (called ORACLE.EXE) for the whole instance, and the Oracle processes run as separate threads within this one process.

 TIP In release 12c, it is in fact possible to run Oracle in a multithreaded model (rather than the default multiprocess model) as it runs on Windows. This is enabled with the THREADED_EXECUTION instance parameter, which is beyond the scope of the OCP exam.

SMON, the System Monitor

SMON initially has the task of mounting and opening a database. The steps involved in this are described in detail in Chapter 13. In brief, SMON *mounts* a database by locating and validating the database controlfile. It then *opens* a database by locating and validating all the datafiles and online log files. Once the database is opened and in use, SMON is responsible for various housekeeping tasks, such as collating free space in datafiles.

PMON, the Process Monitor

A user session is a user process that is connected to a server process. The server process is launched when the session is created and destroyed when the session ends. An orderly exit from a session involves the user logging off. When this occurs, any work they were doing will be completed in an orderly fashion, and their server process will be terminated. If the session is terminated in a disorderly manner (perhaps because the user's PC is rebooted), the session will be left in a state that must be cleared up. PMON monitors all the server processes and detects any problems with the sessions. If a session has terminated abnormally, PMON will destroy the server process, return its PGA memory to the operating system's free memory pool, and roll back any incomplete transaction that may have been in progress.

 EXAM TIP If a session terminates abnormally, what will happen to an active transaction? It will be rolled back by the PMON background process.

DBWn, the Database Writer

Always remember that sessions do not as a general rule write to disk. They write data (or changes to existing data) to buffers in the database buffer cache. It is the database writer that subsequently writes the buffers to disk. It is possible for an instance to have several database writers (up to a maximum of 100) that will be called DBW0 to DBW9 and then DBWa to DBWz; that's why DBWn refers to "the" database writer. Writers beyond 36 are named BW36 to BW99. The default number is one database writer per eight CPUs, rounded up.

PART III

 TIP How many database writers do you need? The default number may well be correct. Adding more may help performance, but usually you should look at tuning memory first. As a rule, before you optimize disk I/O, ask why there is any need for disk I/O.

DBWn writes dirty buffers from the database buffer cache to the datafiles, but it does not write the buffers as they become dirty. On the contrary—it writes as few buffers as it can get away with. The general idea is that disk I/O is bad for performance, so don't do it unless it really is needed. If a block in a buffer has been written to by a session, there is a reasonable possibility that it will be written to again—by that session or a different one. Why write the buffer to disk if it may well be dirtied again in the near future? The algorithm DBWn uses to select dirty buffers for writing to disk (which will clean them) will select only buffers that have not been recently used. So if a buffer is very busy because sessions are repeatedly reading or writing to it, DBWn will not write it to disk for some time. There could be hundreds or thousands of writes to a buffer before DBWn cleans it. It could be that in a buffer cache of a million buffers, a hundred thousand of them are dirty, but DBWn might write only a few hundred of them to disk at a time. These will be the few hundred that no session has been interested in for some time.

 EXAM TIP What will cause DBWn to write? The answer is no free buffers, too many dirty buffers, a three-second timeout, or a checkpoint.

DBWn writes according to a very lazy algorithm: as little as possible and as rarely as possible. Four circumstances will cause DBWn to write: no free buffers, too many dirty buffers, a three-second timeout, and when there is a checkpoint.

The first circumstance is when there are no free buffers. If a server process needs to copy a block into the database buffer cache, it must find a *free buffer*, which is a buffer that is neither dirty (updated and not yet written back to disk) nor pinned (a pinned buffer is one that is being used by another session at that moment). A dirty buffer must not be overwritten because if it were, the changed data would be lost, and a pinned buffer cannot be overwritten because the operating system's memory protection mechanisms will not permit this. If a server process takes "too long" (as determined by Oracle internally) to find a free buffer, it signals DBW*n* to write some dirty buffers to disk. Once this is done, they will be clean—and thus free and available for use.

The second circumstance is when there are too many dirty buffers ("too many" being another internal threshold). No one server process may have had a problem finding a free buffer, but overall, there could be a large number of dirty buffers, which will cause DBW*n* to write some of them to disk.

The third circumstance is the three-second timeout. Every three seconds, DBW*n* will clean a few buffers. In practice, this event may not be significant in a production system because the two previously described circumstances will be forcing the writes, but the timeout does mean that even if the system is idle, the database buffer cache will eventually be cleaned.

Fourth, there may be a checkpoint requested. The three reasons already given will cause DBW*n* to write a limited number of dirty buffers to the datafiles. When a checkpoint occurs, all dirty buffers are written.

Writing buffers for the first three reasons mentioned is referred to as an *incremental checkpoint* or as *advancing the incremental checkpoint position*. This is all that should happen in the course of normal running and is optimized such that buffers will be made available as needed without impacting performance by stressing the I/O system.

The only moment when a full checkpoint is absolutely necessary is when the database is closed and the instance is shut down (a full description of this sequence is given in Chapter 13). A checkpoint writes all dirty buffers to disk; this synchronizes the buffer cache with the datafiles and synchronizes the instance with the database. During normal running, the datafiles are always out of date. They may be missing changes (committed and uncommitted). This does not matter because the copies of blocks in the buffer cache are up to date, and it is these that the sessions work on. But on shutdown, it is necessary to write everything to disk. Automatic checkpoints occur only on shutdown, but a checkpoint can be forced at any time with this statement:

```
alter system checkpoint;
```

The checkpoint described so far is a full checkpoint. Partial checkpoints that force DBW*n* to write all the dirty buffers containing blocks from just one or more datafiles, rather than the whole database, occur more frequently, for example, when a datafile or tablespace is taken offline, when a tablespace is put into backup mode, or when a tablespace is made read-only. These are less drastic than full checkpoints and occur automatically whenever the relevant event happens.

 EXAM TIP Is there a full checkpoint on log switch? No, there hasn't been since release 8*i*. Many DBAs, including some who should know better, have never learned this change in behavior that happened many years ago.

To conclude, DBW*n* writes on a very lazy algorithm—as little as possible and as rarely as possible—except when a full checkpoint occurs. Then, all dirty buffers are written to disk as fast as possible.

LGWR, the Log Writer

LGWR writes the contents of the log buffer to the online log files on disk. A write of the log buffer to the online redo log files is often referred to as *flushing* the log buffer.

When a session makes any change (by executing INSERT, UPDATE, or DELETE commands) to blocks in the database buffer cache, before it applies the change to the block it writes out the change vector that it is about to apply to the log buffer. So that no work is lost, these change vectors must be written to disk with only minimal delay. To this end, the LGWR streams the contents of the log buffer to the online redo log files on disk in near real time. And when a session issues a COMMIT, the LGWR writes in real time; the session hangs while LGWR writes the buffer to disk. Only then is the transaction recorded as committed and therefore nonreversible.

Three circumstances will cause LGWR to flush the log buffer: if a session issues a COMMIT, if the log buffer is one-third full, and if DBW*n* is about to write dirty buffers.

The first circumstance is the write-on-commit. To process a COMMIT, the server process inserts a commit record into the log buffer. It will then hang while LGWR flushes the log buffer to disk. Only when this write has completed is a commit-complete message returned to the session, and the server process can then continue working. This is the guarantee that transactions will never be lost. Every change vector for a committed transaction will be available in the redo log on disk and can therefore be applied to datafile backups. Therefore, if the database is ever damaged, it can be restored from backup, and all work done since the backup was made can be redone.

Second, when the log buffer is one-third full, LGWR will flush it to disk. This is about performance. If the log buffer is small (as it usually should be), this one-third-full trigger will force LGWR to write the buffer to disk in near real time, even if no one is committing transactions. The log buffer for many applications will be optimally sized at only a few megabytes. The application will generate enough redo to fill one-third of this in a fraction of a second, so LGWR will be forced to stream the change vectors to disk continuously, in near real time. Then, when a session does COMMIT, there will be hardly anything to write, so the COMMIT will complete almost instantaneously.

Third, when DBW*n* needs to write dirty buffers from the database buffer cache to the datafiles, it will signal LGWR to flush the log buffer to the online redo log files. This is to ensure that it will always be possible to reverse an uncommitted transaction. The mechanism of transaction rollback is fully explained in Chapter 6. For now, you just need to know that it is perfectly possible for DBW*n* to write an uncommitted transaction to the datafiles. This is fine, so long as the undo data needed to reverse the transaction is guaranteed to be available. Generating undo data also generates change vectors, and because these will be in the redo log files before the datafiles are updated, the undo data needed to roll back a transaction (should this be necessary) can be reconstructed if needed.

Note that it can be said that there is a three-second timeout that causes LGWR to write. In fact, the timeout is on DBW*n*. However, because LGWR will always write just before DBW*n*, in effect there is a three-second timeout on LGWR as well.

 EXAM TIP When will LGWR flush the log buffer to disk? It happens on COMMIT, when the buffer is one-third full and just before DBWn writes.

CKPT, the Checkpoint Process

The CKPT keeps track of where in the redo stream the incremental checkpoint position is and, if necessary, instructs DBW*n* to write out some dirty buffers in order to push the checkpoint position forward. The current checkpoint position is the point in the redo stream at which recovery must begin in the event of an instance crash. CKPT continually updates the controlfile with the current checkpoint position.

MMON, the Manageability Monitor

MMON is the enabling process for many of the self-monitoring and self-tuning capabilities of the database. The database instance gathers a vast number of statistics about activity and performance. These statistics are accumulated in the SGA, and their current values can be interrogated by issuing SQL queries against various V$ views. For performance tuning and also for trend analysis and historical reporting, it is necessary to save these statistics to long-term storage. MMON regularly (by default, every hour) captures statistics from the SGA and writes them to the data dictionary, where they can be stored indefinitely (though, by default, they are kept for only eight days).

Every time MMON gathers a set of statistics (known as a *snapshot*), it also launches the Automatic Database Diagnostic Monitor (ADDM). The ADDM is a tool that analyzes database activity using an expert system developed over many years by many DBAs. It studies two snapshots (by default, the current and previous snapshots) and makes observations and recommendations regarding performance during the period covered. Chapter 18 describes the use of ADDM (and other tools) for performance tuning. As well as gathering snapshots, MMON continuously monitors the database and the instance to check whether any alerts should be raised.

 EXAM TIP   By default, MMON gathers a snapshot and launches the ADDM every hour.

MMNL, the Manageability Monitor Light

MMNL is a process that assists the MMON. There are times when MMON's scheduled activity is not enough. For example, MMON flushes statistical information accumulated in the SGA to the database according to a schedule (by default, every hour). If the memory buffers used to accumulate this information fill before MMON is due to flush them, MMNL will take responsibility for flushing the data.

MMAN, the Memory Manager

MMAN can completely automate memory management. All the DBA needs to do is set an overall target for memory usage, and MMAN will observe the demand for PGA memory and SGA memory and then allocate memory to sessions and to SGA structures, as needed, while keeping the total allocated memory within a limit set by the DBA.

TIP The automation of memory management is one of the major technical advances of the later releases, automating a large part of the DBA's job and giving huge benefits in performance and resource utilization. MMAN does it better than you can.

LREG, the Listener Registration Process

A database instance will attempt to register itself with a database listener. This is to allow users to connect via the listener. In an advanced environment such as a clustered database with several instances offering many services, LREG will also update the listener with information regarding workload and performance. This allows the listener to direct sessions intelligently to appropriate instances. In earlier releases, this function was performed by the PMON process, but in release 12c a dedicated process (namely, LREG) has been added to do this.

ARC*n*, the Archiver

This is an optional process as far as the database is concerned, but it is usually a required process for the business. Without one or more ARC*n* processes (there can be up to 30, named ARC0, ARC1, and so on), it is possible to lose data. The process and purpose of launching ARC*n* to create archive log files is described in detail in Chapter 22. For now, only a summary is needed.

All change vectors applied to data blocks are written out to the log buffer (by the sessions making the changes) and then to the *online* redo log files (by the LGWR). The online redo log files are of fixed size and number. Once they have been filled, LGWR will overwrite them with more redo data. The time that must elapse before this happens is dependent on the size and number of the online log files and the amount of DML activity (and therefore the amount of redo generated) against the database. This means that the online redo log stores change vectors only for recent activity. To preserve a complete history of all changes applied to the data, the online log files must be copied as they are filled and before they are reused. The ARC*n* is responsible for doing this. Provided that these copies, known as *archive* redo log files, are available, it will always be possible to recover from any damage to the database by restoring datafile backups and applying change vectors to them extracted from all the archive log files generated since the backups were made.

 EXAM TIP LGWR writes the online log files; ARC*n* reads them. During normal running, no other processes touch them at all.

 TIP The progress of the ARC*n* processes and the state of the destinations to which they are writing must be monitored. If archiving fails, the database will eventually hang. This monitoring can be done through the alert system.

RECO, the Recoverer Process

A *distributed transaction* is a transaction that involves updates to two or more databases. Distributed transactions are designed by programmers and operate through database links. Consider this example:

```
update employees set salary=salary * 1.1
where employee_id=1000;
update employees@dev set salary=salary * 1.1
where employee_id=1000;
commit;
```

The first update applies to a row in the local database; the second applies to a row in a remote database identified by the database link DEV. The COMMIT command instructs both databases to commit the transaction, which consists of both statements. Distributed transactions require a *two-phase commit*. The commit in each database must be coordinated; if one were to fail and the other were to succeed, the data overall would be in an inconsistent state. A two-phase commit prepares each database by instructing their LGWRs to flush the log buffer to disk (the first phase), and once this is confirmed, the transaction is flagged as committed everywhere (the second phase). If anything goes wrong anywhere between the two phases, RECO takes action to cancel the commit and roll back the work in all databases.

Some Other Background Processes

It is unlikely that processes other than those already described will be examined, but for completeness this section describes the remaining processes usually present in an instance. Figure 12-4 shows a query that lists all the processes running in an instance on a Linux system. Many more processes may exist, depending on certain options being enabled, but those shown in the figure will be present in most instances.

Exercise 12-3: Investigate the Processes Running in Your Instance   In this exercise, you will run queries to see what background processes are running on your instance. You may use either SQL Developer or SQL*Plus. Here are the steps to follow:

1. Connect to the database as user SYSTEM.

2. Determine what processes are running and how many of each.

   ```
   select program,paddr from v$session order by program;
   select program,addr from v$process order by program;
   ```

   These queries will give similar results. Each process must have a session (even the background processes), and each session must have a process. The processes that can occur multiple times will have a numeric suffix, except for the processes supporting user sessions, which will all have the same name.

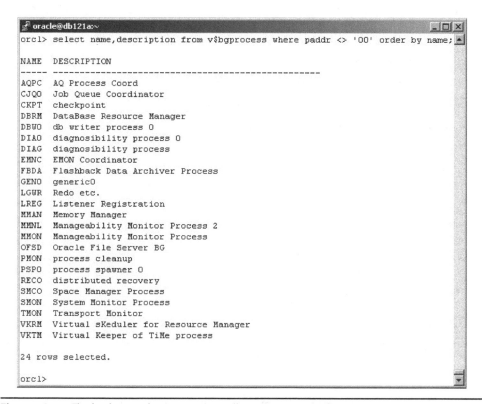

```
 oracle@db121a:~                                              _ □ ×
orcl> select name,description from v$bgprocess where paddr <> '00' order by name;

NAME   DESCRIPTION
-----  --------------------------------------------------
AQPC   AQ Process Coord
CJQ0   Job Queue Coordinator
CKPT   checkpoint
DBRM   DataBase Resource Manager
DBW0   db writer process 0
DIA0   diagnosibility process 0
DIAG   diagnosibility process
EMNC   EMON Coordinator
FBDA   Flashback Data Archiver Process
GEN0   generic0
LGWR   Redo etc.
LREG   Listener Registration
MMAN   Memory Manager
MMNL   Manageability Monitor Process 2
MMON   Manageability Monitor Process
OFSD   Oracle File Server BG
PMON   process cleanup
PSP0   process spawner 0
RECO   distributed recovery
SMCO   Space Manager Process
SMON   System Monitor Process
TMON   Transport Monitor
VKRM   Virtual sKeduler for Resource Manager
VKTM   Virtual Keeper of TiMe process

24 rows selected.

orcl>
```

Figure 12-4   The background processes typically present in a single instance

3. Investigate how many processes could be running.

   The v$bgprocess view has one row for every possible process. Processes that are actually running have an address, which is a join column to the v$process view.

   ```
   select name,description,paddr from v$bgprocess
   order by paddr;
   ```

4. Observe the launching of server processes as sessions are made by counting the number of server processes (on Linux or any Unix platform) or the number of Oracle threads (on Windows). The technique is different on the two platforms. On Linux/Unix, the Oracle processes are separate operating system processes, but on Windows they are threads within one operating system process.

PART III

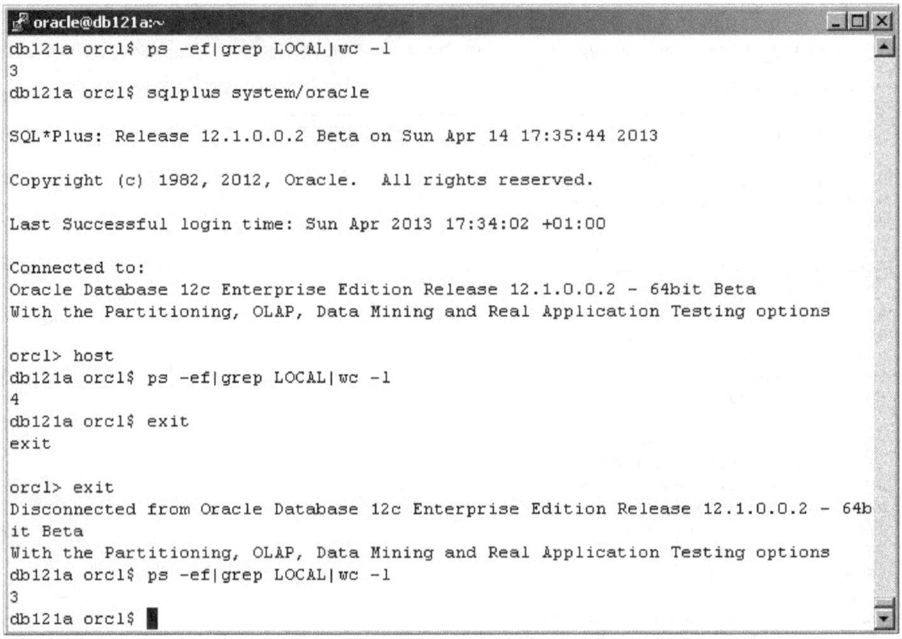

```
oracle@db121a:~                                                      _ □ ×
db121a orcl$ ps -ef|grep LOCAL|wc -1
3
db121a orcl$ sqlplus system/oracle

SQL*Plus: Release 12.1.0.0.2 Beta on Sun Apr 14 17:35:44 2013

Copyright (c) 1982, 2012, Oracle.  All rights reserved.

Last Successful login time: Sun Apr 2013 17:34:02 +01:00

Connected to:
Oracle Database 12c Enterprise Edition Release 12.1.0.0.2 - 64bit Beta
With the Partitioning, OLAP, Data Mining and Real Application Testing options

orcl> host
db121a orcl$ ps -ef|grep LOCAL|wc -1
4
db121a orcl$ exit
exit

orcl> exit
Disconnected from Oracle Database 12c Enterprise Edition Release 12.1.0.0.2 - 64b
it Beta
With the Partitioning, OLAP, Data Mining and Real Application Testing options
db121a orcl$ ps -ef|grep LOCAL|wc -1
3
db121a orcl$ █
```

Figure 12-5 Counting session server processes

On Linux, run this command from an operating system prompt:

```
ps -ef | grep LOCAL | wc -1
```

This will count the number of processes running that have the string LOCAL in their name. This will include all the session server processes.

Launch a SQL*Plus session and then rerun the preceding command. Use the host command to launch an operating shell from within the SQL*Plus session. You will see that the number of processes has increased. Exit the session, and you will see that the number has dropped again. Figure 12-5 demonstrates this.

Observe in the figure how the number of processes changes from 3 to 4 and back again; the difference is the launching and terminating of the server process supporting the SQL*Plus session.

On Windows, launch Task Manager. Configure it to show the number of threads within each process by following these steps: In the View menu, select the Select Columns option and select the Thread Count check box. Look for the ORACLE.EXE process, and note the number of threads. In Figure 12-6, this is currently at 33.

Launch a new session against the instance, and you will see the thread count increment. Exit the session, and it will decrement.

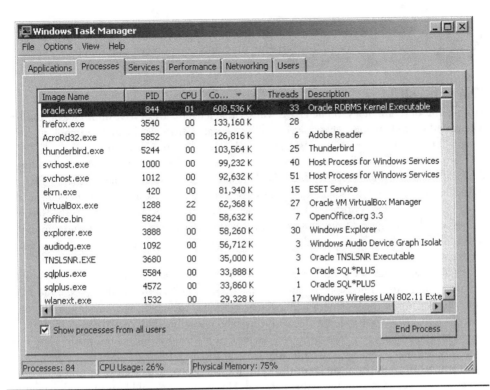

Figure 12-6 Displaying the thread count within the Oracle executable image

Explain the Relationship Between Logical and Physical Storage Structures

The Oracle database provides complete abstraction of the logical storage from the physical. The logical data storage is in *segments*. There are various segment types; a typical segment is a table. The segments are stored physically in datafiles. The abstraction of the logical storage from the physical storage is accomplished through tablespaces. The relationships between the logical and physical structures, as well as their definitions, are maintained in the data dictionary.

You can find a full treatment of database storage, both logical and physical, in Chapter 15.

The Physical Database Structures

Three file types make up an Oracle database, plus a few others that exist externally to the database and are, strictly speaking, optional. The required files are the controlfile, the online redo log files, and the datafiles. The external files that will usually be present (there are others, needed for advanced options) are the initialization parameter file, the password file, the archive redo log files, and the log and trace files.

EXAM TIP What three files types must be present in a database? The controlfile, the online redo log files, and any number of datafiles.

The Controlfile

First a point of terminology: Some DBAs will say that a database can have multiple controlfiles, whereas others will say that it has one controlfile, of which there may be multiple copies. This book will follow the latter terminology. The Oracle documentation is inconsistent.

The controlfile is small but vital. It contains pointers to the rest of the database, including the locations of the online redo log files, the datafiles, and more recently the archive log files (if the database is in archive log mode). It also stores information required to maintain database integrity such as various critical sequence numbers and timestamps, for example. If the Recovery Manager tool is being used for backups, the details of these backups will also be stored in the controlfile. The controlfile will usually be no more than a few megabytes in size, but you can't survive without it.

Every database has one controlfile, but a good DBA will always create multiple copies of the controlfile so that if one copy is damaged, the database will survive. If all copies of the controlfile are lost, it is possible (though perhaps awkward) to recover, but you should never find yourself in that situation. You don't have to worry about keeping multiplexed copies of the controlfile synchronized—Oracle will take care of that. Its maintenance is automatic; your only control is how many copies to have and where to put them.

If you get the number of copies or their location wrong at database creation time, you can add or remove copies later or move them around. However, you should bear in mind that any such operations will require downtime, so it is a good idea to get it right at the beginning. There is no right or wrong answer when determining how many copies to have. The minimum is one; the maximum possible is eight. All organizations should have a DBA standards handbook that states something like "All production databases will have three copies of the controlfile, on three separate devices" (three being a number picked for illustration purposes only but a number with which many organizations are happy). If no such guidelines are in place, someone should write them (and perhaps the "someone" should be you). There is no rule that says two copies are too few or seven copies are too many; there are only corporate standards, and the DBA's job is to ensure that the databases conform to these standards.

Damage to any controlfile copy will cause the database instance to terminate immediately. There is no way to avoid this. Oracle Corporation does not permit operating a database with less than the number of controlfiles requested.

The Online Redo Log Files

The redo log stores a continuous chain in chronological order of every change vector applied to the database. This will be the bare minimum of information required to reconstruct, or redo, all the work that has been done. If a datafile (or the whole database) is damaged or destroyed, these change vectors can be applied to datafile backups to redo the work, bringing them forward in time until the moment that the damage occurred. The redo log consists of two file types: the online redo log files (which are required) and the archive log files (which are optional).

Every database has at least two online redo log files, but like with the controlfile, a good DBA creates multiple copies of each online redo log file. The online redo log consists of groups of online redo log files, each file being known as a member. An Oracle database requires at least two groups of at least one member each to function. You may create more than two groups for performance reasons and more than one member per group for security (as the old joke goes, "This isn't just data security; it is job security"). The requirement for a minimum of two groups is so that one group can be accepting the current changes while the other group is being backed up (or *archived,* to use the correct term).

EXAM TIP Every database must have at least two online redo log file groups to function. Each group should have at least two members for safety.

One of the groups is the *current* group. Changes are written to the current online redo log file group by LGWR. As user sessions update data in the database buffer cache, they also write out the minimal change vectors to the redo log buffer. LGWR continually flushes this buffer to the files that make up the current online redo log file group. Log files are fixed size; therefore, eventually the files making up the current group will fill. LGWR will then perform what is called a *log switch,* which makes the second group current and starts writing to that. If your database is configured appropriately, the ARC*n* process(es) will then archive (in effect, back up) the log file members making up the first group. When the second group fills, LGWR will switch back to the first group, making it current and overwriting it; ARC*n* will then archive the second group. Thus, the online redo log file groups (and therefore the members making them up) are used in a circular fashion, and each log switch will generate an archive redo log file.

As with the controlfile, if you have multiple members per group (and you should!), you don't have to worry about keeping them synchronized. LGWR will ensure that it writes to all of them, in parallel, thus keeping them identical. If you lose one member of a group, as long as you have a surviving member, the database will continue to function.

The size and number of your log file groups are a matter of tuning. In general, you will choose a size appropriate to the amount of activity you anticipate. The minimum size is 50MB, but some active databases will need to raise this to several gigabytes if they are not to fill every few minutes. A busy database can generate megabytes of redo a second, whereas a largely static database may generate only a few megabytes an hour. The number of members per group will be dependent on what level of fault tolerance is deemed appropriate and is a matter to be documented in corporate standards. However, you don't have to worry about this at database creation time. You can move your online redo log files around, add or drop them, and create ones of different sizes as you please at any time later. Such operations are performed "online" and don't require downtime; they are therefore transparent to the end users.

The Datafiles

The third required file type making up a database is the datafile. At a minimum, you must have three datafiles (all to be created at database creation time), one each for the SYSTEM tablespace (which stores the data dictionary), the SYSAUX tablespace (which stores data that is auxiliary to the data dictionary), and the UNDO tablespace (which stores the undo segments required to protect transactions). You will have many more than that when your database goes live and will often create a few more to begin with.

Datafiles are the repository for data. Their size and numbers are effectively unlimited. A small database might have just half a dozen datafiles of only a few hundred megabytes each. A larger database could have thousands of datafiles, whose size is limited only by the capabilities of the host operating system and hardware.

The datafiles are the physical structures visible to the system administrators. Logically, they are the repository for the *segments* containing user data that the programmers see and also for the segments that make up the data dictionary. A segment is a storage structure for data; typical segments are tables and indexes. Datafiles can be renamed, resized, moved, added, or dropped at any time in the lifetime of the database, but remember that some operations on some datafiles may require downtime.

At the operating system level, a datafile consists of a number of operating system blocks. Internally, datafiles are formatted into *Oracle blocks*. These blocks are consecutively numbered within each datafile. The block size is fixed when the datafile is created, and in most circumstances it will be the same throughout the entire database. The block size is a matter for tuning and can range (with limits, depending on the platform) from 2KB up to 32KB. There is no necessary relationship between the Oracle block size and the operating system block size.

Figure 12-7 shows the Oracle storage model in the form of an entity-relationship diagram. The left column shows the logical structures next to the physical structures. For completeness, the diagram also shows the ASM entities in the two rightmost columns, which are covered in Chapter 3. These are an alternative to the file system storage discussed here.

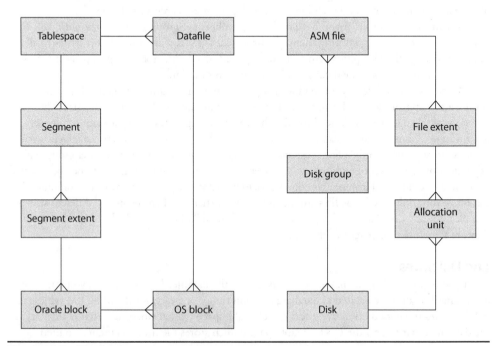

Figure 12-7 The Oracle storage model

TIP Many DBAs like to match the operating system block size to the Oracle block size. For performance reasons, the operating system blocks should never be larger than the Oracle blocks, but there is no reason not to have them smaller. For instance, having a 1KB operating block size and an 8KB Oracle block size is perfectly acceptable.

Within a block is a header section, a data area, and possibly some free space. The header section contains information such as the row directory, which lists the location within the data area of the rows in the block (if the block is being used for a table segment) and also row locking information if there is a transaction (or several concurrent transactions) working on the rows in the block. The data area contains the data itself, such as rows if it is part of a table segment, or index keys if the block is part of an index segment.

EXAM TIP Server processes read from the datafiles; DBW*n* writes to datafiles.

Other Database Files

These files exist outside the database. They are necessary for practical purposes, but are not, strictly speaking, part of the database.

- **Instance parameter file** When an Oracle instance is started, the SGA structures build in memory, and the background processes start according to settings in the parameter file. This is the only file that needs to exist to start an instance. There are several hundred parameters, but only one is required: the DB_NAME parameter. All others have defaults. Therefore, the parameter file can be quite small, but it must exist.

- **Password file** Users establish sessions by presenting a username and password. The Oracle server authenticates these against user definitions stored in the data dictionary. The data dictionary is a set of tables in the database; it is therefore inaccessible if the database is not open. There are occasions when a user needs to be authenticated before the data dictionary is available, such as when they need to start the database or indeed to create it. An external password file is one means of doing this. It contains a small number of (typically less than half a dozen) usernames and passwords that exist outside the data dictionary that can be used to connect to an instance before the data dictionary is available.

- **Archive redo log files** When an online redo log file fills, the ARC*n* process copies it out of the database to an archive redo log file. Once this is done, the archive log is no longer part of the database. It is, however, essential if it's ever necessary to restore a datafile backup, and Oracle does provide facilities for managing the archive redo log files.

- **Alert log and trace files** The alert log is a continuous stream of messages regarding certain critical operations affecting the instance and the database. Not everything is logged; only events that are considered to be really important (such as startup and shutdown), changes to the physical structures of the database, and changes to the parameters that control the instance. Trace files are generated by background processes when they detect error conditions and sometimes to report certain actions.

The Logical Database Structures

The physical structures that make up a database are visible as operating system files to your system administrators. Your users see logical structures such as tables. Oracle uses the term *segment* to describe any structure that contains data. A typical segment is a table, containing rows of data, but there are more than a dozen possible segment types in an Oracle database. Of particular interest (for examination purposes) are table segments, index segments, and undo segments, all of which are investigated in detail later. For now, you don't need to know any more than that tables contain rows of information, that indexes are a mechanism for giving fast access to any particular row, and that undo segments are data structures used for storing the information that might be needed to reverse, or roll back, any transactions you do not want to make permanent.

So, system administrators see physical datafiles, and programmers see logical segments. Oracle abstracts the logical storage from the physical storage by means of the *tablespace,* which is logically a collection of one or more segments and physically a collection of one or more datafiles. Put in terms of relational analysis, there is a many-to-many relationship between segments and datafiles. One table may be cut across many datafiles, and one datafile may contain bits of many tables. By inserting the tablespace entity between the segments and the files, Oracle resolves this many-to-many relationship.

 EXAM TIP The SYSAUX tablespace must be created at database creation time. If you do not specify it, one will be created by default.

A segment will consist of a number of blocks. Datafiles are formatted into blocks, and these blocks are assigned to segments as the segments grow. Because managing space one block at a time would be a time-consuming process, blocks are grouped into extents. An *extent* is a series of Oracle blocks that are consecutively numbered within a datafile, and segments grow by having new extents added to them. These extents need not be adjacent to each other or even in the same datafile; they can come from any datafile that is part of the tablespace within which the segment resides.

Figure 12-7, shown earlier, shows the Oracle data storage hierarchy, with the separation of logical from physical storage. The figure shows the relationships between the storage structures. Logically, a tablespace can contain many segments, each consisting of many extents. Physically, a datafile consists of many operating system blocks assigned by whatever file system the operating system is using. The two parts of the model are connected by the relationships showing that one tablespace can consist of multiple datafiles and at the lowest level that one Oracle block will consist of multiple operating system blocks.

The Data Dictionary

The data dictionary is metadata, which is data about data. It describes the database, both physically and logically, and its contents. User definitions, security information, integrity constraints, and performance monitoring information are all part of the data dictionary. It is stored as a set of segments in the SYSTEM and SYSAUX tablespaces.

In many ways, the segments that make up the data dictionary are segments like any other—just tables and indexes. The critical difference is that the data dictionary tables are generated at database creation time, and you are not allowed to access them directly. There is nothing to stop an inquisitive DBA from investigating the data dictionary directly, but if you do any updates to it, you may cause irreparable damage to your database—and certainly Oracle Corporation will not support you. Creating a data dictionary is part of the database creation process. It is maintained subsequently by Data Definition Language (DDL) commands. When you issue the CREATE TABLE command, you are in fact inserting rows into data dictionary tables, as you are with commands such as CREATE USER and GRANT.

For querying the dictionary, Oracle provides a set of views. The views come in four forms, prefixed CDB_, DBA_, ALL_, or USER_. Any view prefixed USER_ will be populated with rows describing objects owned by the user querying the view. Therefore, no two people will see the same contents. If user SCOTT queries USER_TABLES, he will see information about his tables; if you query USER_TABLES, you will see information about your tables. Any view prefixed ALL_ will be populated with rows describing objects to which you have access. Therefore, ALL_TABLES will contain rows describing your own tables, plus rows describing tables belonging to anyone else you have been given permission to see. Any view prefixed DBA_ will have rows for every object in the database, so DBA_TABLES will have one row for every table in the database, no matter who created it. The CDB views are identical to the DBA views, unless you are working in a multitenant database. These views are created as part of the database creation process, along with a large number of PL/SQL packages that are provided by Oracle to assist database administrators in managing the database and programmers in developing applications. PL/SQL code is also stored in the data dictionary.

 EXAM TIP Which view will show you *all* the tables in the database? The view is DBA_TABLES, not ALL_TABLES.

The relationship between tablespaces and datafiles is maintained in the database controlfile. This lists all the datafiles, stating which tablespace they are part of. Without the controlfile, there is no way an instance can locate the datafiles and then identify those that make up the SYSTEM tablespace. Only when the SYSTEM tablespace has been opened is it possible for the instance to access the data dictionary, at which point it becomes possible to open the database.

Exercise 12-4: Investigate the Storage Structures in Your Database In this exercise, you will create a table segment and then work out where it is physically. Follow these steps:

1. Connect to the database as user SYSTEM.

2. Create a table without nominating a tablespace—it will be created in your default tablespace, with one extent.

```
create table tab34 (c1 varchar2(10))
segment creation immediate;
```

3. Identify the tablespace in which the table resides, the size of the extent, the file number the extent is in, and at which block of the file the extent starts.

```
select tablespace_name, extent_id, bytes, file_id, block_id
from dba_extents where owner='SYSTEM' and segment_name='TAB34';
```

4. Identify the file by name (substitute the file_id from the previous query when prompted).

```
select name from v$datafile where file#=&file_id;
```

5. Work out precisely where in the file the extent is in terms of how many bytes into the file it begins. This requires finding out the tablespace's block size. Enter the block_id and tablespace_name returned by the query in step 3 when prompted.

```
select block_size * &block_id from dba_tablespaces
where tablespace_name='&tablespace_name';
```

Figure 12-8 shows these steps, executed from SQL*Plus.

The figure shows that the table exists in one extent (extent 0) that is 64KB in size. This extent is in the file /u01/app/oracle/oradata/orcl/system01.dbf and begins about 826MB into the file.

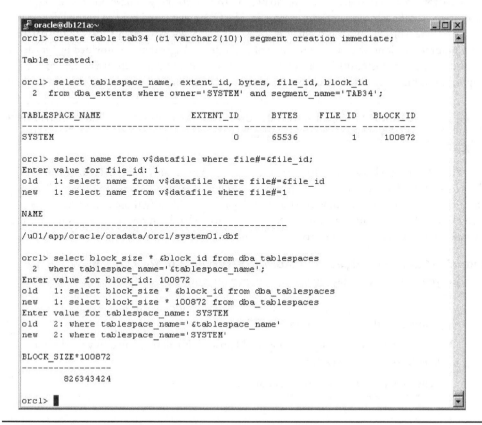

Figure 12-8 Determining the physical location of a logical object

Two-Minute Drill

List the Architectural Components of an Oracle Database

- An Oracle server is an instance connected to a database.
- An instance is a block of shared memory and a set of background processes.
- A database is a set of files on disk.
- A user session is a user process connected to a server process.

Explain the Memory Structures

- The instance shared memory is the System Global Area (the SGA).
- A session's private memory is its Program Global Area (the PGA).
- The SGA consists of a number of substructures, some of which are required (the database buffer cache, the log buffer, and the shared pool) and some of which are optional (the large pool, the Java pool, and the streams pool).
- The SGA structures can be dynamically resized and automatically managed, with the exception of the log buffer.

Describe the Background Processes

- Session server processes are launched on demand when users connect.
- Some background processes are launched at instance startup and persist until shutdown; others start/stop as needed.
- Server processes read from the database; background processes write to the database.
- Some background processes will always be present (in particular SMON, PMON, DBW*n*, LGWR, CKPT, and MMON); others will run depending on what options have been enabled.

Explain the Relationship Between Logical and Physical Storage Structures

- There are three required file types in a database: the controlfile, the online redo log files, and the datafiles.
- The controlfile stores integrity information and pointers to the rest of the database.
- The online redo logs store recent change vectors applied to the database.
- The datafiles store the data.
- External files include the parameter file, the password file, the archive redo logs, and the log and trace files.
- Logical data storage (segments) is abstracted from physical data storage (datafiles) by tablespaces.

- A tablespace can consist of multiple datafiles.
- Segments consist of multiple extents, which consist of multiple Oracle blocks, which consist of multiple operating system blocks.
- A segment can have extents in several datafiles.

Self Test

1. What statements regarding instance memory and session memory are correct? (Choose all correct answers.)

    A. SGA memory is private memory segments; PGA memory is shared memory segments.

    B. Sessions can write to the PGA, not the SGA.

    C. The SGA is written to by all sessions; a PGA is written by one session.

    D. The PGA is allocated at instance startup.

    E. The SGA is allocated at instance startup.

2. How do sessions communicate with the database? (Choose the best answer.)

    A. Server processes use Oracle Net to connect to the instance.

    B. Background processes use Oracle Net to connect to the database.

    C. User processes read from the database and write to the instance.

    D. Server processes execute SQL received from user processes.

3. What memory structures are a required part of the SGA? (Choose all correct answers.)

    A. The database buffer cache

    B. The Java pool

    C. The large pool

    D. The log buffer

    E. The Program Global Area

    F. The shared pool

    G. The streams pool

4. Which SGA memory structures cannot be resized dynamically after instance startup? (Choose all correct answers.)

    A. The database buffer cache.

    B. The Java pool.

    C. The large pool.

    D. The log buffer.

    E. The shared pool.

    F. The streams pool.

    G. All SGA structures can be resized dynamically after instance startup.

5. Which SGA memory structures cannot be resized automatically after instance startup? (Choose all correct answers.)

   A. The database buffer cache.

   B. The Java pool.

   C. The large pool.

   D. The log buffer.

   E. The shared pool.

   F. The streams pool.

   G. All SGA structures can be resized automatically after instance startup.

6. When a session changes data, where does the change get written? (Choose the best answer.)

   A. It gets written to the data block in the cache and the redo log buffer.

   B. It gets written to the data block on disk and the current online redo log file.

   C. The session writes to the database buffer cache, and the log writer writes to the current online redo log file.

   D. Nothing is written until the change is committed.

7. Which of these background processes is optional? (Choose the best answer.)

   A. ARC*n*, the archive process

   B. CKPT, the checkpoint process

   C. DBW*n*, the database writer

   D. LGWR, the log writer

   E. MMON, the manageability monitor

8. What happens when a user issues a COMMIT? (Choose the best answer.)

   A. The CKPT process signals a checkpoint.

   B. The DBW*n* process writes the transaction's changed buffers to the datafiles.

   C. The LGWR flushes the log buffer to the online redo log.

   D. The ARC*n* process writes the change vectors to the archive redo log.

9. An Oracle instance can have only one of some processes but several of others. Which of these processes can occur several times? (Choose all correct answers.)

   A. The archive process

   B. The checkpoint process

   C. The database writer process

   D. The log writer process

   E. The session server process

10. One segment can be spread across many datafiles. How? (Choose the best answer.)

   A. By allocating extents with blocks in multiple datafiles

   B. By spreading the segment across multiple tablespaces

   C. By assigning multiple datafiles to a tablespace

   D. By using an Oracle block size that is larger than the operating system block size

11. Which statement is correct regarding the online redo log? (Choose the best answer.)

   A. There must be at least one log file group, with at least one member.

   B. There must be at least one log file group, with at least two members.

   C. There must be at least two log file groups, with at least one member each.

   D. There must be at least two log file groups, with at least two members each.

12. Where is the current redo byte address, also known as the incremental checkpoint position, recorded? (Choose the best answer.)

   A. In the controlfile

   B. In the current online log file group

   C. In the header of each datafile

   D. In the System Global Area

Self Test Answers

1. ☑ **C, E.** The SGA is shared memory, updated by all sessions; PGAs are private to each session. The SGA is allocated at startup time (but it can be modified later).
   ☒ **A, B,** and **D** are incorrect. **A** is incorrect because it reverses the situation. It is the SGA that exists in shared memory, not the PGA. **B** is incorrect because sessions write both to their own PGA and to the SGA. **D** is incorrect because (unlike the SGA) the PGA is allocated only on demand.

2. ☑ **D.** This is the client-server split. User processes generate SQL, and server processes execute SQL.
   ☒ **A, B,** and **C** are incorrect. **A** and **B** are incorrect because they get the use of Oracle Net incorrect. Oracle Net is the protocol between a user process and a server process. **C** is incorrect because it describes what server processes do, not what user processes do.

3. ☑ **A, D, F.** Every instance must have a database buffer cache, a log buffer, and a shared pool.
   ☒ **B, C, E,** and **G** are incorrect. **B, C,** and **G** are incorrect because the Java pool, the large pool, and the streams pool are needed only for certain options. **E** is incorrect because the PGA is not part of the SGA at all.

4. ☑ **D.** The log buffer is fixed in size at startup time.
   ☒ **A, B, C, E, F,** and **G** are incorrect. **A, B, C, E,** and **F** are incorrect because these are the SGA's resizable components. **G** is incorrect because the log buffer is static.

5. ☑ **D.** The log buffer cannot be resized manually, never mind automatically.

☒ **A, B, C, E, F,** and **G** are incorrect. **A, B, C, E,** and **F** are incorrect because these SGA components can all be automatically managed. **G** is incorrect because the log buffer is static.

6. ☑ **A.** The session updates the copy of the block in memory and writes out the change vector to the log buffer.

☒ **B, C,** and **D** are incorrect. **B** is incorrect because although this will happen, it does not happen when the change is made. **C** is incorrect because it confuses the session making changes in memory with LGWR propagating changes to disk. **D** is incorrect because all changes to data occur in memory as they are made—the COMMIT is not relevant.

7. ☑ **A.** Archiving is not compulsory (although it is usually a good idea).

☒ **B, C, D,** and **E** are incorrect. CKPT, DBW*n*, LGWR, and MMON are all necessary processes.

8. ☑ **C.** On COMMIT, the log writer flushes the log buffer to disk. No other background processes need do anything.

☒ **A, B,** and **D** are incorrect. **A** is incorrect because full checkpoints occur only on request or on orderly shutdown; partial checkpoints are automatic as needed. **B** is incorrect because the algorithm DBW*n* uses to select buffers to write to the datafiles is not related to COMMIT processing but to how busy the buffer is. **D** is incorrect because ARC*n* copies only filled online redo logs; it doesn't copy change vectors in real time.

9. ☑ **A, C, E.** Both **A** and **C** are correct because the DBA can choose to configure multiple archive and database writer processes. **E** is correct because one server process will be launched for every concurrent session.

☒ **B** and **D** are incorrect. An instance can have only one log writer process and only one checkpoint process.

10. ☑ **C.** If a tablespace has several datafiles, segments can have extents in all of them.

☒ **A, B,** and **D** are incorrect. **A** is incorrect because one extent consists of consecutive blocks in any one datafile. **B** is incorrect because one segment can exist in only one tablespace (although one tablespace can contain many segments). **D** is incorrect because although this can certainly be done, one block can exist in only one datafile.

11. ☑ **C.** Two groups of one member is the minimum required for the database to function.

☒ **A, B,** and **D** are incorrect. **A** and **B** are incorrect because at least two groups are always required. **D** is incorrect because although it is certainly advisable to multiplex the members, it is not a technical requirement.

12. ☑ **A.** The checkpoint process writes the redo byte address (RBA) to the controlfile.

☒ **B, C,** and **D** are incorrect. The online logs, the datafiles, and the SGA have no knowledge of where the current RBA is.

CHAPTER 13

Instance Management

Exam Objectives

- 062.3.1 Use Database Management Tools
- 062.3.2 Understand Initialization Parameter Files
- 062.3.3 Start Up and Shut Down an Oracle Database Instance
- 062.3.4 View the Alert Log and Access Dynamic Performance Views

After creating a database and an instance, the instance will start, and the database will be open. Assuming that the database was configured with Enterprise Manager Database Express, this will be available as a management tool. What may not be running is the database listener (which is fully described in Chapter 14). Before a user can connect to Database Express, the listener must be running too.

Database Express requires no configuration. It only has to be created, and that is done at database creation time (or it can be installed later). However, the database instance in most cases will require substantial configuration after creation. This is done by adjusting initialization parameters.

Whichever tool is used to connect to the database, it is necessary at this point to understand the two techniques for connecting to an Oracle instance. A *normal* user is authenticated by presenting a password whose hash is stored within the data dictionary. A *privileged* user is authenticated either by presenting a password whose hash is stored in the external password file or by presenting an operating system identity that Oracle accepts.

Use Database Management Tools

The tools used in this section are the SQL*Plus command-line utility and the Database Express graphical utility. Some sites will have access to Cloud Control as well, which in some ways is a superior management tool but is beyond the scope of the Oracle Certified Professional (OCP) exams.

Working with SQL*Plus

SQL*Plus is just an elementary process for issuing ad hoc SQL commands to a database. On Windows systems, either launch it from a command prompt or use the shortcut to the sqlplus .exe executable file in your Start menu that the standard installation of Oracle will have created. On Unix, it is called sqlplus. On either operating system you will find the executable program in your ORACLE_HOME/bin directory.

A variation you need to be aware of is the NOLOG switch. By default, the SQL*Plus program immediately prompts you for an Oracle username, password, and database connect string. To launch SQL*Plus without a login prompt, use the /NOLOG switch.

```
sqlplus /nolog
```

This will give you a SQL prompt from which you can connect with a variety of syntaxes, to be detailed in the next section.

If SQL*Plus does not launch or throws errors when it does launch, the most likely reason is that your operating system session environment is not set up correctly; the ORACLE_HOME variable or the PATH variable is wrong or missing. Figure 13-1 shows examples of this problem, and how to correct it, for Linux. The same technique is applicable on Windows.

 TIP Many database administrators (DBAs) always work from SQL*Plus when trying to resolve problems. It is a simple tool that does not conceal error messages and is always available.

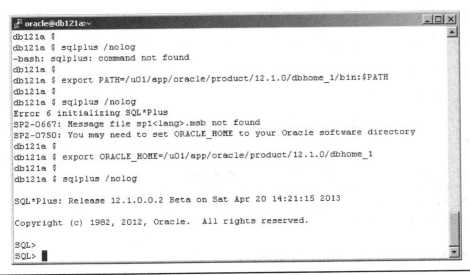

```
  oracle@db121a:~                                              _ □ x
db121a $
db121a $ sqlplus /nolog
-bash: sqlplus: command not found
db121a $
db121a $ export PATH=/u01/app/oracle/product/12.1.0/dbhome_1/bin:$PATH
db121a $
db121a $ sqlplus /nolog
Error 6 initializing SQL*Plus
SP2-0667: Message file sp1<lang>.msb not found
SP2-0750: You may need to set ORACLE_HOME to your Oracle software directory
db121a $
db121a $ export ORACLE_HOME=/u01/app/oracle/product/12.1.0/dbhome_1
db121a $
db121a $ sqlplus /nolog

SQL*Plus: Release 12.1.0.0.2 Beta on Sat Apr 20 14:21:15 2013

Copyright (c) 1982, 2012, Oracle.  All rights reserved.

SQL>
SQL>
```

Figure 13-1   Launching SQL*Plus from an operating system command prompt

Log On as a Normal or Privileged User

Chapter 16 goes through security in detail, but an understanding of how to connect with
SYSDBA privileges is necessary at this point.

A normal user logon requires presenting a username and a password. The username is stored
in the data dictionary, along with a hashed version of the password. This technique for logon
requires the database to be open. If the database were not open, it would not be possible to query
the data dictionary. This raises the question of how one can log on to a database that is not
open—or, indeed, to an instance that has not been started. The answer is that Oracle offers two
techniques for authenticating oneself that do not require the database to be open: password file
authentication and operating system authentication. Both of these give you the option to connect
with the SYSDBA or SYSOPER privilege. Only SYSDBA is discussed here (see Chapter 16
for SYSOPER).

Password file authentication compares a username and the hash of a presented password
with values stored in the external password file. This is the file that was created with the orapwd
utility before the database was created (see Chapter 2 for details). If the values match, the user is
logged on as user SYS.

Operating system authentication delegates the authentication to the operating system. At
install time, an OS group was nominated as the SYSDBA group (see Chapter 12). If your Unix
or Windows user is a member of that group, Oracle will permit you to connect as user SYS with
the SYSDBA privilege without presenting a password at all.

The choice of authentication method is made by the syntax used when connecting. Here's
how to connect as a normal user from a SQL prompt:

```
connect username/password [ @connect_string ]
```

This is how to connect as a privileged user using password file authentication:

```
connect username/password [ @connect_string ] as sysdba
```

And this is how to connect as a privileged user using operating system authentication:

```
connect / as sysdba
```

Figure 13-2 shows all three connection syntaxes. The first example connects as a normal user, over the network. The database must be open (and the database listener must be running) for this to succeed. The second example connects as the privileged user SYS over the network. The database listener must be running, but this would succeed even if the database were shut down. The third example uses operating system authentication to obtain a privileged connection. The SQL*Plus session must be running on the same machine as the database. Neither the database nor the listener need be running for the connection to succeed.

Working with Database Express

Database Express is a Java servlet application. Users communicate with it from a browser over a Hypertext Transfer Protocol (HTTP) connection established by the database listener. The application generates pages of Hypertext Markup Language (HTML) that are sent to browsers; users can use these pages to retrieve information or to send updates back. Because it consists of code stored within the database, Database Express cannot be used to start up or shut down a database.

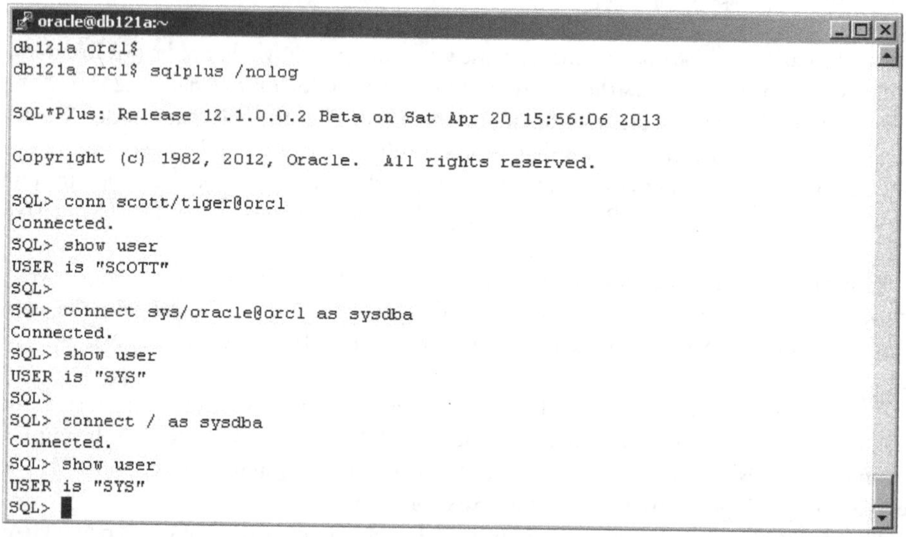

```
oracle@db121a:~                                                    _ □ ×
db121a orcl$
db121a orcl$ sqlplus /nolog

SQL*Plus: Release 12.1.0.0.2 Beta on Sat Apr 20 15:56:06 2013

Copyright (c) 1982, 2012, Oracle.  All rights reserved.

SQL> conn scott/tiger@orcl
Connected.
SQL> show user
USER is "SCOTT"
SQL>
SQL> connect sys/oracle@orcl as sysdba
Connected.
SQL> show user
USER is "SYS"
SQL>
SQL> connect / as sysdba
Connected.
SQL> show user
USER is "SYS"
SQL>
```

Figure 13-2   Syntax for login with SQL*Plus

The uniform resource locator (URL) to access Database Express will have been displayed by the Database Configuration Assistant (DBCA) at the conclusion of the database creation. By default, it will be the following:

```
http://<database-host-name>:5500/em
```

To determine the HTTP listening port if it is not the default of 5500, log on to the database with SQL*Plus and run this query:

```
SQL>
SQL>  select dbms_xdb.gethttpport from dual;
GETHTTPPORT
-----------
      5500
SQL>
```

In this example, the listening port is 5500, and the protocol is HTTP. Use the lsnrctl utility to show the status of the listener, as in Figure 13-3.

In the figure, the lsnrctl utility is run with the status switch. In the STATUS section of the output, you can see that the listener has been running for an hour and a half and that it is listening on two endpoints: port 1521 and port 5500, both on the address db121a.example .com. Port 1521 is the default port for database connections over Oracle Net. Note that port

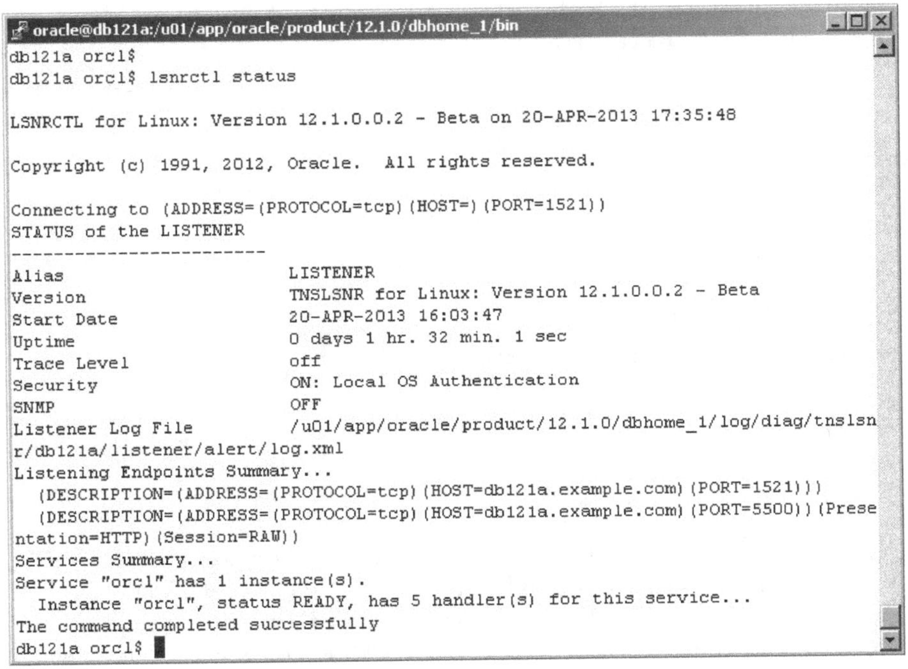

```
oracle@db121a:/u01/app/oracle/product/12.1.0/dbhome_1/bin                    _ □ ×
db121a orcl$
db121a orcl$ lsnrctl status

LSNRCTL for Linux: Version 12.1.0.0.2 - Beta on 20-APR-2013 17:35:48

Copyright (c) 1991, 2012, Oracle.  All rights reserved.

Connecting to (ADDRESS=(PROTOCOL=tcp)(HOST=)(PORT=1521))
STATUS of the LISTENER
------------------------
Alias                     LISTENER
Version                   TNSLSNR for Linux: Version 12.1.0.0.2 - Beta
Start Date                20-APR-2013 16:03:47
Uptime                    0 days 1 hr. 32 min. 1 sec
Trace Level               off
Security                  ON: Local OS Authentication
SNMP                      OFF
Listener Log File         /u01/app/oracle/product/12.1.0/dbhome_1/log/diag/tnslsn
r/db121a/listener/alert/log.xml
Listening Endpoints Summary...
  (DESCRIPTION=(ADDRESS=(PROTOCOL=tcp)(HOST=db121a.example.com)(PORT=1521)))
  (DESCRIPTION=(ADDRESS=(PROTOCOL=tcp)(HOST=db121a.example.com)(PORT=5500))(Prese
ntation=HTTP)(Session=RAW))
Services Summary...
Service "orcl" has 1 instance(s).
  Instance "orcl", status READY, has 5 handler(s) for this service...
The command completed successfully
db121a orcl$ █
```

Figure 13-3   The status of the database listener

5500 is listening for HTTP; therefore, this is the port for Database Express, and it is now possible to deduce what the URL for Database Express is.

```
http://db121a.example.com:5500/em
```

If the lsnrctl status command returns any sort of error, it is probable that the listener has not been started. In this case, start it with this:

```
lsnrctl start
```

The Database Express login window prompts for a username and password, with the option to specify that the connection should be made AS SYSDBA. If you want to connect as a privileged user, give the username SYS and the password and then check the box for AS SYSDBA. Otherwise, give any username and password that are valid for the database.

TIP Database Express requires the Adobe Flash Player plug-in. Without this, it is not possible to log on.

Database Express can be installed in a database at database creation time. The DBCA tool prompts for this. It can also be installed subsequently, either by running scripts or (much easier) by using DBCA and selecting the option Configure Database Options. The prerequisites for using Database Express are as follows: First, an HTTP or HTTPS listening port must have been created. To confirm whether this has been done (and to correct the situation if it has not), use the DBMS_XDB_CONFIG package.

```
orclz>
orclz> select dbms_xdb_config.gethttpport from dual;

GETHTTPPORT
-----------
          0

orclz> exec dbms_xdb_config.sethttpport(5500)

PL/SQL procedure successfully completed.

orclz> select dbms_xdb_config.gethttpport from dual;

GETHTTPPORT
-----------
       5500

orclz>
```

Also, if you prefer to use HTTPS for Database Express, use the procedure DBMS_XDB_CONFIG.SETHTTPSPORT rather than DBM_XDB_CONFIG.SETHTTPPORT.

Finally, all access to Database Express is through the shared server mechanism, described in Chapter 14. This requires the existence of a DISPATCHER process; one will be running by default.

EXAM TIP   What are the prerequisites for using Database Express? The listener must be running, a dispatcher must be running, and the XML DB (XDB) procedure must have been used to enable a listening port.

Exercise 13-1: Use Database Management Tools   In this exercise, you become familiar with the techniques for connecting as a privileged user, with both SQL*Plus and Database Express. Explore the Database Express user interface by following these steps:

1. From an operating system prompt, confirm that your account is in the DBA group. On Linux, use the id command.

```
db121a $ id
uid=54321(oracle) gid=54321(oinstall) groups=54321(oinstall),54322(dba)
db121a $
```

This output shows that the user is logged on as user oracle and is a member of the groups oinstall and dba. These are the default names for the groups that own the Oracle software and have SYSDBA privilege within the database.

On Windows, use the whoami command.

```
c:\>
c:\>whoami /user /groups /fo list
USER INFORMATION
----------------
User Name: jwdell\john
SID:       S-1-5-21-3642582072-1318583595-1076227079-1000
GROUP INFORMATION
-----------------
Group Name: Everyone
Type:       Well-known group
SID:        S-1-1-0
Attributes: Mandatory group, Enabled by default, Enabled
Group Name: jwdell\ora_dba
Type:       Alias
SID:        S-1-5-21-3642582072-1318583595-1076227079-
Attributes: Mandatory group, Enabled by default, Enabled
```

This output shows that the user is a member of the group ora_dba, which is the name of the DBA group on Windows.

2. Set the necessary environment variables. This is a Linux example:

```
export ORACLE_BASE=/u01/app/oracle
export ORACLE_HOME=$ORACLE_BASE/product/12.1.0/dbhome_1
export PATH=$ORACLE_HOME/bin:$PATH
export ORACLE_SID=orcl
```

And this is a Windows example:

```
set ORACLE_BASE=c:\app\oracle
set ORACLE_HOME=%ORACLE_BASE%\product\12.1.0\dbhome_1
set PATH=%ORACLE_HOME%\bin;%PATH%
set ORACLE_SID=orcl
```

Substitute whatever values are appropriate for your installation.

3. Launch SQL*Plus and then connect as a privileged user using operating system authentication.

```
sqlplus /nolog
connect / as sysdba
show user
exit
```

This must show that you are connected as user SYS.

4. Launch a browser and then issue this URL:

```
http://<server_address>:5500/em
```

This will present you with a logon screen. Enter the username **sys** and password **oracle** (or whatever password you specified when creating the database) and select the "as sysdba" check box.

5. Explore the Database Express user interface. Select any tabs or links that look interesting. You will need to become familiar with all of them.

Understand Initialization Parameter Files

An instance is defined by the parameters used to build it in memory. It can be changed after startup by adjusting these parameters—if the parameters are ones that can be changed. Some are fixed at startup time and can be changed only by shutting down the instance and starting it again.

Static and Dynamic Parameter Files

Parameter files come in two flavors: the static parameter file (also known as a pfile or an init file) and the dynamic server parameter file (also known as the spfile). Either way, the initialization parameter file stores values for parameters used to build the instance in memory and to start the background processes. There are three default filenames. On Unix they are as follows:

$ORACLE_HOME/dbs/spfile<SID>.ora
$ORACLE_HOME/dbs/spfile.ora
$ORACLE_HOME/dbs/init<SID>.ora

On Windows they are as follows:

%ORACLE_HOME%\database\SPFILE<SID>.ORA
%ORACLE_HOME%\database\SPFILE.ORA
%ORACLE_HOME%\database\INIT<SID>.ORA

In all cases, <SID> refers to the name of the instance that the parameter file will start. The preceding order is important! Unless a pfile is specified in the startup command, Oracle will work its way down the list, using the first file it finds and ignoring the rest. If none of them exists (and a nondefault pfile is not specified), the instance will not start.

The spfile is a server-side file, and it cannot be renamed or relocated. The only exception to this is when using Grid Infrastructure (GI), in which case a nondefault and location name can be registered in the GI registry. It is read by the System Monitor (SMON) background process when the instance is started. The spfile is a binary file, and it cannot be edited by hand. Any attempt to edit will usually corrupt it and make it unusable. The pfile is a client-side file. It exists by default in the ORACLE_HOME directory, but it is in fact read by the user process that issues the command to start the instance. You can rename or move the pfile as you want, but if you do this, it will not be found by default, and you must specify its name and location on your STARTUP command. The pfile is an ASCII text file; edit it with any text editor you like (perhaps with Windows notepad.exe or the Unix vi editor). The spfile is a binary file and cannot be edited manually. To change any values in it, use the ALTER SYSTEM SET... commands from SQL*Plus or the parameter-editing facilities of Database Express.

To create a pfile, just type in the parameter=value pairs, one per line, and save the file with a name that conforms to the standard. To create an spfile, use this SQL*Plus command:

```
CREATE SPFILE [ = filename ] FROM PFILE [ = filename];
```

This command will read the nominated text pfile and then use its contents to generate the binary spfile. By default, the files read and written will be those with the standard names in the standard directories. To convert an spfile into a text file that can be edited, use the reverse command.

```
CREATE PFILE [ = filename ] FROM SPFILE [ = filename];
```

The CREATE PFILE and CREATE SPFILE commands can be run from SQL*Plus at any time, even before the instance has been started.

 TIP   The file spfile<SID>.ora is undoubtedly the most convenient file to use as your parameter file. Normally, you will use spfile.ora only in a Real Application Clusters (RAC) environment, where one file can be used to start several instances. You will use an init<SID>.ora file only if for some reason you need to make manual edits; spfiles are binary files and cannot be edited by hand.

Static and Dynamic Parameters and the Initialization Parameter File

To view the parameters and their current values, a query such as this will do:

```
select name,value from v$parameter order by name;
```

This query may give slightly different results.

```
select name,value from v$spparameter order by name;
```

The difference is the view from which the parameter names and values are taken. V$PARAMETER shows the parameter values currently in effect in the running instance. V$SPPARAMETER shows the values in spfile on disk. Usually, these will be the same but not always. Some parameters can be changed while the instance is running; others, known as static parameters, are fixed at instance startup time. A change made to the changeable parameters will have an immediate effect and can optionally be written to the spfile. If this is done, the change will be permanent. The next time the instance is stopped and started, the new value will be read from the spfile. If the change is not saved to the spfile, the change will persist only until the instance is stopped. To change a static parameter, the change must be written to the spfile, and then it will come into effect at the next startup. If the output of the two preceding queries differs, this will typically be because the DBA has done some tuning work that he has not yet made permanent, or he has found it necessary to adjust a static parameter and hasn't yet restarted the instance.

If the instance is started with a pfile rather than an spfile, the V$SPPARAMETER view will show a NULL as the value for every parameter. Any attempt to change a parameter in the spfile will return an error. Here's an example:

```
orclz>
orclz> alter system set sga_max_size=8g scope=spfile;
alter system set sga_max_size=8g scope=spfile
*
ERROR at line 1:
ORA-32001: write to SPFILE requested but no SPFILE in use
orclz>
```

You can also see the view through Database Express. From the home page, select the Configuration tab and click the Initialization Parameters link. In the subsequent window, shown in Figure 13-4, are two subtabs. Current shows the values currently in effect in the running instance, and SPFile shows those recorded in the spfile.

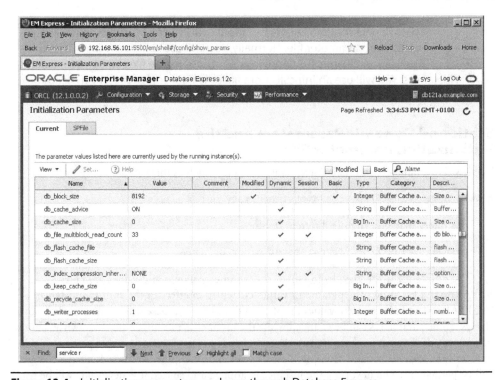

Figure 13-4 Initialization parameters, as shown through Database Express

You can adjust the changeable parameters through the same window. The values for the first parameter shown (DB_BLOCK_SIZE) cannot be changed; it is not a dynamic parameter. But the next three parameters can be changed. To change the static parameters, it is necessary to select the SPFile subtab and make the changes there.

The Basic Parameters

The instance parameters considered to be "basic" are those that should be considered for every database. To view the basic parameters and their current values, a query such as this will do:

```
select name,value from v$parameter
where isbasic='TRUE' order by name;
```

The following query may give slightly different results:

```
select s.name,s.value
from v$spparameter s join v$parameter p on s.name=p.name
where p.isbasic='TRUE' order by name;
```

The difference will be because some parameter changes may have been applied to the instance but not the spfile (or vice versa). The join is necessary because there is no column on V$SPPARAMETER to show whether a parameter is basic or advanced. Table 13-1 summarizes the basic parameters.

Parameter	Purpose
cluster_database	Is the database a RAC or a single instance? That this is basic indicates that RAC is considered a standard option.
compatible	The release that the instance will emulate. Normally this would be the actual release, unless you are nervous about new features.
control_files	The name and location of the controlfile copies.
db_block_size	The default block size for formatting datafiles.
db_create_file_dest	The default location for datafiles.
db_create_online_log_dest_1	The default location for online redo log files.
db_create_online_log_dest_2	The default location for multiplexed copies of online redo log files.
db_domain	The domain name that can be suffixed to the db_name to generate a globally unique name.
db_name	The name of the database (the only parameter with no default).
db_recovery_file_dest	The location of the flash recovery area.
db_recovery_file_dest_size	The amount of data that may be written to the flash recovery area.

Table 13-1   Basic Parameters (*continued*)

Parameter	Purpose
db_unique_name	A unique identifier necessary in a Data Guard environment.
instance_number	Used to distinguish multiple RAC instances opening the same database.
ldap_directory_sysauth	Enables LDAP authentication for SYSDBA connections.
log_archive_dest_1	The destination for archiving redo log files.
log_archive_dest_2	The destination for multiplexed copies of archived redo log files.
log_archive_dest_state_1	An indicator for whether the destination is enabled or not.
log_archive_dest_state_2	An indicator for whether the destination is enabled or not.
nls_language	The language of the instance (provides many default formats).
nls_territory	The geographical location of the instance (which provides even more default formats).
open_cursors	The number of SQL work areas that a session can open at once.
pga_aggregate_target	The total amount of memory the instance can allocate to PGAs.
processes	The maximum number of processes (including session server processes) allowed to connect to the instance.
remote_listener	The addresses of listeners on other machines with which the instance should register (relevant only for RAC).
remote_login_passwordfile	Whether or not to use an external password file, to permit password file authentication.
sessions	The maximum number of sessions allowed to connect.
sga_target	The size of the System Global Area (SGA), within which Oracle will manage the various SGA memory structures.
shared_servers	The number of shared server processes to launch, for sessions that are not established with dedicated server processes.
star_transformation_enabled	Whether to permit the optimizer to rewrite queries that join the dimensions of a fact table.
undo_tablespace	The tablespace where the undo data will reside.

Table 13-1   Basic Parameters

All these basic parameters, as well as some of the advanced parameters, are discussed in the appropriate chapters.

Changing Parameters

To change parameters with SQL*Plus, use the ALTER SYSTEM command. Figure 13-5 shows examples.

The first query in Figure 13-5 shows that the value for the parameter DB_FILE_MULTIBLOCK_READ_COUNT is on by default. It does not exist in the spfile on disk.

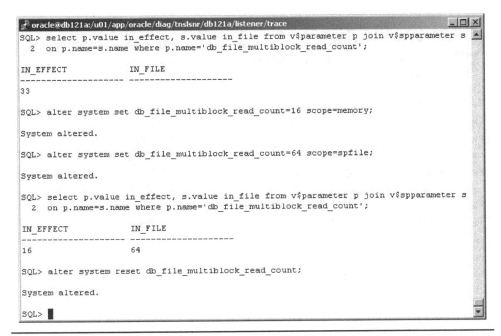

Figure 13-5   Changing and querying parameters with SQL*Plus

The next two commands adjust the parameter in both memory and the spfile to different values, using the SCOPE keyword to determine where the change is made. The results are seen in the second query. The final command uses RESET to remove the stored value from the spfile; it will remain in effect within the instance at its current value until the instance is restarted, at which time it will return to the default. Here is the syntax:

```
ALTER SYSTEM SET <name> = <value> SCOPE = MEMORY | SPFILE | BOTH
```

Note that the default for the scope clause is BOTH, meaning that if you do not specify a SCOPE, the update will be applied to the running instance and written to the spfile. Therefore, it will become a permanent change.

 EXAM TIP   An attempt to change a static parameter will fail unless SCOPE is specified as SPFILE. The default SCOPE is BOTH (the running instance and the spfile). If the instance is started with a pfile, then SCOPE=SPFILE will fail.

An example of a static parameter is LOG_BUFFER. If you want to resize the log buffer to 10MB and issue the following command, it will fail with the message "ORA-02095: specified initialization parameter cannot be modified":

```
alter system set log_buffer=10m;
```

It must be changed with the SCOPE=SPFILE clause, and the instance must be restarted to take effect.

TIP The default log buffer size is probably correct. If you raise it, you may find that COMMIT processing takes longer. If you make it smaller than the default, it may in fact be internally adjusted up to whatever Oracle thinks is necessary.

An example of a parameter that applies to the whole instance but can be adjusted for individual sessions is OPTIMIZER_MODE. This influences the way in which Oracle will execute statements. A common choice is between the values ALL_ROWS and FIRST_ROWS. The value ALL_ROWS instructs the optimizer to generate execution plans that will run statements to completion as quickly as possible, whereas FIRST_ROWS instructs it to generate plans that will get something back to the user as soon as possible, even if the whole statement takes longer to complete. Therefore, if your database is generally used for long DSS-type queries but some users use it for interactive work, you might issue the command

```
alter system set optimizer_mode=all_rows;
```

and let the individual users issue

```
alter session set optimizer_mode=first_rows;
```

if they want.

TIP Logon triggers can be used to adjust session parameters to values suitable for different users, depending on the username with which they log on.

Exercise 13-2: Query and Set Initialization Parameters In this exercise, use either SQL*Plus or Database Express to manage initialization parameters. The examples use SQL*Plus, but only because it is clearer to give exact commands than to provide navigation paths through a graphical user interface (GUI). Here are the steps to follow:

1. Connect to the database (which must be open!) as user SYS, with the SYSDBA privilege. Use either operating system authentication or password file authentication.

2. Display all the basic parameters, checking whether they have all been set or are still at their default, and note the values for PROCESSES and SESSIONS.

   ```
   select name,value,isdefault from v$parameter
   where isbasic='TRUE' order by name;
   ```

   Any basic parameters that are at their default should be investigated to see whether the default is appropriate. In fact, all the basic parameters should be considered. Read up on all of them in the Oracle documentation now. The volume you need is titled "Oracle Database Reference." Chapter 1 in Part 1 has a paragraph describing every initialization parameter.

3. Change the PROCESSES parameter to 200. This is a static parameter. It is therefore necessary to specify a SCOPE value and then to bounce the database.

   Figure 13-6 shows the sequence of commands. The STARTUP FORCE command is explained in the next section.

4. Rerun the query from step 2. Note the new value for PROCESSES and also for SESSIONS. PROCESSES limits the number of operating system processes allowed to connect to the instance, and SESSIONS limits the number of sessions. These figures are related because each session will require a process. The default value for SESSIONS is derived from PROCESSES, so if SESSIONS was on default, it will now have a new value.

5. Change the value for the NLS_LANGUAGE parameter for your session. Choose whatever mainstream language you want (Oracle supports 67 languages at the time of writing), but the language must be specified in English (for example, you would use German, not Deutsch):

   ```
   alter session set nls_language=French;
   ```

6. Confirm that the change has worked by querying the system date.

   ```
   select to_char(sysdate,'day month') from dual;
   ```

   You may want to change your session language back to what it was before (such as English) with another ALTER SESSION command. If you don't, be prepared for error messages to be in the language your session is now using.

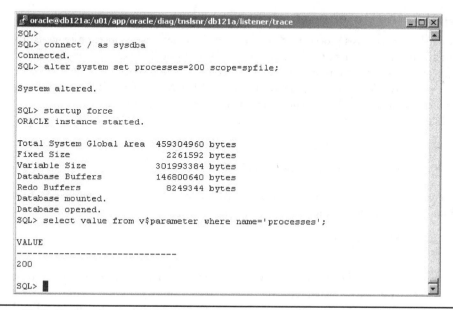

```
oracle@db121a:/u01/app/oracle/diag/tnslsnr/db121a/listener/trace
SQL>
SQL> connect / as sysdba
Connected.
SQL> alter system set processes=200 scope=spfile;

System altered.

SQL> startup force
ORACLE instance started.

Total System Global Area   459304960 bytes
Fixed Size                   2261592 bytes
Variable Size              301993384 bytes
Database Buffers           146800640 bytes
Redo Buffers                 8249344 bytes
Database mounted.
Database opened.
SQL> select value from v$parameter where name='processes';

VALUE
---------------------------
200

SQL>
```

Figure 13-6   How to change a static parameter

7. Change the OPTIMIZER_MODE parameter, but restrict the scope to the running instance only; do not update the parameter file. This exercise enables the deprecated rule-based optimizer, which might be needed while testing some old code, but you would not want the change to be permanent.

```
alter system set optimizer_mode=rule scope=memory;
```

8. Confirm that the change has been effected but not written to the parameter file.

```
select value from v$parameter where name='optimizer_mode'
union
select value from v$spparameter where name='optimizer_mode';
```

9. Return the OPTIMIZER_MODE to its standard value in both the running instance and the parameter file.

```
alter system set optimizer_mode=all_rows scope=both;
```

Note that the scope clause is not actually needed because BOTH is the default.

Start Up and Shut Down an Oracle Database Instance

Oracle Corporation's recommended sequence for starting a database is to start the database listener and then the database. Starting the database is itself a staged process.

Starting the Database Listener

The database listener is a process that monitors a port for database connection requests. These requests (and all subsequent traffic once a session is established) use Oracle Net, Oracle's proprietary communications protocol. Oracle Net is a layered protocol running over whatever underlying network protocol is in use (probably TCP/IP). Managing the listener is fully described in Chapter 14, but it is necessary to know how to start it now.

There are two ways to start the database listener:

- With the lsnrctl utility
- As a Windows service (Windows only, of course)

The lsnrctl utility is in the ORACLE_HOME/bin directory. The key commands are as follows, where <listener> is the name of the listener:

```
lsnrctl start [ <listener> ]
lsnrctl status [ <listener> ]
```

This will have defaulted to LISTENER, which is correct in most cases. You will know if you have created a listener with another name. Figure 13-3, from earlier in the chapter, shows the output of the lsnrctl status command when the listener (which is indeed named LISTENER) is running.

Note that the first DESCRIPTION line of the output in the figure shows the host address and port on which the listener is listening, and the third line from the bottom states that the listener will accept connections for the service orcl, which is offered by an instance called orcl. These are the critical bits of information needed to connect to the database. Following a successful database creation with DBCA, it can be assumed that they are correct. If the listener is not running, the output of lsnrctl status will make this clear.

Under Windows, the listener runs as a Windows service. It is therefore possible to control it through the services interface. To identify the name of the listener service, use the Services management console. Control it either through the Services console or from a command prompt.

```
c:\>
c:\>net stop OracleOraDb12c_home1TNSListener
The OracleOraDb12c_home1TNSListener service is stopping.
The OracleOraDb12c_home1TNSListener service was stopped successfully.

c:\>net start OracleOraDb12c_home1TNSListener
The OracleOraDb12c_home1TNSListener service is starting.
The OracleOraDb12c_home1TNSListener service was started successfully.

c:\>
```

Database Startup and Shutdown

If you are being precise (always a good idea if you want to pass the OCP examinations), you do not start or stop a database. An instance may be started and stopped; a database is *mounted* and *opened* and then dismounted and closed. This can be done with SQL*Plus using the STARTUP and SHUTDOWN commands. On a Windows system, it can also be done by controlling the Windows service under which the instance runs.

Connecting with an Appropriate Privilege

Ordinary users cannot start up or shut down a database. You must therefore connect with some form of external authentication. You must be authenticated either by the operating system, as being a member of the group that owns the Oracle software, or by giving a username/password combination that exists in an external password file. You tell Oracle that you want to use external authentication by using the appropriate syntax in the CONNECT command you give in your user process.

If you are using SQL*Plus, the syntax of the CONNECT command tells Oracle what type of authentication you want to use: the default of data dictionary authentication, password file authentication, or operating system authentication. Here are the possibilities:

- connect user/pass[@connect_alias]
- connect user/pass[@connect_alias] as sysdba
- connect user/pass[@connect_alias] as sysoper
- connect / as sysdba
- connect / as sysoper

In these examples, user is the username, and pass is the password. The connect_alias will be resolved to a connect string, as described in Chapter 14. Either SYSDBA or SYSOPER is needed to perform a STARTUP or SHUTDOWN. Figure 13-7 shows examples of connecting with these privileges.

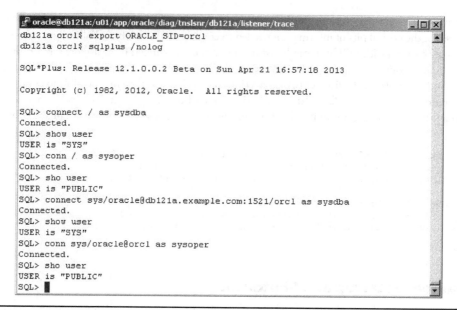

```
oracle@db121a:/u01/app/oracle/diag/tnslsnr/db121a/listener/trace
db121a orcl$ export ORACLE_SID=orcl
db121a orcl$ sqlplus /nolog

SQL*Plus: Release 12.1.0.0.2 Beta on Sun Apr 21 16:57:18 2013

Copyright (c) 1982, 2012, Oracle.  All rights reserved.

SQL> connect / as sysdba
Connected.
SQL> show user
USER is "SYS"
SQL> conn / as sysoper
Connected.
SQL> sho user
USER is "PUBLIC"
SQL> connect sys/oracle@db121a.example.com:1521/orcl as sysdba
Connected.
SQL> show user
USER is "SYS"
SQL> conn sys/oracle@orcl as sysoper
Connected.
SQL> sho user
USER is "PUBLIC"
SQL>
```

Figure 13-7   Use of operating system and password file authentication

 EXAM TIP   SYSDBA and SYSOPER are not users; they are privileges that can be granted to users. By default, only user SYS has these privileges until they are deliberately granted to other users.

Use of the SYSDBA privilege logs you on to the instance as user SYS, the most powerful user in the database and the owner of the data dictionary. Use of the SYSOPER privilege connects you as user PUBLIC. PUBLIC is not a user in any normal sense; they are a notional user with administration privileges, but with no privileges that let them see or manipulate data.

Startup: NOMOUNT, MOUNT, and OPEN

Remember that the instance and the database are separate entities; they can exist independently of each other. The startup process is therefore staged.

1. You build the instance in memory.

2. You enable a connection to the database by mounting the controlfile.

3. You open the database for use.

At any moment, a database will be in one of four states:

- SHUTDOWN
- NOMOUNT
- MOUNT
- OPEN

When the database is in SHUTDOWN mode, all files are closed, and the instance does not exist. In NOMOUNT mode, the instance has been built in memory (the SGA has been created and the background processes started according to whatever is specified in its parameter file), but no connection has been made to a database. It is indeed possible that the database does not yet exist. In MOUNT mode, the instance locates and reads the database controlfile. In OPEN mode, all database files are located and opened, and the database is made available for use by end users. The startup process is staged. Whenever you issue a startup command, it will go through these stages. It is possible to stop the startup partway. For example, if your controlfile is damaged or a multiplexed copy is missing, you will not be able to mount the database, but by stopping in NOMOUNT mode, you may be able to repair the damage.

At any stage, how does the instance find the files it needs, and exactly what happens? Start with NOMOUNT. When you issue a startup command, Oracle will attempt to locate a parameter file, following the naming convention given earlier.

If no parameter file exists, the instance will not start. The only file used in NOMOUNT mode is the parameter file. The parameters in the parameter file are used to build the SGA in memory and to start the background processes.

Where is the alert log? It's in the location calculated from the DIAGNOSTIC_DEST parameter. This will have defaulted to the ORACLE_BASE (remember Optimal Flexible Architecture [OFA] from Chapter 2) directory. Within the DIAGNOSTIC_DEST is a standard directory structure. The alert log will be located and named as follows:

```
<DIAGNOSTIC_DEST>/diag/rdbms/<DBNAME>/<INSTANCE_NAME>/trace/
alert_<instance_name>.log
```

For a database and instance named orcl, the values (Windows and Linux) would typically be the following:

```
c:\app\oracle\diag\rdbms\orcl\orcl\trace\alert_orcl.log
/u01/app/oracle/diag/rdbms/orcl/orcl/trace/alert_orcl.log
```

If the log already exists, it will be appended to. Otherwise, it will be created. If any problems occur during this stage, trace files can also be generated in the same location.

Once the instance is successfully started in NOMOUNT mode, it may be transitioned to MOUNT mode by reading the controlfile. It locates the controlfile by using the CONTROL_FILES parameter, which it knows from having read the parameter file used when starting in NOMOUNT mode. If the controlfile (or any multiplexed copy of it) is damaged or missing, the database will not mount, and you will have to take appropriate action before proceeding. All copies of the controlfile must be available and identical if the mount is to be successful.

As part of the mount, the names and locations of all the datafiles and online redo logs are read from the controlfile, but Oracle does not yet attempt to find them. This will happen during the transition to OPEN mode. If any files are missing or damaged, the database will remain in MOUNT mode and cannot be opened until you take appropriate action. Furthermore, even if all the files are present, they must be synchronized before the database opens. If the last shutdown was orderly, with all database buffers in the database buffer cache being flushed to disk by DBW*n,* then everything will be synchronized. Oracle will know that all committed transactions are safely stored in the datafiles and that no uncommitted transactions are hanging around waiting to be rolled back. However, if the last shutdown was disorderly (such as from a loss of power or from the server being rebooted), Oracle must repair the damage, and the database is considered to be in an inconsistent state. The mechanism for this process (known as *instance recovery*) is described in Chapter 22. The process that mounts and opens the database (and carries out repairs, if the previous shutdown was disorderly) is the SMON process. Only once the database has been successfully opened will Oracle permit user sessions to be established with normal data dictionary authentication.

Shutdown should be the reverse of startup. During an orderly shutdown, the database is first closed and then dismounted, and finally the instance is stopped. During the close phase, all sessions are terminated; active transactions are rolled back, completed transactions are flushed to disk by DBW*n*, and the datafiles and redo log files are closed. During the dismount, the controlfile is closed. Then the instance is stopped by deallocating the SGA and terminating the background processes.

 TIP The startup command STARTUP FORCE can save you time. It is two commands in one: a SHUTDOWN ABORT followed by a STARTUP NORMAL.

Shutdown: NORMAL, IMMEDIATE, TRANSACTIONAL, and ABORT

Here are the options that can be used on the SHUTDOWN command, all of which require either a SYSDBA or a SYSOPER connection:

```
shutdown [ normal | transactional | immediate | abort ]
```

- **Normal** This is the default. No new user connections will be permitted, but all current connections are allowed to continue. Only once all users have (voluntarily!) logged off will the database actually shut down.

- **Transactional** No new user connections are permitted. Existing sessions that are not in a transaction will be terminated; sessions currently in a transaction are allowed to complete the transaction and will then be terminated. Once all sessions are terminated, the database will shut down.

- **Immediate** No new sessions are permitted, and all currently connected sessions are terminated. Any active transactions are rolled back, and the database will then shut down.

- **Abort** As far as Oracle is concerned, this is the equivalent of a power cut. The instance terminates immediately. Nothing is written to disk, and there is no attempt to terminate transactions in progress in any orderly fashion.

 TIP Typically, a normal shutdown is useless because there is always someone logged on, even if it is only a Cloud Control agent, so the command just hangs forever.

The normal, immediate, and transactional shutdown modes are usually referred to as *clean* or *consistent* shutdowns. After all sessions are terminated, PMON will roll back any incomplete transactions. A checkpoint is then issued that forces the DBW*n* process to write all updated data from the database buffer cache down to the datafiles. LGWR also flushes any change vectors still in memory to the log files. Then the file headers are updated and the file handles closed. This means that the database is in a "consistent" state: All committed transactions are in the datafiles, there are no uncommitted transactions hanging about that need to be rolled back, and all datafiles and log files are synchronized.

TIP   If someone were in the middle of a long-running update statement or, for example, were loading tables for a data warehouse when you had to shut down the database, the rollback phase, and therefore the time it takes the database to close and shut down cleanly, could be a *long, long* time.

The abort mode leaves the database in an *inconsistent* state; it is quite possible that committed transactions have been lost because they existed only in memory and DBW*n* had not yet written them to the datafiles. Equally, there may be uncommitted transactions in the datafiles that have not yet been rolled back. This is a definition of a corrupted database. It may be missing committed transactions or storing uncommitted transactions. These corruptions must be repaired by instance recovery (described in Chapter 22). It is exactly as though the database server had been switched off, or perhaps rebooted, while the database was running.

TIP   A shutdown abort will not damage the database, but some operations (such as backups) are not possible after an abort.

An orderly shutdown is a staged process, and it is theoretically possible to control the stages. The SQL*Plus commands are as follows:

```
alter database close;
alter database dismount;
```

These commands will exactly reverse the startup sequence. In practice, however, there is no value to them; a SHUTDOWN is all any DBA will ever use.

Exercise 13-3: Start Up and Shut Down an Oracle Database Instance   Use

SQL*Plus to start an instance and open a database. If the database is already open, do this in the opposite order. Note that if you are working in Windows, the Windows service for the database must be running. It will have a name of the form OracleService*SID*, where *SID* is the name of the instance.

1. Log on to the computer as a member of the operating system group that owns the ORACLE_HOME and then set the environment variables appropriately for ORACLE_HOME and PATH and ORACLE_SID, as described previously.

2. Connect as SYS with operating system authentication.
   ```
   sqlplus / as sysdba
   ```

3. Start the instance only.
   ```
   startup nomount
   ```

4. Mount the database.

```
alter database mount;
```

5. Open the database.

```
alter database open;
```

6. Confirm that the database is open.

```
select open_mode from v$database;
```

This will return READ WRITE if the database is open.

7. Shut down the database.

```
shutdown immediate
```

Figure 13-8 shows the entire sequence of steps 2 through 7.

8. Restart the database.

```
startup
```

Observe that the default startup mode is OPEN.

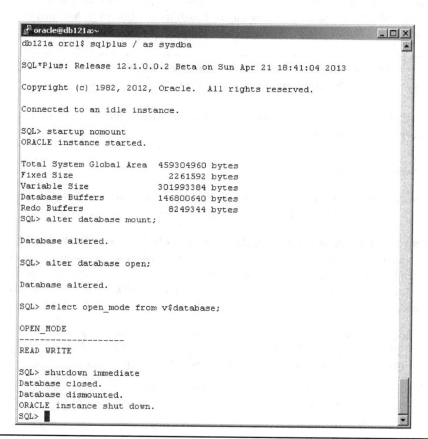

```
oracle@db121a:~                                                     _ □ ×
db121a orcl$ sqlplus / as sysdba

SQL*Plus: Release 12.1.0.0.2 Beta on Sun Apr 21 18:41:04 2013

Copyright (c) 1982, 2012, Oracle.  All rights reserved.

Connected to an idle instance.

SQL> startup nomount
ORACLE instance started.

Total System Global Area  459304960 bytes
Fixed Size                  2261592 bytes
Variable Size             301993384 bytes
Database Buffers          146800640 bytes
Redo Buffers                8249344 bytes
SQL> alter database mount;

Database altered.

SQL> alter database open;

Database altered.

SQL> select open_mode from v$database;

OPEN_MODE
--------------------
READ WRITE

SQL> shutdown immediate
Database closed.
Database dismounted.
ORACLE instance shut down.
SQL>
```

Figure 13-8   Database startup and shutdown

View the Alert Log and Access Dynamic Performance Views

The alert log is a vital source of information regarding important events in the life of the database instance. It is a continuous historical record of events. The dynamic performance views give real-time information, in other words, what is happening right now or in the recent past. In addition to the alert log, there is an optionally enabled Data Definition Language (DDL) log and a debug log generated automatically in the event of certain errors.

The Alert Log

The alert log is a continuous record of critical operations applied to the instance and the database. Its location is derived from the instance parameter DIAGNOSTIC_DEST, and its name is alert_<SID>.log, where <SID> is the name of the instance. The DIAGNOSTIC_DEST defaults to the ORACLE_BASE, and the alert log will be beneath that.

```
DIAGNOSTIC_DEST/diag/rdbms/<dbname>/<instancename>/trace
```

 TIP   The two instance parameters BACKGROUND_DUMP_DEST and USER_ DUMP_DEST give the full path to the location of the alert log. These parameters are officially deprecated, but showing them is the quickest way to locate the trace directory.

A copy of the alert log in Extensible Markup Language (XML) format is also maintained in a different directory.

```
DIAGNOSTIC_DEST/diag/rdbms/<dbname>/<instancename>/alert
```

The critical operations recorded in the alert include the following:

- All startup and shutdown commands, including intermediate commands such as ALTER DATABASE MOUNT
- All errors internal to the instance (the ORA-600 errors, about which the DBA can do nothing other than investigate them using My Oracle Support and report them to Oracle Support if they are new issues)
- Any detected datafile block corruptions
- Any row-locking deadlocks that may have occurred
- All operations that affect the physical structure of the database, such as creating or renaming datafiles and online redo logs
- All ALTER SYSTEM commands that adjust the values of initialization parameters
- All log switches and log archives

The alert log entry for a startup shows all the initialization parameters specified in the parameter file. This information, together with the subsequent record of changes to the instance with ALTER

SYSTEM and to the database physical structures with ALTER DATABASE, means that it is always possible to reconstruct the history of changes to the database and the instance. This can be invaluable when you are trying to backtrack in order to find the source of a problem.

TIP For many DBAs, the first thing they do when they are asked to look at a database for the first time is locate the alert log and scan it, just to get an idea of what has been going on.

Trace files are generated by the various background processes, usually when they hit an error. These files will be located in the trace directory, along with the alert log. If a background process has failed because of an error, the trace file generated will be invaluable in diagnosing the problem.

The DDL Log

Should the DBA choose to enable this, it is possible to record DDL commands in a log file. The statement used (without any supporting information, such as who issued it) is recorded in a text file named ddl_<instancename> in the following directory, with the same information in an XML file named log.xml:

```
DIAGNOSTIC_DEST/diag/rdbms/<dbname>/<instancename>/log
```

To enable DDL logging, the instance parameter ENABLE_DDL_LOGGING must be set to TRUE (the default is FALSE).

TIP DDL logging is of minimal value to the DBA because it captures nothing about who did it. It is of value only to Oracle Support, as part of the Incident Packaging Service. If you need to track DDL, do it by enabling audit of DDL statements.

The Dynamic Performance Views

There are more than 600 dynamic performance views. You will often hear them referred to as the *vee dollar* views because their names are prefixed with V$. In fact, the vee dollar views are not views at all—they are synonyms to views that are prefixed with V_$, as shown in Figure 13-9.

The figure shows V$INSTANCE, which has one row with some summary information about the instance. Most views are populated with information from the instance; the remainder are populated from the controlfile. All of them give real-time information. Dynamic performance views that are populated from the instance, such as V$INSTANCE or V$SYSSTAT, are available at all times, even when the instance is in NOMOUNT mode. Dynamic performance views that are populated from the controlfile, such as V$DATABASE and V$DATAFILE, cannot be queried unless the database has been mounted, which is when the controlfile is read. By contrast, the data dictionary views (prefixed DBA_, ALL_, or USER_) can be queried only after the database—including the data dictionary—has been opened.

```
 oracle@db121a:~                                                    _|□|×|
SQL>
SQL> select owner,object_name,object_type from dba_objects
  2  where object_name like 'V%INSTANCE';

OWNER        OBJECT_NAME        OBJECT_TYPE
----------   ----------------   ------------------
SYS          V_$INSTANCE        VIEW
PUBLIC       V$INSTANCE         SYNONYM

SQL> describe v$instance
 Name                                         Null?       Type
-------------------------------------------   --------    ---------------------------
 INSTANCE_NUMBER                                          NUMBER
 INSTANCE_NAME                                            VARCHAR2(16)
 HOST_NAME                                                VARCHAR2(64)
 VERSION                                                  VARCHAR2(17)
 STARTUP_TIME                                             DATE
 STATUS                                                   VARCHAR2(12)
 PARALLEL                                                 VARCHAR2(3)
 THREAD#                                                  NUMBER
 ARCHIVER                                                 VARCHAR2(7)
 LOG_SWITCH_WAIT                                          VARCHAR2(15)
 LOGINS                                                   VARCHAR2(10)
```

Figure 13-9 A V$ view (or rather, a view and its V$ synonym)

EXAM TIP Dynamic performance views (the V$ views) are populated from the instance or the controlfile, whereas the DBA_, ALL_, and USER_ views are populated from the data dictionary. This difference determines what views can be queried at the various startup stages.

The dynamic performance views are created at startup, updated during the lifetime of the instance, and dropped at shutdown. This means that they will contain values that have been accumulated since startup time; if your database has been open for six months nonstop, they will have data built up over that period. After a shutdown/startup, they will start from the beginning again.

TIP There is some overlap between V$ views and data dictionary views. For instance, V$TABLESPACE has a row for every tablespace, as does DBA_TABLESPACES. Note that as a general rule, V$ views are singular and data dictionary views are plural. But there are exceptions.

Exercise 13-4: Use the Alert Log and Dynamic Performance Views   In this exercise, you will locate the alert log and find the entries for the parameter changes made in Exercise 13-2 and the startups and shutdowns in Exercise 13-3.

1. Connect to your database with SQL*Plus and then display the value of some parameters.

```
select value from v$parameter where name='diagnostic_dest';
select value from v$parameter where name='db_name';
select value from v$parameter where name='instance_name';
select value from v$parameter where name='background_dump_dest';
```

Note that the manner in which the name of the trace directory is derived.

2. Using whatever operating system tool you choose (such as the Windows Explorer or whatever file system browser your Linux session is using), navigate to the directory identified in step 1.

   Open the alert log. It will be a file called alert_<SID>.log, where <SID> is the name of the instance. Use any editor you please (but note that on Windows, Notepad may not be a good choice because of the way carriage returns are handled).

   Go to the bottom of the file. You will see the ALTER SYSTEM commands of Exercise 13-2 and the results of the startups and shutdowns.

3. Use dynamic performance views to determine what datafile and tablespaces make up the database.

   ```
   select t.name,d.name,d.bytes from v$tablespace t join
   v$datafile d on t.ts#=d.ts# order by t.name;
   ```

   Obtain the same information from data dictionary views.

   ```
   select t.tablespace_name,d.file_name,d.bytes from
   dba_tablespaces t
   join dba_data_files d on t.tablespace_name=d.tablespace_name
   order by tablespace_name;
   ```

4. Determine the location of all the controlfile copies, in two ways.

   ```
   select * from v$controlfile;
   select value from v$parameter where name='control_files';
   ```

5. Determine the location of the online redo log file members as well as their size. Because the size is an attribute of the group, not the members, you will have to join two views.

   ```
   select m.group#,m.member,g.bytes from v$log g join v$logfile m
   on m.group#=g.group# order by m.group#,m.member;
   ```

Two-Minute Drill

Use Database Management Tools

- SQL*Plus is always available. Database Express can make administration easy, but it depends on underlying database objects; it is therefore not available until the database is open.

Understand Initialization Parameter Files

- A database instance may be started from either a static parameter file (the init file) or a dynamic server parameter file (the spfile). If both exist, the spfile takes precedence.
- Static parameters cannot be changed without a shutdown/startup.
- Other parameters can be changed dynamically for the instance or a session.
- Parameters can be seen in the dynamic performance views V$PARAMETER and V$SPPARAMETER.

Start Up and Shut Down an Oracle Database Instance

- The stages are NOMOUNT, MOUNT, and OPEN.
- NOMOUNT mode requires a parameter file.
- MOUNT mode requires the controlfile.
- OPEN mode requires the datafiles and online redo log files.

View the Alert Log and Access Dynamic Performance Views

- The alert log is a continuous stream of messages regarding critical operations.
- Trace files are generated by background processes, usually when they hit errors.
- The dynamic performance views are populated from the instance or the controlfile.
- The data dictionary views are populated from the data dictionary.
- Dynamic performance views accumulate values through the lifetime of the instance, and they are reinitialized at startup.
- Data dictionary views show information that persists across shutdown and startup.
- Both the data dictionary views and the dynamic performance views are published through synonyms.

Self Test

1. You issue the URL https://127.0.0.1:5500/em and receive an error. What could be the problem? (Choose all correct answers.)

   A. You have not started the database listener.

   B. Database Express is running on a different port.

   C. You are not logged on to the database server node.

   D. You have not started the Cloud Control agent.

   E. You have not started the database.

2. What protocols can be used to contact Database Express? (Choose all correct answers.)

   A. HTTP

   B. HTTPS

   C. Oracle Net

   D. IPC

3. What will be the setting of the OPTIMIZER_MODE parameter for your session after the next startup if you issue these commands:

```
alter system set optimizer_mode=all_rows scope=spfile;
alter system set optimizer_mode=rule;
alter session set optimizer_mode=first_rows;
```

(Choose the best answer.)

A. all_rows

B. rule

C. first_rows

4. The LOG_BUFFER parameter is a static parameter. How can you change it? (Choose the best answer.)

A. You cannot change it because it is static.

B. You can change it only for individual sessions; it will return to the previous value for all subsequent sessions.

C. You can change it within the instance, but it will return to the static value at the next startup.

D. You can change it in the parameter file, but the new value will come into effect only at the next startup.

5. Which files must be synchronized for a database to open? (Choose the best answer.)

A. Datafiles, online redo log files, and the controlfile.

B. Parameter file and password file.

C. All the multiplexed controlfile copies.

D. None. SMON will synchronize all files by instance recovery after opening the database.

6. During the transition from NOMOUNT to MOUNT mode, which files are required? (Choose the best answer.)

A. Parameter file

B. Controlfiles

C. Online redo logs

D. Datafiles

E. All of the above

7. You shut down your instance with SHUTDOWN IMMEDIATE. What will happen on the next startup? (Choose the best answer.)

A. SMON will perform automatic instance recovery.

B. You must perform manual instance recovery.

C. PMON will roll back uncommitted transactions.

D. The database will open without recovery.

8. You issue the command SHUTDOWN, and it seems to hang. What could be the reason? (Choose the best answer.)

   A. You are not connected as SYSDBA or SYSOPER.

   B. There are other sessions logged on.

   C. You have not connected with operating system or password file authentication.

   D. There are active transactions in the database; when they complete, the SHUTDOWN will proceed.

9. What action should you take after terminating the instance with SHUTDOWN ABORT? (Choose the best answer.)

   A. Back up the database immediately.

   B. Open the database and perform database recovery.

   C. Open the database and perform instance recovery.

   D. None, but some transactions may be lost.

   E. None. Recovery will be automatic.

10. Which of these actions will not be recorded in the alert log? (Choose all correct answers.)

   A. ALTER DATABASE commands

   B. ALTER SESSION commands

   C. ALTER SYSTEM commands

   D. Archiving an online redo log file

   E. Creating a tablespace

   F. Creating a user

11. Which parameter controls the location of background process trace files? (Choose the best answer.)

   A. BACKGROUND_DUMP_DEST.

   B. BACKGROUND_TRACE_DEST.

   C. DB_CREATE_FILE_DEST.

   D. DIAGNOSTIC_DEST.

   E. No parameter. The location is platform specific and cannot be changed.

12. Which of these views can be queried successfully in nomount mode? (Choose all correct answers.)

   A. DBA_DATA_FILES

   B. DBA_TABLESPACES

   C. V$DATABASE

   D. V$DATAFILE

   E. V$INSTANCE

   F. V$SESSION

13. Which view will list all tables in the database? (Choose the best answer.)

   A. ALL_TABLES

   B. DBA_TABLES

   C. USER_TABLES, when connected as SYS

   D. V$FIXED_TABLE

Self Test Answers

1. ☑ **A, B, C,** and **E.** Both the database listener and the database itself must be running to use Database Express. It is also possible the HTTP listening service may not be on the default port of 5500, and the loopback address will function only if you are running the browser on the database server machine.

   ☒ **D** is incorrect. The Cloud Control agent is not needed to use Database Express.

2. ☑ **A** and **B.** Both HTTP and HTTPS can be used, provided that an appropriate listening port has been configured with XDB.

   ☒ **C** and **D** are incorrect. Oracle Net and IPC are the protocols that can be used by user processes to contact the server, not by browsers to contact Database Express.

3. ☑ **B.** The default scope of ALTER SYSTEM is BOTH, meaning memory and spfile.

   ☒ **A** and **C** are incorrect. **A** is incorrect because this setting will have been replaced by the setting in the second command. **C** is incorrect because the session-level setting will have been lost during the restart of the instance.

4. ☑ **D.** This is the technique for changing a static parameter.

   ☒ **A, B,** and **C** are incorrect. **A** is incorrect because static parameters can be changed—but only with a shutdown. **B** and **C** are incorrect because static parameters cannot be changed for a running session or instance.

5. ☑ **A.** These are the files that make up a database, and all must be synchronized if the database is to open.

   ☒ **B, C,** and **D** are incorrect. **B** is incorrect because these files are not, strictly speaking, part of the database. **C** is incorrect because a problem with a controlfile copy would mean that the database could not be mounted, never mind opened. **D** is incorrect because SMON's instance recovery mechanism can fix problems only in datafiles, not anything else.

6. ☑ **B.** Mounting the database is the process of opening the controlfile (all copies thereof).

   ☒ **A, C, D,** and **E** are incorrect. **A** is incorrect because the parameter file is needed only for NOMOUNT. **C, D,** and **E** are incorrect because these file types are needed only for open mode.

7. ☑ **D**. An immediate shutdown is clean, so no recovery will be required.
   ☒ **A**, **B**, and **C** are incorrect. No recovery or rollback will be required; all the work will have been done as part of the shutdown.

8. ☑ **B**. The default shutdown mode is SHUTDOWN NORMAL, which will hang until all sessions have voluntarily disconnected.
   ☒ **A**, **C**, and **D** are incorrect. **A** and **C** are incorrect because these would cause an error, not a hang. **D** is incorrect because it describes SHUTDOWN TRANSACTIONAL, not SHUTDOWN NORMAL.

9. ☑ **E**. No action is required; recovery will be automatic.
   ☒ **A**, **B**, **C**, and **D** are incorrect. **A** is incorrect because this is one thing you should *not* do after an ABORT. **B** is incorrect because database recovery is not necessary, only instance recovery. **C** is incorrect because instance recovery will occur automatically in mount mode at the next startup. **D** is incorrect because no transactions will ever be lost as a result of an ABORT.

10. ☑ **B** and **F**. Neither of these affects the structure of the database or the instance; they are not important enough to generate an alert log entry.
    ☒ **A**, **C**, **D**, and **E** are incorrect. All of these are changes to physical or memory structures, and all such changes are recorded in the alert log.

11. ☑ **D**. This is the parameter used to determine the location of background trace files and indeed the whole of the Automatic Diagnostic Repository.
    ☒ **A**, **B**, **C**, and **E** are incorrect. **A** is incorrect because although this parameter does still exist, it is deprecated. **B** is incorrect because there is no such parameter. **C** is incorrect because this is the default location for datafiles, not trace files. **E** is incorrect because although there is a platform-specific default, it can be overridden with a parameter.

12. ☑ **E** and **F**. These views are populated from the instance and will therefore be available at all times.
    ☒ **A**, **B**, **C**, and **D** are incorrect. **A** and **B** are data dictionary views, which can be seen only in open mode. **C** and **D** are dynamic performance views populated from the controlfile and are therefore available only in mount mode or open mode.

13. ☑ **B**. The DBA views list every appropriate object in the database.
    ☒ **A**, **C**, and **D** are incorrect. **A** is incorrect because this will list only the tables the current user has permissions on—which might be all the tables but probably isn't. **C** is incorrect because it will list only the tables owned by SYS. **D** is incorrect because this is the view that lists all the dynamic performance views, not all the tables.

PART III

CHAPTER 14

Oracle Networking

Exam Objectives

- 062.4.1   Configure Oracle Net Services
- 062.4.2   Use Tools for Configuring and Managing the Oracle Network
- 062.4.3   Configure the Client-Side Network
- 062.4.4   Understand Database Resident Connection Pooling
- 062.4.5   Configure Communication Between Databases

Oracle Net is the enabling technology for Oracle's client-server architecture. It is the mechanism for establishing sessions against a database instance. Several tools can be used for setting up and administering Oracle Net, although it can be done with nothing more than a simple text editor. The end result is a set of files that control a process (the database listener) that launches server processes in response to connection requests and defines the means by which a user process will locate the listener.

Configure Oracle Net Services

Oracle's client-server architecture uses the Oracle Net protocol to establish and maintain the session between the client and the server. It is possible to use this with no configuration at all, but all sites will, in practice, configure it.

Oracle Net and the Client-Server Paradigm

There are many layers between the user and the database. In the Oracle environment, no user ever has direct access to the database—nor does the process that the user is running. Client-server architecture guarantees that all access to data is controlled by the server.

A user interacts with a user process. This is the software running on the user's local terminal. For example, it could be Microsoft Access plus an ODBC driver on a Windows PC, it could be something written in C and linked with the Oracle Call Interface (OCI) libraries, and it could even be your old friend SQL*Plus. Whatever it is, the purpose of the user process is to prompt the user to enter information that the process can use to generate SQL statements. In the case of SQL*Plus, the process merely waits for you to type something in; a more sophisticated user process will paint a proper data-entry screen and validate your input, and then when you click the Submit button, it will construct the statement and send it off to the server process.

The server process is a process running on the database server machine that executes the SQL it receives from the user process. This is the client-server split: a user process generating SQL, a server process executing SQL.

Oracle Net provides the mechanism for launching a server process to execute code on behalf of a user process. This is establishing a session. Then Oracle Net is responsible for maintaining the session, meaning transmitting SQL from the user process to the server process and fetching results from the server process back to the user process.

Figure 14-1 shows the various components of a session. A user interacts with a user process; a user process interacts with a server process, via Oracle Net; a server process interacts with the instance; and the instance, via its background processes, interacts with the database.

The client-server split between the user process and the server process will usually be physical as well as logical. There will be a network between the machines hosting the user processes and the machine hosting the server side, implemented by Oracle Net running on top of whatever communications protocol is supported by your operating system. The supported protocols are Transmission Control Protocol/Internet Protocol (TCP/IP) version 4 and 6, with or without Secure Sockets Layer (SSL); Windows named pipes; and the Sockets Direct Protocol (SDP) designed for InfiniBand networks. All operating systems also have an Inter-Process Communication (IPC) protocol proprietary to the operating system. This, too, is available to Oracle Net for local connections where the user process is on the same machine as the server.

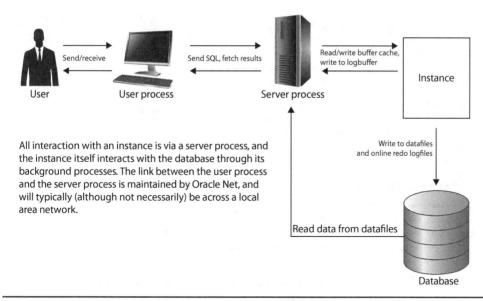

All interaction with an instance is via a server process, and the instance itself interacts with the database through its background processes. The link between the user process and the server process is maintained by Oracle Net, and will typically (although not necessarily) be across a local area network.

Figure 14-1   The database is protected from the user by several layers.

Establishing a Session

When a user, through their user process, wants to establish a session against an instance, the user will issue a command such as this:

```
CONNECT SCOTT/TIGER@ORCL12C
```

What actually happens when that command is processed? First, break down the command into its components. There is a database user name (SCOTT), followed by a database password (TIGER, which is case sensitive), and the two are separated by a delimiter (/). Then there is an @ symbol, followed by a connect string (ORCL12C). The @ symbol indicates to the user process that a network connection is required. If the @ symbol and the connect string are omitted, the user process will assume that the instance the user wants to connect to is running on the local machine and that the always-available IPC protocol can be used. If the @ symbol and a connect string are included, the user process will assume that the user is requesting a network connection to an instance on a remote machine—although, in fact, the user could be bouncing off the network card and back to the machine onto which they are logged.

Connecting to a Local Instance

Even when you connect to an instance running on your local machine, you still use Oracle Net. All Oracle sessions use a network protocol to implement the separation of user code from server code, but for a local connection the protocol is IPC. This is the only type of connection that does not require a database listener; indeed, local connections do not require any configuration at all. The only information needed is to tell your user process which instance you want to

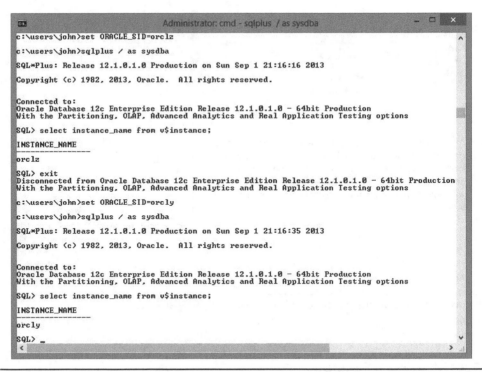

Figure 14-2   Local database connections on Windows

connect to. Remember that several instances could be running on your local computer. You give the process this information through an environment variable. Figure 14-2 shows examples of this on Windows.

Name Resolution

When connecting over a network, the first stage is to work out exactly what it is you want to connect to. This is the process of name resolution. If your connect statement includes the connect string @orcl12c, Oracle Net has to work out what is meant by orcl12c. This means the string has to be resolved into certain pieces of information: the protocol you want to use (assume that this is TCP), the IP address on which the database listener is running, the port that the listener is monitoring for incoming connection requests, and the name of the instance (which need not be the same as the connect string) to which you want to connect. There are variations; rather than an IP address, the connect string can include a hostname, which then gets further resolved to an IP address by the Domain Name System (DNS) resolution mechanism. You can configure a number of ways of resolving connect strings to address and instance names, but one way or another the name resolution process gives your user process enough information to go across the network to a database listener and request a connection to a particular instance.

Launching a Server Process

The database listener, running on the server machine, monitors one or more ports on one or more network interface cards for incoming connection requests. When it receives a connect request, the listener must first validate whether the instance requested is actually available. Assuming that it is, the listener will launch a new server process to service the user process. Thus, if you have a thousand users logging on concurrently to your instance, you will be launching a thousand server processes.

In the TCP environment, each dedicated server process launched by a listener will acquire a unique TCP port number. This will be assigned at process startup time by your operating system's port-mapping algorithm. The port number gets passed back to the user process by the listener (or on some operating systems, the socket already opened to the listener is transferred to the new port number), and the user process can then communicate directly with its server process. The listener has now completed its work and waits for the next connect request.

Creating a Database Listener

A listener is defined in a file, the listener.ora file, whose default location is in the ORACLE_HOME/network/admin directory. At a minimum, the listener.ora file must include a section for one listener that states its name, the protocol, and the listening address it will use. You can configure several listeners in the one file, but they must all have different names and addresses.

 EXAM TIP If the database listener is not running or is stopped, no new server processes can be launched—but this will not affect any existing sessions that have already been established.

This is an example of a listener.ora file:

```
LISTENER =
  (DESCRIPTION =
    (ADDRESS =
         (PROTOCOL = TCP)(HOST = jwlnx1)(PORT = 1521))
  )
LIST2 =
  (DESCRIPTION =
     (ADDRESS_LIST =
     (ADDRESS =
         (PROTOCOL = TCP)(HOST = 127.0.0.1)(PORT = 1522))
     (ADDRESS =
         (PROTOCOL = TCP)(HOST = jwlnx1.sb)(PORT = 1522))
     )
  )
```

The first section of this file defines a listener called LISTENER, monitoring the local hostname on the default port, 1521. The second section defines another listener called LIST2. This listener is monitoring port 1522 on both the hostname address and a loopback address.

To create a listener, you need do nothing more than create an entry in the listener.ora file and then start it. Under Windows, the listener will run as a Windows service, but there is no need to create the service explicitly; it will be created implicitly the first time the listener is started. From then on, if you want, it can be started and stopped like any other Windows service.

TIP You can run a listener completely on defaults, without a listener.ora file at all. It will listen on whatever address resolves to the machine's hostname, on port 1521. Avoid this to prevent confusion. Always configure the listener .ora file to make your Oracle Net environment self-documenting.

Dynamic Service Registration

To launch sessions against an instance, the listener needs to know what instances are currently running on the server. This is the final part of the puzzle. It is possible to hard-code a list of instances in the listener.ora file, but this is not considered best practice. The approved technique is to rely on dynamic service registration.

Every database offers one or more services. A *service* is a logical name to which sessions can attach through the instance. Different services within the database can have different characteristics (for instance, for fault tolerance). There will always be a default service named after the database, which is often the same name as the instance, which is often the same name as the Net service alias defined in a tnsnames.ora file and used in connect strings. When an instance starts, by default it will look for a listener on the address to which the machine's hostname resolves using port 1521. If there is indeed a listener running on that address:port, the database will register its service name (or names) with the listener, and the listener will then be able to connect users. When the database is shut down, it will deregister itself from the listener. This is the process of dynamic registration.

EXAM TIP It is the listener registration (LREG) background process that registers services with the listener.

During the lifetime of the instance, the LREG process repeatedly reregisters with the listener. Thus, if the listener is stopped and started, it will become aware of the database the next time LREG attempts to register.

Shared Server

The network architecture described so far is the *dedicated server* architecture. Each user process is connected to a server process, launched by the listener for servicing that one session. An alternative is the *shared server* architecture, where a relatively small pool of server processes services a much larger number of user sessions.

The Limitations of Dedicated Server Architecture

As more users log on to your instance, more server processes get launched. This is not a problem as far as Oracle is concerned. The database listener can launch as many processes as required, although there may be operating system limits on the speed with which it can launch them. Then, once the sessions are established, there is no limit to the number that the process monitor (PMON) can manage (although your operating system may have limits on the number of processes that it can support related to context switches and memory).

A computer can do only one thing at a time unless it is a symmetric multiprocessing (SMP) machine, in which case each central processing unit (CPU) can do only one thing at a time. The operating system simulates concurrent processing by using an algorithm to share CPU cycles across all the currently executing processes. This algorithm, often referred to as a *time-slicing* or *time-sharing algorithm,* takes care of allocating a few CPU cycles to each process in turn. The switch of taking one process off the CPU to put another process on the CPU is called a *context switch.* Context switches are expensive; the operating system has to do a lot of work to restore the state of each process as it is brought on to the CPU and then save its state when it is switched off the CPU. As more users connect to the instance, the operating system has to context-switch between more and more server processes. Depending on your operating system, this can cause a severe degradation in performance. A decent mainframe operating system can context-switch between tens of thousands of processes without problems, but newer (and simpler) operating systems such as Unix and Windows may not be good at running thousands, or even just hundreds, of concurrent processes. Performance can degrade dramatically because a large proportion of the computer's processing capacity is taken up with managing the context switches, leaving a relatively small amount of processing capacity available for actually doing work.

Also, memory problems may occur as more sessions are established. The actual server processes themselves are not an issue because all modern operating systems use shared memory when the same process is loaded more than once. So, launching a thousand server processes should take no more memory than launching one. The problem comes with the Program Global Area (PGA). The PGA is a block of memory associated with each server process to maintain the state of the session, and is a work area for operations such as sorting rows. Clearly, the PGAs cannot be in shared memory; they contain data unique to each session.

Therefore, in the dedicated server environment, performance may degrade if your operating system has problems managing a large number of concurrent processes, and the problem will be exacerbated if your server machine has insufficient memory. Note that it doesn't really matter whether the sessions are actually doing anything. Even if the sessions are idle, the operating system must still bring them on and off the CPU and possibly page the appropriate PGA into main memory from swap files according to its time-slicing algorithm. There comes a point when no matter what you do in the way of hardware upgrades, performance begins to degrade because of the operating system inefficiencies in managing context switches and paging. These are not Oracle's problems, but to overcome them, Oracle offers the option of the shared server architecture. This allows a large number of user processes to be serviced by a relatively small number of shared server processes, thus reducing dramatically the number of processes that the server's operating system has to manage. As a fringe benefit, memory usage may also reduce.

The Shared Server Architecture

One point to emphasize immediately is that shared server is implemented purely on the server side. The user process and the application software have no way of telling that anything has changed. The user process issues a connect string that must resolve to the address of a listener and the name of a service (or of an instance). In return, it will receive the address of a server-side process that it will think is a dedicated server. It will then proceed to send SQL statements and receive result sets; as far as the user process is concerned, absolutely nothing has changed. But the server side is different.

EXAM TIP Shared server is configured at the server side, but the client can demand either a shared server or a dedicated server by specifying either SERVER=DEDICATED or SERVER=SHARED in the TNS connect string.

Shared server is implemented by additional processes that are part of the instance. They are background processes launched at instance startup time. There are two process types: dispatchers and shared servers. There are also some extra queue memory structures within the System Global Area (SGA), and the database listener modifies its behavior for shared server. When an instance that is configured for shared server starts up, in addition to the usual background processes, one or more dispatcher processes start. The dispatchers, like any other TCP process, run on a unique TCP port allocated by your operating system's port mapper. They contact the listener and register with it. One or more shared server processes also start. These are conceptually similar to a normal dedicated server process, but they are not tied to one session. They will receive SQL statements, parse and execute them, and generate a result set. However, they will not receive the SQL statements directly from a user process; instead, they will read them from a queue that will be populated with statements from any number of user processes. Similarly, the shared servers don't fetch result sets to a user process directly; instead, they put the result sets onto a response queue.

The next questions are how do the user-generated statements get onto the queue that is read by the server processes, and how do results get fetched to the users? This is where the dispatchers come in. When a user process contacts a listener, rather than launching a server process and connecting it to the user process, the listener passes back the address of a dispatcher. If there is only one dispatcher, the listener will connect it to all the user processes. If there are multiple dispatchers, the listener will load-balance incoming connection requests across them, but the end result is that many user processes will be connected to each dispatcher. Each user process will be under the impression that it is communicating with a dedicated server process, but it isn't. It is sharing a dispatcher with many other user processes. At the network level, many user processes will have connections multiplexed through the one port used by the dispatcher.

EXAM TIP A session's connection to a dispatcher persists for the duration of the session, unlike the connection to the listener, which is transient.

When a user process issues a SQL statement, it is sent to the dispatcher. The dispatcher puts all the statements it receives onto a queue. This queue is called the *common queue* because all dispatchers share it. No matter which dispatcher a user process is connected to, all statements end up on the common queue.

All the shared server processes monitor the common queue. When a statement arrives on the common queue, the first available shared server picks it up. From then on, execution proceeds through the usual parse-bind-execute cycle, but when it comes to the fetch phase, it is impossible for the shared server to fetch the result set to the user process; there is no connection between the user process and the shared server. So, instead, the shared server puts the result set onto a response queue that is specific to the dispatcher that received the job in the first place. Each dispatcher monitors its own response queue, and whenever any results are put on it, the dispatcher will pick them up and fetch them back to the user process that originally issued the statement.

EXAM TIP There is a common input queue shared by all dispatchers, but each dispatcher has its own response queue.

A result of the mechanism of dispatchers and queues is that any statement from any user process could be executed by any available shared server. This raises the question of how the state of the session can be maintained. It would be quite possible for a user process to issue, for example, a SELECT FOR UPDATE, a DELETE, and a COMMIT. In a normal dedicated server connection, this isn't a problem because the PGA (which is tied to the one server process that is managing the session) stores information about what the session was doing, and therefore the dedicated server will know what to COMMIT and what locks to release. The PGA for a dedicated server session will store the session's session data, its cursor state, its sort space, and its stack space. But in the shared server environment, each statement might be picked off the common queue by a different shared server process, which will have no idea what the state of the transaction is. To get around this problem, a shared server session stores most of the session data in the SGA, rather than in a PGA. Then, whenever a shared server picks a job off the common queue, it will go to the SGA and connect to the appropriate block of memory to find out the state of the session. The memory used in the SGA for each shared server session is known as the User Global Area (UGA) and includes all of what would have been in a PGA, with the exception of the session's stack space. This is where the memory saving will come from. Oracle can manage memory in the shared pool much more effectively than it can in many separate PGAs.

The following session memory structures are stored in the SGA when shared server is implemented:

- Sort area
- Hash area
- Bitmap creation area
- Bitmap merge area
- Cursor state
- User session data

The following session memory structures remain outside the SGA. These may be thought of as the run-time information for a call in progress:

- Stack space
- Local variables

EXAM TIP In shared server, what PGA memory structures do not go into the SGA? Stack space and local variables.

The part of the SGA used for storing UGAs is the large pool. This can be configured manually with the large_pool_size parameter, or it can be automatically managed.

It is impossible to use a shared server session to start up or shut down the instance. This is because the processes needed to support shared server (dispatchers and shared server processes) are themselves part of the instance.

Configuring Shared Server

Being a server-side capability, there is no need for client configuration at all beyond perfectly normal client-side Oracle Net (the tnsnames.ora and sqlnet.ora files), as detailed previously. On the server side, shared server has nothing to do with the database—only the instance. The listener will be automatically configured for shared server through dynamic instance registration. It follows that shared server is configured through instance initialization parameters. There are a number of relevant parameters, but two are all that are usually necessary: shared_servers and dispatchers.

The first parameter to consider is shared_servers. This controls the number of shared servers that will be launched at instance startup time. Shared server uses a queuing mechanism, but ideally there should be no queuing. There should always be a server process ready and waiting for every job that is put on the common queue by the dispatchers. Therefore, shared_servers should be set to the maximum number of concurrent requests you expect. But if there is a sudden burst of activity, you don't have to worry too much because Oracle will launch additional shared servers, up to the value specified for max_shared_servers. By default, shared_servers is 1 if dispatchers is set. If the parameter max_shared_servers is not set, it defaults to one-eighth of the processes parameter.

The dispatchers parameter controls how many dispatcher processes to launch at instance startup time and how they will behave. This is the only required parameter. There are many options for this parameter, but usually two will suffice: how many to start and what protocol they should listen on. Among the more advanced options are ones that allow you to control the port and network card on which the dispatcher will listen and the address of the listener (or listeners) with which it will register. However, you can usually let your operating system's port mapper assign a port and use the local_listener parameter to control which listener the dispatchers will register. The max_dispatchers parameter sets an upper limit to the number of dispatchers you can start, but unlike with shared servers, Oracle will not start extra dispatchers on demand. You can, however, launch additional dispatchers at any time, up to this limit.

For example, to enable the shared server architecture, adjust the two critical parameters as follows:

```
SQL> alter system set dispatchers='(dispatchers=2)(protocol=tcp)';
SQL> alter system set shared_servers=20;
```

Tuning the shared server is vital. There should always be enough shared servers to dequeue requests from the common queue as they arrive, and there should always be enough dispatchers that they can service incoming requests as they arrive and return results as they are enqueued to the response queues. Memory usage by shared server sessions in the SGA must be monitored. After converting from dedicated server to shared server, the SGA will need to be substantially larger.

When to Use the Shared Server

You will not find a great deal of hard advice in the Oracle documentation on when to use shared server or how many dispatchers and shared servers you'll need. The main point to hang on to is that shared server is a facility you use because you are forced to, not something you use automatically. It increases scalability but perhaps at the cost of reducing performance. It is quite possible that any one statement will take longer to execute in a shared server environment than if it were executing on a dedicated server because it has to go via queues. It may also take more CPU resources because of this enqueuing and dequeuing activity. But overall, the scalability of your system will increase dramatically. Even if each request is marginally slower, you will be able to carry out many more requests per second through the instance.

Consider an online transaction processing (OLTP) environment, with hundreds of telephone operators in a call center. Each operator may spend one or two minutes per call, collecting the caller details and entering them into the user process. Then, when the operator clicks the Submit button, the user process constructs an insert statement and sends it off to the server process. The server process might go through the whole parse/bind/execute/fetch cycle for the statement in just a few hundredths of a second. Clearly, no matter how fast the clerks work, their server processes are idle 99.9 percent of the time. But the operating system still has to switch all those processes on and off the CPU according to its time-sharing algorithm. By contrast, consider a data warehouse environment. Here, users submit queries that may run for a long time. The batch uploads of data will be equally long running. Whenever one of these large jobs is submitted, the server process for that session could be working flat out for hours on just one statement.

It should be apparent that shared server is ideal for managing many sessions doing short transactions, where the bulk of the work is on the client side of the client-server divide. In these circumstances, one shared server will be able to service dozens of sessions. But for batch processing work, dedicated servers are much better. If you submit a large batch job through a shared server session, it will work—but it will tie up one of your small pool of shared server processes for the duration of the job, leaving all your other users to compete for the remaining shared servers. The amount of network traffic involved in batch uploads from a user process and in fetching large result sets back to a user process will also cause contention for dispatchers.

A second class of operations that are better done through a dedicated server is database administration work. Index creation, table maintenance operations, and backup and recovery work through Recovery Manager will perform much better through a dedicated server. And it is logically impossible to issue startup or shutdown commands through a shared server; the shared servers are part of the instance and therefore not available at the time you issue a startup command. So, the administrator should always have a dedicated server connection.

The Default Shared Server Configuration

A 12*c* database instance will run shared server by default, but only for connections through the XDB. These queries show the default configuration, which is adequate for running Database Express (remember from Chapter 13 that Database Express requires XDB to be configured):

```
orcl> select name,value from v$parameter
where name like '%dispatchers';
NAME                    VALUE
-------------------     ------------------------------------
dispatchers             (PROTOCOL=TCP) (SERVICE=orclXDB)
max_dispatchers
orcl>
orcl> select name,value from v$parameter
where name like '%shared_servers';
```

```
NAME                   VALUE
-------------------    ------------------------------------
shared_servers         1
max_shared_servers
orcl>
```

Use Tools for Configuring and Managing the Oracle Network

Configuring Oracle Net is nothing more than creating the configuration files. There are three of them:

- The configuration file listener.ora exists on the server side and defines the operation of the database listener.

- The configuration file tnsnames.ora is a client-side file used for name resolution. There will usually be a copy on the server as well to facilitate running clients on the server machine.

- The configuration file sqlnet.ora is an optional file that may exist on both the client and server sides. It sets various defaults that will affect all clients and listeners.

Two graphical tools are provided for creating and editing these files: the Net Manager and the Net Configuration Assistant.

The Net Manager

To launch the Net Manager, run netmgr from a Unix prompt; on Windows you will find it on the Start menu.

The Net Manager navigation tree has three branches. The Profile branch creates or edits the sqlnet.ora file and is used to set options that may apply to both the client and server sides of Oracle. This is where, for example, you can configure detailed tracing of Oracle Net sessions or (as in Figure 14-3) enable certain name-resolution methods. The Service Naming branch is used to configure client-side name resolution in the tnsnames.ora file. The Listeners branch is used to configure database listeners in the listener.ora file.

The Net Configuration Assistant

Launch netca by running the executable $ORACLE_HOME/bin/netca on Linux or by navigating through the Start menu on Windows. Net Configuration Assistant is simple to use. It does not have all the functionality of the Net Manager and can configure only database listeners and tnsnames connect strings.

The Listener Control Utility

The Listener Control utility is the executable $ORACLE_HOME/bin/lsnrctl on Linux or %ORACLE_HOME%\bin\lsnrctl.exe on Windows. lsnrctl commands can be run directly from an operating system prompt or through a simple user interface. For all the commands, you must specify the name of the listener if it is not the default name of LISTENER. Figure 14-4 shows

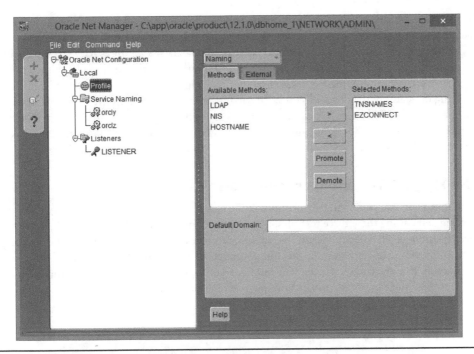

Figure 14-3   Net Manager's Profile editor

Figure 14-4   Starting the default listener

how to check the status of the default listener named LISTENER and start it. Note that the listener starts listening on the address jwvaio on port 1521, but it is not offering a connection to any services. This is because it has only just started, and no database instances have registered with it. The registration will happen automatically within a minute, as instances find that it is started.

The lsnrctl utility does have a simple user interface. Figure 14-5 shows starting the interface, checking the status of the default listener, shutting it down, and exiting from the tool. Note the output of the STATUS command. The listener is listening on port 1521 for incoming TCP connections. These will be logon requests. It is also listening on port 5500 for Hypertext Transfer Protocol (HTTP) over TCPS. This is for connections from browsers to Database Express.

The TNS_ADMIN Environment Variable

Configuring Oracle Net, manually or through the graphical tools, consists of nothing more than creating and editing these three text files: tnsnames.ora, sqlnet.ora, and listener.ora. Where do these files reside? The default location where Oracle processes will look for them is the directory $ORACLE_HOME/network/admin (Linux) or %ORACLE_HOME%\network\admin (Windows). In some circumstances, you will not want to use this directory. For example, if you have several Oracle products installed on one machine (multiple releases of the database, the

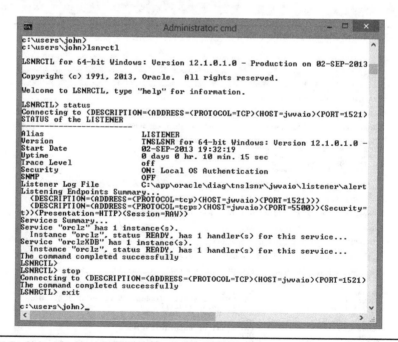

Figure 14-5 Using the lsnrctl user interface to check the status and then stop the listener named LISTENER

Oracle client, and an application server perhaps), each will be in its own Oracle home, and therefore each will have its own copy of the files.

Keeping multiple copies of the files (particularly tnsnames.ora) identical can be awkward. The worst case is when hundreds of client PCs each have their own copy. One answer is to store the files in a central location (which could be a network-mounted file system) and instruct all processes to read the files from this nondefault location. Do this by setting the TNS_ADMIN environment variable. Here is an example on Linux:

```
export TNS_ADMIN=/common/oracle/oraclenet
```

And here is an example on Windows:

```
set TNS_ADMIN=o:\common\oracle\oraclenet
```

Configure Client-Side Network

The client side of Oracle Net is configured in a sqlnet.ora file and (typically) a tnsnames.ora file. The sqlnet.ora file is optional, and many sites will never use it. Most sites will, however, use a tnsnames file.

To establish a session against an instance, your user process must issue a connect string. That string resolves to the address of a listener and the name of an instance or service. Oracle provides four methods of name resolution: easy connect, local naming, directory naming, and external naming. It is probably true to say that the majority of Oracle sites use local naming, but there is no question that directory naming is the best method for a large and complex installation.

Easy Connect Name Resolution

The Easy Connect name resolution method is easy to use—it requires no configuration at all. But it is limited to one protocol: TCP. The other name resolution methods can use any of the other supported protocols, such as TCP with secure sockets or named pipes. Another limitation is that Easy Connect cannot be used with any of Oracle Net's more advanced capabilities, such as load balancing or connect-time failover across different network routes. It is fair to say that Easy Connect is a method you as a database administrator (DBA) will find handy to use, but it is not a method of much use for your end users. Easy Connect is enabled by default. You invoke it with syntax such as the following connect string:

```
SQL> connect scott/tiger@jwvaio:1521/orclz
```

In this example, SQL*Plus will use TCP to go to port 1521 on the IP address to which the hostname jwvaio resolves. Then, if there is a listener running on that port and address, it will ask the listener to spawn a server process against an instance that is offering a service called orclz.

Local Naming Name Resolution

With local naming, the user supplies an alias, known as an Oracle Net service alias, for the connect string, and the alias is resolved by a local file into the full network address (protocol, address, port, and service or instance name). This local file is the infamous tnsnames.ora file, which has caused DBAs much grief over the years. Consider this example of a tnsnames.ora file:

```
orclz =
  (DESCRIPTION =
    (ADDRESS_LIST =
      (ADDRESS =
        (PROTOCOL = TCP)(HOST = jwvaio)(PORT = 1522))
      )
    (CONNECT_DATA =
      (service_name = orclz)
    )
  )
test =
  (DESCRIPTION =
    (ADDRESS_LIST =
      (ADDRESS =
      (PROTOCOL = TCP)
      (HOST = serv2.example.com)
      (PORT = 1521))
      )
    (CONNECT_DATA =
      (sid = testdb)
    )
  )
```

This tnsnames.ora file has two Oracle Net service aliases defined within it: orclz and test. These aliases are what your users will provide in their connect statements. The first entry, orclz, simply says that when the connect string @orclz is issued, your user process should use the TCP protocol to go the machine jwvaio, contact it on port 1521, and ask the listener monitoring that port to establish a session against the instance with the service name orclz. The second entry, test, directs users to a listener on a different machine, serv2.example.com, and asks for a session against the instance called testdb.

 TIP   There need be no relationship between the alias, the service name, and the instance name, but for the sake of your sanity you will usually keep them the same.

Local naming supports all protocols and all the advanced features of Oracle Net, but maintaining tnsnames.ora files on all your client machines can be an extremely time-consuming task. The tnsnames.ora file is also notoriously sensitive to apparently trivial variations in layout. Using the graphical user interface (GUI) tools will help avoid such problems.

Directory Naming and External Naming

Directory naming points the user toward a Lightweight Directory Access Protocol (LDAP) directory server to resolve aliases. LDAP is a widely used standard that Oracle Corporation (and other mainstream software vendors) is encouraging organizations to adopt. To use directory naming, you must first install and configure a directory server somewhere on your network. Oracle provides an LDAP server (the Oracle Internet Directory) as part of the Oracle Application Server, but you do not have to use that—if you already have a Microsoft Active Directory, that will be perfectly adequate. IBM and Novell also sell directory servers conforming to the LDAP standard.

Like local naming, directory naming supports all Oracle Net features—but unlike local naming, it uses a central repository, the directory server, for all your name resolution details. This is much easier to maintain than many tnsnames.ora files distributed across your whole user community.

External naming is conceptually similar to directory naming, but it uses third-party naming services such as Sun's Network Information Services (NIS+) or the Cell Directory Services (CDS) that are part of the Distributed Computing Environment (DCE).

The use of directories and external naming services is beyond the scope of the Oracle Certified Professional (OCP) syllabus.

Testing Oracle Net Connectivity

An invaluable troubleshooting tool is the tnsping utility. This accepts a connect string and then tests whether it works. It will show the name resolution method used, the Oracle Net configuration files being read, the details of what the string resolves to, and whether there is indeed a listener listening on those details. It does not test whether the database is actually running, but it does attempt to hit the listener and will return a suitable error message if it cannot.

Figure 14-6 shows the use of tnsping to test a connect string—first successfully and then unsuccessfully.

The first example tests the tnsconnect string orclz. The utility resolves the string using files located in the directory C:\app\oracle\product\12.1.0\dbhome_1\network\admin, which say that the address is a machine called jwvaio and port 1521. The requested service will be orclz. The test succeeds; there is indeed a listener on that address and port, and the listener does know of a service called orclz. The second test attempts to resolve the name orcla and fails, presumably because there is no such entry in the tnsnames.ora file.

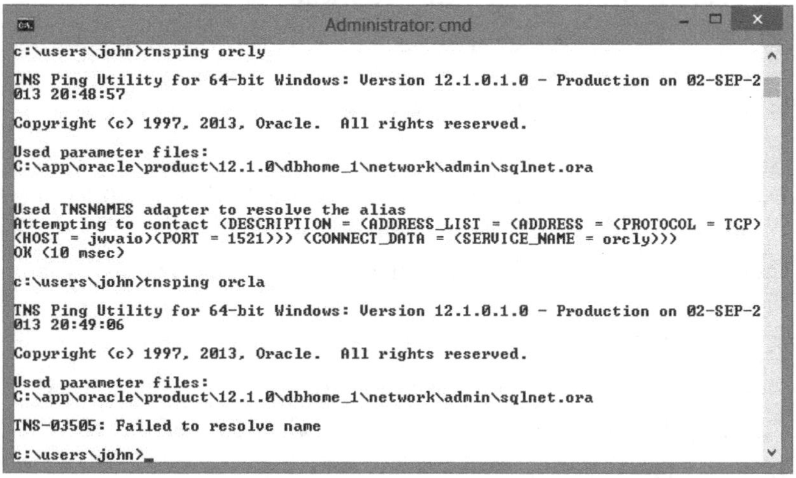

Figure 14-6   Using the tnsping utility to test name resolution

Exercise 14-1: Configure Oracle Net   In this exercise, you will set up a complete Oracle Net environment using graphical and command-line tools. Any differences between Windows and Linux will be pointed out. These are the steps to follow:

1. Create a directory to be used for the Oracle Net configuration files and then set the TNS_ADMIN variable to point to this. It doesn't matter where the directory is, as long as the Oracle user has permission to create, read, and write it.

   Here's an example on Linux:

   ```
   mkdir /u01/oracle/net
   export TNS_ADMIN=/u01/oracle/net
   ```

   Ensure that all work from now is done from a session where the variable has been set.

   Here's an example on Windows:

   ```
   mkdir d:\oracle\net
   ```

   Create and set the key TNS_ADMIN as a string variable in the registry in the Oracle Home branch. This will typically be as follows:

   HKEY_LOCAL_MACHINE\SOFTWARE\ORACLE\KEY_OraDB12Home1

   Check that the variable is being read by using the TNSPING command from an operating system prompt.

   ```
   tnsping orcl
   ```

   This will return the error "TNS-03505: Failed to resolve name" because there are no files in the TNS_ADMIN directory. On Windows, you may need to launch a new command prompt to pick up the new TNS_ADMIN value from the registry.

2. Start the Net Manager. On Linux, run netmgr from an operating system prompt; on Windows, launch it from the Start menu. The top line of the Net Manager window will show the location of the Oracle Net files. If this is not the new directory, the TNS_ADMIN variable has not been set correctly.

   A. Create a new listener by expanding the Local branch of the navigation tree, highlighting Listeners, and clicking +.

   B. Enter a listener name, **NEWLIST**, and click OK.

   C. Click Add Address.

   D. For Address 1, choose TCP/IP as the protocol and enter **127.0.0.1** as the host and **2521** as the port. Figure 14-7 shows this.

3. Create a new service name by highlighting Service Naming in the navigation tree and clicking +.

   A. Enter **NEW** as the net service name and click Next.

   B. Select TCP/IP as the protocol and click Next.

   C. Enter **127.0.0.1** as the hostname and **2521** as the port and then click Next.

   D. Enter **SERV1** as the service name and click Next.

   E. Click Finish. If you try the test, it will fail at this time. Figure 14-8 shows this.

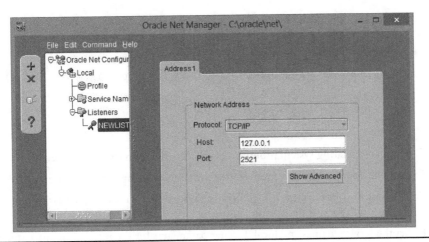

Figure 14-7 Creating a listener with the Net Manager

4. Save the configuration by clicking File and Save Network Configuration. This will create the listener.ora and tnsnames.ora files in the TNS_ADMIN directory.

Use an editor to check the two files.

LISTENER.ORA will look like this:

```
NEWLIST =
  (DESCRIPTION =
    (ADDRESS = (PROTOCOL = TCP)(HOST = 127.0.0.1)(PORT = 2521))
  )
```

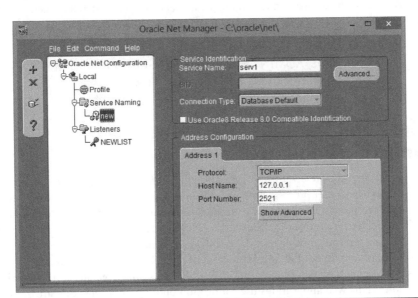

Figure 14-8 Creating a tnsnames service name alias with the Net Manager

TNSNAMES.ora will look like this:

```
NEW =
  (DESCRIPTION =
    (ADDRESS_LIST =
      (ADDRESS = (PROTOCOL = TCP)(HOST = 127.0.0.1)(PORT = 2521))
    )
    (CONNECT_DATA =
      (SERVICE_NAME = SERV1)
    )
  )
```

5. From an operating system prompt, start the listener with lsnrctl start newlist.

6. From an operating system prompt, test the connect string with tnsping new.

7. Connect to your database using operating system authentication, bypassing any listener, with sqlplus / as sysdba.

8. Set the service_names and local_listener parameters for the running instance (memory only, not the parameter file) and register the new service name with the new, nondefault listener.

```
alter system set service_names=serv1 scope=memory;
alter system set local_listener=new scope=memory;
alter system register;
```

9. From an operating system prompt, confirm that the new service has registered with the new listener with lsnrctl services newlist.

10. Confirm that the new network environment is functional by logging on.

```
sqlplus system/oracle@new
```

11. Back out the changes to revert to default operation.

   A. Restart the database to return the parameters changed in step 8 to their default values.

   B. Stop the listener with lsnrctl stop newlist.

   C. Unset the TNS_ADMIN variable. On Linux, export TNS_ADMIN=''. On Windows, remove the TNS_ADMIN registry key.

Understand Database Resident Connection Pooling

The Oracle Net architecture described previously is the *dedicated server* architecture, where each connect request from a user process goes to a listener, and the listener spawns a server process. The server process persists until the session terminates and is dedicated to serving that one session. This architecture is fine for a client-server environment where users log on and stay connected for a long time, making use of the session repeatedly.

Many applications do not follow this model. They have a large number of sessions that may be very short lived and may not log on/off in an orderly fashion. Web applications typify this situation. Many web applications use connection pooling to manage this situation. The application server middle tier software establishes a relatively small number of persistent sessions and passes temporary use of them to users on demand. Using the Database Resident Connection Pool (DRCP) is a technique for implementing similar functionality for middle tier software that cannot do connection pooling, such as some Apache-based products. A DRCP can scale up to tens of thousands of concurrent sessions, which would be beyond the capability of almost any hardware if the dedicated server architecture is being used.

A DRCP is enabled by default, configured to launch a minimum of 4 server processes, up to a maximum of 40. Idle servers will be terminated after 300 seconds. To make use of the pool with Easy Connect name resolution, simply add POOLED to the end of the connect string. Here's an example:

```
sqlplus scott/tiger@jwvaio:1521/orclz:pooled
```

Or you can go through a tnsnames.ora alias such as this:

```
pooled =
    (description =
        (address =
            (protocl=tcp)(host=jwvaio)(port=1521)
        )
        (connect_data=
            (service_name=orclz)(server=pooled)
        )
    )
```

 EXAM TIP When would you use a DRCP? You would use it when many application server sessions connect to the same database schema, but they use it for only short requests.

Configure Communication Between Databases

So far, we've discussed Oracle Net in the context of users connecting to database instances. Oracle Net can also be used for communications between databases. In other words, a user session against one database can execute SQL statements against another database. This is done through a database link. There are several options for creating database links (all to do with security), but a simple example is shown here:

```
create database link prodscott
connect to fred identified by perry using 'prod';
```

This defines a database link from the current database to a remote database identified by the tnsnames.ora connect string PROD and has embedded within it the logon credentials to be used when invoking code through the link. The link exists in the current user's schema, SCOTT, and only SCOTT can use it. When a statement such as the following is issued, the session will transparently launch a session against the remote database, log on to it as the user FRED, and run the query there:

```
select * from score@prodscott;
```

The results will be sent back to the local database session and then returned to the user process. Note that the name resolution occurs on the server, not the client. The client does not need any information regarding the connection details of the remote server; these details will need to be available in a tnsnames.ora file on the server side.

Exercise 14-2: Create and Use a Database Link This exercise assumes that only one database is available, so the link will be a loopback link (out of the one database and back into it). Follow these steps:

1. Connected as user SYSTEM, create a database link.

```
create database link l1
connect to system identified by oracle using 'orcl';
```

(Substitute a working tnsnames alias for 'orcl'. Note that this must be enclosed in single quotes.)

2. Test the link.

```
select * from all_users@l1;
```

3. Troubleshoot.

The most common problems with database links are that the username/password embedded in the link are wrong and that the tnsnames alias does not function. Other possible issues are that the listener is down and that the database dynamic registration with the listener has not yet happened.

Two-Minute Drill

Configure Oracle Net Services

- Oracle Net is configured with a set of three files: tnsnames.ora on the client side, listener.ora on the server side, and (optionally) sqlnet.ora on both sides. The database listener process spawns server sessions in response to connection requests from clients.

- The usual architecture is a dedicated server. There is one server process per user process, and the session consists of a persistent connection between the two. All session data is stored in PGA. An alternative is the shared server architecture, where user processes have persistent connections to dispatchers, which pass requests to a pool of shared server processes. In this architecture, most of the session information is stored in SGA rather than PGA.

Use Tools for Configuring and Managing the Oracle Network

- Two configuration tools are provided: the Net Manager and the simpler Net Configuration Assistant. The listener is controlled with the Listener Control utility, lsnrctl.

Configure Client-Side Network

- Clients need the ability to resolve names into connection details. The details consist of the listening address of the database listener in the form of a hostname or IP address and a port, as well as a database service name or instance name. The usual technique is to use a network alias, resolved by an entry in a tnsnames.ora file.

Understand Database Resident Connection Pooling

- A DRCP can be used for managing the problem of a large number of typically short-lived connections, such as those that come in through a web site. Rather than spawning processes for each session, the DRCP passes out temporary use of one of a fixed number of persistent server processes on demand.

Configure Communication Between Databases

- Database links allow a session against one database to run SQL against another database. In effect, the first database becomes a client to the second. When a query is run through a link, a session is launched over Oracle Net from the first session to the linked database. The name resolution necessary to establish the remote session occurs on the server, not the client.

Self Test

1. Which protocols can Oracle Net 12*c* use? (Choose all correct answers.)

   A. TCP

   B. UDP

   C. SPX/IPX

   D. SDP

   E. TCP with secure sockets

   F. Named pipes

   G. LU6.2

   H. NetBIOS/NetBEUI

2. Where is the division between the client and the server in the Oracle environment? (Choose the best answer.)

   A. Between the instance and the database.

   B. Between the user and the user process.

   C. Between the server process and the instance.

   D. Between the user process and the server process.

   E. The client-server split varies, depending on the stage of the execution cycle.

3. Which of the following statements about listeners is correct? (Choose the best answer.)

   A. A listener can connect you to one instance only.

   B. A listener can connect you to one service only.

   C. Multiple listeners can share one network interface card.

   D. An instance will accept connections only from the listener specified on the local_listener parameter.

4. You have decided to use local naming. Which file (or files) must you create on the client machine? (Choose the best answer.)

   A. tnsnames.ora and sqlnet.ora.

   B. listener.ora only.

   C. tnsnames.ora only.

   D. listener.ora and sqlnet.ora.

   E. None. You can rely on defaults if you are using TCP and your listener is running on port 1521.

5. If you stop your listener, what will happen to sessions that connected through it? (Choose the best answer.)

   A. They will continue if you have configured failover.

   B. They will not be affected in any way.

   C. They will hang until you restart the listener.

   D. You cannot stop a listener if it is in use.

   E. The sessions will error out.

6. Study this tnsnames.ora file:

```
test =
  (description =
    (address_list =
      (address = (protocol = tcp)(host = serv2)(port = 1521))
    )
    (connect_data =
      (service_name = prod)
    )
  )
prod =
  (description =
    (address_list =
      (address = (protocol = tcp)(host = serv1)(port = 1521))
    )
    (connect_data =
      (service_name = prod)
    )
  )
dev =
  (description =
    (address_list =
      (address = (protocol = tcp)(host = serv2)(port = 1521))
    )
```

```
    (connect_data =
      (service_name = dev)
    )
  )
```

Which of the following statements are correct about the connect strings test, prod, and dev? (Choose all correct answers.)

A. All three are valid.

B. All three can succeed only if the instances are set up for dynamic instance registration.

C. The test connection will fail because the connect string doesn't match the service name.

D. There will be a port conflict on serv2 because prod and dev try to use the same port.

7. Consider this line from a listener.ora file:

```
L1=(description=(address=(protocol=tcp)(host=serv1)(port=1521)))
```

What will happen if you issue the following connect string?

```
connect scott/tiger@L1
```

(Choose the best answer.)

A. You will be connected to the instance L1.

B. You will be connected to an instance only if dynamic instance registration is working.

C. You can't tell—it depends on how the client side is configured.

D. If you are logged on to the server machine, IPC will connect you to the local instance.

E. The connection will fail if the listener is not started.

8. Which of these tools can configure a listener.ora file? (Choose two answers.)

A. The Database Configuration Assistant

B. Database Express

C. The lsnrctl utility

D. The Net Configuration Assistant

E. The Net Manager

9. Consider this tnsnames.ora net service name:

```
orcl=(description=
(address=(protocol=tcp)(host=dbserv1)(port=(1521))
(connect_data=(service_name=orcl)(server=dedicated))
)
```

What will happen if shared server is configured and this net service name is used? (Choose the best answer.)

A. The connect attempt will fail.

B. The connect will succeed with a shared server connection.

C. The connect will succeed with a dedicated server connection.

D. The connect will succeed only for SYSDBA or SYSOPER logons.

10. Under what circumstances would a connection through a Database Resident Connection Pool (SERVER=POOLED) connection be suitable?

    A. When an application server needs a pool of persistent connections

    B. When many short-lived connections share a schema

    C. When many short-lived connections connect to different schemas

    D. When many persistent connections make infrequent requests

11. When updating rows locally and through a database link in one transaction, what must you do to ensure a two-phase commit?

    A. Nothing special because two-phase commit is automatic.

    B. Issue a COMMIT locally first and then through the database link.

    C. Issue a COMMIT through the link and then locally.

    D. It is not possible to interleave local and remote updates.

Self Test Answers

1. ☑ **A, D, E, F.** TCP, SDP, TCPS, and NMP are the supported protocols with the current release.
   ☒ **B, C, G,** and **H** are incorrect. **B** and **H** are incorrect because UDP and NetBIOS/NetBEUI have never been supported. **C** and **G** are incorrect because SPX and LU6.2 are no longer supported.

2. ☑ **D.** The client-server split is between the user process and server process.
   ☒ **A, B, C,** and **E** are incorrect. These all misrepresent the client-server architecture.

3. ☑ **C.** Many listeners can share one address, if they use different ports.
   ☒ **A, B,** and **D** are incorrect. **A** is incorrect because one listener can launch sessions against many instances. **B** is incorrect because a listener can connect you to a registered service. **D** is incorrect because the local_listener parameter controls which listener the instance will register with dynamically; it will also accept connections from any listener that has it statically registered.

4. ☑ **C.** This is the only required client-side file for local naming.
   ☒ **A, B, D,** and **E** are incorrect. **A** is incorrect because SQLNET.ORA is not essential. **B** and **D** are incorrect because they refer to server-side files. **E** is incorrect because some configuration is always necessary for local naming (though not for Easy Connect).

5. ☑ **B**. The listener establishes connections but is not needed for their maintenance.
☒ **A, C, D**, and **E** are incorrect. These are all incorrect because they assume that the listener is necessary for the continuance of an established session.

6. ☑ **A** and **B**. All three are valid but will work only if the services are registered with the listeners.
☒ **C** and **D** are incorrect. **C** is incorrect because there doesn't need to be a connection between the alias used in a connect string and the service name. **D** is incorrect because many services can be accessible through a single listening port.

7. ☑ **C**. Some client-side configuration is necessary, and without knowing what it is, you have no idea what will happen.
☒ **A, B, D**, and **E** are incorrect. **A** is incorrect because the connect string could connect to any instance. **B** is incorrect because although the listener L1 must use dynamic registration, this is not enough. **D** is incorrect because the use of IPC to bypass the listener is not relevant. **E** is incorrect because (although certainly true) you don't know if it is relevant.

8. ☑ **D, E**. Both netca and netman offer a graphical interface for editing the listener.ora file.
☒ **A, B**, and **C** are incorrect. **A** is incorrect because the Database Configuration Assistant (DBCA) cannot edit a listener, though it will edit the tnsnames.ora file. **B** is incorrect because Database Express has no capability for editing any file. **C** is incorrect because the lsnrctl utility can control a listener but not configure the listener.ora file.

9. ☑ **C**. The SERVER=DEDICATED directive requests a dedicated server, even if shared server is configured.
☒ **A, B**, and **D** are incorrect. **A** and **B** are incorrect because the client configuration takes precedence over the server configuration. **D** is incorrect because anyone can use this connect string. It will be necessary to use it rather than a shared server connection for SYSDBA connections; otherwise, startup/shutdown commands will fail.

10. ☑ **B**. This is exactly the environment for which DRCP is designed: many short connections to a shared schema.
☒ **A, C**, and **D** are incorrect. **A** is incorrect because an application server would manage the pool itself. **C** is incorrect because a DRCP will pool connections to the same schema. **D** is incorrect because persistent connections would tie up the pooled servers.

11. ☑ **A**. Two-phase commit for distributed transactions is fully automatic.
☒ **B, C**, and **D** are incorrect. **B** and **C** are incorrect because a distributed transaction is, syntactically, committed exactly as a local transaction. **D** is incorrect because distributed transactions are no problem in the Oracle environment.

CHAPTER 15

Oracle Storage

Exam Objectives

- 062.5.1   Describe the Storage of Table Row Data in Blocks
- 062.5.2   Create and Manage Tablespaces
- 062.15.1   Explain How Oracle Database Server Automatically Manages Space
- 062.15.2   Save Space by Using Compression
- 062.15.3   Proactively Monitor and Manage Tablespace Space Usage
- 062.15.4   Use the Segment Advisor
- 062.15.5   Reclaim Wasted Space from Tables and Indexes by Using the Segment Shrink Functionality
- 062.15.6   Manage Resumable Space Allocation

Users never see a physical datafile. All they see are logical segments. System administrators never see a logical segment. All they see are physical datafiles. The Oracle database provides complete abstraction of logical storage from physical. This is one of the requirements of the relational database paradigm. As a database administrator (DBA), you must be aware of the relationship between the logical and physical storage. Monitoring and administering these structures, a task often described as *space management,* used to be a huge part of a DBA's workload. The facilities provided in recent releases of the database can automate space management to a certain extent, and they can certainly let the DBA set up storage in ways that will reduce the maintenance workload considerably. Also, some facilities will permit more efficient use of space, such as compression and segment reorganization through the segment shrink capability.

When a user hits a space limit, an error will be returned, and the statement that hit the limit will fail. This situation should, of course, be avoided, but if it does occur, the user can be protected by enabling the resumable space allocation facility.

Describe the Storage of Table Row Data in Blocks

At the lowest level, rows are stored in blocks. But there are several layers of storage above that, all of which must be understood before drilling down to the level of the row in the block. Start at the top and work down.

The Oracle Data Storage Model

The separation of logical from physical storage is a necessary part of the relational database paradigm. It means that programmers have no way of physically referencing an item of data, thus eliminating any dependency on a specific machine. The relational paradigm states that programmers should address only logical structures and let the database manage the mapping to physical structures. This means that physical storage can be reorganized or the whole database can be moved to completely different hardware and operating system, and the application will not be aware of any change.

Figure 15-1 shows the Oracle storage model sketched as an entity-relationship diagram, with the logical structures to the left and the physical structures to the right.

There is one relationship, shown as a dotted line. This is a many-to-many relationship between segments and datafiles. This relationship is dotted because it shouldn't be there. As good relational engineers, DBAs do not permit many-to-many relationships. Resolving this relationship into a normalized structure is what the storage model is all about.

The tablespace entity resolves the many-to-many relationship between segments and datafiles. One tablespace can contain many segments and be made up of many datafiles. This means that any one segment may be spread across multiple datafiles, and any one datafile may contain all of or parts of many segments. This solves many storage challenges. Some older database management systems used a one-to-one relationship between segments and files; every table or index would be stored as a separate file. This raised two dreadful problems for large systems. First, an application might well have thousands of tables and even more indexes; managing many thousands of files was an appalling task for the system administrators. Second, the maximum size of a table is limited by the maximum size of a file. Even if modern operating

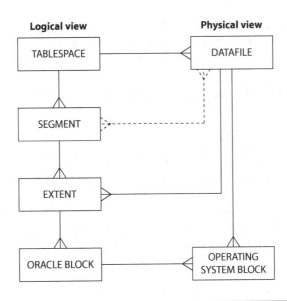

Logical view   **Physical view**

Figure 15-1   The Oracle storage model

systems do not have any practical limits, there may be limitations imposed by the underlying hardware environment. Use of tablespaces bypasses both these problems. Tablespaces are identified by name, unique in the database.

The segment entity represents any database object that stores data and therefore requires space in a tablespace. Your typical segment is a table, but there are other segment types, notably index segments and undo segments. Any one segment can exist in only one tablespace, but the tablespace can spread it across all the files making up the tablespace. This means that the tables' sizes are not subject to any limitations imposed by the environment on maximum file size. Because many segments can share a single tablespace, it becomes possible to have far more segments than there are datafiles. Segments are schema objects, identified by the segment name and qualified with the owning schema name. Note that programmatic schema objects (such as PL/SQL procedures, views, or sequences) are not segments; they do not store data, and they exist as structures within the data dictionary.

The Oracle block is the unit of input/output (I/O) for the database. Datafiles are formatted into Oracle blocks, consecutively numbered. The size of the Oracle blocks is fixed for a tablespace (generally speaking, it is the same for all tablespaces in the database); the default is 8KB. A row might be only a couple hundred bytes, so there could be many rows stored in one block. However, when a session wants a row, the whole block will be read from disk into the database buffer cache. Similarly, if just one column of one row has been changed in the database buffer cache, the database writer (DBWn) will (eventually) write the whole block back into the datafile from which it came, overwriting the previous version. The size of an Oracle block can range from 2KB to 16KB on Linux or Windows and to 32KB on some other operating systems. The block size is controlled by the parameter DB_BLOCK_SIZE. This can never be changed after database creation because it is used to format the datafiles that make up the SYSTEM tablespace. If it becomes apparent later that the block size is inappropriate, the only course of action is to create a new database and transfer everything into it. A block is uniquely identified by its number within a datafile; the block number alone is not enough.

 EXAM TIP The DB_BLOCK_SIZE is set at database creation and can never be changed.

Managing space one block at a time would be a crippling task, so blocks are grouped into extents. An *extent* is a set of consecutively numbered Oracle blocks within one datafile. Every segment will consist of one or more extents, also consecutively numbered. These extents may be in any and all of the datafiles that make up the tablespace. An extent can be identified from either the dimension of the segment (extents are consecutively numbered per segment, starting from zero) or the dimension of the datafile (every extent is in one file, starting at a certain Oracle block number).

A datafile is physically made up of a number of operating system blocks. How datafiles and the operating system blocks are structured is entirely dependent on the operating system's file system. Some file systems have well-known limitations and are therefore not widely used for modern systems (for example, the old MS-DOS FAT file system could handle files up to only 4GB, and only 512 of them per directory). Most databases will be installed on file systems with no practical limits, such as NTFS on Windows and ext3 on Linux. The alternatives to file systems for datafile storage are raw devices or ASM. Raw devices are no longer supported by Oracle for datafile storage. ASM is described in Chapter 3.

An operating system block is the unit of I/O for your file system. A process might want to read only one byte from disk, but the I/O system will have to read an operating system block. The operating system block size is configurable for some file systems (for example, when formatting an NTFS file system, you can choose from 512 bytes to 64KB), but typically system administrators leave it at the default (512 bytes for NTFS, 1KB for ext3). This is why the relationship between Oracle blocks and operating system blocks is usually one-to-many, as shown in Figure 15-1. There is no reason not to match the operating system block size to the Oracle block size if your file system lets you do this. A configuration that should always be avoided is one where the operating system blocks are bigger than the Oracle blocks.

Segments, Extents, Blocks, and Rows

Data is stored in segments. The data dictionary view DBA_SEGMENTS describes every segment in the database. This query shows the segment types in a simple database—the counts are low because there is no real application installed:

```
SQL> select segment_type,count(1) from dba_segments
     group by segment_type
     order by segment_type;
SEGMENT_TYPE        COUNT(1)
------------------ ----------
CLUSTER                  10
INDEX                  3185
INDEX PARTITION         324
LOB PARTITION             7
LOBINDEX                760
```

```
LOBSEGMENT              760
NESTED TABLE            29
ROLLBACK                1
TABLE                   2193
TABLE PARTITION         164
TYPE2 UNDO              10
11 rows selected.
SQL>
```

In brief, and in the order they are most likely to concern a DBA, these segment types are as follows:

- **TABLE**   These are the heap-structured table; they consist of variable-length rows in random order. Even though a typical segment is a table segment, never forget that the table is not the segment and that there are more complex table organizations that use other segment types.

- **INDEX**   Indexes are sorted lists of key values, each with a pointer, the ROWID, to the physical location of the row. The ROWID specifies which Oracle block of which datafile the row is in, as well as the row number within the block.

- **TYPE2 UNDO**   These are the undo segments (no one refers to them as "type2 undo" segments) that store the prechange versions of data necessary for providing transactional integrity: rollback, read consistency, and isolation.

- **TABLE PARTITION**   A table can be divided into many partitions. If this is done, then the partitions will be individual segments, and the table itself will not be a segment at all; it exists only as the total of its partitions. Each table partition of a heap table is itself structured as a heap table in its own segment. These segments can be in different tablespaces, meaning that it becomes possible to spread one table across multiple tablespaces.

- **INDEX PARTITION**   An index will be in one segment by default, but indexes can be partitioned. If you are partitioning your tables, you will usually partition the indexes on those tables as well.

- **LOBSEGMENT, LOBINDEX, LOB PARTITION**   If a column is defined as a large object data type, then only a pointer is stored in the table itself; the pointer is to an entry in a separate segment where the column data actually resides. LOBs can have indexes built on them for rapid access to data within the objects, and LOBs can also be partitioned.

- **CLUSTER**   A cluster is a segment that can contain several tables. In contrast with partitioning, which lets you spread one table across many segments, clustering lets you denormalize many tables into one segment.

- **NESTED TABLE**   If a column of a table is defined as a user-defined object type that itself has columns, then the column can be stored in its own segment as a nested table.

- **ROLLBACK**   Rollback segments should not be used in normal running from release 9*i* onward. Release 9*i* introduced automatic undo management, which is based on undo segments. There will always be one rollback segment that protects the transactions used to create a database (this is necessary because at that point, no undo segments exist), but it shouldn't be used subsequently.

Every segment has one or more extents. When a segment is created, Oracle will allocate an extent to it in whatever tablespace is specified. Eventually, as data is entered, the extent will fill. Oracle will then allocate a second extent in the same tablespace, but not necessarily in the same datafile. If you know that a segment is going to need more space, you can manually allocate an extent. Figure 15-2 shows how to identify precisely where each extent of a segment is.

In the figure, the first command creates the table SCOTT.NEWTAB, relying completely on defaults for the storage. Then a query against DBA_EXTENTS shows that the segment consists of just one extent, extent 0. This extent is in file 6 and is eight blocks long. The first of the eight blocks is block 224. The size of the extent is 64KB, which shows that the block size is 8KB. The next command forces Oracle to allocate another extent to the segment, even though the first extent will not be full. The next query shows that this new extent, extent 1, is also in file 6 and starts immediately after extent 0. Note that it is not clear from this example whether the tablespace consists of multiple datafiles because the algorithm Oracle uses to work out where to assign the next extent does not simply use datafiles in turn. If the tablespace does consist of multiple datafiles, you can override Oracle's choice with this syntax:

```
ALTER TABLE tablename ALLOCATE EXTENT STORAGE (DATAFILE 'filename');
```

The last query in Figure 15-2 goes to the view DBA_DATA_FILES to determine the name of the file in which the extents were allocated and the name of the tablespace to which the datafile belongs. To identify the table's tablespace, you can also query DBA_SEGMENTS.

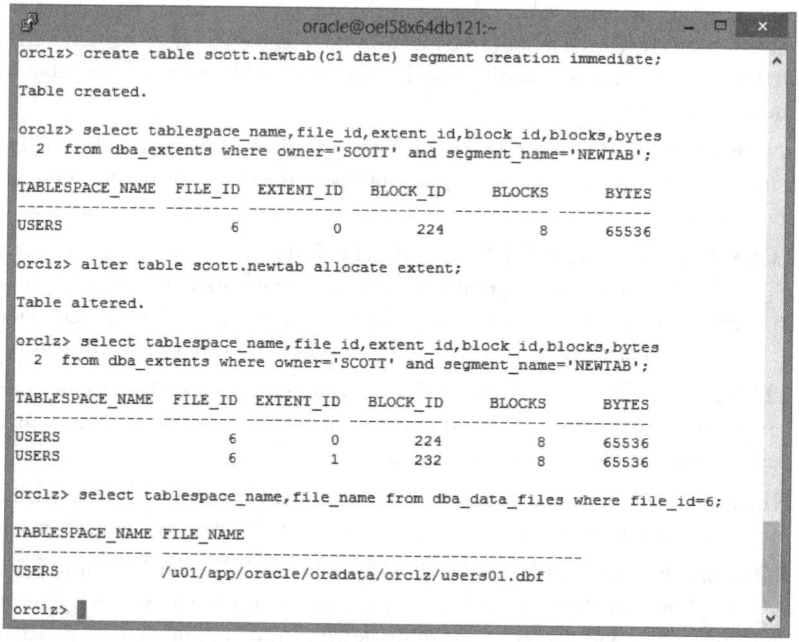

Figure 15-2 Determining the physical location of a segment's extents

TIP   You can query DBA_TABLES to find out in which tablespace a table resides, but this will work only for nonpartitioned tables—not for partitioned tables, where each partition is its own segment and can be in a different tablespace. Partitioning lets one table (stored as multiple segments) span tablespaces.

An extent consists of a set of consecutively numbered blocks. Each block will have a header area and a data area. The header is of variable size and grows downward, if necessary, from the top of the block. Among other things, it contains a row directory that lists where in the block each row begins and row locking information. The data area fills from the bottom up. Between the two there may (or may not) be an area of free space. Events that will cause a block's header to grow include inserting and locking rows. The data area will initially be empty and will fill as rows are inserted (or index keys are inserted, in the case of a block of an index segment). The free space does get fragmented as rows are inserted, deleted, and updated (which may cause a row's size to change), but that is of no significance because all this happens in memory, after the block has been copied into a buffer in the database buffer cache. The free space is coalesced into a contiguous area, when necessary, and always before the DBW*n* writes the block back to its datafile.

Exercise 15-1: Investigate Storage Structures   In this exercise, you will run various queries to determine storage characteristics. Follow these steps:

1. Determine the physical structures of your database.

```
select name from v$controlfile;
select member,bytes from v$logfile
join v$log using (group#);
select t.name,d.name,d.bytes from v$tablespace t
join v$datafile d using (ts#)
union all
select t.name,d.name,d.bytes from v$tablespace t
join v$tempfile d using (ts#);
select tablespace_name,t.contents,d.file_name,d.bytes
from dba_tablespaces t
join dba_data_files d using (tablespace_name)
union all
select tablespace_name,t.contents,d.file_name,d.bytes
from dba_tablespaces t
join dba_temp_files d using (tablespace_name);
```

2. Create a table and determine where it is stored.

```
create table system.mytable as select * from
 all_objects;select tablespace_name from dba_tables
where owner='SYSTEM' and table_name='MYTABLE';
select tablespace_name,segment_type from dba_segments
where owner='SYSTEM' and segment_name='MYTABLE';
select file_name,extent_id,block_id from dba_data_files
join dba_extents using (file_id)
where owner='SYSTEM' and segment_name='MYTABLE';
```

What size are the extents? By default, this is the size that will be used for the first 16 extents of a segment, after which extents of 128 blocks will be allocated.

3. Move the table.

```
alter table system.mytable move tablespace sysaux;
```

Where are the extents now?

4. Tidy up.

```
drop table system.mytable;
```

Create and Manage Tablespaces

Tablespaces are repositories for schema data, including the data dictionary. All databases must have a SYSTEM tablespace and a SYSAUX tablespace, as well as (for practical purposes) a temporary tablespace and an undo tablespace. These four will usually have been created when the database was created. Subsequently, the DBA may create many more tablespaces for user data and possibly additional tablespaces for undo and temporary data.

Creating Tablespaces

To create a tablespace with Database Express, from the database home page click the Storage tab and then the Tablespaces link. Figure 15-3 shows the result for the default database.

There are six tablespaces shown in the figure. For each tablespace, identified by name, the window shows the following:

- **Size**   This is the current size of the datafile (or datafiles) assigned to the tablespace. It is based on the current size, not the maximum size to which it may be allowed to expand.

- **Free space**   The space currently available within the tablespace.

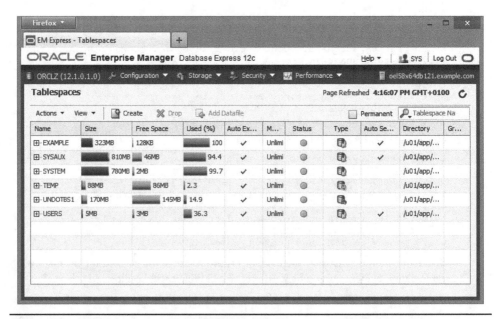

Figure 15-3   The tablespaces in the default General Purpose template database

- **Used (%)**   This is the space occupied by segments in the tablespace that cannot be reclaimed.
- **Auto Extend**   Indicates whether any files of the tablespace have the automatic extension facility enabled (they all do).
- **Maximum size**   If autoextensible, to what limit? In the figure, all are Unlimited, meaning the maximum possible.
- **Status**   Green indicates that the tablespace is online and therefore that the objects within it should be accessible. An offline tablespace would be indicated in red.
- **Type**   An icon indicating whether the tablespace stores permanent objects, temporary objects, or undo segments.
- **Auto segment management**   A check mark indicates that automatic segment space management is used by the tablespace.

You could also glean this information by querying the data dictionary views DBA_ TABLESPACES, DBA_DATA_FILES, DBA_TEMP_FILES, and DBA_FREE_SPACE.

In Database Express, click the Actions button for a drop-down menu including Create to create a tablespace. The Create Tablespace window prompts for a tablespace name as well as the type of data (permanent, temporary, or undo) to be stored within it. The dialog continues with prompts for the datafile (or datafiles) definition and various attributes.

Database Express has a SHOW SQL button in most windows. This means you can use it to construct syntactically correct statements that you can save (and edit) for future, scripted use. This is a typical statement generated by Database Express (line numbers added):

```
1 CREATE SMALLFILE TABLESPACE "JWTS"
2   DATAFILE '/u01/app/oracle/oradata/orclzjwts01.dbf'
3   SIZE 100M AUTOEXTEND ON NEXT 10M MAXSIZE 200M
4   LOGGIN
5   DEFAULT NOCOMPRESS
6   ONLINE
7   EXTENT MANAGEMENT LOCAL AUTOALLOCATE
8   SEGMENT SPACE MANAGEMENT AUTO;
```

Look at this command line by line.

Line 1	The tablespace is a SMALLFILE tablespace. This means it can consist of many datafiles. The alternative is BIGFILE, in which case it would be impossible to add a second datafile later (though the first file could be resized). SMALLFILE is the default.
Line 2	The datafile name and location.
Line 3	The datafile will be created as 100MB but when full can automatically extend in 10MB increments to a maximum of 200MB. By default, automatic extension is not enabled.
Line 4	All operations on segments in the tablespace will generate redo, unless it is explicitly disabled; this is the default. It is possible to disable redo generation for a few operations (such as index generation).
Line 5	Objects in the tablespace will not be compressed. This is the default.
Line 6	The tablespace will be online (available for use) immediately. This is the default.
Line 7	The tablespace will use bitmaps for allocating extents, whose size will be set automatically; this is the default.
Line 8	Segments in the tablespace will use bitmaps for tracking block usage; this is the default.

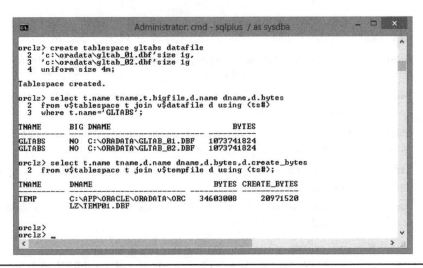

Figure 15-4   Tablespace creation and verification with SQL*Plus

Figure 15-4 shows a typical tablespace creation statement, as executed from the SQL*Plus command line, with a query confirming the result.

The tablespace GLTABS consists of two datafiles, neither of which will autoextend. The only deviation from defaults has been to specify a uniform extent size of 4MB. The first query in the figure shows that the tablespace is not a bigfile tablespace; if it were, it would not have been possible to define two datafiles.

The second query in the figure investigates the TEMP tablespace, used by the database for storing temporary objects. It is important to note that temporary tablespaces use *tempfiles,* not datafiles. Tempfiles are listed in the views V$TEMPFILE and DBA_TEMP_FILES, whereas datafiles are listed in V$DATAFILE and DBA_DATA_FILES. Also note that the V$ views and the DBA views give different information. As the query shows, you can query V$TABLESPACE to find if a tablespace is a bigfile tablespace, and you can query V$TEMPFILE (or V$DATAFILE) to find how big a file was at creation time. This information is not shown in the DBA views. However, the DBA views give the detail of extent management and segment space management. The different information available in the views is because some information is stored only in the controlfile (and therefore visible only in V$ views) and some is stored only in the data dictionary (and therefore visible only in DBA views). Other information is duplicated.

Exercise 15-2: Create, Alter, and Drop Tablespaces   In this exercise, you will create tablespaces and change their characteristics. Follow these steps:

1. Connect to the database as user SYSTEM.

2. Create a tablespace in a suitable directory—any directory on which the Oracle owner has write permission will do. This is an example:

```
create tablespace newtbs
datafile '/home/db12c/oradata/newtbs_01.dbf' size 10m
extent management local autoallocate
segment space management auto;
```

This command specifies the options that are the default. Nonetheless, it may be considered good practice to do this to make the statement self-documenting.

3. Create a table in the new tablespace and determine the size of the first extent.

```
create table newtab(c1 date) tablespace newtbs;
select extent_id,bytes from dba_extents
where owner='SYSTEM' and segment_name='NEWTAB';
```

4. Add extents manually and observe the size of each new extent by repeatedly executing the command

```
alter table newtab allocate extent;
```

followed by the query from step 3. Note the point at which the extent size increases.

5. Take the tablespace offline, observe the effect, and bring it back online.

```
alter tablespace newtbs offline;
delete newtab;
drop newtab;
alter tablespace newtbs online;
```

6. Make the tablespace read-only, observe the effect, and make it read-write again.

```
alter tablespace newtbs read only;
delete newtab;
drop newtab;
alter tablespace newtbs read write;
```

7. Tidy up by issuing the following command:

```
drop tablespace newtbs including contents and datafiles;
```

Altering Tablespaces

These are the changes commonly made to tablespaces after creation:

- Renaming
- Taking online and offline
- Flagging as read-write or read-only
- Resizing

Rename a Tablespace and Its Datafiles

The syntax is as follows:

```
ALTER TABLESPACE oldname RENAME TO newname;
```

This is simple but can cause problems later. Many sites rely on naming conventions to relate tablespaces to their datafiles. All the examples in this chapter do just that; they embed the name of the tablespace in the name of the datafiles. Oracle doesn't care. Internally, it maintains the relationships by using the tablespace number and the datafile (or tempfile) number. These are visible as the columns V$TABLESPACE.TS# and V$DATAFILE.FILE#. If your site does rely on naming conventions, it will be necessary to rename the files as well.

A tablespace can be renamed while it is in use, but to rename a datafile, it must be offline. This is because the file must be renamed at the operating system level, as well as within the

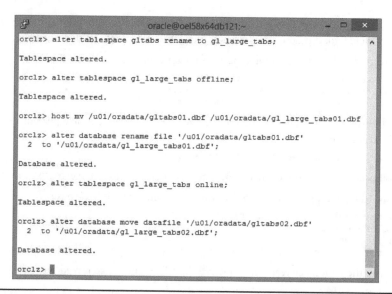

Figure 15-5 Renaming a tablespace and its datafiles

Oracle environment, and this can't be done if the file is open. All the file handles would become invalid. It is, however, possible to move a datafile online.

Figure 15-5 shows an example of the whole process, using the GLTBS tablespace created in Figure 15-4.

In the figure, the first command renames the tablespace. Then the tablespace is taken offline (as described in the next section), and an operating system command renames one of the datafiles in the file system. An ALTER DATABASE command changes the filename as recorded within the controlfile so that Oracle will be able to find it. Finally, the tablespace is brought back online. The last command shows the alternative approach; it physically moves the other file and renames it (both at the file system level and within the controlfile) in one operation with zero downtime.

Taking a Tablespace Online or Offline

An *online* tablespace or datafile is available for use; an *offline* tablespace or datafile exists as a definition in the data dictionary and the controlfile but cannot be used. It is possible for a tablespace to be online but one or more of its datafiles to be offline. This is a situation that can produce interesting results and should generally be avoided. Here is the syntax for taking a tablespace offline:

```
ALTER TABLESPACE tablespacename
OFFLINE [ NORMAL | IMMEDIATE | TEMPORARY];
```

A NORMAL offline (which is the default) will force a checkpoint for all the tablespace's datafiles. Every dirty buffer in the database buffer cache that contains a block from the tablespace will be written to its datafile, and then the tablespace and the datafiles are taken offline.

At the other extreme is IMMEDIATE, which offlines the tablespace and the datafiles immediately, without flushing any dirty buffers. Following this, the datafiles will be corrupted (they may be missing committed changes) and will have to be recovered by applying change vectors from the redo log before the tablespace can be brought back online. Clearly, this is a drastic operation. It would normally be done only if a file has become damaged so that the checkpoint cannot be completed. The process of recovery is detailed in Chapter 22. You cannot take a tablespace offline using IMMEDIATE unless media recovery through archive logging has been enabled.

A TEMPORARY offline will checkpoint all the files that can be checkpointed and then take them and the tablespace offline in an orderly fashion. Any damaged files will be offlined immediately. If just some of the tablespace's datafiles have been damaged, this will limit the number of files that will need to be recovered.

Use the following command to bring the tablespace back online:

```
ALTER TABLESPACE tablespacename ONLINE;
```

Mark a Tablespace as Read-Only

To see the effect of making a tablespace read-only, study Figure 15-6.

The syntax is completely self-explanatory.

```
ALTER TABLESPACE tablespacename [READ ONLY | READ WRITE] ;
```

After a tablespace is made read-only, none of the objects within it can be changed with Data Manipulation Language (DML) statements, as demonstrated in the figure. But they can be dropped. This is a little disconcerting but makes perfect sense when you think it through. Dropping a table doesn't actually affect the table. It is a transaction against the data dictionary that deletes the rows that describe the table and its columns; the data dictionary is in the SYSTEM tablespace, and that is not read-only.

```
orclz> create table test_tab(c1 date) tablespace gl_large_tabs;

Table created.

orclz> alter tablespace gl_large_tabs read only;

Tablespace altered.

orclz> insert into test_tab values(sysdate);
insert into test_tab values(sysdate)
            *
ERROR at line 1:
ORA-00372: file 5 cannot be modified at this time
ORA-01110: data file 5: '/u01/oradata/gl_large_tabs01.dbf'


orclz> drop table test_tab;

Table dropped.

orclz>
```

Figure 15-6 Operations on a read-only tablespace

TIP Making a tablespace read-only can have advantages for backup and restore operations. Oracle will be aware that the tablespace contents cannot change and that it may not therefore be necessary to back up the tablespace repeatedly.

Resizing a Tablespace

You can resize a tablespace either by adding datafiles to it or by adjusting the size of the existing datafiles. You can resize datafiles upward automatically as necessary if the AUTOEXTEND syntax was used at file creation time. Otherwise, you have to do it manually with an ALTER DATABASE command.

```
ALTER DATABASE DATAFILE 'filename' RESIZE n[M|G|T];
```

The M, G, and T refer to the units of size for the file (megabytes, gigabytes, and terabytes, respectively). This is an example:

```
alter database datafile '/oradata/users02.dbf' resize 10m;
```

From the syntax, you do not know whether the file is being made larger or smaller. An upward resize can succeed only if there is enough space in the file system, and a resize downward can succeed only if the space in the file is not already in use by extents allocated to a segment.

To add another datafile of 2GB in size to a tablespace, use the following command:

```
alter tablespace gl_large_tabs
add datafile 'D:\ORADATA\GL_LARGE_TABS_03.DBF' size 2g;
```

You can include clauses for automatic extension when creating the file. To enable automatic extension later, use a command such as this:

```
alter database datafile 'D:\ORADATA\GL_LARGE_TABS_03.DBF'
autoextend on next 100m maxsize 4g;
```

This will allow the file to double in size, increasing 100MB at a time.

A bigfile tablespace can be resized at the tablespace level, rather than the datafile level. This is because Oracle knows that the tablespace can have only one datafile, and therefore there is no ambiguity about which datafile should be resized. Figure 15-7 shows how to create and resize a bigfile tablespace.

Figure 15-7
Working with bigfile
tablespaces

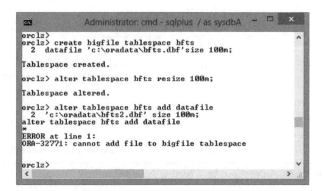

You might think that limiting a tablespace to one file only would limit the storage capacity of the tablespace, but this is not the case. A smallfile tablespace can consist of up to 1,022 datafiles, each of which can be up to 4 million blocks. A bigfile tablespace can be one datafile of up to 4 billion blocks, so there is really no difference.

Dropping Tablespaces

To drop a tablespace, use the DROP TABLESPACE command. The syntax is as follows:

```
DROP TABLESPACE tablespacename
[INCLUDING CONTENTS [AND DATAFILES] ] ;
```

If the INCLUDING CONTENTS keywords are not specified, the drop will fail if there are any objects in the tablespace. Using these keywords instructs Oracle to drop the objects first and then to drop the tablespace. Even this will fail in some circumstances, such as when the tablespace contains a table that is the parent in a foreign key relationship with a table in another tablespace.

If the AND DATAFILES keywords are not specified, the tablespace and its contents will be dropped, but the datafiles will continue to exist on disk. Oracle will know nothing about them anymore, and they will have to be deleted with operating system commands.

Extent Management

The extent management method is set per tablespace and applies to all segments in the tablespace. There are two techniques for managing extent usage: dictionary management and local management. The difference is clear: Local management should always be used; dictionary management should never be used. Dictionary-managed extent management is still supported, but it is just a holdover from previous releases.

Dictionary extent management uses two tables in the data dictionary. SYS.UET$ has rows describing used extents, and SYS.FET$ has rows describing free extents. Every time the database needs to allocate an extent to a segment, it must search FET$ to find an appropriate bit of free space and then carry out DML operations against FET$ and UET$ to allocate it to the segment. This mechanism causes problems with performance because all space management operations in the database (many of which could be initiated concurrently) must serialize on the code that constructs the transactions.

Local extent management was introduced with release 8*i* and became the default with release 9*i*. It uses bitmaps stored in each datafile. Each bit in the bitmap covers a range of blocks, and when space is allocated, the appropriate bits are changed from zero to one. This mechanism is far more efficient than the transaction-based mechanism of dictionary management. The cost of assigning extents is amortized across bitmaps in every datafile that can be updated concurrently, rather than being concentrated (and serialized) on the two tables.

When creating a locally managed tablespace, an important option is *uniform size*. If uniform is specified, then every extent ever allocated in the tablespace will be that size. This can make the space management highly efficient because the block ranges covered by each bit can be larger, namely, only one bit per extent. Consider this statement:

```
create tablespace large_tabs
datafile 'large_tabs_01.dbf' size 10g
extent management local uniform size 160m;
```

Every extent allocated in this tablespace will be 160MB, so there will be about 64 of them. The bitmap needs only 64 bits, and 160MB of space can be allocated by updating just one bit. This is going to be very efficient—provided that the segments in the tablespace are large. If a segment were created that needed space for only a few rows, it would still get an extent of 160MB. Small objects need their own tablespace.

```
create tablespace small_tabs
datafile 'small_tabs_01.dbf' size 1g
extent management local uniform size 160k;
```

Here is the alternative (and default) syntax:

```
create tablespace any_tabs
datafile 'any_tabs_01.dbf' size 10g
extent management local autoallocate;
```

When segments are created in this tablespace, Oracle will allocate an eight-block (64KB) extent. As a segment grows and requires more extents, Oracle will allocate extents of this size up to 16 extents, after which it will allocate 128-block (1MB) extents. Thus, fast-growing segments will tend to be given space in larger chunks.

 TIP Oracle Corporation recommends AUTOALLOCATE, but if you know how big segments are likely to be and can place them accordingly, UNIFORM SIZE may well be the best option. Many applications are designed in this manner.

It is possible that if a database has been upgraded from previous versions, it will include dictionary-managed tablespaces. Check this with the following query:

```
select tablespace_name, extent_management
from dba_tablespaces;
```

Any dictionary-managed tablespaces should be converted to local management with this PL/SQL procedure call:

```
execute dbms_space_admin.tablespace_migrate_to_local(-
'tablespacename');
```

Segment Space Management

The segment space management method is set per tablespace and applies to all segments in the tablespace. There are two techniques for managing segment space usage: manual and automatic. The difference is clear: Automatic management should always be used; manual management should never be used. Manual segment space management is still supported but never recommended. It is a remnant from previous releases.

Automatic segment space management was introduced with release 9i and became the default in release 11g. Every segment created in an automatic management tablespace has a set of bitmaps that describe how full each block is. There are five bitmaps for each segment, and each block will appear on exactly one bitmap. The bitmaps track the space used in bands; there is a bitmap for full blocks, and there are bitmaps for blocks that are 75 percent to 100 percent used, 50 percent to 75 percent used, 25 percent to 50 percent used, and 0 percent to 25 percent used. When searching for a block into which to insert a row, the session server process will look at the size of the row to determine which bitmap to search. For instance, if the block size is 4KB and the row to be inserted is 1,500 bytes, an appropriate block will be found by searching the "25 percent to 50 percent" bitmap. Every block on this bitmap is guaranteed to have at least 2 KB of free space. As rows are inserted, are deleted, or change size through updates, the bitmaps get updated accordingly.

The old manual space management method used a simple list, known as the *freelist,* that stated which blocks were available for insert but without any information on how full they were. This method could cause excessive activity because blocks had to be tested for space at insert time, and it often resulted in a large proportion of wasted space.

To see whether any tablespaces are using manual management, run this query:

```
select tablespace_name,segment_space_management
from dba_tablespaces;
```

The only tablespaces that should be returned by this query are SYSTEM, undo tablespaces, and temporary tablespaces. The segments in these tablespaces are managed by Oracle, which does not require assistance from any automatic mechanism. It is not possible to convert tablespaces from manual to automatic segment space management. The only way is to create a new tablespace using automatic segment space management, move the segments into it (at which point the bitmap will be generated), and drop the old tablespaces.

Oracle Managed Files

Using Oracle Managed Files (OMF) is intended to remove the necessity for the DBA to have any knowledge of the file systems. The creation of database files can be fully automated. To enable OMF, set some or all of these instance parameters:

```
DB_CREATE_FILE_DEST
DB_CREATE_ONLINE_LOG_DEST_1
DB_CREATE_ONLINE_LOG_DEST_2
DB_CREATE_ONLINE_LOG_DEST_3
DB_CREATE_ONLINE_LOG_DEST_4
DB_CREATE_ONLINE_LOG_DEST_5
DB_RECOVERY_FILE_DEST
```

The DB_CREATE_FILE_DEST parameter specifies a default location for all datafiles and online redo log files. The DB_CREATE_ONLINE_LOG_DEST_n parameters specify a default location for online redo log files, taking precedence over DB_CREATE_FILE_DEST. DB_RECOVERY_FILE_DEST sets up a default location for archive redo log files and Recovery Manager (RMAN) backup files; this will be discussed in later chapters on backup and recovery. As well as setting default file locations, OMF will generate filenames and (by default) set the file sizes. Setting these parameters can greatly simplify file-related operations. Once OMF has been enabled, it can always be overridden by specifying a datafile name on the CREATE TABLESPACE command.

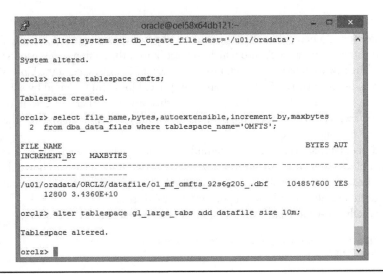

Figure 15-8 Using Oracle Managed Files

Figure 15-8 shows an example of enabling and using OMF.

In the figure, first the parameter is set. Note that the parameter is dynamic; you can change it at any time, and all OMF files created subsequently will be in the new location. Existing OMF files are not affected by any such change. Then the tablespace OMFTS is created, relying completely on the OMF defaults. The query shows what these are.

- **File name** Generated with a leading string (o1_mf), followed by the name of the tablespace, followed by eight random characters (to generate a unique name), and then a suffix (.dbf)

- **File size** 100MB

- **Autoextend** Enabled in units of 12,800 blocks (100MB), up to 32GB

The final example in the figure shows adding an OMF file to an existing tablespace, overriding the OMF default for the file size.

The combination of OMF, bigfile tablespaces, and autoextend can make space management in an Oracle database extremely easy and completely automatic.

Exercise 15-3: Change Tablespace Characteristics In this exercise, you will create a tablespace using the nondefault manual space management to simulate the need to convert to automatic segment space management after an upgrade. Enable OMF first to ease the process. Follow these steps:

1. Enable OMF for datafile creation. Choose any directory that exists and on which the Oracle user has read-write permissions. This is an example on Linux and then Windows:
   ```
   alter system set db_create_file_dest='/home/oradata';
   alter system set db_create_file_dest='c:\users\oracle\oradata';
   ```

2. Create a tablespace, using the minimum syntax now possible.
   ```
   create tablespace omftbs;
   ```

3. Determine the characteristics of the OMF file.

```
select file_name,bytes,autoextensible,maxbytes,increment_by
from dba_data_files where tablespace_name='OMFTBS';
```

Note the file is initially 100MB, autoextensible, with no upper limit.

4. Adjust the OMF file to have more sensible characteristics. Use whatever system-generated filename was returned by step 3.

```
alter database datafile
'/home/oradata/ORCL/datafile/o1_mf_omftbs_3olpn462_.dbf'
resize 500m;
alter database datafile
'/home/oradata/ORCL/datafile/o1_mf_omftbs_3olpn462_.dbf'
autoextend on next 100m maxsize 2g;
```

5. Drop the tablespace and use an operating system command to confirm that the file has indeed gone.

```
drop tablespace omftbs including contents and datafiles;
```

6. Create a tablespace using manual segment space management. Because OMF is enabled, there is no need for any datafile clause.

```
create tablespace manualsegs segment space management manual;
```

7. Confirm that the new tablespace is indeed using the manual technique.

```
select segment_space_management from dba_tablespaces
where tablespace_name='MANUALSEGS';
```

8. Create a table and an index in the tablespace.

```
create table mantab (c1 number) tablespace manualsegs;
create index mantabi on mantab(c1) tablespace manualsegs;
```

9. These segments will be created with freelists, not bitmaps. Create a new tablespace that will (by default) use automatic segment space management.

```
create tablespace autosegs;
```

10. Move the objects into the new tablespace.

```
alter table mantab move tablespace autosegs;
alter index mantabi rebuild online tablespace autosegs;
```

11. Confirm that the objects are in the correct tablespace.

```
select tablespace_name from dba_segments
where segment_name like 'MANTAB%';
```

12. Drop the original tablespace.

```
drop tablespace manualsegs including contents and datafiles;
```

13. Rename the new tablespace to the original name. This is often necessary because some application software checks the tablespace names.

```
alter tablespace autosegs rename to manualsegs;
```

14. Tidy up by dropping the tablespace, first with this command:

```
drop tablespace manualsegs;
```

15. Note the error caused by the tablespace not being empty and fix it.

```
drop tablespace manualsegs including contents and datafiles;
```

Explain How Oracle Database Server Automatically Manages Space

Space is managed at three levels: the tablespace, the segment, and the block. Once these physical structures are in place, management moves to the logical level: how space is assigned to segments and how space is used within segments.

Segment Space Assignment

Space is allocated to a segment in the form of an extent, which is a set of consecutive Oracle blocks. Every datafile has a bitmap that describes the state of the block in the file, whether it is free or part of an extent that has been assigned to a segment. When a segment fills up and needs to extend, Oracle will search the bitmaps of the files of the tablespace for free space, select one file, and create a new extent of an appropriate size by modifying the bitmap. The extent can then be assigned to the segment.

A segment is a container for an object, but the two are not the same thing. It is possible for the object to exist without a segment. When a segment is first created, it will have at least one extent—but it is possible for some objects to exist without a segment. Study the code in Figure 15-9. The first two queries show the tables (four) and indexes (two) in the currently logged-on schema, with the flag that shows whether a segment has been created for them. The third query shows the segments. The table BONUS exists logically but has no segment within which it can be contained.

 TIP Deferred segment creation can have some odd effects. For example, problems with a quota will not show up when creating a table—only when inserting into it.

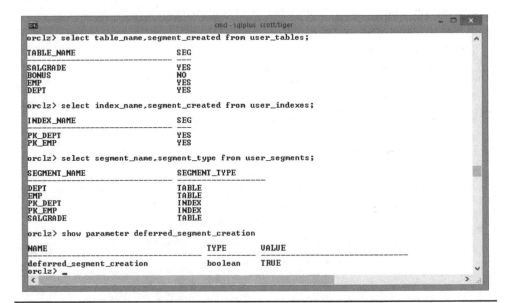

Figure 15-9 Objects and segments

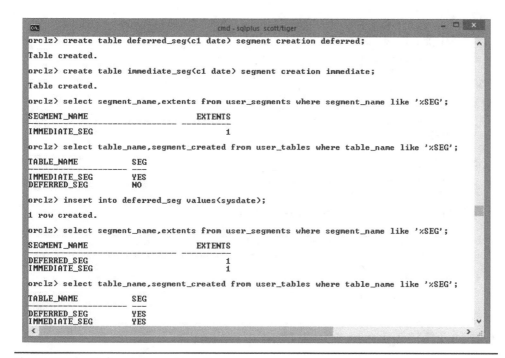

Figure 15-10   Deferred segment creation

The key to understanding this situation is the instance parameter DEFERRED_SEGMENT_
CREATION, which defaults to TRUE. If set to TRUE, this parameter instructs Oracle not to
create a segment until the object actually contains some data. At table creation time, only the data
dictionary structure describing the table is created. Only subsequently, when an attempt is made
to insert a row into the table, is the segment created. It is possible to control this behavior and to
override the parameter setting, with the SEGMENT CREATION clause of the CREATE TABLE
statement. Figure 15-10 demonstrates this, showing that a segment is created consisting of one
extent when a row is inserted into a table.

EXAM TIP   Segment creation is always immediate for objects created by
internal users such as SYS or SYSTEM, no matter what the setting of the
parameter. Attempting to use the SEGMENT CREATION DEFERRED clause as
SYS returns an error.

Exercise 15-4: Manage Segment Space   In this exercise, you observe the allocation of
extents to segments.

1. Connect to the database as user SYSTEM.

2. Create a schema to work in for this exercise and then connect to it.

```
create user ex7 identified by ex7;
grant dba to ex7;
connect ex7/ex7;
```

3. Check that the DEFERRED_SEGMENT_CREATION parameter is set to TRUE, which is the default, and set it if it is not.

```
show parameter deferred_segment_creation
alter session set deferred_segment_creation=true;
```

4. Create tables and indexes as follows:

```
create table ex7a (c1 varchar2(10));
create table ex7b (c1 varchar2(10)) segment creation
deferred;
create table ex7c (c1 varchar2(10)) segment creation
immediate;
create index ex7ai on ex7a(c1);
create index ex7bi on ex7b(c1);
create index ex7ci on ex7c(c1);
```

5. Determine what segments have been created.

```
select segment_name from user_segments;
select table_name,segment_created from user_tables;
select index_name,segment_created from user_indexes;
```

6. Insert a row into EX7A and EX7B.

7. Run the queries from step 5 again.

Automatic Segment Space Management

A table segment consists of multiple blocks in one or more extents. When an attempt is made to insert a row into the table, Oracle must make a decision: Into which block should the row be placed? This is determined by a bitmap that reflects how full each block in the segment is. By inspecting the bitmap, Oracle can determine whether a block has sufficient space to accept the new row. The mapping is not precise but rather works in 25 percent ranges: between 0 and 25 percent free space, 25 to 50 percent free space, 50 to 75 percent free space, and 75 to 100 percent free space. In addition, the bitmap shows whether the block is not actually formatted at all (that is, it is assigned to the segment but has not yet been used) or is classed as full and is therefore not available for inserts no matter how small the new row is. As rows are inserted into blocks and deleted from blocks, the status of the block (in terms of to which of the 25 percent bands it belongs) is adjusted in the bitmap.

A problem related to the selection of a block for an insert is how to manage the situation where a row changes size. Some Oracle data types—principally, the VARCHAR2 data type—are of variable length. If a VARCHAR2 column is updated such that it becomes longer, the row will become longer. Furthermore, if any columns are NULL when a row is inserted, they will take no space at all. Therefore, when UPDATE statements are executed that expand a VARCHAR2 or populate a previously NULL column, the row will become bigger. It will therefore require more space in the block.

By default, Oracle reserves 10 percent of a block for row expansion. This is the PCTFREE (percent free) setting for the segment, set at segment creation time (though it can be modified later). A block whose usage has exceeded the PCTFREE setting for the segment is classed by the Automatic Segment Space Management (ASSM) bitmap as FULL, and therefore the block is not available for insert even though it may in fact still have some free space. So if, on average, the rows in a block increase by no more than 10 percent during their lifetime, there is no problem; enough space will be available for the new versions of the rows. If a row expands such that there is not sufficient space in the block, it must be moved to a block with sufficient space. This is known as *row migration.*

 EXAM TIP   Row migration is caused by UPDATE statements. INSERT and DELETE can never result in row migration.

When a row is migrated, it is removed from the block in which it resides and inserted into a different block with sufficient space. The new block will be located by searching the ASSM bitmap. So in effect, when a user executes an UPDATE, this becomes an INSERT and DELETE, which is a more expensive operation. Furthermore, the ROWID of the row (the physical locator of the row) is not changed. The ROWID still points to the original block, which now stores no more than a "forwarding address" for the row; the forwarding address is the address of the block to which the row has been moved. The fact that the ROWID remains unchanged is good and bad. It is good because there is no need to adjust any indexes; they will still point to the original location. It is bad because when the row is retrieved through an index search, an extra I/O operation will be needed to read the row from its new location. This is, of course, transparent to SQL but may in extreme circumstances result in performance degradation.

Closely related to row migration is the issue of row chaining. A *chained row* is a row that is larger than the block. Clearly, if the block size is 8K and the row is 20K, then the row must be distributed across three blocks. At insert time, all three blocks will be located by searching the ASSM bitmap for blocks available for insertion, and when retrieving the row later, all three blocks may be read (depending on which columns are projected by the query). The ROWID of a chained row points to the first block of the row, as is also the case with a migrated row.

Save Space by Using Compression

Compression comes in various forms, some of which require a separate license: the Advanced Compression option. The primary purpose of compression is to reduce disk space requirements, but there is sometimes a fringe benefit in improved performance for subsequent queries. Compression may, however, cause performance degradation in some circumstances and should therefore be approached with caution. An advisor capability will estimate the space savings that compression can achieve for a table.

Compression comes in three forms:

- Basic table compression compresses data within a block when rows are inserted through a direct load operation. Subsequent DML operations will cause the rows to be uncompressed (and possibly migrated as a result of this).

- Advanced row compression will compress rows no matter how they are inserted and maintain the compression through DML. The compression is still on a block-by-block basis.

- Hybrid Columnar Compression (HCC) restructures data into compression units of several megabytes and is available only on certain storage platforms.

Basic compression (which is the default type) is, in fact, de-duplication. If a repeating pattern of characters occurs within a block, the pattern is stored once only in a symbol table, with a reference to the symbol table stored in each row where the pattern occurs. Advanced row compression uses the same de-duplication technology. Either way, the compression is per block; the symbol tables are not usable outside of the block in which they exist. HCC is true compression, in that it uses compression algorithms to reduce the space needed to store data. HCC is not applied per block but across groups of blocks, which further enhances the achievable compression ratios.

The type of compression is determined at table creation time. Compression can be added or removed after creation, but any such change will not affect existing rows. To bring the change into effect, the table must be reorganized. Typically, this would be accomplished with an ALTER TABLE . . . MOVE statement.

The syntax to create a table with basic or advanced compression is a normal creation statement, with a suffix specifying the compression type.

```
CREATE TABLE.....COMPRESS [ BASIC ];
CREATE TABLE....ROW STORE COMPRESS ADVANCED;
```

Proactively Monitor and Manage Tablespace Space Usage

The database will automatically monitor tablespace usage through the server alert system. Figure 15-11 shows a query against the DBA_THRESHOLDS view.

The first two lines of the output for Figure 15-11 show the system-generated thresholds for a temporary tablespace and the undo tablespace; tablespaces of these types are not monitored. This is because a simple check of free space is useless for tablespaces of these types because they are usually fully occupied by temporary or undo segments. What matters is whether the temporary or undo segments within them are full; this is a more complex metric that is not configured by default.

The third line of the query's output shows the database-wide default alerts for all tablespaces that do not have an alert explicitly configured. The warning alert is set at greater than or equal to 85 percent, and the critical alert is set at greater than or equal to 97 percent.

In addition to the alert system, which will inform you of issues according to preconfigured thresholds, Oracle maintains a history of tablespace usage. This is stored in the Automatic Workload Repository (AWR), the information being gathered as part of the AWR snapshots created by the manageability monitor (MMON) process. You can see this information in the DBA_HIST_TBSPC_SPACE_USAGE view. The second query in Figure 15-11 joins this view to the V$TABLESPACE view (the join is necessary to retrieve the tablespace name) and shows the history of space usage for each tablespace. Note that there is one row per tablespace per snapshot. You can see that the snapshot frequency has been set to every 15 minutes and that (in the few lines displayed) there was no change in the usage within the EXAMPLE tablespace.

 TIP You may want to write your own reporting code that queries DBA_HIST_TBSPC_SPACE_USAGE to gain a picture of how space is being used in the database so that you can add space to tablespaces before alerts are raised.

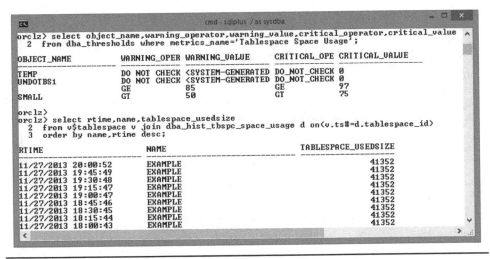

Figure 15-11 Tablespace thresholds and usage

Use the Segment Advisor

The Segment Advisor attempts to generate recommendations regarding reorganizing segments to reclaim space. The issue is that over time, in some circumstances, table and index segments may become larger than is necessary for the amount of data contained within them.

An obvious example is many rows having been deleted. Deletion frees up space within the segment, but the segment itself remains the same size. This will affect the table segment and all associated index segments. In most cases, if space has ever been assigned to a segment, then even if it is not needed now, it will be needed again. For example, the process of loading data into data warehouse tables often involves inserting many rows into a staging table, processing them, and deleting them. But even though the table may be empty at the end of the day's run, all the space will be needed again the next day.

It is therefore not enough to examine the current state of a table to determine whether it is excessively large; you must also consider the history of space usage. The Segment Advisor can do this. It considers data in the AWR as well as the current state of the objects. The recommendations are based on a sampled analysis of the object and historical information used to predict future growth trends.

The Segment Advisor runs, by default, every night as an autotask scheduled job. The autotask does not attempt to analyze every segment. It selects segments on these criteria:

- Segments in tablespaces that have crossed a space usage threshold
- Segments that have had the most activity
- Segments that have the highest growth rate

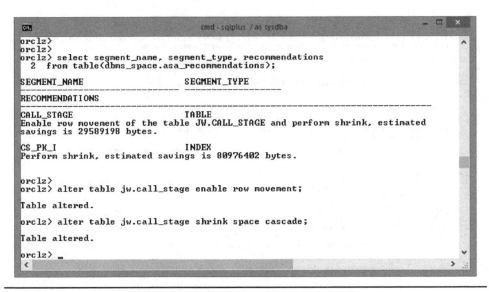

```
                              cmd - sqlplus / as sysdba                    _ ☐ ☓
orclz>
orclz>
orclz> select segment_name, segment_type, recommendations
  2  from table(dbms_space.asa_recommendations);

SEGMENT_NAME                    SEGMENT_TYPE
------------------------------  ------------------
RECOMMENDATIONS
----------------------------------------------------------------------------
CALL_STAGE                      TABLE
Enable row movement of the table JW.CALL_STAGE and perform shrink, estimated
savings is 29589198 bytes.

CS_PK_I                         INDEX
Perform shrink, estimated savings is 80976402 bytes.


orclz>
orclz> alter table jw.call_stage enable row movement;

Table altered.

orclz> alter table jw.call_stage shrink space cascade;

Table altered.

orclz> _
<                                                                     >
```

Figure 15-12   Retrieving and implementing the Segment Advisor's autotask advice

To see the results of the autotask, use the DBMS_SPACE.ASA_RECOMMENDATIONS function. This function returns a table with the results of the last run. Figure 15-12 shows an example of querying the result of the Segment Advisor autotask, followed by the commands that implement its recommendations.

 TIP   The Segment Advisor autotask runs by default. Many DBAs never look at its advice. You should either look at the results or disable the task.

Reclaim Wasted Space from Tables and Indexes by Using the Segment Shrink Functionality

When a row is deleted, the space it was occupying in its block becomes available for reuse when another row is inserted. However, the nature of the activity against a table can result in a significant amount of wasted space within the table. This could be reclaimed with a MOVE operation. Following a move, all the blocks will be consecutively full of freshly reinserted rows. But during the move, the table is locked, and following it all the indexes must be rebuilt. For many environments, this makes using MOVE to reorganize tables impossible. The SHRINK command avoids these problems. It can be run without any impact on end users. A limitation is that the table's tablespace must have been created to use automatic segment space management. Tables in tablespaces that use the older freelist technique for managing segment space usage cannot be shrunk because (unlike the new bitmap method) the freelist does not include sufficient information for Oracle to work out how full each block actually is.

The underlying implementation of a table shrink is to relocate rows from the end of the table into blocks toward the beginning of the table, by means of matched INSERT and DELETE operations, and then, when all possible moves have been done, to bring the high water mark of the table down to the last currently used block and release all the space above this point. There are two distinct phases. The compact phase moves the rows in a series of small transactions, through normal DML that generates both undo and redo and uses row locks. The second phase is a Data Definition Language (DDL) command. As with any DDL command, this is a transaction against the data dictionary; it will execute almost instantaneously but will require a short table lock. This last step is often referred to as "relocating the high water mark (HWM) of the segment."

 EXAM TIP   A table shrink operation generates undo and redo. Indexes are maintained because the shrink is implemented as a set of DML transactions. There is no table lock during the compaction, but individual rows will be locked while they are being moved.

The syntax of the SHRINK SPACE command is as follows:

```
ALTER TABLE <table name> SHRINK SPACE [COMPACT] [CASCADE];
```

Using the keyword COMPACT carries out the first phase but not the second; in other words, the rows are relocated, but the space is not actually released from the segment. The reason for using this is that while the compaction can occur during normal running hours (though it may take many hours to complete on a large table), it is possible that the DDL at the end will hang because of concurrency with other transactions, and it will also invalidate parsed SQL in the library cache. So, it may be necessary to shrink the table with the COMPACT keyword first and then again without COMPACT during a maintenance period. It will be fast because the compaction will have already been done. The CASCADE keyword instructs Oracle also to shrink dependent objects, such as indexes.

 EXAM TIP   The SHRINK SPACE COMPACT command reorganizes the contents of the segment but does not return space to the tablespace.

Before a table can be shrunk, you must enable row movement for the table.

```
ALTER TABLE <table name> ENABLE ROW MOVEMENT;
```

Enabling row movement is necessary because the nature of the operation means that row IDs will be changing. The same row (no change to the primary key) will be in a different physical location and will therefore have a different row ID. This is something that Oracle will not permit unless row movement has been enabled.

 EXAM TIP   A table must be in a tablespace with automatic segment space management, and row movement must have been enabled; otherwise, it cannot be shrunk. If these conditions have not been met, a MOVE may be the only way to reorganize the table.

PART III

Figure 15-12 shows enabling row movement for a table, followed by a SHRINK SPACE that reclaims space from both the table and its index.

 TIP Compression is incompatible with SHRINK SPACE. You will need to uncompress before shrinking. To do this, use ALTER TABLE . . . NOCOMPRESS and ALTER TABLE . . . MOVE.

Manage Resumable Space Allocation

Many operations can fail for reasons of inadequate space. This typically shows up as an inability to add another extent to a segment, which itself can have several causes. A datafile could be full, an auto-extensible datafile or tempfile could be on a disk that is full, an undo segment could be in an undo tablespace that is full, an operation requiring temporary space could be using a temporary tablespace that is full, or a user could have reached their quota limit on a tablespace. Whatever the reason, space-related errors tend to be dreadfully time consuming.

Consider an exercise to load data into a data warehouse. The first time you attempt this, it fails because the destination tablespace runs out of space. The data that did go in must be rolled back (which may take as long as the insert), the tablespace extended, and the load done again. Then it fails because of inadequate undo space; therefore, you roll back, increase the undo tablespace, and try again. Then it fails during index rebuilding because of a lack of temporary space. And so on. Exercises such as this are the bane of many DBAs' lives. The resumable space allocation feature can be the solution.

If you enable resumable space allocation, when an operation hits a space problem (any space problem at all), rather than failing with an error (and in many cases rolling back what it did manage to do), the operation will be suspended. To the user, this will show as the session hanging. When the error condition is resolved, it will continue. All suspended sessions (currently suspended and previously suspended but now running again) are listed in the view DBA_RESUMABLE.

To enable resumable space allocation at the session level, the command is as follows:

```
ALTER SESSION ENABLE RESUMABLE [ TIMEOUT <seconds> ] ;
```

The TIMEOUT option lets you specify for how long the statement should hang. If this time is reached without the problem being resolved, the error is returned, and the statement fails. If there is no specified TIMEOUT, the session will hang indefinitely.

 TIP It is possible for a process to be suspended and resumed many times without your knowledge. The DBA_RESUMABLE view will show you details of the current or last suspension only.

It is also possible to enable resumable space for all sessions by setting an instance parameter. This is a dynamic parameter. For example, here is how to set a timeout of one minute:

```
alter system set resumable_timeout=60;
```

This will cause all sessions that hit a space problem to be suspended for up to one minute.

TIP   The expdb and impdp Data Pump utilities have the command-line switch RESUMABLE=Y (the default is N), which will allow Data Pump jobs to suspend if they hit space problems. This is extremely useful.

There is little point in enabling resumable space allocation for a session or the instance if you don't do anything about the problem that caused a session to be suspended. Suspended sessions will, by default, be reported through the server alert system, be displayed by Database Control, and be listed in the DBA_RESUMABLE data dictionary view. Having spotted a problem, you can fix it interactively from another session. Or you can create an AFTER SUSPEND ON DATABASE trigger, which will run whenever a session is suspended. This trigger could report the problem (perhaps by generating an e-mail), or it could include code to investigate the problem and fix it automatically.

Two-Minute Drill

Describe the Storage of Table Row Data in Blocks

- One tablespace can span many datafiles.
- One tablespace can have many segments.
- One segment is one or more extents.
- One extent is many consecutive blocks in one datafile.
- One Oracle block should be one or more operating system blocks.
- The Oracle block is the granularity of database I/O.
- A SMALLFILE tablespace can have many datafiles, but a BIGFILE tablespace can have only one.
- Tablespaces default to local extent management and automatic segment space management, but not to a uniform extent size.
- OMF datafiles are automatically named, are initially 100MB, and can autoextend without limit.
- A tablespace that contains segments cannot be dropped unless an INCLUDING DATAFILES clause is specified.
- Tablespaces can be online or offline and read-write or read-only.
- Any one tablespace can store only one type of object: permanent objects, temporary objects, or undo segments.

Create and Manage Tablespaces

- Tablespaces can be resized by adding datafiles or by extending existing datafiles.
- Local extent management tracks extent allocation with bitmaps in each datafile.

- The UNIFORM SIZE clause when creating a tablespace forces all extents to be the same size.

- The AUTOALLOCATE clause lets Oracle determine the next extent size, which is based on how many extents are being allocated to a segment.

- Automatic segment space management tracks the free space in each block of an extent using bitmaps.

- It is possible to convert a tablespace from dictionary extent management to local extent management but not from freelist segment management to automatic management.

Explain How Oracle Database Server Automatically Manages Space

- Space is allocated to segments on demand in the form of extents. Extent usage is tracked by bitmaps.

- Space usage within a segment is tracked in 25 percent bands by bitmaps.

Save Space by Using Compression

- Basic compression de-duplicates data when inserted through a direct load.

- Advanced row compression can maintain the de-duplication compression through conventional DML.

Proactively Monitor and Manage Tablespace Space Usage

- The server alert system is preconfigured to raise alerts when a tablespace is 85 percent full (warning) and 97 percent full (critical).

- Alerts are not raised for temporary or undo tablespaces.

- Alert thresholds can be configured at any value for any tablespace individually.

Use the Segment Advisor

- The Segment Advisor runs every night as an autotask.

- The advice will be to shrink a table if doing so would release a significant amount of space.

- The Segment Advisor considers historical usage as well as the current usage.

Reclaim Wasted Space from Tables and Indexes by Using the Segment Shrink Functionality

- A table shrink operation relocates rows toward the front of the segment and (by default) releases free space at the end.

- A shrink is an online and in-place operation; it requires no additional space while running, and the table is not locked against other DML.

Manage Resumable Space Allocation

- Resumable space allocation can be enabled for a session or for the instance.
- If a session hits a space error, it will hang until the problem is fixed—or until a timeout expires.
- A database trigger can be configured to fire whenever a session is suspended.

Self Test

1. Examine the exhibit:

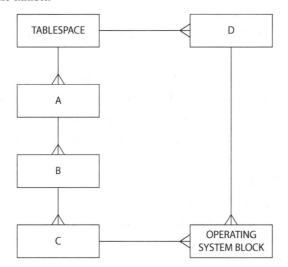

The exhibit shows the Oracle storage model, with four entities having letters for names. Match four of the following entities to the letters *A*, *B*, *C*, and *D*:

   A. Datafile

   B. Extent

   C. Oracle block

   D. Row

   E. Segment

   F. Table

2. What statements are correct about extents? (Choose all correct answers.)

   A. An extent is a grouping of several Oracle blocks.

   B. An extent is a grouping of several operating system blocks.

   C. An extent can be distributed across one or more datafiles.

   D. An extent can contain blocks from one or more segments.

   E. An extent can be assigned to only one segment.

3. Which of these are types of segments? (Choose all correct answers.)

   A. Sequence

   B. Stored procedure

   C. Table

   D. Table partition

   E. View

4. If a tablespace is created with the syntax

   ```
   create tablespace tbs1 datafile 'tbs1.dbf' size 10m;
   ```

   which of these characteristics will it have? (Choose all correct answers.)

   A. The datafile will autoextend, but only to double its initial size.

   B. The datafile will autoextend with MAXSIZE UNLIMITED.

   C. The extent management will be local.

   D. Segment space management will be with bitmaps.

   E. The file will be created in the DB_CREATE_FILE_DEST directory.

5. How can a tablespace be made larger? (Choose all correct answers.)

   A. Convert it from a SMALLFILE tablespace to a BIGFILE tablespace.

   B. If it is a SMALLFILE tablespace, add files.

   C. If it is a BIGFILE tablespace, add more files.

   D. Resize the existing file (or files).

6. Which of these commands can be executed against a table in a read-only tablespace? (Choose the best answer.)

   A. DELETE

   B. DROP

   C. INSERT

   D. TRUNCATE

   E. UPDATE

7. What operation cannot be applied to a tablespace after creation? (Choose the best answer.)

   A. Convert from dictionary extent management to local extent management.

   B. Convert from manual segment space management to automatic segment space management.

   C. Change the name of the tablespace.

   D. Reduce the size of the datafile (or datafiles) assigned to the tablespace.

   E. All the above operations can be applied.

8. When the database is in mount mode, what views can be queried to find what datafiles and tablespaces make up the database? (Choose all correct answers.)

   A. DBA_DATA_FILES

   B. DBA_TABLESPACES

   C. DBA_TEMP_FILES

   D. V$DATABASE

   E. V$DATAFILE

   F. V$TABLESPACE

9. Which views could you query to find out about the temporary tablespaces and the files that make them up? (Choose all correct answers.)

   A. DBA_DATA_FILES

   B. DBA_TABLESPACES

   C. DBA_TEMP_TABLESPACES

   D. DBA_TEMP_FILES

   E. V$DATAFILE

   F. V$TABLESPACE

   G. V$TEMPTABLESPACE

   H. V$TEMPFILE

10. Which statements are correct about extents? (Choose all correct answers.)

   A. An extent is a consecutive grouping of Oracle blocks.

   B. An extent is a random grouping of Oracle blocks.

   C. An extent can be distributed across one or more datafiles.

   D. An extent can contain blocks from one or more segments.

   E. An extent can be assigned to only one segment.

11. Which of these are types of segments? (Choose all correct answers.)

   A. Sequence

   B. Stored procedure

   C. Table

   D. Table partition

   E. View

12. Which form of compression uses compression algorithms rather than de-duplication algorithms? (Choose the best answer.)

    A. Compression implemented with COMPRESS BASIC.

    B. Compression implemented with ROW STORE COMPRESS ADVANCED.

    C. Hybrid columnar compression.

    D. All Oracle compression methods use compression algorithms.

    E. All Oracle compression methods use de-duplication algorithms.

13. You receive an alert warning you that a tablespace is nearly full. What action could you take to prevent this becoming a problem, without any impact for your users? (Choose two correct answers.)

    A. Purge all recycle bin objects in the tablespace.

    B. Shrink the tables in the tablespace.

    C. Shrink the indexes in the tablespace.

    D. Move one or more tables to a different tablespace.

    E. Move one or more indexes to a different tablespace.

14. Which process is responsible for sending the alert when a tablespace usage critical threshold is reached? (Choose the best answer.)

    A. Database Control

    B. The DBMS_SERVER_ALERT package

    C. MMON, the manageability monitor process

    D. The server process of the session that detected the problem

    E. DBW*n*, the database writer, when it detects the problem

15. When will the Segment Advisor run? (Choose two correct answers.)

    A. Every night, as an autotask

    B. On demand

    C. Automatically when a tablespace crosses a threshold for space usage

    D. Automatically when a session is suspended by the resumable space allocation mechanism

16. Which of the following commands will shrink space in a table or index segment and relocate the HWM? (Choose the best answer.)

    A. ALTER TABLE EMPLOYEES SHRINK SPACE COMPACT HWM;

    B. ALTER TABLE EMPLOYEES SHRINK SPACE HWM;

    C. ALTER TABLE EMPLOYEES SHRINK SPACE COMPACT;

    D. ALTER TABLE EMPLOYEES SHRINK SPACE CASCADE;

    E. ALTER TABLE EMPLOYEES SHRINK SPACE;

17. What is required before shrinking a table? (Choose all that apply.)

    A. Triggers must be disabled.

    B. Indexes must be dropped.

    C. Row movement must be enabled.

    D. Automatic segment space management must be enabled.

    E. LOB columns must be dropped.

18. How can you enable the suspension and resumption of statements that hit space errors? (Choose all correct answers.)

    A. Issue an ALTER SESSION ENABLE RESUMABLE command.

    B. Issue an ALTER SYSTEM ENABLE RESUMABLE command.

    C. Set the instance parameter RESUMABLE_STATEMENTS.

    D. Set the instance parameter RESUMABLE_TIMEOUT.

    E. Use the DBMS_RESUMABLE.ENABLE procedure.

19. If a statement is suspended because of a space error, what will happen when the problem is fixed? (Choose the best answer.)

    A. After the resumable timeout has expired, the statement will continue executing from the point it had reached.

    B. After the resumable timeout has expired, the statement will start executing from the beginning again.

    C. The statement will start executing from the beginning immediately after the problem is fixed.

    D. The statement will continue executing from the point it had reached immediately after the problem is fixed.

Self Test Answers

1. ☑   **A** is SEGMENT, **B** is EXTENT, **C** is ORACLE BLOCK, and **D** is DATAFILE.
    ☒   Neither ROW nor TABLE is included in the model.

2. ☑   **A** and **E.** One extent is several consecutive Oracle blocks, and one segment consists of one or more extents.
    ☒   **B, C,** and **D** are incorrect. They misinterpret the Oracle storage model.

3. ☑   **C** and **D.** A table can be a type of segment, as can a table partition (in which case the table itself will not be a segment).
    ☒   **A, B,** and **E** are incorrect. They exist only as objects defined within the data dictionary. The data dictionary itself is a set of segments.

4. ☑ **C** and **D.** Local extent management and automatic segment space management are enabled by default.

☒ **A, B**, and **E** are incorrect. **A** and **B** are incorrect because, by default, autoextension is disabled. **E** is incorrect because providing a filename will override the OMF mechanism.

5. ☑ **B** and **D.** A smallfile tablespace can have many files, and all datafiles can be resized upward.

☒ **A** and **C** are incorrect. **A** is incorrect because you cannot convert between SMALLFILE and BIGFILE. **C** is incorrect because a BIGFILE tablespace can have only one file.

6. ☑ **B.** Objects can be dropped from read-only tablespaces.

☒ **A, C, D**, and **E** are incorrect. All these commands will fail because they require writing to the table, unlike a DROP, which writes only to the data dictionary.

7. ☑ **B.** It is not possible to change the segment space management method after creation.

☒ **A, C, D**, and **E** are incorrect. **A** and **C** are incorrect because a tablespace can be converted to local extent management or renamed at any time. **D** is incorrect because a datafile can be resized downward, although only if the space to be freed up has not already been used. **E** is incorrect because you cannot change the segment space management without re-creating the tablespace.

8. ☑ **E** and **F.** Joining these views will give the necessary information.

☒ **A, B, C**, and **D** are incorrect. **A, B**, and **C** are incorrect because these views will not be available in mount mode. **D** is incorrect because there is no relevant information in V$DATABASE.

9. ☑ **B, D, F**, and **H.** V$TABLESPACE and DBA_TABLESPACE will list the temporary tablespaces, and V$TEMPFILE and DBA_TEMP_FILES will list their files.

☒ **A, C, E**, and **G** are incorrect. **A** and **E** are incorrect because V$DATAFILE and DBA_DATA_FILES do not include tempfiles. **C** and **G** are incorrect because there are no views with these names.

10. ☑ **A** and **E.** One extent is several consecutive Oracle blocks, and one segment consists of one or more extents.

☒ **B, C**, and **D** are incorrect. They misinterpret the Oracle storage model.

11. ☑ **C** and **D.** A table can be a type of segment, and so can a table partition.

☒ **A, B**, and **E** are incorrect. These exist only as objects defined within the data dictionary. The data dictionary itself is a set of segments.

12. ☑ **C.** Hybrid columnar compression is true compression.

☒ **A, B, D**, and **E** are incorrect. **A** and **B** are incorrect because both BASIC and ADVANCED compression are, in fact, based on de-duplication. **D** and **E** are incorrect because Oracle can use either technique.

13. ☑ **A** and **B**. Both purging dropped objects and shrinking tables will release space immediately, with no downtime.
    ☒ **C, D,** and **E** are incorrect. An index can be shrunk, but this will release space within the index, not return it to the tablespace. Relocating either indexes or tables has implications for the availability of the data.

14. ☑ **C**. The MMON background process raises alerts.
    ☒ **A, B, D,** and **E** are incorrect. **A** is incorrect because although Database Control reports alerts, it does not raise them. **B** is incorrect because the DBMS_SERVER_ALERT API is used to configure the alert system—it does not implement it. **D** and **E** are incorrect because foreground and background processes will encounter problems, not warn of their imminence.

15. ☑ **A** and **B**. Unless the autotask has been disabled, it will run in every maintenance window. It can also be invoked on demand.
    ☒ **C** and **D** are incorrect. **C** is incorrect because although a tablespace usage alert will cause the autotask to analyze all objects in the tablespace in the next maintenance window, this does not happen when the alert is raised. **D** is incorrect because the only action triggered by suspension of a session is running the AFTER SUSPEND ON DATABASE trigger.

16. ☑ **D**. SHRINK SPACE both compacts the data and moves the HWM. While the HWM is being moved, DML operations on the table are blocked.
    ☒ **A, B, C,** and **E** are incorrect. **A, B,** and **E** are syntactically incorrect. **C** is incorrect because COMPACT only performs the shrink operation but does not move the HWM after shrinking the segment.

17. ☑ **C** and **D**. Row movement is necessary because a shrink will change row IDs. ASSM is needed to give the necessary information on how full a block is.
    ☒ **A, B,** and **E** are incorrect. **A** is incorrect because triggers will not fire for the operation; they will continue to fire for any other DML. **B** is incorrect because indexes are maintained during a shrink. **E** is incorrect because LOB segments will not block a table shrink. They will be shrunk themselves if CASCADE is specified.

18. ☑ **A** and **D**. These are the only two methods to enable resumable space allocation.
    ☒ **B, C,** and **E** are incorrect. **B** and **C** are incorrect because resumable space allocation is enabled at the system level with the instance parameter RESUMABLE_TIMEOUT. **E** is incorrect because although there is a package called DBMS_RESUMABLE, it does not (rather annoyingly) include a procedure to enable resumable space allocation.

19. ☑ **D**. As "suspended" implies, the statement will continue from the point at which it stopped.
    ☒ **A, B,** and **C** are incorrect. The timeout controls how long the suspension can last before returning an error; it is the period during which the problem can be fixed.

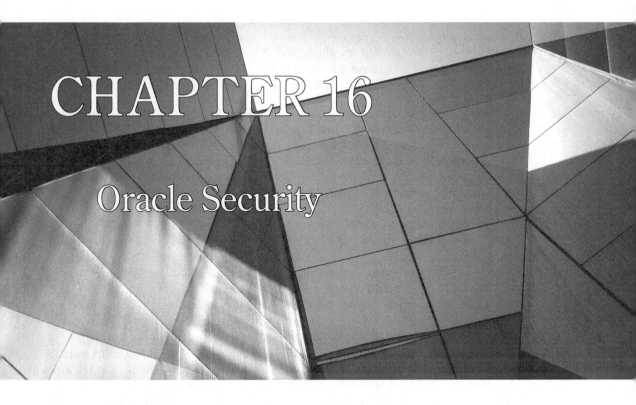

CHAPTER 16

Oracle Security

Exam Objectives

- 062.6.1   Create and Manage Database User Accounts
- 062.6.2   Grant and Revoke Privileges
- 062.6.3   Create and Manage Roles
- 062.6.4   Create and Manage Profiles
- 062.9.1   Explain DBA Responsibilities for Security and Auditing
- 062.9.2   Enable Standard Database Auditing and Unified Auditing

Database security has several aspects. First, there is authentication: Who can connect? How does one identify them? Second, there is authorization: What are users allowed to do? How does one restrict their actions? Finally, there is auditing: Given that users can connect and perform certain actions, how do you track what they are doing? These aspects are covered in this chapter.

When a user logs on to the database, following some means of identification, they connect to a *user account,* which defines their initial access permissions and the attributes of the session. Associated with a user account is a schema. The terms *user, user account,* and *schema* can often be used interchangeably in the Oracle environment, but they are not always the same thing. A *user* is a person who connects to a user account by establishing a session against the instance and logging on with the user account name. A *schema* is a set of objects owned by a user account.

A user account must be granted privileges before a session (or sessions) connected to the account can do anything. Many different privileges can be granted for many different objects and actions, and managing privileges individually is not practical for any but the simplest systems. Privileges are usually grouped into roles, which make privilege administration much easier.

You can use profiles to manage passwords and (to a limited extent) control the resources a user is allowed to consume within the instance and the database.

In many environments, users will have permission to do certain things, but that doesn't mean they should be able to do them without a record being kept. For example, a database administrator (DBA) will (usually) be able to read and write any row in any table in the database. This is part of their job. For example, if a business data corruption occurs (perhaps through user error or through application software issues), the DBA will need to use SQL*Plus or some other tool that can bypass all the application security and rules and edit the data to fix it. But that does not mean the DBA should be diving into tables of sensitive data without good reason. Actions such as this cannot be prevented, but they can, and must, be tracked. This is the purpose of auditing: to record actions that are permitted but potentially harmful.

Create and Manage Database User Accounts

To establish a session against an instance and a database, a user must connect to a user account. The account must be specified by name and authenticated by some means. The way the account was created will set up a range of attributes for the session, some of which can be changed later while the session is in progress.

User Account Attributes

A user account has a number of attributes defined at account creation time. These attributes will be applied to sessions that connect to the account, although some can be modified by the session or the DBA while the session is running. These attributes are as follows:

- Username
- Authentication method
- Default tablespace
- Tablespace quotas

- Temporary tablespace
- User profile
- Account status

All of these should be specified when creating the user, although only username and authentication methods are mandatory; the others have defaults.

Username

The username must be unique in the database and must conform to certain rules. A username must begin with a letter, must be no more than 30 characters, and can consist of only letters, digits, and the dollar sign ($) and underscore (_) characters. A username cannot be a reserved word. The letters are case sensitive but will be automatically converted to uppercase. All these rules (with the exception of the length) can be broken if the username is specified within double quotes, as shown in Figure 16-1.

In the first example in the figure, the username JOHN is created. This was entered in lowercase but will have been converted to uppercase, as shown in the first query. The second example uses double quotes to create the user with a name in lowercase. The third and fourth examples use double quotes to bypass the rules on characters and reserved words; both of these would fail without the double quotes. If a username includes lowercase letters or illegal characters or is a reserved word, then double quotes must always be used to connect to the account subsequently.

 TIP It is possible to use nonstandard usernames, but this may cause dreadful confusion. Some applications rely on the case conversion; others always use double quotes. It may be considered good practice always to use uppercase and only the standard characters; this means that double quotes can be used or not.

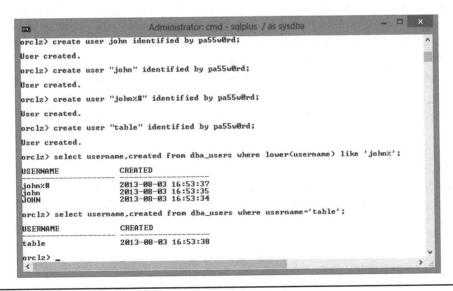

```
Administrator: cmd - sqlplus / as sysdba

orclz> create user john identified by pa55w0rd;

User created.
orclz> create user "john" identified by pa55w0rd;

User created.
orclz> create user "john%#" identified by pa55w0rd;

User created.
orclz> create user "table" identified by pa55w0rd;

User created.
orclz> select username,created from dba_users where lower(username) like 'john%';

USERNAME            CREATED
------------------- -------------------
john%#              2013-08-03 16:53:37
john                2013-08-03 16:53:35
JOHN                2013-08-03 16:53:34
orclz> select username,created from dba_users where username='table';

USERNAME            CREATED
------------------- -------------------
table               2013-08-03 16:53:38
orclz>
```

Figure 16-1 How to create users with nonstandard names

Default Tablespace and Quotas

Every user account has a *default tablespace*, which is the tablespace where any schema objects (such as tables or indexes) created by a user will reside. It is possible for users to own objects in any tablespace on which they have been given a quota, but unless another tablespace is specified when creating the object, it will go into a user's default tablespace.

A database-wide default tablespace will be applied to all user accounts if a default tablespace is not specified when creating the user. The default can be set when creating the database and then changed later with the following:

```
ALTER DATABASE DEFAULT TABLESPACE tablespace_name;
```

If a default tablespace is not specified when the database is created, it will be set to the SYSTEM tablespace.

 CAUTION After creating a database, do not leave the default tablespace as SYSTEM; this is bad practice. Either change it as soon as you have created another tablespace or use a form of the CREATE DATABASE command that creates a default tablespace.

A *quota* is the amount of space in a tablespace that a user is allowed to occupy. The user can create objects and allocate extents to them until the quota is reached. If the user has no quota on a tablespace, the user cannot create any objects at all. Quotas can be changed at any time. If a user's quota is reduced to less than the size of the objects the user already owns (or even reduced to zero), the objects will survive and will still be usable, but they will not be permitted to get any bigger.

Figure 16-2 shows how to investigate and set quotas.

The first query in the figure is against DBA_USERS and determines the default and temporary tablespaces for the user JOHN, created in Figure 16-1. DBA_USERS has one row for every user account in the database. User JOHN has picked up the database defaults for the default and temporary tablespaces, which are shown in the last query against DATABASE_PROPERTIES.

 NOTE Most users will not need any quotas because they will never create objects. They will only have permissions against objects owned by other schemas. The few object-owning schemas will probably have QUOTA UNLIMITED on the tablespaces where their objects reside.

The two ALTER USER commands in Figure 16-2 give JOHN the capability to take up to 10MB of space in the USERS tablespace and to have an unlimited amount of space in the EXAMPLE tablespace. The query against DBA_TS_QUOTAS confirms this; the number −1 is how "unlimited" is represented. At the time the query was run, JOHN had not created any objects, so the figures for BYTES are zeros, indicating that he is not currently using any space in either tablespace.

 EXAM TIP Before you can create a segment, you must have both permission to execute CREATE TABLE and a quota on a tablespace in which to create it.

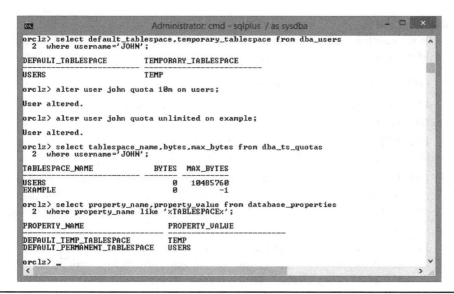

Figure 16-2 Managing user quotas

Temporary Tablespace

Permanent objects (such as tables) are stored in permanent tablespaces; temporary objects are stored in temporary tablespaces. A session will need space in a temporary tablespace if it needs space for certain operations that exceed the space available in the session's Program Global Area (PGA). Every user account is assigned a temporary tablespace, and all user sessions connecting to the account will share this temporary tablespace.

The query against DBA_USERS in Figure 16-2 shows user JOHN's temporary tablespace, which in this case is the database default temporary tablespace because an alternative temporary tablespace was not specified when the user was created. This is shown by the last query in Figure 16-2, against DATABASE_PROPERTIES.

A user does not need to be granted a quota on their temporary tablespace. This is because the objects in it are not actually owned by the user; they are owned by the SYS user, who has an unlimited quota on all tablespaces.

 EXAM TIP Users do not need a quota on their temporary tablespaces.

To change a user's temporary tablespace (which will affect all future sessions that connect to the account), use an ALTER USER command.

```
ALTER USER username TEMPORARY TABLESPACE tablespace_name;
```

 TIP If many users are logging on to the same user account, they will share use of one temporary tablespace. This can be a performance bottleneck, which can be avoided by using temporary tablespace groups.

Account Status

Every user account has a certain status, as listed in the ACCOUNT_STATUS column of DBA_USERS. There are five possibilities:

- **OPEN** The account is available for use.
- **LOCKED** This indicates that the DBA deliberately locked the account. No user can connect to a locked account.
- **EXPIRED** This indicates that the lifetime has expired. Passwords can have a limited lifetime. No user can connect to an EXPIRED account until the password is reset.
- **EXPIRED (GRACE)** This indicates that the *grace period* is in effect. A password need not expire immediately when its lifetime ends; it may be configured with a grace period during which users connecting to the account have the opportunity to change the password.
- **LOCKED (TIMED)** This indicates that the account is locked because of failed login attempts. An account can be configured to lock automatically for a period after an incorrect password is presented a certain number of times.

To lock and unlock an account, use these commands:

```
ALTER USER username ACCOUNT LOCK;
ALTER USER username ACCOUNT UNLOCK;
```

To force a user to change their password, use this command:

```
ALTER USER username PASSWORD EXPIRE;
```

This will immediately start the grace period, forcing the user to change their password at their next login attempt. There is no such command as ALTER ... UNEXPIRE. The only way to make the account fully functional again is to reset the password.

Authentication Methods

A user account must have an authentication method, in other words, some means whereby the database can determine whether the user attempting to create a session connecting to the account is allowed to do so. The simplest technique is by presenting a password that will be matched against a password stored within the database, but there are alternatives. These are the possibilities:

- Operating system authentication
- Password file authentication
- Password authentication
- External authentication
- Global authentication

The first two techniques are used only for administrators; the last requires a Lightweight Directory Access Protocol (LDAP) directory server. The LDAP directory server is the Oracle Internet Directory, shipped as part of the Oracle Fusion Middleware Suite.

Operating System and Password File Authentication

To enable operating system and password file authentication (the two go together) for an account, you must grant the user an administration role. There are six of these:

Admin Role	Group Name	Capabilities
SYSDBA	OSDBA	Startup and shutdown; all system privileges with admin. Total power.
SYSOPER	OSOPER	Startup and shutdown, nothing else. No privileges on users or data.
SYSASM	OSASM	Not relevant to a relational database management system (RDBMS) instance. Automatic Storage Management (ASM) only.
SYSBACKUP	OSBACKUPDBA	Startup and shutdown; create anything; no privileges on data.
SYSDG	OSDGDB	Startup and shutdown; privileges necessary to manage Data Guard.
SYSKM	OSKMDBA	Privileges necessary to manage data security and encryption.

Grant the roles as follows:

```
GRANT [SYSDBA | SYSOPER | SYSASM | SYSBACKUP | SYSDG | SYSKM] TO username;
```

Granting any (or all) of these privileges will copy the user's password from the data dictionary into the external password file, where it can be read by the instance even if the database is not open. Following database creation, the only user with these privileges is SYS. It also allows the instance to authenticate users by checking whether the operating system user attempting the connection is a member of the operating system group mapped to the Oracle group name. On Linux, the operating system groups must be specified when installing the Oracle Home. On Windows, there is no choice. The groups are created implicitly with these names:

Oracle Group	Windows Group
OSDBA	ORA_DBA
OSOPER	ORA_OPER
OSASM	ORA_ASM
OSBACKUPDBA	ORA_%HOMENAME%_SYSBACKUP
OSDGDB	ORA_%HOMENAME%_SYSDG
OSKMDBA	ORA_%HOMENAME%_SYSKM

To use password file authentication, the user can connect with this syntax with SQL*Plus:

```
CONNECT username / password [@db_alias] AS [ SYSOPER | SYSDBA ];
```

Note that you can use password file authentication for a connection to a remote database over Oracle Net. This is a logical impossibility with operating system authentication because when using a remote database, one never logs on to the remote operating system.

To use operating system authentication, the user can connect with this syntax with SQL*Plus:

```
CONNECT / AS [ SYSOPER | SYSDBA ];
```

The operating system password is not stored by Oracle, and therefore there are no issues with changing passwords.

The equivalent of these syntaxes is also available when connecting with Database Express, by selecting the AS SYSDBA check box in the Database Express login window. To determine to whom the SYSDBA and SYSOPER privileges have been granted, query the view V$PWFILE_USERS. A connection with operating system or password file authentication is always possible, no matter what state the instance and database are in, and is necessary to issue STARTUP and SHUTDOWN commands.

EXAM TIP All user sessions must be authenticated. There is no such thing as an "anonymous" login, and some authentication method must be used. There is, however, a user ANONYMOUS, which is the account used by Oracle Application Express (APEX) applications.

Password Authentication

The syntax for a connection with password authentication using SQL*Plus is as follows:

```
CONNECT username / password [@db_alias];
```

When the user connects with password authentication, the instance will validate the password given against the password hash stored with the user account in the data dictionary. For this to work, the database must be open; it is logically impossible to issue STARTUP and SHUTDOWN commands when connected with password authentication. The user SYS is not permitted to connect with password authentication; only password file, operating system, and LDAP authentication are possible for SYS.

Usernames are case sensitive but are automatically converted to uppercase unless specified within double quotes. Passwords are case sensitive, and there is no automatic case conversion. It is not necessary to use double quotes; the password will always be read exactly as entered.

Any user can change their user account password at any time, or a highly privileged user (such as SYSTEM) can change any user account password. The syntax (whether you are changing your own password or another one) is as follows:

```
ALTER USER username IDENTIFIED BY password;
```

External Authentication

If a user account is created with external authentication, Oracle will delegate the authentication to an external service; it will not prompt for a password. If the Advanced Security Option has been licensed, then the external service can be a number of third-party services, such as a Kerberos server or a RADIUS server. When a user attempts to connect to the user account, rather than authenticating the user itself, the database instance will accept (or reject) the authentication according to whether the external authentication service has authenticated the user. For example, if Kerberos is being used, the database will check that the user does have a valid Kerberos token.

Without the Advanced Security Option, the only form of external authentication that can be used is operating system authentication. This is a requirement for SYSDBA and SYSOPER accounts (as already discussed) but can also be used for normal users. The technique is to create an Oracle user account with the same name as the operating system user account but prefixed with a string specified by the instance parameter OS_AUTHENT_PREFIX. This parameter defaults to the string OPS$. To check its value, use a query such as this:

```
select value from v$parameter where name='os_authent_prefix';
```

On Linux or Unix, external operating system authentication is simple. Assuming that OS_AUTHENT_PREFIX is set to the default and that there is an operating system user called jwatson, if you create an oracle user and grant him the CREATE SESSION privilege, he will be able to log in with no password and will be connected to the database user account ops$jwatson.

```
create user ops$jwatson identified externally;
grant create session to ops$jwatson;
sqlplus /
```

Under Windows, when Oracle queries the operating system to find the identity of the user, Windows will usually (depending on the details of Windows security configuration) return the username prefixed with the Windows domain. Assuming that the Windows logon ID is John Watson (including a space), that the Windows domain is JWACER (which happens to be the machine name), and that the OS_AUTHENT_PREFIX is set to the default, the command will be as follows:

```
create user "OPS$JWACER\JOHN WATSON" identified externally;
```

Note that the username must be in uppercase, and because of the illegal characters (a backslash and a space), it must be enclosed in double quotes.

TIP Using external authentication can be useful, but only if the users actually log on to the machine hosting the database. Users will rarely do this, so the technique is more likely to be of value for accounts used for running maintenance or batch jobs.

Creating Accounts

The CREATE USER command has only two required arguments: a username and a method of authentication. Optionally, it can accept a clause to specify a default tablespace and a temporary tablespace, one or more quota clauses, a named profile, and commands to lock the account and expire the password. This is a typical example (with line numbers added):

```
1    create user scott identified by tiger
2    default tablespace users temporary tablespace temp
3    quota 100m on users, quota unlimited on example
4    profile developer_profile
5    password expire
6    account unlock;
```

Only the first line is required; there are defaults for everything else. Here is what the command does, broken down line by line:

1. Provide the username and a password for password authentication

2. Provide the default and temporary tablespaces

3. Set up quotas on the default and another tablespace

4. Nominate a profile for password and resource management

5. Force the user to change the password immediately

6. Make the account available for use (which would have been the default)

Every attribute of an account can be adjusted later with ALTER USER commands, with the exception of the name. This is how to change the attributes:

```
alter user scott identified by lion;
alter user scott default tablespace hr_data temporary tablespace hr_temp;
alter user scott quota unlimited on hr_data, quota 0 on users;
alter user scott profile prod_profile;
alter user scott password expire;
alter user scott account lock;
```

Having created a user account, it may be necessary to drop it.

```
drop user scott;
```

This command will succeed only if the user does not own any objects—if the schema is empty. If you do not want to identify all the objects owned and drop them first, they can be dropped with the user by specifying CASCADE.

```
drop user scott cascade;
```

Exercise 16-1: Create Users   In this exercise, you will create some users to be used for the remaining exercises in this chapter. It is assumed that there is a permanent tablespace called EXAMPLE and a temporary tablespace called TEMP. If these don't exist, either create them or use any other suitable tablespaces. Here are the steps to follow:

1. Connect to your database with SQL*Plus as a highly privileged user, such as SYSTEM or SYS.

2. Create three users.
   ```
   create user alois identified by alois
   default tablespace example password expire;
   create user afra identified by oracle
   default tablespace example quota unlimited on example;
   create user anja identified by oracle;
   ```

3. Confirm that the users have been created with Database Express. From the database home page, the navigation path is the Security tab | Users link. The users should look something like those shown in Figure 16-3.

4. From SQL*Plus, attempt to connect as user ALOIS.
   ```
   connect alois/alois
   ```

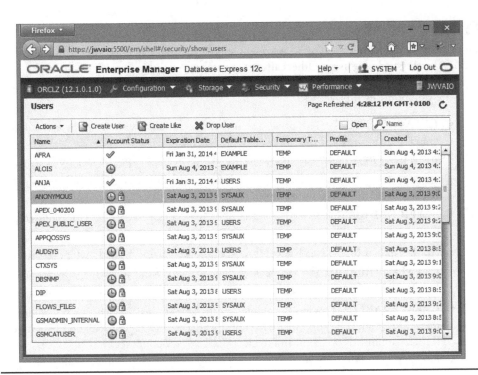

Figure 16-3 Users displayed in Database Express

5. When prompted, select a new password (such as oracle). This won't get you anywhere because ALOIS does not have the CREATE SESSION privilege.

6. Refresh the Database Express window and note that the status of the ALOIS account is no longer EXPIRED (indicated with the clock symbol) but rather OPEN (indicated with a tick) because his password has been changed.

Grant and Revoke Privileges

By default, no one can do anything in an Oracle database. A user cannot even connect without being granted a privilege. And once this has been done, they still can't do anything useful (or dangerous) without being given more privileges. Privileges are assigned to user accounts with a GRANT command and withdrawn with a REVOKE. Additional syntax can give a user the ability to grant any privileges they have to other users. By default, only the DBAs (SYS and SYSTEM) have the right to grant any but the most limited privileges.

Privileges come in two groups: system privileges, which (generally speaking) let users perform actions that affect the data dictionary, and object privileges, which let users perform actions that affect data.

PART III

System Privileges

There are more than 200 system privileges. Most apply to actions that affect the data dictionary, such as creating tables or users. Others affect the database or the instance, such as creating tablespaces, adjusting instance parameter values, and establishing a session. These are some of the more commonly used privileges:

- **CREATE SESSION**   This privilege lets the user connect. Without it, the user cannot even log on to the database.

- **RESTRICTED SESSION**   If the database is started with STARTUP RESTRICT or adjusted with ALTER SYSTEM ENABLE RESTRICTED SESSION, only users with this privilege will be able to connect.

- **ALTER DATABASE**   This gives access to many commands necessary for modifying physical structures.

- **ALTER SYSTEM**   This gives control over instance parameters and memory structures.

- **CREATE TABLESPACE**   This is used along with the ALTER TABLESPACE and DROP TABLESPACE privileges; these privileges will let a user manage tablespaces.

- **CREATE TABLE**   This lets the grantee create tables in his own schema; it includes the ability to alter and drop them, to run SELECT and Data Manipulation Language (DML) commands on them, and to create, alter, or drop indexes on them.

- **GRANT ANY OBJECT PRIVILEGE**   Lets the grantee grant object permissions on all objects, including those he does not own, to others (but not to himself).

- **CREATE ANY TABLE**   The grantee can create tables that belong to other users.

- **DROP ANY TABLE**   The grantee can drop tables belonging to any other users.

- **INSERT ANY TABLE, UPDATE ANY TABLE, DELETE ANY TABLE**   The grantee can execute these DML commands against tables owned by all other users.

- **SELECT ANY TABLE**   The grantee can SELECT from any table in the database, with one provision: Tables owned by SYS, including the data dictionary tables, are not visible.

The syntax for granting system privileges is as follows:

```
GRANT privilege [, privilege...] TO username;
```

After creating a user account, a command such as the following will grant the system privileges commonly assigned to users who will be involved in developing applications:

```
grant create session, alter session,
create table, create view, create synonym, create cluster,
create database link, create sequence,
create trigger, create type, create procedure, create operator
to username;
```

These privileges let the user connect and configure a session and then create objects to store data and PL/SQL objects. These objects can exist only in their own schema; they will have no privileges against any other schema. The object creation will also be limited by the quotas they may (or may not) have been assigned on various tablespaces.

A variation in the syntax lets the grantee pass their privilege on to a third party. This is an example:

```
connect system/oracle;
grant create table to scott with admin option;
connect scott/tiger;
grant create table to jon;
```

This gives SCOTT the ability to create tables in his own schema and also to issue the GRANT CREATE TABLE TO command himself.

 EXAM TIP Revocation of a system privilege will not cascade (unlike revocation of an object privilege).

If a privilege is revoked from a user, any actions the user performed using that privilege (such as creating tables) remain intact. Also, if the user has been granted and has used the ADMIN OPTION, any users to whom the user passed on the privilege will retain it. There is no record kept of the grantor of a system privilege, so it is not possible for a REVOKE to cascade. Figure 16-4 illustrates this.

The ANY privileges give permissions against all relevant objects in the database. Thus, the following will let SCOTT query every table in every schema in the database:

```
grant select any table to scott;
```

It is often considered bad practice to grant the ANY privileges to any user other than the system administration staff.

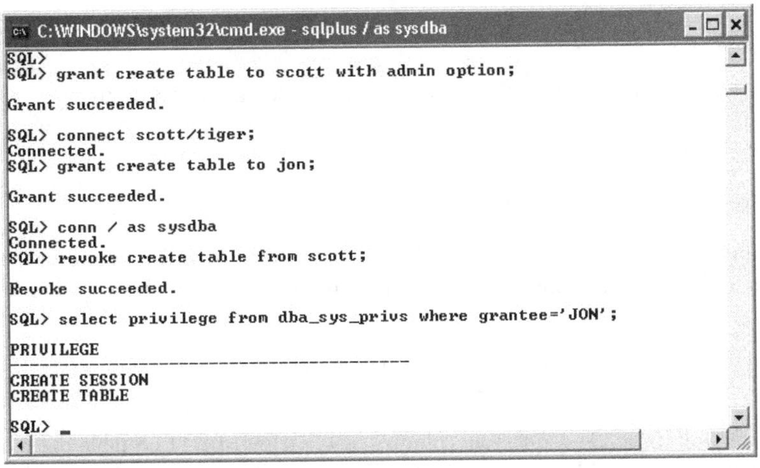

```
C:\WINDOWS\system32\cmd.exe - sqlplus / as sysdba

SQL>
SQL> grant create table to scott with admin option;

Grant succeeded.

SQL> connect scott/tiger;
Connected.
SQL> grant create table to jon;

Grant succeeded.

SQL> conn / as sysdba
Connected.
SQL> revoke create table from scott;

Revoke succeeded.

SQL> select privilege from dba_sys_privs where grantee='JON';

PRIVILEGE
------------------------------------------------
CREATE SESSION
CREATE TABLE

SQL> _
```

Figure 16-4   GRANT and REVOKE from SQL*Plus

CAUTION In fact, ANY is not as dangerous now as it was in earlier releases. It no longer includes tables in the SYS schema, so the data dictionary is still protected. However, ANY should still be used with extreme caution because it removes all protection from user tables.

Object Privileges

Object privileges give the ability to perform SELECT, INSERT, UPDATE, and DELETE commands against tables and related objects as well as to execute PL/SQL objects. These privileges do not exist for objects in the users' own schemas; if a user has the system privilege CREATE TABLE, they can perform SELECT and DML operations against the tables they create with no further need for permissions.

EXAM TIP The ANY privileges, which grant permissions against objects in every user account in the database, are not object privileges; they are system privileges.

The object privileges apply to different types of objects, listed here:

Privilege	Granted On
SELECT	Tables, views, sequences, synonyms
INSERT	Tables, views, synonyms
UPDATE	Tables, views, synonyms
DELETE	Tables, views, synonyms
ALTER	Tables, views, sequences
EXECUTE	Procedures, functions, packages, synonyms

The syntax is as follows:

```
GRANT privilege ON schema.object TO username [WITH GRANT OPTION];
```

Here is an example:

```
grant select on hr.regions to scott;
```

Variations include the use of ALL, which will apply all the permissions relevant to the type of object, and the ability to nominate particular columns of views or tables.

```
grant select on hr.employees to scott;
grant update (salary) on hr.employees to scott;
grant all on hr.regions to scott;
```

This code will let SCOTT query all columns of HR's EMPLOYEES table but write to only one nominated column, SALARY. Then SCOTT is given all the object privileges (SELECT and DML) on HR's REGIONS table.

TIP   Granting privileges at the column level is often said to be bad practice because of the massive workload involved. If it is necessary to restrict people's access to certain columns, creating a view that shows only those columns will often be a better alternative.

Using WITH GRANT OPTION (or with Database Express, navigate to Security | Users | Privileges and Roles | Edit) lets a user pass their object privilege on to a third party. Oracle retains a record of who granted object privileges to whom; this allows a REVOKE of an object to cascade to all those in the chain. Consider this sequence of commands:

```
connect hr/hr;
grant select on employees to scott with grant option;
connect scott/tiger;
grant select on hr.employees to jon with grant option;
conn jon/jon;
grant select on hr.employees to sue;
connect hr/hr;
revoke select on employees from scott;
```

At the conclusion of these commands, neither SCOTT nor JON nor SUE has the SELECT privilege against HR.EMPLOYEES.

EXAM TIP   The revocation of an object privilege will cascade (unlike revocation of a system privilege).

Exercise 16-2: Grant Direct Privileges   In this exercise, you will grant some privileges to the users created in Exercise 16-1 and prove that they work. Follow these steps:

1. Connect to your database as user SYSTEM with SQL*Plus and then grant CREATE SESSION to user ALOIS.

   ```
   grant create session to alois;
   ```

2. Open another SQL*Plus session and connect as ALOIS. This time, the login will succeed.

   ```
   connect alois/oracle
   ```

3. As ALOIS, attempt to create a table.

   ```
   create table t1 (c1 date);
   ```

   This will fail with the message "ORA-01031: insufficient privileges."

4. In the SYSTEM session, grant ALOIS the CREATE TABLE privilege.

   ```
   grant create table to alois;
   ```

5. In the ALOIS session, try again.

   ```
   create table t1 (c1 date) segment creation immediate;
   ```

   This will fail with the message "ORA-01950: no privileges on tablespace 'EXAMPLE'."

6. In the SYSTEM session, give ALOIS a quota on the EXAMPLE tablespace.

   ```
   alter user alois quota 1m on example;
   ```

7. In the ALOIS session, try again. This time, the creation will succeed.

8. As ALOIS, grant object privileges on the new table.

```
grant all on t1 to afra;
grant select on t1 to anja;
```

9. To retrieve information regarding these grants, as SYSTEM, run these queries:

```
select grantee,privilege,grantor,grantable from dba_tab_privs
where owner='ALOIS' and table_name='T1';
select * from dba_sys_privs where grantee='ALOIS';
```

10. Revoke the privileges granted to AFRA and ANJA.

```
revoke all on alois.t1 from afra;
revoke all on alois.t1 from anja;
```

11. Confirm the revocations by rerunning the first query from step 9.

Create and Manage Roles

Managing security with directly granted privileges works but has two problems. First, it can be a huge workload; an application with thousands of tables and users could need millions of grants. Second, if a privilege has been granted to a user, that user has it in all circumstances; it is not possible to make a privilege active only in certain circumstances. Both these problems are solved by using roles. A *role* is a bundle of system and/or object privileges that can be granted and revoked as a unit and, having been granted, can be temporarily activated or deactivated within a session.

Creating and Granting Roles

Roles are not schema objects; they aren't owned by anyone and therefore cannot be prefixed with a username. However, they do share the same namespace as users. It is not possible to create a role with the same name as an already-existing user or to create a user with the same name as an already-existing role.

Create a role with the CREATE ROLE command.

```
CREATE ROLE rolename;
```

Then grant privileges to the role with the usual syntax, including WITH ADMIN or WITH GRANT OPTION, as desired.

For example, assume that the HR schema is being used as a repository for data to be used by three groups of staff: managerial staff have full access, senior clerical staff have limited access, and junior clerical staff have restricted access. First, create a role that might be suitable for the junior clerks; all they can do is answer questions by running queries.

```
create role hr_junior;
grant create session to hr_junior;
grant select on hr.regions to hr_junior;
grant select on hr.locations to hr_junior;
grant select on hr.countries to hr_junior;
grant select on hr.departments to hr_junior;
grant select on hr.job_history to hr_junior;
grant select on hr.jobs to hr_junior;
grant select on hr.employees to hr_junior;
```

Anyone granted this role will be able to log on to the database and run SELECT statements against the HR tables. Next, create a role for the senior clerks, who can also write data to the EMPLOYEES and JOB_HISTORY tables.

```
create role hr_senior;
grant hr_junior to hr_senior with admin option;
grant insert, update, delete on hr.employees to hr_senior;
grant insert, update, delete on hr.job_history to hr_senior;
```

This role is first granted the HR_JUNIOR role (there is no problem granting one role to another) with the syntax that will let the senior users assign the junior role to others. Then it is granted DML privileges on just two tables. Now, create the managers' role, which can update all the other tables.

```
create role hr_manager;
grant hr_senior to hr_manager with admin option;
grant all on hr.regions to hr_manager;
grant all on hr.locations to hr_manager;
grant all on hr.countries to hr_manager;
grant all on hr.departments to hr_manager;
grant all on hr.job_history to hr_manager;
grant all on hr.jobs to hr_manager;
grant all on hr.employees to hr_manager;
```

This third role is given the HR_SENIOR role with the ability to pass it on and then gets full control over the contents of all the tables. But note that the only system privilege this role has is CREATE_SESSION, acquired through HR_SENIOR, which acquired it through HR_JUNIOR. Not even this role can create or drop tables; that must be done by the HR user or an administrator with CREATE ANY TABLE and DROP ANY TABLE system privileges.

Note the syntax WITH ADMIN OPTION, which is the same as that for granting system privileges. As with system privileges, the revocation of a role will not cascade; there is no record kept of who has granted a role to whom.

Finally, grant the roles to the relevant staff. If SCOTT is a manager, SUE is a senior clerk, and JON and ROOP are junior clerks, the flow would be as shown in Figure 16-5.

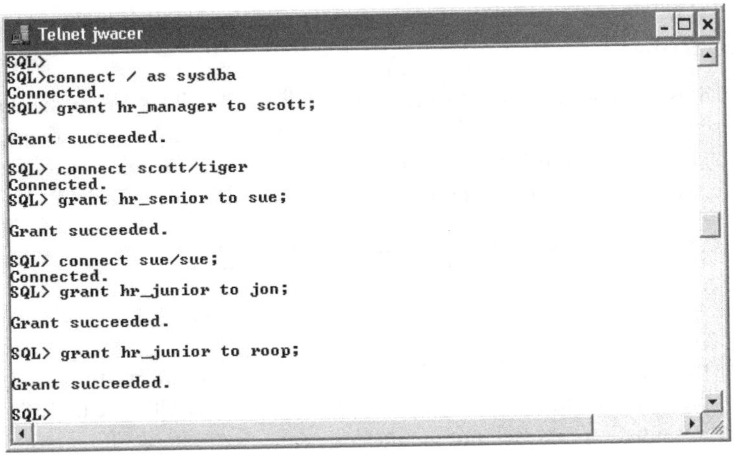

Figure 16-5 Granting roles with SQL*Plus

Predefined Roles

There are dozens of predefined roles in an Oracle database. Here are some that every DBA should be aware of:

- **CONNECT**   This role exists only for backward compatibility. In previous releases, it had the system privileges necessary to create data-storing objects, such as tables; with the current release, it has only CREATE SESSION.

- **RESOURCE**   Also for backward compatibility, this role can create both data objects (such as tables) and procedural objects (such as PL/SQL procedures).

- **DBA**   This has most of the system privileges as well as several object privileges and roles. Any user granted DBA can manage virtually all aspects of the database, except for startup and shutdown.

- **SELECT_CATALOG_ROLE**   This has thousands of object privileges against data dictionary objects but no system privileges or privileges against user data. This is useful for junior administration staff who must monitor and report on the database but not be able to see user data.

- **SCHEDULER_ADMIN**   This has the system privileges necessary for managing the Scheduler job-scheduling service.

Also, the predefined role PUBLIC is always granted to every database user account. It follows that if a privilege is granted to PUBLIC, it will be available to all users. Therefore, after the following command, all users will be able to query the HR.REGIONS table:

```
grant select on hr.regions to public;
```

 NOTE   The PUBLIC role is treated differently from any other role. It does not, for example, appear in the view DBA_ROLES. This is because the source code for DBA_ROLES, which can be seen in the cdsec.sql script called by the catalog.sql script, specifically excludes it.

Enabling Roles

By default, if a user has been granted a role, the role will enabled. This means that the moment a session is established connecting to the user account, all the privileges (and other roles) granted to the role will be active. This behavior can be modified by making the role nondefault. Following the example given in the preceding section, this query shows what roles have been granted to JON:

```
SQL> select * from dba_role_privs where grantee='JON';
GRANTEE                              GRANTED_ROLE      ADM DEF
------------------------------       --------------    --- ---
JON                                  HR_JUNIOR         NO  YES
```

JON has been granted HR_JUNIOR. He does not have administration on the role (so he cannot pass it on to anyone else), but it is a default role—he will have this role whenever he connects. This situation may well not be what you want. For example, JON has to be able to see the HR tables (it's his job), but that doesn't mean you want him to be able to dial in from home, at midnight, and hack into the tables with SQL*Plus. You want to arrange things such that he can see the tables only when he is at a terminal in the personnel office, running the HR application during working hours.

Here is how to change the default behavior:

```
alter user jon default role none;
```

Now when JON logs on, he will not have any roles enabled. Unfortunately, this means he can't log on at all—because it is only HR_JUNIOR that gives him the CREATE SESSION system privilege. This is easily fixed.

```
SQL> grant connect to jon;
Grant succeeded.
SQL> alter user jon default role connect;
User altered.
SQL> select * from dba_role_privs where grantee='JON';
GRANTEE                          GRANTED_ROLE     ADM DEF
-------------------------------- ---------------- --- ---
JON                              HR_JUNIOR        NO  NO
JON                              CONNECT          NO  YES
```

Now when JON connects, only his CONNECT role is enabled, and the current version of CONNECT is not dangerous at all. Within the application, software commands can be embedded to enable the HR_JUNIOR role. The basic command to enable a role within a session, which can be issued by the user at any time, is as follows:

```
SET ROLE rolename;
```

So, there's no security yet. But if the role is created with the following syntax, then the role can be enabled only by running the PL/SQL procedure nominated by *procedure_name*:

```
CREATE ROLE rolename IDENTIFIED USING procedure_name;
```

This procedure can make any number of checks: that the user is working on a particular TCP/IP subnet, that the user is running a particular user process (probably not SQL*Plus), that the time is in a certain range, and so on. Embedding calls to the enabling procedures at appropriate points in an application can switch roles on and off, as required, while leaving them disabled at all times when a connection is made with an ad hoc SQL tool such as SQL*Plus.

Privilege Analysis

It is sometimes difficult to identify what privileges a user has and what privileges the user actually uses, particularly when roles are involved. For this reason, Oracle provides the Privilege Analysis mechanism. The flow is as follows:

1. Define the scope of what should be analyzed, such as privilege usage throughout the entire database, privileges used that were accessed through certain roles, and privileges used by particular applications.

2. Start monitoring activity, allow users to work for a period, and stop monitoring activity.

3. Generate reports on what privileges were used, and what granted privileges were not used, during the analysis period.

The following are the critical procedures:

- dbms_privilege_capture.create_capture
- dbms_privilege_capture.enable_capture
- dbms_privilege_capture.disable_capture
- dbms_privilege_capture.generate_result

The following are the critical views:

- dba_used_privs
- dba_unused_privs

Exercise 16-3: Create and Grant Roles   In this exercise, you will create some roles, grant them to the users, and demonstrate their effectiveness. Follow these steps:

1. Connect to your database with SQL*Plus as user SYSTEM.

2. Create two roles, as follows:

```
create role usr_role;
create role mgr_role;
```

3. Grant some privileges to the roles and then grant USR_ROLE to MGR_ROLE.

```
grant create session to usr_role;
grant select on alois.t1 to usr_role;
grant usr_role to mgr_role with admin option;
grant all on alois.t1 to mgr_role;
```

4. As user SYSTEM, grant the roles to AFRA and ANJA.

```
grant mgr_role to AFRA;
```

5. Connect to the database as user AFRA.

```
connect afra/oracle;
```

6. Grant the USR_ROLE to ANJA and then insert a row into ALOIS.T1.

```
grant usr_role to anja;
insert into alois.t1 values(sysdate);
commit;
```

7. Confirm that ANJA can connect and query ALOIS.T1 but do nothing else.

```
connect anja/oracle
select * from alois.t1;
insert into alois.t1 values(sysdate);
```

8. As user SYSTEM, adjust ANJA so that by default she can log on but do nothing else.

```
connect system/oracle
grant connect to anja;
alter user anja default role connect;
```

9. Demonstrate the enabling and disabling of roles.

```
connect anja/oracle
select * from alois.t1;
set role usr_role;
select * from alois.t1;
```

10. Query the data dictionary to identify their role usage.

```
connect system/oracle
select * from dba_role_privs
where granted_role in ('USR_ROLE','MGR_ROLE');
select grantee,owner,table_name,privilege,grantable
from dba_tab_privs where grantee in ('USR_ROLE','MGR_ROLE')
union all
select grantee,to_char(null),to_char(null),privilege,admin_option
from dba_sys_privs  where grantee in ('USR_ROLE','MGR_ROLE')
order by grantee;
```

Create and Manage Profiles

You can use a profile to enforce a password. Profiles are always used, but the default profile (applied by default to all users, including SYS and SYSTEM) does very little.

Password Profile Limits

These are the limits that can be applied to passwords:

- **FAILED_LOGIN_ATTEMPTS**   Specifies the number of consecutive errors on a password before the account is locked. If the correct password is given before this limit is reached, the counter is reset to zero.

- **PASSWORD_LOCK_TIME**   Specifies the number of days to lock an account after FAILED_LOGIN_ATTEMPTS is reached.

- **PASSWORD_LIFE_TIME**   Specifies the number of days before a password expires. It may still be usable for a while after this time, depending on PASSWORD_ GRACE_TIME.

- **PASSWORD_GRACE_TIME**   Specifies the number of days following the first successful login after the password has expired during which the password can be changed. The old password is still usable during this time.

- **PASSWORD_REUSE_TIME**   Specifies the number of days before a password can be reused.

- **PASSWORD_REUSE_MAX**   Specifies the number of password changes before a password can be reused.

- **PASSWORD_VERIFY_FUNCTION**   Specifies the name of a function to run whenever a password is changed. The purpose of the function is assumed to be checking the new password for a required degree of complexity, but it can do pretty much anything you want.

TIP   You can also use profiles to limit resource usage, but a much more sophisticated tool to accomplish this is Resource Manager.

To see which profile is currently assigned to each user, run this query:

```
select username,profile from dba_users;
```

By default, all users will be assigned the profile called DEFAULT. Then the view that will display the profiles themselves is DBA_PROFILES.

```
select * from dba_profiles where profile='DEFAULT';
```

The DEFAULT profile has these password limits:

Resource Name	Limit
FAILED_LOGIN_ATTEMPTS	10
PASSWORD_LIFE_TIME	180 days
PASSWORD_REUSE_TIME	Unlimited
PASSWORD_REUSE_MAX	Unlimited
PASSWORD_VERIFY_FUNCTION	null
PASSWORD_LOCK_TIME	1 day
PASSWORD_GRACE_TIME	7 days

These restrictions are not too strict; a password can be entered incorrectly ten consecutive times before the account is locked for one day, and a password will expire after about six months with a one-week grace period for changing it after that. There is no check on password complexity.

Creating and Assigning Profiles

The simplest way to enable more sophisticated password management is to run code provided in a supplied script. On Unix or Linux, it is as follows:

```
$ORACLE_HOME/rdbms/admin/utlpwdmg.sql
```

On Windows, it is as follows:

```
%ORACLE_HOME%\rdbms\admin\utlpwdmg.sql
```

On either platform, the script creates a set of functions offering various degrees of password complexity checking.

To create a profile with SQL*Plus, use the CREATE PROFILE command, setting whatever limits are required. Any limits not specified will be picked up from the current version of the DEFAULT profile. For example, it could be that the rules of the organization state that accounts should be locked after five consecutive failed login attempts for one hour, except for administrators, who should be locked after two attempts for a whole day, and that all passwords should be subject to the provided standard password complexity verification algorithm.

Exercise 16-4: Create and Use Profiles   In this exercise, you'll create, assign, and test a profile that forces some password control. Here are the steps to follow:

1. Connect to your database with SQL*Plus as user SYS.

2. Execute the script that will create the supplied verification functions and then apply one to the default profile. Confirm that the function has been created and applied.

   ```
   @?/rdbms/admin/utlpwdmg.sql
   describe sys.ora12c_verify_function
   select * from dba_profiles where resource_name=
   'PASSWORD_VERIFY_FUNCTION';
   ```

3. Create a profile that will lock accounts after two wrong passwords for 10 minutes.

   ```
   create profile two_wrong limit failed_login_attempts 2
   password_lock_time 10/1440;
   ```

4. Assign this new profile to ALOIS.

   ```
   alter user alois profile two_wrong;
   ```

5. Deliberately enter the wrong password for ALOIS a few times.

   ```
   connect alois/wrongpassword
   ```

6. As user SYSTEM, check the status of the ALOIS account and unlock it.

   ```
   select account_status from dba_users where username='ALOIS';
   alter user alois account unlock;
   select account_status from dba_users where username='ALOIS';
   ```

7. Check that ALOIS can now connect.

   ```
   connect alois/oracle
   ```

8. Test the verification function by attempting to change the password a few times.

   ```
   alter user alois identified by oracle;
   ```

9. Tidy up by dropping the profile, the roles, and the users. Note the use of CASCADE when dropping the profile to remove it from ALOIS as well as on the DROP USER command to drop his table. Roles can be dropped even if they are assigned to users. The privileges granted on the table will be revoked as the table is dropped.

   ```
   connect system/oracle
   drop profile two_wrong cascade;
   alter profile default limit password_verify_function null;
   drop role usr_role;
   drop role mgr_role;
   drop user alois cascade;
   drop user anja;
   drop user afra;
   ```

Explain DBA Responsibilities for Security and Auditing

Auditing is necessary to detect suspicious or even downright illegal activity. Auditing is not an area where the DBA makes all the decisions; they do what they are told. If the business states that all access to certain tables must be tracked, the DBA must arrange this. In some jurisdictions, regulatory requirements make auditing certain actions mandatory. Apart from these business needs, two groups of users require special attention: developers and DBAs. Developers have great power within the database; DBAs have even more. Monitoring activity by these groups to ensure that they are not abusing their powers raises the issue of how to audit users who may be able to modify the audit trail (or "Who will guard the guards themselves?" as Juvenal put it (in Latin) nearly 2,000 years ago).

Reasons for Auditing

Why is an audit considered necessary in virtually all databases? The following are typical reasons:

- *To enable accountability for actions.* To hold users responsible for their actions, it is necessary to track what they have done.

- *To deter users from inappropriate activity.* Many users will have the ability to perform actions that are damaging or fraudulent. Knowing that they are monitored will dissuade them from doing this.

- *To investigate suspicious activity.* Security may be set up correctly, but it is still useful to know whether people are trying to access data or run commands that are beyond their authorization.

- *To notify an auditor of unauthorized activity.* In some cases, users may have more capabilities than they need. Auditing can track the use of any privileges considered dangerous and access to sensitive data.

- *Compliance issues.* Many applications have quasi-legal requirements for audit. Typically, these are based around access to personal or financial information.

Auditing Techniques

Several auditing techniques are available in an Oracle environment. The most powerful is the Audit Vault. This is a separately installed and licensed product that is far beyond the scope of the Oracle Certified Professional (OCP) syllabus. Most environments will not need this; the internal techniques described in this section will be sufficient for the majority of business needs. Release 12c introduces a new auditing method: *unified auditing*. It is this technique that is tested.

Standard Database Auditing

Standard database auditing is enabled with one parameter: AUDIT_TRAIL. The default for this parameter is NULL, meaning that standard audit is disabled. However, if the database is created with the Database Configuration Assistant (DBCA), a standard audit will have been enabled by setting this parameter to DB.

Standard auditing is configured with the AUDIT and NOAUDIT commands. Standard auditing can track access to objects, use of privileges, and execution of certain statements. Audit records can be gathered for all users or only some, gathered once per session or once per action in the session, gathered whenever the attempt was made, or filtered by successful or unsuccessful attempts. The audit records are either written to a database table (which is SYS.AUD$) and visible through a set of views or written to the operating system where they are stored as files external to the database.

This technique for auditing is fully supported, but in release 12.1, Oracle Corporation recommends that unified auditing should be used instead.

Fine Grained Auditing

Fine Grained Auditing (FGA) can be configured to focus on precise areas of concern. Rather than auditing access at the object level, FGA can track access to certain rows and columns. Without FGA, an audit tends to produce a large number of "false positives," that is, audit records that report issues of no concern. The following are examples:

- Access to a table of employee data is fine in general, but if a SALARY column is accessed, that should be recorded.

- Perhaps a user has full rights to read a table when running an approved application. But if they query the table from SQL*Plus, that should be known.

- It may not be necessary to record access that occurs through normal means in the working day, but out-of-hours access from a device outside the corporate network should be tracked.

FGA will generate an audit record when certain conditions are met. The condition can be based on a predicate and also on a column list. As well as auditing the event, FGA can execute a user-defined procedure. This is a powerful facility. In effect, it is a trigger on SELECT. It is possible to define different audit policies for different statements. For example, you might want to record changes to data but not reads.

The interface to FGA is a simple-to-use application programming interface (API)—the DBMS_FGA package, with four procedures:

- **DBMS_FGA.ADD_POLICY**   Create a policy for a table.

- **DBMS_FGA.DROP_POLICY**   Drop a previously created policy.

- **DBMS_FGA.DISABLE_POLICY**   Disable the policy. Policies are by default enabled.

- **DBMS_FGA.ENABLE_POLICY**   Enable a policy that had been previously disabled.

The API is reasonably self-explanatory. Consider these examples:

```
execute dbms_fga.add_policy(-
     object_schema=>'scott',-
     object_name=>'emp',-
     policy_name=>'emp_d10_pol',-
     audit_condition=>'deptno=10',-
     statement_types=>'select,insert,update,delete');
execute dbms_fga.add_policy(-
     object_schema=>'scott',-
     object_name=>'emp',-
     policy_name=>'emp_sal_pol',-
     audit_column=>'sal');
execute dbms_fga.add_policy(-
     object_schema=>'scott',-
     object_name=>'emp',-
     policy_name=>'emp_del_pol',-
     handler_schema=>'sec',-
     handler_module=>'empdel',-
     statement_types=>'delete');
```

The previous code defines three policies on one table, SCOTT.EMP. The first policy, EMP_D10_POL, will generate an audit record whenever any statement is executed that accesses an employee in Department 10. Note that the policy does not include MERGE. A MERGE is captured according to the underlying DML statement that the MERGE implements. Using the default of NULL for AUDIT_COLUMNS means that there is no column restriction; no matter what columns are projected, the statement will be audited.

The second policy will capture all SELECT statements (SELECT is the default for the STATEMENT_TYPE argument) that read the SAL column. The default of NULL for AUDIT_CONDITION means that the audit will be made for any row.

The third policy will generate an audit record and will also run a procedure, SEC.EMPDEL, whenever a row is deleted. The procedure must conform to a defined interface. It must accept three VARCHAR2 arguments, which will be populated with the object schema (in this case, SCOTT), the object name (in this case, EMP), and the policy name (in this case, EMP_DEL_POL).

The audit records are visible in the data dictionary view DBA_FGA_AUDIT_TRAIL. This includes the actual SQL statement, along with details such as who executed it and when. The underlying storage for the view is the table SYS.FGA_LOG$, which by default resides in the SYSTEM tablespace.

Value-Based Auditing

The declarative techniques for auditing (standard auditing, FGA, and unified auditing) do not capture the data themselves. They capture the action: who, what, when, and with which privilege. This means the statement executed, not the values that were actually seen or updated. If it is necessary to see the values, you must resort to value-base auditing, which is implemented with triggers.

A DML trigger designed to fire whenever any DML statement is executed can capture the row values and write them out to a user-defined audit table. Consider this example:

```
create or replace trigger emp_val_audit
after update or insert or delete on emp
for each row
begin
case
when updating then insert into sec.emp_aud
     values(user,sysdate,:new.empno,:old.sal,:new.sal);
when inserting then insert into sec.emp_aud
     values(user,sysdate,:new.empno,null,:new.sal);
when deleting then insert into sec.emp_aud
     values(user,sysdate,:new.empno,:old.sal,null);
end case;
end;
```

Depending on the nature of the DML, this trigger will capture appropriate values into a logging table. The trigger will fire as part of the DML, and the insert will be committed (or rolled back) with the calling transaction. It is therefore possible that performance may degrade. This should not be the case with standard or FGA auditing, where the capture is accomplished by routines that are internal to the instance, not by user-defined PL/SQL code.

Unified Auditing

Unified auditing is a new technique that replaces standard auditing, although the two can work concurrently. Unified auditing declares policies, which are then enabled for particular (or all) users. Five preconfigured policies are available to be implemented:

- ORA_SECURECONFIG declares similar audits to the default standard auditing.

- ORA_DATABASE_PARAMETER captures changes implemented with ALTER DATABASE and ALTER SYSTEM commands.

- ORA_ACCOUNT_MGMT captures changes made with ALTER, DROP, and CREATE roles and users, as well as GRANT and REVOKE.

- ORA_RAS_POLICY_MANAGEMENT and ORA_RAS_SESSION_MANAGEMENT have to do with Real Application Security, which is beyond the scope of the OCP examinations.

To confirm whether unified auditing is enabled, query the V$OPTION dynamic performance view. In this example, it is not enabled:

```
orclz>
orclz> select value from v$option where
  2  parameter ='Unified Auditing';

VALUE
--------------------------------------------------
FALSE

orclz>
```

The unified auditing mechanism is efficient. By default, audit records are not written to the audit trail table (in the AUDSYS schema) in real time but via a buffered queue. So, sessions are writing only to a memory structure in the System Global Area (SGA). A background process, the GEN0 generic process, takes the strain of writing the records from the queue to the table asynchronously. This delayed write does raise the possibility of losing audit records in the event of an instance crash. Although enabled by default, this can be changed. To switch from delayed write mode to immediate write mode, use a procedure in the DBMS_AUDIT_MGMT package. This example enables immediate write and then switches back the default queued write:

```
orclz>
orclz> exec dbms_audit_mgmt.set_audit_trail_property(-
> dbms_audit_mgmt.audit_trail_unified,-
> dbms_audit_mgmt.audit_trail_write_mode,-
> dbms_audit_mgmt.audit_trail_immediate_write);

PL/SQL procedure successfully completed.

orclz>
orclz> exec dbms_audit_mgmt.set_audit_trail_property(-
> dbms_audit_mgmt.audit_trail_unified,-
> dbms_audit_mgmt.audit_trail_write_mode,-
> dbms_audit_mgmt.audit_trail_queued_write);

PL/SQL procedure successfully completed.

orclz>
```

Unified audit records are written to a table in the AUDSYS schema. The table has a system-generated name that may be different in every database and is read-only to any regular Data Definition Language (DDL) or DML statements. It can be managed only through DBMS_AUDIT_MGMT.

Mandatory Auditing

A small number of operations are always audited, whether configured or not:

- Execution of the unified auditing commands CREATE/ALTER/DROP AUDIT POLICY
- Execution of the standard audit commands AUDIT/NOAUDIT
- Execution of the FGA package DBMS_FGA
- Execution of the management package DBMS_AUDIT_MGMT

Furthermore, all top-level statements executed by administrative users (sessions connected as SYSDBA, SYSOPER, SYSBACKUP, SYSDG, SYSKM, or SYSASM) while the database is in NOMOUNT or MOUNT mode are audited to the operating system audit trail. On Unix or Linux, the records are written to files in the directory specified by the AUDIT_FILE_DEST parameter; on Windows, they are written to the Windows application log. These statements include connect attempts, startup or shutdown, and any ALTER SYSTEM and ALTER DATABASE commands.

Enable Standard Database Auditing and Unified Auditing

Standard auditing is possible (although may not be enabled or configured) only if the database has not been converted to unified auditing. Unified auditing requires an appropriate dynamic library to be available, which is not the case following installation of the Oracle Home.

Enable Standard Auditing

Figure 16-6 shows a query that displays the current values of the standard auditing parameters as well as two commands to enable auditing.

The parameters are as follows:

audit_sys_operations	Records all SQL executed as an administrative user to the operating system audit trail. Default: false.
audit_file_dest	The location of audit records if auditing is to the operating system. Unix default: $ORACLE_BASE/admin/$ORACLE_SID/adump. Windows: always to the application log.
audit_syslog_level	Enables writing to the syslog daemon. Set according to your system administrator's instruction. Default: null (disabled).
audit_trail	Enables or disables standard auditing to the operating system or the database, in various formats. Default: null (disabled).

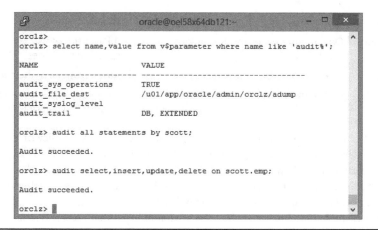

Figure 16-6   Standard auditing configuration

The values in Figure 16-6 are typical of many installations. Once the parameters have been set (all of which are static), the AUDIT command enables auditing of the execution of certain statements, the use of certain privileges, or the access to certain objects.

Enable Unified Auditing

If unified auditing is not enabled (which it is not, following a standard installation), it is necessary to enable it within the Oracle executable code; you relink the Oracle executables for Linux or copy in a dynamic link library for Windows.

Here is how to relink the executables:

```
cd $ORACLE_HOME/rdbms/lib
make -f ins_rdbms.mk uniaud_on ioracle ORACLE_HOME=$ORACLE_HOME
```

On Windows, stop the Windows services for the database and the listener and then copy in the appropriate dynamic link library.

```
net stop oracleserviceORCL
net stop OracleOraDB12Home1TNSListener
cd %ORACLE_HOME%\bin
copy orauniaud12.dll.dbl orauniaud12.dll
net start oracleserviceORCL
net start OracleOraDB12Home1TNSListener
```

Restart the listener and database instance and then confirm in V$OPTION that unified auditing is now enabled.

To configure unified auditing, first grant the necessary roles to a user. These roles are AUDIT_ADMIN to administer unified auditing and AUDIT_VIEWER to view and analyze audit data. Then, as an AUDIT_ADMIN user, enable the supplied policies or create your own. A policy consists of specifying one (or more) of the three categories to audit.

Category	What to Specify	What Is Audited
PRIVILEGES	One or more system and/or object privileges	All events that use any of the specified privileges
ACTIONS	One or more SQL commands	All invocations of the command
ROLES	One or more roles	Use of any privileges used through a direct grant to the role

Figure 16-7 shows creating policies of each type, followed by a mixed policy that combines the three types. Finally, it shows an example of an ACTION policy that will apply to just one table.

Having created the policy, it must be activated, either globally or for individual users. By default, an audit record is generated whenever the audit condition is met, whether the result was successful or not. Figure 16-8 shows activating policies in various ways.

The first example in the figure enables the privpol policy for all users. Every attempt to use either of the privileges, whether successful or not, will be recorded. The next example enables the actpol policy but will record only successful attempts to execute the statements. The third example will activate the rolepol policy for just two users, recording every time they use a privilege acquired through the nominated role. Then mixedpol is enabled for all users when attempts fail. The syntax to disable a policy is NOAUDIT POLICY *<policy name>*.

The last example in Figure 16-8 uses the DBMS_AUDIT_MGMT.FLUSH_UNIFIED_ AUDIT_TRAIL procedure to flush all records currently buffered in the SGA to the audit trail within the database.

Exercise 16-5: Use Unified Auditing   In this exercise, you will enable unified auditing. The method differs between Linux and Windows. Then you will create and configure audit policies as well as query the results. Connect as SYSDBA unless otherwise directed. Here are the steps to follow:

1. Determine whether unified auditing is enabled by running this query:

```
select value from v$option where parameter='Unified Auditing';
```

Following a standard install, this will return FALSE.

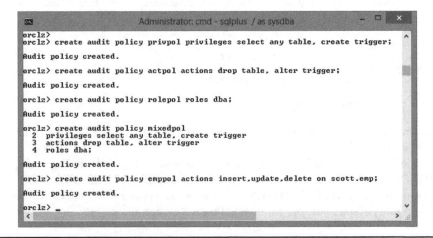

Figure 16-7   Defining unified auditing policies

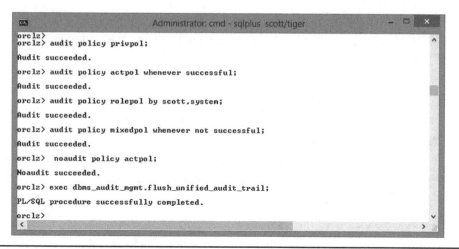

```
Administrator: cmd - sqlplus  scott/tiger                    —  □  ✕

orclz>
orclz> audit policy privpol;

Audit succeeded.

orclz> audit policy actpol whenever successful;

Audit succeeded.

orclz> audit policy rolepol by scott,system;

Audit succeeded.

orclz> audit policy mixedpol whenever not successful;

Audit succeeded.

orclz>  noaudit policy actpol;

Noaudit succeeded.

orclz> exec dbms_audit_mgmt.flush_unified_audit_trail;

PL/SQL procedure successfully completed.

orclz>
```

Figure 16-8   Enabling and disabling policies

2. Shut down the Oracle services.

   Shut down all database instances and listeners. On Windows, also stop all Oracle-related Windows services.

3. Enable unified auditing.

   In Linux, relink the executables to include the unified auditing libraries.
   ```
   cd $ORACLE_HOME/rdbms/lib
   make -f ins_rdbms.mk uniaud_on ioracle ORACLE_HOME=$ORACLE_HOME
   ```
   In Windows, copy in the unified auditing dynamic link library:
   ```
   cd %ORACLE_HOME%\bin
   copy orauniaud12.dll.dbl orauniaud12.dll
   ```

4. Confirm that unified auditing is now enabled.

   Start the instance and listener (on Windows, start the relevant services) and rerun the query from step 1. This will return TRUE.

5. Enable a presupplied audit policy and then create and enable your own.
   ```
   audit policy ora_account_mgmt;
   create audit policy aud_dba_role roles dba;
   audit policy aud_dba_role by system;
   ```
   a. Confirm what has been configured:
   ```
   select policy_name, enabled_opt, user_name from
   audit_unified_enabled_policies;
   ```
   b. Note for whom the policies have been enabled. Are any policies enabled by default?

6. Confirm that unified auditing records are generated.

    a. Connect as user SYSTEM and perform a few actions. Here is an example:

```
create user x identified by y;
alter system set open_cursors=300 scope=memory;
```

    b. Query the unified audit trail.

```
exec dbms_audit_mgmt.flush_unified_audit_trail
select dbusername,sql_text from unified_audit_trail;
```

7. Attempt to tamper with the audit trail.

Connected as SYSDBA, identify the name of the audit trail table, and attempt to delete it.

```
select table_name from dba_tables where owner='AUDSYS';
delete from audsys."&audit_table_name";
truncate table audsys."&audit_table_name";
```

8. Clean the audit trail.

Execute a procedure to clear out the unified audit trail. This may throw an error message regarding initialization but will function nonetheless.

```
select count(*) from unified_audit_trail;
execute dbms_audit_mgmt.clean_audit_trail(-
dbms_audit_mgmt.audit_trail_all,false);
select count(*) from unified_audit_trail;
```

Two-Minute Drill

Create and Manage Database User Accounts

- Users connect to a user account, which is connected to a schema.
- Some form of authentication is always required.
- A user must have a quota on a tablespace before they can create any objects.
- A user who owns objects cannot be dropped, unless the CASCADE keyword is used.

Grant and Revoke Privileges

- Privileges are of two types: object privileges and system privileges.
- By default, a user can do nothing. They can't even log on.
- A revocation of a system privilege does not cascade; a revocation of an object privilege does.

Create and Manage Roles

- Roles are not schema objects.
- Roles can contain both system and object privileges as well as other roles.
- A role can be enabled or disabled for a session.

Create and Manage Profiles

- Profiles can enforce password policies.
- Every user always has a profile (by default, the DEFAULT profile).

Explain DBA Responsibilities for Security and Auditing

- The DBA should configure auditing according to the organization's requirements.
- Unified auditing is the recommended approach.
- Value-based auditing can also be used, based on DML triggers.

Enable Standard Database Auditing and Unified Auditing

- Standard auditing is still supported and is enabled with instance parameters.
- Configure standard auditing with the AUDIT and NOAUDIT commands.
- Unified auditing requires linking appropriate modules into the Oracle executables.
- Unified auditing is configured by declaring audit policies.
- It is not possible to edit the unified audit trail with SQL commands.

Self Test

1. How can you permit users to connect without requiring them to authenticate themselves? (Choose the best answer.)

   A. Grant CREATE SESSION to PUBLIC.

   B. Create a user such as this, without a password:
      ```
      CREATE USER ANON IDENTIFIED BY '';
      ```

   C. Create a profile that disables password authentication and assign it to the users.

   D. You cannot do this because all users must be authenticated.

2. You create a user with this statement:
   ```
   create user jon identified by oracle default tablespace example;
   ```
   What more must be done before the user can create a table in the EXAMPLE tablespace? (Choose all correct answers.)

   A. Nothing more is necessary.

   B. Give him a quota on EXAMPLE.

   C. Grant him the CREATE TABLE privilege.

   D. Grant him the CREATE SESSION privilege.

   E. Grant him the MANAGE TABLESPACE privilege.

3. If a user owns tables in a tablespace, what will be the effect of attempting to reduce the user's quota on the tablespace to zero? (Choose the best answer.)

    A. The tables will survive, but INSERTS will fail.

    B. The tables will survive but cannot get bigger.

    C. The attempt will fail unless the tables are dropped first.

    D. The tables will be dropped automatically if the CASCADE keyword is used.

4. If you create a user without specifying a temporary tablespace, what temporary tablespace will be assigned? (Choose the best answer.)

    A. You must specify a temporary tablespace.

    B. SYSTEM.

    C. TEMP.

    D. The database default temporary tablespace.

    E. The user will not have a temporary tablespace.

5. You issue these commands:

```
a.        grant select on hr.regions to jon;
b.        grant all on hr.regions to jon;
c.        grant dba to jon;
d.        grant select on hr.regions to public;
```

Which grants should be revoked to prevent JON from seeing the contents of HR.REGIONS? (Choose the best answer.)

    A. a, b, c, and d

    B. a, c, and d

    C. a and b

    D. c and d

    E. a, b, and c

6. Which of these statements about system privileges are correct? (Choose all correct answers.)

    A. Only the SYS and SYSTEM users can grant system privileges.

    B. If a system privilege is revoked from a user, it will also be revoked from all users to whom the user granted it.

    C. If a system privilege is revoked from a user, it will not be revoked from all users to whom the user granted it.

    D. CREATE TABLE is a system privilege.

    E. CREATE ANY TABLE is a system privilege.

7. Study this script (line numbers have been added):

```
1      create role hr_role identified by pass;
2      grant create table to hr_role;
3      grant select table to hr_role;
4      grant connect to hr_role;
```

Which line will cause an error? (Choose the best answer.)

A. Line 1, because only users, not roles, have passwords.

B. Line 2, because only users, not roles, can create and own tables.

C. Line 3, because SELECT TABLE is not a privilege.

D. Line 4, because a role cannot have a system privilege in addition to table privileges.

8. Which of these statements is incorrect regarding roles? (Choose the best answer.)

A. You can grant object privileges and system privileges as well as roles to a role.

B. A role cannot have the same name as a table.

C. A role cannot have the same name as a user.

D. Roles can be enabled or disabled within a session.

9. If a password profile is dropped, what will be the effect on users to whom it is assigned? (Choose the best answer.)

A. You cannot drop the profile until it is unassigned from the users.

B. The profile will be removed if you use the CASCADE keyword.

C. The users will revert to the default profile.

D. Users to whom it is assigned will continue to use it, but it can no longer be assigned to anyone else.

10. Which of these can be controlled by a password profile? (Choose all correct answers.)

A. Two or more users choosing the same password

B. Preventing the reuse of a password by the same user

C. Forcing a user to change the password

D. Enabling or disabling password file authentication

11. You want to use unified auditing, and you run this query:

```
orclz> select value from v$option
where parameter='Unified Auditing';
VALUE
-----------------------------------------------------------------
TRUE
orclz>
```

What should you do to enable unified auditing? (Choose the best answer.)

A. Run ALTER SYSTEM SET AUDIT_TRAIL=DB,EXTENDED SCOPE=SPFILE; and then restart the database.

B. Relink the Oracle executables with the unified auditing libraries.

C. Create and enable one or more unified auditing policies.

D. Disable standard auditing.

12. It is necessary to track all executions of SELECT by any users against a particular table. Which auditing tool will do this? (Choose the best answer.)

    A. Standard auditing

    B. Fine Grained Auditing

    C. Unified auditing

    D. All of the above

13. What types of activity are mandatorily audited? (Choose three answers.)

    A. Creating, altering, or dropping an audit policy

    B. Creating, altering, or dropping a user

    C. Execution of the AUDIT and NOAUDIT commands

    D. All statements executed while connected as SYSDBA

    E. SYSDBA top-level statements in MOUNT or NOMOUNT

    F. DDL against the data dictionary

14. Is it possible for the unified audit trail to lose audit records? (Choose the best answer.)

    A. The unified audit trail is always protected in all circumstances.

    B. Records cannot be lost, but they can be deleted or modified with DML commands.

    C. The audit trail is protected against DML, but DDL (such as TRUNCATE) can lose records.

    D. It is possible for records to be lost in the event of an instance failure.

Self Test Answers

   1. ☑ **D.** All users must be authenticated.
     ☒ **A, B,** and **C** are incorrect. **A** is incorrect because although this will give all users permission to connect, they will still have to authenticate. **B** is incorrect because a NULL is not acceptable as a password. **C** is incorrect because a profile can only manage passwords, not disable them.

   2. ☑ **C** and **D.** All these actions are necessary.
     ☒ **A, B,** and **E** are incorrect. **A** is incorrect because without privileges and a quota, JON cannot connect and create a table. **B** is not necessary because an unlimited quota is implicitly granted on the EXAMPLE tablespace to user JON. **E** is incorrect because this privilege lets you manage a tablespace, not create objects in it.

   3. ☑ **B.** It will not be possible to allocate further extents to the tables.
     ☒ **A, C,** and **D** are incorrect. **A** is incorrect because inserts will succeed as long as there is space in the extents already allocated. **C** is incorrect because there is no need to drop the tables. **D** is incorrect because CASCADE cannot be applied to a quota command.

4. ☑ **D.** There is always a database-wide default, which (by default) is SYSTEM. In many cases, it will have been set to TEMP.

☒ **A, B, C,** and **E** are incorrect. **A** is incorrect because there is a default. **B** is incorrect because the default temporary tablespace may have been changed. **C** is incorrect because although TEMP is frequently used by default, it may not be. **E** is incorrect because all user accounts must have a temporary tablespace.

5. ☑ **B.** The grant of the DBA role and the grant to PUBLIC must be removed, as well as the directly granted SELECT privilege.

☒ **A, C, D,** and **E** are incorrect. **C, D,** and **E** are incorrect because they all leave one grant in place that must be revoked. **A** is incorrect because it is not necessary to revoke ALL as well as SELECT; either would be sufficient.

6. ☑ **C, D,** and **E.** Answer **C** is correct because the revocation of a system privilege does not cascade. **D** and **E** are correct because any action that updates the data dictionary is a system privilege.

☒ **A** and **B** are incorrect. **A** is incorrect because system privileges can be granted by any user who has been granted the privilege WITH ADMIN OPTION. **B** is incorrect because the revocation of a system privilege does not cascade.

7. ☑ **C.** There is no such privilege as SELECT TABLE; it is granted implicitly with CREATE TABLE.

☒ **A, B,** and **D** are incorrect. **A** is incorrect because roles can be password protected. **B** is incorrect because even though tables must be owned by users, permission to create them can be granted to a role. **D** is incorrect because a role can have any combination of object and system privileges.

8. ☑ **B.** Roles are not schema objects and therefore can have the same names as tables.

☒ **A, C,** and **D** are incorrect. **A** is incorrect because roles can have any combination of system, object, and role privileges. **C** is incorrect because roles cannot have the same names as users. **D** is incorrect because roles can be enabled and disabled at any time.

9. ☑ **C.** Dropping a profile implicitly reassigns all relevant users to the default profile.

☒ **A, B,** and **D** are incorrect. **A** is incorrect because of the implicit reassignment of users. **B** is incorrect because there is no CASCADE keyword in the DROP PROFILE command; it isn't necessary. **D** is incorrect because the effect of dropping a profile is immediate.

10. ☑ **B** and **C.** These are both password limits.

☒ **A** and **D** are incorrect. **A** is incorrect because it is not possible to control this. Oracle has no knowledge of the actual password, only knowledge of the hash of the password. **D** is incorrect because this is controlled through the REMOTE_LOGIN_PASSWORDFILE instance parameter, not through profiles.

11. ☑ **B.** It is necessary to link in the unified auditing libraries to the Oracle binaries.

☒ **A, C,** and **D** are incorrect. **A** is incorrect because the AUDIT_TRAIL parameter enables standard auditing, not unified auditing. **C** is necessary but not sufficient. **D** is incorrect because standard and unified auditing can coexist.

12. ☑ **D**. Any of the auditing methods can do this.

☒ **A**, **B**, and **C** are incorrect. Each of these methods can track such access, although each has different means for configuration and different destinations for the audit records.

13. ☑ **A**, **C**, and **E**. Commands that configure auditing are themselves audited, as well as all top-level statements executed before the database is opened.

☒ **B**, **D**, and **F** are incorrect. These classes of commands are not mandatorily audited. Most DBAs will want to audit them, but this must be explicitly configured.

14. ☑ **D**. By default, records may be buffered in the SGA before being written to the audit trail. Therefore, an instance failure could lose records.

☒ **A**, **B**, and **C** are incorrect. **A** is incorrect because the audit trail can in fact lose records—if not configured to write them in real time. **B** and **C** are incorrect because the audit trail is protected against both DML and DDL.

CHAPTER 17

Moving and Re-organizing Data

Exam Objectives

- 062.17.1   Describe Ways to Move Data
- 062.17.2   Create and Use Directory Objects
- 062.17.3   Use SQL*Loader to Load Data from a Non-Oracle Database
- 062.17.4   Use External Tables to Move Data via Platform-Independent Files
- 062.17.5   Explain the General Architecture of Oracle Data Pump
- 062.17.6   Use Data Pump Export and Import to Move Data between Oracle Databases
- 063.15.1   Use Data Pump in a Multitenant Environment
- 063.15.2   Use SQL*Loader in a Multitenant Environment

A common need in a database environment is to move data from one database to another. Oracle provides two facilities for this: Data Pump and SQL*Loader. Data Pump can transfer data between Oracle databases (across versions and platforms), whereas SQL*Loader can read datasets generated by non-Oracle systems. The chapter ends with a discussion of using these two facilities in a multitenant environment. Multitenant container and pluggable databases are discussed in Chapter 32. Using Data Pump and SQL*Loader in a multitenant environment are measured in the Advanced Administration exam.

Describe Ways to Move Data

There are many situations where bulk transfers of data into a database or between databases are necessary. Common cases include populating a data warehouse with data extracted from transaction processing systems and copying data from live systems to test or development environments. Because entering data with standard INSERT statements is not always the best way to do large-scale operations, the Oracle database comes with facilities designed for bulk operations. These are SQL*Loader and Data Pump. Database administrators also have the option of reading data without ever actually inserting it into the database; this is accomplished through the use of external tables.

Create and Use Directory Objects

Oracle directory objects allow sessions against the database to read and write operating system files. Some Oracle utilities (such as Data Pump) require directories.

Oracle directories provide a layer of abstraction between the user and the operating system. You as the database administrator (DBA) create a directory object within the database, which points to a physical path on the file system. Permissions on these Oracle directories can then be granted to individual database users. At the operating system level, the Oracle user (the operating system account under which the Oracle instance is running) will need permissions against the operating system directories to which the Oracle directories refer.

Directories can be created from a SQL*Plus prompt with the CREATE DIRECTORY command. To see information about directories, query the view DBA_DIRECTORIES. Each directory has a name and the physical path to which it refers. Note that Oracle does not verify whether the path exists when you create the directory; if it does not exist or if the operating system user who owns the Oracle software does not have permission to read and write to it, there will be an error only when an attempt is made to use the directory. Having created a directory, you must give the Oracle database users who will be making use of the directory permission to read from and write to it, just as your system administrators must give the operating system users permission to read from and write to the physical path.

 EXAM TIP Directories are always owned by user SYS, but any user to whom you have granted the CREATE ANY DIRECTORY privilege can create them.

Figure 17-1 demonstrates how to create directories using SQL*Plus. In the figure, user SCOTT attempts to create a directory pointing to his operating system home directory on the database server machine. This fails because, by default, users do not have permission to do this. After being granted permission, he tries again. He then grants read permission on the directory (and therefore any files within it) to all users and grants read and write permission to one user.

The query of ALL_DIRECTORIES in the figure shows that the directory (like all directories) is owned by SYS; directories are not schema objects. This is why SCOTT cannot drop the directory even though he created it. Dropping a directory requires another privilege: DROP ANY DIRECTORY.

TIP An Oracle directory always points to an operating system directory on the database server. There is no way to write to a directory on the client.

Figure 17-1 Managing directories with SQL*Plus

Use SQL*Loader to Load Data from a Non-Oracle Database

In many cases you will be faced with a need to do a bulk upload of datasets generated from some third-party system. This is the purpose of SQL*Loader. The input files can be generated by anything, but as long as the layout conforms to something that SQL*Loader can understand, it will upload the data successfully. Your task as the DBA is to configure a SQL*Loader controlfile that can interpret the contents of the input datafiles; SQL*Loader will then insert the data.

Using SQL*Loader

Architecturally, SQL*Loader is a user process like any other. It connects to the database via a server process, issuing a connect string that identifies a database listener, or if SQL*Loader is running on the database server machine, it can connect using the ORACLE_SID environment variable. To insert rows, it can use one of two techniques: conventional or direct path. A conventional insert uses absolutely ordinary INSERT statements. The SQL*Loader user process constructs an INSERT statement with bind variables in the VALUES clause and then reads the source datafile to execute the INSERT once for each row to be inserted. This method uses the database buffer cache and generates undo and redo data; these are INSERT statements like any others, and normal commit processing makes them permanent.

The direct path load bypasses the database buffer cache. SQL*Loader reads the source datafile and sends its contents to the server process. The server process then assembles blocks of table data in its Program Global Area (PGA) and writes them directly to the datafiles. The write is above the high water mark of the table and is known as a *data save*. The high water mark is a marker in the table segment above which no data has ever been written; the space above the high water mark is space allocated to the table that has not yet been used. Once the load is complete, SQL*Loader shifts the high water mark up to include the newly written blocks, and the rows within them are then immediately visible to other users. This is the equivalent of a COMMIT. No undo is generated, and if you want, you can switch off the generation of redo as well. For these reasons, direct path loading is extremely fast, and furthermore it should not impact your end users because interaction with the System Global Area (SGA) is kept to a minimum.

Direct path loads are fast, but they do have drawbacks:

- Referential integrity constraints must be dropped or disabled for the duration of the operation.
- Insert triggers do not fire.
- The table will be locked against DML from other sessions.
- It is not possible to use direct path for clustered tables.

These limitations are a result of the lack of interaction with the SGA while the load is in progress.

EXAM TIP Only UNIQUE, PRIMARY KEY, and NOT NULL constraints are enforced during a direct path load. INSERT triggers do not fire, and the table is locked for DML.

SQL*Loader uses a number of files. The input datafiles are the source data that it will upload into the database. The controlfile is a text file with directives telling SQL*Loader how to interpret the contents of the input files and what to do with the rows it extracts from them. Log files summarize the success (or otherwise) of the job, with details of any errors. Rows extracted from the input files may be rejected by SQL*Loader (perhaps because they do not conform to the format expected by the controlfile) or by the database (for instance, insertion might violate an integrity constraint); in either case, they are written to a bad file. If rows are successfully extracted from the input but rejected because they did not match some record-selection criterion, they are written to a reject file.

The controlfile is a text file instructing SQL*Loader on how to process the input datafiles. It is possible to include the actual data to be loaded in the controlfile, but you would not normally do this; usually, you will create one controlfile and reuse it, on a regular basis, with different input datafiles. The variety of input formats that SQL*Loader can understand is limited only by your ingenuity in constructing a controlfile.

EXAM TIP All files related to SQL*Loader are client-side files, not server-side files.

Consider this table:

```
SQL> desc dept;
 Name                            Null?    Type
 ------------------------------- -------- --------------
 DEPTNO                          NOT NULL NUMBER(2)
 DNAME                                    VARCHAR2(14)
 LOC                                      VARCHAR2(13)
```

Then consider this source datafile, named DEPT.DAT:

```
60,CONSULTING,TORONTO
70,HR,OXFORD
80,EDUCATION,
```

A SQL*Loader controlfile (with line numbers added) that could load this data is DEPTS.CTL, shown here:

```
1      load data
2      infile 'dept.dat'
3      badfile 'depts.bad'
4      discardfile 'depts.dsc'
5      append
6      into table dept
7      fields terminated by ','
8      trailing nullcols
9      (deptno integer external(2),
10      dname,
11      loc)
```

To perform the load, run this command from an operating system prompt:

```
sqlldr userid=scott/tiger@orcl control=depts.ctl
```

This command launches the SQL*Loader user process, connects to the local database as user SCOTT password TIGER, and then performs the actions specified in the controlfile DEPTS.CTL. Adding a DIRECT=TRUE argument would instruct SQL*Loader to use the direct path rather than a conventional insert (which is the default). The following explains the controlfile line by line:

Line	Purpose
1	Start a new load operation.
2	Nominate the source of the data.
3	Nominate the file to write out any badly formatted records.
4	Nominate the file to write out any unselected records.
5	Add rows to the table (rather than, for example, truncating it first).
6	The table into which to insert the rows.
7	Specify the field delimiter in the source file.
8	If there are missing fields, insert NULL values.
9, 10,11	The columns into which to insert the data.

This is a simple example. The syntax of the controlfile can handle a wide range of formats with intelligent parsing to fix any deviations in format, such as length and data types. In general, you can assume that it is possible to construct a controlfile that will understand just about any input datafile. However, do not think that it is always easy.

 TIP   It may be difficult to get a controlfile right, but once you have it, you can use it repeatedly, with different input datafiles for each run. It is then the responsibility of the feeder system to produce input datafiles that match your controlfile, rather than the other way around.

SQL*Loader Express Mode

There is a simple way to use SQL*Loader that requires no controlfile. This is the express mode, demonstrated (on Windows) in Figure 17-2.

The directory listing in Figure 17-2 shows that there is one file present: dept.dat. This has been created according to the description given previously. Then the sqlldr.exe executable is launched, connecting as user SCOTT with the connect string orclz and nominating the DEPT table and nothing else. The output shows that two rows were loaded, even though there are three in the datafile. The next directory listing shows that a file suffixed BAD has been generated that, when typed, contains one row from the input datafile. This is the third row, which was incomplete because there is no value for the LOC column of the table.

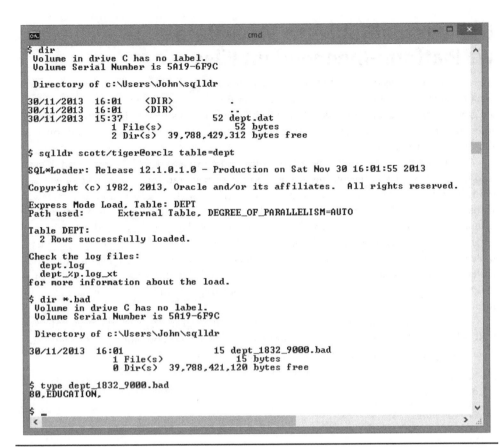

```
$ dir
 Volume in drive C has no label.
 Volume Serial Number is 5A19-6F9C

 Directory of c:\Users\John\sqlldr

30/11/2013  16:01    <DIR>          .
30/11/2013  16:01    <DIR>          ..
30/11/2013  15:37                52 dept.dat
               1 File(s)             52 bytes
               2 Dir(s)  39,788,429,312 bytes free

$ sqlldr scott/tiger@orclz table=dept

SQL*Loader: Release 12.1.0.1.0 - Production on Sat Nov 30 16:01:55 2013

Copyright (c) 1982, 2013, Oracle and/or its affiliates.  All rights reserved.

Express Mode Load, Table: DEPT
Path used:      External Table, DEGREE_OF_PARALLELISM=AUTO

Table DEPT:
  2 Rows successfully loaded.

Check the log files:
   dept.log
   dept_xp.log_xt
for more information about the load.

$ dir *.bad
 Volume in drive C has no label.
 Volume Serial Number is 5A19-6F9C

 Directory of c:\Users\John\sqlldr

30/11/2013  16:01                15 dept_1832_9000.bad
               1 File(s)             15 bytes
               0 Dir(s)  39,788,421,120 bytes free

$ type dept_1832_9000.bad
80,EDUCATION,

$ _
```

Figure 17-2   SQL*Loader running in express mode

Express mode is easy to use but is demanding in its requirements:

- There must be a datafile with the same name as the table to be loaded, suffixed with .DAT.
- The columns must be a scalar data type: character, number, or date.
- The fields in the file must be comma delimited and not enclosed in quotes.
- The input rows must have values for every column of the table.
- The user must have the CREATE ANY DIRECTORY privilege.

The log files generated by express mode can be instructive. Among other things, they include a SQL*Loader controlfile definition, which can be used (or edited) for subsequent jobs.

Use External Tables to Move Data via Platform-Independent Files

An external table is visible to SELECT statements like any other table, but you cannot perform Data Manipulation Language (DML) statements against it. This is because it does not exist as a segment in the database. It exists only as a data dictionary construct, pointing toward one or more operating system files. The operating system files of external tables are located through Oracle directory objects.

A common use of external tables is to avoid needing to use SQL*Loader to read data into the database. This can give huge savings in the extract-transform-load (ETL) cycle typically used to update a decision support system (DSS) with data from a feeder system. Consider the case where a feeder system regularly generates a dataset as a flat American Standard Code for Information Interchange (ASCII) file, which should be merged into existing database tables. One approach would be to use SQL*Loader to load the data into a staging table and then use a separate routine to merge the rows from the staging table into the DSS tables. This second routine cannot start until the load is finished. Using external tables, the merge routine can read the source data from the operating system files without having to wait for it to be loaded.

To create an external table, use the CREATE TABLE command with the keywords ORGANIZATION EXTERNAL. This tells Oracle that the table does not exist as a segment. Then specify the layout and location of the operating system file. Here is an example:

```
create table new_dept
  (deptno number(2),
  dname varchar2(14),
  loc varchar2(13))
organization external (
  type oracle_loader
  default directory ext_dir
  access parameters
    (records delimited by newline
    badfile 'depts.bad'
    discardfile 'depts.dsc'
    logfile 'depts.log'
    fields terminated by ','
    missing field values are null)
  location ('depts.dat'));
```

This command creates an external table that will be populated by the DEPTS.DAT file shown in the section "Using SQL*Loader," earlier in this chapter. The syntax for ACCESS PARAMETERS is virtually identical to the SQL*Loader controlfile syntax and is used because TYPE has been set to ORACLE_LOADER. The specification for DEFAULT DIRECTORY gives the Oracle directory where Oracle will look for the source datafile and where it will write the log and other files.

External tables can be queried in the same way as internal tables. Any SQL involving a SELECT will function against an external table; external tables can be used in joins, views, and subqueries. They cannot have indexes, constraints, or triggers.

Exercise 17-1: Use Directories, SQL*Loader, and External Tables   In this exercise, you will install and use SQL*Loader to insert data into a table and also to generate the CREATE TABLE script for an external table.

1. Connect to your database as user SYSTEM (in the examples, the SYSTEM password is oracle) with SQL*Plus.

2. Create a table to use for the exercise.

```
create table names(first varchar2(10),last varchar2(10));
```

3. Using any editor that will create plain-text files, create a file called names.txt with these values (or similar):

```
John,Watson
Roopesh,Ramklass
Sam,Alapati
```

4. Using the editor, create a controlfile called names.ctl with these settings:

```
load data
infile 'names.txt'
badfile 'names.bad'
truncate
into table names
fields terminated by ','
trailing nullcols
(first,last)
```

Note that this controlfile will truncate the target table before carrying out the insert.

5. From an operating system prompt, run SQL*Loader as follows:

```
sqlldr system/oracle control=names.ctl
```

6. Study the log file names.log that is generated.

7. With SQL*Plus, confirm that the rows have been inserted.

```
select * from names;
```

8. To generate a statement that will create an external table, you can use SQL*Loader and an existing controlfile.

```
sqlldr userid=system/oracle control=names.ctl
external_table=generate_only
```

9. This will have generated a CREATE TABLE statement in the log file names.log, which will look something like this:

```
CREATE TABLE "SYS_SQLLDR_X_EXT_NAMES"(
  "FIRST" VARCHAR2(10),
  "LAST" VARCHAR2(10))
ORGANIZATION external(
  TYPE oracle_loader
  DEFAULT DIRECTORY SYS_SQLLDR_XT_TMPDIR_00000
  ACCESS PARAMETERS(
    RECORDS DELIMITED BY NEWLINE CHARACTERSET WE8MSWIN1252
    BADFILE 'SYS_SQLLDR_XT_TMPDIR_00000':'names.bad'
    LOGFILE 'names.log_xt'
    READSIZE 1048576
    FIELDS TERMINATED BY "," LDRTRIM
    MISSING FIELD VALUES ARE NULL
```

```
        REJECT ROWS WITH ALL NULL FIELDS(
          "FIRST" CHAR(255)
            TERMINATED BY ",",
          "LAST" CHAR(255)
            TERMINATED BY ","))
   location(
     'names.txt'))
   REJECT LIMIT UNLIMITED
```

10. From your SQL*Plus session, create an Oracle directory pointing to the operating system directory where your names.txt file is. Here is an example:

    ```
    create directory system_dmp as '/home/oracle';
    ```

11. Make any edits you want to the command shown in step 9. For example, you might want to change the name of the table being created (SYS_SQLLDR_X_EXT_NAMES isn't very useful) to something more meaningful. You will need to change both the DEFAULT DIRECTORY and BADFILE settings to point to the directory created in step 10.

12. Run the statement created in step 11 from your SQL*Plus session.

13. Query the table with a few SELECT and DML statements. You will find that a log file is generated for every SELECT and that DML is not permitted.

14. Tidy up by deleting the names.txt and names.ctl files, dropping the tables, and, as SYS, dropping the directory.

Explain the General Architecture of Oracle Data Pump

Data Pump is a server-side utility. You initiate Data Pump jobs from a user process, but all the work is done by server processes. This improves performance dramatically over the old Export/Import utilities because the Data Pump processes running on the server have direct access to the datafiles and the SGA; they do not have to go via a session. Also, it is possible to launch a Data Pump job and then detach from it, leaving it running in the background. You can reconnect to the job to monitor its progress at any time.

Involved in a Data Pump job are a number of processes, two queues, a number of files, and one table. The user processes are expdp and impdp (for Unix) or expdp.exe and impdp.exe (for Windows). These are used to launch, control, and monitor Data Pump jobs. The expdp or impdp user process establishes a session against the database through a normal server process, either locally or via a listener. This session then issues commands to control and monitor Data Pump jobs. When a Data Pump job is launched, at least two processes are started: a Data Pump master process (the DM*nn*) and one or more worker processes (named DW*nn*). If multiple Data Pump jobs are running concurrently, each will have its own DM*nn* process and its own set of DW*nn* processes. As the name implies, the master process controls the workers.

Two queues are created for each Data Pump job: a control queue and a status queue. The DM*nn* divides up the work to be done and places individual tasks that make up the job on the control queue. The worker processes pick up these tasks and execute them—perhaps making use of parallel execution servers. This queue operates on a deliver-exactly-once model: Messages are enqueued by the DM*nn* and dequeued by the worker that picks them up. The status queue is for monitoring purposes; the DM*nn* places messages on it describing the state of the job. This queue operates on a publish-and-subscribe model; any session (with appropriate privileges) can query the queue to monitor the job's progress.

The files generated by Data Pump come in three forms: SQL files, dump files, and log files. SQL files are Data Definition Language (DDL) statements describing the objects included in the job. You can choose to generate them (without any data) as an easy way of getting this information out of the database, perhaps for documentation purposes or as a set of scripts to re-create the database. Dump files contain the exported data. This is formatted in a fashion resembling Extensible Markup Language (XML) tags. This means that there is considerable overhead in dump files for describing the data. A small table like the REGIONS table in the HR sample schema will generate a 94KB dump file, but although this overhead may seem disproportionately large for a tiny table like that, it becomes trivial for larger tables. The log files describe the history of the job run.

 EXAM TIP   Data Pump can be invoked by a client, but it runs on the server. All the files are server-side files, with nothing on the client side.

Finally, there is the control table. This is created for you by the DM*nn* when you launch a job and is used both to record the job's progress and to describe it. It is included in the dump file as the final item of the job.

Data Pump has two methods for loading and unloading data: the direct path and the external table path. The direct path bypasses the database buffer cache. For a direct path export, Data Pump reads the datafile blocks directly from disk, extracts and formats the content, and writes it out as a dump file. For a direct path import, Data Pump reads the dump file, uses its content to assemble blocks of table data, and writes them directly to the datafiles. The write is above the high water mark of the table, with the same benefits as those described earlier for a SQL*Loader direct load.

The external table path uses the database buffer cache. Even though Data Pump is manipulating files that are external to the database, it uses the database buffer cache as though it were reading and writing an internal table. For an export, Data Pump reads blocks from the datafiles into the cache through a normal SELECT process. From there, it formats the data for output to a dump file. During an import, Data Pump constructs standard INSERT statements from the content of the dump file and executes them by reading blocks from the datafiles into the cache, where the insert is carried out in the normal fashion. As far as the database is concerned, external table Data Pump jobs look like absolutely ordinary (though perhaps rather large) SELECT or INSERT operations. Both undo and redo are generated, like they would be for any normal DML statement. Your end users may well complain while these jobs are in progress. Commit processing is absolutely normal.

So, what determines whether Data Pump uses the direct path or the external table path? You as DBA have no control; Data Pump itself makes the decision based on the complexity of the objects. Only simple structures, such as heap tables without active triggers, can be processed through the direct path; more complex objects such as clustered tables force Data Pump to use the external table path because it requires interaction with the SGA in order to resolve the complexities. In either case, the dump file generated is identical.

Use Data Pump Export and Import to Move Data Between Oracle Databases

Data Pump is commonly used for extracting large amounts of data from one database and inserting it into another, but it can also be used to extract other information such as PL/SQL code or various object definitions. There are several interfaces: command-line utilities, Enterprise Manager Cloud Control, and a PL/SQL application programming interface (API). Whatever purpose and technique are used, the files are always in the Data Pump proprietary format. It is not possible to read a Data Pump file with any tool other than Data Pump.

Capabilities

Whatever interface is used, Data Pump has these capabilities:

- Fine-grained object and data selection facilities mean that Data Pump can export either the complete database or any part of it. It is possible to export table definitions (with or without their rows), PL/SQL objects, views, sequences, or any other object type.

- If exporting a table, it is possible to apply a WHERE clause to restrict the rows exported (although this may make the direct path impossible) or to instruct Data Pump to export a random sample of the table expressed as a percentage.

- Parallel processing can speed up Data Pump operations. Parallelism can come at two levels: the number of Data Pump worker processes and the number of parallel execution servers each worker process uses.

- An estimate facility can calculate the space needed for a Data Pump export, without actually running the job.

- The Network Mode allows transfer of a Data Pump dataset from one database to another without ever staging it on disk. This is implemented by a Data Pump export job on the source database writing the data over a database link to the target database, where a Data Pump import job reads the data from the database link and inserts it.

- Remapping facilities mean that objects can be renamed or transferred from one schema to another and, in the case of data objects, moved from one tablespace to another as they are imported.

- When data is being exported, the output files can be compressed and encrypted.

Using Data Pump with the Command-Line Utilities

The executables expdb and impdp are installed into the ORACLE_HOME/bin directory. The following are several examples of using them. Note that in all cases the command must be a single one-line command; the line breaks are purely for readability.

Here is how to export the entire database:

```
expdp system/manager@orcl12g full=y
parallel=2
dumpfile=datadir1:full1_%U.dmp,datadir2:full2_%U.dmp
filesize=2g
compression=all
```

This command will connect to the database as user SYSTEM and launch a full Data Pump export, using two worker processes working in parallel. Each worker will generate its own set of dump files, uniquely named according to the %U template, which generates unique strings of eight characters. Each worker will break up its output into files of 2GB (perhaps because of underlying file system restrictions) of compressed data.

A corresponding import job (which assumes that the files generated by the export have all been placed in one directory) would be as follows:

```
impdb system/manager@dev12g full=y
directory=data_dir
parallel=2
dumpfile=full1_%U.dmp,full2_%U.dmp
```

This command makes a selective export of the PL/SQL objects belonging to two schemas.

```
expdp system/manager schemas=hr,oe
directory=code_archive
dumpfile=hr_oe_code.dmp
include=function,
include=package,
include=procedure,
include=type
```

This command will extract everything from a Data Pump export that was in the HR schema and import it into the DEV schema.

```
impdp system/manager
directory=usr_data
dumpfile=usr_dat.dmp
schema=hr
remap_schema=hr:dev
```

Tablespace Export and Import

A variation on Data Pump export/import is the tablespace transport capability. This is a facility whereby entire tablespaces and their contents can be copied from one database to another. This is the routine:

1. Make the source tablespaces read-only.
2. Use Data Pump to export the metadata describing the tablespaces and the contents.
3. Copy the datafiles and Data Pump export file to the destination system.
4. Use Data Pump to import the metadata.
5. Make the tablespaces read-write on both the source and the destination.

An additional step that may be required when transporting tablespaces from one platform to another is to convert the endian format of the data. A big-endian platform (such as Solaris on SPARC chips) stores a multibyte value such as a 16-bit integer with the most significant byte first. A little-endian platform (such as Windows on Intel chips) stores the least significant byte first. Transporting tablespaces across platforms with a different endian format requires converting the datafiles. You do this with the Recovery Manager (RMAN) command CONVERT.

PART III

To determine the platform on which a database is running, query the column PLATFORM_ NAME in V$DATABASE. Then to see the list of currently supported platforms (which will vary depending on your exact release) and their endianness, query the view V$TRANSPORTABLE_ PLATFORM.

```
orcl > select * from v$transportable_platform order by
platform_name;
PLATFORM_ID PLATFORM_NAME                       ENDIAN_FORMAT
----------- ------------------------------     --------------
          6 AIX-Based Systems (64-bit)         Big
         16 Apple Mac OS                       Big
         19 HP IA Open VMS                     Little
         15 HP Open VMS                        Little
          5 HP Tru64 UNIX                      Little
          3 HP-UX (64-bit)                     Big
          4 HP-UX IA (64-bit)                  Big
         18 IBM Power Based Linux              Big
          9 IBM zSeries Based Linux            Big
         13 Linux 64-bit for AMD               Little
         10 Linux IA (32-bit)                  Little
         11 Linux IA (64-bit)                  Little
         12 Microsoft Windows 64-bit for AMD   Little
          7 Microsoft Windows IA (32-bit)      Little
          8 Microsoft Windows IA (64-bit)      Little
         20 Solaris Operating System (AMD64)   Little
         17 Solaris Operating System (x86)     Little
          1 Solaris[tm] OE (32-bit)            Big
          2 Solaris[tm] OE (64-bit)            Big
19 rows selected.
```

When transporting tablespaces, there are certain restrictions:

- The tablespaces should be self-contained. This means that the objects within the tablespaces must be complete, in other words, not dependent on any other objects. For instance, if tables are in one tablespace and indexes on the tables in another, both tablespaces must be included in the set to be transported.

- The destination database must use the same (or a compatible) character set as the source database.

- The schemas that own the objects in the tablespaces must exist in the destination database, or the operation will fail.

- Any objects in the destination database with the same owner and object name as objects in the transportable tablespace set will not be lost; they will be ignored during the import.

- A tablespace of the same name must not already exist. Remember that it is possible to rename tablespaces.

Figure 17-3 shows the steps to generate a transport set. In Figure 17-3, the first command is the PL/SQL procedure call to confirm that a set of tablespaces (in the example, just one tablespace: TS1) is self-contained. Then the tablespace is made read-only. The Data Pump job, launched with the expdp command-line utility, connects as user SYSTEM and then specifies the tablespace to be transported. This will generate a dump file with metadata describing the

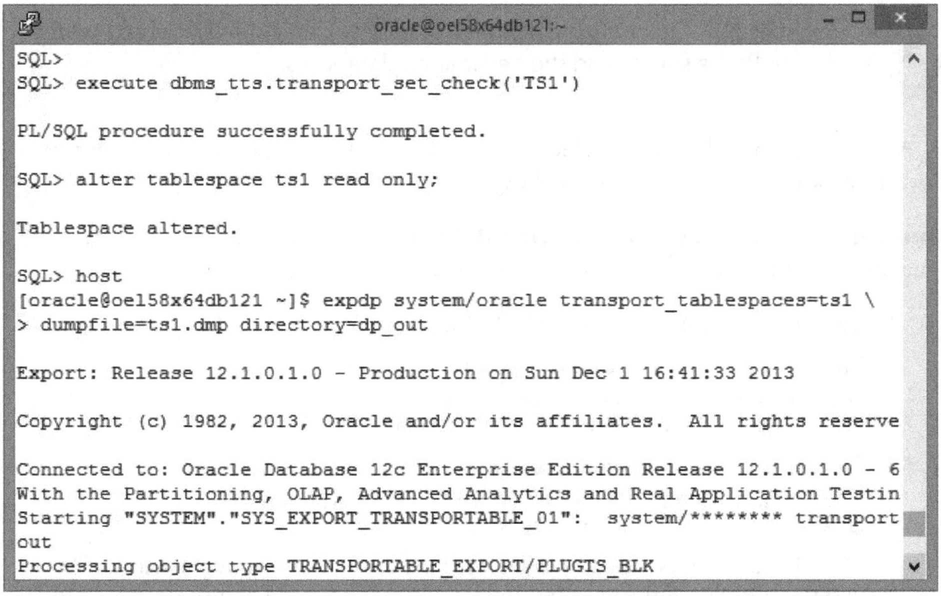

Figure 17-3 Using command-line utilities to create a transportable tablespace set

contents of the TS1 tablespace in the Oracle directory DP_OUT. Then, while the tablespace is still read-only, copy its datafiles and the Data Pump dump file to a suitable location on the destination database server.

If the destination database is on a platform with a different endianness from the source, the files must be converted. To do this on the source, connect to the source database with RMAN and run a command such as this:

```
convert datafile '/u02/oradata/ts1.dbf' to platform
'Solaris[tm] OE (64-bit)' format '/to_solaris/ts1.dbf';
```

This command will write out a copy of the file with the endianness changed. Alternatively, copy the unchanged file to the destination database, connect with RMAN, and run a command such as this:

```
convert datafile '/from_linux/ts1.dbf' from platform
'Linux IA (64-bit)' format '/u02/oradata/ts1.dbf';
```

This command will read the nominated datafile and convert it from the named platform format to a new file in the format that is required for the destination database.

To import the tablespaces on the destination system, use a command such as that shown in Figure 17-4.

The impdp command in Figure 17-4 reads a dump file to determine the name and contents of the tablespace consisting of the nominated datafile (previously converted, if necessary).

CAUTION Do not forget the final step! Make the tablespace read-write in both the source and the destination databases.

A generalization of the transportable tablespace feature makes it possible to transport an entire database from one machine to another.

Exercise 17-2: Use Data Pump Export/Import In this exercise, use the Data Pump command-line utilities to copy a table from one schema to another.

1. Connect to the database as user SYSTEM.

2. Create two schemas to use for this exercise.

   ```
   grant dba to artem identified by artem;
   grant dba to ivana identified by ivana;
   ```

3. Create a table and index in one schema.

   ```
   create table artem.users as select * from all_users;
   create index artem.ui on artem.users(user_id);
   ```

4. There is a directory created by default for the use of Data Pump, named DATA_ PUMP_DIR, which the Data Pump clients will use if no other directory is specified. Confirm its existence with this query and create it (using any suitable operating system path) if it does not exist.

   ```
   select directory_path from dba_directories
   where directory_name='DATA_PUMP_DIR';
   ```

```
oracle@oel58x64db121:~

[oracle@oel58x64db121 ~]$
[oracle@oel58x64db121 ~]$ impdp system/oracle dumpfile=ts1.dmp \
> directory=dp_in transport_datafiles=/u02/oradata/ts1.dbf

Import: Release 12.1.0.1.0 - Production on Sun Dec 1 17:32:32 2013

Copyright (c) 1982, 2013, Oracle and/or its affiliates.  All rights reserved.

Connected to: Oracle Database 12c Enterprise Edition Release 12.1.0.1.0 - 64bi
With the Partitioning, OLAP, Advanced Analytics and Real Application Testing o
Master table "SYSTEM"."SYS_IMPORT_TRANSPORTABLE_01" successfully loaded/unload
Starting "SYSTEM"."SYS_IMPORT_TRANSPORTABLE_01":  system/******** dumpfile=ts1
Processing object type TRANSPORTABLE_EXPORT/PLUGTS_BLK
Processing object type TRANSPORTABLE_EXPORT/TABLE
Processing object type TRANSPORTABLE_EXPORT/TABLE_STATISTICS
Processing object type TRANSPORTABLE_EXPORT/STATISTICS/MARKER
Processing object type TRANSPORTABLE_EXPORT/POST_INSTANCE/PLUGTS_BLK
Job "SYSTEM"."SYS_IMPORT_TRANSPORTABLE_01" successfully completed at Sun Dec 1

[oracle@oel58x64db121 ~]$
```

Figure 17-4 Using the impdp utility to import a transported tablespace

5. Export the ARTEM schema with this command:

```
expdp system/<password> schemas=artem dumpfile=artem.dmp
```

6. Import the ARTEM schema into the IVANA schema:

```
impdp system/<password> remap_schema=artem:ivana
dumpfile=artem.dmp
```

7. Confirm that the objects have been imported.

```
select object_name,object_type from dba_objects
where owner='IVANA';
```

Use Data Pump in a Multitenant Environment

In Oracle Database 12c, Data Pump fully supports import to and export from previous versions of Oracle Database (those that aren't container databases [CDBs]) and Oracle Database 12c non-CDBs and pluggable databases (PDBs). Since Data Pump is a logical export and import tool, the only operation not supported in a multitenant environment is import into or export from a container database (CDB$ROOT).

The key to using Data Pump in a multitenant environment is to use the PDB service name as the source or target of the Data Pump operation. In this way, the type of database (non-CDB or PDB) is not a factor in the operation. Figure 17-5 shows several scenarios using Data Pump in a multitenant environment.

Export from Non-CDB and Import into PDB

Using Data Pump export from a non-CDB to a PDB is an easy way to convert a non-CDB from Oracle Database 11g or earlier to a PDB in Oracle Database 12c without upgrading the non-CDB to Oracle Database 12c and then converting the database to a PDB. If the target

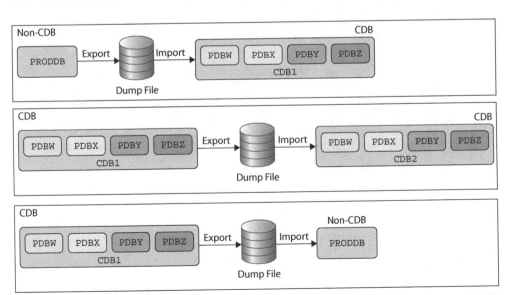

Figure 17-5 Oracle Data Pump scenarios in a multitenant environment

PDB does not exist, you must create it first. In this example, you have a non-CDB called HR, and you want to migrate the users and tablespaces to a PDB in the container CDB01.

The basic steps are as follows:

1. Create the Oracle and OS directory for the Data Pump dump file.

2. Export the database.

3. Create the target PDB if it does not already exist.

4. Import the database from the dump file into the PDB.

```
$ cd /u01/app/oracle
$ mkdir datapump
$ sqlplus / as sysdba
SQL> create directory dpump as '/u01/app/oracle/datapump';

Directory created.
SQL> select name from v$tablespace;

NAME
------------------------------
SYSTEM
SYSAUX
UNDOTBS1
USERS
TEMP
ACCT_PAY
ACCT_REC

7 rows selected.

SQL> quit

$ expdp rjb@hr full=y directory=dpump dumpfile=hr_exp.dmp
Starting "RJB"."SYS_EXPORT_FULL_01":  rjb/********@hr full=y
    directory=dpump dumpfile=hr_exp.dmp
Estimate in progress using BLOCKS method...
Processing object type DATABASE_EXPORT/EARLY_OPTIONS/VIEWS_AS_TABLES/
TABLE_DATA
Processing object type DATABASE_EXPORT/NORMAL_OPTIONS/TABLE_DATA
Processing object type DATABASE_EXPORT/NORMAL_OPTIONS/VIEWS_AS_TABLES/
TABLE_DATA
Processing object type DATABASE_EXPORT/SCHEMA/TABLE/TABLE_DATA
Total estimation using BLOCKS method: 4.890 MB
Processing object type DATABASE_EXPORT/PRE_SYSTEM_IMPCALLOUT/MARKER
Processing object type DATABASE_EXPORT/PRE_INSTANCE_IMPCALLOUT/MARKER
Processing object type DATABASE_EXPORT/TABLESPACE
Processing object type DATABASE_EXPORT/PROFILE
. . .
. . exported "SYS"."NACL$_WALLET_EXP"                       0 KB
0 rows
. . exported "SYSTEM"."SCHEDULER_JOB_ARGS"                  0 KB
0 rows
. . exported "SCOTT"."DEPT"                             6.007 KB
4 rows
. . exported "SCOTT"."EMP"                              8.757 KB
14 rows
. . exported "SCOTT"."SALGRADE"                         5.937 KB
```

```
5 rows
. . exported "SCOTT"."BONUS"                                          0 KB
0 rows
Master table "RJB"."SYS_EXPORT_FULL_01" successfully loaded/unloaded
************************************************************************
********
Dump file set for RJB.SYS_EXPORT_FULL_01 is:
  /u01/app/oracle/datapump/hr_exp.dmp
Job "RJB"."SYS_EXPORT_FULL_01" successfully completed at
     Tue Jun 24 07:49:10 2014 elapsed 0 00:01:55

$ . oraenv
ORACLE_SID = [hr] ? cdb01

$ sqlplus / as sysdba

SQL> create pluggable database hr admin user hr_admin
     identified by hr_admin49 roles=(connect);

Pluggable database created.

SQL> alter session set container=hr;

Session altered.

SQL> alter pluggable database hr open;

Pluggable database altered.

SQL> create directory dpump as '/u01/app/oracle/datapump';

Directory created.
SQL> quit
$ impdp rjb@hr full=y directory=dpump dumpfile=hr_exp.dmp

Master table "RJB"."SYS_IMPORT_FULL_01" successfully loaded/unloaded
Starting "RJB"."SYS_IMPORT_FULL_01":  rjb/********@hr full=y
     directory=dpump dumpfile=hr_exp.dmp
Processing object type DATABASE_EXPORT/PRE_SYSTEM_IMPCALLOUT/MARKER
Processing object type DATABASE_EXPORT/PRE_INSTANCE_IMPCALLOUT/MARKER
Processing object type DATABASE_EXPORT/TABLESPACE
. . .
Processing object type DATABASE_EXPORT/AUDIT_UNIFIED/AUDIT_POLICY_
ENABLE
Processing object type DATABASE_EXPORT/AUDIT
Processing object type DATABASE_EXPORT/POST_SYSTEM_IMPCALLOUT/MARKER
Job "RJB"."SYS_IMPORT_FULL_01" completed with 21 error(s) at Tue Jun
24 08:06:41 2014 elapsed 0 00:01:16
```

During the import, any tablespaces that already exist will not be re-created. In the target PDB, all users from the non-CDB are re-created as local users in the new PDB.

Export and Import Between PDBs

Exporting from an existing PDB to a new PDB, either in the same container or in a new container, follows most of the steps as in the previous section. If the target PDB does not exist, you create it ahead of time in the target CDB. For both the source and target PDBs, you need to create a directory object for the dump file. The directory object must be at the PDB, not CDB, level because the new PDB will not have visibility to that directory object; as you'd expect, the same directory name can exist at the CDB level and in every PDB.

When you export from an existing PDB, you may have common users who own objects in the source PDB. That user and their objects won't be imported successfully into a new target PDB because the Data Pump import is at the PDB level and you can't create local users in a PDB with the C## prefix as part of the Data Pump import. For example, if an existing PDB's common user C##RJB owns objects, the import to a new PDB in a different CDB without the common user C##RJB will fail with this error message:

```
ORA-65094: invalid local user or role name
```

To fix this issue, you can do one of two things. The first option is to create the same common user in the target CDB before starting the Data Pump import. If you don't want to have the same common user in the target CDB, use the REMAP_SCHEMA option on the impdp command line to create a local user who will own the objects from the common user in the source PDB.

```
impdp rjb@hr full=y directory= . . . remap_schema=c##rjb:jan_d
```

On a similar note, if you have tablespace name conflicts and you don't want the source PDB's objects to end up in the tablespace with the same name, use the REMAP_TABLESPACE option.

Export from PDB and Import into Non-CDB

Importing an export from a PDB into a non-PDB is supported for all types of exports: full, conventional, schema, and transportable. The only exception is that you cannot import a common user's objects into a non-CDB. You would get the same error message as if you were trying to import another PDB's common users into a new PDB. The workaround is the same: Use the REMAP_SCHEMA option.

If you are importing a PDB export into an Oracle 11g non-CDB, however, you *will* get the common users' schemas and objects imported successfully. The # character is valid in schema names; therefore, you can create the user C##RJB in an Oracle 11g database, and it will be treated no differently than any other user in that database since the multitenant option exists only from Oracle Database 12c on.

Full Transportable Export and Import

As you recall, one of the new features of Oracle Database 12c is full transportable export and import. This operation is more like a transportable tablespace operation than a Data Pump operation. The expdp command creates only the metadata for the database, and the actual datafiles are copied or moved as-is to the target destination.

In a multitenant environment, you can leverage full transportable export/import both to move tablespaces quickly and to avoid upgrading an existing database in place; instead, you use an existing PDB or create a new PDB and transport the datafiles from an 11g database (or newer) to the PDB.

Of course, since full transportable export/import would normally include the SYSTEM and SYSAUX tablespaces, those are not included in a transportable import operation if the target is a PDB.

Transporting a Database Over the Network

When using transportable export/import over the network to transport a database into a PDB, you follow these steps:

1. Create the new PDB in the target container.

2. Create a database link in the target PDB to the source database with the appropriate permissions granted to the user defined in the database link.

3. Change the status of the nonsystem tablespaces (SYSTEM and SYSAUX) in the source database to READ ONLY.

4. Copy the datafiles from the source location to the target location accessible to the new PDB.

5. Convert the datafiles if necessary (for endian conversion).

6. Import into the target database.

Change the source database's tablespaces back to READ WRITE.
Your impdp operation will look something like this:

```
impdp rjb@hr full=y network_link=remote_hrdb transportable=always
    transport_datafiles=. . . version=12
```

In Oracle Database 11*g* Data Pump, you could perform import/export over the network as well, and the same applies to Oracle Database 12*c* Data Pump in a multitenant scenario. No dump file is required, saving both time and disk space. Only the metadata file for the source database is created on the file system.

Use SQL*Loader in a Multitenant Environment

Using SQL*Loader in a multitenant environment is just as easy as using SQL*Loader in a non-CDB environment. The key to ensuring success is to specify the service name of the new or existing PDB when loading data into one or more tables.

Two-Minute Drill

Describe Ways to Move Data

- Data Pump can transfer data between Oracle databases.
- SQL*Loader can read files generated by third-party products.

Create and Use Directory Objects

- An Oracle directory maps a database object to an operating system path.
- The Oracle OS user must have permissions on the OS directory.
- Database users must be granted permissions on the Oracle directory.

Use SQL*Loader to Load Data from a Non-Oracle Database

- SQL*Loader reads operating system text files generated by any third-party system.
- Express mode simplifies usage.

Use External Tables to Move Data via Platform-Independent Files

- External tables are operating system text files defined with SQL*Loader syntax.
- No segment exists for an external table.
- External tables can be queried, but DML or indexes are not possible.

Explain the General Architecture of Oracle Data Pump

- Data Pump processes run on the instance, not the client.
- All files are accessed through Oracle directory objects.
- Direct path bypasses the buffer cache; external table path goes through the cache.

Use Data Pump Export and Import to Move Data Between Oracle Databases

- Data Pump dump files are compatible across versions and platforms.
- Network mode avoids the need to stage data on disk.
- Tablespace transport mode permits copying of datafiles between databases.

Use Data Pump in a Multitenant Environment

- Using the database instance's service name is the key to shielding the export/import process from the details of the CDB.
- Data Pump export and import are supported from non-CDB to PDB, PDB to PDB, and 11g to non-CDB or PDB, respectively.
- Full transportable export and import from a non-CDB to a PDB copies all tablespaces except for SYSTEM and SYSAUX.

- For common users with objects in a Data Pump export from a non-CDB or PDB in Oracle Database 12c, the impdp command line must include an REMAP_SCHEMA clause to ensure that schemas starting with C## will be imported into the target database.

Use SQL*Loader in a Multitenant Environment

- SQL*Loader works as in previous versions when you use the database's service name.

Self Test

1. Which of these methods of moving data can transfer data from one platform to another? (Choose all correct answers.)

   A. Using CREATE TABLE AS with a SELECT statement that reads from a database link

   B. A Data Pump network mode export/import

   C. A Data Pump tablespace transport

   D. Using the legacy exp and imp export/import utilities

   E. Using RMAN backup and restore with backup sets, not image copies

2. You create a directory with the statement

   ```
   create directory dp_dir as 'c:\tmp';
   ```

   but when you try to use it with Data Pump, there is an error. Which of the following could be true? (Choose three answers.)

   A. The Oracle software owner has no permissions on c:\tmp.

   B. The Oracle database user has no permissions on dp_dir.

   C. The path c:\tmp does not exist.

   D. The path c:\tmp must exist or else the CREATE DIRECTORY statement would have failed.

   E. If you use Data Pump in network mode, there will be no need for a directory.

   F. Issuing the command grant all on 'c:\tmp' to public; may solve some permission problems.

3. What is a necessary condition to import a Data Pump file from a client? (Choose the best answer.)

   A. A directory object must be created pointing to the operating system directory where the file exists.

   B. A controlfile must exist that accurately describes the format of the file.

   C. The client and server operating systems must use the same endian format.

   D. It is not possible to import a file from a client.

4. Which of the following is not a SQL*Loader file? (Choose the best answer.)

   A. Bad file

   B. Controlfile

   C. Discard file

   D. Good file

   E. Log file

5. You run SQL*Loader on your PC to insert data into a remote database. Which of the following is true? (Choose the correct answer.)

   A. The input datafiles must be on your PC.

   B. The input datafiles must be on the server.

   C. Direct load is possible only if the input datafiles are on the server.

   D. Direct load is possible only if you run SQL*Loader on the server, not on the PC.

6. Study this SQL*Loader command:

```
sqlldr scott/tiger table=emp
```

What will be the result? (Choose the best answer.)

   A. The load will fail unless there is a controlfile present named EMP.CTL.

   B. The load will succeed if there is a file present named EMP.DAT.

   C. The EMP table will be created if it does not exist or appended to if it does.

   D. The user will be prompted for missing arguments, such as the datafile name.

7. Which of these SQL commands can reference an external table? (Choose two answers.)

   A. SELECT

   B. INSERT, UPDATE, DELETE

   C. CREATE VIEW

   D. CREATE INDEX

8. Which of the following is not a Data Pump file type? (Choose the best answer.)

   A. Dump file

   B. Log file

   C. Controlfile

   D. SQL file

9. You are using Data Pump to upload rows into a table, and you want to use the direct path. Which of the following statements is correct? (Choose two answers.)

A. You must include the DIRECT keyword in the Data Pump controlfile.

B. This is not possible if the table is in a cluster.

C. You have no control over this; Data Pump will use the direct path automatically if it can.

D. Direct path is slower than the external table path because it doesn't cache data in memory.

10. You intend to transport a tablespace from database A on Windows to database B on AIX. These are the steps:

a. Convert the files from little endian to big endian.

b. Copy the files from A to B.

c. Export the metadata describing the tablespace.

d. Import the metadata describing the tablespace.

e. Make the tablespace read-only in A.

f. Make the tablespace read-write in B.

In what order could the steps be carried out?

A. c, e, b, f, a, d

B. e, c, b, a, d, f

C. e, c, d, a, b, f

D. c, e, b, a, d, f

11. Which of the following operations are supported with Oracle Database 12*c* Data Pump export and import in a multitenant environment? (Choose all that apply.)

A. You must always upgrade a pre-12c database to version 12c before performing an export and importing to a 12c non-CDB.

B. An Oracle 11g database can be exported and imported into an Oracle 12c PDB as a full transportable database operation.

C. Only PDBs can be exported and imported into another PDB.

D. Only PDBs can be exported and imported into the root container (CDB$ROOT).

E. Only non-CDBs can be imported into another non-CDB.

F. You can export a PDB and import it into a different PDB within the same CDB.

Self Test Answers

1. ☑ **A, B, C,** and **D**. All of these techniques have a cross-platform capability. **C** (tablespace transport) may require converting the files if the target platform is a different endian from the source.
   ☒ **E** is incorrect. This is incorrect because backup sets are not portable across platforms, although image copies may be.

2. ☑ **A, B,** and **C**. These conditions could all cause problems when using the directory, but not when creating it.
   ☒ **D, E,** and **F** are incorrect. **D** is incorrect because the existence of the directory is not checked at creation time. **E** is incorrect because although network mode does not need a directory for the dump files, it will need a directory for the log files. **F** is incorrect because it confuses the issue of Oracle permissions on directories with operating system permissions on physical paths.

3. ☑ **D**. It is not possible to import a file from the client; the dump must exist on the server.
   ☒ **A, B,** and **C** are incorrect. **A** is incorrect because a directory object can point only to a directory on the server. **B** is incorrect because a controlfile is used by SQL*Loader, not by Data Pump. **C** is incorrect because endianness is relevant to transportable tablespaces, not data import.

4. ☑ **D**. There is no "good" file—the acceptable rows are inserted into the table and are not logged by SQL*Loader.
   ☒ **A, B, C,** and **E** are incorrect. These are the file types that SQL*Loader can generate.

5. ☑ **A**. SQL*Loader is a client-server process; the input files must be local to the user process.
   ☒ **B, C,** and **D** are incorrect. **B** is incorrect because the input files must be on the PC, accessible to the client-side process. **C** and **D** are incorrect because direct load is not relevant to the location of the files.

6. ☑ **B**. Express mode relies on many defaults, one of which is that the datafile name must be the table name suffixed with .DAT.
   ☒ **A, C,** and **D** are incorrect. **A** is incorrect because express mode does not use a controlfile. **C** is incorrect because express mode cannot create a table; it can only append to an existing table. **D** is incorrect because express mode does not prompt.

7. ☑ **A** and **C**. Anything related to SELECT, including creating a view, can be executed against an external table.
   ☒ **B** and **D** are incorrect. DML is impossible against an external table, as is indexing.

8. ☑ **C**. SQL*Loader can use a controlfile; Data Pump does not.
   ☒ **A, B,** and **D** are incorrect. Data Pump export generates a dump file, an import can generate a SQL file, and both export and import generate log files.

9. ☑ **B** and **C**. Clusters are complex structures that cannot be directly loaded. Data Pump determines whether a direct load is possible automatically.
   ☒ **A** and **D** are incorrect. There is no DIRECT keyword because the choice is automatic. Direct is faster because it bypasses the SGA.

10. ☑ **B**. This is the correct sequence.

   ☒ **A**, **C**, and **D** are incorrect. All these sequences are wrong. The only acceptable alternative would have been to convert the endianness on step a before copying to step b.

11. ☑ **B** and **F**. You can perform an export of any type (schema, tablespace, full transportable) from database version 11*g* and import it into a PDB. Also, you can use Data Pump export/import with the full transportable option to copy a PDB within the same CDB.

   ☒ **A**, **C**, **D**, and **E** are incorrect. **A** is incorrect because you do not need to upgrade a database before using Data Pump export/import as long as the version of Oracle Database is 11*g* or newer. **C** is incorrect because you can always import a non-CDB into a new PDB as long as you use the service name when connecting to the PDB. **D** is incorrect because you cannot use Data Pump import into the root container of a CDB. **E** is incorrect because non-CDBs can be imported into another non-CDB or a PDB as long as the source database version is 11*g* or newer.

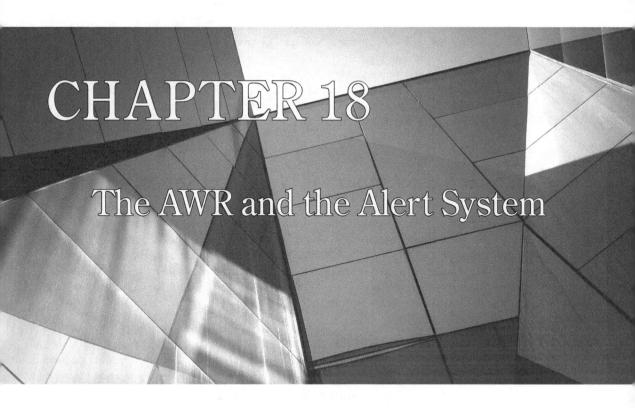

CHAPTER 18

The AWR and the Alert System

Exam Objectives

- 062.10.1 Manage the Automatic Workload Repository (AWR)
- 062.10.2 Use the Automatic Database Diagnostic Monitor (ADDM)
- 062.10.3 Describe and Use the Advisory Framework
- 062.10.4 Set Alert Thresholds
- 062.10.5 Use Automated Tasks

A 12c database is largely self-managing. Maintenance tasks run automatically (unless disabled), and diagnostic information is gathered at regular intervals. With earlier releases, monitoring the database to pick up developing problems before they become critical took much time. Identifying and diagnosing performance issues was not only time consuming but also required much skill. Use of the Alert system and the diagnostic advisors, installed as standard in every 12c database, frees the database administrator (DBA) from the necessity of devoting a large amount of effort to this work.

Manage the Automatic Workload Repository

Oracle collects a vast amount of statistical information regarding performance and activity. This information is accumulated in memory and periodically written to disk, specifically, to the tables that make up the Automatic Workload Repository (AWR). The AWR exists as a set of tables and other objects in the SYSAUX tablespace. The AWR is related to the data dictionary, but unlike the data dictionary, the AWR is not essential for the database to function (although it may be necessary for it to function well). Data is written to the AWR, stored for a while, and eventually overwritten with more recent information.

Gathering AWR Statistics

The level of statistics gathered is controlled by the instance parameter STATISTICS_LEVEL. This can be set to BASIC, TYPICAL (which is the default), or ALL. The TYPICAL level will force the collection of all the statistics needed for normal tuning, without collecting any that would adversely impact performance. The BASIC level will disable virtually all statistics, all performance-tuning advisors, and the server-generated Alert system—with no appreciable run-time performance benefit. The ALL level will collect extremely detailed statistics on SQL statement execution; these may occasionally be necessary if you are doing advanced SQL statement tuning, but they may cause a slight performance drop while being collected.

 EXAM TIP   Setting STATISTICS_LEVEL=BASIC will disable all advisors and the server-generated Alert system.

Statistics are accumulated in memory in data structures within the System Global Area (SGA). This causes no performance impact because the statistics merely reflect what the instance is doing anyway. Periodically (by default, once an hour) they are flushed to disk, specifically, to the AWR. This is known as an *AWR snapshot*. The flushing to disk is done by the Manageability Monitor (MMON) background process. This use of a background process is the key to the efficiency of the statistics collection process. In earlier releases of the database, accessing performance-tuning statistics was possible only by running queries against various views—the dynamic performance V$ views. Populating these views is an expensive process. The DBA must launch a session against the database and then issue a query. Executing this query forces Oracle to extract data from the SGA and present it to the session in a view. This approach is still possible—all the old views, and many more, are still available—but the AWR approach is far more efficient.

TIP No third-party tool can ever have the direct memory access to the instance that MMON has. If your instance is highly stressed, you should think carefully before using any tuning products other than those provided by Oracle.

MMON has direct access to the memory structures that make up the SGA and therefore the statistics within them. It can extract data from the SGA without the need to go via a session or to execute SQL. The only overhead involved is writing the snapshot of the data to the AWR. By default, this occurs only once an hour and therefore should not have a noticeable effect on run-time performance.

EXAM TIP AWR statistics are saved as a snapshot to the AWR by the MMON process (by default, every 60 minutes). By default, the snapshots are stored for eight days before being overwritten.

The AWR is a set of tables, owned by SYS and located in the SYSAUX tablespace. These tables cannot be relocated. Oracle Corporation supports access to the AWR tables only through the various application programming interfaces (APIs) provided in the form of database management system (DBMS) packages or through various views.

You can think of an AWR snapshot as a copy of the contents of many V$ views at the time the snapshot was taken. However, never forget that the mechanism for copying the information is not to query the V$ views; the information is extracted directly from the data structures that make up the instance. The process that makes the copy is MMON. In addition to information from the dynamic performance (or V$) views, the AWR stores information from the DBA views, populated from the data dictionary. This category of information includes a history of object statistics. Without the AWR, the database would have no long-term record of how objects were changing. The statistics gathered with DBMS_STATS give current information, but it may also be necessary to have a historical picture of the state of the database objects. The AWR can provide this.

Managing the AWR

Snapshots of statistics data are kept in the AWR, by default, for eight days. This period is configurable, and it is also possible to mark a pair of snapshots as a baseline, to be kept indefinitely. Baseline snapshots are not automatically purged. As a rough guide for sizing, if the snapshot collection is left on every hour and the retention time is left on eight days, then the AWR may well require between 200MB and 300MB of space in the SYSAUX tablespace. But this figure is highly variable and will, to a large extent, depend on the number of sessions. Adjusting the AWR settings to save snapshots more frequently will make problem diagnosis more precise. If the snapshots are several hours apart, you may miss peaks of activity (and consequent dips in performance). But gathering snapshots too frequently will increase the size of the AWR and could possibly impact performance because of the increased workload of collecting and saving the information.

TIP It is important to monitor the size and growth of the SYSAUX tablespace and the AWR within it. The Alert system will assist with the first task, and the view V$SYSAUX_OCCUPANTS should be used for the second.

PART III

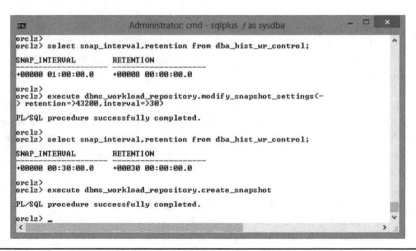

Figure 18-1 How to display and adjust the AWR snapshot settings

Adjusting the AWR snapshot frequency and retention is done with the PL/SQL API called DBMS_WORKLOAD_REPOSITORY. Figure 18-1 shows examples of using this package. First, a query against the DBA_HIST_WR_CONTROL view shows the current values for snapshot retention and frequency. The values (which are of data type INTERVAL) are the default values. Then a call to the MODIFY_SNAPSHOT_SETTINGS procedure changes them to 30 days and half an hour; the units are minutes. Finally, the CREATE_SNAPSHOT procedure forces the snapshot, which will be made in addition to the regularly scheduled collections. Forcing a snapshot would typically be done immediately before and after launching a job of some kind so that reports can be generated focusing on a particular time frame.

EXAM TIP   By default, AWR snapshots are taken every hour and saved for eight days. The AWR is located in the SYSAUX tablespace and cannot be relocated to other tablespaces.

Exercise 18-1: Monitor the Automatic Workload Repository   In this exercise, you will determine the size of the AWR and monitor its growth as it stores more snapshots. Follow these steps:

1. Connect to your database with SQL*Plus as user SYSTEM.

2. The view V$SYSAUX_OCCUPANTS shows all the components installed into the SYSAUX tablespace. Find out how much space the AWR is taking up.

   ```
   select occupant_desc,space_usage_kbytes from v$sysaux_occupants
   where occupant_name='SM/AWR';
   ```

   Note the size returned.

3. Take an AWR snapshot.

   ```
   execute dbms_workload_repository.create_snapshot
   ```

4. Rerun the query from step 2 and then calculate the increase in size caused by taking the manual snapshot.

5. Find out how many snapshots there are as well as what date range they cover.

```
select min(begin_interval_time), max(begin_interval_time),
count(snap_id) from dba_hist_snapshot;
```

Use the Automatic Database Diagnostic Monitor

The database comes preconfigured with a set of advisors. First among these is the Automatic Database Diagnostic Monitor (ADDM). Studying ADDM reports, which are generated automatically whenever an AWR snapshot is taken, will usually be a regular part of the DBA's routine. The ADDM reports are of great value in themselves and will highlight problems within the database and suggest solutions, but in many cases the recommendations will include suggesting that you run one or more other advisors. These advisors can give much more precise diagnostic information and advice than the ADDM.

The ADDM looks at data stored in two AWR snapshots. By comparing them, it can summarize the activity during the period between these snapshots and generate a report. The report attempts to detect any possible performance issues and make recommendations that will alleviate them. The issues that the ADDM can identify include the following:

- CPU bottlenecks

- Contention issues such as row locking

- Stress on the I/O system

- High-load SQL

The ADDM runs automatically whenever an AWR snapshot is generated, and it will analyze activity between that snapshot and the preceding snapshot. Therefore, by default, reports are available per hour. It is also possible to generate a report on demand covering the time between any two snapshots. ADDM reports can be retrieved or generated either by using Database Express (click the Performance Hub link on the Performance tab and then select the ADDM subtab) or by running the addmrpt.sql script. This script resides in the ORACLE_HOME/rdbms/admin directory. It presents all available snapshots and prompts for the two snapshot periods over which the report should be generated.

 EXAM TIP   ADDM reports are generated on demand as well as whenever a snapshot is gathered. A report requires two snapshots.

ADDM reports will sometimes give precise advice (such as to change a parameter) but will more often identify particular statements and advise running another advisor against them. ADDM may also suggest restructuring objects, for example, perhaps to implement partitioning. It will always give reasons for its recommendations, which can be instructive, even if you decide not to implement the advice.

CAUTION   ADDM will often recommend using facilities for which you may not be licensed, such as the SQL Tuning Advisor or partitioning. This can be somewhat irritating and in breach of your software license contract.

Exercise 18-2: Generate an ADDM Report   In this exercise, you will generate an ADDM report. Follow these steps:

1. Connect to the database as user SYSTEM.

2. Generate the report by running this command from a SQL prompt:

   `@?/rdbms/admin/addmrpt.sql`

   When prompted, select any two snapshots.

3. Study the report. Note that it is possible that the time frame does not include enough activity to perform any meaningful analysis—if so, try again with a different period.

Describe and Use the Advisory Framework

The advisors rely on activity statistics accumulated by the instance in memory and written to the AWR as snapshots. You can access ADDM and the SQL Tuning Advisor through Database Express (go to the Performance tab of the database home page). The other advisors have PL/SQL interfaces or are visible as data dictionary views. All the advisors are detailed in Chapter 19. For now, the following sections summarize them.

The Memory Advisors

The memory advisors predict the effect of varying the size of memory structures, reporting the estimates in terms of processing time saved (the Shared Pool, Java Pool, and Streams Pool Advisors), disk activity reductions (the Database Buffer Cache Advisor), or both (the PGA Advisor). There is no advisor for the Large Pool. There is, however, an SGA Advisor, which will report on the effect of varying the size of the entire SGA. If memory management has been automated via the parameter MEMORY_TARGET and all other memory parameters have been left at their defaults, an overall memory advisor gives a single point from which to gauge whether allocating more memory to the instance would improve performance.

The memory advisors are exposed through these views:

- **V$DB_CACHE_ADVICE**   The DB Cache advisor
- **V$JAVA_POOL_ADVICE**   The Java Pool advisor
- **V$MEMORY_TARGET_ADVICE**   The Automatic Memory Management advisor
- **V$PGA_TARGET_ADVICE**   The PGA advisor
- **V$SGA_TARGET_ADVICE**   The Shared Memory Management advisor
- **V$SHARED_POOL_ADVICE**   The Shared Pool advisor
- **V$STREAMS_POOL_ADVICE**   The Streams Pool advisor

The SQL Advisors

There are two SQL advisors: the SQL Access Advisor and the SQL Tuning Advisor. The SQL Access Advisor will observe a workload of SQL statements and make recommendations regarding segments so that the workload will run more quickly. The workload can be a hypothetical workload, or it can be derived from the SQL actually executed during a certain time frame. The recommendations can be to create or drop indexes and materialized views and to make use of segment partitioning. The SQL Tuning Advisor can analyze individual statements, as well as recommend schema changes (like the SQL Access Advisor does). It can recommend generating additional statistics on the statement's execution that will assist the optimizer in choosing the best execution plan and recommend rewriting the statement to eliminate some inefficiencies inherent in some SQL structures.

You can access the SQL advisors through the PL/SQL APIs called DBMS_ADVISOR and DBMS_SQLTUNE. The SQL Tuning Advisor is also accessible through Database Express.

The Automatic Undo Advisor

As discussed in Chapter 6, the Undo Advisor (exposed through the V$UNDOSTAT view) will observe the rate of undo data generation and the length of queries being run, and it will recommend a minimum size for the undo tablespace, which will ensure that queries do not fail with a "snapshot too old" error and that Data Manipulation Language (DML) statements do not fail because of insufficient undo space.

The Mean Time to Recover Advisor

The mechanism for instance recovery after a failure is detailed in Chapter 22. In summary, if the instance terminates in a disorderly fashion (such as a power cut or server reboot while the database is open or just a SHUTDOWN ABORT), then on the next startup it is necessary to reinstate all work in progress that had not been written to the datafiles at the time of the crash. This will happen automatically, but until it is done, users cannot log on. The Mean Time to Recover (MTTR) Advisor (exposed in the V$INSTANCE_RECOVERY view) estimates how long this period of downtime for crash recovery will be, given the current workload.

The Data Recovery Advisor

If the database has been damaged in some way (such as files deleted or data blocks corrupted), it may take some time to identify the problem. Then there will often be several ways of recovering from the situation. For example, if a number of datafiles have been damaged by corruptions appearing on a disk, it will be necessary to find out which files as well as which blocks require recovery. Then a decision must be made as to whether to restore entire files or only the damaged blocks. If the database is protected by a physical standby, switching over to that would also be a possibility.

Following a failure, any DBA (no matter how experienced) will need time to determine the nature and extent of the problem and then need more time to decide upon the course of action that will repair the damage with the minimum disruption to work. The Data Recovery Advisor follows an expert system to advise the DBA on this. The expert system is essentially what the

DBA would follow anyway, but the advisor can do it much faster. It is accessed with the DBMS_SQLDIAG package, invoked either through SQL*Plus or from the RMAN Recovery Manager tool.

The Segment Advisor

Segments grow automatically. As rows are inserted into table segments and index keys are inserted into index segments, the segments fill—and then Oracle will allocate more extents as necessary. But segments do not shrink automatically as data is removed or modified with DELETE and UPDATE commands; this happens only when the segment is deliberately reorganized. The Segment Advisor observes tables and indexes—both their current state and their historical patterns of use—and recommends appropriate reorganization when necessary. Invoke the Segment Advisor with the DBMS_ADVISOR package.

The SQL Repair Advisor

Occasionally, a SQL statement can fail because of an internal Oracle error. This will be reported with the ORA-600 error message. If the error condition (which is a polite name for a bug) is encountered only for a particular execution plan, it follows that using a different execution plan could avoid the failure. The SQL Repair Advisor can investigate this and generate a patch to the statement that will force the optimizer to choose a safe plan, rather than a plan that hits the problem.

Set Alert Thresholds

The Alert system is why the Oracle database can now be described as self-managing. In earlier releases, the DBA had to spend a great deal of effort on humdrum work that was essential but not always that interesting. They also had to devise methods of picking up exceptional conditions as they occurred. The Alert system can automate a large amount of work that previously fell into the DBA domain.

Alert Condition Monitoring and Notifications

A typical example of the humdrum work is space management, which, at its most basic, involves monitoring tablespaces to see when they are about to fill up. This could be done with scripts, such as this one:

```
SQL> select d.tablespace_name,sum(d.bytes) total,sum(f.bytes) free
  2  from dba_data_files d left outer join dba_free_space f
  3  on d.tablespace_name=f.tablespace_name
  4  group by d.tablespace_name;
TABLESPACE_NAME                              TOTAL        FREE
------------------------------------  ----------  ----------
SYSAUX                                807337984    38928384
USERS                                  24641536     1507328
SMALL                                    401408
SYSTEM                               1509949440     4390912
EXAMPLE                               314572800    23396352
UNDO1                                 209715200   208338944
```

But these scripts are prone to error—or at least, misinterpretation. For example, the view DBA_FREE_SPACE has one row for every bit of free space in every tablespace. But if a tablespace were full, there would be no rows at all. That's why you need OUTER JOIN, without which the SMALL tablespace would not be listed, even though it is in a critical state. Then consider the effect of enabling AUTOEXTEND on the datafiles. Also, an UNDO tablespace will usually be 100 percent full, but this is not a problem because a large part of the undo data will be inactive and can be overwritten. And what about temporary tablespaces? The query would have to be in a UNION with another query against DBA_TEMP_FILES. This second query would have to work out whether the space occupied by temporary segments is in use or merely waiting to be used.

Many DBAs have written suites of SQL code to report on space usage and raise warnings before error conditions occur. This is fine, but the scripts have to be written, they have to be run regularly, and they have to be updated to take account of changes in technology. Many companies have written and marketed tools to do the same thing. The Alert system replaces a vast amount of this humdrum work. It will monitor many conditions that can cause problems and will send notifications by a variety of methods. With regard to space management, it is by default configured to raise a warning alert when a tablespace reaches 85 percent full and a critical alert when a tablespace is 97 percent full, with account being taken of autoextension and the nature of the contents.

Alerts comes in two forms. *Stateful* alerts are based on conditions that persist and can be fixed. Examples include tablespace space usage, the number of sessions hanging, and the average time it takes to complete SQL statement execution. *Stateless* alerts are based on events; they happen and are gone. A query failing with "snapshot too old" and two transactions deadlocking are examples.

To configure the Alert system, you set thresholds. The thresholds are stored in the AWR. Then the MMON background process will monitor the database and the instance, in near real time, and compare the current state with the thresholds. If a threshold is crossed, it will raise the alert. The mechanism by which an alert is raised is simply to put an entry on the alert queue. A *queue* is a table of messages that other processes can read. What happens to the alert message next is a matter for further configuration. The default behavior is that Enterprise Manager Cloud Control will (if an agent has been installed) dequeue the message and display it on the database home page, but Enterprise Manager can be configured to send e-mails or SMS messages when it finds that an alert has been raised.

You can view the alerts by querying the view DBA_OUTSTANDING_ALERTS, and it is possible to write an alert handler in PL/SQL that will dequeue the messages and take any action desired.

 EXAM TIP Alerts are raised by the MMON process, not by Enterprise Manager. Enterprise Manager reads alerts, as can other event handlers written by you or by third parties.

Setting Thresholds

You can set more than 200 metrics for thresholds. They are documented in the view V$METRICNAME, which gives the name of the metric, the units in which it is measured, and the ID number by which it is identified.

There is an API (the DBMS_SERVER_ALERT package) for setting thresholds. Here is an example:

```
 1    execute dbms_server_alert.set_threshold(-
 2    metrics_id=>dbms_server_alert.redo_generated_sec,-
 3    warning_operator=>dbms_server_alert.operator_ge,-
 4    warning_value=>'1048576',-
 5    critical_operator=>dbms_server_alert.operator_ge,-
 6    critical_value=>'2097152',-
 7    observation_period=>1,-
 8    consecutive_occurrences=>5,-
 9    instance_name=>'ORCLZ',-
10     object_type=>dbms_server_alert.object_type_system,-
11     object_name=>null);
```

Taking this PL/SQL execution call line by line, here is what happens:

1. The procedure SET_THRESHOLD will create or update an alert threshold.

2. In PL/SQL you may pass either literals or a result returned by a function using the => operator to named parameters (arguments). Here, the metric being set is the rate of redo generation, measured in bytes per second. This is specified by passing the value returned by the dbms_server_alert.redo_generated_sec function to the metrics_id parameter using the => operator.

3. The comparison operator for the warning level, which is "greater than or equal to" is passed to the warning_operator parameter.

4. The value for a warning alert, which is 1MB per second, is passed to the warning_value parameter.

5. The comparison operator for the critical level, which is "greater than or equal to" is passed to the critical_operator parameter.

6. The value for a critical alert, which is 2MB per second, is passed to the critical_value parameter.

7. The observation period, in minutes, is passed to the observation_period parameter.

8. The number of consecutive occurrences before the alert is raised. The literal 5 is passed to the consecutive_occurrences parameter.

9. The instance for which the alert is being configured, ORCLZ, is passed to the instance_name parameter.

10. The type of object to which the alert refers. The result from the function dbms_server_alert.object_type_system is passed to the object_type parameter.

11. The name of the object to which the alert refers. In this case a NULL is provided since an object name is not meaningful to a metric that measures rate of redo generation.

Note that not all the arguments are relevant for all alerts.

The preceding example configures an alert for the rate of redo generation; a warning will be raised if this exceeds 1MB per second, and a critical warning will be raised if it goes over 2MB per second. The observation period is set to a minute and consecutive occurrences to five; this means that if the redo generation happens to hit a high level just a couple of times, it will not be reported—but if it stays at a high level consistently (for five consecutive minutes), it will be reported. Because this metric is one that could vary between instances in a Real Application Clusters (RAC) environment, the instance name must be specified, but the object name is not relevant. If the alert were for tablespace usage, the instance name would not be specified, the object type would be tablespace, and the object name would be set to the name of the tablespace.

When stateful alerts are raised, they are visible as rows in the DBA_OUTSTANDING_ ALERTS view. They will remain visible until they are cleared. They may be cleared because the DBA has fixed the problem, or in some cases the problem will go away in the natural course of events. For instance, a tablespace-usage alert would usually require DBA action (such as adding another datafile), whereas an activity-related alert, such as the rate of redo generation, might clear automatically when the activity reduces. When an alert is cleared, it is removed from the DBA_OUTSTANDING_ALERTS view and written to the DBA_ALERT_HISTORY view. Stateless alerts go straight to the history view.

Thresholds are configured by default for tablespace usage and blocking sessions. A space usage warning will be raised when a tablespace is 85 percent full and a critical warning when it is 97 percent full. The warning and critical values for blocked sessions are 2 and 4.

Exercise 18-3: Configure Alerts   In this exercise, you will enable an alert for the commit rate and demonstrate its use. Follow these steps:

1. Connect to your database with Database Control as user SYSTEM.

2. Create a rather small tablespace, as follows:

```
create tablespace small datafile 'small.dbf' size 1m
uniform size 128k;
```

   Given that the datafile will (by default) not autoextend and that each extent is a fixed size, it is impossible for this tablespace to contain more than eight extents.

3. Set a space usage alert that will raise a warning when the tablespace is half-full and a critical warning when three-quarters full. Confirm that the threshold has been set.

```
execute DBMS_SERVER_ALERT.SET_THRESHOLD(-
    metrics_id => DBMS_SERVER_ALERT.TABLESPACE_PCT_FULL,-
    warning_operator => DBMS_SERVER_ALERT.OPERATOR_GT,-
    warning_value => '50',-
    critical_operator => DBMS_SERVER_ALERT.OPERATOR_GT,-
    critical_value => '75',-
    observation_period => 1,-
    consecutive_occurrences => 1,-
    instance_name => NULL,-
    object_type => DBMS_SERVER_ALERT.OBJECT_TYPE_TABLESPACE,-
    object_name => 'SMALL')
select * from dba_thresholds where object_name='SMALL';
```

4. Create a table and fill the tablespace.

```
create table big (c1 date) tablespace small;
```

5. Fill the tablespace by allocating extents repeatedly until you receive the error "ORA-01653: unable to extend table SYSTEM.BIG by 16 in tablespace SMALL."

```
alter table big allocate extent;
```

6. Query the DBA_OUTSTANDING_ALERTS view. Note that it may take up to 10 minutes for the alert to be raised. This is because the timing of the space management alert is programmed internally and cannot be changed.

```
select * from dba_outstanding_alerts;
```

7. Resolve the problem by adding more space to the tablespace.

```
alter tablespace small add datafile 'small2.dbf' size 1m;
```

8. Confirm that the alert is cleared by querying the DBA_OUTSTANDING_ALERTS and DBA_ALERT_HISTORY views. Again, it may take up to 10 minutes for this to happen.

Use Automated Tasks

The autotask system is a mechanism whereby certain maintenance jobs run automatically. These are jobs that Oracle recommends should be run regularly on all databases.

The Autotasks

There are three autotasks:

- Gathering optimizer statistics
- Running the SQL Tuning Advisor
- Running the Segment Advisor

Optimizer statistics are needed if the optimizer is to generate efficient plans for executing SQL statements. These statistics include information such as how big tables are and the number of distinct values in columns. If these statistics are missing or inaccurate, code will certainly run, but performance may degrade because the execution plans will not be appropriate to the state of the data. For example, using an index to retrieve rows rather than scanning an entire table may or may not be the best way to run a query, depending on the size of the table and the predicate; statistics will let the optimizer make the best decision. Statistics such as these are not static. As the application is used, they will become out of date and should be refreshed. The autotask that gathers statistics will do this. By default, any fresh statistics are made available for use immediately.

The SQL Tuning Advisor autotask identifies high-load SQLs that have been run, using information written to the AWR by snapshots, and attempts to tune them. The results of the tuning are stored in a *profile,* which is additional information on how best to run the statement that can be used by the optimizer the next time the statement is executed. By default, profiles are generated but are not actually brought into use. If this default is not changed, the DBA should check for any profiles that have been generated and decide whether to implement them. To see the profiles, query the DBA_SQL_PROFILES view.

The Segment Advisor identifies table and index segments that contain a large amount of unused space, which could be released from the segment and returned to the tablespace by reorganizing the segment. Its recommendations cannot be implemented automatically.

Interpreting and implementing the result of the advisors is covered in later chapters on tuning the database and SQL.

Controlling the Autotasks

A prerequisite for running the autotasks is that the STATISTICS_LEVEL parameter should be set to either TYPICAL or ALL. The autotasks are launched by a background process, namely, the ABP0 process. The tasks, if enabled, run within defined windows. The timing of the windows is to open at 22:00 on weekdays and remain open for four hours and to open at 06:00 on weekend days and remain open for 20 hours. These windows are managed by the Scheduler, as described in Chapter 21. The intention is that the autotasks should run at times when the database is less likely to be in use by users. To limit further the impact on users, the resources used by the autotasks are restricted by the Resource Manager (detailed in Chapter 20) such that if the system is stressed, they will take up no more than 25 percent of CPU capacity.

> **TIP** The standard windows for the autotasks assume that your users are American and may not be appropriate in a multinational environment. Just because it is nighttime in the database time zone does not mean that it is nighttime elsewhere. Furthermore, Saturday and Sunday are working days in some parts of the world.

The DBA_AUTOTASK_CLIENT view will show whether the tasks are enabled, and the DBMS_AUTO_TASK_ADMIN package has procedures to enable and disable them, as shown in Figure 18-2.

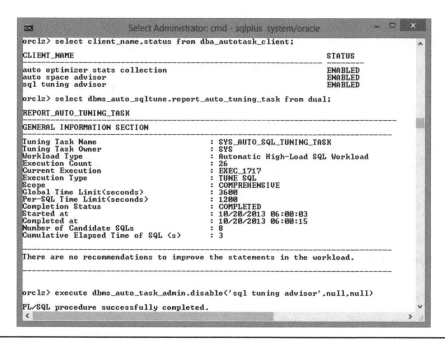

```
Select Administrator: cmd - sqlplus  system/oracle

orclz> select client_name,status from dba_autotask_client;

CLIENT_NAME                                        STATUS
-------------------------------------------------- --------
auto optimizer stats collection                    ENABLED
auto space advisor                                 ENABLED
sql tuning advisor                                 ENABLED

orclz> select dbms_auto_sqltune.report_auto_tuning_task from dual;

REPORT_AUTO_TUNING_TASK
--------------------------------------------------------------------------------
GENERAL INFORMATION SECTION
--------------------------------------------------------------------------------
Tuning Task Name                   : SYS_AUTO_SQL_TUNING_TASK
Tuning Task Owner                  : SYS
Workload Type                      : Automatic High-Load SQL Workload
Execution Count                    : 26
Current Execution                  : EXEC_1717
Execution Type                     : TUNE SQL
Scope                              : COMPREHENSIVE
Global Time Limit(seconds)         : 3600
Per-SQL Time Limit(seconds)        : 1200
Completion Status                  : COMPLETED
Started at                         : 10/20/2013 06:00:03
Completed at                       : 10/20/2013 06:00:15
Number of Candidate SQLs           : 8
Cumulative Elapsed Time of SQL (s) : 3
--------------------------------------------------------------------------------
There are no recommendations to improve the statements in the workload.
--------------------------------------------------------------------------------

orclz> execute dbms_auto_task_admin.disable('sql tuning advisor',null,null)

PL/SQL procedure successfully completed.
```

Figure 18-2   Controlling the autotasks

The first query in the figure shows that all three autotasks are enabled. Then the results of the last run of the SQL Tuning Advisor are shown. The advisor identified eight SQL statements as being worthy of attention but decided not to make any recommendations. Finally, the task is disabled.

 CAUTION Many databases are running the SQL Tuning autotask every night for no purpose because no one ever looks at the results.

Two-Minute Drill

Manage the Automatic Workload Repository

- By default, snapshots are taken every hour and stored for eight days.
- Additional snapshots can be taken on demand.
- MMON is responsible for creating snapshots and launching the ADDM.
- The AWR consists of tables (and related objects) in the SYS schema, in the SYSAUX tablespace.
- The STATISTICS_LEVEL parameter must be set to TYPICAL or ALL; otherwise, the snapshots will not be made.

Use the Automatic Database Diagnostic Monitor

- The ADDM runs automatically whenever a snapshot is taken and manually on demand.
- ADDM reports will give advice directly and may also recommend running other advisors.
- The ADDM requires two snapshots, generating reports on activity between them.

Describe and Use the Advisory Framework

- A set of advisors is provided for tuning purposes.
- The advisors depend on statistics stored as snapshots in the AWR.
- Access to some advisors is through Enterprise Manager, and all are accessible through views and PL/SQL APIs. By default, the SQL Tuning Advisor and the Segment Advisor will run automatically in the maintenance windows.

Set Alert Thresholds

- Stateful alerts must be configured with thresholds.
- If a stateful alert is raised, it will remain until the situation is cleared; stateless alerts are reported and do not need to be cleared.
- Thresholds are stored in the AWR.

- It is the MMON background process that raises an alert.
- Setting STATISTICS_LEVEL to BASIC will disable server alerts.

Use Automated Tasks

- The autotask framework automates execution of critical maintenance jobs.
- The three autotasks are gathering optimizer statistics, running the SQL Tuning Advisor, and running the Segment Advisor.
- By default, new statistics are published, but the advisor tasks' recommendations are not implemented.
- The running of the autotasks is controlled by the Scheduler and the Resource Manager.

Self Test

1. The AWR is located in the SYSAUX tablespace. If you suspect that it is growing to such a size that it will fill the SYSAUX tablespace, what actions could you take to reduce the likelihood of this happening? (Choose all correct answers.)

    A. Relocate the AWR to a tablespace created specifically for storing it.

    B. Reduce the time between snapshots so that less data will be generated by each one.

    C. Increase the time between snapshots so that fewer snapshots will be generated.

    D. Adjust the scheduling of the automatic maintenance tasks so that they will run less frequently.

2. By default, snapshots are removed from the AWR on a regular basis, making comparisons of activity over a long period of time (such as contrasting this year's year-end processing with last year's) impossible. What should you do to make this possible? (Choose the best answer.)

    A. Save the year-end snapshots as a baseline.

    B. Adjust the snapshot-retention period to the whole period: a little over a year.

    C. Set the datafiles that make up the SYSAUX tablespace to AUTOEXTEND so that snapshots will not be purged.

    D. Disable purging of snapshots by setting STATISTICS_LEVEL to ALL.

3. When will the ADDM run? (Choose the best answer.)

    A. Whenever an alert is raised by the server alert system

    B. During the maintenance windows that run the autotasks

    C. Following the gathering of an AWR snapshot

    D. Only when explicitly requested

4. With regard to the collection of monitoring information, put these steps in the correct order:

A. Data accumulates in the SGA.

B. MMON generates an ADDM report.

C. MMON writes data to the AWR.

D. Reports are purged.

E. Snapshots are purged.

5. Which advisors are run by the autotask system in the maintenance windows? (Choose all correct answers.)

A. The ADDM

B. The memory advisors

C. The Segment Advisor

D. The SQL Access Advisor

E. The SQL Tuning Advisor

F. The Undo Advisor

6. Under which circumstances would the advisors not be available? (Choose the best answer.)

A. If the optimizer statistics-gathering autotask has been disabled

B. If the STATISTICS_LEVEL parameter is set to BASIC

C. If the AWR snapshots have been purged

D. If Enterprise Manager has not been configured

7. Which process raises alerts? (Choose the best answer.)

A. MMON, the Manageability Monitor

B. Enterprise Manager (Database Express or Cloud Control)

C. The server process that detects the problem

D. SMON, the System Monitor

8. End users are complaining that they receive "snapshot too old" error messages when running long queries. You look at the DBA_OUTSTANDING_ALERTS view and don't see any. Why might this be? (Choose the best answer.)

A. The STATISTICS_LEVEL parameter is set to BASIC.

B. The snapshots for the periods when the errors occurred have been purged.

C. No alert has been configured for "snapshot too old."

D. "Snapshot too old" is reported in DBA_ALERT_HISTORY.

9. How can you best automate the collection of optimizer statistics? (Choose the best answer.)

   A. The MMON process will collect them if STATISTICS_LEVEL is set to TYPICAL or to ALL.

   B. An automatic maintenance job will collect them if STATISTICS_LEVEL is set to TYPICAL or to ALL.

   C. Enterprise Manager Cloud Control will collect them if the agent is running.

   D. Schedule a job to execute the DBMS_STATS.GATHER_DATABASE_STATISTICS procedure.

10. Where are the object statistics used by the query optimizer stored? (Choose the best answer.)

   A. With the objects themselves.

   B. In the data dictionary.

   C. In the AWR.

   D. They are accumulated in the shared pool of the SGA.

11. You notice that the autotasks do not appear to be running. Why might this be? (Choose all correct answers.)

   A. The STATISTICS_LEVEL parameter is set to BASIC.

   B. The tasks have been explicitly disabled.

   C. The Enterprise Manager Agent is not running.

   D. The tasks have not been scheduled with the DBMS_SCHEDULER package.

   E. The tasks have not been scheduled with the DBMS_JOB package.

Self Test Answers

1. ☑   **C.** Increasing the time between snapshots will reduce the number stored and therefore the space needed.
   ☒   **A**, **B**, and **D** are incorrect. **A** is incorrect because it is not possible to relocate the AWR. **B** is incorrect because the space needed to store a snapshot is not related to the snapshot frequency; this would actually have the opposite effect to that desired. **D** is incorrect because the automatic maintenance tasks do not control snapshots, and it is snapshots that take up the bulk of the space in the AWR.

2. ☑   **A.** This is exactly the type of situation for which baselines are intended.
   ☒   **B**, **C**, and **D** are incorrect. **B** would work, but you would need a SYSAUX tablespace the size of Jupiter; it is not a good solution. **C** is incorrect because the available space has no effect on the retention time. **D** is incorrect because STATISTICS_LEVEL controls how much information is gathered, not for how long it is kept.

3. ☑ **C.** The ADDM runs automatically whenever a snapshot is generated, contrasting that snapshot with the previous snapshot.

☒ **A, B,** and **D** are incorrect. **A** is incorrect because there is no integration between the alert system and ADDM. **B** is incorrect because ADDM is not an autotask. **D** is incorrect because although you can request ADDM reports explicitly, they are also generated automatically.

4. ☑ **A, C, B, E, D** is the correct sequence.

☒ All other sequences are wrong.

5. ☑ **C** and **E.** These run in every maintenance window, but implementing the recommendations is up to the DBA.

☒ **A, B, D,** and **F** are incorrect. **A** is incorrect because MMON invokes the ADDM. **B, D,** and **F** are incorrect because they are advisors that must be invoked manually.

6. ☑ **B.** The advisors are dependent on the STATISTICS_LEVEL.

☒ **A, C,** and **D** are incorrect. **A** is incorrect because optimizer statistics are not required by the advisors, although they may recommend collecting them. **C** is incorrect because the advisors can always be invoked using the information currently available in the instance. **D** is incorrect because although Enterprise Manager can invoke the advisors, there is no dependency between them.

7. ☑ **A.** MMON raises alerts by writing a message to the alert queue.

☒ **B, C,** and **D** are incorrect. **B** is incorrect because Enterprise Manager does not raise alerts; it reports them. **C** and **D** are incorrect because neither server sessions nor the SMON are part of the Alert system.

8. ☑ **D.** "Snapshot too old" is a stateless alert and therefore goes directly to the alert history.

☒ **A, B,** and **C** are incorrect. **A** is incorrect because the STATISTICS_LEVEL refers to statistics, not alerts. **B** is incorrect because outstanding alerts do not get purged on any schedule, only by being resolved. **C** is incorrect because "snapshot too old" is a stateless alert, and thresholds can apply only to stateful alerts.

9. ☑ **B.** A job will run in the maintenance windows unless STATISICS_LEVEL is set to BASIC.

☒ **A, C,** and **D** are incorrect. **A** and **C** are incorrect because they specify the wrong component to carry out the task. **D** is incorrect because although you could schedule a job yourself, letting the autotask facility do this is the best option.

10. ☑ **B.** The optimizer uses the latest published statistics, which are stored in the data dictionary.

☒ **A, C,** and **D** are incorrect. **A** is incorrect because the statistics are stored independently of the actual segments. **C** is incorrect because the AWR stores historical values, which are not used for real-time parsing. **D** is incorrect because the SGA stores the execution plan itself, not the information used to generate it.

11. ☑ **A** and **B.** Setting STATISTICS_LEVEL=BASIC will disable the autotasks (and a few other things). The tasks can also be disabled with the DBMS_AUTO_TASK_ ADMIN.DISABLE procedure.

☒ **C, D,** and **E** are incorrect. **C** is incorrect because Enterprise Manager is not required to run autotasks. **D** and **E** are incorrect because although the Scheduler and the Resource Manager control when and how autotasks will run, they do not enable or disable them.

CHAPTER 19

Performance Tuning

Exam Objectives

- 062.11.1 Use Enterprise Manager to Monitor Performance
- 062.11.2 Use Automatic Memory Management
- 062.11.3 Use the Memory Advisor to Size Memory Buffers
- 062.12.1 Manage Optimizer Statistics
- 062.12.2 Use the SQL Tuning Advisor
- 062.12.3 Use the SQL Access Advisor to Tune Workload

Performance tuning is a huge subject. The treatment given in the core Oracle Certified Professional (OCP) syllabus is little more than an introduction. As an Oracle database administrator (DBA), you will study performance monitoring and enhancement techniques throughout your whole career. Indeed, you may want "Don't worry, I'll find the problem soon" inscribed on your tombstone. The topics discussed here include using Enterprise Manager to monitor performance, followed by an in-depth discussion of memory management. Sorting out memory management will solve many performance issues, and it is a prerequisite step to tuning SQL statements.

Generally speaking, the approach to take toward SQL tuning is to trust the optimizer. Oracle's Cost Based Optimizer (CBO) may well be the most complex piece of software with which you will ever work. Many DBAs have spent years studying the operation of the CBO. Clearly, a comprehensive knowledge of the CBO is beyond the scope of the OCP—and the Oracle Certified Master (OCM)—examination. But one aspect is discussed: the need to supply the CBO with the statistical information it needs to make decisions. These decisions are about how best to execute SQL statements, and if this information is missing or inaccurate, performance may degrade drastically. Developing execution plans based on statistics is known as *cost-based optimization* and is one of the hottest topics in computer science.

Two advisors are relevant to SQL performance: the SQL Tuning Advisor, which looks at how a given statement runs, and the SQL Access Advisor, which looks at the segment structures against which the statement runs. Both these advisors are licensed as part of the Tuning Pack, available for Enterprise Edition installations.

Use Enterprise Manager to Monitor Performance

Enterprise Manager has some nice facilities for displaying the results of monitoring queries, but before investigating them, it is necessary to appreciate what performance management is all about and how it should be approached.

A Performance Tuning Methodology

Tuning has one purpose only: to reduce response time for end users. Or to put it another way, all tuning should be oriented toward fixing a business problem. For example, no end user has ever telephoned the help desk to complain that "the shared pool is too small" or that "the indexing strategy is not correct." They telephone with complaints such as "the order-entry screen does not refresh quickly enough" or "the overnight batch jobs didn't finish until lunchtime." It is easy for a DBA to become sidetracked into tuning particular aspects of database operation, without considering whether they actually matter. It may well be that the memory structures or the indexes are not optimal for a given workload, but if end users are not facing any quantifiable problems related to this, there is no reason to expend effort on attempting to improve them.

Once you accept that tuning should be focused on business needs, it becomes apparent that a top-down approach is required. Start by analyzing, and if necessary re-engineering, the business processes. A performance tuning methodology should concentrate on business needs, and performance should be considered at all stages. Consider this as a possible application development life cycle:

- **Business analysis**   Define the organization's business processes, in other words, what it needs to do.

- **Systems analysis**   Model the business processes as an ideal system, using techniques such as entity-relationship modeling and data flow diagramming.

- **System design**   Adapt the ideal system to reality. Consider the environment within which the application will run (including the fact that it is an Oracle database).

- **Application design**   Write the SQL.

- **Implementation**   Create the database and deploy the application.

- **Maintenance**   Monitor and make adjustments during use.

A mistake made early on may be hard to fix subsequently. For example, if the business analysis assumes that a customer name is unique and therefore at systems analysis time "customer name" is used as a primary key, it will be difficult to adjust the application when at implementation time it turns out that several customers can have the same name. Similarly, performance should be considered right at the beginning. For example, systems analysts will model the data structures (typically) to third normal form. But although third normal form may be ideal theoretically, it is rarely optimal for performance. Selective denormalization should occur at the system design stage. If this is not done, the problems of managing over-normalized data will be hard to fix later.

A tuning methodology should therefore have two major characteristics. First, it should be applied from the top down. Second, it should concentrate on business needs.

 NOTE   To say that tuning should be top down is all very well, but in many cases the DBA is presented with a finished product and is forced to tune it from the bottom up, reacting to issues as they occur that perhaps were never properly considered earlier.

Performance Monitoring Data

Oracle collects a vast amount of information regarding activity and performance. This information is accumulated throughout the lifetime of the instance in a set of V$ views and periodically flushed to the Automatic Workload Repository (AWR) by the Manageability Monitor (MMON) background process (as described in Chapter 18). Two terms must be defined: *statistics* and *metrics*. In the Oracle world, a statistic is a figure that is meaningless by itself, whereas a metric is two or more statistics correlated together—and often correlated with time. For example, the number of disk reads is a statistic. Let's say this statistic is at 100,000,000. So what? That is useless. What you need to know is disk reads per second, disk reads per execution of a statement, or disk reads per transaction this week compared with disk reads per transaction last week. The conversion of statistics to metrics is to a large extent done by Oracle on the DBA's behalf, and the results are exposed through a set of views.

Execution of a SQL statement is rarely a continuous process. Usually, it is a set of stop-start events. For example, a statement such as SELECT COUNT(*) FROM EMP might require reading every block of the segment containing the EMP table. This could be many thousands of blocks. To accomplish this, the session's server process must ask the operating system to deliver a set of blocks—but not all of them in one go. The session will then hang while the operating system's input/output (I/O) subsystem locates and delivers the blocks. Then the session can wake up, process the rows in the blocks, and issue another read request. It will hang until the next set of blocks is delivered. Many reasons are possible for a session to hang during execution of a statement. The reasons for hanging are known as *wait events*.

It is never possible to eliminate wait events completely (they are part of the normal SQL execution cycle), but if certain wait events are consuming an inordinate amount of time, the cause of the wait event should be investigated and, if possible, removed (or at least reduced). In the example of the query just given, the most significant wait event would probably be *db file scattered read*. This is the event that occurs during a full table scan as groups of blocks are read for insertion into the buffer cache. Other wait events could also occur: *free buffer wait* as the server process searches for buffers in the cache into which to place the blocks, or *buffer busy wait,* which means that the block is already in the cache but temporarily inaccessible because another session is working on it.

Performance monitoring data is accumulated and metrics calculated on several dimensions. Here are some of the critical views:

- **V$STATNAME** A documentation view, listing every statistic gathered, grouping them into classes

- **V$SYSSTAT** The current value of each statistic for the entire instance, accumulated since the instance was started

- **V$SESSTAT** The current value of each statistic for each currently logged-on session, accumulated since the session started

- **V$MYSTAT** The statistics for your currently logged-on session

- **V$EVENT_NAME** A documentation view, listing every wait event, grouping them into classes

- **V$SYSTEM_EVENT** The number of times each wait event has occurred and the total time spent waiting on the event for the entire instance, accumulated since the instance was started

- **V$SESSION_EVENT** The number of times each wait event has occurred for each currently logged-on session and the total time spent by that session waiting on the event, accumulated since the session started

The Database Express Performance Pages

Enterprise Manager Database Express provides limited access to performance monitoring information. From the database home page, the Performance tab links to what is called Performance Hub. When you are navigating around the Performance Hub, the first step is to choose the time frame. By default, this is real time, showing data for the last hour. The historical view lets you choose any time up to the limit of data within the AWR.

The following tabs on the Performance Hub page give access to this information:

- **Summary**   This tab shows an overall view of the performance activity of the system over the selected time period.

- **Activity**   This tab displays currently active sessions, showing the SQL they are running and the wait events they are experiencing.

- **Workload**   This tab displays charts showing the pattern of user calls, the logon rate, the redo generation, and the SQL being executed.

- **Monitored SQL**   All statements that consume more than five seconds of central processing unit (CPU) or I/O time are monitored, with data regarding I/O, wait events, and the execution plan.

- **ADDM**   This tab gives access to ADDM reports over whatever time period has been selected.

Exercise 19-1: Use Enterprise Manager to Monitor Activity   In this exercise, you generate a workload and inspect activity in Enterprise Manager. Follow these steps:

1. Connect to the database as user SYSTEM with SQL*Plus.

2. Determine the Hypertext Transfer Protocol (HTTP) or HTTP Secure (HTTPS) listening port and set one if necessary. The following two function calls will list the port (returning zero if it has not been set). At least one, either HTTP or HTTPS, is needed. These two example procedure calls will create a listening endpoint and register it with the listener. Use either protocol on any free port you want. Confirm that the port is active by rerunning the function calls and checking the status of the database listener— which will display the listening address and the protocol (either Transmission Control Protocol [TCP] or TCP Secure [TCPS]).

```
select dbms_xdb_config.gethttpport from dual;
select dbms_xdb_config.gethttpsport from dual;
exec dbms_xdb_config.sethttpport(5500);
exec dbms_xdb_config.sethttpsport(5501);
lsnrctl status
```

3. Connect to Database Express, logging on as user SYSTEM, with the appropriate URL. Here are two examples:

    http://127.0.0.1:5500/em

    https://127.0.0.0:5501/em

4. In the SQL*Plus session, launch a long-running query that should put some stress on the system.

```
select count(*) from
(select a.*,b.* from all_objects a,all_objects b);
```

5. In Database Express, observe the activity build up on the database home page. Then navigate to the Performance Hub, on the Performance tab, and investigate all the subtabs.

Use Automatic Memory Management

Memory usage in the Oracle instance falls into two categories: Program Global Areas (PGAs) that are private to each session and the System Global Area (the SGA) that is shared by all the Oracle processes. From release 9*i* it has been possible to automate the management of the PGA. From release 10*g* it has been possible to automate the management of the SGA. Releases 11*g* and 12*c* can manage both the PGA and the SGA together, fully automatically.

 CAUTION All Oracle memory usage is virtual memory. The Oracle processes have no way of knowing whether the memory to which they are connecting is in random access memory (RAM) or has been swapped (or paged) to disk. However, swapping will cripple performance and should be avoided.

PGA Memory Management

A user session against an Oracle instance consists of a user process connected to a server process. The user process generates SQL statements and sends them to the server process for execution. This is the client-server split. Associated with the server process is a block of nonsharable memory: the PGA. When executing SQL, the server process makes use of the PGA to store session-specific data, including the following:

- Sorting rows
- Merging bitmaps
- Variables
- The call stack

For some data in the PGA, use of memory is nonnegotiable. For example, if the session needs memory for its call stack, that memory must be made available. For other structures (such as sort space), use of PGA is preferable but not essential because if necessary the data can be written out to a disk-based storage structure—although this will impact adversely on performance.

Every SQL statement uses memory in the SGA (specifically, the shared SQL area in the shared pool) and also will require a minimum amount of PGA memory (sometimes referred to as the private SQL area), without which it cannot execute. Making more PGA memory available will often reduce execution time, but the reduction is not linear. Typically, there will be three stages of memory allocation: these are known as optimal, one-pass, and multipass. The optimal memory allocation will allow the statement to execute purely in memory, with no requirement to make use of temporary storage on disk. The optimal memory allocation is sufficient to accommodate all the input data and any auxiliary data structures that the statement must create. The one-pass memory allocation is insufficient for optimal execution and therefore forces an extra pass over the data. The multipass memory allocation is even smaller and means that several passes over the data will be needed.

As an example, consider a sort operation. The ideal situation is that all the rows to be sorted can be read into the PGA and sorted there. The memory required for this is the optimal memory allocation. If the optimal memory allocation is not available, then the rows must be separated into batches. Each batch will be read into memory, sorted, and written out to disk. This results in a set of sorted batches on disk, which must then be read back into memory and merged into a final sorted list of all the rows. The PGA memory needed for this is the one-pass allocation; the sort operation has had to become multiple sorts followed by a merge. If the one-pass memory allocation is not available, then the merge phase as well as the sort phase will require use of temporary disk storage. This is a multipass execution.

EXAM TIP A statement's shared SQL area is in the shared pool of the SGA; its private SQL area is in the session's PGA.

The ideal situation is that all SQL statements should execute optimally, but this goal may be impossible to reach. In data warehouse operations, the optimal memory allocation can be many gigabytes if the queries are addressing vast tables. In such environments, one-pass executions may be the best that can be achieved. Multipass executions should be avoided if at all possible. For example, sorting 10GB of data may require more than 10GB of memory to run optimally but only 40MB to run with one pass. Only if less than 40MB is available will the sort become multipass, and execution times will then increase substantially.

Managing PGA memory can be automatic, and Oracle Corporation strongly recommends that it should be. The older manual management techniques are supported only for backward compatibility and will not be discussed here. To implement automatic PGA memory management, you set a target for the total PGA memory allocation, summed up for all sessions. The Oracle instance will then pass out memory from this total to sessions on demand. When a session has finished executing its statement, the PGA it was using can be allocated to another session. This system relies on the fact that at any one moment only some of the connected sessions will need any negotiable PGA memory. They will all need a certain amount of PGA memory to retain the state of the session, even when the session is idle, but this will leave enough from the total so that those sessions actually running statements can have what they need. At least, that is what one hopes.

NOTE It is sometimes impossible to achieve optimal memory allocations because the memory requirements can be huge. One-pass executions are bad but may be unavoidable. Multipass executions are disastrous, and if these are occurring, you should talk to the system administrators about available hardware and to the programmers about tuning their SQL.

Automatic PGA memory management is enabled with three instance parameters:

- WORKAREA_SIZE_POLICY
- PGA_AGGREGATE_TARGET
- PGA_AGGREGATE_LIMIT

The WORKAREA_SIZE_POLICY parameter will default to AUTO, meaning that Oracle can assign PGA to sessions on demand, while attempting to keep the total allocated PGA within the PGA_AGGREGATE_TARGET parameter. This parameter defaults to the greater of 10MB, or 20 percent of the size of the SGA, and should be adjusted upward until a satisfactory proportion of statements is executing optimally, but it shouldn't be set so high that memory is over-allocated and the operating system has to page virtual memory to disk. Note that this is only a target—a soft limit. If set to a value that is too low for sessions to function (perhaps because the total of nonnegotiable memory requirements exceeds the target), the target will be broken and more memory will be allocated.

EXAM TIP What happens to sessions if the PGA_AGGREGATE_TARGET value is exceeded? Nothing—that is, until the PGA_AGGREGATE_LIMIT value is also exceeded, at which point statements will fail.

The PGA_AGGREGATE_LIMIT value is a hard limit on the total PGA that can be used. The default is the greater of 2GB, or double the PGA_AGGREGATE_TARGET, or 3MB multiplied by the PROCESSES parameter. It cannot be set to less than 2GB. If this limit is exceeded, Oracle will terminate calls in progress in order to bring the PGA usage down below the limit.

CAUTION If your PGA_AGGREGATE_TARGET is not sufficient for optimal and one-pass operations, your database will be performing badly. If the PGA_AGGREGATE_LIMIT is ever reached, the situation is disastrous. As a matter of urgency, tune the SQL to require less memory, and if possible, add more memory to the system.

SGA Memory Management

The SGA contains several memory structures that can be sized independently:

- The shared pool
- The database buffer cache (default pool)
- The large pool
- The streams pool
- The Java pool
- The log buffer

As a general rule, the memory allocation to the large pool, the Java pool, and the streams pool is not a matter for negotiation—either the memory is needed or it isn't. If these structures are undersized, there will be errors; if they are oversized, there will be no performance improvement. The memory allocation to the shared pool, the database buffer cache, and the log buffer is negotiable; if it's less than optimal, there will not be errors but performance will degrade. The exception is the shared pool; if this is chronically undersized, errors will occur.

TIP Do not throw memory at Oracle unnecessarily. An oversized shared pool or log buffer can be bad for performance. An oversized buffer cache is less likely to be a problem, unless it is so oversized that the system is having to swap.

SGA memory management can be automatic (and Oracle Corporation advises that it should be), with the exception of the log buffer and the nonstandard buffer cache pools. The DBA sets a total size for the SGA, and the instance will apportion this total to the various structures, thus ensuring that there are no errors from SGA components being undersized and that memory above this minimum is allocated where it will do the most good. The components will be resized on demand, so if a component needs more memory, it will be taken from a component that can spare it. The log buffer is the one SGA component whose size is fixed at instance startup and that cannot be automatically managed.

 EXAM TIP The log buffer is the only SGA structure that cannot be adjusted dynamically. It cannot therefore be automatically managed.

The parameters for manual management of the SGA are as follows:

- SHARED_POOL_SIZE
- DB_CACHE_SIZE
- LARGE_POOL_SIZE
- STREAMS_POOL_SIZE
- JAVA_POOL_SIZE

To enable automatic shared memory management (ASMM), leave all of these set to the default (or set to zero) and set one parameter instead: SGA_TARGET. Optionally, set SGA_MAX_SIZE as well.

When ASMM is used, the instance will monitor demand for memory in the various SGA components and pass out memory to the components as required, downsizing components if this is necessary to keep the total allocated memory within the target. Also included within the target is the log buffer. This is sized with the LOG_BUFFER parameter, which is static; the log buffer is created at instance startup and cannot be resized subsequently.

 TIP The default for LOG_BUFFER is probably correct. You can set the parameter to higher than the default, but this may well cause a degradation in performance. If you set it to less than the default, your setting will often be ignored.

If you set any of the parameters that control the automatically managed SGA components, the value given will act as the minimum size below which ASMM will never reduce that component. Depending on activity, the size at any given moment may be above that requested by the parameter.

 EXAM TIP The DBA can set minimum values for the automatically managed memory structures but not maximum values.

The SGA_TARGET parameter is dynamic; it can be adjusted to a lower value, and the instance will resize the variable components downward to meet the new target. It can also be raised, provided it is not raised above the value of the SGA_MAX_SIZE parameter. The SGA_MAX_SIZE parameter defaults to the SGA_TARGET value and is a static parameter. Therefore, by default, you can never make the total SGA larger than it was at instance startup time.

Automatic Memory Management

The Automatic Memory Management (AMM) mechanism lets the Oracle instance manage server memory usage as a whole via one parameter: MEMORY_TARGET. Optionally, you can set MEMORY_MAX_TARGET as well. This takes the automatic PGA management (enabled with PGA_AGGREGATE_TARGET) and the Automatic Shared Memory Management (ASMM) (enabled with SGA_TARGET) a step further by letting Oracle transfer memory between PGAs and SGA on demand.

TIP To make your life easy, set the parameter MEMORY_TARGET only and do not set any of the other parameters listed previously. Set MEMORY_MAX_TARGET to, perhaps, 20 percent higher—to give yourself some wiggle room if you need to tune later.

AMM is not just a tool to make database administration easy. It will often provide noticeable performance benefits as well. Many databases will experience different patterns of activity at different times, which could benefit from different memory configurations. For example, it is not uncommon for a database used for order processing to experience a high transaction processing workload during most of the month and then a heavy query processing workload during month-end reporting runs. Transaction processing will typically not be demanding on PGA memory but will require a large database buffer cache. Query processing will often require large PGA allocations but not much buffer cache.

EXAM TIP The MEMORY_TARGET parameter is dynamic—it can be adjusted without shutting down the instance—but only within a limit set by another parameter: MEMORY_MAX_TARGET. This is static, so it can be raised only by adjusting with the SCOPE=SPFILE clause and restarting the instance.

Manually transferring memory between SGA and PGA in response to changing patterns of activity is not a practical option, and many systems will not be able to allocate enough memory to both concurrently to satisfy their peak demands. Automatic Memory Management is able to transfer memory between SGA and PGA as necessary to optimize performance within an overall memory constraint. This overall constraint must be determined by the DBA and the system administrator together. There is little point in the DBA setting an upper limit that is so large that the operating system has to page SGA and PGA to a swap device; the system administrator will be able to advise on a suitable maximum value.

EXAM TIP If you set the parameters PGA_AGGREGATE_TARGET and SGA_TARGET when AMM is enabled, the values you specify are a minimum size beneath which AMM will never reduce the PGA or SGA.

Generally speaking, memory allocations will stabilize within an instance after an application has been running for a while, until there is some dramatic change in the pattern of activity. Two views will be useful to monitor this:

- V$MEMORY_DYNAMIC_COMPONENTS shows the current sizes of the structures.
- V$MEMORY_RESIZE_OPS shows the history of the last 800 resizing operations.

AMM is implemented by the *memory broker,* which consists of two background processes. The MMON process monitors activity and, when advisable, instructs the Memory Manager (MMAN) process to reassign memory between components. Memory transfers should occur at most only every few minutes for tuning purposes and will usually occur much less frequently—perhaps never—once the system has stabilized. There will, however, be an immediate transfer in the event of an error condition being raised by a session. Rather than the statement failing, the session will hang while memory is made available and will then resume.

 NOTE AMM does have platform variations. For example, on Linux it is not possible to enable AMM if HugePages is in use. On Solaris, adequate Dynamic Intimate Shared Memory segments must be configured for the project under which the instance is running.

Exercise 19-2: Set the Memory Management Parameters In this exercise, you will disable Automatic Memory Management (if it is enabled) and set the SGA and PGA targets independently. Make all the changes using syntax that will affect only the running instance; do not propagate the changes to the spfile, unless you are prepared to reverse them later. Here are the steps to follow:

1. Connect to your database with SQL*Plus as user SYSTEM.

2. Ensure that none of the parameters for managing the dynamic SGA memory structures manually are set.
```
alter system set db_cache_size=0 scope=memory;
alter system set shared_pool_size=0 scope=memory;
alter system set large_pool_size=0 scope=memory;
alter system set java_pool_size=0 scope=memory;
```

3. Disable Automatic Memory Management.
```
alter system set memory_target=0 scope=memory;
```

4. Set the parameters to size PGA and SGA independently, using very low values.
```
alter system set pga_aggregate_target=10m scope=memory;
alter system set sga_target=256m scope=memory;
```

The second command may take a few minutes to complete, and it may fail if Oracle cannot reduce the SGA to the minimum. In this case, try a larger value.

5. Determine the actual size of the currently allocated PGAs by summing up the value for the statistic "session pga memory" across all sessions.
```
select sum(value) from v$sesstat natural join v$statname
where name='session pga memory';
```

The figure will be significantly in excess of the 10MB requested in step 4. This is because 10MB is a value that is so low that Oracle cannot keep to it. The PGA target is only a target, not a hard limit.

6. Determine the actual size of the SGA.

```
select sum(bytes) from v$sgastat;
```

This figure, too, may be greater than that requested in step 4.

Use the Memory Advisor to Size Memory Buffers

The Oracle instance collects a vast amount of information regarding activity and performance. These statistics enable the memory advisors, which are tools that calculate the effect of varying the sizes of the SGA and PGA memory structures. The Automatic Memory Management facility uses the advisors to make decisions about memory allocation, and they are also visible to the DBA through various views and through Enterprise Manager. Figure 19-1 shows three queries that display memory advisor information.

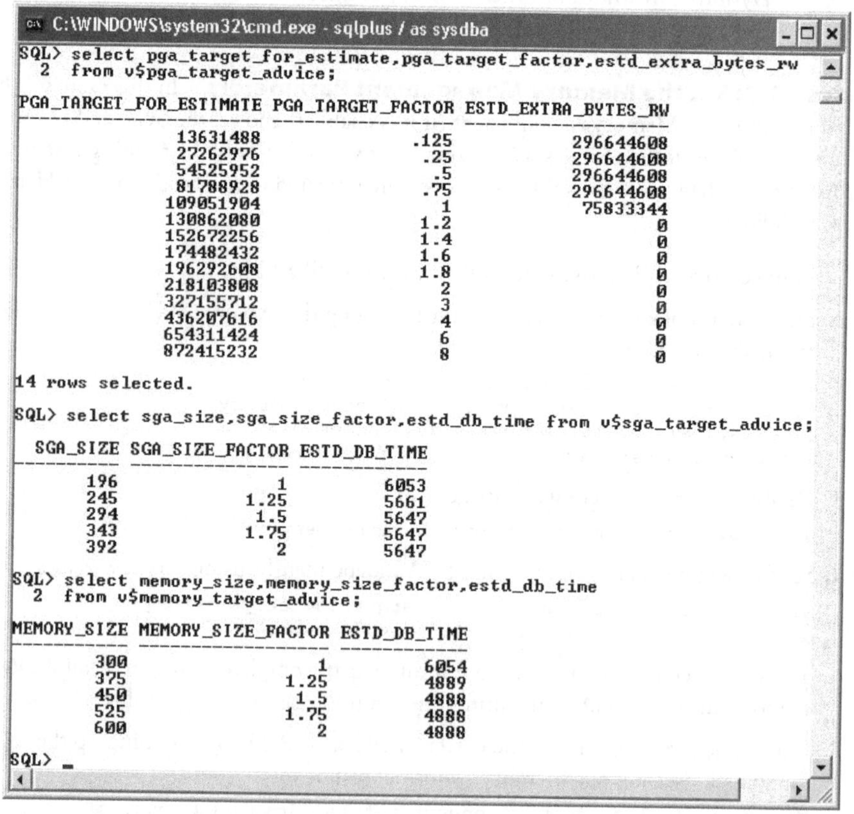

Figure 19-1 Three memory advisors queried with SQL*Plus

The first query in Figure 19-1 shows the PGA advisor. The third selected column shows an estimate for the amount of disk I/O that would be needed if the PGA target were set to the figure shown in the first column. The second column expresses this figure as a proportion of the actual setting. The fifth row of the output is the current setting: a PGA_TARGET_FACTOR of 1. As you can see, if another 30MB of memory were added to the target, less I/O would be needed, but adding more than this would give no further benefit.

The second query in Figure 19-1 shows the SGA advisor. This relates the size of the SGA to a projected value for DB_TIME, which is an overall figure for the amount of time taken by the database to execute SQL; minimizing DB_TIME is the overall objective of all tuning. As you can see, if the SGA were raised from its current value of 196MB to 294MB, DB_TIME would reduce, but there would be no point in going further.

The third query is against the memory target advisor, which gives advice on the total (SGA plus PGA) memory allocation. This shows that the optimal value is 450MB, as opposed to the current value of 300MB. If Automatic Memory Management is in use (enabled with the MEMORY_TARGET parameter), then this last query is all that would be needed. As you can see, virtually all of the DB_TIME saving could be achieved by raising the target to 375MB, and if the system administrators say sufficient memory is not available to allocate the optimal amount, then this is what the DBA should ask for.

 EXAM TIP   The advisors will not be enabled unless the STATISTICS_LEVEL parameter is set to TYPICAL or ALL.

In all, there are seven memory advisors. Each is exposed through a dynamic performance (or V$) view populated with current information in the SGA, as well as a DBA view populated with historical data from tables in the AWR.

Advisor	V$ View	DBA View
PGA	V$PGA_TARGET_ADVICE	DBA_HIST_PGA_TARGET_ADVICE
SGA	V$SGA_TARGET_ADVICE	DBA_HIST_SGA_TARGET_ADVICE
Memory	V$MEMORY_TARGET_ADVICE	DBA_HIST_MEMORY_TARGET_ADVICE
DB cache	V$DB_CACHE_ADVICE	DBA_HIST_DB_CACHE_ADVICE
Java pool	V$JAVA_POOL_ADVICE	DBA_HIST_JAVA_POOL_ADVICE
Streams pool	V$STREAMS_POOL_ADVICE	DBA_HIST_STREAMS_POOL_ADVICE
Shared pool	V$SHARED_POOL_ADVICE	DBA_HIST_SHARED_POOL_ADVICE

Exercise 19-3: Use the Memory Advisors   In this exercise, you will gather advice about memory allocation by querying the relevant views. This exercise assumes that Exercise 19-2 has been completed. Here are the steps to follow:

1. Connect to your database as user SYSTEM with SQL*Plus.

2. Run this query to see the results of the SGA advisor:
```
select sga_size,sga_size_factor,estd_db_time,estd_physical_reads
from v$sga_target_advice;
```

The value for SGA_SIZE_FACTOR=1 will be that specified in Exercise 19-2, step 6. Note the point at which there is no significant anticipated benefit to adding more memory.

3. Run this query to see the results of the PGA advisor:

```
select
pga_target_for_estimate,pga_target_factor,estd_extra_bytes_rw,
estd_pga_cache_hit_percentage,estd_overalloc_count
from v$pga_target_advice;
```

This query will show the anticipated effect of various values for PGA_AGGREGATE_TARGET. As the target increases, ESTD_EXTRA_BYTES_RW will reduce. This is the amount of physical I/O necessary because SQL work areas do not need to be written out to temporary storage. The ESTD_PGA_CACHE_HIT_PERCENTAGE value will tend toward 100 percent because queries can run optimally rather than one-pass or multipass. ESTD_OVERALLOC_COUNT is the number of times Oracle would not be able to keep to the PGA target; this will tend toward zero if PGA is available.

4. Return your instance to the state it was in before Exercise 19-2 by restarting it.

Manage Optimizer Statistics

Any one SQL statement can be executed in a number of ways. For example, it may be possible to join tables in different orders, there may be a choice of whether to use indexes or table scans, or some execution methods may be more intensive in their use of disk I/O and CPU resources. The method of executing a statement is known as the *execution plan,* and the choice of execution plan is critical for performance. In an Oracle database, execution plans are developed dynamically by the optimizer. The optimizer relies heavily on statistics to evaluate the effectiveness of many possible execution plans and to choose which plan to use. For good performance, it is vital that these statistics are accurate. There are many types of statistics, but chief among them are the object statistics that give details of the tables that the SQL statements address.

 TIP　Statistics are not relevant to PL/SQL, only to SQL—so gathering statistics will not improve PL/SQL performance. But most PL/SQL code will include calls to SQL statements; statistics are as important for these statements as for any others.

Object Statistics

Analyzing a table gathers statistics on the table that will be of use to the optimizer. Some of the statistics are visible in the DBA_TABLES view; they include the following:

- The number of rows in the table
- The number of blocks (used and not yet used) allocated to the table
- The amount of free space in the blocks that are being used

- The average length of each row
- The number of "chained" rows—rows that cut across two or more blocks, either because they are very long or because of poor storage settings

Apart from statistics regarding the table as a whole, each column of the table is also analyzed. Column statistics are visible in the DBA_TAB_COLUMNS view; they include the following:

- The number of distinct values
- The highest and lowest values
- The number of nulls
- The average column length

When a table is analyzed, its indexes are analyzed implicitly. It is also possible to gather index statistics explicitly. The statistics on indexes are shown on the DBA_INDEXES view; they include the following:

- The depth of the index tree
- The number of distinct key values
- The clustering factor—how closely the natural order of the rows follows the order of the keys

These statistics, which are stored within the data dictionary, give the optimizer the information it needs to make vital decisions about how best to execute statements. If statistics are missing or incorrect, performance may degrade dramatically.

Object statistics are often imperfect, first, because they are static—until they are gathered again. This means that they become *stale*, or out of date, as a result of Data Manipulation Language (DML) against the objects. Second, object statistics are often imperfect because, as a general rule, statistics are gathered through a sampling process. If an object is many gigabytes big, a complete analysis will take much time and resources and possibly have an impact on other work. Analyzing a sample of the object will usually give statistics that are representative of the whole at a much lower cost. In many cases, stale or sampled statistics are perfectly adequate. For example, if a table has a billion rows, you may be able to add millions more without disturbing the efficiency of execution plans, provided that the column values in the new rows fit within the frequency distributions already discovered. But in other cases, a relatively small amount of DML may have a significant effect.

 EXAM TIP Object statistics are static. They must be regenerated regularly to pick up changes in the state of the data.

How the Optimizer Uses Statistics

It is common for there to be several ways of running any given statement. Consider this trivial example: There is a table EMP with one row for each employee that includes a column for SAL with the employee's salary, and this column is indexed. A query retrieves the name of every employee whose salary is higher than a certain figure. To run this statement, Oracle could scan the entire table, checking each row against the criterion, or Oracle could search the index to identify those employees who meet the criterion and then use the index to retrieve exactly those employee rows. Consider these queries:

```
select ename from emp where sal > 1000000;
select ename from emp where sal > 0;
```

The first query will (almost certainly) be quicker if executed using the index method. Assuming that there are few employees who meet the criterion, there is no point in reading the entire table to find them. Searching the index to find the relevant employees will be faster. The second query, however, is going to be faster (assuming everyone does have a positive salary) if the entire table is scanned. All employees will be retrieved, so there is no point in using the index.

In making this choice of access method, you are using *object statistics*. Object statistics tell Oracle how many rows are in the table, how many blocks the table segment is occupying, the maximum and minimum values of the columns, the depth of the indexes, and much more. If the object statistics are missing or inaccurate, the optimizer will develop an inappropriate plan. To take this (somewhat contrived) example a step further, consider the situation where the object statistics say that the table is very small—that it contains only one row and occupies only one block. In this case, there is no point in using the index. The entire table can be read by a single block read. Accessing the index would mean at least one read of the index, possibly followed by another read of the table. This could never be faster, so the optimizer would always choose to scan the table no matter what the criterion was. But if the statistics were, in fact, wrong and the table consists of several million rows occupying many megabytes of space, this decision would be disastrous for some criteria. It becomes apparent that statistics should be both present and accurate if the optimizer is to develop efficient execution plans.

The optimizer bases its decisions on *cardinality estimates*. Using the available statistics, it makes guesses about how many rows and blocks will be accessed by various execution methods. The accuracy of these guesses is critical for performance and is generally dependent on the frequency of gathering statistics and the size of the sample. In some cases, these estimates will turn out to be wrong. Why? Typically because the statistics are either stale or based on an inadequate sample. Oracle has two facilities that allow it to correct this: SQL plan directives and adaptive execution plans.

During the execution of a statement, the CBO monitors how many rows are returned at each step and compares this figure for actual cardinality to the estimated cardinality used to derive the execution plan. If the figures deviate sufficiently, the CBO will generate a SQL plan directive for future use. A *directive* is an instruction to the optimizer to gather additional information regarding the objects through a mechanism known as *dynamic sampling*. A simple example would be that used previously: The statistics say that the EMP table has one row, but when querying it the optimizer finds that, in fact, it has millions of rows. In this case, Oracle will generate a directive that, in the future, will instruct the optimizer to check the size of the table when deciding upon an execution plan. A more complex example might be retrieving employees by city, state, and country. Humans know that Munich is the capital of Bavaria and that Bavaria is in Germany. But Oracle does not. This will distort its assumptions about the number of rows returned if a predicate specifies values for all three columns. The directive would instruct the CBO to generate additional statistics regarding the correlation of values between columns. The directives are saved to the AWR in the SYSAUX tablespace and associated with the table to which they refer and will thus be of benefit to any statements that hit the table from then on.

 EXAM TIP SQL plan directives are tied to tables, not to statements. They are persisted in the AWR.

The adaptive execution plan facility affects just one statement at run-time. If a choice has to be made between execution plans that would be more or less efficient depending on the number of rows retrieved, the CBO will determine a crossover point. If there are fewer than X rows, use plan A; if there are more than X rows, use plan B. Oracle will start to run the statement using the plan determined by the object statistics to be optimal, but if this turns out to be incorrect, it will switch to the alternative plan during running. For example, if the crossover point were 100 rows and the cardinality estimate is 1,000, the statement would start with plan B and then switch to plan A if only 50 rows were returned by the first step of the plan. Adaptive execution is possible only if the plans have the same, or similar, initial operations. Data is buffered until the crossover point is (or is not) reached, and then the final choice of plan is made.

 TIP The adaptive execution plan allows switching between the join methods: either nested loop join or hash join. Both of these can start by scanning, and counting, rows from one table. It can also switch the row distribution method for a parallel query.

Gathering Statistics Manually

Object statistics are not real time; they are static, which means that they become out of date as DML operations are applied to the tables. It is therefore necessary to gather statistics regularly to ensure that the optimizer always has access to statistics that reflect reasonably accurately the current state of the database. Statistics can be gathered manually by executing procedures in the DBMS_STATS package, as in Figure 19-2.

In Figure 19-2, first the table REGIONS is analyzed, using the DBMS_STATS package. Setting the argument ESTIMATE_PERCENT to 100 instructs Oracle to analyze the entire table, not just a sample of it. The following query shows that there are four rows in the table. Then a row is inserted, but the statistics haven't been updated, so the number of rows is incorrect until the table is analyzed again—this time with the ESTIMATE_PERCENT set to enable sampling using Oracle's default sample size. Numerous arguments can be supplied to the GATHER_TABLE_STATS procedure to control what it does; this is the simplest form of its use.

Gathering statistics will improve performance, but the actual gathering may impose a strain on the database that will have a noticeable effect on performance while the analysis is in progress. This paradoxical situation raises two questions. First, how frequently should statistics be gathered? The more frequently this is done, the better performance may be; however, if it is done more

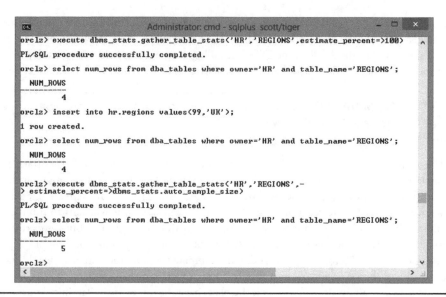

```
Administrator: cmd - sqlplus  scott/tiger

orclz> execute dbms_stats.gather_table_stats('HR','REGIONS',estimate_percent=>100)

PL/SQL procedure successfully completed.

orclz> select num_rows from dba_tables where owner='HR' and table_name='REGIONS';

   NUM_ROWS
----------
          4

orclz> insert into hr.regions values(99,'UK');

1 row created.

orclz> select num_rows from dba_tables where owner='HR' and table_name='REGIONS';

   NUM_ROWS
----------
          4

orclz> execute dbms_stats.gather_table_stats('HR','REGIONS',-
> estimate_percent=>dbms_stats.auto_sample_size)

PL/SQL procedure successfully completed.

orclz> select num_rows from dba_tables where owner='HR' and table_name='REGIONS';

   NUM_ROWS
----------
          5

orclz>
```

Figure 19-2 Gathering statistics from the SQL*Plus prompt

frequently than necessary, performance will suffer needlessly. Second, what proportion of an object needs to be analyzed to gain an accurate picture of it? Analyzing a huge table will be a long and resource-intensive process; it may well be that analyzing a representative sample of the object would be enough for the optimizer and would not impose such a strain on the database.

EXAM TIP Object statistics are not real time; they are static until refreshed by a new analysis. If this is not done with sufficient frequency, they will be seriously out of date, and the optimizer may consequently develop inappropriate execution plans.

Object statistics can be gathered at various levels. These are the relevant procedures in the DBMS_STATS package:

- **gather_database_stats** Analyzes the entire database
- **gather_schema_stats** Analyzes all objects in one schema
- **gather_table_stats** Analyzes one table
- **gather_index_stats** Analyzes one index

When statistics are gathered at any level, a number of arguments can be passed. These can be specified in the procedure call or set as saved preferences at each level. Consider the following procedure call, which specifies the commonly used arguments giving the default value:

```
execute dbms_stats.gather_schema_stats(-
ownname=>'HR',-
cascade=>dbms_stats.auto_cascade,-
```

```
estimate_percent=>dbms_stats.auto_sample_size,-
degree=>dbms_stats.auto_degree,-
no_invalidate=>dbms_stats.auto_invalidate,-
granularity=>'auto',-
method_opt=>'for all columns size auto',-
options=>'gather');
```

Taking these arguments in turn, here is what takes place:

- CASCADE will analyze indexes as well as tables. The setting given lets Oracle decide which indexes (if any) should be analyzed.

- ESTIMATE_PERCENT controls how much of each table to analyze. The setting given instructs Oracle to make an intelligent guess at the amount needed for a meaningful sample.

- DEGREE specifies whether to perform the analysis with parallel processing. The setting given lets Oracle decide the number of parallel processes according to the environment and the size of each table.

- NO_INVALIDATE controls whether to reparse any SQL with dependencies on the objects analyzed immediately. The setting given lets Oracle decide.

- GRANULARITY refers to how best to analyze objects consisting of a number of subobjects, such as a table that is divided into partitions. The setting given lets Oracle decide.

- METHOD_OPT controls for which columns to build up histograms and how many buckets they should have. The setting given lets Oracle decide, according to the nature of the SQL being executed and the distribution of values in the data.

- OPTIONS determines which objects to analyze. The setting given instructs Oracle to analyze all objects.

The remaining point to consider is how frequently to run the command. An automatic statistics-gathering task will do this every day during the maintenance window. The maintenance window runs for four hours every weekday night (starting at 2200) and for 20 hours on Saturday and Sunday (starting at 0600), though usually only a small proportion of this time will be needed. Many databases will run well with statistics gathered by the automatic task, obviating any need to gather statistics manually.

Use the SQL Tuning Advisor

The SQL Tuning Advisor analyzes one or more SQL statements and potentially recommends gathering fresh object statistics, creating a SQL profile, creating additional indexes, or creating a revised SQL statement. You can run the SQL Tuning Advisor manually; however, it is run automatically during every maintenance window on the most resource-intensive SQL statements identified within the production workload. Optionally, you can specify that the analysis performed during the maintenance window automatically implements recommended SQL profiles.

The Capabilities of the SQL Tuning Advisor

Whether the SQL Tuning Advisor runs automatically or you run it on one or more SQL statements, it performs the same types of analyses:

- **Statistics analysis**   Checks for stale or missing statistics and recommends refreshing or creating them
- **SQL profiling**   Collects auxiliary statistics on a SQL statement along with partial execution statistics and stores them in a SQL profile
- **Access paths**   Analyzes the impact of creating new indexes
- **Structure analysis**   Restructures the SQL statements to see whether better execution plans are generated

When profiling a SQL statement, the optimizer partially runs the statement, experimenting with various execution plans. The execution statistics generated during this process update the profile. Information on how the statement actually ran can be used by the optimizer subsequently when the statement is encountered during normal database operation. Note that the SQL Tuning Advisor considers each SQL statement individually. If it recommends an index for a SELECT statement, it may help the performance of the query but may reduce the performance of DML activity against the table in a heavy online transaction processing (OLTP) environment. Thus, the SQL Access Advisor, discussed later in this chapter, may be a better tool to analyze all operations against one or more tables in a workload.

The SQL Tuning Advisor can use a number of sources for its analysis:

- The SQL statements currently cached in the library cache of the shared pool
- A precreated set of statements
- Statements retrieved from the AWR
- An individual ad hoc statement

There is a graphical interface to the SQL Tuning Advisor and also a set of PL/SQL APIs.

 EXAM TIP   The Tuning Advisor's segment advice is limited to index creation.

The SQL Tuning Advisor API: The DBMS_SQLTUNE Package

Database Express has an interface to the results of the SQL Tuning Advisor. Navigate to the SQL Tuning Advisor link on the Performance tab to reach this.

If you need to have more control over your tuning tasks or want to run a specific set of tuning tasks repeatedly, you can use the DBMS_SQLTUNE PL/SQL package to create, run, and monitor a SQL Tuning Advisor job.

For a basic analysis of a SQL statement, you will use the following procedures within DBMS_SQLTUNE:

- **CREATE_TUNING_TASK**   Creates a tuning task for a SQL statement or a SQL Tuning Set

- **EXECUTE_TUNING_TASK**   Executes a tuning task created with CREATE_TUNING_TASK

- **REPORT_TUNING_TASK**   Shows the results and recommendations from the SQL Tuning Advisor

In addition, you can use the following data dictionary views to query the name and status of tuning jobs:

- **DBA_ADVISOR_LOG**   Task names, status, and execution statistics for all tasks

- **DBA_ADVISOR_TASKS**   More detailed information about advisor tasks, such as advisor name, user-specified description, and execution type for the current user

- **V$ADVISOR_PROGRESS**   More detailed information about the completion status and time remaining for an advisor task

Exercise 19-4: Run the SQL Tuning Advisor for a SQL Statement   In this exercise, you will use DBMS_SQLTUNE to generate recommendations for a SQL statement.

1. Connect to the database with SQL*Plus as user SYSTEM.

2. Create the schema and table to be used in this exercise.

```
create user user13 identified by user13;
grant dba to user13;
connect user13/user13
create table object_analysis as select * from all_objects;
```

3. These commands, executed at the SQL prompt, will create a variable to store the name of the task, create a task to tune one statement, and then run the task.

```
variable vtask varchar2(100);
execute :vtask := dbms_sqltune.create_tuning_task(-
sql_text=>'select max(object_id) from object_analysis');
execute dbms_sqltune.execute_tuning_task(:vtask);
```

The illustration shows steps 2 and 3.

4. Retrieve the recommendations from the tuning task, first setting up SQL*Plus to display them.

```
set long 10000
set longchunksize 10000
select dbms_sqltune.report_tuning_task(:vtask) from dual;
```

5. Study the output of the tuning task, as retrieved in step 4. Following the detail of the task, there will be a recommendation to create an index and an example of a suitable index-creation statement. Note that the rationale for the index creation will include this phrase (which, in the current release, includes a minor typing error):

```
Creating the recommended indices significantly improves
the execution plan of this statement. However, it might
be preferable to run "Access Advisor" using a representative
SQL workload as opposed to a single statement. This will
allow to get comprehensive index recommendations which takes
into account index maintenance overhead and additional space
consumption.
```

6. Tidy up as follows:

```
connect system/oracle

drop user user13 cascade;
```

Use the SQL Access Advisor to Tune Workload

The SQL Access Advisor performs an analysis of overall SQL performance using a workload specification, concentrating on the segment structures. The Tuning Advisor may give basic advice on indexes, but the Access Advisor advice is much more comprehensive.

The Capabilities of the SQL Access Advisor

The workload specification can be one of the following:

- A single SQL statement
- A SQL statement tuning set
- Current SQL cache contents
- A hypothetical workload imputed from the Data Definition Language (DDL) of a set of objects

A SQL statement tuning set is a stored set of statements. This set can be populated from a variety of sources, such as statements captured by an AWR snapshot or the recently executed code currently in the library cache of the shared pool. Statements are looked at individually, but reports will cover the entire set. Recommendations from the SQL Access Advisor include the following:

- Indexes (B*Tree, bitmap, and function based)
- Materialized views and materialized view logs
- Partitioning strategies

It is always possible that recommendations that improve some aspect of the workload may have an adverse impact on another. This should be highlighted in the reports.

TIP An advisor will never give advice that is definitively wrong, but often you can do better. Run the advisors, and when looking at the reports, always consider whether the recommendations could be further improved.

The Tuning Advisor has its own API: DBMS_SQLTUNE. The Access Advisor does not. To invoke the Access Advisor, use either the Enterprise Manager interface or the DBMS_ADVISOR API. The DBMS_ADVISOR package is a generic API for running any of the advisors.

Using the SQL Access Advisor with DBMS_ADVISOR

Using the SQL Access Advisor via the DBMS_ADVISOR package can get quite complex. There is, however, one procedure designed to make the job easy.

DBMS_ADVISOR.QUICK_TUNE is straightforward and takes as input a single SQL statement to tune. As a result, it performs much like the SQL Tuning Advisor but can perform a much more in-depth analysis, producing more recommendations than the SQL Tuning Advisor, such as materialized view recommendations. The procedure requires (at a minimum) three arguments: the name of the advisor, the name of the task to be run, and the statement. Here's an example:

```
SQL> execute dbms_advisor.quick_tune(-
  3      dbms_advisor.sqlaccess_advisor,-
  4      'task1',-
  5      'select distinct object_id from object_analysis'-
  6      )
PL/SQL procedure successfully completed.

SQL>
```

The results of the tuning effort reside in the data dictionary view USER_ADVISOR_ACTIONS, but the output is not very readable. Therefore, you can use the procedure CREATE_FILE to create the script you use to implement the recommendations generated by the QUICK_TUNE procedure. First, create a directory object to point to a file system directory to hold the script.

```
SQL> create directory tune_scripts as '/u06/tune_scripts';

Directory created.

SQL>
```

Next, use CREATE_FILE to create the script containing the implementation recommendations.

```
SQL> begin
  2      dbms_advisor.create_file
  3          (dbms_advisor.get_task_script('task1'),
  4          'TUNE_SCRIPTS',
```

```
5           'tune_fts.sql'
6          );
7  end;
8  /

PL/SQL procedure successfully completed.

SQL>
```

In this example, the file tune_fts.sql looks like this:

```
Rem  SQL Access Advisor: Version 12.1.0.1.0 - Production
Rem
Rem  Username:        SCOTT
Rem  Task:            task4
Rem  Execution date:
Rem

CREATE MATERIALIZED VIEW LOG ON
    "SCOTT"."OBJECT_ANALYSIS"
    WITH ROWID, SEQUENCE("OBJECT_ID")
    INCLUDING NEW VALUES;

CREATE MATERIALIZED VIEW "SCOTT"."MV$$_03B80000"
    REFRESH FAST WITH ROWID
    ENABLE QUERY REWRITE
    AS SELECT MAX("SCOTT"."OBJECT_ANALYSIS"."OBJECT_ID") M1,
COUNT(*) M2 FROM SCOTT.OBJECT_ANALYSIS;

begin
  dbms_stats.gather_table_stats('"SCOTT"','"MV$$_03B80000"',
NULL,dbms_stats.auto_sample_size);
end;
/
```

The recommendations include creating a materialized view log, creating a materialized view that can be used for query rewrite, and collecting statistics on the materialized view. This advice is very different from that generated by the SQL Tuning Advisor for the same statement. Both advice sets would need to be tested to determine which is optimal.

CAUTION   You cannot run the Access Advisor against objects owned by internal users, such as SYSTEM. If you try to do this, you will receive the error "QSM-00794: the statement cannot be stored due to a violation of the invalid table reference filter."

Two-Minute Drill

Use Enterprise Manager to Monitor Performance

- Statistics are accumulated in memory, and metrics are calculated from these.
- Database Express exposes certain key statistics and metrics, represented graphically.

Use Automatic Memory Management

- All SGA structures except the log buffer can be dynamically resized.
- PGA is passed out, on demand, to sessions.
- AMM can transfer memory between SGA and PGA, within an overall target.
- Individual structures can be given minimum sizes with their own parameters.

Use the Memory Advisor to Size Memory Buffers

- There are seven memory advisors.
- The advisors are enabled if STATISTICS_LEVEL is set to TYPICAL or ALL.
- The memory broker uses the advisors to tune memory allocations.

Manage Optimizer Statistics

- Object statistics are static until gathered again.
- An autotask gathers needed statistics every night.
- Statistics can be gathered manually for the database, a schema, a table, or an index.

Use the SQL Tuning Advisor

- The Tuning Advisor recommends the restructuring of SQL, gathering statistics, or B*Tree index creation.
- The Tuning Advisor is run every night by an autotask against detected high-load SQL.
- Invoke the Tuning Advisor with Enterprise Manager or the DBMS_SQLTUNE package.
- The Tuning Advisor considers statements individually, not as a set.

Use the SQL Access Advisor to Tune Workload

- The Access Advisor can recommend all types of indexes, materialized views, and partitioning.
- Invoke the Access Advisor with Enterprise Manager or the DBMS_ADVISOR package.
- The Access Advisor can consider a set of SQL statements together.

Self Test

1. Which advisors can be invoked through Database Express? (Choose two answers.)
   A. The SQL Access Advisor
   B. The SQL Tuning Advisor
   C. The Undo Advisor
   D. The memory advisors

2. Where are private SQL areas stored? (Choose the best answer.)

   A. In each session's PGA, always

   B. In each session's PGA, unless a PGA Aggregate Target value has been set

   C. In the PGA, unless Automatic Memory Management has been enabled

   D. In the shared pool of the SGA, always

3. Which memory structure is fixed in size at instance startup? (Choose the best answer.)

   A. The shared pool.

   B. The large pool.

   C. The Java pool.

   D. The log buffer.

   E. None are fixed if Automatic Memory Management has been enabled.

4. When Automatic Memory Management is enabled, what is not possible? (Choose the best answer.)

   A. Transfer of memory between sessions' PGAs.

   B. Transfer of memory between structures within the SGA.

   C. Transfer of memory from SGA to PGA, and vice versa.

   D. Increasing the total memory usage after instance startup.

   E. All of the above are possible.

5. Storage of what structures can exist in the PGA? (Choose all correct answers.)

   A. Shared SQL areas

   B. Private SQL areas

   C. Global temporary tables

   D. Sort areas

   E. Bitmap merge areas

   F. Cached object definitions

6. Which instance parameter can disable the memory advisors? (Choose the best answer.)

   A. DB_CACHE_ADVICE

   B. MEMORY_TARGET

   C. STATISTICS_LEVEL

   D. TIMED_STATISTICS

7. Identify the true statement about Automatic Memory Management. (Choose the best answer.)

    A. MEMORY_TARGET and MEMORY_MAX_TARGET must both be set to enable AMM.

    B. MEMORY_TARGET enables AMM, and it is a static parameter.

    C. MEMORY_MAX_TARGET enables AMM, and it is a static parameter.

    D. MEMORY_TARGET enables AMM, and it is a dynamic parameter.

8. How can you best automate the collection of optimizer statistics? (Choose the best answer.)

    A. The MMON process will collect them if STATISTICS_LEVEL is set to TYPICAL or ALL.

    B. An automatic maintenance job will collect them if STATISTICS_LEVEL is set to TYPICAL or ALL.

    C. Enterprise Manager (Database Express or Cloud Control) will collect them if STATISTICS_LEVEL is set to TYPICAL or ALL.

    D. Execute the DBMS_STATS.GATHER_DATABASE_STATISTICS procedure with OPTIONS=>'GATHER AUTO'.

9. You notice that the statistics on a table are not correct. The NUM_ROWS figure does not include any rows inserted in the day so far. Why might this be? (Choose the best answer.)

    A. The STATISTICS_LEVEL parameter is not set to TYPICAL or ALL.

    B. The statistics have been locked by the DBMS_STATS.LOCK_TABLE_STATS procedure.

    C. The statistics will not change until the table is next analyzed.

    D. The automatic maintenance tasks are not running.

10. Where are the object statistics used by the query optimizer stored? (Choose the best answer.)

    A. With the objects themselves.

    B. In the data dictionary.

    C. In the AWR.

    D. They are accumulated in the shared pool of the SGA.

11. The SQL Tuning Advisor performs all but which of the following analyses? (Choose the best answer.)

    A. Structure analysis

    B. SQL Profile analysis

    C. Access paths

    D. Changes to materialized views

    E. Statistics analysis

12. Which of the following can you use as input for the SQL Tuning Advisor? (Choose all that apply.)

   A. A single SQL statement provided by a user

   B. An existing SQL Tuning Set (STS)

   C. A preprocessed Database Replay workload

   D. A schema name

   E. A SQL statement identified in EM as using excessive resources

13. Which of the following can you use as input for the SQL Access Advisor? (Choose all that apply.)

   A. A single SQL statement provided by a user

   B. An existing SQL Tuning Set (STS)

   C. A preprocessed Database Replay workload

   D. A schema name

   E. Current SQL cache contents

14. Which of the following changes can the SQL Access Advisor recommend? (Choose two answers.)

   A. Restructuring one or more SQL statements

   B. Gathering statistics for selected SQL statements

   C. Adding a materialized view log

   D. Enabling query rewrite

Self Test Answers

1. ☑   **B** and **C**. The Tuning Advisor is available on the Performance tab, and the Undo Advisor is available on the Storage tab.
    ☒   **A** and **D** are incorrect. The Access Advisor and the various memory advisors can be reached through Cloud Control but not through Database Express.

2. ☑   **A**. Private SQL areas are private to each session in the session's PGA.
    ☒   **B**, **C**, and **D** are incorrect. **B** is incorrect because automatic PGA management is not relevant to where the private SQL area is stored, only to how it is managed. **C** and **D** are incorrect because private SQL areas are always in the PGA.

3. ☑   **D**. The log buffer cannot be changed after startup.
    ☒   **A**, **B**, **C**, and **E** are incorrect. **A**, **B**, and **C** are incorrect because all these structures can be resized. **E** is incorrect because not even Automatic Memory Management makes the log buffer resizable.

4. ☑ **E.** Memory can be transferred between all structures (except the log buffer), and the total can be increased.

☒ **A**, **B**, **C**, and **D** are incorrect. These are incorrect because all are possible—although **D** (the increase of total memory usage) is possible only up to the value specified by the MEMORY_MAX_TARGET parameter.

5. ☑ **B**, **C**, **D**, and **E.** These are all PGA memory structures, although they may spill to a temporary segment in the users' temporary tablespace.

☒ **A** and **F** are incorrect. These structures both exist in the shared pool of the SGA.

6. ☑ **C.** STATISTICS_LEVEL must be on TYPICAL or FULL; otherwise, the advisors will not run.

☒ **A**, **B**, and **D** are incorrect. **A** and **D** are incorrect because these parameters (which still exist only for backward compatibility) are controlled by STATISTICS_LEVEL. **B** is incorrect because MEMORY_TARGET determines whether implementing the advice is automatic or manual.

7. ☑ **D.** MEMORY_TARGET enables AMM; it is a dynamic parameter and cannot be more than MEMORY_MAX_TARGET.

☒ **A**, **B**, and **C** are incorrect. **A** is incorrect because the MEMORY_MAX_TARGET can be left on default. **B** is incorrect because MEMORY_TARGET is dynamic. **C** is incorrect because although MEMORY_MAX_TARGET provides a limit for AMM, it does not enable it.

8. ☑ **B.** A job will run in the maintenance windows unless STATISICS_LEVEL is set to BASIC.

☒ **A** and **C** are incorrect because they specify the incorrect component to carry out the task. **D** is incorrect because the 'GATHER AUTO' option controls what objects to analyze, not whether to analyze at all.

9. ☑ **C.** Optimizer statistics are not maintained in real time, only refreshed when the object is analyzed.

☒ **A**, **B**, and **D** are incorrect. **A** and **D** are incorrect because they would affect the nightly refresh of the statistics, not a refresh during the day. **B** is incorrect because it would freeze the statistics permanently, not just for the day.

10. ☑ **B.** The optimizer uses the latest statistics, which are stored in the data dictionary.

☒ **A**, **C**, and **D** are incorrect. **A** is incorrect because the statistics are stored independently of the actual segments. **C** is incorrect because the AWR stores historical values, which are not used for real-time parsing. **D** is incorrect because the SGA stores the execution plan itself, not the information used to generate it.

11. ☑ **D.** Only the SQL Access Advisor recommends changes to materialized views, including creating materialized view logs.

☒ **A**, **B**, **C**, and **E** are incorrect. The SQL Tuning Advisor performs statistics analysis, SQL profiling, access paths, and structure analysis.

PART III

12. ☑ **A**, **B**, and **E**. The SQL Tuning Advisor can use currently running SQL statements, a single statement provided by any user, an existing SQL Tuning Set, or historical SQL statements from AWR snapshots.

☒ **C** and **D** are incorrect. **C** is incorrect because you cannot use Database Replay workloads to specify SQL for SQL Tuning Advisor. **D** is incorrect because you cannot specify a schema or table names; you can specify only SQL statements.

13. ☑ **A**, **B**, **D**, and **E**. In addition to a single SQL statement (using QUICK_TUNE), an existing STS, a schema name, and the current SQL cache contents, the SQL Access Advisor uses statistics to analyze overall SQL performance.

☒ **C** is incorrect. You cannot use the captured Database Replay information as a source for the SQL Access Advisor.

14. ☑ **C** and **D**. The SQL Access Advisor recommends materialized views, materialized view logs, and enabling query rewrite. In addition, the SQL Access Advisor will recommend new indexes or partitions.

☒ **A** and **B** are incorrect. The SQL Tuning Advisor recommends SQL statement restructuring and statistics gathering, not the SQL Access Advisor.

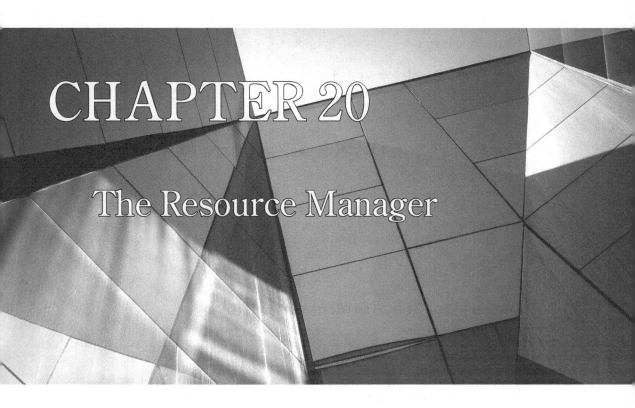

CHAPTER 20

The Resource Manager

Exam Objectives

- 062.13.1 Configure the Database Resource Manager
- 062.13.2 Access and Create Resource Plans
- 062.13.3 Monitor the Resource Manager

Many computer systems will have several groups of users, each with different standards for the level of service it requires. If the system as a whole is highly stressed, it may be impossible to deliver the desired level of service to all groups. But if a priority structure can be negotiated, it should be possible to guarantee a certain level of service to certain groups—perhaps at the expense of other groups.

Configure the Database Resource Manager

In a mainframe environment, the operating system handles allocating resources to tasks. But simpler operating systems such as Unix and Windows may not have proper resource-scheduling capabilities. Oracle's Resource Manager brings mainframe-style resource management capabilities to all supported Oracle platforms, meaning that you as database administrator (DBA) can guarantee that certain groups of database users will always receive a certain level of service, no matter what the overall workload on the database may be. Configuring the Resource Manager is often easy, but testing its effect and monitoring what it is doing may be difficult.

The Need for Resource Management

Operating systems such as Linux and Windows use a simple algorithm to assign resources to different processes: round-robin time slicing. To the operating system, there is really no difference between any of the background processes that make up the Oracle instance and any of the many server processes that support user sessions. As far as the operating system is concerned, a process is a process; it will be brought onto the central processing unit (CPU), given a few cycles of CPU time, and then switched off the CPU so that the next process can be brought on. The operating system has no way of knowing that one server process is supporting a session doing completely trivial work while another server process is supporting a session doing work critical to the survival of the organization. The Resource Manager provides a mechanism whereby the operating system's time-slicing algorithm can be adjusted to ensure that some users receive more processing capacity than others—and to ensure that any single query does not destroy performance for everyone else. The underlying mechanism is to place a cooperative multitasking layer controlled by Oracle on top of the operating system's preemptive multitasking system.

Throughout this chapter, the environment is assumed to be that of a telesales organization. There are several groups of users, and of particular interest are the data-entry clerks and the management accountants. There may be 200 data-entry clerks in the call center taking orders over the telephone. If their database sessions are running slowly, this is disastrous for the company. Customers will dial in only to be told, "You are number 964 in the queue. Your call is important to us. Please do not hang up." This is happening because the data-entry clerks cannot process calls fast enough. They take an order, they click the Submit button, and then they wait…and wait… and wait…for the system to respond. This is costing money.

On the other hand, the management accountants' work is not so urgent. Perhaps an advertisement has been run on one local radio station, and the response in terms of sales inquiries needs to be evaluated before running the advertisement nationwide. This is important work, but it doesn't have to be real time. If the reports take 10 minutes to run instead of 5, does it really matter?

CAUTION Do not adjust the priorities of Oracle processes by using the Unix renice command or the Windows equivalent. Oracle assumes that the operating system is treating all processes equally, and if you interfere with this, there may be unexpected (and disastrous) side effects.

What is needed is a technique for ensuring that if the database sessions supporting the data-entry clerks need computing resources, they get them—no matter what. This could mean that at certain times of day when the call center is really busy, the clerks need 100 percent of computing resources. Resource Manager can handle this, and during that time of peak usage the sessions supporting the management accountants may hang completely. But during other times of day, when the call center is not busy, plenty of resources will be available to be directed to the management accountants' work. At month end, another task will become top priority, specifically, the end-of-month billing runs and the rollover of the ledgers into the next accounting period. Resource Manager needs to be versatile enough to manage this too.

Clearly, Resource Manager is necessary only in highly stressed systems, but when you need it, there is no alternative. In fact, you are using Resource Manager whether you know it or not; it is configured by default in all databases to control the resources used by the Autotask system, but the default configuration has a minimal effect on normal work.

The Resource Manager Architecture

Users are placed in Resource Manager consumer groups, and Resource Manager plans, consisting of a set of directives, control the allocation of resources across the groups. Each session is assigned to a group, depending on attributes defined when the session was established and possibly modified subsequently. The underlying architecture places a cooperative multitasking layer on top of the preemptive multitasking provided by the operating system. The server process of a session in a low-priority group will, when brought onto the CPU by a context switch, voluntarily relinquish the CPU earlier than it would have done if relying purely on the operating system's preemptive multitasking algorithm.

Consumer Groups

A Resource Manager consumer group is a set of users with similar resource requirements. One group may contain many users, and one user may be a member of many groups, but at any given moment, each session will have one group as its effective group. When a user first creates a session, his default consumer group membership will be active, but if he is a member of multiple groups, he can switch to another group, activating his membership of that group. The switch can be manual or automatic, depending on a number of factors.

In the telesales example, the 200 data-entry clerks could be in a group called OLTP, and the half-dozen management accountants could be in a group called DSS. Some users could be in both groups; depending on what work they are doing, they will activate the appropriate group membership. Other groups might be BATCH, to be given top priority for month-end processing, and LOW, for people who happen to have accounts on the system but are of no great significance.

PART III

Eighteen groups are created by default when a database is created:

- **SYS_GROUP** This group is intended for the database administrators. By default, only the SYS and SYSTEM users are in this group.

- **DEFAULT_CONSUMER_GROUP** This group is for all users who have not been specifically assigned to any other group. By default, all sessions other than SYS and SYSTEM are in this group, and this membership is active when they first create a session.

- **OTHER_GROUPS** All users are members of this group. It is used as a catchall for any sessions that are in groups not explicitly mentioned in the active Resource Manager plan.

- **Demonstration groups** The following groups are intended for separating different types of work: BATCH_GROUP, DSS_CRITICAL_GROUP, DSS_GROUP, ETL_GROUP, INTERACTIVE_GROUP, and LOW_GROUP.

- **ORA$AUTOTASK** The sessions running the autotasks will run under this group.

- **ORA$APPQOS_0 through ORA$APPQOS_7** These eight groups are used if Quality Of Service has been enabled; this is applicable only to clustered systems.

To view the groups in your database, query the views DBA_RSRC_CONSUMER_GROUPS and DBA_USERS. The latter shows the initial consumer group set for each session at connect time (see Figure 20-1).

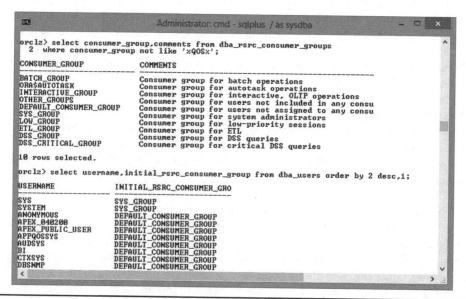

Figure 20-1 Resource Manager consumer groups

Resource Manager Plans

A Resource Manager plan is of a certain type. The most basic (and most commonly used) type of plan is one that allocates CPU resources, but there are other resource allocation methods. Many plans can exist within the database, but only one plan is active at any one time. This plan applies to the whole instance; all sessions are controlled by it.

The following are the resources that can be controlled by a plan:

- Total CPU usage for all sessions in a group
- Degree of parallelism available to each session in a group
- Number of active sessions permitted per group
- Volume of undo space permitted per group
- Time before terminating idle sessions
- Maximum length of execution time for a call in a session, which can also trigger the switch of a session into another group

In the telesales example, there could be three plans based on CPU usage. A daytime plan would give top priority to the OLTP group. At times of peak activity, with the system working to full capacity, it is possible that the sessions of users in other groups would hang. At night, a different plan would be activated that guarantees the DSS jobs will run, though perhaps still not with the priority of the OLTP group. A month-end plan would give 100 percent of resources to the BATCH group, if it requires this.

A plan consists of a number of directives. Each directive assigns resources to a particular group at a particular priority level. Eleven plans are configured at database creation time:

- The INTERNAL_PLAN is not for normal use; it disables the Resource Manager.
- The DEFAULT_PLAN has three directives (see Figure 20-2). The first states that at priority level 1, the highest priority, any sessions connected to the SYS_GROUP consumer group can take 90 percent of CPU resources. OTHER_GROUPS sessions are guaranteed at least 9 percent, and the ORA$AUTOTASK group 1 percent.
- The DEFAULT_MAINTENANCE_PLAN (shown in Figure 20-2) raises the proportion of resources guaranteed to maintenance tasks and other users to 25 percent.
- The INTERNAL_QUIESCE plan has a particular purpose covered later in this chapter; it will freeze all sessions except those of the SYS_GROUP members.
- The MIXED_WORKLOAD_PLAN (also shown in Figure 20-2) gives top priority to the SYS_GROUP, then the INTERACTIVE_GROUP, and then the BATCH_GROUP. Other demonstration plans are DSS_PLAN and ETL_CRITICAL_PLAN.
- The ORA$AUTOTASK_PLAN is used by the Autotask system and cannot be adjusted.
- The ORA$ROOT_PLAN is relevant only to the multitenant container database.
- The ORA$QOS_PLAN is used by the Quality Of Service system.

To enable a plan, set the RESOURCE_MANAGER_PLAN instance parameter. This can be set automatically by the Scheduler (described in Chapter 21), manually with an ALTER SYSTEM

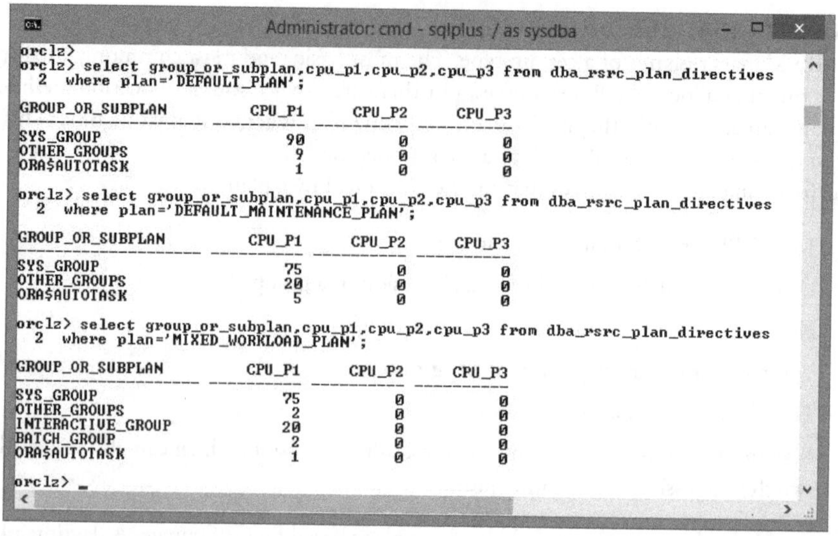

Figure 20-2   The directives of the DEFAULT_PLAN, the DEFAULT_MAINTENANCE_PLAN, and the MIXED_WORKLOAD_PLAN

command, or programmatically with the DBMS_RESOURCE_MANAGER.SWITCH_PLAN procedure. Following creation of a database with the Database Configuration Assistant (DBCA), the Scheduler will be configured to activate the DEFAULT_PLAN during normal working hours and the DEFAULT_MAINTENANCE_PLAN at night and weekends. It is assumed that these plans will be appropriate for most sites. They give the DBA staff top priority, followed by users, and restrict the resources that can be taken by maintenance jobs.

EXAM TIP   The instance parameter RESOURCE_LIMITS has nothing to do with Resource Manager. It pertains to the older method of controlling resources through database profiles.

Resource Manager works on a "trickle-down" model. All resources not utilized at one priority level are available to the level lower down, and within a level any resources not needed by one group are available to the other groups. So, if the DEFAULT_PLAN is enabled and no member of the SYS_GROUP is doing anything, the entire machine is available to the OTHER_GROUPS sessions, except for 1 percent, which may be used by the ORA$AUTOTASK group if it needs it.

Resource Manager Configuration

A PL/SQL API can be used to administer Resource Manager. This application programming interface (API) consists of two packages: DBMS_RESOURCE_MANAGER_PRIVS and DBMS_RESOURCE_MANAGER. DBMS_RESOURCE_MANAGER_PRIVS is used to put users into consumer groups and also to grant the system privilege necessary to administer Resource Manager (see Figure 20-3).

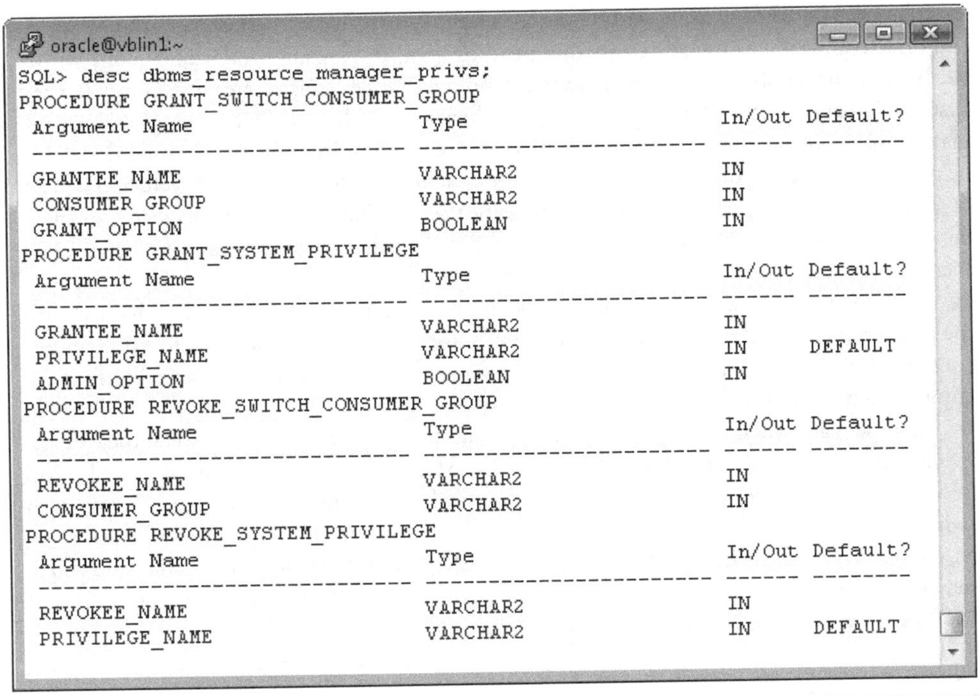

Figure 20-3   The DBMS_RESOURCE_MANAGER_PRIVS package

Here is how to give user JOHN the capability of administering Resource Manager, with the ability to pass on the privilege to other users:

```
SQL> execute dbms_resource_manager_privs.grant_system_privilege(-
grantee_name=>'JOHN',admin_option=>true);
```

This procedure call grants the system privilege ADMINISTER RESOURCE MANAGER. You can see this grant by querying the DBA_SYS_PRIVS view. To add a user to a group, use a call such as this:

```
SQL> exec dbms_resource_manager_privs.grant_switch_consumer_group(-
'ROOPESH','OLTP',false);
```

This call adds ROOPESH to the group OLTP, but without giving him the ability to add other users to the group. If ROOPESH is now a member of several groups, you should nominate one as his default group. This requires a procedure in a different package.

```
exec dbms_resource_manager.set_initial_consumer_group(-
user=>'ROOPESH',consumer_group=>'OLTP');
```

The DBMS_RESOURCE_MANAGER package is used to create consumer groups, plans, and directives. It is also used to create the "pending area." Before any work can be done with Resource Manager objects, you must create a pending area, which is an area of memory in the System Global Area (SGA) used for storing the objects while they are being configured. A plan may consist of many directives, and each directive is created independently; it would therefore be possible to create a totally impossible plan, one that might, for example, allocate 500 percent of CPU. The pending area is provided to prevent this possibility. The plan is created in the pending area, and then when complete, it is validated to check that it does make sense. Only then does the plan get saved to the data dictionary.

At connect time, a session will pick up the initial consumer group assigned to that user. If the user is a member of multiple consumer groups, the session can be switched to a different consumer group later. This can be done either manually or by using more advanced techniques automatically, according to the work that the session is doing.

Any user can switch their active consumer group to any of the groups of which they are a member by using the SWITCH_CURRENT_CONSUMER_GROUP procedure in the DBMS_SESSION package. Alternatively, a user with the privilege to administer Resource Manager can switch another session over by using one of two procedures in the DBMS_RESOURCE_MANAGER package. The SWITCH_CONSUMER_GROUP_FOR_USER procedure will switch all sessions logged on with a particular username, or SWITCH_CONSUMER_GROUP_FOR_SESS will switch one particular session, identified by SID and SERIAL#.

```
SQL> exec dbms_resource_manager.switch_consumer_group_for_sess(-
session_id=>29,session_serial=>123,consumer_group=>'OLTP');
```

Access and Create Resource Plans

A plan consists of a set of directives dividing resources between consumer groups. The following principles can be used to control this:

- CPU method
- Number of active sessions
- Degree of parallelism
- Operation execution time
- Idle time
- Volume of undo data

CPU Method

Continuing the telesales example, the daytime plan would give maximum resources to the OLTP group. All other sessions will hang if the OLTP users really do need the whole machine. The only exception is the SYS_GROUP. You should always give the SYS_GROUP priority over anything else. If you, the DBA, need to do something on the production system (such as rebuilding a broken index or doing a restore and recover), you should be able to do it as fast as possible. The plan could look like this:

Priority Level	Group	CPU %
1	SYS_GROUP	100
2	OLTP	100
3	DSS	50
	BATCH	50
4	OTHER_GROUPS	100

There are eight possible priority levels; this plan uses four of them. All CPU resources not used at one level trickle down to the next level. When this plan is active, the SYS_GROUP at level 1 can, if necessary, take over the whole machine; all other sessions will hang. But this shouldn't happen; in normal running, no CPU cycles will be taken by the SYS_GROUP, so the whole machine will be available at level 2, where the OLTP users can use it all. Any CPU resources they do not need drop down to level 3, where they are divided 50/50 between the DSS and the BATCH sessions. If, after the OLTP, DSS, and BATCH users have taken what they need, some capacity is still left, it will be available to members of other groups. It is possible, at times when the OLTP users are working nonstop and CPU usage has hit 100 percent, that the DSS and BATCH sessions will hang.

EXAM TIP The total CPU allocated at each level cannot exceed 100 percent. If it does, the pending area will fail to validate, and the plan will not be saved to the data dictionary. It is possible to have a plan that allocates less than 100 percent at a level, but there is little purpose in doing this.

The nighttime plan will have different settings.

Priority Level	Group	CPU %
1	SYS_GROUP	100
2	OLTP	50
	DSS	25
	BATCH	25
3	OTHER_GROUPS	100

As with the daytime plan, if the SYS_GROUP needs to do something, it will get top priority. But at level 2, the DSS and BATCH users are guaranteed processing time. They still do not have as high a priority as the OLTP group, but their sessions will not hang. The month-end plan might change this further.

Priority Level	Group	CPU %
1	SYS_GROUP	100
2	BATCH	100
3	DSS	50
	OLTP	50
4	OTHER_GROUPS	100

When this plan is active, the BATCH jobs will take priority over everyone else, taking the whole machine if necessary. This would be advisable if the month-end processing actually means that the system is not usable, so it is vital to get it done as fast as possible.

 TIP   If the CPU is not running at 100 percent usage, these plans will have no effect. They have an impact only if the CPU capacity cannot satisfy the demands on it.

A variation on the CPU method is that the "group" can itself be a plan. It is possible by this method to set up a hierarchy, where a top-level plan allocates resources between subplans. These subplans can then allocate resources between consumer groups. A case where this might be applicable would be an application service provider. Perhaps you have installed an application such as an accounting suite, and you lease time on it to several customers. Each customer will have their own groups of users. Your top-level plan will divide resources between subplans for each customer, perhaps according to the amount they are paying for access to the service. Then, within that division, the customers can each allocate resources between their consumer groups.

 EXAM TIP   Every plan must include a directive for the group OTHER_GROUPS; otherwise, the validation will fail, and you cannot save the plan from the pending area to the data dictionary.

Creating a plan such as the daytime plan just described requires a series of procedure calls through the API. The first step is to create the pending area.

```
SQL> exec dbms_resource_manager.create_pending_area;
```

You then create the plan.

```
SQL> exec dbms_resource_manager.create_plan(-
plan=>'DAY',comment=>'plan for normal working hours');
```

Then you create the directives within it.

```
SQL> exec dbms_resource_manager.create_plan_directive(-
plan=>'DAY',group_or_subplan=>'SYS_GROUP',mgmt_p1=>100,-
comment=>'give sys_group users top priority');
SQL> exec dbms_resource_manager.create_plan_directive(-
plan=>'DAY',group_or_subplan=>'OLTP',mgmt_p2=>100,-
comment=>'give oltp users next priority');
```

```
SQL> exec dbms_resource_manager.create_plan_directive(-
plan=>'DAY',group_or_subplan=>'DSS',mgmt_p3=>50,-
comment=>'dss users have half at level 3');
SQL> exec dbms_resource_manager.create_plan_directive(-
plan=>'DAY',group_or_subplan=>'BATCH',mgmt_p3=>50,-
comment=>'batch users have half at level 3');
SQL> exec dbms_resource_manager.create_plan_directive(-
plan=>'DAY',group_or_subplan=>'OTHER_GROUPS',mgmt_p4=>100,-
comment=>'if there is anything left, others can have it');
```

Finally, validate the pending area and (if the validation returns successfully) save the plan to the data dictionary.

```
SQL> exec dbms_resource_manager.validate_pending_area;
SQL> exec dbms_resource_manager.submit_pending_area;
```

Here is how to activate the plan:

```
SQL> alter system set resource_manager_plan=day;
```

Use of the Ratio CPU Method

There is an alternative technique for allocating CPU resources. Rather than coding CPU usage as a percentage, you can specify ratios—and let Oracle work out the percentages. In the telesales example in the preceding section, the CPU resources at level 2 for the nighttime plan were as follows:

- OLTP 50%
- DSS 25%
- BATCH 25%

If you decide to add a fourth group (call it WEB) and want to make it equal in priority to OLTP and to double DSS and BATCH, you will have to change all the directives to achieve this.

- OLTP 33%
- WEB 33%
- DSS 17%
- BATCH 17%

The ratio method lets you specify proportions. The absolute values have no significance. For example, the original ratios could have been as follows:

- OLTP 20
- DSS 10
- BATCH 10

Now, to add the WEB group with a priority equal to OLTP, you have to add only one new directive—WEB 20—and leave the others unchanged.

The Active Session Pool Method

It may be that investigation has shown that a certain number of jobs can be run concurrently by one group of users with no problems but that if this number is exceeded, other groups will have difficulties. For example, it might be that the telesales company has six management accountants, logging on with Oracle usernames in the DSS group. If one, two, or even three of them generate reports at the same time, everything is fine, but if four or more attempt to run reports concurrently, the OLTP users begin to suffer.

The active session pool method of Resource Manager lets the DBA limit the number of statements that will run concurrently for one group, without restricting the actual number of logins. To continue the example, all six accountants can be connected, and if three of them submit reports, they will all run, but if a fourth submits a job, it will be queued until one of the other three finishes. The nighttime plan would remove all restrictions of this nature.

An *active session* is defined as a session that is running a query or as a session that is in an uncommitted transaction. If parallel processing has been enabled, the individual parallel processors do not count against the session pool; rather, the entire parallel operation counts as one active session. By default, a session will be queued indefinitely, but if you want, you can set a time limit. If a session from the pool does not become available within this limit, the statement is aborted, and an error is returned to the session that issued it. This call will adjust the DAY plan to limit the DSS group to three active sessions, queuing requests for one minute before returning an error.

```
execute dbms_resource_manager.update_plan_directive(-
plan=>'DAY',-
group_or_subplan=>'DSS',-
new_active_sess_pool_p1=>3,-
new_queueing_p1=>60);
```

 EXAM TIP A session that is not actually doing anything will still count against the active session pool for the group if it has made a change and not committed it.

To monitor the effect of the active session pool, the column CURRENT_QUEUE_ DURATION in V$SESSION will show for every queued session the number of seconds it has been waiting. The view V$RSRC_CONSUMER_GROUP gives a global picture, showing how many sessions for each group are queued at any given moment.

What if the active session pool were set to zero for all groups? The result would be that all sessions would hang. This is, in fact, a useful capability, and it is used by the command ALTER SYSTEM QUIESCE RESTRICTED. This command activates the Resource Manager plan INTERNAL_QUIESCE, which sets the active session pool for all groups other than the SYS_ GROUP to zero. The effect is that statements in progress will continue until they finish but that no one (other than members of the SYS_GROUP) can issue any more statements. If they do, the session will hang. In effect, the database is frozen for all but the administrators. This can be invaluable to get a stable system for a moment of maintenance work.

To cancel the quiesce, issue ALTER SYSTEM UNQUIESCE.

TIP   Quiesce is invaluable for DDL operations that require a short exclusive object lock, such as an online index rebuild: quiesce the database, launch the operation, and then unquiesce. The rebuild operation will continue, and users may not have noticed that they were ever blocked.

Limiting the Degree of Parallelism

Parallel processing, both for SELECT statements and for DML, can greatly enhance the performance of individual statements, but the price you pay may be an impact on other users. It may be that your management accountants have discovered that if they run a query with the degree of parallelism set to 50 (and you cannot control this—it is done by hints in the code they write), the report generates faster. But do you really want one session to take 50 parallel execution servers from the pool? That may not leave enough for other work. Furthermore, the query may now run faster but cripple the performance of the rest of the database. Resource Manager can control this by setting a hard limit on the number of parallel processes that each session of any one group is allowed to use. In the daytime plan, for instance, you might limit the DSS and BATCH groups to no more than 4 per session, even if they ask for 50, and not permit OTHER_GROUPS sessions to use parallel processing at all. The nighttime plan could remove these restrictions. Here is an example:

```
execute dbms_resource_manager.update_plan_directive(-
plan=>'DAY',-
group_or_subplan=>'DSS',-
new_parallel_degree_limit_p1=>4,-
new_queueing_p1=>60);
```

Controlling Jobs by Execution Time

The problem of one large job killing performance for everyone else is well known in the database world. Resource Manager solves this by providing a mechanism whereby large jobs can be completely eliminated from the system at certain times. Alternatively, a session can be allowed to launch the job, but if it exceeds (or is likely to exceed) a time threshold, the session can be switched to a lower-priority group. This will allow the statement to run but with reduced impact on other users. The following are the relevant arguments to the DBMS_RESOURCE_MANAGER.CREATE_PLAN DIRECTIVE procedure:

- SWITCH_GROUP
- SWITCH_TIME (measured as CPU time)
- SWITCH_ELAPSED_TIME (measured as wall-clock execution time)
- SWITCH_ESTIMATE
- MAX_EST_EXEC_TIME

The SWITCH_GROUP nominates a consumer group, probably one with lower priority in the plan, to which a session will be switched if a call takes longer than the number of seconds specified by the SWITCH_TIME or SWITCH_ELAPSED_TIME to complete. If SWITCH_

ESTIMATE is TRUE, the session will be switched before the statement starts running if the optimizer thinks it might take more than that number of seconds. The MAX_EST_EXEC_ TIME argument will block all statements that the optimizer believes would take longer than that number of seconds.

Terminating Sessions by Idle Time

Sessions that are not doing anything waste machine resources. Every session consists, on the server side, of a server process and a Program Global Area (PGA). Even if the session is not executing a statement, the operating system must still bring it onto the CPU according to its round-robin time-slicing algorithm. This is known as a *context switch*. Every context switch forces the computer to do a lot of work as registers are loaded from main memory, the state of the session is checked, and then the registers are cleared again. If the PGA has been paged to disk, that, too, must be reloaded into main memory. The shared server mechanism, detailed in Chapter 14, will help to reduce idle processes, but it can't do anything about the number of sessions. The User Global Areas (UGAs)—in the SGA, remember—will still be taking up memory, and Oracle still has to check the state of the session on a regular basis.

Resource Manager can disconnect sessions that are not working, according to two criteria. The first is simply based on idle time: How long has it been since the session executed a statement? The second is more sophisticated: It checks not only how long since a session executed a statement but also whether the session is holding any row or table locks that are blocking other sessions, which is a much more serious problem. Remember from Chapter 6 that a row lock enqueue held by one session will cause another session that needs to lock the same row to hang indefinitely; this can cause the whole database to stop working if the problem escalates from session to session. It is possible for the DBA to detect this problem, identify the session that is holding the lock, and kill it, but this is a tricky procedure. By using Resource Manager, you can configure automatic killing of any sessions that block other sessions for more than a certain length of time.

An important point is that "idle time" is time that the server process has been idle, not time that the user process has been idle. For example, your management accountant might be using a spreadsheet as his user process. He will have downloaded some information to it to work on locally before saving it back to the database. While this is going on, the server process is indeed idle, but the user could be working flat out in the spreadsheet. He will not be pleased if, when he tries to pass the information back, he finds that you have disconnected him and perhaps lost all his work in progress.

The following are the arguments to the DBMS_RESOURCE_MANAGER.CREATE_ PLAN DIRECTIVE procedure that will enable idle session termination:

- MAX_IDLE_TIME
- MAX_IDLE_BLOCKER_TIME

TIP It is also possible to disconnect sessions by using profiles assigned to named users, which you must enable with the instance parameter RESOURCE_LIMITS. However, Resource Manager is a better tool for this.

Restricting Generation of Undo Data

Management of undo data was covered in Chapter 6. All Data Manipulation Language (DML) statements must generate undo data, and this data must be stored until the transaction has been committed or rolled back. Oracle has no choice about this; it is according to the rules of a relational database. If you have configured the UNDO_RETENTION instance parameter and set the RETENTION GUARANTEE attribute for your undo tablespace, the undo data may well be kept for some considerable time after the transaction has committed.

All your undo data will be written to a single undo tablespace. A potential problem is that one badly designed transaction could fill this storage area, the undo tablespace. Programmers should not design large, long-running transactions. In business terms, though, huge transactions may be necessary to preserve the integrity of the system. For example, an accounting suite's nominal ledger cannot be partly in one accounting period and partly in the next, which is an impossibility in accountancy. So, the rollover from one period to the next could mean updating millions of rows in thousands of tables over many hours and then committing. This will require an undo tablespace the size of Jupiter and will also cause record-locking problems as the big transaction blocks other work. The answer is to break up the one business transaction into many small database transactions programmatically. If this is a problem, go back to the developers; there is nothing you as DBA can do to fix it.

As DBA, however, you can prevent large transactions by one group of users from filling up the undo tablespace. If your batch routines do not commit regularly, they will write a lot of undo data that cannot be overwritten. If too many of these batch jobs are run concurrently, the undo tablespace can fill up with active undo. This will cause all transactions to cease, and no more transactions can start until one of them commits. Resource Manager provides a mechanism whereby the undo tablespace can in effect be partitioned into areas reserved for different consumer groups.

Your calculations on undo generated per second and your desired undo retention (as derived from the V$UNDOSTAT view and your requirements for long-running queries and the flashback query capability) might show that the undo tablespace should be, for example, 8GB. To be safe, you size it at 12GB. But to ensure that the small OLTP transactions will always have room for their undo data, you can limit the space used by the BATCH group to, say, 6GB during normal working hours by assigning an undo pool in a Resource Manager plan. To calculate the undo space necessary for individual transactions, you can query the view V$TRANSACTION while the transaction is in progress. The column USED_UBLK shows how much undo is being used by each active transaction.

 EXAM TIP   The undo pool per group has nothing to do with tablespace quotas, which are assigned per user. You cannot even grant quotas on undo tablespaces.

When the amount of active undo data generated by all sessions of a certain consumer group hits its pool limit, it will no longer be possible for members of that group to add more undo to current transactions or to start new transactions. They will hang until one transaction commits, thus freeing up space within the pool. Meanwhile, other groups can continue working in the remainder of the undo tablespace. This restricts the effect of generating too much undo to one group, rather than having it impact all users. The argument to the DBMS_RESOURCE_MANAGER.CREATE_PLAN DIRECTIVE procedure that will define an undo pool is UNDO_POOL.

Exercise 20-1: Create and Implement a Resource Manager Plan   There is a shortcut to creating a Resource Manager plan: a single procedure call, CREATE_SIMPLE_PLAN. Use this to enable resource management in your database.

1. Connect to the database as user SYSTEM.

2. Create some users and grant them the CONNECT role.

   ```
   grant connect to clerk identified by clerk;
   grant connect to acct identified by acct;
   grant connect to batch identified by batch;
   grant connect to mgr identified by mgr;
   ```

3. Create two consumer groups. It is necessary to create a pending area first.

   ```
   execute dbms_resource_manager.create_pending_area;
   execute dbms_resource_manager.create_consumer_group('OLTP');
   execute dbms_resource_manager.create_consumer_group('DSS');
   execute dbms_resource_manager.submit_pending_area;
   ```

4. Assign the users to groups and set their initial consumer group.

   ```
   execute
   dbms_resource_manager_privs.grant_switch_consumer_group-
   ('CLERK','OLTP',false);
   execute
   dbms_resource_manager_privs.grant_switch_consumer_group-
   ('MGR','OLTP',false);
   execute
   dbms_resource_manager_privs.grant_switch_consumer_group-
   ('ACCT','DSS',false);
   execute
   dbms_resource_manager_privs.grant_switch_consumer_group-
   ('BATCH','DSS',false);
   execute dbms_resource_manager.set_initial_consumer_group-
   ('CLERK','OLTP');
   execute dbms_resource_manager.set_initial_consumer_group-
   ('ACCT','DSS');
   execute dbms_resource_manager.set_initial_consumer_group-
   ('BATCH','DSS');
   execute dbms_resource_manager.set_initial_consumer_group-
   ('MGR','OLTP');
   ```

5. Create the plan.

   ```
   execute dbms_resource_manager.create_simple_plan(-
   simple_plan=>'my_plan',-
   consumer_group1=>'OLTP',group1_percent=>80,-
   consumer_group2=>'DSS',group2_percent=>20);
   ```

6. Activate the plan.

   ```
   alter system set resource_manager_plan=my_plan
   scope=memory;
   ```

Monitor the Resource Manager

The Resource Manager configuration is documented in a set of DBA views, principally the following:

- **DBA_RSRC_PLANS**   Plans and status
- **DBA_RSRC_PLAN_DIRECTIVES**   Plan directives
- **DBA_RSRC_CONSUMER_GROUPS**   Consumer groups

The current situation is documented in V$ views:

- **V$SESSION**   The active consumer group of each session
- **V$RSRC_PLAN**   The currently active plan
- **V$RSRC_CONSUMER_GROUP**   Statistics for the groups

If a session has been impacted by Resource Manager, this shows up as the wait event resmgr:cpu quantum, which will be visible in the V$SESSION.EVENT column while the session is actually waiting, as well as in the V$SESSION_EVENT view for the cumulative time waited since the session started.

 NOTE   It is difficult to test the effect of a Resource Manager configuration because until the system becomes stressed, it will have no effect. This can mean that you see no occurrence of the resmgr:cpu quantum wait event for months, and then one day everyone gets it.

Exercise 20-2: Test and Monitor a Resource Manager Plan   This exercise continues from Exercise 20-1, testing the effect of the plan.

1. Connect to the database as user SYSTEM.

2. Restrict the database instance to using only one CPU core to ensure contention when multiple sessions work concurrently.

   ```
   alter system set cpu_count=1 scope=memory;
   ```

3. In two more SQL*Plus sessions, log in as the ACCT and CLERK users.

   ```
   sqlplus acct/acct
   sqlplus clerk/clerk
   ```

4. In the SYSTEM session, run this query to confirm the group memberships of your sessions:

   ```
   select username,resource_consumer_group from v$session
   where username is not null;
   ```

5. In the SYSTEM session, run this query to show the CPU usage by each group so far:

   ```
   select name, active_sessions, consumed_cpu_time
   from v$rsrc_consumer_group;
   ```

   The figures for the DSS and OLTP groups will be low and nearly identical.

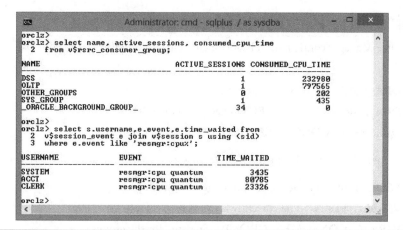

Figure 20-4 Monitoring the effect of a Resource Manager plan

6. In both the CLERK and ACCT sessions, run this query concurrently, and let it run for a while:

```
select count(*) from all_objects,all_objects;
```

7. Repeat the query from step 5. Note that the OLTP group has used approximately four times as much CPU as the DSS group.

8. Run this query to see the wait time in sessions caused by Resource Manager:

```
select s.username,e.event,e.time_waited from
v$session_event e join v$session s using (sid)
where e.event like 'resmgr:cpu%';
```

Figure 20-4 shows typical results from steps 7 and 8, specifically, a much higher wait time for the ACCT user than the CLERK user.

9. Tidy up by dropping the users and then returning the database to its default Resource Manager and CPU configuration by restarting the instance.

Two-Minute Drill

Configure the Database Resource Manager

- Configure Resource Manager with two APIs: DBMS_RESOURCE_MANAGER and DBMS_RESOURCE_MANAGER_PRIVS.

- Enable Resource Manager by setting the RESOURCE_MANAGER_PLAN instance parameter, either interactively or through the Scheduler.

- A plan is a set of directives allocating resources to consumer groups.
- To configure Resource Manager, do the following: First, create consumer groups; second, create a plan; third, create the plan directives that allocate resources to groups.

Access and Create Resource Plans

- A plan can limit several resources: CPU, active sessions, SQL statement execution time, use of parallel query, and undo space.
- The default plan (named DEFAULT_PLAN) gives top priority to the SYS_GROUP and lowest priority to the ORA$AUTOTASK group.

Monitor the Resource Manager

- The Resource Manager configuration is documented in a set of data dictionary views, DBA_RSRC_%. To monitor Resource Manager, query the dynamic performance views.
- Resource Manager will not appear to have any effect until the system comes under stress.

Self Test

1. There are several steps involved in setting up Resource Manager:

   a. Assign users to consumer groups.

   b. Create consumer groups.

   c. Create directives.

   d. Create the pending area.

   e. Create the plan.

   f. Submit the pending area.

   g. Validate the pending area.

   What is the correct order for accomplishing these steps? (Choose the best answer.)

   A. d, e, g, f, c, b, a

   B. d, b, a, e, c, g, f

   C. d, b, a, c, e, g, f

   D. e, c, d, b, a, f, g

   E. b, a, d, e, c, f, g

2. Which of the following statements are correct about users and consumer groups? (Choose all correct answers.)

A. One user can be a member of only one consumer group.

B. One user can be a member of many consumer groups.

C. The SYS_GROUP is reserved for the user SYS.

D. By default, the initial group for all users is DEFAULT_CONSUMER_GROUP.

3. Some actions in the Resource Manager API are done with procedures in the package DBMS_RESOURCE_MANAGER_PRIVS, and others are done with procedures in the package DBMS_RESOURCE_MANAGER. Which package is needed for each of these actions? (Choose the best answer.)

A. Granting the privilege to administer Resource Manager

B. Placing users in groups

C. Removing users from groups

D. Switching a session's effective group

E. Creating consumer groups

F. Configuring how to map sessions to groups

4. Resource Manager plans can use a number of methods to control resources. Which of the following are possible? (Choose three correct answers.)

A. CPU usage

B. Tablespace quota usage

C. Number of active sessions

D. Number of idle sessions

E. Volume of redo data generated

F. Volume of undo data generated

5. A CPU method plan allocates resources at two levels, as follows:

Level 1: SYS_GROUP, 50% OLTP, 50%

Level 2: DSS, 50% BATCH, 50%

If the only users logged on are from the BATCH group, what percentage of CPU can they use? (Choose the best answer.)

A. They can use 12.5 percent.

B. They can use 25 percent.

C. They can use 50 percent.

D. They can use 100 percent.

E. The plan will not validate because it attempts to allocate 200 percent of CPU resources.

6. You create a Resource Manager plan limiting the active session pool for the group DSS to 3. What will happen if three members of the group are logged on and a fourth member attempts to connect? (Choose the best answer.)

   A. The new session will not be able to connect until an existing session disconnects.

   B. The new session will be able to connect but will hang immediately.

   C. The new session will be able to connect but will be able to run only queries, not DML statements.

   D. Any statements the new session issues may hang, depending on other activity.

7. If the active Resource Manager plan specifies that sessions belonging to a particular group may have only four parallel execution servers, what will happen if a session in that group issues a statement that requests six parallel execution servers? (Choose the best answer.)

   A. The statement will not run.

   B. The statement will run with four parallel servers.

   C. It will depend on the setting of the PARALLEL_MIN_PERCENT instance parameter.

   D. It will depend on the setting of the PARALLEL_AUTOMATIC_TUNING instance parameter.

8. When you use Resource Manager to define an undo pool, what happens? (Choose the best answer.)

   A. If a user exceeds their quota on the undo tablespace, their session will hang.

   B. If a user exceeds their quota on the undo tablespace, the statement running will be rolled back, but the rest of the statement will remain intact.

   C. If a group fills its undo pool, all the group's transactions will hang until one session commits, rolls back, or is terminated.

   D. The effect depends on whether RETENTION GUARANTEE is enabled for the undo tablespace.

9. How can you determine what is the active Resource Manager plan? (Choose two answers.)

   A. Use SHOW PARAMETER RESOURCE_LIMIT.

   B. Use SHOW PARAMETER RESOURCE_MANAGER_PLAN.

   C. Query the DBA_RSRC_PLANS view.

   D. Query the V$RSRC_PLAN view.

10. You notice that sessions have been waiting on the resmgr:cpu quantum wait event. What might this indicate? (Choose the best answer.)

    A. That no Resource Manager plan has been enabled

    B. That the system has hit 100 percent CPU usage

    C. That the number of sessions has reached the limit imposed by the SESSIONS parameter

    D. That the CPU_COUNT has been exceeded

Self Test Answers

1. ☑ **C.** This is the correct sequence, although d, b, e, c, g, f, a will also work.
   ☒ **A, B, D,** and **E** are incorrect. None of these sequences will work because the pending area must be active when working with groups and plans and cannot be validated after it has been submitted.

2. ☑ **B.** One user can be a member of many groups, although only one membership is active at any time.
   ☒ **A, C,** and **D** are incorrect. **A** is incorrect because there can be a many-to-many relationship between users and groups. **C** is incorrect because it is possible to put other users in the SYS group. **D** is incorrect because SYS and SYSTEM are, by default, in the SYS_GROUP group.

3. ☑ **A, B,** and **C:** DBMS_RESOURCE_MANAGER_PRIVS; **D, E,** and **F:** DBMS_RESOURCE_MANAGER. The DBMS_RESOURCE_MANAGER_PRIVS package handles security, whereas the DBMS_RESOURCE_MANAGER package manages everything else.
   ☒ All other possibilities are incorrect.

4. ☑ **A, C,** and **F.** The emphasis method controls CPU usage. Active sessions and the volume of undo data are two of the absolute methods.
   ☒ **B, D,** and **E** are incorrect. Tablespace usage can be limited by quotas, not by Resource Manager. Idle sessions can be timed out, but not limited in number. Redo volume is not a possible limit.

5. ☑ **D.** If no other sessions are connected, all CPU resources will be available to the connected sessions.
   ☒ **A, B, C,** and **E** are incorrect. **A, B,** and **C** are incorrect because they misinterpret the "trickle-down" nature of resource allocation. **E** is incorrect because it fails to appreciate that CPU is allocated at each priority level, not across priority levels.

6. ☑ **D.** The session pool does not limit the number of sessions, only the number of active sessions.
   ☒ **A, B,** and **C** are incorrect. **A** is incorrect because it describes the effect of session limits in profiles, not Resource Manager. **B** is incorrect because this result would occur only if the active session pool were full. **C** is incorrect because Resource Manager makes no distinction between the types of SQL statements.

7. ☑ **B.** The limit will override the request.
   ☒ **A, C,** and **D** are incorrect. **A** is incorrect because the intent of Resource Manager is not to block statements but to control them. **C** and **D** are incorrect because they refer to the instance parameters that drive the optimizer, not Resource Manager.

8. ☑ **C.** Undo pools refer to whole groups, not to individual users or sessions. If a group fills its pool, all sessions that are part of the group will hang until one issues a COMMIT or a ROLLBACK.
   ☒ **A, B,** and **D** are incorrect. Tablespace quotas are relevant to neither undo in general nor Resource Manager. RETENTION GUARANTEE does not apply either.

9. ☑ **B** and **C**. The active plan is set with the RESOURCE_MANAGER_PLAN parameter and displayed in the V$RSRC_PLAN dynamic performance view.
   ☒ **A** and **D** are incorrect. **A** is incorrect because the RESOURCE_LIMIT parameter is relevant to profiles, not to Resource Manager. **D** is incorrect because the DBA_RSRC_PLANS data dictionary view shows the configuration of Resource Manager, not its current state.

10. ☑ **B**. Once a system reaches 100 percent CPU usage, a CPU plan will come into effect and start limiting sessions' usage.
    ☒ **A, C,** and **D** are incorrect. **A** is incorrect because if no plan is enabled, there can be no waits on this event. **C** and **D** are incorrect because although these parameters do control resource usage, they do not do this through the Resource Manager plan.

CHAPTER 21

The Scheduler

Exam Objectives

This chapter introduces the Scheduler, which is a facility to automate the running of jobs. These jobs may be procedures that execute within the database, or they may be operating system commands and scripts. They can run locally or on remote machines and databases. They can run according to a schedule, according to the results of a previous job, or in response to events. The Scheduler is integrated with Resource Manager.

An alternative (and older) scheduling mechanism is DBMS_JOB. However, the Scheduler is far more capable (and complex). A job-scheduling facility is also provided by Enterprise Manager, and of course your operating system will have a job scheduler. The Scheduler is probably more sophisticated than any alternative solution.

Use Oracle Scheduler to Simplify Management Tasks

You can configure the Scheduler by creating various objects. At a minimum, a job is all that is needed. But usually, more objects will be involved, at least programs and schedules. In many environments, job classes, windows, and chains are also useful. And at the instance level, the background processes control the environment and run the jobs.

The Scheduler Architecture

The data dictionary includes a table that is the storage point for all Scheduler jobs. You can query this table through the DBA_SCHEDULER_JOBS view. The job queue coordinator background process (the CJQ0 process) monitors this table and, when necessary, launches job queue processes (the J*nnn* processes) to run the jobs. The CJQ0 process is launched automatically if there are any defined and active Scheduler jobs. The J*nnn* processes are launched on demand, although the maximum number is limited by the JOB_QUEUE_PROCESSES instance parameter, which can have any value from 0 to 1000 (the default). If set to zero, the Scheduler will not function.

The job queue coordinator picks up jobs from the job queue table and passes them to job queue processes for execution. It also launches and terminates the job queue processes on demand. To see the processes currently running, query the V$PROCESS view.

```
SQL> select program from v$process
where program like '%J%';
PROGRAM
-------------------------------------------------
oracle@vblin1.example.com (CJQ0)
oracle@vblin1.example.com (J000)
oracle@vblin1.example.com (J001)
```

This query shows that the job queue coordinator and two job queue processes are running. In a Unix instance, the processes will be separate operating system processes (as in this query); in a Windows instance, they execute as threads within the ORACLE.EXE process.

 EXAM TIP The JOB_QUEUE_PROCESSES instance parameter must be greater than zero or the Scheduler cannot run. It is 1000 by default. The job queue coordinator will always be running if there any defined and active jobs.

Jobs defined as procedures run within the database. Jobs can also be defined as operating system commands or shell scripts; these will run as external operating system tasks. The triggering factor for a job can be a time or an event. Time-based jobs can run once or repeatedly according to a schedule. Event-based jobs run when certain conditions arise. There are some preconfigured events, or you can use user-defined events. Jobs can be connected into a chain using simple rules for branching depending on a job's success or failure.

An advanced feature of the Scheduler is to associate it with Resource Manager. It may be that certain jobs should be run with certain priorities, and this can be achieved by linking a job to a Resource Manager consumer group via a job class. It is also possible to use the Scheduler to activate a Resource Manager plan, rather than having to activate a plan manually by changing the RESOURCE_MANAGER_PLAN instance parameter or using the DBMS_RESOURCE_MANAGER.SWITCH_PLAN procedure call.

The application programming interface (API) to administer the Scheduler is the DBMS_SCHEDULER package. Also, Enterprise Manager provides a graphical interface.

Scheduler Objects

The most basic object in the Scheduler environment is a job. A job can be completely self-contained, defining the action to be taken and when to take it. In a more advanced configuration, the job is only part of the structure consisting of a number of Scheduler objects of various types.

Jobs

A job specifies what to do and when to do it. The "what" can be an anonymous PL/SQL block (which could consist of just a single SQL statement), a PL/SQL stored procedure (which could invoke a Java stored procedure or an external procedure), or any executable file stored in the server's file system (either a binary executable or a shell script). A particularly powerful capability (beyond the scope of the Oracle Certified Professional [OCP] curriculum) is the remote external job, which runs on a separate machine. The "when" specifies either the timestamp at which to launch the job and a repeat interval for future runs or the triggering event.

You have several options when creating a job, as shown from looking at the DBMS_SCHEDULER.CREATE_JOB procedure. This procedure is overloaded; it has no fewer than six forms. Figure 21-1 shows part of the output from a DESCRIBE of the DBMS_SCHEDULER package, with the first two forms of CREATE_JOB.

All forms of the CREATE_JOB procedure must specify a JOB_NAME. This must be unique within the schema where the job is created. Note that jobs are schema objects. Then, taking the first form of the procedure, the JOB_TYPE must be one of the following:

- **PLSQL_BLOCK**   An anonymous PL/SQL block
- **STORED_PROCEDURE**   A named PL/SQL procedure
- **EXECUTABLE**   Anything executable from an operating system (OS) prompt
- **CHAIN**   A named job chain object
- **EXTERNAL_SCRIPT**   A script launched by the OS's command interpreter

```
oracle@oel58x64db121:~                    -  □  ×

PROCEDURE CREATE_JOB
Argument Name                    Type                          In/Out Default?
-------------------------------  ----------------------------  ------ --------
JOB_NAME                         VARCHAR2                      IN
JOB_TYPE                         VARCHAR2                      IN
JOB_ACTION                       VARCHAR2                      IN
NUMBER_OF_ARGUMENTS              BINARY_INTEGER                IN     DEFAULT
START_DATE                       TIMESTAMP WITH TIME ZONE IN         DEFAULT
REPEAT_INTERVAL                  VARCHAR2                      IN     DEFAULT
END_DATE                         TIMESTAMP WITH TIME ZONE IN         DEFAULT
JOB_CLASS                        VARCHAR2                      IN     DEFAULT
ENABLED                          BOOLEAN                       IN     DEFAULT
AUTO_DROP                        BOOLEAN                       IN     DEFAULT
COMMENTS                         VARCHAR2                      IN     DEFAULT
CREDENTIAL_NAME                  VARCHAR2                      IN     DEFAULT
DESTINATION_NAME                 VARCHAR2                      IN     DEFAULT
PROCEDURE CREATE_JOB
Argument Name                    Type                          In/Out Default?
-------------------------------  ----------------------------  ------ --------
JOB_NAME                         VARCHAR2                      IN
JOB_TYPE                         VARCHAR2                      IN
JOB_ACTION                       VARCHAR2                      IN
NUMBER_OF_ARGUMENTS              BINARY_INTEGER                IN     DEFAULT
START_DATE                       TIMESTAMP WITH TIME ZONE IN         DEFAULT
EVENT_CONDITION                  VARCHAR2                      IN     DEFAULT
QUEUE_SPEC                       VARCHAR2                      IN
```

Figure 21-1   The specification of the CREATE_JOB procedure

- **SQL_SCRIPT**   A SQL*Plus script
- **BACKUP_SCRIPT**   An RMAN script

The JOB_ACTION is the command or script or chain to be run. The NUMBER_OF_ARGUMENTS parameter states how many arguments the JOB_ACTION should take.

The remaining arguments of the first form of the procedure shown in Figure 21-1 are details of when and how frequently to run the job. The first execution will be on the START_DATE; the REPEAT_INTERVAL defines a repeat frequency, such as daily, until END_DATE. JOB_CLASS has to do with priorities and integration of the Scheduler with Resource Manager. The ENABLED argument determines whether the job can actually be run. Perhaps surprisingly, this defaults to FALSE. If a job is not created with this argument on TRUE, it cannot be run (either manually or through a schedule) without being enabled first. Finally, AUTO_DROP controls whether to drop the job definition after the END_TIME. This defaults to TRUE. If a job is created with no scheduling information, it will be run as soon as it is enabled and then dropped immediately if AUTO_DROP is on TRUE, which is the default.

The second form of CREATE_JOB shown in Figure 21-1 creates an event-based job. The EVENT_CONDITION is an expression based on the definition of the messages enqueued to the queue table nominated by the QUEUE_SPEC argument. Between the start and end dates, Oracle will monitor the queue and launch the job whenever a message arrives that conforms to the condition.

Programs

Programs provide a layer of abstraction between the job and the action it will perform. They are created with the DBMS_SCHEDULER.CREATE_PROGRAM procedure.

```
PROCEDURE CREATE_PROGRAM
Argument Name          Type                  In/Out Default?
---------------------- --------------------- ------ --------
PROGRAM_NAME           VARCHAR2              IN
PROGRAM_TYPE           VARCHAR2              IN
PROGRAM_ACTION         VARCHAR2              IN
NUMBER_OF_ARGUMENTS    BINARY_INTEGER        IN     DEFAULT
ENABLED                BOOLEAN               IN     DEFAULT
COMMENTS               VARCHAR2              IN     DEFAULT
```

By pulling the "what" of a job out of the job definition itself and defining it in a program, you can reference the same program in different jobs and thus associate it with different schedules and job classes, without having to define it many times. Note that (as for a job) a program must be ENABLED before it can be used; the default for this is FALSE.

Schedules

A schedule is a specification for when and how frequently a job should run. The basic principle of a schedule is to pull the "when" portion out of a job, thus associating it with different jobs. It is created with the DBMS_SCHEDULER.CREATE_SCHEDULE procedure.

```
PROCEDURE CREATE_SCHEDULE
Argument Name      Type                       In/Out Default?
------------------ -------------------------- ------ --------
SCHEDULE_NAME      VARCHAR2                   IN
START_DATE         TIMESTAMP WITH TIME ZONE   IN     DEFAULT
REPEAT_INTERVAL    VARCHAR2                   IN
END_DATE           TIMESTAMP WITH TIME ZONE   IN     DEFAULT
COMMENTS           VARCHAR2                   IN     DEFAULT
```

The START_DATE defaults to the current date and time. This is the time that any jobs associated with this schedule will run. The REPEAT_INTERVAL specifies how frequently the job should run until the END_DATE. Schedules without a specified END_DATE will run forever.

The REPEAT_INTERVAL argument can take a wide variety of calendaring expressions. These consist of up to three elements: a frequency, an interval (defaulting to 1), and possibly several specifiers. The frequency may be one of these values:

- YEARLY
- MONTHLY
- WEEKLY
- DAILY
- HOURLY
- MINUTELY
- SECONDLY

The specifiers can be one of these:

- BYMONTH
- BYWEEKNO
- BYYEARDAY
- BYMONTHDAY
- BYHOUR
- BYMINUTE
- BYSECOND

Using these elements of a REPEAT_INTERVAL makes it possible to set up schedules that should satisfy any requirement. For example, the following will run the job every 12 hours, starting at the START_DATE:

```
repeat_interval=>'freq=hourly; interval=12'
```

The next example will run the job on the second day of each of the named three months, starting as early in the day as resources permit:

```
repeat_interval=>'freq=yearly; bymonth=jan,mar,may;
bymonthday=2'
```

The final example will run the job at ten past six on alternate Mondays:

```
repeat_interval=>'freq=weekly; interval=2; byday=mon;
byhour=6; byminute=10'
```

Using programs and schedules normalizes the job structure, allowing reuse of predefined programs and schedules for many jobs, as shown in Figure 21-2. Note that the figure includes other Scheduler objects and also refers to Resource Manager objects Groups, Directives, and Plans.

A Self-Contained Job

To create and schedule a job with one procedure call, use the CREATE_JOB procedure. For example, the following will create an enabled job that calls the procedure HR.REFRESH_SUMMARIES at 11 P.M. on Mondays and Fridays, starting today:

```
begin
dbms_scheduler.create_job(
job_name=>'hr.refresh_sums',
job_type=>'stored_procedure',
job_action=>'hr.refresh_summaries',
start_date=>trunc(sysdate)+23/24,
repeat_interval=>'freq=weekly;byday=mon,fri;byhour=23',
enabled=>true,
auto_drop=>false,
comments=>'update summary tables');
end;
```

The job is created in the HR schema.

Figure 21-2
A normalized
view of the
Scheduler
and Resource
Manager objects

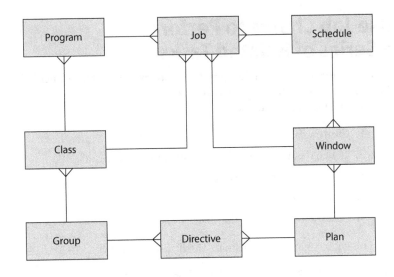

Exercise 21-1: Create a Job with the Scheduler API   Use the DBMS_
SCHEDULER package to create a job and confirm that it is working.

1. Connect to your database as user SYSTEM using SQL*Plus.

2. Create a table to store times and set your date format to show the date and time.

```
create table times (c1 date);
alter session set nls_date_format='dd-mm-yy hh24:mi:ss';
```

3. Create a job to insert the current time into the table every minute.

```
execute dbms_scheduler.create_job(-
job_name=>'savedate',-
job_type=>'plsql_block',-
job_action=>'insert into times values(sysdate);',-
start_date=>sysdate,-
repeat_interval=>'freq=minutely;interval=1',-
enabled=>true,-
auto_drop=>false);
```

4. Query the job table a few times to see that the job is scheduled and running.

```
select job_name,enabled,
to_char(next_run_date,'dd-mm-yy hh24:mi:ss'),run_count
from user_scheduler_jobs;
```

Query the times table to demonstrate that the inserts are occurring.

```
select * from times;
```

5. Disable the job.

```
exec dbms_scheduler.disable('savedate');
```

6. Rerun the queries from step 4 to confirm that the job is disabled and that no more inserts are occurring.

7. Drop the job.

```
exec dbms_scheduler.drop_job('savedate');
```

Use Job Chains to Perform a Series of Related Tasks

A chain represents a set of linked programs with execution dependencies. The logic connecting the steps in a chain is branching based on a success/failure test.

Here are the steps to follow to use job chains:

1. Create a chain object.

2. Define the steps (the individual programs) of the chain.

3. Define the rules connecting the steps.

4. Enable the chain.

5. Create a job to launch the chain.

This code fragment demonstrates the first four steps:

```
exec dbms_scheduler.create_chain(chain_name=>'mychain');
exec dbms_scheduler.define_chain_step(chain_name => 'mychain',-
step_name => 'step1',program_name => 'prg1');
exec dbms_scheduler.define_chain_step(chain_name => 'mychain',-
step_name => 'step2',program_name => 'prg2');
exec dbms_scheduler.define_chain_step(-
chain_name => 'mychain',-
step_name => 'step3',program_name => 'prg3');
exec dbms_scheduler.define_chain_rule(-
chain_name => 'mychain',-
rule_name => 'rule1',condition => 'step1 succeeded',-
action => 'start step2');
exec dbms_scheduler.define_chain_rule(-
chain_name => 'mychain',-
rule_name => 'rule2',condition => 'step1 failed',-
action => 'start step3');
exec dbms_scheduler.enable('mychain');
```

These commands create and enable a simple chain of three steps. The execution of either the second or third step is dependent on the outcome of the first step. The syntax for creating rules permits the use of keywords such as SUCCEEDED and FAILED, which will test the outcome of another step. In this example, it is assumed that the programs have already been created with CREATE_PROGRAM procedure calls.

To launch the chain, you must create a job. This could be based on a schedule or an event. This job will run the chain on the last Tuesday of alternate months:

```
exec dbms_scheduler.create_job(job_name=>'run_mychain',-
job_type=>'chain',-
job_action=>'mychain',-
start_date=>next_day(last_day(sysdate)-7,'tuesday'),-
repeat_interval=>'freq=monthly;interval=2',-
enabled=>true);
```

Use Scheduler Jobs on Remote Systems

It is possible to schedule and run jobs on remote systems. These jobs can be database jobs (typically calling a PL/SQL procedure) or external jobs (typically shell scripts). The job definition exists in the calling database, but the procedure or shell script must reside at the remote site.

Every machine on which a remote job is to run requires a Scheduler Agent. Install this agent from the Oracle Client CD, selecting the Custom Install option. The agent process will, by default, listen on port 1500, although any port can be selected at install time. The protocol between agent and database is Hypertext Transfer Protocol (HTTP). The database and listener will already be configured to accept HTTP if Database Express has been configured. To confirm the listening port and set it if it has not been configured, use procedures in the DBMS_XDB_CONFIG package.

```
orclz>
orclz> select dbms_xdb_config.gethttpport from dual;
GETHTTPPORT
-----------
          0
orclz> exec dbms_xdb_config.sethttpport(new_port=>5500)
PL/SQL procedure successfully completed.
orclz>
```

Once communications have been established between database and agent, create jobs that specify the DESTINATION_NAME argument of the CREATE_JOB procedure, giving the network name of the remote machine.

Use Advanced Scheduler Features to Prioritize Jobs

The more advanced capabilities of the Scheduler enable you to integrate it with Resource Manager to control and prioritize jobs. These are the relevant components:

- **Job classes**   Jobs can be assigned a class, and a class can be linked to a Resource Manager consumer group. Classes also control the logging level for their jobs.

- **Consumer groups**   Resource Manager consumer groups are restricted in the resources they can use, being limited in, for instance, central processing unit (CPU) usage or the number of active sessions.

- **Resource plans**   A Resource Manager plan defines how to apportion resources to groups. Only one plan is active in the instance at any one time.

- **Windows**   A window is a defined (probably recurring) period of time during which certain jobs will run and a certain plan will be active.

- **Window groups**   It is possible to combine windows into window groups for ease of administration.

Prioritizing jobs within a window is done at two levels. Within a class, jobs can be given different priorities by the Scheduler, but because all jobs in a class are in the same consumer group, Resource Manager will not distinguish between them. But if jobs in different classes are scheduled within the same window, Resource Manager will assign resources to each class according to the consumer groups for that class.

Using Job Classes

Create a class with the DBMS_SCHEDULER API. Here is an example:

```
SQL> exec dbms_scheduler.create_job_class(-
job_class_name=>'daily_reports',-
resource_consumer_group=>'dss',-
logging_level=>dbms_scheduler.logging_full);
```

Then assign the jobs to the class, either at job creation time by specifying the JOB_CLASS attribute or by modifying the job later. To assign a job to a class after creation, you must use the SET_ATTRIBUTE procedure. Here is how to create a job called REPORTS_JOB and place it in the class just created:

```
SQL> exec dbms_scheduler.create_job(job_name=>'reports_job',-
job_type=>'stored_procedure',-
job_action=>'run_reports')
SQL> exec dbms_scheduler.set_attribute(-
name=>'reports_job',-
attribute=>'job_class',-
value=>'daily_reports')
```

If there are several jobs in the one class, prioritize them with further SET_ATTRIBUTE calls.

```
SQL> exec dbms_scheduler.set_attribute(-
name=>'reports_job',-
attribute=>'job_priority',-
value=>2);
```

If several jobs in the same class are scheduled to be executed at the same time, the job priority determines the order in which jobs from that class are picked up for execution by the job coordinator process. It can be a value from 1 to 5, with 1 being the first to be picked up for job execution. The default for all jobs is 3. This could be critical if, for example, the class's consumer group has an active session pool that is smaller than the number of jobs; those jobs with the highest priority will run first, while the others are queued.

 EXAM TIP   It is not possible to assign priorities when creating jobs with the CREATE_JOB procedures; you must use the SET_ATTRIBUTE procedure of the API subsequently.

Logging levels are also controlled by the job's class. There are three options:

- **DBMS_SCHEDULER.LOGGING_OFF**   No logging is done for any jobs in this class.
- **DBMS_SCHEDULER.LOGGING_RUNS**   Information is written to the job log regarding each run of each job in the class, including when the run was started and whether the job ran successfully.

- **DBMS_SCHEDULER.LOGGING_FULL**   In addition to logging information about the job runs, the log will record management operations on the class, such as creating new jobs.

To view logging information, query the DBA_SCHEDULER_JOB_LOG view.

```
SQL> select job_name,log_date,status from
dba_scheduler_job_log;
JOB_NAME     LOG_DATE                      STATUS
------------ ----------------------------- ------------
PURGE_LOG    21-OCT-13 13-00-03            SUCCEEDED
TEST_JOB     21-OCT-13 11-00-00            FAILED
NIGHT_INCR   21-OCT-13 01-00-13            SUCCEEDED
NIGHT_ARCH   21-OCT-13 01-00-00            SUCCEEDED
```

More detailed information is written to the DBA_SCHEDULER_JOB_RUN_DETAILS view, including the job's run duration and any error code it returned. Logging information is cleared by the automatically created PURGE_LOG job. By default, this runs daily according to the preconfigured schedule DAILY_PURGE_SCHEDULE and will remove all logging information more than 30 days old.

Using Windows

Create windows with the CREATE_WINDOW procedure. Here is an example:

```
SQL> exec dbms_scheduler.create_window(-
window_name=>'daily_reporting_window',-
resource_plan=>'night_plan',-
schedule_name=>'weekday_nights',-
duration=>'0 04:00:00',-
window_priority=>'low',-
comments=>'for running regular reports');
```

This window activates a Resource Manager plan called NIGHT_PLAN. This might be a plan that gives priority to the DSS consumer groups over the OLTP group. It opens according to the schedule WEEKDAY_NIGHTS, which might be Monday through Friday at 20:00. The window will remain open for four hours; the DURATION argument accepts an INTERVAL DAY TO SECOND value, as does the REPEAT_INTERVAL for a schedule. Setting the priority to LOW means that if this window overlaps with another window, the other window will be allowed to impose its Resource Manager plan. This would be the case if you created a different window for your end-of-month processing and the end-of-month happened to be on a weekday. You could give the end-of-month window HIGH priority to ensure that the end-of-month Resource Manager plan, which could give top priority to the BATCH group, does come into effect.

EXAM TIP   Even if a job has priority 1 within its class, it might still run only after a job with priority 5 in another class—if the second job's class is in a consumer group with a higher Resource Manager priority.

If two windows with equal priority overlap, the window with the longest duration will open (or remain open). If both windows have the same time to run, the window currently open will remain open.

CAUTION Oracle Corporation advises that you should avoid using overlapping windows.

Exercise 21-2: Use Scheduler Windows to Control Resource Manager In this exercise, you will use the Scheduler to automate the activation of the Resource Manager plan MY_PLAN created in Exercise 20-1.

1. Connect to your database as user SYSTEM with SQL*Plus.

2. Run this query to determine whether a window is currently open:
   ```
   select WINDOW_NAME,ACTIVE from dba_scheduler_windows;
   ```

3. Run this query to determine which Resource Manager plan is currently active:
   ```
   select * from v$rsrc_plan;
   ```

4. Temporarily clear whatever Resource Manager plan may be currently active.
   ```
   alter system set resource_manager_plan='' scope=memory;
   ```

5. Confirm that there is no Resource Manager Plan active.

   Rerun the query from step 3. This will show that the INTERNAL_PLAN is active, which is the plan used when no other has been set.

6. Execute this procedure call to create a window named MY_WINDOW that will activate the MY_PLAN plan:
   ```
   execute dbms_scheduler.create_window(-
   window_name=>'daytime',resource_plan=>'my_plan',-
   start_date=>trunc(systimestamp) + 6/24,-
   repeat_interval=>'freq=daily',-
   duration=>'0 12:00:00',-
   comments=>'daily at 6AM');
   ```

   This will open the window from now onward every day at 6 A.M. for 12 hours.

7. Force the database to open the new window immediately.
   ```
   exec dbms_scheduler.open_window(-
   window_name=>'daytime',duration=>'0 00:05:00',force=>true);
   ```

   This procedure call will open the window immediately and activate its plan but only for five minutes.

8. Rerun the queries from steps 2 and 3 to confirm that the DAYTIME window is open and the MY_PLAN plan is active.

9. After five minutes, repeat step 8. You will see that the window has closed and that no plan is active. This situation will persist until the next scheduled opening of a window.

10. Tidy up.
    ```
    exec dbms_scheduler.drop_window('daytime');
    ```

Two-Minute Drill

Use Oracle Scheduler to Simplify Management Tasks

- A job can specify what to do and when to do it, or it can point to a program or a schedule.
- A job (or its program) can be an anonymous PL/SQL block, a stored procedure, or an external operating system command or script.
- Jobs are launched by the CJQ0 background process and executed by J*nnn* processes.
- J*nnn* processes are launched on demand, up to the limit set by the JOB_QUEUE_PROCESSES parameter. Setting this to zero disables the job system.

Use Job Chains to Perform a Series of Related Tasks

- A chain object consists of a number of steps.
- Each step can launch a program.
- Simple logic (such as the success or failure of a previous step) can control the flow of execution through a job chain with branching steps.
- The chain itself is launched by a job, triggered by either an event or a schedule.

Use Scheduler Jobs on Remote Systems

- Remote jobs can run in remote databases or on remote hosts.
- Every system where a remote job may run must run a Scheduler Agent.
- Remote jobs are defined in the source database and sent to the remote agent with credentials.
- Create a remote job by specifying the DESTINATION argument of CREATE_JOB.

Use Advanced Scheduler Features to Prioritize Jobs

- Jobs can be prioritized at two levels: Resource Manager will allocate resources via consumer groups to all the jobs in a class, and the class will prioritize the jobs within it according to the job priority set by the Scheduler.
- Scheduler priority varies between levels 1 and 5 (highest to lowest).

Self Test

1. When a job is due to run, what process will run it? (Choose the best answer.)

   A. A CJQ*n* process

   B. A J*nnn* process

   C. A server process

   D. A background process

2. Which of the following is a requirement if the Scheduler is to work? (Choose the best answer.)

   A. The instance parameter JOB_QUEUE_PROCESSES must be set.

   B. A Resource Manager plan must be enabled.

   C. A schedule must have been created.

   D. All of the above.

   E. None of the above.

3. A Scheduler job can be of several types. (Choose all that apply.)

   A. An anonymous PL/SQL block

   B. An executable operating system file

   C. A PL/SQL stored procedure

   D. A Java stored procedure

   E. An operating system command

   F. An operating system shell script (Unix) or batch file (Windows)

4. How can jobs best be chained together? (Choose the best answer.)

   A. Put them in the same class and use priorities to control the running order.

   B. Create them as programs, connected in a chain.

   C. Assign them to different schedules, timed to start consecutively.

   D. Run them within a window, giving them window priorities.

5. Which process runs a remote database job? (Choose the best answer.)

   A. A job queue process on the originating machine

   B. A job queue process on the destination machine

   C. The Scheduler Agent on the destination machine

   D. The Enterprise Manager agent on the destination machine

6. You create a job with the syntax

```
exec dbms_scheduler.create_job(-
job_name=>'j1',-
program_name=>'p1',-
schedule_name=>'s1',-
job_class=>'c1');
```

and find that it is not running when expected. What might be a reason for this? (Choose the best answer.)

    A. The schedule is associated with a window, which has not opened.

    B. The job has not been enabled.

    C. The class is part of a Resource Manager consumer group with low priority.

    D. The permissions on the job are not correct.

7. What are the possible priority levels of a job within a class? (Choose the best answer.)

    A. 1 to 5.

    B. 1 to 999.

    C. HIGH or LOW.

    D. It depends on the Resource Manager plan in effect.

8. You want a job to run every 30 minutes. Which of the following possibilities for the REPEAT_INTERVAL argument are correct syntactically and will achieve this result? (Choose three answers.)

    A. 'freq=minutely;interval=30'

    B. 'freq=hourly;interval=1/2'

    C. '0 00:30:00'

    D. 'freq=minutely;byminute=30'

    E. 'freq=byminute;interval=30'

9. You create a job class, and you set the LOGGING_LEVEL argument to LOGGING_RUNS. What will be the result? (Choose the best answer.)

    A. There will be a log entry for each run of each job in the class but no information on whether the job was successful.

    B. There will be a log entry for each run of each job in the class and information on whether the job was successful.

    C. There will be a single log entry for the class whenever it is run.

    D. You cannot set logging per class, only per job.

Self Test Answers

1. ☑   **B.** Jobs are run by job queue processes.
   ☒   **A, C,** and **D** are incorrect. The job queue coordinator does not run jobs; it assigns them to job queue processes. These are ephemeral processes, not background processes that run continuously, and they are not server processes.

2. ☑   **E.** The Scheduler is available by default, with no preconfiguration steps needed.
   ☒   **A, B, C,** and **D** are incorrect. **A** is incorrect because the JOB_QUEUE_PROCESSES instance parameter defaults to 1000; therefore, it does not need to be set. **B** and **C** are incorrect because Resource Manager is not required, and neither are schedules. Therefore, **D** is incorrect also.

3. ☑ **A, B, C, D, E**, and **F**. The JOB_TYPE can be PLSQL_BLOCK, STORED_
PROCEDURE (which can be PL/SQL or Java), EXECUTABLE (which includes
executable files and OS commands), or EXTERNAL_SCRIPT (either a shell script
or a SQL*Plus script).
   ☒ All the answers are correct.

4. ☑ **B**. This is the best way, connecting them with branches based on success or failure.
   ☒ **A, C**, and **D** are incorrect. **A** and **C** are incorrect because although they might work,
there is no guarantee of this. **D** is incorrect because window priorities control which
window will open, not which job runs within a window.

5. ☑ **B**. PL/SQL jobs are always run by job queue processes in the instance where the
job runs.
   ☒ **A, C**, and **D** are incorrect. **A** is incorrect because a job queue process can run
jobs only within its local instance. **C** is incorrect because although the agent launches
the job, it does not actually run it. **D** is incorrect because the Enterprise Manager job
system is not part of the Scheduler job system.

6. ☑ **B**. The job will, by default, not be enabled and therefore cannot run.
   ☒ **A, C**, and **D** are incorrect. **A** is incorrect because the job is not controlled by a
window but by a schedule. **C** is incorrect because although Resource Manager can
control job priority, it would not in most circumstances block a job completely.
D is incorrect because although permissions might cause a job to fail, they would not
stop it from running.

7. ☑ **A**. Job priorities are 1 to 5 (highest to lowest).
   ☒ **B, C**, and **D** are incorrect. **B** is incorrect because it is the wrong range. **C** is the
choice for window priority, not job priority. **D** is incorrect because Resource Manager
controls priorities between classes, not within them.

8. ☑ **A, B**, and **D**. These will provide a half-hour repeat interval.
   ☒ **C** and **E** are incorrect. **C** is incorrect because it is the syntax for a window's duration,
not a repeat interval. **E** is syntactically incorrect.

9. ☑ **B**. With logging set to LOGGING_RUNS, you will get records of each run of
each job, including the success or failure.
   ☒ **A, C**, and **D** are incorrect. **A** is incorrect because LOGGING_RUNS will include
the success or failure. **C** and **D** are incorrect because even though logging is set at the
class level, it is applied at the job level. Note that logging can also be set at the job level.

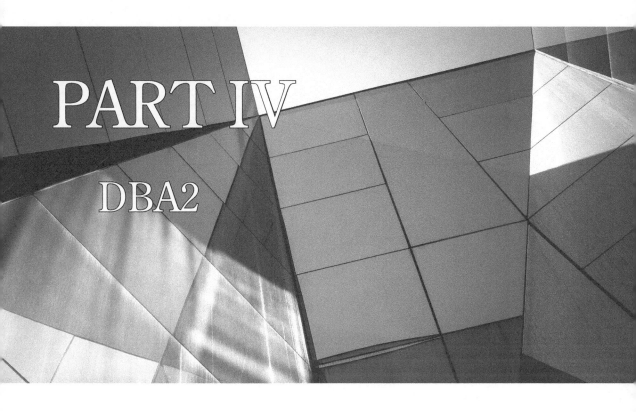

PART IV

DBA2

CHAPTER 22

Configuring the Database
for Backup and Recovery

Exam Objectives

This chapter summarizes what can go wrong in an Oracle database and the steps necessary to ensure that data will never be lost. This requires an understanding of the instance recovery mechanism and the usage of certain files.

Possible Failures and Their Resolution

Eventually your database will have some kind of failure whether it be a network failure, user error, disk drive failure, or memory corruption issue causing an instance failure. To prepare for this nearly inescapable occurrence, it is necessary to have a backup and recovery plan in place. This backup and recovery plan should be tested on a regular basis to make sure that the recovery techniques will be successful if they are ever needed.

To create a successful backup and recovery strategy, you must first understand the types of failures and how Oracle responds to each of them. Some require no user or database administrator (DBA) intervention, and others do. Which backup and recovery solutions you leverage depend on many factors, including how fast you need to recover from a failure and how many resources you want to dedicate to the solution. Your investment in recovery infrastructure is proportional to the cost of lost productivity or business income if the database is unavailable for a day, an hour, or a minute.

Failure Categories

The types of failures or errors you may encounter fall into two general categories: physical and logical. Physical errors are generally hardware errors or software errors in the applications using the database, while logical errors are typically at the end-user level (database users or administrators). The categories of failures are as follows:

- **Statement failure**   A user's SELECT or Data Manipulation Language (DML) statement failed because of permissions, syntax, or resource limits.
- **User error**   The user mistakenly dropped a table or deleted the wrong rows in a table.
- **User process failure**   The connection to the database failed because of a client disconnect or unexpected shutdown.
- **Network failure**   As the name implies, the network connection between the client and the server (database) failed because of network hardware or protocol errors.
- **Instance failure**   The database instance crashed because of a bug, operating system (OS) errors, memory corruption, or even power loss to the server.
- **Media failure**   There were disk drive physical errors or a controller hardware failure.

These failure categories are in order of least serious and easiest to recover from to the most serious and harder to recover from. Specifically, statement failures are the easiest to recover from since they are almost always user managed: you rewrite the SELECT or INSERT statement so it does not generate a syntax error. Accidentally dropping an important table can be recovered by the user or by the database administrator depending on whether the dropped table is still in the recycle bin or whether the DBA has given the user privileges to use various flashback features. Recovery from network, instance, or media failure will necessitate varying actions, the choice of which will depend on the criticality and severity of any lost data.

Your backup and recovery strategy will need to account for all of these failures, even though some of these failures are easier to recover from than others. For example, an instance failure may be because of a power outage. The recovery of committed transactions is relatively painless and automatic as long as your online redo log files are intact and multiplexed.

Oracle Backup and Recovery Solutions

Your *recovery time objective* (RTO) is the target in which a recovery operation must be completed to meet your customer's or client's service level agreement (SLA). Various Oracle tools and technologies will apply depending on the RTO:

- **Days or hours**   Recovery Manager (RMAN), and optionally Oracle Secure Backup, can recover your database in days or hours if the entire database is lost because of natural disaster or disk failures.

- **Hours or minutes**   Various flashback technologies, either user initiated or DBA initiated, can recover database objects usually while the database is still available to other users. Although the database needs to be temporarily shut down, by using a flashback database the DBA can roll back the entire database to a point in time earlier in the day or even weeks ago depending on the storage available in the Fast Recovery Area and the restore points defined.

- **Minutes or seconds**   If the database must be available continuously with downtimes no longer than a few minutes, Oracle solutions such as Data Guard or Real Application Cluster (RAC) can fail over to a backup database or an alternative running instance with minimal or no intervention from the DBA.

- **Recovery analysis**   Regardless of the type of failure or RTO, the Oracle Data Recover Advisor makes it easy to quickly determine the type of failure and the fastest way to recover from a specific type of failure.

Recovery Manager

Recovery Manager is the primary tool you use to back up, restore, and recover database objects from the table level (new to Oracle Database 12*c*) to the datafile, tablespace, and, of course, database level. RMAN has many uses outside of backup and recovery, including the cloning or duplication of a database to another location.

A key component of RMAN is a special location for backup and recovery objects called the *Fast Recovery Area* (FRA). While this area is ideally a disk group in ASM, it can also be located in an operating system (OS) file system. Regardless of location, it is a centralized place for all backup and recovery objects. The FRA is managed based on size and your recovery objectives, whether that's based on the recovery window or on the number of backups you need to retain. Using an FRA is optional but is considered to be best practice.

Oracle Secure Backup

In conjunction with RMAN, Oracle Secure Backup (OSB) will take RMAN backups and copy them to a tape device or to cloud storage to prevent loss of data from a catastrophic failure at a data center. OSB also provides an extension to RMAN at the OS level to back up Linux servers as well as any attached storage such as in a network attached storage (NAS) appliance.

Oracle Data Guard

Oracle Data Guard is one of Oracle's high-availability (HA) solutions to ensure near-real-time availability because of a failure of the primary database or to prevent database corruptions. A standby database (several of which may be created) is instantiated from a copy of the primary database and receives redo from the primary database and applies this redo to update its datafiles. Thus, the standby is kept synchronized with the primary. A standby database can also play the temporary role of a read-only copy of the database for reporting purposes and therefore free up resources on the primary database for better response time in an online transaction processing (OLTP) environment.

Another type of standby database is called a *logical standby database*. Instead of continuously applying redo to a physical copy of the primary database, a logical standby database converts the redo into equivalent DML SQL. Therefore, the standby database is *logically* equivalent to the standby database but will almost certainly not have the identical *physical* structure of the primary database. A logical standby is not really part of a fault-tolerant environment; it is a separate database optimized as a data warehouse that happens to contain the same data as the primary.

Instance Recovery and the Impossibility of Database Corruption

An instance failure could be caused by a power outage, rebooting the server, issuing a SHUTDOWN ABORT command, or anything that causes the instance background processes to terminate and the System Global Area (SGA) to be destroyed—all this without any attempt to flush changed buffers in the cache to the datafiles or to roll back any in-flight transactions. In principle, instance recovery is nothing more than using the contents of the online log files to rebuild the database buffer cache to the state it was in before the crash. This will replay all changes extracted from the online redo log files that refer to blocks that had not been written to disk at the time of the crash. Once this has been done, the database can be opened. This phase of recovery, known as the *roll forward,* reinstates all changes—changes to data blocks and changes to undo blocks—for both committed and uncommitted transactions. Each redo record has the bare minimum of information needed to reconstruct a change: the block address and the new values. During a roll forward, each redo record is read, the appropriate block is loaded from the datafiles into the database buffer cache, and the change is applied. Then the block is written back to disk.

Once the roll forward is complete, it is as though the crash had never occurred. But at that point, there will be uncommitted transactions in the database; these must be rolled back, and Oracle will do that automatically in the rollback phase of instance recovery. However, that happens after the database has been opened for use. If a user connects and hits some data that needs to be rolled back and hasn't yet been, this is not a problem; the roll forward phase will have populated the undo segment that was protecting the uncommitted transaction, so the server can roll back the change in the normal manner for read consistency.

Instance recovery is automatic and unavoidable, so how do you invoke it? By issuing a STARTUP command. When starting an instance, after mounting the controlfile and before opening the database, the System Monitor process (SMON) checks the file headers of all the datafiles and online redo log files. At this point, if there had been an instance failure, it is apparent because the file headers are all out of sync. So, SMON goes into the instance recovery routine, and the database is opened only after the roll-forward phase has completed.

Tuning the instance recovery process can (theoretically) be done by setting the RECOVERY_PARALLELISM instance parameter to specify the number of processes that will participate in the instance recovery operation. Setting this explicitly to 0 or 1 will disable parallel recovery. However, from release 10.1, leaving this parameter on the default will allow Oracle to launch whatever number of processes are appropriate. That actual number used is written out to the alert log. This is an excerpt from an alert log following a SHUTDOWN ABORT command:

```
Sun Jan 11 18:42:49 2015
Beginning crash recovery of 1 threads
 parallel recovery started with 7 processes
Sun Jan 11 18:42:49 2015
Started redo scan
Sun Jan 11 18:42:49 2015
Completed redo scan
 read 13 KB redo, 9 data blocks need recovery
Sun Jan 11 18:42:49 2015
Started redo application at
 Thread 1: logseq 20, block 78667
Sun Jan 11 18:42:49 2015
Recovery of Online Redo Log: Thread 1 Group 2 Seq 20
```

TIP   You never have anything to lose by issuing a STARTUP command. After any sort of crash, try a STARTUP and see how far it gets. It might get all the way.

It should now be apparent that there is always enough information in the redo log stream to reconstruct all work done up to the point at which the crash occurred and furthermore that this includes reconstructing the undo information needed to roll back transactions that were in progress at the time of the crash. But for the final proof, consider the following scenario.

User JOHN has started a transaction. He has updated one row of a table with some new values, and his server process has copied the old values to an undo segment. But before these updates were done, his server process wrote out the changes to the log buffer. User ROOPESH has also started a transaction. Neither has committed; nothing has been written to disk. If the instance crashed now, there would be no record whatsoever of either transaction, not even in the redo logs. So, neither transaction would be recovered—but that is not a problem. Neither was committed, so they should not be recovered; uncommitted work must never be saved.

Then user JOHN commits his transaction. This triggers LGWR to flush the log buffer to the online redo log files, which means that the changes to both the table and the undo segments for both JOHN's transaction and ROOPESH's transaction are now in the redo log files, together with a commit record for JOHN's transaction. Only when the write has completed is the "commit complete" message returned to JOHN's user process. But there is still nothing in the datafiles.

If the instance fails at this point, the roll forward phase will reconstruct both the transactions, but when all the redo has been processed, there will be no commit record for ROOPESH's update; that signals SMON to roll back ROOPESH's change but leave JOHN's in place.

But what if DBWR has written some blocks to disk before the crash? It might be that JOHN (or another user) was continually requerying his data but that ROOPESH had made his uncommitted change and not looked at the data again. DBW*n* will therefore decide to write ROOPESH's changes to disk in preference to JOHN's; DBW*n* will always tend to write inactive blocks rather than active blocks. So now, the datafiles are storing ROOPESH's uncommitted transaction but missing JOHN's committed transaction. This is as bad a corruption as you can have. But think it through. If the instance crashes now—a power cut, perhaps, or a SHUTDOWN ABORT—the roll forward will still be able to sort out the mess. There will always be enough information in the redo stream to reconstruct committed changes; that is obvious, because a commit isn't completed until the write is done. But because LGWR flushes all changes to all blocks to the log files, there will also be enough information to reconstruct the undo segment needed to roll back ROOPESH's uncommitted transaction.

To summarize, because LGWR always writes ahead of DBW*n* and because it writes in real time on commit, there will always be enough information in the redo stream to reconstruct any committed changes that had not been written to the datafiles and to roll back any uncommitted changes that had been written to the data files. This instance recovery mechanism of redo and rollback makes it absolutely impossible to corrupt an Oracle database—so long as there has been no physical damage to the redo log.

 EXAM TIP Can a SHUTDOWN ABORT corrupt the database? Absolutely not! It is impossible to corrupt the database. The instance recovery mechanism will always repair any damage as long as the online log files are available.

Checkpoints and the Redo Log

Blocks in the buffer cache that have been changed are checkpointed to disk by the database writer (DBW*n*) process (or processes). The change vectors that were applied to these blocks will have already been written to the redo stream by the LGWR process. The DBW*n* writes according to a lazy algorithm, and the LGWR writes according to an aggressive algorithm that is near real time and is real time on COMMIT.

The Checkpointing Mechanism

The checkpoint position (the point in the redo stream from which instance recovery must start following a crash) is advanced automatically by the DBW*n*. This process is known as *incremental checkpointing*. In addition, there may be full checkpoints and partial checkpoints.

An *incremental checkpoint* is part of normal database activity. The DBW*n* processes decide there are sufficient blocks in the cache that have been updated (these are known as *dirty buffers*) and that it is time to write a few of them to disk. The algorithm to select which changed buffers to write is based on how long ago the change was made and how active the buffer is. In general, a buffer will be written only if it has been changed (there is no point in writing a buffer that has not been changed) and idle (there is no point in writing a buffer if it is continually being used). Never forget that there is no correlation between committing changes and writing blocks to disk and that DBW*n* writes only the minimum number of blocks necessary.

A *full checkpoint* occurs when all dirty buffers are written to disk. In normal running, there might be 100,000 dirty buffers in the cache, but the DBW*n* would write just a few hundred of them for the incremental checkpoint. For a full checkpoint, it will write the lot. This entails a great deal of work, including high CPU and disk usage while the checkpoint is in progress and reduced performance for user sessions. Full checkpoints are bad for business. Because of this, there will never be a full checkpoint except in two circumstances: an orderly shutdown and at the DBA's request.

TIP   Manually initiated checkpoints should never be necessary in normal running, although they can be useful when you want to test the effect of tuning. There is no full checkpoint following a log switch. This has been the case since release 8*i*, though to this day many DBAs do not realize this.

When the database is shut down with the NORMAL, IMMEDIATE, or TRANSACTIONAL option, there is a checkpoint; all dirty buffers are flushed to disk by the DBW*n* before the database is closed and dismounted. This means that when the database is opened again, no recovery will be needed. A clean shutdown is always desirable and is necessary before some operations (such as enabling archivelog mode). A full checkpoint can be signaled at any time with this command:

```
alter system checkpoint;
```

A *partial checkpoint* is necessary and occurs automatically as part of certain operations. Depending on the operation, the partial checkpoint will affect different buffers. These operations are detailed here:

Operation	What Buffers Will Be Flushed to Disk
Taking a tablespace offline	All blocks that are part of the tablespace
Taking a datafile offline	All blocks that are part of the datafile
Dropping a segment	All blocks that are part of the segment
Truncating a table	All blocks that are part of the table
Putting a tablespace into backup mode	All blocks that are part of the tablespace
Backing up a datafile with RMAN	All blocks that are part of the datafile

EXAM TIP   Full checkpoints occur only with an orderly shutdown or by request. Partial checkpoints occur automatically as needed.

PART IV

Protecting the Online Redo Log Files

Remember that an Oracle database requires at least two online log file groups to function so that it can switch between them. You may need to add more groups for performance reasons, but two are required. Each group consists of one or more members, which are the physical files. Only one member per group is required for Oracle to function, but at least two members per group are required for safety.

 TIP Always have at least two members in each log file group for security. This is not just data security—it is job security, too.

The one thing that a DBA is not allowed to do is to lose all copies of the current online log file group. If that happens, you will lose data. The only way to protect against data loss when you lose all members of the current group is to configure a Data Guard environment for zero data loss, which is not a trivial exercise. Why is it so critical that you not lose all members of the current group? Think about instance recovery. After a crash, SMON will use the contents of the current online log file group for roll-forward recovery to repair any corruptions in the database. If the current online log file group is not available, perhaps because it was not multiplexed and media damage has destroyed the one member, then SMON cannot do this. And if SMON cannot correct corruptions with roll forward, you cannot open the database.

If a member of a redo log file group is damaged or missing, the database will remain open if there is a surviving member. This contrasts with the controlfile, where damage to any copy will crash the database immediately. Similarly, groups can be added or removed and members of groups can be added or moved while the database is open, as long as there are always at least two groups and each group has at least one valid member.

 EXAM TIP The online redo log can be reconfigured while the database is open with no downtime, whereas operations on the controlfile can be carried out only when the database is in nomount mode or completely shut down.

If you create a database with the Database Configuration Assistant (DBCA), by default you will have three groups, but unless you instructed DBCA to use Oracle Managed Files and a Fast Recovery Area, they will have only one member each. Two views will tell you the state of your redo logs: V$LOG will have one row per group, and V$LOGFILE will have one row per log file member. Figure 22-1 shows an example of online redo log configuration.

The first query shows that this database has three log file groups. The current group—the one LGWR is writing to at the moment—is group 2; the other groups are inactive, meaning first that the LGWR is not writing to them and second that in the event of an instance failure SMON would not require them for instance recovery. In other words, the checkpoint position has advanced into group 2. The SEQUENCE# column tells you that there have been 497 log switches since the database was created (or since the log sequence was reset using ALTER DATABASE OPEN RESETLOGS). This number is incremented with each log switch. The MEMBERS column shows that each group consists of only one member—and that is seriously bad news and should be corrected as soon as possible.

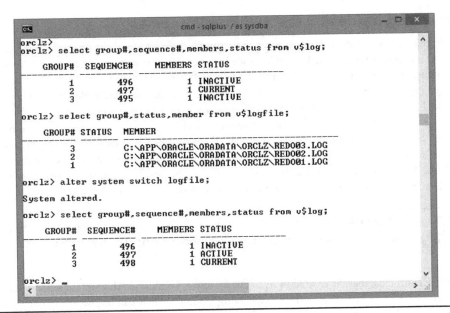

```
orclz>
orclz> select group#,sequence#,members,status from v$log;

   GROUP#   SEQUENCE#    MEMBERS STATUS
   _____ _____ _____ _____
          1        496         1 INACTIVE
          2        497         1 CURRENT
          3        495         1 INACTIVE

orclz> select group#,status,member from v$logfile;

   GROUP# STATUS   MEMBER
   _____ _____ _____
        3                C:\APP\ORACLE\ORADATA\ORCLZ\REDO03.LOG
        2                C:\APP\ORACLE\ORADATA\ORCLZ\REDO02.LOG
        1                C:\APP\ORACLE\ORADATA\ORCLZ\REDO01.LOG

orclz> alter system switch logfile;

System altered.

orclz> select group#,sequence#,members,status from v$log;

   GROUP#   SEQUENCE#    MEMBERS STATUS
   _____ _____ _____ _____
          1        496         1 INACTIVE
          2        497         1 ACTIVE
          3        498         1 CURRENT

orclz> _
```

Figure 22-1   Online redo log file configuration

The second query shows the individual online redo log files. Each file is part of one group (identified by GROUP#, which is the join column back to V$LOG) and has a unique name. The STATUS column should always be null, as shown. If the member has not yet been used, typically because the database has only just been opened and no log switches have occurred, the status will be INVALID; this will be there only until the first log switch. If the status is persistently INVALID, you have a problem.

TIP   As with the controlfile and datafiles, Oracle does not enforce any naming convention for log files, but most organizations will have standards for this.

Then there is an ALTER SYSTEM SWITCH LOGFILE command to force a log switch. The log switch would happen automatically, eventually, if there were any DML statements in progress. The previous query shows that after the log switch, group 3 is now the current group that LGWR is writing to, at log switch sequence 498. The previously current group, group 2, has status ACTIVE. This means that it would still be needed by SMON for instance recovery if the instance failed now. In a short time, as the checkpoint position advances, it will become INACTIVE. Issuing an ALTER SYSTEM CHECKPOINT command would force the checkpoint position to come up to date, and group 2 would then become inactive immediately.

To protect the database against loss of data in the event of damage to an online redo log file group, multiplex it. Following the example in Figure 22-1, to add multiplexed copies to the online log, you would use a command such as this for each log file group:

```
alter database add logfile member
'D:\APP\ORACLE\ORADATA\ORCLZ\REDO01A.log' to group 1;
```

Archivelog Mode and the Archiver Processes

Oracle guarantees that your database is never corrupted through use of the online redo log files to repair any corruptions caused by an instance failure. This is automatic and unavoidable. But to guarantee no loss of data following a media failure, it is necessary to have a record of all changes applied to the database since the last backup of the database; this is not enabled by default. The online redo log files are overwritten as log switches occur, so the history of change vectors is, by default, not kept—but the transition to archivelog mode ensures that no online redo log file is overwritten unless it has been copied to an archive log file first. So, there will be a series of archive log files that represent a complete history of all changes ever applied to the database. If a datafile is damaged at any time, it will then be possible to restore a backup of the datafile and apply the changes from the archive log redo stream to bring it up to date.

 EXAM TIP An online redo log file can be overwritten only if it is inactive and (if the database is in archivelog mode) if it has been archived.

By default, a database is created in *noarchivelog mode*. This means that online redo log files are overwritten by log switches with no copy being made first. It is still impossible to corrupt the database, but data would be lost if the datafiles were damaged by media failure. Once the database is transitioned to *archivelog mode,* it is impossible to lose data—provided that all the archive log files generated since the last backup are available.

Once a database is converted to archivelog mode, a new background process will start automatically. This is the archiver process, ARC*n*. By default Oracle will start four of these processes, but you can have up to 30. In earlier releases of the database, it was necessary to start this process either by using a SQL*Plus command or by setting the initialization parameter LOG_ARCHIVE_START, but from release 10*g* onward Oracle automatically starts the archiver processes if the database is in archivelog mode.

 TIP In archivelog mode, recovery is possible with no loss of data up to and including the last commit. As a general rule, all databases where you cannot afford to lose data should run in archivelog mode. Don't exclude test and development systems from this rule; they are important too.

The archiver processes will copy the current online redo log file to an archive log file after each log switch, thus generating a continuous chain of log files that can be used for recovering a backup. The name and location of these archive log files are controlled by initialization parameters. For safety, the archive log files can be multiplexed, just as the online log files can be multiplexed—but eventually they should be migrated to offline storage, such as a tape library. The Oracle instance takes care of creating the archive logs with the ARC*n* process, but the migration to tape must be controlled by the DBA, either by using operating system commands or by using the Recovery Manager utility RMAN.

 EXAM TIP Archiver processes launch automatically if the database is in archivelog mode.

The transition to archivelog mode can be done only while the database is in mount mode after a clean shutdown, and it must therefore be done by a user with a SYSDBA connection. It is also necessary to set the initialization parameters that control the names and locations of the archive logs generated. Clearly, these names must be unique or archive logs could be overwritten by other archive logs. To ensure unique filenames, it is possible to embed variables such as the log switch sequence number in the archive log filenames. These variables may be used to embed unique values in archive log filenames:

Variable	Description
%d	A unique database identifier, necessary if multiple databases are being archived to the same directories.
%t	The thread number, visible as the THREAD# column in V$INSTANCE. This is not significant, except in a RAC database.
%r	The incarnation number. This is important if an incomplete recovery has been done, which will reset the log switch sequence number.
%s	The log switch sequence number. This will guarantee that the archives from any one database incarnation do not overwrite each other.

The minimum archiving necessary to ensure that recovery from a restored backup will be possible is to set one archive destination. But for safety, it will usually be a requirement to multiplex the archive log files by specifying two or more destinations, ideally on different disks served by different controllers. It is possible to specify up to 31 archive destinations, giving you that many copies of each filled online redo log file. This is perhaps excessive for safety.

One archive destination? Good idea. Two destinations? Sure, why not? But *30?*

The reason for so many possible destinations is distributed systems. For the purposes of this book and the OCP exam, an archive log destination will always be a directory on the machine hosting the database—and two destinations on local disks will usually be sufficient. But the destination can be an Oracle Net alias, specifying the address of a listener on a remote computer. This is the key to zero data loss: The redo stream can be shipped across the network to a remote database, where it can be applied to give a real-time backup. This is the Data Guard mechanism.

Backup and Recovery: Configuration

Configuring a database for recoverability means ensuring that certain critical files are multiplexed. These files are the online redo log files and the controlfile. Adjusting the online redo log file configuration is an online operation, whereas adjusting the controlfile configuration requires a shutdown/startup.

 TIP A point of terminology: some DBAs say that a database should have multiple controlfiles, whereas others will say that it should have multiple copies of the controlfile. This book uses the latter terminology. The Oracle documentation is inconsistent.

To determine the names and locations of the controlfile copies, query either a view or a parameter.

```
orclz> select name from v$controlfile;
NAME
----------------------------------------------------
C:\APP\ORACLE\ORADATA\ORCLZ\CONTROL01.CTL
C:\APP\ORACLE\FAST_RECOVERY_AREA\ORCLZ\CONTROL02.CTL

orclz> select value from v$parameter2
where name='control_files';
VALUE
----------------------------------------------------
C:\APP\ORACLE\ORADATA\ORCLZ\CONTROL01.CTL
C:\APP\ORACLE\FAST_RECOVERY_AREA\ORCLZ\CONTROL02.CTL
orclz>
```

The preceding queries show that this database is running with two copies of the controlfile.

Exercise 22-1: Investigate and Adjust the Redo Log Configuration In this exercise, you will investigate the configuration of the redo log.

1. Connect to your database as user SYSTEM using SQL*Plus.

2. Document the configuration of redo log with this query:
   ```
   select * from v$log join v$logfile using (group#);
   ```
   This will show the log file members, their status, their size, and the group to which they belong. If your database is the default database, it will have three groups each of one member, with a size of 50MB.

3. Determine the archivelog mode of the database and whether ARC*n* is running with these commands:
   ```
   select log_mode from v$database;
   select archiver from v$instance;
   ```
   Note that the mode is an attribute of the database, but archiving is an attribute of the instance.

4. Add another member to each of the online log file groups. Choose any directory and filename suitable for your operating system. For example, following the situation described in Figure 22-1, the commands could be as follows:
   ```
   alter database add logfile member
   'c:\app\oracle\oradata\orclz\redo01a.log' to group 1;
   alter database add logfile member
   'c:\app\oracle\oradata\orclz\redo02a.log' to group 2;
   alter database add logfile member
   'c:\app\oracle\oradata\orclz\redo03a.log' to group 3;
   ```

5. Run this query to check the status of your log file members:
   ```
   select * from v$logfile;
   ```
   Note that the new members will be INVALID.

6. Cycle through the log file groups by executing this command a few times:
   ```
   alter system switch logfile;
   ```

7. Rerun the query from step 5. The status of each member should now have cleared. If it is still invalid, something is wrong. Look at the database instance alert log to diagnose what the problem might be.

Configure the Fast Recovery Area

The Fast Recovery Area is a disk destination used as the default location for recovery-related files. It is controlled with two instance parameters:

- db_recovery_file_dest
- db_recovery_file_dest_size

The first of these parameters nominates the location. This can be a file system directory or an Automatic Storage Management (ASM) disk group. It is possible for several databases to share a common destination; each database will have its own directory structure (created automatically) in the destination. The second parameter limits the amount of space in the destination that the database will occupy; it says nothing about how much space is actually available in the destination. The configuration and usage of the Fast Recovery Area are shown in two views:

- v$recovery_file_dest
- v$recovery_area_usage

TIP   Release 10.*x* introduced the *Flash* Recovery Area. In release 11.2.*x*, it was renamed to the *Fast Recovery Area* (a major upgrade). Some old views (and some old DBAs) still use the original name.

The files that will be written to the Fast Recovery Area (unless specified otherwise) include the following:

- Recovery Manager backups
- Archive redo log files
- Database flashback logs

RMAN, the Recovery Manager, can manage space within the flash recovery area; it can delete files that are no longer needed according to its configured policies for retaining copies and backup of files. In an ideal situation, the Fast Recovery Area will be large enough to store a complete copy of the database, plus any archive logs and incremental backups that would be necessary to recover the copy plus multiplexed copies of the online redo log files and the controlfile.

The database backup routines should also include backing up the Fast Recovery Area to tape, thus implementing a strategy of primary, secondary, and tertiary storage.

- Primary storage is the live database, on disk.
- Secondary storage is a disk-based copy of the database plus files needed for fast recovery.
- Tertiary storage is long-term backups, usually in a tape library.

RMAN can manage the whole cycle, namely, backup of the database from primary to secondary and migration of backups from secondary to tertiary storage. Such a system can be implemented in a fashion that will allow near-instant recovery following a failure, combined with the ability to take the database back in time if this is ever necessary.

The Fast Recovery Area can be reconfigured at any time, without affecting any files within it. Changes will apply only to files created subsequently. Figure 22-2 shows how to determine the Fast Recovery Area configuration, followed by statements to adjust both its location and its size.

Configure ARCHIVELOG Mode

A database is, by default, created in noarchivelog mode. The transition to archivelog mode is straightforward, but it does require downtime. The process is as follows:

1. Shut down the database cleanly.

2. Start up in mount mode.

3. Issue the command ALTER DATABASE ARCHIVELOG;.

4. Open the database.

5. Perform a full backup.

Following a default installation, the archive logs will be written to only one destination, which will be the Fast Recovery Area. This is specified by an implicit setting for the LOG_ARCHIVE_DEST_1 parameter, visible in the V$ARCHIVE_DEST view. If the parameters that enable the

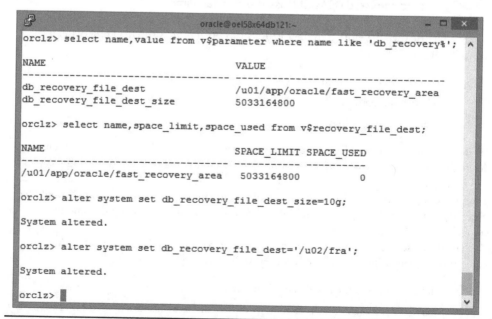

```
oracle@oel58x64db121:~
orclz> select name,value from v$parameter where name like 'db_recovery%';

NAME                                      VALUE
---------------------------------------   ------------------------------------
db_recovery_file_dest                     /u01/app/oracle/fast_recovery_area
db_recovery_file_dest_size                5033164800

orclz> select name,space_limit,space_used from v$recovery_file_dest;

NAME                                      SPACE_LIMIT SPACE_USED
---------------------------------------   ----------- ----------
/u01/app/oracle/fast_recovery_area        5033164800           0

orclz> alter system set db_recovery_file_dest_size=10g;

System altered.

orclz> alter system set db_recovery_file_dest='/u02/fra';

System altered.

orclz>
```

Figure 22-2   Determining the Fast Recovery Area configuration

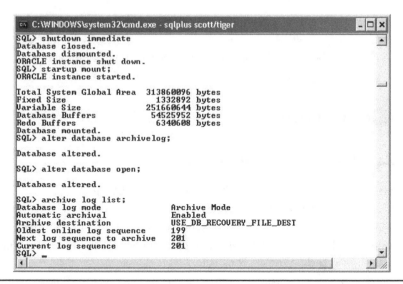

```
C:\WINDOWS\system32\cmd.exe - sqlplus scott/tiger                    _ □ ×
SQL> shutdown immediate
Database closed.
Database dismounted.
ORACLE instance shut down.
SQL> startup mount;
ORACLE instance started.

Total System Global Area   313860096 bytes
Fixed Size                    1332892 bytes
Variable Size               251660644 bytes
Database Buffers             54525952 bytes
Redo Buffers                  6340608 bytes
Database mounted.
SQL> alter database archivelog;

Database altered.

SQL> alter database open;

Database altered.

SQL> archive log list;
Database log mode              Archive Mode
Automatic archival             Enabled
Archive destination            USE_DB_RECOVERY_FILE_DEST
Oldest online log sequence     199
Next log sequence to archive   201
Current log sequence           201
SQL> _
```

Figure 22-3   Enabling and verifying archivelog mode with SQL*Plus

Fast Recovery Area have not been set, they will go to a platform-specific destination (the $ORACLE_HOME/dbs directory for Unix systems). The final command in Figure 22-3, ARCHIVE LOG LIST, shows summary information about the archiving configuration, including that the database is running in archivelog mode, that the ARC*n* process is running, and that the archive log files are being written to the fast recovery area.

 EXAM TIP   The change to archivelog mode can be done only in mount mode after a clean shutdown.

A full backup is an essential step for the transition to archivelog mode. Following the transition, all backups made earlier are useless. The backup can be made while the database is open or closed, but until it is made, the database is not protected at all.

 TIP   If the shutdown is not clean (for instance, SHUTDOWN ABORT), the transition will fail. That's not a problem—open the database and shut it down again, this time cleanly.

Exercise 22-2: Enable Archivelog Mode   In this exercise, you will transition your database into archivelog mode. This is an essential procedure for completing later chapters on backup and recovery.

1. Connect to your database with Database Control as user SYS. (Why SYS? Because you will have to stop and start the instance.)

2. Follow the steps shown in Figure 22-3 to enable archivelog mode.

3. Confirm that archiving is working by forcing a log switch and an archive.

```
alter system archive log current;
```

4. Confirm that the archive log file has been generated in the fast recovery area.

```
select name,is_recovery_dest_file from v$archived_log;
```

Two-Minute Drill

Possible Failures and Their Resolution

- SQL failures will usually be repaired by the users and developers.
- Instance failure may result in data corruptions, but the automatic instance recovery process will always repair these—as long as the online redo log files are available.
- Damage to files requires DBA action to repair. This will usually be restoring the database from backup and applying redo.
- Recovery from instance failure is automatic and unstoppable. If it fails (typically because of a problem with the online log files), then the database cannot be opened.

Checkpoints and the Redo Log

- Checkpointing refers to the writing of buffers from buffer cache to datafiles by the DBWn proesses. A full checkpoint writes all changed (aka dirty) buffers to disk.
- Full checkpoints occur only on demand or as part of an orderly shutdown. Partial checkpoints (all dirty buffers of a datafile or a segment) occur automatically in response to various events.
- Incremental checkpoints are part of normal database operation. The DBWn writes buffers to disk to make the buffers available for reuse, using an algorithm optimized to minimize the writing workload.
- The online redo log files contain change vectors applied recently to buffers in cache. They are required for instance recovery. When an online log file group is filled, it will be copied to an archive log file. At that point, it becomes available for reuse.
- Archive log files are not reused. They are an unbroken record of all changes applied to data blocks and used for database recovery following a restore operation.

Configure the Fast Recovery Area

- The Fast Recovery Area is an optional disk destination used for storing recovery-related files. These include multiplexed copies of online log files and the controlfile, archive log files, and RMAN backups.
- Space within the FRA is (to an extent) automatically managed. It will usually stabilize in an almost full state, and Oracle will then, when necessary, delete older files that are no longer required for recovery as more space is required for newer files.

- The FRA is configured with two instance parameters. DB_RECOVERY_FILE_DEST_SIZE sets a space budget, and DBA_RECOVERY_FILE_DEST specifies the root of the FRA directory. The parameters must be set in this order.

- Within the FRA, no manual management is possible. Oracle takes full control of creating and removing files and directories.

- The parameters are dynamic, meaning that the FRA can be resized or relocated at any time.

Configure ARCHIVELOG Mode

- The transition to archivelog mode must be done while the database is mounted, following a clean shutdown.

- In archive log mode, when the database is opened, archive processes will copy filled online log files to archive log files.

Configure Control Files and Redo Log Files for Recoverability

- The controlfile is small but vital. It contains pointers to all other database files and the archive log files, as well as critical information regarding the state of the database.

- The location is specified by the CONTROL_FILES instance parameter. The parameter is static and can therefore be changed only with a SCOPE=SPFILE clause; the change will come into effect after the next shutdown/startup.

- To add a controlfile copy, the database must be shut down. It is not possible to copy the controlfile while it is in use.

- If the online redo log is damaged following an instance failure, it will not be possible to open the database. This is because the online redo log is used to repair an instance failure.

- It is vitally important to multiplex the online log, in other words, to create multiple copies of the members that make up the online log file groups.

- Members can be added to an online log file group at any time while the database is open. Members can be removed, as long as there is always at least one member of each group.

Self Test

1. When will a full checkpoint occur? (Choose all correct answers.)

   A. As part of a NORMAL shutdown

   B. As part of an IMMEDIATE shutdown

   C. When a tablespace is taken offline

   D. When a log switch occurs

2. Which of these operations cannot be accomplished while the database is open? (Choose all correct answers.)

A. Adding a controlfile copy

B. Adding an online log file member

C. Changing the location of the flash recovery area

D. Changing the archivelog mode of the database

3. Which of these files is *not* required for instance recovery? (Choose the best answer.)

A. Archive log files

B. Controlfile

C. Datafiles

D. Online log files

4. If the database is in archivelog mode, what will happen if the archiving fails for any reason? (Choose the best answer.)

A. The instance will abort.

B. All non-SYSDBA sessions will hang.

C. DML operations will hang.

D. The database will revert to noarchivelog mode.

5. To configure the database for recoverability, which files types can (and should) be multiplexed? (Choose three answers.)

A. Archive redo log file

B. Controlfile

C. Online redo log file

D. Server parameter file

E. System tablespace datafile

F. Undo tablespace datafile

6. What file types will, by default, be stored in the flash recovery area if it has been defined? (Choose all correct answers.)

A. Archive redo log files

B. Background process trace files

C. RMAN backup sets

D. RMAN image copies

E. Undo data

7. Several steps are involved in transitioning to archivelog mode. Put these in the correct order:

    1   alter database archivelog
    2   alter database open
    3   alter system archive log start
    4   full backup
    5   shutdown immediate
    6   startup mount

    A. 5, 6, 1, 2, 4; 3 not necessary

    B. 5, 4, 6, 1, 2, 3

    C. 6, 1, 3, 5, 4, 2

    D. 1, 5, 4, 6, 2; 3 not necessary

    E. 5, 6, 1, 2, 3; 4 not necessary

8. What conditions must hold before an online log file member can be reused if the database is operating in archivelog mode? (Choose all correct answers.)

    A. It must be inactive.

    B. It must be multiplexed.

    C. It must be archived.

    D. The archive must be multiplexed.

9. Which of the following tablespaces are required in an installation of Oracle Database 12*c*? (Choose all that apply.)

    A. USERS

    B. SYSTEM

    C. SYSAUX

    D. TEMP

    E. UNDOTBS1

    F. RMAN

10. What is the maximum number of database writer processes (DBW*n*) in an Oracle database instance?

    A. 1.

    B. 100.

    C. 20.

    D. None; database writer processes exist only in an ASM instance.

11. Which of the following failures would be considered user errors? (Choose all that apply.)

    A. The intern just got a user account on the database and tries to update her own salary in the HR.EMPLOYEES table.

    B. Because of a power outage, the report server goes down during the overnight report batch window and is not able to generate most of the daily reports.

    C. Several users think the database has been upgraded to Oracle Database 12c and try to create a table with a VARCHAR2 column of more than 4,000 characters.

    D. The Linux administrator accidentally kills an OS process belonging to a database user who is trying to run a SELECT statement against the data warehouse.

    E. A data warehouse programmer enters the server room and removes a network card from the primary database server.

12. Which Oracle HA technology would be best suited for near-real-time failover in the case of a complete media failure of all disks in the primary database?

    A. Logical standby database

    B. Oracle Active Data Guard read-only access

    C. Oracle flashback database

    D. Oracle Active Data Guard physical standby

Self Test Answers

1. ☑ **A** and **B**. Any orderly shutdown will trigger a full checkpoint.
    ☒ **C** and **D** are incorrect. **C** is incorrect because this would trigger only a partial checkpoint. **D** is incorrect because log switches do not trigger checkpoints.

2. ☑ **A** and **D**. Anything to do with the controlfile can be done only in nomount or shutdown mode. Changing the archivelog mode can be done only in mount mode.
    ☒ **B** and **C** are incorrect. **B** is incorrect because the online redo log can be configured while the database is open. **C** is incorrect because DB_RECOVERY_FILE_DEST is a dynamic parameter.

3. ☑ **A**. Archive log files are used for media recovery, not instance recovery.
    ☒ **B**, **C**, and **D** are incorrect. **B** is incorrect because the controlfile stores the critical values needed to determine the checkpoint position and control the recovery. **C** and **D** are incorrect because during instance recovery change vectors from the online log files are used to update blocks read from the datafiles.

4. ☑ **C**. Once all the online log files need archiving, DML commands will be blocked.
    ☒ **A**, **B**, and **D** are incorrect. **A** is incorrect because the instance will remain open. **B** is incorrect because only sessions that attempt DML will hang; those running SELECTs can continue. **D** is incorrect because this cannot happen automatically.

5. ☑ **A**, **B**, and **C**. These file types can all be multiplexed, with Oracle ensuring that copies are identical.
   ☒ **D**, **E**, and **F** are incorrect. These files cannot be multiplexed by Oracle (although you can, of course, mirror them with operating system facilities or with ASM).

6. ☑ **A**, **C**, and **D**. These will go to the flash recovery area, unless directed elsewhere.
   ☒ **B** and **E** are incorrect. **B** is incorrect because background trace files will go to a directory in the DIAGNOSTIC_DEST directory. **E** is incorrect because undo data is stored in the undo tablespace.

7. ☑ **A**. This is the correct sequence.
   ☒ **B**, **C**, **D**, and **E** are incorrect. **B**, **C**, and **E** are incorrect because enabling archiving is not necessary (it will occur automatically). **D** is incorrect because the database must be in mount mode to issue the ALTER DATABASE ARCHIVELOG statement.

8. ☑ **A** and **C**. These are the two conditions.
   ☒ **B** and **D** are incorrect. Although these are certainly good practices, they are not requirements.

9. ☑ **B** and **C**. Both the SYSTEM and SYSAUX tablespaces are required.
   ☒ **A**, **D**, **E**, and **F** are incorrect. While the USERS tablespace is highly desirable for placing application tables in its own tablespace, it is not required; TEMP, USERS, and UNDOTBS1 are created in a default installation of Oracle Database 12c. No RMAN tablespace is created, nor is it required in an installation of Oracle Database 12c.

10. ☑ **B**. The database writer processes are DBW0 through DBW9 and, if needed, DBWa through DBWz and BW36 through BW99 (for a total of 100) on most operating system platforms.
    ☒ **A**, **C**, and **D** are incorrect. Database writers exist only in an RDBMS instance.

11. ☑ **A** and **C**. User errors are typically logical errors with SQL syntax, permissions on database objects, or trying to use features not available in the current version of the database.
    ☒ **B**, **D**, and **E** are incorrect. **B** is a process failure since the client (in this case, the batch report generator) has failed and disconnects from the database. **D** is a user process failure except that the user's process fails because an OS administrator killed the incorrect process. If the OS administrator had killed a global database process, the failure would likely be considered an instance failure instead. **E** is a hardware or network failure, not a user failure. The user will likely be looking for a job somewhere else.

12. ☑ **D**. Oracle Active Data Guard physical standby continuously applies archived redo log files on one or more (up to 30) remote locations (standby locations) and can be configured to almost instantaneously take over the role of the primary database in case of a catastrophic failure of the primary database. Any standby location can be configured to apply the archived redo logs after a predefined delay to avoid potential

logical corruptions to the database even if there is not a catastrophic failure of the primary database.

☒   **A**, **B**, and **C** are incorrect. **A** is suitable for read-write access to report writers or developers but will not be an exact physical copy of the primary database. **B** is incorrect because using an Active Data Guard database for read-only queries is not providing a failover after a catastrophic failure, but instead supplements the primary database for offloading some or all of the reporting workload. **C** is a viable option for recovering a database, tablespace, or individual database object to a previous state, but does not provide real-time failover from a failure of the primary database.

CHAPTER 23

Back Up with RMAN

Exam Objectives

- 63.1.1.1 Explain Oracle Backup and Recovery Solutions
- 63.1.2.1 Back Up and Recover a NOARCHIVELOG Database
- 63.1.3.1 Configure and Manage RMAN Settings
- 63.1.4.1 Create and Use an RMAN Recovery Catalog
- 63.1.5.1 Use Various RMAN Backup Types and Strategies
- 63.1.6.1 Perform Full and Incremental Backups
- 63.1.6.2 Manage Backups
- 63.1.7.1 Use Techniques to Improve Backups

Even though the list of exam objectives for this chapter is long, most of the objectives involve adding just one or two keywords to your BACKUP command. Using the Recovery Manager (RMAN) tool is straightforward, and with a little practice you will become familiar with all its functions.

Backup Theory and Basic Syntax

There are a few simple choices to be made when performing a database backup, including what you want to back up and how you will do it. Then to perform the backup, you must run the appropriate RMAN commands. It is possible to perform backups without using RMAN. Such techniques are known as *user-managed* backups as opposed to RMAN's server-managed backups. User-managed backups are perfectly valid and fully supported but are not covered in the examinations because Oracle's approved tool for backup and recovery is RMAN.

Using RMAN can be simple or somewhat complex. To reduce the complexity, most database administrators (DBAs) will make use of stored configuration parameters. These set defaults for all operations and means that complex jobs can be performed with simple commands.

Backup Concepts

The database on which backup or restore operations are to be carried out is known as the *target*. In some environments there will be many databases and therefore many RMAN targets. You will connect to each database in turn. Every backup of a target will have certain attributes:

- Open or closed
- Whole or partial
- Full or incremental
- To disk or to tape
- Copy or backupset

Any combination of these attributes is possible, but depending on the environment and configuration, you may be limited to only a subset of these attributes. In all cases, the backup is accomplished by Oracle server processes launched in response to commands issued within the RMAN executable user process.

RMAN Architecture

The RMAN executable is a user process like any other. It logs on to an Oracle database (the target database) either locally using interprocess communication (IPC) or remotely using Transmission Control Protocol (TCP) and a database listener. Once connected, the user can issue commands to carry out backup and restore operations. These operations are performed by additional Oracle server processes launched as necessary, known as *channels*. A channel is a server process like any other, but its function is restricted to copying files.

A major feature of RMAN is its use of a *repository*. The RMAN repository consists of metadata regarding backups. This includes details of what has been backed up, where the backup files are, what archive logfiles exist, what persistent configuration settings have been made, and everything RMAN will ever need to understand the database and the backups such that restore and recovery operations can be fully automated. The repository exists in either one or two places. A copy of the repository is always stored on the target database controlfile. Relying solely on this can potentially have two issues. First, information can be stored for only a limited period. Specifically, this is the number of days specified by the CONTROLFILE_ RECORD_KEEP_TIME instance parameter, which defaults to seven days. If you are using only the controlfile-based repository, you will probably want to adjust this to allow RMAN to "remember" information for a longer period. For example, to raise this period to a month, you'd use the following:

```
SQL>
SQL> sho parameter keep_time
NAME                                 TYPE        VALUE
------------------------------------ ----------- --------------------
control_file_record_keep_time        integer     7
SQL>
SQL> alter system set control_file_record_keep_time=30;
System altered.
SQL>
```

RMAN can also use a secondary storage location for the repository in the form of an Oracle database. This requires creating a schema in the database known as the RMAN *catalog*. The catalog should be created in a database used solely for this purpose. The catalog can record metadata for many targets and acts as a central repository of all backup information. When using a catalog, there is no effective limit to the time frame for which backup information can be stored. Using a catalog also enables some of the more advanced RMAN features.

An RMAN backup can be directed to a disk location or to a tape location. Backup to disk is always available and requires no configuration. To use a tape device, RMAN needs assistance from the hardware manufacturer. This is in the form of a dynamically linked library, provided (and almost certainly charged for) by the hardware vendor. For example, if you are going to use an automated tape library manufactured by IBM, you will need to buy IBM's Tivoli Storage Manager agent for Oracle. This code will allow RMAN to drive the tape library. Within the RMAN environment, there is minimal difference when using tape devices. RMAN conceals all the complexity of managing third-party hardware from the DBA.

RMAN can create two types of backup: *image copies* and *backupsets*. An image copy backup generates an output file that is byte-for-byte identical to the input file. A backupset is a more intelligent structure. It can combine several input files into one output file, it will not include blocks of the input files that have never been used, it can be compressed and encrypted, and it can be divided into multiple *pieces*. The pieces are the physical files that make up the backupset.

Backing Up in One Page

An open (aka *hot* or *inconsistent*) backup is performed while the database is in use. It is impossible to perform an open backup unless the database is in archivelog mode. This is because any backup of an open file will be inconsistent. It will take an appreciable period of time to read the file and write the copy, and during this time the file is being updated. Therefore, the copy will not represent a stable version of the file. In archive log mode, this is not a problem because the redo log stream will have a record of all changes applied to the file in the form of the change vectors that were applied to the Oracle blocks while the backup was in progress. If it is ever necessary to restore the file from the backup, the information in the redo stream can be used to make the inconsistent backup usable by applying these changes. If the database were not in archivelog mode, the redo from the time the backup was made would not be available. A closed (aka *cold* or *consistent*) backup is performed while the database is in mount mode. The controlfile must be mounted for RMAN to have access to its repository. Closed backups are consistent; the datafiles are stable. Closed backup is the only type of backup possible if the database is in noarchivelog mode.

A whole backup is the entire set of datafiles and the controlfile. A partial backup is a subset of the database. Whole backup is the only type of backup possible in noarchivelog mode. This is because to open a database, all datafiles must be consistent up to the same system change number (SCN). If the backup consists of several partial backups, each partial backup will be at a different SCN, and following a restore, redo data is required to bring all the backups up to the same SCN. This redo data would not be available in noarchivelog mode.

A full backup contains every used block of every file. An incremental backup has only those blocks that have been changed since the last backup. An incremental backup strategy must start with a full backup, followed by as many incrementals as you like, but a restore will always require first restoring the full backup (known as the *level 0* backup) and then applying the incremental backups to bring the files up to date. Only after a new level 0 backup is taken can any of the previous backups be discarded.

RMAN Basic Syntax

The RMAN executable connects to the target database and (optionally) to a catalog database, if it has been configured. Consider these commands, executed from an operating system prompt:

```
rman target /
rman target sys/oracle
rman target sys/oracle@orclz
```

All three will log on to a target database as user SYS with the SYSDBA privilege. In the first case, the target will be a local database instance running on the same machine, identified by the ORACLE_SID environment variable, and the user is authenticated by their operating system account. The second example also connects to a local database instance but authenticates using the database password file. The third example connects to a remote database across a network using a tnsnames service name and will also use password file authentication.

Once connected, you can issue ad hoc SQL commands against the target database just as you would within a SQL*Plus session (though the display of results may not be the same, and some SQL*Plus commands, such as those for formatting columns, are not available) or issue RMAN commands for backup and restore operations.

Backing Up in Noarchivelog Mode

Backing up in noarchivelog mode can be accomplished only in mount mode. Consider the example in Figure 23-1.

In the figure, from a Windows operating system prompt the user launches the RMAN executable, connecting to a local database using operating system authentication. Once connected

```
 ▫      —  ⊡  ×
                          Command Prompt

C:\Users\john>
C:\Users\john>rman target /

Recovery Manager: Release 12.1.0.2.0 - Production on Sat Jan 17 18:02:04 2015

Copyright (c) 1982, 2014, Oracle and/or its affiliates.  All rights reserved.

connected to target database: ORCLZ (DBID=2090971366)

RMAN> shutdown immediate;

using target database control file instead of recovery catalog
database closed
database dismounted
Oracle instance shut down

RMAN> startup mount;

connected to target database (not started)
Oracle instance started
database mounted

Total System Global Area    1048576000 bytes

Fixed Size                     3053584 bytes
Variable Size                734005232 bytes
Database Buffers             306184192 bytes
Redo Buffers                   5332992 bytes

RMAN> backup database;

Starting backup at 2015-01-17:18:03:40
allocated channel: ORA_DISK_1
channel ORA_DISK_1: SID=241 device type=DISK
channel ORA_DISK_1: starting full datafile backup set
channel ORA_DISK_1: specifying datafile(s) in backup set
input datafile file number=00007 name=C:\APP\ORACLE\ORADATA\ORCLZ\DATAFILE\O1_MF_E
input datafile file number=00003 name=C:\APP\ORACLE\ORADATA\ORCLZ\DATAFILE\O1_MF_S
input datafile file number=00001 name=C:\APP\ORACLE\ORADATA\ORCLZ\DATAFILEZSYSTEM1
input datafile file number=00005 name=C:\APP\ORACLE\ORADATA\ORCLZ\DATAFILE\O1_MF_U
input datafile file number=00006 name=C:\APP\ORACLE\ORADATA\ORCLZ\DATAFILE\USRES.D
channel ORA_DISK_1: starting piece 1 at 2015-01-17:18:03:40
channel ORA_DISK_1: finished piece 1 at 2015-01-17:18:04:05
piece handle=C:\APP\ORACLE\FAST_RECOVERY_AREA\ORCLZ\BACKUPSET\2015_01_17\O1_MF_NNN
117T180340 comment=NONE
channel ORA_DISK_1: backup set complete, elapsed time: 00:00:25
channel ORA_DISK_1: starting full datafile backup set
channel ORA_DISK_1: specifying datafile(s) in backup set
including current control file in backup set
including current SPFILE in backup set
channel ORA_DISK_1: starting piece 1 at 2015-01-17:18:04:07
channel ORA_DISK_1: finished piece 1 at 2015-01-17:18:04:08
piece handle=C:\APP\ORACLE\FAST_RECOVERY_AREA\ORCLZ\BACKUPSET\2015_01_17\O1_MF_NCS
117T180340 comment=NONE
channel ORA_DISK_1: backup set complete, elapsed time: 00:00:01
Finished backup at 2015-01-17:18:04:08

RMAN> alter database open;

Statement processed

RMAN> exit


Recovery Manager complete.

C:\Users\john>_
<                                                                    >
```

Figure 23-1   A closed, whole, full backup with RMAN

and at the RMAN> prompt, the user shuts down the database with the IMMEDIATE option and restarts in mount mode. Then the BACKUP DATABASE command (which is run completely on defaults) automatically launches a channel process named ORA_DISK_1 that will generate backupsets on disk, identifies the five datafiles that make up the database, backs them up into a single piece located in the Fast Recovery Area, and backs up the controlfile and the spfile into a second backupset. Then the user opens the database and exits from the tool. This is an example of a whole-closed full backup. Incremental backup is a possibility, but all noarchivelog mode backups must be whole and closed.

Backup Possibilities in Archivelog Mode

The following are some simple backup commands:

```
BACKUP DATAFILE 1,2;
BACKUP TABLESPACE USERS,EXAMPLE;
BACKUP CURRENT CONTROLFILE;
BACKUP DATABASE;
BACKUP ARCHIVELOG ALL;
```

A partial backup specification can be a list of one or more datafiles (identified either by filename or by file number), one or more tablespaces, or the controlfile. A whole backup is the entire database. Archive logfiles can (and should) also be backed up, meaning either all of the archive logfiles or a subset of the archive logfiles. It is also possible (as in the example following) to remove the archive logfiles as they are backed up. The default backup destination is to disk, specifically, to files (the backup pieces of backupsets) in the Fast Recovery Area.

Usually single-line commands will not be sufficient. To chain several commands together, you must group them into a block. A block is preceded by RUN and enclosed with {}. Consider the example in Figure 23-2.

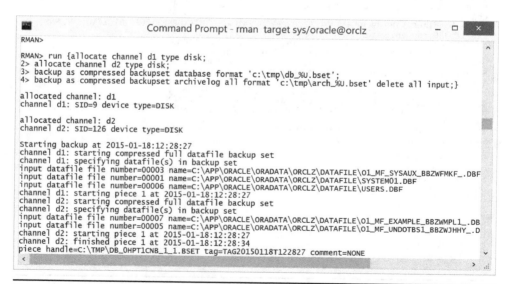

Figure 23-2 An open, whole, full backup—including archive logfile backup and deletion

The first two commands in the run block are ALLOCATE CHANNEL. Allocating a channel launches a server process. Each channel needs a name (just an arbitrary string, in this example D1 and D2) and must specify whether it will be using tape or disk as the backup destination (in the example, disk). Launching multiple channels enables parallelism for the backup. RMAN will distribute the workload across the channels, as shown later in the output: Datafiles 3, 1, and 6 are being backed up by channel D1, while channel D2 backs up datafiles 7 and 5. The third line in the run block specifies a whole database backup, using FORMAT to nominate the output piece name. The fourth line specifies that all the archive logfiles should be backed up and deleted. The FORMAT specification includes %U. This is a variable that will be expanded into a name that includes an eight-character random string to ensure that if the block is run many times, different piece names will always be generated. The type of backup is COMPRESSED BACKUPSET. Compression will generally not only reduce the size of the backup pieces but also improve the speed of the operation. In most circumstances, the bottleneck in backup is writing the backup pieces, and compression means that there is much less data to write.

The default backup type is a backupset. The alternative is the image copy. To create copies, use commands such as these:

```
BACKUP AS COPY DATAFILE '/u01/oradata/orcl/system1.dbf'
FORMAT '/u02/backup/orcl/system01.dbf';
BACKUP AS COPY DATABASE;
```

The first command shown copies one datafile to a named destination. The second command copies the entire database to the default destination, which is the Fast Recovery Area.

Any backup command (whether creating backupsets or image copies) can be parallelized if it is executed within a run block that launches multiple channels. Note that the parallelism is only within a backup command, not across backup commands. So in Figure 23-2, the backup of the database is parallelized, and only when that is completed will the archive logfiles be backed up, again by two processes in parallel. If multiple files are specified for one channel, the files are read concurrently and interleaved in the backupset, but there is no parallelism at that level; the channel process cycles through its list of files, reading blocks from each in turn.

Backing up to tape rather than to a disk destination requires configuring the Media Management Layer (MML). This is the dynamic link library provided by the hardware manufacturer and will be product specific. Then within RMAN, you must launch tape channels. For example:

```
RUN { ALLOCATE CHANNEL T1 TYPE SBT;
ALLOCATE CHANNEL T2 TYPE SBT
BACKUP DATABASE; }
```

This block will launch two tape channels (the SBT keyword stands for System Backup to Tape and instructs RMAN to link the MML library into the channel process) that will back up the database to the tape library. You would usually relate the number of channels to the number of tape drives in the library. In most cases, using tape devices is considerably more complicated than this, with many platform-specific options that must be specified.

PART IV

Persistent RMAN Settings

RMAN run blocks (and stored scripts) can get quite long and awkward, if the defaults are not adequate. The ability to store persistent configuration settings lets the DBA modify the defaults. They can then run simple commands, which RMAN will automatically modify at run-time.

Setting and Clearing Default Values

To see the default settings, use the SHOW ALL command. For example:

```
RMAN> show all;
RMAN configuration parameters for database with db_unique_name ORCLZ are:
CONFIGURE RETENTION POLICY TO REDUNDANCY 1; # default
CONFIGURE BACKUP OPTIMIZATION OFF; # default
CONFIGURE DEFAULT DEVICE TYPE TO DISK; # default
CONFIGURE CONTROLFILE AUTOBACKUP OFF; # default
CONFIGURE CONTROLFILE AUTOBACKUP FORMAT FOR DEVICE TYPE DISK TO '%F'; #
default
CONFIGURE DEVICE TYPE DISK PARALLELISM 1 BACKUP TYPE TO BACKUPSET; # default
CONFIGURE DATAFILE BACKUP COPIES FOR DEVICE TYPE DISK TO 1; # default
CONFIGURE ARCHIVELOG BACKUP COPIES FOR DEVICE TYPE DISK TO 1; # default
CONFIGURE MAXSETSIZE TO UNLIMITED; # default
CONFIGURE ENCRYPTION FOR DATABASE OFF; # default
CONFIGURE ENCRYPTION ALGORITHM 'AES128'; # default
CONFIGURE COMPRESSION ALGORITHM 'BASIC' AS OF RELEASE 'DEFAULT' OPTIMIZE FOR
LOAD TRUE ; # default
CONFIGURE RMAN OUTPUT TO KEEP FOR 7 DAYS; # default
CONFIGURE ARCHIVELOG DELETION POLICY TO NONE; # default
CONFIGURE SNAPSHOT CONTROLFILE NAME TO 'C:\APP\ORACLE\PRODUCT\12.1.0\
DBHOME_1\DATABASE\SNCFORCLZ.ORA'
RMAN>
```

Consider these defaults in order:

- RETENTION POLICY specifies what backups RMAN should attempt to create and when they can be deleted. The default is one copy of every file.

- OPTIMIZATION determines whether RMAN should back up files on request, even if sufficient backups already exist. The default is to back them up anyway.

- DEFAULT DEVICE TYPE TO DISK means that unless directed otherwise, RMAN will launch only disk channels and will not write to tape.

- CONTROLFILE AUTOBACKUP OFF prevents RMAN from automatically backing up the controlfile as part of any other backup operation.

- AUTOBACKUP FORMAT generates a name and location for the controlfile autobackups, if they have been enabled.

- DEVICE TYPE DISK PARALLELISM 1 BACKUP TYPE TO BACKUPSET means that by default only one channel will be launched when performing a backup to disk and that the backup will be to an uncompressed backupset.

- BACKUP COPIES specifies how many copies of backupsets should be generated when backing up datafiles and archive logfiles.

- MAXSETSIZE can restrict the size of each backupset. If this size is reached, the backupset piece(s) will be closed, and the backup will continue into a new backupset.

- ENCRYPTION of backupsets is disabled by default.

- COMPRESSION (if requested) will use the BASIC algorithm, which is license free.

- RMAN OUTPUT controls how long to keep the results of an RMAN job in tables in the RMAN repository.

- ARCHIVELOG DELETION POLICY allows RMAN to delete automatically archivelogs that are no longer needed, according to various criteria.

- SNAPSHOT CONTROLFILE specifies a name and location to be used for a temporary copy of the controlfile created as part of the controlfile backup mechanism.

When designing a backup strategy, an example of the requirements could be as follows: It must always be possible to restore the database to any time in the last two weeks; do not create any more backups than are needed to achieve this goal; backups will go to disk, using degree of parallelism of four channels; the controlfile must always be included with any backup; backups will be as compressed backupsets, stored in the directory c:\db_backups; backupset pieces will be named according to the name of the database, the date of the backup, and a unique string; and archivelogs will be deleted when they have been backed up to disk twice. To configure this requirement, these are the commands to run:

```
configure retention policy to recovery window of 14 days;
configure backup optimization on;
configure controlfile autobackup on;
configure device type disk parallelism 4 backup type to compressed backupset;
configure channel device type disk format 'c:\db_backups\%d_%T_%u';
configure archivelog deletion policy to backed up 2 times to disk;
```

Using SHOW ALL will then display the new values. These two simple commands are now all that is necessary to meet the requirement:

```
backup database;
backup archivelog all delete input;
```

Persistent configuration settings are configured for each target database and stored in the RMAN repository, specifically, in the target database's controlfile and the recovery catalog if one has been created. To return them to the defaults, connect to the target and issue CLEAR commands.

```
configure retention policy clear;
configure backup optimization clear;
configure controlfile autobackup clear;
configure device type disk clear;
configure channel device type disk clear;
configure archivelog deletion policy clear;
```

Using a Retention Policy

Backups can be automatically retained and managed using a *recovery window* or using *redundancy*. Using a recovery window, RMAN will retain as many backups as necessary to bring the database to any point in time within the recovery window. For example, with a recovery window of seven days, RMAN will maintain enough image copies, incremental backups, and archived redo logs to ensure that the database can be restored and recovered to any point in time within the last seven days. Any backups that are not needed to support this recovery window are marked as OBSOLETE and are automatically removed by RMAN if you are using a Fast Recovery Area and disk space is needed for new backups.

In contrast, a redundancy retention policy directs RMAN to retain the specified number of backups. Any extra copies or backups beyond the number specified in the redundancy policy are marked as OBSOLETE. As with a recovery window, obsolete backups are automatically removed if disk space is needed and the Fast Recovery Area is used. Otherwise, you can use the DELETE OBSOLETE command to manually remove backup files and update the catalog.

If the retention policy is set to NONE, no backups or copies are ever considered obsolete, and the DBA must manually remove unneeded backups from the catalog and from disk. By default, the retention policy is a single copy (with the retention policy set to 1). You can set the retention policy to two copies using the following RMAN command:

```
RMAN> configure retention policy to redundancy 2;
```

The following example sets the retention policy to a recovery window of four days:

```
RMAN> configure retention policy to recovery window of 4 days;
old RMAN configuration parameters:
CONFIGURE RETENTION POLICY TO REDUNDANCY 2;
new RMAN configuration parameters:
CONFIGURE RETENTION POLICY TO RECOVERY WINDOW OF 4 DAYS;
new RMAN configuration parameters are successfully stored
RMAN>
```

Oracle best practices recommend using a recovery window (a period of time in which it is possible to uncover any problems with the database, such as an inadvertently dropped table or deleted rows in a table) and performing a point-in-time recovery at just before the error occurred.

In some environments, you may want to disable the retention policy completely. This is useful in an environment where a backup system outside of RMAN stores the disk backups to tape and deletes them. As a result, RMAN does not need to decide when a backup is obsolete, and therefore no retention policy is needed. As a result, the details of RMAN backups are maintained up to the time specified by the initialization parameter CONTROL_FILE_RECORD_KEEP_TIME. Here is how you can disable the retention policy:

```
RMAN> configure retention policy to none;
```

Format Specifiers

Usually, you will want to automate the naming of backupset pieces. This will allow you to run the same scripts repeatedly, generating different output filenames every time. You will not know the names (though you can decode them), but RMAN will. This is an important part of automating the backup process. To generate names, configure persistent format specifiers, using a combination of literals (such as directory names) and variables. The variables are as follows:

- **%d**   Database name.
- **%e**   Archived log sequence number.
- **%f**   Absolute file number.

- **%F**   Combines the database identifier (DBID), day, month, year, and sequence number, separated by dashes.

- **%c**   Copy number for multiple copies in a duplexed backup.

- **%I**   DBID.

- **%N**   Tablespace name padded to eight characters.

- **%t**   Backupset timestamp.

- **%p**   Piece number within the backupset.

- **%s**   Backupset number.

- **%t**   Backupset timestamp.

- **%u**   In effect, eight random characters. This is derived from the backupset number and the time.

- **%U**   System-generated unique filename (the default). For a backupset, it is equivalent to %u_%p_%c; for a datafile image copy, it is data-D-%d_id-%I_TS-%N_FNO-%f_%u; for an archivelog image copy, it is arch-D_%d-id-%I_S-%e_T-%h_A-%a_%u; and for a controlfile image copy, it is cf-D_%d-id-%I_%u.

Exercise 23-1: Configure RMAN and Perform a Backup   For this exercise, it is assumed that the database is in archivelog mode. Should it not be, complete the exercises in Chapter 22.

1. Connect to the database using the RMAN executable client, from the operating system command line.

   ```
   rman target /
   ```

2. Show the configured parameters. They should all be on their defaults.

   ```
   RMAN> show all;
   ```

3. From the RMAN prompt, set some parameters as you might on a production system. When nominating the directory for the default backup destination, be sure to nominate a directory on which the oracle user has full privileges.

   ```
   configure retention policy to recovery window of 14 days;
   configure backup optimization on;
   configure controlfile autobackup on;
   configure device type disk parallelism 4 backup type to compressed
   backupset;
   configure channel device type disk format '/u01/backups';
   configure archivelog deletion policy to backed up 2 times to disk;
   show all;
   ```

4. Back up the database and archivelogs.

   ```
   backup database;
   backup archivelog all delete input;
   ```

   Observe the automatic channel allocation and the manner in which files are apportioned to channels, the filenames of the output pieces, and the autobackup of the controlfile and spfile. Note that the deletion of archive logfiles does not occur until you run the archive logfile backup command a couple more times.

5. Override the configured defaults.

Run a backup that does not permit RMAN to use the configured defaults by specifying some values and using a run block.

```
run {
allocate channel d1 type disk;
backup as copy datafile 1;
backup as backupset datafile 1;
backup as compressed backupset datafile 1;
}
```

Note the names of the output files and compare their sizes with each other and with the source datafile.

Some Advanced RMAN Capabilities

To get the best out of RMAN, most sites will want to use a recovery catalog for the RMAN repository. While not essential, a catalog enhances RMAN's capabilities significantly. RMAN has many other backup capabilities beyond the basic functionality described so far.

The Recovery Catalog

If you manage more than one database in your environment and you want to keep your recovery information for a longer time than CONTROLFILE_RECORD_KEEP_TIME, then you need a recovery catalog to store the RMAN repository. A single recovery catalog can store RMAN information for a virtually unlimited number of target databases.

Using stored scripts is another reason to use a recovery catalog; you cannot store scripts in the target database's controlfile. You can save a sequence of commands as a single script to make it easy to run the sequence of commands on demand or perhaps on a specific schedule. A script can be tied to a specific target database (a local script), or it can be available to all target databases (a global script).

Because you can put the metadata from several databases into a single recovery catalog, the RC_ views, such as RC_ARCHIVED_LOG, RC_BACKUP_FILES, and RC_DATABASE, are created in the recovery catalog database to retrieve metadata for all target databases. Otherwise, when you're using the target database controlfile, you must connect to each target database separately and query the V$ views based on the target database's controlfile.

Finally, using a recovery catalog permits you to use the following RMAN commands:

- **BACKUP ... KEEP UNTIL TIME**   Keep a backup for a period of time that differs from the configured retention policy.

- **BACKUP ... KEEP FOREVER**   Keep a backup indefinitely or until you manually remove it.

- **REPORT SCHEMA ... AT**   Show the structure of the database at a specific time in the past.

Configure the Recovery Catalog Database

Connect to the repository database (in this case the RCAT database) with SYSDBA privileges and create the recovery catalog in the RMAN tablespace as follows:

```
[oracle@tettnang ~]$ . oraenv
ORACLE_SID = [oracle] ? rcat
The Oracle base remains unchanged with value /u00/app/oracle
[oracle@tettnang ~]$ sqlplus / as sysdba

SQL*Plus: Release 12.1.0.1.0 Production on Tue Feb 18 14:46:11 2014
Copyright (c) 1982, 2013, Oracle.  All rights reserved.
Connected to:
Oracle Database 12c Enterprise Edition Release 12.1.0.1.0 - 64bit Production
With the Partitioning, Automatic Storage Management,
   OLAP, Advanced Analytics and Real Application Testing options
SQL> create tablespace rman datafile '+data' size 150m
  2  autoextend on next 50m;
Tablespace created.
SQL>
```

Create the Recovery Catalog Owner

Creating the recovery catalog owner is as easy as creating any database user. In this example, you create the user RMAN to manage the recovery catalog. You could just as easily create a user called FRED to own the recovery catalog. Using RMAN as the catalog owner makes it easier to identify the purpose of the account.

```
SQL> create user rcat_owner identified by Rcat9095
  2  default tablespace rman
  3  quota unlimited on rman;
User created.
SQL> grant recovery_catalog_owner to rcat_owner;
Grant succeeded.
SQL>
```

The predefined role RECOVERY_CATALOG_OWNER includes these system privileges:

- ALTER SESSION
- CREATE CLUSTER
- CREATE DATABASE LINK
- CREATE PROCEDURE
- CREATE SEQUENCE
- CREATE SESSION
- CREATE SYNONYM
- CREATE TABLE
- CREATE TRIGGER
- CREATE TYPE
- CREATE VIEW

PART IV

Create the Recovery Catalog

Now that the RMAN user account exists in the repository database, you can start RMAN, connect to the catalog, and initialize the repository with the CREATE CATALOG command.

```
[oracle@tettnang ~]$ rman catalog rcat_owner/Rcat9095@rcat
Recovery Manager: Release 12.1.0.1.0 -
   Production on Tue Feb 18 14:55:14 2014
Copyright(c) 1982, 2013, Oracle and/or its affiliates. All rights reserved.
connected to recovery catalog database
RMAN> create catalog;
recovery catalog created
RMAN>
```

From this point on, using a repository is as easy as specifying the repository username and password on the RMAN command line with the CATALOG parameter or using the CONNECT CATALOG command in an RMAN session.

Synchronize the Recovery Catalog

Now that you've set up your recovery catalog, you can register one or more of your databases with the recovery catalog. The registration process propagates backup information and the target database structure to the recovery catalog. In general, RMAN saves most information from the controlfile to the recovery catalog; however, a few operations require you to update the metadata manually in the recovery catalog.

For each database for which RMAN will perform a backup or recovery, you must register the database in the RMAN repository; this operation records information such as the target database schema and the unique DBID of the target database. The target database needs to be registered only once; subsequent RMAN sessions that connect to the target database will automatically reference the correct metadata in the repository. The database must be in the MOUNT or OPEN state to be successfully registered.

The following example connects to the target database using operating system authentication and connects to the repository with password authentication:

```
[oracle@tettnang ~]$ rman target / catalog rcat_owner/Rcat9095@rcat
Recovery Manager: Release 12.1.0.1.0 -
     Production on Tue Feb 18 21:20:26 2014
Copyright (c)1982, 2013, Oracle and/or its affiliates. All rights reserved.
connected to target database: RPT12C (DBID=1766066998)
connected to recovery catalog database
RMAN> register database;
database registered in recovery catalog
starting full resync of recovery catalog
full resync complete
RMAN>
```

All databases registered with the repository must have unique DBIDs; trying to register the database again yields the following error message:

```
RMAN> register database;
RMAN-00571: ===========================================================
RMAN-00569: =============== ERROR MESSAGE STACK FOLLOWS ===============
RMAN-00571: ===========================================================
```

```
RMAN-03009: failure of register command on
    default channel at 02/18/2014 21:22:40
RMAN-20002: target database already registered in recovery catalog
RMAN>
```

In some situations, you need to resynchronize the metadata in the target database's controlfile with the recovery catalog. For example, the recovery catalog database might be unavailable for one or more of your backups because of a network problem or because the recovery catalog database is down. In this situation, RMAN records the backup information only in the target database controlfile. RMAN always records backup information in the controlfile even when the recovery catalog is unavailable!

 EXAM TIP The RMAN recovery catalog records information about target database structures, archived redo logs, and backups when you run an RMAN BACKUP command or perform a manual resynchronization.

In addition, you may perform infrequent backups and rely on archived redo logfiles for a recovery scenario. This is not a problem per se, but the list of recent archived redo logfiles is not recorded automatically in the recovery catalog.

Finally, you may occasionally make changes to the physical structure of the target database. This information is automatically recorded in the target database controlfile but not in the recovery catalog.

Manually resynchronizing the recovery catalog is a straightforward process. After you start RMAN (and connect to a recovery catalog, of course), run the RESYNC CATALOG command, as in this example:

```
RMAN> resync catalog;
starting full resync of recovery catalog
full resync complete
RMAN>
```

Create and Use RMAN Stored Scripts

Stored scripts help you automate repetitive groups of RMAN commands. The scripts are stored in the recovery catalog. A stored script can be tied to a single target database or be visible to all target databases registered in the recovery catalog.

You create an RMAN script with the CREATE SCRIPT or CREATE GLOBAL SCRIPT command. The GLOBAL parameter specifies that the script is available to all RMAN target databases sharing this recovery catalog. To create a script (either global or local), you must be connected to the target database and the recovery catalog.

This example creates a global script called GLOBAL_BACKUP_DB that creates a full backup including archived logfiles:

```
RMAN> CREATE GLOBAL SCRIPT
2>      global_backup_db { BACKUP DATABASE PLUS ARCHIVELOG; }

created global script global_backup_db

RMAN>
```

If you wanted the script to be available to only one specific target database, you would omit the GLOBAL keyword. If you already have an RMAN script in a text file on a file system, you can import the script into an RMAN global or local script using this syntax:

```
RMAN> create script local_backup_db from file
2>        '/home/oracle/dbscripts/local_bak.rman';
```

Running a global or local RMAN stored script is straightforward; however, you must execute the script within a run block. The syntax is as follows:

```
RUN
{  ...other commands...;
   EXECUTE [GLOBAL] SCRIPT scriptname;
   ...other commands...;
}
```

Here is how to run the global script you created in the previous section:

```
RMAN> run { execute script global_backup_db; }
```

You can also use parameters within an RMAN stored script. In other words, if one or two values will change within a script, such as the value for a particular channel or the value of an object to back up, then you can use the & character as a substitution indicator, much like you would in a SQL*Plus script.

You can retrieve the contents of RMAN stored scripts using the PRINT and LIST commands. The PRINT command shows the contents of an individual script, and the LIST command shows the names of global scripts or both global and local scripts.

This example uses the LIST SCRIPT NAMES command to show both the local and global scripts:

```
RMAN> list script names;

List of Stored Scripts in Recovery Catalog

    Scripts of Target Database COMPLREF

       Script Name
       Description
       -----------------------------------------------------------
       local_backup_db

    Global Scripts

       Script Name
       Description
       -----------------------------------------------------------
       backup_ts

       global_backup_db

RMAN>
```

LIST GLOBAL SCRIPT NAMES returns only the global script names.

To show the actual contents of a script, use the PRINT command. Because a global script and a local script can have the same name, you qualify the PRINT command with the GLOBAL option if you want to print the global version instead of the local version. This example retrieves the contents of the global_backup_db script:

```
RMAN> print global script global_backup_db;

printing stored global script: global_backup_db
{ BACKUP DATABASE PLUS ARCHIVELOG; }

RMAN>
```

You can spool the contents of a global or local script to a file using the TO FILE option of the PRINT command.

```
RMAN> print global script global_backup_db
2>          to file '/tmp/save_script.rman';

global script global_backup_db written to file /tmp/save_script.rman

RMAN>
```

It's also easy to delete or replace stored scripts. To replace a stored script, use the REPLACE [GLOBAL] SCRIPT command. In this example, you want to modify the global script backup_ts to back up the SYSTEM tablespace in addition to the desired tablespace:

```
RMAN> replace global script backup_ts
2>     {
3>         backup tablespace system, &1;

Enter value for 1: users
4>     }

replaced global script backup_ts

RMAN>
```

As you might expect, you use the DELETE SCRIPT command to delete a global or local script.

```
RMAN> delete script local_backup_db;

deleted script: local_backup_db

RMAN>
```

Incremental Backups

An incremental backup can be one of two types: level 0 or level 1. A level 0 incremental backup includes all blocks in the specified datafiles except for blocks that have never been used. A level 0 backup is physically identical to a full backup of the same datafiles, except that a full backup cannot be used in an incremental backup strategy—it stands alone. A level 1 backup can be one of two types: either a differential backup that backs up changed blocks since the last backup at level 0 or level 1 or a cumulative backup that backs up all changed blocks since the last level 0 backup. A level 0 backup can be either a backupset or an image copy; a level 1 can be only a backupset.

You use the following keywords in the RMAN BACKUP command to specify an incremental level 0 or level 1 backup:

```
INCREMENTAL LEVEL [0|1]
```

You'll learn how to set up an incremental backup strategy for the USERS tablespace in the following sections.

Level 0 Incremental Backups

A level 0 backup includes all blocks in a database object except for blocks that were never used above the high water mark (HWM). Subsequent level 1 backups use the most recent level 0 backup as the base for comparison when identifying changed blocks.

How often you perform a level 0 backup depends on how much the database object, such as a tablespace, changes between backups. A tablespace containing tables that are completely replaced on a weekly basis would most likely have more frequent level 0 backups than a tablespace containing tables that your applications change infrequently—for example, only 5 percent of the table's rows every week, but the changes might depend on the block distribution of those rows.

In this example, you perform the first level 0 backup of the USERS tablespace in your incremental backup strategy:

```
RMAN> backup incremental level 0 tablespace users;

Starting backup at 25-FEB-14
using channel ORA_DISK_1
using channel ORA_DISK_2
using channel ORA_DISK_3
using channel ORA_DISK_4
channel ORA_DISK_1: starting compressed incremental level 0
    datafile backup set
channel ORA_DISK_1: specifying datafile(s) in backup set
input datafile file number=00005
    name=+DATA/RPT12C/DATAFILE/users.269.826931347
channel ORA_DISK_1: starting piece 1 at 25-FEB-14
channel ORA_DISK_2: starting compressed incremental level 0
    datafile backup set
channel ORA_DISK_2: specifying datafile(s) in backup set
input datafile file number=00006
    name=+DATA/RPT12C/DATAFILE/users.259.826650843
channel ORA_DISK_2: starting piece 1 at 25-FEB-14
channel ORA_DISK_1: finished piece 1 at 25-FEB-14
piece handle=+RECOV/RPT12C/BACKUPSET/2014_02_25/
    nnndn0_tag20140225t093233_0.288.840447153 tag=TAG20140225T093233
    comment=NONE
channel ORA_DISK_1: backup set complete, elapsed time: 00:00:01
channel ORA_DISK_2: finished piece 1 at 25-FEB-14
piece handle=+RECOV/RPT12C/BACKUPSET/2014_02_25/
nnndn0_tag20140225t093233_0.268.840447153 tag=TAG20140225T093233
    comment=NONE
channel ORA_DISK_2: backup set complete, elapsed time: 00:00:01
Finished backup at 25-FEB-14

RMAN>
```

Subsequent level 1 backups will use this backup as the starting point for identifying changed blocks.

Differential Incremental Backups

A *differential* backup is the default type of incremental backup that backs up all changed blocks since the last level 0 or level 1 incremental backup. Again using the USERS tablespace, here's how you perform an incremental backup:

```
RMAN> backup incremental level 1 tablespace users;

Starting backup at 25-FEB-14
using channel ORA_DISK_1
using channel ORA_DISK_2
using channel ORA_DISK_3
using channel ORA_DISK_4
channel ORA_DISK_1: starting compressed incremental level 1
   datafile backup set
channel ORA_DISK_1: specifying datafile(s) in backup set
input datafile file number=00005
    name=+DATA/RPT12C/DATAFILE/users.269.826931347
channel ORA_DISK_1: starting piece 1 at 25-FEB-14
channel ORA_DISK_2: starting compressed incremental level 1
   datafile backup set
channel ORA_DISK_2: specifying datafile(s) in backup set
input datafile file number=00006
    name=+DATA/RPT12C/DATAFILE/users.259.826650843

channel ORA_DISK_2: starting piece 1 at 25-FEB-14
channel ORA_DISK_1: finished piece 1 at 25-FEB-14
piece handle=+RECOV/RPT12C/BACKUPSET/2014_02_25/
nnndn1_tag20140225t093513_0.315.840447313 tag=TAG20140225T093513
    comment=NONE
channel ORA_DISK_1: backup set complete, elapsed time: 00:00:01
channel ORA_DISK_2: finished piece 1 at 25-FEB-14
piece handle=+RECOV/RPT12C/BACKUPSET/2014_02_25/
nnndn1_tag20140225t093513_0.284.840447313 tag=TAG20140225T093513
    comment=NONE
channel ORA_DISK_2: backup set complete, elapsed time: 00:00:01
Finished backup at 25-FEB-14

RMAN>
```

 TIP Differential is the default incremental backup type. Unlike most Oracle commands that allow you to use a keyword that is the default, DIFFERENTIAL cannot be specified for the RMAN BACKUP command.

Cumulative Incremental Backups

Cumulative incremental backups back up all changed blocks since the last level 0 incremental backup. You perform a cumulative incremental level 1 backup the same way you perform a differential level 1 backup, except that you specify the CUMULATIVE keyword, as in this example:

```
RMAN> backup incremental level 1 cumulative tablespace users;

Starting backup at 25-FEB-14
using channel ORA_DISK_1
```

```
using channel ORA_DISK_2
using channel ORA_DISK_3
using channel ORA_DISK_4
channel ORA_DISK_1: starting compressed incremental level 1
    datafile backup set
channel ORA_DISK_1: specifying datafile(s) in backup set
input datafile file number=00005
    name=+DATA/RPT12C/DATAFILE/users.269.826931347
channel ORA_DISK_1: starting piece 1 at 25-FEB-14
channel ORA_DISK_2: starting compressed incremental level 1
    datafile backup set
channel ORA_DISK_2: specifying datafile(s) in backup set
input datafile file number=00006
    name=+DATA/RPT12C/DATAFILE/users.259.826650843
channel ORA_DISK_2: starting piece 1 at 25-FEB-14
channel ORA_DISK_1: finished piece 1 at 25-FEB-14
piece handle=+RECOV/RPT12C/BACKUPSET/2014_02_25/
    nnndn1_tag20140225t093821_0.283.840447501 tag=TAG20140225T093821
    comment=NONE
channel ORA_DISK_1: backup set complete, elapsed time: 00:00:01
channel ORA_DISK_2: finished piece 1 at 25-FEB-14
piece handle=+RECOV/RPT12C/BACKUPSET/2014_02_25/
    nnndn1_tag20140225t093821_0.282.840447501 tag=TAG20140225T093821
    comment=NONE
channel ORA_DISK_2: backup set complete, elapsed time: 00:00:01
Finished backup at 25-FEB-14

RMAN>
```

The decision whether to use a cumulative or differential backup is based partly on where you want to spend the central processing unit (CPU) cycles and how much disk space is available. Using cumulative backups means that each incremental backup will become progressively larger and take longer until another level 0 incremental backup is performed. This can be beneficial in that only two backupsets will be required during a restore and recovery operation. On the other hand, differential backups record only the changes since the last backup, so each backupset might be smaller or larger than the previous one, with no overlap in data blocks backed up. However, a restore and recovery operation can take longer if you have to restore from several backupsets instead of just two.

Exercise 23-2: Take an Incremental Backup   In this exercise, you will investigate the use of incremental backups.

1. Connect to the database using the RMAN executable client, from the operating system command line.

   ```
   rman target /
   ```

2. It is not possible to perform a level 1 backup if there is no level 0. So far, all you have is a full backup. Attempt to perform a level 1 backup.

   ```
   Backup incremental level 1 database;
   ```

3. Study the output of step 2. What type of backup was carried out?

4. Repeat the command from step 2. What type of backup do you get this time?

Other Capabilities

RMAN provides a number of options to make multiple copies of your backup simultaneously, to create backups of your existing backupsets, and to skip unnecessary backups of read-only tablespaces. As your database grows in size, you inevitably have some really big datafiles that will take a long time to back up as part of a full database backup if backed up as a whole. Therefore, RMAN supports multisection backups so that a large datafile can be backed up in pieces in parallel. Archival backups give you the flexibility to take a snapshot of the database and retain it indefinitely or for a specific period of time. Lastly, read-only tablespaces may require special consideration.

Creating Duplexed Backupsets

To make multiple backups of the same backupset simultaneously, you can configure RMAN to make up to four duplexed copies of each backup piece. As with most RMAN commands, you can specify a default value for the COPIES parameter using the CONFIGURE command, as in this example:

```
RMAN> configure datafile backup copies
2>        for device type sbt to 3;

new RMAN configuration parameters:
CONFIGURE DATAFILE BACKUP COPIES FOR DEVICE TYPE 'SBT_TAPE' TO 3;
new RMAN configuration parameters are successfully stored
starting full resync of recovery catalog
full resync complete

RMAN>
```

Duplexing has a few restrictions. You cannot duplex backups to the fast recovery area, and you cannot duplex image copies—only backupsets. For duplexed disk backups, you specify multiple locations for a backup using the FORMAT clause. You can specify multiple locations either in the BACKUP command or when setting default values for device type DISK in the CONFIGURE command.

In this example, you back up the USERS tablespace to two different disk locations simultaneously:

```
RMAN> backup as compressed backupset
2>      device type disk
3>      copies 2
4>      tablespace users
5>      format '/u01/oradata/bkup/%U', '/u04/oradata/bkup/%U';
```

Note that even though you have the same format for each copy of the backupset, RMAN's format specifier %U will generate unique names for each piece.

Creating Backups of Backupsets

One option for creating a second copy of a backup is to create a backup of existing backupsets. If your backupsets are on disk (you cannot back up existing backupsets that are on tape), you can use the BACKUP . . . BACKUPSET command to copy all backupsets on one disk to another disk or to tape. This command copies all existing disk-based backupsets to the default tape device and channel:

```
RMAN> backup device type sbt backupset all;
```

If you want to keep recent backupsets on disk and older backupsets on tape, you can use the COMPLETED and DELETE INPUT options. In the following example, all backupsets older than two weeks are backed up to tape and deleted from the disk:

```
RMAN> backup device type sbt backupset
2>        completed before 'sysdate-14'
3>        delete input;
```

Backing Up Read-Only Tablespaces

As you might expect, backing up a read-only tablespace needs to happen often enough to satisfy the retention period configured in RMAN. You can force RMAN to skip a read-only tablespace by using the SKIP READONLY option of the BACKUP command. If you have configured RMAN for backup optimization, RMAN backs up read-only tablespaces only when there are not enough backups of the tablespace to satisfy the retention policy.

Use of read-only tablespaces may be particularly important in a data warehouse environment, where a high proportion of the data is static. Careful use of partitioning (typically range partitioning based on date) may mean that many table segments (and index segments, if the indexes are locally partitioned) can be moved to read-only tablespaces, hugely reducing the time and space needed for backup.

Creating Archival Backups

By default, RMAN keeps your backups and archived logfiles not only to satisfy the configured retention policy but also to provide a mechanism to restore your database to any point in time between the backup and the present. RMAN uses a combination of full backups, incremental backups, and archived redo logfiles.

In certain situations, you may want only a snapshot of the database at a certain point in time for archival or regulatory purposes. This causes two complications with the default RMAN configuration. First, your snapshot will most likely fall outside of your retention policy, and you certainly don't want your yearly database snapshot to disappear before the end of the week. Second, you don't want RMAN to maintain one, two, or more years' worth of archived redo logfiles if you are not going to restore your database to a point in time between the snapshot and the current time.

RMAN addresses the need for a database snapshot by supporting an *archival backup*. If you label a backup as an archival backup, RMAN does not consider the backup to be obsolete using the configured retention policy; instead, RMAN marks an archival backup as obsolete after the amount of time you specify. Alternatively, you can specify that RMAN keep the archival backup indefinitely.

TIP   You can use an archival backup to migrate a copy of the database to another system for testing purposes without affecting the retention policy of the original database. Once you have created the database on the test system, you can delete the archival backup.

A restriction for archival backups is that you cannot use the fast recovery area to store an archival backup. If you have a fast recovery area configured, you will have to use the FORMAT parameter to specify an alternative disk location for the backup. Additionally, a tape device might be the best option for long-term storage of archival backups.

This example creates an archival backup to be retained for one year using the KEEP UNTIL clause:

```
RMAN> backup as compressed backupset
2>      database format '/u02/oradata/rman/archback/%U'
3>      tag save1yr
4>      keep until time 'sysdate+365'
5>    ;

Starting backup at 25-FEB-14
starting full resync of recovery catalog
full resync complete
current log archived

using channel ORA_DISK_1
backup will be obsolete on date 25-FEB-15
archived logs required to recover from this backup will be backed up
. . .
channel ORA_DISK_1: backup set complete, elapsed time: 00:00:02

using channel ORA_DISK_1
using channel ORA_DISK_2
using channel ORA_DISK_3
using channel ORA_DISK_4
backup will be obsolete on date 25-FEB-15
archived logs required to recover from this backup will be backed up
channel ORA_DISK_1: starting compressed full datafile backup set
channel ORA_DISK_1: specifying datafile(s) in backup set
including current control file in backup set
channel ORA_DISK_1: starting piece 1 at 25-FEB-14
channel ORA_DISK_1: finished piece 1 at 25-FEB-14
piece handle=/u02/oradata/rman/archback/2bp1gfdd_1_1
     tag=SAVE1YR comment=NONE
channel ORA_DISK_1: backup set complete, elapsed time: 00:00:01
Finished backup at 25-FEB-14

RMAN>
```

Since the RPT12C database has a fast recovery area defined, you use the FORMAT clause to specify a location in which to store the archival backup. Note also that RMAN backs up any archived logs, which would be required to use the backup in a possible future recovery scenario.

Alternatively, you can perform the same backup but retain it indefinitely.

```
 RMAN> backup as compressed backupset
2>      database format '/u02/oradata/rman/archback/%U'
3>      tag saveforever
4>      keep forever;
. . .
using channel ORA_DISK_1
backup will never be obsolete
archived logs required to recover from this backup will be backed up
. . .
```

PART IV

In some situations, you might want to change the status of a backup. For example, you might want to change an archival backup's retention period, change an archival backup to a standard backup, or change a consistent backup to an archival backup. As you might expect, you can use the CHANGE command to accomplish this task. Although the CHANGE command has many other uses (such as to change the availability of a backup or to change the priority of failures in the database), the CHANGE command in relation to archival backups is covered here.

This example changes the backup created earlier with the tag SAVEFOREVER to fall under the existing retention policy instead:

```
RMAN> change backup tag 'saveforever' nokeep;

starting full resync of recovery catalog
full resync complete
using channel ORA_DISK_1
keep attributes for the backup are deleted
backupset key=3321 RECID=26 STAMP=654037077
keep attributes for the backup are deleted
backupset key=3344 RECID=27 STAMP=654037106
keep attributes for the backup are deleted
backupset key=3345 RECID=28 STAMP=654037128
keep attributes for the backup are deleted
backupset key=3346 RECID=29 STAMP=654037151

RMAN>
```

Depending on the retention policy and the other older or newer backups for this database, the backup could be deleted the next time RMAN starts. The backup could be retained longer if the configured retention policy needs this backup to fulfill the retention policy.

You can also use the CHANGE command to change all backups of a certain type. For example, if you want to remove the archive flag from all image copies of the database, you use the NOKEEP parameter.

```
change copy of database nokeep;
```

Creating a Multisection Backup

Creating a multisection backup is easy, but you must specify the section size with each BACKUP command. In addition, you can run the RMAN VALIDATE command by section. New data dictionary views, both the V$ and RC_ views, help you to identify which backups are multisection and how many blocks are in each section of a multisection backup.

To create a multisection backup, you add the SECTION SIZE parameter to the BACKUP command. The section size can be specified in kilobytes, megabytes, or gigabytes. Here is the general syntax for specifying a multisection backup:

```
BACKUP <backup options> SECTION SIZE <size> [K|M|G]
```

In this example HR database, the USERS tablespace is approximately 250MB, and you want to back it up with a section size of 100MB:

```
RMAN> backup tablespace users
2>      section size 100m;
```

```
Starting backup at 25-FEB-14
using channel ORA_DISK_1
using channel ORA_DISK_2
using channel ORA_DISK_3
using channel ORA_DISK_4
channel ORA_DISK_1: starting compressed full datafile backup set
channel ORA_DISK_1: specifying datafile(s) in backup set
input datafile file number=00005
    name=+DATA/RPT12C/DATAFILE/users.269.826931347
backing up blocks 1 through 12800
channel ORA_DISK_1: starting piece 1 at 25-FEB-14
channel ORA_DISK_2: starting compressed full datafile backup set
channel ORA_DISK_2: specifying datafile(s) in backup set
input datafile file number=00006
    name=+DATA/RPT12C/DATAFILE/users.259.826650843
channel ORA_DISK_2: starting piece 1 at 25-FEB-14
channel ORA_DISK_3: starting compressed full datafile backup set
channel ORA_DISK_3: specifying datafile(s) in backup set
input datafile file number=00005
    name=+DATA/RPT12C/DATAFILE/users.269.826931347
backing up blocks 12801 through 25600
channel ORA_DISK_3: starting piece 2 at 25-FEB-14
channel ORA_DISK_4: starting compressed full datafile backup set
channel ORA_DISK_4: specifying datafile(s) in backup set
input datafile file number=00005
    name=+DATA/RPT12C/DATAFILE/users.269.826931347
backing up blocks 25601 through 32000
channel ORA_DISK_4: starting piece 3 at 25-FEB-14
channel ORA_DISK_1: finished piece 1 at 25-FEB-14
piece handle=+RECOV/RPT12C/BACKUPSET/2014_02_25/
    nnndf0_tag20140225t101644_0.278.840449805 tag=TAG20140225T101644
    comment=NONE
channel ORA_DISK_1: backup set complete, elapsed time: 00:00:01
channel ORA_DISK_2: finished piece 1 at 25-FEB-14
piece handle=+RECOV/RPT12C/BACKUPSET/2014_02_25/
    nnndf0_tag20140225t101644_0.277.840449805 tag=TAG20140225T101644
    comment=NONE
channel ORA_DISK_2: backup set complete, elapsed time: 00:00:01
channel ORA_DISK_3: finished piece 2 at 25-FEB-14
piece handle=+RECOV/RPT12C/BACKUPSET/2014_02_25/
    nnndf0_tag20140225t101644_0.276.840449807 tag=TAG20140225T101644
    comment=NONE
channel ORA_DISK_3: backup set complete, elapsed time: 00:00:01
channel ORA_DISK_4: finished piece 3 at 25-FEB-14
piece handle=+RECOV/RPT12C/BACKUPSET/2014_02_25/
    nnndf0_tag20140225t101644_0.275.840449807 tag=TAG20140225T101644
    comment=NONE
channel ORA_DISK_4: backup set complete, elapsed time: 00:00:01
Finished backup at 25-FEB-14

RMAN>
```

This backup created three backup pieces; the first two were 100MB each, and the third piece was approximately 50MB, which is the remainder of the datafile. Multisection backups permit parallelism for the backup of a single datafile. If the operation is performed by multiple channels (as in the previous example), then sections will be read and written concurrently.

TIP Don't use a high value for parallelism in your multisection backups to back up a large file on a small number of disks. The input/output (I/O) contention of multiple RMAN channels hitting the same file on the same disk can erase any time savings gained by using a high value for parallelism.

Compressing Backups

In addition to skipping unused blocks during a backup, RMAN can also apply a compression method to the used blocks in a backup when you specify the COMPRESSED parameter with one of four values:

- **BASIC** Similar to MEDIUM compression but uses more CPU
- **LOW** Fastest but lower compression ratios
- **MEDIUM** Moderate CPU usage; good for network bandwidth constraints
- **HIGH** Most CPU usage; ideal for network bandwidth constraints

The default compression level is set to BASIC.

```
CONFIGURE COMPRESSION ALGORITHM 'BASIC'; # default
```

All compression methods except for BASIC require the Advanced Compression option.

The HIGH algorithm, as you might expect, creates much smaller backups but requires more CPU time to compress the blocks. If not too many other server processes are demanding CPU resources when your backups run, use MEDIUM or HIGH. On the other hand, if a lot of disk space is available and the network path from the database to your backup location is not congested, it might take less time overall not to use compression.

Regardless of what compression method you use, restoring a compressed backup requires no knowledge of the compression method used during the original backup. RMAN automatically detects the compression method used and decompresses accordingly.

Verifying that the Repository Is Up to Date

The RMAN repository is crucial for the automation of backup and restore operations. It is therefore important that it should be accurate: that the backupsets and archive logfiles that are registered in the repository do in fact exist. When a backup is made or an archive logfile is created following a log switch, this information is, of course, registered automatically. If a backup piece or an archive logfile is subsequently removed by an operating system utility rather than by an RMAN operation, the repository will no longer be correct. A typical reason for this sort of event is that the files are stored on a device such a tape library that has its own automatic file deletion policy. This script will first perform a reality check with CROSSCHECK commands, and then delete references to files that no longer exist with the DELETE EXPIRED command:

```
run{
crosscheck backupset;
crosscheck archivelog all;
delete expired backupset;
delete expired archivelog all;
}
```

The CROSSCHECK commands pass through the repository checking whether files registered within it do in fact exist. If any files are found to be missing, they are flagged as being EXPIRED. The DELETE EXPIRED command removes the detail of any expired files from the repository. If there is any possibility that files could be removed without RMAN's knowledge, it is important to run a maintenance script such as that above regularly in order to update the repository.

Two-Minute Drill

Create Consistent Database Backups

- Consistent (aka closed or cold) backups are taken by RMAN when in mount mode.
- A full closed backup is the complete set of datafiles plus the controlfile.

Back Up Your Database Without Shutting It Down

- Open (aka hot) backups are taken by RMAN while the database is in use.
- Open backups are possible only if the database is running in archivelog mode.
- Archive logfiles must also be backed up or an open backup of the database will be useless.

Create Incremental Backups

- A level 0 incremental backup consists of the whole datafile and can be used as the base for subsequent level 1 backups.
- A level 1 incremental backup consists of all blocks changed since the last level 1 backup or the level 0 backup if no level 1 has yet been taken.
- A level 1 cumulative backup consists of all blocks changed since the last level 0 backup.

Automate Database Backups

- Enterprise Manager can schedule automatic backups.
- Scheduled backups use RMAN, invoked by the Enterprise Manager agent.

Manage Backups and the RMAN Repository

- RMAN uses a repository. This is stored in the target database controlfile and (optionally) in a recovery catalog database.
- The repository stores information regarding all backups that have been made and is vital for automating restore and recovery operations.

- The repository can be written out to a catalog database, which permits long-term storage of backup metadata.

- The catalog schema is created and owned by a catalog owner who must be granted the RECOVERY CATALOG OWNER role.

Use Various RMAN Backup Types and Strategies

- RMAN backups can be full or incremental.

- Incremental backups can be level 0 or 1. Level 0 backups are full backups that you can use as part of a differential, incremental, or cumulative incremental level 1 backup strategy.

- RMAN image copies are exact copies of datafiles. Using RMAN to make copies of datafiles has the additional advantage of checking for corruption in each block read.

- RMAN can use backup compression to save space on the destination device, and RMAN automatically decompresses the backup during a recovery operation.

- Using a fast recovery area for RMAN has two advantages: RMAN automatically names backup files in the fast recovery area, and it automatically deletes obsolete backup files when there is space pressure in the fast recovery area.

- More than one database can use the fast recovery area.

- The RMAN command SHOW ALL lists all persistent RMAN settings.

- Use CONFIGURE CONTROLFILE AUTOBACKUP ON to ensure that a backup copy of the target database controlfile exists after each backup.

Perform Full and Incremental Backups

- RMAN backups are either backupsets or image backups.

- Backupsets can be created only by RMAN and can be read only by RMAN.

- The FORMAT clause of the BACKUP command specifies the substitution variables for the destination backup filename.

- You can create image copies of datafiles, archived redo logfiles, and controlfiles.

- Image copies can be written only to disk.

- You can use the SWITCH command to quickly and easily switch between a datafile and its image copy during a recovery operation.

- A whole-database backup includes all datafiles plus the controlfile.

- A full backup of a datafile is a logical subset of a whole-database backup.

- A full backup cannot be used as the basis for an incremental backup strategy.

- An incremental backup is level 0 or level 1.

- An incremental level 0 backup can be used as the basis for an incremental backup strategy.
- Differential backups back up all changed blocks since the last level 0 or level 1 incremental backup.
- Cumulative incremental backups back up all changed blocks since the last level 0 backup.
- An archival backup is a snapshot of the database at a certain point in time created to satisfy archival or regulatory purposes.
- Archival backups make it easy to migrate a copy of the database to another system without affecting the retention policy of the original database.
- To create an archival backup, you specify either the KEEP UNTIL TIME or KEEP FOREVER option in the BACKUP command.
- An RMAN archival backup also includes any archived logs required to use the backup in a recovery scenario.
- You can use the CHANGE command to change the status of an archival backup.
- Multisection RMAN backups can significantly reduce the time it takes to back up large datafiles to multiple destinations.
- You can run the VALIDATE command in multisection mode.
- The SECTION SIZE parameter determines the size for each section of a file to be read in a multisection backup. Sections can be read in parallel.
- RMAN can compress backups of used blocks using four compression levels: BASIC, LOW, MEDIUM, and HIGH.
- All compression methods except for BASIC require the Advanced Compression option.

Use Techniques to Improve Backups

- Channels can be persisted with the CONFIGURE command or assigned within the run block using the ALLOCATE CHANNEL command.
- Using DISK as the default device type does not require any channel allocation.
- RMAN uses backup optimization to skip backups of one or more files if identical files have already been backed up to disk or tape.
- Backup optimization takes into account duplexing and retention policies before skipping a source file.
- You set backup optimization in RMAN with the command CONFIGURE BACKUP OPTIMIZATION ON.

Self Test

1. What file types can be backed up by RMAN? (Choose all correct answers.)

   A. Archive logfiles

   B. Controlfile

   C. Online logfiles

   D. Password files

   E. Permanent tablespace datafiles

   F. Server parameter files

   G. Static parameter files

   H. Temporary tablespace tempfiles

2. Why are RMAN backupsets smaller than RMAN image copies? (Choose the best answer.)

   A. They always use compression.

   B. They always skip unused blocks.

   C. They never include tempfiles.

   D. They can be written directly to tape.

3. Which of the following statements is correct about RMAN offline backup? (Choose all correct answers.)

   A. The database must be in NOMOUNT mode.

   B. The database must be in MOUNT mode.

   C. The backup will fail if the shutdown mode was SHUTDOWN IMMEDIATE.

   D. Noarchivelog databases can be backed up only offline.

   E. Archivelog databases cannot be backed up offline.

   F. Offline backups can be incremental.

4. You need to back up the controlfile while the database is open. What will work? (Choose the best answer.)

   A. The controlfile can be included in an RMAN backupset but not backed up as an image copy.

   B. The ALTER DATABASE BACKUP CONTROLFILE TO TRACE command will make an image copy of the controlfile.

   C. You cannot back up the controlfile while it is in use—it is protected by multiplexing.

   D. None of the above.

5. You are setting up an incremental backup strategy. Which of these statements is correct? (Choose the best answer.)

    A. Before running an incremental level 1 backup, you must run an incremental level 0 backup.

    B. Either a full backup or an incremental level 0 backup can be the basis for an incremental level 1 backup.

    C. When restoring and recovering with incremental backups, archive logfiles are not needed.

    D. You cannot make an incremental backup of a database in NOARCHIVELOG mode.

    E. Running an incremental level 1 backup will automatically perform an incremental level 0 if none exists.

6. What processes must be running if an RMAN backup scheduled within the Oracle environment is to run? (Choose all correct answers.)

    A. The database instance must be started.

    B. The Cloud Control management server must be running.

    C. The Enterprise Manager agent must be running.

    D. The operating system scheduler must be running.

7. What is true about the crosscheck command? (Choose the best answer.)

    A. Crosscheck will check the validity of the backup pieces.

    B. Crosscheck will delete references to files that no longer exist.

    C. Crosscheck will verify the existence of backupset pieces.

    D. Crosscheck works only with backupsets, not image copies.

8. If the volume of data in the fast recovery area has reached the limit defined by DB_RECOVERY_FILE_DEST_SIZE, what will happen when RMAN attempts to write more data to it? (Choose the best answer.)

    A. If AUTOEXTEND has been enabled and the MAXSIZE value has not been reached, the fast recovery area will extend as necessary.

    B. The operation will fail.

    C. This will depend on whether warning and critical alerts have been enabled for the fast recovery area.

    D. RMAN will automatically delete OBSOLETE backups.

    E. RMAN will automatically delete EXPIRED backups.

9. You run the following RMAN command:

   RMAN> configure controlfile autobackup on;

   Under what conditions does RMAN back up the controlfile and the spfile? (Choose all that apply.)

   A. When an RMAN backup completes

   B. When you start RMAN

   C. When you connect to a target database

   D. When you back up the SYSTEM tablespace

   E. When you run the command BACKUP CURRENT CONTROLFILE;

   F. When any of the DBA passwords change

   G. When you change the size of the fast recovery area

   H. When you add a tablespace

10. Which of the following objects cannot be backed up by RMAN using the RMAN BACKUP command? (Choose all that apply.)

    A. DATAFILE

    B. DATABASE

    C. INSTANCE

    D. CURRENT CONTROLFILE

    E. SPFILE

    F. TABLESPACE

    G. ARCHIVELOG

    H. CONTROLFILE

    I. REDOLOG

11. Identify the statements in the following list that are true about managing RMAN persistent settings. (Choose all that apply.)

    A. SHOW ALL lists all current settings for the connected target database.

    B. You can use the CONFIGURE . . . CLEAR command to set a configuration value to an empty string.

    C. SHOW ALL shows the configuration values that apply to all target databases.

    D. You can use the CONFIGURE . . . CLEAR command to set a configuration value to its default value.

    E. SHOW ALL lists all RMAN settings that are different from the default value.

12. Which of the following is the default substitution variable for the FORMAT clause of the BACKUP command? (Choose the best answer.)

    A. %t

    B. %d

   C. %u

   D. %U

   E. %I

13. Which of the following are candidates for RMAN image copies? (Choose two answers.)

   A. Datafiles

   B. Archived redo logfiles

   C. Online redo logfiles

   D. Password files

14. You run the following command to create a whole-database backup:
RMAN> backup as copy database spfile plus archivelog delete input;
What does the DELETE INPUT clause do? (Choose the best answer.)

   A. After the backup completes, RMAN deletes the archived logfiles from all archived logfile destinations except for the fast recovery area.

   B. After the backup completes, RMAN deletes the archived logfiles from the fast recovery area only.

   C. After the backup completes, RMAN deletes the archived logfiles from the fast recovery area and any other archived logfile destinations.

   D. RMAN deletes all obsolete copies of database backups after the backup completes.

15. What is the difference between a full backup and a whole-database backup? (Choose the best answer.)

   A. A whole-database backup can be used as the basis for an incremental backup strategy, but a full database backup cannot.

   B. A full database backup can be used as the basis for an incremental backup strategy, but a whole-database backup cannot.

   C. A whole-database backup can be only an image copy. A full backup can be an image copy or a backupset.

   D. A full backup consists of a backup of one or more datafiles or tablespaces, whereas a whole-database backup contains all datafiles for all tablespaces plus the controlfile.

16. What is true about a level 0 incremental backup? (Choose all correct answers.)

   A. A level 0 backup includes all blocks in a datafile, including blocks that have never been used.

   B. A level 0 backup includes all blocks in a datafile, except for blocks that have never been used.

   C. A level 0 backup can be used with a level 1 cumulative backup.

   D. A level 0 backup can be used with a level 1 differential backup.

   E. A level 0 backup of a datafile has additional information that differentiates it from a full backup of the same datafile.

17. Identify the true statement regarding incremental and differential backups. (Choose the best answer.)

    A. A differential backup is the default type of incremental backup and backs up all changed blocks since the last level 0 or level 1 incremental backup.

    B. A cumulative backup is the default type of incremental backup and backs up all changed blocks since the last level 0 or level 1 incremental backup.

    C. A differential backup is the default type of incremental backup and backs up all changed blocks since the last level 0 incremental backup.

    D. A cumulative backup is the default type of incremental backup and backs up all changed blocks since the last level 1 incremental backup.

18. When you want to create a duplexed backupset, what is the maximum number of copies of each backup piece you can create with one BACKUP command? (Choose the best answer.)

    A. Two for disk locations and four for tape destinations.

    B. A maximum of four.

    C. Two for tape locations and four for disk locations.

    D. The maximum is limited only by the number of destination disks or tape drives.

19. Identify the true statements regarding archival backups. (Choose all correct answers.)

    A. Archival backups can be retained indefinitely.

    B. You can drop an archival backup using the CHANGE . . . DROP command.

    C. Archival backups include all archived redo logs from the archival date to the present.

    D. Once you create an archival backup, you must either keep it for the retention period specified or drop it.

    E. You can use an archival backup to migrate a copy of the database without affecting the retention policy.

    F. You can change the retention period of an archival backup once it has been created.

20. You have a datafile from the smallfile tablespace USERS that has a size of 90MB, and you run the following RMAN command:

    RMAN> backup tablespace users section size 40m;

    How many sections does this backup create? (Choose the best answer.)

    A. The command does not run because multisection backups apply only to bigfile tablespaces.

    B. Two sections of 45MB each.

    C. Two sections of 40MB each and one section of 10MB.

    D. The command does not run because you can back up the entire database only as a multisection backup.

21. What happens when you run the following RMAN commands?

RMAN> run
{ configure channel ch2 device type disk;
  backup database; }

(Choose the best answer.)

A. A full database backup is created in the Fast Recovery Area.

B. The database is backed up to all default channels configured outside of the run block plus the additional channel within the run block.

C. The command fails because you cannot use CONFIGURE within a run block.

D. The command fails because you cannot use BACKUP within a run block.

22. You have configured backup optimization for your database using CONFIGURE BACKUP OPTIMIZATION ON. For which of the following commands will RMAN not skip a backup if the files are identical?

A. BACKUP DATABASE;

B. BACKUP TABLESPACE USERS;

C. BACKUP ARCHIVELOG ALL;

D. BACKUP BACKUPSET ALL;

Self Test Answers

1. ☑ **A, B, E,** and **F.** These are the database file types that the Recovery Manager can back up and restore.
☒ **C, D, G,** and **H** are incorrect. RMAN will never back up online redo logs or tempfiles because it is not necessary to back them up, and it cannot back up a static parameter file or the external password file.

2. ☑ **B.** A backupset will never include blocks that have never been used.
☒ **A, C,** and **D** are incorrect. **A** is incorrect because compression is an option, not enabled by default. **C** is incorrect because it applies to image copies as well as backupsets. **D** is incorrect because it is not relevant; an image copy can't go to tape; if it did, it wouldn't be an image.

3. ☑ **B, D,** and **F.** Offline backups must be done in mount mode. This is the only backup type for a noarchivelog mode database, but it can be incremental.
☒ **A, C,** and **E** are incorrect. **A** is incorrect because the database must be mounted; otherwise, RMAN won't be able to connect to its repository or find the location of the datafiles. **C** is incorrect because an IMMEDIATE shutdown is clean—it is only an ABORT that would cause problems. **E** is incorrect because an archivelog mode database can certainly be backed up offline—it just isn't necessary.

4. ☑ **D**. In this case, none of the answers will work.

☒ **A**, **B**, and **C** are incorrect. **A** is incorrect because a copy of the controlfile can be created while the database is open, via a read-consistent snapshot. **B** is incorrect because this command will generate a CREATE CONTROLFILE script, not a file copy. **C** is incorrect because the file multiplexing is an additional precaution, not the only one.

5. ☑ **E**. RMAN will detect the absence of a suitable backup on which to base the incremental and will therefore make a level 0 backup.

☒ **A**, **B**, **C**, and **D** are incorrect. **A** is incorrect because this will occur automatically. **B** is incorrect because FULL cannot be used as the base for any incremental backup. **C** is incorrect because redo is required to fill the gap between the last incremental backup and the current time. **D** is incorrect because an incremental strategy can be used with NOARCHIVELOG mode, so long as the backup is made while the database is closed.

6. ☑ **A**, **B**, and **C**. Enterprise Manager will instruct the agent to run the backup. The database instance must be running, or the agent will not be able to contact it and start RMAN.

☒ **D** is incorrect. Oracle-scheduled backups do not use the operating system scheduler.

7. ☑ **C**. The crosscheck command verifies that the repository does accurately reflect reality.

☒ **A**, **B**, and **D** are incorrect. **A** is incorrect because crosscheck does not validate whether the backups are good—only whether they exist. **B** is incorrect because crosscheck doesn't delete references to missing backups; it only flags them as expired. **D** is incorrect because crosscheck confirms the existence of both backupsets and image copies.

8. ☑ **D**. Backups that are OBSOLETE according to RMAN's retention policy will be removed.

☒ **A**, **B**, **C**, and **E** are incorrect. **A** is incorrect because this describes datafiles, not the fast recovery area. **B** is incorrect because the operation will not necessarily fail—it may be possible to free up space automatically. **C** is incorrect because the alert system will only report the problem; it won't fix it. **E** is incorrect because EXPIRED refers to the status of the backup record in the repository, not the backup itself.

9. ☑ **A**, **E**, and **H**. RMAN backs up the current controlfile and the spfile (if you use one) after a successful backup, when you explicitly back up the current controlfile, and when the structure of the database changes.

☒ **B**, **C**, **D**, **F**, and **G** are incorrect. RMAN does not back up the controlfile under any of these circumstances.

10. ☑ **C**, **H**, and **I**. INSTANCE cannot be backed up because RMAN backs up databases; an instance comprises the Oracle memory structures and cannot be backed up. CONTROLFILE cannot be backed up because it is not a valid option; you must use CURRENT CONTROLFILE to back up the controlfile. REDOLOG cannot be backed up because you should never back up the online redo logfiles, and therefore BACKUP REDOLOG is syntactically incorrect.

☒ **A**, **B**, **D**, **E**, **F**, and **G** are incorrect because they can all be backed up. All other objects listed (the current controlfile, the spfile, the entire database, an individual datafile, an individual tablespace, or one or more archived redo logfiles) can be backed up by RMAN.

11. ☑ **A** and **D**. The SHOW ALL command shows all settings for the connected target; you can use CONFIGURE . . . CLEAR to reset a configuration value to its default.

☒ **B, C,** and **E** are incorrect. **B** is incorrect because CONFIGURE . . . CLEAR resets the configuration setting to its default value. **C** is incorrect because SHOW ALL works only when you are connected to a target database. **E** is incorrect since SHOW ALL lists all configuration values regardless of whether they have been changed from the default.

12. ☑ **D**. %U is the default and is a system-generated unique filename that is equivalent to %u_%p_%c.

☒ **A, B, C,** and **E** are incorrect. These choices are valid in the FORMAT command but are not the default.

13. ☑ **A** and **B**. In addition to datafiles and archived redo logfiles, you can create image copies of controlfiles.

☒ **C** and **D** are incorrect because they cannot be backed up as image copies. In fact, they cannot be backed up using RMAN.

14. ☑ **C**. When the backup completes successfully, RMAN deletes all archived redo logfiles from all destinations, including the fast recovery area.

☒ **A, B,** and **D** are incorrect. **A** and **B** are incorrect because RMAN deletes archived redo logfiles from all destinations. **D** is incorrect because the DELETE INPUT command applies only to archived redo logfiles that apply to this backup.

15. ☑ **D**. A whole-database backup can also include archived redo logfiles and the spfile.

☒ **A, B,** and **C** are incorrect. **A** and **B** are incorrect because either of these can be the basis for an incremental backup strategy as long as you use the INCREMENTAL LEVEL 0 parameter in the BACKUP command. **C** is incorrect because both a whole-database backup and a full backup can be image copies or backupsets.

16. ☑ **B, C,** and **D**. A level 0 backup includes all blocks in a datafile, except for blocks that have never been used. It also can be used with both cumulative and incremental level 1 backups.

☒ **A** and **E** are incorrect. **A** is incorrect because a level 0 backup excludes blocks that have never been used. **E** is incorrect because a level 0 backup is physically identical to a full backup of the same datafile; the differentiation is the metadata stored in the recovery catalog.

17. ☑ **A**. A differential backup is the default and backs up all changed blocks since the last level 0 or level 1 backup. You cannot specify the DIFFERENTIAL keyword, which is the default.

☒ **B, C,** and **D** are incorrect. **B** is incorrect because a cumulative backup is not the default and it backs up only changed blocks since the last level 0 backup. **C** is incorrect because differential backups also back up changed blocks from the last level 1 incremental backup. **D** is incorrect because a cumulative backup is not the default type of incremental backup and it backs up only changed blocks since the last level 0 backup.

18. ☑ **B**. RMAN creates a maximum of four copies for disk or tape locations.

☒ **A, C,** and **D** are incorrect. There is no differentiation between tape and disk for duplexed backups, and the range is from two to four.

19. ☑ **A, E,** and **F.** Archival backups can be kept for an indefinite period of time or retained for a specific period of time using the KEEP UNTIL clause. In addition, you can use an archival backup to migrate a database, and you can change the retention period as many times as you need to after you create it.

☒ **B, C,** and **D** are incorrect. **B** is incorrect since the correct clause is CHANGE . . . NOKEEP. **C** is incorrect because only the archived redo logs necessary for the snapshot are included in the backup. **D** is incorrect because you can easily change the retention period for any archival backup.

20. ☑ **C.** RMAN backs up the datafile in multiples of the section size, and any remainder resides in the last section.

☒ **A, B,** and **D** are incorrect. **A** is incorrect because you can use multisection backups for any type of tablespace. **B** is incorrect because RMAN does not round up the section size to create equal section sizes in the output. **D** is incorrect because you can back up either an individual tablespace or the entire database as a multisection backup.

21. ☑ **C.** You can use CONFIGURE only at the RMAN command prompt to set default values, and it cannot be used within a run block.

☒ **A, B,** and **D** are incorrect. **A** is incorrect because the CONFIGURE command cannot be used within a run block. **B** is incorrect for the same reason; additionally, any channels allocated within a run block override the default channel. **D** is incorrect since you can use BACKUP either as a stand-alone command or within a run block.

22. ☑ **B.** Backup optimization is not used for backing up individual tablespaces.

☒ **A, C,** and **D** are incorrect. Backup optimization is used for all of these commands.

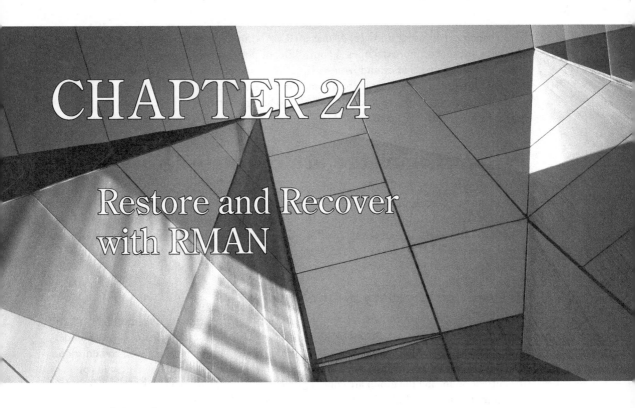

CHAPTER 24

Restore and Recover with RMAN

Exam Objectives

- 63.1.10.2 Perform Complete and Incomplete Recovery
- 63.1.1.12 Recover Files Using RMAN
- 63.1.12.1 Perform Recovery for Spfile, Password file, Controlfile, and Redo Log Files
- 63.1.12.2 Perform Table Recovery from Backups
- 63.1.12.3 Perform Recovery of Index and Read-only Tablespaces, Tempfile
- 63.1.12.4 Restore a Database to a New Host

This chapter details using Recovery Manager (RMAN) in a recovery scenario. This is required if you have lost one or more datafiles, a controlfile, or possibly the entire database. Two terms must be defined first: *restore* and *recover*. To restore a file means to replace the damaged or missing file with a copy extracted from some form of backup. To recover a file means to apply redo change vectors to the restored file in order to bring it forward in time, ideally to the state it was in before the damage occurred. RMAN automates the entire restore and recover process.

Perform Complete and Incomplete Recovery

In the following sections, you'll learn how to use the RESTORE and RECOVER commands for a database running in ARCHIVELOG mode. First, you'll read about the basic functions of RESTORE and RECOVER and how they work. Next, you'll see how to recover both a noncritical and a critical datafile successfully. You'll use incomplete recovery when either more recent archived redo logs are not available or you want to restore and recover to a time in the past before some kind of logical error occurred.

Restore and Recovery in One Page

Restore and recovery can be *complete* (meaning no loss of data) or *incomplete* (meaning you do lose data). The first decision a database administrator (DBA) makes after a problem is whether to try complete or incomplete recovery. Ninety-nine times out of a hundred, you should try for compete recovery. Loss of any number of any files is no reason to lose data—unless all copies of the current online log file group are gone. In that case, incomplete recovery is the only option.

Complete recovery following datafile damage requires four steps:

1. Take the damaged or missing file (or files) offline.
2. Restore it (or them).
3. Recover it (or them).
4. Bring it (or them) online.

Incomplete recovery also requires four steps:

1. Mount the database.
2. Restore all datafiles.
3. Recover the database until some point.
4. Open the database with RESETLOGS.

These are the differences: Complete recovery can (usually) be done while the database is open; incomplete recovery is done in mount mode. The granularity of restore for complete recovery is the damaged file (or files); the granularity of incomplete recovery is the entire database. Incomplete recovery uses the UNTIL keyword to stop recovery at a certain system change number (SCN), time, or log switch sequence number; complete recovery does not. Following complete recovery, no further action is required, it is as though nothing had ever gone wrong; incomplete recovery finishes by re-creating the online redo log files, with the RESETLOGS command.

Using the RMAN RESTORE and RECOVER Commands

In general, recovering from a database failure is a two-step process: restoring one or more database files from a backup location, which is the restore phase, and applying archived and online redo log files to bring the entire database or individual datafile up to the specified SCN (usually the most recent SCN, or the last committed transaction), which is the recovery phase.

The RESTORE command is the first step in any recovery process. When you issue a RESTORE command, RMAN retrieves one or more datafiles from disk or tape along with any archived redo log files required during the recovery operation. If your backup files are on tape, you will need to allocate the necessary tape channels as well.

When you issue the RECOVER command, RMAN applies the changes in the archived and online redo log files to the restored datafiles. The process can be as simple as the following example (the command output is excluded for clarity):

```
SQL> shutdown immediate;
SQL> startup mount;
[oracle@srv04 ~]$ rman target / catalog rman/rman@rcat
RMAN> restore database;
RMAN> recover database;
RMAN> sql 'alter database open';
```

The recovery process is slightly different, depending on whether you lose a critical or a noncritical datafile. If you lose a critical datafile, you must shut down and start up the database in MOUNT mode before you can recover the database. For a noncritical datafile, you can perform the recovery while users are connected and using other available datafiles. Note that many operations can be accomplished at either the tablespace level or the datafile level but that tablespace operations are possible only if the database is open.

Performing Complete Recovery of a Noncritical Datafile

If you lose a datafile that is not part of the SYSTEM or UNDO tablespace, the datafile is considered noncritical (although the users of the lost datafile might disagree with this assessment). When the database is in ARCHIVELOG mode, a corrupted or missing datafile that is not part of the SYSTEM or UNDO tablespace affects only objects in that datafile, and the database can remain open.

The general steps to recover a datafile from a noncritical tablespace are as follows:

1. If the database is open, take the tablespace containing the corrupted or missing datafile offline with the ALTER TABLESPACE command.

2. Use the RMAN RESTORE command to load the datafiles for the tablespace from the backup location.

3. Use the RMAN RECOVER command to apply archived and online redo log files to the restored datafiles.

4. Bring the tablespace back online.

Because the database is in ARCHIVELOG mode, recovery up to the last committed transaction is possible. In other words, users do not have to reenter any data for previously committed transactions. Note that it is, strictly speaking, not necessary to take the whole tablespace offline. If the tablespace consists of multiple datafiles and only one of the datafiles is damaged, it is possible to take only that one datafile offline. This will result in only some objects in the tablespace (those that have extents in the damaged file) being unavailable. How your software will react to this situation is hard to predict.

Exercise 24-1: Restore and Recover the USERS Tablespace   In this exercise, the datafile for the USERS tablespace was accidentally deleted by the system administrator. Restore and recover the tablespace while the database is still open for access to the other tablespaces. It is assumed that previous exercises have been completed.

1. Connect to RMAN and take the USERS tablespace offline.

   ```
   RMAN> sql "alter tablespace users offline immediate";
   ```

 TIP   Starting with Oracle Database 12c, you can run most SQL commands within RMAN without using the RMAN sql command. However, you may still choose to use the sql command to make it clear that you are running a non-RMAN command.

   Any users trying to access the tablespace while it is offline will receive a message similar to the following:

   ```
   SQL> select * from sales_data;
                      *
   ERROR at line 1:
   ORA-00376: file 4 cannot be read at this time
   ORA-01110: data file 4: '/u01/app/oracle/oradata/hr/users01.dbf'

   SQL>
   ```

2. Restore the USERS tablespace.

   ```
   RMAN> restore tablespace users;
   ```

3. Recover the USERS tablespace to apply the archived and online redo log files.

   ```
   RMAN> recover tablespace users;
   ```

4. Bring the USERS tablespace back online.

   ```
   RMAN> sql "alter tablespace users online";
   ```

5. Confirm that users can once again access the USERS tablespace.

   ```
   SQL> select * from sales_data;

   SALES_ID SALE_DATE TRAN_AMT
   -------- --------- --------
        202 11-MAR-14  1402.12
   . . .
   ```

6. Repeat the exercise, performing restore and recover at the datafile level.

   These are the commands:

   ```
   alter database datafile '…' offline;
   restore datafile '…' ;
   recover datafile '…' ;
   alter database datafile '…' online ;
   ```

Performing Complete Recovery of a Critical Datafile

The procedure for recovering a critical datafile is similar to that of a noncritical datafile, except that the database must be shut down and opened in the MOUNT state to perform the recovery operation. If the lost datafile is from the SYSTEM tablespace, the instance will most likely crash or shut down automatically. Here are the steps you use to recover a critical datafile:

1. Shut down the database with SHUTDOWN ABORT if it is not already shut down.

2. Reopen the database with STARTUP MOUNT.

3. Use the RMAN RESTORE command to copy (restore) the datafile (or datafiles) for the critical tablespace from the backup location.

4. Use the RMAN RECOVER command to apply any archived or online redo log files.

5. Reopen the database for users with ALTER DATABASE OPEN.

All committed transactions are recovered up until the time of failure, so users will not have to reenter any data.

In mount mode (necessary when repairing damage to a critical file), ALTER TABLESPACE commands are not available, so restore and recovery must be done at the file level. The ALTER TABLESPACE commands can be used only when the database is open.

Performing Incomplete Recovery Using RMAN

On occasion, you might need to restore a database to a point of time in the past. For example, applications could have made numerous erroneous changes to the database in the last 24 hours, and you may not be able to reverse errors easily with a table flashback, or you do not have flashback configured for the database.

Using restore points makes it easier to perform point-in-time recovery, whether you're performing incomplete recovery in RMAN or Flashback Database. After you learn about restore points, you'll perform an incomplete recovery using a restore point.

Creating Restore Points

You can create two types of restore points—either as of a specific time or with an SCN number in the past. Which type you use depends on your environment and which option is the more convenient. If you do not specify either option, Oracle uses the current SCN and assumes you want the restore time to be the current time. Remember that you can retrieve the current SCN from V$DATABASE.

```
SQL> select current_scn from v$database;

CURRENT_SCN
-----------
   34674668

SQL>
```

PART IV

To create a restore point for the present time or SCN, use this format of the CREATE RESTORE POINT command:

```
SQL> create restore point good_for_now;

Restore point created.

SQL>
```

To create a restore point for a particular SCN, use the AS OF syntax.

```
SQL> create restore point good_for_now as of scn 34674668;

Restore point created.

SQL>
```

Restore points are also useful when you want to use Oracle's flashback technology to flash back the database to a point in time in the past.

Oracle keeps restore points for at least as long as the time specified in the CONTROL_FILE_RECORD_KEEP_TIME initialization parameter. If you explicitly want to keep a restore point longer, use the PRESERVE keyword when you create the restore point.

```
SQL> create restore point good_for_now preserve;

Restore point created.

SQL>
```

As you might expect, you can explicitly remove a restore point with the DROP RESTORE POINT command.

```
SQL> drop restore point good_for_now;

Restore point dropped.

SQL>
```

Performing Server-Managed Incomplete Recovery

To perform server-managed (RMAN) incomplete recovery (user-managed recovery is not recommended and deprecated in Oracle Database 12c), use the following steps:

1. Determine the target point for the restore (SCN, time, restore point, or log sequence number).

2. Set the NLS variables at the operating system prompt if you are using time-based incomplete recovery.

   - NLS_LANG
   - NLS_DATE_FORMAT

3. Stop and restart the database in MOUNT mode.

4. Using an RMAN run block, use the SET UNTIL, RESTORE, and RECOVER commands.

5. Optionally, open the database in READ ONLY mode to verify that the restore point was the desired restore point.

6. Open the database using RESETLOGS.

It's important to specify the correct NLS variables so that RMAN will interpret the date strings you provide correctly; here are some sample values:

```
$ export NLS_LANG = american_america.us7ascii
$ export NLS_DATE_FORMAT = "Mon DD YYYY HH24:MI:SS"
```

Also note that opening the database as READ ONLY after your incomplete recovery gives you the opportunity to run another incomplete recovery for a different SCN or time. Once you open the database for read-write with RESETLOGS, the current log sequence is set to 1, and any redo information not applied during recovery is discarded. This prevents you from performing another recovery using a redo generated after the SCN or timestamp of your incomplete recovery.

Exercise 24-2: Perform Incomplete Recovery to Restore the USERS Tablespace
In this exercise, you will create a restore point and use it later to recover from the inadvertent deletion of tables and views in the EXAMPLE tablespace.

1. Connect with SQL*Plus and create a restore point for the current SCN.

   ```
   SQL> create restore point before_disaster_strikes;
   ```

2. "Accidentally" drop some tables and views in the EXAMPLE tablespace.

   ```
   SQL> drop table hr.job_history;

   SQL> drop view hr.emp_details_view;
   ```

3. Shut down the instance and restart the database in MOUNT mode.

   ```
   SQL> shutdown immediate
   SQL> startup mount
   ```

4. At the RMAN prompt, create a run block that uses the restore point created earlier to restore and recover the database to the time of the restore point.

   ```
   RMAN> run
   2>    {
   3>       set until restore point before_disaster_strikes;
   4>       restore database;
   5>       recover database;
   6>    }
   ```

5. Open the database with RESETLOGS.

   ```
   SQL> alter database open resetlogs;
   ```

6. Verify the existence of the dropped table.

   ```
   SQL> select * from hr.job_history;
   ```

Note that several less draconian methods are available to restore and recover these tables and views, such as using Flashback Database, restoring and recovering each tablespace while the database is still online, or retrieving the tables from the recycle bin. Each recovery situation must be evaluated separately, balancing these factors:

- The time required to obtain the backup files needed for recovery. If backup files are on a tape offsite, then the time required could be unacceptable.
- The time to restore and recover the entire database once the recovery files are available.
- The time the DBA must spend to perform the recovery.
- The time the users must spend to reenter lost data.
- The tolerance of users for database downtime.

Recovering Using Incrementally Updated Backups

Using image copies in your backup and recovery strategy significantly reduces the time it takes to restore a datafile or the entire database. Image copies are already in the native Oracle datafile format and do not need to be re-created from a compressed or uncompressed RMAN backupset. RMAN can improve on this even more because you can incrementally update an image copy using an incremental backup. In the following sections, you'll learn more about how to recover an image copy, and you'll review a sample image copy strategy.

To clarify, you're creating image copies, but going forward you're keeping that image copy up to date incrementally. You're not actually using this image copy to recover your live database but instead using online and archived redo log files to recover the *copy* of a datafile so it's ready to use if and when disaster strikes.

The "Oracle-suggested backup strategy" that Enterprise Manager can implement is based on an incrementally updated backup.

Recovering Image Copies

When you update an image copy with an incremental backup, any recovery scenario that uses the image copy needs to apply only the archived and online redo log files since the last incremental backup. There is no longer any need to perform another full image copy of the datafile or database. The incremental recovery of each datafile is indistinguishable from a full image copy.

If more than one image copy of a datafile exists, RMAN automatically determines which one to use—usually the most recently created or incrementally updated version. If the recovery process for an image copy fails when applying an incremental backup, such as the temporary unavailability of the incremental backup, just restart the recovery process when the incremental backup is available again. RMAN picks up where it left off.

Implementing an Image Copy Strategy

Here is a sample RMAN script to implement an incrementally updated image copy strategy on a daily basis:

```
run {
      recover copy of database
         with tag 'inc_upd';
      backup incremental level 1
         for recover of copy
         with tag 'inc_upd'
         database;
}
```

Here's a breakdown of what happens in this run block. The first time you run it, there is no level 0 image copy to restore and, similarly, no level 0 incremental backup yet, so you get these messages:

```
Starting recover at 13-MAR-14
using channel ORA_DISK_1
no copy of datafile 1 found to recover
no copy of datafile 2 found to recover
no copy of datafile 3 found to recover
no copy of datafile 4 found to recover
no copy of datafile 5 found to recover
Finished recover at 13-MAR-14

Starting backup at 13-MAR-14
using channel ORA_DISK_1
no parent backup or copy of datafile 2 found
no parent backup or copy of datafile 1 found
no parent backup or copy of datafile 3 found
no parent backup or copy of datafile 5 found
no parent backup or copy of datafile 4 found
channel ORA_DISK_1: starting datafile copy
. . .
```

RMAN automatically creates a level 0 backup whenever a level 1 backup occurs and there is no level 0 backup. The next time you run the script, the level 0 backup exists, but no incremental level 0 backup exists yet. So, the RECOVER command in the run block still generates these messages:

```
Starting recover at 13-MAR-14
using channel ORA_DISK_1
no copy of datafile 1 found to recover
no copy of datafile 2 found to recover
no copy of datafile 3 found to recover
no copy of datafile 4 found to recover
no copy of datafile 13-MAR-14

Starting backup at 13-MAR-14
using channel ORA_DISK_1
channel ORA_DISK_1: starting incremental level 1 datafile backup set
. . .
```

On the third and successive invocation of this run block, the RECOVER command updates the image copy with the latest level 1 backup, and another level 1 incremental backup occurs. This will be applied the next time this run block is executed. As a result, any recovery operation after the third invocation of this script will involve no more than the image copies, one incremental backup, and any archived and online redo logs generated since the last level 1 incremental backup.

Switching to Image Copies for Fast Recovery

Once you've starting making image copies, and even incrementally updating them, you can use them in a restore and recover operation to quickly recover some or your entire database. To recover your database even faster, you can perform a fast switch to image copies. In other words, you can use the image copies directly, skip the restore step, and apply only the recovery step. After the original datafiles are repaired or restored, you can easily switch back with little or no impact to users who are using other datafiles. The database does not need to be shut down unless you are switching to the image copies of the critical SYSTEM or UNDO tablespace datafiles.

Using the SET NEWNAME command within the run block to specify an alternative location for the replacement image copy allows RMAN to make the switch to image copies even easier.

Performing a Fast Switch to Image Copies

When disaster strikes and you lose a single datafile or even all datafiles, having image copies available significantly reduces the time required to recover your database. Once you've switched to an image copy, you will most likely want to switch back to the original datafile locations after the media failure has been repaired.

The steps to switch to a datafile copy are straightforward. This assumes, of course, that you have image copies of the damaged or lost datafile, as well as all archived and online redo log files since the image copy was created (or incrementally updated). Here are the steps:

1. Take the missing datafiles offline. You can use one of the dynamic performance views V$RECOVER_FILE, V$DATAFILE_HEADER, or V$TABLESPACE to identify which datafiles need recovery.

2. Use RMAN SWITCH . . . TO COPY to point to the image copy of the missing datafiles.

3. Recover the datafiles using the RMAN RECOVER command.

4. Bring the datafiles back online.

 EXAM TIP The RMAN SWITCH command is equivalent to the SQL command ALTER DATABASE RENAME FILE.

Exercise 24-3: Use the SWITCH Command to Recover a Datafile Quickly   The datafile for the USERS tablespace mysteriously disappears. Users start to complain immediately, reporting this message when they try to create or update a table:

```
ERROR at line 1:
ORA-01116: error in opening database file 4
ORA-01110: data file 4: '/u01/app/oracle/oradata/hr/users01.dbf'
ORA-27041: unable to open file
Linux Error: 2: No such file or directory
Additional information: 3
```

In addition, you see this message in the alert log. This alert should also be visible as an alert on the Enterprise Manager home page.

```
Fri Mar 14 19:45:13 2014
Checker run found 1 new persistent data failures
```

Find out what datafile number you need to restore, switch to an image copy, and then recover the datafile and bring the tablespace back online.

1. Prepare for the exercise by creating an image copy of the database to the fast recovery area. From the RMAN prompt, use this:

```
backup as copy database;
```

Use an operating system command to delete the datafile.

2. Since you already know that datafile #4 is having problems, query V$TABLESPACE to confirm that the USERS tablespace is the culprit.

```
SQL> select ts#, name
  2  from v$tablespace
  3  where ts# = 4;

      TS# NAME
--------- --------------------
        4 USERS

SQL>
```

The dynamic performance view V$DATAFILE_HEADER shows the error as well but does not always identify the tablespace name.

```
SQL> select file#, status, error, recover, tablespace_name, name
  2  from v$datafile_header
  3  where recover = 'YES'
  4     or (recover is null and error is not null);

    FILE# STATUS  ERROR              REC TABLESPACE_NAME NAME
--------- ------- ------------------ --- --------------- ------
        4 ONLINE  CANNOT OPEN FILE

SQL>
```

3. Take the datafile offline at the SQL> prompt.

```
SQL> alter database datafile 4 offline;
```

Alternatively, you can take the datafile offline from within an RMAN session.

4. Switch to the datafile copy for the USERS tablespace.

```
RMAN> switch datafile 4 to copy;


RMAN>
```

> **NOTE** You can use the SWITCH command with either the DATAFILE or TABLESPACE parameter, whichever is easier or more convenient. Also, you don't need to know where your datafile copy is. RMAN knows where it is and will switch it and update the controlfile and recovery catalog automatically with the new location.

5. Recover the datafile using the recent archived and online redo log files.

```
RMAN> recover datafile 4;
```

6. Bring the datafile back online.

```
RMAN> alter database datafile 4 online;
```

Alternatively, you can bring the datafile back online using the SQL> prompt.

Once your database is back up and running after switching to an image copy, you will likely want to switch the datafile back to its original location after the source disk has been repaired.

This is especially true if the image copy you switched to resides in the fast recovery area. To move the datafiles back to the original location, follow these steps:

1. Create an image copy of the datafiles in the original location.

2. Take the datafiles offline.

3. Use the SWITCH TO . . . COPY command to switch back to the restored (re-created) datafile.

4. Recover the datafiles.

5. Bring the datafiles back online.

Exercise 24-4: Use the SWITCH Command After Creating the USERS Tablespace's Datafile in the Original Location In this exercise, you'll switch the datafile for the USERS tablespace back to its original location after the source disk has been repaired (or you have figured out why datafiles are disappearing from the source disk). This time, do the work at the tablespace level. The datafile locations for each tablespace are currently as follows:

```
SQL> select file#, df.name, ts#, ts.name
  2  from v$datafile df join v$tablespace ts using(ts#);

     FILE# NAME                            TS# NAME
---------- ------------------------- ---------- -------------
         1 /u01/app/oracle/oradata/h       0 SYSTEM
           r/system01.dbf
         2 /u01/app/oracle/oradata/h       1 SYSAUX
           r/sysaux01.dbf
         3 /u01/app/oracle/oradata/h       2 UNDOTBS1
           r/undotbs01.dbf
         4 /u01/oradata/bkup/data_D-        4 USERS
           HR_I-3318356692_TS-USERS_
           FNO-4_37jhmn1m
         5 /u01/app/oracle/oradata/h       6 EXAMPLE
           r/example01.dbf
SQL>
```

1. Create an image copy of the datafile at the original location.

```
RMAN> backup as copy tablespace users
2>       format '/u01/app/oracle/oradata/hr/users01.dbf';

Starting backup at 14-MAR-14
using channel ORA_DISK_1
channel ORA_DISK_1: starting datafile copy
input datafile file number=00004
   name=/u01/oradata/bkup/data_D-HR_I-3318356692_TS-USERSoutput file
name=/u01/app/oracle/oradata/hr/users01.dbf
tag=TAG20080530T211450 RECID=36 STAMP=656111726
channel ORA_DISK_1: datafile copy complete, elapsed time: 00:00:16
Finished backup at 14-MAR-14

RMAN>
```

Note that you can name the image copy anything you want. In this case, you'll use the original name of the datafile to be consistent with the other datafile names.

2. Take the USERS tablespace offline in preparation for the SWITCH command.

```
RMAN> alter tablespace users offline;

sql statement: alter tablespace users offline
starting full resync of recovery catalog
full resync complete

RMAN>
```

3. Switch to the newly created copy.

```
RMAN> switch tablespace users to copy;

datafile 4 switched to datafile copy
        "/u01/app/oracle/oradata/hr/users01.dbf"
starting full resync of recovery catalog
full resync complete

RMAN>
```

4. Recover the datafile in its new location.

```
RMAN> recover tablespace users;

Starting recover at 14-MAR-14
using channel ORA_DISK_1

starting media recovery
media recovery complete, elapsed time: 00:00:00

Finished recover at 14-MAR-14

RMAN>
```

5. Bring the USERS tablespace back online.

```
RMAN> alter tablespace users online;

sql statement: alter tablespace users online
starting full resync of recovery catalog
full resync complete

RMAN>
```

6. Confirm that the datafile for the USERS tablespace is back in its original location.

```
SQL> select file#, df.name, ts#, ts.name
  2  from v$datafile df join v$tablespace ts using(ts#)
  3  where ts.name = 'USERS';

    FILE# NAME                            TS# NAME
---------- -------------------------- ---------- -------------
        4 /u01/app/oracle/oradata/h      4 USERS
          r/users01.dbf

SQL>
```

7. Create a new image copy to be ready when or if the datafile disappears again, although you could also use the image copy you just switched from.

```
RMAN> backup as copy tablespace users;

Starting backup at 14-MAR-14
starting full resync of recovery catalog
full resync complete
using channel ORA_DISK_1
channel ORA_DISK_1: starting datafile copy
input datafile file number=00004
name=/u01/app/oracle/oradata/hr/users01.dbf
output file name=/u01/oradata/bkup/  data_D-HR_I-3318356692_TS-USERS_
FNO-4_39jhn16a channel ORA_DISK_1: datafile copy complete, elapsed
time: 00:00:26
Finished backup at 14-MAR-14

RMAN>
```

Perform Recovery for Spfiles, Controlfiles, and Online Redo Log Files

In rare instances, you may lose all copies of the current controlfile. This is rare because you should have the controlfile multiplexed to several locations. Even if you do lose all copies of the current controlfile, you should have at least one autobackup of the controlfile from the most recent RMAN backup. In addition, if you are using a recovery catalog, all metadata within your most recent controlfile resides in the recovery catalog. The spfile is also susceptible to loss if it does not reside on a mirrored external file system or on a mirrored Automatic Storage Management (ASM) disk group. When RMAN performs a controlfile autobackup, both the current controlfile and the spfile are backed up.

Damage to online redo log files cannot be repaired by RMAN because RMAN never backs up online redo log files. They are intended to be protected by multiplexing. To repair damage to them, use SQL commands. These can be executed from SQL*Plus or from within an RMAN session, but in either case the recovery does not in any way involve RMAN channel processes.

Restoring the Spfile from the Autobackup

To restore the spfile from the autobackup, first set the database ID (DBID) if the instance is not running when the spfile is lost.

```
RMAN> set dbid 3318356692;
```

The DBID should be part of your most basic documentation and will have been displayed every time you connected with RMAN. Next, restart the database with a default spfile (you will do something similar later in the chapter when recovering to a new host).

```
RMAN> startup force nomount;
```

Next, restore the spfile from the autobackup to the original location.

```
RMAN> restore spfile from autobackup;
```

Finally, start the database.

```
RMAN> startup force;
```

Restoring the Controlfile

If the controlfile is multiplexed (as it should be), recovery from loss of one copy is trivial; simply copy a surviving controlfile copy over the damaged or missing controlfile copy. This must be done while the database is shut down or in NOMOUNT mode (which will always be the case because the instance will have failed when the controlfile copy was damaged and cannot subsequently be mounted). Then mount and open the database. Only if all copies of the controlfile are lost is anything more complex required. The routine is as follows:

1. Start up the instance in NOMOUNT mode.

2. Restore the controlfile from backup.

3. Mount the database.

4. Recover the database.

5. Open the database with RESETLOGS.

The awkward part is the second step. Because the database cannot be mounted, RMAN has no access to its repository and does not therefore know where the backup pieces that contain your controlfile backups actually are. There are three ways around this.

First, use the RESTORE CONTROLFILE FROM AUTOBACKUP command. The autobackups go to a well-known filename, based on the DBID, and RMAN can find them automatically.

Second, use a recovery catalog. The catalog contains a copy of the RMAN repository, so if you are connected to it, RMAN can interrogate the repository to find the backup locations. Then use the command RESTORE CONTROLFILE;.

Third, nominate a backup piece that you know includes a controlfile backup. Provided you have kept the output of your previously executed backup commands, you will have this information: RESTORE CONTROLFILE FROM '......' ;.

Restoring the controlfile from an autobackup is similar to the steps you use to restore an spfile from an autobackup. Here are the sample RMAN commands:

```
RMAN> startup nomount;
RMAN> restore controlfile from autobackup;
RMAN> alter database mount;
RMAN> recover database;
RMAN> alter database open resetlogs;
```

Note that since there is no controlfile, you have to open the database with NOMOUNT and then restore the controlfile. After you mount the database with the restored backup controlfile, you must recover the database because the backup controlfile contains information about an older version of the database. For the same reason, you must open the database with RESETLOGS.

RMAN restores the controlfile to all locations specified by the initialization parameter CONTROL_FILES. If one or more of those locations are still not available, you will have to edit the CONTROL_FILES parameter to specify alternative locations or temporarily restore the controlfile to a different location.

```
RMAN> restore controlfile to '/u06/oradata/rest_cf.dbf' from autobackup;
```

Exercise 24-5: Restore the Controlfile from an Autobackup   In this exercise, all copies of the controlfile were accidentally deleted by an overly eager system administrator trying to free up disk space. Restore and recover the database with a controlfile restored from a controlfile and spfile autobackup.

1. Identify the controlfile locations where all copies of the controlfile used to reside.

   ```
   SQL> show parameter control_files
   ```

   Use an operating system command to delete all copies of the controlfile.

2. Shut down the instance (if it is not already down) and reopen it in NOMOUNT mode.

   ```
   SQL> connect / as sysdba
   SQL> shutdown immediate;
   SQL> startup force nomount;
   ```

3. Start RMAN and restore the controlfile from autobackup to the original locations.

   ```
   rman target /
   ```

   ```
   RMAN> restore controlfile from autobackup;
   ```

   A few points are worth noting here. RMAN can connect to the instance even if it is not mounted. In fact, RMAN has to connect to an unmounted database to be able to restore the controlfile. RMAN finds the controlfile autobackup in the fast recovery area and writes it to the three controlfile destinations specified by the CONTROL_FILES initialization parameter.

4. Mount the database, recover the database (to synchronize the datafiles with the restored controlfile), and open the database with RESETLOGS.

   ```
   RMAN> alter database mount;
   ```

   ```
   RMAN> recover database;
   ```

   ```
   RMAN> alter database open resetlogs;
   ```

Recovering from a Lost Redo Log Group

The loss of a redo log group or a redo log group member can mean data loss and a significant recovery effort. It can also mean no data loss and a minimal recovery effort, depending on the status of the redo log group and whether you lose the entire log group or only a member of a log group. The following sections review how log groups work and how the different log group statuses change as redo is written to the group, how the database switches to the next log group, and how a filled log group is copied to an archive location. In most scenarios, data loss is nonexistent, especially if you mirror your log groups.

Log File Status	Status Description
CURRENT	Oracle is writing to this log group, and this group is needed for instance recovery.
ACTIVE	This log group is needed for instance recovery, but Oracle is not writing to this log group. It may or may not be archived yet.
INACTIVE	The log group is not needed for instance recovery and may or may not be archived.
UNUSED	The log group has not been used yet.
CLEARING	The log is being cleared by ALTER DATABASE CLEAR LOGFILE. After being cleared, the status changes to UNUSED.
CLEARING_CURRENT	An error has occurred during ALTER DATABASE CLEAR LOGFILE.

Table 24-1   Log File Status in V$LOG

A redo log group can have one of six statuses in the view V$LOG.

At any given point in time, the most common statuses are CURRENT, ACTIVE, and INACTIVE. A redo log group is in the UNUSED state after creation, and once it's used, it will never return to that state. The CLEARING and CLEARING_CURRENT states exist when you re-create a corrupted log file, which ideally will not occur often!

The sample database has three redo log file groups, and this query of V$LOG shows the status of each log:

```
SQL> select group#, sequence#, archived, status
  2  from v$log;

   GROUP#  SEQUENCE# ARC STATUS
---------- ---------- --- ----------------
        1         88 NO  CURRENT
        2         86 YES INACTIVE
        3         87 YES INACTIVE
SQL>
```

The two log file groups with a status of INACTIVE have been archived. Depending on the input/output (I/O) load of the system and other factors, the ARCHIVED status will be NO until the log file has been successfully written to all mandatory archived log file destinations.

Recovering from Log Group Member Failures

If one member of a log group becomes damaged or is lost, the Log Writer (LGWR) process continues to write to the undamaged member, and no data loss or interruption in service occurs. However, it is imperative that you correct this problem as soon as possible because the log group with only one member is now the single point of failure in your database. If it is lost, your recovery efforts will increase, and loss of committed transactions is likely.

PART IV

In this example, the second member of the third redo log file group becomes damaged. These error messages should appear in the alert log. You will see similar messages on the Enterprise Manager Database Control home page if it is configured.

```
Fri Mar 14 11:13:16 2014
Errors in file /u01/app/oracle/diag/rdbms/hr/hr/trace/hr_arc2_5718.trc:
ORA-00313: open failed for members of log group 3 of thread 1
ORA-00312: online log 3 thread 1: '/u06/app/oracle/oradata/hr/redo03.log'
ORA-27046: file size is not a multiple of logical block size
Additional information: 1
```

You can also identify the lost or damaged redo log file member using the V$LOGFILE view:

```
SQL> select group#, status, member from v$logfile;

     GROUP# STATUS  MEMBER
---------- ------- ----------------------------------------
         3         /u01/app/oracle/oradata/hr/redo03.log
         2         /u01/app/oracle/oradata/hr/redo02.log
         1         /u01/app/oracle/oradata/hr/redo01.log
         1         /u06/app/oracle/oradata/hr/redo01.log
         2         /u06/app/oracle/oradata/hr/redo02.log
         3 INVALID /u06/app/oracle/oradata/hr/redo03.log

6 rows selected.
SQL>
```

The solution to this problem is straightforward. Drop the invalid member and add a new member to the group, as in this example:

```
SQL> alter database drop logfile member
  2       '/u06/app/oracle/oradata/hr/redo03.log';

Database altered.

SQL> alter database add logfile member
  2       '/u06/app/oracle/oradata/hr/redo03a.log'
  3       to group 3;

Database altered.

SQL>
```

Note that the redundancy provided by the repaired redo log file group will not be available until the next time this log file group is active. If the destination disk itself is not damaged and the original redo log file is logically corrupted from user error or a rogue process, you can reuse the original redo log file by specifying the REUSE clause as follows:

```
alter database add logfile member
  '/u06/app/oracle/oradata/hr/redo03.log'
  reuse to group 3;
```

Recovering from Loss of an Entire INACTIVE Redo Log Group

The loss of all members of a redo log group marked INACTIVE is the most benign redo log group failure, although you must act quickly before the Oracle database processes need to use the redo log group again. If Oracle needs to use the redo log group before it is repaired, the database halts until the problem is fixed. The group is not needed for crash recovery because it is INACTIVE. Therefore, you can clear the group using the ALTER DATABASE CLEAR LOGFILE command.

A damaged redo log group with a status of INACTIVE may or may not be archived yet. The archival status determines which form of the ALTER DATABASE CLEAR LOGFILE command to use.

If a damaged inactive redo log group has been archived, you can identify the group number of the damaged group from the alert log or from the dynamic performance view V$LOGFILE. Remember that you can look at the ARCHIVED column in the dynamic performance view V$LOG to determine whether the log group has been archived yet.

In this example, redo log group #1 is damaged but has been archived. Use the ALTER DATABASE command as follows:

```
SQL> alter database clear logfile group 1;

Database altered.

SQL>
```

If the instance is down, start the database in MOUNT mode and run this command. Otherwise, you can run the command when the database is OPEN. All members of the redo log file group are reinitialized. If any or all of the redo log group members are missing, they are then re-created, provided that the destination directories are available.

The redo log group has been archived. Thus, no data loss will result, and all backups in combination with archived redo log files can be used for complete recovery of the database. Until the database reuses the redo log file group, it has a status of UNUSED, as you can see in this query:

```
SQL> select group#, sequence#, archived, status from v$log;

   GROUP#  SEQUENCE# ARC STATUS
---------- ---------- --- ----------------
        1          0 YES UNUSED
        2         98 NO  CURRENT
        3         96 YES INACTIVE

SQL>
```

If you have a damaged nonarchived inactive redo log group, you will not lose any committed transactions. However, you must perform a full backup after clearing the redo log group to ensure that you can perform a complete recovery. If you do not, you will have a gap in archived redo log files. Therefore, you will be able to perform only incomplete recovery up to the SCN of the last transaction in the archived redo log file created before the missing log file.

To clear the second unarchived log group, start the database in MOUNT mode (if it is not already up) and use the following command:

```
alter database clear unarchived logfile group 2;
```

Note the UNARCHIVED keyword in this command. It performs the same action that occurs when you cleared an archived redo log group, but this is Oracle's way of forcing you to acknowledge that you will have a gap in your archived redo log files.

After clearing the log file group, perform a full backup. This provides a backup that you can use for complete recovery, along with all successive archived redo log files.

A complicating factor to consider when you're clearing a damaged nonarchived inactive redo log group is whether an offline datafile needs the cleared log file group before it can be brought online. If it does, you may have to drop the datafile. Segments in the tablespace containing the offline datafile may exist in other online datafiles that belong to this tablespace and may be relocated to other tablespaces. The tablespace may have to be re-created using logical backups or some other method. You cannot recover the datafile, and therefore the tablespace containing the datafile, because the redo required to bring the datafile back online is gone. Oracle makes you acknowledge that your datafile is unrecoverable in this scenario as well, and you must use the UNRECOVERABLE DATAFILE keywords when you clear the log file group:

```
alter database clear logfile unarchived group 2 unrecoverable datafile;
```

Recovering from a Lost ACTIVE Redo Log Group

If a damaged redo log group is in the ACTIVE state, Oracle is not currently writing to it, but it is needed for instance recovery. Execute ALTER SYSTEM CHECKPOINT to force the database writer process (DBWn) to write all changed buffers from buffer cache to datafiles, and the group will then become inactive. Clear the redo log file group as you did with an inactive redo log group. You will not lose any transactions. In addition, your archived redo log file stream will be intact, if the group had been archived at the time the problem occurred.

Recovering from a Lost CURRENT Redo Log Group

This is the one situation where you will lose data. A lost redo log group in the CURRENT state is currently being written to by the LGWR process—or it *was* being written to at the time of failure. The instance will crash, and your only option is to perform incomplete recovery applying archived and online redo log files up to but not including the damaged redo log group.

After performing incomplete recovery with the database in MOUNT mode, open the database with RESETLOGS.

```
alter database open resetlogs;
```

If the location for the damaged online redo log file group is available, Oracle will reinitialize the log file group along with all other groups, resetting the log sequence number to 1 and starting a new incarnation. If the location is no longer available, rename the online redo log files and point them to a new location as in this example, while the database is mounted and before opening the database with RESETLOGS:

```
alter database rename file '/u01/app/oracle/oradata/hr/redo02.log'
    to '/u02/app/oracle/oradata/hr/redo02.log';
alter database rename file '/u06/app/oracle/oradata/hr/redo02.log'
    to '/u07/app/oracle/oradata/hr/redo02.log';
```

When you open the database with RESETLOGS, Oracle re-creates and initializes any missing online redo log files.

Backing Up and Restoring the Password File

The password file cannot be managed by RMAN. To protect it, copy it with any appropriate operating system utility. Ideally, this should be done after any grant or revoke of the administrative privileges (which are SYSDBA, SYSOPER, SYSBACKUP, SYSDG, and SYSKM in a database instance; SYSASM in an ASM instance) and subsequently after any change of password for any user granted these privileges. In practice, it usually sufficient simply to rely on whatever backups are made by your system administrator of the Oracle Home file system. Because the default location of the password file is in the ORACLE_HOME/dbs directory (or ORACLE_HOME\database directory on Windows), it will be included in any such backup. It is possible to store the password file on an ASM disk group by specifying this when you run the ORAPWD utility to create the file. In this case, you cannot copy the file using an operating system utility, and it will not, of course, be included in an Oracle Home backup. In this case, use the ASMCMD utility to copy the file from the disk group to a file system.

If the password file is ever damaged, simply copy it back.

An alternative to backing up and restoring the password file is to re-create it. This takes only a couple of seconds. If users other than SYS have been granted administrative privileges, these grants will have to be made again because they will not exist in a freshly created file.

Recovering from a Lost Tempfile

Recovering from the loss of one or more tempfiles is a straightforward process. Remember that a tempfile is identical to a datafile except that it belongs to a temporary tablespace. The impact to a running database is minimal depending on the query mix. In all cases, you can recover the tempfile while the database is up, even if the original file location is not available.

Losing a Tempfile

One of the consequences of losing a tempfile is that any SQL statements that need temporary disk space for sorting (in other words, insufficient memory is available in Oracle's memory space) will fail. If one or all of the datafiles for the TEMP tablespace is deleted at the operating system level, you can create a new tempfile in the same directory as the original one using the ALTER TABLESPACE command. If the original directory location is not available, you can create it in a different location. After that you can drop the original tempfile using a similar ALTER TABLESPACE command.

Exercise 24-6: Create a Replacement Tempfile for the TEMP Tablespace   In this exercise, the tempfile for the TEMP tablespace was accidentally deleted, so you must create another tempfile to replace it while the database is still running.

1. Identify the name of the tempfile for the TEMP tablespace.

```
SQL> select file#, name from v$tempfile;

      FILE# NAME
---------- -------------------------------------------------------
          1 /u01/app/oracle/oradata/hr/temp01.dbf

SQL>
```

2. Create a new tempfile with a different name for the TEMP tablespace.

```
SQL> alter tablespace temp add tempfile
  2    '/u01/app/oracle/oradata/hr/temp02.dbf'
  3    size 25m;

Tablespace altered.

SQL>
```

3. Drop the previous tempfile. This will update only the controlfile because the original tempfile is missing.

```
SQL> alter tablespace temp drop tempfile
  2    '/u01/app/oracle/oradata/hr/temp01.dbf';

Tablespace altered.

SQL>
```

4. Confirm that the TEMP tablespace contains only the newly created tempfile.

```
SQL> select file#, name from v$tempfile;

     FILE# NAME
---------- ---------------------------------------------------
         2 /u01/app/oracle/oradata/hr/temp02.dbf

SQL>
```

Starting a Database Without a Tempfile

Recovering from the loss of a tempfile is even easier if you start the database with a missing tempfile. The database starts, and if the original disk directory location is available, Oracle re-creates all missing tempfiles, as you can see in this excerpt from the alert log:

```
Re-creating tempfile /u01/app/oracle/oradata/hr/temp02.dbf
Re-creating tempfile /u01/app/oracle/oradata/hr/temp03.dbf
```

If the original disk directory location is no longer available, the database still starts, and you can use the steps from the preceding section to re-create the tempfiles manually for the TEMP tablespace.

Two-Minute Drill

Perform Complete and Incomplete Recovery

- Use RMAN RESTORE and RECOVER for complete recovery from a critical and noncritical datafile loss.
- Datafiles from the SYSTEM and UNDO tablespaces are critical datafiles.
- When restoring and recovering a critical datafile, the database must be in MOUNT mode.
- You can completely recover any datafile if the database is in ARCHIVELOG mode.
- You use restore points to recover a database to an SCN or a time in the past.

- Use CREATE RESTORE POINT to create a restore point.
- You must open the database with RESETLOGS if you perform incomplete recovery.
- You can recover image copies with more recent incremental level 1 backups.
- RMAN automatically determines the best image copy to use if more than one is available.
- Use tags with an incrementally updated image copy strategy to ensure that the correct incremental backup updates the image copy.
- Using image copies skips the restore step and saves overall recovery time.
- Use the RMAN command SWITCH TO . . . COPY to switch to the most recent image copy for a datafile, tablespace, or database.
- RMAN automatically applies incremental backups and archived redo log files when you recover with an image copy.
- Use the dynamic performance views V$TABLESPACE and V$DATAFILE_HEADER to determine the tablespace and datafile number needing recovery.
- After switching to an image copy, you can switch back to an image copy at the original location when it becomes available.
- You use the SET NEWNAME command in RMAN to identify new locations for restored datafiles.
- After restoring one or more datafiles with RESTORE, you use the SWITCH command to update the controlfile and recovery catalog with the new datafile locations.
- You can use an RMAN autobackup to restore either an spfile or controlfile when all online copies are lost.
- RMAN restores the controlfile to all locations specified by the initialization parameter CONTROL_FILES.
- If the spfile is lost, RMAN uses a default spfile when you start the database with NOMOUNT.
- Use RESTORE SPFILE FROM AUTOBACKUP to restore the spfile.
- Use RESTORE CONTROLFILE FROM AUTOBACKUP to restore the controlfile.
- When restoring a controlfile from autobackup, you must open the database with RESETLOGS.
- You can optionally restore a copy of the controlfile to an alternative location.

Perform Recovery for Spfiles, Controlfiles, and Online Redo Log Files

- A redo log group can have six statuses: CURRENT, ACTIVE, INACTIVE, UNUSED, CLEARING, or CLEARING_CURRENT. The most common statuses are CURRENT, ACTIVE, and INACTIVE.
- You can use the dynamic performance view V$LOG to query the status of each redo log group.

- If one member of a log group becomes damaged or is lost, the LGWR process continues to write to the undamaged member, and no data loss or interruption in service occurs.

- The dynamic performance view V$LOGFILE shows the status of each individual member of each log file group.

- If the status of a log file group member is INVALID in the view V$LOGFILE, it is damaged or unavailable and must be re-created.

- Losing an inactive log file group that has not been archived will result in a gap in the archived redo log files and necessitates a full backup after recovering the log file group.

- Losing a redo log file group with a status of ACTIVE will not cause the loss of committed transactions if you can successfully perform ALTER SYSTEM CHECKPOINT. If the checkpoint fails, you must perform incomplete recovery.

- Losing a redo log file group with a status of CURRENT will crash the instance, and you must perform incomplete recovery.

- Losing a password file prevents DBAs from connecting to an open or closed instance with the SYSDBA, SYSOPER, SYSASM, SYSBACKUP, SYSDG, or SYSKM privilege, unless using operating system authentication.

- You use the orapwd command at an operating system prompt to re-create the password file.

- The default location for the password file is $ORACLE_HOME/dbs on Linux and %ORACLE_HOME%\database on Windows.

- The dynamic performance view V$PWFILE_USERS lists all the database users who have SYSDBA, SYSOPER, or SYSASM privileges.

- If you want to back up your controlfile while the database is open, you can do it with two different SQL commands: ALTER DATABASE BACKUP CONTROLFILE TO <filename> and ALTER DATABASE BACKUP CONTROLFILE TO TRACE.

- ALTER DATABASE BACKUP CONTROLFILE TO < filename > creates an exact binary copy of the controlfile at the specified location.

- ALTER DATABASE BACKUP CONTROLFILE TO TRACE creates an editable script that re-creates the controlfile in the directory $ORACLE_BASE/diag/rdbms/<database>/<instance>/trace.

- Losing all copies of the online controlfile does not lose any committed transactions if you have a recent backup copy of the controlfile and both the datafiles and online redo log files are intact.

- You do not have to open the database with RESETLOGS after restoring your controlfile if you manually create the replacement controlfile using CREATE CONTROLFILE or you use a version of the controlfile script that you created with ALTER DATABASE BACKUP CONTROLFILE TO TRACE.

Perform Recovery of Tempfiles

- A tempfile can be recovered while the database is open.

- The impact of a lost tempfile is noticed when users attempt to sort large result sets.

- When a tempfile is lost, you can re-create it in the original location or specify a new location.

- If the database starts without tempfiles, it creates them in the location specified in the controlfile.

Self Test

1. What is the difference between a critical and a noncritical datafile in a recovery scenario? (Choose the best answer.)

   A. To recover a critical datafile, only the tablespace containing the critical datafile must be offline.

   B. To recover a noncritical datafile, both the SYSTEM tablespace and the tablespace containing the critical datafile must be offline.

   C. To recover a critical datafile, the database must be in NOMOUNT mode. To recover a noncritical datafile, the database must be in MOUNT mode.

   D. To recover a critical datafile, the database must be in MOUNT mode. To recover a noncritical datafile, the database can be open.

2. Which tablespaces contain critical datafiles that must be recovered when the database is offline? (Choose the best answer.)

   A. SYSTEM and SYSAUX

   B. SYSTEM and UNDO

   C. SYSTEM, SYSAUX, and UNDO

   D. SYSTEM and USERS

3. During complete recovery of a noncritical datafile, which of the following steps are not required? (Choose two answers.)

   A. Use the RMAN RESTORE command to load the missing datafiles from backup.

   B. Reopen the database with RESETLOGS.

   C. Shut down the database and reopen in MOUNT mode.

   D. Bring the damaged datafiles offline before the recovery operation and online after recovery is complete.

   E. Use the RMAN RECOVER command to apply committed transactions from archived and online redo log files.

4. Which of the following methods can you use to retrieve the current system change number (SCN)? (Choose the best answer.)

   A. Query the CURRENT_SCN column from the V$DATAFILE_HEADER.

   B. Query the CURRENT_SCN column of the V$INSTANCE view.

   C. Query the LAST_SCN column of the V$DATABASE view.

   D. Query the CURRENT_SCN column of the V$DATABASE view.

   E. Start RMAN and connect to the target database; the current SCN and the DBID are displayed.

5. Which of the following CREATE RESTORE POINT commands will preserve the restore point past the time specified by the initialization parameter CONTROL_FILE_RECORD_KEEP_TIME? (Choose the best answer.)

   A. CREATE RESTORE POINT SAVE_IT_PAST KEEP

   B. CREATE RESTORE POINT SAVE_IT_PAST AS OF SCN 3988943

   C. CREATE RESTORE POINT SAVE_IT_NOW PRESERVE

   D. CREATE RESTORE POINT SAVE_IT_NOW UNTIL FOREVER

6. Which operating system environment variables should be set when you use RMAN time-based incomplete recovery? (Choose two answers.)

   A. ORACLE_SID

   B. NLS_LANG

   C. ORACLE_BASE

   D. NLS_DATE_FORMAT

   E. NLS_TIME_FORMAT

7. You are implementing an incrementally updated backup strategy using the following RMAN script:

```
run {
      recover copy of database
         with tag 'inc_upd';
      backup incremental level 1
         for recover of copy
         with tag 'inc_upd'
         database;
   }
```

   How many times do you need to run this script before the image copy will have been updated with an incremental level 1 backup? (Choose the best answer.)

   A. Once

   B. Twice

   C. Three times

   D. At least four times

8. The RMAN SWITCH command is equivalent to what SQL command? (Choose the best answer.)

   A. ALTER DATABASE RENAME FILE

   B. ALTER DATABASE ARCHIVELOG

   C. ALTER DATABASE OPEN RESETLOGS

   D. ALTER SYSTEM SWITCH LOGFILE

9. What is the correct order of the following commands for restoring a controlfile from an RMAN autobackup? (Choose the best answer.)

   1. RECOVER DATABASE
   2. ALTER DATABASE OPEN RESETLOGS
   3. STARTUP NOMOUNT
   4. ALTER DATABASE MOUNT
   5. RESTORE CONTROLFILE FROM AUTOBACKUP

   A. 5, 3, 4, 1, 2

   B. 3, 5, 4, 1, 2

   C. 3, 5, 4, 2, 1

   D. 5, 1, 3, 4, 2

10. When you run the RMAN RESTORE CONTROLFILE command, where does RMAN put the previous version of the controlfile? (Choose the best answer.)

    A. In all available locations defined by the CONTROL_FILES initialization parameter

    B. In the Fast Recovery Area

    C. In all locations defined by the CONTROL_FILES initialization parameter unless overridden with the TO '*<filename>*' clause

    D. In the first location defined by the CONTROL_FILES initialization parameter

11. Which of the following is not a valid status for an online redo log group? (Choose the best answer.)

    A. CURRENT

    B. ACTIVE

    C. INVALID

    D. UNUSED

    E. CLEARING

12. What is the difference between the V$LOG and V$LOGFILE views? (Choose the best answer.)

   A. V$LOG contains the status of all archived redo log files, and V$LOGFILE contains the status of all online redo log files.

   B. V$LOG contains the status of the online redo log group members, and V$LOGFILE contains the status of individual online redo log groups.

   C. V$LOG contains the status of all online redo log files, and V$LOGFILE contains the status of all archived redo log files.

   D. V$LOG contains the status of the online redo log groups, and V$LOGFILE contains the status of individual redo log group members.

13. Which methods can you use to recover a lost or damaged password file? (Choose all that apply.)

   A. Use the orapwd command at an operating system prompt to re-create the password file.

   B. Restore the password file from backup and apply any archived and online redo log files to bring its contents to the present time.

   C. Use the orapwd SQL command to re-create the password file.

   D. Restore the password file from an operating system backup.

14. Which of the following commands does not back up the current controlfile? (Choose the best answer.)

   A. SQL> ALTER DATABASE BACKUP CONTROLFILE TO TRACE;

   B. SQL> ALTER SYSTEM BACKUP CURRENT CONTROLFILE;

   C. RMAN> BACKUP CURRENT CONTROLFILE;

   D. SQL> ALTER DATABASE BACKUP CONTROLFILE TO '/U08/BACKUP/CTL.BAK';

15. If you lose all of the tempfiles from your temporary tablespace, what is the most likely result noticed by your users? (Choose the best answer.)

   A. The database becomes unavailable and users cannot connect.

   B. The users can't perform SELECT statements.

   C. The users cannot add or delete rows in any table.

   D. The users can't use ORDER BY or GROUP BY in their queries.

16. Which is the best method for recovering a tempfile? (Choose the best answer.)

   A. Drop the TEMP tablespace and re-create it with a datafile in a new location.

   B. Add another tempfile to the TEMP tablespace and drop the corrupted or missing tempfile while the database is running.

   C. Shut down the database, restore the tempfile from a backup, and recover it using archived and online redo log files.

   D. Add another tempfile to the TEMP tablespace and drop the corrupted or missing tempfile after the database has been shut down and restarted in MOUNT mode.

Self Test Answers

1. ☑   **D.** When you restore and recover a critical datafile, the entire database must be shut down and reopened in MOUNT mode to open the controlfile and make the datafile locations available to RMAN.
   ☒   **A, B,** and **C** are incorrect. **A** is incorrect because the entire database must be offline when recovering a critical datafile. **B** is incorrect because recovering a noncritical datafile requires only the damaged datafile to be offline. **C** is incorrect because the database must be in MOUNT mode to recover a critical datafile and can be in OPEN mode to recover a noncritical datafile.

2. ☑   **B.** The SYSTEM and UNDO tablespaces contain critical datafiles and therefore require the database to be in MOUNT mode during the recovery process.
   ☒   **A, C,** and **D** are incorrect because the SYSAUX and USERS tablespaces do not contain critical datafiles.

3. ☑   **B and C.** The database does not need to be opened with RESETLOGS because you are not performing incomplete recovery. For a noncritical datafile, only the tablespace containing the missing or damaged datafile needs to be offline.
   ☒   **A, D,** and **E** are incorrect. These steps are all required.

4. ☑   **D.** V$DATABASE contains the most recent SCN in the CURRENT_SCN column.
   ☒   **A, B, C,** and **E** are incorrect. **A** and **B** are incorrect because the column CURRENT_SCN does not exist in either V$DATAFILE_HEADER or V$INSTANCE. **C** is incorrect because V$DATABASE does not have a column named LAST_SCN. **E** is incorrect because when RMAN starts, it shows only the DBID and not the current SCN.

5. ☑   **C.** The keyword PRESERVE keeps the restore point past the time specified by CONTROL_FILE_RECORD_KEEP_TIME.
   ☒   **A, B,** and **D** are incorrect. **A** is incorrect because the keyword KEEP is not valid for the command. **B** is incorrect because PRESERVE was not specified. **D** is incorrect because UNTIL FOREVER is not valid for the command.

6. ☑   **B and D.** Both NLS_LANG and NLS_DATE_FORMAT must be set so that RMAN will correctly interpret date strings provided during a recovery operation.
   ☒   **A, C,** and **E** are incorrect. ORACLE_SID and ORACLE_BASE are required to connect to the correct database and database software, but they are not directly related to RMAN time-based recovery. NLS_TIME_FORMAT is not a valid environment variable.

7. ☑   **C.** The first time the script runs, there is no level 0 image copy or a level 1 incremental backup. The second time the script runs, the level 0 image copy exists, but there is no incremental level 1 backup to apply to it. The third successive time, the first incremental level 1 backup is applied to the image copy.
   ☒   **A, B,** and **D** are incorrect. They all specify the incorrect number of executions.

8. ☑ **A.** Both the RMAN SWITCH and the SQL ALTER DATABASE RENAME FILE commands update the location of the datafile in both the controlfile and the recovery catalog.

☒ **B, C,** and **D** are incorrect. **B** is incorrect because this command puts the database into ARCHIVELOG mode. **C** is incorrect because the command is used only after incomplete recovery. **D** is incorrect because the command switches online redo log files, not datafile names.

9. ☑ **B.** The specified order is correct. You must open the database with RESETLOGS since your restored controlfile has information about an older version of the database.

☒ **A, C,** and **D** are incorrect because they specify an incorrect sequence of commands.

10. ☑ **C.** The command restores the controlfile from autobackup to all locations defined by the initialization parameter CONTROL_FILES. If any of those locations are unavailable, change the value of CONTROL_FILES or use the TO '*<filename>*' option.

☒ **A, B,** and **D** are incorrect. **A** is incorrect because the command fails if any of the locations defined by CONTROL_FILES are not available. **B** is incorrect because the autobackup of the controlfile will most likely originate from the fast recovery area. **D** is incorrect because RMAN restores the controlfile to all locations defined by CONTROL_FILES.

11. ☑ **C.** The status INVALID is valid only for an online redo log group member, not for the entire group.

☒ **A, B, D,** and **E** are incorrect. They are valid statuses for an online redo log group.

12. ☑ **D.** V$LOG contains the status of redo log groups, including whether the group is currently being written to. V$LOGFILE contains the status of individual redo log group members.

☒ **A, B,** and **C** are incorrect. The views V$LOG and V$LOGFILE do not contain information about archived redo log files, although the view V$LOG has a column to indicate whether the redo log file group has been archived or not.

13. ☑ **A** and **D.** Either method can be used to recover the password file, but using the **orapwd** command requires that you re-create the privileged user accounts that need SYSDBA, SYSOPER, SYSADM, SYSBACKUP, SYSDG, and SYSKM privileges.

☒ **B** and **C** are incorrect. **B** is incorrect because you do not apply redo log files to the password file. **C** is incorrect because orapwd is valid only at an operating system command prompt.

14. ☑ **B.** There is no such command.

☒ **A, C,** and **D** are incorrect. **A** is incorrect because it creates a text-based file containing two different CREATE CONTROLFILE commands, depending on the availability of your datafiles and online redo log files. **C** is incorrect because it is one of many ways that RMAN backs up the controlfile. **D** is incorrect because it creates a binary copy of the controlfile at the specified location.

15. ☑ **D.** Temporary tablespaces provide sort space for queries that use ORDER BY and GROUP BY when the sort operation will not fit in memory. Other operations cause sorts as well: SELECT DISTINCT, index creations, and index rebuilds.

☒ **A, B,** and **C** are incorrect. **A** is incorrect because the database remains available for some queries and most DML activity even if the TEMP tablespace is unavailable. **B** is incorrect because users can still perform SELECT statements that don't need sorting or the sort operation will fit into memory. **C** is incorrect because most DML activity does not require the TEMP tablespace.

16. ☑ **B.** Once the missing tempfile is dropped and a new one added, the TEMP tablespace is automatically available to users.

☒ **A, C,** and **D** are incorrect. **A** is incorrect because dropping the tablespace is not necessary, and you cannot drop the default temporary tablespace. **C** is incorrect because you cannot recover a temporary tablespace; there are no permanent objects in a temporary tablespace. **D** is incorrect because the database does not need to be shut down to recover a temporary tablespace.

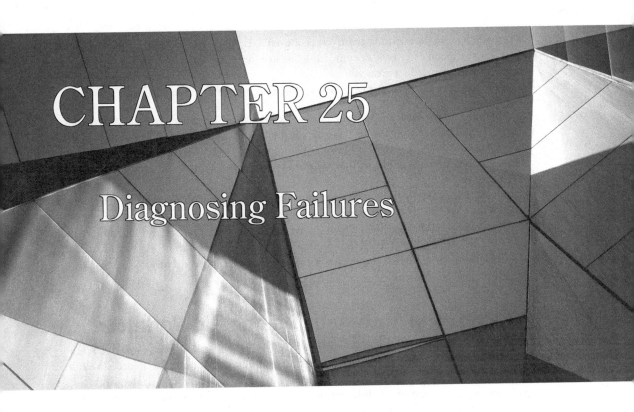

CHAPTER 25

Diagnosing Failures

Exam Objectives

- 63.1.9.1 Describe the Automatic Diagnostic Workflow
- 63.1.9.2 Handle Block Corruption

When you have to deal with database errors or even a database that is completely down, you don't want to spend extra time documenting one or more database error conditions for Oracle Support. This chapter first gives you a brief overview of how Oracle reports problems with the database and then shows how it categorizes errors into problems and incidents.

In addition, the Health Monitor framework provides both proactive and reactive tools to deal with database errors. The database administrator (DBA) can run a proactive health check manually using Enterprise Manager Cloud Control 12c (Cloud Control) or PL/SQL packages. In contrast, the Health Monitor can run diagnostic checks in response to critical database errors.

Finally, the chapter will switch from reporting, managing, and submitting service requests for database problems and incidents to recovering individual blocks after you have identified the problem. Recovery Manager (RMAN) supports the detection and recovery of individual blocks using the DB_BLOCK_CHECKING initialization parameter and the RMAN RECOVER . . . BLOCK command. RMAN also makes it easy to identify failures and implement repairs using the Data Recovery Advisor.

Describe the Automatic Diagnostic Workflow

The key to the automatic diagnostic repository (ADR) is the first word: *automatic*. ADR is an always-on facility that captures errors in trace and dump files the first and any successive times they occur (which is the reason for the *diagnostic* part of the Oracle feature name). The third part, *repository*, is a location on disk that stores the diagnostic information on disk and comes with a tool that makes it easy to query the repository even when the database is unavailable.

The following sections provide more details about the structure of the repository, how to retrieve information from the repository, and how to find the diagnostic information you're looking for in the repository using initialization parameters and data dictionary views. In addition, you'll see how to easily and quickly package the diagnostic information from the ADR and send it to Oracle support for problem resolution.

Understanding the ADR

The ADR is a file-based repository of diagnostic and other noncritical information for all products in your environment. Each database instance and Automatic Storage Management (ASM) instance has its own directory structure called an *ADR home* within a top-level directory known as the *ADR base*. In a Real Application Clusters (RAC) environment, each instance has its own subdirectory, which not only makes it easy to view diagnostics for an individual instance, but also makes it easy for the diagnostic tools to analyze data across instances for cluster-wide problems.

The ADR base directory is also known as the *ADR root directory*. The location for the ADR base is set depending on the values of initialization parameters and environment variables. If the initialization parameter DIAGNOSTIC_DEST is set, the ADR base directory is set to this value, and all other file locations are set relative to this location. If DIAGNOSTIC_DEST is not set,

Figure 25-1 ADR directory structure for the COMPLREF database

then DIAGNOSTIC_DEST is set to the environment variable ORACLE_BASE. Figure 25-1 shows the ADR directory structure for the COMPLREF database.

For the database in Figure 25-1, the initialization parameter DIAGNOSTIC_DEST is not set, so Oracle sets DIAGNOSTIC_DEST to the value of the environment variable ORACLE_BASE, which in this case is /u01/app/oracle.

```
[oracle@dw ~]$ echo $ORACLE_BASE
/u01/app/oracle
[oracle@dw ~]$ echo $ORACLE_HOME
/u01/app/oracle/product/12.1.0/dbhome_1
[oracle@dw ~]$
```

You can retrieve the values for each diagnostic directory using the dynamic performance view V$DIAG_INFO, as in this example:

```
SQL> select inst_id,name,value from v$diag_info;
INST_ID NAME                         VALUE
------- ------------------------     ------------------------------------
      1 Diag Enabled                    TRUE
      1 ADR Base                     /u01/app/oracle
      1 ADR Home                     /u01/app/oracle/diag/rdbms/complref
                                     /complref

      1 Diag Trace                       /u01/app/oracle/diag/rdbms/complref
                                     /complref/trace

      1 Diag Alert                       /u01/app/oracle/diag/rdbms/complref
                                     /complref/alert

      1 Diag Incident                    /u01/app/oracle/diag/rdbms/complref
                                     /complref/incident

      1 Diag Cdump                       /u01/app/oracle/diag/rdbms/complref
                                     /complref/cdump

      1 Health Monitor                   /u01/app/oracle/diag/rdbms/complref
                                     /complref/hm

      1 Default Trace File           /u01/app/oracle/diag/rdbms/complref
                                     /complref/trace/complref_ora_30559.
                                     trc

      1 Active Problem Count      0
      1 Active Incident Count     0

11 rows selected.
```

Note the column INST_ID. In a RAC environment, this value differentiates the value of each directory by node. For example, if COMPLREF were the database name and the database contained the three instances COMPLREF1, COMPLREF2, and COMPLREF3, the value for the second instance's diagnostic trace directory would be as follows:

```
INST_ID NAME                         VALUE
------- ------------------------     ------------------------------------
      2 Diag Trace                   /u01/app/oracle/diag/rdbms/complref
                                     /complref2/trace
```

Compared to previous releases of Oracle, the diagnostic information is better partitioned. In other words, all nonincident trace files are stored in the trace subdirectory, all core dumps are in the cdump directory, and all incident dumps are stored as individual directories within the incident subdirectory. Table 25-1 shows the ADR location for each type of diagnostic data.

Note the differentiation between trace and dump files. Trace files contain continuous output to diagnose a problem with a running process. A dump file is a one-time diagnostic output file resulting from an incident. Similarly, a core dump is a one-time platform-specific binary memory dump. Note also that there is no initialization parameter or environment variable

Diagnostic Data Type	Location Within the ADR
Foreground process trace files	ADR_HOME/trace
Background process trace files	ADR_HOME/trace
Alert log	ADR_HOME/alert (Extensible Markup Language [XML] format) ADR_HOME/trace (plain-text format)
Core dumps	ADR_HOME/cdump
Incident dumps	ADR_HOME/incident/incdir_n
Health Monitor	ADR_HOME/hm

Table 25-1   ADR Diagnostic Information Directory Locations

named ADR_HOME. You can determine the value of ADR_HOME from the row in V$DIAG_INFO containing the name ADR Home.

```
1 ADR Home                    /u01/app/oracle/diag/rdbms/complref/complref
```

Using the ADRCI Tool

The ADR Command Interpreter (ADRCI) tool makes it easy to query the contents of the ADR. You can use the tool in command mode or create scripts to run in batch mode. You can use ADRCI even when the database is down—remember that the ADR is completely file system based. In addition to querying the contents of the ADR with ADRCI, you can package incident and problem information into a compressed ZIP file that you can send to Oracle Support.

Note that ADRCI does not require a login or any other authorization. The contents of the ADR are protected only by operating system permissions on the directory containing the ADR file structures. For a default installation of Oracle Database 12c, this means that the ADR has the same permissions as the ORACLE_BASE directory and its subdirectories. You can alter the permissions further if you want, but you must make sure the user owning the Oracle processes (usually the oracle user) has full read-write access to the ADR.

When you start ADRCI, you see the current ADR base directory. Type **help** for a list of commands.

```
[oracle@dw ~]$ adrci

ADRCI: Release 12.1.0.1.0 - Production on Fri Mar 7 07:31:29 2014

Copyright (c) 1982, 2013, Oracle and/or its affiliates.  All rights reserved.

ADR base = "/u01/app/oracle"
adrci> help

 HELP [topic]
   Available Topics:
        CREATE REPORT
        ECHO
        EXIT
```

```
        HELP
        HOST
        IPS
        PURGE
        RUN
        SET BASE
        SET BROWSER
        SET CONTROL
        SET ECHO
        SET EDITOR
        SET HOMES | HOME | HOMEPATH
        SET TERMOUT
        SHOW ALERT
        SHOW BASE
        SHOW CONTROL
        SHOW HM_RUN
        SHOW HOMES | HOME | HOMEPATH
        SHOW INCDIR
        SHOW INCIDENT
        SHOW LOG
        SHOW PROBLEM
        SHOW REPORT
        SHOW TRACEFILE
        SPOOL

    There are other commands intended to be used directly by Oracle, type
    "HELP EXTENDED" to see the list
adrci>
```

Even when there are no incidents or problems to view, you can perform more mundane tasks such as viewing the alert log from ADRCI.

```
adrci> show alert
Choose the home from which to view the alert log:
1: diag/rdbms/rcat/rcat
2: diag/rdbms/cdb01/cdb01
3: diag/rdbms/complref/complref
Q: to quit

Please select option: 3
Output the results to file: /tmp/alert_1768_14054_complref_1.ado
. . .
2014-03-06 22:00:00.221000 -06:00
Setting Resource Manager plan

SCHEDULER[0x420F]:DEFAULT_MAINTENANCE_PLAN via scheduler window
Setting Resource Manager plan DEFAULT_MAINTENANCE_PLAN via parameter
Starting background process VKRM
VKRM started with pid=27, OS id=12750
. . .
Please select option: q
adrci>
```

Notice that the ADRCI tool tracks all ADR home directories within the ADR root directory. Therefore, you must select which database, ASM, or listener directory you want to view with ADRCI.

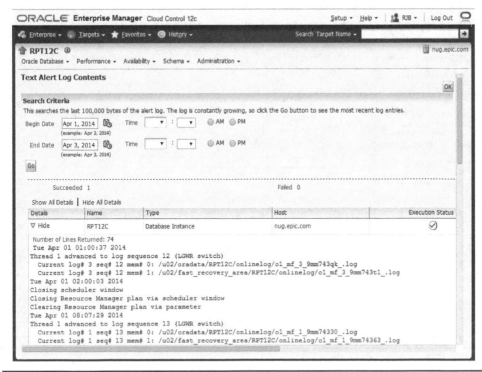

Figure 25-2   Viewing alert log contents from Cloud Control

Of course, you can perform the same task from Cloud Control 12c. At the bottom of the Cloud Control home page, click the Alert Log Contents link. Then select the number of lines at the end of the alert log you want to see and click Go. You'll see the page shown in Figure 25-2.

Understanding Alerts, Problems, and Incidents

Although the alert log (either text format or XML format) contains all alerts for the instance, you see the alerts at the warning and critical levels on the Enterprise Manager (EM) home page. You can view specific incidents in the Incident Manager in Cloud Control 12c. In Figure 25-3, you see several recent incidents. In the oldest incident (at the bottom), Cloud Control reported that a user was trying to access an object without the proper privileges. In the most recent incident, the database reports that a user connected to the SYS user or another user with SYSDBA privileges.

A *problem,* defined by the Support Workbench framework, is a critical error in the database, such as the internal error ORA-00600 or some other serious event such as running out of memory in the shared pool or an operating system exception. An *incident* is a single occurrence of a problem. Each problem has a *problem key,* which is a text string that contains the error code and optionally other problem characteristics. A problem may have one or many incidents.

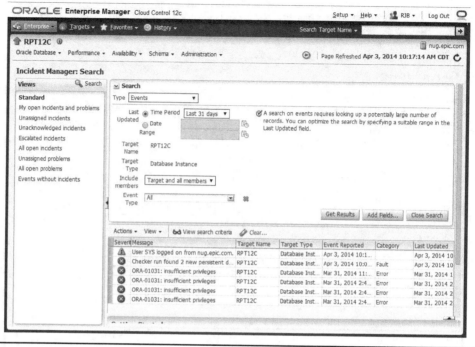

Figure 25-3   Viewing error alerts in EM

Each incident is identified by a numeric incident ID and is stored in its own subdirectory of the ADR (ADR_HOME/incident/incdir_n). When an incident occurs, the database performs the following steps:

1. Adds an entry to the alert log (both text and XML based)

2. Sends an incident alert to EM

3. Sends an alert via e-mail to administrators (if configured)

4. Gathers trace files and other incident information

5. Tags all incident information with the incident ID

6. Creates an incident directory under ADR_HOME for the incident and stores incident information and trace files in the directory

Using the Health Monitor

You can use the Oracle Health Monitor framework to proactively or reactively assess the health of your database. Health Monitor checks the status of various database components, including the following:

- Datafiles
- Memory

- Transaction integrity

- Metadata

- Process usage

You can run health checks using Cloud Control via the Support Workbench, or you can manually run a health check using the DBMS_HM PL/SQL package. Some checks can be run only when the database is open. Other checks are available when the instance is running but the database is in NOMOUNT mode. You can list the checks available and whether they are available in offline or online mode by querying the dynamic performance view V$HM_CHECK.

```
SQL> select id,name,offline_capable,internal_check from v$hm_check;

        ID NAME                            O I
---------- ------------------------------- - -
        27 ASM Allocation Check            Y N
        25 CF Block Integrity Check        Y N
         2 DB Structure Integrity Check    Y N
         3 Data Block Integrity Check      Y N
        24 Dictionary Integrity Check      N N
         4 Redo Integrity Check            Y N
        10 Transaction Integrity Check     N N
        11 Undo Segment Integrity Check    N N
        37 ASM DG Force Dismount Check      Y Y
        36 ASM DGFDM Check No DG Name       Y Y
        28 ASM Disk Visibility Check        Y Y
        29 ASM File Busy Check              Y Y
        33 ASM Insufficient Disks Check    Y Y
        35 ASM Insufficient Mem Check       Y Y
        26 ASM Mount Check                  Y Y
        38 ASM Sync IO Fail Check           Y Y
        32 ASM Toomanyoff Check             Y Y
        14 All Datafiles Check              Y Y
        18 Archived Log Check               Y Y
        21 Block IO Revalidation Check     Y Y
        13 CF Member Check                  Y Y
        34 Failover Check                   Y Y
        23 Failure Simulation Check         Y Y
         1 HM Test Check                    Y Y
        20 IO Revalidation Check            Y Y
        16 Log Group Check                  Y Y
        17 Log Group Member Check           Y Y
         5 Logical Block Check             N Y
        31 Mount CF Check                   Y Y
        12 No Mount CF Check                Y Y
        19 Redo Revalidation Check          Y Y
        15 Single Datafile Check            Y Y
        30 Tablespace Check Check           Y Y
        22 Txn Revalidation Check          N Y

34 rows selected.

orclz>
```

Note that all but eight of the checks are INTERNAL_CHECK='Y'. The DBA cannot invoke the internal checks. You can view the results of health checks from the ADRCI tool with the show hm_run command. In the following examples, you retrieve the results of a Health Monitor run first in text format, and then you generate a Health Monitor report in XML format.

```
adrci> show hm_run -p "run_id=36961"

*************************************************************
HM RUN RECORD 1607
*************************************************************
    RUN_ID                     36961
    RUN_NAME                   HM_RUN_36961
    CHECK_NAME                 DB Structure Integrity Check
    NAME_ID                    2
    MODE                       2
    START_TIME                 2014-02-25 09:37:20.403101 -05:00
    RESUME_TIME                <NULL>
    END_TIME                   2014-02-25 09:37:20.658541 -05:00
    MODIFIED_TIME              2014-02-25 09:37:20.658541 -05:00
    TIMEOUT                    0
    FLAGS                      0
    STATUS                     5
    SRC_INCIDENT_ID            0
    NUM_INCIDENTS              0
    ERR_NUMBER                 0
    REPORT_FILE                <NULL>

adrci> create report hm_run hm_run_36961
adrci> show report hm_run hm_run_36961
<?xml version="1.0" encoding="US-ASCII"?>
<HM-REPORT REPORT_ID="HM_RUN_36961">
    <TITLE>HM Report: HM_RUN_36961</TITLE>
    <RUN_INFO>
        <CHECK_NAME>DB Structure Integrity Check</CHECK_NAME>
        <RUN_ID>36961</RUN_ID>
        <RUN_NAME>HM_RUN_36961</RUN_NAME>
        <RUN_MODE>REACTIVE</RUN_MODE>
        <RUN_STATUS>COMPLETED</RUN_STATUS>
        <RUN_ERROR_NUM>0</RUN_ERROR_NUM>
        <SOURCE_INCIDENT_ID>0</SOURCE_INCIDENT_ID>
        <NUM_INCIDENTS_CREATED>0</NUM_INCIDENTS_CREATED>
        <RUN_START_TIME>2014-02-25 09:37:20.403101 -05:00</RUN_START_TIME>
        <RUN_END_TIME>2014-02-25 09:37:20.658541 -05:00</RUN_END_TIME>
    </RUN_INFO>
    <RUN_PARAMETERS/>
    <RUN-FINDINGS/>
</HM-REPORT>
adrci>
```

To run a check manually, use the DBMS_HM package. For example, this is a run of the Data Dictionary Integrity check, ID 24 in the previous listing:

```
orclz>
orclz> exec dbms_hm.run_check(check_name=>'Dictionary Integrity Check',-
> run_name=>'my_dd_check')

PL/SQL procedure successfully completed.

orclz>
orclz> set long 10000
orclz>
orclz> select dbms_hm.get_run_report('my_dd_check') from dual;
```

```
DBMS_HM.GET_RUN_REPORT('MY_DD_CHECK')
---------------------------------------------------------------------
Basic Run Information
  Run Name                   : my_dd_check
  Run Id                     : 10221
  Check Name                 : Dictionary Integrity Check
  Mode                       : MANUAL
  Status                     : COMPLETED
  Start Time                 : 2015-02-08 14:44:59.553000 +00:00
  End Time                   : 2015-02-08 14:45:04.102000 +00:00
  Error Encountered          : 0
  Source Incident Id         : 0
  Number of Incidents Created : 0
```

Handle Block Corruption

Many of the errors you will encounter will be related to bad blocks in your database datafiles because of either media failures, server memory errors, or logical corruption caused by Oracle bugs (not that Oracle has bugs—merely anomalous and undocumented behavior). Once you've identified these problems using the diagnostic methods provided earlier in this chapter, you can use the tools in the following sections to fix the problems.

As with nearly every Oracle feature, you can adjust the level of control and monitoring that Oracle performs; data block checking is no exception. Regardless of the settings you'll learn about shortly, Oracle always performs the following checks on a data block when it is read from or written to a datafile:

- Checks that the block version matches the version of the database
- Checks that data block address (DBA) in the cache is the same as the DBA value in the block buffer
- Checks that, by default, the block checksum is correct

You can repair a corrupt block either by recovering the block or by dropping the object containing the bad block. The following sections tell you more about block corruption, how to control the amount of overhead Oracle will use to ensure the integrity of blocks, and how to fix a corrupted block.

Block Corruption

When Oracle detects a corrupted block, it registers an ORA-01578 error in the alert log and on the EM home page. Included in the error message are the absolute file number and block number of the bad block. In addition, the session reading or writing the bad block sees the same error message. Here is an example of a block corruption error message:

```
ORA-01578: ORACLE data block corrupted (file # 6, block # 403)
ORA-01110: data file 6: '/u09/oradata/ord/oe_trans01.dbf'
```

Most often, corruption is caused by operating system or disk hardware failures such as faulty input/output (I/O) hardware or firmware, operating system caching problems, memory or paging problems, or errors caused by disk repair utilities.

Two instance parameters control the checks for block corruption: DB_BLOCK_CHECKSUM and DB_BLOCK_CHECKING.

DB_BLOCK_CHECKSUM has three possible values:

- **OFF or FALSE**   No checksums are computed.

- **TYPICAL**   This is the default value. Checksums are computed when writing a block to disk and validated on reading it from disk.

- **FULL**   Checksums are computed and checked every time a block is changed. Checksums are also added to redo blocks on writing.

Note that even if this parameter is OFF, checksums are still computed for all blocks in the SYSTEM tablespace.

The initialization parameter DB_BLOCK_CHECKING controls how thoroughly Oracle checks the logical structure of every data block. The level of checking you enable depends on the level of failure tolerable in your environment balanced against the overhead required to perform the continuous block checks. The possible values for DB_BLOCK_CHECKING are as follows:

- **OFF or FALSE**   This is the default value; no block checking is performed.

- **LOW**   Basic block checks are performed after blocks are changed in memory or read from disk, including interinstance block transfers in RAC environments.

- **MEDIUM**   This includes all LOW checks plus block checking for all non-index-organized table blocks.

- **FULL or TRUE**   This includes all LOW and MEDIUM checks plus checks for index blocks.

DB_BLOCK_CHECKING is known to have a performance overhead, and by default it is therefore not enabled. However, FULL block checking for the SYSTEM tablespace is always enabled and cannot be stopped.

The default value for DB_BLOCK_CHECKSUM means that Oracle will be able to detect damage to a block that occurred while it was on disk. Good idea! Enabling DB_BLOCK_CHECKING lets Oracle detect problems that occur while the block is in memory. Usually this is not necessary and would be enabled only on instruction from Oracle Support when trying to resolve a problem.

 EXAM TIP   Check sums and logical block validation are always enabled for the SYSTEM tablespace but can be enabled or disabled for the rest of the database.

Using Block Media Recovery

If you discover only a small handful of blocks to recover in a database from the aforementioned health checks or results discovered in the alert log, RMAN can perform *block media recovery* rather than a full datafile recovery. Block media recovery minimizes the time required to apply the redo logs (since only a small part of each redo log is needed or possibly no redo logs are required!) and drastically reduces the amount of I/O required to recover only the block or blocks in question. While block media recovery is in progress, the affected datafiles can remain online and available to users.

 EXAM TIP Block media recovery is available only from within the RMAN application.

In addition to the block verification performed by Oracle as defined by the DB_BLOCK_ CHECKING initialization parameter, an RMAN BACKUP or BACKUP VALIDATE command can add information about corrupted blocks to the dynamic performance view V$DATABASE_ BLOCK_CORRUPTION.

You'll need to know the advantages and disadvantages of block media recovery; as you might expect, there are many more advantages than disadvantages. In addition to touting the benefits of RMAN block media recovery, the following sections cover the prerequisites for block media recovery and provide some real-world use cases.

Advantages of Block Media Recovery

Recovering one or a small number of blocks using RMAN has some obvious and some not-so-obvious advantages. First, recovering one block using a recent backup, together with archived and online redo log files, will almost certainly take much less time than restoring and recovering one or more datafiles. In addition, during block media recovery, the entire datafile remains online and available during the recovery process; only the blocks being recovered are unavailable. Therefore, only a small part of one table, index, or other database object remains unavailable during block media recovery.

When you use the RMAN RECOVER . . . BLOCK command, RMAN first searches the flashback logs for a good copy of the corrupted block (if Flashback Database is enabled). Otherwise, RMAN uses the latest level 0 or full backup, restores the bad blocks, and performs media recovery on the bad blocks using the redo stream. Note that RMAN cannot use incremental level 1 backups for block media recovery.

You can use the dynamic performance view V$DATABASE_BLOCK_CORRUPTION to view the bad blocks in the database. This view contains blocks that are both physically and logically corrupted. Here are the tools or commands that can populate this view when they find bad blocks:

- RMAN backup commands
- ANALYZE
- dbv operating system utility
- SQL queries that try to access a corrupted block

Prerequisites for Using Block Recovery

Before you can use block media recovery, your database must fulfill a few prerequisites. First, the target database must be in ARCHIVELOG mode. Unless your database is for testing or is a read-only database, your database should be in ARCHIVELOG mode for maximum recoverability anyway!

Second, the backups of datafiles with bad blocks must be full backups or level 0 incremental backups. RMAN cannot use level 1 incremental backups for block recovery. Thus, you must have all archived redo log files since the last full backup or level 0 incremental backup.

Alternatively, you can use flashback logs in the flash recovery area for retrieving uncorrupt versions of bad blocks if you have Flashback Database enabled. Unless the number of bad blocks is large, recovering a block from the flashback logs will certainly be faster than starting with a level 0 incremental or full backup.

Using the RMAN RECOVER . . . BLOCK Command

You can use the RMAN RECOVER . . . BLOCK command in response to an alert or other notification of a bad block. Typically, block corruption is reported in the following locations:

- Output from the RMAN LIST FAILURE, VALIDATE, or BACKUP . . . VALIDATE commands

- The V$DATABASE_BLOCK_CORRUPTION dynamic performance view

- Error messages during a SQL*Plus or other client session

- The alert log or user trace files

- Results from the SQL commands ANALYZE TABLE or ANALYZE INDEX

- Results from the DBVERIFY command-line utility (dbv)

To recover one or more data blocks, RMAN must know the datafile number and block number within the datafile. As mentioned previously, this information is available in a user trace file, as in the following example:

```
ORA-01578: ORACLE data block corrupted (file # 6, block # 403)
ORA-01110: data file 6: '/u09/oradata/ord/oe_trans01.dbf'
```

In addition, the block information will appear in the view V$DATABASE_BLOCK_CORRUPTION; the columns FILE# and BLOCK# provide the information needed to execute the RECOVER command. The column CORRUPTION_TYPE identifies the type of corruption in the block, such as FRACTURED, CHECKSUM, or CORRUPT. Fixing the block is easily accomplished in RMAN.

```
RMAN> recover datafile 6 block 403;

Starting recover at 04-FEB-14
using channel ORA_DISK_1

starting media recovery
media recovery complete, elapsed time: 00:00:01

Finished recover at 04-FEB-14

RMAN>
```

A corrupted block must be recovered completely. In other words, all redo operations up to the latest SCN against the data block must be applied before the block can be considered usable again.

If all bad blocks are recorded in V$DATABASE_BLOCK_CORRUPTION, you can easily recover all of them at once. Using the following command, RMAN will recover all physically corrupted blocks in V$DATABASE_BLOCK_CORRUPTION:

```
RMAN> recover corruption list;
```

After RMAN recovers the blocks, they are removed from V$DATABASE_BLOCK_CORRUPTION.

Using the Data Recovery Advisor

The Data Recovery Advisor is part of the Oracle advisor framework and automatically gathers information about a failure when an error is encountered. If you run the Data Recovery Advisor proactively, you are often able to detect and repair a failure before a user query or backup operation detects it. The Data Recovery Advisor can detect relatively small errors such as corrupted blocks. At the other end of the spectrum, it will detect errors that would otherwise prevent successful startup of the database, such as missing online redo log files. Your database may continue running for a short amount of time without online redo log files, but it will not start the next time you shut down and restart. Data Recovery Advisor will catch this error proactively.

Identifying Failures

As with most advisors and Oracle features, you can use either Cloud Control or command-line tools to run the Data Recovery Advisor, show the errors, and repair the failures.

Once the Data Recovery Advisor has identified a failure, you can review the details of the failure using the EM or RMAN interface. From RMAN, you can use the LIST FAILURE, ADVISE FAILURE, REPAIR FAILURE, and CHANGE FAILURE commands. Table 25-2 summarizes the purpose of these commands.

The LIST FAILURE command has a number of options, depending on what types of errors you want to see:

- *Failure#* Lists an individual failure's details (by failure number).
- **ALL** Lists all failures.
- **CRITICAL** Lists failures that make the database unavailable.
- **HIGH** Lists serious failures that make parts of the database unavailable, such as a missing datafile.

RMAN Command	Description
LIST FAILURE	Lists failures recorded by the Data Recovery Advisor
ADVISE FAILURE	Shows recommended repair option
REPAIR FAILURE	Repairs and closes failure using RMAN's recommendations
CHANGE FAILURE	Changes the status or closes a failure

Table 25-2 RMAN Failure Advisory and Repair Commands

PART IV

- **LOW**   Lists intermittent or lower-priority failures that can wait until more serious problems are fixed. For example, this can include corrupted blocks in infrequently used tablespaces.

- **CLOSED**   Lists only closed failures.

For example, LIST FAILURE 2097 lists the details for a failure with an identifier of 2097. Also, LIST FAILURE ALL lists all open failures of any priority.

Implementing Repairs

Once the Data Recovery Advisor has identified a failure, you can use the RMAN ADVISE FAILURE command to recommend a repair option for the specified failure. RMAN will suggest a repair and create a script with the recommended repair. If the repair is acceptable (in terms of downtime or other factors), you can then run REPAIR FAILURE (within the same RMAN session) to perform the recommended action. After the repair action completes successfully, the failure is automatically closed. The commands must always be run in the correct order: LIST, then ADVISE, then REPAIR.

You can also change the priority of a failure using CHANGE FAILURE. For example, a corrupted block will be recorded as a HIGH failure, but if it is in an infrequently used tablespace, then you can change its priority to LOW so that you see only other more serious failures in the LIST FAILURE command. However, you cannot change the priority of a CRITICAL failure. You can change the priority of a failure only from HIGH to LOW, or vice versa. Here is how you can change the priority of failure number 307 from HIGH to LOW:

```
RMAN> change failure 307 priority low;
```

Data Recovery Advisor Views

You can use several dynamic performance views to retrieve information about failures detected by the Data Recovery Advisor:

- **V$IR_FAILURE**   Lists all failures, including closed failures
- **V$IR_MANUAL_CHECKLIST**   Lists of manual advice
- **V$IR_REPAIR**   Lists of repairs
- **V$IR_REPAIR_SET**   Cross-references failure and advises on identifier numbers

For example, to retrieve the information for the failure with an ID of 37305, query V$IR_FAILURE as follows:

```
SQL> select failure_id, parent_id, description, status
  2  from v$ir_failure
  3  where failure_id = 37305;

FAILURE_ID  PARENT_ID DESCRIPTION                             STATUS
----------  --------- ------------------------------------    ------------
    37305       1345 Datafile 10: '/u05/oradata/xpo CLOSED
                     rt_dw.dbf' is corrupt

SQL>
```

Exercise 25-1: Use the DRA to Diagnose and Resolve Problems   In this exercise, you will cause a problem with the database and use the DRA to report on and fix it.

1. From an operating system prompt, launch the RMAN executable.

   ```
   rman target /
   ```

2. Confirm that there is a whole full backup of the SYSAUX tablespace.

   ```
   list backup of tablespace sysaux;
   ```

   If this does not return at least one backup set of type FULL, create one.

   ```
   backup as backupset tablespace sysaux;
   ```

3. Shut down the instance and exit from RMAN.

   ```
   shutdown immediate;
   exit;
   ```

4. Using an operating system utility, delete the datafile (or datafiles) for the SYSAUX tablespace that were listed in step 2. If using Windows, you may have to stop the Windows service under which the instance is running to release the Windows file lock before the deletion is possible.

5. Connect to the database with SQL*Plus and attempt a startup.

   ```
   startup;
   ```

   This will stop in mount mode, with an error regarding the missing file. If using Windows, make sure the service has been started.

6. Launch the RMAN executable and connect, as in step 1.

7. Diagnose the problem.

   ```
   list failure;
   ```

   This will return a message to the effect that one or more nonsystem datafiles are missing.

8. Generate advice on the failure.

   ```
   advise failure;
   ```

   This will suggest that you should restore and recover the datafile and generate a repair script. Open the script with any operating system editor and study its contents.

9. Run the commands in the generated script to restore the missing file, recover it, and bring it online.

Two-Minute Drill

Describe the Automatic Diagnostic Workflow

- ADR is an always-on facility that captures errors in trace and dump files the first and any subsequent times they occur.
- ADR uses a location on disk to store the diagnostic information and comes with a tool that makes it easy to query the repository even when the database is unavailable.

- Each database instance or Automatic Storage Management instance has its own directory structure called an *ADR home* within a top-level directory known as the *ADR base*.

- The ADR base directory is also known as the *ADR root directory*.

- If the initialization parameter DIAGNOSTIC_DEST is set, the ADR base directory is set to this value, and all other file locations are set relative to this location.

- If DIAGNOSTIC_DEST is not set, then DIAGNOSTIC_DEST is set to the environment variable ORACLE_BASE.

- If ORACLE_BASE is not set, DIAGNOSTIC_DEST is set to the value $ORACLE_HOME/log.

- The ADR diagnostic information is partitioned. All nonincident traces are stored in the trace subdirectory, all core dumps are stored in the cdump directory, and all incident dumps are stored as individual directories within the incident subdirectory.

- The ADR Command Interpreter tool makes it easy to query the contents of the ADR. You can use ADRCI even when the database is down.

- ADRCI does not require a login or any other authorization. The contents of the ADR are protected only by operating system permissions on the directory containing the ADR file structures.

- A *problem,* as defined by the Support Workbench framework, is a critical error in the database. An example is the internal error ORA-00600 or some other serious event such as running out of memory in the shared pool or perhaps an operating system exception.

- An *incident* is a single occurrence of a problem.

- Each problem has a *problem key,* which is a text string that contains the error code and optionally other problem characteristics.

- Health Monitor checks the status of various database components, including datafiles, memory, transaction integrity, metadata, and process usage.

- You can run health checks using EM via the Support Workbench, or you can manually run a health check using the DBMS_HM PL/SQL package.

Handle Block Corruption

- When Oracle detects a corrupted block, it registers an ORA-01578 error in the alert log and on the EM home page.

- The initialization parameter DB_BLOCK_CHECKING controls how thoroughly Oracle checks the integrity of every data block that is read or written.

- If you discover only a small handful of blocks to recover in a database from the aforementioned health checks or results discovered in the alert log, then RMAN can perform *block media recovery* rather than a full datafile recovery.

- When you use the RMAN RECOVER . . . BLOCK command, RMAN first searches the flashback logs for a good copy of the corrupted block (if Flashback Database is enabled).

- You can use the dynamic performance view V$DATABASE_BLOCK_CORRUPTION to view the bad blocks in the database.

- The target database must be in ARCHIVELOG mode to use RMAN block recovery.

- Alternatively, you can use flashback logs in the flash recovery area for uncorrupt versions of bad blocks.

- The Data Recovery Advisor is part of the Oracle advisor framework and automatically gathers information about a failure when an error is encountered.

- Once the Data Recovery Advisor has identified a failure, you can review the details of the failure using the EM or RMAN interface.

- Once the Data Recovery Advisor has identified a failure, you can use the RMAN ADVISE FAILURE command to recommend a repair option for the specified failure.

Self Test

1. The value of the initialization parameter DIAGNOSTIC_DEST is NULL, the environment variable ORACLE_HOME is set to /u01/app/oracle/product/12.1.0/db_1, and the value of the environment variable ORACLE_BASE is set to /u01/app/oracle. At startup, what value is assigned by Oracle to DIAGNOSTIC_DEST? (Choose the best answer.)

   A. /u01/app/oracle/diag

   B. /u01/app/oracle/log

   C. /u01/app/oracle/product/12.1.0/db_1/log

   D. /u01/app/oracle

2. Which of the following tasks can you accomplish using the ADRCI tool? (Choose all that apply.)

   A. Package incident information into a ZIP file to send to Oracle Support

   B. View diagnostic data within ADR

   C. Perform a health check on the database while it is running

   D. Run recommended fixes from the most recent health check on the database

3. The V$DIAG_INFO view shows the location of various files. Which of the following file types are not identified in V$DIAG_INFO? (Choose the best answer.)

   A. Diagnostic trace files

   B. Diagnostic incident files

   C. Diagnostic problem files

   D. The database XML alert log

4. Which of the following basic consistency checks are performed by default when a block is written or read? (Choose all that apply.)

   A. Block checksum.

   B. Data block address in cache matches the address on disk.

   C. Block version.

   D. The data block is below the high water mark when reading or updating a block.

5. What is a prerequisite for using block media recovery? (Choose the best answer.)

   A. Flashback Database must be enabled.

   B. The database must be in ARCHIVELOG mode.

   C. A full (or level 0) backup from before the damage must be available.

   D. DB_BLOCK_CHECKING must be set to LOW, MEDIUM, or FULL.

6. You can use the RMAN CHANGE FAILURE command to change the priority of which types of failures? (Choose all that apply.)

   A. OPEN

   B. HIGH

   C. CRITICAL

   D. LOW

   E. CLOSED

7. When using the Data Recovery Advisor, you run the LIST FAILURE command, and it reports an issue with a datafile. Then after a second datafile is damaged, you run ADVISE FAILURE. For which issues will the advisor generate advice? (Choose the best answer.)

   A. Only the first file

   B. Only the second file

   C. Both files

   D. Neither file, because ADVISE must be immediately preceded by LIST

Self Test Answers

1. ☑ **D**. The ADR root directory (also known as the ADR base) is set by the parameter DIAGNOSTIC_DEST. If it is not set, Oracle sets DIAGNOSTIC_DEST to the environment variable ORACLE_BASE.

   ☒ **A**, **B**, and **C** are incorrect. All three locations are not assigned, given the values of DIAGNOSTIC_DEST, ORACLE_BASE, and ORACLE_HOME.

2. ☑ **A** and **B**. The ADRCI tool allows you to view diagnostic information in the ADR root directory in addition to packaging both problem and incident information for Oracle Support.

☒ **C** and **D** are incorrect. The ADRCI tool cannot initiate health checks or run fixes recommended by other Oracle diagnostic tools.

3. ☑ **C**. The view V$DIAG_INFO does not specify a directory for problems, only incidents. Each incident is labeled with a text string representing the problem identifier.

☒ **A**, **B**, and **D** are incorrect. They are listed in V$DIAG_INFO with the operating system–specific path name. Note that the text version of the database alert log is not specifically mentioned; it exists with the trace files. The XML version of the database alert log is specifically given.

4. ☑ **A**, **B**, and **C**. Oracle performs all of these checks with the default value of DB_BLOCK_CHECKSUM=TYPICAL.

☒ **D** is incorrect because Oracle does not check whether a block is below the high water mark when updating or reading a block.

5. ☑ **B**. A complete chain of redo is required to recover the restored block to the present point.

☑ **A, C,** and **D** are incorrect. **A** and **C** are incorrect because the block can be extracted from either a full (level 0) backup or from the flashback log; either is sufficient, but only one is necessary. **D** is incorrect because DB_BLOCK_CHECKING does not have to be enabled at all to use block recovery, though it may help with detecting damage.

6. ☑ **B** and **D**. You can change the priority of a HIGH failure to LOW, and vice versa.

☒ **A, C,** and **E** are incorrect. **A** is incorrect because OPEN is not a failure status. **C** is incorrect because you cannot change the priority of a CRITICAL failure. **E** is incorrect because once closed, it cannot be further adjusted.

7. ☑ **A**. Advice is generated only for problems previously detected with LIST.

☒ **B, C,** and **D** are incorrect. **B** and **C** are incorrect because advice cannot be generated for a problem that has not been listed. **D** is incorrect because there is no time limit between LIST and ADVISE.

CHAPTER 26

Flashback

Exam Objectives

- 63.1.14.1 Describe the Flashback Technologies
- 63.1.14.2 Use Flashback to Query Data
- 63.1.14.3 Perform Flashback Table Operations
- 63.1.14.4 Perform Table Recovery from Backups
- 63.1.14.5 Describe and Use Flashback Data Archive
- 63.1.14.6 Perform Flashback Database

To protect against loss of data because of physical damage to the database, you use backups and archive logging. If they are appropriately managed, you can guarantee that your database will never lose one row of committed data. But what about damage caused by users? What if someone has accidentally (or deliberately) committed a bad transaction? Dropped a table? Any such actions are not errors as far as the database is concerned, and the *D* (for durability) of the ACID test means that Oracle is not allowed to reverse these actions. However, the various flashback technologies let the database administrator (DBA) do just that: take the entire database, or perhaps just one table or even one transaction, back in time to reverse the effect of the error. A related capability is the ability to query the database as it was at some time in the past.

Describe the Flashback Technologies

Four distinct flashback technologies are available, each implemented with a different underlying architecture. Each technology has different capabilities and limitations, but there is overlapping functionality between them. The typical reason for using any type of flashback technology is to correct mistakes—it is vital to understand what type of flashback technology is appropriate for correcting different types of errors.

Flashback Database

Flashback Database is, by analogy, like pressing a rewind button on the database (if you cannot remember the concept of a rewind button, research the use of tape recorders). The current database is taken as the starting point, and it is taken back in time, change by change, reversing all work done sequentially. The end result is as if you had done an incomplete recovery: all work subsequent to the flashback point is lost, and the database must be opened with RESETLOGS. Clearly, this is a drastic thing to do. It allows you to back out changes that resulted in logical corruptions (in a business sense) such as inappropriate transactions (for example, running your year-end archive-and-purge routines before running your end-of-year reports).

 EXAM TIP Flashback Database will not back out physical corruption, only logical corruption caused by user error.

Flashback Query, Transaction, and Table

Three flashback techniques are based on the use of undo segments. The first flashback capability was initially introduced with release 9*i* of the database and has been substantially enhanced subsequently.

Flashback Query (the release 9*i* feature) lets you query the database as it was at some time in the past, either for one select statement or by taking your session temporarily back in time so that all its queries will be against a previous version of the database. This can be used to see the state of the data before a set of transactions was committed. What did the tables look like half an hour ago? This can be invaluable in tracking down the cause of business data corruptions and can also be used to correct some mistakes. By comparing the current and previous versions of a table, you can identify what was done that was wrong. It is even possible to select all versions of a row over a period of time to show a history of what has happened to the row, when it happened, who did it, and the identifiers of the transactions that made each change.

Flashback Transaction automates the repair process. Once you have used Flashback Query to identify which transaction it was that caused the problem, Oracle can construct SQL statements that will reverse the changes. This is not the same as rolling back a committed transaction! It is impossible to roll back a committed change because the rules of a relational database do not permit this. But it is possible to construct another transaction that will reverse the effect of the first, erroneous transaction. Unlike Flashback Database, Flashback Transaction does not imply data loss; all other work done remains in effect, and the database stays current.

The third flashback technique based on undo data is Flashback Table. Having determined that inappropriate work has been committed against one table, you can instruct Oracle to reverse all changes made to that table since a particular point in time, while leaving all other tables current.

Throughout any Flashback Query, Flashback Transaction, or Flashback Table operation, the database remains open, and all objects (including those involved in the flashback) are available for use. Transactional integrity and constraints are always enforced, which means that the flashback operation might fail. For example, if a flashback of a transaction requires an insert into a primary key column, that value must not be in use. Flashing back one table may not be possible if it has foreign key constraints—you will have to flash back all the related tables in one operation.

 EXAM TIP Flashback Query, in its three variations, relies on the use of undo segments.

Flashback Drop

It is now possible to "undrop" a table. This is implemented by mapping the DROP command onto a RENAME command. Rather than dropping the table, the table is renamed to a system-generated name and only dropped later, when its storage space is needed for a live object. If necessary and if its storage space has not been reused, the object can be renamed back to its original name and thus restored. Without this capability, the only way to get a table back after a drop would be to do an incomplete recovery to the point in time just before the table was dropped. This was usually time consuming, and it meant the loss of all work done subsequently. The new Flashback Database capability achieves the same result as incomplete recovery and should be much faster, but work done on other tables following the drop is lost, and the database will be unavailable until the operation is completed.

Flashback Drop lets you reinstate the table as it was at the time that it was dropped, with no loss of data whatsoever; the database remains current. This does not require any use of backups, and neither is there any downtime for users. Note that Flashback Drop is specifically for the DROP command; you cannot flash back a TRUNCATE command. Along with the table itself, any associated indexes, constraints, triggers, and permissions will also be restored.

 EXAM TIP You cannot flash back a table truncation, only a table drop.

Flashback Data Archive

The Flashback Data Archive provides the ability to view tables as they were at any time in the past. The forms of flashback described so far all have time limits: Flashback Database is restricted by the size of the flashback logs, Flashback Query by the undo retention, and Flashback Drop by the available space in tablespaces. A Flashback Data Archive can be configured to store before images of rows indefinitely. It must, however, be configured. Unlike Flashback Query and Flashback Drop, it is not enabled by default.

Enabling a table for Flashback Data Archive creates another table (and a few other objects) that will store all previous versions of rows, storing them forever if desired. When Data Manipulation Language (DML) is committed against the table, a background process called the Flashback Data Archive (FBDA) process will capture the necessary data and save it to the archive. From there, it can be queried with the same syntax used for a regular Flashback Query—but the flashback can go back years.

When a Flashback Data Archive is created, you specify a time limit (which may be years), and the FBDA will make sure that all data is saved until that time has passed and will then remove it. The FBDA is responsible for creating the objects in the archive, populating them with rows as necessary, and purging data that has passed the expiry date.

When to Use Flashback Technology

Human error has always been the most difficult type of error from which to recover. This is because as far as the database is concerned, human error is not an error at all. Depending on the nature of the error, the different flashback technologies may help you to recover while minimizing downtime and loss of data.

The most drastic flashback technique is Flashback Database. Consider using this only when you would also consider using incomplete recovery—the effect is the same, though the downtime will typically be much less. An example is when dropping a schema on the production system when you thought you were connected to the test system. A critical table truncation (though not a table drop) would also be a time to use Flashback Database.

Flashback Drop will restore a table (together with various dependent objects) to the state it was in at the time of the drop. Note that this will not restore a truncated table—only one that has been completely dropped. There is no downtime involved, other than the obvious fact that until the table is undropped, no one can get to it, and no work will be lost. Unlike Flashback Database, Flashback Drop does not require any configuration—it is always available, unless you specifically disable it.

For finer granularity of recovery, consider Flashback Table and Flashback Transaction. These should not affect the users at all, other than that the work reversed is gone—which is presumably the desired outcome. Like Flashback Drop, the Flashback Query, Transaction, and Table facilities are always available without any configuration other than granting appropriate privileges. They may, however, require some tuning of undo management.

The Flashback Data Archive is for long-term storage. Typically, this will be for legal reasons; in many jurisdictions there are requirements for keeping data for years and then for destroying it (sometimes known as *digital shredding*). A Flashback Data Archive can enable this transparently. The DBA can thus guarantee legal compliance without the need for any programming effort.

In some cases, you will have a choice of flashback technologies. Consider an example where a batch job is run twice. Perhaps you import a few hundred thousand invoices into your accounting system from your billing system every day, and through some mistake and lack of validation, the same billing run is imported twice. If the import is done as one huge transaction, then Flashback Transaction will reverse it. But if it is done as many small transactions, rather than reversing them all, it may be easier to do a table-level flashback of all the tables affected. It may be that some of the billing system interface tables are dropped after the run—Flashback Drop will recover them. But if the run involves a truncation, the only option is Flashback Database. Also, it may be that the error was not discovered for some time and a significant amount of work has been done based on the erroneously imported data; then Flashback Database may be the only way to ensure that you end up with a database that is consistent in business terms.

When choosing a flashback technique, always remember that Oracle will guarantee transactional integrity but that the results in business terms may not be what you want. Flashback Database, or indeed incomplete recovery, is the only way to guarantee absolutely the integrity of the database and conformity with your business rules—but the price in lost time and data may be very high.

EXAM TIP   In the case of media damage, such as losing a datafile, no flashback technology can help. That is what the standard backup, restore, and recovery procedures are for.

Use Flashback to Query Data

The basic form of Flashback Query lets you query the database as it was at some time in the past. The principle is that your query specifies a time, which is mapped onto a system change number (SCN), and whenever the query hits a block that has been changed since that SCN, it will go to the undo segments to extract the undo data needed to roll back the change. This rollback is strictly temporary and is visible only to the session running the Flashback Query. Clearly, for a Flashback Query to succeed, the undo data must be available. More sophisticated techniques can be used to retrieve all versions of a row, to reverse individual transactions, or to reverse all the changes made to a table since a certain time. It is also possible to guarantee that a flashback will succeed—but there is a price to be paid for enabling this: It may cause transactions to fail.

EXAM TIP   All forms of Flashback Query rely on undo data to reconstruct data as it was at an earlier point in time.

Basic Flashback Query

Any SELECT statement can be directed against a previous version of a table. Consider this example:

```
SQL> select sysdate from dual;
SYSDATE
----------------
27-12-14 16:54:06
SQL> delete from regions where region_name like 'A%';
```

```
2 rows deleted.
SQL> commit;
Commit complete.
SQL> select * from regions;
REGION_ID REGION_NAME
--------- ------------------------
        1 Europe
        4 Middle East and Africa
SQL> select * from regions as of timestamp

to_timestamp('27-12-14 16:54:06','dd-mm-yy hh24:mi:ss');
REGION_ID REGION_NAME
--------- ------------------------
        1 Europe
        2 Americas
        3 Asia
        4 Middle East and Africa
SQL> select * from regions as of timestamp

to_timestamp('27-12-14 16:54:06','dd-mm-yy hh24:mi:ss')

minus select * from regions;
REGION_ID REGION_NAME
--------- ------------------------
        2 Americas
        3 Asia
```

First, note the time. Then delete some rows from a table and commit the change. A query confirms that there are only two rows in the table and no rows where the REGION_NAME begins with *A*. The next query is directed against the table as it was at the earlier time (back when there were four rows, including those for *Asia* and *Americas*). Make no mistake about this—the two rows beginning with *A* are gone; they were deleted, and the delete was committed. This cannot be rolled back. The deleted rows you are seeing have been constructed from undo data. The final query combines real-time data with historical data to see what rows have been removed. The output of this query could be used for repair purposes to insert the rows back into the table.

Although being able to direct one query against data as of an earlier point in time may be useful, there will be times when you want to make a series of selects. It is possible to take your whole session back in time by using the DBMS_FLASHBACK package.

```
SQL> execute dbms_flashback.enable_at_time(-
> to_timestamp('27-12-08 16:54:06','dd-mm-yy hh24:mi:ss'));
PL/SQL procedure successfully completed.
SQL>
```

From this point on, all queries will see the database as it was at the time specified. All other sessions will see real-time data, but this one session will see a frozen version of the database until the flashback is cancelled.

```
SQL> execute dbms_flashback.disable;
PL/SQL procedure successfully completed.
SQL>
```

While in flashback mode, it is impossible to execute DML commands. They will throw an error. Only SELECT statements are possible.

How far back you can take a Flashback Query (either one query or by using DBMS_ FLASHBACK) depends on the contents of the undo segments. If the undo data needed to construct the out-of-date result set is not available, then the query will fail with an ORA-08180, "No snapshot found based on specified time," error.

The syntax for enabling Flashback Query will accept either a timestamp or an SCN. If you use an SCN, then the point to which the flashback goes is precise. If you specify a time, it will be mapped onto an SCN with a precision of three seconds.

EXAM TIP   You can query the database as of an earlier point in time, but you can never execute DML against the older versions of the data.

Flashback Table Query

Conceptually, a table flashback is simple. Oracle will query the undo segments to extract details of all rows that have been changed and then construct and execute statements that will reverse the changes. The flashback operation is a separate transaction, which will counteract the effect of all the previous transactions—if possible. The database remains online and normal work is not affected, unless row locking is an issue. This is not a rollback of committed work; it is a new transaction designed to reverse the effects of committed work. All indexes are maintained, and constraints are enforced; a table flashback is just another transaction, and the usual rules apply. The only exception to normal processing is that, by default, triggers on the table are disabled for the flashback operation.

A table flashback will often involve a table that is in a foreign key relationship. In that case, it is almost inevitable that the flashback operation will fail with a constraint violation. To avoid this problem, the syntax permits flashback of multiple tables with one command, which will be executed as a single transaction with the constraint checked at the end.

The first step to enabling table flashback is to enable row movement on the tables. This is a flag set in the data dictionary that informs Oracle that row IDs may change. A row ID can never actually change, but a flashback operation may make it appear as though it has. For instance, in the case of a row that is deleted, the flashback operation will insert it back into the table. It will have the same primary key value but a different row ID.

In the example that follows, there are two tables: EMP and DEPT. There is a foreign key relationship between them, stating that every employee in EMP must be a member of a department in DEPT.

First, insert a new department and an employee in that department and note the time.

```
SQL> insert into dept values(50,'SUPPORT','LONDON');
1 row created.
SQL> insert into emp

values(8000,'WATSON','ANALYST',7566,'27-DEC-14',3000,null,50);
1 row created.
SQL> commit;
Commit complete.
SQL> select sysdate from dual;
SYSDATE
-----------------
27-12-14 18:30:11
```

PART IV

Next, delete the department and the employee, taking care to delete the employee first to avoid a constraint violation.

```
SQL> delete from emp where empno=8000;
1 row deleted.
SQL> delete from dept where deptno=50;
1 row deleted.
SQL> commit;
Commit complete.
```

Now attempt to flash back the tables to the time when the department and employee existed.

```
SQL> flashback table emp to timestamp

to_timestamp('27-12-14 18:30:11','dd-mm-yy hh24:mi:ss');
flashback table emp to timestamp

to_timestamp('27-12-14 18:30:11','dd-mm-yy hh24:mi:ss')
               *
ERROR at line 1:
ORA-08189: cannot flashback the table because row movement is not enabled
```

This fails because, by default, row movement, which is a prerequisite for table flashback, is not enabled for any table, so enable it for both tables.

```
SQL> alter table dept enable row movement;
Table altered.
SQL> alter table emp enable row movement;
Table altered.
```

Now try the flashback again.

```
SQL> flashback table emp to timestamp

to_timestamp('27-12-14 18:30:11','dd-mm-yy hh24:mi:ss');
flashback table emp to timestamp

to_timestamp('27-12-14 18:30:11','dd-mm-yy hh24:mi:ss')
*
ERROR at line 1:
ORA-02091: transaction rolled back
ORA-02291: integrity constraint (SCOTT.FK_DEPTNO) violated
```

This time the flashback fails for a more subtle reason. The flashback is attempting to reverse the deletion of employee 8000 by inserting him, but employee 8000 was in department 50, which has been deleted and so does not exist. So, there is a foreign key violation. You could avoid this problem by flashing back the DEPT table first, which would insert department 50. But if your flashback involves many tables and many DML statements, it may be logically difficult to find a sequence that will work. The answer is to flash back both tables together.

```
SQL> flashback table emp,dept to timestamp

to_timestamp('27-12-14 18:30:11','dd-mm-yy hh24:mi:ss');
Flashback complete.
```

This succeeds because both the tables are flashed back in one transaction, and the constraints are checked only at the end of that transaction by which time the data is logically consistent.

The flashback could still fail for other reasons:

- Primary key violations will occur if a key value has been reused between a delete and the flashback.

- An ORA-08180, "No snapshot found based on specified time," error will be raised if there is not enough undo information to go back to the time requested.

- If any rows affected by the flashback are locked by other users, the flashback will fail with ORA-00054: "Resource busy and acquire with NOWAIT specified."

- The table definitions must not change during the period concerned; flashback cannot go across Data Definition Language (DDL) statements. Attempting to do this will generate ORA-01466: "Unable to read data—table definition has changed."

- Flashback does not work for tables in the SYS schema. Try to imagine the effect of flashing back part of the data dictionary.

If a table flashback fails for any reason, the flashback operation will be cancelled. Any parts of it that did succeed will be rolled back, and the tables will be as they were before the flashback command was issued.

Variations in the syntax allow flashback to a system change number and the firing of DML triggers during the operation.

```
SQL> flashback table emp,dept to scn 6539425 enable triggers;
```

Flashback Versions Query

A row may have changed several times during its life. Flashback Versions Query lets you see all the committed versions of a row (but not any uncommitted versions), including the timestamps for when each version was created and when it ended. You can also see the transaction identifier of the transaction that created any given version of a row, which can then be used with Flashback Transaction Query. This information is exposed by a number of pseudocolumns that are available with every table. Pseudocolumns are columns appended to the row by Oracle internally; they are not part of the International Organization for Standardization (ISO) standards for a relational database, but they can be useful. One pseudocolumn is the row ID. This is the unique identifier for every row in the database that is used in indexes as the pointer back to the table. The pseudocolumns relevant to flashback are as follows:

- **VERSIONS_STARTSCN**   The SCN at which this version of the row was created, either by INSERT or by UPDATE

- **VERSIONS_STARTTIME**   The timestamp at which this version of the row was created

- **VERSIONS_ENDSCN**   The SCN at which this version of the row expired, because of either DELETE or UPDATE

- **VERSIONS_ENDTIME**   The timestamp at which this version of the row expired

- **VERSIONS_XID** The unique identifier for the transaction that created this version of the row

- **VERSIONS_OPERATIONS** The operation done by the transaction to create this version of the row, either INSERT or UPDATE or DELETE

To see these pseudocolumns, you must include the VERSIONS BETWEEN keywords in your query. For example, Figure 26-1 shows all versions of the row for employee 8000.

The versions are sorted in descending order of existence; they must be read from the bottom up. The bottom row shows that employee 8000 was inserted (the *I* in the last column) at SCN 95828152 by transaction number 01000E0002180000. The employee was given the ENAME of RAMKLASS and the SAL of 3000. This version of the row existed until SCN 95828273, which takes you to the third row. At this SCN, the row was updated (the *U* in the last column) with a new salary. This version of the row persisted until SCN 95828279, when it was deleted, as shown in the second row. The VERSIONS_ENDSCN column is always null for a deletion. The top row of the result set shows a new insertion, which reuses the employee number. For this row, the VERSIONS_ENDSCN is also null because the row still exists in that version at the end of the time range specified in the query.

In the example in Figure 26-1, the VERSIONS BETWEEN clause uses two constants for the SCN. MINVALUE instructs Oracle to retrieve the earliest information in the undo segments; MAXVALUE will be the current SCN. In other words, the query as written will show all versions that can possibly be retrieved, given the information available. The syntax will also accept a range specified with two timestamps.

```
SQL> select empno,ename,sal,versions_xid,versions_starttime,
versions_endtime,versions_operation from emp versions between
timestamp (systimestamp - 1/24) and systimestamp
where empno=8000;
```

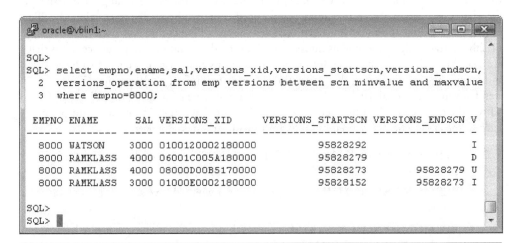

Figure 26-1 Flashback Versions Query

The preceding example will select all versions of employee number 8000 that existed during the last hour.

 EXAM TIP Flashback Version Query cannot work against external tables or V$ views. Why not? Because changes to these objects do not generate undo.

Flashback Transaction Query

Flashback Table Query and Flashback Versions Query use undo data for an object. Flashback Transaction Query analyzes the undo by a different dimension. It will retrieve all the undo data for a transaction, no matter how many objects it affects. The critical view is FLASHBACK_TRANSACTION_QUERY, described here:

```
SQL> describe flashback_transaction_query
 Name                                     Null?    Type
 --------------------------------------- -------- --------------------
 XID                                               RAW(8)
 START_SCN                                         NUMBER
 START_TIMESTAMP                                   DATE
 COMMIT_SCN                                        NUMBER
 COMMIT_TIMESTAMP                                  DATE
 LOGON_USER                                        VARCHAR2(30)
 UNDO_CHANGE#                                      NUMBER
 OPERATION                                         VARCHAR2(32)
 TABLE_NAME                                        VARCHAR2(256)
 TABLE_OWNER                                       VARCHAR2(32)
 ROW_ID                                            VARCHAR2(19)
 UNDO_SQL                                          VARCHAR2(4000)
```

Because the data in this view may be sensitive, it is protected by a privilege. You must be granted SELECT ANY TRANSACTION before you can query it. By default, this privilege is granted to SYS and to the DBA role. There will be one or more rows in this view for every transaction whose undo data still exists in the undo segments, and every row will refer to one row affected by the transaction. Table 26-1 describes the columns.

A one-line SQL statement might generate many rows in FLASHBACK_TRANSACTION_QUERY. This is because SQL is a set-oriented language. One statement can affect many rows. But each row affected will have its own row in the view. The view will show committed transactions and also transactions in progress. For an active transaction, the COMMIT_SCN and COMMIT_TIMESTAMP columns are NULL. Rolled-back transactions are not displayed.

Take an example where a salary was multiplied by 11 rather than being incremented by 10 percent.

```
SQL> update emp set sal = sal*11 where empno=7902;
1 row updated.
SQL> commit;
Commit complete.
```

Column	Description
XID	The transaction identifier. This is the join column to the pseudocolumn VERSIONS_XID displayed in a Flashback Version Query.
START_SCN	The system change number at the time the transaction started.
START_TIMESTAMP	The timestamp at the time the transaction started.
COMMIT_SCN	The system change number at the time the transaction was committed.
COMMIT_TIMESTAMP	The timestamp at the time the transaction was committed.
LOGON_USER	The Oracle username of the session that performed the transaction.
UNDO_CHANGE#	The undo system change number. This is not likely to be relevant to most work.
OPERATION	The DML operation applied to the row: INSERT, UPDATE, or DELETE.
TABLE_NAME	The table to which the row belongs.
TABLE_OWNER	The schema to which the table belongs.
ROW_ID	The unique identifier of the row affected.
UNDO_SQL	A constructed statement that will reverse the operation. For example, if the OPERATION were a DELETE, then this will be an INSERT.

Table 26-1   The Columns of the FLASHBACK_TRANSACTION_QUERY View

Later, it is suspected that a mistake was made. So, you query the versions of the row.

```
SQL> select ename,sal,versions_xid from emp versions between scn
  2  minvalue and maxvalue where empno=7902;
ENAME             SAL VERSIONS_XID
---------- ----------- ----------------
FORD            33000 06002600B0010000
FORD             3000
```

This does indicate what happened and gives enough information to reverse the change. But what if the transaction affected other rows in other tables? To be certain, query FLASHBACK_TRANSACTION_QUERY, which will have one row for every row affected by the transaction. A minor complication is that the XID column is type RAW, whereas the VERSIONS_XID pseudocolumn is hexadecimal, so you must use a type casting function to make the join.

```
SQL> select operation,undo_sql from flashback_transaction_query
where xid=hextoraw('06002600B0010000');
OPERATION  UNDO_SQL
---------- -----------------------------------------------------------
UPDATE     update "SCOTT"."EMP" set "SAL" = '3000' where ROWID =
           'AAAM+yAAEAAAAAeAAM';
```

This query returns only one row, which confirms that there was indeed only one row affected by the transaction and provides a statement that will reverse the impact of the change. Note the use of a ROWID in the UNDO_SQL statement. Provided that there has been no reorganization of the table, this will guarantee that the correct row is changed.

The view FLASHBACK_TRANSACTION_QUERY will construct undo statements to reverse a transaction, but executing them individually would be an awful task for a large transaction. This is where the DBMS_FLASHBACK package is again useful. It includes procedures to back out transactions. To execute the transaction backout procedures, you must have been granted the FLASHBACK ANY TABLE privilege.

Consider this example:

```
SQL> execute dbms_flashback.transaction_backout(-
numtxns=>2,-
xids=>sys.xid_array('0900010059100000','02000700920F0000'),-

options=>dbms_flashback.cascade);
```

This procedure call will reverse all the work done by the two nominated transactions. Here are the arguments in order:

- NUMTXNS is the number of transactions that should be reversed; in this example, two.

- XIDS is a list of transaction identifiers, passed as an XID_ARRAY variable. This list would have been identified with a Flashback Query.

- OPTIONS can take various values in the form of package constants. The CASCADE option will attempt to order the changes to avoid conflicts.

It is impossible to roll back a committed transaction. The rules of a relational database forbid this. So when the backout procedure reverses one or more transactions, it must construct and attempt to execute more DML in another transaction, which will reverse the effect of the original transactions. This process is fraught with difficulty because of the possibility of dependencies between the transactions and conflicts with work done subsequently. This will typically show up as constraint violations. The OPTIONS argument controls what to do if there is a problem. These are the possible values:

- NOCASCADE (the default) will apply undo changes with no attempt to identify dependencies. This may well fail if, for instance, the transactions listed affect tables in foreign key relationships.

- CASCADE attempts to undo the transactions logically such that constraint violations will not occur.

- NONCONFLICT_ONLY backs out only changes to rows that do not cause problems. The database will remain consistent, but some transactions may be incomplete.

- NOCASCADE_FORCE will undo SQL statements in reverse order of commit times.

Whatever changes the DBMS_FLASHBACK.BACKOUT_TRANSACTION manages to accomplish are left uncommitted. This gives you an opportunity to investigate what it managed to achieve before committing (or rolling back).

Figure 26-2 shows an example of combining Flashback Query with Flashback Transaction. The first query shows a row, which is then updated and committed. A Flashback Version Query retrieves the identifier of the transaction that made the change, and passing this to

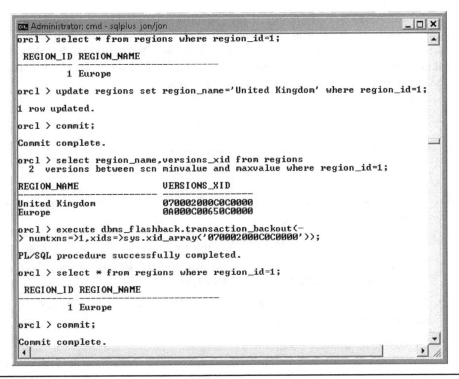

Figure 26-2   Using the Flashback Transaction facility

DBMS_FLASHBACK.BACKOUT_TRANSACTION reverses the change. Finally, the reversal must be committed.

Flashback and Undo Data

Flashback Query in its various forms relies entirely on undo data. You are asking Oracle to present you a version of the data as it was some time ago. If the data has been changed since that time, Oracle must roll back the changes. To do this, Oracle needs the undo data that protected the change. Whether the query will succeed will depend on whether that undo data is still available. Consider Figure 26-3.

The first query asks for a view of the table as it was 40 minutes ago, and it succeeds. This is because there is at least 40 minutes of undo data available in the undo segments. The second query attempts to go back 40 days, and it fails. In virtually all databases, it would be completely unrealistic to expect Flashback Query to work over such a long period. You would need an undo tablespace the size of Jupiter to store that much undo data.

To guarantee that a Flashback Query will always succeed for a given period, set the RETENTION GUARANTEE attribute for the undo tablespace in conjunction with the UNDO_RETENTION instance parameter. This will ensure that you can always flash back

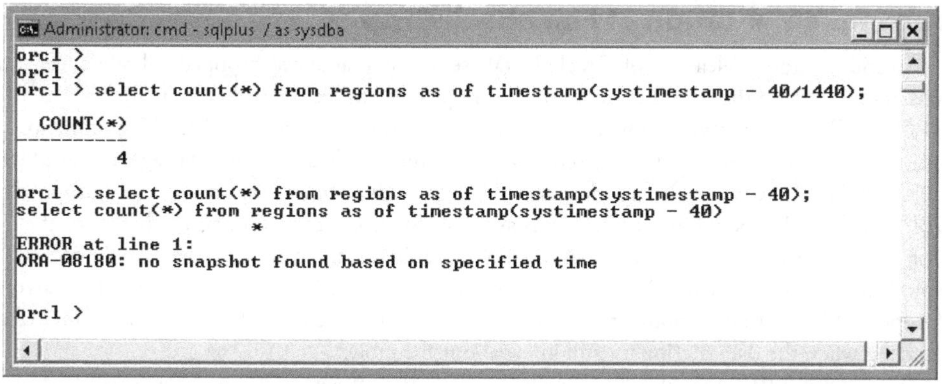

```
Administrator: cmd - sqlplus / as sysdba                    _ □ ×
orcl >
orcl >
orcl > select count(*) from regions as of timestamp(systimestamp - 40/1440);

  COUNT(*)
  ----------
         4

orcl > select count(*) from regions as of timestamp(systimestamp - 40);
select count(*) from regions as of timestamp(systimestamp - 40)
                       *
ERROR at line 1:
ORA-08180: no snapshot found based on specified time

orcl >
```

Figure 26-3   Flashback Query and undo data

the number of seconds specified—but the price you will pay is that if your undo tablespace is not sized adequately for the transaction workload, then the database may hang while performing DML.

Perform Flashback Table Drop Operations

Accidentally dropping a table is easy to do. It is not just that you can drop the wrong table because of a typing error—it could be the right table, but you are connected to the wrong schema or logged onto the wrong instance. You can reduce the likelihood of this by setting your SQL*Plus prompt. Here's an example:

```
SQL> set sqlprompt "_user'@'_connect_identifier>"
SYSTEM@orcl12c>
```

TIP   To set your sqlprompt automatically for all SQL*Plus sessions, put the preceding command into the glogin.sql file in the ORACLE_HOME/sqlplus/admin directory.

Flashback Drop lets you reinstate a previously dropped table (but not a truncated table) exactly as it was before the drop. All the indexes will also be recovered and also any triggers and grants. Unique, primary key, and not-null constraints will also be recovered—but not foreign key constraints.

EXAM TIP   The Flashback Drop command applies only to tables, but all associated objects will also be recovered—except for foreign key constraints.

The Implementation of Flashback Drop

Up to and including release 9i of Oracle Database, when a table was dropped, all references to it were removed from the data dictionary. If it were possible to see the source code for the old DROP TABLE command, you would see that it was actually a series of DELETE commands against the various tables in the SYS schema that define a table and its space usage, followed by a COMMIT. There was no actual clearing of data from disk, but the space used by a dropped table was flagged as being unused and thus available for reuse. Even though the blocks of the table were still there, there was no possible way of getting to them because the data dictionary would have no record of which blocks were part of the dropped table. The only way to recover a dropped table was to do a point-in-time recovery, restoring a version of the database from before the drop when the data dictionary still knew about the table.

From release 10g onward of the Oracle database, the implementation of the DROP TABLE command has changed. Tables are no longer dropped at all; they are renamed.

In Figure 26-4, you can see that a table, OLD_NAME, occupies one extent of 64KB, which starts 38,281 blocks into file 4. After the rename to NEW_NAME, the storage is the same; therefore, the table is the same. Querying the view DBA_OBJECTS would show that the table's object number had not changed either.

The DROP TABLE command has been mapped internally onto a RENAME command, which affects the table and all its associated indexes, triggers, and constraints, with the

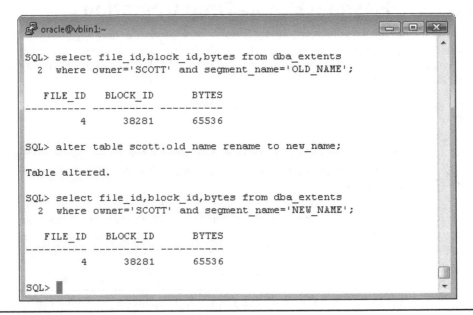

Figure 26-4 Renaming tables with SQL*Plus

exception of foreign key constraints, which are dropped. Foreign key constraints have to be physically dropped. If they were maintained, even with a different name, then DML on the nondropped parent table would be constrained by the contents of a dropped table, which would be absurd.

Grants on tables do not have names, so they can't be renamed. When you grant an object privilege, you specify the object by name, and the underlying storage of the grant references the object by its object number. Because the object numbers don't get changed by a RENAME operation, the grants remain valid.

As far as normal SELECT and DML statements are concerned, a dropped table is definitely dropped. There is no change to any other commands, and all your software will assume that a dropped table really is gone. But now that DROP is in fact RENAME, it becomes possible to undrop—by renaming the table back to its original name. However, this is not guaranteed to succeed. It may be that the space occupied by the dropped table has been reused. There are also complications if in the interim period another table has been created, reusing the same name as the dropped table.

The dropped objects can be queried by looking at the "recycle bin" to obtain their new names. This is a listing of all objects that have been dropped, mapping the original table and index names onto the system-generated names of the dropped objects. There is a recycle bin for each user, visible in the USER_RECYCLEBIN data dictionary view, or for a global picture you can query DBA_RECYCLEBIN. The space occupied by the recycle bin objects will be reused automatically when a tablespace comes under space pressure (after which time the objects cannot be recovered), or you can manually force Oracle to really drop the objects with the PURGE command.

 TIP There are no guarantees of success with Flashback Drop, but it may well work. The sooner you execute it, the greater the likelihood of success.

Using Flashback Drop

Consider the example in Figure 26-5. This is the most basic use of Flashback Drop. The DROP command renames the table to a system-generated name, and Flashback Drop brings it back.

Variations in syntax are as follows:

```
SQL> drop table <table_name> purge;
SQL> flashback table <table_name> to before drop rename to <new_name> ;
```

The first command really will drop the table. The PURGE keyword instructs Oracle to revert to the original meaning of DROP: all references to the table are deleted, and it can never be brought back. The second command will flash back the table but give it a new name. This would be essential if between the drop and the flashback another table had been created with the same name as the dropped table. Note that although a table can be renamed during a flashback, it cannot change schemas; all flashback operations occur within the schema to which the object belongs. The indexes, triggers, and constraints that are flashed back along with

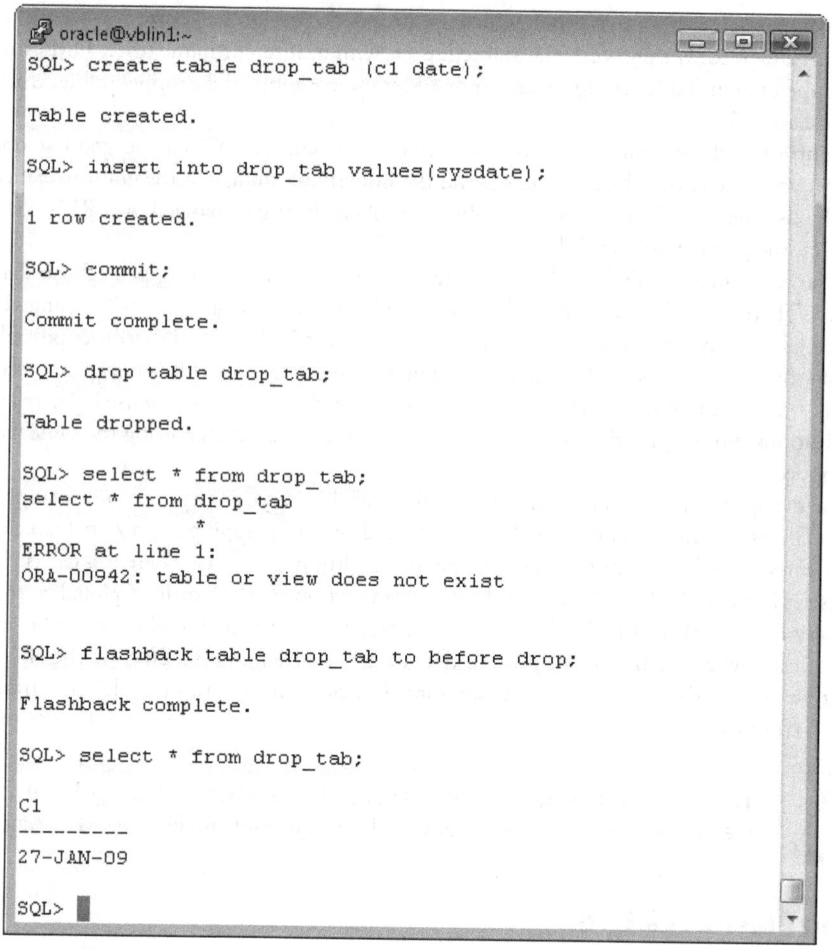

```
oracle@vblin1:~

SQL> create table drop_tab (c1 date);

Table created.

SQL> insert into drop_tab values(sysdate);

1 row created.

SQL> commit;

Commit complete.

SQL> drop table drop_tab;

Table dropped.

SQL> select * from drop_tab;
select * from drop_tab
              *
ERROR at line 1:
ORA-00942: table or view does not exist


SQL> flashback table drop_tab to before drop;

Flashback complete.

SQL> select * from drop_tab;

C1
---------
27-JAN-09

SQL>
```

Figure 26-5   Using Flashback Drop

the table keep their recycle bin names. If you want to return them to their original names, you must rename them manually after the flashback.

There are two points to emphasize here. First, Flashback Drop can recover only from a DROP. It cannot recover from a TRUNCATE. Second, if you drop a user with, CASCADE as shown here, you will not be able to recover any of SCOTT's tables with a flashback:

```
SQL> drop user scott cascade;
```

The drop of the schema means that Oracle cannot maintain the objects at all, even in the recycle bin, because there is no schema to contain them.

The SQL*Plus command SHOW RECYCLEBIN will display the dropped objects, with their original names and their recycle bin names. The view DBA_RECYCLEBIN provides the same information, and more.

If a table is dropped and then another table is created with the same name and then also dropped, there will be two tables in the recycle bin. They will have different recycle bin names but the same original name. By default, a Flashback Drop command will always recover the most recent version of the table, but if this is not the version you want, you can specify the recycle bin name of the version you want recovered, rather than the original name. Here's an example:

```
SQL> flashback table "BIN$sn0WEwXuTum7c1Vx4dOcaA==$0" to before drop;
```

Exercise 26-1: Use Flashback Drop with SQL*Plus   Create a new schema and a table within it. Drop the table and then recover it with Flashback Drop.

1. Connect to your database as user SYSTEM with SQL*Plus.

2. Create a user for this exercise.
   ```
   SQL> create user dropper identified by dropper;
   SQL> grant create session, resource, unlimited tablespace

   to dropper;
   SQL> connect dropper/dropper;
   ```

3. Create a table, with an index and a constraint, and insert a row.
   ```
   SQL> create table names (name varchar2(10));
   SQL> create index name_idx on names(name);
   SQL> alter table names add (constraint name_u unique(name));
   SQL> insert into names values ('John');
   SQL> commit;
   ```

4. Confirm the contents of your schema.
   ```
   SQL> select object_name,object_type from user_objects;
   SQL> select constraint_name,constraint_type,table_name

   from user_constraints;
   ```

5. Drop the table.
   ```
   SQL> drop table names;
   ```

6. Rerun the queries from step 4. Note that the objects have been removed from USER_OBJECTS, but the constraint does still exist with a system-generated name.

7. Query your recycle bin to see the mapping of the original name to the recycle bin names.
   ```
   SQL> select object_name,original_name,type from user_recyclebin;
   ```
   Note that this view does not show the constraint.

8. Demonstrate that it is possible to query the recycle bin but that you cannot do DML against it, as the next illustration shows. Note that the table name must be enclosed in double quotes to allow SQL*Plus to parse the nonstandard characters correctly.

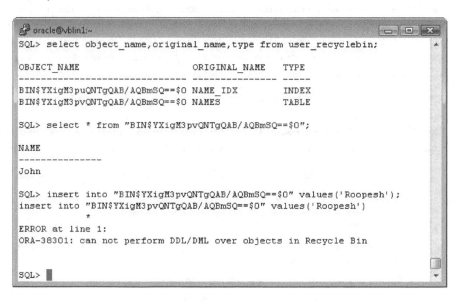

```
SQL> select object_name,original_name,type from user_recyclebin;

OBJECT_NAME                      ORIGINAL_NAME    TYPE
-------------------------------- ---------------- -----
BIN$YXigM3puQNTgQAB/AQBmSQ==$0 NAME_IDX         INDEX
BIN$YXigM3pvQNTgQAB/AQBmSQ==$0 NAMES            TABLE

SQL> select * from "BIN$YXigM3pvQNTgQAB/AQBmSQ==$0";

NAME
---------------
John

SQL> insert into "BIN$YXigM3pvQNTgQAB/AQBmSQ==$0" values('Roopesh');
insert into "BIN$YXigM3pvQNTgQAB/AQBmSQ==$0" values('Roopesh')
            *
ERROR at line 1:
ORA-38301: can not perform DDL/DML over objects in Recycle Bin

SQL>
```

9. Recover the table with Flashback Drop.

```
SQL> flashback table names to before drop;
```

10. Rerun the queries from steps 4 and 7. Note that the index and the constraint have retained their recycle bin names.

11. Rename the index and constraint to the original names. In the examples that follow, substitute your own recycle bin names:

```
SQL> alter index "BIN$YXigM3puQNTgQAB/AQBmSQ==$0"

rename to name_idx;
SQL> alter table names rename constraint
"BIN$YXigM3ptQNTgQAB/AQBmSQ==$0" to name_u;
```

12. Confirm the success of the operation by rerunning the queries from steps 4 and 7.

13. Connect as user SYSTEM and drop the DROPPER schema.

```
SQL> connect system/oracle;
SQL> drop user dropper cascade;
```

14. Query the DBA_RECYCLEBIN view to demonstrate that all the objects owned by user DROPPER really are gone.

```
SQL> select count(*) from dba_recyclebin where owner='DROPPER';
```

Managing the Recycle Bin

The recycle bin is a term given to the storage space used by dropped objects. You can ignore the recycle bin completely; its management is automatic, both in terms of transferring objects into it when they are dropped and removing them permanently when the space is needed in the tablespace for live objects. But there may be circumstances when you will need to be aware of the contents of the recycle bin and how much space they are taking up.

The recycle bin can be disabled with the instance parameter RECYCLEBIN. This defaults to ON, meaning that all schemas will have a recycle bin. The parameter is dynamic and can be set to OFF for a session or for the entire system.

Querying the Recycle Bin

Each user has their own recycle bin and can always view dropped tables in their own schema. The simplest way is the SHOW RECYCLEBIN command.

```
SQL> show recyclebin;
ORIGINAL NAME   RECYCLEBIN NAME                 OBJECT TYPE   DROP TIME
-------------   ------------------------------  -----------   -----------
DROP_TAB        BIN$vWMhmt3sTcqJ9WhSREM29g==$0  TABLE         2014-12-27:09:18:42
TEMP_DEPT       BIN$OLp3r9zPRRe6KSjs7Ee3gQ==$0  TABLE         2014-12-27:11:15:50
TEMP_EMPS       BIN$DKaQ10DDSty8hXQH2Xniwg==$0  TABLE         2014-12-27:11:15:36
```

This shows that the current user has three dropped tables: their original names, their recycle bin names, and the time they were dropped. For more detailed information, query the data dictionary view USER_RECYCLEBIN or query DBA_RECYCLEBIN for a global view.

```
SQL> select owner,original_name,type,droptime,can_undrop, space

from  dba_recyclebin;
OWNER       ORIGINAL_NAME    TYPE    DROPTIME               CAN   SPACE
----------  ---------------  ------  -------------------    ---   -------
SYS         T1               TABLE   2014-12-04:12:44:05    YES       8
DROPPER     T1               TABLE   2014-12-27:11:23:21    YES       8
HR          DROP_TAB         TABLE   2014-12-27:09:18:42    YES       8
HR          TEMP_EMPS        TABLE   2014-12-27:11:15:36    YES       8
HR          TEMP_DEPT        TABLE   2014-12-27:11:15:50    YES       8
```

The critical column is CAN_UNDROP. Oracle is under no obligation to keep dropped tables or indexes. The Flashback Drop facility is purely a convenience that Oracle provides; it is not part of the relational database standard. If Oracle needs the space being occupied by a dropped object to allocate more space to a live object, it will take it. From that point, the dropped object can no longer be recovered with Flashback Drop, and it will be removed from the view. The SPACE column (in units of datafile blocks) shows how much space is taken up by the dropped object.

Having identified the dropped table's name in the recycle bin, it can be queried like any other table, though you will have to enclose its name in double quotes because of the nonstandard characters used in recycle bin names. But always remember that you have a limited (and unpredictable) time during which you can do this. If you think it is likely that a dropped table will be needed, you should undrop it immediately.

EXAM TIP Flashback Drop is not enabled for tables stored in the SYSTEM tablespace. Such tables will not be reported by the queries described here because they are dropped and purged immediately.

Reclaiming Space from the Recycle Bin

Space taken up by dropped objects is in an ambiguous state. It is assigned to the object, but Oracle can overwrite it at will. The normal diagnostics regarding space usage will ignore space occupied by the recycle bin. This means that your "tablespace percent full" alerts will not fire until the warning and critical space usage levels are reached by live objects. Furthermore, if your datafiles have the AUTOEXTEND attribute enabled, Oracle will not in fact autoextend the datafiles until all space occupied by dropped objects has been reassigned. It will overwrite the recycle bin in preference to increasing the datafile size.

Perform Table Recovery from Backups

Recovery Manager (RMAN) table recovery is not a flashback technology, but the result is similar: a table is returned to the state it was in at some time in the past. It is therefore dealt with at this point. Using an RMAN backup to recover a table bypasses the issues of table flashback, in that the time frame is not constrained by the availability of undo data or whether the table's space has been reused but rather by the availability of backups of datafile and archive logfiles. This may mean that you can recover a table to the state it was in weeks or months ago.

This is the process:

1. Create an auxiliary instance. This is an instance started off a default parameter file with a system-generated name.

2. Restore the SYSTEM, SYSAUX, and UNDO tablespaces to the auxiliary instance from a sufficiently old backup and recover to the desired time.

3. Restore the datafiles of the tablespace containing the table and recover to the desired time.

4. Use Data Pump to export the table from the auxiliary instance and import it into the target instance.

5. Drop the auxiliary instance and database.

   This technique has always been possible, but in the current release RMAN can automate the entire process.

Exercise 26-2: Recover a Table from a Backup   In this exercise, you will create a tablespace and a table, backup the tablespace, drop the table, and recover it from the backup. Note that if working on Windows, you may need to run RMAN with elevated privileges in order to create the auxiliary instance. It is necessary for the database to be in archivelog mode, and a full backup must already exist.

1. Create a tablespace and a table.

```
create tablespace ex262ts datafile 'ex262' size 10m;
create table system.ex262tab tablespace ex262ts as

select * from all_users;
```

2. Back up the tablespace with RMAN.

```
backup tablespace ex262ts;
```

3. Note the current system change number and drop the table.

```
select current_scn from v$database;
drop table system.ex262tab;
```

4. Recover the table with RMAN.

The RECOVER TABLE command lets you specify a location for the auxiliary database. Choose any suitable directory; in this case (a Windows example), it is c:\tmp. Substitute the SCN for that in step 3.

```
recover table system.ex262tab until scn 2904974
auxiliary destination 'c:\tmp';
```

5. Observe the recovery.

Study the output of the recovery command. Do not skip this; it is extremely instructive. When you can understand each line, you are well on the way to passing the final Oracle Certified Professional (OCP) examination.

6. Confirm the success of the operation and tidy up.

```
select count(*) from system.ex262tab;
drop tablespace ex262ts including contents and datafiles;
```

Describe and Use Flashback Data Archive

The flashback technologies discussed so far can be useful, but they all have limited flashback capability. A Flashback Data Archive can be configured to guarantee the ability to flash back a table to any time—perhaps to a time years ago. It can also guarantee that data is removed when it has expired.

Architecturally, Flashback Data Archive requires one or more tablespaces, various segments for each protected table, and a new background process: the FBDA process. The DBA must create the tablespaces and the archives within them, specifying a retention period for each archive, and then nominate tables to be protected by an archive. The necessary segments will be created automatically, and the FBDA will start when required. Users and application software will not be aware of any change so far as DML is concerned. Some DDL commands will be affected. For example, TRUNCATE will be slow, and a DROP is not possible. Flashback Query commands (such as a SELECT with the AS OF clause) will execute successfully against versions of the table within the time frame specified for the archive protecting the table.

To create a Flashback Data Archive, first create a tablespace. It is technically possible to create the archives in a preexisting tablespace, but it makes sense to separate them from regular data. Then create the archive, specifying the tablespace, a retention time, and (optionally) a quota. Here's an example:

```
create flashback archive default hrarch tablespace fbda1
quota 10g retention 5 year;
```

This command includes the DEFAULT keyword, which means that it will be used as the archive for all tables unless specified otherwise. The default archive can be also be set later.

```
alter flashback archive hrarch set default;
```

The QUOTA clause limits the space the archive can occupy in the tablespace. If an archive fills, more space can be added either in the original tablespace or in another tablespace. For example, this command will extend the archive into another tablespace:

```
alter flashback archive hrarch add tablespace fbda2 quota 10g;
```

It is also possible to adjust the retention.

```
alter flashback archive hrarch modify retention 7 year;
```

Data is removed from an archive automatically by the FBDA background process once it is older than the nominated retention period, but it can be removed manually before the period has expired. Here's an example:

```
alter flashback archive hrarch
purge before timestamp to_timestamp('01-01-2015','dd-mm-yyyy');
```

Because there will often be legal implications to the ability to manage an archive, it is protected by privileges. The FLASHBACK ARCHIVE ADMINISTER system privilege grants the ability to create, alter, or drop an archive, as well as control the retention and purging. You must grant FLASHBACK ARCHIVE on the archive to a user who will nominate tables to be archived.

```
grant flashback archive administer to fbdaadmin;
grant flashback archive on hrarch to hr;
```

Finally, to enable archive protection for a table, use this command:

```
alter table hr.employees flashback archive hrarch;
```

There are three data dictionary views that document the Flashback Data Archive configuration:

- **DBA_FLASHBACK_ARCHIVE**   Describes the configured archives
- **DBA_FLASHBACK_ARCHIVE_TS**   Shows the quotas assigned per archive per tablespace
- **DBA_FLASHBACK_ARCHIVE_TABLES**   Lists the tables for which archiving is enabled

Exercise 26-3: Create a Flashback Data Archive   In this exercise, you will investigate the structures of a Flashback Data Archive.

1. Create a tablespace to be used for the Flashback Data archive.
   ```
   create tablespace fda datafile 'fda1.dbf' size 10m;
   ```

2. Create a Flashback Data Archive in the tablespace, with a retention of seven years.
   ```
   create flashback archive fla1 tablespace fda retention 7 year;
   ```

3. Create a schema to use for this exercise and grant it the DBA role.

```
grant dba to fbdauser identified by fbdauser;
```

4. Grant the user the necessary privilege on the archive.

```
grant flashback archive on fla1 to fbdauser;
```

5. Connect as the FBDAUSER. Create a table and enable the Flashback Data Archive for this table.

```
connect fbdauser/fbdauser
create table t1 as select * from all_users;
alter table t1 flashback archive fla1;
```

6. Run these queries to determine the objects created by the archive. You may have to wait several minutes because the objects are not created immediately.

```
select object_name,object_type from user_objects;
select segment_name,segment_type from dba_segments
where tablespace_name='FDA';
```

7. Perform some DML against the protected table.

```
delete from t1;
commit;
```

8. Perform a Flashback Query against the protected table using standard Flashback Query syntax. Here's an example:

```
select count(*) from t1 as of timestamp(sysdate - 5/1440);
```

9. Attempt some DDLs that would affect the protected table:

```
drop table t1;
drop user fbdauser cascade;
drop tablespace fda including contents and datafiles;
```

Note that these commands all generate errors related to the existence of the archive and the protected table.

10. Remove the archive protection from the table.

```
alter table fbdauser.t1 no flashback archive;
```

11. Drop the Flashback Data Archive.

```
drop flashback archive fla1;
```

12. Rerun all the commands from step 9.

Perform Flashback Database

Flashing back an entire database is functionally equivalent to an incomplete recovery, but the method and the enabling technology are completely different.

Flashback Database Architecture

Once Flashback Database is enabled, images of altered blocks are copied from time to time from the database buffer cache to a memory area within the System Global Area (SGA), the flashback buffer. This flashback buffer is flushed to disk, to the flashback logs, by a new background process:

the Recovery Writer (RVWR). There is no change to the usual routine of writing changes to the log buffer, which the LGWR then flushes to disk; flashback logging is additional to this. Unlike the redo log, flashback logging is not a log of changes—it is a log of complete block images.

 EXAM TIP Unlike redo logs, the flashback logs cannot be multiplexed and are not archived. They are created and managed automatically.

Critical to performance is that not every change is copied to the flashback buffer—only a subset of changes. If all changes to all blocks were copied to the buffer, then the overhead in terms of memory usage and the amount of extra disk input/output (I/O) required to flush the buffer to disk would be crippling for performance. Internal algorithms limit which versions of which blocks are placed in the flashback buffer in order to restrict its size and the frequency with which it will fill and be written to disk. These algorithms are intended to ensure that there will be no negative performance hit when enabling Flashback Database; they guarantee that even very busy blocks are logged only infrequently.

When conducting a database flashback, Oracle will read the flashback logs to extract the versions of each changed database block and copy these versions back into the datafiles. As these changes are applied to the current database in reverse chronological order, this has the effect of taking the database back in time by reversing the writes that the DBWn process has done. Since not every version of every changed block is copied into the flashback buffer and hence to the flashback logs, it is not possible to flash back to an exact point in time. It may be that a block was changed many times but that the flashback log has only a subset of these changes. Consider the case where block A was changed at 10:00 and again at 10:05 but that only the 10:00 version is in the flashback log. Block B was changed at 10:05 and at 10:20, and both versions are in the flashback log. All the changes have been committed. It is now 11:00, and you want to flash back to 10:15. The flashback operation will restore the 10:00 version of block A and the 10:05 version of block B; it will take each changed block back as close as it can to, but no later than, the desired time. Thus, Flashback Database constructs a version of the datafiles that is just before the time you want. This version of the datafiles may well be totally inconsistent. As in this example, different blocks will be at different system change numbers, depending on what happened to be available in the flashback log. To complete the flashback process, Oracle then uses the redo log. It will recover all the blocks to the exact time requested (in the example, only block A needs recovery), thus synchronizing all the datafiles to the same SCN. The final stage is to roll back any transactions that were uncommitted at the point, exactly as occurs at the last stage of an incomplete recovery.

So, Flashback Database is, in fact, a combination of several processes and data structures. First, you must allocate some memory in the SGA (which will be automatic—you cannot control how large the buffer is) and some space on disk to store the flashback data and start the RVWR process to enable flashback logging. When doing a flashback, Oracle will use the flashback logs to take the database back in time to before the time you want and then apply redo logs (using whatever archive redo log files and online redo log files are necessary) in the usual fashion for incomplete recovery to bring the datafiles forward to the exact time you want. Then the database can be opened with a new incarnation, in the same manner as following a normal incomplete recovery.

EXAM TIP Flashback Database requires archivelog mode and the use of ALTER DATABASE OPEN RESETLOGS to create a new incarnation of the database.

Flashback Database requires archive log mode because without the availability of the archive log stream, it would not be possible to convert the inconsistent version of the database produced by the application of flashback logs to a consistent version that can be opened. So, what is the benefit of Flashback Database over incomplete recovery, which also requires archive log mode? It is in the speed and convenience with which you can take the database back in time.

An incomplete recovery is always time consuming because part of the process is a full restore. The time for an incomplete recovery is, to a large extent, proportional to the size of the database. By contrast, the time needed for a database flashback is largely proportional to the number of changes that need to be backed out. In any normal environment, the volume of changed data will be tiny when compared to the total volume of data, so a flashback should be many times faster. Furthermore, Flashback Database is easy to use. Once configured, flashback logging will proceed completely unattended, and a database can be flashed back easily with one command. There are none of the possibilities for error inherent in a traditional restore and recover operation.

Configuring Flashback Database

Configuring a database to enable Flashback Database will require downtime if the database is not already in archive log mode. Otherwise, it is an online operation. To configure Flashback Database, follow these steps:

1. Ensure that the database is in archive log mode.

   Archive log mode is a prerequisite for enabling Flashback Database. Confirm this by querying the V$DATABASE view.
   ```
   SQL> select log_mode from v$database;
   ```

2. Set up a Fast Recovery Area.

   The Fast Recovery Area is the location for the flashback logs. You have no control over them other than setting the Fast Recovery Area directory and limiting its size. It is controlled with two instance parameters: DB_RECOVERY_FILE_DEST specifies the destination directory, and DB_RECOVERY_FILE_DEST_SIZE restricts the maximum amount of space in bytes that it can take up. Remember that the Fast Recovery Area is used for purposes other than just flashback logs, and it will need to be sized appropriately. Here's an example:
   ```
   SQL> alter system set db_recovery_file_dest='/fast_recovery_area';
   SQL> alter system set db_recovery_file_dest_size=8G;
   ```

3. Set the flashback retention target.

   This is controlled by the DB_FLASHBACK_RETENTION_TARGET instance parameter, which is in minutes, and the default is one day. The flashback log space is reused in a circular fashion, with older data being overwritten by newer data. This parameter instructs Oracle to keep flashback data for a certain number of minutes before overwriting it:

```
SQL> alter system set db_flashback_retention_target=240;
```

It is only a target (four hours in the preceding example), and if the Fast Recovery Area is undersized, Oracle may not be able to keep to it. But in principle, you should be able to flash back to any time within this target.

4. Enable flashback logging.

```
SQL> alter database flashback on;
```

This will start the RVWR process and allocate a flashback buffer in the SGA. The process startup will be automatic from now on.

5. Open the database.

```
SQL> alter database open;
```

Logging of data block images from the database buffer cache to the flashback buffer will be enabled from now on.

Monitoring Flashback Database

The flashback retention target is only a target—there is no guarantee that you could actually flash back to a time within it. Conversely, you might be able to flash back to beyond the target. The possible flashback period is a function of how much flashback logging information is being generated per second and how much space is available to store this information before overwriting it with more recent data.

The most basic level of flashback monitoring is to confirm that it is actually enabled.

```
SQL> select flashback_on from v$database;
```

On Unix you can see the RVWR process as an operating system process; on Windows it will be another thread within ORACLE.EXE.

To monitor the current flashback capability and estimate the space needed for flashback logs to meet your target, query the V$FLASHBACK_DATABASE_LOG view. V$FLASHBACK_DATABASE_STAT gives a historical view of the rate of disk I/O for the datafiles, the online redo log files, and the flashback log files.

In Figure 26-6, the first query shows the setting for the retention target in minutes, as specified by the DB_FLASHBACK_RETENTION_TARGET instance parameter; this is on the default of one day. Then there is the actual space being taken up by the flashback log files, as well as the exact time to which the flashback logs could take the database back. If the Fast Recovery Area is sized appropriately and the retention target is realistic, then there will be a sensible relationship between the time shown in this query and the current time less the retention target.

The second query shows the price you are paying for enabling Flashback Database in terms of the bytes of I/O that it necessitates per hour. The top row will always be an incomplete hour,

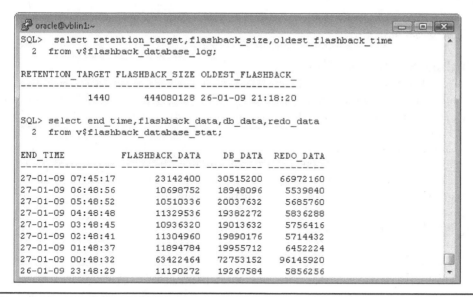

```
oracle@vblin1:~
SQL> select retention_target,flashback_size,oldest_flashback_time
  2  from v$flashback_database_log;

RETENTION_TARGET FLASHBACK_SIZE OLDEST_FLASHBACK_
---------------- -------------- -----------------
            1440      444080128 26-01-09 21:18:20

SQL> select end_time,flashback_data,db_data,redo_data
  2  from v$flashback_database_stat;

END_TIME          FLASHBACK_DATA    DB_DATA  REDO_DATA
----------------- -------------- ---------- ----------
27-01-09 07:45:17       23142400   30515200   66972160
27-01-09 06:48:56       10698752   18948096    5539840
27-01-09 05:48:52       10510336   20037632    5685760
27-01-09 04:48:48       11329536   19382272    5836288
27-01-09 03:48:45       10936320   19013632    5756416
27-01-09 02:48:41       11304960   19890176    5714432
27-01-09 01:48:37       11894784   19955712    6452224
27-01-09 00:48:32       63422464   72753152   96145920
26-01-09 23:48:29       11190272   19267584    5856256
```

Figure 26-6   Monitoring Flashback Database

up to the current time. In the example, the database was generating about 10MB of flashback data per hour through the night, with higher rates in the late evening and morning. The impact of this on performance will need to be discussed with your system administrators, bearing in mind whether the system is I/O bound or not. For comparison, the view also shows the I/O related to normal database activity. The view will have one row per hour.

The size of the flashback buffer is outside the DBA's control, but to see the current size, you can query the V$SGASTAT view.

```
SQL> select * from v$sgastat where name = 'flashback generation buff';
POOL         NAME                      BYTES
-----------  ------------------------- ----------
shared pool  flashback generation buff 3981204
```

Using Flashback Database

Flashback Database can be used from SQL*Plus or RMAN. Whichever tool you choose to use, the method is the same.

1. Shut down the database.
2. Mount the database.
3. Flash back to a time, an SCN, or a log sequence number.
4. Open the database with RESETLOGS.

Provided that all archive logs required are available, a flashback operation will proceed completely automatically.

Flashback with SQL*Plus

The SQL*Plus flashback syntax will accept either a timestamp or a system change number argument. If you are not sure exactly what time you need to go back to (you will be fortunate if you know the exact timestamp or SCN), you can have several attempts by combining flashback with recovery.

Consider this scenario: It is December 20, 2014. At about 10:00 A.M. a junior DBA drops an important schema on the production database. This is terrifyingly easy to do; perhaps it happened during an upgrade of software on a development system when connected to the production database by mistake. The error is noticed within 10 minutes, but it is a big, busy database in a call center, used for taking orders, and every second lost will cost money. The first step is to shut down the database.

```
SQL> shutdown abort;
```

There is no point in using any other type of shutdown; all work in progress is going to be lost anyway, and you need to minimize the downtime. Then take the database back to 10:00 as follows:

```
SQL> startup mount;
SQL> flashback database to timestamp
to_timestamp('20-12-14 10:00:00','dd-mm-yy hh24:mi:ss');
SQL> alter database open read only;
```

Note that unlike RECOVER DATABASE UNTIL TIME, this command is sensitive to NLS settings for the timestamp format. While in READ ONLY mode, you can run a query against the dropped schema. If you discover that the schema is still there, perhaps you can recover a bit more user data.

```
SQL> shutdown abort;
SQL> startup mount;
SQL> recover database until time '2014-12-20:10:02:00';
SQL> alter database open read only;
```

You run your test query again, and you discover that after recovering 2 more minutes of data, the schema is gone. It must have been dropped between 10:00 and 10:02. So, you split the difference.

```
SQL> shutdown abort;
SQL> startup mount;
SQL> flashback database to timestamp
to_timestamp('20-12-14 10:01:00','dd-mm-yy hh24:mi:ss');
SQL> alter database open read only;
```

If the schema is not there now, flash back a few seconds earlier. If it is there, do a few seconds of recovery. You can repeatedly issue flashback and recover commands until you find the time that you want, testing by running queries while in READ ONLY mode. When you get to a point you are satisfied with, do one final shutdown and open with RESETLOGS to create a new incarnation of the database that can be opened for normal use.

```
SQL> shutdown abort;
SQL> startup mount;
SQL> alter database open resetlogs;
```

This method will minimize the loss of data, and it may take only a few minutes. An incomplete recovery might take hours, particularly if you need to have several tries before you get to the right time.

 TIP Many sites name machines following conventions such as sun1p1 for the production server, sun1d1 for the development server, sun1t1 for the test server, and so on. The various databases and instances may have exactly the same names. Get one key wrong, and you are connected to the wrong database. Always check where you are before doing anything.

Flashback with RMAN

Within the Recovery Manager environment you have three options: you can flash back to a time, to an SCN, or to a log sequence number, as in these examples:

```
RMAN> flashback database to time =
to_date('14-12-20 10:00:00','dd-mm-yy hh24:mi:ss');
RMAN> flashback database to scn=2728665;
RMAN> flashback database to sequence=2123 thread=1;
```

Apart from the minor changes in syntax, RMAN flashback is the same as SQL*Plus flashback. In particular, you can use the same technique of repeatedly applying flashback and recovery until you find the optimal point to open the database.

Exercise 26-4: Use Flashback Database Enable database flashback. Simulate a user error and flash back the database to before the transaction.

1. Connect to the database as user SYSTEM and enable database flashback.

    ```
    sqlplus system
    alter database flashback on;
    select flashback_on from v$database;
    ```

2. Note the time and simulate an error.

    ```
    create table t1 as select * from all_users;
    select to_char(sysdate,'yyyy-mm-dd:hh24:mi:ss') from dual;
    truncate table t1;
    ```

3. Attempt recovery using various techniques. Substitute the time from step 2.

    ```
    select * from t1 as of timestamp
    to_timestamp('2015-02-16:11:45:29','yyyy-mm-dd:hh24:mi:ss');
    flashback table t1 to timestamp
    to_timestamp('2015-02-16:11:45:29','yyyy-mm-dd:hh24:mi:ss');
    flashback table t1 to before drop;
    ```

PART IV

4. Why are these techniques not applicable?

5. Recover the table using database flashback.

```
connect / as sysdba
shutdown abort
startup mount
flashback database to timestamp

to_timestamp('2015-02-16:11:45:29','yyyy-mm-dd:hh24:mi:ss');
alter database open resetlogs;
select count(*) from system.t1;
```

Two-Minute Drill

Describe the Flashback Technologies

- Flashback is for correcting user (or DBA) error.
- Physical damage requires use of restore and recover.

Use Flashback to Query Data

- Flashback Query relies on the use of undo data.
- Basic Flashback Query uses a modified SELECT statement or DBMS_FLASHBACK.
- It is also possible to flash back a transaction or all changes to a table or set of tables.

Perform Flashback Table Operations

- Flashback Drop relies on the fact that, by default, objects are renamed when dropped.
- Control the availability to Flashback Drop with the RECYCLEBIN instance parameter and override the default with the PURGE keyword.
- All dependent objects are recovered with the exception of foreign key constraints.

Perform Table Recovery from Backups

- RMAN can extract a table from a backupset.
- Data Pump is used to transfer the table from an auxiliary database into the target database.

Describe and Use Flashback Data Archive

- Flashback Data Archive is not available by default. It must be explicitly configured and enabled for nominated tables.

- An archive retains data for a defined period, permanently removing it once that period has passed.
- Query the archive with the usual Flashback Query syntax.

Perform Flashback Database

- Flashback Database is not enabled by default. Once enabled, it relies on a memory structure (the flashback buffer), a disk structure (the flashback logs), and a background process (the RVWR).
- Flashback Database is functionally equivalent to an incomplete recovery.

Self Test

1. Which of the following flashback technologies use data from the current undo tablespace? (Choose all that apply.)

   A. Flashback Table

   B. Flashback Transaction Query

   C. Flashback Query

   D. Flashback Version Query

   E. Flashback Drop

   F. Flashback Database

   G. Flashback Data Archive

2. Which of the following parameters directly affect the behavior and proper functioning of Flashback Table? (Choose all that apply.)

   A. DB_RECOVERY_FILE_DEST

   B. UNDO_MANAGEMENT

   C. DB_RECOVERY_FILE_DEST_SIZE

   D. UNDO_TABLESPACE

   E. UNDO_RETENTION

3. When using the VERSIONS BETWEEN clause for Flashback Version Query, what can't you use to restrict the number of rows returned by the query? (Choose the best answer.)

   A. A timestamp

   B. An SCN

   C. A WHERE clause on any column in the table

   D. A guaranteed restore point

4. Which of the following statements is true about the recycle bin? (Choose the best answer.)

   A. When you drop an object, the space allocated by the object is not immediately reflected in DBA_FREE_SPACE and counts against the user's quota.

   B. When you drop an object, the space allocated by the object is immediately reflected in DBA_FREE_SPACE and does not count against the user's quota.

   C. When you drop an object, the space allocated by the object is immediately reflected in DBA_FREE_SPACE but still counts against the user's quota.

   D. When you drop an object, the space allocated by the object is not immediately reflected in DBA_FREE_SPACE and does not count against the user's quota.

5. The column CAN_UNDROP is set to YES for an object in the view DBA_RECYCLEBIN. Which of the following is true for this object? (Choose all that apply.)

   A. The object is a table.

   B. The object can be undropped by the user who owns the object.

   C. The object can be undropped by any user with DBA privileges.

   D. The object does not have any dependent objects in the recycle bin.

   E. No existing object with the same name exists outside of the recycle bin.

6. Which of the following columns is not in the data dictionary view FLASHBACK_TRANSACTION_QUERY? (Choose the best answer.)

   A. UNDO_SQL

   B. XID

   C. OPERATION

   D. ORA_ROWSCN

7. What happens to the rows in FLASHBACK_TRANSACTION_QUERY when part of the transaction is no longer available in the undo tablespace? (Choose the best answer.)

   A. The user ID number replaces the username in the LOGON_USER column.

   B. The OPERATION column contains the value UNKNOWN.

   C. The object number replaces the table name in the TABLE_NAME column.

   D. The OPERATION column contains the value UNAVAILABLE.

   E. All rows for the transaction are no longer available in FLASHBACK_TRANSACTION_QUERY.

8. What methods can you use in the AS OF clause of a Flashback Table operation to specify the time in the past to which you want to recover the table? (Choose all that apply.)

   A. A timestamp

   B. A filter condition in the WHERE clause

   C. An SCN

   D. A restore point

   E. A guaranteed restore point

9. You create the table VAC_SCHED on Monday with a primary key index; the SCN right after table creation was 5680123. On Wednesday, you drop the index. On Thursday, you accidentally delete most of the rows in the database. On Friday, you execute this command:

```
SQL> FLASHBACK TABLE VAC_SCHED TO SCN 5680123;
```

You have set guaranteed undo retention to one week. What is the result of running this command? (Choose the best answer.)

   A. The table is recovered to SCN 5680123 without the index.

   B. The table is recovered using the data in the undo tablespace, and the index is re-created using the dropped index in the recycle bin.

   C. The table is recovered, and all rows deleted on Thursday are restored using archived and online redo log files.

   D. The command fails because FLASHBACK TABLE cannot recover a table before a change to a dependent object.

10. Which of the following conditions will prevent recovery of a table or table partition using table recovery from backups? (Choose all that apply.)

   A. The database is in read-only mode.

   B. COMPATIBLE is set to 12.1.

   C. You are recovering a table owned by SYS in the USERS tablespace.

   D. The table is partitioned, and the indexes are in a different partition.

   E. The database is in NOARCHIVELOG mode.

11. Identify the true statement about Flashback Data Archive. (Choose the best answer.)

   A. You cannot specify more than one Flashback Data Archive.

   B. If you do not specify a RETENTION clause for a Flashback Data Archive, you must specify it when assigning a table to the Flashback Data Archive.

   C. The QUOTA parameter is required when creating a Flashback Data Archive to limit the amount of space used in the tablespace.

   D. A Flashback Data Archive can exist in multiple tablespaces, including undo tablespaces and temporary tablespaces.

12. Which of the following data dictionary views contains a list of the tables using a Flashback Data Archive? (Choose the best answer.)

   A. DBA_FLASHBACK_ARCHIVE_TABLES

   B. DBA_FLASHBACK_ARCHIVE

   C. DBA_FLASHBACK_ARCHIVE_TS

   D. DBA_FLASHBACK_DATA_ARCHIVE_TABLES

PART IV

13. Which of the following initialization parameters is not required to configure Flashback Database operations? (Choose the best answer.)

    A. DB_RECOVERY_FILE_DEST_SIZE

    B. UNDO_RETENTION

    C. DB_FLASHBACK_RETENTION_TARGET

    D. DB_RECOVERY_FILE_DEST

14. What is the difference between a regular restore point and a guaranteed restore point? (Choose all that apply.)

    A. A regular restore point does not require that a Fast Recovery Area be configured.

    B. A guaranteed restore point can be used only with Flashback Database.

    C. A guaranteed restore point cannot be dropped.

    D. A guaranteed restore point will never be aged out of the controlfile.

    E. You must have flashback logging enabled to use guaranteed restore points.

Self Test Answers

1. ☑ **A, B, C,** and **D.** All of these technologies rely on the undo data in the undo tablespace.
☒ **E, F,** and **G** are incorrect. Flashback Drop relies on the recycle bin, Flashback Database relies on flashback logs in the Fast Recovery Area, and Flashback Data Archive relies on history tables based on a permanent table in tablespaces designated for flashback data archives.

2. ☑ **B, D,** and **E.** For Flashback Query, Flashback Table, Flashback Transaction Query, and Flashback Version Query, you must have automatic undo management configured, an undo tablespace defined, and an undo retention value to specify how long undo data is retained in the undo tablespace.
☒ **A** and **C** are incorrect. The parameters DB_RECOVERY_FILE_DEST and DB_RECOVERY_FILE_DEST_SIZE are used to configure Flashback Database, not Flashback Query.

3. ☑ **D.** Guaranteed restore points are used only in recovery scenarios such as Flashback Database.
☒ **A, B,** and **C** are incorrect. All three can be used. You can restrict the results of a Flashback Version Query by SCN or timestamp. You can further filter the rows by using a WHERE clause on the table columns.

4. ☑ **C.** A dropped object's space is immediately reflected in DBA_FREE_SPACE but still counts against the user's quota until it is purged from the recycle bin.
☒ **A, B,** and **D** are incorrect. All three reflect incorrect statements about free space management and quota management for objects in the recycle bin.

5. ☑ **A**, **B**, and **C**. Table objects in the recycle bin can be undropped, and they can be undropped by the original owner or a user with DBA privileges.

☒ **D** and **E** are incorrect. **D** is incorrect because a table in the recycle bin may or may not have dependent objects in the recycle bin. **E** is incorrect because the undrop syntax does permit recovering a table even if an object exists with the same original name as an object in the recycle bin.

6. ☑ **D**. ORA_ROWSCN is a pseudocolumn that is available for all tables and contains the last SCN that modified or created the row.

☒ **A**, **B**, and **C** are incorrect. UNDO_SQL is the SQL you can use to reverse the change to the row, XID is the transaction ID, and OPERATION is the DML operation performed.

7. ☑ **B**. The OPERATION column in FLASHBACK_TRANSACTION_QUERY contains UNKNOWN for data no longer in the UNDO tablespace.

☒ **A**, **C**, **D**, and **E** are incorrect. **A** is incorrect because the user ID replaces the username in the LOGON_USER column when the user no longer exists. **C** is incorrect because the object number replaces the table name in the TABLE_NAME column when the table no longer exists. **D** is incorrect because the OPERATION column contains UNKNOWN, not UNAVAILABLE, when the information is no longer available in the UNDO tablespace. **E** is incorrect because part of a transaction might still be available in the UNDO tablespace.

8. ☑ **A**, **C**, **D**, and **E**. You can use the AS OF clause with the TIMESTAMP or SCN qualifier to specify a time to which you want to recover the table. In addition, you can specify a restore point or a guaranteed restore point for Flashback Table. Guaranteed restore points are also useful in Flashback Database operations to ensure that flashback logs are maintained in the Fast Recovery Area at least as far back as the earliest guaranteed restore point.

☒ **B** is incorrect. You cannot use a WHERE clause to specify the time in the past for the FLASHBACK TABLE operation.

9. ☑ **A**. The table is recovered to its original state right after creation and without the index.

☒ **B**, **C**, and **D** are incorrect. **B** is incorrect because FLASHBACK TABLE does not leverage the recycle bin. **C** is incorrect because the table is recovered as of the SCN but not rolled forward. **D** is incorrect because a dropped index does not affect the recoverability of a table; however, a change to the structure of the table itself prevents a flashback operation to before the DDL change to the table.

10. ☑ **A**, **C**, and **E**. To successfully perform table recovery from backups (TRFB), the database must be in read-write mode, you cannot recover objects owned by SYS, regardless of which tablespace they reside in, and the database must be in ARCHIVELOG mode. In addition, the COMPATIBLE parameter must be set to 12.0 or higher, and you cannot recover objects to the SYSTEM or SYSAUX tablespace.

☒ **B** and **D** are incorrect. The COMPATIBLE parameter must be at least 12.0, and the table to be recovered need not be contained in a single tablespace or group of tablespaces as it would be required with traditional tablespace point in time recovery (TSPITR).

11. ☑   **B.** You must either specify a default retention period for the Flashback Data Archive itself or specify a retention period when adding the table to the archive.

☒   **A, C,** and **D** are incorrect. **A** is incorrect because you can have several Flashback Data Archives. **C** is incorrect because the QUOTA parameter is needed only if you want to limit the amount of space used by the Flashback Data Archive in the tablespace; otherwise, it can grow to use all available space in the tablespace. **D** is incorrect because you can create Flashback Data Archives only in permanent, non-UNDO tablespaces.

12. ☑   **A.** DBA_FLASHBACK_ARCHIVE_TABLES contains a list of tables currently using a Flashback Data Archive.

☒   **B, C,** and **D** are incorrect. **B** is incorrect because DBA_FLASHBACK_ARCHIVE contains a list of the archives but not the tables within. **C** is incorrect because DBA_FLASHBACK_ARCHIVE_TS contains the archive to tablespace mapping. **D** is incorrect because DBA_FLASHBACK_DATA_ARCHIVE_TABLES is not a valid data dictionary view.

13. ☑   **B.** The initialization parameter UNDO_RETENTION is required for other flashback features but not for Flashback Database.

☒   **A, C,** and **D** are incorrect. The parameters DB_RECOVERY_FILE_DEST_SIZE and DB_RECOVERY_FILE_DEST are required to define the location and size of the Fast Recovery Area, and DB_FLASHBACK_RETENTION_TARGET is needed to define a desired upper limit for the Flashback Database recovery window.

14. ☑   **A** and **D.** A regular restore point does not require a Fast Recovery Area, and it can be aged out of the controlfile; a guaranteed restore point will never be aged out of the controlfile unless it is explicitly dropped.

☒   **B, C,** and **E** are incorrect. **B** is incorrect because a guaranteed restore point can be referenced for other flashback features, not just Flashback Database. **C** is incorrect because you can explicitly drop any type of restore point. **E** is incorrect because you can define guaranteed restore points without flashback logging enabled; however, you must still have a Fast Recovery Area enabled.

CHAPTER 27

Duplicating a Database

Exam Objectives

- 63.1.16.1   Describe and Use Transportable Tablespaces and Databases
- 63.1.17.1   Choose a Technique for Duplicating a Database
- 63.1.17.2   Create a Backup-Based Duplicate Database
- 63.1.17.3   Duplicate a Database Based on a Running Instance

The transportable tablespace feature can quickly copy one or more tablespaces from one database to another without using the much more time-consuming export/import. An extension to transportable tablespaces, transportable databases, makes it easy to create a new database and move all non-SYSTEM tablespaces to the new database. Related to this are techniques for duplicating an entire database. If you must have your source database open on a continuous basis, you can clone your database while it is open and available to users. Because you are copying from an open database, you don't need an intermediate Recovery Manager (RMAN) backup, which can save a lot of time and disk space.

Describe and Use Transportable Tablespaces and Databases

There are many ways to move data from one database to another, such as database links, Data Pump export/import, and transportable tablespaces. For large volumes of data, using transportable tablespaces is by far the fastest method. In a nutshell, you export just the metadata for the objects in the tablespace using Data Pump, copy the datafiles comprising the tablespace to the destination database, and import the tablespace's metadata into the destination database. Even platforms with different hardware architectures are candidates for transportable tablespaces.

Configuring Transportable Tablespaces

The tablespace transport feature has many uses, such as quickly distributing data from a data warehouse to data marts in other databases or converting an entire database from one platform to another. When transporting between platforms, both the source and destination platforms must be on Oracle's list of supported platforms. All commonly used 64-bit server platforms running on Intel, SPARC, or PowerPC hardware are supported.

Determining Compatibility Requirements

Oracle Database feature compatibility is controlled by the COMPATIBLE initialization parameter, which enables or disables the use of certain features in the database. For the purposes of discussing transportable tablespaces, these are features that require specific structures within the datafiles. For example, if you want to upgrade to Oracle Database 12c from Oracle Database 11g R2, you may want to set COMPATIBLE to 11.2.0 for a short time. Thus, you can downgrade to version 11g R2 if you encounter problems in production, without requiring a restore and recover from backup because the datafile formats for version 12c are not usable on version 11g R2. Even though you may have tested the upgrade on a backup server, problems might not arise for some time.

When you create a transportable tablespace set, Oracle determines the minimum compatibility level of the target database and stores this value in the metadata for the transportable tablespace set. Starting with Oracle Database 11g, you can always transport a tablespace to another database with the same or higher compatibility level, regardless of the target platform.

TIP Regardless of the similarities or differences in hardware platforms between the source and target databases, both must be using the same character set.

In other words, even if you are running Oracle Database 12c with COMPATIBLE set to 11.0.0, you can transport in a tablespace from a database on a different platform that has COMPATIBLE set to 10.0.0.

Determining Endian Requirements

Oracle's transportable tablespace feature may require an extra step depending on the underlying hardware platform. For example, on systems based on Intel processors, the value 2 is stored as 0x0200. This byte ordering is known as *little-endian* because the least significant byte is first. In contrast, a *big-endian* system stores bytes in order of most significant to least significant byte. Therefore, on a big-endian hardware platform, such as Oracle SPARC or IBM PowerPC, the value 2 is stored as 0x0002. Understandably, a conversion must be done on column data transported between platforms with different endian formats.

To determine the endian formats of all supported platforms, you can query the dynamic performance view V$TRANSPORTABLE_PLATFORM, as in this example:

```
SQL> select platform_id, platform_name, endian_format
  2  from v$transportable_platform;

PLATFORM_ID PLATFORM_NAME                                      ENDIAN_FORMAT
----------- -------------------------------------------------- -------------
          1 Solaris[tm] OE (32-bit)                            Big
          2 Solaris[tm] OE (64-bit)                            Big
          7 Microsoft Windows IA (32-bit)                      Little
         10 Linux IA (32-bit)                                  Little
          6 AIX-Based Systems (64-bit)                         Big
          3 HP-UX (64-bit)                                     Big
          5 HP Tru64 UNIX                                      Little
          4 HP-UX IA (64-bit)                                  Big
         11 Linux IA (64-bit)                                  Little
         15 HP Open VMS                                        Little
          8 Microsoft Windows IA (64-bit)                      Little
          9 IBM zSeries Based Linux                            Big
         13 Linux x86 64-bit                                   Little
         16 Apple Mac OS                                       Big
         12 Microsoft Windows x86 64-bit                       Little
         17 Solaris Operating System (x86)                     Little
         18 IBM Power Based Linux                              Big
         19 HP IA Open VMS                                     Little
         20 Solaris Operating System (x86-64)                  Little
         21 Apple Mac OS (x86-64)                              Little

20 rows selected.

SQL>
```

This query also shows you all supported platforms for transportable tablespaces. If the value of ENDIAN_FORMAT is different, then you must use RMAN commands at the source or target database to convert the datafiles to the target database's endian format. The required RMAN commands will be discussed later in this chapter. To determine the endian format of your platform, you can join V$DATABASE to V$TRANSPORTABLE_PLATFORM.

```
SQL> select platform_name my_platform,
  2         endian_format my_endian_format
  3  from v$transportable_platform
  4     join v$database using(platform_name)
  5  ;

MY_PLATFORM               MY_ENDIAN_FORM
------------------------- --------------
Linux x86 64-bit          Little

SQL>
```

To convert datafiles from one endian format to the other, use the RMAN command CONVERT. This example, run in a Windows system, will read a datafile and write it out to a new name with an endian format appropriate for the named platform:

```
RMAN> convert datafile 'c:\tmp\ts_trans01.dbf' to platform
'AIX-Based Systems (64-bit)' format 'c:\tmp\towin.dbf';
```

The converted file would then be manually copied to the destination system. Alternatively, files can be copied using procedures in the DBMS_FILE_TRANSFER package. This will detect the endian rules for the source and destination platforms and convert the files as they are copied.

The Tablespace Transport Set Must Be Self-Contained

All objects in the tablespaces to be copied from one database to another must be complete. If the object includes references to other objects, they must all be included. The supplied procedure DBMS_TTS can test for this. Examples of possible violations of this rule would be partitioned tables that are distributed across several tablespaces or indexes that are meaningless unless the table to which they refer is also included.

Transporting Tablespaces

Whether you use SQL commands or Cloud Control to transport a tablespace, the general steps are the same:

1. Make the tablespace (or tablespaces) read-only on the source database.
2. Use Data Pump export to extract the tablespace metadata from the source database.
3. If the target does not have the same endian format, convert the datafiles. This can be done on either the source or destination platform.
4. Copy the tablespace datafiles and metadata dump file from the source to the destination.
5. Use Data Pump to import tablespace metadata into the target tablespace.
6. Make the tablespace (or tablespaces) read-write on both the source and target databases.

Step 4 in the previous list can be accomplished with the DBMS_FILE_TRANSFER package. This contains procedures that can copy files between file systems, between ASM disk groups, between file systems and ASM disk groups, and from one server to another. A particular advantage in the context of tablespace transport is that if endian conversion is needed when copying from one server to another, the DBMS_FILE_TRANSFER procedures GET_FILE and PUT_FILE detect this and perform the conversion while copying the files.

Exercise 27-1: Transport a Tablespace Using SQL and PL/SQL   In this exercise, you will simulate transporting a tablespace by creating a tablespace, copying it, dropping it, and transporting it back into the database. You will need to connect with SYSDBA privileges.

1. Create a tablespace and some objects within it. Name the datafile (in this case, a Windows filename; adjust this accordingly for Linux) rather than using Oracle Managed Files (OMF).

   ```
   create tablespace trans datafile 'c:\tmp\trans1.dbf' size 10m;
   create table transtab tablespace trans as select * from all_users;
   ```

2. Check for tablespace self-consistency and query the transport violations view.

   ```
   SQL> execute dbms_tts.transport_set_check('trans')
   SQL> select * from transport_set_violations;
   ```

   The view is populated every time the check is run, reporting any issues such as dependent objects in other tablespaces. If there are no rows, then the transport can proceed.

3. Make the tablespace read-only.

   ```
   SQL> alter tablespace trans read only;
   ```

4. Use the expdp utility to export the metadata describing the tablespace and its contents. You will need to provide a username and password of a highly privileged user, such as SYSTEM. The dump file will go to the default DATA_PUMP_DIR directory.

   ```
   expdp dumpfile=trans.dmp transport_tablespaces=trans
   ```

5. Drop the tablespace (without deleting the datafile).

   ```
   drop tablespace trans including contents;
   ```

6. Rename the datafile to make the simulation more realistic. Examples for Windows and Linux are as follows, respectively:

   ```
   ren c:\tmp\trans1.dbf ts_trans01.dbf
   mv /tmp/trans1.dbf /tmp/ts_trans01.dbf
   ```

7. Transport the tablespace into the database using the impdp utility from the operating system command line. This example uses a Linux path for the datafile:

   ```
   impdp directory=data_pump_dir dumpfile=trans.dmp \
   transport_datafiles='/tmp/ts_trans01.dbf';
   ```

8. Confirm that the tablespace has been transported in and make it usable.

   ```
   select tablespace_name,status from dba_tablespaces;
   alter tablespace trans read write;
   ```

Transporting a Database

It is possible to transport an entire database. Conceptually, the technique is the same as tablespace transport: You copy the datafiles, converting them if necessary to take into account platform variations. The difference is that there is no preexisting destination database into which to import the transported tablespace. A limitation of this technique is that it cannot function across platforms with different endian-ness. The conversion method can handle the logical differences in structures between Oracle implementations on different platforms but not the physical difference of endian-ness.

These are the high-level steps:

1. Open the source database in read-only mode.

   The database must be consistent, with no incomplete transactions, and all datafiles must be synchronized to the same system change number (SCN). To ensure this state, the database must be shut down cleanly and then opened in read-only mode. Note that it is not possible to open in read-only mode following a SHUTDOWN ABORT.

2. Copy the full set of datafiles.

   A decision must be made on whether to convert the files on the source system or the destination system. For conversion on the source, the conversion process will create a new set of files in the new format, which will then be copied to the destination. For conversion on the destination, they will be copied before conversion. Note that the controlfile and the online log files must not be copied because new ones will be created at the destination.

3. Convert the files to the destination format.

   RMAN will perform the conversion. If the conversion is at the source, RMAN will use channels against the running source instance to write out the converted files. If the conversion is to be at the destination, this must be done after the following step.

4. Start an instance for the destination database.

   An instance requires a parameter file and a password file. Once these are created, the instance can be started in NOMOUNT mode. It is possible at this point to convert the datafiles, if that has not already been done.

5. Create a controlfile for the destination instance.

   The CREATE CONTROLFILE command will specify the names and locations of all the converted datafiles, the characteristics of the destination database's online redo log, and the new database name. Then it will mount the newly created controlfile.

6. Open the destination database with RESETLOGS.

   Initialize the online redo log with ALTER DATABASE OPEN RESETLOGS.

   This process can be accomplished manually, but RMAN provides a facility that may help: the CONVERT command. This command, to be run against the source, generates scripts for steps 3 and 5 and generates a parameter file for step 4. There are variations depending on whether the conversion is to be done on the source or the destination.

Exercise 27-2: Generate Database Transport Scripts   In this exercise, generate the scripts for transporting a database to another platform. It is assumed that the source platform (and therefore destination platform) is little-endian.

1. Open the database in read-only mode.

   Using SQL*Plus, connect AS SYSDBA.

   ```
   shutdown immediate
   startup mount
   alter database open read only;
   ```

2. Generate the scripts for conversion at the destination.

   Using RMAN, connected as SYS, run this command:

   ```
   convert database on target platform convert script 'cnvt_sundb.sql'
   transport script 'crdb_sundb.sql' new database 'sundb'
   to platform 'Solaris Operating System (x86-64)' format 'c:\tmp\%U';
   ```

   The suggested path assumes that the source is a Windows system. Study the output of the command. It is very instructive.

3. Study the generated scripts.

   In the nominated directory, you will find the scripts crdb_sundb.sql and cnvt_sundb .sql and a pfile. Study them carefully. They would, of course, need substantial editing to match the destination file system.

4. Prepare for transport with conversion on the source.

   This command (which assumes a Linux source system) will write out converted datafiles to the nominated directory:

   ```
   convert database transport script 'crdb_sundb.sql'
   new database 'sundb'
   to platform 'Solaris Operating System (x86-64)' format '/tmp/%U';
   ```

   Study the command's output closely.

5. Study the generated scripts.

   In the nominated directory, you will find copies of the datafiles converted for use at the destination site, a parameter file for starting the destination instance, and the crdb_sundb.sql script. Study them closely.

Duplicate a Database

You can use several methods to duplicate an entire database on the same server or to a different server. The method you use depends on several factors, including the destination for the database copy, whether the target server is of the same operating system (OS) and endian-ness, and the requirements for database availability. The methods are to duplicate by copying datafiles or to duplicate by using backupsets. The duplication can rely on existing backups or image copies, or it can create the duplicate from the active source database. In contrast to the database transport method, there is no requirement for any downtime on the source system. Using a recovery catalog is not essential but may make the process easier.

PART IV

The terminology is that the source database is known as the *target,* and the duplicate database to be created is the *auxiliary.*

Using a Duplicate Database

A duplicate database can be used for many things, including the following:

- Testing backup and recovery procedures without disrupting the production database.
- Testing a database upgrade.
- Testing the effect of application upgrades on database performance.
- Generating reports that would otherwise have a detrimental effect on the response time for an online transaction processing (OLTP) production system.
- Exporting a table from a duplicate database that was inadvertently dropped from the production database and then importing it back into the production database; this assumes that the table is static or read-only. As of Oracle Database 12*c,* you can recover a single table from RMAN backups, but this method is preferable if you need more than just a few individual tables.

At a high level, these are the five possibilities for database duplication:

From the active database:	"Push" image copies	
	"Pull" backupsets	
From existing backups:	With a target connection	
	Without a target connection:	With a catalog connection
		Without a catalog connection

The choice of technique is dependent on the availability of a preexisting backup (which must be visible at the auxiliary site) and the availability of network connectivity between the target and the auxiliary.

Duplicate from the Active Database

This method requires a connection from the RMAN executable to both the target database and the auxiliary database. Connection to a recovery catalog is optional. There is no requirement for a backup to exist. The duplicate is created by copying the target datafiles to the auxiliary over Oracle Net.

The "push" method is based on image copies; the actual datafiles are copied from target to auxiliary. The "pull" method creates a backupset that is copied to the auxiliary. Generally, the push method requires more resources on the target, and the volume of data transferred is greater than when using a pull method. When you use one of these clauses in the DUPLICATE command, RMAN uses the "pull" method:

- USING BACKUPSET
- SECTION SIZE

- Encryption clause
- Compression clause

The following are the high-level steps to create a duplicate database on another host from the active database:

1. Create a password file for the auxiliary instance.
2. Create an initialization parameter file for the auxiliary instance.
3. Start the auxiliary instance in NOMOUNT mode.
4. Configure network connectivity between the target and the auxiliary.
5. Run the RMAN DUPLICATE command.

Configure the Auxiliary Instance

Some preparation on the destination server is required before you perform the database duplication. First, you must create a password file for the auxiliary instance. Create the password file with the same SYS password as the target database (or simply copy the target password file) and name it according to the necessary convention with the auxiliary database name embedded within the password filename.

The next step is to create an initialization parameter file for the auxiliary instance. Only the DB_NAME parameter is required; all other parameters are theoretically optional. In most cases, you will create a parameter file based on a copy of the target parameter file and edit it according to the auxiliary environment. Table 27-1 lists the parameters you can specify in the auxiliary initialization file along with their descriptions and under what circumstances they are required; these are the parameters you would usually consider carefully.

Note that the DB_FILE_NAME_CONVERT options for generating filenames at the auxiliary can also be specified when you run the DUPLICATE command, which will take precedence over any values in the parameter file.

Initialization Parameter	Values
DB_NAME	The name you specify in the DUPLICATE command, which must be unique among databases in the destination ORACLE_HOME.
CONTROL_FILES	All controlfile locations.
DB_BLOCK_SIZE	The block size for the duplicate database. This size must match the source database.
DB_FILE_NAME_CONVERT	Pairs of strings for converting datafile and tempfile names.
LOG_FILE_NAME_CONVERT	Pairs of strings to rename online redo log files.
DB_CREATE_%_DEST	Locations for OMF files (if using OMF)
DB_RECOVERY_FILE_DEST	Location of the fast recovery area.

Table 27-1 The Minimum Parameters that will Usually be Specified for an Auxiliary Instance

Using the initialization parameter file just created, create an spfile and start the instance in NOMOUNT mode. If working on Windows, it will be necessary to use the ORADIM utility to create the Windows service under which the instance will run.

Establish Network Connectivity

The target database will (you can assume) already be registered with the database listener on the target's host. The auxiliary host must also run a database listener, which will need to be configured with a static registration for the auxiliary instance. You cannot rely on dynamic instance registration because RMAN may have to stop and start the auxiliary. Both target and auxiliary servers will need a TNS resolution mechanism, usually a tnsnames.ora file with entries for both the target and the auxiliary instances.

Run the RMAN DUPLICATE Command

Here is the moment you've been waiting for: starting RMAN and performing the duplication process. There are variations in syntax for connecting concurrently to the target and the auxiliary and (optionally) to the catalog. This would be a typical connect string:

```
rman target sys/oracle@orcl auxiliary sys/oracle@dupdb catalog rman/rman@rcat
```

This example uses Oracle Net and password file authentication to connect to both the target and the auxiliary and to a catalog. Alternatively, you could use operating system authentication to connect to one of the databases and perhaps not use a catalog.

```
rman target / auxiliary sys/oracle@dupdb
```

The DUPLICATE command can be simple. Here's an example:

```
duplicate target database to dupdb from active database;
```

This command will create the duplicate and name it dupdb by copying the target's datafiles as image copies. It says nothing about what filenames should be used at the auxiliary and will succeed only if one of these circumstances applies:

- Oracle Managed Files are used to generate filenames.
- The *_FILE_NAME_CONVERT parameters can generate meaningful names.
- The directory structures are identical at both sites.

If none of these conditions applies, then the duplicate command will need to be more complex. Here's an example:

```
run{set newname for datafile 1 to '/u01/oradata/dupdb/system.dbf';

set newname for datafile 2 to '/u01/oradata/dupdb/sysaux.dbf';
set newname for datafile 3 to '/u01/oradata/dupdb/undo.dbf';
set newname for datafile 4 to '/u01/oradata/dupdb/uses.dbf';
duplicate target database to dupdb from active database
logfile
group 1 ('/u01/dupdb/redo1.log') size 50m,
group 2 ('/u01/dupdb/redo2.log') size 50m;}
```

In summary, here is what the DUPLICATE command does:

1. Creates a controlfile for the duplicate database, using the names specified in the CONTROL_FILES instance parameter

2. Copies the target datafiles to the auxiliary database from the running database

3. Recovers the auxiliary using the target's online (and if necessary archived) redo

4. Opens the auxiliary database with the RESETLOGS option

5. Generates a new DBID for the auxiliary database

Here are some other options available with the DUPLICATE command:

- **SKIP READONLY**   Exclude read-only tablespaces from the copy operation.

- **SKIP TABLESPACE**   Exclude specific tablespaces, except for SYSTEM and UNDO.

- **NOFILENAMECHECK**   Don't check for duplicate filenames between the source and destination databases.

- **OPEN RESTRICTED**   When the destination database is ready, open it immediately with the RESTRICTED SESSION option.

- **NOOPEN**   Do not open the auxiliary after creation

Active Duplication Using Backupsets

To enable the "pull" method, you must instruct RMAN to generate and transfer a backupset from the target, rather than transferring image copies of datafiles. This requires adding one or more keywords to the duplicate command. Here's an example:

```
connect target "backupadmin/oracle@orcl as sysbackup";
connect auxiliary "backupadmin/oracle@dupdb as sysbackup";
set encryption algorithm 'aes256';
set encryption on identified by pa55w0rd;
duplicate target database to dupdb
    from active database
    using compressed backupset
    section size 10g;
```

This example connects to the databases with the SYSBACKUP privilege rather than SYSDBA, using password file authentication. Then it specifies that the transfer of data should be encrypted, the key being protected by a password. The backupset will be compressed and divided into sections no larger than 10GB. The transfer of sections will be parallelized according to the number of configured channels on the target.

Duplicate from Backup

The key to backup-based duplication is that all necessary backups of datafiles and archive log files must be visible to the auxiliary instance, ideally in the same path as on the target. If the backups are stored in a network-attached device, this should be no problem. Otherwise, they must be copied to the auxiliary server. If it is not possible to expose the backups in the same path, the syntax does permit nominating the path where they exist.

If a target connection is possible, then RMAN can interrogate the target for all necessary information about the location of backups and the structure and state of the database. If a target connection is not possible but a catalog connection is possible, then RMAN can retrieve this information from the catalog. If neither a target nor a catalog connection is possible, then all this information must be provided in the duplicate command. When using backups for the duplication process, you need to configure RMAN channels to be used on the auxiliary database instance. The channel on the auxiliary instance restores the backups, so you need to specify the ALLOCATE command in the run block, as in this example:

```
RMAN> run
      { allocate auxiliary channel aux0 device type disk;
        allocate auxiliary channel aux1 device type disk;
        . . .
        duplicate target database . . .
      }
```

Exercise 27-3: Duplicate a Database   This exercise assumes that you have a database named orcl that is running in archivelog mode and that it is an OMF database, which includes all datafiles, online log files, and controlfile copies named by OMF. It will be duplicated to a database named dupdb, running on the same server. Be aware of variations for Linux and Windows, and, of course, substitute names and paths and other literals as necessary.

1. Create a password file for the auxiliary by copying the target password file.

   Here's how to do it on Linux:

   ```
   cp $ORACLE_HOME/dbs/orapworcl $ORACLE_HOME/dbs/orapwdupdb
   ```

   Here's how to do it on Windows:

   ```
   copy %ORACLE_HOME%\database\PWDorcl.ora  %ORACLE_HOME%\database\
   PWDdupdb.ora
   ```

2. Create a dummy parameter file, with these parameters:

   ```
   db_name=dupdb
   db_file_name_convert='orcl','dupdb','ORCL','DUPDB'
   log_file_name_convert='orcl','dupdb','ORCL','DUPDB'
   ```

   Here's the Linux filename:

   ```
   $ORACLE_HOME/dbs/initdupdb.ora
   ```

   Here's the Windows filename:

   ```
   %ORACLE_HOME%\database\initdupdb.ora
   ```

3. Start the auxiliary instance.

   Here's how to do it on Linux:

   ```
   export ORACLE_SID=dupdb
   sqlplus / as sysdba
   create spfile from pfile;
   startup nomount
   ```

   Here's how to do it on Windows:

   ```
   oradim -new -sid dupdb
   set ORACLE_SID=dupdb
   sqlplus / as sysdba
   create spfile from pfile;
   startup nomount
   ```

4. Configure Oracle Net.

Add this entry to the listener.ora file:

```
sid_list_listener=
(sid_list=
 (sid_desc=(sid_name=orcl))
 (sid_desc=(sid_name=dupdb))
 )
```

Restart the listener.

Add these entries to the tnsnames.ora file:

```
orcl=(description=(address=(protocol=tcp)(host=localhost)(port=1521))
(connect_data=(sid=orcl)))
dupdb=(description=(address=(protocol=tcp)(host=localhost)(port=1521))
(connect_data=(sid=dupdb)))
```

Test the configuration.

```
tnsping orcl
tnsping dupdb
```

5. Connect to the target and auxiliary with RMAN.

```
rman target sys/oracle@orcl auxiliary sys/oracle@dupdb
```

6. Duplicate the database.

```
duplicate target database to dupdb from active database;
```

Observe the manner in which memory scripts are generated and executed. The scripts are instructive.

7. It is almost inevitable that you will need several tries to get this exercise completed successfully. That is part of a database administrator's life! Following a failed attempt, be aware that the duplication may have partially succeeded, and you may therefore need to delete various files before trying again, as well as restart the auxiliary instance.

Two-Minute Drill

Describe and Use Transportable Tablespaces and Databases

- When transporting between platforms, both the source and destination platforms must be on Oracle's list of supported platforms.

- Oracle Database feature compatibility is controlled by the COMPATIBLE initialization parameter.

- When you create a transportable tablespace set, Oracle determines the minimum compatibility level of the target database and stores this value in the metadata for the transportable tablespace set.

- A conversion process must be performed for data columns transported between platforms with different endian formats.

- To determine the endian formats of all supported platforms, you can query the dynamic performance view V$TRANSPORTABLE_PLATFORM.

- When transporting a tablespace, the source tablespace must be read-only during the copy process and changed to read-write after import to the target database.

- You use expdp and impdp to copy metadata describing a tablespace from one database to another.

- The DBMS_FILE_TRANSFER PL/SQL package can perform endian conversion as it copies files.

Choose a Technique for Duplicating a Database

- Cross-platform data transport requires tablespaces to be in READ ONLY mode to copy the tablespaces' datafiles to the target system.

- Only the metadata for a tablespace or entire database needs to be created for Data Pump export/import since the image copies themselves will be copied to the target database.

- Use RMAN backupsets for file transfer speed, compression, and minimal downtime of the source tablespace or database.

Create a Backup-Based Duplicate Database

- When you duplicate a database, the source database is copied to the duplicate database.

- The source database is also known as the target database.

- The duplicate database is also known as the auxiliary database.

- Preparing to create a duplicate database includes creating a password file, ensuring network connectivity, and creating an initialization parameter file for the auxiliary instance.

- At a minimum, you need to specify the DB_NAME value in the auxiliary instance's initialization parameter file. You must also specify DB_BLOCK_SIZE if it is set explicitly in the target database.

- The initialization parameter DB_FILE_NAME_CONVERT specifies the file system mapping for datafile and tempfile names.

- The initialization parameter LOG_FILE_NAME_CONVERT specifies the file system mapping for online redo log files.

- The initialization parameter CONTROL_FILES specifies the new names for all controlfiles, unless you are using Oracle Managed Files because OMF will name files for you.

- The RMAN command for performing database duplication is DUPLICATE TARGET DATABASE.

- The duplicate database has a new DBID, even if it has the same database name as the source database.

Duplicate a Database

- You use the RMAN DUPLICATE command to duplicate a database.
- You can use the "push" method to duplicate the database, which is based on image copies.
- The "pull" method generates an RMAN backupset that permits use of compression and encryption.
- You can specify FROM ACTIVE DATABASE in the DUPLICATE command to create the copy from an online database instead of from a database backup.

Self Test

1. You are running Oracle Database 12*c* with the COMPATIBLE initialization parameter set to 12.0.0. What is the minimal compatibility level for transporting a tablespace from a database on a different platform? (Choose the best answer.)

   A. 8.0

   B. 10.0

   C. 12.0

   D. 11.0

   E. All of the above

2. When transporting a tablespace, what is the purpose of DBMS_TTS.TRANSPORT_ SET_CHECK? (Choose the best answer.)

   A. It ensures that the COMPATIBILITY level is high enough for the transport operation.

   B. It compares the endian level for the source and target databases and runs RMAN to convert the datafiles before transportation.

   C. It validates that the metadata for the tablespace does not have any naming conflicts with the target database schemas.

   D. It checks for tablespace self-consistency.

3. You want to duplicate a database but maximize availability for the source database and all its tablespaces. What is the best method to use for this type of database duplication? (Choose the best answer.)

   A. Image copies

   B. Data Pump export with FULL=Y

   C. RMAN backupsets because then the downtime will be zero

   D. RMAN backupsets because then the downtime will be close to zero

4. Identify the correct statement regarding duplicate databases created with RMAN. (Choose the best answer.)

   A. RMAN copies the source database to the target database, and both can have the same name.

   B. RMAN creates an auxiliary instance for the duration of the copy operation and drops it after the copy operation is complete.

   C. The auxiliary database is the same as the target database.

   D. RMAN copies the database from the target to the duplicate database, and both can have the same name.

   E. The source database must be shut down before you can start up the destination database.

5. To create a duplicate database, put the following steps in the correct order:

   1. Start the auxiliary instance as NOMOUNT.
   2. Allocate auxiliary channels if necessary.
   3. Run the RMAN DUPLICATE command.
   4. Create a password file for the auxiliary instance.
   5. Ensure network connectivity to the auxiliary instance.
   6. Open the auxiliary instance.
   7. Start the source database in MOUNT or OPEN mode.
   8. Create an initialization parameter file for the auxiliary instance.
   9. Create backups or copy existing backups and archived log files to a common location accessible by the auxiliary instance.

   A. 5, 4, 8, 1, 7, 9, 3, 2, 6

   B. 4, 5, 8, 1, 7, 9, 2, 3, 6

   C. 4, 5, 8, 1, 7, 9, 3, 2, 6

   D. 5, 4, 1, 8, 7, 9, 2, 3, 6

6. Which of the following clauses is not valid for the RMAN DUPLICATE command? (Choose the best answer.)

   A. SKIP OFFLINE

   B. SKIP READONLY

   C. SKIP TABLESPACE

   D. NOFILENAMECHECK

   E. OPEN RESTRICTED

7. Identify the true statement regarding the status of the source database and the auxiliary database instance when duplicating a database based on a running instance. (Choose the best answer.)

    A. The active database must be in MOUNT mode, and the auxiliary instance must be in MOUNT mode.

    B. The active database must be in MOUNT or OPEN mode, and the auxiliary instance must be in NOMOUNT mode.

    C. The active database must be in OPEN mode, and the auxiliary instance must be in NOMOUNT mode.

    D. The active database must be in NOMOUNT mode, and the auxiliary instance must be in MOUNT mode.

Self Test Answers

1. ☑ **B.** If the source and target databases are on different platforms, both the source and target must have a compatibility level of at least 10.0.
    ☒ **A, C, D,** and **E** are incorrect. For transporting between identical platforms, you need only COMPATIBLE=8.0. For transporting between databases with different block sizes, you need only COMPATIBLE=9.0.

2. ☑ **D.** DBMS_TTS.TRANSPORT_SET_CHECK checks to ensure that there are no objects in the tablespace to be transported that have dependencies on objects in other tablespaces in the source database.
    ☒ **A, B,** and **C** are incorrect. They are not valid uses for DBMS_TTS .TRANSPORT_SET_CHECK.

3. ☑ **D.** Using RMAN for duplicating a database with backupsets has the advantage of keeping the tablespaces available as much as possible (in READ WRITE mode). Successive incremental backups will get smaller and smaller until the last backup in which you must make the tablespaces read-only to perform the last incremental backup to be applied to the target database.
    ☒ **A, B,** and **C** are incorrect. **A** is incorrect because image copies are a valid method for transporting a tablespace or database, but the tablespace's datafiles must be in READ ONLY mode to perform the image copy. **B** is incorrect because Data Pump can back up an entire database, but it is a logical backup, not a physical backup. **C** is incorrect because there will still be some unavailability of the tablespace to perform the last incremental backup to be applied to the target database's copy of the tablespace.

4. ☑ **D.** You can keep the same name because RMAN creates a new DBID, and therefore you can use the same recovery catalog for both databases.
    ☒ **A, B, C,** and **E** are incorrect. **A** is incorrect because the target database is the same as the source database. **B** is incorrect because RMAN does not drop the auxiliary instance or database after the copy operation is complete. **C** is incorrect because the target database is the source database and the auxiliary database is the destination database. **E** is incorrect because both databases can be open at the same time, even on the same host and with the same recovery catalog.

PART IV

5. ☑ **B.** These steps are in the correct order.

☒ **A, C,** and **D** are incorrect because they are in the wrong order.

6. ☑ **A.** The SKIP OFFLINE option is not valid for the DUPLICATE command.

☒ **B, C, D,** and **E** are incorrect. **B** is incorrect because the SKIP READONLY clause excludes read-only tablespaces. **C** is incorrect because SKIP TABLESPACE excludes one or more tablespaces from the copy operation; you cannot skip the SYSTEM or UNDO tablespace. **D** is incorrect because NOFILENAMECHECK doesn't check for duplicate filenames between the source and destination. **E** is incorrect because OPEN RESTRICTED opens the destination database with the RESTRICTED SESSION option.

7. ☑ **B.** To duplicate a database based on a running instance, the source database can be in either MOUNT or OPEN mode; since the auxiliary database does not yet have even a controlfile, it must be opened in NOMOUNT mode.

☒ **A, C,** and **D** are incorrect. **A** is incorrect because the auxiliary instance does not have a controlfile right away, so it cannot be started in MOUNT mode. **C** is incorrect because the active database can also be in MOUNT mode. **D** is incorrect because the database can't be duplicated if the source database is in NOMOUNT mode, and the auxiliary instance can't be in MOUNT mode either!

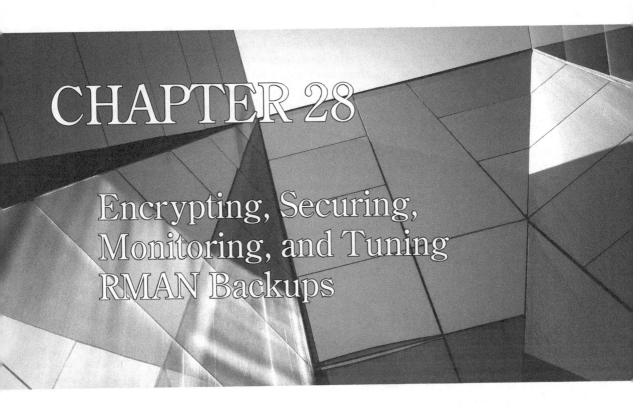

CHAPTER 28

Encrypting, Securing, Monitoring, and Tuning RMAN Backups

Exam Objectives

- 63.1.8.1   Create RMAN-Encrypted Backups
- 63.1.13.1   Configure and Use Oracle Secure Backup
- 63.1.18.1   Tune RMAN Performance

This chapter describes some advanced techniques for managing backups that relate to encryption and tuning. It also covers Oracle Secure Backup (OSB). Oracle Database 12c provides two types of encrypted backups to ensure that enterprise data is not compromised or seen by the wrong person. The backup method you use (via either Oracle Advanced Security or Oracle Secure Backup) depends on the types of data you're backing up and its destination. As you've seen in previous chapters, Recovery Manager (RMAN) can back up large datafiles as a multisection backup, leveraging multiple output devices (multiple channels either to disk or to tape) to reduce dramatically the time it takes to back up the datafile, among other advantages. RMAN's alternative compression techniques and encryption methods further reduce backup size and make the backups unavailable to unauthorized parties by using stand-alone passwords or the database's encryption wallet.

Oracle Secure Backup is based on a global client-server model where both Oracle databases and file systems can be encrypted and backed up via an enterprise tape library system while still using the familiar RMAN interface. You use the command-line tool obtool in addition to a web interface to manage Oracle Secure Backup.

Create RMAN-Encrypted Backups

To ensure the security and privacy of your backups, you can encrypt them in one of three ways: transparent encryption, password encryption, or dual-mode encryption. By default, encryption is turned off.

```
CONFIGURE ENCRYPTION FOR DATABASE OFF; # default
CONFIGURE ENCRYPTION ALGORITHM 'AES128'; # default
```

In the following sections, you'll learn how to enable each type of encryption (transparent or password). To create a successful backup and recovery strategy, you must first understand the types of failures and how Oracle responds to each of them. Some require no user or database administrator (DBA) intervention, and others do. Which backup and recovery solutions you leverage depends on many factors, including how fast you need to recover from a failure and how many resources you want to dedicate to the solution. Your investment in recovery infrastructure is proportional to the cost of lost productivity or business income if the database is unavailable for a day, an hour, or a minute.

Configuring and Using Transparent Encryption

You can set transparent (wallet-based) encryption as the default RMAN encryption method using the CONFIGURE command as follows:

```
RMAN> configure encryption for database on;
new RMAN configuration parameters:
CONFIGURE ENCRYPTION FOR DATABASE ON;
new RMAN configuration parameters are successfully stored
starting full resync of recovery catalog
full resync complete
RMAN>
```

Keep in mind that your database wallet must be open as well. If it is not open, you might think that everything is going as planned—until the encryption process attempts to start. This is shown by the backup failure error message in the following output:

```
RMAN> backup as compressed backupset tablespace users;
Starting backup at 20-MAR-14
allocated channel: ORA_DISK_1
channel ORA_DISK_1: SID=137 device type=DISK
channel ORA_DISK_1: starting compressed full datafile backup set
channel ORA_DISK_1: specifying datafile(s) in backup set
input datafile file number=00006
name=+DATA/COMPLREF/DATAFILE/users.259.821312559
channel ORA_DISK_1: starting piece 1 at 20-MAR-14
RMAN-00571: ===========================================================
RMAN-00569: =============== ERROR MESSAGE STACK FOLLOWS ===============
RMAN-00571: ===========================================================
RMAN-03009: failure of backup command on ORA_DISK_1 channel
at 03/20/2014 21:39:32
ORA-19914: unable to encrypt backup
ORA-28365: wallet is not open
RMAN>
```

Setting up an encryption wallet for the instance is easy. Your sqlnet.ora file points to the location of the encryption wallet with an entry similar to the following:

```
ENCRYPTION_WALLET_LOCATION=
(SOURCE=
(METHOD=FILE)
(METHOD_DATA=
(DIRECTORY=/u01/app/oracle/product/12.1.0/dbhome_1/
network/admin/wallet)))
```

Within the $ORACLE_HOME/network/admin/wallet directory are the database encryption keys. Using an account with the SYSKM or ADMINISTER KEY MANAGEMENT system privilege, or via operating system (OS) authentication as in this example, create the keystore with the ADMINISTER KEY MANAGEMENT facility:

```
SQL> administer key management
2 create keystore '/u01/app/oracle/product/12.1.0/dbhome_1/
network/admin/wallet'
3 identified by "fre#3dXX0";
```

Don't lose the contents of the files in the wallet directory—back it up. You won't be able to decrypt encrypted tablespaces or encrypted RMAN backups without it.

Opening the wallet at the SQL> prompt (and, as of Oracle Database 12c, at the RMAN> prompt) and creating a master encryption key makes everything work a lot more smoothly.

```
SQL> connect / as sysdba
Connected.
SQL> administer key management
2 set keystore open
3 identified by "fre#3dXX0";
```

```
keystore altered.
SQL> administer key management
2 set key identified by "XX407$9!@"
3 with backup using 'master_key_1';
keystore altered.
. . .
RMAN> backup as compressed backupset tablespace users;
Starting backup at 20-MAR-14
allocated channel: ORA_DISK_1
channel ORA_DISK_1: SID=254 device type=DISK
channel ORA_DISK_1: starting compressed full datafile backup set
channel ORA_DISK_1: specifying datafile(s) in backup set
input datafile file number=00006

name=+DATA/COMPLREF/DATAFILE/users.259.821312559
channel ORA_DISK_1: starting piece 1 at 20-MAR-14
channel ORA_DISK_1: finished piece 1 at 20-MAR-14
piece handle=+RECOV/COMPLREF/BACKUPSET/2014_03_20
/nnndf0_tag20140320t233149_0.273.842743911
tag=TAG20140320T233149 comment=NONE
channel ORA_DISK_1: backup set complete, elapsed time: 00:00:01
Finished backup at 20-MAR-14
RMAN>
```

As you might expect, even if transparent encryption is not the default, you can turn it on just for the duration of a single backup. As in the previous example, the database wallet must be open. Here is an example:

```
RMAN> set encryption on;
executing command: SET encryption
RMAN> backup as compressed backupset tablespace sysaux;
Starting backup at 20-MAR-14
using channel ORA_DISK_1
channel ORA_DISK_1: starting compressed full datafile backup set
channel ORA_DISK_1: specifying datafile(s) in backup set
. . .
842743985 tag=TAG20140320T233305 comment=NONE
channel ORA_DISK_1: backup set complete, elapsed time: 00:01:25
Finished backup at 20-MAR-14
RMAN> set encryption off;
executing command: SET encryption
RMAN>
```

To restore or recover from an encrypted backup, the database wallet must be open, and either the encryption default must be ON or you must use SET ENCRYPTION ON before the recovery operation.

For password-based keystores, you had to specify WITH BACKUP in the earlier example when generating the master encryption key. A new master key needs to be generated only when you think that security has been compromised. Better yet, change it on a regular basis as a preventive measure.

If you need to restore an older copy of the keystore, you can recover old data only up to the point at which you changed the master encryption key.

Using Password Encryption

To enable password encryption for a specific backup, use the SET ENCRYPTION command as follows:

```
RMAN> set encryption identified by "F45$Xa98";
executing command: SET encryption
RMAN> backup as compressed backupset tablespace users;
```

Password encryption is inherently less secure and reliable than transparent (wallet-based) encryption because a password can be lost, forgotten, or intercepted easily. Use password encryption only when backups must be transportable to a different database.

When you want to restore this backup, either to the same database (if wallet-based encryption is off) or to a different database, you must specify the decryption password with SET DECRYPTION.

```
RMAN> set decryption identified by "F45$Xa98";
executing command: SET decryption
RMAN>
```

If you are recovering one or more tablespaces or the entire database from backups that have different passwords, you can conveniently specify all the passwords at once with SET DECRYPTION.

```
RMAN> set decryption identified by "F45$Xa98", "XX407$9!@";
executing command: SET decryption
RMAN>
```

RMAN will try each password in turn for every encrypted backup until it finds a match. RMAN will terminate with an error only if no passwords match any of the passwords in any of the backups.

Using Dual-Mode Encryption

You can use both transparent encryption and password encryption at the same time. This is useful if your backup might be used to restore or recover within the same database, and on occasion it can be used to recover another database. When both methods are in effect, you can use either the password or the database wallet to restore the backup. When recovering to a remote database, you must specify the password before recovering, as follows:

```
RMAN> set encryption on identified by "F45$Xa98";
executing command: SET encryption
RMAN>
```

If you want to use only password-based encryption for a backup, add the ONLY clause to SET ENCRYPTION.

```
RMAN> set encryption on identified by "F45$Xa98" only;
```

As a result, even if ENCRYPTION defaults to ON (and therefore uses the wallet), all subsequent backups use password encryption only until you turn off password encryption or exit RMAN altogether.

Configure and Use Oracle Secure Backup

Oracle Secure Backup enhances the privacy of the data in your backup by encrypting backups using several new methods. In addition, the range of objects you can back up goes beyond just the database files. OSB is a tool that can back up file systems on servers and on client PCs as well as databases.

The three main components in an OSB environment are as follows:

- **Administrative server**   A server somewhere within the enterprise that has the OSB software installed. This could be installed on a database server, but is usually on a dedicated server.

- **Media server**   A server that manages tiered storage such as disks, tape libraries, and optical media.

- **Client**   The target for OSB backups. This can be an Oracle database or a file system on another server.

OSB can be leveraged in several ways: via Enterprise Manager Cloud Control, seamlessly through RMAN via the existing SBT (System Backup to Tape) interface, via the OSB web tool, and via the command-line obtool utility.

Installing and Configuring Oracle Secure Backup

To install OSB, start by downloading the latest version, which as of this writing is 12.1. Designate a directory on the server where you want to install OSB (must be done with a privileged account) and unzip the file. Then run the setup script. OSB must be installed on all nodes in the environment. During the run of the setup script, you specify which role the particular installation should fulfill: administrative server, media server, or client.

You can configure details of the tape libraries or disk pools to be used at install time or any time subsequently. Note that OSB comes with the capability to manage all of the commonly used devices on the market. OSB includes its own catalog, which is not an Oracle database but rather a structure proprietary to OSB. This catalog stores details of all devices, of all backups, and of OSB users and their passwords.

Included in the install is the command-line utility obtool, and the administrative install includes a web server hosting a Hypertext Markup Language (HTML) administration interface.

Using RMAN with Oracle Secure Backup

RMAN (or any other client that needs its data backed up) cannot automatically use OSB on the backup server and will not explicitly invoke the obtool command. Instead, RMAN will connect to OSB via the SBT interface. Here are the four requirements for using OSB via RMAN:

- RMAN must be pre-authorized on that host using the obtool command.
- The OS user identity of the Oracle instance must match the authorized user.
- The RMAN user must be assigned the pertinent OSB classes to perform Oracle backups and restores.
- The SBT library must be available.

For example, here is how you would use obtool to create an OSB user called pa_rman on the host oel63 to allow RMAN to perform backups under the OS user oracle:

```
ob> mkuser pa_rman --class oracle --preauth oel63:oracle+rman
```

From this point on, any RMAN job running under the oracle user on the server oel63 can perform backups of any database objects accessible by the RMAN session.

The SBT library is installed on the database server as part of the database installation. On Unix and Windows, the files are as follows:

```
$ORACLE_HOME/lib/libosbws12.so
%ORACLE_HOME%\bin\oraosbws12.dll
```

To back up to OSB, use a script that specifies the library as a parameter to be passed to the channel allocation statement.

```
run{allocate channel t1 type sbt parms "SBT_LIBRARY=

/u01/app/oracle/product/12.1.0/dbhome_1/lib/libosbws12.so";
backup as compressed backupset database plus archivelog delete all input;}
```

When an RMAN backup begins, the database name, content type, and copy number are sent to OSB, which translates to a given storage selector that defines the devices and media families to use for the backup.

Miscellaneous obtool Commands

Dozens of obtool commands are available, but only a handful will be used on a daily basis. Most of these commands look and act like a Linux command with similar switches. In fact, many of these commands begin with ls.

Here's how to show OSB host information:

```
ob> lshost -l
oel63:
Access mode: OB
IP names: oel63
Disable RDS: not set (system default)
TCP/IP buffer size: not set (global policy)
Algorithm: aes192
Encryption policy: allowed
Rekey frequency: 1 month
Key type: transparent
In service: yes
Roles: admin,client
Trusted host: yes
Certificate key size: 1024
UUID: 3131737a-9359-1031-b4f1-080027356346
ob>
```

Here's how to show detailed user information:

```
ob> lsuser -l
admin:
Password: (set)
User class: admin
Given name: [none]
```

PART IV

```
UNIX name: root
UNIX group: root
Windows domain/acct: [none]
NDMP server user: no
Email address: [none]
UUID: 313f7aec-9359-1031-b4f1-080027356346
Preauthorized access: [none]
pa_rman:
Password: (not set)
User class: oracle
Given name: [none]
UNIX name: [none]
UNIX group: [none]
Windows domain/acct: [none]
NDMP server user: no
Email address: [none]
UUID: c58b97a8-9363-1031-b781-080027356346
Preauthorized access:
Hostname: oel63
Username: oracle
Windows domain: [all]
RMAN enabled: yes
Cmdline enabled: no
ob>
```

Here's how to list dataset backup contents:

```
ob> lsds
Top level dataset directory:
NEW_CLIENTS/
OSB-CATALOG-DS
ob>
```

Monitor and Tune RMAN Performance

Tuning RMAN backup and recovery operations is frequently an afterthought. If you run a full backup once a week and incremental backups daily, you might not think you need to optimize your backup and recovery operations because they take up only about four hours of your time every week. This logic seems to make sense, until any of the following events occur in your organization:

- Your company expands its offices worldwide, users will be accessing the database at all times of the day and night, and you don't want a backup operation reducing response time.

- New applications increase demand for the tape library system.

- Management demands improvements in the database recovery time to meet service level agreements (SLAs).

Optimizing your RMAN backup and recovery operations will mitigate the effects of these events. You need to understand the importance of tuning RMAN and be able to identify bottlenecks in the different phases of an RMAN backup.

First, you'll learn about the dynamic performance views you can use to monitor an RMAN backup in progress, such as V$SESSION and V$PROCESS. RMAN makes it easy to identify a specific backup job in V$SESSION.

Next, you'll dive into some tuning exercises, using techniques such as multiple channel allocation to improve the performance of your backup operations. You'll also learn where RMAN bottlenecks occur and how to measure a bottleneck with views such as V$BACKUP_SYNC_IO and V$BACKUP_ASYNC_IO. The RMAN BACKUP command offers you a lot of flexibility by letting you control the size of each backup piece, determine how many files to put into a backupset, and decrease the load on the system by defining a desired backup duration.

Monitoring RMAN Sessions and Jobs

At any given point in time, you may have multiple backup jobs running, each with one or more channels. Each channel utilizes one operating system process. If you want to identify which channel is using the most central processing unit (CPU) or input/output (I/O) resources at the operating system level, you can join the dynamic performance views V$SESSION and V$PROCESS to identify the operating system processes associated with each RMAN channel.

In addition to identifying the processes associated with each RMAN job, you can determine the progress of a backup or restore operation. You can use the dynamic performance view V$SESSION_LONGOPS to identify how much work an RMAN session has completed and the estimated total amount of work.

Finally, RMAN provides troubleshooting information in a number of ways, above and beyond the command output at the RMAN> prompt, when something goes wrong. You can also enable enhanced debugging to help you and Oracle Support identify the cause of a serious RMAN problem.

In the following sections, you'll be introduced to the dynamic performance views V$SESSION, V$PROCESS, and V$SESSION_LONGOPS that can help you identify and monitor RMAN backup and restore jobs. Also, you'll learn where to look when a backup or restore job fails.

Using V$SESSION and V$PROCESS

The dynamic performance view V$PROCESS contains a row for each operating system process connected to the database instance. V$SESSION contains additional information about each session connected to the database, such as the current SQL command and the Oracle username executing the command. These sessions include RMAN sessions. As a result, you can monitor RMAN sessions using these views as well.

RMAN populates the column V$SESSION.CLIENT_INFO with the string rman and the name of the channel. Remember that each RMAN channel corresponds to a server process, and therefore V$SESSION will have one row for each channel.

To retrieve information from V$SESSION and V$PROCESS about current RMAN sessions, join the views V$SESSION and V$PROCESS on the PADDR and ADDR columns, as you will see in the exercise.

Exercise 28-1: Monitor RMAN Channel Processes   In this exercise, you'll start an RMAN job that uses two or more channels and retrieve the channel names from V$SESSION and V$PROCESS.

1. Create an RMAN job that backs up the USERS tablespace using two disk channels.

```
RMAN> run {
2> allocate channel ch1 type disk;
3> allocate channel ch2 type disk;
4> backup as compressed backupset tablespace users;
5> }
starting full resync of recovery catalog
full resync complete
released channel: ORA_DISK_1
allocated channel: ch1
channel ch1: SID=130 device type=DISK
starting full resync of recovery catalog
full resync complete
allocated channel: ch2
channel ch2: SID=126 device type=DISK
. . .
Finished Control File and SPFILE Autobackup at 20-MAR-14
released channel: ch1
released channel: ch2
RMAN>
```

2. While the RMAN job is running, join the views V$PROCESS and V$SESSION to retrieve the CLIENT_INFO column contents.

```
SQL> select sid, spid, client_info
2 from v$process p join v$session s on (p.addr = s.paddr)
3 where client_info like '%rman%'
4 ;
SID SPID CLIENT_INFO
---------- ------------------------ ------------------------
126 25070 rman channel=ch2
130 7732 rman channel=ch1
SQL>
```

Note that RMAN's user processes will still exist in V$SESSION until you exit RMAN or start another backup operation.

If you have multiple RMAN jobs running, some with two or more channels allocated, it might be difficult to identify which process corresponds to which RMAN backup or recovery operation. To facilitate the desired differentiation, you can use the SET COMMAND ID command within an RMAN run block, as in this example:

```
run {
set command id to 'bkup users';
backup tablespace users;
}
```

When this RMAN job runs, the CLIENT_INFO column in V$SESSION contains the string id=bkup users to help you identify the session for each RMAN job.

Exercise 28-2: Monitor Multiple RMAN Jobs In this exercise, you'll start two RMAN jobs and identify each job in V$SESSION and V$PROCESS using the SET COMMAND option in RMAN.

1. Create two RMAN jobs (in two different RMAN sessions) that back up two tablespaces and use the SET COMMAND option.

```
/* session 1 */

RMAN> run {
2> set command id to 'bkup system';
3> backup as compressed backupset tablespace system;
4> }
/* session 2 */

RMAN> run {
2> set command id to 'bkup sysaux';
3> backup as compressed backupset tablespace sysaux;
4> }
```

2. While the RMAN job is running, join the views V$PROCESS and V$SESSION to retrieve the CLIENT_INFO column contents.

```
SQL> select sid, spid, client_info
2 from v$process p join v$session s on (p.addr = s.paddr)
3 where client_info like '%id=%';
```

Using V$SESSION_LONGOPS

The dynamic performance view V$SESSION_LONGOPS isn't specific to RMAN either. Oracle records any operations that run for more than 6 seconds (in absolute time), including RMAN backup and recovery operations, statistics gathering, and long queries in V$SESSION_LONGOPS.

This example queries V$SESSION_LONGOPS while a datafile backup is in progress:

```
SQL> select opname,sofar,totalwork,units,time_remaining
 2 from v$session_longops where time_remaining > 0;

OPNAME                      SOFAR   TOTALWORK UNITS   TIME_REMAINING
-------------------------   ------  ---------- ------  --------------
RMAN: full datafile backup  677191     747680 Blocks               4
```

Tuning RMAN Performance

You can tune RMAN operations in many ways. You can tune the overall throughput of a backup by using multiple RMAN channels and assigning datafiles to different channels. Each channel is assigned to a single process, so parallel processing can speed the backup process. Conversely, you can multiplex several backup files to the same backup piece. For a particular channel, you can use the MAXPIECESIZE and MAXOPENFILES parameters to maximize throughput to a specific output device. The BACKUP command uses these parameters in addition to FILESPERSET and BACKUP DURATION to optimize your backup operation.

PART IV

You can also use BACKUP DURATION to minimize the effect of the backup on response time if your database must be continuously available and you have to contend with stringent SLAs. Finally, you can also use database initialization parameters to optimize backup and recovery performance, especially for synchronous I/O operations.

If you understand how each tuning method works, you can keep the user response time fast, optimize your hardware and software environment, and potentially delay upgrades when budgets are tight. A throughput bottleneck will almost always exist somewhere in your environment. A bottleneck is the slowest step or task during an RMAN backup.

The next section reviews the basic steps that a channel performs during a backup operation. The techniques presented in the following sections will help you identify where the bottleneck is within the channel's tasks and how to minimize its impact on backup and recovery operations.

Identifying Backup and Restore Steps

RMAN backup performs its tasks within a channel in one of three main phases:

- **Read phase**   The channel reads data blocks into the input buffers.
- **Copy phase**   The channel copies blocks from the input buffers to the output buffers and performs additional processing, if necessary.
  - **Validation**   Check blocks for corruption, which is not CPU intensive.
  - **Compression**   Use BZIP2 or ZLIB to compress the block, which is CPU intensive.
  - **Encryption**   Use an encryption algorithm (transparent, password-protected, or both) to secure the data, which is CPU intensive.
- **Write phase**   The channel writes the blocks from the output buffers to the output device (disk or tape).

Using dynamic performance views, you can identify which phase of which channel operation is the bottleneck and address it accordingly.

In some scenarios, you may want to increase the backup time to ensure that the recovery time will be short. Creating image copies and recovering the image copies on a daily or hourly basis will add to the backup time but will dramatically reduce recovery time.

Parallelizing Backupsets

One of the simplest ways to improve RMAN performance is to allocate multiple channels (either disk or tape). The number of channels you allocate should be no larger than the number of physical devices; allocating two or more channels (and therefore processes) for a single physical device will not improve performance and may even decrease performance. If you're writing to a single Automatic Storage Management (ASM) disk group or a file system striped by the operating system, you can allocate more channels and improve throughput since the logical ASM disk group or striped file system maps to two or more physical disks. You can allocate up to 255 channels, and each channel can read up to 64 datafiles in parallel. Each channel writes to a separate backup copy or image copy.

If the number of datafiles in your database is relatively constant, you can allocate a fixed number of channels and assign each datafile to a specific channel. Here is an example:

```
run {
allocate channel dc1 device type disk;
allocate channel dc2 device type disk;
allocate channel dc3 device type disk;
backup incremental level 0
(datafile 1,2,9 channel dc1)
(datafile 3,8,7 channel dc2)
(datafile 4,6,7 channel dc3)
as compressed backupset;
}
```

Note also that you can specify the path name for a datafile instead of the datafile number, as in this example:

```
(datafile '/u01/oradata/users02.dbf' channel dc2)
```

To automate this process further, you can use the CONFIGURE command to increase the parallelism for each device type.

```
CONFIGURE DEVICE TYPE DISK PARALLELISM 3 ;
```

Understanding RMAN Multiplexing

You can improve RMAN performance and throughput by multiplexing backup and recovery operations. Multiplexing enables RMAN to read from multiple files simultaneously and write the data blocks to the same backup piece. You cannot multiplex image copies. If you did, the output would not be an image of the input.

Using multiplexing as an RMAN tuning method is one way to reduce bottlenecks in backup and recovery operations. The level of multiplexing is primarily controlled by two parameters: FILESPERSET and MAXOPENFILES. The FILESPERSET parameter of the RMAN BACKUP command determines the number of datafiles to put in each backupset. If a single channel backs up ten datafiles and the value of FILESPERSET is 4, RMAN will back up only four files per backupset, and three sets will be generated. The parameter FILESPERSET defaults to 64.

The level of multiplexing (the number of input files that are read and written to the same backup piece) is the minimum of MAXOPENFILES and the number of files in each backupset. The default value for MAXOPENFILES is 8. RMAN allocates a different number and size of disk I/O buffers depending on the level of multiplexing in your RMAN job. Once the level of multiplexing is derived by RMAN using the FILESPERSET and MAXOPENFILES parameters, the number and size of buffers are as follows:

Level of Multiplexing	Size and Number of Buffers
Less than 5	16 buffers of 1MB each divided among all input files
5 to 8	A variable number of 512MB buffers to keep total buffer size under 16MB
More than 8	Total of 4 buffers of 128KB for each (512KB) for each input file

Tuning RMAN Channels

You can further tune your RMAN backup performance by tuning individual channels with the CONFIGURE CHANNEL and ALLOCATE CHANNEL commands. Each CHANNEL command accepts the following parameters:

- **MAXPIECESIZE**   The maximum size of a backup piece
- **RATE**   The number of bytes per second read by RMAN on the channel
- **MAXOPENFILES**   The maximum number of input files that a channel can have open at a given time

The MAXPIECESIZE parameter is useful when you back up to disk and the underlying operating system limits the size of an individual disk file or when a tape media manager cannot split a backup piece across multiple tapes.

Note that the RATE parameter doesn't improve performance, but throttles performance intentionally to limit the disk bandwidth available to a channel. This is useful when your RMAN backups must occur during periods of peak activity elsewhere in the database.

MAXOPENFILES was reviewed in the preceding section, but it is worth revisiting when you want to optimize the performance of an individual channel. For example, you can use MAXOPENFILES to limit RMAN's use of operating system file handles or buffers.

Tuning the BACKUP Command

Just like the CONFIGURE CHANNEL command, the BACKUP command has parameters that can help you improve performance or limit the computing resources that a channel uses for an RMAN backup. Here are the key tuning parameters for the BACKUP command:

- **MAXPIECESIZE**   The maximum size of a backup piece per channel
- **FILESPERSET**   The maximum number of files per backupset
- **MAXOPENFILES**   The maximum number of input files that a channel can have open at a given time
- **BACKUP DURATION**   The time to complete the backup

You've seen the parameters MAXPIECESIZE, FILESPERSET, and MAXOPENFILES before. Note that MAXPIECESIZE and MAXOPENFILES have the same purpose as in the CHANNEL commands, except that they apply to all channels in the backup.

BACKUP DURATION specifies an amount of time to complete the backup. You can qualify this option with MINIMIZE TIME to run the backup as fast as possible or with MINIMIZE LOAD to use the entire time frame specified in the BACKUP DURATION window. In addition, you can use the PARTIAL option, as you might expect, to save a partial backup that was terminated because of time constraints. For example, to limit a full database backup to two hours, run it as fast as possible, and save a partial backup, use this command:

```
RMAN> backup duration 2:00 partial database;
```

If the backup does not complete in the specified time frame, the partial backup is still usable in a recovery scenario after a successive BACKUP command finishes the backup and you use the PARTIAL option.

Two-Minute Drill

Create RMAN-Encrypted Backups

- Transparent encryption uses a database wallet to encrypt a backup, and the backup can be restored only to the source database.
- Password encryption uses a password to encrypt a backup, and the backup can be restored either to the source database or to another database.
- You can use both transparent encryption and password encryption on the same backup.
- Transparent encryption can be enabled for a single backup using the SET ENCRYPTION command.

Configure and Use Oracle Secure Backup

- Oracle Secure Backup is hosted on an administrative server and provides the interface between RMAN and media servers for both databases and file systems across the enterprise.
- An OSB storage selector consists of a database name, content type, and copy number. RMAN passes the storage selector to OSB and processes the backup job.
- OSB maintains its own backup catalog.
- Typical OSB obtool commands perform tasks such as showing registered hosts (lshost), devices (lsdev), backup datasets (lsds), and volumes (lsvol).

Tune RMAN Performance

- You can join V$SESSION with V$PROCESS to identify the operating system processes associated with each RMAN channel.
- The RMAN command SET COMMAND ID helps you distinguish processes for different backup jobs in V$SESSION.
- Use V$SESSION_LONGOPS to monitor the status of RMAN jobs that run for more than 6 seconds.
- Parallelization (allocating multiple channels) can improve backup performance. You can allocate up to 255 channels per RMAN session, and each channel can read up to 64 datafiles in parallel.
- Multiplexing is primarily controlled by the RMAN parameters FILESPERSET and MAXOPENFILES.

- You tune RMAN channels by using the MAXPIECESIZE, RATE, and MAXOPENFILES parameters.

- The BACKUP parameter BACKUP DURATION can be set to MINIMIZE TIME to perform the backup as quickly as possible, or can be set to MINIMIZE LOAD to reduce the I/O demands on the database.

Self Test

1. You have a datafile from the smallfile tablespace USERS that has a size of 90MB, and you run the following RMAN command:

   ```
   RMAN> backup tablespace users section size 40m;
   ```

   How many sections does this backup create? (Choose the best answer.)

   A. The command does not run because multisection backups apply only when multiple channels are used.

   B. Two sections of 45MB each.

   C. Two sections of 40MB each and one section of 10MB.

   D. It is not possible to predict the size of the sections.

2. Which of the following attributes or characteristics are passed by RMAN to OSB when performing a backup? Assume that the RMAN client has already been registered with OSB. (Choose all that apply.)

   A. Content type

   B. Unique hostname

   C. Database ID

   D. Database name

   E. Copy number

   F. Requested media group number

3. What RMAN retention policy should you use if the RMAN backups leverage OSB? (Choose the best answer.)

   A. RMAN inherits the OSB retention policy.

   B. RECOVERY WINDOW.

   C. COPIES.

   D. OSB inherits the RMAN retention policy.

4. Which of the following two dynamic performance views can you use to identify the relationship between Oracle server sessions and RMAN channels? (Choose the best answer.)

   A. V$PROCESS and V$SESSION

   B. V$PROCESS and V$BACKUP_SESSION

C. V$PROCESS and V$BACKUP_ASYNC_IO

D. V$BACKUP_ASYNC_IO and V$SESSION

E. V$BACKUP_SYNC_IO and V$BACKUP_ASYNC_IO

5. You create three RMAN sessions to back up three different tablespaces. Your third RMAN session runs this command:

```
run {
set command id to 'user bkup';
backup tablespace users;
}
```

What values does the column V$SESSION.CLIENT_INFO have for this command? (Choose all that apply.)

A. rman channel=ORA_DISK_1, id=user bkup.

B. id=user bkup, rman channel=ORA_DISK_1.

C. id=user bkup, cmd=backup tablespace users.

D. id=user bkup.

E. The column CLIENT_INFO is in V$PROCESS, not V$SESSION.

6. Identify the location where RMAN message output and troubleshooting information can be found. (Choose all that apply.)

A. The Oracle server trace file

B. The RMAN trace file

C. The view V$PROCESS

D. The database alert log

E. RMAN command output

F. The vendor-specific file sbtio.log

G. The table SYS.AUDIT$

7. These instance parameters in your database are set as follows:

BACKUP_TAPE_IO_SLAVES = TRUE
LARGE_POOL_SIZE = 200M
JAVA_POOL_SIZE = 200M
PGA_AGGREGATE_TARGET = 200M

Which is the correct statement regarding where RMAN allocates the memory buffers for tape backup? (Choose the best answer.)

A. RMAN uses the Java pool in the SGA.

B. RMAN uses the shared pool in the SGA.

C. RMAN allocates memory from the large pool in the PGA.

D. RMAN allocates memory from the large pool in the SGA.

8. Which of the following are bottlenecks that affect RMAN backup and recovery operations? (Choose all that apply.)

   A. Reading data from the database

   B. Writing data to disk

   C. Writing data to tape

   D. Validating data blocks

   E. Using SGA memory buffers versus PGA memory buffers

9. Which RMAN parameter controls multiplexing to disk and tape? (Choose the best answer.)

   A. FILESPERSET from the BACKUP command

   B. FILESPERSET from the BACKUP command and MAXOPENFILES from the CONFIGURE command

   C. FILESPERSET from the CONFIGURE command and MAXOPENFILES from the BACKUP command

   D. MAXOPENFILES from the CONFIGURE command

Self Test Answers

1. ☑ **D.** The section size divides the input datafile, not the output backup piece.
   ☒ **A, B,** and **C** are incorrect. **A** is incorrect because you can use multisection backups without parallelism (though there may not be much point to this). **B** and **C** are incorrect because the size of the output pieces cannot be predicted because it will depend on how many blocks of the datafile sections actually contain data.

2. ☑ **A, C, D,** and **E.** When RMAN sends a backup request to OSB, you must specify the database name (or ID), the content type, and the copy number. Given this information, OSB will use the stored backup storage selector and send the backup to the appropriate backup devices and media family.
   ☒ **B** and **F** are incorrect. **B** is incorrect because the hostname is used to register the RMAN client with the OSB administration server, but is not needed for each backup. **F** is incorrect because RMAN does not select the media group number; OSB does.

3. ☑ **B.** You should use a RECOVERY WINDOW retention policy when using RMAN with OSB. You will use a certain amount of disk space in the Fast Recovery Area for meeting the recovery needs for a certain number of hours each day; longer recovery operations will also leverage tape backups managed by OSB. You will use an obtool command to create a media family for RMAN backups.
   ☒ **A, C,** and **D** are incorrect. **A** and **D** are incorrect because there is no inheritance of backup retention policies between RMAN and OSB. **C** is incorrect because you will not be able to leverage the contents of the Fast Recovery Area as much as you could with a recovery window-based policy.

4. ☑ **A.** You join the views V$PROCESS and V$SESSION on the ADDR and PADDR columns and select rows where the beginning of the column CLIENT_INFO contains the string RMAN.

   ☒ **B, C, D,** and **E** are incorrect. **B** is incorrect because there is no such view V$BACKUP_SESSION. **C, D,** and **E** are incorrect because you use V$BACKUP_ASYNC_IO and V$BACKUP_SYNC_IO to monitor the performance of RMAN jobs for asynchronous and synchronous I/O, respectively.

5. ☑ **B** and **D.** The view V$SESSION has two rows for each backup process, both of them with the value specified in the RMAN command SET COMMAND ID.

   ☒ **A, C,** and **E** are incorrect. **A** is incorrect because the values for CLIENT_INFO are in the incorrect order. **C** is incorrect because the actual RMAN command is not included in CLIENT_INFO. **E** is incorrect because CLIENT_INFO is, in fact, in the view V$SESSION.

6. ☑ **A, B, D, E,** and **F.** RMAN debugging information and other message output can be found in the Oracle server trace files, the RMAN trace file, the database alert log, output from the RMAN command itself, and the vendor-specific file sbtio.log (for tape libraries).

   ☒ **C** and **G** are incorrect. RMAN does not record any debugging or error information in the view V$PROCESS or in the table SYS.AUDIT$.

7. ☑ **D.** If you set BACKUP_TAPE_IO_SLAVES to TRUE, then RMAN allocates tape buffers from the shared pool unless the initialization parameter LARGE_POOL_SIZE is set, in which case RMAN allocates tape buffers from the large pool.

   ☒ **A, B,** and **C** are incorrect. The parameters JAVA_POOL_SIZE and PGA_AGGREGATE_TARGET have no effect on the location of the RMAN buffers.

8. ☑ **A, B, C,** and **D.** All of these options are potential bottlenecks.

   ☒ **E** is incorrect. The location of the RMAN data buffers is not a factor that can cause a bottleneck and reduce RMAN throughput.

9. ☑ **B.** Both FILESPERSET and MAXOPENFILES control the level of multiplexing during an RMAN backup operation.

   ☒ **A, C,** and **D** are incorrect. **A** is incorrect because MAXOPENFILES in the CONFIGURE command also controls the level of multiplexing, not just FILESPERSET. **C** is incorrect because FILESPERSET is not a valid option for the CONFIGURE command, and MAXOPENFILES is not a valid option for the BACKUP command. **D** is incorrect because MAXOPENFILES of the CONFIGURE command is not the only parameter that controls the level of multiplexing.

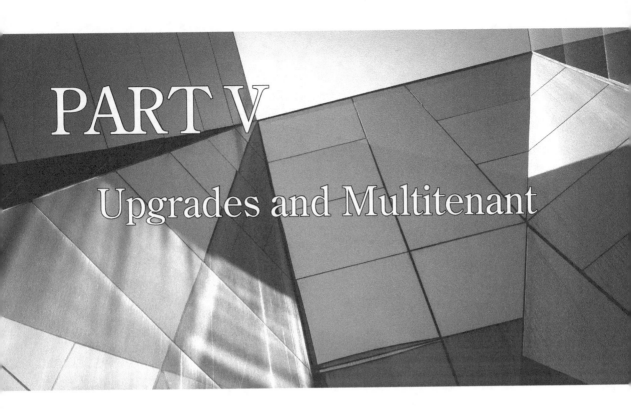

PART V

Upgrades and Multitenant

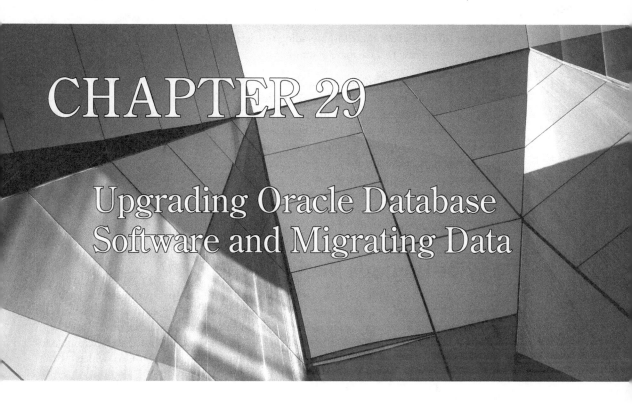

CHAPTER 29

Upgrading Oracle Database Software and Migrating Data

Exam Objectives

- 062.2.6.1   Describe Upgrade Methods
- 062.2.6.2   Describe Data Migration Methods
- 062.2.6.3   Describe the Upgrade Process
- 062.2.10.1 Migrating Data by Using Oracle Data Pump

This chapter covers the technique for upgrading the database software and migrating data from a database of one release to a database of another.

From release 11.2.*x*, the routine for upgrade is the same whether you are applying a patchset (to move from, for example, release 12.1.0.1 to release 12.1.0.2) or performing a major release upgrade (from, for example, 11.2.0.3 to 12.1.0.1). In either case, it is necessary to install a new Oracle Home. Before release 11.2.*x*, a major release required a new Oracle Home, but a patchset was applied to the existing Oracle Home. Now, only individual patches or patchset updates are applied, in place, to an existing home.

Having upgraded the database software, you must either upgrade the database itself or create a new database with the new software and move the data into it. Database upgrade is described in the following chapter. Data migration to a new database using the Data Pump utility is described in this chapter.

Describe Upgrade Methods

Moving from one release of the database to another involves two distinct processes: upgrading the database software and upgrading the database. The software and the database must always be at the same release level, except for the short period while the database is being upgraded. The software upgrade is accomplished with the Oracle Universal Installer (OUI). Then there are two options for the database upgrade: using the Database Upgrade Assistant (DBUA), which automates most of the steps, and performing all the steps manually.

Software Upgrade

Oracle products have a multifaceted release number, with five elements:

- Major release number
- Database maintenance release number
- Application server release number (always zero for a database)
- Component-specific release number
- Platform-specific release number

To determine the release of your database, query the V$VERSION view. Within the database, it is possible for some installed components to be at different releases. To determine what is installed at what release, query the DBA_REGISTRY view. Figure 29-1 shows these queries on a database running on 64-bit Windows.

In the figure, the database release is 12.1.0.1.0, which was the first 12*c* production version, specifically, release 12, the first maintenance release. The fourth digit indicates the patchset. Patchset 1 is included in the first production release (the final beta release, used for developing much of this book, was 12.1.0.0.0). The second query in the figure shows that all the components installed in the database are also at release 12.1.0.1.0, with the exception of Application Express (APEX). APEX has its own upgrade routine, and the release of APEX is largely independent of the release of the database.

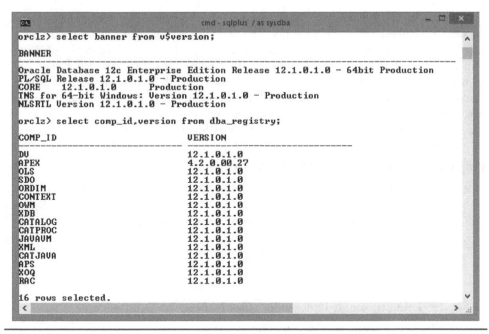

Figure 29-1   Determining the release of the database

 TIP   Terms such as 12c and 11g are pretty meaningless in a technical context; they are little more than marketing labels. You will find that professional DBAs always identify their version with the release number to four decimals.

The method for software upgrade is to use the OUI. A patchset (identified by the fourth element of the release number) of the database is delivered as a self-contained installable image that includes a copy of OUI that is appropriate for the patchset. Launch OUI by running the runInstaller.sh script (Linux) or the setup.exe file (Windows) that is included with the patchset, and follow exactly the installation routine detailed in Chapter 1. The software must be installed into a newly created Oracle Home. OUI will prompt for the location. Best practice is to create the new home beneath the Oracle Base directory, next to the existing Oracle Home. To start using the newly installed version of the software, adjust your ORACLE_HOME and PATH environment variables to point to the new home. Then create (or upgrade) a database.

 EXAM TIP   It is not necessary to install a base release of the product before installing a patchset. Patchsets are complete installlable software images.

When using OUI to install an Oracle database home (whether a base release or a patchset), the OUI will detect all previous installations. It can do this by reading the content of the OUI Inventory, which will have been created during the first installation. If OUI detects a previous installation, it will prompt for whether any existing databases should be upgraded. Should you answer "yes," following the installation OUI will launch the DBUA to perform these database upgrades. Alternatively, you can answer "no" and run the DBUA later. This approach means that you can separate the tasks of software upgrade and database upgrade. It also means that you can upgrade databases manually, by running scripts, rather than using the DBUA.

Database Upgrade: DBUA or Manual

DBUA can be launched by the OUI or as a stand-alone tool at any time. It is a graphical interface that guides you through the database upgrade process, although it can also be driven through a command-line interface, in which case no prompts need be answered.

The DBUA functionality is as follows:

- Automates the entire process
- Supports single-instance and clustered environments
- Upgrades databases and Automatic Storage Management (ASM) storage
- Checks and (where possible) fixes prerequisites
- Logs errors and generates a Hypertext Markup Language (HTML) report of the upgrade process

Using the DBUA is undoubtedly the easiest way to upgrade and is less prone to error than a manual technique. But it is not always appropriate. For example, if downtime is critical, it may be faster to upgrade manually. DBUA generally does all steps sequentially, many of them while the database is not available for use. A manual upgrade may be able to perform some steps in parallel and others either before or after the essential downtime period.

A manual upgrade will typically involve these tasks:

- Space check of the SYSTEM and SYSAUX tablespaces
- Adjust newly obsoleted or deprecated parameters
- Run scripts to upgrade the data dictionary and installed components
- Recompile all stored code

Whether you are using DBUA or a manual method, direct upgrade to 12.1 is possible from these releases:

- 10.2.0.5 (the terminal release of 10g)
- 11.1.0.7 (the terminal release of 11g R1)
- 11.2.0.2 or later

All other releases must be upgraded to one of those listed before you upgrade to 12.1.

Describe Data Migration Methods

A database upgrade has two major restrictions. First, it must be performed on the same platform. You cannot move from, for example, Windows to AIX during an upgrade. Second, you cannot carry out any form of reorganization or implementation of new features during the upgrade. After it has completed, nothing has really changed beyond the fact that you are running the database off new binaries. Data migration gets around both these limitations.

A migration is the process of transferring data from one database into another. In the context of upgrade, this means creating a new database of the new release and copying the entire user dataset from the old database into the new. The new database can be configured, in advance, with all the new features enabled that you want to use. Then as the data is inserted, it will take on the characteristics of the new release. Furthermore, the new database can be on a different platform. The downside of data migration as an upgrade technique is the necessary downtime. An upgrade of a database with DBUA might involve downtime of less than an hour; a migration could take hours or even days, depending on the volume of data to be moved.

TIP   Many DBAs prefer migration to upgrade because it results in a new, "clean" data dictionary, with no rubbish left behind by years of (ab)use.

Data migration is usually accomplished with the Data Pump export/import utility. Particular advantages are as follows:

- Data Pump can work across platforms.
- Source and destination character sets need not be the same.
- The source can be any release from 10.0 upward.
- It is not necessary to transfer the entire database if only a subset is needed.
- Data segments will be reorganized as part of the process.

If the migration is from a pre-10*g* database, it can still be accomplished from any release by using the legacy exp/imp utilities.

Describe the Upgrade Process

Database upgrade is an operation that is fraught with peril. Theoretically, an upgrade can do nothing but good, but there is always the possibility that the behavior of the applications using the database will change. For that reason, testing is vital. There are typically six steps to an upgrade:

1. Prepare to upgrade. Choose an upgrade method, install the new Oracle Home, develop a test plan, and determine what new features to implement.

2. Upgrade a test database. Test the upgrade process on a nonproduction clone of the database. In particular, note the necessary downtime.

3. Test the upgraded database. Complete the planned tests. In particular, ensure that performance has not regressed. Iterate steps 2 and 3 as necessary until all issues are resolved.

4. Prepare the production database. Stop all user activity according to an agreed schedule for downtime and then take a full backup.

5. Upgrade the production database. Follow the tried-and-tested upgrade procedure. Take a full backup after completion. The downtime will now be over.

6. Tune the upgraded database. As the system comes back into use, monitor performance and carry out normal proactive and reactive tuning work.

Migrate Data by Using Oracle Data Pump

The use of Data Pump for transferring individual tables, schemas, and various object types between databases was discussed in Chapter 17. Data Pump can also be used to copy an entire database; all user objects can be read from one database and created in another. Because the objects are represented in a Data Pump dump file logically rather than physically, there is no reason why they cannot be read from a database of one release on one platform and written into a database of another release, possibly on another platform. Thus, the database can (in effect) be upgraded by the export/import process. It is possible to downgrade through the same technique, but only if the objects in the source database do not require any features that are not available in the destination.

If the new database is configured with various features enabled, the data will take on these features during the import. If run completely on defaults, a full import will create tablespaces, schemas, and objects as they were in the source before inserting data—but they can be pre-created. For example, the tablespaces in the source database might be using the old storage mechanisms of dictionary-managed extents and freelist-managed segments; the destination tablespaces would be created, in advance, with the current defaults of local extent management and automatic segment space management.

One issue with using Data Pump for upgrade is the space requirement. A large database will require a great deal of space for the dump files generated by the export. Furthermore, if the upgrade is to a destination database on a different machine, the dump will have to be copied to the remote machine—where the same amount of space will be required again. There is also a time penalty; the export must complete before the copy can begin, and the copy must complete before the import can begin. A *network mode* import avoids both the space and the time issues.

To use the network mode of Data Pump, a database link must exist from the destination database to the source database. This link must connect to a user with the DATAPUMP_EXP_FULL_DATABASE role. Then, running the import on the destination database (as a user with the DATAPUMP_IMP_FULL_DATABASE role) will launch worker processes on the source database that read the data and write it through the database link to the destination database, where more worker processes write the data to the database. This mechanism avoids the need to stage the data on disk as a dump file and also means that the export, the copy, and the import all run concurrently. Figure 29-2 shows the initiation of this operation.

In Figure 29-2, the user is connected to a database named orclb. This is a release 12.1.0.1 database. The database link orcla connects to an 11.2.0.3 database. Then the impdp command starts a job that will perform a complete migration of all user data from orcla into orclb, through the database link. Schemas and tablespaces will be created as they were in the source database, although they can be pre-created with appropriate characteristics if desired. During the import there will be many messages of the form "ORA-31684: Object ... already exists" as the import

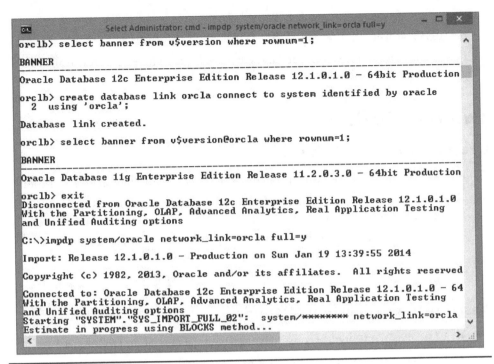

Figure 29-2 Launching a full import in network mode

encounters objects that are part of Oracle's seeded schemas. These can safely be ignored. The end result will be a complete migration of all user data.

 TIP A network mode export/import cannot use the direct path; the reading and writing of tables must go through the database buffer cache, using the eternal table path. This may mean that it is not as fast as one might expect.

Exercise 29-1: Perform a Data Pump Full Database Migration

In this exercise, you will simulate a data migration from one database to another. It is assumed that the source database is a database created from the General Purpose template, with the sample schemas installed.

1. Create a full export of the database, using the default DATA_PUMP_DIR directory.

   ```
   expdp system/oracle full=y dumpfile=full_exp.dmp
   ```

2. Drop any tablespaces and schemas that hold user data. These commands will be needed:

   ```
   drop tablespace users including contents and datafiles;
   drop tablespace example including contents and datafiles;
   drop user scott cascade;
   drop user hr cascade;
   drop user sh cascade;
   drop user oe cascade;
   drop user pm cascade;
   drop user ix cascade;
   ```

   At this point, you have a database that is devoid of user data.

3. Import the user data into the database.

```
impdp system/oracle full=y dumpfile=full_exp.dmp
```

4. Confirm that the tablespaces and users dropped in step 2 have been created and that the schemas are populated with tables and other objects.

Two-Minute Drill

Describe Upgrade Methods

- The Database Upgrade Assistant automates the upgrade and all before and after checks.
- A manual upgrade gives the DBA full control of all steps, which is a more complex process but possibly faster.
- An upgrade is an in-place operation; it is not possible to change platform, physical location, character set, or indeed anything except the release.
- Upgrade is possible only from a defined list of previous releases.

Describe Data Migration Methods

- A Data Pump migration exports from one database and imports into another.
- A migration can go across platforms as well as releases.
- The source database can be any release from 10.0 onward.
- A network mode import obviates the need to stage a dump file on disk.

Describe the Upgrade Process

- A new Oracle Home, of the new release, must be installed with the OUI.
- Determine whether to use DBUA or a manual upgrade.
- Design and implement a test plan.
- Perform the production upgrade.
- Verify the success of the operation.

Migrate Data by Using Oracle Data Pump

- A new Oracle Home, of the new release, must be installed with the OUI.
- Create a new database.
- Create any objects that you want to configure (such as tablespaces).
- Perform a full export of the source database.
- Transfer the dump file to the destination database.

- Import the dump file.
- Redirect users to the new database.

Self Test

1. What can be accomplished during an upgrade when using the Database Upgrade Assistant? (Choose two answers.)

    A. Conversion from a legacy character set to Unicode

    B. Direct upgrade from any release of 11*g* to 12*c*

    C. Direct upgrade from the terminal release of 10*g* to 12*c*

    D. Verification of prerequisite conditions

2. What considerations are needed for space usage during an upgrade? (Choose the best answer.)

    A. None: an upgrade is an in-place operation and requires no significant additional storage.

    B. It is possible that the SYSTEM and SYSAUX tablespaces will expand during an upgrade.

    C. Up to double the space needed for data will be needed during the upgrade.

    D. No archivelogs will be generated because an upgrade is not recoverable and no redo is generated.

3. Which of the following can be accomplished with a Data Pump migration? (Choose all correct answers.)

    A. Upgrade from any release of 10*g* or 11*g*

    B. Character set conversion

    C. A move from a 32-bit to a 64-bit platform

    D. Direct upgrade from the terminal release of 9*i*

4. Which of these correctly describes a network mode Data Pump operation? (Choose the best answer.)

    A. Create database links in both the source and destination databases, and run expdp on the source and impdp on the destination.

    B. Create a database link in the source pointing to the destination, and run expdp on the source.

    C. Create a database link in the destination pointing to the source, and run impdp on the destination.

    D. Run expdp in the source, writing a dump file to a pipe, and run impdp on the destination, reading the dump file from the pipe.

5. What does the Database Upgrade Assistant upgrade? (Choose the best answer.)

   A. Oracle database software and databases

   B. Oracle database software

   C. Oracle databases

   D. User data storage structures and user data logical attributes

6. Under which circumstance must a Data Pump export be performed when carrying out a database migration? (Choose the best answer.)

   A. The database must be open read-only.

   B. The database must be in mount mode.

   C. The database must have restricted session enabled.

   D. The database must be open.

7. If a full database import operation attempts to import objects into a tablespace that does not exist, what will happen? (Choose the best answer.)

   A. The tablespace must be pre-created, or the operation will fail.

   B. The tablespace will be created if Oracle Managed Files has been enabled in the destination database.

   C. The import will succeed if the tablespace is specified with the TABLESPACES parameter.

   D. The objects will be imported into the database's default permanent tablespace.

Self Test Answers

1. ☑ **C** and **D**. Direct upgrade is possible from the terminal release of 10g but not from earlier releases. The DBUA runs verification scripts before and after the upgrade.
   ☒ **A** and **B** are incorrect. **A** is incorrect because character set conversion is not part of DBUA's functionality; you must use other utilities for this. **B** is incorrect because direct upgrade from 11g is possible only for the terminal release of 11.1 or any release from 11.2.0.2.

2. ☑ **B**. It is usual for data dictionary objects to increase in size as a result of an upgrade (Oracle keeps getting bigger...).
   ☒ **A**, **C**, and **D** are incorrect. **A** is incorrect because space will often be required for data dictionary objects. **C** is incorrect because user data is not affected by an upgrade. The changes are usually limited to metadata. **D** is incorrect because an upgrade involves executing a large number of DML and DDL queries against the data dictionary, which does generate redo.

3. ☑ **A**, **B**, and **C**. Data Pump is compatible across all versions that support it, from 10.0 onward. It can move data across any supported platforms, performing character set conversion as it does so.

☒ **D** is incorrect. This is incorrect because Data Pump was introduced with release 10*g*. To migrate from 9*i*, you must use the legacy exp/imp utilities.

4. ☑ **C.** A network mode import is initiated by impdp, although worker processes will run at both the source and the destination.

☒ **A, B,** and **D** are incorrect. **A** and **B** are incorrect because a network mode operation is managed from the destination only. **D** is incorrect because it is not possible to import a dump file until it has been completed. The technique described does, however, function with the legacy imp/exp utilities.

5. ☑ **C.** The DBUA upgrades databases—and nothing else.

☒ **A, B,** and **D** are incorrect. **A** and **B** are incorrect because the software must be upgraded with the OUI, not the DBUA. **D** is incorrect because restructuring storage and objects is a task that must be done after the upgrade, not during the upgrade.

6. ☑ **D.** The export is a perfectly normal export operation with no special requirements.

☒ **A, B,** and **C** are incorrect. **A** and **B** are incorrect because the database must be open read-write; otherwise, it is not possible for Data Pump to create its master table. **C** is incorrect because although restricted mode might be a good idea, it is not a requirement.

7. ☑ **B.** If Oracle Managed Files (OMF) has been enabled, tablespaces will be created accordingly.

☒ **A, C,** and **D** are incorrect. **A** is incorrect because the import will attempt to create the tablespace, using either OMF or the datafile definition from the source database. **C** is incorrect because the TABLESPACES parameter identifies a list of tablespaces to import; it is not relevant for a full import. **D** is incorrect because if a suitable tablespace neither exists nor can be created, there will be an error.

PART V

CHAPTER 30

Upgrading an Oracle Database

Exam Objectives

- 062.2.7.1   Describe Upgrade Requirements When Certain Features or Options Are Used in Oracle Database
- 062.2.7.2   Use the Pre-Upgrade Information Tool Before Performing an Upgrade
- 062.2.7.3   Prepare the New Oracle Home Prior to Performing an Upgrade
- 062.2.8.1   Upgrade the Database to Oracle Database 12c by Using the Database Upgrade Assistant (DBUA)
- 062.2.8.2   Perform a Manual Upgrade to Oracle Database 12c by Using Scripts and Tools
- 062.2.9.1   Migrate to Unified Auditing
- 062.2.9.2   Perform Post-Upgrade Tasks

This chapter describes the process of upgrading an Oracle database. This could be an upgrade to a new major release (such as from 11.2.0.4 to 12.1.0.1) or could be applying a patchset update within a release (such as from 12.1.0.1 to 12.1.0.2). Either way, the principle is the same. Assuming that the software has already been upgraded (by using the Oracle Universal Installer [OUI] to create a new Oracle Home), certain steps must be followed before, during, and after the upgrade process.

Describe Upgrade Requirements when Certain Features or Options Are Used in Oracle Database

An upgrade involves running scripts against the data dictionary that will upgrade various database features and options. Depending on what options have been installed and configured, some preparatory work may be needed.

Oracle Label Security and Oracle Data Vault

These options are beyond the scope of the Oracle Certified Professional (OCP) curriculum, but their impact on upgrade may be tested. In summary, Oracle Label Security (OLS) is a technique for filtering access by users to rows. This is in addition to the usual mechanism of privileges. Two users may have the same SELECT or Data Manipulation Language (DML) privileges on a table, but even though they run identical SQL statements, they will see a different subset of the table. The filtering is based on session attributes over which the users have no control, and they will not be aware that the filtering has occurred.

Oracle Data Vault adds another layer to Oracle's privilege and role model. Users can be placed in groups, and policies can be designed that control groups' access to user objects even though they may have the requisite privilege. These policies apply to all users, including those with the SYSDBA privilege. This is the only way to limit access to data by the otherwise all-powerful database administrators.

To determine whether either OLS or Data Vault has been installed in the database, run this query:

```
select * from v$option where parameter in
('Oracle Database Vault','Oracle Label Security');
```

If either option is installed, then it is possible that the SYS.AUD$ table will need to be relocated. A script is provided in the new 12.x Oracle Home to accomplish this:

```
ORACLE_HOME/rdbms/admin/olspreupgrade.sql
```

The script is well documented and includes precise instructions on what to do if either OLS or Data Vault or both are installed, with variations depending on the exact release of the database to be upgraded. Copy the script from the newly installed 12.x Oracle Home to the Oracle Home currently in use, study the instructions in the script, and then run it while connected as SYSDBA.

Oracle Warehouse Builder

Oracle Warehouse Builder (OWB) is a graphical tool for designing, building, managing, and maintaining data integration processes in business intelligence systems. It is beyond the scope of the OCP curriculum. OWB is not shipped with the 12c database; therefore, if it is installed in the database to be upgraded, the upgrade routine will not upgrade it, and it will no longer be usable. It is, however, possible for a 12c database to interoperate with a separate release 11.2.0.3 (nothing earlier) OWB installation. There are three techniques for this:

- Give the upgraded 12c database access to an existing stand-alone (that is, not installed as part of an 11g database) OWB installation.

- Retain an already configured OWB installation in an 11g database running off the 11g Oracle Home, and continue to use this.

- Configure a new stand-alone OWB installation.

All these methods come down to the same thing: you can no longer use OWB in the database after upgrade and must therefore provide an OWB installation external to the upgraded database.

To determine whether OWB is installed in the database, run this query:

```
select comp_name,version,status from dba_registry
where comp_id='OWB';
```

Use the Pre-Upgrade Information Tool Before Performing an Upgrade

Following the installation of the new 12c database Oracle Home, you will have access to the Pre-Upgrade Information Tool. This is a script, preupgrd.sql, installed into the ORACLE_HOME/rdbms/admin directory. Run this script against the database to be upgraded. It will generate a report detailing any issues, as well as a "fix-up" script that will fix some issues; other issues will have to be addressed manually.

Figure 30-1 shows an example of running this script on a Windows database.

In the figure, the database is currently at release 11.2.0.3. The script is run from the newly installed (but not yet used) 12c Oracle Home. It produces three files, generated in a directory (cfgtoollogs\<db_name>\preupgrade) below the Oracle Base directory:

- preupgrade.log details all the checks that were run with advice on items that should be addressed.

- preupgrade_fixups.sql contains commands that should be run in the database before commencing the upgrade to fix any problems.

- postupgrade_fixups.sql contains commands that should be run in the database after the upgrade has completed.

The log file and the scripts should be studied with care; they give information and instructions that may make the upgrade run more smoothly.

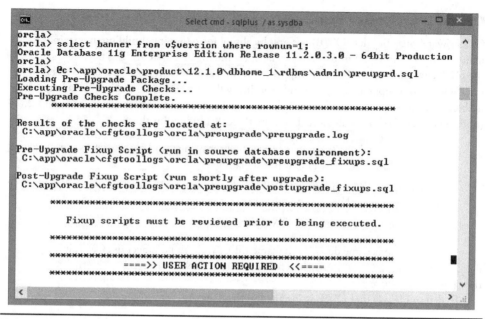

Figure 30-1   Running the Pre-Upgrade Information Tool

Prepare the New Oracle Home Prior to Performing an Upgrade

The new Oracle Home must be installed, using the OUI. This installation (either interactive or a silent install driven by a response file) should be a software-only install, as shown in Figure 30-2.

Do not take the option to create a database. It is possible to select the option to upgrade an existing database. This will chain the software install to a run of the Database Upgrade Assistant (DBUA). There is nothing wrong with this in theory, but most database administrators (DBAs) will want to separate these two processes in order to take the time to run the Pre-Upgrade Information Tool manually and consider thoroughly its advice. There is also the issue of downtime. Doing the install plus upgrade in one operation will usually involve a longer period of downtime than separating these actions.

At this point, consider the database listener. If you are using a database listener running from a Grid Infrastructure (GI) home, no further action is needed. A GI listener can support connections to any release of the database. But if your database listener is running off the database Oracle Home, you will want to shut down the listener running off the old Oracle

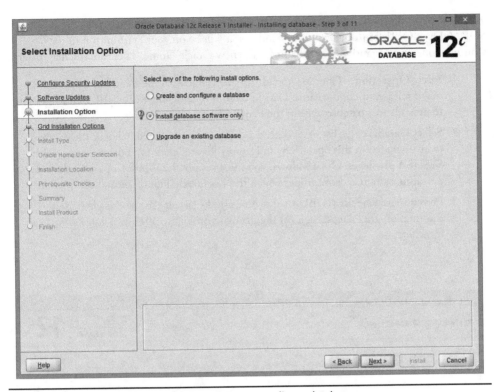

Figure 30-2   Installing an Oracle Home prior to upgrading a database

Home and replace it with a listener from the new Oracle Home. This listener upgrade need not be related to the database upgrade and can be carried out before or after. The process is to copy the Oracle Net configuration files from the old home to the new and make any edits that may be necessary to entries that include directory paths.

Upgrade the Database to Oracle Database 12c by Using the Database Upgrade Assistant

The DBUA is a guided wizard that automates the process of configuring an existing database to run with the new release of the software. It can also be run noninteractively by a single statement supplied with appropriate command-line arguments that answer all the questions.

For an interactive upgrade, in a graphical terminal connect to the newly installed release 12c Oracle Home by setting the ORACLE_BASE, ORACLE_HOME, and PATH

872

variables appropriately. Then launch the DBUA executable. On Linux, this is the file $ORACLE_HOME/bin/dbua, and on Windows, it will be on your Start button in the Configuration and Migration Tools menu for the new Oracle Home. These are the major steps:

1. **Select Operation** Choose Upgrade Oracle Database to upgrade from a previous major release, or choose Move Database From A Different Release 12.1 Oracle Home to upgrade to a patchset within the major release.

2. **Select Database** A list of all detected databases is presented. Choose the database to be upgraded in this operation, and supply logon details for a database user with SYSDBA privileges. On Windows, you must supply the Windows password for the operating system account under which the 12c Oracle Home is installed.

3. **Prerequisite Checks** DBUA runs some checks (similar to the Pre-Upgrade Information Tool checks) against the database. In Figure 30-3, two issues have been identified.

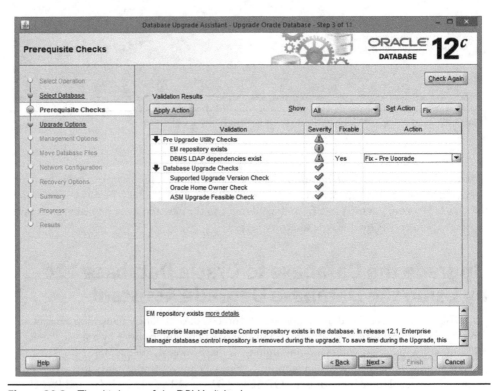

Figure 30-3 The third step of the DBUA dialog box

The first issue shown in Figure 30-3 is informative. DBUA has detected that Enterprise Manager Database Control (the management facility shipped with release 10*g* and 11*g* databases) is installed. This will be removed during the upgrade. The second issue is that the database has been configured to work with a Lightweight Directory Access Protocol (LDAP) directory, and some adjustments to this will be needed. DBUA can do this during the upgrade, or it can be ignored for now and dealt with later.

4. **Upgrade Options**   There are some choices that give a limited amount of control over the upgrade process and how long it will take. The defaults are usually correct. The following are choices to consider:

   - **Select Upgrade Parallelism**   The default is based on the number of central processing units (CPUs) detected. You might think it is too high and would flood the machine with work or that it's too low and that a higher value would push the upgrade through faster.

   - **Recompile Invalid Objects During Post Upgrade, Recompilation Parallelism** Allowing DBUA to recompile during the upgrade will make the operation comprehensive but will also delay the postupgrade restart. You may want to recompile manually afterward instead.

   - **Upgrade Timezone Data**   Depending on what is already installed, you may need to update the database's time zone files, either as part of the upgrade or later.

   - **Gather Statistics Before Upgrade**   If you have already gathered statistics for the database, this will not be necessary.

5. **Management Options**   Select whether to configure the database with Database Express (default), to register it with Cloud Control, or neither.

6. **Move Database Files**   DBUA can physically relocate the database and the Fast Recovery Area during the upgrade. This could be useful if, for example, you want to take the opportunity to convert from file system storage to Automatic Storage Management (ASM) storage. It will, of course, increase the duration of the operation significantly.

7. **Network Configuration**   This is a prompt for registering the database with an LDAP directory and with a database listener.

8. **Recovery Options**   Should DBUA perform a full offline backup before upgrading? The default is Yes, but if you already have a backup, considerable time can be saved by disallowing this.

9. **Summary**   This is a description of what will be done.

10. **Progress**   This is a display of what is happening, updated as the upgrade proceeds.

Following completion, DBUA will display the result, as shown in Figure 30-4.

The Results screen may give some instructions (such as that regarding time zone files, as shown in Figure 30-4), as well as the status of the upgrade. Follow them, as well as any steps advised by the Pre-Upgrade Information Tool.

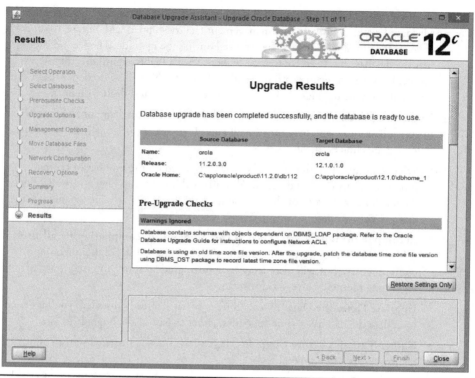

Figure 30-4   The completion of a DBUA upgrade exercise

Perform a Manual Upgrade to Oracle Database 12c by Using Scripts and Tools

A manual upgrade is perhaps a little more work than using DBUA, but it does give more control to the DBA. These are the steps to follow:

1. While connected to the old Oracle Home and with the database open, log on to the database and run the Pre-Upgrade Information Tool provided with the new software. Study the log file and scripts it generates and take any appropriate action.

2. Back up the source database.

3. Prepare the newly installed Oracle Home. Copy the password file and the instance parameter file into the new Oracle Home. If any parameters need to be adjusted (the Pre-Upgrade Information Tool will have informed you of this), make the adjustments first, using the SCOPE=SPFILE clause of ALTER SYSTEM.

4. Shut down the source database.

   On Windows, it is necessary to remove the old Windows service under which the database runs and to create a new one. For example, for the database named ORCLA, run these commands from the old Oracle Home:

   ```
   net stop OracleServiceORCLA
   oradim -delete -sid ORCLA
   ```

   Run this command from the new Oracle Home:

   ```
   oradim -new -sid ORCLA
   ```

5. Set your environment to connect to the new Oracle Home and open the database with SQL*Plus. Use the command STARTUP UPGRADE. The UPGRADE mode disables logons that do not use the SYSDBA privilege, disables system triggers, and, most importantly, permits connections to a database that has a data dictionary in an indeterminate state: neither one release nor another.

6. Execute the parallel upgrade script, which is provided in the ORACLE_HOME/ rdbms/admin directory. This is a Perl script that invokes parallelism to reduce the necessary downtime. A suitable Perl interpreter is provided in the Oracle Home. Here is the code for Windows:

   ```
   cd %ORACLE_HOME%\rdbms\admin
   %ORACLE_HOME%\perl\bin\perl catctl.pl catupgrd.sql
   ```

   Here is the code for Linux:

   ```
   cd $ORACLE_HOME/rdbms/admin
   $ORACLE_HOME/perl/bin/perl catctl.pl catupgrd.sql
   ```

7. The parallel upgrade script finishes by shutting down the database. Open it as normal.

8. Run the Post-Upgrade Status Tool to generate a summary of the result of the upgrade exercise. If it shows any errors or any components as not VALID, take appropriate action. To run the tool, execute the script utlu121s.sql.

   ```
   SQL> @?/rdbms/admin/utlu121s.sql
   ```

9. Run scripts to complete the postupgrade operations. The catuppst.sql script attempts to fix any problems encountered by the upgrade, and the ultrp.sql script recompiles all invalid PL/SQL. Here is a Linux example:

   ```
   SQL> @?/rdbms/admin/ctuppst.sql
   SQL> @?/rdbms/admin/utlrp.sql
   ```

   Re-run the Post-Upgrade Status Tool to ensure that there are no remaining issues.

Migrate to Unified Auditing

Chapter 16 covered how to configure and enable unified audit. Here is a summary:

- By default, the 12*c* unified audit facility is not enabled.

- All previous auditing (standard audit, fine-grained audit, and component-specific audit) will continue to function unchanged in the upgraded database.

- Grant the AUDIT_ADMIN and AUDIT_VIEWER roles as necessary.

- Configure unified audit policies that match the existing audit regime.

- During a period of downtime, enable unified audit. On Linux, relink the executables; on Windows, copy in the appropriate dynamic link library.

Perform Postupgrade Tasks

In addition to the steps identified by the Pre-Upgrade Information Tool and documented in the postupgrade_fixups.sql script, various actions may or may not be necessary depending on the environment and whether the upgrade was manual or done with DBUA. All these items should, however, be considered:

- Update environment variables in all relevant scripts. Critical variables are ORACLE_HOME, PATH, and ORACLE_SID.

- On Linux, update the /etc/oratab file.

- On Windows, check all registry settings for the database.

- If a Recovery Manager (RMAN) catalog database is in use, connect with the RMAN executable and upgrade the catalog (it is not necessary to upgrade the catalog database itself).

- If Database Express has been installed as part of the upgrade, confirm and (if necessary) configure its listening ports. The routine for this is as follows:

```
select dbms_xdb_config.gethttpport from dual;
select dbms_xdb_config.gethttpsport from dual;
execute dbms_xdb_config.sethttpport(<your desired port>)
execute dbms_xdb_config.sethttpsport(<your desired port>)
```

- Enable the Database Vault (if installed).

```
execute dvsys.dbms_macadm.enable_dv
```

- Reset all passwords. If the upgrade is from release 10.x, all passwords should be changed to take on the password attributes of the current release.

- Set thresholds for tablespace usage alerts. Tablespace alerts are disabled by the upgrade and will need to be reestablished.

- Implement new features as appropriate.

Exercise 30-1: Simulate Some Upgrade Tasks For this exercise, it is assumed that there is not, in fact, a database that needs to be upgraded. It is, however, possible to run some of the tasks that would be required.

1. Determine what components are installed in the database.

```
select comp_name,version,status from dba_registry;
```

2. Run the Pre-Upgrade Information Tool.

```
SQL> @?/rdbms/admin/preupgrd.sql
```

Study the output and the files generated. These are the log file preupgrade.log and the fix-up scripts preupgrade_fixups.sql and postupgrade_fixups.sql.

3. Open the database in UPGRADE mode, confirm this, and attempt to connect as a non-SYSDBA user. Restart the database. Use commands such as these:

```
connect / as sysdba
shutdown immediate
startup upgrade
select status from v$instance;
connect scott/tiger
connect / as sysdba
startup force
```

4. From a command prompt, display all the options for running DBUA.

```
dbua -help
```

Observe the wide range of options that can be applied when running DBUA—many more than are prompted for when running it interactively.

5. Run the script to identify and recompile all invalid objects.

```
@?/rdbms/admin/utlrp.sql
```

Study the output of the script.

Two-Minute Drill

Describe Upgrade Requirements when Certain Features or Options Are Used in Oracle Database

- Installed components, their version, and status are listed in the DBA_REGISTRY view.
- Some components (such as APEX) have their own upgrade mechanisms; others (such as Oracle Warehouse Builder, Label Security, and Data Vault) have particular requirements.

Use the Pre-Upgrade Information Tool Before Performing an Upgrade

- The Pre-Upgrade Information Tool is a SQL script provided with the new software that is run while still using the previous release.
- The tool inspects the database and generates a report that describes the necessary actions and provides fix-up scripts with commands to be run before and after the upgrade.

Prepare the New Oracle Home Prior to Performing an Upgrade

- The new Oracle Home must be instantiated before you upgrade the database.
- If performing a manual upgrade, you must copy certain configuration files (such as the instance parameter file and the password file) to the new home.

PART V

Upgrade the Database to Oracle Database 12c by Using the Database Upgrade Assistant

- The DBUA is run from the new Oracle Home and automates the entire upgrade process.
- DBUA can be run interactively, or for silent upgrade, it can be executed from the command line with arguments that replace the dialog box.

Perform a Manual Upgrade to Oracle Database 12c by Using Scripts and Tools

- A manual upgrade follows the same steps as the DBUA, but they are invoked individually from the command line.

Migrate to Unified Auditing

- Following upgrade to 12c, unified auditing is not enabled.
- To enable unified auditing, configure appropriate audit policies and then relink the Oracle executable.

Perform Post-Upgrade Tasks

- The Pre-Upgrade Information Tool (run either manually or by DBUA) will have generated instructions on necessary post-upgrade tasks.
- Optional (but advisable) post-upgrade tasks include gathering statistics for the database and recompiling all invalid objects.
- Bringing new features into use is a step that can be done at any time after the upgrade.

Self Test

1. Which of these components is no longer available in the database following an upgrade to 12c? (Choose the best answer.)

   A. Data Vault

   B. Oracle Label Security

   C. Oracle Warehouse Builder

   D. Standard database auditing

2. Before running the Pre-Upgrade Information Tool, preupgrd.sql, how should you start the database? (Choose the best answer.)

   A. Start the database with STARTUP UPGRADE from the old Oracle Home.

   B. Start the database with STARTUP OPEN from the old Oracle Home.

   C. Start the database with STARTUP UPGRADE from the new Oracle Home.

   D. Start the database with STARTUP OPEN from the new Oracle Home.

3. What is the output of the Pre-Upgrade Information Tool, preupgrd.sql? (Choose the best answer.)

   A. Fix-up scripts with commands to be run before and after upgrade

   B. Scripts to run during the upgrade

   C. Instructions for how to run the upgrade

   D. The script prompts for what reports and scripts should be generated

4. When you are upgrading a database manually, what files would usually be copied from the old Oracle Home to the new? (Choose all correct answers.)

   A. Database controlfile

   B. Instance parameter file

   C. Password file

   D. Time zone files

   E. The AUDIT_FILE_DEST directory

5. What is the correct method for using the DBUA? (Choose the best answer.)

   A. Start the database in UPGRADE mode from the new Oracle Home and then run DBUA from the new Oracle Home.

   B. Start the database in UPGRADE mode from the old Oracle Home and then run DBUA from the new Oracle Home.

   C. Start the database in OPEN mode from the old Oracle Home and then run DBUA from the new Oracle Home.

   D. Shut down the database and then run DBUA from the new Oracle Home.

6. To minimize downtime for your users, which of these operations can be carried out while the database is open for use? (Choose all correct answers.)

   A. The backup before starting the upgrade

   B. Running the Pre-Upgrade Information Tool, the script preupgrd.sql

   C. Running the catctl.pl Perl script that parallelizes the upgrade process

   D. Recompiling all invalid PL/SQL after upgrade

   E. Gathering statistics on the data dictionary after upgrade

   F. Running the Post-Upgrade Status Tool, the utlu121s.sql script

7. You are performing a manual upgrade of a database and have opened the database in UPGRADE mode. If a user attempts to connect to the database at this time, what will be the result? (Choose the best answer.)

   A. The connection will succeed but may compromise the success of the upgrade.

   B. The connection will succeed, but all DML and Data Definition Language (DDL) will be blocked.

   C. The connection will fail because the database listener will not spawn sessions against a database in UPGRADE mode.

   D. The connection will fail unless the user has the SYSDBA privilege.

PART V

8. What options do you have following the 12c upgrade, if you have configured both standard audit and fine-grained audit in the source 11g database? (Choose the best answer.)

  A. You must disable both standard and fine-grained audit before the upgrade and configure unified audit after the upgrade.

  B. After upgrade, you can enable unified audit and leave the standard and fine-grained audit running in parallel for a while to ensure that the results are the same.

  C. After upgrade, the standard audit and fine-grained audit will continue to run until you enable unified audit, at which time they will cease to function.

  D. After upgrade, you can migrate first the standard audit to unified auditing and then the fine-grained audit to unified auditing.

9. Some of the post-upgrade tasks are time consuming, and you may want to perform them after opening the database for use. If you choose to open the database for use before recompiling invalid PL/SQL with the utlrp.sql script, what may result? (Choose the best answer.)

  A. The database will not open if any of the SYS-owned supplied PL/SQL packages are invalid.

  B. The database will open, but if any users attempt to use invalid PL/SQL that has not yet been recompiled, they will receive errors.

  C. The database will open, but if any users attempt to use invalid PL/SQL that has not yet been recompiled, it will be compiled automatically.

  D. The database will open, but if any users attempt to use invalid PL/SQL that has not yet been recompiled, it will run in interpreted mode rather than native mode.

10. Following a successful upgrade with the DBUA, you find that remote users can no longer connect to the database. What might be the problem? (Choose two correct answers.)

  A. You are running your database listener off the Grid Infrastructure home, and it must be reconfigured to point to the new release of the database.

  B. You have shut down the database listener running off the old home and have not started a listener from the new home.

  C. You have omitted copying the tnsnames.ora file from the old home to the new home.

  D. You have omitted copying the password file from the old home to the new home.

  E. You did not restart the database after the upgrade.

Self Test Answers

1. ☑   **C.** Following an upgrade, Oracle Warehouse Builder can still be used, but it must be installed externally.

☒   **A, B,** and **D** are incorrect. **A** and **B** are incorrect because although Data Vault and OLS have special requirements for upgrade, they are still available. **D** is incorrect because standard auditing is enabled after upgrade, although you may want to convert to unified auditing instead.

2. ☑   **B.** The tool is supplied with the new Oracle Home but run against a database opened from the old Oracle Home.

☒   **A, C,** and **D** are incorrect. **A** and **C** are incorrect because STARTUP UPGRADE (from the new Oracle Home) is used for the upgrade itself, not the preparatory steps. **D** is incorrect because the database cannot be opened from the new Oracle Home at this point.

3. ☑   **A.** The scripts are preupgrade_fixups.sql and postupgrade_fixups.sql.

☒   **B, C,** and **D** are incorrect. **B** and **C** are incorrect because the tool is concerned with steps before and after upgrade, not during. **D** is incorrect because the tool is not interactive; there are no prompts.

4. ☑   **B** and **C.** The parameter file and password file must be copied because their default location is derived from the Oracle Home.

☒   **A, D,** and **E** are incorrect. **A** is incorrect because no datafiles should be moved; an upgrade is an in-place operation. **D** is incorrect because the new Oracle Home will have new time zone files. **E** is incorrect because the AUDIT_FILE_DEST remains unchanged following upgrade.

5. ☑   **C.** The DBUA must be run from the new home and will take care of all the necessary startups and shutdowns.

☒   **A, B,** and **D** are incorrect. **A** and **B** are incorrect because the DBUA will manage the start in UPGRADE mode. **D** is incorrect because the DBUA automates the whole process, including the shutdown before upgrade.

6. ☑   **A, B, D, E,** and **F.** All of these steps can be performed against an open database.

☒   **C** is incorrect. The catctl.pl script can be run only when the database is in UPGRADE mode, during which time no regular users can connect.

7. ☑   **D.** A database instance started in UPGRADE mode will not accept any logons other than those with the SYSDBA privilege.

☒   **A, B,** and **C** are incorrect. These are incorrect because a database in UPGRADE mode is protected against all non-SYSDBA connections.

8. ☑   **C.** There is no necessity to enable unified auditing, but when you do, other audits will stop.

☒   **A, B,** and **D** are incorrect. **A** is incorrect because you can continue to use older methods of audit after upgrade. **B** and **D** are incorrect because it is not possible to run the older methods in conjunction with the new.

PART V

9. ☑ **C.** Invalid packages are recompiled when necessary, but they will be a performance hit on the session that does this.

☒ **A, B,** and **D** are incorrect. **A** and **B** are incorrect because recompilation is automatic when needed. **D** is incorrect because whether the PL/SQL is set for native compilation or interpretation, it will still be recompiled on demand.

10. ☑ **B** and **E. B** is correct because if you stop the old listener, you must configure and start a replacement. **E** is correct because following upgrade, DBUA leaves the database shut down.

☒ **A, C,** and **D** are incorrect. **A** is incorrect because the new release of the database will register with the GI listener, as it did before the upgrade. **C** and **D** are incorrect because although failing to copy these files may cause problems for the DBA, it should not be relevant to users.

CHAPTER 31

Multitenant Container and Pluggable Database Architecture

Exam Objectives

- 063.2.1   Describe the Multitenant Container Database Architecture
- 063.2.2   Explain Pluggable Database Provisioning

The Oracle Multitenant option (also known as *pluggable databases*) allows database administrators (DBAs) to consolidate many databases into one. To a large extent, the previously separate databases can still be used and administered independently following conversion to the multitenant environment. While end users and developers should not be aware of any change, Oracle Multitenant can at first be somewhat confusing for DBAs. Fear not. Once you have a firm understanding of the architecture, everything will fall into place.

Although not examined, it is certainly helpful to understand the licensing implications of the Oracle Multitenant architecture and its future importance. To use the headline functionality of database consolidation, you must purchase Enterprise Edition licenses plus the Oracle Multitenant option. This is not cheap. However, the Multitenant Single Tenancy functionality is included at no charge in all editions and does offer considerable benefits. The Upgrade Guide release 12.1.0.2 includes this statement: "The non-CDB architecture is deprecated in Oracle Database 12c, and may be desupported and unavailable in a release after Oracle Database 12c Release 2. Oracle recommends use of the CDB architecture." This unequivocal statement of direction makes it clear that from now on, DBAs should consider Oracle Multitenant for all installations.

Describe the Multitenant Container Database Architecture

Many Oracle sites have a large number of databases. The workload of administering many databases and the hardware and license costs lead many users toward a strategy of server consolidation. This can be done at several levels, such as many databases on one machine, many schemas in one database, or perhaps a virtualized environment of many operating system images, each supporting one database running on a single physical machine. Multitenant is simpler to implement than any of these: There is, physically, one database on one machine. But logically, there are many databases that can be accessed and managed independently. This can solve a number of business problems quickly and simply.

Multitenant Concepts

An Oracle Multitenant environment consists of a *container database* (CDB) and one or more *pluggable databases* (PDBs). A *container* is a set of tablespaces exposed to the world as a logical database. On creation, a CDB will contain a minimum of two containers. The *root container,* named CDB$ROOT, is the management container for the environment. Generally speaking, no one other than the DBA will ever connect to the root container. The *seed container* (named PDB$SEED) is a supplied, read-only container that can be cloned to create pluggable containers (named whatever you please).

Here are some important points:

- There is one database, the CDB.
- There is one database instance, with one System Global Area (SGA) and one set of background processes.

- A PDB is nothing more than a set of tablespaces and a service.

- The PDB services are exposed to users by the database listener.

- When you connect to a PDB service, the scope of your session is limited to the tablespaces associated with the PDB.

- Objects defined in the root container may be shared and visible to all PDBs.

- Objects (including users) defined in a PDB are private to their PDB.

- Each PDB has its own data dictionary, defining its local objects, with pointers to shared objects defined in the root container's data dictionary.

A pluggable database is a set of tablespaces, including a SYSTEM tablespace with a data dictionary. This data dictionary defines the objects local to the container, which are users and their schema objects (such as tables). All PL/SQL, SELECT, DML, and DDL commands executed while connected to the container affect only these local objects. When connected to the root container, it is possible (if you have appropriate permissions) to see the whole picture by querying the data dictionaries of all the containers. In the root container, you can create users and roles that are propagated to all containers. The privileges these users have in any one container may, however, be different.

There are some considerations when using Oracle Multitenant with other options:

- All containers must use the same character set. This is a natural limitation of the fact that there is only one database, the CDB.

- Data Guard must be configured at the CDB level because there is only one stream of redo. It is, however, possible to exclude some PDBs from standby databases. Note that this is possible only from release 12.1.0.2.

- Database Vault must be configured individually in each PDB. There is no overlap of realms across PDBs.

- Encryption must be configured individually per PDB. Each PDB generates and manages its own keys, stored in a shared wallet.

- Unified audit can be configured at the CDB and PDB levels. When creating a policy in the root container, appending CONTAINER=ALL to the CREATE AUDIT POLICY command will propagate it to all PDBs. In a PDB, any policies created are local to the PDB.

- GoldenGate and XStream replication are multitenant aware; they can capture and apply changes per PDB. Streams, however, is not supported in a multitenant environment.

While the Oracle Multitenant option is primarily intended for consolidating many previously separate non-CDB databases into one CDB, there is another option: Multitenant Single Tenancy. This uses the CDB/PDB architecture, but has only one pluggable database per CDB. A case can be made for creating *all* databases in this way. The reason is that while some sites may not need the server consolidation features of Oracle Multitenant, all sites face problems of downtime because of patching and upgrade that can be alleviated in an Oracle Multitenant environment. Patches need to be applied to the root container only; the pluggable container does not need to be patched.

TIP The Oracle Multitenant option is licensed on top of Enterprise Edition, but Multitenant Single Tenancy is included in all editions of the database.

To understand a multitenant environment, you must become familiar with a set of views. In a non-CDB environment, the data dictionary views used are prefixed with USER_, ALL_, and DBA_. The USER views show all objects owned by the user who is querying them. The ALL views show all objects on which the user has privileges, regardless of the schema in which they reside. The DBA views show all objects in the database. There is a fourth set of views, prefixed with CDB_. The CDB views exist in all databases, but they have meaning only in the root container of a CDB. In the root container, the CDB views show all objects in the CDB. In effect, they are a UNION ALL of the DBA views in every container, namely, the root container, the seed container, and all pluggable containers. In a non-CDB database or a pluggable database, the CDB views show the same rows as the DBA views. The column CON_ID in a CDB view identifies the container from which the row came. Containers are uniquely identified by the container ID and also by name. Figure 31-1 shows a query that lists the tablespaces associated with each container. Note that the query was executed while connected to the root container.

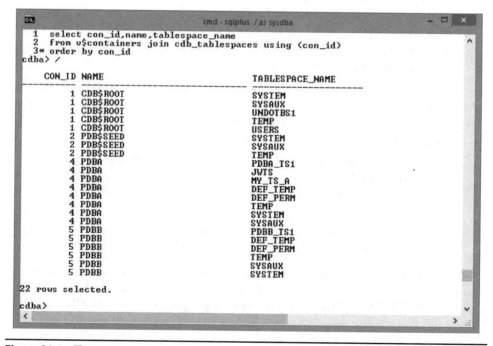

Figure 31-1 The mapping of tablespaces to containers in a CDB

Figure 31-1 shows that the CDB contains four containers:

- Container 1 is the root container, CDB$ROOT. It has five tablespaces: SYSTEM, SYSAUX, UNDOTBS1, TEMP, and USERS.

- Container 2 is the seed container, PDB$SEED. This has three tablespaces: SYSTEM, SYAUX, and TEMP.

- Containers 4 and 5 are pluggable containers named PDBA and PDBB. They each have tablespaces named SYSTEM, SYSAUX, TEMP, and other tablespaces for user data.

The unique identifier for a tablespace in a CDB is not its name. It is the name qualified with the container ID. The views joined in the query are V$CONTAINERS, which has one row for every container, and CDB_TABLESPACES, which has one row for every tablespace. The join column is CON_ID. Similar queries against (for example) CDB_DATA_FILES, CDB_USERS, and CDB_TABLES would show the datafiles, users, and tables that exist in each container.

The Drivers for Multitenant

The Oracle Multitenant option is primarily intended to be of use for server consolidation. Many sites have a plethora of databases. This may be because there are many applications and each is running in its own database, or perhaps it is because there are separate databases for production, test, development, and other purposes. In some cases, it may be that these databases do not use the full capacity of the hardware on which they are deployed and do not require full-time administration support. But they do each require storage, memory, CPU resources, and administration time, particularly for patching and upgrades. There may also be licensing implications if the databases are distributed across many machines.

In a non-CDB environment, each database instance has its own SGA, background processes, and data dictionary. They may have their own Oracle Home, or they may be running on different machines. This is potentially a significant overhead. Creating one CDB and running each database as a pluggable container will yield savings; you have only one set of background processes, one SGA (which will usually be much smaller than the total of the individual SGAs), one copy of many data dictionary structures, and one Oracle Home. The CDB architecture enables sharing of these resources with consequent savings.

When consolidating servers, it is vital that there should be no requirement for application changes and that each previously isolated database should remain completely separate from the other databases. If these conditions cannot be met, the consolidation exercise may cost more than it saves. The Oracle Multitenant architecture guarantees that no application changes will be needed and that the previously separate applications are completely isolated from each other. End users and developers will have no way of determining that the database has been converted from a non-CDB database into a pluggable container. The separation of duties between the various application administrators and users is maintained; in addition, to a large extent each PDB can have its own DBA and be administered as though it were a non-CDB.

Perhaps most important is the administration workload. Many experienced DBAs prefer to manage one big database rather than many small ones. This is relevant to one issue in particular: patching and upgrade. Patches and upgrades (henceforth referred to as *updates*) make changes either to the binaries that run the Oracle instance or to the data dictionary (or to both). If an update affects only the binaries (the simplest form of patch), then Oracle Multitenant hugely reduces the workload; patching the one Oracle Home off which the CDB runs will in effect patch all the PDBs within it. If the update includes scripts that change the data dictionary, then usually no work is required in the PDBs; however, sometimes this is not the case. Shared objects are defined in the root container, with pointers to them in each pluggable container. If these references require updating, this occurs automatically. In the worst case (such as a major upgrade), objects in the PDB may be invalidated. In that case, they must be recompiled. This can be done manually, or it will occur automatically when the object is accessed by a user session. In all cases, Oracle guarantees that applying any sort of update will never leave a previously valid user object in an irrevocably invalid state.

The fact that critical data dictionary structures are defined once only, in the root container, opens the way for an extraordinarily fast and easy method of upgrade. Consider the situation where a CDB is at release 12.1.0.1 and contains many PDBs. To apply the 12.1.0.2 patchset, the DBA can install the new Oracle Home on the same machine and create a new release 12.1.0.2 CDB. Then the DBA can unplug the PDBs from the old 12.1.0.1 CDB and plug them into the new 12.1.0.2 CDB. The downtime involved in this operation may be in single-digit minutes for each PDB. The PDBs can be moved individually, according to whatever schedule is convenient for the DBA and the users. The technique for plugging and unplugging will be detailed in Chapter 32.

The CDB and the Root Container

The CDB is the database, mounted and opened by the instance. The root container is the container from which all the shared resources are managed. Principal among these are as follows:

- The controlfile
- The undo tablespace
- The redo log
- The instance SGA and background processes
- The data dictionary
- Common users and roles

The root container will have a minimum of four tablespaces: SYSTEM, SYSAUX, UNDO, and TEMP. It will also have the common users and roles that are propagated to all the PDBs, and it will have all the Oracle-supplied objects that every PDB requires. These objects include, for example, all the supplied PL/SQL packages. Operations affecting these shared resources can be accomplished only through a session attached to the root container.

The root container is the only container to which you can connect without going via a database listener. If you are logged on to the server machine and you set your ORACLE_SID environment variable to the name of the CDB instance, you can connect to the root container. It is not possible to connect to a PDB in this way because there is only one instance, with only one name. Following a connection to the root container, it is possible to move your session to another container. Figure 31-2 demonstrates this.

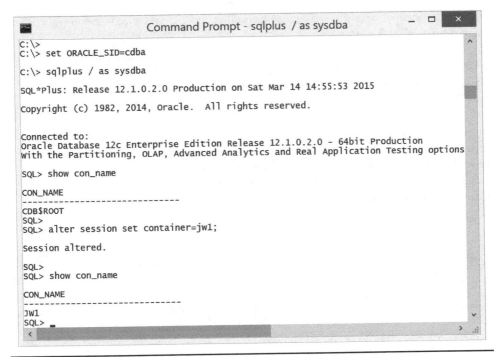

Figure 31-2   Moving your session from one container to another

Figure 31-2 shows a Windows user setting the ORACLE_SID environment variable to the name of an instance CDBA and then connecting to this with interprocess communication (IPC), bypassing the database listener. SQL*Plus includes a command SHOW CON_NAME, which shows the name of the container to which the session is currently connected, which is initially the root container. Then the ALTER SESSION command is used to move the session to a pluggable container named JW1.

PDBs: Pluggable Containers

A pluggable container, also referred to as a *pluggable database,* is a set of tablespaces and objects to be used by developers and end users as though it were an independent database.

PDBs have a SYSTEM tablespace just like non-CDBs. Only the user metadata specific to the PDB is stored in the PDB's SYSTEM tablespace. In addition, there are logical links to the common objects defined in the root container. The object names are the same in a PDB as in a non-CDB or a CDB, such as OBJ$, TAB$, and SOURCE$. Thus, the PDB appears to an application as a stand-alone database. The DBA for an application in a PDB will, as a general rule (to which there are a few exceptions), not be aware that there may be one or many other PDBs sharing resources in the CDB.

Every PDB has a unique container ID number and container name. These are recorded in the controlfile and exposed through the views V$CONTAINERS and V$PDBS. When connected to a pluggable container, rows referring to containers other than the current container are filtered out. From the root, all containers are visible.

 TIP The V$PDBS view is identical to the V$CONTAINERS view, except that it excludes the row for the root container.

Every pluggable database has a unique global name. This is the name of the container and is used as the default service to be registered with the database listener. Figure 31-3 shows connections to PDBs named JW1 and JW5 through their default service and the listener (using the EZCONNECT syntax) with queries showing that the hosting database and instance, named CDBA, are always the same.

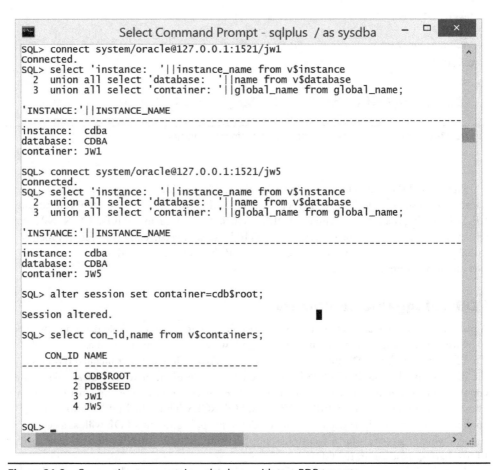

Figure 31-3 Connecting to a container database with two PDB tenants

Explain Pluggable Database Provisioning

A major advantage of moving to Oracle Multitenant architecture is the ease with which pluggable databases can be created, copied, and relocated. This is the process of *provisioning*.

Techniques for Provisioning Pluggable Containers

There are four techniques for provisioning a container:

- Create a new PDB from the seed container. This method creates a new PDB consisting of nothing more than the SYSTEM, SYSAUX, and TEMP tablespaces. This would typically be used for a new application implementation.

- Create a new PDB from a non-CDB. This method takes an existing database, which must be release 12.*x*, converts it into a pluggable container, and plugs it into a CDB. This would typically be part of a consolidation exercise. It is not possible to convert back to non-CDB.

- Clone a PDB to another new PDB. The source can be a PDB in the same or a different CDB. This could be used for creating test or development environments from a production PDB.

- Plug in an unplugged PDB. A PDB can be unplugged from one CDB and then plugged into the same or a different CDB. This can be used to relocate or to upgrade a PDB.

Whichever technique is appropriate, all are usually fast. The clone technique requires copying the datafiles that make up the PDB's tablespaces. The time for this will be dependent on the size of the datafiles. The other techniques are typically single-digit minutes.

Communications Between Containers

When databases are deployed as non-CDB databases, there will often be reasons to share data between them, whether the databases are on separate servers or even on the same server. This is usually accomplished by using database links to access tables in other databases. Following provisioning them into the same CDB as PDBs, the same method can be used. But since the objects in two PDBs reside within the same container, it is possible to create a fast version of a database link (known as a *fast intra-CDB link*) under the covers. Usually, a database link will use Transmission Control Protocol (TCP). In an Oracle Multitenant environment, it is possible to optimize database link communications by using IPC. Remember that a PDB does not know where another PDB or non-CDB database resides, so the definition and use of a database link are the same, regardless of where both databases reside. All application users will make use of links as the only way to communicate between containers.

From within the root container, it is possible to query objects in all PDBs, but only in a strictly controlled manner. A common user can be defined in the root and will be propagated to all containers. If this user in each container (including the root) owns a table or a view or synonym with the same definition, all copies of this object can be queried from the root by using the CONTAINERS clause in a SELECT statement. This example queries the DUAL table, which exists in the common SYS schema:

```
SQL>
SQL> show user
USER is "SYS"
SQL>
SQL> show con_name

CON_NAME
------------------------------
CDB$ROOT
SQL>
SQL> select con_id,name,dummy


from containers(sys.dual) natural join v$containers;

    CON_ID NAME                           D
---------- ------------------------------ -
         4 JW5                            X
         3 JW1                            X
         1 CDB$ROOT                       X

SQL>
```

Two-Minute Drill

Describe the Multitenant Container Database Architecture

- The Oracle Multitenant architecture helps use server resources more efficiently by sharing instance memory and processes as well as SYSTEM tablespace common objects.

- Upgrading a multitenant container database upgrades all PDBs within the container.

- A CDB at any point in time can contain zero, one, or up to 252 user-defined PDBs.

- A CDB is a single instance, regardless of the number of PDBs within the CDB.

- Across all PDBs within a CDB, the redo log files, undo tablespace, controlfiles, and temporary tablespace are shared.

- An individual PDB may have its own temporary tablespace.

- Each PDB has its own SYSTEM tablespace with private metadata. The SYSTEM tablespace has pointers to common Oracle metadata stored in the SYSTEM tablespace within the CDB.

- The data dictionary views prefixed with DBA_ have corresponding views with the CDB_ prefix. When queries are run in the root container, these show the entire environment.

Explain Pluggable Database Provisioning

- The CDB is initially provisioned with the root container CDB$ROOT and the seed container PDB$SEED.

- PDBs can be created from the seed container by cloning an existing PDB, by plugging in a non-CDB database, or by plugging in a previously unplugged PDB.

- Non-CDBs can be converted to a PDB only once they have been upgraded to Oracle Database 12c. This process cannot be reversed.

- Table data can be shared between PDBs within a CDB by using an intra-CDB link.

- An intra-CDB link behaves just like a pre-12c database link and requires no application changes.

Self Test

1. Identify the correct statements about Oracle Database versions and their compatibility with container databases. (Choose all correct answers.)

   A. Oracle Databases created in 12c are automatically pluggable into any existing CDB.

   B. An Oracle 12c database can be a non-CDB, a CDB, or a PDB.

   C. Oracle 11g databases can be plugged into a container database if you create an XML database description file.

   D. Oracle 11g databases can be easily upgraded to Oracle Database 12c by plugging it into a CDB created with Oracle Database 12c release 1 or newer.

   E. A CDB created with Oracle Database 12c can be converted to a PDB by removing the PDB$SEED user container.

2. Which of the following database objects are always shared across all PDBs within a system container? (Choose three correct answers.)

   A. The temporary tablespace

   B. The undo tablespace

   C. The database global name

   D. The controlfile

   E. Online redo logfiles

3. Which of these is a necessary condition for a non-CDB to be plugged into a CDB? (Choose the best answer.)

   A. The CDB and non-CDB must use the same database character set.

   B. GoldenGate replication must not be configured.

   C. All the non-CDB tablespaces with the same names as already existing CDB tablespaces must be renamed to prevent conflicts.

   D. The non-CDB must be release 12c or the terminal release of 11g.

4. What method is appropriate for a user to establish a session against a PDB? (Choose two correct answers.)

A. Local users can set their ORACLE_SID environment variable to the PDB name and connect over IPC.

B. Logon to a PDB is possible only through a database listener.

C. The user can log on to the root container and then alter the session to connect to an application schema in the PDB.

D. When connected to one PDB, the user can connect to another PDB in the same CDB through a database link.

Self Test Answers

1. ☑ **B.** A 12c database can be a container database, a pluggable database, or a traditional non-container database.
☒ **A, C, D** and **E** are incorrect. **A** is incorrect because there are restrictions on whether a non-CDB is compatible with a given CDB, such as the character set. **C** and **D** are incorrect because an 11g database must be upgraded before plugging in. **E** is incorrect because there is no way to reverse the conversion to the multitenant environment.

2. ☑ **B, D,** and **E.** The undo tablespace, the controlfile, and the redo log are used by sessions against all containers and managed only from the root container.
☒ **A** and **C** are incorrect. **A** is incorrect because each container can create and manage its own temporary tablespaces. **C** is incorrect because each container always has its own global name.

3. ☑ **A.** The database character set must be same, or the plug-in will fail
☒ **B, C,** and **D** are incorrect. **B** is incorrect because GoldenGate is compatible with Oracle Multitenant. **C** is incorrect because the tablespace name is not a unique identifier. **D** is incorrect because all 11g databases must be upgraded before plugging in.

4. ☑ **B** and **D. B** is correct because establishing a session against a PDB can be done only through a service exposed by a listener. **D** is correct because once one has a session against one PDB, a session against another can be established through a database link, which will also be established by the listener.
☒ **A** and **C** are incorrect. **A** is incorrect because only the root container can be contacted using the IPC protocol. **C** is incorrect because while you can move your session from one container to another, you cannot change the schema as you do so.

CHAPTER 32

Creating and Managing Multitenant Container and Pluggable Databases

Exam Objectives

- 063.3.1   Configure and Create a CDB
- 063.3.2   Create a PDB Using Different Methods
- 063.3.3   Unplug and Drop a PDB
- 063.3.4   Migrate a Non-CDB Database to a PDB
- 063.4.1   Establish Connections to CDB/PDB
- 063.4.2   Start Up and Shut Down a CDB and Open and Close PDBs
- 063.4.3   Evaluate the Impact of Parameter Value Changes

This chapter describes the process of creating a container database (CDB) and the various techniques for creating the pluggable databases (PDBs) that will reside within it. Generally speaking, administration of a multitenant environment is similar to administering a non-CDB environment. That is the whole point: many non-CDBs can be consolidated into a single CDB with no changes for the users and developers and with only minimal changes for the administrators.

Create a Container Database

A container database and instance are distinguished from a non-CDB by two attributes that must be specified at creation time and can never be changed subsequently. After database creation, it is not possible to convert a non-CDB into a CDB, or the other way around. These attributes are a memory structure in the instance, which is enabled by starting the instance with the instance parameter ENABLE_PLUGGABLE_DATABASE=TRUE, and a controlfile structure, which is enabled by adding the clause ENABLE PLUGGABLE DATABASE to the CREATE DATABASE command. As when creating a non-CDB, the easiest way is undoubtedly to use the Database Creation Assistant (DBCA).

Use DBCA to Create a CDB

The Database Creation Assistant is usually the tool you would use to create a new container database. In fact, it gives you the options to create a non-CDB database, just a container database, or a container database with one or more new pluggable databases. Figure 32-1 shows using the

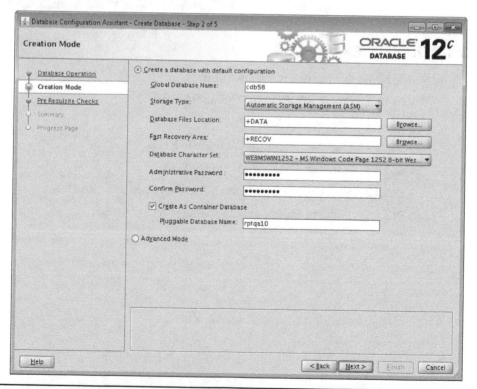

Figure 32-1 Creating a container database using DBCA

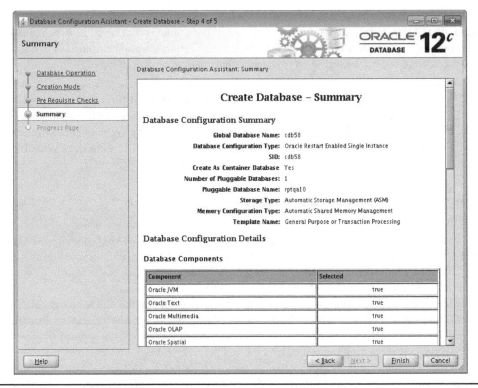

Figure 32-2 Create database – Summary page

"express" method to create a new container database called CDB58, which will reside in the existing Automatic Storage Management (ASM) disk group +DATA. The recovery files will reside in +RECOV. An initial pluggable database called RPTQA10 will be created along with the container.

In the next window, you can review the summary of the container database to be created. Note in Figure 32-2 that creating a container database can create a pluggable database as well.

But how do you contact the initial pluggable database? For clues, you can check the listener.

```
[oracle@oel63 ~]$ lsnrctl status
LSNRCTL for Linux: Version 12.1.0.1.0 - Production on 27-MAY-2013 20:47:02
. . .
Service "cdb58" has 1 instance(s).
Instance "cdb58", status READY, has 1 handler(s) for this service...
. . .
Service "complrefXDB" has 1 instance(s).
Instance "complref", status READY, has 1 handler(s) for this service...
Service "rptqa10" has 1 instance(s).
Instance "cdb58", status READY, has 1 handler(s) for this service...
The command completed successfully
[oracle@oel63 ~]$
```

The previous code shows that any requests for the service RPTQA10 will be handed off to the instance CDB58, which is the instance that has opened the container database. These requests will launch sessions against the PDB. Requests for the service CDB58 will also be connected to the instance CDB58 but will be logged on to the root container rather than to the PDB.

> **TIP** Run the DBCA many times, taking different options each time, and at the end of the dialog select the check box to Generate Database Creation Scripts. Study the scripts, which are instructive. Many experienced database administrators (DBAs), including the authors of this book, usually create databases by generating DBCA scripts and then editing them if necessary.

Using SQL*Plus to Create a CDB

A CDB is distinguished from a non-CDB by memory structures and physical structures. To enable the necessary memory structures, start an instance with the parameter ENABLE_PLUGGABLE_DATABASE set to TRUE. Then in the CREATE DATABASE command, include ENABLE PLUGGABLE DATABASE to create the necessary disk-based structures in the controlfile and the data dictionary.

Additional instance parameters and keywords can specify names for the seed container datafiles, or they can be generated automatically by the Oracle Managed Files (OMF) mechanism. Starting the instance with OMF enabled automates all filename creation in directories beneath whatever directory or ASM disk group is specified by the DB_CREATE_FILE_DEST parameter. This will apply to the datafiles for the root container, the seed container, and all subsequent pluggable containers. Alternatively, specifying the PDB_FILE_NAME_CONVERT parameter will generate names for the seed and pluggable containers by remapping the names specified for the root container. This parameter consists of matched pairs of strings, suffixed and prefixed with an implicit wildcard. Consider this setting:

```
pdb_file_name_convert='/u01/oradata/cdba','/u02/oradata/seed'
```

If the CDB root container has files for SYSTEM or SYSAUX or TEMP in the directory /u01/oradata/cdba, the seed container will have its files created in /u02/oradata/seed'. Alternatively, you could specify this in the CREATE DATABASE command.

```
create database cdba
logfile
group 1 ('/u01/oradata/cdba/redo1a.log') size 50m,
group 2 ('/u01/oradata/cdba/redo2a.log') size 50m
datafile '/u01/oradata/cdba/system01.dbf' size 500m
sysaux datafile '/u01/oradata/cdba/sysaux01.dbf' size 500m
default temporary tablespace temp
tempfile '/u01/oradata/cdba/temp01.dbf' size 500m
undo tablespace undotbs datafile '/u01/oradata/cdba/undotbs01.dbf' size 100m
enable pluggable database
seed file_name_convert = ('cdba','seed');
```

Exercise 32-1: Create a Container Database In this exercise, you will create a container database using SQL*Plus.

1. Create a simple parameter file named initcdba.ora, with just these four lines:

```
control_files='/u01/oradata/cdba/control.ctl'
db_name=cdba
memory_target=1g
enable_pluggable_database=true
```

Note that the path for the controlfile is a suggested Linux path; adjust according to your environment (or for Windows) as necessary. Place the file in the $ORACLE_HOME/dbs directory (Linux) or %ORACLE_HOME%\database directory (Windows).

2. Start the CDBA instance.

Set your ORACLE_SID environment variable.

Here is the code for Linux:

```
export ORACLE_SID=cdba
```

Here is the code for Windows:

```
set ORACLE_SID=cdba
```

On Windows, create the Windows service for the instance.

```
oradim -new -sid cdba
```

Connect to SQL*Plus and start up.

```
sqlplus / as sysdba
create spfile from pfile;
startup nomount
```

3. Create directories for the root container and the seed container.

Here is a Linux example:

```
mkdir -p /u01/oradata/cdba
mkdir /u01/oradata/seed
```

Here is a Windows example:

```
md c:\oradata\cdba
md c:\oradata\seed
```

4. Create the container database.

Run the CREATE DATABASE command.

Here is a Linux example:

```
create database cdba
logfile
group 1 ('/u01/oradata/cdba/redo1a.log') size 50m,
group 2 ('/u01/oradata/cdba/redo2a.log') size 50m
datafile '/u01/oradata/cdba/system01.dbf' size 500m
sysaux datafile '/u01/oradata/cdba/sysaux01.dbf' size 500m
default temporary tablespace temp
tempfile '/u01/oradata/cdba/temp01.dbf' size 500m
undo tablespace undotbs
datafile '/u01/oradata/cdba/undotbs01.dbf' size 100m
enable pluggable database
seed file_name_convert = ('cdba','seed');
```

Note the explicit naming of all the files and adjust according to your environment.

5. Run the scripts CATALOG.SQL and CATPROC.SQL, which will create the data dictionary views and the supplied packages. In a CDB environment, it is not sufficient simply to run the SQL scripts from a SQL*Plus session as you would in a non-CDB database. They must be invoked through a supplied Perl script, run from an operating system prompt, that understands the nature of a CDB and can create the objects in both the root and seed containers.

Here's an example on Unix:

```
$ORACLE_HOME/perl/bin/perl $ORACLE_HOME/rdbms/admin/catcon.pl
-b catalog $ORACLE_HOME/rdbms/admin/catalog.sql
$ORACLE_HOME/perl/bin/perl $ORACLE_HOME/rdbms/admin/catcon.pl
-b catproc $ORACLE_HOME/rdbms/admin/catproc.sql
```

Here's an example on Windows:

```
%ORACLE_HOME%\perl\bin\perl %ORACLE_HOME%\rdbms\admin\catcon.pl
-b catalog %ORACLE_HOME%\rdbms\admin\catalog.sql
%ORACLE_HOME%\perl\bin\perl %ORACLE_HOME%\rdbms\admin\catcon.pl
-b catproc %ORACLE_HOME%\rdbms\admin\catproc.sql
```

Note that the previous two commands should not include any line breaks.

6. Investigate the CDB physical structures.

From your SQL*Plus session, run these queries:

```
select name,cdb from v$database;
select name,con_id,open_mode from v$containers;
select con_id,name from v$datafile;
select con_id,name from v$tempfile;
select * from v$controlfile;
select con_id,member from v$logfile;
select sys_context('userenv','con_name') from dual;
show con_name;
```

Note how the filenames for the seed container have been calculated by applying a conversion to the root container's filenames and that the controlfile and log files are not (unlike the datafiles and tempfiles) associated with any one container.

7. Create a CDB with DBCA.

To become completely familiar with the CDB creation process, use the DBCA as well. Follow the options to create a container database (using both the templates that include datafiles and the "custom" template that does not) and in the last window select the check box to generate database creation scripts. Study them! They are instructive.

Create Pluggable Containers

There are four techniques for creating a pluggable database:

- Clone the seed container.
- Clone an already extant PDB.
- Plug in a previously unplugged PDB.
- Plug in a non-CDB database.

Using PDB$SEED to Create a New PDB

Every container database has a read-only seed database container called PDB$SEED used for quickly creating a new pluggable database. When you create a new PDB from PDB$SEED, the following things happen, regardless of whether you use SQL*Plus, SQL Developer, or Enterprise Manager Cloud Control 12c. Each of these steps is performed with a CREATE PLUGGABLE DATABASE statement, either manually or via DBCA:

- Datafiles in PDB$SEED are copied to the new PDB.
- Local versions of the SYSTEM and SYSAUX and TEMP tablespaces are created.
- A local metadata catalog is initialized (with pointers to common read-only objects in the root container).
- The common users (including SYS and SYSTEM) are created.
- A local user is created and is granted the local PDB_DBA role. This is the PDB administrator and is used to create the PDB.
- A new default service for the PDB is created and is registered with the listener.

Given the relatively small amount of data creation and movement in those steps, the creation of the PDB is fast. Generating filenames for the new PDB will depend on the environment. The simplest way is to enable OMF. If, for some reason, that cannot be done, the PDB_FILE_NAME_CONVERT instance parameter (consisting of matched pairs of strings) can generate new names from the seed PDB's datafile names. As a last resort, filename mappings or fully qualified filenames can be specified in the CREATE PLUGGABLE DATABASE command.

Exercise 32-2: Create a Pluggable Database from the Seed   In this exercise, you'll create a PDB by cloning the seed PDB. It is assumed that a CDB exists named cdba, that you have the ORACLE_SID environment variable set to cdba, and that a database listener is running on the default address and port.

1. Connect to the root container as user SYS and enable OMF.

```
sqlplus / as sysdba
alter system set db_create_file_dest='c:\oradata';
```

The previous example is for Windows; adjust according to your environment.

2. Create a PDB named pdba, with an admin user named pdba_admin.

```
create pluggable database pdba admin user pdba_admin identified by
oracle;
select con_id,name,open_mode from v$pdbs;
select con_id,name,open_mode from v$containers;
select con_id,pdb_id,pdb_name,status from cdb_pdbs;
select con_id,file_name from cdb_data_files;
select con_id,name from v$datafile;
```

3. Open the new PDB.

```
alter pluggable database pdba open;
select con_id,name,open_mode from v$containers;
select con_id,pdb_id,pdb_name,status from cdb_pdbs;
```

4. Note the services registered with the database listener, which will include a service for the root container and a service for the PDB, as in the following illustration:

```
oracle@db12102:~                                                      –   □   ×

[oracle@db12102 ~]$ lsnrctl status

LSNRCTL for Linux: Version 12.1.0.2.0 - Production on 29-MAR-2015 18:25:25

Copyright (c) 1991, 2014, Oracle.  All rights reserved.

Connecting to (DESCRIPTION=(ADDRESS=(PROTOCOL=TCP)(HOST=db12102.example.com)(PORT=1521)))
STATUS of the LISTENER
------------------------
Alias                     LISTENER
Version                   TNSLSNR for Linux: Version 12.1.0.2.0 - Production
Start Date                29-MAR-2015 18:23:54
Uptime                    0 days 0 hr. 1 min. 31 sec
Trace Level               off
Security                  ON: Local OS Authentication
SNMP                      OFF
Listener Parameter File   /u01/app/oracle/product/12.1.0/dbhome_1/network/admin/listener.ora
Listener Log File         /u01/app/oracle/diag/tnslsnr/db12102/listener/alert/log.xml
Listening Endpoints Summary...
  (DESCRIPTION=(ADDRESS=(PROTOCOL=tcp)(HOST=db12102.example.com)(PORT=1521)))
  (DESCRIPTION=(ADDRESS=(PROTOCOL=ipc)(KEY=EXTPROC1521)))
Services Summary...
Service "cdba" has 1 instance(s).
  Instance "cdba", status READY, has 1 handler(s) for this service...
Service "pdba" has 1 instance(s).
  Instance "cdba", status READY, has 1 handler(s) for this service...
The command completed successfully
[oracle@db12102 ~]$
```

Cloning a PDB to Create a New PDB

If you need a new database that's similar to one that already exists, you can clone an existing database within the CDB. The new PDB will be identical to the source except for the PDB name. In this example, you'll use the DBA features of SQL Developer to clone the PDB. You don't have to worry about what's going on under the covers; each step of the way you can see the DDL that SQL Developer runs to create the clone.

Before cloning an existing PDB, you must close it and reopen it in READ ONLY mode.

```
SQL> alter pluggable database qa_2014 close;
Pluggable database altered.
SQL> alter pluggable database qa_2014 open read only;
Pluggable database altered.
SQL>
```

You can browse the DBA connections for the container database CDB01 and its PDBs. Right-click the QA_2014 PDB and select Clone Pluggable Database, as shown in Figure 32-3.

In the dialog box that opens, as shown in Figure 32-4, change the database name to QA_2015. All other features and options of QA_2014 are retained for QA_2015.

The SQL tab shows the command that SQL Developer will run to clone the database:

```
CREATE PLUGGABLE DATABASE QA_2015 FROM QA_2014
STORAGE UNLIMITED
FILE_NAME_CONVERT=NONE;
```

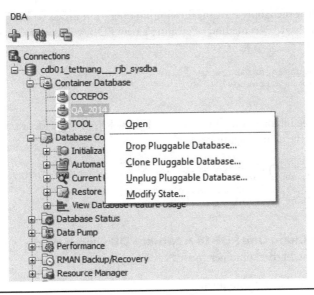

Figure 32-3   Selecting a database to clone in SQL Developer

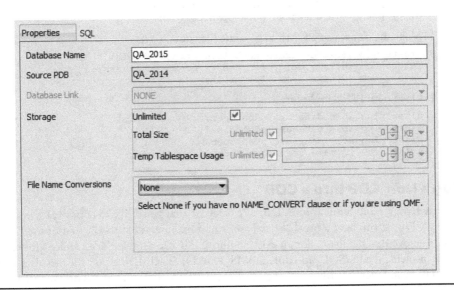

Figure 32-4   Specifying PDB clone characteristics

Once you click the Apply button, the cloning operation proceeds and creates the new PDB. As with the SQL*Plus method of creating a new PDB, you have to open the new PDB as READ WRITE.

```
SQL> alter pluggable database qa_2015 open read write;
Pluggable database altered.
SQL>
```

Finally, you need to open the QA_2014 database as READ WRITE again since it was set to READ ONLY for the clone operation.

```
SQL> alter pluggable database qa_2014 close;
Pluggable database altered.
SQL> alter pluggable database qa_2014 open read write;
Pluggable database altered.
SQL>
```

Exercise 32-3: Clone One PDB to Another PDB   In this exercise, you will create a PDB by cloning the PDBA container created earlier.

1. Connect to the root container.

   ```
   sqlplus / as sysdba
   show con_name
   ```

2. Open PDBA read-only.

   ```
   alter pluggable database pdba close immediate;
   alter pluggable database pdba open read only;
   ```

3. Make the clone, using OMF to generate filenames.

   ```
   create pluggable database pdbb from pdba;
   select con_id,name,guid,open_mode from v$containers;
   select con_id,name from v$datafile;
   ```

4. Open both PDBs read-write.

   ```
   alter pluggable database pdbb open;
   alter pluggable database pdba close;
   alter pluggable database pdba open;
   select con_id,name,open_mode from v$containers;
   ```

Plug a Non-CDB into a CDB

You may have a stand-alone (non-CDB) 12c database that you'd like to consolidate into an existing CDB. If you have a pre-12c database, you must upgrade it to 12c first or use Data Pump to move that database. For an existing non-CDB 12c database, it's a straightforward process involving the PL/SQL procedure DBMS_PDB.DESCRIBE to export the metadata for a non-CDB to an Extensible Markup Language (XML) OS file. In this example, on the tettnang server, there are three instances: +ASM, CDB01, and RPTQA12C:

```
[oracle@tettnang ~]$ cat /etc/oratab
+ASM:/u01/app/oracle/product/12.1.0/grid:N:
cdb01:/u01/app/oracle/product/12.1.0/dbhome_1:N:
rptqa12c:/u01/app/oracle/product/12.1.0/dbhome_1:N:
```

Here is how you would export the metadata for the RPTQA12C database. Connect to the target database (the database that will be assimilated into CDB01), change its status to READ ONLY, and run the procedure.

```
SQL> startup mount
ORACLE instance started.
Total System Global Area 2622255104 bytes
Fixed Size 2685024 bytes
Variable Size 1644169120 bytes
Database Buffers 956301312 bytes
Redo Buffers 19099648 bytes
Database mounted.
SQL> alter database open read only;
Database altered.
SQL> exec dbms_pdb.describe('/tmp/rptqa12c.xml');
PL/SQL procedure successfully completed.
SQL>
```

The file contains information describing the datafiles of the database, which components are installed, and certain critical instance parameters. Note that the undo tablespace, the controlfile, and the redo logfiles are discarded. The XML looks like this:

```
<?xml version="1.0" encoding="UTF-8"?>
<PDB>
<pdbname>rptqa12c</pdbname>
<cid>0</cid>
<byteorder>1</byteorder>
<vsn>202375168</vsn>
<dbid>1288637549</dbid>
<cdbid>1288637549</cdbid>
<guid>F754FCD8744A55AAE043E3A0080A3B17</guid>
<uscnbas>3905844</uscnbas>
<uscnwrp>0</uscnwrp>
<rdba>4194824</rdba>
<tablespace>
<name>SYSTEM</name>
<type>0</type>
<tsn>0</tsn>
<status>1</status>
<issft>0</issft>
<file>
<path>+DATA/RPTQA12C/DATAFILE/system.261.845207525</path>
. . .
</options>
<olsoid>0</olsoid>
<dv>0</dv>
<ncdb2pdb>1</ncdb2pdb>
<APEX>4.2.0.00.27:1</APEX>
<parameters>
<parameter>processes=300</parameter>
<parameter>shared_pool_size=805306368</parameter>
<parameter>sga_target=2634022912</parameter>
<parameter>db_block_size=8192</parameter>
<parameter>compatible=12.1.0.0.0</parameter>
<parameter>shared_servers=0</parameter>
<parameter>open_cursors=300</parameter>
<parameter>star_transformation_enabled=TRUE</parameter>
```

```
<parameter>pga_aggregate_target=524288000</parameter>
</parameters>
<tzvers>
<tzver>primary version:18</tzver>
<tzver>secondary version:0</tzver>
</tzvers>
<walletkey>0</walletkey>
</optional>
</PDB>
```

If the existing non-CDB database is on the same machine as the destination CDB, connect to the container database CDB01 and import the XML for RPTQA12C.

```
[oracle@tettnang ~]$ . oraenv
ORACLE_SID = [rptqa12c] ? cdb01
The Oracle base remains unchanged with value /u01/app/oracle
[oracle@tettnang ~]$ sqlplus / as sysdba
SQL*Plus: Release 12.1.0.1.0 Production on Wed May 28 12:40:34 2014
Copyright (c) 1982, 2013, Oracle. All rights reserved.
Connected to:
Oracle Database 12c Enterprise Edition Release 12.1.0.1.0 - 64bit Production
With the Partitioning, Automatic Storage Management, OLAP, Advanced Analytics
and Real Application Testing options
SQL> create pluggable database rptqa12c using '/tmp/rptqa12c.xml';
Pluggable database created.
SQL>
```

In many cases, it will be necessary to transfer the non-CDB's datafiles and the XML file to the machine where the DB is running. No problem. Edit the XML file to take account of any changes in file and directory names before running the CREATE PLUGGABLE DATABASE command.

The plugging-in operation may take as little as a minute or two. Some final cleanup and configuration are needed before the plugged-in database can be used. The script noncdb_to_pdb.sql cleans up unnecessary metadata not needed in a multitenant environment. In addition, you must open the newly plugged-in database just as you would with a clone operation.

```
SQL> alter session set container=rptqa12c;
SQL> @$ORACLE_HOME/rdbms/admin/noncdb_to_pdb.sql
. . .
6 IF (sqlcode <> -900) THEN
7 RAISE;
8 END IF;
9 END;
10 END;
11 /
PL/SQL procedure successfully completed.
SQL>
SQL> WHENEVER SQLERROR CONTINUE;
SQL> SQL> alter pluggable database rptqa12c open read write;
Pluggable database altered.
SQL>
```

Plug an Unplugged PDB into a CDB

You may have several unplugged databases at any given time. An unplugged database can't be opened outside of a CDB, so you'll likely plug an unplugged database (PDB) back into a CDB at some point. In this example, the PDB CCREPOS is currently unplugged and has its XML file located in /tmp/ccrepos.xml on the server. The steps to plug a currently unplugged PDB into a CDB are both straightforward and finish quickly, just as most multitenant operations do. All you have to do is run one command to plug it in and another command to open it. Connect as a common user with the ALTER PLUGGABLE DATABASE privilege as follows (connecting as SYSDBA to CDB01 with operating system [OS] authentication works great):

```
SQL> create pluggable database ccrepos using '/tmp/ccrepos.xml' nocopy;
Pluggable database created.
SQL> alter pluggable database ccrepos open read write;
Pluggable database altered.
SQL>
```

Note that a PDB must be dropped, and not just unplugged, from a CDB before it can be plugged back in. Using the NOCOPY option saves time if the PDB's datafiles are already in the correct location.

Unplug and Drop a PDB

Since a PDB is, by nature, highly mobile, it's likely that you'll move it to another CDB on the same or another server. You may just unplug it to make it unavailable to users. You may also unplug it to drop it completely. Or, perhaps most importantly, you may want to upgrade it by unplugging from one CDB at a certain patch level and plugging it into a CDB at a higher patch level. This is a way to upgrade with minimal downtime. SQL Developer has an option to unplug, or you can use SQL*Plus.

```
SQL> alter pluggable database ccrepos close;
Pluggable database altered.
SQL> alter pluggable database ccrepos unplug into '/tmp/ccrepos.xml';
Pluggable database altered.
SQL>
```

This routine generates an XML file equivalent to that generated by the DBMS_PDB .DESCRIBE procedure, and it can be used in the same way to plug the PDB into any other CDB.

When you drop a PDB, all references to the PDB are removed from the CDB's controlfile. By default, the datafiles are retained; therefore, if you had previously unplugged that PDB, you can use the XML file to plug that PDB back into the same or another CDB. In this example, you will drop the QA_2014 PDB along with its datafiles. It will no longer be available to plug into another database even if you still have the XML metadata.

```
SQL> alter pluggable database qa_2014 close;
Pluggable database altered.
SQL> drop pluggable database qa_2014 including datafiles;
Pluggable database dropped.
SQL>
```

Migrate a Pre-12.1 Non-CDB Database to CDB

Converting Oracle Database 12*c* non-CDBs to a PDB is fast and straightforward, but what if your database is a previous version such as 11*g* or even 10*g*? There are two approaches: You can upgrade, or you can use Data Pump.

EXAM TIP   Only release 12.x non-CDB databases can be converted into PDBs. Any earlier databases must be upgraded first.

If your application is not sensitive or dependent on the version of the database (which you should have verified by now), then your cleanest option is to upgrade the non-CDB in place up to version 12c (12.1.0.1 or later) and then plug it in to the CDB using the methods mentioned earlier in this chapter. The advantages to this method are that you don't need to allocate any extra space for the migration as you would for the other two methods and that it is fast.

To use the Data Pump method, you'll use Data Pump export/import as you would in a non-CDB environment. Create a new PDB from the seed database in the CDB, and adjust the initialization parameters to be comparable to those in the existing database. One of the advantages with this method is that you can leave the current non-CDB in place to ensure compatibility with Oracle Database 12c before dropping the original database. It will also allow you to perform a platform migration, or to move from file system storage to ASM storage, as part of the consolidation. But if the database is large, this may take some time.

 TIP   The upgrade and plug-in method is usually much faster because the time needed is (generally speaking) independent of the size of the database. An export-import of a large database may take many hours. Or days.

Establish Connections to CDBs and PDBs

You connect to a PDB or CDB much as you connect to a non-CDB. You can connect to a CDB via OS authentication and the common user SYS. Otherwise, you will connect to either a CDB or one of the PDBs within the CDB using a service name. The service name is referenced either using an EasyConnect string or within a tnsnames.ora entry. This method is the same whether you are using SQL*Plus or SQL Developer.

By default, a service name is created for each new, cloned, or plugged-in PDB. If that is not sufficient in your environment, you'll use the DBMS_SERVICE package or the srvctl utility to create additional services for the PDB.

Understanding CDB and PDB Service Names

In a non-CDB environment, a database instance is associated with at least one service managed by at least one listener. One listener can manage a combination of non-CDB and PDB services. The database server oel63 has two databases: DBAHANDBOOK and CDB01. As you might suspect, the database CDB01 is a multitenant database, and DBAHANDBOOK is a non-CDB, but they are both Oracle Database version 12c and are managed by a single listener called LISTENER.

```
[oracle@oel63 ~]$ lsnrctl status

LSNRCTL for Linux: Version 12.1.0.1.0 - Production on 02-JUL-2014 22:47:35

Copyright (c) 1991, 2013, Oracle.  All rights reserved.
```

```
. . .
Services Summary...
Service "+ASM" has 1 instance(s).
  Instance "+ASM", status READY, has 1 handler(s) for this service...
Service "cdb01" has 1 instance(s).
  Instance "cdb01", status READY, has 1 handler(s) for this service...
Service "cdb01XDB" has 1 instance(s).
  Instance "cdb01", status READY, has 1 handler(s) for this service...
Service "dbahandbook" has 1 instance(s).
  Instance "dbahandbook", status READY, has 1 handler(s) for this service...
Service "dbahandbookXDB" has 1 instance(s).
  Instance "dbahandbook", status READY, has 1 handler(s) for this service...
Service "dw17" has 1 instance(s).
  Instance "cdb01", status READY, has 1 handler(s) for this service...
Service "qatest1" has 1 instance(s).
  Instance "cdb01", status READY, has 1 handler(s) for this service...
The command completed successfully
[oracle@oel63 ~]$
```

The container database CDB01 has two PDBs, DW17 and QATEST1, and the same listener manages connections for both PDBs.

Every container in a CDB has its own service name. The CDB itself has the default service name that's the same as the CDB name plus the domain, if any. For each PDB created or cloned, a new service is created and managed by the default listener unless otherwise specified. As you might expect, the only exception to this rule is the seed container (PDB$SEED). Since it is read-only and used only to create new PDBs, there is no reason to create a service and connect to it.

In addition to using the service name to connect to the CDB or any PDBs contained within, you can use OS authentication and connect as SYSDBA just as you would with a non-CDB. You'll be connected as the SYS user—a common user with privileges to maintain all PDBs within the CDB.

The transparency of a PDB and how it appears as a non-CDB to nonprivileged users extends to how you connect using entries in tnsnames.ora or using Oracle EasyConnect. As you may recall, the format for an EasyConnect connect string is as follows:

```
<username>/<password>@<hostname>:<port_number>/<service_name>
```

Therefore, for connecting to the user RJB in the PDB named DW17 in the CDB named CDB01 on the server oel63, you would use the following when starting SQL*Plus:

```
[oracle@oel63 ~]$ sqlplus rjb/rjb@oel63:1521/dw17

SQL*Plus: Release 12.1.0.1.0 Production on Thu Jul 3 21:56:44 2014

Copyright (c) 1982, 2013, Oracle.  All rights reserved.


Connected to:
Oracle Database 12c Enterprise Edition Release 12.1.0.1.0 - 64bit Production
With the Partitioning, Automatic Storage Management, OLAP, Advanced Analytics
and Real Application Testing options

SQL>
```

Notice that no reference to CDB01 is necessary. The PDB's service name masks the existence of the CDB or any other PDBs in the CDB.

Creating Services for CDBs or PDBs

If you're using a stand-alone server environment with Oracle Restart or a clustered environment using Oracle Clusterware, you'll automatically get a new service created with every new or cloned PDB or non-CDB (database instance). If you want additional services for a PDB, use the srvctl command like this:

```
[oracle@oel63 ~]$ srvctl add service -db cdb01 -service dwsvc2 -pdb dw17
[oracle@oel63 ~]$ srvctl start service -db cdb01 -service dwsvc2
[oracle@oel63 ~]$ lsnrctl status
. . .
Service "dwsvc2" has 1 instance(s).
  Instance "cdb01", status READY, has 1 handler(s) for this service...
. . .
[oracle@oel63 ~]$
```

In a nonrestart or nonclustered environment, you can use the DBMS_SERVICE package to create and start the service. To create the same new service as in the previous example with srvctl but instead using DBMS_SERVICE, you would connect to the PDB and then do the following:

```
SQL> begin
  2     dbms_service.create_service(
  3         service_name => 'dwsvc2',
  4         network_name => 'dwsvcnew');
  5     dbms_service.start_service(service_name => 'dwsvc2');
  6  end;
  7  /

PL/SQL procedure successfully completed.

SQL>
```

Note the slight difference in the example with DBMS_SERVICE: The actual service name is still dwsvc2, but the service name exposed to end users is dwsvcnew and would be used in the connection string for clients accessing this service.

Switching Connections Within a CDB

As you may infer from examples in previous chapters, you can switch containers within a session if you either are a common user with the SET CONTAINER system privilege or have a local user in each container and you connect using the service name.

```
[oracle@oel63 ~]$ sqlplus / as sysdba

SQL*Plus: Release 12.1.0.1.0 Production on Sat Jul 5 22:09:41 2014

Copyright (c) 1982, 2013, Oracle.  All rights reserved.
```

```
Connected to:
Oracle Database 12c Enterprise Edition Release 12.1.0.1.0 - 64bit Production
With the Partitioning, Automatic Storage Management, OLAP, Advanced Analytics
and Real Application Testing options

SQL> show con_name

CON_NAME
-----------------------------
CDB$ROOT
SQL> alter session set container=qatest1;

Session altered.

SQL> show con_name

CON_NAME
-----------------------------
QATEST1
SQL> connect rjb/rjb@oel63/dw17
Connected.
SQL> show con_name

CON_NAME
-----------------------------
DW17
SQL>
```

You can have a pending transaction in the first container, switch to a new container, and then switch back to the first container, and you still have the option to commit or roll back the pending transaction.

EXAM TIP   Common users who have the SET CONTAINER system privilege or local users who switch containers using CONNECT *local_user@PDB_NAME* do not automatically commit pending transactions when switching containers.

Start Up and Shut Down a CDB and Open and Close PDBs

Starting up and shutting down a CDB or opening and closing a PDB will seem familiar to any Oracle DBA who starts up and shuts down a non-CDB. The point that is often missed is that a CDB is ultimately a single database instance, and each PDB shares the resources of the CDB's instance. This is to be expected since each PDB is logically partitioned from all other PDBs using the CON_ID column in every table that is shared among the root and each PDB. This logical partitioning extends to user accounts and security as well; thus, it appears to noncommon users that the PDB has its own dedicated instance.

TIP   As you might expect, in a Real Application Cluster (RAC) environment, a CDB will usually have one instance on each node of the cluster. PDB services can fail over between the instances.

Since the CDB is a database instance, anything running within the CDB is shut down or disconnected when the CDB is shut down. This means that a PDB is not open for users until the CDB has been started and explicitly opened (either manually by the DBA or via a trigger), and similarly the PDB is closed when the CDB instance is shut down.

In the following sections, I'll show you how CDBs and PDBs are started up and shut down, as well as how to automate the process. You'll also want to know how to change parameters that are specific to a PDB, as well as database objects such as temporary tablespaces that can be created specifically for a PDB if the default global temporary tablespace does not meet the needs of the PDB's application.

CDB Instance Startup

The CDB instance is most like a traditional non-CDB instance. Figure 32-5 shows the five possible states for CDBs and PDBs in a multitenant environment.

From the shutdown state, you can perform a STARTUP NOMOUNT (connecting as SYSDBA using OS authentication) to start a CDB instance by opening the spfile and creating the processes and memory structures, but not yet opening the controlfile.

```
SQL> startup nomount
ORACLE instance started.

Total System Global Area 2622255104 bytes
Fixed Size                  2291808 bytes
Variable Size            1140852640 bytes
Database Buffers         1459617792 bytes
Redo Buffers               19492864 bytes
SQL> select con_id,name,open_mode from v$pdbs;

no rows selected

SQL>
```

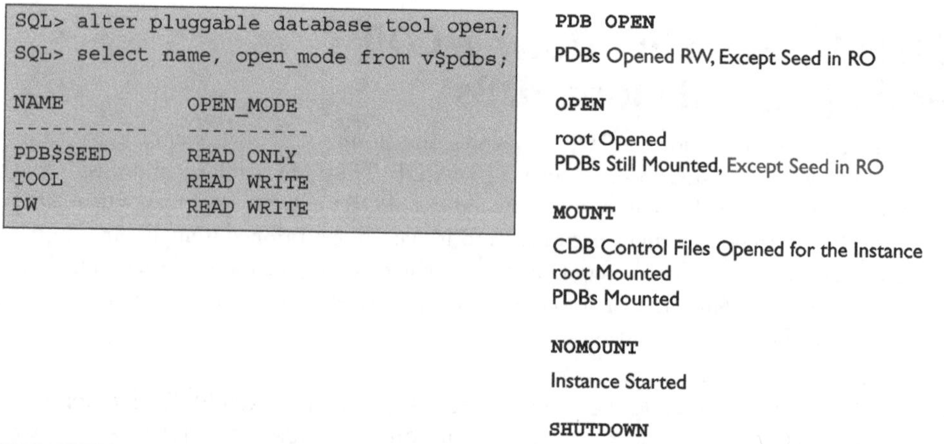

```
SQL> alter pluggable database tool open;
SQL> select name, open_mode from v$pdbs;

NAME            OPEN_MODE
-----------     ----------
PDB$SEED        READ ONLY
TOOL            READ WRITE
DW              READ WRITE
```

PDB OPEN

PDBs Opened RW, Except Seed in RO

OPEN

root Opened
PDBs Still Mounted, Except Seed in RO

MOUNT

CDB Control Files Opened for the Instance
root Mounted
PDBs Mounted

NOMOUNT

Instance Started

SHUTDOWN

Figure 32-5   CDB and PDB states

At this point in the startup process, the instance has no information about the PDBs within the CDB yet. You would typically perform a STARTUP NOMOUNT when you need to re-create or restore a missing controlfile for the CDB instance.

A lot of things happen when you move a CDB to the MOUNT state, as you can see in Figure 32-5. Not only are the CDB's controlfiles opened for the instance, but both the CDB$ROOT and all PDBs are changed to the MOUNT state.

```
SQL> alter database mount;

Database altered.

SQL> select con_id,name,open_mode from v$pdbs;

    CON_ID NAME                                OPEN_MODE
---------- --------------------------------    ----------
         2 PDB$SEED                            MOUNTED
         3 QATEST1                             MOUNTED
         5 DW17                                MOUNTED

SQL>
```

If any datafile operations are necessary (restore and recover, for example), this is where you would perform those, especially if those operations are required on the SYSTEM tablespace. The final step to make the root container available for opening PDBs is to change the CDB's state to OPEN. After CDB$ROOT is OPEN, it's available for read and write operations. The PDBs are still mounted with the seed database PDB$SEED mounted as READ ONLY.

```
SQL> alter database cdb01 open;

Database altered.

SQL> select con_id,name,open_mode from v$pdbs;

    CON_ID NAME             OPEN_MODE
---------- ---------------- ----------
         2 PDB$SEED         READ ONLY
         3 QATEST1          MOUNTED
         5 DW17             READ WRITE

SQL>
```

Because I created a second service for the PDB named DW17 earlier in the chapter and Oracle Restart is installed in this environment, DW17 is automatically opened in READ WRITE mode. The seed database PDB$SEED is always opened READ ONLY.

Once the CDB is opened (in other words, the root's datafiles are available along with the global temporary tablespace and the online redo log files), the PDBs are mounted but not yet open and available to users. Unless a PDB is opened with a trigger or via Oracle Restart, it remains by default in the MOUNTED state.

At this point, the CDB instance behaves much like a non-CDB instance. In the next section, you'll see how individual PDBs are opened and closed.

Open and Close a PDB

Once you have the root (CDB$ROOT) container of a CDB open, you can perform all desired operations on the PDBs within the CDB, including but not limited to cloning PDBs, creating a new PDB from the seed, unplugging a PDB, or plugging in a previously unplugged PDB. Remember that the seed container, PDB$SEED, is always open when CDB$ROOT is open but with an OPEN_MODE of READ ONLY.

There are quite a few options when you want to open or close a PDB. You can use ALTER PLUGGABLE DATABASE when connected as SYSDBA or SYSOPER, or if you're connected as SYSDBA within a PDB, you can use the same commands without having to specify the PDB name. In addition, you can selectively open or close one or more PDBs with the ALL or EXCEPT ALL option.

Using the ALTER PLUGGABLE DATABASE Command

You can open or close a PDB from any container by specifying the PDB name; alternatively, you can change the session context to a specific PDB and perform multiple operations on that PDB without qualifying it, as in these examples. Regardless of the current container, you can open and close any PDB by explicitly specifying the PDB name.

```
SQL> select con_id,name,open_mode from v$pdbs;

    CON_ID NAME                             OPEN_MODE
---------- -------------------------------- ----------
         2 PDB$SEED                         READ ONLY
         3 QATEST1                          MOUNTED
         5 DW17                             READ WRITE

SQL> alter pluggable database dw17 close;

Pluggable database altered.

SQL> alter pluggable database dw17 open read only;

Pluggable database altered.

SQL> alter pluggable database qatest1 open;

Pluggable database altered.

SQL>
```

Alternatively, you can set the default PDB name at the session level.

```
SQL> alter session set container=dw17;

Session altered.

SQL> alter pluggable database close;

Pluggable database altered.

SQL> alter pluggable database open read write;

Pluggable database altered.

SQL>
```

To set the default container back to the root container, use CONTAINER=CDB$ROOT in the ALTER SESSION command.

Selectively Opening or Closing PDBs

Even if you configure the PDBs in your CDB to open automatically with triggers, what if you have dozens of PDBs in your CDB and you want to open all of them except for one? You can use ALL EXCEPT to accomplish this in one command.

```
SQL> select con_id,name,open_mode from v$pdbs;

    CON_ID NAME                            OPEN_MODE
---------- ------------------------------- ----------
         2 PDB$SEED                        READ ONLY
         3 QATEST1                         MOUNTED
         4 DEV2015                         MOUNTED
         5 DW17                            MOUNTED

SQL> alter pluggable database all except qatest1 open;

Pluggable database altered.

SQL> select con_id,name,open_mode from v$pdbs;

    CON_ID NAME                            OPEN_MODE
---------- ------------------------------- ----------
         2 PDB$SEED                        READ ONLY
         3 QATEST1                         MOUNTED
         4 DEV2015                         READ WRITE
         5 DW17                            READ WRITE

SQL>
```

If you want to close all PDBs at once, just use ALL.

```
SQL> alter pluggable database all close;

Pluggable database altered.

SQL> select con_id,name,open_mode from v$pdbs;

    CON_ID NAME                            OPEN_MODE
---------- ------------------------------- ----------
         2 PDB$SEED                        READ ONLY
         3 QATEST1                         MOUNTED
         4 DEV2015                         MOUNTED
         5 DW17                            MOUNTED

SQL>
```

Opening or closing all PDBs leaves the root container in its current state, and as noted earlier, the seed container PDB$SEED is always READ ONLY and is in the MOUNT state only when the CDB is in the MOUNT state.

 TIP Within a PDB, you can use SHUTDOWN, with IMMEDIATE or TRANSACTIONAL or ABORT. The result is always the same as CLOSE.

When you close one or more PDBs, you can add the IMMEDIATE keyword to roll back any pending transactions within the PDB. If you leave off the IMMEDIATE keyword, the PDB is not shut down until all pending transactions have been either committed or rolled back, just as in a non-CDB database instance and all user sessions are disconnected by the user. If your session context is in a specific PDB, you can also use the SHUTDOWN IMMEDIATE statement to close the PDB, but note that this does not affect any other PDBs and that the root container's instance is still running.

CDB Instance Shutdown

When you are connected to the root container, you can shut down the CDB instance and close all PDBs with one command, much like you would shut down a non-CDB database instance.

```
SQL> shutdown immediate
Database closed.
Database dismounted.
ORACLE instance shut down.
SQL>
```

When specifying IMMEDIATE, the CDB instance does not wait for a COMMIT or ROLLBACK of pending transactions, and all user sessions to any PDB are disconnected. Using TRANSACTIONAL waits for all pending transactions to complete and then disconnects all sessions before terminating the instance.

As described in the previous section, you can use the same command to shut down a specific PDB, but only that PDB's datafiles are closed, and its services will no longer accept connection requests until it is opened again.

Automating PDB Startup

New options are available in database event triggers for a multitenant environment. One of these triggers is persistent, while two others are not; the reason for this will be clear shortly.

By default, after a CDB instance starts, all PDBs within the CDB are in MOUNT mode. If your PDB is not automatically opened by any other method (such as Oracle Restart), you can create a database trigger to start up all PDBs or just a few or just one. In the container database CDB01, the pluggable database DW17 starts up automatically via Oracle Restart; for the DEV2015 pluggable database, you'll create a trigger to change its status to OPEN READ WRITE when the container database is open, as shown here:

```
SQL> select con_id,name,open_mode from v$pdbs;

    CON_ID NAME                           OPEN_MODE
---------- ------------------------------ ----------
         2 PDB$SEED                       READ ONLY
         3 QATEST1                        MOUNTED
         4 DEV2015                        MOUNTED
         5 DW17                           READ WRITE
```

```
SQL> create trigger open_dev
  2    after startup on database
  3  begin
  4    execute immediate 'alter pluggable database dev2015 open';
  5  end;
  6  /

Trigger created.

SQL>
```

Next, shut down and restart the container CDB01 and see what happens.

```
SQL> shutdown immediate
Database closed.
Database dismounted.
ORACLE instance shut down.
SQL> startup
ORACLE instance started.

Total System Global Area 2622255104 bytes
Fixed Size                   291808 bytes
Variable Size            1140852640 bytes
Database Buffers         1459617792 bytes
Redo Buffers               19492864 bytes
Database mounted.
Database opened.
SQL> select con_id,name,open_mode from v$pdbs;

    CON_ID NAME                           OPEN_MODE
---------- ------------------------------ ----------
         2 PDB$SEED                       READ ONLY
         3 QATEST1                        MOUNTED
         4 DEV2015                        READ WRITE
         5 DW17                           READ WRITE

SQL>
```

 EXAM TIP By default, PDBs are closed after CDB startup. However, release 12.1.0.2 does allow you to instruct Oracle to preserve the state of the PDB so that if it was open on CDB shutdown, it will be opened on CDB startup.

The AFTER STARTUP ON DATABASE trigger is persistent unless you drop or disable it. Two new database event triggers for Oracle Database 12c, AFTER CLONE and BEFORE UNPLUG, are more dynamic. Both of those triggers must be specified with ON PLUGGABLE DATABASE; otherwise, the trigger will be invalid and will not fire.

You would use a trigger such as AFTER CLONE for a PDB that you'll frequently clone in a testing or development environment. The trigger itself exists in the source PDB and will persist unless you explicitly drop it. However, when you create a new PDB by cloning the existing PDB that contains this trigger, you can perform one-time initialization tasks in the cloned PDB right after it is cloned. Once those tasks are completed, the trigger is deleted so that any clones of the already cloned database won't perform those initialization tasks.

Changing PDB Status

In a non-CDB environment you often have reason to restrict access to a database for either maintenance tasks or to prepare it for a transportable tablespace or database operation. This is also true in a CDB environment. Previously in this chapter you saw how to open a PDB as READ ONLY. For any PDB that you want restricted to users with SYSDBA privileges (granted to either a global user or a local user), you use the RESTRICTED clause just as you would in a non-CDB environment.

```
SQL> alter pluggable database qatest1 close;

Pluggable database altered.

SQL> alter pluggable database qatest1 open restricted;

Pluggable database altered.

SQL> select con_id,name,open_mode from v$pdbs;

    CON_ID NAME                            OPEN_MODE
---------- ------------------------------- ----------
         2 PDB$SEED                        READ ONLY
         3 QATEST1                         RESTRICTED
         4 DEV2015                         READ WRITE
         5 DW17                            READ WRITE

SQL>
```

To turn off RESTRICTED mode, you close and reopen the PDB without the RESTRICTED keyword.

There are several operations you can perform on a PDB that do not require restarting the PDB in RESTRICTED mode:

- Take PDB datafiles offline or bring them back online
- Change the PDB's default tablespace
- Change the PDB's default temporary tablespace (local tablespace)
- Change the maximum size of a PDB:
  ```
  alter pluggable database storage (maxsize 50g);
  ```
- Change the name of a PDB

These dynamic settings help to maximize the availability of a PDB and allow you to make changes to a PDB much more quickly than the same changes you would make to a non-CDB that would require shutting down and restarting the database.

Evaluate the Impact of Parameter Value Changes

Although the application developer or database user of a PDB will not see any difference in how a PDB operates compared to a non-CDB, some of the differences require careful consideration by the global and local DBAs. A subset of parameters can be changed at the PDB level, but for the most part, a PDB inherits the parameter settings of the CDB. In addition, some ALTER

SYSTEM commands behave slightly differently depending on the context in which they are run by the DBA.

Understanding the Scope of Parameter Changes

Because a CDB is a database instance and PDBs share this instance, some of the CDB's parameters (stored in an spfile, of course) apply to the CDB and all PDBs and cannot be changed for any given PDB. You can identify the parameters that can be changed at the PDB level by looking at the ISPDB_MODIFIABLE column of V$PARAMETER. The data dictionary view PDB_SPFILE$ shows the nondefault values for specific parameters across all PDBs.

```
SQL> select pdb_uid,name,value$
  2  from pdb_spfile$
  3  where name='star_transformation_enabled';

  PDB_UID NAME                           VALUE$
---------- ------------------------------------- --------------------
2557165657 star_transformation_enabled          'FALSE'
3994587631 star_transformation_enabled          'TRUE'

SQL>
```

The settings local to a PDB stay with the PDB even when the PDB has been cloned or unplugged.

Using ALTER SYSTEM in a Multitenant Environment

Many of the ALTER SYSTEM commands you would use in a non-CDB environment work as you'd expect in a multitenant environment with a few caveats and exceptions. Some of the ALTER SYSTEM commands affect only the PDB or the CDB in which they are run. In contrast, some ALTER SYSTEM commands can be run only in the root container.

Within a PDB (as a local DBA or global DBA with a PDB as the current container), the following ALTER SYSTEM commands affect objects, parameters, or sessions specific to the PDB with no effect on any other PDBs or the root container:

- ALTER SYSTEM FLUSH SHARED_POOL
- ALTER SYSTEM FLUSH BUFFER_CACHE
- ALTER SYSTEM ENABLE RESTRICTED SESSION
- ALTER SYSTEM KILL SESSION
- ALTER SYSTEM SET

There are a few ALTER SYSTEM commands that you can run at the PDB level but affect the entire CDB. For example, running ALTER SYSTEM CHECKPOINT affects datafiles across the entire container unless the datafiles belong to a PDB that is opened as READ ONLY (such as the seed) or are OFFLINE.

Some ALTER SYSTEM commands are valid only for the entire container *and* must be run by a common user with SYSDBA privileges in the root container. For example, running ALTER SYSTEM SWITCH LOGFILE switches to the next online redo log file group. Since the online redo log files are common to all containers, this is the expected behavior.

Two-Minute Drill

Create a Container Database

- Every CDB is created with a seed database and a root container.
- To create a new CDB, you must use the ENABLE PLUGGABLE DATABASE clause of the CREATE DATABASE statement.
- If you are not using OMF (ideally with ASM), you must use the SEED FILE_NAME_CONVERT clause to specify the location and names for the database files of the seed container.
- Creating a CDB using CREATE DATABASE requires that you run catalog scripts to enable other Oracle features and create data dictionary objects through the catcon.pl script.

Create Pluggable Containers

- Creating a new PDB clones the PDB$SEED database within the same container.
- The new PDB has its own metadata catalog, local versions of SYSTEM and SYSAUX, and common users SYS and SYSTEM.
- Existing PDBs can be cloned, but only while they are open in read-only mode.
- A non-CDB (which must be release 12.x) can be plugged in by generating and running an XML file that describes the non-CDB.
- A non-CDB of release less than 12.x cannot be plugged in, but its contents can be imported into a new PDB.
- After starting the new PDB, the new default service name is registered with the listener.

Migrate a Pre-12.1 Non-CDB Database to CDB

- Only release 12.x databases can be converted to PDBs and plugged into a CDB
- Data Pump can transfer the contents of a pre-12.x non-CDB into a newly created PDB

Establish Connections to CDBs and PDBs

- You can connect to the root container as SYSDBA with OS authentication.
- Each PDB has at least one service published by a database listener.
- Services can be created with the srvctl utility or the DBMS_SERVICE package.
- Connections to PDBs can use EasyConnect or tnsnames.ora entries.
- A new PDB service created with Oracle Restart will automatically open a PDB when the CDB opens.
- To switch between PDBs and the CDB within a SQL*Plus session, use the ALTER SESSION SET CONTAINER command.

Start Up and Shut Down a CDB and Open and Close PDBs

- A container database (root container) starts up and shuts down in much the same way as a non-CDB.

- When the container database is in the OPEN state, all PDBs are initially in the MOUNT state unless automatically started via a trigger or Oracle Restart.

- The seed container PDB$SEED stays in READ ONLY state even when all other PDBs are open and cannot be set to READ WRITE.

- For a local user with SYSDBA privileges, a PDB can be closed with the usual SHUTDOWN syntax.

- PDBs support both the AFTER CLONE and BEFORE UNPLUG triggers, but these triggers are dropped after being executed once for the PDB target.

Evaluate the Impact of Parameter Value Changes

- The data dictionary view PDB_SPFILE$ contains the contents of the PDB instance's spfile, with the PDB_UID column identifying parameters specific to a PDB.

- Several ALTER SYSTEM commands, run by a user with DBA privileges in a PDB, operate only on the PDB, such as flushing the shared pool, flushing the buffer cache, killing sessions, and setting parameters specific to the PDB.

- ALTER SYSTEM CHECKPOINT in a PDB performs a checkpoint on the container database and therefore across all PDBs.

Self Test

1. Which of the following clauses are required in the CREATE DATABASE command to create a container database? (Choose all that apply.)

   A. ENABLE PLUGGABLE DATABASE

   B. CHARACTER SET

   C. SEED FILE_NAME_CONVERT

   D. ENABLE CONTAINER DATABASE

2. To unplug a database, which of the following conditions must be true? (Choose all that apply.)

   A. The database must be exported with Data Pump before dropping a PDB.

   B. There must be a full RMAN backup of the container.

   C. The PDB must be shut down.

   D. You must create an XML file with the metadata for the PDB.

3. Which of the following methods are viable options for migrating a pre-12.1 database to a PDB within an existing CDB? (Choose all that apply.)

   A. Upgrade the pre-12.1 database in place to version 12.1.0.1 or newer and plug it into an existing CDB.

   B. For Oracle Database versions 11g and 10g, you can use the DBMS_PDB .DESCRIBE PL/SQL procedure to create the XML file that will allow you to migrate the database to a CDB environment.

   C. Leave the existing database in place and perform a logical migration of the data using Data Pump export/import into a new PDB.

   D. Leave the existing database in place and perform a logical migration of the data using database links between the existing database and a new PDB.

4. Which of the following methods can you use to create a service for a new PDB or add another service to an existing PDB? (Choose all that apply.)

   A. A new service is created when the PDB is created or cloned; only one service is allowed per PDB.

   B. Use the srvctl add service command for an existing PDB.

   C. Use the DBMS_SERVICE package.

   D. Add a new listener to the configuration and add services with lsnrctl.

5. You execute the following commands for container CDB01:

```
SQL> shutdown immediate;
SQL> startup mount;
SQL> alter database open;
```

What is the default state of the CDB and its PDBs? (Choose the best answer.)

   A. All PDBs remain in a MOUNT state, including the root container.

   B. After STARTUP MOUNT, all PDBs are opened as READ WRITE but still in the MOUNT state.

   C. Only the root container is OPEN, and each PDB must be opened with a STARTUP command from the root container.

   D. The PDBs are opened if a trigger is defined or you use Oracle restart; the root container is opened in RESTRICTED mode.

   E. The root container is open, the seed database is open READ ONLY, and any PDBs with a trigger are opened.

6. What is the best way to find out whether an initialization parameter is modifiable at the PDB level? (Choose the best answer.)

   A. Change the session context to a specific PDB and use ALTER SYSTEM SET . . . .

   B. The TYPE column in V$PARAMETER will be PDB.

   C. Check the column ISPDB_MODIFIABLE in V$PARAMETER.

   D. Check the column ISCDB_MODIFIABLE in V$PARAMETER.

Self Test Answers

1. ☑ **A.** For creating a container database, the only required clause is ENABLE PLUGGABLE DATABASE. If you are not using OMF and you do not have the parameter DB_CREATE_FILE_DEST set (for example, to an ASM disk group), then you need to use the optional SEED FILE_NAME_CONVERT to specify where the seed database (PDB$SEED) files will reside.

   ☒ **B, C,** and **D** are incorrect. **B** is incorrect because the database character set is not related to whether the database is a CDB. **C** is incorrect because SEED FILE_NAME_CONVERT is required only if you are not using OMF for your database files. **D** is incorrect because there is no such clause ENABLE CONTAINER DATABASE in the CREATE DATABASE command.

2. ☑ **C** and **D.** To unplug a PDB from a CDB, it must first be shut down with the ALTER PLUGGABLE DATABASE . . . CLOSE command; you must also create the XML metadata file with DBMS_PDB.DESCRIBE so that the PDB can be plugged in later to this or another CDB in the future.

   ☒ **A** and **B** are incorrect. Neither a Data Pump export nor an RMAN backup of the PDB is required to unplug a PDB. When a PDB is unplugged, its datafiles are not dropped unless you explicitly drop the PDB and specify the INCLUDING DATAFILES clause.

3. ☑ **A, C,** and **D.** If you upgrade the database to version 12.1.0.1 or newer, you can run DBMS_PDB.DESCRIBE to create the XML file and plug the database into an existing CDB. Both Data Pump and database links are viable options for database migration in particular because both methods leave the original database intact at its original version.

   ☒ **B** is incorrect. You cannot directly plug a pre-12.1 Oracle Database into a CDB using this method since the DBMS_PDB package exists only in Oracle Database 12*c* container databases.

4. ☑ **B** and **C.** A listener service is automatically added when you create, clone, or plug in a PDB, but if you want an additional listener for a PDB, you can either use the **srvctl** command in an Oracle Restart or clustered environment or use the DBMS_SERVICE package with calls to CREATE_SERVICE and START_SERVICE to create and start the service.

   ☒ **A** and **D** are incorrect. **A** is incorrect because even though a service is automatically created when a PDB is created, cloned, or plugged in, you can have more than one service per PDB. **D** is incorrect because all services can share the default listener if desired.

PART V

5. ☑ **E.** When a CDB is in the OPEN state, the root container is available for connections, and the seed database is open but as READ ONLY. Any PDBs that have a trigger defined or are managed with Oracle Restart are opened automatically.

☒ **A, B, C**, and **D** are incorrect. **A** is incorrect because once the CDB is OPEN, the root container is open for READ WRITE, the seed database is open for READ ONLY, and all PDBs with a trigger or Oracle Restart service are opened as well. **B** is incorrect because the seed PDB is READ ONLY. **C** is incorrect because even if no PDBs are automatically opened, you can open them from the root container with the ALTER PLUGGABLE DATABASE command one at a time or all at once. You can use the STARTUP command to open a PDB only if you set the session parameter CONTAINER to the name of the PDB. **D** is incorrect because the root container must be explicitly opened in RESTRICTED mode when required.

6. ☑ **C.** The column ISPDB_MODIFIABLE is TRUE in V$PARAMETER if you can change this parameter for a single PDB.

☒ **A, B**, and **D** are incorrect. **A** is incorrect because even though you'll find out whether the parameter is modifiable, it is much easier to look in V$PARAMETER. **B** is incorrect because the TYPE column in V$PARAMETER indicates the data type of the parameter value. **D** is incorrect because there is no such column ISCDB_MODIFIABLE in V$PARAMETER.

CHAPTER 33

Managing Storage, Security, Availability, and Performance in a CDB and PDBs

Exam Objectives

- 063.5.1   Manage Permanent and Temporary Tablespaces in CDB and PDBs
- 063.6.1   Manage Common and Local Users
- 063.6.2   Manage Common and Local Privileges
- 063.6.3   Manage Common and Local Roles
- 063.6.4   Enable Common Users to Access Data in Specific PDBs
- 063.7.1   Perform Backups of a CDB and PDBs
- 063.7.2   Recover PDB from PDB Datafiles Loss
- 063.7.3   Use Data Recovery Advisor
- 063.7.4   Duplicate PDBs Using RMAN
- 063.8.1   Monitor Operations and Performance in a CDB and PDBs
- 063.8.3   Manage Allocation of Resources Between PDBs and Within a PDB
- 063.8.4   Perform Database Replay

This chapter covers a daunting list of objectives. Not to worry—many of them are straightforward if you understand the equivalent objective for environments that don't have container databases (CDBs). All that is necessary to translate that knowledge to a CDB environment is an understanding of the CDB architecture covered in previous chapters. There is, however, potential for confusion. Be prepared for some odd effects (typically when attempting to do something in the root container that should be done in a pluggable container) and always be aware of which container your session is currently attached to.

Space Management in a Multitenant Environment

In a multitenant environment, tablespaces and the datafiles that comprise them are associated with either the root container or one of the pluggable databases (PDBs) within the CDB. Within a container (either the root or a PDB), the database administrator (DBA) can issue absolutely normal commands to create and manage tablespaces and datafiles. The fact that a database is running in a multitenant environment should not have any effect.

Tablespace Architecture

The unique identifier for a tablespace is the tablespace name qualified with the container number. There is no problem with several PDBs having tablespaces with the same name. Indeed, every PDB will have a tablespace named SYSTEM (to store the definitions of the objects defined within the PDB) and a tablespace named SYSAUX that contains Oracle-defined objects such as the Automatic Workload Repository (AWR) that can be configured and populated independently in each PDB. Datafiles must of, course, be uniquely named, but they are still associated with only one PDB and can be administered only from within that PDB.

The following query shows the tablespace and datafile structure of a CDB with two pluggable containers named jw1 and jw5:

```
cdba> select con_id,c.name c,t.name t,d.name d from
  2  v$containers c join v$tablespace t using (con_id)
  3  join v$datafile d using (con_id,ts#) order by 1,2,3;
CON_ID C          T          D
------ ---------- ---------- --------------------------------
     1 CDB$ROOT   SYSAUX     C:\ORADATA\CDBA\SYSAUX01.DBF
     1 CDB$ROOT   SYSTEM     C:\ORADATA\CDBA\SYSTEM01.DBF
     1 CDB$ROOT   UNDOTBS1   C:\ORADATA\CDBA\UNDOTBS01.DBF
     1 CDB$ROOT   USERS      C:\ORADATA\CDBA\USERS01.DBF
     2 PDB$SEED   SYSAUX     C:\ORADATA\CDBA\SEED\SYSAUX_01.DBF
     2 PDB$SEED   SYSTEM     C:\ORADATA\CDBA\SEED\SYSTEM_01.DBF
     3 JW1        MYTS       C:\ORADATA\CDBA\JW1\MYTS1.DBF
     3 JW1        MYTS       C:\ORADATA\CDBA\JW1\MYTS2.DBF
     3 JW1        MYTS       C:\ORADATA\CDBA\JW1\MYTS3.DBF
     3 JW1        SYSAUX     C:\ORADATA\CDBA\JW1\SYSAUX01.DBF
     3 JW1        SYSTEM     C:\ORADATA\CDBA\JW1\SYSTEM01.DBF
     3 JW1        TSJW1      C:\ORADATA\CDBA\JW1\TSJW101.DBF
     3 JW1        USERS      C:\ORADATA\CDBA\JW1\USERS_01.DBF
     4 JW5        JW3TS      C:\ORADATA\CDBA\JW5\JW3TS.DBF
     4 JW5        SYSAUX     C:\ORADATA\CDBA\JW5\SYSAUX01.DBF
     4 JW5        SYSTEM     C:\ORADATA\CDBA\JW5\SYSTEM_01.DBF
     4 JW5        SYSTEM     C:\ORADATA\CDBA\JW5\SYSTEM02.DBF
     4 JW5        USERS      C:\ORADATA\CDBA\JW5\USERS01.DBF
19 rows selected.
cdba>
```

The only major enhancement to space management in a multitenant environment is that it is possible to set a space budget for each PDB, in other words, a limit for the total size of all datafiles and tempfiles that make up the container. To limit the overall size of a container, connect to the PDB and issue a command such as this:

```
alter pluggable database jw5 storage(maxsize 500g);
```

Any attempt to add a datafile or to extend an existing datafile that would take the total over the limit should fail.

Using CREATE TABLESPACE

The procedure for creating and modifying a tablespace in a CDB (root) container with CREATE TABLESPACE is the same as creating a tablespace in any PDB. If you are connected to CDB$ROOT, then the tablespace is visible and usable only in the root container; similarly, a tablespace created when connected to a PDB is visible only to that PDB and cannot be used by any other PDB unless connected with a database link. When connected to the root container, the CDB_TABLESPACES and CDB_DATA_FILE views will show the whole picture, as will V$TABLESPACE and V$DATAFILE. When connected to a PDB, these views will show the tablespaces and datafiles that are part of the PDB and the common undo tablespace.

For ease of management, Oracle recommends using separate directories to store datafiles for each PDB and the CDB. Even better, if you use Automatic Storage Management (ASM) or Oracle Managed Files (OMF), you'll automatically get your datafiles and other database objects segregated into separate directories by container ID. Here is how the datafiles for the container database CDB01 are stored in an ASM disk group:

```
SQL> select con_id,name,open_mode from v$pdbs;

    CON_ID NAME                              OPEN_MODE
---------- ------------------------------- ---------- ----------
         2 PDB$SEED                          READ ONLY
         3 QATEST1                           READ WRITE
         4 DEV2015                           READ WRITE
         5 DW17                              READ WRITE

SQL> quit
Disconnected from Oracle Database 12c Enterprise Edition

Release 12.1.0.1.0 - 64bit Production
With the Partitioning, Automatic Storage Management, OLAP, Advanced Analytics
and Real Application Testing options
[oracle@oel63 ~]$ . oraenv
 ORACLE_SID = [cdb01] ? +ASM
The Oracle base has been changed from /u01/app/oracle to /u01/app
[oracle@oel63 ~]$ asmcmd
ASMCMD> ls
DATA/
RECOV/
ASMCMD> cd data
ASMCMD> ls
ASM/
CDB01/
```

PART V

```
DBAHANDBOOK/
orapwasm
ASMCMD> cd cdb01
ASMCMD> ls
CONTROLFILE/
DATAFILE/
DD7C48AA5A4404A2E04325AAE80A403C/
EA128C7783417731E0434702A8C08F56/
EA129627ACA47C9DE0434702A8C0836F/
FAE6382E325C40D8E0434702A8C03802/
FD8E768DE1094F9AE0434702A8C03E94/
ONLINELOG/
PARAMETERFILE/
TEMPFILE/
spfilecdb01.ora
ASMCMD> cd datafile
ASMCMD> ls
SYSAUX.272.830282801
SYSTEM.273.830282857
UNDOTBS1.275.830282923
USERS.274.830282921
ASMCMD>
```

The container's datafiles are stored in the DATAFILE subdirectory; each of the PDBs has its own set of datafiles in one of those subdirectories with the long string of hexadecimal digits. You use OMF with ASM in this scenario; you don't need to know or care what those directory paths and filenames are since the locations of the datafiles are managed automatically.

Default Permanent and Temporary Tablespaces in a PDB

Changing the default tablespace in a CDB or PDB is identical to changing the default tablespace in a non-CDB. For both CDBs and PDBs, you use the ALTER DATABASE DEFAULT TABLESPACE command. In the following example, you set the container to QATEST1, create a new tablespace within QATEST1, and change the default tablespace to be the tablespace you just created:

```
SQL> alter session set container=qatest1;

Session altered.

SQL> create tablespace qa_dflt datafile size 100m
  2        autoextend on next 100m maxsize 1g;

Tablespace created.

SQL> alter database default tablespace qa_dflt;

Pluggable database altered.

SQL>
```

Going forward, any new users (local or common) within QATEST1 that don't have a specific default permanent tablespace will use the tablespace QA_DFLT.

For any CDB you can have one default temporary tablespace or temporary tablespace group defined at the CDB level that can be used by the root container. Every PDB should also have a temporary tablespace. This will be created automatically if the PDB is created from the seed container and would usually already exist in any non-CDB database that is plugged in. A PDB can have multiple temporary tablespaces to be used by different users, as well as one default temporary tablespace. In the following example, you create a new temporary tablespace called QA_DFLT_TEMP in the PDB QATEST1 and make it the default temporary tablespace for QATEST1:

```
SQL> create temporary tablespace qa_dflt_temp
  2  tempfile size 100m autoextend on
  3  next 100m maxsize 500m;

Tablespace created.

SQL> alter database
  2  default temporary tablespace qa_dflt_temp;

Pluggable database altered.

SQL>
```

A temporary tablespace created within a PDB stays with that PDB when it's unplugged and plugged back into the same or a different CDB. If a user is not assigned a specific temporary tablespace, then that user is assigned the default temporary tablespace for the PDB.

Exercise 33-1: Administering Tablespaces in a Multitenant Database   This exercise assumes you have a CDB named cdba with two pluggable containers called pdba and pdbb, opened in read-write mode, and that there is a tnsnames.ora file with entries for each PDB and the root container.

1. Enable Oracle Managed Files for pdba, giving it its own location. Create the nominated directory first, and ensure that the Oracle owner has read-write permissions on it. The following example is for Linux:

   ```
   sqlplus sys/oracle@pdba as sysdba
   alter system set db_create_file_dest='/u01/oradata/pdba';
   alter session set container=cdb$root;
   select  value,con_id from v$system_parameter
   where name='db_create_file_dest';
   ```

   Note that the OMF parameters are PDB modifiable.

2. In each PDB, create a new permanent tablespace. Use OMF for pdba and nominate files for pdbb. The following example is for Windows:

   ```
   sqlplus sys/oracle@pdba as sysdba
   create tablespace defa datafile size 100m;
   create temporary tablespace tmpa tempfile size 100m;
   alter database default tablespace defa;
   alter database default temporary tablespace tmpa;
   alter session set container=pdbb;
   create tablespace defb datafile 'c:\oradata\defb.dbf' size 100m;
   create temporary tablespace tmpb tempfile 'c:\oradata\tmpb.dbf' size 100m;
   alter database default tablespace defb;
   alter database default temporary tablespace tmpb;
   ```

3. Investigate the structures created.

```
alter session set container=cdb$root;
select con_id,property_value from cdb_properties where property_
name='DEFAULT_PERMANENT_TABLESPACE';
select con_id,property_value from cdb_properties where property_
name='DEFAULT_TEMP_TABLESPACE';
select con_id,ts#,name from v$tablespace;
select con_id,ts#,name from v$datafile;
select con_id,ts#,name from v$tempfile;
```

Manage Common and Local Users, Roles, and Privileges

Users and roles can be defined in the root container, in which case they are *common* and propagated to every PDB in the CDB, or they can be defined in a PDB, in which case they are *local* and exist only in that PDB. Common and local roles can be granted to local users or to common users. Direct grants of privileges are always local to the container where the grant was made.

Common and Local Users

In a multitenant environment, there are two types of users: *common* users and *local* users. A common user in a CDB (root container) has an account available in the root container and automatically in each PDB within the CDB. Common users' names must start, by default, with C##, which makes it easy to distinguish a common user from a local user in each PDB.

Creating a local user in a PDB is exactly like creating a user in a non-CDB. You can create a local user either with a common user or with another local user with the CREATE USER privileges.

```
SQL> alter session set container=qatest1;

Session altered.

SQL> create user qa_fnd1 identified by qa901;

User created.

SQL> grant create session to qa_fnd1;

Grant succeeded.

SQL> connect qa_fnd1/qa901@oel63:1521/qatest1
Connected.
SQL>
```

The root container (CDB$ROOT) cannot have local users, only common users. Common users have the same identity and password in the root container and every PDB, both current and future. Having a common user account doesn't automatically mean you have the same privileges across every PDB, including the root container. The accounts SYS and SYSTEM are common users who can set any PDB as their default container. For new common users, the username must begin with C## unless the instance parameter COMMON_USER_PREFIX has been changed from the default. Note that the Oracle-supplied common users do not have the C## prefix in order to maintain compatibility with non-CDB environments.

When you create a common user with the CREATE USER command, you can add CONTAINER=ALL to the command, as in this example:

```
SQL> create user c##secadmin identified by sec404 container=all;

User created.

SQL> grant dba to c##secadmin;

Grant succeeded.

SQL>
```

If you are connected to the root container and have the CREATE USER privilege, the CONTAINER=ALL clause is applied by default. The same applies to a local user and the CONTAINER=CURRENT clause. The C##SECADMIN user now has DBA privileges in the root container. This user has an account set up in each PDB but no privileges in any PDB unless explicitly assigned.

```
SQL> connect c##secadmin/sec404@oel63:1521/cdb01
Connected.
SQL> alter session set container=qatest1;
ERROR:
ORA-01031: insufficient privileges


SQL>
```

To allow the user C##SECADMIN to at least connect to the QATEST1 database, grant the appropriate privileges as follows:

```
SQL> grant create session, set container to c##secadmin;

Grant succeeded.

SQL> connect c##secadmin/sec404@oel63:1521/cdb01
Connected.
SQL> alter session set container=qatest1;

Session altered.

SQL>
```

When using CREATE USER, you can optionally specify the default tablespace, the default temporary tablespace, and the profile. These three attributes must exist in each PDB; otherwise, those values will be set to the PDB defaults for those items.

What if a common user is created while one of the PDBs is currently not OPEN or is in READ ONLY mode? The new common user's attributes are synced the next time the PDB is opened in READ WRITE mode.

PART V

Grant Privileges Commonly and Locally

Common and local privileges apply to common and local users. If a privilege is granted across all containers to a common user, it's a common privilege. Similarly, a privilege granted in the context of a single PDB is a local privilege, regardless of whether the user is local or common.

In the previous section, the user C##SECADMIN, a common user, was granted the CREATE SESSION privilege but only on the QATEST1 container. If C##SECADMIN needs access to all PDBs by default, use the CONTAINER=ALL keyword to grant that privilege across all current and new PDBs in the CDB.

```
SQL> connect / as sysdba
Connected.
SQL> show con_id

CON_ID
------------------------------
1
SQL> grant create session to c##secadmin container=all;

Grant succeeded.

SQL> connect c##secadmin/sec404@oel63:1521/dw17
Connected.
SQL>
```

From a security perspective, you can grant common users privileges in the root container but no other containers. Remember that only common users can connect to the root container, regardless of the privileges granted; for a common user to connect to the root container, the user will need the CREATE SESSION privilege in the context of the root container, as you can see in the following example:

```
SQL> connect / as sysdba
Connected.
SQL> alter session set container=cdb$root;

Session altered.

SQL> create user c##rootadm identified by adm580;

User created.

SQL> connect c##rootadm/adm580@oel63:1521/cdb01
ERROR:
ORA-01045: user C##ROOTADM lacks CREATE SESSION privilege; logon denied


Warning: You are no longer connected to ORACLE.
SQL>
```

To fix this issue for C##ROOTADM, you need to grant the CREATE SESSION privilege in the context of the root container.

```
SQL> grant create session to c##rootadm container=current;

Grant succeeded.
```

```
SQL> connect c##rootadm/adm580@oel63:1521/cdb01
Connected.
SQL>
```

You revoke privileges from users and roles using the REVOKE command, as in previous releases and non-CDBs. The key difference using GRANT and REVOKE in a multitenant environment is the addition of the CONTAINER clause where you specify the context of the GRANT or REVOKE. Here are some examples of the CONTAINER clause:

- CONTAINER=QATEST1 (privileges valid only in the PDB QATEST1)
- CONTAINER=ALL (privileges valid across all PDBs, current and future)
- CONTAINER=CURRENT (privileges granted or revoked in the current container)

To grant a privilege with CONTAINER=ALL, the grantor must have the SET CONTAINER privilege along with the GRANT ANY PRIVILEGE system privilege.

Manage Common and Local Roles

Roles, just like system and object privileges, work much the same in a multitenant environment as they do in a non-CDB environment. Common roles use the same conventions as common users and start with C##; a common role can have the same privileges across all containers or specific privileges or no privileges in a subset of containers. You use the CONTAINER clause to specify the context of the role.

```
SQL> connect / as sysdba
Connected.
SQL> create role c##mv container=all;

Role created.

SQL> alter session set container=dw17;

Session altered.

SQL> create user dw_repl identified by dw909;

User created.

SQL> grant c##mv to dw_repl;

Grant succeeded.

SQL>
```

Note in the example that a common role (C##MV) was granted to a local user (DW_REPL) in DW17. The user DW_REPL inherits all the privileges in the role C##MV but only in the DW17 PDB. The reverse is also possible: A common user (such as C##RJB) can be granted a local role (such as LOCAL_ADM) in a specific PDB (such as QATEST1), and therefore the privileges granted via LOCAL_ADM are available only in QATEST1 for C##RJB.

PART V

Enable Common Users to Access Data in Specific PDBs

Just as in a non-CDB environment, you may want to share objects with users in other PDBs. By default, any tables created by a common or local user are nonshared and are accessible only in the PDB where they were created.

Shared tables, on the other hand, have some restrictions. Only Oracle-supplied common users (such as SYS or SYSTEM) can create shared tables, and these can be created only by running the supplied scripts that create the component in which they are used. Common users that the DBA creates (even with DBA privileges such as CREATE USER, DROP ANY TABLE, and so forth) cannot create shared tables.

The two types of shared objects are "links": object links and metadata links. Object links connect every PDB to a table in the root container, and each PDB sees the same rows. A good example of this is AWR data in tables like DBA_HIST_ACTIVE_SESS_HISTORY, which has the column CON_ID so you can identify which container the row in DBA_HIST_ACTIVE_ SESSION_HISTORY applies to.

In contrast, metadata links allow access to tables in the root container plus their own private copies of the data. Most of the DBA_xxx views use this method. For example, looking at the DBA_USERS view in the PDB QATEST1, there is no CON_ID column from the PDB perspective.

```
SQL> select username, common from dba_users;

USERNAME                          COMMON
------------------------------    ----------
C##KLH                            YES
PDBADMIN                          NO
AUDSYS                            YES
GSMUSER                           YES
SPATIAL_WFS_ADMIN_USR             YES
C##RJB                            YES
SPATIAL_CSW_ADMIN_USR             YES
APEX_PUBLIC_USER                  YES
RJB                               NO
SYSDG                             YES
DIP                               YES
QA_FND1                           NO
```

However, from the same table in the root container, you can look at CDB_USERS and see the local and common users across all containers.

```
SQL> select con_id,username,common from cdb_users
  2  order by username,con_id;

   CON_ID USERNAME                       COMMON
---------- ------------------------------  ----------
        1 ANONYMOUS                       YES
. . .
        5 AUDSYS                          YES
        1 C##KLH                          YES
        3 C##KLH                          YES
        4 C##KLH                          YES
        5 C##KLH                          YES
```

```
1 C##RJB                     YES
3 C##RJB                     YES
4 C##RJB                     YES
5 C##RJB                     YES
1 C##ROOTADM                 YES
3 C##ROOTADM                 YES
. . .
4 DVSYS                      YES
5 DVSYS                      YES
5 DW_REPL                    NO
1 FLOWS_FILES                YES
2 FLOWS_FILES                YES
. . .
5 OUTLN                      YES
3 PDBADMIN                   NO
3 QAFRED                     NO
3 QA_FND1                    NO
3 RJB                        NO
4 RJB                        NO
5 RJB                        NO
1 SI_INFORMTN_SCHEMA         YES
2 SI_INFORMTN_SCHEMA         YES
. . .
198 rows selected.

SQL>
```

The common users such as C##RJB exist for every PDB (other than the seed database). Users such as QAFRED exist only in the PDB with CON_ID=3 (QATEST1). Note also that the common users you create must start with C##; Oracle-supplied common users do not need this prefix.

Exercise 33-2: Manage Common and Local Users and Roles This exercise demonstrates how to manage users and roles in a multitenant environment. It is assumed the CDB is named cdba, with pluggable containers pdba and pdbb.

1. Run queries to determine what users exist.
   ```
   conn system/oracle@cdba
   select con_id,username,common,oracle_maintained
   from cdb_users order by 1,2;
   select con_id,username,common,oracle_maintained
   from cdb_users order by 2,1;
   ```
   Note which users are common and which are local.

2. Create users in the root container and grant a common role.
   ```
   conn system/oracle@cdba
   create user user1 identified by oracle;
   create user c##user1 identified by oracle;
   show parameter common_user_prefix
   create user c##user2 identified by oracle container=all;
   grant dba to c##user1;
   grant dba to c##user2 container=all;
   ```
   Note that it is not possible to create a common user unless the prefix is used.

PART V

3. Connect as a newly created common user.

```
conn c##user1/oracle@cdba;
conn c##user1/oracle@pdba;
conn c##user2/oracle@pdba;
```

Note that the connection to a PDB fails if the user has not been granted the appropriate role or privilege with an appropriate scope.

4. Create a local user.

```
conn c##user2/oracle@pdba;
create user locala identified by oracle container=current;
grant dba to locala;
connect locala/oracle@pdba
select * from session_roles;
conn sys/oracle@cdba as sysdba;
select con_id,username,common,oracle_maintained

from cdb_users order by 1,2;
```

Observe that the new users are not "Oracle maintained."

5. Use common and local roles.

Only common roles can be created in the root, and they can be granted commonly or locally. Any attempt to create a local role in the root or to grant it to a user in a particular PDB will fail.

```
conn system/oracle@cdba
select role,common,oracle_maintained,con_id

from cdb_roles order by role;
create role myrole1 container=current;
create role c##myrole1 container=current;
create role c##myrole1 container=all;
create role c##myrole2 container=all;
grant c##myrole1 to c##user2 container=all;
grant c##myrole2 to c##user2 container=pdba;
conn system/oracle@pdba
grant c##myrole2 to c##user2 container=current;
conn system/oracle@cdba
select grantee,granted_role,common,con_id from cdb_role_privs
where grantee like 'C##%' order by 1,2,3;
conn c##user2/oracle@pdba
select * from session_roles;
```

What syntax is valid for local and common roles? What is the scope of the various role grants?

EXAM TIP   In the root container, only common users and roles can be created. Appending CONTAINER=ALL to the CREATE statement is optional; CONTAINER=CURRENT is not permitted.
In a pluggable container, only local users and roles can be created. Appending CONTAINER=CURRENT to the CREATE statement is optional; CONTAINER=ALL is not permitted.

Audit in the Multitenant Environment

Traditional audit (as enabled with the AUDIT_% instance parameters and the AUDIT command) does not change when moving to a multitenant environment. It is configured in each PDB as in previous releases. Unified Audit is multitenant aware and is the recommended technique.

The syntax for creating and enabling unified Audit policies was discussed in Chapter 16. This syntax is unchanged in a multitenant environment. What does change is the visibility of the audit policies. If a policy is defined in the root container, it can be enabled in all CDBs. It cannot be enabled (or disabled) from within a PDB. This means that the senior DBA, who has access to the root container, can configure auditing of any action by any user in the entire environment. A policy defined while connected to a PDB is visible only within that PDB and can be managed by the DBA of that PDB.

To view audit records, query the UNIFIED_AUDIT_TRAIL view. This will show the audit records generated by your currently connected container, either the root or a PDB. When connected to the root, you can also query the CDB_UNIFIED_AUDIT_TRAIL view. This is a consolidated view of the unified Audit trail in every container.

The following example creates and enables a CDB-wide audit policy that will capture all actions by users who have connected with DBA privileges assigned by operating system or password file authentication:

```
cdba>
cdba> conn / as sysdba
Connected.
cdba> show con_name
CON_NAME
------------------------------
CDB$ROOT
cdba> create audit policy audit_sys actions all
  2    when 'sys_context(''userenv'',''isdba'')=''TRUE'''
  3    evaluate per statement;
Audit policy created.
cdba> audit policy audit_sys whenever successful;
Audit succeeded.
```

A user now connects to the pluggable container JW1 with the SYSDBA privilege, but he cannot disable (or even see) the audit policy.

```
cdba> conn sys/oracle@jw1 as sysdba
Connected.
jw1> noaudit policy audit_sys;
noaudit policy audit_sys
*
ERROR at line 1:
ORA-46357: Audit policy AUDIT_SYS not found.
jw1> select * from scott.emp where ename='KING';
    EMPNO ENAME      JOB              MGR HIREDATE                   SAL
--------- ---------- --------- ---------- -------------------- ----------
     7839 KING       PRESIDENT            1981-11-17:00:00:00         5000
```

Nonetheless, in the root container the audit records can be seen as having been generated in the pluggable container.

```
cdba> select con_id,dbusername,sql_text from cdb_unified_audit_trail
  2  where unified_audit_policies='AUDIT_SYS' and sql_text like '%emp%';
   CON_ID DBUSERNAME SQL_TEXT
---------- ---------- --------------------------------------------------------
        3 SYS        select * from scott.emp where ename='KING'
```

Multitenant Backup and Recovery

In a multitenant environment, you use the same tools for backup and recovery as in a non-CDB environment. You can back up and restore the entire CDB, a single PDB, a tablespace, a datafile, or even a single block anywhere in the CDB. Many operations can be performed from within a PDB, and some can be performed only at the CDB level from the root container. You can also duplicate a PDB using Recovery Manager (RMAN). Using RMAN gives you more flexibility than when cloning a PDB with the CREATE PLUGGABLE DATABASE . . . FROM . . . option. For example, you can use the RMAN DUPLICATE command to copy all PDBs or a subset of PDBs within a CDB or to a new CDB, including the root and the seed containers.

The Data Recovery Advisor is usable in a CDB in the same way as in a non-CDB. Follow the routine within an RMAN session.

```
list failure;
advise failure
repair falure;
```

This will report on detected problems, generate a script to fix them, and run the script.

Back Up a CDB and Individual PDBs

For multitenant databases, the RMAN syntax has been modified, and new clauses have been added. You need to be careful when connecting with RMAN because the ORACLE_SID environment variable will refer to the instance, which is managed from the root. Connecting using operating system authentication will therefore connect you to the root container, as shown in Figure 33-1. Note that the RMAN session can see the tablespaces and datafiles of all the containers and that (with the exception of the root) the tablespaces are prefixed with the container name.

From a session such as that depicted in Figure 33-1, you can back up the entire CDB or individual PDBs with commands such as these:

```
backup database;
backup pluggable database jw5;
```

The second command in the previous code will identify the tablespaces that make up the nominated container and back them up using what RMAN defaults have been configured. It is also possible to back up individual tablespaces of pluggable databases from the root by using the container name as a prefix. Here's an example:

```
backup tablespace jw1:users,jw5:users
```

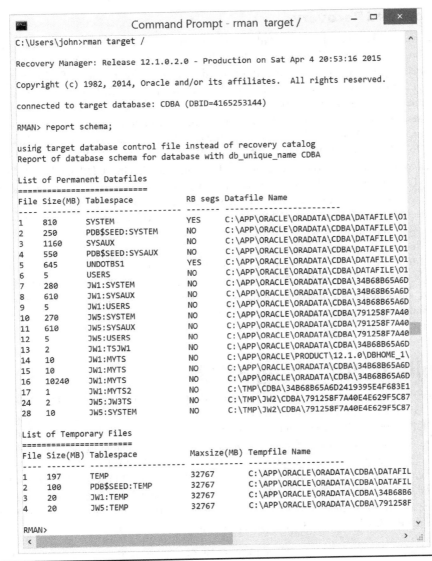

Figure 33-1   An RMAN session against the root container of a CDB

To connect to a pluggable container, you must use password file authentication and connect through a TNS service name. Here's an example:

```
rman target sys/oracle@jw5
```

The scope of a session launched in this way will be limited to the tablespaces that make up the pluggable database, and there are no changes in syntax from what you would use in a non-CDB.

Restore and Recovery

In the event of any sort of instance failure, instance recovery will occur automatically in the transition from mount mode to open mode, in the same manner as for a non-CDB. Once this is completed, any in-flight transactions will be rolled back when the individual PDBs are opened. Recovering from loss of a controlfile is also identical to a non-CDB: In nomount mode, the controlfile must be restored or re-created.

To restore and recover the entire CDB, start the instance in nomount mode, connect to the root container (which is the only accessible container in this mode), and issue the usual RESTORE CONTROLFILE, RESTORE DATABASE, and RECOVER DATABASE commands that are used for complete or incomplete recovery. The critical datafiles in a CDB are the SYSTEM and UNDO tablespaces of the root container. Damage to these will force the CDB instance to terminate, and they must be restored and recovered in mount mode. Thus far, there are no differences between CDB and non-CDB. The differences are when applying restore and recover operations to individual PDBs.

Within a PDB, the SYSTEM tablespace is critical. If this is damaged, the entire container will be brought down to mount mode, and until the tablespace is restored and recovered, it cannot be opened. Other PDBs will be unaffected by this. Any other tablespaces can be offlined, restored, and recovered individually while the PDB remains open. These operations can be accomplished from the root container by prefixing the tablespace name with the container name or from within the PDB using the usual non-CDB commands.

Duplicate PDBs Using RMAN

Chapter 32 showed you how to clone a PDB using the CREATE PLUGGABLE DATABASE . . . FROM command. RMAN gives you more flexibility and scalability when duplicating one or more PDBs within a CDB or the entire CDB. As in any RMAN DUPLICATE operation, you must create an auxiliary instance for the destination CDB. The auxiliary instance must be started with the initialization parameter ENABLE_PLUGGABLE_DATABASE=TRUE.

When duplicating a CDB, the syntax lets you nominate which PDBs should or should not be included in the duplicate. The duplicate will always include the root and seed containers. To duplicate a CDB to another CDB with just one PDB called TOOL to a new CDB called NINE, you use the RMAN DUPLICATE command like this:

```
RMAN> duplicate database to nine pluggable database tool;
```

If you want to copy two or more pluggable databases, you just add them to the end of the DUPLICATE command.

```
RMAN> duplicate database to nine pluggable database qa_2015,tool;
```

Exclusions are allowed in the DUPLICATE command. If you want to clone an entire CDB but without the CCREPOS PDB, do this:

```
RMAN> duplicate database to nine skip pluggable database ccrepos;
```

Finally, you can duplicate not only pluggable databases, but also individual tablespaces, to a new CDB.

```
RMAN> duplicate database to nine
2>              pluggable databases qa_2015,ccrepos tablespace tool:users;
```

Mulitenant Performance Monitoring and Tuning

Generally speaking, instance and database tuning may be best done from the root container, from where the instance and the database as a whole can be observed. SQL tuning will usually be done from within the container where the SQL is running. In either case, the same methodology that you would use in a non-CDB environment applies.

1. Identify the problem and a goal.

2. Determine a possible cause of the problem.

3. Apply a solution.

4. Confirm whether the solution has been effective.

5. Repeat as necessary until the goal is reached.

The same techniques and tools that you would use in a non-CDB are available, usually at both the CDB and PDB levels. One issue that is unique to a CDB environment is the possibility that activity generated by sessions against one PDB could impact adversely activity in another PDB. To manage this, the Resource Manager has enhancements to control what resources are available to each PDB.

Tuning the Instance

Adjusting parameters at the CDB is much like tuning a single instance in a non-CDB environment that has several applications with different resource and availability requirements. It's worth mentioning again that a CDB *is* a single database instance; however, with the added features of the multitenant environment, you have much more control over resource consumption among the several applications (each in their own PDB) in addition to the strong isolation between the applications from a security perspective.

Tuning the memory in a CDB means you're changing the same memory areas as in a non-CDB:

- Buffer cache (SGA)
- Shared pool (SGA)
- Program Global Area (PGA)

When you calculate the memory requirements for a CDB, your first estimate can be the sum of all corresponding memory requirements for each non-CDB that will become a PDB. Of course, you will eventually want to reduce the total memory footprint for the CDB based on a number of factors. For example, not all PDBs will be active at the same time; therefore, you will likely not need as much total memory allocated to the CDB.

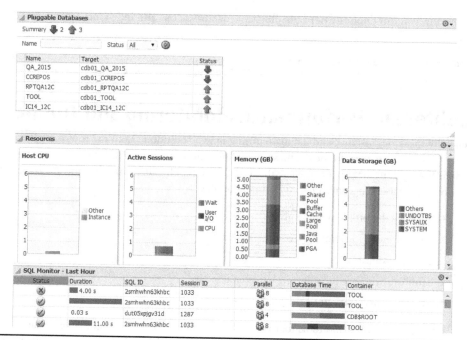

Figure 33-2   Viewing PDB resource usage within a CDB using Cloud Control 12c

Using Enterprise Manager Cloud Control 12c is a good way to see resource usage across the CDB. In Figure 33-2, the container CDB01 has three active PDBs and two inactive ones.

The total memory allocated for the CDB is approximately 5GB. Three non-CDB databases would likely use 5GB or more each; all five PDBs in CDB01 may perform just fine in a total of 5GB.

There are a few different approaches to resource allocation among PDBs within a CDB:

- **None**   Let each PDB use all the resources of the CDB if no other PDB is active; when multiple PDBs need resources, they are divided equally.

- **Minimum**   Each PDB gets a minimum guaranteed resource allocation.

- **Minimum/maximum**   Each PDB gets both a minimum guaranteed resource allocation and a maximum.

Resource usage allocation in a CDB is measured in *shares*. By default, all PDBs can consume all resources allocated to the CDB. We cover more details on how shares are allocated and calculated later in the chapter.

There is only one spfile per CDB instance. All database parameters are stored in the CDB's spfile, but many of those parameters can be changed at the PDB level. The column ISPDB_MODIFIABLE is an easy way to see which parameters you can change at the PDB level.

```
SQL> select ispdb_modifiable,count(ispdb_modifiable)
  2  from v$parameter
  3  group by ispdb_modifiable;
```

```
ISPDB COUNT(ISPDB_MODIFIABLE)
----- --------------------
TRUE                     171
FALSE                    196

SQL>
```

When you unplug a PDB, its customized parameters stay with the unplugged PDB and are set when that PDB is plugged back in, regardless of which PDB it is plugged into. When a PDB is cloned, the custom parameters are cloned as well. At the container level, you can also look at the data dictionary view PDB_SPFILE$ to see which parameters are different across PDBs.

```
select pdb_uid,pdb_name,name,value$
from pdb_spfile$ ps
   join cdb_pdbs cp
      on ps.pdb_uid=cp.con_uid;

   PDB_UID PDB_NAME        NAME                                  VALUE$
---------- --------------- ------------------------------------- ----------
1258510409 TOOL            sessions                              200
1288637549 RPTQA12C        cursor_sharing                        'FORCE'
1288637549 RPTQA12C        star_transformation_enabled           TRUE
1288637549 RPTQA12C        open_cursors                          300
```

In the TOOL PDB, the SESSIONS parameter is different from the default (at the CDB level); the RPTQA12C PDB has three nondefault parameters set.

Using Memory Advisors

The buffer cache in a CDB, shared across all PDBs, behaves much like the buffer cache in a non-CDB; the same least recently used (LRU) algorithms are used to determine when and if a block should stay in the buffer cache. Because the buffer cache is shared, the PDB's container ID (CON_ID) is also stored in each block. The same container ID is stored in the other SGA and PGA memory areas such as the shared pool in the SGA and the global PGA. The memory advisors from previous versions of Oracle Database work in much the same way in a multitenant environment; sizing recommendations are at the CDB (instance) level. Individual memory parameters that can be adjusted at the PDB are limited to SORT_AREA_SIZE and SORT_AREA_RETAINED_SIZE.

Figure 33-3 shows the output from the SGA Memory Advisor launched from Cloud Control 12c.

Even with several PDBs in the CDB01 container, it appears that the total memory for the CDB can be reduced by at least 1GB and retain good performance for all PDBs.

To accommodate a potentially larger number of sessions in a CDB, the parameter PGA_AGGREGATE_LIMIT was added to place a hard limit on the amount of PGA memory used. The existing parameter PGA_AGGREGATE_TARGET was useful in previous releases as a soft limit but only for tunable memory. Several sessions using untunable memory (such as PL/SQL applications that allocate large memory arrays) could potentially use up all available PGA memory, causing swap activity at the OS level and affecting performance across all instances on

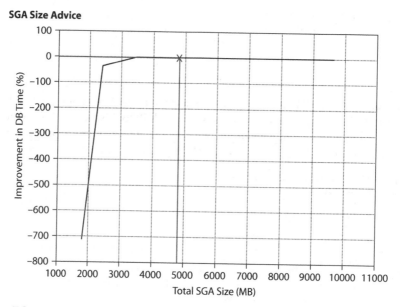

SGA Size Advice

■ Percentage Improvement in DB Time for Various Sizes of SGA

Figure 33-3 CDB SGA Memory Advisor in Cloud Control 12c

the server. Thus, the parameter PGA_AGGREGATE_LIMIT was added to abort PGA memory requests by one or more nonsystem connections to get under this limit.

Manage Allocation of Resources Between PDBs and Within a PDB

Within a PDB, the DBA can (generally speaking) configure the Resource Manager exactly as in a non-CDB; there are only a few capabilities that are not available. The change in use of the Resource Manager is at the CDB level, where a plan must be created that will allocate resources between PDBs.

Using Shares to Manage Inter-PDB Resources

Each PDB that's plugged into a CDB competes for the resources of a CDB—primarily central processing units (CPUs), parallel servers, and, in the case of Oracle Exadata, input/output (I/O). How much of each resource a PDB gets depends on how many *shares* that PDB was assigned when it was created.

EXAM TIP Neither consumer groups (using Resource Manager) nor shares can be defined for the root container.

PDB Name	Shares	CPU Percent (Maximum)
HR	1	16.67 percent
BI	3	50 percent
REPOS	1	16.67 percent
TOOL	1	16.67 percent

Table 33-1 PDBs and Share Allocation for Four PDBs

By default, each PDB gets one share unless otherwise specified. When a new PDB is added or an existing PDB is unplugged, the number of shares each PDB has remains the same. Table 33-1 shows a CDB with four PDBs: HR, BI, REPOS, and TOOL. The BI PDB has three shares, and the rest have one each, the default.

The TOOL database, for example, is guaranteed 16.67 percent of the server's CPU resources if needed. If one or more of the other PDBs are not active, their share is available to active PDBs.

In Table 33-2, you create a PDB called NCAL and don't specify the number of shares, so it defaults to 1.

The minimum CPU guaranteed for each PDB is automatically recalculated based on the new total number of shares. Each PDB with one share now gets 14.29 percent of the CPU resources, and the CPU resources available (at a minimum) for the BI PDB are now 42.86 percent.

Creating and Modifying Resource Manager Plans

To refine the resource consumption further, you can set limits within each PDB using Resource Manager. From the perspective of the PDB, all resources are controlled by directives created using DBMS_RESOURCE_MANAGER. The amount of CPU, Exadata I/O, and concurrent parallel servers used by the PDB default to 100 percent, but can be adjusted down to 0 percent depending on the time of day or other circumstances.

The resource plan itself is created at the CDB level, and you create directives for each PDB within the CDB. You can also specify a set of default directives for those PDBs that do not have an explicit set of directives.

Identifying Parameters to Limit PDB Resource Usage

As part of the utilization plan for each PDB, there are two key limits you can control: the utilization limit for CPU, Exadata I/O, and parallel servers, as well as a parallel server limit. These plan directive limits are UTILIZATION_LIMIT and PARALLEL_SERVER_LIMIT, respectively.

PDB Name	Shares	CPU Percent (Maximum)
HR	1	14.29 percent
BI	3	42.86 percent
REPOS	1	14.29 percent
TOOL	1	14.29 percent
NCAL	1	14.29 percent

Table 33-2 PDBs and Share Allocation for Five PDBs After Adding a New One

The resource directive UTILIZATION_LIMIT defines the percentage of CPU, I/O, and parallel servers available to a PDB. If UTILIZATION_LIMIT is set at 30, then the PDB can use no more than 30 percent of the resources available to the CDB, even if no other PDBs are active.

To further refine the resource limits, you can use PARALLEL_SERVER_LIMIT to define the maximum percentage of the CDB's PARALLEL_SERVERS_TARGET value; this value overrides the UTILIZATION_LIMIT directive, but only for parallel resources. The default is 100 percent.

Creating the CDB Resource Plan

The steps for creating a CDB resource plan are similar to creating a resource plan in a non-CDB, but with additional steps for each PDB. You create and manage the resource plan from the root container only. Table 33-3 lists the steps and corresponding DBMS_RESOURCE_MANAGER calls needed to create and configure the CDB resource plan.

Other key procedures in DBMS_RESOURCE_MANAGER include UPDATE_CDB_PLAN to change the characteristics of the CDB resource plan and DELETE_CDB_PLAN to delete the resource plan and all of its directives. To update and delete individual CDB plan directives, use UPDATE_CDB_PLAN_DIRECTIVE and DELETE_CDB_PLAN_DIRECTIVE.

Exercise 33-3: Creating a CDB Resource Plan with PDB Directives In this exercise, you'll create a CDB resource plan for the CDB01 container and define plan directives for two of the PDBs in the CDB.

1. Create a pending area for the CDB plan.

```
SQL> connect / as sysdba
Connected.
SQL> exec dbms_resource_manager.create_pending_area();

PL/SQL procedure successfully completed.
```

Step	Description	DBMS_RESOURCE_MANAGER Procedure
1	Create a pending area.	CREATE_PENDING_AREA
2	Create a CDB resource plan.	CREATE_CDB_PLAN
3	Create PDB directives.	CREATE_CDB_PLAN_DIRECTIVE
4	Update default PDB directives.	UPDATE_CDB_DEFAULT_DIRECTIVE
5	Update default autotask directives.	UPDATE_CDB_AUTOTASK_DIRECTIVE
6	Validate the pending area.	VALIDATE_PENDING_AREA
7	Submit the pending area.	SUBMIT_PENDING_AREA

Table 33-3 Steps to Create a Resource Plan with DBMS_RESOURCE_MANAGER Calls

2. Create a resource plan that manages the TOOL and CCREPOS PDBs to minimize CPU and other resource usage.

```
SQL> begin
  2      dbms_resource_manager.create_cdb_plan(
  3      plan     => 'low_prio_apps',
  4      comment  => 'TOOL and rep database low priority');
  5  end;
  6  /

PL/SQL procedure successfully completed.
SQL>
```

3. Create a plan directive that gives PDBs different shares. In this, the PDBs named TOOL and CCREPOS have one share each. The utilization limit for TOOL should be 50 percent, and for CCREPOS it will be 75 percent.

```
SQL> begin
  2      dbms_resource_manager.create_cdb_plan_directive(
  3          plan => 'low_prio_apps',
  4          pluggable_database => 'tool',
  5          shares => 1,
  6          utilization_limit => 50,
  7          parallel_server_limit => 50);
  8  end;
  9  /

PL/SQL procedure successfully completed.

SQL> begin
  2      dbms_resource_manager.create_cdb_plan_directive(
  3          plan => 'low_prio_apps',
  4          pluggable_database => 'ccrepos',
  5          shares => 1,
  6          utilization_limit => 75,
  7          parallel_server_limit => 75);
  8  end;
  9  /

PL/SQL procedure successfully completed.

SQL>
```

4. Validate and submit the pending area.

```
SQL> exec dbms_resource_manager.validate_pending_area();

PL/SQL procedure successfully completed.

SQL> exec dbms_resource_manager.submit_pending_area();

PL/SQL procedure successfully completed.

SQL>
```

5. Finally, make this Resource Manager plan the current plan.

```
SQL> alter system set resource_manager_plan='low_prio_apps';
System altered.
SQL>
```

Viewing Resource Plan Directives

In Oracle Database 12c you have a data dictionary view called DBA_CDB_RSRC_PLAN_DIRECTIVES to see all of the current resource plans. Querying that view, you can see the resource plans you just created for TOOL and CCREPOS.

```
SQL> select plan, pluggable_database, shares,
  2      utilization_limit, parallel_server_limit
  3  from dba_cdb_rsrc_plan_directives
  4  order by plan,pluggable_database;

PLAN                         PLUGGABLE_DATABASE SHARES UTILIZA PARALLEL_
-----------------------      ------------------ ------ ------- ---------
DEFAULT_CDB_PLAN             ORA$AUTOTASK                   90       100
DEFAULT_CDB_PLAN             ORA$DEFAULT_PDB_DI      1     100       100
                             RECTIVE
DEFAULT_MAINTENANCE_PLAN     ORA$AUTOTASK                   90       100
DEFAULT_MAINTENANCE_PLAN     ORA$DEFAULT_PDB_DI      1     100       100
                             RECTIVE

LOW_PRIO_APPS                CCREPOS                 1      75        75
LOW_PRIO_APPS                ORA$AUTOTASK                   90       100
LOW_PRIO_APPS                ORA$DEFAULT_PDB_DI      1     100       100
                             RECTIVE
LOW_PRIO_APPS                TOOL                    1      50        50
ORA$INTERNAL_CDB_PLAN        ORA$AUTOTASK
ORA$INTERNAL_CDB_PLAN        ORA$DEFAULT_PDB_DI
                             RECTIVE
ORA$QOS_CDB_PLAN             ORA$AUTOTASK                   90       100
ORA$QOS_CDB_PLAN             ORA$DEFAULT_PDB_DI      1     100       100
                             RECTIVE
```

In previous releases of Oracle Database and for non-CDBs in Oracle Database 12c, the corresponding data dictionary view is DBA_RSRC_PLAN_DIRECTIVES.

Managing Resources Within a PDB

Resource plans can manage workloads within a PDB as well. These resource plans manage workloads just as they do in a non-CDB and, not surprisingly, are called *PDB resource plans*. There are a few restrictions and differences with PDB plans. Table 33-4 shows the parameter and feature differences between non-CDB and PDB resource plans.

Resource Plan Feature	Non-CDB	PDB
Multilevel plans	Yes	No
Consumer groups	Maximum: 32	Maximum: 8
Subplans	Yes	No
CREATE_PLAN_DIRECTIVE parameter	N/A	SHARE
CREATE_PLAN_DIRECTIVE parameter	MAX_UTILIZATION_LIMIT	UTILIZATION_LIMIT-
CREATE_PLAN_DIRECTIVE parameter	PARALLEL_TARGET_PERCENTAGE	PARALLEL_SERVER_LIMIT

Table 33-4 Differences Between Non-CDB and PDB Resource Plans

Regardless of the container type, you still view resource plans using the V$RSRC_PLAN dynamic performance view. To find the active CDB resource plan, select the row in V$RSRC_PLAN with CON_ID=1.

Migrating Non-CDB Resource Plans

You will likely convert and plug in many non-CDBs as new PDBs. This process is straightforward, and all of your applications should work as expected. If the non-CDB has a resource plan, it will be converted as well, as long as it meets these conditions:

- There are no more than eight consumer groups.
- There are no subplans.
- All resource allocations are on level 1.

In other words, the migrated resource plan must be compatible with a new PDB resource plan that follows the rules in the previous section. If the plan violates any of these conditions, the plan is converted during the plug-in operation to a plan that is compatible with a PDB. This plan may be unsuitable; you can drop, modify, or create a new resource plan. The original plan is saved in DBA_RSRC_PLAN_DIRECTIVES with the STATUS column having a value of LEGACY.

Perform Database Replay

The Database Replay functionality from previous Oracle Database releases has also been enhanced in Oracle Database 12c to include simultaneous workload replays as a planning tool for estimating how multiple non-CDBs will perform in a CDB environment. You can take production workloads from multiple servers in a non-CDB environment and play them back in various configurations on a single new server to simulate how well they would coexist in a multitenant environment.

Capture Source Database Workloads

When you capture workloads for potential multitenant deployment, the workloads are typically in different business units and locations; the peak load for each application is likely at different times of the day, which makes these applications ideal candidates for consolidation. Figure 33-4 shows a typical set of workloads from applications currently on different servers.

You can also analyze existing PDBs and capture workloads to see how they would perform as a PDB of another CDB on a different server. The general steps you'll follow as part of this analysis phase are as follows:

1. Capture the workload of an existing non-CDB or PDB.
2. Optionally export the AWR snapshots for the database.
3. Restore the candidate database onto the target system.
4. Make changes to the imported candidate database as needed, such as upgrading to Oracle Database 12c.

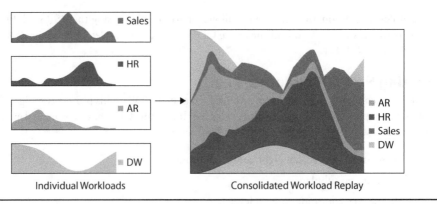

Figure 33-4 Candidate workloads for multitenant consolidation

5. Copy the generated workload files to the target system.

6. Process the workload as a one-time prerequisite step.

7. Repeat steps 1–6 for all other candidate databases.

8. Configure the target system for replay (such as the workload replay client processes).

9. Replay the workloads for all PDBs within the single CDB on the target system.

On the source database server, you'll capture the workload for a typical 8-hour or 24-hour period. You'll want all captured workloads to cover the same time period. To optimize the performance of the replay test, you can optionally export AWR snapshots, SQL profiles, and SQL tuning sets.

Process Workloads on the Target System

After you import the candidate database into a PDB of the new CDB, you import the workload generated on the source server. You preprocess the workload files in preparation for the replay, which needs to happen only once for each imported workload. It's recommended that you replay each imported workload individually to ensure that there are no extreme variations in performance compared to that database's performance on the original server.

Replay Workloads on Target CDB: Consolidated Replay

After all PDBs have been created and preprocessed, remap any connections that might refer to objects that don't exist on the target system. Create a replay schedule that will replay each workload at the same time and rate that it does on the source system. You can create multiple schedules to see how workloads can be shifted to optimize the CDB's overall performance. This is the *consolidated replay* capability, which will replay all the work from all the source non-CDBs concurrently.

After the replay session is complete, you review the reports generated by Consolidated Database Replay to see, for example, if the response time and overall service level agreement

(SLA) of the databases on their original servers can be met by this consolidation platform. If there are severe regressions, then you can use the tuning methodologies discussed earlier in this chapter and run the replay again. Even after tuning, you may find that the server needs more CPUs or memory. Ideally, you'll find out that each database runs just as fast or faster than it did on the original server.

One set of processed capture files can be replayed as often as desired, perhaps with different settings for the CDB instance or with different Resource Manager plans. To compare replay runs, the entire CDB may need to be reverted to a known point before each consolidated replay. Database Flashback or point-in-time recovery is useful for this to ensure that each run starts from a known state. During the replay, generate AWR snapshots and reports as you would for a production database.

Two-Minute Drill

Manage Permanent and Temporary Tablespaces in CDB and PDBs

- The CREATE TABLESPACE command creates a tablespace whose visibility is limited to the container in which it was created, either the CDB or any of the PDBs.

- Using ASM and OMF for tablespaces in a multitenant environment automatically keeps datafiles for each PDB in a separate directory for ease of maintenance.

- Each PDB can have its own default permanent tablespace and temporary tablespace or temporary tablespace group.

Manage Common and Local Users

- The two types of users in a multitenant environment are common and local.

- Common users not created during an Oracle installation must begin with a specified prefix, which is the default of C##.

- The root container cannot have local users, only common users.

- Non-Oracle-maintained common users have no privileges in any container until explicitly granted.

Manage Common and Local Privileges

- Non-Oracle-maintained common users need the CREATE SESSION privilege to connect to any container, including CDB$ROOT.

- The GRANT and REVOKE commands work as in a non-CDB environment with the addition of the CONTAINER clause.

- The CONTAINER clause can specify a specific container, all containers (ALL), or the currently connected container (CURRENT).

Manage Common and Local Roles

- Common roles begin with a specified prefix, which is a default of C##.

- Common roles can have different privileges in each PDB.

- The CONTAINER clause specifies the scope of the changes to the role with GRANT or REVOKE.

Enable Common Users to Access Data in Specific PDBs

- The two shared object types are object links and metadata links.

- The CDB_USERS data dictionary view has the same columns as DBA_USERS with the addition of the CON_ID column.

- Each container manages its own security, granting roles and privileges locally to local and common users.

Perform Backups of a CDB and PDBs

- RMAN includes the new clause PLUGGABLE to back up and recover a PDB from the root.

- You can back up the root container as a PDB with the name CDB$ROOT.

- The REPORT SCHEMA command shows each tablespace and datafile within a CDB or PDB, depending on how you connected to RMAN.

- The PLUGGABLE keyword is available in other RMAN commands such as DUPLICATE, SWITCH, and DELETE.

- You can back up an individual PDB as the container owner with SYSDBA privileges or as a local (noncommon) user with SYSDBA or SYSBACKUP privileges.

Recover PDB from PDB Datafiles Loss

- Instance recovery occurs only at the CDB level.

- Missing temporary datafiles (tempfiles) are re-created automatically at container open.

- Flashback Database is available only at the CDB level.

- PDB PITR recovery works similarly to a tablespace recovery in a non-CDB.

- Tablespace PITR is available for any tablespace other than SYSTEM, UNDO, and SYSAUX.

- Controlfile loss is handled the same way as a non-CDB: Either replace the missing or damaged controlfile with a multiplexed copy or restore from an RMAN autobackup.

- Recovery of the root SYSAUX datafile can occur with the CDB and all PDBs online.

Use Data Recovery Advisor

- The Data Recovery Advisor supports single-instance CDBs and non-CDBs, but not clustered (RAC) databases.
- You use the LIST FAILURE command to see any outstanding data failures within RMAN.
- ADVISE FAILURE shows one or more options to repair the database error.
- REPAIR FAILURE PREVIEW shows you the steps RMAN will take to repair the corrupt or lost datafiles.
- REPAIR FAILURE implements one of the recommendations provided with ADVISE FAILURE.
- Media failure can be repaired using PITR at either the PDB or PDB tablespace level.
- Flashback CDB rewinds both the CDB and all PDBs within the CDB.
- You cannot flashback a CDB to a system change number (SCN) before any PDB's database point-in-time recovery (DBPITR).

Duplicate PDBs Using RMAN

- You use the RMAN DUPLICATE command with new clauses that specify one or more PDBs to include in the duplicate.
- Using the SKIP keyword, you can duplicate all PDBs within a CDB except for the specified PDBs.
- The TABLESPACE keyword with a qualified tablespace name will duplicate a single tablespace, along with any other complete PDBs, in a single DUPLICATE command.

Monitor Operations and Performance in a CDB and PDBs

- A CDB and its PDBs are tuned as a single instance since, well, a CDB is a single instance.
- CDB tuning methodologies are identical to well-established tuning methodologies for non-CDB environments.
- When consolidating multiple non-CDBs into a single CDB, start by adding together the resource usage of each non-CDB.
- Resource usage allocations between PDBs are measured in shares.
- Parameters that can be changed within a PDB are identified by the column ISPDB_ MODIFIABLE in V$PARAMETER.
- The buffer cache in the CDB's instance is shared by all PDBs, and each block in the buffer cache has a container ID.
- The new parameter PGA_AGGREGATE_LIMIT is a hard limit on total PGA usage across all PDBs.

PART V

Manage Allocation of Resources Between PDBs and Within a PDB

- You use DBMS_RESOURCE_MANAGER to create resource allocations both at the CDB and PDB levels.

- A share is the basic unit of minimum resource required for the PDB and defaults to 1.

- The minimum number of resources for a PDB is a percentage calculated by its share value divided by the total number of shares across all PDBs in the CDB.

- Adding new PDBs to a CDB does not change the share value of other PDBs; however, the percentage of resources allocated for other PDBs will decrease proportionally.

- Using Resource Manager, you cannot define consumer groups or shares at the CDB level.

- The utilization limit for CPU, Exadata I/O, and parallel servers is defined by the UTILIZATION_LIMIT directive in a PDB resource plan.

- The parallel server limit in a PDB can be set in a resource plan using the PARALLEL_SERVER_LIMIT directive.

- The data dictionary view DBA_CDB_RSRC_PLAN_DIRECTIVES contains all CDB resource plans.

- PDB resource plans are limited to one level and eight consumer groups and cannot have subplans.

- You can find the active CDB resource plan by querying V$RSRC_PLAN with a CON_ID of 1.

- When you plug in a non-CDB as a new PDB, all existing resource plans are migrated as is unless the plan has more than eight consumer groups, has subplans, or is multilevel.

- Imported resource plans from a non-PDB are converted if they violate the resource plan restrictions for a PDB.

- A noncompliant resource plan for an imported non-CDB is saved in DBA_RSRC_PLAN_DIRECTIVES with STATUS='LEGACY'.

Perform Database Replay

- Consolidated Database Replay uses Oracle Database Replay to measure the performance of multiple databases in a new server environment.

- For each source database, capture workload data for replay.

- Optionally, you can export AWR snapshots and SQL profiles to optimize performance in the target CDB.

- You need to preprocess each imported workload only once on the target CDB.

- Replay the consolidated workloads multiple times with tuning steps for major performance regression.

- The CDB should be flashed back or restored between each consolidated replay run.

Self Test

1. You are logged on to a pluggable database as SYSDBA and need to create a datafile. Which view will show you all the datafiles that already exist in the container database? (Choose the best answer.)

   A. DBA_DATA_FILES.

   B. CDB_DATA_FILES.

   C. V$DATAFILE.

   D. When connected to a pluggable container, it is not possible to see all the datafiles in the CDB.

2. In a multitenant database, which tablespace that is part of the root container can be used by sessions connected to pluggable containers? (Choose the best answer.)

   A. The default permanent tablespace.

   B. The default temporary tablespace.

   C. The undo tablespace.

   D. No tablespace that is part of the root container can be used by sessions connected to pluggable containers.

3. Study this code snippet:

   ```
   cdba>
   cdba> show user
   USER is "SYS"
   cdba> show con_name
   CON_NAME
   ------------------------------
   CDB$ROOT
   cdba> create user c##jw identified by jw;
   User created.
   cdba> grant connect to c##jw;
   Grant succeeded.
   cdba>
   ```

   Following the execution of these commands, what can be said regarding the C##JW user?

   A. The user exists only in the root container.

   B. The user exists in the root and all pluggable containers but can connect only to the root.

   C. The user exists in the root and all pluggable containers and can connect to the root and to all pluggable containers.

   D. The user will not be able to log in to a pluggable container until their password has been set in the pluggable container.

4. Which of the following GRANT commands, executed in the root container, will give the common user C##RWR the ability to access any table across all PDBs and the root container? (Choose the best answer.)

   A. grant select any table to c##rwr container=current;

   B. grant select any table to c##rwr container=all;

   C. grant select any table to c##rwr;

   D. grant select any table to c##rwr container=cdb$root;

5. Which of the following statements is incorrect regarding local and common roles?

   A. Common roles can be granted to local roles.

   B. Local roles can be granted to common roles.

   C. Common roles can be granted only to common users.

   D. Local roles can be granted to local or common users.

6. Which of the following are correct regarding multitenant (CDB and PDB) and RMAN? (Choose all that apply.)

   A. You can back up the controlfile only when connected to the root container.

   B. Tablespace backups can include multiple tablespaces from different PDBs.

   C. PDBs can be backed up individually only by connecting to the target PDB in RMAN.

   D. You can enforce division of responsibility by granting the privilege SYSBACKUP to local users within individual PDBs.

   E. The SYSBACKUP privilege can be granted commonly, to a common user.

7. RMAN is configured for autobackup of the controlfile and spfile. You perform a whole PDB backup with RMAN like this:

   ```
   RMAN> connect target /
   RMAN> backup pluggable database ccrepos;
   ```

   Shortly afterward, you lose all copies of the controlfile. Consider these steps:

   1 Connect to each container and open it with RESETLOGS.

   2 Connect to the pluggable container ccrepos.

   3 Connect to the root container.

   4 Open the database with RESETLOGS.

   5 Open all pluggable containers.

   6 Restore the controlfile from autobackup.

   7 Recover the database.

   8 Start up the CDB instance in nomount mode.

What is a correct course of action to follow?

A. 8, 2, 6, 3, 7, 1

B. 2, 8, 6, 7, 1

C. 8, 2, 6, 7, 3, 4, 5

D. 8, 6, 7, 4, 5

8. Identify the correct statements about initialization parameters in a multitenant environment. (Choose all that apply.)

   A. A subset of parameters set at the container level can be overridden at the PDB level.

   B. Pluggable databases can have parameters that cannot be set at the container level.

   C. Unplugging a PDB and plugging it back into the same container database preserves the customized parameters set in the PDB.

   D. Unplugging a PDB and plugging it into a different container database preserves the customized parameters set in the PDB.

9. Which of the following is true about allocating resources between PDBs in a CDB? (Choose the best answer.)

   A. Using a minimal allocation plan, the shares allocated to a PDB prevent other PDBs from using those shares even if the PDB is not busy.

   B. Using no resource plan in a CDB environment is the default and lets PDBs compete equally for all resources.

   C. In a minimum/maximum allocation scheme, a PDB can still go over the maximum if no other PDBs are busy.

   D. The "share" amount is the percentage of overall resources that a PDB can use within the CDB.

   E. The tiered allocation plan gives some users in one PDB a higher priority than users in another PDB.

10. You are plugging in a non-CDB into a container database, and the non-CDB has several resource plans. Which of the following conditions will invalidate the imported resource plan? (Choose the best answer.)

    A. The original plan has 12 consumer groups.

    B. The resource allocations are on only the first level.

    C. The imported resource plan has the same name as an existing resource plan.

    D. The imported resource plan already has a status of LEGACY.

    E. The resource plan directive PARALLEL_SERVER_LIMIT is higher than the value of the CDB initialization parameter PARALLEL_MAX_SERVERS.

    F. The number of shares in the original resource plan is more than the total shares of all PDBs already in the container.

11. When performing a consolidated workload replay, which of the following steps are optional when exporting or importing the workload for the databases that are candidates for multitenant consolidation?

   A. Exporting AWR snapshots from every candidate database

   B. Exporting SQL tuning sets from the candidate database

   C. Capturing and exporting the workload for a candidate database

   D. Creating a replay schedule

   E. Creating a PDB for each database

Self Test Answers

1. ☑   **D.** When connecting to a pluggable container, the scope of all views is limited to that container.
   ☒   **A**, **B**, and **C** are incorrect. **A** is incorrect because DBA views show only rows relevant to the current container. **B** and **C** are incorrect because the V$ and CDB views will show the full picture only when connected to the root container.

2. ☑   **C.** The undo tablespace is administered from the root container and used by all sessions in all containers.
   ☒   **A**, **B**, and **D** are incorrect. None of the root container's tablespaces, with the exception of the undo tablespace, are visible to any PDB.

3. ☑   **B.** The user will have been created as a common user in every container, but the grant of the role is effective only for the local container, which is the root.
   ☒   **A**, **C**, and **D** are incorrect. **A** is incorrect because all users created in the root are common users. **C** is incorrect because unless the grant is made with the CONTAINERS=ALL clause, the grant is only local. **D** is incorrect because a common user's password is always the same in all containers.

4. ☑   **B.** The GRANT statement must include CONTAINER=ALL.
   ☒   **A**, **C**, and **D** are incorrect. **A** is incorrect because specifying CONTAINER= CURRENT gives privileges only to C##RWR in the current container. **C** is incorrect because without a CONTAINER keyword, the privilege is granted locally. **D** is incorrect because the values for CONTAINER must be either CURRENT or ALL; you cannot specify a PDB or root container name.

5. ☑   **C.** Common roles can be granted to either common or local users.
   ☒   **A**, **B**, and **D** are incorrect. They are all valid role assignments, either local or common, to either local or common users or roles.

6. ☑   **B**, **D**, and **E.** When connected to the root container, the RMAN syntax lets you specify any tablespaces from any container. The SYSBACKUP privilege can be granted commonly to a common user or locally to a local user.
   ☒   **A** and **C** are incorrect. The controlfile can be backed up from any container, and a PDB can be backed up either from within the PDB or from the root.

7. ☑ **D.** This sequence will perform complete recovery of all containers.

☒ **A, B,** and **C** are incorrect. The controlfile restore can be done only in nomount mode, when only the root container is available. The OPEN RESETLOGS is executed from the root and applies to all containers.

8. ☑ **A, C,** and **D.** When you create a PDB, it automatically inherits all of the parameters at the CDB level. A subset of parameters can be set at the PDB level. These parameter values persist even if the PDB is unplugged and plugged back into the same or another container.

☒ **B** is incorrect because there are no parameters at the PDB level that do not exist at the CDB level.

9. ☑ **B.** The default resource allocation in a CDB is none. One PDB can use all CDB resources.

☒ **A, C, D,** and **E** are incorrect. **A** is incorrect because a PDB can use all remaining resources in a CDB even if another PDB with a higher number of shares is not active. **C** is incorrect because a PDB cannot exceed the maximum number of shares even if no other PDBs are busy. **D** is incorrect because shares are relative resource quantities and not percentages. **E** is incorrect because there is no such tiered resource allocation plan across PDBs in a multitenant environment, although the Resource Manager can control resource usage between users in a single PDB.

10. ☑ **A.** When importing a non-CDB and plugging it into a PDB of an existing container (CDB), any existing Resource Manager plans must have no more than eight consumer groups, must all be at level 1, and must have no subplans.

☒ **B, C, D, E,** and **F** are incorrect. **B** is incorrect because existing resource plans will import just fine with only one level. **C** is incorrect because the resource plans are qualified with the PDB name, and thus there is no name conflict. **D** is incorrect because a non-CDB's resource plan will never have a STATUS of LEGACY since only PDBs can have imported resource plans with that status. **E** is incorrect because an existing non-CDB resource plan will not have a plan directive of PARALLEL_SERVER_LIMIT, which is valid only in a multitenant environment. **F** is incorrect because a non-CDB will not have a resource plan with a share directive.

11. ☑ **A** and **B.** You do not need to export AWR snapshots and SQL tuning sets from the source databases, but they would be helpful when tuning the combined workloads in the target CDB.

☒ **C, D,** and **E** are incorrect. **C** is incorrect because you cannot use Consolidated Database Replay on a target server without a workload capture. **D** is incorrect because you won't be able to replay the workloads side-by-side in the new CDB without the configured schedule. **E** is incorrect because each candidate database must be converted (if necessary) and plugged into the new CDB as a PDB to test the consolidated workload.

PART V

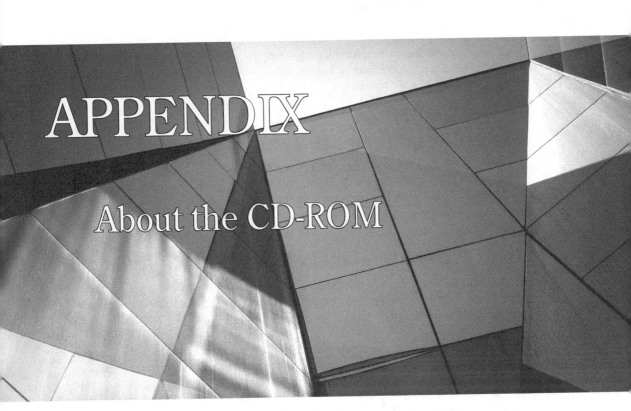

APPENDIX

About the CD-ROM

The CD-ROM included with this book comes complete with Total Tester customizable practice exam software, including question packs for exam 1Z0-061, exam 1Z0-062, and exam 1Z0-063, in addition to a PDF copy of the book.

System Requirements

The software requires Windows XP or higher and 30MB of hard disk space for full installation, in addition to a current or prior major release of Chrome, Firefox, Internet Explorer, or Safari. To run, the screen resolution must be set to 1024 × 768 or higher. The PDF copy of the book requires Adobe Acrobat, Adobe Reader, or Adobe Digital Editions.

Total Tester Premium Practice Exam Software

Total Tester provides you with a simulation of the live exam. You can also create custom exams from selected certification objectives or chapters. You can further customize the number of questions and time allowed.

The exams can be taken in either Practice Mode or Exam Mode. Practice Mode provides an assistance window with hints, references to the book, explanations of the correct and incorrect answers, and the option to check your answers as you take the test. Exam Mode provides a simulation of the actual exam. The number of questions, the types of questions, and the time allowed are intended to be an accurate representation of the exam environment. Both Practice Mode and Exam Mode provide an overall grade and a grade broken down by certification objectives.

To take a test, launch the program and select the exam from the Installed Question Packs list. You can then select Practice Mode, Exam Mode, or Custom Mode. After making your selection, click Start Exam to begin.

Installing and Running Total Tester Premium Practice Exam Software

From the main screen you may install the Total Tester by clicking the Total Tester Practice Exams button. This will begin the installation process and place an icon on your desktop and in your Start menu. To run Total Tester, navigate to Start | (All) Programs | Total Seminars, or double-click the icon on your desktop.

To uninstall the Total Tester software, go to Start | Settings | Control Panel | Add/Remove Programs (XP) or Programs And Features (Vista/7/8), and then select the Total Tester program. Select Remove, and Windows will completely uninstall the software.

PDF Copy of the Book

The entire contents of the book are provided in a PDF on the CD-ROM. This file is viewable on your computer and many portable devices. Adobe Acrobat, Adobe Reader, or Adobe Digital Editions is required to view the file on your computer. A link to Adobe's web site, where you can download and install Adobe Reader, has been included on the CD-ROM.

NOTE   For more information on Adobe Reader and to check for the most recent version of the software, visit Adobe's web site at www.adobe.com and search for the free Adobe Reader or look for Adobe Reader on the product page. Adobe Digital Editions can also be downloaded from the Adobe web site.

To view the PDF copy of the book on a portable device, copy the PDF file to your computer from the CD-ROM, and then copy the file to your portable device using a USB or other connection. Adobe offers a mobile version of Adobe Reader, the Adobe Reader mobile app, which currently supports iOS and Android. For customers using Adobe Digital Editions and an iPad, you may have to download and install a separate reader program on your device. The Adobe web site has a list of recommended applications, and McGraw-Hill Education recommends the Bluefire Reader.

Technical Support

Technical Support information is provided in the following sections by feature.

McGraw-Hill Education Content Support

For questions regarding the Total Tester content or the PDF copy of the book, e-mail techsolutions@mhedu.com or visit http://mhp.softwareassist.com.

For questions regarding book content, e-mail customer.service@mheducation.com. For customers outside the United States, e-mail international_cs@mheducation.com.

Total Seminars Technical Support

For questions regarding the Total Tester software or operation of the CD-ROM, visit www.totalsem.com or e-mail support@totalsem.com.

Glossary

ACID Atomicity, Consistency, Isolation, and Durability. Four characteristics that a relational database must be able to maintain for transactions.

ADDM Automatic Database Diagnostic Monitor. A tool that generates performance-tuning reports based on snapshots in the AWR.

ADR Automatic Diagnostic Repository. Default location for the alert log, trace files, and other information useful for fault finding.

ADRCI The ADR command-line interface.

AES Advanced Encryption Standard. A widely used data encryption method.

AL16UTF16 A Unicode fixed-width 2-byte character set, commonly specified for the NLS character set used for NVARCHAR2, NCHAR, and NCLOB data types.

alias (1) In Oracle SQL, an alternative name for a table, a view, or a set of data used in a query. (2) In Oracle Net, a pointer to a connect string. An alias must be resolved into the address of a listener and the name of a service or instance.

AMM Automatic Memory Management. The technique for allowing Oracle full control over sizing SGA and PGA structures.

ANSI   American National Standards Institute. A U.S. body that defines a number of standards relevant to computing.

API   Application programming interface. A defined method for manipulating data, typically implemented as a set of PL/SQL procedures in a package.

ARBn   Background processes that perform extent movement between disks in an Automatic Storage Management (ASM) disk group.

ASA   Automatic Segment Advisor. An Oracle advisory tool that can recommend segments (tables or indexes) that are candidates for segment shrink.

ASCII   American Standard Code for Information Interchange. A standard (with many variations) for coding letters and other characters as bytes.

ASH   Active Session History. A category of information in the AWR that records details of session activity.

ASM   Automatic Storage Management. An LVM provided with the Oracle database.

asmcmd   A command-line utility used to query and maintain objects in an ASM disk group.

ASMM   Automatic Shared Memory Management. The technique for allowing Oracle full control over sizing SGA structures.

ASSM   Automatic Segment Space Management. The method of managing space within segments by use of bitmaps.

attribute   One element of a tuple (aka a column).

AWR   Automatic Workload Repository. A set of tables in the SYSAUX tablespace, populated with tuning data gathered by the MMON process.

background process   A process that is part of the instance that is launched at startup.

bfile   A large object data type that is stored as an operating system file. The value in the table column is a pointer to the file.

bind variable   A value passed from a user process to a SQL statement at statement execution time.

BLOB   Binary large object. A LOB data type for binary data, such as photographs and video clips.

block   The units of storage into which datafiles are formatted. The size can be 2KB, 4KB, 8KB, 16KB, 32KB, or 64KB.

BMR   Block Media Recovery. An RMAN technique for the restoration and recovery of individual data blocks, rather than complete datafiles.

Cartesian product   Sometimes called a cross join. A mathematical term that refers to the set of data created by multiplying the rows from two or more tables.

CDB_xxx views   Data dictionary views that include metadata across all containers in a container database. Similar to the corresponding DBA_xxx views but has an additional column CON_ID to identify which container this row applies to.

CDB$ROOT   The root container in a multitenant environment. All other pluggable databases share the resources defined in CDB$ROOT.

CET   Central European time. A time zone used in much of Europe (though not Great Britain) that is one hour ahead of UTC, with daylight saving time in effect during the summer months.

character set   The encoding system for representing data within bytes. Different character sets can store different characters and may not be suitable for all languages. Unicode character sets can store any character.

check constraint   A simple rule enforced by the database that restricts the values that can be entered into a column.

checkpoint   An event that forces the DBWn to write dirty buffers from the database buffer cache to the datafiles.

CKPT   The Checkpoint process. The background process responsible for recording the current redo byte address—the point in time up to which the DBWn has written changed data blocks to disk—and for signaling checkpoints, which forces the DBWn to write changed blocks to disk immediately.

client-server architecture   A processing paradigm where the application is divided into client software that interacts with the user and server software that interacts with the data.

CLOB   Character large object. A LOB data type for character data, such as text documents, stored in the database character set.

cluster   A hardware environment where more than one computer shares access to storage.

cluster segment   A segment that can contain one or more tables, denormalized into a single structure.

COALESCE   A function that returns the first non-null value from its parameter list. If all its parameters are null, then a null value is returned.

column   An element of a row; tables are two-dimensional structures, divided horizontally into rows and vertically into columns.

commit   To make a change to data permanent.

common privileges   A system or object privilege granted to a common user in a multitenant environment and is therefore in effect for that user in all containers.

common profile   A database profile that exists for all current and future pluggable databases in a CDB.

common role   A database role that is defined in the root container and therefore propagated to all containers. Common roles must be prefixed (by default) with C## and can be granted "commonly" to a common user in all containers or locally to have effect in only the current container.

common user   A user account in a container database (CDB) that exists across all pluggable databases (PDB) in a container database. The same user may have different privileges in each PDB. Non-Oracle-maintained common users must be prefixed with (by default) C##.

complete recovery   Following a restore of damaged database files, a complete recovery applies all redo actions to bring the database up to date with no loss of data.

connect identifier   An Oracle Net service name.

connect role   A preseeded role retained only for backward compatibility.

connect string   The database connection details needed to establish a session, namely, the address of the listener and the service or instance name.

consistent backup   A backup made while the database is closed.

Consolidated Database Replay   An enhancement to Oracle Database Replay to replay individual workloads from multiple non-CDBs and play them back within a single multitenant environment. Using Consolidated Database Replay helps to measure resource requirements for the new CDB.

constraint   A mechanism for enforcing that a column value must be unique or may contain only certain values. A primary key constraint specifies that the column must be both unique and not null.

container database   A database in a multitenant environment that hosts zero, one, or more pluggable databases (PDBs). It will always host the root container and the seed container.

controlfile   The file containing pointers to the rest of the database, critical sequence information, and the RMAN repository.

CPU   Central processing unit. The chip that provides the processing capability of a computer, such as an Intel i7 or an Oracle SPARC M7.

CTWR   Change Tracking Writer. The optional background process that records the addresses of changed blocks to enable fast incremental backups.

data blocks   The units into which datafiles are formatted.

data dictionary   The tables owned by SYS in the SYSTEM tablespace that define the database and the objects within it.

data dictionary views   Views on the data dictionary tables that let the DBA investigate the state of the database.

Data Guard   A facility whereby a copy of the production database is created and updated (possibly in real time) with all changes applied to the production database.

Data Pump   A facility for transferring large amounts of data at high speed into, out of, or between databases.

database buffer cache   An area of memory in the SGA used for working on blocks copied from datafiles.

database event trigger   An Oracle program code block that fires when a specific database event occurs such as startup, shutdown, or some other database-wide event. Database event triggers have been enhanced in Oracle Database 12c to automate the opening of pluggable databases when the root container (CDB) starts up.

database link   A connection from one database to another, based on a username and password and a connect string.

Database Replay   An Oracle monitoring feature that can help to assess the change in performance on a test system by capturing the workload on a production server and replaying the workload on a test system.

datafile   The disk-based structure for storing data.

DBA   Database administrator. The person responsible for creating and managing Oracle databases—this could be you.

DBA role   A preseeded role provided for backward compatibility that includes all the privileges needed to manage a database, except those needed to start up and shut down.

DBCA   The Database Configuration Assistant. A GUI tool for creating, modifying, and dropping instances and databases.

DBID   Database identifier. A unique number for every database, visible in the DBID column of the V$DATABASE dynamic performance view.

DBMS   Database management system. Often used interchangeably with RDBMS.

DBNEWID   A command-line utility (usually nid) that can change the value of the DBID for a database.

DBWn or DBWR   The Database Writer. The background process responsible for writing changed blocks from the database buffer cache to the datafiles. An instance may have up to 100 Database Writer processes: DBW0–DBW9, DBWa–DBWz, and BW36–BW99.

DDL   Data Definition Language. The subset of SQL commands that change object definitions within the data dictionary: CREATE, ALTER, DROP, and TRUNCATE.

PART V

deadlock   A situation where two sessions block each other, such that neither can do anything. Deadlocks are detected and resolved automatically.

DECODE   A function that implements if-then-else conditional logic by testing two terms for equality and returning the third term if they are equal or, optionally, returning some other term if they are not.

DHCP   Dynamic Host Configuration Protocol. The standard for configuring the network characteristics of a computer, such as its IP address, in a changing environment where computers can be moved from one location to another.

DIA0   The diagnosability process that detects hang and deadlock situations.

DIAG   The diagnosability process that generates diagnostic dumps.

direct path   A method of I/O on datafiles that bypasses the database buffer cache.

directory object   An Oracle directory, specifically, an object within the database that points to an operating system directory.

dirty buffer   A buffer in the database buffer cache that contains a copy of a data block that has been updated and not yet written back to the datafile.

DML   Data Manipulation Language. The SQL commands that change data within the database: INSERT, UPDATE, DELETE, and MERGE.

DMnn   Data Pump master process. The process that controls a Data Pump job—one will be launched for each job that is running.

DNS   Domain Name System. The TCP mechanism for resolving network names into IP addresses.

domain   The set of values an attribute is allowed to take. Terminology: tables have rows, and rows have columns with values. Alternatively, relations have tuples, and tuples have attributes with values taken from their domain.

DSS   Decision support system. A database, such as a data warehouse, optimized for running queries rather than OLTP work.

DWnn   The Data Pump Worker process. There will be one or more of these launched for each Data Pump job that is running.

Easy Connect   A method of establishing a session against a database by specifying the address on the listener and the service name, without using an Oracle Net alias.

EBCDIC   Extended Binary Coded Decimal Interchange Code. A standard developed by IBM for coding letters and other characters in bytes.

Enterprise Manager Database Express   A lightweight monitoring and query tool for an Oracle database instance on a single server. Replaces Enterprise Manager Database Control in Oracle Database 12*c*.

environment variable   A variable set in the operating system shell that can be used by application software and by shell scripts.

equijoin   A join condition using an equality operator.

fact table   The central table in a star schema, with columns for values relevant to the row and columns used as foreign keys to the dimension tables.

fast incremental backup   An incremental backup that uses a block change tracking file to identify only changed blocks since the last backup.

Fast Recovery Area (previously known as the flash recovery area)   A default location for all recovery-related files.

FGA   Fine-grained auditing. A facility for tracking user access to data, based on the rows that are seen or manipulated.

Flashback Data Archive   A database container object that retains historical data for one or more database objects for a specified retention period.

Flashback Database   A flashback feature that recovers the entire database to a point in time in the past using Flashback Database logs.

Flashback Database logs   Changed database blocks that are stored in the fast recovery area and used for Flashback Database.

Flashback Drop   A flashback feature that makes it easy to recover dropped tables if they are still in a tablespace's recycle bin.

Flashback Query   A flashback feature that enables you to view one or more rows in a table at a time in the past.

Flashback Table   A Flashback Query that recovers a single table and its associated objects to a point in time that has passed.

fractured block   A database block that is simultaneously being read by an operating system copy command and modified by the DBWR process.

full backup   A backup containing all blocks of the files backed up, not only those blocks changed since the last backup.

GMT   Greenwich mean time. Now referred to as UTC, this is the time zone of the meridian through Greenwich Observatory in London.

PART V

Grid computing   An architecture where the delivery of a service to end users is not tied to certain server resources but can be provided from anywhere in a pool of resources.

GUI   Graphical user interface. A layer of an application that lets users work with the application through a graphical terminal, such as a PC with a mouse.

HTTP   Hypertext Transfer Protocol. The protocol that enables the World Wide Web (both invented at the European Organization for Nuclear Research in 1989); this is a layered protocol that runs over TCP/IP.

HWM   High water mark. This is the last block of a segment that has ever been used; blocks above this are part of the segment but are not yet formatted for use.

IBM   International Business Machines. A well-known computer hardware, software, and services company.

image copy   An RMAN copy of a file.

inconsistent backup   A backup made while the database was open.

incremental backup   A backup containing only blocks that have been changed since the last backup was made.

INITCAP   A function that accepts a string of characters and returns each word in title case.

inner join   When equijoins and nonequijoins are performed, rows from the source and target tables are matched. These are referred to as inner joins.

instance recovery   The automatic repair of damage caused by a disorderly shutdown of the database.

INSTR   A function that returns the positional location of an occurrence of a specified string of characters in a source string.

I/O   Input/output. The activity of reading from or writing to disks—often the slowest point of a data processing operation because it's the slowest piece of hardware when compared with CPU and RAM.

IOT   Index organized table. A table type where the rows are stored in the leaf blocks of an index segment.

IP   Internet Protocol. Together with the Transmission Control Protocol, IP makes up the de facto standard communication protocol (TCP/IP) used for client-server communication over a network.

IPC   Interprocess Communications Protocol. The platform-specific protocol, provided by your OS vendor, used for processes running on the same machine to communicate with each other.

ISO   International Standards Organization. A group that defines many standards, including SQL.

JEE   Java Enterprise Edition. The standard for developing Java applications.

job   A row in a scheduler table that specifies what to do and when to do it. The "what" can be a single SQL statement, a PL/SQL block, a PL/SQL stored procedure, a Java stored procedure, an external procedure, or any executable file stored in the server's file system.

job chain   A database object that contains a named series of programs linked together for a combined objective.

job class   A scheduler object that is used to associate one or more jobs with a Resource Manager consumer group and to control logging levels.

join   The process of connecting rows in different tables, based on common column values.

JOIN...ON   A clause that allows the explicit specification of join columns, regardless of their column names. This provides a flexible joining format.

JOIN...USING   A syntax that allows a natural join to be formed on specific columns with shared names.

JVM   Java Virtual Machine. The run-time environment needed for running code written in Java. Oracle provides a JVM within the database, and there will be one provided by your operating system.

large pool   A memory structure within the SGA used by certain processes, such as principally shared server processes and parallel execution servers.

LAST_DAY   A function used to obtain the last day in a month given any valid date item.

LDAP   Lightweight Directory Access Protocol. The TCP implementation of the X25 directory standard, used by the Oracle Internet Directory for name resolution, security, and authentication. LDAP is also used by other software vendors, including Microsoft and IBM.

LENGTH   A function that computes the number of characters in a string, including spaces and special characters.

level 0 incremental backup   A full RMAN backup that can be used as the basis for an incremental backup strategy.

level 1 cumulative incremental backup   An RMAN backup of all changed blocks since the last level 0 incremental backup.

level 1 differential incremental backup   An RMAN backup of all changed blocks since the last level 0 or level 1 incremental backup.

LGWR   The Log Writer. The background process responsible for flushing change vectors from the log buffer in memory to the online redo log files on disk.

library cache A memory structure within the shared pool, used for caching SQL statements parsed into their executable form.

lightweight job A scheduler job that has many of the same characteristics of a standard job, except that a lightweight job is ideal for running many short-duration jobs that run frequently.

LISTAGG A function that returns a string aggregation of column values.

listener The server-side process that listens for database connection requests from user processes and launches server processes to establish sessions.

LOB Large object. A data structure that is too large to store within a table. LOBs (Oracle supports several types) are defined as columns of a table but physically are stored in a separate segment.

local privileges A system or object privilege granted to a local user and is therefore in effect for that user in only a single container.

local profile A database profile that exists only in a single PDB and can be assigned only to local users.

local role A database role that is created in a single PDB and granted to a local user and therefore is available to that user in only one container.

local user A user account that is created and exists only in a pluggable database (PDB). The root container (CDB$ROOT) cannot have local users, only common users.

Locale Builder A graphical tool that can create a customized globalization environment by generating definitions for languages, territories, character sets, and linguistic sorting.

log switch The action of closing one online logfile group and opening another: typically triggered by the LGWR process filling the current group.

logical backup A backup that reads a set of database rows and writes them to a file in the operating system or to another tablespace.

LREG The background process responsible for registering database services with the listener.

LRU Least recently used. LRU lists are used to manage access to data structures, using algorithms that ensure the data that has not been accessed for the longest time is the data that will be overwritten.

LVM Logical volume manager. A layer of software that abstracts the physical storage within your computer from the logical storage visible to an application.

MMAN The Memory Manager background process, which monitors and reassigns memory allocations in the SGA for automatically tunable SGA components.

MML Media management layer. Software that lets RMAN make use of automated tape libraries and other SBT devices.

MMNL Manageability Monitor Light. The background process responsible for flushing ASH data to the AWR if MMON is not doing this with the necessary frequency.

MMON The Manageability Monitor background process, responsible for gathering performance-monitoring information and raising alerts.

MOD The modulus operation, a function that returns the remainder of a division operation.

MONTHS_BETWEEN A function that computes the number of months between two given date parameters.

mounted database A situation where the instance has opened the database controlfile but not the online redo logfiles or the datafiles.

MTBF Mean time between failure. A measure of the average length of running time for a database between unplanned shutdowns.

MTS Multithreaded server. Since release 9*i*, renamed to shared server. This is the technique whereby a large number of sessions can share a small pool of server processes, rather than requiring one server each.

MTTR Mean time to recover. The average time it takes to make the database available for normal use after a failure.

multiplexing To maintain multiple copies of files.

multitenant architecture An architecture that hosts many logical databases within one larger database instance to more efficiently use server resources such as memory, CPU, and I/O.

namespace A logical grouping of objects within which no two objects may have the same name.

natural join A join performed using the NATURAL JOIN syntax when the source and target tables are implicitly equijoined using all identically named columns.

NCLOB National character large object. A LOB data type for character data, such as text documents, stored in the alternative national database character set.

NLS National language support. The capability of the Oracle database to support many linguistic, geographical, and cultural environments—now usually referred to as globalization.

node A computer attached to a network.

non-CDB A stand-alone database that does not use the multitenant architecture. The non-CDB architecture was the only type of architecture available before release 12.

nonequijoin   Performed when the values in the join columns fulfill the join condition based on an inequality expression.

null   The absence of a value, indicating that the value is not known, missing, or inapplicable.

NULLIF   A function that tests two terms for equality. If they are equal, the function returns null; else it returns the first of the two terms tested.

NVL   A function that returns either the original item unchanged or an alternative item if the initial term is null.

NVL2   A function that returns a new if-null item if the original item is null or an alternative if-not-null item if the original term is not null.

OC4J   Oracle Containers for Java. The control structure provided by the Oracle Application Server for running Java programs. Still supported but replaced by the WebLogic server.

OCA   Oracle Certified Associate. You need to pass two exams to achieve this: one on SQL, the other on basic DB admin.

OCI   Oracle Call Interface. An API, published as a set of C libraries, that programmers can use to write user processes that will use an Oracle database.

OCP   Oracle Certified Professional. The qualification you are working toward.

OCM   Oracle Certified Master. The qualification you are ultimately working toward.

ODBC   Open Database Connectivity. A standard developed by Microsoft for communicating with relational databases. Oracle provides an ODBC driver that will allow clients running Microsoft products to connect to an Oracle database.

offline backup   A backup made while the database is closed.

OLAP   Online analytical processing. Select, intensive work involving running queries against a (usually) large database. Oracle provides OLAP capabilities as an option in addition to the standard query facilities.

OLTP   Online transaction processing. A pattern of activity within a database typified by a large number of small, short transactions.

online backup   A backup made while the database is open.

online redo log   The files to which change vectors are streamed by the LGWR.

ORACLE_BASE   The root directory into which Oracle products are installed.

ORACLE_HOME   The root directory of any one Oracle product.

Oracle Net   Oracle's proprietary communications protocol, layered on top of an industry-standard protocol.

OS   Operating system. Typically, in the Oracle environment this will be a version of Unix (perhaps Linux) or Microsoft Windows.

outer join   A join performed when rows, which are not retrieved by an inner join, are included for retrieval.

parallelization   Using multiple slave processes managed by a single coordinator process to perform queries or DML operations in parallel across multiple CPUs and I/O channels simultaneously. RMAN backups take advantage of parallelism by allocating multiple channels and improving backup performance by executing partitioned chunks of I/O in parallel.

parse   To convert SQL statements into a form suitable for execution.

PDB   *See* pluggable database.

PDB$SEED   A read-only pluggable database within a root container (CDB) used as a template to create new PDBs within the CDB.

PFILE   A text-based file containing initialization parameters and initial values that are set when an Oracle instance starts.

PGA   Program Global Area. The variable-sized block of memory used to maintain the state of a database session. PGAs are private to the session and controlled by the session's server process.

PL/SQL   Procedural Language/Structured Query Language. Oracle's proprietary programming language, which combines procedural constructs, such as flow control, and user interface capabilities with the ability to call SQL statements.

pluggable database   Also known as a PDB or a pluggable container. A logical database that exists within a container database and shares the memory, process slots, and other resources with other logical databases within the CDB but is isolated from all other logical databases in the same container. Pluggable databases can be unplugged (removed) from the container database and plugged back in later to the same or different container.

PMON   The Process Monitor. The background process responsible for monitoring the state of users' sessions against an instance.

primary key   The column (or combination of columns) whose values can be used to identify each row in a table.

program   A scheduler object that provides a layer of abstraction between the job and the action it will perform; it is created with the DBMS_SCHEDULER.CREATE_PROGRAM procedure.

projection   The restriction of columns selected from a table. Using projection, you retrieve only the columns of interest and not every possible column.

RAC   Real Application Cluster. Oracle's clustering technology, which allows several instances in different machines to open the same database for scalability, performance, and fault tolerance.

RAID   Redundant array of inexpensive disks. Techniques for enhancing performance or fault tolerance by using a volume manager to present a number of physical disks to the operating system as a single logical disk.

RAM   Random access memory. The chips that make up the real memory in your computer hardware, as opposed to the virtual memory presented to software by the operating system.

raw device   An unformatted disk or disk partition.

RBAL   Rebalance process. A background process in an Automatic Storage Management (ASM) instance that coordinates disk activity for disk groups. In an RDBMS instance, it performs the opening and closing of the disks in the disk group.

RDBMS   Relational database management system. Often used interchangeably with DBMS.

recovery catalog   Objects in a database schema that contain metadata and other backup information for RMAN backups of one or more databases.

recovery window   An RMAN parameter and time period that defines how far back in time the database can be recovered.

referential integrity   A rule defined on a table specifying that the values in a column (or columns) must map onto those of a row in another table.

relation   A two-dimensional structure consisting of tuples with attributes (aka a table).

REPLACE   A function that substitutes each occurrence of a search item in the source string with a replacement term and returns the modified source string.

resource consumer groups   Groups of users or sessions that have similar resource needs.

Resource Manager   An Oracle feature that can allocate resources based on CPU usage, degree of parallelism, number of active sessions, undo space, CPU time limit, and idle time limit.

resource plan   A set of rules in Resource Manager that assign various resources at specific percentages or relative priorities to a resource group.

resource plan directives   Rules within Resource Manager that associate consumer groups with a resource plan and specify how the resources are divided among the consumer groups or subplans.

restore point   A database object containing either a system change number (SCN) or a time in the past used to recover the database to the SCN or timestamp.

resumable space allocation   An Oracle feature that suspends instead of terminating large database operations that require more disk space than is currently available. A suspended operation can be restarted from where it finished off at a later point in time, when the space issues have been resolved. It saves time.

retention policy   The number of copies of all objects that RMAN will retain for recovery purposes.

RMAN   Recovery Manager. Oracle's backup and recovery tool.

root container   The control structure (named CDB$ROOT) in a container database that hosts pluggable databases. All initialization parameters are set in the root container and are inherited by each pluggable database unless overridden. Only a smaller subset of parameters defined in the root container can be changed in a pluggable database along with the default temporary tablespace.

rowid   The unique identifier of every row in the database, used as a pointer to the physical location of the row.

RVWR   The Recovery Writer background process. An optional process responsible for flushing the flashback buffer to the flashback logs.

SBT   System backup to tape. An RMAN term for a tape device.

schema   The objects owned by a database user.

SCN   System change number. The continually incrementing number used to track the sequence and exact time of all events within a database.

seed container   Also known as the seed database in a multitenant environment. The seed container is a special instance of a pluggable database named PDB$SEED, is always read-only, and is used as a template for creating a new pluggable database in the current root container.

segment   A database object within a schema that contains a data object (such as a table or index).

segment shrink   A database operation that makes the free space in a segment available to other segments in the tablespace by compacting and releasing the empty, unused data blocks in a segment.

selection   The extraction of rows from a table. Selection includes the further restriction of the extracted rows based on various criteria or conditions. This allows you to retrieve only the rows that are of interest and not every row in the table.

self-join   A join required when the join columns originate from the same table. Conceptually, the source table is duplicated, and a target table is created. The self-join then works as a regular join between two discrete tables.

sequence   A database object within a schema that generates unique numbers.

service name   A logical name registered by an instance with a listener, which can be specified by a user process when it issues a connect request.

session   A user process and a server process, connected to the instance.

SGA   System Global Area. The block of shared memory that contains the memory structures that make up an Oracle instance.

share   A portion of resources granted to a single PDB. Each PDB will have at least one share, and the total resources available to a PDB are based on the ratio of the PDB's shares to the total number of shares allocated to all PDBs within a CDB.

shared object   An object created in the root container that is available to all current and new PDBs in the container. Only Oracle-supplied common users (such as SYS and SYSTEM) can create shared objects.

SID   System identifier. The name of an instance, which must be unique on the computer the instance is running on.
    Alternatively, session identifier. The number used to identify uniquely a session logged on to an Oracle instance.

SMON   The System Monitor. The background process responsible for opening a database and monitoring the instance.

spfile   The server parameter file, which contains the parameters used to build an instance in memory.

SQL   Structured Query Language. An international standard language for extracting data from and manipulating data in relational databases.

SQL Tuning Advisor   An Oracle advisor that performs statistics analysis, SQL Profile analysis, access path analysis, and structure analysis.

SSL   Secure Sockets Layer. A standard for securing data transmission using encryption, checksumming, and digital certificates.

STDDEV   A function that returns the square root of the variance.

SUBSTR   A function that extracts and returns a segment from a given source string.

SUM   A function that returns an aggregated total of all the non-null numeric expression values in a group.

synonym   An alternative name for a database object.

SYSASM   A system privilege in an ASM instance that facilitates the separation of database administration and storage administration.

sysdba   The privilege that lets a user connect with operating system or password file authentication and create or start up and shut down a database.

SYSDG   System privilege for Data Guard operations.

SYSKM   System privilege for managing Transparent Data Encryption (TDE) keystore operations.

sysoper   The privilege that lets a user connect with operating system or password file authentication and start up and shut down (but not create) a database.

system   A preseeded schema used for database administration purposes.

table   A logical two-dimensional data storage structure, consisting of rows and columns.

tablespace   The logical structure that abstracts logical data storage in tables from physical data storage in datafiles.

TCP   Transmission Control Protocol. Together with the Internet Protocol, TCP makes up the de facto standard communication protocol (TCP/IP) used for client-server communication over a network.

TCPS   TCP with SSL. The secure sockets version of TCP.

tempfile   The physical storage that makes up a temporary tablespace, used for storing temporary segments.

TNS   Transparent Network Substrate. The heart of Oracle Net, TNS is a proprietary layered protocol running on top of whatever underlying network transport protocol you choose to use—probably TCP/IP.

TO_CHAR   A function that performs date-to-character and number-to-character data type conversions.

TO_DATE   A function that explicitly transforms character items into date values.

TO_NUMBER   A function that changes character items into number values.

transaction   A logical unit of work, which will complete in total or not at all.

TSPITR   Tablespace point-in-time recovery. A recovery method that is ideal for recovering a set of objects isolated to a single tablespace.

tuple   A one-dimensional structure consisting of attributes (in other words, a row).

UGA   User Global Area. The part of the PGA stored in the SGA for sessions running through shared servers.

UI   User interface. The layer of an application that communicates with end users; nowadays it is frequently graphical: a GUI.

URL   Uniform resource locator. A standard for specifying the location of an object on the Internet, consisting of a protocol, a hostname and domain, an IP port number, a path and filename, and a series of parameters.

user-managed recovery   Using tools or commands outside of RMAN to recover a database or tablespace.

PART V

UTC   Coordinated Universal Time, previously known as Greenwich mean time (GMT). UTC is the global standard time zone; all others relate to it as offsets, ahead or behind.

VARIANCE   A function that returns the distance from the mean of each number in the set.

virtual private catalog   A logical partitioning of an RMAN catalog to facilitate the separation of duties among several DBAs.

whole-database backup   A database backup that includes all datafiles plus the controlfile.

window   A scheduler construct that extends the concept of schedules by giving Oracle more freedom on deciding when to run a job within a specific start and begin time—for a single day or every day of the week.

X   As in X-Windows, the standard GUI environment used on most computers—except those that run Microsoft Windows instead.

XML   Extensible Markup Language. A standard for data interchange using documents, where the format of the data is defined by tags within the document.

INDEX

Join the Largest Tech Community in the World

 Download the latest software, tools, and developer templates

 Get exclusive access to hands-on trainings and workshops

 Grow your professional network through the Oracle ACE Program

 Publish your technical articles – and get paid to share your expertise

Join the Oracle Technology Network
Membership is free. Visit oracle.com/technetwork

🐦 @OracleOTN f facebook.com/OracleTechnologyNetwork

ORACLE®

Reach More than 700,000 Oracle Customers with Oracle Publishing Group

Connect with the Audience that Matters Most to Your Business

Oracle Magazine
The Largest IT Publication in the World
Circulation: 550,000
Audience: IT Managers, DBAs, Programmers, and Developers

Profit
Business Insight for Enterprise-Class Business Leaders to
Help Them Build a Better Business Using Oracle Technology
Circulation: 100,000
Audience: Top Executives and Line of Business Managers

Java Magazine
The Essential Source on Java Technology, the Java
Programming Language, and Java-Based Applications
Circulation: 125,000 and Growing Steady
Audience: Corporate and Independent Java Developers,
Programmers, and Architects

For more information
or to sign up for a FREE
subscription:
Scan the QR code to visit
Oracle Publishing online.

Beta Test Oracle Software

Get a first look at our newest products—and help perfect them. You must meet the following criteria:

- ✓ **Licensed Oracle customer or Oracle PartnerNetwork member**

- ✓ **Oracle software expert**

- ✓ **Early adopter of Oracle products**

Please apply at: pdpm.oracle.com/BPO/userprofile

If your interests match upcoming activities, we'll contact you. Profiles are kept on file for 12 months.

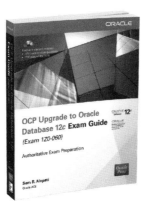